THE CONCISE ENCYCLOPÆDIA OF ISLAM

REVISED EDITION

CYRIL GLASSÉ

INTRODUCTION BY
PROFESSOR HUSTON SMITH

STACEY INTERNATIONAL

Dedicated to Tom Stacey,
my publisher,
and all the scholars in the field of Islamic studies
who made this work possible

Photographic Acknowledgements
Ahuan Islamic Art, London ii, iii (bottom); S.M. Amin (Aramco World) xvii (bottom right); Baco Contracts Ltd/Maju Tekno Adn Bhd xii (bottom left); Ira Block (The Image Bank) x (bottom right); Maximilien Bruggmann iv, xi (bottom right), xxiii; Jusuf Buchinger xvii (top), xx (bottom), xxi (bottom); Camerapix Picture Library viii (top), xvii (bottom), xviii (bottom left); John Egan (Hutchison Library) xxii (bottom left); Peter Fraenkel v (bottom left), ix, xvi (bottom); Cyril Glassé xx (top); IPA/TRIP v (top right), viii (right), x (top right, bottom left), xi (top, bottom left), xii (top left, bottom right; Middle East Archives i, vi, vii, xiv; Christopher Mould (NAAS Picture Library) xviii (top), xix, xxi (top); Peter Sanders (TRIP) viii (left), xxii (bottom right); Reg Seale (TRIP) xiii; Sotheby's xv (right); Tony Stone Photo Library, London xvi (top); Wim Swaan v (top left); Neil Turner (NAAS Picture Library) xxiv(5); By Courtesy of the Board of Trustees of the Victoria and Albert Museum xv (left); Nik Wheeler viii (bottom right), xxii (top).

Consultant Editor J. Peter Hobson
Editors Nicholas Drake and Elizabeth Davis
Art Director Keith Savage

The Concise Encyclopaedia of Islam
Stacey International
128 Kensington Church Street
London W8 4BH
Tel: +44 (0)20 7221 7166; Fax: +44 (0)20 7792 9288
E-mail: stacey.international@virgin.net

Printed and bound in Singapore by Tien Wah Press

ISBN: 1 900988 062

CONTENTS

AUTHOR'S PREFACE

My debt to all the scholars in Islamic studies, past and present, is so vast as to be incalculable. Without their painstaking, and dedicated labors of research and translation it would have been impossible to present the outlines of a subject as complex as a religious civilization in a form as brief as this book. Keys for the understanding of traditional metaphysics and thought have been found in the works of René Guenon.

I am grateful for assistance with the manuscript to: Marguerite N. Howe, Youmna Adal, Kevin Cohalan, Beverly Swabb, Whitall N. Perry, Zaynab Istrabadi, Terry Moore, Lawrence Meehan, Dr. William Stoddart, Alexandra Bonfante-Warren, and to my final editors, J. Peter Hobson and Nicholas Drake.

I am especially indebted to Dr. Victor Danner who was generous with his time and advice.

In matters of interpretation, I have sought to present views which would not be at variance with those of orthodox Sunnī Islam. If I have strayed, the responsibility is my own.

Cyril Glassé
P.O. Box 25009
Columbia University Station
New York
New York 10025 USA

Autumn 1988

INTRODUCTION

by Professor Huston Smith

One can wonder whether in all the human sciences there is greater need for a reference work than for this one in hand. The question risks hyperbole, but there is reason to take it seriously. The world, especially the Western world towards which this encyclopedia is primarily directed, desperately needs to understand Islam better, and in the face of this need previous reference works are woefully inadequate.

At the height of the US-Iranian crisis in 1979, a journalist called attention to the seriousness of our ignorance in words that are likely to retain their force for some time. "We are heading", Meg Greenfield wrote in *Newsweek*,

> into an expansion of the American relationship with that complex of religion, culture and geography known as Islam. There are two things to be said about this. One is that no part of the world is more important to our own well-being at the moment – and probably for the foreseeable future. The other is that no part of the world is more hopelessly and systematically and stubbornly misunderstood by us.

Towards alleviating this misunderstanding previous reference works did what they could, but they do not come close to meeting the present need. Hughes' *Dictionary of Islam* dates back to the nineteenth century and has a missionary bias that forces Pakistani editions to white-out objectionable passages on almost every page. The four-volume *Encyclopaedia of Islam* which appeared between 1913 and 1938 (and its condensed version, cut down to 600 entries from 10,000, the *Shorter Encyclopaedia of Islam* which appeared in 1961) is more objective; its new edition, which is in progress, will serve specialists well, but only half of the fascicules in which it is being issued have appeared, and the price of the eventual multi-volume set will be beyond the reach of the general public. There is a good work in German, *Lexikon der Islamischen Welt*, but (aside from two volumes by the Ronart husband and wife team that deal exclusively with the Arab world) in English this is the picture.

To return to the Greenfield quote, why is it that Islam is so "hopelessly and systematically and stubbornly" – three exceptionally severe adjectives – misunderstood by the West? One answer is that the West's separation of church and state makes it next to impossible for it to understand people who lodge religious belief not only at the center of their individual conduct, but also at the center of their politics.

This is indeed a major obstacle, but there are two others, the first of which again relates to politics. It is ironic that of the major faiths outside Christendom, Islam stands closest to the Judaeo-Christian West both geographically and religiously – geographically, Christianity and Islam have shared common borders for thirteen hundred years, while religiously both are descended from Abraham – yet is the one that is least understood. On reflection, though, while this is indeed ironic, it is not surprising. Common borders provoke border disputes, and these can easily escalate into raids, blood-feuds, and full scale wars. During most of their history, Muslims and Christians have been at odds, and rivals are not known for having the most objective views of each other.

Once we think of them, these two causes of misunderstanding are obvious; but the third one is not. Religiously, people tend to fall into two categories. Some find the meaning they seek in religious forms – commandments, observances, and texts straightforwardly, largely literally, interpreted – while others, without bypassing or abandoning these, sense their provisional character and reach out for meanings that the forms contain but which cannot be equated with those forms. If we call the first type of person exoteric, out of his concern for meanings that attach to outward or manifest forms, the second type that is drawn to the meanings that underlie those forms is conveniently designated esoteric.

Both types turn up in all the historical religions and very likely in tribal ones as well, but nowhere does the difference surface quite as clearly as in Islam. Exoterically – outwardly, and explicitly – Islam is the *sharī'ah*, a revealed, canonic law by which the faithful should live. Concomitantly, though, the Koran and Ḥadīth, or authoritative Traditions that were instituted by Muḥammad, abound in references, frequently veiled, to profound, metaphysical truths which the forms of Islam enfold and protect in the way husks protect and conceal their kernels. Esoterics see these references as invitations to search out those deeper truths and make them the center of their lives. At their best, Sufi orders are associations of such esoterics.

Every reference work on Islam will take note of this esoteric/exoteric distinction somewhere, but in others it turns up only in isolated pockets: a handful of entries such as those on Sufism, Mysticism, *taṣawwuf* – perhaps a dozen items in all. It is a remarkable feature of this new encyclopedia that it takes as its starting point that almost everything in Islam can be viewed in these two persepectives. Beginning with that premise, it proceeds to compile a resource that tries intentionally to do justice to both. A glance at its very first entry, on "Aaron", will make this clear.

What is in hand, therefore, is more than just a new reference work on Islam that is up-to-date and has been kept to manageable compass, i.e. a single volume. By virtue of the "binocular", esoteric/exoteric vision that it trains on its entries throughout, a new dimension of depth comes into view. The result is an encyclopedia that does more than bring reliable information into reach. In the long run it can help its users to see the phenomenon of Islam in a new light.

It seems almost redundant to say that its able and devoted author, Cyril Glassé, deserves our heartfelt thanks.

Huston Smith
Thomas J. Watson Professor of Religion and
Distinguished Adjunct Professor of Philosophy, Emeritus, Syracuse University.
Adjunct Professor, Graduate Theological Union, Berkeley, California.

NOTES TO THE FIRST EDITION

1. The principal abbreviations used are as follows:

A.D.	Anno Domini	Lit.	Literally
A.H. (italicized)	Anno Hegirae	Pers.	Persian
Ar.	Arabic	Pl.	Plural
Fr.	French	Sing.	Singular
Gr.	Greek	Turk.	Turkish

2. In most cases, dates are given according to both Hegirian and Gregorian Calendars. The Hegirian date is given first, in italics.

3. The following system of Arabic transliteration has been used:

Transliteration	Arabic Letter	Transliteration	Arabic Letter
'	ء	ṭ	ط
b	ب	ẓ	ظ
t	ت	'	ع
th	ث	gh	غ
j	ج	f	ف
ḥ	ح	q	ق
kh	خ	k	ك
d	د	l	ل
dh	ذ	m	م
r	ر	n	ن
z	ز	ah/at	ه
s	س	w	و
sh	ش	y	ي
ṣ	ص	t	ة
ḍ	ض		

short vowels (represented by orthographical signs placed above or below Arabic letters)

a	´ (above) eg. ba=	بَ
u	' (above) eg. bu=	بُ
i	´ (below) eg. bi=	بِ

long vowels

ā	اَ
ū	وُ
ī	يَ

dipthongs

aw	وَ
ay	يَ
iyy	يِّ
uww	وُّ

4. The numbering of the Koranic passages is according to Arberry.

بِسْمِ ٱللَّهِ ٱلرَّحْمَٰنِ ٱلرَّحِيمِ

IN THE NAME OF GOD, THE MERCIFUL, THE COMPASSIONATE

A

Aaron (Ar. *Hārūn*). The brother of Moses. In the Koran, Moses says:

> 'Lord, open my breast...
> ... and do Thou ease for me my task.
> Unloose the knot upon my tongue,
> that they may understand my words.
> Appoint for me of my folk a familiar,
> Aaron, my brother; by him confirm
> my strength, and associate him with me
> in my task.' (20:25-35)

The Koran accords Aaron an important place alongside Moses, and he is sometimes deemed a Prophet in his own right representing the esoteric dimension as Moses represents the exoteric. Moses is identified with exoterism because his revelation consists above all of the Mosaic law. The outwardness of Moses' mission is emphasized in the story of his encounter with al-Khiḍr, the personification of esoteric wisdom. Moses does not see beyond the facts of al-Khiḍr's actions to understand their ultimate nature.

> Moses said to him, 'Shall I follow thee
> so that thou teachest me, of what
> thou hast been taught, right judgment?'
> Said he, 'Assuredly thou wilt not
> be able to bear with me patiently.
> And how shouldst thou bear patiently
> that thou has never encompassed
> in thy knowledge?' (18:65-69)

Exoterism is the domain of rituals, of moral precepts, of institutions; esoterism, that of transcendent wisdom and mystical union, of realization through direct knowledge of the Divine. While in exceptional cases such knowledge may, through Divine grace, irrupt spontaneously within the soul, it is much more often the fruit of a sustained effort to actualize doctrine or theoretical truth through a method of concentration, which is found in a Way. As such, it is knowledge which the soul has experienced, and thus confirmed for itself. Ultimately, this process implies a transcendental union between the soul and the truth.

Islam designates the exoteric and esoteric aspects respectively by the terms *sharī'ah* (the religious law) and *ṭarīqah* (the path of mystical realization) or by *aẓ-ẓāhir* ("the outer"), and *al-bāṭin* ("the inner"). Esoterism is also called the "kernel" (*al-lubb*), and the Koran sometimes addresses itself to "those who possess the kernels" (*ulū-l-albāb*).

Another, different, aspect of the relationship between exoterism and esoterism is manifested in the Koranic episode of the golden calf. While Moses is on Mount Sinai, the people make, and pay homage to, an idol. Aaron says to them:

> 'My people, you have been tempted
> by this thing, no more; surely
> Your Lord is the All-merciful; therefore
> follow me, and obey my commandment!'
> 'We will not cease,' they said, 'to cleave
> to it, until Moses returns to us.' (20:92-93)

When Moses returns he reproaches his brother:

> 'What prevented thee,
> Aaron, when thou sawest them in error,
> so that thou didst not follow after me?
> Didst thou then disobey my commandment?'
> 'Son of my mother,' Aaron said,
> 'take me not by the beard, or the head!
> I was fearful that thou wouldst say,
> "Thou has divided the Children of Israel,
> and thou hast not observed my word."' (20:94-96)

Because it opens onto the formless, esoterism threatens to shatter dogma, and the *sharī'ah;* nonetheless, its presence inevitably depends upon exoterism's revealed forms. When exoterism is absent, as symbolized in this episode by Moses' absence on the mountain, orthodoxy is lost and disintegration follows: when the formal hold of religious dogmas weakens, fissiparous heresy is given free rein. It can therefore be said that the test of orthodox esoterism is that it does not contradict exoterism. The realization towards which esoterism is directed implies rather the transcending of form through form. The higher the spiritual aspiration, the more important and strict the observance of religious law becomes. Esoterism depends upon exoterism in yet another way: without exoterism, the truth is "invisible". Light in itself is a revelation, but unless it illuminates forms it "shineth in darkness, and the darkness comprehended it not". It is only through form, in the sense of exoterism and also of a defined corpus of revelation, that it is possible to attain to formless truth: "I am the door..." On the other hand, without esoterism the form becomes empty and a dead letter: "They have no wine."

As al-Hujwīrī says:

> The exoteric aspect of Truth without the esoteric is hypocrisy, and the esoteric without the exoteric is heresy. So, with regard to the Law, mere formality is defective, while mere spirituality is vain.

While the dichotomy between esoterism and exoterism is thus adumbrated in the Koran by the figures of Aaron and Moses (and developed more explicitly in oral tradition which has spun innumerable didactic tales of Moses), we find in the person of the Prophet the two ways joined in one and embodied in their fullness. He was a lawgiver but also the channel for an outpouring of *riḍwān* ("felicitous union"), as took place in the event of the Pact of Ḥudaybiyyah. Among his two hundred names are *Miftāḥ ar-Raḥmah* ("the Key of Mercy"), *Sayyid al-Kawnayn* ("Lord of the Two Worlds"), "the Fount of Grace", "the Master of the Lofty Degree". Many of the Ḥadīth, such as "who has seen me has seen the truth" (*man ra'ānī faqad rā' al-ḥaqq*), completely elude being coherently enclosed in any purely exoteric interpretation. Indeed, Islam, of all religions, is remarkably balanced in this respect.

In Judaism, the esoteric and exoteric were originally one. The "inner", being inseparable from the outer, manifested itself in God's historic acts towards the nation; and the Torah itself was mysticism and sacrament, as, indeed, was the tribe's very history. This could not continue indefinitely, however, since the unmanifest cannot coincide with, or forever be reduced to, the manifest and specific. The tension culminated in the rending of the veil of the Temple, and finally in the destruction of the earthly Temple itself. There remained in Judaism a tendency to transform the esoteric into the exoteric and to make ritual of it. Thus the *Qabbalah* (the post-Christian mysticism which succeeded the *Merkava* or *Heikhalot* school) readily becomes an intensified exoterism or a pietistic fervor; moreover, the *Qabbalah* sees the *sephiroth* as the body or substance of Judaism, and of Jews, but considers the rest to be of a "demonic" substance, as if it were not God's creation.

While Judaism's esoterism is today relatively inaccessible – for what could replace the loss of the pronunciation of the Divine Name? – Christianity, by contrast, is so essentially esoteric in nature that it had to adopt the forms of the Roman Empire as its outer, or exoteric shell. It thus exhibited the opposite tendency to that of Judaism, by esoterizing the outer and the horizontal planes of existence. Christian fervor attempted to actualize the descent of the heavenly Jerusalem in its worldly institution. Byzantium sought to accumulate all of the gold in the world, not only out of ordinary human avarice, but because the Bible says that the streets of the New Jerusalem are paved with gold. In Byzantium, the very weights and measures reflected a heavenly perfection, and a baker could be put to death for selling a loaf which deviated from the ideal dimension.

Full-blown esoterism with a minimum of exoterism is the most subtle of dangers, for it can lead to an "absolutizing" of the relative. The French Revolution, which exalted the merely human and rational, made a shrine in Paris out of a length of metal which it called the "standard" – the absolute – meter bar. The Christian notion that God had become man, in order that man raise his nature to conform with the ideally real, became, particularly after the Renaissance, the idea that man as such, i.e. fallen man, was God. With this came the gradual transformation of the world itself; it led to the invention of "progress" – and the modern world. Man splices genes, and inevitably the idea implants itself that man is God.

Islam, however, from the outset has presented a balance between exoterism and esoterism. It does not demand spiritual heroism of man; it only asks him to be truly man. Nor does God bind himself to man in an historic covenant with a particular people. His covenant is with man as such, and in it God "returns to his throne" (*istawā 'ala-l-'arsh*, Koran 7:54; 10:3; 13:2; 25:59; 57:4) after creating the world in six days. In Islam God "resumes" (with respect to man's knowledge of God, which hangs upon Revelation) His nature of Absolute, as man resumes his primordial nature, symbolized by "the return to the religion of Abraham" and that of Adam. Islam is both a law to ensure social stability, and a transcendent truth; the latter, its esoterism, is found in the *shahādah* (the testimony of faith), the "seeing" that only God is Reality, which truth is itself the means of salvation. This is one sense of the Ḥadīth: "I [the Prophet] have brought both the good things of this world, and the good things of the next world." *See* al-KHIḌR; MOSES; RIḌWĀN; SHAHĀDAH; ṬARĪQAH.

'Abā'. The sleeveless garment, open in the front, which is worn by men in the Arabian peninsula. In Saudi Arabia this male attire is more often called a *busht*, while the generic terms *'abā'* or *'abayah* are commonly used to designate a similar cloak which is worn in black over the head by most women when appearing in public.

al-'Abbās ibn 'Abd al-Muṭṭalib (d. *32*/652). An uncle of the Prophet, noted as a rich and shrewd merchant. Throughout the early struggle of Islam he maintained a cautious balance between the Muslims and the Meccans. He protected the Prophet against the other clans while the latter was in Mecca, but fought on the Meccan side after the Hijrah.

Al-'Abbās entered Islam while held as a captive in Medina after the Battle of Badr. When he protested that he had no means to ransom himself, the Prophet confronted him with miraculous knowledge of a secret conversation that had taken place in Mecca concerning the disposition of al-'Abbās' fortune if he died in war. That the Prophet knew this proved to al-'Abbās that he must indeed be inspired.

However, al-'Abbās returned to Mecca and only joined the Muslims at the last moment as the Prophet advanced upon Mecca for the final conquest. This flight to the Medinan side at the final hour marked the end of the period of the Hijrah, and the Prophet named al-'Abbas "last of the refugees", (*muhājirūn*). Typical of his good fortune in life, these words entitled al-'Abbās and his descendants to stipends from the spoils of war according to the elevated rank of *muhājirūn* as prescribed by the tables of rank and merit, the *diwān*, established in the Caliphate of 'Umar.

Al-'Abbās had the privilege of supplying Zamzam water to pilgrims. This his descendants kept. His son 'Abd Allāh Ibn al-'Abbās became a celebrated interpreter of the Koran, who offered, among his other commentaries, explanations for the meanings of the mysterious isolated letters which are found heading certain Sūrahs. From al-'Abbās sprang the 'Abbāsid dynasty (*132-656*/749-1258), which followed the Umayyads, yet another example of al-'Abbās' enduring good fortune. The 'Abbasids, as cousins, laid claim to the prestige of being of the Prophet's family, while their rivals the 'Alids, the direct descendants of the Prophet, were, for most of history, obliged to lie low.

'Abbāsids (Ar. *ad-dawlah al-'abbāsiyyah*). The second dynasty of the Islamic Empire which succeeded the Umayyads in *132*/749. The rule of the Umayyads was in many ways a prolongation of the old secular and ethnocentric ways of the Arabs. Many of the later trappings of the 'Abbāsids, such as the sudden concealment of the ruler behind a curtain during audiences – his exaltation – which prompted an ambassador of the Fāṭimids to ask during a particularly impressive ceremony at the time of the Buyids if he were being shown God, were in the grand style of an Eastern potentate and a heritage of the Sassanids. But if the Umayyads were like desert kings, with the 'Abbāsids there was a definite consciousness of a supra-national world order. Under the 'Abbāsids, the genius of the Persians fused with Arab-Islamic civilization to reach a first high point. Outstanding accomplishments in the fields of medicine, science, literature, and art date from this epoch. The growing importance of Persia in the Islamic Empire was signaled in *145*/762, in the transfer of the capital eastward, near the Ctesiphon of the Sassanids, to Baghdad, which had been newly founded by the second 'Abbāsid Caliph, al-Manṣūr. (See BAGHDAD.) The reign of the 'Abbāsids, although for the most part they did not actually control the Empire, lasted over five hundred years until the coming of the Mongols in *656*/1258.

The Umayyads had been notorious for their despotism, and rising discontent with their harsh rule led to their downfall. The 'Abbāsids were helped to power by their lieutenant Abū Muslim. Of obscure origins, perhaps from Kufah, Abū Muslim set in motion the propaganda in Khorasan, of which Nasr, the Umayyad Governor wrote to the Caliph Marwān: "I see coals glowing among the embers, they want but little to burst into blaze. Fire springs from the rubbing of sticks, and warfare from the wagging of tongues." The word had been spread: *ar-Riḍā min Āl Muḥammad* ("Felicity is from the Family of Muḥammad"; i.e. the 'Abbāsids). The war-cry of Abū Muslim was: "O Muḥammad, O helped of God". And when the time came for open insurrection, he unfurled the Black Standard of the family of al-'Abbās which was inscribed with the words: "Leave is given to those who fight because they were wronged." (Koran 22:39; which continues: "Surely God is able to help them".)

The last ruling Umayyad was the Caliph Marwān II who was defeated at the Battle of the Zab river. However, 'Abd ar-Raḥmān, who was to be called ad-Dākhil ("the Intruder"), an Umayyad who escaped from the subsequent persecution of the deposed clan, went on to found a kingdom in Cordoba. Following the example of the Fāṭimids, the rulers of Cordoba later also took the title of Caliphs and their kingdom became known as the Umayyad Caliphate of Spain.

The 'Abbāsid dynasty was founded by Abū-l-'Abbās, called as-Saffāḥ, "the Spiller" (of Umayyad blood). The 'Abbāsids were the descendants of al-'Abbās, an uncle of the Prophet. While not directly descended from the Prophet, the family relationship helped to rally nascent Shī'ite sympathies to their side. Eventually, however, the Shī'ites, who wished to see a descendant of the Prophet, the progeny of 'Alī and Fāṭimah, as ruler, came to look upon the 'Abbāsids as persecutors of Shī'ism.

The 'Abbāsid dynasty ruled with the help of the Barmecides, a prominent Persian family from Balkh who, before their conversion, had been priests in the Buddhist monastery of Naubahar. The skilled administration of several generations of this family as Viziers or ministers fostered the flowering of Arab-Persian Islamic civilization, which reached its imperial peak during the reign of Hārūn ar-Rashīd (*170*/786-*194*/809), and its cultural peak soon after that. For reasons which are obscure, Hārūn ar-Rashīd disgraced the Barmecides towards the end of his life, putting to death his former Vizier Ja'far ibn Yaḥyā Barmak in *187*/803. Faḍl, the brother of Ja'far, and his father Yaḥyā, were thrown into prison where they died.

This crucial episode marks the turning point in the 'Abbāsid reign; soon afterwards actual power slipped from their hands. Two of Hārūn ar-Rashīd's sons, al-Amīn and al-Ma'mūn, who inherited respectively the west and the east of the Empire (a third, Qasim, was governor in the south), fought a brief but bloody civil war over the succession which brought al-Ma'mūn to the throne. Al-Ma'mūn's reign opens a curious episode in 'Abbāsid history. As prosperity declined from the opulence of Hārūn ar-Rashīd's reign, ever more threats emerged to the Caliph's power; at every turn complex ideologies surged up, along with the ghosts of old religions, to confuse the allegiance of the masses. To secure the sympathies of the Shī'ites, al-Ma'mūn designated the Shī'ite Imām Alī-r-Riḍā as his successor and married his daughter to him. The black banners of the 'Abbāsids were changed for 'Alid green. This did not produce the desired results; the Iraqis turned and set up, for a short time, another member of the 'Abbāsid family, Ibrāhīm, as Caliph. Then 'Alī-r-Riḍā died, perhaps indeed poisoned – the Shī'ites insist that each Imām died a tragic martyr's death – and was buried by the tomb of Hārūn ar-Rashīd, in today's Mashhad in Iran.

A noted intellectual who took an active interest in theological questions and contributed to their development, al-Ma'mūn adopted the Mu'tazilite, or rationalist, philosophy in *212*/827. This opens another turbulent period in the history of Islamic thought marked by the *mihnah*, or inquisition into the beliefs of religious scholars. The *mihnah* was instituted in *218*/833, shortly before the death of al-Ma'mūn. The Mu'tazilite period lasted twenty years from *212*/827 until the Caliph al-Mutawakkil restored orthodoxy in *232*/847.

Al-Mu'taṣim, the brother and successor of al-Ma'mūn, installed a Turkish guard around him. Feeling uneasy in Baghdad, he founded a new heavily fortified capital at Samarra', 60 miles north of Baghdad. There the capital remained until the Caliph al-Mu'tamid returned to Baghdad. This defensive move to Samarra' foreshadowed the political decline of the 'Abbāsids for, from then on, Turkish soldiers in the armies beginning with al-Wāthiq, began to exercise their own will over the Caliphs, who increasingly ruled in name only. As the Caliphs withdrew into the military camp-city of Samarra', they became more prisoners than princes. Finally, factions in the Turkish guard supplanted the Caliphs as the real political power. Al-Mutawwakil took the title *ẓill Allāh fi-l-arḍ* ("Shadow of God on earth") but was murdered by the Turkish guards, as were the four Caliphs who followed in quick succession.

During this period, North Africa slipped from the grasp of the 'Abbāsid Caliphs to the Aghlabids of Kairouan/Qayrawān (who continued a no more than nominal allegiance to 'Abbāsid suzerainty by sending the Caliphs frequent gifts from the booty of conquest), and then to the Fāṭimids. Parts of Persia fell under Ṭāhirid rule. Although the 'Abbāsids retained their title for four more centuries, the real power fell into the hands of military leaders of a Turkic people called the Daylamites from the Caspian region. Inclined to a political Shī'ism of the Zaydi kind, the Daylamite dynasty, which ruled de facto in the name of the Caliphs, was known as the Buyids (or Buwayhids). The Saljuq Turks replaced them as the ruling power in *447*/1055.

Towards the end of the 'Abbāsid dynasty, although some of the later Caliphs such as an-Nāṣir showed initiative and the possibility of resurgence, the Caliphate no longer exercised direct political power but played a different role symbolizing political continuity and the principle of legitimacy. In the incessant power struggles of the eastern Empire, no ruler could ever be certain that control was firmly in his grasp. In these circumstances, formal recognition by the Caliph, in the guise of an investiture, came to be sought as confirmation of claims which had, in any case, to be maintained by constant application of military force. When the Mongols appeared on the scene in the middle of the *7th*/13th century they were much more powerful than any of the rulers they encountered. Not yet converted to Islam, and unimpressed by the Caliphate's residual authority, the Mongols simply swept the Caliphate away. The Shī'ites among the Caliph's subjects increasingly resented 'Abbāsid rule and offered the Mongols no resistance. Indeed many of them helped the Mongol invaders, at least as advisors. Thus the Mongols were not stopped until they came up against the Mamluks of Egypt, a political and military force which was not fragmented.

Under the 'Abbāsids, Arab-Islamic civilization attained its greatest development in the eastern Empire. Centers of learning flourished, among them, the *Bayt al-Ḥikmah* ("House of Wisdom"), an academy founded by the Caliph al-Ma'mūn for the translation of works of Greek science into Arabic. In part, the endowment of educational institutions was stimulated during the Saljuq suzerainty by the need to counter religious propaganda emanating from Fāṭimid Egypt. Advances were made in medicine and the natural sciences, while the arts, philosophy and literature reached new heights. The location of the capital at Baghdad made it the focal point of influences from as far apart as the Mediterranean and the Far East. Islam also drew upon a rich cultural and intellectual heritage from Byzantium, Persia, India, and even China. The coming of the Mongol Hordes shattered this sophisticated culture and sank its libraries in the Tigris. Yet, as was so often the case with the Mongols, their success against the kingdoms and empires of East and West was really due to the weakness of their enemies.

The 'Abbāsid Caliphs are:

Abū 'Abbās as-Saffāḥ ("the Spiller")	*132-136*/749-754
al-Manṣūr	*136-158*/754-775
al-Mahdī	*158-169*/775-785
al-Hādī	*169-170*/785-786
Hārūn ar-Rashīd	*170-193*/786-809
al-Amin	*193-198*/809-813
al-Ma'mun	*198-218*/813-833
al-Mu'taṣim	*218-227*/833-842
al-Wāthiq	*227-232*/842-847
al-Mutawakkil	*232-247*/847-861
al-Muntaṣir	*247-248*/861-862
al-Musta'īn	*248-252*/862-866
al-Mu'tazz	*252-255*/866-869
al-Muhtadī	*255-256*/869-870
al-Mu'tamid	*256-279*/870-892
al-Mu'tadīd	*279-289*/892-902
al-Muktafi	*289-295*/902-908
al-Muqtadir	*295-320*/908-932

Buyid Suzerainty *320-447*/932-1055

al-Qāhir	*320-322*/932-934
ar-Rāḍī	*322-329*/934-940
al-Muttaqī	*329-333*/940-944
al-Mustakfī	*333-334*/944-946
al-Muṭī'	*334-363*/946-974
at-Tā'i'	*363-381*/974-991
al-Qāir	*381-422*/991-1031
al-Qāim	*422-476*/1031-1075

Saljuq Suzerainty from 447/1055 to *590*/1194

al-Muqtadī	*476-487*/1075-1094

al-Mustaẓhir	*487-512*/1094-1118
al-Mustarshid	*512-529*/1118-1135
al-Rashīd	*529-530*/1135-1136
al-Muqtafi	*530-555*/1136-1160
al-Mustanjid	555-566/1160-1170
al-Mustadī'	*566-575*/1170-1180
an-Nāsir	575-622/1180-1225
az-Ẓahir	*622-623*/1225-1226
al-Muṣtanṣir	*623-640*/1226-1242
al-Musta'ṣīm	*640-656*/1242-1258

The Mongols sacked Baghdad in *656*/1258 and put al-Musta'ṣim to death. However, the Mamlūk soldier Baybars, then lieutenant to the Egyptian ruler Qutuz, defeated the Mongols at Ayn Jalūt in Syria in 6*58*/1260, brought an uncle of the last 'Abbāsid ruler to Cairo, and installed him as Caliph. This Caliph, al-Muṣtanṣir, was killed in the following year *659*/1261 leading an army in an unsuccessful attempt to recover Baghdad from the Mongols. The line of figurehead 'Abbāsids in Cairo continued, however, and added prestige to Mamlūk rule until Egypt was conquered by the Ottomans in *923*/1517. Thereafter, no 'Abbāsid laid claim to the title of Caliph and the Ottomans were later to maintain that the last 'Abbāsid in Cairo, al-Mutawakkil III, ceded the rights of the Caliphate to Selim I, the Ottoman Sultan of Turkey. *See* BAGHDAD; CALIPH; KHURRAMIYYAH; MONGOLS; OTTOMANS; PATRIARCHAL CALIPHS; UMAYYADS; ZANJ.

'Abd (lit. "slave"). One of several terms for "slave" and also that element of many Muslim personal names which is combined with one of the Divine Names. Thus, *'Abd Allāh* means "slave of God", *'Abd ar-Raḥmān* means "slave of the Merciful One", and so forth. "Slave" in this sense refers to a state of complete dependence upon God and conformity to His Will. One of the epithets of the Prophet, along with that of "Messenger of God", is *'abd,* "slave" of God, indeed the "perfect" slave. *See also* SLAVERY.

Abdāl (lit. "substitutes"; sing. *badal*). In Sufi lore, a set of seventy Saints, of whom a certain number are the *ṣiddīqūn* ("truthful ones", similar to the Jewish *tsadeqs*). One *ṣiddīq* is the *quṭb* ("axis" or "pole"), the center of human sanctity on earth. Another four are called *awtād* ("pegs"). The symbolism is that of tent-pegs without which the tent, that is, the world, would collapse.

These Saints are called *Abdāl* because when one dies his function is carried on by another person. This resembles the doctrine of tulkus among the Tibetans, but in transference of spiritual function only, not of personality. (It may be mentioned in passing that it is a widespread popular Sufi belief, of unknown but doubtless extraneous origin, that the number of Saints in Islam at any one moment is constant throughout history up until the last days.)

Although it frequently happens that the disciples of a spiritual Master eulogize him as the *quṭb,* or even *quṭb al-aqṭāb* ("the Pole of Poles"), the identity of the *Abdāl* is considered to be one of God's secrets. Although the *Abdāl* are replaced through history, at the end of time there are less saintly men to fill the role, and when the number lapses below a certain figure, or there are no more at all, it is said that the world will come to an end. *See* QUTB.

'Abd Allāh ibn Maymūn al-Qaddāḥ (d. *261*/875). The obscure but pivotal figure who is the connection between Ja'far as-Ṣadīq (who for Shī'ites is the sixth Imām), the ultimate origins of the Seveners, and the Ismā'īlīs, who became the Fāṭimid dynasty. The family of 'Abd Allāh ibn Maymūn is thought to have originated in Iraq or Ahwāz in southwest Persia; later he moved to Syria. The name al-Qaddāh is thought to refer either to the profession, or to some characteristic, of his father, Maymūn; it may mean an "oculist", from *qadaḥ,* a "bowl", such as would be used for making up a collyrium, that is, "someone whose preparations would lead to clearer sight"; this could well be an allegorical name. Or again, it may simply be the word *qaddāḥ* ("flint") used attributively. 'Abd Allāh and his father Maymūn are thought to have been connected with Muḥammad al-Baqīr and Ja'far as-Ṣādiq, the fifth and sixth Imāms, and are credited with transmitting (as *rāwis*) – or perhaps creating – certain sayings of Ja'far aṣ-Ṣādiq which are fundamental, in different degrees of interpretation, to the Sevener and Twelve-Imām Shī'ite doctrines of the Imām.

The Fāṭimids were accused in violent and caustic terms in the 'Alid Manifesto of *402*/1011, composed by the leader of the Sharīfs of Baghdad al-Murtaḍā, his brother ar-Rāḍi, and certain 'Abbāsid jurists, of having invented their descent from 'Alī through Fāṭimah. They were also accused of being descendants of Maymūn al-Qaddah. The Manifesto alleged that they were in reality the descendants of Daysan (i.e. Bardesanes, a Hellenist Gnostic teacher in the Valentinian tradition). The Fāṭimid Caliph al-Mu'izz li-Dīn Allāh (d. *365*/975) referred cryptically to these allegations in a *sijill,* or rescript, to the Chief Dā'i (Fāṭimid propagandist) of Sind, with a play on word-etymologies to the effect that it was true that he was the son of the "Divinely blessed with success in his affairs" (Ar. *al-maymūn an-naqībāt*) and the "striker of sparks of guidance" kindling the light of Divine Wisdom *(al-qaddaḥ). See* 'ALĀ ad-DĪN 'ATĀ' MALĪK; FĀṬIMIDS; JUWAYNĪ, 'ALĀ ad-DĪN 'ATA' MALĪK; NŪR MUḤAMMADĪ; SEVENERS.

'Abd Allāh ibn az-Zubayr (d. *73*/692). The son of the Companion az-Zubayr ibn al-'Awwām and Asmā' bint Abī Bakr. 'Abd Allāh led a conservative, non-Shī'ite, revolt against the Umayyad tyranny. He declared himself Caliph and seized control of Mecca in *64*/683. The following year in a siege of Mecca, the Ka'bah was hit by a flaming arrow and burned. 'Abd Allāh rebuilt it on a larger scale to include the *Ḥijr Ismā'īl.* This new Ka'bah was pulled down and rebuilt as before by al-Ḥajjāj ibn Yūsuf. When Mecca was captured, the body of 'Abd Allāh was hung from a gibbet and his head then sent to Damascus. *See* ASMĀ'; KA'BAH.

'Abd al-'Azīz, King, *see* IBN SA'ŪD.

'Abd al-Muṭṭalib ibn Ḥāshim. The grandfather of the Prophet and head of the Banū Ḥāshim clan of the Quraysh tribe. His real name was Shaybah and his mother was Salma bint 'Amr of the Najjar clan of the Khazraj tribe of the city of Yathrib, later known as Medina. 'Abd al-Muṭṭalib was born and raised in Medina. When his uncle, Muṭṭalib, brought him to Mecca after the death of Ḥāshim, his father, he acquired the name 'Abd al-Muṭṭalib ("the slave of Muṭṭalib") because he arrived sitting on the back of his uncle's camel and was mistaken for his servant. He later became the most respected man of the tribe Quraysh, who had no chief since a division of privileges had been made between their ancestors 'Abd ad-Dār and 'Abd Manāf. A prophetic dream, seen by 'Abd al-Muṭṭalib while sleeping in the *Ḥijr Ismā'īl* next to the Ka'bah, led him to rediscover the well of Zamzam by digging under the spot where the Quraysh had traditionally conducted their sacrifices. The location of the well had remained unknown after being buried by the Jurhumites who inhabited Mecca before the Quraysh. By rediscovering the well, 'Abd al-Muṭṭalib acquired the rights of supplying water to pilgrims to Mecca. His son al-'Abbās inherited these rights.

At the time he discovered the well of Zamzam, 'Abd al-Muṭṭalib had only one son, Ḥārith. He prayed to the Lord of the Ka'bah to grant him ten sons and promised in return to sacrifice one of them. His prayers were answered and when the time came, the youngest, 'Abd Allāh, was chosen for sacrifice. However, the protests of his family moved 'Abd al-Muṭṭalib to consult a woman soothsayer who lived near the Jewish settlement of Khaybar, in order to ask whether God would accept a substitute for the sworn sacrifice. When the soothsayer's informing spirit confirmed this, 'Abd al-Muṭṭalib cast the divining arrows at Mecca to learn how many camels would be acceptable as a surrogate sacrifice. The answer was "one hundred camels". These being sacrificed, 'Abd Allāh's life was ransomed.

'Abd Allāh was the father of the Prophet Muḥammad, but died before the child was born, so that 'Abd al-Muṭṭalib became guardian. 'Abd al-Muṭṭalib died when Muḥammad was still young, leaving the eight-year-old orphan to the care of one of his sons, Abū Ṭālib, uncle of Muḥammad and later head of the Hāshimite clan.

When Abrahah of the Yemen attacked Mecca with the Army of the Elephant in the year 570, the year in which the Prophet was born, Abd al-Muṭṭalib negotiated with the attacker on behalf of the Quraysh and asked for the return of his camels which Abrahah had seized. Abrahah was set upon destroying the Ka'bah. When questioned about the Ka'bah, 'Abd al-Muṭṭalib is said to have answered that, as his camels had a master that cared for them, so did the Ancient House, and its Lord would protect it. Sudden death and destruction came upon the army of Abrahah when birds with pebbles in their beaks and claws attacked it. This Divine portent drove off the invader. *See* ABRAHAH.

'Abd al-Qādir, Emir (*1223-1300*/1808-1883). The leader of the struggle against the French in Algeria from 1832 until his surrender in 1847. He was famous not only as a military leader, whose exploits were epic, but as a scholar, a poet and above all, a man of religion. 'Abd al-Qādir was interned for three years in the Château d'Amboise in France and finally exiled first to Bursa and then to Damascus where he eventually died in 1883. In Damascus in 1860 he was noted for saving a large number of Christians when their lives were threatened by rioters by giving them refuge in his house, and others, several thousand, by extending his protection.

Being himself a *faqir* (a disciple in a Sufi *tariqah*), 'Abd al-Qādir was entombed next to Ibn 'Arabī in Damascus whom he regarded as his spiritual master; his remains were moved to Algeria in 1968.

During his exile at Bursa 'Abd al-Qādir wrote a book for the Société Asiatique to which he asked admission. This was translated into French by Gustave Dugat and was published in 1858. It is a general overview of philosophy, history and theology, and social questions, in the old Arab tradition, probably the last work of its kind. 'Abd al-Qādir makes an analogy between a game of chess, in which the players are free within the frame of immutable rules, and the exercise of free will. He says that faith is above reason, but both come from God and there need be no incompatibility between them and that reason should be exercised in service of faith; he says that the poor are to be maintained at the charge of the rich; that the law of Moses regards matter, the law of Jesus the spirit, and that of Islam combines them both. He says that the prophets are men with the same father but different mothers.

On 14 June 1830, as the Bourbon dynasty was coming to an end, a French force of 37,000 led by General Louis de Bourmont landed at Sidi Ferruch near Algiers and put to an end the 300 year old Turkish Regency which had ruled the country. In some areas Rayah tribes who had paid taxes to Makhzen tribes for the benefit of the Turkish rulers revolted and anarchy spread in Algeria. Attempts by the Sultan of Morocco to impose himself in Oran were ended by the threat of French naval pressure on the Moroccan coast. Before the Moroccans left Oran, they appointed Muhyi ad-Dīn, a marabout, or venerated religious figure and father of Emir 'Abd al-Qādir, as governor of the province.

On 22 November 1832, his father, and other members of his family, and the notables of three tribes, the Hashim, Gharabah, and Beni Amar made a *bayah* or pact of fealty with 'Abd al-Qādir under a tree near Mascara. 'Abd al-Qādir was given the title of Amir al-Mu'minin which was used by the Caliphs. This event was a deliberate re-enactement of the Pact of Hudaybiyyah made with the Prophet at a dangerous moment in the history of nascent Islam. Although some Arab historians said the Emir was of Berber ancestry from the Ifferen tribe, the official established belief was that he was a *Sharīf*, or Hasani descendent of the Prophet, and moreover descended from the Idrīsi dynasty of Morocco. His grandfather had been made a representative of a Qādiriyyah Sufi Shaykh whom he had met while on pilgrimage. This led to a position of prestige which granted his village, Guetna Oued al-Hammam, immunity from Turkish jurisdiction, and his son Muhyi ad-Dīn eventually became head of the Qādiriyyah for all of Algeria.

On a pilgrimage with his father to Mecca in the year 1826 'Abd al-Qādir, who had been an eager student, came in contact with centers of Islamic learning in Tunisia, the Zeituna university, and in Damascus. During a visit to Baghdad where 'Abd al-Qādir Jīlānī is buried, both father and son were given *ijāzahs*, or permission to instruct, by the chief of the Qādiriyyah Sufi order there. A hagiographical legend says that during the visit to Baghdad a mysterious old man addressed the pilgrims calling the Emir Sultan thereby identifying him with the founder of the Qādiriyyah and also prophesying his future role. Stories of the events in Baghdad circulated in Algeria even before the French incursion. On the return through Egypt, 'Abd al-Qādir studied at the al-Azhar. The return of father and son to Algeria became the occasion for extended festivities which further added to their reputation, which was already that of the most prestigious marabouts in the country.

In the spring of 1832 Muhyi ad-Dīn, after inviting General Boyer to enter Islam, declared holy war on the French in Oran. 'Abd al-Qādir led the attacks and earned a reputation for courage and leadership. He severely punished those who supplied the French by ordering amputation of the right hand, the nose, and ears. (It should be noted that although amputation of the right hand is a threat rarely carried out for theft, even in early times, this kind of mutilation, and mutilation as political punishment, is considered forbidden in Islamic law.) To pay for the fighting, non-combatants in the tribes were assessed special taxes of a certain number of sheep.

'Abd al-Qādir took control of Mascara as seat of government and pronounced a khutbah or Friday religious address in the mosque. He continued to unite the tribes, Berber and Arab, against an outside enemy in the name of religion, constantly invoking a rigorous adherence to Islamic law. His accession to power was accompanied by the propagation of prophetic dreams, on the part of other religious figures and the dream visitations of departed Saints affirming 'Abd al-Qādir's mission.

At first reluctant to recognize the Emir for fear of the French, the Sultan of Morocco eventually lent support and allowed sales of arms for what became a policy of guerrilla warfare. Income came first from gifts, fees for military appointments, and finally only from *zakat* and *'ushr*, traditional taxes; circumstances, however, forced the Emir to impose a non-traditional tax which he called *maunah*. By harassing the French the Emir led them to conclude a peace treaty in February 1834, a tactic which, like the treaty the Prophet Muḥammad made at Hudaybiyyah, won him recognition. The peace treaty contained a secret convention in Arabic supplied by 'Abd al-Qādir and signed later by General Desmichels. The General hid the existence of this convention even from the French government; its articles in effect recognized 'Abd al-Qādir as legitimate sovereign over Oran with the exception of the coastal towns; the French had to obtain visas from 'Abd al-Qādir for travel in Oran, while Muslims did not; thereby French jurisdiction was denied, even in occupied areas, in this and also in other particulars. While General Desmichels presented the treaty as an extension of French authority in Oran, 'Abd al-Qadir did the opposite in regard to the Algerian tribes, presenting it as a recognition of his own government. On the other hand, 'Abd al-Qādir exposed himself to criticism of having dropped the *jihād,* forcing him to resort to force and to use the Makhzen tribes the way the Turks had done to continue collecting taxes.

As an Algerian coalition formed against him, 'Abd al-Qādir actually received military help from the French, which led him to establish a regular army. With the appointment of General Trézel in Oran in 1835 a new policy emerged causing a realignment of forces which culminated in the Figuier convention with other factions in Algeria, the Zmalah and Dawa'ir who joined the French. A battle with 'Abd al-Qādir on the 26th of June was won by the French; but on the 28th the battle of Macta was one of the worst defeats; although it cost 'Abd al-Qādir 500 casualties, the French losses were 2,000. Thereafter, French efforts grew decisively earnest and Mascara was occupied whereupon 'Abd al-Qādir's allies abandoned him leaving him desolate having robbed him even of his personal effects.

However, unexpectedly in Algerian eyes, the French left Mascara three days after occupying it. This must have created a deep psychological impression that a Divine Will was at work, and that this Will was on the side of 'Abd al-Qādir: the Algerians who had abandoned 'Abd al-Qādir returned and begged his forgiveness. In subsequent military operations 'Abd al-Qādir exhibited great shrewdness in using the means at his disposal; he relied heavily on intelligence information obtained clandestinely and by overt means at his disposal, such as reading French newspapers. He got the Moroccans to take part, and in general obtained much help from the Sultan of Morocco who largely succeeded in dissimulating his support for 'Abd al-Qādir by disinformation to French representatives in Morocco. Efforts to involve England and the United States by offering them ports in Algeria failed, but they demonstrated his pragmatism in attempting any avenue that would further his political goals.

The Battle of Sikkak in 1836 was the only pitched, European-style battle that 'Abd al-Qādir fought. It was a great defeat, and again he was abandoned by his followers, an example of the liability of having power based upon possessing baraka, or divine favor, rather than upon social structures of continuity. Again, failure of the French, this time under General Bugeaud, to follow up and aid from Morocco allowed 'Abd al-Qādir to regain his position. This time he relocated further inland. An incident arose in which he punished the Borjia tribe which had maintained friendly relations with the French. In his actions in this case, and in several similar ones, he again deliberately imitated the Prophet's actions, this time the Prophet's reprisals against the treacherous Jewish tribes of the Bani Qurayzah, and the Bani Nadir. Extremely pragmatic, as the Prophet himself was when purely practical questions were involved, 'Abd al-Qādir, on the other hand, was sometimes harsh for political and opportunistic goals whereas the Prophet was not, his actions rigorous only when it was a question of religious principles.

In 1837 the Tafna peace treaty was concluded; it also included secret protocols in which arms were supplied to 'Abd al-Qādir from French Army depots, arms whose payment went to improve roads in the *département* from which General Bugeaud was now an elected deputy, and engagements were undertaken to move tribes not cooperative to the Emir out of Oran. The Emir on the other hand had to make concessions regarding his sovereignty and these he kept hidden from his allies and subjects. The new treaty led to a period of good relations with 'Abd al-Qādir and a moment of quiet while the French consolidated their positions; the Turkish Bey of Constantine was also left in peace.

He received a fatwah, or religious decision, from the *'ulamā'* of Fez which supported the actions he had taken. Some 400 European deserters had joined 'Abd al-Qādir, some of them converted to Islam. In the meantime, however, French policy changed through the occupation of Constantine. 'Abd al-Qādir attempted to bring other parts of Algeria under his control through military means and diplomatic maneuvers, preparing material stockpiles for total war, and even building fortresses, all of which, however, were to fall to the French within three years of the renewal of hostilities at the end of 1839, precipitated by the march of a French force led by the Duc d'Orléans and Governor General Valée from Constantine to Algiers. In the meantime, 'Abd al-Qādir caused himself a serious setback by attacking the marabout Muhammad as-Saghir at-Tijani in order to seize Ain Madhi in the Sahara. He perhaps needed the town as a further fall back position in the future struggle, but the pro-French politics of the Tijanis must have been a prime consideration. Nevertheless, it was a serious division within the Algerian coalition, one which also cost him dearly in men, materials, and prestige.

While the French had consolidated their holdings in Algeria, 'Abd al-Qādir had built himself a state. Within this state the precepts of Islam were upheld; a hierarchy existed from 'Abd al-Qādir to Khalifas to Aghas who administered Khalifaliks and Aghaliks down to Caids. A significant improvement was the existence of salaried Judges; under the Turks the Judges exacted their income from bribes of those judged. He could command perhaps 70,000 troops, but regular adherence could not be depended upon, although there was a regular army of some 6,000. This was an innovation as far as Arabs and Berbers were concerned, although the example could be found in the Turkish Janissary forces which was in fact the model, down to the institution of travelling Army Judges. There were attempts to create factories whose results were rudimentary and ultimately unsuccessful.

The campaign against him which began in 1840 eventually forced him to take refuge in Morocco. Because of harsh oppression by the French in the newly won territories, a widespread resistance came into being in 1845. This gave 'Abd al-Qādir new impetus for a while and led to some military successes. But eventually his situation became untenable; Moroccan support was withdrawn, and in 1847 'Abd al-Qādir, refusing to escape if it meant leaving his family behind instead surrendered to General de Lamoriciäre upon condition of being allowed to go to Alexandria, a commitment violated by the French government. He was imprisoned in the Château d'Amboise, France until 1852 when he was released by Louis-Napoléon and went into exile.

'Abd al-Qādir al-Jīlānī (*470-561*/1077-1166). One of the most celebrated Saints in Islam, 'Abd al-Qādir is the founder of the Qādiriyyah order of Sufis. He was born in the region of Jīlān in Persia but lived in Baghdad, where his tomb stands today.

A legend relates that when 'Abd al-Qādir's mother sent him to Baghdad, she enjoined him to be always truthful. She sewed gold pieces into his coat as a provision for his religious studies. When his band of fellow-travelers was stopped by robbers along the way he was asked – his poor appearance offering no promise of gain – if he had any money. To the astonishment of the robbers he told them the truth about the hidden gold. Later 'Abd al-Qādir told the robber chief that he despaired of attaining truth himself if, at the beginning of the search, he had lied. And this brought the robber chief to repent.

Another story, or allegory, tells that a sick man

called upon 'Abd al-Qādir to help him to sit upright. When the Saint helped him, the sick man miraculously grew to a great size, and explained that he was Islam itself, who had grown weak with the times but was now restored to health by 'Abd al-Qādir. (The idea that Islam needed Jīlānī rather than the reverse is curious because it places a Messianic emphasis upon a person.)

'Abd al-Qādir did not begin public preaching until after the fiftieth year of his life. He went on to found the *ṭarīqah* ("Sufi order" pl. *ṭuruq*), which bears his name. Al-Jīlāni was called the *quṭb* ("spiritual axis") of his age, and even the *Ghawīth al-A'ẓam* ("the greatest succor"), no doubt because he promised to come out from the unseen to the spiritual aid of any disciple who called upon him. The most famous words of 'Abd al-Qādir Jīlānī are to the effect: "in distress call upon me, and I will come on a white horse to help you". These are, in fact, words of Mithra in Yasht 10, line 55 of the Zoroastrian Gathas: "if they invoke me by name I will come to help them". Mithra was always mounted on a white horse. His most famous written work is a collection of exhortations called the *Futūḥ al-Ghayb* ("Revelations of the Unseen").

With al-Jīlānī the tradition begins of a group of Sufis holding a particular great man or Saint to be the founder of their way. Thus the Qādiriyyah is the first *ṭarīqah* to take on a distinct character, or, simply, the first *ṭarīqah* as such.

In the *Futūḥ al-Ghayb*, 'Abd al-Qādir said:

> Die, then, to creatures, by God's leave, and to your passions, by His command, and you will then be worthy to be the dwelling place of the knowledge of God. The sign of your death to creatures is that you detach yourself from them and do not look for anything from them. The sign that you have died to your passions is that you no longer seek benefit for yourself, or to ward off injury, and that you are not concerned about yourself, for you have committed all things to God. The sign that your will has been merged in the Divine Will is that you seek nothing of yourself or for yourself – God's Will is working in you. Give yourself up into the hands of God, like the ball of the polo-player, who sends it to and fro with the mallet, or like the dead body in the hands of the one who washes it, or like the child in its mother's bosom.

'Abd al-Wahhāb, Muḥammad, *see* WAHHĀBĪS.

'Abd ar-Raḥmān ibn 'Awf. A Companion of the Prophet and one of the ten to whom the Prophet explicitly promised paradise. 'Abd ar-Raḥmān led the dawn prayer on the expedition to Tabuk when the Prophet was late in coming to the congregation. When the Prophet arrived, he joined the prayer behind 'Abd ar-Raḥmān; the Prophet also prayed behind Abū Bakr in the last days of his mortal illness.

'Abduh, Muḥammad (*1265-1323*/1849-1905). An Egyptian religious reformer who sought to "modernize Islam" and rectify it through reason. He did not take all of the Koran to be Divinely inspired; what the Koran says of human institutions 'Abduh ascribed to the Prophet's thinking. He also advocated the precedence of reason over the literal meaning of the Koran in case of conflict between the two. This is, to say the least, completely un-traditional; the orthodox view is that all of the Koran is Divinely inspired, from beginning to end; not only Divinely inspired but the uncreated Word of God. But in the climate of Islam's casting about for "renaissance" (*naḥḍah*) in the face of material backwardness in regard to the West, 'Abduh's ideas appealed to those who wished to imitate the West without abandoning their heritage. The movement which embodied this reform was called the *Salafiyyah,* and Muḥammad 'Abduh was its most influential figure.

'Abduh had studied in Paris during a period of political exile. There, he associated briefly with the political agitator Jamāl ad-Dīn al-Afghānī and they founded a political/religious society called *al-'Urwah al-Wuthqa* ("The Unbreakable Bond") and published a periodical called *al-Manār* ("The Minaret"). In 1885 'Abduh and al-Afghānī parted company, when 'Abduh went to Beirut and taught theology at the Madrasah Sulṭāniyyah. He returned to Egypt in 1888 and became Grand Mufti of Egypt in 1889. In 1894 'Abduh became a member of the Supreme Council of the al-Azhar University and in 1897 published his book on theology and law entitled *Risālat at-Tawḥīd* ("The Message of Unity"). *See* SALAFIYYAH.

Abenragel, *see* AR-RIJĀL.

Abjad. A traditional system of calculation based upon the correspondence of each letter of the Arabic alphabet with a number. The letters representing numbers are placed into a diagram of squares which make up a larger square (the figure is related to a "magic square"). The letters are then transposed from one square to another in the diagram according to a certain algorithm or procedure which results in an arithmetical operation of multiplication or division. The square is also used for divination since the letters, while signifying numbers, also produce words. In another approach, the substitution of numbers for letters and then other letters of the same numerical value is a method of mystical exegesis known as the *'Ilm al-Ḥurūf*, similar to the Hebrew Gematria. (*See* 'ILM al-ḤURŪF.)

Abjad order rather than alphabetical order is used when the letters are used as ordinals. That is, a, b, c, d, as ordinals would in Arabic be *alif, ba', jim, dal* (instead of *alif, ba', ta', tha'*, which is Arabic alphabetical order today).

The *abjad* values are:

1	2	3	4	5	6	7	8
أ	ب	ج	د	ه	و	ز	ح
9	10	20	30	40	50	60	70
ط	ي	ك	ل	م	ن	س	ع
80	90	100	200	300	400	500	600
ف	ص	ق	ر	ش	ت	ث	خ
700	800	900	1000				
ز	ض	ظ	غ				

The mnemonic formula is:

أبجَدْ هَوَّزَ حُطّي كَلَمنْ
سَعْفَصْ قرشَتْ ثخذ ضَطَغْ

Ablutions. There are three kinds of ablution which symbolically restore the believer to a state of equilibrium or purity and, for the purposes of ritual, do so effectively.

The first is *ghusl* ("greater ablution"). This involves a ritual washing of the whole body, which removes the impurities (called *junub* or *janābah*) that are the consequences of: sexual intercourse; intromission; ejaculation with or without coitus; menstruation; childbirth; major bloodletting; and contact with a corpse. The performance of *ghusl* also accompanies conversion to Islam and the putting on of *iḥrām* (consecration for pilgrimage). One must also be in a state of *ghusl* before one can enter a mosque or an area purified for prayer (*see* PURIFICATION), or touch an Arabic Koran.

The second kind of ablution is the *wuḍū'* ("lesser ablution") which removes the impurities which are called *aḥdāth*. These include impurities in the state of the individual caused by: the bodily functions, breaking wind, touching a dog, minor bleeding (but not as small as insect bites), and by loss of consciousness or an interval of sleep. It is the *wuḍū'*, a brief washing of the hands, face, and feet, which is performed before the canonic prayer (*ṣalāt*), but only if the state conferred by *ghusl* has not been lost.

The third kind of ablution is *tayammum* where – through lack of, or legitimate aversion to, water – a substitute of sand, earth, or unfashioned stone, is used in the place of water in a single, special ritual which replaces either the *wuḍū'*, or *wuḍū'* and *ghusl* together. For descriptions, see GHUSL; WUḌŪ'; TAYAMMUM.

Abortion. This is acceptable in Islam, according to most theologians, as long as the foetus is not fully formed; a state which is said to occur 120 days after conception, as described by the fourth ḥadīth of Nawāwī which summarizes the states of foetal development:

> Verily the creation of each one of you is brought together in his mother's belly for forty days in the form of a seed (*nuṭfah*), then he is a clot of blood (*'alaqah*) for a like period, then a morsel of flesh for a like period (*mudhghah*), then there is sent to him the angel who blows the breath of life into him.

The breath of life is the ensoulment which was the critical issue for medieval theologians. To call the foetus a human being before this point would have been the same as to equate a possibility with an actuality, or to equate non-existence with existence. It is against this that Aristotle's law of non-contradiction, the first law of reality is set. Or as the theologian Sa'd ad-Dīn at-Taftāzānī (d. *175*/791) insisted: possibility is not a thing. The Ḥanafīs permitted abortion until the fourth month and many Shāfi'īs and Ḥanbalīs did also. The Mālikīs make abortion before the fourth month discouraged (*makrūh*) but most did not make it prohibited (*ḥarām*) until after the fourth month.

The doctrine of ensoulment after 120 days was held by the Catholic Church as well, but in the 19th century was de-emphasized as inopportune precisely because it was recognized it would be used to justify abortion. The idea is consistent with the traditional view, expressed as early as Aristotle, that the soul attaches itself to the foetus out of the unseen at a precise moment around 120 days after conception, and that only with the soul attached has the foetus become a human being. Abortions performed before the term of 120 days are therefore acceptable; others would prolong the term still further. In any case, no objections are raised to abortions performed after this moment if their aim is to safeguard the health or safety of the mother. There is an increase in vociferous anti-abortion polemics in the Islamic world, just as in the Christian world, because Fundamentalism corresponds to a rebirth of Mu'tazilite-like or dualist tendencies that can be seen in all religions at the present time. *See* BIRTH CONTROL.

Abrahah. The Christian viceroy of the Negus of Abyssinia, who ruled the Yemen in the middle of the 6th century A.D. He undertook a campaign against the North Arabians and marched against Mecca. Because he brought an elephant with his army, the year of the campaign became known among the Arabs as the "Year of the Elephant", traditionally identified as the year 570, and as the year of the Prophet's birth. Al-Ma'sūdī says that three years after the campaign against Mecca, the Persians invaded the Yemen and Abrahah was killed by a Persian general named Wahriz "in the 45th year of the reign of Anushirwan" (Chosroe I), which corroborates the date within three years. However, some modern scholars believe that the campaign must have taken place a decade or more earlier. In any case, as far as Abrahah's campaign is concerned, the date is likely to be no more than approximate which, as a significant event, became nonetheless a reference point in time. Such reference points were not treated with precision, and many other events were cumulated around the one which stood out in memory.

The invasion by the "Army of the Elephant" is mentioned in Sūrah 105:

> Hast thou seen how thy Lord did with the Men
> of the Elephant?
> Did He not make their guile go astray?
> And He loosed upon them birds in flight
> Hurling against them stones of baked clay
> and He made them like green blades devoured.

(The stones of baked clay may refer to ancient cuneiform tablets, which the Arabs must have come upon frequently.) Before Abrahah's army was driven off, 'Abd al-Muṭṭalib, the grandfather of the Prophet, came out of Mecca to parley with him. Tradition relates that he asked only for the return of his camels which had been captured, saying: "as for the Holy House [the Ka'bah] it has its Master who will protect it."

Abrahah had built a magnificent church in Sa'na', the chief city of the Yemen, which was called *al-Qalīs* (from the Greek *ekklesia,* also Arabized as al-*Qulays*). A possible motive for the campaign against Mecca may have been to remove the Ka'bah as a rival to his church. After the unexpected failure of his campaign, the Persians regained control of the Yemen until the advent of Islam.

Columns from this church were used by 'Abd Allāh ibn az-Zubayr in the rebuilding of the Ka'bah in 64/683. *See* 'ABD al-MUṬṬALIB.

Abraham (Ar. *Ibrāhīm*). Abraham is the ancient patriarch of Islam, as he is of Judaism. He is also the ancestor of the Prophet, who is his descendant through Abraham's son Ishmael (*Ismā'īl*). The Koran names both Abraham and Ishmael as Divine Messengers (*rasūl*, pl. *rusul*), and together they rebuilt the Ka'bah in Mecca (traditionally founded first by Adam). Abraham established the pilgrimage to Mecca calling mankind to the "ancient house" (*al-bayt al-'atīq*).

The Koran says:

> And when We appointed the House to be
> a place of visitation for the people,
> and a sanctuary,
> and: 'Take to yourselves Abraham's station
> for a place of prayer.' And We made covenant
> with Abraham and Ishmael: 'Purify
> My House for those that shall go about it
> and those that cleave to it, to those who bow
> and prostrate themselves.' (2:118-119)

> And when Abraham, and Ishmael with him,
> raised up the foundations of the House:
> 'Our Lord, receive this from us; Thou art
> the All-hearing , the All-knowing;
> and, our Lord, make us submissive to Thee,
> and of our seed a nation submissive
> to Thee; and show us our holy rites, and
> turn towards us; surely 'Thou turnest, and art
> All-compassionate.' (2:122-123)

The Koran (3:67) says that Abraham was neither Jew, nor Christian, but a submitted *ḥanīf* ("adherent to perennial Monotheism"), and he was not of the "idolators". According to this description, Abraham represents primordial man in universal surrender to the Divine Reality before its fragmentation into religions separated from each other by differences in form. This religion of Abraham is a reconsecration, a restoration of the *fiṭrah,* or primordial "norm", a spontaneous and sacred conformity to reality that is not externalized – and thus necessarily reduced – to the level of a law; it is called in the Koran *millat Ibrāhīm* ("the creed of Abraham").

Islam necessarily has a form because it has a codified law, established ritual, creed, dogma, and so forth, but inwardly, in its essence, Islam sees itself as a restoration of the primordial tradition of Abraham. For example, when the believer performs the canonical prayer (*aṣ-ṣalat*), he does so not as an individual but as a patriarch, or rather, in the name of the entire human species. In other words, in ritual the individual acts not as this or another man, but becomes the representative of mankind, or "universal man".

The primordiality of Abraham abolishes idolatory. The Koran says:

> When he said to his father and his people,
> 'What are these statues unto which
> you are cleaving?'
> They said, 'We found our fathers
> serving them.'
> He said, 'Then assuredly you
> and your fathers have been in
> manifest error.'
> They said, 'What, hast thou come to us
> with the truth, or art thou one of
> those that play?'
> He said, 'Nay, but your Lord
> is the Lord of the heavens and the earth
> who originated them, and I
> am one of those that bear witness
> thereunto.'
> So he broke them into fragments. (21:53-58)

The traditional commentary to the story in Koran 21:53-70 is that before a festival to idols Abraham went to his people's temple and cut off the limbs and heads of some of the idols and set the sword he had used by the side of the largest idol. When the destruction was discovered Abraham accused the largest idol of the act and told the people: "But this, their chief has done it, so question them if they can speak." But the people threw Abraham into a fire from which he emerged unharmed because God said: "O fire, be coolness and peace for Abraham" (cf. Genesis 15:17: "And it came to pass, that, when the sun went down, and it was dark, behold a smoking furnace, and a burning lamp that passed between those pieces").

The Arabs, as descendants of Abraham, inherited his monotheism, as did the Jews. They continued to practice this monotheism, unchanged by the revelations of Moses and Jesus until, figuratively speaking, the "water in the goatskin" which Abraham gave to Hagar, the mother of Ishmael, the mother of the Arabs, was spent (Genesis 21:15). But as "God heard" Ishmael (the name means "God hears"), and the spring of Zamzam gushed from the earth saving the mother and child from death by thirst, God also "heard" Muḥammad, when the Abrahamic spirituality had "dried up", and idolatry had overtaken the Arab spirit. At the lament of the descendant of Ishmael, Muḥammad, who was wont to go for month-long retreats on a mountain near Mecca, the spring of revelation gushed forth again, the Koran was revealed and Islam came into the world as the restoration, and extension of Abraham's religion. *See* HAGAR; ḤANĪF; ISMĀʿĪL; PROPHETS; TALBIYYAH.

Abrogation, *see* NASKH.

Abū Ayyūb. One of the Companions of the Prophet, Abū Ayyūb was a standard bearer of the Prophet who, at a very advanced age and long after the Prophet's death, took part in an attack on Constantinople in *49*/669 (the date *59*/678 is also sometimes given), where he was killed. In Turkey he is known as Eyüp Sultan. His tomb on the outskirts of Istanbul is greatly venerated.

When, in 857/1453, the Turks under Mehmet Nāṣir laid siege to the city, a legend grew up that they were rallied by a light coming from the tomb, which was discovered in a vision by Shaykh ash- Shams ad-Dīn at the outset of the final siege.

The Ottoman Sultans were girded at the tomb with the sword of ʿUthmān or Osman, the founder of the dynasty, who had been himself girded with a sword by his father-in-law Shaykh Edebali, a dervish. The ceremony of the investiture of office was performed by the Imām of the mosque of Ayyūb and the

Buyuk Chelebi, the head of the Mevlevi Dervish order.

Abubacer, *see* IBN TUFAYL.

Abū Bakr. The first Caliph, who held together the Muslim community after the death of the Prophet and consolidated Islam's victories in Arabia. Originally a rich merchant of Mecca he was the second, after Khadījah, to believe in the mission of the Prophet and accompanied him on his escape from Mecca (see HIJRAH). Celebrated as being the closest personal friend of the Prophet and as having an unswerving loyalty to him and an unshakeable belief in every aspect of the prophetic mission, he was known as *Aṣ-Ṣiddīq* ("the faithful"), he replaced the Prophet as Imām to lead the prayers during the Prophet's last illness. His daughter, 'Ā'ishah was the favorite wife of the Prophet. During the early days of Islam, Abū Bakr used his wealth to help the Muslim community through its difficult times and brought freedom for slaves who were persecuted for their belief in Islam. One such ransomed slave, Bilāl, later became famous as the muezzin of the Prophet.

Long before his conversion Abū Bakr had been well respected among the Quraysh and was known to possess the art of interpreting dreams, for which the Meccans often turned to him. His real name was 'Abd Allāh; Abū Bakr ("father of the maiden") is a *kunyah,* a paternity name, in virtue of its indirectness, a respect name. He is mentioned in the Koran as the "second of the two who lay in the cave", in reference to the cave in Mount Thawr where he and the Prophet hid from the Meccan search party on the Hijrah. Of the Prophet's contemporaries, the Koran makes such direct reference only to the Prophet, Abū Bakr and a blind man who importuned the Prophet.

After Abū Bakr was elected Caliph in *11*/632, 'Umar (who became the second Caliph) saw him going to the market place to sell cloth, which was his commerce as a merchant. 'Umar assured him that in view of his office as the head of the Muslim nation it was no longer necessary for him to pursue his trade, and that the public treasury would provide a "middling pension...a winter garment and one for summer..." and a sheep's side a day for provender. Abū Bakr died in the second year of his Caliphate in *13*/634. He is considered to be one of the two who transmitted from the Prophet the esoteric doctrines later know as Taṣawwuf, the other being 'Alī ibn Abī Ṭālib.

Abū Ḥanīfah al-Nu'mān ibn Thābit ibn Zūṭā (*81-150*/700-767). The founder of the Ḥanafī School of Law, which today has the largest following among the Muslim community. Abū Ḥanīfah, a Persian, was one of the great jurists of Islam and one of the historic Sunnī *Mujtahids.* He was born in Kufah in Iraq, and died in Baghdad. Like Mālik ibn Anas, founder of the Mālikī School of Law, Abū Ḥanīfah studied with Ja'far as-Sādiq in Medina, as well as with other teachers elsewhere.

Abū Ḥanīfah was the grandson of a slave captured during the conquest of Kabul, and set free as a *mawlā* ("client") by his captor, who was a member of the Taymallah tribe. Abū Ḥanīfah lived by trading silk in Kufah in Iraq, where he taught religious studies. Although the school of law which bears his name is known for the breadth of its interpretations, he himself may have been a rather more strict traditionalist. Probably because he had been a supporter of a Zaydi revolt, Abū Ḥanīfah died in prison. His followers later ascribed to him a geneology which made him a descendant of the ancient Persian Kings; he is pictured as refusing an invitation to serve the Umayyads as religious judge. Under the 'Abbāsids, however, his followers readily entered government service, and gained favour by a willingness to accommodate the needs of the ruling princes in matters of law. Abū Yūsuf, who wrote a treatise on the law of land tax, became the first Supreme Judge (*Qāḍī 'l Quḍāh*) in Islam under the Caliph Hārūn ar-Rashīd, and gained official sanction for what became known as the Ḥanīfi School of Law. *See* SCHOOLS of LAW; SHARĪ'AH.

Abū Ḥimār, *see* BŪ ḤAMĀRAH; DHŪ-l-ḤIMĀR.

Abū Hurayrah (lit. "the father of the kitten"). A Companion of the Prophet, very fond of cats, whose real name was 'Abd ar-Raḥmān ad-Dawsi. He is the source of more Ḥadīth than any other individual, and is the link in a number of initiatic chains.

Abū Jahl (lit. "father of ignorance"). A prominent enemy of Islam among the Quraysh.

His hostility earned him the apellation of father of ignorance from the Muslims, but his real name was 'Amr ibn Hisham. He was killed in the Battle of Badr in *2*/624.

Abū Lahab (lit. "father of flame"). His real name was 'Abd al-'Uzzā. Although he was an uncle of the Prophet, he was, nevertheless, a violent enemy of Islam. Before the Prophet's mission, however, Abū Lahab's sons, 'Utbah and 'Utaybah, had married the Prophet's daughters, Ruqayyah and Umm Kulthūm. With the advent of Islam, these marriages were annulled because neither son accepted the religion.

At the death of Abū Ṭālib, Abū Lahab became the head of the Banu Hāshim clan and withdrew clan protection from the Prophet, thus precipitating the Hijrah, the Prophet's migration to Medina. Abū Lahab died shortly after the Battle of Badr.

Abū Madyan, Shuayb ibn al-Ḥusayn al-'Ansārī (*520-594*/1126-1198). A famous Sufi Saint born near Seville and buried in the village of al-'Ubbād, also called "Sidi Boumedienne", on the outskirts of Tlemcen, Algeria. He came from a poor family in Spain; when young he was a shepherd; in Morocco, to learn a trade, he became apprenticed to a weaver. It was only much later in life that he fulfilled his wish to learn to read and write.

To search for teachers of esoteric doctrine, he went first to Tangiers and later to Fez, where his master was Abū-l-Ḥasan ibn Harzihim. In Fez he supported himself by weaving but lived in such extreme poverty that a story is told of how his fellow disciples made a contribution of money which they hid in his clothes. At night he went, as was his custom, to meditate on the side of the Zalagh mountain outside Fez, a spot called today the *Khalwah* ("retreat") of Abū Madyan. A gazelle would always come to him there. On the night that the money had been sewn into his robe, the gazelle avoided him and the village dogs barked. Thus alerted, he discovered the money and threw it away saying: "it was because of this uncleanness that the gazelle fled." The famous story, if somewhat an exaggeration – money is the means of the living for which he labored – depicts Abū Madyan's independence of things of this world and his identification with the *fiṭrah*, or primordial norm.

Abū Madyan then became the disciple of a master called Abū Ya'zzah Yalannur ibn Maymūn al-Gharbī (d. *572*/1177), a Dukkala Berber, who lived at Fez and at Taghyah. The famous Sufi 'Abd al-Qādir al-Jīlānī whom, it is said, Abū Madyan met in Mecca, is also numbered among Abū Madyan's teachers. Abū Madyan eventually settled in Bijayah (Bougie) in present day Algeria where a circle of disciples gathered around him. He became famous for miraculous knowledge of the Unseen, both in the world at large and within men. He wrote poetry in the style of his native Andalusia.

Abū Madyan is called the *Qutb al-Ghawth*, which means the (spiritual) "Axis of Succor". The "Pole" or "Axis" is a person who is the expression of a central spiritual presence in the world. Even in the 19th century, the tradition of turning in need to Abu Madyan was exemplified by the instruction of the Shaykh al-Buzīdī (the Darqawi Shaykh of the Shaykh al-'Alawī): "If you cannot find a spiritual master go and pray at the tomb of Abū Madyan." Ibn Arabi referred to him as "his master" and "the proclaimer of the spiritual path in the West". Today he can be considered a "patron saint" of Algeria. *See* QUṬB.

Abū Muslim (d. *134*/755). The leader of the Khorasan coalition that brought the 'Abbāsids to power by overthrowing the Umayyads. He was a Persian, probably from Isfahan. Shahrastani said that Abū Muslim was a Kaysani, that is, an adherent of an earlier revolutionary movement of the end of the 7th century that centered on Kufah. In Kufah Abū Muslim took Islam and became the client of Ibrahim ibn Muḥammad and was sent back to Khorasan as his propagandist (*dā'i*). Because of Abū Muslim many in Khorasan took Islam, or appeared to, since he apparently had another, secret doctrine, which was quite different. After the success of the 'Abbāsid revolution he appears to have declared his own divinity to his followers. He had a follower named Hāshim al-Muqanna who did the same, Many legends describe his entry into paradise after death with a ritual of basil and butter, which is related to Zoroastrianism or Persian popular belief.

Abū Muslim unfurled the black flag of the 'Abbāsids in Khorasan with the motto "Felicity will come from the People of the House". The revolt was declared before the end of Ramadan. (The breaking of a fast is symbolically the pronouncing of a secret). The 'Abbāsids became so closely associated with Khorasan that the litterateur al-Jahiz and others called the 'Abbāsids a foreign Khorasanian dynasty (*dawlah ajami khorasani*). The term "People of the House" could be a translation of a Manichean Buddhist term (Balkh in Khorasan was a center of Buddhism) *Buddhagotra*, family or house of the Buddha, from Sanskrit *gotra*, house or family; this term is given to the light suffering in this world, the "Living Soul" – *viva anima* in Augustine, a designation which can be traced back to 1 Corinthians 15;45 "The first man Adam, became a living soul."

"On the night of 25 Ramadan 129 (10 June 747), the inhabitants of Safidhanj, a village on the outskirts of Merv, witnessed a remarkable spectacle, part religious convocation and part political demonstration. The Khuzaṭi shaykh of the village, Sulayman b. Kathir, led a group of men dressed completely in black to a place of assemblage near his residence. There they proceeded to raise two large black banners, one which they named 'the shadow' on a pole fourteen cubits long and another, called 'the clouds,' on a pole thirteen cubits long. As they did so, a newcomer in the village known as Abū Muslim chanted a verse from the Koran: 'Leave is given to those who fight because they were wronged; surely God is able to help them' (22:39). They then kindled bonfires, and in response, men from surrounding villages, also robed in black, left their homes to join their comrades in Safidhanj."

After the 'Abbāsids came to power, al-Mansur invited Abū Muslim to Iraq and had him murdered. Favorable legends surrounded him in Iran. *See* 'ABBĀSIDS.

Abū Nuaym al-Isbahānī, *see* ḤILYAT al-AWLIYĀ'.

Abū Nuwās (d. *195*/810). A poet, whose real name was Ḥasan ibn Hānī. He was a Persian who became a protégé of Hārūn ar-Rashīd, the famous 'Abbāsid Caliph. Abū Nuwās was a *bon vivant* who, enjoying drinking and high living, has become famous in folklore as a kind of "court jester" to the Caliph. Various stories, jokes, and irreverent remarks are attributed to his wit, in addition to the poetry he actually composed.

Abū Sa'id Aḥmad ibn 'Īsā-l-Kharrāz (d. *286*/899). A famous Sufi of Baghdad who wrote one of the first systematic expositions of Sufism, the *Kitāb as-Ṣidq* ("The Book of Truthfulness"), which takes the form of questions to a master and his answers.

> I said: "Is love according to the number of blessings?"
> He replied: "The beginning of love is the recollection of blessings: then it proceeds according to the capacity of its recipient, that is, according to his deserts. For the true lover of God loves God both when receiving His blessings, and when His blessings are withheld: in every state he loves Him with a true love, whether He withholds or grants, afflicts or spares him. Love invariably attaches to his heart, according to his compact [with God]: except that it is nearer to superfluity [it is better to love more than to love less]. For if love went according to the number of blessings received, it would diminish when the blessings diminish, in times of hardship and when affliction befalls. But he is God's lover whose mind is distraught for his Lord, and who is only concerned to please Him: when he is grateful to God, and when he recollects Him, he is bewildered, as though no blessing ever descended on any man but it descended on him also. His love for God distracts him from all [concern with] creation. The love of God has banished from his heart all pride, rancor, envy, iniquity, and much that concerns his advantage in the affairs of this world – and how much more the recollection of what concerns him not!"

Abū Sufyān. The prominent and wealthy Meccan merchant who led the opposition to the Prophet and conducted some of the military campaigns against him. His wife Hind was also numbered among the fiercest opponents of Islam, and she and Abū Sufyān were among the last to be converted when Mecca was finally occupied by the Muslims. Ironically, it was the descendants of Abū Sufyān who constituted the first dynasty, the Umayyads, who ruled the Islamic Empire after the death of the four "rightly guided Caliphs" (*al-Khulafā' ar-Rāshidūn*).

Abū Ṭālib. An uncle of the Prophet and father of 'Alī ibn Abī Ṭālib, the fourth Caliph. Abū Ṭālib became the head of the clan of the Banū Hāshim, to which the Prophet belonged, at the time of the

Prophet's mission. As clan chief, Abū Ṭālib extended the clan's protection to the Prophet against the enmity of the Quraysh. He had also been the guardian of the Prophet after the death of 'Abd al-Muṭṭalib.

When Abū Ṭālib died in 619, another uncle, Abū Lahab, became the chief of the clan. Abū Lahab, an implacable enemy of the Prophet, withdrew the clan's protection from him, thus exposing the life of the Prophet to danger. This change in his circumstances forced the Prophet to emigrate to Mecca for his safety.

Abyssinia (Ar. *Ḥabashah*). Modern day Ethiopia. The Abyssinians are related to the Semites and their language, Amharic, is ultimately cognate with Arabic. The Abyssinians are an ancient Christian nation whose church is Monophysite, as is the Coptic church of Egypt; the Abyssinian Patriarch formerly resided in Alexandria and now in Addis Ababa. In the sixth century, when the Jewish Himyaritic King Dhū Nuwās (Yusūf As'ar) destroyed the Christians of Najrān in southern Arabia, the Negus, or King, of Abyssinia Ella Aṣbeḥa assembled an army to punish him on behalf of the Byzantine Emperor, whose natural role was protector of all Christians.

The Prophet said of Abyssinia that it was "a land of sincerity in religion". Before the Hijrah, some eighty Muslims, including the Prophet's daughter Ruqayyah and her husband 'Uthmān, emigrated to Abyssinia, where they were received by the Negus and given refuge. The Quraysh sent two emissaries to persuade the Negus to reject the Muslim emigrants as outlaws. To confound the accusations of the Quraysh against them, the leader of the emigrants, Ja'far ibn Abī Ṭālib, recited to the Negus the verses of the Koran which speak of Mary (19:16-24):

> And mention in the Book Mary
> when she withdrew from her people
> to an eastern place,
> and she took a veil apart from them;
> then We sent unto her Our Spirit
> that presented himself to her
> a man without fault.
> She said, 'I take refuge in
> the All-merciful from thee!
> If thou fearest God ...'
> He said, 'I am but a messenger
> come from thy Lord, to give thee
> a boy most pure.'
> She said, 'How shall I have a son
> whom no mortal has touched, neither
> have I been unchaste?'
> He said, 'Even so thy Lord has said:
> "Easy is that for Me; and that We
> may appoint him a sign unto men
> and a mercy from Us; it is
> a thing decreed."'
> So she conceived him, and withdrew with him
> to a distant place.

This recitation convinced the Abyssinians that the Muslims had received a revelation akin to their own.

The sanctuary the Abyssinians gave the Muslim refugees has been cited as the reason why the Arabs in their conquests to spread Islam did not invade that country. Certainly, there is much historical evidence that great sympathy existed between the Negus and the Prophet. In 625, the Negus performed a ceremony in Abyssinia marrying Ḥafsah, daughter of the Companion 'Umar, to the Prophet by proxy; she then went to Medina. Later, when news that the Negus had died reached Medina, the Prophet performed the Muslim funeral prayer for him.

'Ād. A great and ancient people frequently mentioned in the Koran, "who built monuments upon high places". They were the recipients of a Divine Message brought to them by the Prophet Hūd (7:63 and 26:123-135), upon the rejection of which, they were destroyed by God. Their city, or perhaps their tribe was also called "Iram of the pillars" (or perhaps "tent-poles"). Whether 'Ād and "Iram of the pillars" are one and the same depends upon one's interpretation of the Koran 89:6-7; the identification cannot be definitively established.

'Ād is usually placed in the south of Arabia but commentators on the Koran say, doubtless in a symbolical sense, that the Israelites had to fight remnants of the tribe of 'Ād when they entered the Holy Land. 'Ād is considered to be one of the tribes of the original Arabs, the so-called "lost Arabs" (*'Arab al-bāidah*). *See* ARABS.

Adab (lit. "courtesy", "politeness", "propriety", "morals"; also "literature"). An important subject in traditional literature. Al-Hujwīrī wrote as follows:

> The Apostle of God said:
> "Good breeding is a part of faith."
> The beauty and propriety of all affairs, religious as well as temporal, depends on a certain discipline of breeding. Humanly, it consists in noble-mindedness; religiously, in observing the Sunnah; in love, good breeding is reverence. A person who neglects this discipline cannot ever possibly be a saint, for the Prophet said:
> "Good breeding is a mark of those God loves."
> Towards God, one must keep oneself from disrespect in one's private as well as one's public behavior. We have it from a sound Ḥadīth that once, when God's Apostle was sitting with his legs akimbo, [the Angel] Gabriel appeared and said: "Muḥammad, sit as servants sit before a master."
> For forty years Muhasibi never sat, but always knelt.
> "I am ashamed", he replied when questioned, "to sit otherwise than as a servant while I think of God."
> Towards oneself, one must avoid what would be improper with a fellow creature or with God. For instance, a man must not lie, representing himself to himself as what he is not... In social intercourse the best rule is to act nobly and observe the Sunnah. Human companionship must be for God's sake, not for the soul's sake nor for interest. He is a bad companion, said Razi, to whom you have to say:
> "Remember me in your prayers". And he is a bad companion with whom you must flatter or apologize.

In modern times, no less than in the past, great importance is placed in Islam upon proper greetings on meeting and parting. "When you enter houses greet one another" (24:61). The shaking of hands, sitting in such a way as to avoid pointing the soles of one's feet at anyone, not laughing raucously, and a general sobriety of attitude are also insisted upon.

Arabs of the desert – as opposed to sedentary Arabs – normally avoid any physical contact other than handshaking. *Adab* also requires a person to join in the carrying of a bier in a funeral procession, to visit the sick, and to assist those in distress. In general, it is also a part of *adab* that the right side of the body be given precedence over the left in all things. Especially, it is the left hand which is used for unclean things and it is imperative that only the right hand be offered in greetings and used in eating.

Arab rules of hospitality – not specifically Islamic – make it a dishonor to refuse lodging and food to anyone presenting themselves at one's door; but, by custom, such obligations end after three days. When a guest is received by someone it is unthinkable for the guest to refuse at least one cup of tea or coffee. Later glasses may be subtly declined by putting a finger over the cup and rocking it from side to side. In the Arab West, a third glass of tea may be, according to context, a signal from the host that the visit has reached its end. In Arab societies and some others, one offers an invitation to come, to partake, or to do something, three times at one session and the recipient refuses twice, the first two invitations being considered *pro forma*, and of politeness only, and the third, serious.

As refusal can cause acute embarrassment in many traditional societies, requests of others are often made through go-betweens. This practice allows frank discussions to be held through third parties which otherwise would be difficult face-to-face between persons actually involved. *See* GREETINGS.

Adam (Ar. *Ādam*). The first man and father of mankind. All Arab genealogies go back to the Prophets and finally to Adam and then say: "and God made him of clay". Adam is also vicegerent of God on earth (*khalīfatu Llāhi fī-l-arḍ*; *see* CALIPH). He is the first Prophet and builder of the original Ka'bah.

Created by God in His Image (*alā ṣūratihi* according to the Ḥādith related by Ibn Ḥanbal in the *Musnad*), and from earth, Adam was taught the names of all things, which the Angels themselves did not know (2:28-31). As the central being within manifestation, or creation, he actually contained manifestation within himself; this is symbolized by his knowledge of the names; the Angels, not being "central", did not "know" the names.

Adam dwelt at first in the Garden of Eden with his wife Eve (Ar. *Ḥawwā'*), who had been created from a rib taken from his left side. They disobeyed the Divine command and ate the fruit of the forbidden tree. In Islam, however, the responsibility of this sin lies not with man but with *Iblīs*, the Devil, who tempted Adam.

In Christianity, the redemption of the Fall – the sin of wishing to see the world as contingency, in its limitation, rather than in its essence as a prolongation of the Absolute – is effectual through Jesus; the Fall is seen as a fault of the will. By Jesus's sacrifice for man and by man's for Jesus, in denying himself in order to accept Jesus, the Fall is redeemed. In Islam, the Fall is the error of seeing the world and the ego as real instead of God, who alone is Real. Thus the redemption from the Fall lies within the *shahādah,* in realizing the truth that there is no god, or autonomous reality, but Allāh. The affirmation of the *shahādah* in principle corrects virtually the effect of the Fall, and its complete realization within the soul restores man effectively to his original state, that of Adam before the Fall. The Fall clouds the grasp of reality; it introduces reasoning in the place of direct knowledge; the *shahādah* restores the lost direct awareness of the absoluteness of God; it places man back in the Garden of Eden.

> We created you, then We shaped you,
> then We said to the angels: 'Bow yourselves
> to Adam'; so they bowed themselves,
> save Iblis – he was not of those
> that bowed themselves.
> Said He, 'What prevented thee to
> bow thyself, when I commanded thee?'
> Said he, 'I am better than he; Thou
> createdst me of fire, and him Thou
> createdst of clay.'
> Said He, 'Get thee down out of it;
> it is not for thee to wax proud here,
> so go thou forth; surely thou art
> among the humbled.'
> Said he, 'Respite me till the day
> they shall be raised.'
> Said He, 'Thou art among the ones
> that are respited.'
> Said he, 'Now, for Thy perverting me,
> I shall surely sit in ambush for them
> on Thy straight path;
> then I shall come on them from before them
> and from behind them, from their right hands
> and their left hands; Thou wilt not find
> most of them thankful.'
> Said He, Go thou forth from it, despised
> and banished. Those of them that follow
> thee – I shall assuredly fill Gehenna
> with all of you.'
>
> 'O Adam, inherit thou and thy wife,
> the Garden, and eat of where you will,
> but come not nigh this tree, lest you be
> of the evildoers.'
> Then Satan whispered to them, to reveal
> to them that which was hidden from them
> of their shameful parts. He said, 'Your Lord
> has only prohibited you from this tree
> lest you become angels or lest you
> become immortals.'
> And he swore to them, 'Truly, I am for you
> a sincere adviser.'
> So he led them on by delusion; and when
> they tasted the tree, their shameful parts
> revealed to them, so they took to stitching
> upon themselves leaves of the Garden.
> And their Lord called to them, 'Did not I
> prohibit you from this tree, and say
> to you, "Verily Satan is for you
> a manifest foe"?'
> They said, 'Lord, we have wronged ourselves,
> and if Thou dost not forgive us, and
> have mercy upon us, we shall surely be
> among the lost.' (7:10-23)

Adat. (lit. "normative custom" a Malay word derived from Ar.*'ādah*). In Indonesia, Malaysia, and the Philippines, adat denotes those regional customs and practices which are usually unwritten, but which nonetheless have the force of social law alongside Islamic law (*sharī'ah*), and the civil code. Customary laws exist everywhere in the Islamic world, to some degree. The form *'ādah* is common in other parts of the Islamic world for such customary laws. *See* SHARĪ'AH.

Adhān. The call to prayer, which is made one or more times by the muezzin from a minaret, a rooftop, or simply from the door of the place of prayer about a quarter of an hour before the prayer begins. The words of the *adhān* are:
1. *Allāhu Akbar* ("God is greater") – four times.
2. *Ashhadu an[l] lā 'ilāha illā-Llāh* ("I witness that there is no god but Allāh") – twice.
3. *Ashhadu anna Muḥammadān rasūlu-Llāh* ("I witness that Muḥammad is the Messenger of God") – twice.
4. *Ḥayya 'ala-ṣ-ṣalāh* ("Rise up for prayer") – twice.
5. *Ḥayya 'ala-l-falāḥ* ("Rise up for salvation") – twice.
6. *Allāhu Akbar* ("God is greater") – twice.
7. *Lā ilāha illa-Llāh* ("There is no god but God") – once.

The word "Akbar" means "greater than all" and can be translated as "Most great"; there is no specific superlative from the adjective in Arabic.

[1]The rules of euphony in Arabic, as in Koran chanting, call for the *nun* or *n* to be assimilated to a following letter having the same point of articulation. Thus the *an lā* in the*shahādah* is pronounced *al-lā* and*Muḥammadan rasūlu-Llah* is pronounced *Muḥammadar-rasūlu-Llāh.*

For the *ṣubḥ* (early morning) prayer the words: *aṣ-ṣalātu khayrun mina-n-nawm* ("Prayer is better than sleep") are inserted between *Hayya 'ala-l-falāḥ* and *Allāhu Akbar* (that is, between 5. and 6. above). Shī'ites, however, omit this because they believe it was added to the adhān by the Caliph 'Umar.

On the other hand, the Twelve-Imām and Zaydi Shī'ites add to every *adhān: Ḥayya 'alā khayri-l-amal,* "rise up for the best of works" (twice) which they believe was originally part of the call to prayer but was supressed by the Caliph 'Umar. And at the end, Twelve-Imām Shī'ites add: *'Alī walī Allāh,* "'Alī is the Saint of God" (once) and sometimes other formulas as well.

Once the believers have assembled inside the mosque, another call is given within as a signal to rise up and form rows immediately before the prayer begins. This interior call is known as the *iqāmah,* or "raising up". It differs from the *adhān* in that *Allāhu Akbar* (see 1. above) is repeated twice, rather than four times, and *Ḥayya 'ala-ṣ-ṣalāh* and *Ḥayya 'ala-l-falāḥ* (4. and 5.) are recited once each rather than twice. After this, and before the final two *Allāhu Akbar* (between 5. and 6.) the words: *qad qāmati-ṣ-ṣalātu, qad qāmati-ṣ-ṣalāh* ("the prayer is established, the prayer is established") are inserted.

In addition to the call, many mosques will display a white flag as a signal that the prayer is being called; at night, a lamp is lit on the top of the minaret to serve the same purpose.

'Adnān. A descendent of Ismā'īl and traditional ancestor of the North Arabian tribes: the Beduins of the northern and central deserts of the Arabian peninsula who called themselves the "sons of Adnān". The ancestor of the South Arabians is Qaḥṭān, the Joktan of the Bible.

Adultery, see ZĪNA.

Aesop, see LUQMĀN.

al-Afghānī, Jamāl ad-Dīn (*1254-1314*/1838-1897). A modernist, reformer, and political agitator. He was born in Iran but raised in Afghanistan, where he first attached himself to the royal court and rose to become a minister. After his patron fell, his political career became an Odyssey that led through lands as far apart as India and America, and gravitated towards fashionable society circles and centers of power in European and Oriental capitals. He was received by the heads of state in Cairo and Istanbul several times, where he was awarded government subsidies. An inveterate intriguer, al-Afghānī several times was forced to leave those courts which had shown him favor. His political aims were opportunistic rather than consistent. At one time or another he advocated the union of the Islamic countries under one Caliph; pressed for secular republican governments; sought the largesse of princes; called for their overthrow. He swam with the current, wherever it went. He twice ingratiated himself with the then Shah of Iran, Nāṣir ad-Dīn, and twice was expelled, the second time under military escort and in chains.

For a time he collaborated with Muḥammad 'Abduh in Paris in the publication of reformist Islamic periodicals. However, 'Abduh eventually broke with him. Right up until the end of his life al-Afghānī continued to exercise a fascination over the powerful. Shortly before his death in 1897 he received a pension and a house from the Ottoman Sultan 'Abd al-Ḥamīd, an autocrat who certainly did not respond favourably to the revolutionary proposals of al-Afghānī.

This political chameleon involved himself in perpetual intrigues, of which he always painted himself as the victim. The fascination he exercised as a politician derived from his skillful admixture and manipulation of religion and anarchy, conservatism and radical liberalism. Although he was accused of involvement in the murder of Shah Nāṣir ad-Dīn and of wishing to subvert the rule of his final patron, the Ottoman Sultan, al-Afghānī avoided human punitive retribution, succumbing to death by natural causes.

Afghanistan. Population 14,448,000 of which the overwhelming majority are Sunnī Muslims of the Ḥanafī rite. Twelve-Imām Shī'ites make up perhaps 15% of the population and there is a very small minority of Ismāʿīlīs, several thousands, mostly in the remote northern province of Badakshan. The Pashtun make up the ethnic majority and comprise over half of the population; a great many Pashtun live in northwest Pakistan where they are called Pathans. Other peoples within the Afghani population are the Baluchis, Tadjiks, Mongolian Hazaras, and Turkic peoples such as the Kirghiz, Turkmen, and Uzbeks. The most numerous Sufi *ṭarīqah* in Afghanistan is the Naqshbandiyyah, although the Qādiriyyah and Chishtiyyah are also widespread.

The so-called "Kāfirs" (unbelievers) of Afghanistan were actually remnants of an ancient Indo-European paganism. Once they were presumed to be converted their region was called Nūristān. Groups belonging to them can still be found in isolated places in Pakistan where they usually claim to be Muslims towards outsiders. The Hazaras are Turko-Mongols in Afghanistan and Central Asia whose name probably comes from Jenghiz Khan's division of his hord into companies of a thousand (Persian *hazar*). See MAḤMŪD of GHAZNAH.

Afsharids. An interim dynasty which ruled in Persia between *1148-1210*/ 1736-1795. As the previous Ṣafavid power declined and Persia was threatened by invasions from Afghanistan and the Ottomans, a leader appeared from a Turkmen tribe, the Afshar , one of the original tribes of the Qizil Bash. Nādir Shāh (d. *1154*-1741) was at first regent for the last Ṣafavids. A remarkably successful military leader, he preserved the territorial integrity of Persia from possible invaders, the Ottomans and the Afghans. Nādir Shāh captured Bukhara and Khiva and led campaigns against the Moghuls in India where he seized territory, pillaged mercilessly, and captured the peacock throne which he brought back from Delhi. After driving out the Ottoman Turks from Persia, Nādir Shāh had himself declared Shah by an assembly in *1149*/1736 which he called to nominate a ruler.

As a condition of his rule, Nādir Shāh attempted to make the Persians abandon what he called the "heresy of Ismāʿīl" (the first Ṣafavid ruler, who made Twelve-Imām Shiʿism the state religion). Nādir Shāh proposed to the Ottoman Turks that if the Persians eliminated the Imāmī element, becoming thereby Sunnī, the Ottomans should recognize Persian Islam as a fifth school of law (*madhhab*). The legitimacy of this Jaʿfarī School of Law would be confirmed by being accorded a maqām, or symbolic station, around the Kaʿbah in Mecca. In addition, the Persians would be allowed to lead a pilgrimage caravan along with the Syrians and the Egyptians. This plan was accepted neither by the grandees in Persia nor by the Ottomans.

Nādir Shāh was from a Shīʿite family, but Turkic by race, and thus not subject to the ancestral attraction that Shīʿism, whose doctrine of the Imāms echoes ancient and indigenous Persian concepts of religious authority and revelation, exercises upon Persians of Indo-European origin. He tried to restore Sunnism perhaps because he saw himself as being potentially a great Asian conqueror, although personal religious conviction cannot be precluded. While the Ṣafavids were able to exploit Shīʿism in order to rally support for their conquest of Persia, it would have been a liability for Nādir Shāh if he attempted to create an empire beyond Persia. Perhaps it was his failure in this respect and the frustration of his imperial designs that led to the instability of the last years of his reign. He blinded his own son who was involved in a plot against him, and was himself assassinated by courtiers. Political instability of one kind or another characterized the reigns of his successors, the brevity and frequency of which soon led to the accession of the Zand dynasty. See AKHBĀRĪS; IRAN; QIZĪL BASH; ṢAFAVIDS; ZANDS.

Aga Khan. The Imām, or spiritual leader, of the Nizari branch of Ismāʿīlīs. The title *Aga Khan* was bestowed on Abū-l-Ḥasan ʿAlī Shah in 1818 by the then Shah of Persia, Fatḥ ʿAlī. In 1841, Aga Khan I fled Persia after an unsuccessful rebellion against the Shah and emigrated first to the city of Kandahar in Afghanistan and thence to Bombay.

The present Aga Khan, Karim (b. 17 December 1936) is the fourth to bear the title and the 49th Nizari Ismāʿīlī Imām, in the belief of his followers, in unbroken succession of descent. He is the grandson of Muḥammad, the third Aga Khan, who selected Karīm to be his successor, passing over the eldest son ʿAlī, father of Karīm, and ʿAlī's half-brother Ṣadruddīn. The present Aga Khan was educated at Harvard and resides near Paris. He is noted for carrying on his grandfather's tradition of charitable work both within the Ismā'īlī community and outside it. See ISMĀ'ĪLĪS; SHĪ'ISM.

"Age of Ignorance", *see* JĀHILIYYAH.

Agha (also Aga and Aqa). A title of honor and military distinction among the Turks. As an honorific, it is also the title of any of the eunuchs who supervised the woman's sections of the Grand Mosques of Mecca and Medina.

Aghlabids. A dynasty that ruled in Ifrīqīya, the region centered around present-day Tunisia, from *184*/800 until *296*/909 when they were overthrown by the Fāṭimids. Founded by Ibrāhīm ibn al-Aghlab from Khorasān, the Aghlabids ostensibly ruled in the name of the 'Abbāsids of Baghdad, but actually were an independent power. Under their dynastic rule, Muslim civilization flourished in Tunisia and Algeria with Kairouan/Qayrawan as its regional center. Having captured and conquered Sicily from the Byzantines, the Aghlabids incorporated the island into their own empire in *217*/832. Malta was seized and added to their own territories in *255*/868.

Aḥkām. The categories into which all actions fall under Islamic law: forbidden (*ḥarām*), obligatory (*farḍ*), recommended (*mustaḥabb*), discouraged (*makrūh*), permitted (*mubāḥ*). *See* FARḌ; ḤARĀM; MAKRŪH; SHARĪ'AH.

Ahl al-Bayt (lit. "People of the House"). A term for the descendants of the Prophet through his daughter Fāṭimah and his cousin and son-in-law, 'Alī. They had three sons, Ḥasan, Ḥusayn, and Muḥsin (who died in infancy). From Ḥasan and Ḥusayn descend the *sharīfs*, who hold an honored position in Muslim society. Modern day descendants of the Prophet number many tens of thousands. In some countries, such as Egypt, a register is maintained of the Prophet's descendants.

The Shī'ites believe that 'Alī had an intermediary role between man and God which was inherited by Ḥusayn and particular descendants out of suceeding generations. Thus, for the Shī'ites the notion of the Ahl al-Bayt has a special meaning. The term may have originally suggested itself because of its resemblance to the Iranian term vispuhr ("son of the house") which appears in Manichean literature, and "prince of the house", a title of Manī himself. See SHĪ'ISM.

Ahl al-Ḥadīth (lit. "People of the Traditions"). A name given to various conservative traditionalists, especially to those who withheld from theological speculation, during the development of Mu'tazilitism and the Ash'arite reaction. At the present time there are groups in India who, not following any *madhhab,* or school of law, call themselves *Ahl-i Ḥadīth.*

One could say that from the beginning of Islam there has been a current which could be called *Ahl ar-Ra'y*, "people of opinion" or speculation, and a current called *Ahl al-Ḥadīth*, those who hold to literal interpretation and who claim to eschew opinion. Of the schools of law, the Ḥanafis made the most liberal use of opinion, and the Hanbalis the least. The Kharijis and the Zahiris are *Ahl al-Ḥadīth.* Ibn Hazm is the foremost philosopher-theologian of the *Ahl al-Ḥadīth.* In modern times some of the most fundamentalist movements to emerge have been called *Ahl-i Ḥadīth* by themselves and by others. These are the movements which say that a man's beard must be longer than what can be grasped in his fist, that if the gown is not lower than mid-calf it is also a transgression. Generally, *Ahl-i Ḥadīth* do not accept a triple divorce pronounced on one occasion; that "non-compulsion in religion" concerns non-Muslims, but that Muslims can be forced to pray, for example. They say that rightful government is by Emir elected by the 'Ulama, and that Islamic rule over the whole world can be established by Jihad.

Ahl-i Ḥaqq (lit. "People of the Absolute, the Real, God"). One of several sects called collectively *'Alī Ilāhis* ("The Deifiers of 'Alī"). The Ahl-i Ḥaqq are a minor, heretical, dualist cult found among some Persians, Kurds and Turkmens of Iraq and Iran. In Iran, they are concentrated in the west of the country, especially around Tabrīz, but small groups can be found everywhere. They are closely related to the Yazīdis of Iraq, and more distantly with the other dualist sects in the Middle East. Their doctrine teaches that there were seven Divine Manifestations beginning with a figure called Khawandagar; they believe that the Prophet's cousin 'Alī ibn Abī Ṭālib was one of these manifestations, and that the series culminated in the direct founder of the cult, a figure called Sultan Sohak (Ishāq) who lived in the *9th*/15th century.

The cult practices the sacrifice of cocks, an animal which represents the liminal moment of daybreak. Thus the cock appears as a popular symbol in religions with light/darkness polarizations. The Ahl-i Ḥaqq have a ceremony called sabz namudar ("making green") which may hearken back to the beliefs of the Manicheans that the Divine light is hidden in the world in greatest concentrations in plants (which is why the Manicheans were vegetarians). The beliefs of the Ahl-i Ḥaqq, which vary from group to group, incorporate elements typical of the Gnostic or Manichean deviations found on the fringes of Islam, as indeed, around all religions. The Ahl-i Ḥaqq believe in the transmigration of souls, and even in reincarnation; like the Yazīdīs and the 'Alawīs, they seem to be a by-product of the Sevener movement, but without the Islamic clothing. See MANICHEANISM; SEVENERS.

Ahl al-Kisā' (lit. "People of the Cloak"). In the 10th year of the Hijrah a delegation of sixty representatives of the Christian community of Najrān arrived in Medina. Among them were the Bishop Abū-l-Ḥārith and the vicar 'Abd al-Masīḥ. The Christians sought to make a treaty with the Prophet and agreed to pay tribute to the Islamic state which was by then gaining ascendancy over Arabia. During their stay they were allowed to conduct mass in the Prophet's Mosque in Medina.

Theological discussions took place concerning the nature of Jesus, who for the Christians is Divine and for the Muslims a Prophet only, which resulted in the revelation of this verse of the Koran:

Truly, the likeness of
Jesus, in God's sight
is as Adam's likeness;
He created him of dust,
then said He unto him,
'Be,' and he was.
The truth is of God;
be not of the doubters.
And whoso disputes with thee
concerning him, after the
knowledge that has come to thee,
say: 'Come now, let us call
our sons and your sons,
our wives and your wives,
our selves and your selves,
then let us humbly pray
and so lay God's curse
upon the ones who lie.' (3:53-54)

The Prophet invited the Christians to meet with him the next day to settle their dispute in this way. When the Christians came, they found that 'Alī was with the Prophet, and Fāṭimah and their two sons. The Prophet was wearing a large cloak which he drew over all of them. It is from this event that the members of the family were called the "People of the Cloak". The Christians declined to go through with the imprecation, but obtained a treaty of protection against the payment of the *jizyah*, or tax.

Ahl al-Kitāb (lit. "People of the Book"). Those whom the Koran cites as having received revealed scriptures: "Surely they that believe, and those of Jewry, and the Christians, and those Sabians, whoso believe in God and the Last Day, and work righteousness – their wage awaits them with their Lord, and no fear shall be on them, neither shall they sorrow" (2:58 and similar to 5:69). In virtue of 22:17, Magians (*al-majūs*) – that is Zoroastrians, also called Mazdaeans and, in India, Parsis – are sometimes (but not by all authorities) considered to be "People of the Book" along with Christians, Jews and the Sabians.

As for the Sabians, their identity has never been definitively established, although certain religious groups have been suggested. The fact that one Revelation should name others as authentic is an extraordinary event in the history of religions.

The Ahl al-Kitāb could not be forcibly converted, as could pagans or disbelievers. They are entitled to protection within the Islamic state which was granted against payment of a tax called the dhimmah.

The Koran also states that revelations have been made to others whom God does not name: "Every nation has its Messenger" (10:47); "We sent Messengers before thee; of some We have related to thee, and some We have not related to thee"(40:78). And:

To every one
of you We have appointed a right way

and open road.
If God had willed, He would have made you
one nation; but that He may try you
in what has come to you. So be you forward
in good works; unto God shall you
return, all together; and He will tell you
of that whereon you were at variance. (5:51)

Such is the Koranic perspective; however, it is almost too much to ask that a man hold another's religion as equal to his own. In the actual beliefs of the overwhelming majority of Muslims, Christianity has "lost its truth" and is simply "tolerated" by heaven. Thus, some Muslims believe as a matter of course that Christians do not attain to heaven, while others concede that Christians achieve salvation. In the latter case, the question arises (but is not addressed): if the efficacy of Christianity has been suspended, in virtue of what are Christians saved? Even more out of the question for the average Muslim is it to identify Buddhism, Hinduism, Confucianism, Shintoism, or the indigenous religions of the Americas, for example, as one of the Revelations of which God says: "and about some have We not told you."

Naturally, there are exceptions to religious "nationalism" within Islam as within other religions. There is the story, by no means unique, of a Sufi, Ibrāhīm ibn Adham, who when starting upon the mystic path, and having failed to find a Muslim master at the outset, unhesitatingly took spiritual instruction from a Christian. See SABIANS.

Ahl-i Ḥadīth *see* Ahl al-ḤADĪTH

Aḥmad of Ra'e Bareli (Aḥmad Barilwi or Brelvi and also known as Aḥmad ibn Muḥammad 'Irfan) (*1201-1246*/1786-1831). Indian religious reformer, a sharif or descendant of the Prophet, also known as Aḥmad Shahīd, born in Bareilly but educated at Lucknow. He militated against British domination and against Sikhs; thus he was an early figure in the nationalist movement. Having gathered several thousand followers in a Jihad, he died in the Battle of Balākot against Sikhs in what is now the North West Frontier Province of Pakistan. His sayings are contained in a text in Urdu called the Sirāt-i Mustaqīm collected by his nephew. He was the disciple of Shāh 'Abd al-'Aziz, the eldest son of Shāh Walī Allāh. Aḥmad Barilwi was also a reformer with views related to the Wahhabi movement. *See* BARILWĪS.

Aḥmadiyyah. A heterodox sect founded by Mirzā Ghulām Aḥmad (*1251-1326*/1835-1908), a Punjabi. Reacting against the efforts of Christian missionaries, he declared himself a *mujaddid*, a "renewer" (of the faith) in 1882. He identified the Christian West, and particularly the economic, political, and religious colonialism, which was the dominant characteristic in the 19th century, as the manifestation of the *dajjāl* (the "imposter" i.e. apocalyptic Antichrist). Mirzā Ghulām did not judge the Occident to be anti-traditional, but simply denounced it for its domination of Islamic countries. However, he ruled out holy war (*jihād*) as a course of action against the colonial powers, awaiting instead an "awakening" of the Islamic world.

He went on to enunciate a doctrine that Jesus had escaped death on the cross and had attained the age of 120 before dying and being buried in Srinagar. (In Islam, Jesus' death on the cross was only apparent; according to the Islamic perspective regarding the crucifixion, Jesus did not die and is still in a principial state, that is, in Being, from which he will return to this world to destroy the *dajjāl* and bring the world to its end.) Mirzā Ghulām finally claimed that he was the *mahdī*, as well as the Second Coming of Jesus, and moreover, the last avatāra of Vishnu.

After Mirzā Ghulām's death, the Aḥmadiyyah split into two subsects, the Qadianis and Lahorites. The Qadianis (after Qadian, birthplace of Mirzā Ghulām) are called the *Jama'at-i Aḥmadiyyah*, maintain his doctrines, more or less as they were propounded, and consider him a *nabī'*, or Prophet. By this, they establish a gulf between those who do not accept Mirzā Ghulām as a Prophet, whom the Qadianis therefore consider to be *Kāfirūn*, or non-believers; the Sunnīs in turn have been obliged to repudiate, by the pronouncements of religious courts, the Qadianis as non-Muslims. The Qadianis make the distinction that Mirzā Ghulām was a Prophet, but not a law-prescribing Prophet (*ghayr tashrī'ī*). To this end they call him a *ẓillī nabī* ("shadow Prophet") or *burūzī nabī* ("a manifesting Prophet").

The Lahorites (*Anjumān-i Insha'at-i Islām*), less heterodox, hold Mirzā Ghulām to be a *mujaddid*, or "renewer" only, and have not wished to lose solidarity with the rest of the Islamic world. They were led by "Maulvi" (or "Mawlānā", a title) Muḥammad ‘Alī. He also translated the Koran into English, which was published along with Aḥmadiyyah inspired interpretations and commentaries, and also wrote *The Religion of Islam.*

Both Aḥmadiyyah subsects were noted for energetic proselytizing through missionaries – a technique adopted from Protestants – the establishment of mosques abroad, and publication of propaganda materials, particularly in English, long before such activities were adopted by the Sunnīs. As a result, the Ahmadiyyah gained footholds in Europe and America, and above all, in West Africa, where they organized schools and hospitals. But while accepting the methods of the Christian missionaries and the ideas of Western civilization, both groups are stridently anti-Christian. Their opposition to Christianity lies in their claim that it has deviated from its original beliefs and can no longer be considered a "Religion of the Book" (a revealed religion), and that it is, moreover, the great force for unbelief throughout the world. Among the first claims of Mirzā Ghulām to eminence, was that "it was a sign of the Mahdi" to recognize the *Dajjāl,* or Antichrist, as Ghulām recognised him, in Christianity.

After the partition of India and Pakistan in 1947, the Qadiani branch moved to Rabwa in Pakistan and is headed by a leader entitled the "Viceroy of the Messiah" (*khalīfatu-l-masīḥ*). The Qadianis are evidently a departure from Islam, but the Lahorites are also considered with extreme reservation by the Sunnī World for their sometimes novel and un-traditional interpretations of Islamic doctrine and practices, which include "conversion rituals" resembling Christian baptism. Nevertheless, there are approximately 500,000 Aḥmadis, mostly in West Africa.

Aḥzāb, ("confederates"). *See* BATTLE of the TRENCH.

‘Ā’ishah (613-678). Daughter of Abū Bakr, and the favorite wife of the Prophet. She was betrothed to the Prophet at the age of six or seven, after the death of Khadījah. The marriage was consummated after the Hijrah when she had come of age according to the custom of the society. ‘Ā’ishah was eighteen when the Prophet died.

During the campaign against the Banū Musta‘liq, ‘Ā’ishah accompanied the Prophet, riding in a litter. At one halt she lost her necklace; she set off alone to find it only to return and discover that the caravan had left without her, the camel drivers thinking she was in her litter. She was later found wandering alone by a young man called Ṣafwān, who brought her back to the caravan. There followed a scandal and ‘Ā’ishah's fidelity was questioned.

When asked counsel by the Prophet, ‘Alī advised him to divorce her, and contributed to ‘Ā’ishah's subsequent antipathy towards ‘Alī later. However, a revelation of the Koran cleared ‘Ā’ishah and established the law by which accusations of adultery are not valid unless there are four witnesses of the actual act. If four cannot be produced, the accusers themselves are liable to the same punishment for false accusation.

Because it was evident that the Prophet preferred her above his other wives, there was some jealousy in his household. In regard to this jealousy the Prophet said to Umm Salāmah: "Trouble me not concerning ‘Ā’ishah, for verily inspiration does not come to me when I am beneath the coverlet of a wife, except that wife be ‘Ā’ishah."

After the death of the Prophet, in the early days of the Caliphate of ‘Alī, an insurrection was led against the Caliph by the Companions Ṭalḥāh and az-Zubayr; ‘Ā’ishah joined them. During the battle between the rebels and the forces of ‘Alī she was mounted on a camel. The fighting raged until it came up to her camel and then died down; hence the name: the Battle of the Camel. The rebels were defeated, and Ṭalḥāh and az-Zubayr killed in the fighting. ‘Ā’ishah was captured but allowed to retire to Medina.

Towards the end of her life she was often consulted on matters of Ḥadīth and Sunnah. As a wife of the Prophet she had the title *Umm al-Mu'minīn* ("Mother of the Believers"). She is buried in the al-Baqī‘ Cemetery in Medina. Some 2,000 Ḥadith are attributed to her; only 75 are *ṣaḥīḥ* ("sound"). One of her comments in particular deserves especial attention: she said if someone tells you that there is a secret teaching in Islam, he is a liar. As it is in Bukhari: "Verily, he who tells you that the Prophet has concealed a part of the Divine Revelation and that he has not delivered it to his people, lies."

On a tradition from Ibn Iṣhāq, which had been disputed because the narrator from the family of Abū Bakr was not named, 'Ā'ishah said that during the mirāj the body of the Messenger of Allāh did not disappear (from his bed at the time) and that he was made to travel heavenwards spiritually only. See IBN HISHĀN.

Akbar (*949-1014*/1542-1605). The third Timurid emperor of Hindustan, son of Humāyūn, and grandson of Bābur, the founder of this Moghul (Mongol) dynasty. Akbar, (his imperial name means the "Greatest") achieved distinction as both soldier and administrator. Based upon his study of other religions as well as Islam, including Hinduism and Christianity, he founded his own syncretistic cult which was known as *Tawhīd-i-Ilāhī* ("Divine Unity"); apparently it did not spread outside his own court.

Despite his intellectual interests, Akbar never learned to read or write; he acquired his ideas through the spoken word. He even had works translated for himself, to be read to him, to satisfy his desire to learn.

Akhbārīs. Among the Shī'ites, Ḥadīth ("Traditions") recording the acts and sayings of the Prophet are referred to as *Akhbār* ("tidings"); the Akhbārīs are the school among the Shī'ite theologians which corresponds to the *ahl al-ḥadīth* among the Sunnīs, that is, traditionalists who eschew speculation. The division arose at the time of the Buyids and has existed ever since, but the Akhbārīs are outnumbered by the Uṣūlīs, who favor theological speculation and extrapolation in the light of religious principles (*uṣūl*).

In the *12th*/18th century the Akhbārīs were driven out of Najaf and Kerbala by the vigorous attacks of an Uṣūlī Mulla named Vahid Bihbahānī (d. *1207*/1792) who made a declaration of *takfīr* against them, declaring them unbelievers. This was backed up by the use of force and violence administered by Bihbahānī's *mirghadabs,* or religious guards. Thereafter Persia became dominated by the Uṣūlī School which, by permitting speculation, made possible a tremendous growth in the power of the Mullas, or religious authorities. The Akhbārīs still exist, however, in India, in Baḥrayn, and in southern Iraq; an Akhbāri leader, Mirzā Muḥammad Akhbārī, resides in Basra; the Akhbārī school also exists in the Khurramshahr region of Iran.

The Akhbārīs restrict the authority and prerogatives of the '*ulamā'*, in the belief that jurisprudence should be limited to the application of existing tradition. Because they are Shī'ites, this body of tradition goes back to Shī'ite Imāms; nevertheless, the Akhbārīs use an approach related to Ash'arite theology and Sunnī principles of jurisprudence. They do admit the existence of *kashf,* rational intuition, in the solution of questions. The great exponent of the School was the Mulla Muḥammad Amīn Astarābādī (d. *1033*/1623) and it reached its high point in Persia during the reign of the Afsharid ruler Nādir Shāh (*1160*/1747) who tried to bring Persia back to Sunnī Islam.

The Akhbārīs restrict the sources of religious authority to the Koran and Sunnah, and insist, moreover, that the Koran must be interpreted through the inspired traditions of the Imāms. They do not accept, as do the Uṣūlīs, "consensus" (*ijmā*), and "intellect" (*aql*). They consider the Shī'ite "Four Books of Ḥadīth" to be reliable, whereas the Uṣūlīs consider the Four Books to contain unreliable Ḥadīth requiring discriminating interpretation. The Akhbārīs allow traditions from Sunnī sources, recognize only two categories of Ḥadīth, namely "sound" (*ṣaḥiḥ*) and "weak" (*ḍa'īf*); the Uṣūlīs accept as authoritative only the Four Books, but assign four categories of dependability, namely, "sound" (*ṣaḥiḥ*), "good" (*ḥasan*), "derived" (*mutawātir*), and "weak" (*ḍa'īf*). The Akhbārīs consider that "transmitted" (*naqlī*) sources have precedence over reason; whereas the Uṣūlīs hold that naqlī sources, which include the Koran and Sunnah, cannot contradict what can be concluded by reasoning from principles.

The Akhbārīs reject *ijtihād,* or the coming to original and unprecedented conclusions as the result of the investigation of sources, reasoning, and endeavoring to understand, whereas the Uṣūlīs accept both *ijtihād* and even conjecture (*ẓann*) should assured knowledge (*'ilm*) not be available from tradition. The Akhbārīs consider it obligatory to refer to the Imāms, even through intermediary but explicit sources; legal decisions can be made only on the basis of the relevant traditions of the Imāms. The Uṣūlīs accept as *'ilm* only that which was reported by those who were in the presence of the Imāms; after the Occulation of the Hidden Imām, which made direct consultation impossible, the Uṣūlīs hold it necessary to resort to *ijtihād*, even to arbitrate tradition. The Akhbārīs restrict competence to the Imām, and make all men *muqallid*, that is to say obliged to follow the established precedent of the Imām; the Uṣūlīs maintain that there are authorities who are *marja at-taqlīd* ("reference for emulation"), i.e. authorities who are relatively independent of tradition and capable of originating doctrine. Therefore the Uṣūlīs divide their community into the Mujtahid, who sets the precedent, and those who follow it, namely, the *muqallidūn;* for them to follow the Mujtahid results in heavenly reward, even if the Mujtahid is wrong.

For the Akhbārīs, to promulgate any decision except upon the basis of tradition is blameworthy. *See* AYATOLLAH; BIHBAHĀNĪ; SHĪ'ISM; UṢŪLĪS.

Akhund. An honorific title given to some religious authorities. It is used in the Indo-Persian world.

Al-'Alawī, Shaykh, *see* al-'ALAWĪ, ABŪ-L-'ABBAS AḤMAD IBN MUṢṬAFĀ.

'Alawī (lit. "of 'Alī") *'Alawi* is a common family name in the Arab world.

1. The name of the Moroccan royal family who are *sharīfs* descended from Ḥasan ibn 'Alī ibn Abī Ṭālib.

2. A Sufi *ṭarīqah*, the 'Alawiyyah, named after the Algerian Shaykh Aḥmad al-'Alawī. It is widespread in North Africa and elsewhere in the Arab world, especially in Syria where the members of the 'Alawī *ṭarīqah* prefer to be called Shādhilis in order to avoid confusion with the 'Alawīs who adhere to the religion (*see below*) of that name. (*See* al-'ALAWĪ, ABŪ-L-'ABBĀS AḤMAD IBN MUṢṬAFĀ.)

3. A religion, signifying the "followers of 'Alī", professed by an ethnic group of the same name, the 'Alawīs, found mainly in Syria, but also in Lebanon and parts of Turkey, particularly around Antakya where they are called Alevis. The Alevis of Turkey may in fact be far greater in number – possibly in the millions – than was previously believed in the times of official Sunnism and later official Laicism. The beliefs of different 'Alawī groups may vary widely.

In Syria they were at one time thought to be different by virtue of being descendants of South Arabian tribal groups who emigrated to the north and mingled with the native population. The total 'Alawī population in Syria is numbered in hundreds of thousands or approximately 6% of the national population. In the past they have usually been called Nuṣayris after one of their most important leaders, Abū Shuayb Muḥammad ibn Nuṣayr (d. circa *267*/880). Because of this name they are sometimes confused with the Nasoreans, or Mandaeans, of Iraq. It is likely that the 'Alawīs are a relic of the Sevener movement, or simply of pre-Islamic Christian Gnosticism, and that they were closely related to the Syrian branch of the revolutionary Qarmatians (Carmathians) of the *4th*/10th century.

After the withdrawal of the Turks from Syria, and during the French Mandate (*1339-1366*/1920-1946), there has sporadically existed an "'Alawī State" in the region of Latakiah with its center around the Jabal Anṣāriyyah, the principal 'Alawī homeland. The existence of the 'Alawī state has been suppressed several times by the Sunnī majority of Syria. (Over 75% of the population of Syria are Sunnīs; the rest consist of Twelve-Imām Shī'ites, Christians, 'Alawīs, Druzes, and Ismā'īlīs.) In the course of one of these power struggles in 1946, a leader of an 'Alawī bid for political supremacy, Sulaymān al-Murshid, whose followers believed him to be a Divine manifestation, was hanged in Damascus. As the result of a series of *coups d'État* in the 1960s, however, the 'Alawīs came into control of the country and in 1971 Hafez Asad was installed as the head of state and government.

The 'Alawīs are often called Shī'ītes but, despite the reference to 'Alī in their preferred name today, their doctrines do not correspond in any way to Shī'ism as such. Their doctrine bears an unmistakable resemblance to Ismā'īlī teachings, with their characteristic Gnostic, or dualist ideas. Their peculiar schema of Muḥammad as *ism*, or "name", 'Alī as *bāb*, or "door", and Salmān al-Farsī as *ma'nā*, or "meaning", with both Muḥammad and 'Alī considered to be emanations of Salmān al-Farsī, point to roots in the earliest stirrings of the Sevener movement, proto-Ismā'īlism, as found in the book called the *Umm al-Kitab*, which dates from the *2nd*/8th century. The initials *'ayn mim sad*, standing for the "Divine Reality" of Salmān and "its two hypostases Muḥammad and

'Alī", constitute one of the 'Alawī religious symbols. Additional Ismā'īlī influence (which provided a veneer of Islamic colouring to the 'Alawīs) was probably absorbed from the Qarmatians and later from the Ismā'īlī Assassin sect when it was active in Syria during the Crusades, as well as from Ibn Nusayr. However, despite any influences they may have received from later Ismā'īlīsm, the 'Alawīs, like the Druzes, stand outside of the Ismā'īlīsm mainstream.

The beliefs and practices of the 'Alawīs, as is the case in similar sects, are extremely heteroclite, and vary from group to group. The 'Alawīs have a collection of writings called the *Kitāb al-Majmū'* ("The Book of the Collection") which constitute their "holy book" and this contains, among other things, it is said, scraps of a corrupt version of the Nicomachean Ethics of Aristotle. The eclecticism of their doctrines goes far back in time; besides theories of Divine emanations, they include elements of astral religion which are ultimately of Babylonian origin (among these is the use of astral phenomena, such as eclipses, as supports of theurgy; there is a belief that the Milky Way is made up of the deified souls of the true believers). They also have elements of Christianity; the 'Alawīs use certain Christian names and mark, in their own way, certain Christian holidays; it is reported that the religious services of the *khāṣṣah* (the initiate elect) – the rest, being "profane", are called the *'āmmah* – include a mass-like ceremony, with a blessing (if not consecration) of the species of communion, and even includes reference to "body and blood" which are "eternal life". In many ways the ceremony resembles the *agapes* of some early Christian sects. They also practice a religious feast called by a Persian name, *naw ruz* ("new year") which clearly points to an Iranian influence. This mixture suggests that, as a small, historically beleaguered ethnic group living in remote mountain regions, with a strong feeling of clan solidarity (the *'asabiyyah* of Ibn Khaldūn), they have absorbed elements from all the religions which have passed by them since Hellenistic times, including the pagan and Christian Gnosticism of Roman antiquity. Whilst maintaining their own beliefs, they have pretended to adhere to the dominant religion of the age in order to escape persecution, in the style of Shī'ite *taqiyyah* (defensive dissimulation).

'Alawī religious practices are carried out in secret, in their own places of congregation, which are not open to outsiders. These practices involve progressive initiations in which the novice ascends by degrees into the inner knowledge of the sect; at the same time he may then be accepted into the ruling oligarchy of the community which is dominated by family clans. The 'Alawīs believe that women do not have souls (which is absolutely contrary to Islamic doctrine). Like the Druzes, the 'Alawis believe that their real number does not change, probably through reincarnation, and that this is 112,000. (A similar belief is found among Sufis in North Africa and perhaps elsewhere, namely that the number of Saints is always constant in Islam from the beginning to the present.)

Observers have noted that 'Alawī religious practices do not include any of the rites of Islam although, for public relations purposes, 'Alawi leaders have performed *ṣalāt* (Muslim canonical prayer) in the Grand Umayyad Mosque of Damascus with visiting dignitaries from the Islamic world, and have taken part in the pilgrimage to Mecca. The 'Alawīs requested, and received, a religious proclamation from the late Twelve-Imām Shī'ite leader in Lebanon, Imām Musā aṣ-Ṣadr, to the effect that they are a legitimate branch of Islam. *See* QARMATIANS, ISMĀ'ĪLĪS; SEVENERS.

al-'Alawī, Abu-l-'Abbās Aḥmad ibn Muṣṭafā (*1286-1353*/1869-1934). He was also known as Ibn 'Aliwah. Al-'Alawī was born and died at Mostaghanem in Algeria. At a young age he entered into the "popular" or "folk Sufi" *ṭarīqah* of the dervishes known as the *Isayyiwah*, whose practices include the performance of such prodigious feats as stabbing oneself with daggers and the like. He also learned to charm snakes, but abandoned all these in favor of a spiritual discipline under the direction of the Shaykh al-Buzīdī, a master of the Darqawī *ṭarīqah*. On the death of this master, al-'Alawī became the Shaykh of many of the latter's former disciples in Algeria and founded his own order. He was highly esteemed and hailed by many as the Islamic *mujaddid*, or "renewer", of his age (an identification which derives from a Ḥadīth that "every hundred years God will send a renewer for the community").

As a foremost exponent of Islamic esoterism, or Sufism, he attracted disciples to his teachings from many countries and, by the end of his life, the Shaykh al-'Alawī had 200,000 disciples, including a handful of Europeans. His representatives established many *zāwiyahs,* or lodges, outside Algeria, notably in Syria and in the Yemen. The Yemenis, many of whom were seamen, established further *zāwiyahs* in foreign parts, including New York, Marseilles, and Cardiff in Wales.

His doctrine stressed the practice of khalwah, or systematic spiritual retreats, but above all insisted on *dhikr Allāh,* or invocation of the Divine Name.

Coming from a poor family, the Shaykh al-'Alawī learned the trade of cobbler in his youth. Although his formal schooling was limited, he sought out and assimilated the sense of many philosophies and spiritual teachings, including the doctrines of other religions, beyond the orbit of what was immediately at hand in the Muslim milieu. He is the author of a collection of poems, his Diwān, several treatises on mystical subjects, and an unfinished commentary on the Koran. He wrote of the *dhikr:*

> The invocation of God is like a coming and going which realizes a communication ever more and more complete till there is identity between the glimmers of consciousness and the dazzling lightnings of the infinite.

Albania. (Population: 3.3 million; 70% are Muslim; 30% are Eastern Orthodox and Catholic.) A country of the Balkans, it was conquered by the Turks in 1415. Many Albanians attained high positions of leadership under the Ottomans, including Muhammad 'Ali. Between 1673-1676 Shabbatai Zevi, the Jewish messiah who converted to Islam in 1666 as Aziz Mehmed Effendi, was deported to Dulcingo in Albania where he died on the Day of Atonement in 1676. Many of his Donmeh followers accompanied him there. Mustafa Kemal Ataturk was of Albanian origin. In 1928 the country became the seat of Bektashism when mystical organizations were prohibited in Turkey.

Alevis. *See* 'ALAWĪS,

Alexander the Great (Ar. *Iskandar*). The Koran appears to be referring to him when, in the Sūrah of the Cave (*Sūrat al-Kahf*), "he of the two horns" (*Dhū-l-Qarnayn*) is mentioned. The widely current coinage of the conqueror, and of the successor states, generally depicted him in the guise of the horned god, Jupiter-Ammon; hence the popular designation customarily used in the age of the Prophet. However, it also has a symbolical interpretation: "He of the two Ages", which reflects the eschatological shadow that Alexander casts from his time, which preceded Islam by many centuries, until the end of the world. The Arabian word *qarn* means both "horn" and "period" or "century".

The Koran accords the Macedonian warrior a remarkable role; in order to protect a people, until the last days, from the depredations of the hosts of Gog and Magog (*Jūj wa Majūj*) – representing symbolically the forces of chaos – Alexander builds them a barrier of iron and copper between two mountains as a "mercy from my Lord" (18:98). This barrier is interpreted esoterically as being the Revealed Law, i.e. the *Sharī'ah,* which will apply until the Last Days.

In addition to the above Koranic story and its popular elaborations (rather like the Jewish midrash tales of the *Haggadah*), there is a folklore, particularly in Central Asia, which portrays Alexander in a mythic light. For example, legend relates that upon his death his testament decreed that his body be carried through the Empire until the meaning of its open hands should be understood. It was finally a humble cobbler who perceived the meaning, namely that Alexander left everything behind him when he left the world.

The position of Alexander, or *Iskandar,* in Islam may be compared to that of Julius Caesar in Christianity: both fulfilled a destiny as forerunners providentially conquering, and so preparing, or "making straight the way", for the establishment of a world religion, like plowmen preparing the way for the coming of a prophetic sower. It was Alexander who cleared the way for the geographic expansion of Islam, just as Caesar brought the Germanic and Celtic tribes of Europe into the Roman Empire, thus indirectly preparing them to receive Christianity. In recognition of this function Alexander is enshrined both in the Koran and in Muslim memory as a prophet-like figure, if not, as he was to the pagan world, a god-like one. *See* ESCHATOLOGY; GOG AND MAGOG.

"Alexander's Wall." (*Sadd-i Iskandar* or *Qizil*

Yilan, "red snake".) The Sassanids, especially under Anushirwan the Just (Chosroes, d. 579) built defensive walls in Hyrcania south of the Caspian against the nomads from the northern steppes. The most famous of the Sassanid defensive walls was at Derbend. The name "Alexander's Wall", however, must have been given to it long after Islam appeared, when its actual origins were forgotten to the Persians. Since it was built less than a century before the revelation of the Koran, it is likely that this wall was also known to the Arabs as a Sassanid construction. It was of importance for the defense of the Byzantines also and they contributed to its upkeep.

Idrissi's map made for Roger of Sicily shows the land of Gog and Magog to which the Koran refers as being in Mongolia; the Great Wall of China was known to the Roman historian of Greek origin Ammianus Marcellinus (d. c. 391). Thus the wall built by Alexander (*Dhu-l-Qarnayn*) in the Koran (18:95), an ancient and distant wall, may well be an echo of the Great Wall of China, or a conflation of the Sassanid Wall with the Chinese one.

There were also trench defenses in Iraq against the Bedouins (called in Arabic *khandaq sabur*). One was designed to protect Ḥirā'. Ya'qut says that Shapur II had the moat dug and a wall built as well as frontier watchtowers, and that he ordered a khandaq to be dug from the lower region of the Badiya to what is before Basra and is joined to the sea. Others say it was Chosroes. Baladhuri adds that the Arabs who lived by the *khandaq* guarded it and had the use of the land as a fief without paying a land tax. With the absorption of the Lakhmid state into the Sassanid empire about 602, the Sassanian defenses against the Arabs fell apart.

Algerian Democratic Republic. The population of 22,106,000 in 1986 is composed of Arabs and Berbers. 99% are Muslim, almost all being of the Malīkī School of Law (*madhhab*); a very small minority, less than 100,000, are 'Ibadite Muslims living in the M'zab region. The Shādhilī ṭuruq (sing. *ṭarīqah*) are most strongly represented, along with the Qādiriyyah. In the desert villages, it is customary to find that all the adult males belong to a ṭarīqah, most often the Wazzaniyyah, whose center is at Ouezzane in Morocco. *See* 'ABD al-QĀDIR, EMIR; ABŪ MADYAN.

Alhambra (from the Ar. *al-qal'ah al-hamrā'*, "the red palace"). The palace of the Naṣrid princes of Granada, Spain. Largely of *8th*/14th century construction, the Alhambra marks the high point of Islamic architecture in the West. Intricate plaster and tile decorations adorn the walls with elegant calligraphic motifs that repeat the words: "there is no victor except God". These words are attributed to the Spanish Umayyad Prince 'Abd ar-Raḥman III, who was hailed as victor by his subjects on returning from a battle.

Among the more renowned apartments of the palace are the Court of Lions, with its stylized statues of lions around a fountain, the Hall of Ambassadors, and the Hall of the Two Sisters. Next to the palace are the Generalife Gardens (from the Ar. *jannatu-l-'arīf*, "garden of the knower"). Their fountains are fed with water from the Sierra Nevada mountains, whence Machado's description of Granada as *aqua oculta que llora* ("hidden water that weeps").

'Alī ibn Abī Ṭālib (*598-40*/598-661). A member of the house of Hāshim, a cousin of the Prophet, who was to become his son-in-law, and eventually the fourth Caliph. One of the first converts to Islam. Early in his mission, after the Koran enjoined him: "And warn thy clan, thy nearest of kin" (26:214), the Prophet called his clan together and preached to them saying: "O sons of 'Abd al-Muṭṭalib, I know of no Arab who has come to his people with a nobler message than mine. I bring you the best of this world and the next. God has commanded me to call you unto Him. Which of you, then, will help me in this, and be my brother, my executor and my successor among you?" The only one who responded was 'Alī, then thirteen years old, and of whom the Prophet then said: "This is my brother, my executor and my successor among you. Hearken unto him and obey him", whereupon the Hashimites left, saying in derision to Abū Ṭālib: "He has ordered you to hearken to your son and obey him." Following this meeting, however, several aunts of the Prophet and other women of the Hāshimites entered Islam.

'Alī became renowned as a warrior during Islam's struggle for survival, often leading the army. He married the Prophet's daughter Fāṭimah, and it is from their two sons Ḥasan and Ḥusayn that the *sharīfs*, or progeny of the

Prophet, descend. A third son, Muḥsin, died in infancy; they also had a daughter, Zaynab. After Fāṭimah died, 'Alī had another son by a concubine. This son, Muḥammad ibn Ḥanafiyyah, became the figurehead leader of a revolt against the Umayyads. (*See* KAYSANIS.)

The Prophet's son-in-law played a minor role during the first three Caliphates. He disagreed with 'Umar's plan that a portion of the income from the enormous spoils of conquest sent back by the victorious armies of Islam should be set aside as a reserve for unforeseen eventualities. This income, less the prudent reserve, was distributed to the Muslims according to the national register, the *diwān.* 'Alī, for his part, said that all this income should be given away to the nation; presumably his point of view was that the Islamic community need make no provisions of its own but should rely only upon God. Whatever disagreements 'Alī may have had with the Caliph, he was not completely ignored, for he was put in charge of Medina when 'Umar visited Jerusalem after its conquest.

Aṭ-Ṭabarī the historian reports 'Umar as having said to 'Alī that the Quraysh did not want both Prophethood and the Caliphate combined in the house of Hāshim (the Prophet's and 'Alī's clan). This assertion shows a reserved attitude on the part of 'Alī's contemporaries towards according him greater leadership in the expanding and increasingly important political affairs of the Quraysh. Their reluctance may have been due to 'Alī's idiosyncratic and independent character which was little given to the arts of social diplomacy and compromise. At 'Umar's death the Caliphate was offered to 'Alī on condition that he respect the precedents set by the first two Caliphs. 'Alī either refused this condition, or appeared to refuse it whilst in fact modestly making little of his own abilities; there was, if not outright refusal, at least ambiguity. Thereupon the Caliphate was offered to 'Uthmān who unequivocally agreed to abide by the precedents, and was thus named Caliph.

In *35*/656 'Uthmān was assassinated in a rebellion against his nepotism and the despotism of his clansmen who had been made Governors of the conquered provinces. 'Alī was thus elected Caliph at a time of unrest and mounting difficulties. He immediately had to face a rebellion led by the Companions Ṭalḥāh and az-Zubayr in which 'Ā'ishah, the widowed favorite wife of the Prophet, also took part. 'Alī defeated the rebels at the Battle of the Camel. Then Mu'āwiyah, Governor of Damascus and relative of 'Uthmān, made a bid for the Caliphate in an insurrection culminating in the prolonged Battle of Ṣiffīn, which was dragged out inconclusively over several months. In the midst of the stalemate or, as some sources contend, when 'Alī was on the point of winning, he accepted the proposal of Mu'āwiyah, actually conceived by 'Amr ibn al-'Āsī, to arbitrate the conflict as a legitimate dispute, because 'Alī allegedly wished to avoid further bloodshed; in any case, 'Alī did not, or could not, conclude the struggle decisively. This agreement to arbitrate led to the secession from 'Alī's army of a bloc of strict traditionalists, some 4,000, a faction thereafter called the Khārijites ("Seceders"), who believed that the question at issue was so vital and indeed sacred, that it could only be decided by the will of God and not by negotiation.

Mu'āwiyah manipulated the negotiations with cunning. 'Alī's negotiator, who may well have wanted to see his own son-in-law elected Caliph, was deceived by a ruse into going along with Mu'āwiyah's partisans. He deposed 'Alī in a public announcement, on the understanding that an agreement had been made to set aside both contenders. However, Mu'āwiyah's negotiator, instead of then repudiating Mu'āwiyah's claims, declared him Caliph, making this appear to be the agreed outcome of the negotiations. Nevertheless, 'Alī refused to surrender his authority and established himself at Kufah in Iraq.

The Khārijites now posed a separate threat, and went on to sack Ctesiphon. At the subsequent Battle of Nahrawān, 'Alī overwhelmingly defeated them, but did not succeed in completely crushing the movement. In *40*/661, as 'Alī was preparing to lead the morning prayer at the mosque of Kufah, he was assassinated by a surviving Khārijite, Ibn Muljam, who carried out the deed at the demand of a woman who had made 'Alī's assassination a condition of marriage.

'Alī's elder son Ḥasan succeeded his father as Caliph for half a year, but was then forced by threat of arms to cede the Caliphate to Mu'āwiyah. Ḥasan died a few years later, poisoned, it is said, by his wife who had received a promise of marriage from Yazīd, Mu'āwiyah's son. After the death of Mu'āwiyah and the accession of Yazid to the Caliphate, Ḥusayn attempted to lead an insurrection but could not rally support. His tragic death at the hands of the troops of Mu'āwiyah's son was to become the focal point in Twelve-Imām Shī'ism.

'Alī is highly revered by the Sufis as the fountainhead of esoteric doctrine; more generally, he is remembered for his piety, nobility and learning. Often the champion of the Muslims on the field of battle during Islam's struggle for life against the Meccans, he is the model for *futuwwah,* or chivalry. Besides being courageous, he acted towards his enemies with generosity and magnanimity. Before himself becoming Caliph, he had acted as counselor to the Caliphs preceding him.

It is certain that 'Alī's personal relationship to the Prophet was special; the Prophet referred to him at least twice as "my brother" and three times as "my heir" (*wāṣi'*). The Prophet blessed the marriage union of 'Alī and Fāṭimah in an extraordinary way by anointing them both on their marriage night. As far as is known, the Prophet did this for no-one else, and anointing is not a feature of Islamic ritual.

In Shī'ism the position of 'Alī is radically different from what it is in Sunnī Islam, and this is the seed of Shī'ism's fundamental doctrinal divergence. In Shī'ism, 'Alī is the first Imām, in the special sense in which they understand this term, that is, an intermediary between man and God in this world, unique in his age, necessary for salvation. As such, according to them, 'Alī had exclusive, Divine, right to the Caliphate which the preceding three Caliphs sinfully usurped from him, and the others from his heirs.

In Shī'ism, 'Alī and the Imāms who descend from him are beings of superhuman virtue possessing miraculous gifts and absolute spiritual and temporal authority. 'Alī's tomb in Najaf, Iraq, is a place of pilgrimage.

The sayings and sermons of 'Alī, and those utterances attributed to him, are collected in a book called the *Nahj al-Balāghah* ("The Way of Eloquence") which has long served as a model for the use of Arabic much as the speeches of Cicero once did for Latin. It was 'Alī who first laid down the rules of formal Arabic grammar, notably describing language as made up nouns, verbs and particles. As this was first done in the West by Aristotle, it is perhaps to 'Alī that the Greek philosopher has been assimilated in this respect. Similarly, 'Alī became the spokesman and mirror of other ideas and ideologies thereby assuming the epic role finally created for him. *See* SHĪ'ISM, GHADĪR KHUMM, ḤASAN, ḤUSAYN, IMĀM.

'Alī Ilāhīs (lit. "Deifiers of 'Ali"). A spectrum of heterodox sects whose members are found in Iran and Iraq and for whom 'Alī is a Divine hypostasis, being seen as a manifestation and human receptacle of the Godhead. These sects are more or less closely related to each other, and are similar to other ethno-sects found in the Levant and Syria, such as the Druzes who substitute the Fāṭimid Caliph al-Ḥākim for 'Alī.

The origins of these sects lie outside of Islam. They are superficial accommodations with Islam as the dominant religion on the part of belief systems which have survived from antiquity, fossils of ancient religions. *See* AHL-I-ḤAQQ.

'Alids. The descendants of 'Alī ibn Abī Ṭālib and the Prophet's daughter Fāṭimah. The term 'Alid is:

1. A generic adjective describing all families of such descent.

2. A particular term for those figures that the Shī'ites supported for the Caliphate. However, the name does not imply Shī'ism; some 'Alid dynasties, such as the ruling family of Jordan, or that of Morocco, are Sunnī, and enjoy the prestige that descendants of the Prophet have among the Sunnīs – without the overtones inherent to Shī'ism.

Aligarh. A secondary school patterned after European models, founded in India in *1292*/1875 by Sir Sayyid Ahmad Khan. Aligarh College was later added to the Aligarh High School. In 1920 the college became a university. Because of the ideological outlook behind the school, the name Aligarh became associated with a modernizing movement in India that advocated the adoption of Western ideas, or the reform of Islam in that direction. Among its proponents were 'Amīr 'Alī and Sir Muḥammad Iqbal, the President of the Muslim League.

'Alī ibn Abī Ṭālib, see after ALHAMBRA.

'Alī Shīr Navā'i (also written Navo'i and Nawa'i; 845-907/1441-1501). Turkic poet born in Herat, statesman and patron of the arts under Babur and Sultan Bayqara.

Allāh. The Name (*al-ism*) of Majesty (*jalālah*), and the Supreme Name (al-ism al-azam). Allāh is the Name of the Essence, or the Absolute. It is possibly a contraction of *al-ilāh* ("the Divinity"); nevertheless, the word Allāh cannot be reduced to theoretical grammatical components. If it is, so to speak, a synthesis of two words, the article *al* and the word *ilāh* ("Divinity") that synthesis, which took place in this world out of the inner logic of the Arabic language, was a revelation hidden in the origin of the Arabic language itself. It re-constituted in language a Reality that surpasses incomparably the dimension of the words it apparently contains. The word Allāh is a proper and true Name of God, through which man calls upon Him *personally.* It is an opening onto the Divine Essence, beyond language and the world itself.

The Name was known and used before the Koran was revealed; for example, the name of the Prophet's father was 'Abd Allāh, or the servant of God. The Name Allāh is not confined to Islam alone; it is also the Name by which Arabic-speaking Christians of the Oriental churches call upon God. When written, the Name is usually followed by the formula *'azza wa jall* ("Great and Majestic"), or by *jalla jalāluh* ("Great is His Majesty").

The Koran speaks of God in innumerable verses of great beauty and penetration:

God
there is no god but He, the
Living, the Everlasting.
Slumber seizes Him not, neither sleep;
to Him belongs
all that is in the heavens and the earth.
Who is there that shall intercede with Him
save by His leave?
He knows what lies before them
and what is after them,
and they comprehend not anything of His
knowledge
save such as He wills.
His Throne comprises the heavens and earth;
the preserving of them oppresses Him not;
He is the All-high, the All-glorious.
(Verse of the Throne 2:256)

He is God;
there is no god but He.
He is the knower of the Unseen and the Visible;
He is the All-merciful, the All-compassionate.
He is God;
there is no god but He.
He is the King, the All-holy, the All-peaceable,
the All-faithful, the All-preserver,
the All-mighty, the All-compeller,
the All-sublime.
Glory be to God, above that they associate!
He is God,
the Creator, the Maker, the Shaper.
To Him belong the Names Most Beautiful.
All that is in the heavens and the earth magnifies
Him;
He is the All-mighty, the All-wise. (59:22-24)

It is God who splits the grain and the date-stone,
brings forth the living from the dead; He
brings forth the dead too from the living.
So that then is God; then how are you perverted?
He splits the sky into dawn,
and has made the night for a repose,
and the sun and moon for a reckoning.
That is the ordaining of the All-mighty, the All-
knowing.
It is He who has appointed for you the stars, that
by them you might be guided in
the shadows of land and sea.
We have distinguished the signs for a people who
know.

It is He who produced you from one living soul,
and then a lodging place,
and then a repository.
We have distinguished the signs for a people who
understand. (6:95-98)

To God belongs all that is in the heavens and
earth. Whether you publish what is in your hearts
or hide it, God shall make reckoning with you
for it. He will forgive whom He will,
and chastise whom He will; God is powerful
over everything. (2:284)

Say: 'He is God, One,
God, the Everlasting Refuge,
who has not begotten, and has not been begotten,
and equal to Him is not any one.' (112)

With Him are the keys of the Unseen;
none knows them but He.
He knows what is in land and sea;
not a leaf falls, but He knows it.
Not a grain in the earth's shadows,
not a thing, fresh or withered,

but it is in a Book Manifest. (6:59)

His command, when He desires a thing, is to say to
it
'Be,' and it is.
So glory be to Him, in whose hand is the dominion
of everything,
and unto whom you shall be returned. (36:82)

We [God] are nearer to him [man] than the
jugular vein. (50:16)

He created the heavens and the earth with the truth,
and He shaped you, and shaped you well;
and unto Him
is the homecoming. (64:3)

All that is in the heavens and the earth magnifies
God;
He is the All-mighty, the All-wise.
To Him belongs the Kingdom of the heavens and
the earth;
He gives life, and He makes to die, and He is
powerful
over everything.
He is the First and the Last, the Outward and the
Inward;
He has knowledge of everything. (57:1-3)

God is the Light of the heavens and the earth;
the likeness of His Light is as a niche
wherein is a lamp
(the lamp in a glass,
the glass as it were a glittering star)
kindled from a Blessed Tree,
an olive that is neither of the East nor of the West
whose oil wellnigh would shine, even if no fire
touched it;
Light upon Light;
(God guides to His Light whom He will.)
(And God strikes similitudes for men,
and God has knowledge of everything.) (24:35-40)

No affliction befalls, except it be
by the leave of God. Whosoever
believes in God, He will guide his
heart. And God has knowledge of
everything.

And obey God, and obey the Messenger;
but if you turn your backs, it is
only for the Messenger to deliver
the Manifest Message.
God –
there is no god but He.
And in God let the believers
put their trust. (64:11-13)

Your wealth and your children are
only a trial; and with God is
a mighty wage.
So fear God as far as you are able,
and give ear, and obey, and expend
well for yourselves. And whosoever
is guarded against the avarice
of his own soul, those – they are
the prosperers.
If you lend to God a good loan, He
will multiply it for you, and will
forgive you. God is All-thankful,
All-clement,
Knower He of the Unseen and the Visible,
the All-mighty, the All-wise. (64:15-18)

God is
the All-sufficient; you are the needy ones. (47:40)

Written, the Name is *alif, lam, lam* (with *shaddah*), *hā'*. This is a contraction of its full orthography, which is *alif, lam, lam, lam, hā'*. Between the final *lam* and the *ha'* there is a "dagger" *alif*. This is written suspended between the final *lam* and the *hā'*, or decoratively sometimes above the *shaddah*, and sometimes horizontally above the Name, especially above the ligature between the final *lam* and the *hā'*. Often, the "dagger" *alif* is not shown at all. The first *lam* is not voiced, but, in the words of one commentator, inserted (*mudghamah*) into the following *lam*, causing it to carry the *shaddah*, or doubling. The daggar *alif* in the Name has the unique characteristic that when the Name stands by itself this *alif* of prolongation is pronounced with velarization making the preceding *lam* sound heavy (*takhfīm*). When the Name is preceded by a consonant with a *kasrah*, as in *Lillāh*, that *alif* is develarized and the *lam* becomes "light" (*tarqīq*). When it is velarized, the pronunciation of the double *lam* is a heavy "l" sound found in no other word in Arabic, although the combination of letters exists in other words as well. According to *abjad*, or the mystical science of letters, the visible letters of the Divine Name Allāh add up to the number sixty-six, which, tradition points out, is the sum of the letters in Ādam wa Hawwā', or the words Adam and Eve. (*See* ABJAD.)

The initial *alif* is a support (*kursī*, "a seat") for the *hamzah*, a letter which is a transition between silence and sound; or, one could also say, between non-manifestation and manifestation. This *hamzah* is a *hamzat al-waṣl*, and is elided with preceding vowels, such that Yā Allāh is pronounced Yallah. According to Ibn 'Arabi's *Treatise on the Name of Majesty*, the voiced *lam*, and the voiced "dagger" *alif*, represent manifestation in relation to the Absolute.

The last letter, the *hā'*, is ultimately an expiration of breath ending in silence. Symbolically, it is a return to non-manifestation. As such it is also reintegration; a return to Beyond-Being (God as the Absolute) on the part of Being (God as Creator), or, on another level, a return to Being on the part of creation. In the nominative form, *Allāhu*, this final hā' also leads to the Name *Huwa*. *Huwa* is at once simply the third-person pronoun in Arabic, but also at the same time a Divine Name of the Ipseity, or the Divine Essence. Spoken softly, the Name Allāh sounds like a thunderbolt; the first syllable wells suddenly out of silence like an explosion, it peaks its crescendo with the sudden attack of the double *ll*, and then fades slowly like thunder rolling on into the distance.

In the words of Muḥammad Bushārah, a representative of a Moroccan Darqawī Shaykh of the beginning of this century:

> The Name is made up of four letters which are read Allāh; if you remove the first letter those which remain are read *Lillāh* ("to God"); if you remove another letter – the first *lam* – what remains is read *Lahu* ("to Him"). Finally, there remains only the letter *Ha'*, which, vocalized, is the Name "He" (*Huwa*: the Name of the Essence). In the same way, when we invoke the Name of God, its form gradually melts into the breath itself. The same happens to the dying man whose soul is resolved into breathing alone and leaves the body with the last breath.

In Islam, God is known also by ninety-nine other Names collectively called the Most Beautiful Names (*al-asmā' al-ḥusnā*). These are divided into Names of the Essence (*asmā' adh-dhāt*) and Names of the Qualities (*asmā' aṣ-ṣifāt*). The Names are also divided into Names of Majesty (*jalāl*), or rigor, and Names of Beauty (*jamāl*), or mercy. (*See* DIVINE NAMES.)

The Name ar-Raḥmān, "the Merciful One", a Name of the Essence, appears in the Koran almost as a synonym for Allāh. Historically, the reaction of the pagan Meccans to this Name (notably their refusal to recognize it when the consecration "In the Name of God [Allāh] the Merciful [*ar-Raḥmān*] the Compassionate [*ar-Raḥīm*] was written in drawing up the Treaty of Ḥudaybiyyah) shows that while Allāh was known and used by them, as it was to all speakers of Arabic, *ar-Raḥmān* was not. They saw the Name *ar-Raḥmān* as emblematic of the new revelation, and refused to acknowledge it as long as they were unbelievers.

Among other names mentioned in the Koran are: "The First" (*al-Awwal*), "The Last" (*al-Ākhir*), "The Outwardly Manifest" (*aẓ-Ẓāhir*), "The Inward" (*al-Bāṭin*), "The Holy One" (*al-Quddūs*), "The Integral Peace" (*as-Salām*). Among the Names of God as Creator (*al-Khāliq*) are: "The Producer" (from nothing) (*al-Bāri'*) and "The Shaper" (*al-Musawwir*). And He is also called "The Mighty" (*al-'Azīz*) and "The Ruler" (*al-Hakīm*).

In addition to the descriptions of God found in the Koran, there are those found in pious writings. A litany of the Isawiyyah *ṭarīqah* of Morocco says:

> God was alone; around him was the Void. He created the universe to make His power known; He created the world that He might be worshiped. He is the Deity, the excellent Master, the necessary Being. The creature disappears; the excellent Master alone is Eternal; the creature is born perishable, the excellent Master remains. The excellent Master is Immense; Full; the creature is empty; the Master is Glorious, Sublime, Knowing, Perfect; the creature is small, ignorant, incomplete; the excellent Master is Exalted and resembles nothing. The excellent Master is in the heart of those who know...

See ARABIC; BASMALAH; DHIKR; DIVINE NAMES; FIVE DIVINE PRESENCES.

'Allāma Hillī see HILLĪ, 'ALLĀMA.

Almagest. The Latinized form of the Arabic *al-Majisti*, which itself was the Arabization, from the Greek *Megalē Syntaxis*. This is Ptolemy's

2nd century work on astronomy which explained the apparent motion of the planets through the theory of epicycles and deferents.

In departing from the purely mystical theories of Pythagoras concerning the motion of the planets, the *Megalē Syntaxis* represented an important step towards the empiricism of modern science. Yet its empirical tendency was not a divorce from the perception that the heavens were above all a symbol of a higher reality; the physical world was still contained in an ideal, or spiritual world. Ptolemy, like other Greek philosophers, may have known that the earth went around the sun (it is now known that some peoples of antiquity used both geocentric and heliocentric systems for calculations), but he knew above all that the world came from the Spirit, and his planetary model reflected that knowledge, accommodating the data of observed motion as facts of secondary importance.

Islamic astronomy was based upon the theories of Ptolemy as expounded in the Almagest, and it was through the Arabic translation that the Ptolemaic theory was reintroduced as medieval Europe resumed the study of ancient sciences. The word Almagest also served, in European languages, as a generic term for any of the many and great medieval works on such subjects as astrology, alchemy and science. *See* ASTRONOMY.

Almohads (*524-667*/1130-1269). Spanish name of a Moorish dynasty and religious movement called in Arabic *al-Muwaḥḥidūn* ("the Unitarians"), who ruled in Morocco and Spain. The Almohads brought renewed piety and fervor to the Arab West through a powerful sense of religion not just as rules (in any case laxly observed towards the end of the Almoravid epoch) but as spiritual interiority. This interiority, or awareness that the world exists in a sacred dimension, gave the Almohads their name which means "The Upholders of (Divine) Unity", for the profound sense that God is One means that this world and this life are plunged in God.

The movement grew out of the teachings of a reformer called Ibn Tūmart (*470-524*/1077-1130), a Berber from the Maṣmūda tribe in the Atlas mountains in Morocco. After making the pilgrimage to Mecca, Ibn Tūmart remained in the East to study in Damascus and Baghdad. He returned to Morocco imbued with both the vigorous theology of al-Ash'arī and the mystical ideas of al-Ghazālī. Wherever Ibn Tūmart went he attempted to reform morals and religious beliefs, sometimes violently. In Fez, he threw the sister of the Almoravid prince from her horse for not wearing a veil. Although such an act could easily earn death, Ibn Tūmart evidently commanded enough respect or even awe for his righteous audacity, that he was not punished.

Ibn Tūmart returned to Aghmat where he converted Atlas Berbers (who, although nominally Muslims, knew next to nothing about their religion). As for those who were believers, he reformed their hitherto superficial faith. In Tinmal he founded a *ribāṭ*, or religious-military community, which was run as a religious dictatorship. From Tinmal he waged holy war upon his neighbors. According to Ibn Khaldun, Ibn Tūmart, who was called a Mahdi, was descended from the Faṭimids. This does not necessarily mean by birth but could mean intellectually; on the other hand North African Berbers had married into the family of Shī'ite Imams very early on, for example. One North African, Abū Hilal ad-Dayhuri is known to have become Archegos in Ctesiphon at the time of the Caliph al-Manṣur. In any case, he says: 'Al-Mahdi's power did not depend exclusively on his Faṭimid descent [which] had become obscured and knowledge of it disappeared among the people, although it remained alive in him and his family through tradition'. After Ibn Tūmart's death (which some say had been kept secret by the leadership for two years to prolong the sway of Ibn Tūmart's charismatic authority), his lieutenant 'Abd al-Mu'min suceeded him as ruler and brought North Africa as far as the Libyan desert under Almohad control by *544*/1149. This expansion took place at the same time as the Almoravid dynasty was collapsing through its own decadence. In *566*/1170 Muslim Spain fell into Almohad hands and for a time Seville became the Almohad capital, although the rulers eventually returned to Morocco to govern from Marrakesh.

The Almohads' resounding victory over the Spanish at the Battle of Alarcos in *592*/1195 marked a peak of political power. However, it was soon followed by the single most important defeat the Muslims ever received in the history of Moorish Spain: the Battle of Las Navas de Tolosa in *609*/1212. A Christian army strengthened by knights from Portugal and from outside the Iberian peninsula, unified by the spirit of the knightly orders created out of the Crusades, devastated the Moorish armies and made the complete reconquest of Muslim Spain by the Christians no more than a question of time.

The Almohad period saw the heights, and the end, of Muslim philosophy in the West in the persons of Ibn Tufayl (d. *585*/1185) and Ibn Rushd (d. *595*/1198). (*See* PHILOSOPHY.) It was also the period of Ibn 'Arabī (d. *638*/1240), the metaphysician from Murcia in southern Spain. In craftsmanship and architecture the Almohads introduced a powerful style which marked a new beginning for Moorish art. It is outstanding for its direct expression, in the language of art, of a metaphysical conviction, as is to be seen particularly in the Almohad arch, such as those in the Kutubiyyah mosque in Marrakesh, whose amplitude and sense of spiritual fullness, convey visually the *inshirāḥ* ("expansion"), which is the mystical transformation of the physical body that accompanies surrender to (*Islām*) God. The Almohad arch is, as it were, the architectural image of that which the Koran speaks of in Sūrah 94:

> Did We not expand thy breast for thee
> and lift from thee thy burden,
> the burden that weighed down thy back?
> Did We not exalt thy fame?
> so truly with hardship comes ease;
> truly with hardship comes ease.
> So when thou art empty, labor,
> and let thy Lord be thy Quest.

The directness and vigor of the Almohad style influenced Islamic art to some degree everywhere. The monumental legacies of the Almohads are the Giralda, now the vast cathedral of Seville (originally the Grand Mosque), the Kutubiyyah mosque of Marrakesh, the Ḥasan mosque of Rabāṭ (never completed and shattered by the earthquake of 1756 which also destroyed Lisbon), and what remains of the Almohad mosque at Tlemcen.

The Almohad emphasis on acknowledging the Unity of God which, as a call to action in Islamic history, points either to an interiorizing of spiritual life, or to an emphasis on rigor, since the Unity, or Oneness, of God was never in question, and was to some degree a reaction against the tendencies of their predecessors, the Almoravids. As the Almoravids lost their initial zeal, they tended to externalize religion and to reduce it to rules and simplistic conceptions; at the same time, they succumbed to the temptations of hedonism, always present in Moorish Spain. It is true, nonetheless, that the Almohad's integration of all things into the Unity of God reflected, to a greater or lesser degree, the general renewal of spiritual fervor which was then pervading the Islamic East. The Almohads flourished for a short time; by *667*/1269 they were replaced in Morocco by the Merinid dynasty, while in Spain the declining Muslim kingdoms yielded gradually to Christian reconquest. *See* RECONQUISTA.

Almoravids (*448-541*/1056-1147). The Spanish name of a dynasty and its supporting political, military and ethnic organization called in Arabic *al-Murābiṭūn*, those who stand together for the defense of religion (*see* RIBĀṬ). The Almoravids were an imperial movement arising out of an originally religious impetus which enthused and set in motion the Berber tribes of the Ṣanhāja group in the western Sudan, also called the Lemtuna (from *al-Mutalaththimun*, "the veiled ones", because they covered their faces like the Tuareg, to whom they are related). The tribes rose up from the Sahara and the Niger and Mali region to conquer North Africa and then Spain.

One of the chiefs of the Ṣanhāja, Yaḥyā ibn Ibrāhīm, was returning from the pilgrimage to Mecca at the beginning of the *5th*/11th century when he was introduced by the rulers of Kairouan/Qayrawan to a noted scholar, a missionary called 'Abd Allāh ibn Yāsīn. The mission of 'Abd Allāh was to improve the rudimentary religious knowledge of Yaḥyā's people. Upon arrival in the western Sudan 'Abd Allāh took matters firmly into his hands, ordered the penitential scourging of all new converts and imposed a generally zealous regimen. His preaching sparked a movement which spread from a *ribāṭ* (fortress for the defense of Islam) located on an island in the Niger in which religion and conquest joined hands; soon, after the death of 'Abd Allāh ibn Yāsīn, an empire was created and then divided between a leader called Abū Bakr, who held control over the movement from *448*/1056, and his cousin Yūsuf ibn Tāshufīn, who seized Morocco as his portion in *453*/1061. Yūsuf ibn Tāshufīn founded Marrakesh as his capital in *454*/1062.

The Spanish Muslims, divided after the decline of the Caliphate of Cordoba into small princedoms, and beset by the Christians, called on Yūsuf ibn Tāshufīn for help. This he gave by bringing an army of Moroccans and Africans across the straits, and he defeated Alfonso VI at az-Zallaqah (Sagrajas) near Badajoz in *479*/1086. This victory, however, produced the seeds of the ultimate defeat of the Muslims in Spain by changing the nature of the political alignments. Until az-Zallaqah, wars in Spain were internecine struggles between Spanish rulers, both Christian and Muslim; however, when the North African reinforcements entered the field, the struggle became one between Christian Europe and Islam. This led to the turning point for the Muslims in the defeat of the Almohads at Las Navas de Tolosa in *609*/1212.

In *483*/1090, four years after he had been invited to fight there, Yūsuf ibn Tāshufīn returned to Muslim Spain and captured the country for himself. He conquered in the name of the restoration of orthodoxy, reforming the lax and enervating luxury of the Andalusian courts. Ibn Tāshufīn accepted the authority of the 'Abbāsid Caliphate, in name at least. However, he adopted the title of Amīr al-Muslimīn ("Prince of the Muslims") similar to the Caliph's Amīr al-Mu'minīn ("Prince of the Believers"), one of the titles used today by the King of Morocco.

Yūsuf died at the age of one hundred in *500*/1106. His empire extended across southern Iberia and included Valencia, which had been wrested from the widow of al-Cid, and North Africa from the Atlantic to Algiers.

The Almoravid domination lasted a bare century until *541*/1147, and then gave way to another Berber movement, that of the Almohads, with a far higher ideological motivation. The Almoravids are a perfect example of Ibn Khaldūn's theory of Muslim history, according to which periodic nomad invasions from the desert to the settled areas are inevitable; they come to sweep away the decadence of sedentary life, before themselves succumbing to its temptations, once they have escaped the natural discipline of the wastelands. *See* ALMOHADS; IBN KHALDŪN.

Alms, *see* BEGGING; SADAQAH; WAQF; ZAKĀH.

Aloes, Fragrant (Greek *aloē*, cf. Hebrew *ahalīm;* ultimately from Tamil *akil.*) An incense widely used in the Islamic world for religious and special occasions. In Arabic, the incense is called *al-'ūd al-qumari* or *al-qamari,* which is understood to mean "the wood of the moon". However, this is a corruption, for as al-Mas'ūdī says in the "Meadows of Gold", it is *'ūd al-Qimari,* that is, from the "Kingdom of Qimar" which is Cambodia (Khmer).

The wood of aloes (not to be confused with "bitter aloes", a medicinal shrub called *sabrah* in Arabic) is the precious wood of a tree, *Aquilaria muscaria* and *Aquilaria agallocha,* found in Asia. Some 10% of the trees are infected by a fungus disease; the tree reacts to the fungus by producing a resin. When burned, in very small pieces over charcoal, the resin in the wood of the infected tree produces a remarkable and subtle fragrance. The incense is mentioned in the Bible (Ps. 45.8; Prov 7.17; Cant 4.14; John 19:39) and was brought by Nicodemus for Jesus. Aloes is also called Eaglewood (from Portuguese *pao d'Aquila*). In Malay it is called *kayu gahru* (or *gaharu*). The Portuguese epic poet Luis de Camoes called it "the odorous wood"; it was once imported into Europe and well known.

Alyasa'. The Biblical Elisha, the disciple of Elijah. He is mentioned in the Koran in Sūrah 6:86.

Amal (lit. "hope"). The condition of expectation of the soul. It is also the name of a political organization founded in Lebanon in 1974 by Mūsā aṣ-Ṣadr. Imām Mūsā aṣ-Ṣadr was an Iranian Mulla who came to Lebanon in 1959 and became the leader of most of Lebanon's Twelve-Imām Shī'ites. The purpose of Amal was to provide the Shī'ites of the Baqā' Valley and southern Lebanon with a political means of action and self-expression, which, with continuing civil unrest in the country, took on a para-military role in the face of other contending factions, all of which were armed. In 1978 Imām Mūsā aṣ-Ṣadr disappeared while on a visit to Libya. Presumably he was assassinated, a fact which Lebanese Shī'ites have steadfastly refused to admit. *See* LEBANON; METAWILA.

Ameer 'Ali (Sayyid Amir 'Ali; 1849-1928). Modern Indian authority on Islam, author of the *Spirit of Islam.* Like Sir Muḥammad Iqbal, he was strongly affected by the humanist and secular European outlook of the nineteenth century and took an apologetic and rationalist approach to Islam, treating evil, for example, figuratively, and referring to the "parabolic nature of Koranic expressions."

Amen, *see* ĀMĪN.

Āmīn The Arabic form of Amen, meaning assent, "verily", "truly", and "so be it"). "And all the people shall answer and say, Amen" (Deuteronomy 28:14); and "Blessed be the Lord forevermore, Amen and Amen (Psalm 89); and Amen, Amen, I say unto thee, except a man be born again, he cannot see the Kingdom of God" (John 3:3).

In Islam Āmīn is used in the same way as among the Jews and the Christians; it is always uttered at the end of the *fātiḥah,* whether within the ritual prayer (*ṣalāt*), or as *du'ā',* and as an assent to the prayers uttered by others, the preacher at the Friday prayer, for example. It has been suggested that Āmīn is a Divine Name. *See* FĀTIḤAH.

al-Amīn. A name of the Prophet, given to him by the Quraysh before the revelation of Islam, meaning the "Trustworthy One". The word is used as a title for an organization official in a position of trust, such as the treasurer of a charitable organization, a guild, and so forth. *See* FĀTIḤAH.

Amīnah. Mother of the Prophet. She was the daughter of Wahb ibn 'Abd-Manāf. Most sources put her burial place at al-Abwa.

> 'Abd ar-Raḥmān son of 'Awf narrates that his mother Shifah declared as follows:
>
> "I was a midwife to the Prophet's mother Amīnah; and in the night when her labor pains seized her, and Muḥammad Muṣṭafā fell into my hands at his birth, a voice out of the Other World came to my ears, saying: 'Thy Lord show Mercy to thee!' And from the east to west the face of earth became so illuminated that I could see some of the palaces of Damascus by the light of it."
>
> And it is reported that Amīnah declared:
>
> "In that night a flight of birds turned in to my house, so many that the whole house was filled with them. Their beaks were of emerald, their wings of ruby."

See MUḤAMMAD.

Amīr (or Emir, lit. "commander" pl. *umarā',* from the root *amara,* "to command".) In the past *amīr* was usually a military title, now used to mean a prince or as a title for various rulers or chiefs. *Amīr al-Mu'minīn,* or "Prince of the believers", is a title of the Caliph. *Amīr al-Muslimīn,* or "Prince of the Submitted" was used by Yūsuf ibn Tāshufīn of the Almoravids, and has remained a title sometimes used by princes in the Maghreb, or Arab West. The title *Amīr al-Umarā'* ("Prince of Princes") was used by the Buyids who ruled under the nominal control of the 'Abbāsids. *See* CALIPH.

Amir Khusraw Dihlawi (651-727/1253-1325). One of the most famous Muslim literary figures of India, he wrote lyrical and epic poetry in Persian. Amir Khusraw used national material in his writings, and described customs and festivals. He was a disciple of Nizam ad-Dīn Awliya, the most noted mystic of Delhi.

al-Amr (lit. "the command"). In mystical theology the command given by God: *kun,* "Be!" which creates, translating possibilities from the unmanifest to the manifest. As the Word of God it corresponds to an aspect of the idea of the *logos.*

"They will ask thee about the Spirit; say to them: the Spirit proceeds from the Command [*al-amr*] of my Lord..." (17:8). *Al-amr* has thus been one of the terms used for the active pole (in Aristotle *eidos*) of the polarization within Being into act and potency, that is, the Yang and Yin polarization from which creation takes place. The polar opposite of *al-amr* (act, form, power, Yang), is potentiality, the passive pole (Yin), which is also called universal nature (*at-ṭabī'ah*), or primordial substance (in Aristotle, *hyle*). *See* FIVE DIVINE PRESENCES; al-MUMKINĀT; NAFAS ar-RAḤMĀN.

'Amr ibn al-'Āṣī (d. 42/663). A Qurayshī who converted to Islam shortly before the conquest of Mecca and went on to become one of the most successful Muslim military leaders. He took part in the campaign in Syria in *14*/635 and conquered Egypt in *20*/641 during the Caliphate of 'Umar.

'Amr's army of 4,000, reinforced by az-Zubayr with 5,000, defeated the Egyptians at 'Ayn ash-Shams (Heliopolis) in *19*/640. Thereafter, months of fighting led to the conquest of the Egyptian fortress of Bābilūn the following year, which forced Alexandria to surrender without further bloodshed.

'Amr became the governor of Egypt and founded a camp city at Fuṣṭāṭ on the eastern bank of the Nile, near present-day Cairo. There he built a mosque which bears his name and still stands today. 'Amr was removed from office by the Caliph 'Uthmān (the head of the Umayyad clan) but, nevertheless, sensing the victory of the Umayyads in the struggle that ensued after the assassination of 'Uthmān, he joined the army of Mu'āwiyah and fought against 'Alī at the Battle of Ṣiffīn in *37*/657. 'Amr is said to have devised the idea of having Mu'āwiyah's troops attach leaves of the Koran to their lances. When Mu'āwiyah's forces were seen to be losing the struggle this act suddenly proved an irresistible call to both sides to turn to God's Word to decide the quarrel. This led to a mediation between 'Alī and Mu'āwiyah which was manipulated in Mu'āwiyah's favor.

When Mu'āwiyah the Umayyad became Caliph he reinstated 'Amr as governor of Egypt. 'Amr died in Egypt holding office at a very advanced age. *See* CAIRO.

Amulets. Magical charms are widely used everywhere in the Islamic world, but especially in North and West Africa, and in the Sahara. Most often the amulets are calligraphed passages of the Koran which are sealed in a leather case, worn around the neck or on the body. Sometimes they take the form of jewelry, such as the "hand of Fāṭimah", and inscriptions on silver. The wearer hopes in this way to ward off evil by the incantations written on the amulets, and at its best, through the intention of seeking refuge in God, which they express. In Arabic they are called *ḥijab, ḥamā'il* and in West Africa *gri-gri.*

In the Middle East amulets are a domain which preserves obscure beliefs; in amulets and talismans one can find residues of past religions. In Africa it is common for such amulets to incorporate elements of animistic religions. Thus Koranic passages are found side by side with invocations of long names which are purported by those who believe in them to be "names of Angels", in Hausa and the like. *See* HAND of FĀṬIMAH; REFUGE.

Analogy, legal, *see* QIYAS.

Anas ibn Mālik. A famous Companion and personal servant of the Prophet. He should not be confused with Mālik ibn Anas, founder of the Mālikī School of Law (*Madhhab*).

Andarūn. The private interior of an Iranian home occupied by the women and off limits to visitors. The term corresponds to the *ḥaramlik* amongst Turks, and the *ḥarīm* amongst Arabs.

Andarz. Persian wisdom literature which includes such genres as the "mirrors for princes" or "advice for rulers".

Angels (Ar. sing. *malak* or *mal'ak*, from *la'aka*, "to send on a mission"). The doctrine of Angels within the Semitic religions is related to that of the guardian spirits of Babylonia and the *daena* and *fravarti* (*fravarshi*) of the ancient Iranian religions. The elaboration of the concepts of the Archangels in particular, and especially the polarization of Michael and the fallen Archangel, Satan, is influenced by Iranian antecedents. The Angels, who are celestial beings in the supraformal world, called *Jabarūt*, are subordinated in a hierarchy at the head of which stand the four Archangels: Jibrā'īl or Jibrīl (Gabriel, called in Iran by his Zoroastrian name, Sraosh), the Angel of Revelation, Mīkā'īl or Mīkāl (Michael), Isrāfīl, whose blast from the "horn" of primordial sound will shatter forms and creation at the end of time, and Izrā'īl, the Angel of Death. These are of the class of Angels called the *Qarībiyyun*, cognate with Hebrew *Kerūbhīm* ("cherubim") and interpreted to mean "those who are near (to God)"; and like the *Mal'ak Yāhwēh* of the Old Testament, they "act" in the place of the Divinity. The Archangels' centrality as expressions of Divine aspects, or as protagonists of God, sets them apart from the other Angels. Except for the Archangels who, as Divine functionaries, partake of a certain ambiguity expressed in Michael's name which is a question in Hebrew: "Who is like God?", the Angels do not possess a central state (a state with objective self-knowledge and capacity to know the Essence), and unlike man, the Angels do not possess free will. Therefore, although closer to God, they are not superior to man in the perfection of his unfallen primordiality (*fiṭrah*), because man can truly know God, whereas Angels cannot. In the story of the *Mir'āj*, the Prophet's ascent to heaven and the Divine Presence, as told by tradition, the

Prophet is carried upwards by Gabriel. There comes a point, however, beyond which Gabriel cannot approach and the Prophet must go on alone.

When Adam was created, God commanded the Angels to bow down to him, and Adam's superiority to them was made evident by the fact that he knew the *names* of the Angels and objects in creation, while the Angels did not. Adam knew the names because human knowledge is possible through an identity in the center of one's being with the Intellect, the center of Being itself. Of this Intellect, which can also be called Spirit, Meister Eckhart said: "there is something in the soul which is uncreated and not creatable; this is the Intellect." The "Intellect" in this metaphysical sense, partakes at the same time of created form within man, and of the uncreated within Being. Its center is not the mind but the heart; in Arabic it is called *aql* ("intellect"), and also *sirr* ("secret").

Traditionally, the true name of something is itself the object named on a higher plane; the true name contains the object, just as Plato's Ideas contain their "shadows", or the objects of existence. Adam's knowledge of the names showed that he was, in fact, the synthesis of creation, and at the same time its center. Because Adam was defined by physical form, and therefore bounded by limitation, it would seem that this would make him inferior to the station of the Angels, who are formless. But the extreme limitation of the spirit which corporeal existence (as form, not as "matter") represents is itself the means whereby that which lies beyond form – and even Angelic formlessness – may be known.

Because Adam knew directly through the Intellect (one could say that he knew because he contained the object of knowledge within himself as subject), form permitted him to grasp what was beyond form. Our life, which is in the world of forms teaches us to understand death, which is outside the world of forms, it is limitation which brings to our awareness that which is beyond limitation, and it bestows the supreme ability namely, to conceive of the Absolute as Absolute. The Angel's knowledge of the Absolute is necessarily indirect, or "blind", that is, as animals know us, rather than as we know each other.

One of the Angels, Iblīs, refused to recognize, because of pride, the superiority of Adam and was banished, falling from the state of an Angel to that of the jinn, a being in the subtle world. This is the symbolical story of the origin of evil. It expresses clearly, however, the inability of evil, or Satan, to "see" in form, anything but form, limitation, and not through or beyond form to the essence. It could be said the Angels could not see it either, but they obeyed God. Ibn Māja the traditionalist (born *209*/824) says of Angels:

> 'It is believed that Angels are of a simple substance (created of light), endowed with life, speech and reason; and that the differences between them, the *jinn* and *shayṭān*, is a difference of species. Know that the Angels are sanctified from carnal desire and the disturbance of anger; they never disobey God in what He hath commanded them, but do what they are commanded. Their food is the celebration of his glory; their drink is the proclaiming of His holiness; their conversation, the commemoration of God, whose Name be exalted; their pleasure is his worship; and they are created in different forms and with different powers.'

See also ADAM; FIVE DIVINE PRESENCES; HARUT and MARUT; IBLĪS; JINN; MUNKAR and NAKIR.

Anṣār (Ar. "helpers"). The name given by the Prophet to the believers among the people of Medina as an honorific, and to distinguish them from the *muhājirūn,* or immigrants from Mecca. Descendants of the original Anṣār families sometimes still include the title "Anṣārī" in their family name to indicate their origins.

al-Anṣārī, Abū Ismā'īl 'Abd Allāh (*396-481*/1006-1089). Scholar, Sufi, and theologian, at first of the Shāfi'ite school and then a Ḥanbalī. In Persia he is known as Pir-i Anṣār. He was born near Herat and spent most of his life there. Anṣarī's teacher in religious studies was Abū 'Abd Allāh Taqī; his master in Sufism Abū-l-Ḥasan Kharaqānī.

Al-Anṣārī is the author of the devotional *Munājāt* ("Intimate Conversations"), the *Ṭabaqāt as-Sufiyyah* ("The Chronicles of Sufis"), *Dhamm al-Kalām wa Ahlih* ("Shame of Theology and Theologians"), a Ḥanbalī polemic; a book on Sufi theory called *Manāzil aṣ-Ṣā'irin,* and other works.

In his *Munājāt,* al-Anṣārī says:

> O God, seek me out of Thy Mercy that I may come to Thee; and draw me on with Thy Grace that I may

turn to Thee.
O God, I shall never lose all hope of Thee even though I disobey Thee, and my knowledge of Thy Bounty has brought me to stand before Thee.
O God, how shall I be disappointed seeing that Thou art my hope; or how shall I be despised seeing that in Thee is my trust?
O Thou Who art veiled in the shrouds of Thy Glory, so that no eye can perceive Thee! O Thou Who shinest forth in the perfection of Thy splendor, so that the hearts (of the mystics) have realized Thy Majesty! How shalt Thou be hidden, seeing that Thou art ever Manifest; or how shalt Thou be absent, seeing that Thou art ever Present, and watchest over us?

Antichrist, *see* DAJJĀL.

Antinomianism (from Greek *anti,* "against" and *nomos* "law"). In philosophy an antinomy is the mutual contradiction of two principles or inferences resting on premises of equal validity; in philosophy the matter ends there. When religion enters the picture some mutual contradictions can and must be resolved, in the presence of faith, on a higher plane. Not all contradictions can be resolved in this way, however, and notable among them is theodicy or the existence of evil. When the existence of evil is ascribed to two principles, the resolution of contradictory absolutes into a higher principle, which is necessary by the very idea of reality, becomes literally impossible. The way out is to affirm that ultimate reality as such is unreachable and unfathomable. This appears as a doctrine of the unknowability of God. This is found, for example, in the Mu'tazilite separation of God from His Attributes, and was attacked by al-Ash'arī (d. *324*/945) and many others until the Mu'tazilite doctrine was pushed out of Sunni Islam.

Those Hellenist pre-Islamic sects which were fatally committed to this course, called such a contradictory God the *Bythos,* or the "Abyss". The Fāṭimids who held this belief translated and transposed the term into Arabic as *al-ghayb t'ala* ("the Great Otherness"). This is what they called God, relegating Allāh as a name for the first emanation out of the unknowable invisible which was called the First Intellect. This emanation, according to their teaching, was itself created, and limited, thus demiurgic, and lamented its own exile from the Abyss although itself the direct creator of the world. (They said that the Name Allāh derived from a verb – *walaha* – meaning "to lament": which is impossible.)

The orthodox answer to the problem is to explain the existence of evil as an absence of good, not as another kind of substance resulting from another kind of principle. According to the orthodox theodicy, what actually happens when evil enters the world, is that it is a mistake made by consciousness in taking non-existence to be a different form of existence, a kind of anti-existence. Since such an anti-existence would have to have a principle from which it arose (if it is not already God Himself), evidently the essence of such a hypothetical principle for evil would be absolute contradiction. The Creed of Sa'd ad-Dīn at-Taftāzānī (d. *175*/791) found it necessary to affirm that "the non-existent is not a thing".

Antinomianism is specifically religious behavior which is contrary to the law. It is related to philosophical and religious antinomy or dualism because it makes an identity between good and evil and thus between what is permitted and the forbidden. That which is within the limitation from which creation results and that which is beyond limitation, or nothingness, are turned into equal realities, and the sum of the two realities becomes principial or divine. Antinomian sects exist in all religious climates; sometimes the antinomianism expresses itself only as a tendency which stops short of actually transgressing religious prohibitions; at other times it consists of deliberately violating religious prescriptions, as for example, the breaking of the fast of Ramaḍān at the declaration of the *Qiyamah* ("resurrection") at the Assassin stronghold of Alamut in 1164.

It also exists as various degrees of libertinism of which Gnostic sects have frequently been accused, rightly or wrongly. The practice of *mut'ah,* or temporary marriage for a period as short as a day, prohibited by Sunni Islam, is sometimes at the base of these accusations. Elsewhere there were sects called in Persian "the extinguishers of lamps" which may have been radically libertine. In the West the Cathares, for example, were strictly ascetic until they reached a stage which they considered to be purity or perfection of the individual. Thereafter they believed that that they were incapable of sin and that whatever they did was good. They had surmounted the law which still existed for the profane.

Antinomian currents in Islam, in addition to the *ghulat,* or extremist sects who divinized their pontiffs (which for Islam is the greatest of sins) are still to be found in Sufism in many forms. They are concentrated in some well-known sayings which are passed on as being Ḥadīth. The most famous is usually attributed to Abū Hurayrah, although sometimes 'Alī is also cited as the source: "I have two bodies of knowledge from the Prophet; one you know; if I were to tell you the other, you would slit my throat." The other body of knowledge is never specified; it is left as an obscure spot reserved for the awakening of a spontaneous anti-truth. A variant is that there was something Ali could not tell anyone "which he had to whisper in a well".

Another well known pseudo-Ḥadīth of this type says that the Prophet retired during a session into a grove, that 'Alī followed him and when he returned was questioned by 'Umar regarding what the Prophet had said. When 'Umar heard the report he said this must be kept secret otherwise no-one will strive for salvation. The grove theme figures in a series of other rather obscure accounts which refer to an Anti-christ figure appearing in Medina. These are evidently traces of later attempts to neutralize the original forgery by attaching onto it additional elements or evolving it into a third entity.

Some interesting examples of antinomian ideas are among those sayings known as *Ḥadīth qudsi,* or God speaking through the Prophet. Many of the so-called *Ḥadīth qudsi* are simply the Koran itself paraphrased. A number of others, however, are antinomian when presented, as they are in practice, in the context of an acroamatic, or secret, oral teaching. One of these is I [God] was a hidden treasure, I wanted to be known, therefore I created the world. This saying may appear recorded for the first time in the *Mathnawi* of Rūmī; by itself there is nothing necessarily objectionable in it. However, as it is actually transmitted orally, explicitly or by implication, the import is that the world is an emanation of God, and thereby God Himself.

Among Algerian Sufis there is the affirmation that the Prophet frequently asked his disciples "is there a stranger among us" meaning that he was about to teach something which could not be told to everyone, in other words, a secret teaching. The secret teaching is rarely made explicit, the follower being left to reconstruct it for himself, which is the more effective since it takes the form, when it arises, under the effect of the original antinomy, as a sudden realization from within.

The device of a secret teaching is at the heart of Mahayana Buddhism, and appears at one point or another in virtually every other religion as well. It is a simple method to introduce an antinomian idea wherever one wishes. In itself this was used early enough for Bukhārī's *Ṣaḥiḥ* to affirm that 'Ā'ishāh, the Prophet's widow said to Masruq: "Verily, he who tells you that the Prophet has concealed a part of Divine Revelation and that he has not delivered it to his people, lies." The secret teaching idea persists and is repeated among otherwise pious and even strict Muslims even though the Koran itself says "O Messenger! Make known that which has been revealed to you from your Lord, for if you do not, you will not have conveyed the message" (5:67).

Behind this stand two doctrines to which the antinomian allusions lead; these are found amongst many Sufis, and among minor sects related to Islam or at its fringes. The first is the divinization of man. A direct example is the case of a well known saying widely accepted today as a Ḥadīth, namely, "Who knows his soul knows his Lord, who has seen me [the Prophet] has seen the Truth". The first part is simply classical Gnosis, and is in any case relative; the second draws an identity between man and God. The central teaching of the Koran is that only God is God, and that nothing created is God; nevertheless the divinization of man (*hulūl*) remains one of the key ideas that appears and reappears in Sufism even after having been extirpated, as happens from time to time, by reformers. The revealing touchstone is how al-Ḥallāj and the other drunken Sufis are treated by a particular Sufi group; usually the leading figure of the Sufi order affirms that he could have corrected al-Ḥallāj, or that al-Ḥallāj was rightly punished for going too far (namely making the secret of man's essential divinity public), but not that al-Ḥallāj was wrong or that the idea is false. Another touchstone is the emphasis on past masters who, by becoming intermediaries, become assimilated to God Himself by function. This takes the form of a ritual invocation of the figures in the *silsilah* or initiatic chain of the order. Antinomianism and divinization of the created are inseparable pairs; the one makes the forbidden, or what lies beyond the limit, licit, and the other makes the limited into an absolute.

The other doctrine is that of the redemption of Satan (and along with him the rehabilitation of other villains of the Koran, in particular, Pharaoh.) Al-Ḥallāj writes in the *Tāwāsīn* that Iblīs and Pharaoh were his teachers. The idea that Satan is the perfect Muslim who would not bow to Adam as commanded because he would only worship God may have begun with Sahl at-Tustarī. It was taken up also by Ibn 'Arabi, Attar, 'Abd al-Karīm al-Jilī and by others. Ultimately the redemption of Satan was a Trojan Horse brought into Islam, an attempt to elevate an anti-principle or evil to the same status or reality as God.

In the Sunni world this antinomianism lies hidden even today within the folds of Sufism; this is not to say that all Sufis are unorthodox; many condemned it. 'Abū-l Mawahib ash-Shadhilī said of al-Ḥallāj: "Had he attained the reality of annihilation he would have been saved from the errors incurred through saying I am He." Yet it persists nevertheless. Perhaps antinomianism's reason for existence, like the fall of man in the first place, is that by its very contradiction it draws a depth out of consciousness. One could also say that in order to know what we are, we have to know what we are not, and antinomianism teaches this. But it has been condemned by all the religions because by its nature it more often destroys the same consciousness in the process, creating solipsism and an all enclosing subjectivism, not to mention subverting a religion at its base. It was even al-Ḥallāj himself who said: "God threw a man into the sea with his arms tied behind his back, and said to him: Careful! Careful! or you will get wet in the water!" *See* BOUJLOUD; DÖNMEH; "SECRET SOCIETY"; DRUNKEN SUFIS; DUALISM; ḤALLĀJ; MANICHEISM; "SATANIC VERSES"; SAHL TUSTARI; UMM al-KITAB.

Antinomy, see Al-KINDĪ.

Apocatastasis (Greek: "full restoration" from the verb *apokathistēmi* "to restore"). The first appearance of this doctrine is with Zoroastrianism where it is the third time of creation, the *wizarishn* when evil is destroyed at *frashokereti* and the world is restored to its state in the beginning before it was attacked by the evil spirit. This inspires the idea of the descent of the heavenly Jerusalem and other expectations of a blessed time to come. It also appears in a different form, that of the metaphysical doctrine that there is a moment in which there is no creation, no manifestation. In this version of the apocatastasis, beside God the Absolute, there is nothing. Because creation is inherent in the Divine Nature, this interval must be followed by the creation of other worlds anew. However, at this moment between creations, or between worlds, both the paradises and the hells of the previous creation disappear and existence is restored to the perfection which it possesses in the Principle.

In the West this doctrine is associated with the Stoic philosophers; it was later inherited by Christianity and was upheld by Clement of Alexandria, Origen, and St. Gregory of Nyssa. It was not understood in the same sense by all; Origen for example, believed that creation was eternal (which is directly contradictory to the principle at the root of the apocatastasis doctrine), and for him, the apocatastasis simply meant universal salvation; it is this theological interpretation of the apocatastasis doctrine which kept it from becoming a dogma of the early Christian Church, for fear that no-one would then strive for salvation. In Judaism the apocatastasis appears as the ultimate return of all things to the One.

In Hinduism, the apocatastasis is called the *mahā-pralaya.* The *Srīmad Bhagavatam* refers to it when Brahma says: "My play is ended, my day is done". The doctrine also exists in other traditions, notably in Buddhism in the moment in which there is no *samsāra* and all creatures realize Nirvāāa, and in Judaism's "Be with Me".

There are allusions to such a doctrine in Islam among metaphysicians who point to this saying (which is so respected as to be often cited as a Ḥadīth): *Kāna-Lāhu wa lā shay'a mahu, wa Huwa-l-'ān kamā kān* ("God alone was and with Him nothing was; and He is now as He was"). Allusions to the doctrine appear again in another kind of story, found in different versions and often quoted by the Sufis, in which the Prophet leaves his close Companions; first 'Alī goes to look for him and finds him in meditation in a grove. 'Alī holds speech with him and leaves the grove; he meets 'Umar who asks him what the Prophet said, and when 'Alī discloses the Prophet's words (which are not related), 'Umar says that no one must know of this because then no one would strive for paradise. These words of the Prophet are understood to refer to such a doctrine, which must be kept secret. This is similar to the history of the doctrine of the apocatastasis in the early Eastern church, where it was held that the doctrine could not be made general knowledge for the very reason adduced by 'Umar.

The question of the apocatastasis is also at the root of the classical debate between theologians and Muslim Aristotelian philosophers. The philosophers, such as Avicenna, (Ibn Sīnā) argued that the world was eternal; the theologians argued that it was created in an event *ex nihilo.* The metaphysical perspective of the doctrine of the apocastastasis resolves the issue because in its light creation is eternal because, whether manifest or not, it is a permanent and necessary possibility eternally within the Absolute. On the other hand, the theological Absoluteness of God as Creator is maintained because there is, in a manner of speaking, a "moment", a time (an unmeasurable time because there is no reference), when the possibility of creation is *only* inherent and *not* manifest. There is nothing beside the Absolute. Then, when creation begins anew, it begins *ex nihilo,* out of nothing.

The import of this doctrine is that the paradises come to an end and that those who dwell in them are restored to a principal state, namely, possibilities from which all beings issue in the first place. The hells also come to an end, which, for those who have not already been annihilated, is equivalent to a full pardon. Yet, rather than universal salvation it is, so to speak, a reset of manifestation – which includes the paradises and hells, and an affirmation of the Absoluteness of the Absolute. As a further Ḥadīth says: "By the God in Whose hands is my soul, there will be a time when the gates of hell will be closed and watercress will grow therein". *See* ESCHATOLOGY; FIVE DIVINE PRESENCES; al-KINDĪ; PHILOSOPHY.

Apostasy. Although conversion from other religions to Islam is welcomed, apostasy from Islam is not admitted under Islamic law. However, punishment for apostasy (in any case, extremely rare) was not in practice enforced in later times and was completely abolished by the Turks by a decree of the Ottoman government in *1260*/1844. In Arabic, apostasy is called *irtidād* (or *riddah*) and an apostate is called a *murtadd. See* RIDDAH.

Apostasy, Wars of, *see* RIDDAH.

'Aqabah. A hill in Mina just outside Mecca. In June 620, following the Prophet's "year of sadness", six men of the tribe of Khazraj of the town of Yathrib (later to be called Medina), accepted Islam from the Prophet at the hill of 'Aqabah during the Meccan pilgrimage. The following year, five of the original group returned to perform the pilgrimage in consort with seven others, including two men of the Aws, the other leading tribe of Yathrib. These twelve entered Islam and pledged fealty to the Prophet at night in the very place where the original five had entered Islam the year before.

They swore not to associate anything with God, not to steal, not to commit fornication, nor slay their offspring (see MAWŪDAH), nor utter slanders. They promised to obey the Prophet in that which is right. This oath became known as the First 'Aqabah. The Prophet accepted their allegiance saying:

> If you fulfill this pledge, then paradise is yours. If you commit one of the sins and then receive punishment for it in this world, that shall serve as expiation. And if you conceal it until the Day of Resurrection, then it is for God to punish or forgive as He wishes.

Mus'ad of the clan 'Abd ad-Dār went with the men to Yathrib and stayed with them eleven months to teach them the Koran and their religion. The following year, again during the pilgrimage, seventy-three men and two women (eleven of the men from the Aws, the rest from the Khazraj) took a similar oath at 'Aqabah. This time the men also pledged to fight and defend the Prophet. This was the oath of the Second 'Aqabah; the women at the Second 'Aqabah took the oath of the year before, without the pledge to fight, and this form of the oath became a model known as the "Oath of Women".

The Prophet's uncle al-'Abbās was present at the oath as a witness, even though he was then still a pagan. A Sūrah revealed before this event speaks of a mounting incline, a steep, which is in Arabic *al-'aqabah.*

No! I swear by this land,
and thou art a lodger in this land;
by the begetter, and that he begot,
indeed, We created man in trouble.
What, does he think none has power over him,
saying, 'I have consumed wealth abundant'
What, does he think none has seen him?

Have We not appointed to him two eyes,
and a tongue, and two lips,
and guided him on the two highways?
Yet he has not assaulted the steep;
and what shall teach thee what is the steep?
The freeing of a slave,
or giving food upon a day of hunger
to an orphan near of kin
or a needy man in misery;
then that he become of those who believe
and counsel each other to be steadfast,
an counsel each other to be merciful.

Those are the Companions of the Right Hand.
And those who disbelieve in Our signs,
they are the Companions of the Left Hand;
over them is a Fire covered down.
(Koran 90; an early Meccan Sūrah).

In September of 622 the Prophet emigrated to Yathrib. *See* HIJRAH; MUḤAMMAD.

'Aqīdah, *see* CREED.

'Aqīqah. A non-obligatory tradition of shaving the hair of a child on the seventh day after birth. Thereupon a sheep is sacrificed and the weight of the hair in silver is distributed to the poor. It is an old Arab practice confirmed by the Sunnah, or example, of the Prophet.

al-'Aql (lit. "intellect"). Sometimes used to mean "reason' or "thinking", but its highest and metaphysical sense, as used in Islamic philosophy, corresponds to the *intellect,* or *nous,* as understood in Platonism and Neoplatonism. It is the faculty which, in the microcosm or in man, is the embodiment of Being or Spirit. It is in this sense that the Rhenish mystic Meister Eckhart said: "There is something in the soul which is not created and not creatable, and this is the Intellect."

It is also what the Koran calls *ar-Rūḥ* (lit. "spirit"). The "Unity of the Intellect", or the essential identity of the Intellect in the metacosm (what is beyond the created world), the microcosm (man), and the macrocosm (the world, which is the manifestation of the possibilities of the metacosm), was expressed as a theory by Ibn Rushd (Averroes, d. *595*/1198), the philosopher and chief interpreter of Aristotle. But it is also implicit in most Islamic metaphysics when the question of *'aql* arises, even where there is little or no apparent connection with philosophy or mysticism.

This "Intellect", in the Eckhartian sense, is veiled behind discursive thought or reason; nevertheless, it is essentially the same – or not other – than its celestial prototype, the Divine Intellect. Through this transcendent Intellect man is capable of the "recognition" of Reality and of knowing the world, because the world is in fact contained within him, as the world is contained in Being. The Intellect makes possible direct knowledge, or *intellection,* which amounts to "revelation" on the plane of the microcosm, where the subject – because of his capacity for perfect objectivity – *comprehends* the object, seizes or "assimilates" it, and realizes an *identity* between the subject (his own mind) and the object. It is thus that Plato, and later St. Augustine, described knowing as remembering.

It is the presence of the Intellect within man which sets him apart from animals who participate in the cosmic Intellect peripherally, but do not contain it, since they do not occupy the "center" as does man. It is thus also that Adam knew the names of the objects of creation, whereas the Angels did not, being also peripheral, that is, not containing the projection of the Divine Intellect within them. The Angels, it is true, were superior to Adam in that they were less limited in their form; yet they bowed to him because he was truly vicegerent of God on earth, *khalīfatu 'Llāhi fi-l arḍ*: "Adam, tell them their names..." 2:33. *See* FIVE DIVINE PRESENCES.

Aq Qoyunlu. The "White Sheep" Turkmen confederation, so called from the emblem on their standards. The Aq Qoyunlu were a branch of the Ghuzz (or Oghuz, a division of the the Turkic peoples), a steppe tribe who originally formed a part of the Golden Horde of the Mongol Khans.

The Aq Qoyunlu were rivals to the "Black Sheep" confederation or Qara Qoyunlu. The Aq Qoyunlu dominated a region centered around Diyarbakir in Anatolia. At times their control extended into Iraq and Persia. They ruled from *780*/1378 until *913*/1507 when their domains were whittled away by the Ottoman Turks on the one side, and the Safavids on the other.

'Aqrabah, Battle of, *see* MUSAYLAMAH.

al-Aqṣā' (lit. "the farthest [mosque]"). The name the Koran gives to the Temple Mount in Jerusalem and to the Temple of Solomon (also called *al-Bayt al-Muqaddas*, the Holy House. The sanctuary known as the Dome of the Rock (*Qubbat aṣ-Ṣakhrah*, often called the "Mosque of 'Umar") dominates the Temple Mount today. From the rock, which was probably the site of the "Holy of Holies", the Prophet was carried by the Angel Gabriel through the heavens to the presence of God. (*See* NIGHT JOURNEY). At the other end of the Temple Mount stands the mosque called al-Aqṣā (*Masjid al-Aqṣā*), distinguished by its silver dome from the gold of the Dome of the Rock. The Aqṣā mosque, one of the most important in Islam, is famous for its elaborately decorated walls. It was built at the end of the 7th century A.D. and is the largest mosque in Jerusalem. *See* DOME of the ROCK.

Aqsaqalism (from Turkish, "white beard"). A modern propaganda term that had been used in the former Soviet Union to deride traditional respect for elders as found in Central Asia.

Arabian Nights, *see* THE THOUSAND AND ONE NIGHTS.

Arabic. The language of the Koran, and the Arabs, today the most important language of the Semitic group, spoken by over 100 million people and understood by many more. The Arabic writing system has an alphabet of 28 consonants. It developed from Canaanite script (from which the later, square Hebrew letters are also derived) through Nabatean. The various Canaanite scripts evolved from a so-called "demotic", i.e. cursive, versions of Egyptian hieroglyphs. The Arabic writing system was introduced into Mecca not long before the revelation of the Koran. It underwent necessary refinements for some time after that, notably the creation of the vowel points. In South Arabia there existed another writing system found in Himyarite inscriptions; this disappeared from use in Arabia although it survives in an attenuated and barely recognisable form in Ethiopic script.

The Arabic of the Koran is similar to the koine used by the poets of the age, the *lingua franca* of its time, but cannot be equated with it, as the Koran is in every respect, unique. This *lingua franca* differed somewhat from the various tribal dialects and these gave rise to the different Koranic readings (*See* QIRĀ'AH.) Koranic Arabic is today a sacred language used only for reading the holy book and for prayer. So-called classical Arabic, as established by the usages found in the Koran and the Ḥadīth, is still used for composing books. It is also retained, with a very restricted and modified vocabulary, for journalism, broadcasting, conferences and so forth. The vernacular has, however, branched out into several principal dialects, mutually comprehensible for the most part as are, say, Spanish and Italian.

Arabic has provided most of the special vocabulary of Islam in use all over the world. In addition to religious vocabulary, vast numbers of Arabic words have been adopted into such African and Asian languages as Swahili, Hausa, Persian, Turkish, Urdu, and Malay. Arabic is also the liturgical language, not only of Islam, but of some Christian churches.

Muslims consider the Koran to be holy scripture only in the original Arabic of its revelation. The Koran, while it may be translated, is only ritually valid in Arabic. This is connected with the notion of Arabic as a "sacred language". Language itself is sacred, because of its miraculous power to communicate and to externalize thought. In this sense, language is essentially the same as the Divine power of creation. In order to create, God speaks a Word in the Spirit; similarly, man externalizes what is within his mind by formulating words with the breath, by giving breath form in sound. The power of words to transmit to another consciousness the knowledge of the speaker lies in the fact that true words *are* themselves what they mean, or were at their origin; they are the object itself in sound. (*See* NAFAS ar-RAḤMĀN.) Sacred languages preserve this original power of language to an eminent degree; liturgical languages like Latin, the older forms of Greek, and Church Slavonic, have also preserved this power to a lesser degree.

Modern languages have, for the most part, lost this "sacred" quality; the identity between word, or "name", and the object named has become obscured; it is no longer direct, but indirect, through convention, or sign. This obscuration reflects the passage on the part of man from direct knowledge, or intellection, to reason, or indirect knowledge. The Biblical "mark of Cain", placed upon Cain's forehead, as much to protect him as to punish him, has been interpreted to signify this obscuration which took place at the dawn of time.

Arabic was the language of desert nomads, the most conservative of all peoples; it could be said that the desert protected the primordiality of Arabic over other languages by limiting phonetic decay, and by preventing confusion with other languages, loss of the meaning and the power of words, and syntactic degeneration. When it became the fabric of Islam, Arabic was protected further by the need to preserve the Koran unaltered. Thus classical Arabic has retained an ancient quality into modern times.

The nature of Arabic grammar and syntax, which avoids subordination and architectonic complexity (which are the distinctive qualities of Indo-European languages), assures a directness of style. The fact that Arabic (as some other languages such as Russian) does not need the copulative verb "to be" in definitions of being (*al-wujūd*) means that God can easily be referred to in a supra-ontological sense. The phrase *Allāh Huwa adh-Dhāt al-Mutlaqah* ("God is the Absolute Essence"), not involving the verb "to be" in Arabic, does not imply conceptual confinement to being, even pure Being. The case endings make possible great flexibility in sentence structure; the words of a sentence can be presented in more than one order; the meaning remains the same but points of emphasis can be varied. There is a highly developed system of verbal modes, which, by the introduction of prefixes and infixes, generate additional verbs from a given root with meanings which are for the most part predictable from the form of the verbal mode.

In Arabic, almost every word is derived from a "simple root", usually of three letters, most clearly visible in the verbal noun (*masdar*). The root corresponds to an abstract act. The act may be existential such as that expressed by the triliteral root *b-r-k* ("to settle") whence a deposit of water, such as a well (*birkah*), a blessing or spiritual influence (*barakah*, that is, that which comes down from above), or, again, the kneeling of a camel – all are settling. Or it may represent a state: *k-b-r* ("to be big") or *r-ḥ-m* ("to be merciful") whence also *raḥim* or riḥm ("womb"). The letters or phonemes correspond to *al-a'yān ath-thābitah* ("immutable archetypes") in Being (tradition says the letters were taught to Adam by the Angel Gabriel). But the act of which the verbal root is a mysterious incarnation in sound takes place in consciousness: thus the tree of meaning branches from the verbal act-root – the nouns being derived from verbal forms – and the images that the language brings forth are ultimately to be traced back to awareness itself. The words are understood as concepts but they can also shatter concepts or submerge them and return to a threshold between the world and pure mind, where the vibration of sound faces creation on the side of perception, and the uncreated on the side of cognition. The Arabic grammarian Suyuti in the *Kitab al-Muzhir* compared the triliteral roots to fixed stars in the firmament beyond which is the empyrean of Being and said their number was 3,276.

While a given word has a specific meaning determined by convention, it also has a universal sense which is evoked by its "root"; language merges with reality. Thanks to the relationship of words to their roots, as if to a supraformal archetype, a deeper and more universal sense often superimposes itself upon a particular meaning in a phrase in classical Arabic. Simple statements, which are the rule in the Koran, open, under the right conditions of receptivity, into astonishing and vast horizons; the world is reduced to ripples in consciousness. These and other qualities make Arabic an incomparable medium for dialogue between man and God in prayer.

There is a saying that Persian is the language of Paradise, but Arabic is the language of God. The Koran is recited only in Arabic, and even people who cannot read at all, in any tongue, keep Arabic Korans for the blessing of the Koranic presence. In Arabic, the Koran has a sublime beauty at which translations can only allude. Arabic is also the obligatory language of the canonical prayers (*ṣalāh*).

In the Middle Ages, Arabic was also the

intellectual language of the Islamic East and was used by many nationalities and religions for literary and scientific compositions. The Persians in particular were great masters of Arabic. The scientist and scholar Abū Rayḥān al-Birūnī, who was born in Central Asia and not an Arab, wrote:

> Our religion and our empire are Arab...subject tribes
> have often joined together to give the state a non-Arab character. But they have not been able to achieve their aim, and as long as the call to prayer continues to echo in their ears five times a day, and the Koran in lucid Arabic is recited among the worshipers standing in rows behind the *Imām,* and its refreshing message is preached in the mosques, they will needs submit; the bond of Islam will not be broken nor its fortresses vanquished.
>
> Branches of knowledge from all countries in the world have been translated into the tongue of the Arabs, embellished and made seductive, and the beauties of the language have infused the veins and arteries of the peoples of those countries, despite the fact that each considers its own language beautiful, since it is accustomed to it and employs it in its daily offices. I speak from experience, for I was reared in a language in which it would be strange to see a branch of knowledge enshrined. Thence I passed to Arabic and Persian, and I am a guest in both tongues, having made an effort to acquire them, but I would rather be reproved in Arabic than complimented in Persian.

See also ABJAD; ALLĀH; ARABS; 'ILM al-ḤURUF; KORAN; QIRĀ'AH; as-SŪRYĀNIYYAH.

Arabs. The Semitic people indigenous to the Arabian peninsula. The name Arab is now applied to all peoples who speak Arabic as a mother tongue, including Muslims and Christians, but not Druzes and Arabic-speaking Jews. However, many Arab speakers have little or no Arab blood; they are instead descendants of the other ethnic families of the Middle East and North Africa.

When the Arabs came out of the Arabian peninsula with the expansion of Islam, their language was adopted by all those peoples who already spoke a cognate, Semitic (or, in some cases, Hamitic) tongue. Arab custom too was adopted far and wide, despite the fact that in many countries the Arabs themselves were a small minority who were absorbed and submerged into local populations. Peoples who are Arabs by blood as well as language are found in the Arabian peninsula from Yemen, and the African coast near Yemen, throughout the Syrian desert and southern Iraq. After the expansion of Islam they also emigrated in numbers large enough to maintain a tribal identity, like the Banū Ḥilāl in North Africa. In Algeria, Morocco and Mauritania Arabs make up less than half the population, while the majority is Berber; in Mauritania there is also a variety of West African peoples with close connections with Senegal. Communities of descendants of Arab emigrants, chiefly from the Ḥadramaut, are also found in Indonesia and Malaysia.

Geographers of antiquity divided Arabia into Arabia Felix – the Yemen, which receives the rains of the monsoon from the Indian Ocean and is luxuriously fertile, and Arabia Deserta – North Arabia. This also corresponds to the traditional division of the Arabs into two major groups: the South Arabians who believe that they are descended from a patriarch named Qaḥṭān, identified with Joktan of the Bible, and the North Arabians, who claim descent from a patriarch named 'Adnān, and through him, from Ishmael (Ismā'īl), son of Abraham. Both northern and southern groups were also divided further into two social groups: the *ahl al-madar,* or house dwellers, and the *ahl al-wabar* ("the people of goat-hair"), tent-dwellers, or Beduins (from *badiya,* "wilderness").

The name Arab means "nomad". The North Arabs are considered *'Arab al-musta'ribah,* "Arabized Arabs", while the Qaḥṭānis of the south consider themselves *'Arab al-muta 'arribah,* or tribes resulting from mixing with the *'Arab al-'aribah,* original, or "true Arabs". From the Qaḥṭānis, through a traditional ancestor called Himyar, descend the Arabs of the ancient South Arabian or "Himyaritic" kingdoms. The completely "true Arabs", descendants of Aram son of Shem son of Noah, (son-in-law of the Arabic-speaking Jurhum who, according to Arab tradition, was with Noah in the Ark) are called the *'Arab al-bā'idah,* "the lost Arabs", who, like the "lost tribes of Israel", are "lost", or rather "remote", because their names, while remembered by posterity, are lost to them: their identity has been submerged in that of other peoples. These are the tribes of 'Abil, 'Ād, Imlik, Jadis, Jurhum, Tasm, Thamūd, Umaiyim, and Wabir. The Koranic "Thamūd", who were destroyed by God for turning away from His revelations made through the Prophet Ṣāliḥ, are identified with the Nabateans. Koranic commentators make the people against whom the Jews fought coming out of the Desert after the captivity in Egypt remnants of the tribe of 'Ād (symbolically so, for 'Ād is traditionally located in the south of Arabia, a people the Koran says were destroyed for repudiating the Prophet Hūd).

The distinction between South and North Arabian tribes, and a certain opposition due to different traditions, caused tension in later Arab history, as long as the groups maintained a consciousness of their identities. One example is the differences which erupted in Medina on the death of the Prophet, between the *Muhājirūn*, North Arabians from Mecca, and the *Anṣār*, native Medinans who were originally of South Arabian origin. After the death of Yazīd I, strife broke out in Syria and Iraq between the North Arab tribal group of the Qays, and the South Arab Kalb, a conflict which persisted throughout the Umayyad Caliphate.

Two trees grow in the Yemen which were crucial to the economy of the ancient Arabs and influenced their history. One tree produces frankincense which was burned as a fragrance in large quantities in pagan religious ceremonies. The other, myrrh, was used in cosmetics and the embalming of the dead. In antiquity before Christianity became dominant, these substances were in such demand that they made the Yemen a source of wealth to those who ruled it. Besides the incense trade and agriculture in those areas which could support it, the Beduins lived by the raising of camels and livestock which were traded in the markets of Syria and Egypt.

In ancient times the incense trade of the Yemen attracted settlers from the fertile crescent. On the other hand, population pressures in the Yemen forced some clans into the desert to wander in a pattern which progressed northward often bringing them to settle, finally, after wanderings over the course of centuries, in the north. The Kindah tribe, of which the famous poet 'Imru'-l-Qays was chief, left the Yemen in the fifth century B.C. and wandered in the Syrian desert before returning to the Yemen shortly before the revelation of Islam.

The time before Islam was called the *Jāhiliyyah* ("the Age of Ignorance"). Its great events were the feuds and raids between desert Arabs. These were recorded in poetic lays called the *Ayyām al-'Arab*, the "Days of the Arabs", that were handed down orally. The importance of poetry to the Arabs persists to this day. It is the principal art form of the nomad, as pictures are the principal art form of sedentary peoples, because poetry recreates the dimension of time by the succession of sounds. Poetry thus manifests time, the complement to space, which is the dominant life dimension of the hunter-nomad, who meets his prey in space in the destiny of an instant, or pastures his flocks in the endless wilds. Similarly, the picture manifests simultaneity, or space, the complement to the dominant life dimension of the sedentary-farmer whose existence is based on the cycles of planting and harvesting, and thus time.

In the Age of Ignorance great markets existed, such as that at 'Ukāẓ, in which an important attraction was the declaiming of poetry. The most acclaimed poems were written in gold letters and hung in the Ka'bah at Mecca. The idea of one God, inherent in the very Name Allāh ("the God") was ancient among the Arabs. Christianity and Judaism were practiced throughout the peninsula. Through Byzantine influence, Christian communities arose in such places as Najrān in the south of Arabia, which was important enough to be the seat of a bishop. Christian hermits also lived in the deserts, and there were isolated Christians in the midst of otherwise pagan tribes. Besides tribes of Jewish origin living in Arabia, there were also Jewish converts from among the Arabs. In the Yemen in 525 A.D., the King Dhū Nuwās, who had been converted to Judaism, tried also to convert the Christians of Najrān to Judaism by force, and when they refused, he had them thrown into a burning pit. The martyrs of Najrān are honored in the Koran (85:4-8).

Another religious group before Islam were the *hunafā'* (sing. *hanīf*), a word of uncertain origin indicating the generally hermitic adherents of a primordial – or perennial – monotheism that went back to Ismā'īl and Abraham. By the seventh century this Abrahamic monotheistic consciousness among the Arabs had all but disappeared. In its place there was a proliferation of idols. The sanctuary of the Ka'bah, originally dedicated to the one God, was filled with objects made of wood and stone representing deities brought from all the lands with which the Meccans traded. Drinking, boasting and feuding prevailed; worship at the Ka'bah became mere whistling and clapping of hands (Koran 8:35). Within twenty years all was to change when the Center irrupted into the history of the Arabs and the world was accorded the last divine message: the revelation of Islam.

The revelation of the Koran began around the year 612; by 636 the whole peninsula was converted. Islam has since been adopted by men and women from every people and nation. Its universality is evident, but at the same time Islam everywhere has been marked by the Arab soul. It incarnates something of the purity of the desert, a liberation from time into space, and from form into act; an awakening from the past and a discovery of the eternal in the present, and the nomad's sense of life as a unique journey. According to Aristotle (and, for that matter, in the doctrine of the Tao), the absence of a quality contains potentially its opposite. The desert is the prototype of existence reduced to its essential, to a kind of void. In its emptiness the desert calls forth plenitude, in its receptivity it calls forth the Absolute. *See* 'ABBĀSIDS; ARABIC; ABRAHAH; 'ĀD; BAGHDAD; DAMASCUS; DHŪ NUWĀS; HŪD; IBN KHALDŪN; 'IMRU'-l-QAYS; ISMĀ'ĪL; JĀHILIYYAH; MA'RIB DAM; MECCA; MEDINA; MUḤAMMAD; NAJRĀN; QURAYSH; SABA'; ṢĀLIḤ; SHU'AYB; THAMŪD; 'UKAZ; UMAYYADS.

al-A'rāf. Ar. the "heights", or high ground (from which a clear view is possible of the sky and the low-lying land) and hence a symbolical place between heaven and earth, a limbo for those who do not merit hell but cannot enter heaven. This other-wordly locus may also be considered a kind of purgatory but a beneficent one, with privation but without suffering. This interpretation is based upon several verses in Sūrah al-A'rāf, notably verses 46 and 47.

> And between them is a veil, and
> on the Ramparts are men knowing
> each by their mark,
> who shall call to the inhabitants
> of Paradise: "Peace be upon you!
> They have not entered it, for all
> their eagerness."
> And when their eyes are turned
> towards the inhabitants of the Fire
> they shall say, "Our Lord, do not
> Thou assign us with the people
> of the evildoers."

There exists also the concept of a purgatory of suffering, in the sense that many theologians, such as Ibn Hazm, have maintained that if a believer went to hell it would be for a limited and not an indefinite duration; he would be released into paradise when the sins which brought him there were exhausted. Non-believers, however, would remain in hell indefinitely, that is, until the awareness of an individual self disappeared. Massignon believed that the Christian concept of an eschatological limbo (*limbus*) may have come from the Muslim interpretation of the al-A'rāf of the Koran. *See* CHILDREN; ESCHATOLOGY.

'Arafāt. A plain 12 miles/19 kilometers southwest of Mecca which lies partly outside the restricted area of the *ḥaram*. One of the culminating stations of the great pilgrimage (*ḥajj*) takes place here. On the 12th Dhu-l-Ḥijjah, or *yawm 'Arafāt*, the pilgrims assemble on the plain, continually repeating the talbiyyah formula. Attendance at 'Arafāt, at least for a short time – most pilgrims stay from noon to sunset – is obligatory for the accomplishment of the rites of the pilgrimage.

In the 19th century a Christian disguised as a Muslim, John Fryer Keane (Ḥajj Muḥammad Amīn) visited 'Arafāt. His experience is described thus: "The sides of 'Arafāt were thickly clothed with men, and thence they extended one mile and a half to the south, and half a mile across, a rippling sea of black heads and white bodies. The distant countries from which they came, and the object which brought them, filled him with awe. Could all this be of no avail, and all this faith be in vain? If so, it was enough to make a man lose faith in everything of the kind." (*See* PILGRIMAGE).

The name 'Arafāt, is variously interpreted. It came from the root *'arifa* "to know", "to recognise", and is most commonly taken to refer to Adam and Eve, separated from each other by the Fall from Eden, and, according to tradition, reunited here and recognising one another. At one end of 'Arafāt is a prominence called the Mount of Mercy (*Jabal ar-Raḥmah*), which is the place of choice to pass the day of the pilgrimage.

The massive gathering of humanity which takes place here in the *ḥajj*, a million or more from all over the world, is unique. It has been interpreted symbolically as a foretaste of the Day of Judgement.

al-Arba'ayn (lit. "the forty"). A family ceremony to commemorate the death of one of the members forty days after the event. The practices vary, but often include inviting religious dignitaries for the reading of the Koran, prayers, and a meal. Another commemoration may be held on the first anniversary of the death. It is common in Arab countries for the women to visit the graves of family members on Fridays. *See* FUNERALS.

'Arīf or 'Ārif (lit. "a knower"). Formerly a term applied to someone who was expert in some field, such as an architect. The gardens of the Generalife in Granada are so called from the Arabic *jannatu-l-'arīf*, "the garden of the architect", or, "the knower". *'Ārif* has the technical meaning in Sufism: "someone possessed of direct knowledge of God". The highest station of Sainthood is an *'Ārif bi'Llāh* or "knower by (or through) God", the equivalent of the Sanskrit *jīvanmukta* in Vedanta (someone not only saved, or admitted to a superior condition of existence, but liberated, in this case "liberated in life"; that is, liberated from all becoming). *Ma'rifah* describes this state of knowing and is generally translated "gnosis".

Ibn 'Aṭā'Allāh says in the Ḥikam: "Not all who are most certainly amongst the chosen go on to perfect their liberation." *See* SAINTS.

Arkān ad-dīn, *see* FIVE PILLARS.

Arqam (d. *55*/674). A Companion and early convert to Islam. Arqam was one of the *muhājirūn* who emigrated to Medina because of religious persecution in Mecca. He took part in the great battles of Islam's struggle for survival, and lived to an old age.

His house in Mecca stood at the foot of the hill of Ṣafā near the Ka'bah (because he was from one of the important families, one of the "Quraysh of the Hollow"). The house of Arqam was one of the most important early meeting places of the Muslims before the conversion of 'Umar. The site is now incorporated into the present Grand Mosque of Mecca.

al-'Arsh (lit. "throne"). The Koran speaks often of the "throne" of God (7:54; 9:129 and others). One interpretation is that the throne symbolizes Being. According to tradition, God's throne is inscribed with the words "My Mercy outstrips My Wrath" (*inna raḥmatī sabaqat ghaḍabī*). The Koran also refers to *al-kursī*, which is synonymous with *al-'arsh*. In the human microcosm it corresponds to "the heart".

An 'Isawa litany says: "My Master! place me in the shadow of Your throne the Day when there will be no shadow but Thine." *See* al-KURSĪ; FIVE DIVINE PRESENCES.

Artifice, legal, *see* ḤĪLAH.

'Asabiyyah (from *'asab*, "stalks that bind together"). Tribal or group solidarity in the face of those outside the group. Ibn Khaldūn's observations on society in the Prolegomena made the term famous.

Ascetic, *see* ZĀHID.

Aṣḥāb an-Nabī, *see* COMPANIONS.

Aṣḥāb al-Ukhdūd (lit. "people of the ditch"). The Christians of Najrān who were burned alive in 525 A.D. by Dhū Nuwās, a tyrant from the Yemen who tried to convert them forcibly to Judaism. The people of the ditch are extolled by the Koran as martyrs (85:4). *See* NAJRĀN.

Aṣḥāb aṣ-Ṣuffāḥ (lit. "the people of the bench"). Poor Muslims who flocked to Medina and were to be found sitting on a bench near the Prophet's house, hoping to receive sustenance. At this time the Prophet himself lived in extreme poverty, yet he gave to the people of the bench and said "The food of one is enough for four, and the food of four is enough for eight."

Of the early period in Medina the histories say:

> In those days the Prophet would go to the room of one or the other of his wives and ask: "Is there anything to eat?" And the answer might be "No." "Then I fast today," he would say.
>
> "We used to be as long as forty days on end and never lit a fire, in those times", 'Ā'ishah said.

"Believers", the Prophet said "are content in all

circumstances" (*Al-Mu'minūna fī kulli ḥālin bi-khayr*).

The straitened circumstances of the Muslims' lives lasted until the conquest of Khaybar, and improved continually thereafter. When he became Caliph, 'Umar once laughed in disbelief when he was told that half of the year's revenue from Baḥrayn amounted to a million dirhams. But he found out afterwards that it was true. When the people gathered in the mosque for prayer, 'Umar spoke to them: "I have got from Baḥrayn a huge sum of money: will ye take your shares weighed out? Or must I count it over to you coin by coin?"

Asharah Mubāsharah (lit. "ten well-betided ones"). Ten Companions to whom the Prophet foretold they would enter Paradise. They were: Abū Bakr, 'Umar, 'Uthmān, 'Alī, Ṭalḥāh, az-Zubayr, 'Abd ar-Raḥmān, Sa'd ibn Abī Waqqās, Sa'īd ibn Zayd, Abū 'Ubaydah ibn al-Jarrāh.

al-Ash'arī, Abū-l-Ḥasan 'Alī ibn Ismā'īl (*260-324*/873-935). He is considered to be the founder of Sunnī Kalām, or theology. Born and raised in Baṣra, until the age of forty al-Ash'arī was a Mu'tazilite and the student of al-Jubba'ī (d. *303*/915; see MU'TAZILITES). At that point he put this famous question (here paraphrased from the many versions recorded of al-Ash'arī's thought-experiment) to his teacher: "Take the case of three brothers, one a believer who did good works, one a sinner, and one who died in infancy. What would happen to them?" His teacher answered that the believer went to paradise, the sinner to hell, and the infant to limbo. "Well", asked al-Ash'arī, "since according to the Mu'tazilite doctrine of *al-aṣlaḥ*, God always chooses the best for his creatures, why did the infant die?" "Because", the teacher answered, "God knew the infant would go on to be a sinner, and so ended his life at the stage which avoided hell, the most advantageous solution." "Then", asked al-Ash'arī, "why did God let the sinner grow to the age of responsibility and be punished for his sin?" (*Regarding salvation of children,* see CHILDREN.)

To this, Mu'tazilite rationalism had no answer, and with this episode al-Ash'arī abandoned their school, became a Ḥanbalī Sunnī, and made public repentance and repudiation in the mosque of Baṣra for his errors. (Although al-Ash'arī considered himself a Ḥanbalī, the Ḥanbalīs themselves accord little place to theology. Like the Ḥanbalīs, al-Ash'arī asserted that the Koran was completely uncreated, even in its letters and sounds; in the school of theology which bears his name, however, the Koran is uncreated in its essence, but created when it takes on a form in letters and sounds, when, that is, it is written or recited.) Despite his repudiation, however, al-Ash'arī went on to apply the Mu'tazilite use of dialectic and rational methods to the dogmas of orthodox Islam, except that whereas they used logic to bring everything down to a horizontal plane, he accepted the transcendent aspects of divinity but, as it were, set them "off limits" to speculation by the use of the formula *bilā kayfa,* "without asking how". He assumed the acts of God to be inscrutable and beyond accountability. In particular, he exalted God's Will to be so far beyond human comprehension that it became absolute in itself, beyond coherence, and even purely arbitrary. According to al-Ash'arī, God could punish good if He so willed, and send the pious to hell. This is clearly a reaction to the Mu'tazilite desire to reduce the vertical dimension of Divine transcendence and mystery to that of horizontal, and human, logic. But it was al-Ash'arī who actually legitimized the use of some of the Mu'tazilite methods in many domains because he became one of the most accepted authorities in theology. Thus, in the end, he achieved precisely a reformed rationalism, or even, one could say, a reformed Mu'tazilitism.

Al-Ash'arī, denying the existence of secondary causes, is also known for the doctrine of *kasb* (lit. "acquisition") regarding action. According to him, any act such as the mere raising of the hand, is created by God, but *acquired* by the creature who thus takes responsibility for it. This is a device to ascribe free will for man and therefore responsibility, but to reserve all power of action to God alone. In other words, it is an attempt to resolve the opposition between freedom and determinism without resorting to antinomy or to formulations which are contradictory on one plane and resolved on a higher plane. (Although it could be said that what al-Ash'arī actually produced was a reverse antimony.)

Within the Ash'arīte scheme of things it is technically impossible to make a statement about the present without saying "if God wills" whereas normally this proviso – *in shā'a-Llāh* –

is only applied to the future. The great achievement of Ash'arīsm was to establish an orthodox dogmatic guideline. A mystic such as Ḥasan of Baṣra could resolve metaphysical problems intuitively, but it required the integration of philosophy into Islamic thought in order to provide the tools and concepts to deal with metaphysical thought precisely and flexibly. In theology, Ash'arism laid down a line of defense against reductive reasoning; inevitably it could also be used against philosophy, and was, by al-Ghazālī. (*For the Creed of al-Ash'arī, see* CREED.).

Through his followers, al-Ash'arī's influence became considerable. Although Ash'arīsm was at first opposed by the Saljuqs, and Ash'arītes were even persecuted, as the ideological struggle with the Fāṭimids became more important, Ash'arīsm revealed itself as a useful weapon, and the Saljuq Vizier Niẓām al-Mulk named Ash'arītes to teaching posts, namely al-Juwaynī, al-Ghazālī, and others. Ash'arīsm also became a cornerstone of the Almohad movement. The Ash'arīte school of theology is widespread in the Islamic West while that of al-Maturidi, which is in practice very similar, is the preferred theology in the East.

Among al-Ash'arī's many works, the most famous are the *al-Ibānah 'an Uṣūl ad-Diyānah* ("The Elucidation of the Foundations of Religion"); *Maqālāt al-Islāmiyyīn* ("The Discourses of the Islamicists") and the *Risālah fī istiḥsān al-khawḍ fī-l-Kalām* ("Treatise on Theology"); *Kitāb ash-Sharḥ wa-t-Tafṣīl* ("The Book of Commentary and Explanation"). Al-Ash'ari played in Islam the role the great councils played in early Christianity, by correcting major doctrinal errors and for this reason, he was credited with "singlehandedly saving Islam". *See* CHILDREN; CREED; KALĀM; MU'TAZILITES; QADARIYYAH.

Ashraf. The word means "nobles" in Arabic. In India, it has in addition a technical meaning and refers to what is *de facto* a caste system amongst Muslims. Belonging to the *ashraf*, in descending order, are *Sayyids*, also called by the title *Mir*, who are real and purported descendants of the Prophet; *Shaykhs*, that is, descendants of Companions, as well as holders of the title by virtue of leadership; *Mughals* who are Chagathay Turks, and *Pathans*, often called by the surname Khan. That false claims of ancestry are often made is indicated by this saying; "Last year I was a weaver; this year I am a shaykh, next year I will be a Sayyid."

'Āshūrā'. The tenth of the month of Muḥarram, the first month of the Islamic year. The 'Āshūrā', which is derived from Jewish holy days, was observed as an optional fast day by the Prophet. It is a holy day of beneficent character for the Sunnīs. Among the Shī'ites it is the terrible anniversary of the murder of Ḥusayn by the troops of the Caliph Yazīd. Shī'ites fast the ninth of Muḥarram; on the tenth, certain Shī'ite groups wander the cities and publicly inflict wounds upon themselves. This mortification is an expression of guilt among the Shī'ites for having abandoned the Imāms in their moment of need. In the days preceding the tenth of Muḥarram the *ta'azīyah* martyrdom plays are performed in Iran.

As a Sunnī holy day the 'Āshūrā' has been observed since the time of the Prophet because it is, precisely, Sunnah. As the anniversary of the death of Ḥusayn, the public observance was instituted by the Buyid ruler al-Muizz ad-Dawlah, a Shī'ite, in *351*/962.

Asiyah (wife of Pharaoh), *see* PHARAOH.

Asmā' bint Abī Bakr (d. *73*/692). A daughter of Abū Bakr and older sister of 'Ā'ishah, the Prophet's wife. When the Prophet and Abū Bakr hid in a cave in the mountain of Thawr outside Mecca, Asmā' brought them food and water in secret, which she carried suspended from two belts that went over the shoulders. Because of this she was called "she of the two belts" (*Dhāt an-Nitaqayn*).

Asmā' became the wife of one of the Prophet's closest Companions, az-Zubayr ibn al-'Awwām, and the father of 'Abd Allāh ibn az-Zubayr. 'Abd Allāh raised an opposition to the Umayyad tyranny, declared himself Caliph, and held Mecca from *64*/683. When Mecca was conquered in *73*/692 by the Umayyad general al-Hajjāj ibn Yusuf, 'Abd Allāh's body was suspended from a gibbet for several days. Asmā' came to al-Hajjāj and told him to cut down the body, which he did. She died shortly thereafter. She had been, in fact, a driving force in the old conservative (non-Shī'ite or non-'Alid) opposition to the Umayyads. Asmā' lived to be around one hundred years old.

'Asmah ("sinlessness"), *see* 'ISMAH.

al-Asmā' al-Ḥusnā, (adh-Dhāt; aṣ-Ṣifāt) *see* DIVINE NAMES.

Assassins (from the Arabic *ḥashshāshīn*, "consumers of hashish", through Medieval Latin *assassini*). The name was adapted, from local usage, by the Crusaders for members of the Nizārī branch of the Ismā'īlīs at a period when the sect was characterized by extreme militancy. This phase in the history of the Nizārīs extended from *483*/1090 until the fall of Alamūt fortress in *654*/1256. The association with hashish is obscure; it may come from stories that drugs were used as part of an indoctrination intended to produce perfect obedience to the leaders. Or simply, it may be a disparaging reference to the sect's ideas on the part of Sunnis. In Syria, where the Assassins occupied a string of fortresses, their chief was known to the Crusaders as *le vieux de la montagne*, "the old man of the mountain" (*shaykh al-jabal*). The most famous of the the Syrian leaders was Rashīd ad-Dīn Sinān, but the movement was actually headed by the Masters of the castle of Alamūt in Persia. The first of these was Ḥasan aṣ-Ṣabbāḥ who took over the leadership of of the main branch of the Ismā'īlīs when a schism occurred in Fāṭimid Egypt.

Ḥasan aṣ-Ṣabbāḥ was an Ismā'īlī propagandist or dā'i of Persian origin. Around the year *479*/1086 he traveled to Egypt, then the center of Ismā'īlī activity under the Fāṭimid dynasty, and subsequently returned to Persia to carry on propaganda in the name of Nizār, the expected successor to the Fāṭimid throne and the Ismā'īlī Imāmate. However, in *487*/1094 a struggle erupted in which Nizār was imprisoned and supplanted by his younger brother al-Must'alī, at the instigation of the leader of the armies, al-Afḍal. Ḥasan aṣ-Ṣabbāḥ, who was committed to upholding Nizār, took the occasion to break with the Fāṭimids, and by *483*/1090 he had seized the fortress of Alamūt, "the eagle's nest" in the north of Persia near the Caspian Sea. With Alamūt as his center of operations, aṣ-Ṣabbāḥ succeeded in establishing a power base among the outer tribes in mountainous regions far removed from the centers of political influence.

He built his empire through the propagation of Ismā'īlism, a Gnostic-dualist creed which teaches that out of an unknowable God, because of "an inner conflict" between good and evil within the Divinity Itself, a series of emanations called "intellects" emerged which culminated in the creation of the world. The mythic backdrop from which the doctrines of Ismā'īlism derive declares that the world and the body are evil because in them light and darkness are mixed; however, there is within some men a spark of knowledge, imprisoned and cut off from its source. It is said that at the end of the world, light and darkness, which in themselves are neither evil nor good, are resolved into their separate domains; meanwhile, the chosen ones who possess the spark hear the secret call, awaken to the realization of their true nature of light and, at the end of time, they are saved. The quotation attributed to Ḥasan aṣ-Ṣabbāḥ, a kind of paraphrase of the *shahādah*, "nothing is true, everything is permitted" comes from a book by Hammer-Purgstall who based himself on a line in Maqrizi's Topography of Egypt (*Muhawal Dar al-Ḥikmah*).

The Assassins won disciples by claiming to possess the secret knowledge which is the core of Ismā'īlism, known through the *Imām*, himself a hypostasis of the unknowable God and an intermediary to salvation. The Fāṭimid Caliphs were held by the Ismā'īlis to be the *Imāms*, and thus the spiritual heads of the sect.

Marco Polo passed through the region in *670*/1271, and recorded in the account of his travels what he heard about the Assassins. The castle of Alamūt was conquered by the Mongols in *654*/1256; thus stories told in Morocco that Marco Polo encountered the master of Alamūt are factually impossible (and a blending of recent European influence with what may be authentically indigenous material). But the Moroccan stories are revealing in substance: they say that the leader of the sect set upon Marco Polo's head a helmet made of crystal. He could bear to wear it for only a moment because, when it was struck, the crystal produced the "sound of pure evil itself".

Ḥasan aṣ-Ṣabbāḥ's "Assassins" were known in the Islamic world at the time as the *Ta'līmiyyah*, ("people of the teaching"), the *Bāṭiniyyah* ("the people of the inner truth"), or the *Fidā'iyyah* ("the self-sacrificers"). Marco Polo gave this description of how the Assassins created completely submitted followers: as part of their initiation, novices destined to become self-destructive *fidā'iyyūn* were drugged; they awoke to find themselves in a garden of delights complete with fountains flowing with wine, milk, and honey, and *houris*, the maidens of paradise. After this heady taste of the "afterlife", the new recruits were drugged again and when they returned to their normal state that were told that they had indeed visited paradise, which would be theirs without fail if they obeyed.

Taken allegorically, and not literally, this could be termed a fair description of the process of intellectual indoctrination into the reality system of, say, a cult or a radical political movement; it is the glimpsing of a different and mysterious way of seeing the world, the unveiling of "hidden truths" which constitute the system's typically subjective explanation of theological, political, or even economic phenomena. This has a psychological impact which, once experienced, changes one's perceptions forever, so that it is usually difficult, if not impossible, to de-program completely. Marco Polo's story (to which there is a parallel in the "Universal History" of Rashīd ad-Dīn aṭ-Ṭabīb) is a traditional model of the process of deliberately modifying someone's perception of reality; in modern times it has come to be called "brain-washing".

To illustrate the Assassins' complete domination over their adepts, Ibn al-Jawzi reported that the followers of Assassin chiefs had been seen to hurl themselves to their deaths by leaping off precipices at their leader's command. More than likely this was a staged piece of theater intended to frighten their enemies, but it was effective and typical of the Assassin style. In any case, the *fidā'iyyūn* were certainly prepared to sacrifice their lives. Their mission was to sow fear of the sect through terrorism and at the same time to weaken their enemies by the murder of key political figures.

The Assassins infiltrated the ranks of their adversaries, often in the guise of dervishes and religious teachers. When they attained to positions of trust they would kill their selected victims, always through the use of a knife. Apparently by design, they usually perished themselves when they carried out their orders. Among their victims were the famous Saljuqid vizier Niẓām al-Mulk (the first to attempt to put down the Assassins), as well as his brother and his son; the Sultan Mālik Shah; al-Amīr, son of al-Musta'lī, the Fāṭimid who put Nizār to death; two 'Abbāsid Caliphs, and hundreds, if not thousands, of others. In Syria, Crusader leaders were among their targets and the Assassins succeeded in murdering Conrad of Montferrat, King of Jerusalem. Saladin himself narrowly escaped Assassin attempts on his life and always had to be on his guard.

Through the profound ideological hold the leaders maintained over their followers, and the political destabilization brought about by their program of murder, the Assassins were able to exist as an invisible kingdom within kingdoms. Their castles in northern Persia and Syria were almost impregnable to siege and attack by reason of their well chosen situations. Ultimately, the opponents of the Assassins preferred compromise to the risk of a fatal dagger stroke at the hands of a trusted servant who turned out to be a member of the dreaded sect.

Al-Ghazālī combatted the teachings of the sect (under the name of *Ta'līmiyyah*) by writing polemics against them. Fakhr ad-Dīn Rāzī denounced them until he was warned at knife-point to desist along with the gift of a bag of gold if he complied. When he ceased to attack them, his students asked why, and he replied, "I do not wish to speak evil of men whose demonstrations are so pointed and whose proofs are so weighty".

The power of the Assassins came to an end when the Mongols under Hūlāgū Khān advanced on Alamūt in *654*/1256 with "an army", writes the historian al-Juwaynī, "of such numbers that Gog and Magog themselves would have been destroyed by waves of its battalions". The last Grand Master, Rukn ad-Dīn, surrendered and was sent to Qaraqorum where he was put to death. The Egyptian Mamlūks conquered the Syrian strongholds soon after. Even earlier, as their power declined, the Syrian Assassins had offered to ally themselves with the Crusaders and to become Christians. This offer was declined by the Christians, who may well have realised that, whatever religion the Assassins professed, it would be no more than an outer garment, and that their "conversion" could not be expected to affect their inner and secret beliefs.

There was more to the Assassins, however, than mere terrorism: true to the serious pursuit of knowledge that marked the first centuries of Ismā'īlism, they amassed libraries and acquired scientific instruments, and did not hesitate, if one is to believe the case of Nāṣir ad-Dīn aṭ-

Ṭūsī, to kidnap such scholars as could increase their store of cosmological science. The Nestorians and Shī'ites who accompanied the Mongol horde found books and instruments which showed that Alamūt was not only a center of murder but, strangely, of learning as well. The Assassins' fascination with science can be traced to the nature of Ismā'īlism. The metaphysics of dualism, in Ismā'īlism as in Valentinian Gnosticism, is inseparable from cosmology because the physical universe is considered to be, in a certain sense, itself Divine, a kind of shadow of the metaphysically unknowable "Abyss".

Ḥasan aṣ-Ṣabbāḥ, murdered his own sons for disobedience. When he was dying he appointed his lieutenant, Kiya Buzurg Ummīd, the master of the Assassin fortress of Lamasar, to be the new chief of Alamūt and the Ismā'īlīs. Aṣ-Ṣabbāḥ had called his own propaganda the New Preaching", (*ad-dawah al-jadīdah*). It marked a break with the Ismā'īlīs of Cairo, the Fāṭimids. The inheritors of Alamūt carried on the tradition of aṣ-Ṣabbāḥ. Then, Ḥasan, the grandson of Buzurg Ummīd, declared himself the Ismā'īlī Imām, making himself the secret descendant through mysterious and improbable means, of Nizār, the deposed Fāṭimid.

While alive, Ḥasan's father Muḥammad repudiated the claims of his son and put 250 of his followers to death, or so it is said. Nevertheless, when Ḥasan assumed control he continued to affirm his claim to the Imāmate. Two years after his accession, during the month of Ramaḍān in *559*/1164, he declared to Nizārī leaders from Khorasan, Iraq, Syria, and the Caspian regions, assembled in the courtyard of Alamūt, and to "*jinn*, Angels and men", that their salvation lay in following his commands and that the religious law of Islam, the *sharī'ah*, was abrogated. Thereupon Ḥasan performed two *raka'āt* or bows of prayer signifying the premature end of the month of fasting, calling the day the *'Īd al-Qiyāmah*, that is, "Festival of Resurrection" – not just of the end of Ramaḍān. Those who were present joined him in eating, drinking, and festivities to mark the formal shattering of the sacred law. A traveler reported that on the door of the library of Alamūt were written the words: "With the aid of God, the ruler of the universe destroyed the fetters of the law; '*alā dhikrihi-s-salām*" ("blessings be upon his memory"). (In Gnostic theosophy the religious law is often considered to be evil.)

Not long after, Ḥasan himself was murdered, but his son Muḥammad continued his policies. His grandson Jalāl ad-Dīn, however, made a complete turnabout. He reinstated the practice of the law of Islam, declared himself a Sunnī, publicly cursed his forefathers, and for good measure burned the books of Ḥasan aṣ-Ṣabbāḥ. He allied himself with the 'Abbāsid Caliph and put his own military power at the Caliph's disposal. When he died his son 'Alā' ad-Dīn, a shadowy and corrupt figure, returned temporarily to the principles of his great-grandfather, in which the law of Islam, like the "cosmic illusion" itself was merely "clothing" which could be put on and off at will.

With Ḥasan, and the doctrine of the *Qiyāmah*, the curtain had been drawn back from the Assassin's inner doctrines. With Jalāl ad-Dīn the curtain was closed again, and the period known as the *Satr* ("veiling") resumed, with a brief interruption during the time of 'Alā' ad-Dīn.

The break between the Nizārīs and the Fāṭimids of Cairo was made complete by the establishment of the schism in the line of Imāms. The original sect in Egypt followed Nizār's brother and were called Musta'lī Ismā'īlīs. Nizār himself, his son and perhaps his grandson died in Egypt, but several explanations were devised to explain the sudden reappearance of the Nizārī line at Alamūt. One was that a pregnant concubine of Nizār's, or of Nizār's son, brought the yet unborn Imām there who, when he came into the world, was substituted for a son of the master of the Assassins.

With the death of al-Musta'lī's son al-Amīr, assassinated presumably on orders from Alamūt, the Must'alī line came to an end. However, some Musta'lī Ismā'īlīs believe that a putative grandson of al-Amīr called aṭ-Ṭayyib is alive in the unseen world, like the Hidden Imām of the Twelve-Imām Shī'ites, and they await his return as Mahdī at the end of time. Others believe that there exist descendants of aṭ-Ṭayyib who carry on the Mustal'ī line in secret. Musta'lī Ismā'īlīs in the Yemen and the Bohoras of India continue this branch of Ismā'īlīsm without manifest Imāms. Instead they are led by a figure called the *Dā'i Muṭlaq* ("Absolute Preacher").

Nor was the New Preaching snuffed out in the destruction of Alamūt by the Mongols; its old names faded away but the sect survived, rediscovered its Imāms, and eventually found a new life in Persia, and above all, through the success of its proselytizing, among the Khojas in India. *See* ISMĀ'ĪLĪS; SEVENERS; SHĪ'ISM; TA'WĪL.

Astrolabe. The astrolabe was a Greek invention and dates from 200 B.C. It is a projection of the observed heavens as seen from the earth within a defined region upon a flat surface. The astrolabe was used as navigation aid. The art of making astrolabes was preserved in the city of Harrān and from there spread throughout the Islamic world where it was refined. The astronomer 'Abd ar-Rahmān aṣ-Ṣufī said that the astrolabe was capable of performing some 350 mathematical functions. There were different styles of astrolabes, in particular the Maghribi from Morocco, and the Persian. Until 1960, a *mu'aqqit,* (the mosque functionary charged with determing prayer times), in Fez still made astrolabes by hand.

Astrology (Ar. *ilm at-tanjīm*). Astrology as a symbolism attached to heavenly bodies – "the heavens reveal the glory of God" – was accepted in the Middle Ages and was not prohibited. One would be hard put to find any astronomer, East or West, up to modern times who was not also an astrologer, that is, a student of cosmological symbolism. As divination, however, predicting the future, astrology is condemned in Islam, as in most religions, because it is misleading to the soul. The theologian Sad ad-Dīn at-Taftāzānī (d. *175*/791) made a distinction between astrology as a symbolic science and astrology as divination. In his *Creed* he says, after condemning divination, the "astrologer whenever he pretends to know approaching events is like the diviner."

The danger inherent in astrology, despite what value it may have as a mythological system, is that it may trap the soul in some existential illusion or error; that is to say, divination can throw up some illusion which is actually the projection of a subjective flaw. If what is foreseen by divination then appears to be confirmed by events, the soul is snared in an unreality of its own making. As the Ḥadīth says: "Even when the soothsayers tell the truth, they lie". And: "Let no-one malign fate for God says, 'I am destiny.'"(found in the Muwatta').

Moreover, Islam commends surrender to fate, and the importance of this attitude precludes from the outset recourse to predictions. In Judaism for example, a practising Jew is considered to have no astrological sign; that is, a sacred identity as a bondsman of God replaces the individual identity; the Talmud says: "Israel has no constellation".

Nevertheless, astrology for the purposes of divination has been widely practiced. In antiquity virtually all mathematicians were astronomers, and all astronomers were astrologers. Such men as Naṣīr ad-Dīn āṭ-Ṭūsī and al-Bīrūnī were famous astrologers. The latter attacked astrologers for poor calculations rather than for their science. Thābit ibn Qurrā said:

> Aristotle said that whoever reads philosophy and geometry and every science and is without experience of astrology, will be hindered and obstructed, because the science of talismans is more precious than geometry and more profound than philosophy.

Astrology was used for political purposes; prophecies around astrological events were spread abroad to destabilize regimes. The seveners arranged political events timed to coincide with planetary conjunctions and such prophecies. The Astrologer Shādhan al-Balkhi predicted the collapse of the Caliphal empire for 922 at the time of the rise of Qarmatians; Abu Mashar (d. 886) predicted the end of the Abbasids for 1213. A certain Daniali came to the Caliph al-Muqtadir and told him that he had found books of Daniel predicted that al-Muqtadir would solve his financial problems by using a banker whose description Daniali gave and who was an accomplice. In Baghdad in the unsettled 10th century, there were many anxieties and preoccupations with political events. Oracles and books of apocalyptic interpretations of the future were current. The Seveners and their successors the Qarmatians and Fāṭimids took advantage of this by spreading a prophecy which said that with the seventh conjunction of Saturn and Jupiter starting from a date which al-Biruni said was a Zoroastrian cyclic anniversary, there would be a new world order: the advent of the true religion. These conjunctions took place in the years 809, 829, 848, 868, 888, 908, 928, 948, 967.

For the year 928 a great victory had been predicted for the Faṭimids which did not take place. However, a raid by the Qarmatians of Abu Ṭāhir (who were a dissident sister movement) seized the Black Stone from the Ka'bah in Mecca (*17 Hijra 317*/Jan 21) and took it to al-Ḥasā' (al-Aḥsā') or to Bahrayn, This was probably planned to create waves as a fulfillment of the prophecy. Perhaps the founding of Cairo (which means the "Victorious") was also built around these deliberate prophecies. But where they succeeded completely on schedule, despite great difficulties, was the installation of their leader in Tunisia and the declaration of the Faṭimid Caliphate in the year 908.

Arab astrology is derived from the Greco-Egyptian tradition and the *Tetrabiblos* of Claudius Ptolemy. The Arabs added the points on the individual horoscope known as the Arabian Parts. These are derived by taking the arcs which separate planets such as the sun and moon, adding or subtracting other arcs, and mapping the resulting arc on a horoscope starting from the horizon in order to determine sensitive points, such as "the part of fortune", "the point of spirit" etc. This system may indeed have given rise, or at least be related to, a traditional Arab system of fortune-telling, still practiced in the market place, which involves measuring distances on the body of an individual – the arm, the head, leg and so forth – and adding and subtracting the measures to produce a divination. Other methods of divination used sand.

The Arabs assigned to the Moon twenty-eight houses (*manāzil*), one for each day of its cycle. In Arabic the signs are called *burūj*, towers or mansions. Individual stars played a greater role in interpretation than they do in the West, especially, the pairs of *naw'ī* stars, which, at a given moment, are observed on the rising and sinking horizons, corresponding to the ascendant and the descendant. This defined the horizontal axis, or the individual nature. The non-individual, or ontological axis, was the vertical between the *samt ar-ra's* ("the highest point" from which zenith is derived; also called the *Media Coeli*) and *samt an-naẓīr* (whence "nadir", *Imum Coeli*).

Naw'ī is derived from *naw'*, "the appearance of the first light", and it refers also to the entrance of the moon into each of its twenty-eight mansions, the *manāzil al-qamar*. The study of the progressions of the moon is called the *'ilm al-anwā'* and constitutes traditional Arab agricultural meteorology. The best known book on this science is the *Kitāb al-Anwā'* of Ibn Qutaybah al-Dinawārī.

Other systems of divination existed among the Arabs, such as the *mandalah*, the *ilm ar-raml* (drawing figures on sand), magic squares (*al-wafq*) combined with interpretations derived from the *ilm al-ḥurūf* ("science of letters").

In addition to predictions, or perhaps above all, astrology was used as a basis for cosmological theory to understand the secrets of creation in the sense that: "the heavens declare the glory of God". The cycles of events, or of lives, were made intelligible by sacred symbolism in the cycles of the planets. In traditional astrological or astronomical diagrams, the divisions of the zodiac, and even each degree (which represents one revolution of the earth) are assigned to an Angel; the identity of the Angel is the link, or the correspondence, between a celestial mechanics and a higher, supra-individual order of reality. Such diagrams of traditional Arab astrology as are available to us today are not easily comprehensible; some aspects may appear to be arbitrary because they are inadequately conceptualized; nevertheless, they cannot be dismissed, for while they are not systematic, they were intended to be guideposts to an individual contemplation which would yield up an understanding within the scope of a personal experience.

The cycles of the planets were applied to manifestations on the human plane, that is, events and history. These cycles (Ar. *akwār* or *adwār)* range from the precession of the equinoxes, a cycle of slightly less than 25,700 years (a number known to most traditional cosmologies, not from measurements, an impossibility which gives rise to fantastical suppositions, but by induction from ideal proportions in mathematics, or as among the Pythagoreans and al-Farābī, from music) to the cycles of the moon, and the daily turning of the earth.

Among the many stories of fate and astrology that are told in the lands of the *Thousand and One Nights* is the following: legend foretold that Islam would rule in Spain as long as the star Canopus (Ar. *Suhayl*) was visible. In the 8th century it could be seen as far north as Saragossa. By 1492, due to the precession of the equinoxes, it was barely visible in Europe. Today it is below the horizon as seen from the southernmost point in Spain.

It is also related that when Naṣīr ad-Dīn aṭ-Ṭūsī was with the Assassins at their castles in the north of Persia, the Mongols invaded the land and besieged them. The last master of Alamūt, Rukn ad-Dīn, asked Naṣīr ad-Dīn aṭ-Ṭūsī to cast a horoscope in order to determine the best course of action. Naṣīr ad-Dīn's horoscope advised Rukn ad-Dīn to surrender, which he did. Rukn ad-Dīn was first well received by the Mongols, but after a short time beheaded on the orders of Hūlāgū Khān. Aṭ-Ṭūsī, on the other hand, became astrologer and astronomer to Hūlāgū Khān, joining the Shī'ites in the Mongol train, being appointed astronomer at the Maragha observatory, and thus contributing to the sparing of Shī'ite holy places by the Mongols. *See* ALMAGEST; ASTRONOMY; 'ILM al-ḤURŪF; MANDALAH.

Astronomy (Ar. *'ilm an-nujūm*; also *'ilm al-hay'ah, 'ilm al-falak*). "Surely in the creation of the heavens and the earth, and the alternation of night and day... are signs for a people having understanding" (2:159). In the Middle Ages, the Muslims built a great number of observatories, such as the observatory of the *Bayt al-Ḥikmah* ("House of Wisdom") founded by the Caliph al-Ma'mūn (d. *218*/833). His astronomer was the mathematician Ḥabash al-Ḥāsib, as were also the "Banū Mūsā" (the "sons of Mūsā Shākir"). Other obervatories were those of the Fāṭimids in Cairo, the observatory of Maragha founded by Hūlāgu Khān (d. *663*/1265) in *657*/1259 for Naṣīr ad-Dīn aṭ-Ṭūsī, the observatory of Samarkand (c. *823*/1420) founded by Ulug Beg, the observatory of Istanbul established in *983*/1575 by Taqī ad-Dīn, and the observatories of Jai Singh at Delhi, Jaipur and Ujjain founded in the *12th*/18th centuries. Apart from observatories as such, there were many lookout towers to study the motions of the stars; often minarets were used for this purpose.

Muslim astronomers created accurate tables (*zīj*) of planetary motion: the *Zīj aṣ-Ṣābi'* of Abū 'Abd Allāh al-Battānī (called Albategnius in Europe), the *zīj* of al-Khwarizmi, the *zīj al-Ḥākimī* of the Fāṭimids made by the astronomer Ibn Yūnus from his observatory on the Muqattam hills outside Cairo, the *Zij il-Khānid* of Maragha, and many others. These often served for the creation of special calendars such as the *Jalālī*, which were noted for their accuracy. Major works on astronomy were written by al-Bīrūnī: *Qānūn al-Masūdī* ("the Masudic Canon"), and the *Kitāb at-Tafhīm* ("Book of Elucidation"); by Qutb ad-Dīn ash-Shīrāzī: *Nihāyat al-Idrāk* ("the Limit of Comprehension"); by Abū Mashar al-Balkhī: *Kitāb al-Ulūf* ("the Book of Thousands"); by al-Farghānī (in Latin *Alfraganus*): *Kitāb fi-l-Harakāt as-Samāwiyyah wa Jawāmi' 'Ilm an-Nujūm* ("On the Celestial Motions and General Principles of Astronomy"), and so forth.

Islamic astronomy was based upon Greek knowledge and Ptolemaic astronomy (*see* ALMAGEST), the sciences of the Harranians and of the Nestorians of Jundishāpūr; later, through Persia, it drew upon Indian science, notably the works of Brahmagupta and Aryabhāta, and the Mahāsiddhānta. A Chinese astronomer called Fao-Mun-Ji was associated with the observatory of Maragha in Persia.

The influence of Islamic astronomy upon Europe was very considerable. It made its first impact through the work of Arab astronomers in Spain, such as az-Zarqalī (Azarquiel in Europe) who edited the Toledan Tables, and then showed a direct reflection in the first European books on astronomy such as the *Libros del Saber de Astronomia* of King Alfonso X el Sabio ("the Wise"). Islamic observatories must also have influenced the work of the later European astronomers, Tycho Brahe and Kepler.

The early dominance of Islamic astronomy is indicated by the preponderance of words of Arabic derivation in the technical vocabulary of modern astronomy: the index of the light reflection of a celestial body is called albedo (Arabic *al-baiḍā*, "whiteness"); the zenith (Arabic *samt ar-ra's*, "the direction of the head"); nadir (Arabic *an-naẓīr*, "the opposite"); azimuth (Arabic *as-samt*, the direction"); the star Vega (Arabic *an-nasr al-wāqi'*, "the falling eagle"); the star Betelgeuse (Arabic *bayt al-jawzah*, "arm-pit of the centre"); the star Algol (Arabic *al-ghūl*, "the ghoul"); the star Rigel (Arabic *ar-rijl*, "the foot" of Orion); the star Deneb (Arabic *adh-dhanb*, "the tail"); the star Aldebaran (Arabic *ad-dabarān*, "the follower" of the Pleiades) and so forth.

The precise astronomical knowledge of the Muslims also permitted them to make perfected astrolabes which were a vital contribution to the voyages of the age of European exploration. The pre-eminence of Muslims in astronomy gave them a lead in navigation, and it is for this reason that the school founded by Prince Henry the Navigator in the Algarve in Portugal contained Arab astronomers, and it was Arab navigators who guided the Portuguese in many of their voyages: Aḥmad ibn Mājid an-Najdī, who wrote treatises on navigation in verse (to aid memorization) and prose, was pilot in the voyage of Vasco da Gama to India.

As is true of all traditional astronomy, as for example, the *jyøtividyā* of Hinduism, the science in Islam was inseparable from an interpretation of celestial phenomenon as a symbolic cosmology, or what is now called astrology. *See* ASTROLOGY; al-BĪRŪNĪ; al-KHWARIZMĪ; NAṢĪR ad-DĪN aṭ-ṬŪSĪ; MŪSĀ SHĀKIR; UMAR KHAYYĀM.

al-Aswad. ("the black one") A false prophet who appeared in South Arabia and the Yemen towards the end of the Prophet's life. He was known as *Dhu-l-Khimār*, "the veiled one". He claimed to have revelations from ar-Raḥmān ("The All-merciful"), a Name of God which was revealed, apparently for the first time, in Islam. For a brief time, al-Aswad seized control of the Yemen, much of which was then under Persian suzerainty, and made Sanā'a' his capital until his assassination in an internal power struggle. *See* MUSAYLAMAH; RIDDAH.

Atabāt ("the thresholds"). The Shī'ite Holy Places in Iraq: Kerbala (tomb of Husayn), Najaf (tomb of 'Ali), Kazimayn and Samarra (tombs of Imams).

Atatürk, Mustafa Kemal, see KEMAL, MUSTAFA.

Atjeh. A Muslim Sultanate at the north-western tip of the island of Sumatra in what is now Indonesia. When Marco Polo visited it at the end of the *7th*/13th century Islam was already established in Sumatra; by the *12th*/17th century it had attained to a highpoint of culture and politically dominated most of the island. From *1290*/1873 the region resisted Dutch conquest, succumbing only in *1322*/1904.

In Sumatra, Islam was distinctly marked by esoterism of the school of Ibn 'Arabī. A teacher named Hamzah Fansūrī taught the Ṣūfī doctrine of *waḥdat al-wujūd* ("the metaphysical unity of Being") under the name of the *wujūdiyyah* order; his successor Shams ad-Dīn (d. *1040*/1630) became the spiritual master of the King of Atjeh, Iskandar Muda (d. *1046*/1636), under whose rule Atjeh saw the summit of its cultural development. The great metaphysicians of the Shādhilī *ṭarīqah*, especially Ibn Atā'Allah (d. *709*/1309) were well known and earnestly studied in Atjeh. A later Ṣūfī of Atjeh named 'Abd ar-Ra'ūf of Singkel typified the mystical cast of Sumatran Islam in these words:

> We were lofty sounds [yet] unuttered, held in
> abeyance on the highest peaks of the mountains.
> I was in Him and we were you, and you were He
> and in Him was He; ask those who have attained.

See INDONESIA; SLAMETAN; SULUK.

Atheist, *see* DAHRI.

'Aṭṭār, Farīd ad-Dīn (d. circa *627*/1229). Persian mystic of Nayshabūr and author of the celebrated *Mantiq aṭ-Ṭā'ir* ("The Language of the Birds"; the name is a Koranic reference to Solomon's powers of communicating with the spiritual world, and David's hymning of the praises of God). This is an allegory of the spiritual path in which the birds, led by the *Hudhud*, or Hoopoe, go off in search of their King, the Simurgh. (The starting point of the allegory is the Koran 38:19: "And the birds assembled; all were turning unto Him".)

'Aṭṭār also wrote the *Tadhkirāt al-Awliyā'* ("Recollections of the Saints"), a collection of biographies and anecdotes about famous Sufis.

Attributes. Sunnī theology, among the Divine Names and Attributes mentioned in the Koran, places a particular emphasis upon the seven "Attributes", namely: Life (*Ḥayāh*), Knowledge (*'Ilm*), Power (*Qudrah*), Will (*Īrādah*), Hearing (*Sam*), Sight (*Baṣr*), Speech (*Kalām*).

Avempace, *see* IBN BAJJAH.

Avenzoar, *see* IBN ZUHR.

Averroes, *see* IBN RUSHD.

Avicebron, *see* IBN GABIROL.

Avicenna, *see* IBN SĪNĀ.

Awliya', *see* SAINTS.

Axis, Spiritual, *see* QUTB.

Āyat al-Kursī (lit. the "Verse of the Throne"). A single verse of the Koran (2:256) of more than average length, it is one of the principal verses of refuge and protection", which are known as *āyāt al-ḥifẓ*:

God
there is no god but He, the
Living, the Everlasting.
Slumber seizes Him not, neither sleep;
to Him belongs
all that is in the heavens and the earth.
Who is there that shall intercede with Him
save by His leave?
He knows what lies before them
and what is after them,
and they comprehend not anything of His
knowledge
save such as He wills.
His Throne comprises the heavens and earth;
the preserving of them oppresses Him not;
He is the All-high, the All-glorious.

It is recited in Arabic as a means of entrusting one's self to God's care and is often written on amulets. The power of the Verse of the Throne is praised in Ḥadīth. *See also* REFUGE.

Ayatollah (Ar. *Āyat Allāh* "A Sign of God"). An honorific title for high-ranking Shī'ite religious authorities in Iran. There is also an Ayatollah in Iraq, who resides in Najaf. The title came into being only in this century. The handful of Ayatollahs, who are associated with religious centers such as Tabrīz, Qūm, and Mashhad, constitute a kind of theological "college", or synod. Newcomers are admitted to the ranks on the basis of recognition and acceptance by existing Ayatollahs, and by popular acclamation. Like all high-ranking Shī'ite Mullas, the Ayatollahs have personal followings.

This grandiose title is an innovation of the 20th century. It arose out of the victory in Persia (but not in southern Iraq or Baḥrayn) of the Uṣūlī school of Twelve-Imām Shī'ism over the Akhbārī school in the *12th*/18th century. This cleared the way for a development in the authority of the Mullas. Thereafter, the Uṣūlī religious authorities aggrandized power to themselves, in a way reminiscent of the Priestly class of Mazdeism in the days of the ancient Persian dynasties.

The Uṣūlīs maintain that, despite the absence of the Shī'ite Imām, highly qualified teachers have the capacity to make autonomous religious judgements as Mujtahids and that such an authority is a *marja at-taqlīd,* "a reference of emulation". The Uṣūlī doctrine teaches that a Shī'ite must be the follower of such a Mujtahid; furthermore, the Mujtahid must be living; one is even forbidden to follow a dead Mujtahid. Moreover, the Mujtahids claim the allegiance of lesser Mullas who are not Mujtahids and receive the religious *zakāt* tax, and the special tax perpetuated in Shī'ism known as the khums.

In the early 19th century there were only three or four Mujtahids; by the end of the century the numbers had grown considerably, and those who could claim large followings adopted the title *Ḥujjat al-Islam* ("Proof of Islam") to mark their higher status. In this century, with the ranks of the Mujtahids now swollen to several hundred, in addition to a large number of *Ḥujjat al-Islam,* the rank was introduced of the Ayatollah, or "Divine Sign". But then, as the number of Ayatollahs grew apace, there came the need for a further distinguishing title, namely that of the Ayatollah al-Uẓmā ("the greatest sign of God"). Past Shī'ite history has been reinterpreted to show that such an authority, a *marja at-taqlīd al-muṭlaq,* an "absolute point of reference", has always existed, and those who represented this authority have been named. After the revolution of 1979, the Ayatollah Khomeini gave up using the title and adopted the title of "Imām". Since he could not claim to be, in his own person, the Hidden Imām returned, this signaled a new development in Persian Twelve-Imām Shī'ism. At the same time, the Ayatollah Sharīat Madarī was down-graded to the title of *Ḥujjat al-Islam* for his role in political events, an unprecedented event. *See* AKHBĀRĪ; BIHBAHĀNĪ; HIDDEN IMĀM; SHĪ'ISM; UṢŪLĪ.

Ayup Sultan, *see* ABŪ AYYŪB.

Ayyūb. The prophet Job. He and the trials he underwent are mentioned in the Koran in 4:163; 21:83; 38:42. *See* PROPHETS.

Ayyūbids (*564-658*/1169-1260; a Sunnī dynasty which lasted in Diyarbakir until *866*/1492), it was founded by Ṣalāḥ ad-Dīn al-Ayyūbī (d. *589*/1193), called Saladin in Europe. Ṣalāḥ ad-Dīn, the great heroic figure of the Crusades, was a Kurd who started his career in the service of Nūr ad-Dīn, the Emir of Syria. After supplanting the Shī'ite Fāṭimids, Ṣalāḥ ad-Dīn established his family as rulers in Egypt and Syria (he was confirmed as Sultan by the Caliph in *570*/1174 upon the death of Nur ad-Dīn). He consolidated his control of Aleppo and Damascus, and then directed a series of wars against the Crusader kingdoms in Palestine, recovering Jerusalem in *583*/*1*187 after defeating the Crusaders at the Battle of the Horn of Hattin, when he captured the Christian King and the Grand Masters of the Knightly Orders.

For a time, Egypt, Jerusalem, Damascus, parts of the Yemen, and Diyarbakir, were under Ayyūbid control. The Ayyūbid empire ended in the West at the hands of the Mamlūks; in Syria, the Ayyūbids were overwhelmed by the Mongols. *See* MAMLŪKS; ṢALĀḤ ad-DĪN al-AYYŪBĪ.

Āzād, Abū al-Kalām (1888-1958) Indian journalist writing in Urdu and political figure of the anti-colonial movement. He was born in Mecca of an Indian father who was a Sufi, married to the daughter of the Mufti of Medina. Āzād was open to the influences of his time, the Khilāfat movement, Sir Sayyid Ahmad Khan the modernist reformer, and imbibed the ideas of the other politicians the Islamic world, but went on to become an opponent of the partition of India and instead the advocate of a multi-cultural Indian state.

He became a journalist at an early age publishing *al-Hilāl* ("the Crescent"), and joined the Congress party becoming one of its influential leaders and a colleague of Mohandas Gandhi. In 1940 he was elected president of the All-India National Congress, a post he held until 1946, and in 1947 became Minister of Education in the government of independent India, a post he held until his death. He wrote partial translation and commentary on the Koran, his *Tarjumān al-Quran.*

Azerbaijan. Republic: population 7,789,886. Azeris 83%, Russian 6%, Armenian 6%. The principal religion is Islam with a Shi'ite majority. The religious leader is Shaykh al-Islam Shukur Allah Pashazadeh. The capital is Baku. In the neighboring republic of Iran there is a northwest region also called Azerbaijan whose capitals are Tabriz and Rezaiyeh. *See* AZERI.

Azeri. A Turkic people, numbering about five million, who live in the Republic of Azerbaijan and in neighboring regions of Iran. Their language is Azeri Turkish and they are the only Turkic group which is predominantly Shī'ite. The Azeris were much influenced by Iran, to the extent of absorbing many Zoroastrian elements into their culture.

al-Azhar (Ar. the "resplendent"). The most famous university of the Islamic world, in Cairo, Egypt. It was founded by the general al-Jawhar shortly after the founding of Cairo itself in *358*/969. Originally it was an institution of the Faṭīmids to train preachers, or *da'ī's,* to propagate Ismā'īlī doctrines. The existence of such a centre for the teaching of a special ideology threatening to Abbāsid authority forced the Sunni Saljuqs to create their own schools of orthodox theology as a counterforce. Thus the Vizier Nizām al-Mūlk (d. *485*/1092) founded several "Nizamiyyah" Madrasahs in Iraq and Persia while Saladin and other Syrian rulers founded schools in Syria and Palestine and provided upkeep for others. In this way the al-Azhar gave an important impetus to the development of higher education in the Islamic world.

The al-Azhar also had an important effect upon the development of educational institutions in Europe. The wearing of black academic gowns, traditions of public disputations, divisions into undergraduate and graduate faculties, derive from the al-Azhar and point to an influence that must have made itself felt in other deeper ways. After the Ayyūbids conquered Egypt, the Fāṭimid dynasty came to an end and the al-Azhar became a Sunni university. It acquired a great prestige and reputation for authority in religious domains which it has kept to the present day.

B

Bāb (lit. "door" or "gate"). The Shī'ites often quote this Ḥadīth: "I [the Prophet] am the city of knowledge and 'Alī is the gate (*bāb*)". From this, the term *bāb* lent itself to be used in Shī'ism as the title of a person claiming to vehicle special knowledge. The most famous use of the title *bāb* is that of the spiritual leader of the *Bābīs*, a 19th century branch of the Shaykhis, who were themselves an offshoot of Twelve-Imām Shī 'ism. In *1260*/1844, Mirzā 'Alī Muḥammad, the leader of a branch of the Shaykhīs, claimed to be the *bāb*, or living door to the Hidden Imām. He later went on to claim to be the Mahdī, and finally, a Divine Messenger. Mirzā 'Alī Muḥammad composed a book called the *Bayān* ("Explanation"). His followers caused revolts in Iran and he was shot by a firing squad in Tabrīz in *1267*/1850. *See* BĀBĪS; HIDDEN IMĀM; SHAYKHĪS.

Bābīs. The followers of a small sect which sprang up in Iran in the middle of the last century, as a schism within the Shaykhis. Its leader, Mirzā 'Alī Muḥammad called himself the *Bāb*, or door to the Hidden Imām, but later declared himself the revealer of a new religion. A small number of Bābīs still exist today, but the sect was mainly a springboard to another religion, with a wider appeal, the Bahā'is. *See* BĀB; BAHĀ'ĪS; HIDDEN IMĀM; SHAYKHIS.

Badā' (lit. "priority"). A doctrine of changes in the Divine Will which was advanced by the Kaysaniyyah to explain why certain expected prophecies did not come true. Traces of the doctrine of *badā'* have a very relative and unimportant place in the theology of Twelve-Imām Shī'ism. *Badā'* is very different from the principle of *naskh*, or abrogation of certain verses of the Koran. *See* KAYSĀNIYYAH; NASKH.

Badr, *see* BATTLE of BADR.

Baghdad. The capital of the 'Abbāsid Caliphate. The unrest arising from the province of Khorasan directed against the Umayyad tyranny led to frequent revolts which culminated in the defeat of Marwān II at the battle of the Zab river in *132*/750. The victors established the 'Abbāsid dynasty, and the new capital reflected the shift away from the influence of Byzantium towards that of Persia.

The city was founded by the Caliph al-Manṣūr on the west side of the Tigris river, on the site of an ancient Babylonian town. The date of founding was chosen by astrologers for July 23 *762*/145 under the sign of Leo with Sagittarius rising. But most significant is that the site was next to the Sassanid capital of Ctesiphon-Seleucia (Madā'in).

> Manṣūr rode through Iraq seeking the site for a new capital. At the little village of Baghdad on the Tigris (where Euphrates flows near) he was counselled: "We think it best to settle here, midway between these four agricultural districts of Buq, Kalwadha, Qutrabbul, and Baduria. Thus you will have palm plantations on every side of you and water near at hand; if harvest fails or is late from one district, you can get relief from another. You can get provisions by the Sarat canal from the Euphrates river traffic; Egyptian and Syrian caravans will come here by the desert roads, and all kinds of China goods upriver from the sea, and Byzantine and Mosul produce down the Tigris. And with rivers on both sides, no enemy can approach except by ship or bridge".
>
> "The site is excellent for a military camp", Manṣūr said. And here he built the city of Baghdad, called the Round City by reason of its plan and City of Peace.

Ctesiphon had been reduced to a village around the ruins of the Sassanid Palace. One resident who must have rejoiced at the location of the new capital near the village was the Archegos, the head of the Manichean religion, who was obliged by tradition to remain in the former Persian capital, the way the Pope is tied to the city of Rome. The Arab invasion had devastated Ctesiphon in 636; now it was to come back to life; indeed Baghdad means "Gift of God". The original city built by the 'Abbāsids was called *Dār as-Salām* ("House of Peace"), a circular city in the Parthian-Sassanid tradition, with three concentric walls, pierced at the four cardinal directions by gates opening towards Basra, Syria, Kufah, and Khorasan, and surrounded by a deep moat. *Mas'ūdī* remarked that the Gate of Khorasan was in the old days often called the *Bab ad-Dawlah*, because the dynasty (*dawlah*) or state power of the 'Abbāsids had come to them out of Khorasan. (Because of this support the 'Abbāsids were also called the "foreign Khorasani state".) The circle of the outer wall had a diameter of 1.6 miles/2.6 km. The gigantic Caliphal palace, with an immense throne room modeled after the Sassanid palace of Ctesiphon, and a grand mosque nearby formed the city's center, surrounded by vast gardens 1 mile/1.5 km in diameter. The city lay upon the great routes of communication with Persia and India, and was the cultural and political focus of Islam in the eastern empire, as Cordoba was in the west. Its glory is reflected in the splendor of the stories of the *Thousand and One Nights*, whose Arab form crystallized the memory of the legendary height of the 'Abbāsid dynasty under Hārūn ar-Rashīd (d. *194*/809). A historian wrote that Baghdad was:

> the market to which the wares of the sciences and arts were brought, where wisdom was sought as a man seeks after his stray camels, and whose judgement of values was accepted by the whole world.

Baghdad was destroyed by the Mongol invasion in *656*/1258. In keeping with the religious law of the Mongols, the *Yasa*, which prohibited the spilling of royal blood onto the ground, the last 'Abbāsid Caliph, al-Mustaṣim, was executed by being rolled up in carpets and trodden to death by horses. The Mongol Il-Khanid dynasty, which replaced the 'Abbāsids in Persia, made Tabrīz and Maragha their capitals. However, Ḥasan Buzurg, of a rival Mongol tribe within the Golden Horde, becoming the chief of the Jalayrid successor state, turned to Baghdad to make it again a royal residence in *741*/1340. This was the prelude to a fresh catastrophe for the city in the form of its sacking by Timur in *795*/1393. The Mongol invasions and, in addition, the establishment of trade routes by sea in the Age of Explorations made the city's decline inevitable. Under the Ottomans, however, who took possession under Murād IV in *1048*/1638, Baghdad again assumed a certain importance but lacked a prosperous economic base.

Today, Kazimayn, in a suburb to the north, is a Shī'ite shrine of the first magnitude (whose present architecture dates to the last century). As the tomb of the seventh and ninth Shī'ite Imāms Mūsā ibn Ja'far and Muḥammad ibn 'Alī al-Jawād, it draws many pilgrims. The city also boasts the tomb of 'Abd al-Qādir al-Jīlānī, one of the great Saints of Islam, the tomb of the famous Sufi Marūf al-Karkhī (originally a Mandaean who was instrumental in establishing religious toleration for his former religion, d. *200*/815), and the tomb of the founder of the Ḥanafī School of Law, Abū Ḥanīfah. Baghdad and its environs also possess a number of Jewish shrines, notably the reputed tomb of Joshua, and those of Ezra and Ezekiel. Until 1451 Baghdad was the seat of the Exilarch, or chief of the Babylonian Jewish community. In different periods, the Exilarch (*Resh Galuta*) was accorded sometimes substantial independent authority by the 'Abbāsids, even to the extent of passing sentence on Muslims involved in disputes with Jews. The Exilarch, who was a descendant of David, has sometimes been called the Jewish Caliph. Although in 'Abbāsid times his authority was civil, once he also had religious authority before this devolved upon the Rabbis. Although the Jews have left, there are other ancient ethnic groups who remain, such as the Mandaeans, and Nestorian Christians, all of whom are a living link with the Mesopotamian past.

One of the neighborhoods of Baghdad, at-Tabiah, gave its name to the cloth "tabby", once a kind of richly colored silk imported into Europe from the city. *See* 'ABBĀSIDS; CALIPHATE; HĀRŪN ar-RASHĪD; IRAQ; MANDAEANS; NESTORIANS; SHĪ'ISM; THOUSAND and ONE NIGHTS.

Bahā'īs. A religion of modern times; an offshoot of the Bābī sect of Persia (itself an offshoot of the Shaykhīs, who broke away from Twelve-Imām Shī'ism). In the middle of the last century the Bābīs split three ways: original Bābīs, Azalī Bābīs, and Bahā'īs. The Azalis are now almost extinct. After the death of the Bāb, Mirzā 'Alī Muḥammad, in *1267*/1850, one branch of the Bābī movement followed a young man called by the Bābī name of Ṣubḥ-i Azal ("the Eternal Dawn"). After three Bābī followers attempted to assassinate Shah Nāṣir ad-Dīn in *1269*/1852, the Bābīs were repressed by the government. The talented Bābī poetess Zarrin Tāj, called Qurrat al-Ayn, or "Coolness of the Eye" was executed, with others, and Ṣubḥ-i Azal left Persia for Baghdad.

Ṣubḥ-i Azal's leadership was successfully challenged by his much older half-brother Bahā' Allāh ("the Splendor of God" *1233-1310*/1817-1892) whose former, pre-Bābī name was Mirzā Husayn 'Alī Nūrī. Bahā' Allāh declared himself the promised one of the Bāb's prophecies and founded Bahā'ism, taking many of the Bābī followers with him.

In *1280*/1863 at the request of the Persian government, the Ottomans first imprisoned the Bahā'ī chiefs, first in Edirne (Adrianople), and then sent Ṣubḥ-i Azal to Cyprus, and Bahā' Allāh to Acre (Akko) in Palestine. There was intrigue between the two factions; the Azalis went into decline. The Bahā'ī branch flourished, despite a heavy 19% levy (*huququ'Llāh*) on the surplus revenue (after exempted basic expenses) of its followers. After the death of Bahā' Allāh in internment at Acre in 1892, there were many schisms, first between his sons. The leadership of Abbās Effendi (1844-1921), who took the name 'Abd al-Bahā', ("Slave of Bahā' Allāh") was contested by his younger brother, Muḥammad 'Alī, and was willed to 'Abd al-Bahā's grandson, Shoghi Effendi (d. 1957), but passed effectively to a council of nine and then to an elected Universal House of Justice in 1963.

The shrine of Bahā'ism is in Haifa, Israel. The religion, propounding a mixture of humanism, world peace, and brotherly love, has gained a following of over five million. Nearly two million are converts from Hinduism in India. There are a million and a half Bahā'īs in sub-Saharan Africa and Latin America, and 120,000 in America and 25,000 in Europe. In Iran, the Bahā'īs are now looked upon as heretical and are often persecuted. *See* BĀB.

Baḥīrāh. A Christian monk of the 7th century who lived in Bostra, Syria. His dwelling lay along the route followed by the Meccan caravans. One of the caravans which stopped there was accompanied by the Prophet, then twelve years old, and his uncle Abū Ṭālib. The monk saw portents which led him to recognize in Muḥammad the Prophet-to-come. Al-Mas'ūdī said that the monk's name was Sergius and that he belonged to the tribe of 'Abd al-Qays. There are various versions of the story.

Baḥrayn. (Ar. "The Two Seas") Emirate in the Persian Gulf; an archipelago named after the principal island. The population numbers over 409,000 of whom 98% are Muslim. Somewhat less than half are Arabs and Sunnīs, mostly of the Mālikī rite, with some Ḥanbalīs; the other half is an indigenous people called the Baḥarīnī, who are of Indo-European origin and Twelve-Imām Shī'ite. The Shī'ites are mostly of the Akhbārī school of Jurisprudence (unlike Iran which is Uṣūlī). There is also a minority of Indians, Pakistanis, and Persians.

Bakhtiār. A semi-nomadic people of south-western Iran related to the Lūrs, who speak a Lūrī dialect. They are Shī'ite and number over half a million. The Bakhtiārī are divided into the Haft-Lang and Chahar-Lang, tribal groupings which were once called the "Great Lūrs" and the "Little Lūrs".

al-Balādhurī, Aḥmad ibn Yaḥyā (d. *279*/892). Historian of Persian origin who wrote the *Kitāb Futūh al-Buldān* describing the early Arab conquests, and *Kitāb Ansāb al-Ashrāf,* a book of geneologies and biographies.

Balewa, Sir Abubakar Tafawa (1912-1966). A member of the Fulānī tribe, he was born Maham Abubakar, in a village in northern Nigeria, and later became a schoolteacher. He was one of the founders of the Northern People's Party, which developed into one of the most important political parties in Nigeria during the colonial period. When the Federation of Nigeria became independent, Sir Abubakar was elected the first Prime Minister. Along with Sir Ahmadou Bello, Dr. Naamde Azikiwe and Chief Obatemi Awolowe, Sir Abubakar was one of Nigeria's most outstanding leaders.

Sir Abubakar brought traditional Muslim values to his post and conducted himself with the pious simplicity of a believer. His assassination in a *coup d'état* in 1966 represented the passing of an age.

Balkh. *See* MAZĀR-I SHARĪF.

Baloch. A Sunnī people who number over three million; they are part shepherds and part farmers, who live in Balochistan in Pakistan, in eastern Iran, and also in Afghanistan. Some Baloch are complete nomads.

Bangladesh. Republic. Estimated population 102,000,000 of whom 80% are Muslim and 15%

Hindu. There are also Christian and Buddhist minorities. Of the Muslims 90% are Ḥanafī Sunnīs and 10% Twelve-Imām Shī'ites. The most important Sufi *ṭuruq* are the Qādiriyyah, the Suhrawardiyyah, and the Chishtiyyah.

Banking, Islamic, *see* ISLAMIC BANKING.

Banū Isrā'īl (lit. the "Children of Israel"). The name by which the Koran most commonly calls the Jews whom it calls also *alladhīna hādū* ("those that practice Jewish rites"). In Arabia, before Islam, the Jews lived in oases, and practiced crafts such as silver-smithing and agriculture, through which they traded with the Beduins. There were few Jews at Mecca, but half of the population of Medina was Jewish, and there had also been Jewish kingdoms in the Yemen.

The influence of Judaism on Islam is very great and well documented. To begin with, the Arabs and the Jews have a common traditional ancestor in Abraham; besides the Abrahamic heritage, Mosaic Judaism was familiar to the Arabs. Many of the laws of Judaism are also found in Islam, and in the first century of the Hijrah, Jews who were converted to Islam brought the Haggadah literature to bear upon Koranic commentary.

What is much less well documented is the influence of Islam upon Judaism. In the light of the Koranic re-affirmation of God as Absolute, and as He was known to Adam, Islamic thought redefined the Aristotelian concept of the First Mover in its assimilation of Hellenist philosophy. This revelation or renewal of the primordial awareness of God probably influenced Jewish mysticism in Moorish Spain to emerge as the *Ain Sof* ("Without Limit") of the Qabbalah. While the framework of the doctrine of the Sephiroth could also have come from Neoplatonism directly, the fact that Islam, a Semitic monotheism, produced a massive synthesis of Hellenist metaphysics, probably inspired parallels within Judaism, derived from the Islamic model.

Banū Mūsā, *see* MŪSĀ SHĀKIR.

Baqā' (lit. "residue"). A Sufi technical term. According to the Sufis, through the practice of spiritual discrimination, concentration, and virtue, the unreality of the worshiper, the mortal and corruptible elements of his soul, fade away (*fanā'*) with the help of Divine grace, and there remains an adamantine and immortal nature, beyond appearances. The origin of the term *baqa'* is in the Koran (55:26-27):

> All that dwells upon the earth is perishing, yet still abides the Face of thy Lord, majestic, splendid.

Al-Ghazālī wrote:

> Each thing has two faces, a face of its own, and a face of its Lord; in respect of its own face it is nothingness, and in respect of the Face of God it is Being. Thus there is nothing in existence save only God and His Face, for everything perisheth but His Face.

This "remainder" is called *baqā'*. As in the words of al-Junayd: "*Tawḥīd* (unification with God) is the removal of the temporal from the eternal."

al-Baqī'. The cemetery in Medina, located near the *Masjid ash-Sharīf*, where many of the famous figures of Islam, Companions of the Prophet, scholars, Saints, and heroes, from its beginnings to recent times, are buried. The cemetery's full name is *baqī' al-gharqad,* or "roots of the lote-tree".

al-Baqillānī, Abū Bakr Muḥammad ibn aṭ-Ṭayyib (d. *403*/1013). A Judge and a theologian, born in Baṣra, Iraq. Trained as a Maliki jurist, he was energetic and effective in spreading and establishing the Ash'arite school of *kalām* (theology). He is the author of the *I'jāz al-Qur'ān* ("The Incomparability of the Koran"). This was connected with another work of his that treated the notion discussed in al-Baqillānī's time, of the "apologetic miracle" that is, miracles substantiating claims to Divine mission. Al-Baqillānī says that an authentic miracle (and not mere trickery) must be a suspension of natural laws. *See* al-ASH'ARI.

Baqqā', Buqqā', *see* "Weeping Sufis".

Barabanshchiki. A name given by Russians to the followers of the Chim Mirza Sufi brotherhood, a branch of the Qadiriyyah *tariqah* in the Caucasus. An old Sufi order, also called the Jilālah in Morocco, it expanded in the

Caucuses after 1850 under the leadership of a Daghestani, Kunta Haji Kishiev. *See* QADIRIYYAH.

Barakah. From the root *baraka*, meaning "to settle", whence *birkah*, or "well", and, in a derived meaning of the word, the act of kneeling by a camel. The primary meaning of *barakah*, however, is "grace" – in the sense of a blessing or a spiritual influence which God sends down. *Barakah* may be found in persons, places, and things. Certain actions and circumstances may also be a vehicle for blessing, as other actions and circumstances can dispel grace. Many religious greetings and expressions include the idea of *barakah*, such as *bāraka 'Llāhu fīk* ("May God bless you"), the most common and traditional way of saying thanks.

Bareilly. City west of Delhi in India, halfway to Lucknow. The theological school, Dar al-Ulum of Bareilly, is characterized by its tolerance of folk beliefs among Indian Muslims carried over with their conversions from Hinduism in earlier times. The school of Bareilly extends its influence through the political party in Pakistan known as the Jama'at-i Ulama-i Pakistan. *See* BARILWIS.

Barīd (from the Persian *burīdah dum*, "having a docked tail". Hence a "mule" and, finally any post-horse or mounted messenger system or postal system. Or possibly from Latin *veredus* "mule", but doubtfully so). The 'Abbāsids inherited the famous Persian system of postal couriers, already described by Herodotus in those famous lines paraphrased as "Neither rain, nor sleet, nor dark of night stays them from the completion of their appointed rounds". The Caliph al-Manṣūr (d. *158*/775) set the precedents for the 'Abbāsid system of government, and like the Umayyads, used the Byzantine and Sassanid chanceries to carry out the operations of the state. To keep a check on his provincial administration, al-Manṣūr made full use of the institution of the postal directorate and its directors to stay informed. They were thus an intelligence service to the Caliph, supplying information about the conduct and activities of provincial Governors, as well as about agricultural conditions and the state of the crops. Out of the registers of the postal stations came one impetus for the science of geography among the Arabs.

Barilwīs. 1. Barilwī 'alims, teachers and students of the Madrasah of Bareilly in India.

2. A Muslim sect in India, followers of Mawlānā Aḥmad Riḍā Khān (*1273-1340*/1856-1921), who concentrate on experiencing the presence of the Prophet Muḥammad during worship, and believe they find it in ecstasies which sometimes render them insensible.

3. The followers of Sayyid Aḥmad Barilwi (*1201-1246*/1786-1831; also known as Aḥmad of Rā'e Bareli, and as Aḥmad Shahīd), and followers of other leaders with the name Barilwi, Barelwi, and Brelvi. *See* BAREILLY; AḤMAD of RA'E BARELI.

Barnabas, Gospel of. An "apocryphal" account of the life of Jesus in which Jesus is not crucified, but instead Judas Iscariot miraculously takes his form and is crucified in his place. The disciples steal the dead body of Judas, and Jesus reappears.

This story has became popular as a result of its propagation in the Islamic Middle East in recent times because it is taken to be the "suppressed", "true" gospel which does not conflict with the description of Jesus in the Koran. While the so-called "Gospel of Barnabas" does not actually conflict with the Koran, neither can it be taken in the sense of the Koranic passages in question – for it is clear from the Koran that God willed the people to *see* what they saw – and is pointless as far as Christianity itself is concerned, making nonsense of God's acts towards man.

Of the crucifixion, the Koran (4:155-158) says:

> ...and for their unbelief, and their uttering
> against Mary a mighty calumny,
> and for their saying, 'We slew the Messiah,
> Jesus, son of Mary, the Messenger of God' -
> yet they did not slay him, neither crucified him,
> only a likeness of that was shown to them.
> Those who are at variance concerning him surely
> are in doubt regarding him; they have no
> knowledge of him, except the following of surmise;
> and they slew him not of a certainty -
> no indeed; God raised him up to Him; God is
> All-mighty, All-wise.
> There is not one of the People of the Book
> but will assuredly believe in him before his
> death, and on the Resurrection Day he will be
> a witness against them.

Jesus is thus considered to be still alive in a

principial state from which he will return at the end of time. The Koran does not further explain the nature of the crucifixion, nor the difference between its outward appearance – the death of a man – and its inner truth, which is that Jesus was not killed. The Koran does say that the crucifixion of Jesus is what the people saw, and does not go into the reasons why God let the event take place and let the people see what they saw.

The Koranic passage in question is part of a series of accusations against the Jews, namely, of breaking the covenant, of disbelieving in God's revelations, slaying of the Prophets, and claiming, as it puts it: "We slew the Messiah Jesus son of Mary". It is the claim that they slew Jesus which the Koran refutes; it then cites sanctions for this and other transgressions.

As regards the "Gospel of Barnabas" itself, there is no question that it is a medieval forgery. A complete Italian manuscript exists which appears to be a translation from a Spanish original (which exists in part), written to curry favor with Muslims of the time. It contains anachronisms which can date only from the Middle Ages and not before, and shows a garbled comprehension of Islamic doctrines, calling the Prophet "the Messiah", which Islam does not claim for him. Besides its farcical notion of sacred history, stylistically it is a mediocre parody of the Gospels, as the writings of Bahā' Allāh are of the Koran. *See* BIBLE; JESUS.

Barzakh (Ar. a "barrier", an "obstruction" between two things or places; specifically, an "isthmus"). A point of transition where entities similar yet different come together. The word has many applications in metaphysics. The Koran in 25:55 states:

> And it is He who let forth the two seas, this one sweet,
> grateful to taste, and this
> salt, bitter to the tongue,
> and He set between them a barrier, and a ban forbidden.

and in 55:20:

> He let forth the two seas that meet together,
> between them a barrier they do not overpass.

Thus the isthmus, or *barzakh* between the salt and sweet seas (metaphors for this world and the next) beyond which one cannot cross without permission, is a barrier. There is another barrier (also *barzakh*) at death which prevents return, or reincarnation, to this world (23:100):

> Till, when death comes to one of them, he says,
> 'My Lord, return me;
> haply I shall do righteousness in that
> I forsook.' Nay, it is but a word
> he speaks; and there, behind them,
> is a barrier until the day that they
> shall be raised up.

A Saint who spans the chasm of human and Divine knowledge may also be called a *barzakh.* Indeed man in general, in view of his conjunction of body and soul, matter and intellect, and above all individual and Divine consciousness, is also a *barzakh.* Because the *barzakh* touches the two worlds it is not only a separation, but also a bridge; thus it is very similar to the concept of man as *pontifex.*

Basmachis. ("Bandits"). The revolt of the Basmachis or Bandits was what the Bolsheviks called the Islamic resistance to Communism in Central Asia in the 1920s and 1930s. One Tatar who did become a Bolshevik and was extolled by the Revolution was Mir Sultangaliev. In 1921 the Tartar nationalist and Communist Sultangaliev called for the creation of an international organization of colonial and semi-colonial nations and for its dictatorship over the advanced industrial states.

Basmalah. The formula *bismi-Llāhi-r-Raḥmāni-r-Raḥīm*: "In the Name of God, the Merciful, the Compassionate". The *basmalah* is spoken by Muslims many times each day as a consecration before undertaking any lawful action. It is never omitted before a meal, where it is the equivalent of "saying grace". The meal is ended with the uttering of the *ḥamdalah.* When beginning ritual action the basmalah is preceded by the *ta'awwudh.* When performing ritual slaughter the words *ar-Raḥmāni 'r-Raḥīm* are replaced by *Allāhu akbar.*

The *basmalah* has a clear predecessor in the Pahlavi Zoroastrian formula of the 4th century: *pa nām i yazdan i xvorromand i rāyomand* ("in the name of the blessing and bountiful

Divinity"). *See* ḤAMDALAH; PIOUS EXPRESSIONS; TA'AWWUDH.

Basṭ. An expansion or dilation of the soul which is experienced as joy. *Basṭ* is related to the Divine Name *al-Bāsiṭ*, the "Expander" or "He who gives joy". In Sufism, *basṭ* is a technical term for an expanding state of the soul that is inevitably followed, sooner or later, by its opposite which is contraction (*qabḍ*). As it is written in the *Ḥikam* of Ibn Aṭā'Allāh:

> Through the existence of joy the soul obtains its portion in expansion, but in contraction there is no portion for the soul.

And al-Hujwīrī said:

> John (the Baptist) was in straitness (*qabḍ*), Jesus in joyous expansion (*basṭ*); for John, according to a well-known Ḥadīth, wept from the day he was born, and Jesus from the day he was born smiled. When they met, John used to say: "Jesus hast thou no fear thou wilt be cut off from God?"
>
> "John, hast thou no hope of mercy?" Jesus would reply. "Neither thy tears nor my smiling will change decree".

The concepts are similar to the medieval alchemical notions of *solve* (a spiritual, as well as physical, entering into solution, or a dissolving) and *coagula* (fixation in form). But it is the phase of coagulation (*qabḍ*), paradoxically, which offers the possibility of release through the "narrow gate" of form, while solution (*basṭ*) actually entraps because the essence becomes compounded with the conditional. As Ibn 'Aṭā' Allāh says:

> It is more dreadful for gnostics to be expanded than to be contracted, for only a few can stay within the limits of proper conduct in expansion.

There is also this Ḥadīth which demonstrates the benefits of qabḍ, or straitening: "Sins fall from a sick man, like leaves from a tree." *See* QABḌ.

Ba'th. The Arab Resurrection Socialist Party founded in Syria by both Muslims and Christians held its first congress in Damascus in 1947. It was based upon principles of Arab nationalism and was not religious. After 1963 it split into Syrian and Iraqi branches which are inimical to each other and rule those two countries today. The party is organized in both countries as revolutionary organization with a cell structure and strict hierarchy that has brought control of the parties into the hands of narrow elites.

Bāṭin (lit. "inward"). One of the Names of God, *al-Bāṭin*, "the Inner" (57:3). *Bāṭin* also means that which is secret and, in particular, denotes esoteric knowledge.

Bāṭini. Any doctrine which is esoteric, secret, or initiatic. It also denotes someone who belongs to a group of such nature. Sometimes, but not always, it is used reproachfully, indicating a doctrine of dubious nature.

al-Battānī, Abū 'Abd Allāh Muḥammad. (*244-317*/858-929). Astronomer and mathematician. Al-Battānī was from Harrān (today Altinbasak in Turkey, near Urfa), and belonged to the Hellenist pagan religion of that city, but became a Muslim. He studied in Raqqa in Syria on the Euphrates and died in Samarra'. In medieval and renaissance Europe (where he was known as Albatenius) he was accounted one of the most important authorities on astronomy; indeed his calculations (*az-Zīj aṣ-Ṣābi'*) of planetary motion were remarkably accurate, and he also made original contributions to mathematics, notably in spherical trigonometry.

Battle of Aqrabah, *see* MUSAYLAMAH.

Battle of 'Ayn Jalūt ("Battle of Goliath's Spring"; *658*/1260). At this battle near Nablūs in Palestine, the Mamlūks led by Qutuz and his lieutenant Baybars decisively defeated the Mongols (a much smaller force), thus saving Egypt from Mongol expansion. This battle also brought Syria under Mamlūk control.

Battle of Badr (*19th Ramadan 2*/Friday 17th March 623). The first major encounter between the Muslims and the Meccans (after the skirmish of Nakhlah). Badr lies 90 miles/125 km to the south of Medina. The Muslim force numbered 305 (before the battle one Meccan joined the Muslims; there were besides him, seventy-four original emigrants (*muhājirūn*). The rest were "Companions" (*anṣār*), or Medinans. The force of the Meccans was close to a thousand.

The Muslims had set out to attack a Meccan caravan led by Abū Ṣufyān who, however, learned of the danger from scouts and sent a message to Mecca asking for reinforcements. The caravan itself then hastened around Badr to avoid the attackers completely, but the Meccan army of reinforcement encountered the Muslims.

At the beginning of the battle the Prophet threw a handful of pebbles at the Meccans, saying "abased be those faces". A later revelation of the Koran said that it was not he, but God Who threw (8:17). Angels, led by Gabriel, joined the Muslims; one of two men observing on a hill related that they heard the neighing of stallions that swept past them as if in a moving cloud; the other man died on the spot of sudden fear.

After initial challenges to individual combats, the Muslims fought, under the orders of the Prophet, in a style revolutionary to the Arabs; instead of indulging in sporadic and disorganised hit-and-run skirmishes, the Muslims fought as a disciplined body with an order of battle. To this the Koran attached merit when it says "God loves those who fight in His way in ranks" (61:4). The Muslim casualties were fourteen, those of the Meccans fifty, among them Abū Jahl. Fifty Meccans were captured; of these Umayyah, Nadr, and 'Uqbah, bitter enemies of Islam, were put to death, the rest being held for ransom. After the battle, the Prophet addressed the fallen infidels in their common grave, and when those around him expressed surprise, he explained that the recently dead can still hear the living. (The doctrine in Islam, in respect of the nature of hearing and sound, is that the dead may continue hearing for as long as three days).

The battle amounted to an astonishing victory for the Muslims, and one that gained them political credibility for their cause among other tribes. It became one of the greatest marks of glory for survivors to say that they had fought at Badr. *See* MUḤAMMAD.

Battle of the Camel (*10th Jumada II 36*/4th December 656). The decisive encounter of the army of the Caliph, 'Alī, and the army of rebels led by the Companions Ṭalḥāh and az-Zubayr, who were joined by 'Ā'ishah. 'Alī won, Ṭalḥāh and az-Zubayr were killed in the battle and 'Ā'ishah was sent back to Medina without sanctions. 'Ā'ishah was in a litter on a camel; the battle raged up to her camel and then stopped; from this the battle got its name. *See* 'ALĪ.

Battle of Goliath's Spring, *see* BATTLE of 'AYN JALŪT.

Battle of Ḥunayn (*8*/630). After their conquest of Mecca, the Muslims fought a battle against the allied tribes of Ḥawāzin and Thaqīf at a point between Mecca and Ṭā'if. The Muslim army, although very numerous, at first panicked and fled when the Hawāzin came down upon it in the defile of Ḥunayn. The Prophet drew to one side with his Companions and some of the Anṣār, turned to al-'Abbās who had a strong voice, and had him cry out "Companions of the Tree! Companions of the Acacia!" (of the Pact of Hudaybiyyah). Thereupon from all sides the Companions responded "*Labbayk*" ("At thy service!"), and rallied to the Prophet. The Prophet stood up in the stirrups and prayed "God! I ask of Thee Thy promise". Then he took some pebbles and flung them in the face of the enemy as he had done at Badr, whereupon the tide of battle turned. Afterwards the revelation came:

> God has already helped you on many fields, and on
> the day of Hunain, when your multitude was
> pleasing to you, but it availed you naught, and the
> land
> for all its breadth was strait for you, and you
> turned about, retreating.
> Then God sent down upon his Messenger His
> Shechina,
> and upon the believers, and He sent down
> legions you did not see, and He chastised
> the unbelievers; and that is the recompense
> of the unbelievers;
> then God thereafter turns towards whom He will;
> God is All-forgiving, All-compassionate. (9:25-27)

The routed enemy took refuge in Ṭā'if which was besieged unsuccessfully; but the Muslim victory persuaded the desert tribes to accept Islam and shortly thereafter the rebel tribes and Ṭā'if also surrendered and entered Islam. *See also* RIḌĀ'.

Battle of Nahrawan (*38*/658). (Ar. *waq'at an-nahr* "The Encounter at the River"). Following the Battle of Ṣiffīn (*37*/657) and the arbitration which followed, a group seceded from the army of the Caliph 'Ali and became known as Khārijites (from Arabic *Kharaja:* "to secede"). They embarked on a military campaign, taking Ctesiphon (Madā'īn). 'Alī attacked them at Nahrawan and annihilated all but a handful. In revenge he was assassinated by a surviving Khārijite, Ibn Muljam. *See* 'ALĪ; KHĀRIJITES.

Battle of Nihawand (*22*/642). This marked the final defeat of the Persians during the Arab expansion which followed the revelation of Islam. The Persians were led by the General Firozān; the Muslims, at first by Nu'mān ibn Muqarran, who was killed and replaced by Hudhayfah ibn al-Yaman. The battle took place near Hamadan. Afterwards the last Sassanid, Yazdagird, fled into Khorasān, and then to Merv, where he was betrayed by one of his satraps and killed while he hid in the house of a miller. *See* YAZDAGIRD.

Battle of Qādisiyyah (*15*/636). This took place near Kufah (which became an Arab camp-city, founded after the battle). The Persian army of the emperor Yazdagird, the last Sassanid, under the general Rustum, was decisively defeated by the Muslims led by Sa'd ibn Abī Waqqās. The legendary Persian war flag, the *Drafsh-i Kavianeh*, made of leather and precious stones, was captured, cut up, and divided among the victors.

Persian resistance continued until their final defeat at the Battle of Nihawand, south of Hamadān, in *22*/642.

Battle of Ṣiffīn, *see* 'ALĪ ibn ABĪ ṬĀLIB.

Battle of the Trench. (Also known as the *Khandaq*, lit. "the trench", and the "War of the Confederates"). In *5*/627 the Meccan Quraysh prepared to attack the Muslims in a massed battle with an army, called afterwards the "Confederates" (*al-aḥzāb*). The Quraysh had made an alliance with certain desert tribes, the Banū Ghatafan, and Jews of the Banū Nādir who had emigrated from Medina to Khaybar. The Prophet, however, forewarned of these plans, perhaps by his cousin al-'Abbās from Mecca, ordered a defensive trench to be dug around Medina. This stratagem had not been used before by the Arabs but was known to the Sassanids; they had built a trench against Arab incursions near Hirah which was maintained for them by their clients the Lakhmids. (There had also been a three meter deep ditch around a Sumerian city near present day Samarra'.) By a later tradition it was Salmān al-Fārsī, the Persian, who gave the idea to the Prophet. Tradition says the trench took six days of feverish work to dig since the warning came only a week before the attack. This is, however, too short a time to make such a trench; it was probably the result of a longer term strategy following the defeat of the Muslims at the Battle of Uḥud.

The Meccan army was made up of 4,000 from Mecca and 5,000 or more from the allies, with a total of 1,000 cavalry. The Medinans numbered 3,000. The Meccan cavalry was stopped by the trench, and the attackers laid siege for two weeks. The Meccan general Khālid ibn al-Walīd, attempted several times to cross the trench with horsemen at its narrowest point near the Jabal Sal' but succeeded only once. 'Alī fought in single combat with one of the attackers and slew him. Another tried to escape, fell into the trench, and was also killed.

Nu'aym of the Ashjā was one of the leaders of the Confederates, who before the battle, had been sent to Medina to sow discord and apprehension; instead, he then began inclining towards Islam. During the battle, he again made his way into Medina, in secret. He entered Islam and then proceeded to stir up the Banū Qurayzah. This was a Jewish tribe in Medina who had broken their pact with the Prophet and secretly conspired to give assistance to the Confederates. Nu'aym set the Banū Qurayzah against the Quraysh by telling them that they would be abandoned by the Meccans and should refuse to help unless they were given hostages from the Quraysh. To the Quraysh, on the other hand, he said that the Banū Qurayzah would not fulfill their promise to help and would attempt to stall by asking for Qurayshi hostages to share their plight in the case of defeat. Nu'aym's ruse succeeded. Dissension among the Confederates grew and was exacerbated by the tribulation of a violent wind from the sea which blew for three days and nights, unleashing torrents of rain. Discouraged, the Quraysh abandoned the siege. Abū Ṣufyān, the Meccan leader, left precipitously, almost before all the others.

After the battle, the Medinans executed the Banū Qurayzah for their treachery. The most notable casualty on the Medinan side was Sa'd ibn Mu'ādh, chief of one of the clans of the tribe of Aws. *See* QURAYZAH.

Battle of Uḥud. Uḥud on the western outskirts of Medina is a volcanic hill with a plain stretching before it. The Quraysh soundly defeated the Muslims here in the third year of the Hijrah (625). The Meccan army, led by Abū Ṣufyān, numbered three thousand men, including seven hundred in coats of mail and two hundred horse. On the morning of the battle three hundred Medinans under 'Abd Allāh ibn Ubayy (the leader of the "hypocrite" faction in Medina), deserted the Prophet as the troops rode out of the city, leaving the Muslims only seven hundred strong.

Nevertheless, the Muslims were close to victory when forty archers whom the Prophet had stationed on the hill to remain there and guard the flank, saw that the Muslims were winning. Afraid to lose their share of the booty, most of them abandoned their post. This left the way open for a counter-attack by a detachment of the Meccan cavalry led by Khālid ibn al-Walīd. The ten Muslim archers who had remained faithful to their orders proved too small a number to hold back the cavalry and were cut down.

Caught by the breakthrough of the Meccan cavalry, the Prophet's army was routed and the Prophet himself was wounded and momentarily knocked unconscious. The rumor of his death caused the Meccans to withdraw thinking the battle won. When the Meccans learned that the Prophet had survived it was too late to launch a counter-attack.

In this battle, Hamzah, an uncle of the Prophet and one of Islam's most formidable warriors, was killed, speared by a slave named Waḥshī. Hind, wife of Abū Ṣufyān, thirsting to revenge her kinsman killed at Badr, had set her slave to this exploit with promises of reward. The Prophet greatly mourned Hamzah, foremost of the Martyrs of Uḥud. Another hero is Anās ibn Naḍr who fought so valiantly that he succumbed to eighty wounds. Seventy-two Muslims were killed on the battlefield (and are buried there) and several died afterwards. One man, Usayrim, had not believed in Islam until the morning of the battle. When belief suddenly overtook him he set out alone to join the Medinan army. He is notable for having died a martyr on that day and therefore having entered paradise without ever praying a single ritual prayer.

Two women, Umm Sulaym and Nuṣaybah, followed the army from Medina to tend the wounded on the battlefield; of these, Nuṣaybah had participated in the Pact of the Second 'Aqabah.

Bay'ah ("a pact"). The installation or recognition of a ruler in his office takes the form of a pact, a *bay'ah*, which is an oath of fealty or allegiance. This is made with the ruler by the subjects, or, on their behalf, by the body of religious scholars, the *'ulamā'*, and political chiefs. Initiation into a Sufi order is also in the form of pact made by the novice with God through the spiritual master. *See* ḤUDAYBIYYAH; RIḌWĀN.

Bayat ar-Riḍwān, *see* RIḌWĀN.

Baybars I (al-Mālik aẓ-Ẓāhir Rukn ad-Dīn; *632-676*/1233-1277). The greatest of the Mamlūk Sultans of Egypt. He began his career as a Turkish slave who was sold into the bodyguard of the Ayyūbid Sultan of Damascus, al-Mālik aṣ-Ṣāliḥ. Baybars took part in the assassination of the Sultan's son, Turanshah, and fled, entering the service of Qutuz, the Mamlūk Sultan of Egypt.

As Qutuz's lieutenant, Baybars defeated the Mongols at 'Ayn Jalūt in *660*/1260. Then, angry at being denied governorship of Aleppo, he murdered Qutuz, seized the Sultanate for himself, and led the Baḥrī Mamlūks to many victories against the Crusaders, reducing the Crac des Chevaliers castle in Syria (*Qal'at al-ḥiṣn*) and other fortresses. Baybars crushed the last Assassin strongholds in Syria and extended Mamlūk rule to its historic limits.

Baybars installed Abū-l-Qāsim Aḥmad as a figurehead 'Abbāsid in Cairo under the name al-Mustanṣir bi-Llāh. Abū-l-Qāsim, an uncle of the last 'Abbāsid Caliph who was killed by the Mongols when they captured Baghdad, was himself killed in an attempt to recapture Baghdad in *659*/1261; but the dynasty maintained itself in Cairo until the Ottoman conquest in *923*/1517. The presence of a figurehead Caliph in Egypt gave Baybars and his Mamlūk successors a greater prestige and enhanced legitimacy.

Baybars recognized the authority of all four Schools of Law and established the custom of naming *qāḍis* (Judges) for each school in his territories, a practice which the Ottomans continued. Baybars was thus able also to play off the schools against one another when it suited him. He was an energetic if ruthless ruler, noted for his military exploits but also for his public works and patronage of splendid architecture. A power struggle followed his death, as was customary with the Mamlūks, and Baybars' infant son was deposed by another contender, Qala'ūn.

al-Bayḍāwī, 'Abd Allāh ibn Umar (d. *691*/1291). A Persian religious scholar, who was *Qāḍī* (Judge) in Shīrāz. He wrote a commentary on the Koran entitled *Anwār at-Tanzīl wa Asrār at-Ta'wīl* ("The Lights of Revelation and the Secrets of Interpretation"). Although he takes many opinions from az-Zamakasharī (d. *538*/1144), a Mu'tazilite, al-Bayḍāwī represents a sifting of all previous commentaries, and is regarded as the soundest and most authoritative commentator. *See* COMMENTARIES on the KORAN.

Bayram. A Turkish name for the festivals of 'Īd al-Adhā (in Turkish: *kurban bayram*) and the 'Īd al-Fiṭr. *See* 'ĪD al-AḌHĀ.

Bayt al-Ḥikmah, *see* HOUSE of WISDOM.

"Beatific Vision". The Koran speaks of men's "meeting with their Lord" as in the last verse of the Sūrah of the Cave:

> So let him, who hopes for
> the encounter with his Lord,
> work righteousness, and not associate with his
> Lord's service anyone. (18:110)

and it speaks of souls "gazing upon their Lord" as in the Sūrah of the Resurrection:

> Upon that day faces shall be radiant,
> gazing upon their Lord. (75:22-23)

Again, there are references in the Koran, to God's "Face", as in the Sūrah of the Night:

> ...even he who gives his wealth to purify himself
> and confers no favour on any man for recompense,
> only seeking the Face of his Lord the Most High;
> and he shall surely be satisfied. (92:18-20)

The Mu'tazilites, or Rationalists, denied that it could be possible to see God, and said that such passages had to be interpreted symbolically or allegorically. The Twelve-Imām Shī'ites, whose theology perpetuates many rationalist ideas of the Mu'tazilites, also deny the Beatific Vision, interpreting it symbolically. The traditionalists responded with a Ḥadīth in which the Prophet answers his Companions' questions about "seeing" God in Paradise by saying He will be seen as we "see the full moon against the dark night", that is, indirectly, as the moon reflects the light of the sun.

Al-Ash'arī, himself a former and repented Mu'tazilite and the greatest authority on *kalām*, or theology, went on to say that the seeing of God in paradise was the greatest joy that the Blessed enjoyed there.

The importance of the "Beatific Vision", is not a question of sight, but of awareness or knowledge. Or, to put it another way, "seeing God" is a participation, even indirectly, in the Divine Essence. The Mu'tazilites, in denying the "Beatific Vision" deny the possibility of knowing God; an unknowable God does not have even a merciful relation with creation; it is this which constitutes the importance of this Mu'tazilite heresy. Christian theologians, notable St. Thomas Aquinas, also emphasize the importance of the contemplation of God, the intellectual "vision" of God – even though God is invisible – in paradise. *See* MU'TAZILITES.

Bedug. A drum used in Indonesia to call the prayer in forested areas where the human voice does not carry well.

Begging. A practice frowned upon by Islamic law; on the other hand, the giving of alms (*ṣadaqah*), is a religious duty which purifies the soul. It is not legal to beg as long as one has sustenance for a day and a night. Nevertheless, dervishes sometimes took to begging for a livelihood. As al-Hujwīrī said:

> There are three allowable motives for begging, as more than one Shaykh has said: first, for the sake of mental liberty, since no anxiety is so engrossing as worry about getting something to eat; second, for the soul's discipline: Sufis beg because it is so humiliating and helps them to realize how little they are worth in other men's opinion, so that they escape self-esteem; third to beg from men out of

> reverence for God, regarding all as His agents – a servant who petitions an agent is humbler than one who makes petition to God Himself.
>
> The begging rule is this: if you beg and get nothing, be more cheerful than if you get something; never beg of women or people who hang about the bazaar; as far as possible, beg in a selfless spirit; never using what you get for self-adornment or housekeeping, or buying property with it. You should live in the present; never let a thought of tomorrow enter your mind, or you are lost. A final rule is never to let your piety be seen in the expectation of more liberal alms on that account.
>
> I once saw a venerable old Sufi who had lost his way in the desert come starving into the market place at Kufah with a sparrow perched on his hand crying: "Give me something, for the sparrow's sake!"
>
> "Why do you say that?" People asked. "I can't say: for God's sake", he replied; "one must let an insignificant creature plead for worldly things."

Being (Ar. *al-wujūd*). In Islamic metaphysics this is *Lāhūt,* the second of the "Five Divine Presences", (*al-ḥaḍarāt al-ilāhiyyah al-khams*). Being is what religions call the "personal God"; the first differentation of the Absolute, which is Itself Divine but not Absolute. It is Divine in relation to existence because it contains all existence in perfection; it is Divine in relation to the Absolute because it is nothing other than the Absolute, "reflected", but a perfect mirror, nonetheless. The Essence, Beyond-Being, which is the Absolute, *Allāh,* is All-Possibility; which must also embrace the possibility of Its own limitation. This necessary possibility is a perfection of the Absolute, no less than the Omnipotence of the Absolute is a perfection. It is Being which is the first movement in the unfolding of this possibility of self-negation.

What is One, indivisible, All-Possibility in the Absolute, becomes differentiated possibilities in Being. And Being translates the All-Possibility of Beyond-Being into existence and generates the creation of the world. Within Being a polarization takes place into Act (or Power) and Receptivity (or Substance, which is often used as a synonym for Being). Aristotle, and after him the Scholastics, called this polarization *eidos* and *hyle,* form and materia. It is what the Koran calls the "pen" (*al-qalam*) and the guarded tablet (*al-lawḥ al-mahfūẓ*). This polarization corresponds to Yang (Power) and Yin (Receptivity) in Taoism. Manifestation or creation takes place "between" this polarization, as the result of its union. Being is the "locus" of the higher paradises, and the degree of the Divine Names of the Qualities such as *ar-Raḥīm* (but not the Names of the Essence, or the Absolute, such as *ar-Raḥmān*).

Being corresponds to what Neoplatonism calls the *logos,* or the *nous.* Seen from different perspectives, Being is also called in Arabic *al-'amr, al-'aql al-awwal,* and many more terms as well. *Moksha,* or *mukti,* or "deliverance", is release from all contingency into Being, whereas salvation is conformity with a higher, but still contingent, degree of existence.

The Scholastics of Medieval Europe spoke of existence (from *ex-sistere,* "to stand out") as "accidents in relation to substance", or Being. "Accidents", metaphysically, are that which is contingent, or dependent, upon something else. Ibn 'Arabī (d. *638*/1240), and metaphysicians of his school, used exactly the same terminology; that which existed he called accidents (*araḍ*) emerging from substance (*jawhar*). Similarly Jāmī' (d. *898*/1491) and other poets said that beings in this world are "foam" on the waves of the ocean. (Water, which takes any shape, and is virtually a universal solvent, is the immediate symbol of substance; the ocean, in Arabic *al-Muḥīṭ,* "the encircling", an immediate symbol of Being.) The foam, the "accidents" come into existence because of privation, or an absence (*'adam*); the world "exists" because it is something removed from Being, from that which really IS, just as a color is the result of the removal of the other colors from colorless light, from light as such.

A Chinese Muslim named Ma Fu-Ch'u writing in the 18th century described Being thus in a treatise called *The Three Character Rhymed Classic on the Ka'bah:*

> Being's great attribute
> is called Consciousness-Potency,
> Consciousness foreshadowing the intelligence of things
> and Potency implying forms;
> creative change begins
> when the archetypes are born;
> the Great Command [Ar. *kun,* 'Be!'; cf. Koran 16:40]
> is given
> which is the gate to all marvels;

natures and intelligences are separated out
prefiguring their forms;
the myriad intelligences muster
and the subtle substance forms;
what one calls the Primal Spirit [Ar. *ruḥ*)
is truly all-pervasive
from the limits of the Previous Heaven [the unmanifest; *al-ghayb*]
to the roots of the Later Heaven [creation: *ad-dunyā*]
the male and female principles emerge
and the four elements are manifested
and their celestial and chthonic aspects fixed;
when the myriad forms are complete
they make Man.
Now Man
is the Essence of Heaven and earth;
among the ten thousand transformations
his is a special creation;
the quintessence of Heaven
is Man's heart;
the glory of earth
is his body;
the ten thousand intelligent principles
are Man's essential Nature.

See FANĀ'; FIVE DIVINE PRESENCES; al-INSĀN al-KĀMIL; al-KINDĪ.

Bektashī. A heterodox sect found in Turkey and to a lesser extent in countries formerly part of the Ottoman Empire. The Bektashis are sometimes considered to be a Sufi *ṭarīqah,* since they are organized as such. Rather than an esoterism, however, they represent instead a mixture of beliefs and practices which includes elements from Shī'ism, Christianity, and other sources, including possibly Buddhism.

The sect was widespread among the Janissaries, the military corps composed of boys taken from Christian families in the Balkans and converted to Islam, which accounts for the eclectic syncretism of Bektashi practices, reflecting certain vestiges of Christianity. *See* JANISSARIES.

Beloshaposhniki. A Russian name for the followers of the *Vis* (from the name "Uways") *Haji* brotherhood, a branch of the Caucasus Qadiriyyah tariqah, derived from the Chim Mirza branch ("Barabanshchiki"). The *Vis Haji* were founded in Kazakhstan by Chechen exiles. *See* QĀDIRIYYAH.

Bench, People of the, *see* AṢHĀB aṣ-ṢUFFĀH.

Berbers. A Mediterranean people found in North Africa from Libya to the Atlantic, and from the Mediterranean to regions just below the Sahara. They include nomads such as the Tuaregs of the Sahara, Mali and Niger, as well as settled farmers in the Atlas mountains of Morocco, of the Souss, the Rīfī, the Kabyles of Algeria. They also include the Guanches of the Canary Islands. Berbers speak a number of related languages such as Targui, Tamanzikht, Rīfī, etc. which belong to the Hamitic group; the Tuaregs possess a script which was once widely used by the other Berbers.

The Berbers were partly Islamicized in the course of the first Arab invasions and participated in the conquest of Spain. Some Berber groups were left behind after the retreat of the Arabs from Spain and today survive as Spanish ethnic groups such as the Maragatos of Astorga in Leon.

With the help of Berbers in Tunisia, the Fāṭimids carved out their Kingdom, as did the Idrissids with Berbers in Morocco. The Almoravids, the Almohads and the Merinids were Berber movements that established empires and dynasties. Today the Berbers constitute the majority of the population in Morocco and Algeria, and constitute important minorities elsewhere.

Bey. Formerly, a Turkic title for a chief. Today it is a title of respect in social intercourse. Its alternate form is Beg.

Beylerbey. "Bey of Beys", the Ottoman title for a provincial governor. Today in Arabic the equivalent title is usually *walī.*

Originally, there were two Beylerbeys, one for Anadolu (Anatolia) with headquarters at Ankara (from 1451 at Ktahya), and one for Rumeli (Europe) with headquarters at Sofia. The Anatolian Beylerbey had the higher rank and his standard bore three horse's tail pennants (Turkish: *tugh*) while that of the Rumeli Beylerbey had two. In campaigns in Asia, the Anatolian Beylerbey had precedence, while in campaigns in Europe, the Rumeli. The Beylerbeys were also called Pasha. Towards the end of the Ottoman period the number of Beylerbeys had grown to twenty.

The domain under a Beylerbey's control was a

sanjak ("banner"). From the original two *sanjaks* there grew to be 290, governed by Beys. These were progressively reorganized to form *pashaliks* and *vilayets,* of which there were more than seventy at the end of the Ottoman period after World War I.

Under Selim I, a Beylerbey of the sea, or Admiral, was appointed with the title of Kapudanpasha. Other important Ottoman officials included the *Defterdar,* a kind of Comptroller or accountant, an imperial treasurer, the Shaykh al-Islam, the highest religious authority, and the Viziers, or ministers, who conducted the business of government and held the imperial seal with the *tughra,* or Sultan's monogram. The office of the Grand Vizier was called the *Bāb-i 'Alī* ("the High Gate"), from a gate nearby it, which gave rise to the term "Sublime Porte" for the Ottoman Government. *See* OTTOMANS.

Bhakti marga, *see* MAḤABBAH.

Bible. Three sections of the Bible are cited by the Koran as being Divinely revealed: the Pentateuch, or Books of Moses (*Tawrāt*); the Psalms of David (*Zabur*); and the Gospels of Jesus (*Injīl*). These provide the basis for the identification, "People of the Book" (*ahl al-kitāb*), meaning those with revealed religions. These are Jews, Christians, Muslims, and others. However, the Gospels and Psalms have found no place in an Islamic canon and their contents are mostly ignored and unknown to Muslims. Moreover, the Gospel poses particular difficulties in Islam. Leaving aside the distinction between direct revelation from God which is the case of the Koran (in Arabic *tanzīl,* which corresponds to shruti in Sanskrit), and secondary inspiration (in Arabic *ilhām,* the equivalent of *smriti* in Sanskrit), which is the case of the Gospels, the Christian Gospel clashes with Islamic understanding of doctrine on several points, most importantly regarding the nature of Jesus.

Firstly, although in Islam Jesus has no earthly father and is the Spirit of God breathed into Mary, he is not the *son* of God. (*See* JESUS). Secondly, in the Koran, the death of Jesus on the cross is an *appearance* (4:154); that is, he did not die, but was taken up to God, where he will remain until he returns to earth at the end of time.

A third point of contention is the foretelling in the Gospel of the coming of the Prophet. Taking John 16:7:

> Nevertheless I tell you the truth; it is expedient for you that I go away, for if I go not away the Comforter will not come unto you; but if I depart I will send him unto you.

A slight change in the Greek word *paraclete* of the original text ("Comforter", or "Holy Ghost") turns the word into *paracleitos* ("Praised One") which is the meaning in Arabic of the name Muḥammad and its cognate *Aḥmad,* also used of the Prophet. The Gospel would then echo the words of the Koran:

> And when Jesus son of
> Mary said, 'Children of
> Israel, I am indeed the
> Messenger of God to you,
> confirming the Torah
> that is before me, and
> giving good tidings of
> a Messenger who shall
> come after me, whose
> name shall be Ahmad.' (61:6)

Muslims believe that the New Testament as used by Christians is incorrect and has, somehow, been falsified. Because the Koran affirms Christianity as a Divinely revealed religion, Muslims expect Christianity to be exactly like the Divine revelation that is Islam. Naturally, Muslims assume that Islam is the essence of true, or universal religion, and as Christianity is also a revealed religion, then the assumption that the two must coincide is inevitable. In practice, however, the religions do not, and cannot, coincide. Because comparison between the two is usually made on the basis of their outward forms, not finding the equivalent of the "Five Pillars", not finding exoteric Islam in Christianity, and finding rather a doctrine of Jesus which contradicts the basis of Islam as salvation through the recognition of God as Absolute, Muslims readily came to the conclusion, now established as dogma, that Christianity has somehow been altered; and this alteration can most easily be ascribed to some corruption (*taḥrīf*) of the original text of the Gospels by later editors. Thus what is a symbolical or virtual corruption of the Biblical text (from the Islamic point of view) as regards the Greek reference to the "Comforter"/"Praised One" is extended to cover and explain the metaphysical problem (for Muslims) of the meaning of the crucifixion, and the whole discrepancy between the two religions. *See* BARNABAS, GOSPEL of; JESUS; KORAN; PEOPLE of the BOOK; REVELATION.

Bid'ah ("innovation"). A practice or a belief which was not present in Islam as it was revealed in the Koran, and established by the Sunnah on the basis of the Prophetic traditions; hence something possibly contrary to Islam. For some Muslims *bid'ah* includes any practice, or religious fixture, that was not present at the time of early Islam, such as the construction of minarets on mosques, and which is thus to be rejected. For the majority, the introduction of something new is *bid'ah* only when it contradicts the spirit of Islam.

Since the possibilities of Islam can never be exhausted, anticipated in advance, or made entirely explicit in any one epoch, most exponents of Islamic law allow for the concept of *bid'ah ḥasanah,* or "good innovation", that is, an innovation which does not contradict the essence of the religion. Such an innovation may be, for example, the building of the additional storey onto the Grand Mosque of Mecca to permit the larger numbers of pilgrims in the present day to circumambulate the Ka'bah at one time.

Bihbahānī, Vahid (Aqa Muḥammad Baqir ibn Muḥammad Akmal; *1118-1207*/1706-1792). A descendant of the Shī'ite scholar Shaykh al-Mufīd, born near Isfahan. Bihbahānī defined the Uṣūlī system of Shī'ite jurisprudence, which stressed the application of principles to current religious questions in order to arrive at original and unprecedented answers, as opposed to the Akhbārī, or traditionalist school which stressed the application of precedent only.

By taking an extremely militant stance, declaring the Akhbārīs categorically to be *kāfirūn,* or unbelievers, as Muḥammad ibn 'Abd al-Wahhāb had done in Arabia towards his opponents, Bihbahānī drove the Akhbārīs out of Persia. (Akhbārīs still exist in southern Iraq, especially in Baṣra, as well as in Baḥrayn). He also used force to impose his ideas, surrounding himself with *mirghadabs,* or "executors of wrath" (a kind of forerunner of the *pasdarān,* or "revolutionary guards" of modern times), who physically intimidated and punished his opponents, on the spot, if necessary. Thus Bihbahānī, as the ultimately successful proponent, came to be considered the founder of the Uṣūlī school. He made it possible, particularly by his example of how he dealt with his opponents, for the superior Mullas to declare themselves Mujtahids and establish themselves as the absolute arbiters of religious authority in Persia, as the *nāibs* or representatives of the Hidden Imām.

Bihbahānī had studied at Kerbala and made Kerbala the center of Shī'ite scholarship in his time. He wrote the *Risālat al-Ijtihād wa-l-Akhbār,* and *Sharḥ al-Mafātiḥ.* He was also categorical with Sufis, as a competing group; for this he was known as *Sufi Kush,* or "Sufi Terminator". *See* AKHBĀRĪS; AYATOLLAH; SHĪ'ISM; UṢŪLĪ.

Bila kayfā ("without [asking] how"). A theological principle of not questioning revelation when it may perplex or defy human understanding. This concept is most closely associated with al-Ash'arī, but has been also used by others, such as Ibn Ḥanbal. Al-Ash'arī invoked the notion of *bilā kayfā wa lā tashbīh* ("without asking how or making comparison") most notably in respect of the Koran's so-called anthropomorphizing expressions which speak of God as having human attributes – such as the "Hand of God" or the "Face of God", or God's being "seated" on a throne. Although God could not physically have a hand, according to al-Ash'arī and Ibn Ḥanbal, these expressions have to be accepted literally as they are, "without asking how".

These expressions have also been interpreted not literally, but figuratively, today as in the past. The use of the term "anthropomorphizing" in Western writings on the subject of Islam may be misleading, because the references are isolated and do not actually entail anything beyond the level of certain concepts; they do not in fact imply an "anthropomorphic" idea of God. The device of *bilā kayfā* reflects the need felt by theologians in the past to reconcile the fact that if the Koran has symbolic planes of meaning, it must first of all be accepted as true on the literal plane. Because there was the equal imperative to acknowledge God as completely incomparable, solutions had to be sought of which *bilā kayfā* was the closest at hand.

Resorting to the principle *bilā kayfā* is similar to the recourse to "divine mystery" in Catholicism when dogma and metaphysics cannot be reconciled on the purely theological plane without surpassing theology itself by antimony. *See* ISTAWĀ'.

Bilāl. The first *muezzin* (Ar. *mua'dhadhin,*) or caller to prayer. A black slave from Abyssinia, Bilāl was an early convert to Islam who, because his master severely mistreated him for his religious beliefs, was ransomed and freed by his fellow-convert Abū Bakr. When the call to prayer – rather than a summons by bells – was instituted, Bilāl was chosen for his fine voice and despite his imperfect pronunciation of Arabic. He made the call from the top of the Ka'bah when the Prophet entered Mecca in the pilgrimage of *8*/629 as allowed by the treaty of Ḥudaybiyyah, and again the following year when the Prophet entered the city in triumph. He served the Prophet and was the chamberlain to the first Caliphs. Bilāl accompanied the armies to Syria and some accounts say he is buried there.

Bilalians. A name adopted by some members of the "Nation of Islam" in America when Elijah Muhammad was succeeded by his son Wallace Warith Deen Muhammad. Bilāl was the first renowned Muslim who was black. (*See* BILĀL; "BLACK MUSLIMS").

Bilqīs. The Queen of Sheba (or Ar. *Sabā'*), a pre-Islamic kingdom in South Arabia. She became a consort of King Solomon and entered his religion. Stories describe how the *jinn* brought her throne to Solomon in Jerusalem from Sheba. The Koran relates that when Bilqīs visited Solomon, she mistook the polished floor of the throne room for water and raised her skirt to cross it. When she realized her error, and thereby the power of illusion, she accepted the *shahādah,* or testimony of Islam, and surrendered to God.

Bilqīs has come to symbolize the nature of woman as infinitude, in complement to man as center and Intellect, which Solomon represented. That magical and mysterious feminine nature that Bilqīs represents is expressed by the Arab legend that her father was not human, but a *jinn,* a being from the subtle world. Ibn 'Arabī in the *Tarjuman al-Ashwāq* mentions her and comments:

> On the day of parting they did not saddle the full-grown reddish-white camels, until they had mounted the peacocks upon them,
>
> Peacocks with murderous glances and sovereign power: thou wouldst fancy that each of them was a Bilqīs on her throne of pearls.
>
> When she walks on the glass pavement thou seest a sun, a celestial sphere in the bosom of Idrīs.
>
> When she kills with her glances, her speech restores to life, as though she, in giving life thereby, were Jesus.
>
> Commentary:
>
> The full-grown camels, i.e. the actions inward and outward, for they exalt the good word to Him who is throned on high, as He hath said: 'And the good deed exalts it' (Koran 25:11). 'The peacocks' mounted on them are his loved ones: he likens them to peacocks because of their beauty. The peacocks are the spirits of those actions, for no action is acceptable or good or fair until it hath a spirit consisting in the intention or desire of its doer.
>
> 'With murderous glances and sovereign power': he refers to the Divine Wisdom which accrues to a man in his hours of solitude, and which assaults him with such violence that he is unable to behold his personality.
>
> 'A Bilqīs on her throne of pearls': he refers to that which was manifested to Gabriel and the Prophet during his night journey upon the bed of pearl and jacinth in the terrestrial heaven. The author calls the Divine wisdom 'Bilqīs' on account of its being the child of theory, which is subtle, and practice, which is gross, just as Bilqīs was both spirit and woman, since her father was of the Jinn and her mother was of mankind.
>
> The mention of Idrīs alludes to her lofty and exalted rank. 'In the bosom of Idrīs', i.e. under his control, in respect of his turning her wheresoever he will, as the Prophet said: 'Do not bestow wisdom on those who are unworthy of it, lest ye do it wrong'. The opposite case is that of one who speaks because he is dominated by his feeling (*ḥāl*), and who is therefore under the control of an influence (*warīd*). In this verse the author calls attention to his puissance in virtue of a prophetic heritage, for the prophets are masters of their spiritual feelings (*aḥwāl*), whereas most of the saints are mastered by them.

'She kills with her glances': referring to the station of passing away in contemplation (*al-fanā' fī-l-mushāhadah*). 'Her speech restores to life': referring to the the contemplation of the moldering of man when the spirit was breathed into him.

Birth. Upon birth it is customary to whisper the *shahādah,* or testimony of the faith, into the ears of the newborn. One can also make the call to prayer, which includes the *shahādah.* Ceremonies which may follow, according to local customs, include the sacrifice of the *'aqīqah,* and celebrations of the giving of a name to the newborn child, after seven days. *See* 'AQĪQAH; NAMES.

Birth control. It has been practiced in the past in Islam, and most methods of contraception are generally admitted upon condition of being acceptable to both parties. In recent times there have been *fatwas* (legal decisions) to this effect, issued by councils of *'ulama',* reaffirming legal opinions formed centuries ago. *See* ABORTION.

al-Bīrūnī, Abū Rayḥān (*362-442*/973-1048). Born of Persian-speaking parents in what today is Uzbekistan, al-Bīrūnī was a universal genius and polymath who turned his attention to every available field of learning. Called *al-ustādh,* "the teacher", the scope of al-Bīrūnī's enquiries was vast and profound, and he is a great luminary in the history of world science.

When attached to the court of Maḥmūd of Ghaznah, he traveled with the Sultan to India, where he learned Sanskrit and became a bridge between the world of Hindu learning and Arabic-speaking Islamic civilization. For twelve years he concentrated on studying the wisdom of India and the resulting encyclopedic *Book of India* (*Kitāb al-Hind*) described Hindu systems of philosophy, cosmological theories, and customs. Al-Bīrūnī not only translated the *Patanjāli Yoga* from Sanskrit to Arabic, he also translated Euclid's Elements and his own works into Sanskrit. His knowledge of the sacred books of Hinduism gave al-Bīrūnī an unusually broad framework for his study of history. Hindu notions of cyclic time led him to a remarkable awareness of the vast ages of the geologic past.

In *387*/997 he exchanged letters on Aristotle's *Physics* with Ibn Sīnā (Avicenna), then living in Bukhāra and was no more than seventeen years old. The two later met, when al-Bīrūnī disputed with him some of Aristotle's scientific reasoning, in particular the notion of the "eternity of the world". (*See* PHILOSOPHY.)

Al-Bīrūnī's work on astronomy, the *Mas'ūdic Canon,* is dedicated to the successor of Maḥmūd of Ghaznah. He listed 1029 stars and calculated latitude and longitude using instruments of his own making. His treatise on pharmacology, the *Kitāb aṣ-Ṣaydalah,* lists names of substances in Greek, Persian, Arabic, and Sanskrit. As for botany, al-Bīrūnī described five times as many plants as Dioscorides. He calculated the specific gravity of various substances, wrote on the properties of gems in the *Kitāb al-Jawāhir,* and on the history of nations in *Athar al-Baqiyah.*

In *409*/18, at the fortress of Nandana near present day Islamabad in Pakistan, al-Bīrūnī calculated the radius and circumference of the earth. Using the height of a mountain and its angular relationship to the horizon, he arrived at a figure for the radius of the earth which has been equated to be 6,338 km, only 15 km from the estimate of today. His figures for the circumference of the earth are less than 200 km from today's calculations. One of the proofs he gave for the sphericity of the earth is its round shadow on the moon during lunar eclipses (an observation made more than once even by ancient philosophers).

Al-Bīrūnī's field of study embraced the human world, plants and animals, the physical world, and the abstractions of physics and mathematics. Moreover, he showed a profound interest in the subject of religion and, whilst being fully aware of the differences between his own Islamic faith and others which had resort to radically different forms, he did not conclude that the various creeds were no more than subjective systems, or that one was wrong and the other right. Nor did al-Bīrūnī reduce physical reality to what can be ascertained by empirical observations, lose sight of the Presence of God in what he studied, or put dogma between himself and his researches. He was thus a true scientist in the broadest sense of the term.

al-Bisṭāmī, Abū Yazīd (Bāyazīd) Ṭaifūr (d. *260*/874). A Sufi, sometimes referred to as the first of the "drunken Sufis", because he went so far as to speak in terms which implied Divinity in himself. Al-Bisṭāmī was born in Bisṭām in northern Persia and is buried there. He was the son of a Magian, and this "deifying" thread in mysticism, (which is even found in exoterism, as some of the early Persian converts to Islam proposed deification of the ruler), probably arose out of the characteristic influences of certain of the indigenous religions of Iran.

> "The vestiges of knowledge", said Bāyazīd, are effaced; its essence is noughted by the Essence of Another, its track lost in the Track of Another. Thirty years God was my mirror. But now I am my own mirror; that which used to be I, I am no more. To say I and God denies the Unity of God. I say I am my own mirror, but it is God that speaks with my tongue – I have vanished. I glided out of my Bāyazīdhood as a snake glides from a cast skin. And then I looked. And what I saw was this: lover and Beloved and Love are One. Glory to Me!" (Ar. *Subḥānī,* a play on the customary *Subḥān Allāh* , "Glory to God!")

Such notions are not shared by all Sufis, by any means, and al-Junayd of Baghdad, in response to precisely this phenomenon, was the spokesman of rigor and "dryness" (*ṣawḥ*), that is, of "union without deification".

Al-Bisṭāmī left no writings and what is known of his sayings (sometimes referred to as *shataḥāt,* or ecstatic utterances; phrases like "How great is my majesty!") come from later compilations such as the *Kitāb al-Lumā* ("The Book of Illumination") of as-Sarrāj. Many of these sayings are orthodox, and may represent the attribution of anonymous mystic teachings to a famous Sufi name in order to position their contents; (a question of origin complicated by the apparent existence of another Sufi of exactly the same name, a transmitter of sayings, called al-Bisṭāmī-l-Asghar, "al-Bisṭāmī the lesser". The obscurity of this other Bisṭāmī may be the result of orthodoxy splitting the figure into two, a problematic "greater" Bistami, and a more easily acceptable "lesser").

But of the scandalous stories regarding Bistami there is one in the Masnavi which recounts that Bāyazīd was on his way to the Ka'bah when he met a holy man who asked him how much money he had for the journey. Then the holy man advised Bāyazīd to go around himself seven times and give him the money instead because "into this house that is I none but the Living God has gone. In seeing me you have seen God; you have circled about the Ka'bah of Truthfulness."

It is curious that many Sufis of impeccable repute, such as al-Hujwīrī, came and visited the tomb of al-Bisṭāmī, and other marks of respect were accorded him; but this does not mean that they accepted his formulations without reservation. Indeed, some of his sayings are so problematic that he is even reported to have scoffed at believers for their belief. Abū Yazīd was also reported to have said that "I used to keep company with Abū 'Alī al-Sindī and I used to show him how to perform the obligatory duties of Islam, and in exchange he would give me instruction in the divine unity (*tawḥīd*) and in the ultimate truths (*ḥaqā'iq*)". This Abū 'Ali may have been a co-religionist of Bisṭāmīs before they professed Islam and they were probably discussing the tenets of their previous religion. To say that he learned *tat tvam asi* from Sindi, is to overlook that very similar doctrines had long been professed by Iranian religions. *See* al-JUNAYD; ZINDIQ.

"Black Muslims". A sect among blacks in America with its center in Chicago, the original name of which was the "Nation of Islam". The founder was Elijah Muḥammad; but it was the dynamic leadership of Malcolm X, originally Malcolm Little, (later al-Ḥajj Mālik ash-Shabazz), murdered in 1965, that brought the organization to international prominence.

The roots of the sect reach back to movements among American blacks in the early years of this century. Marcus Garvey's promotion of solidarity with Africa connected the quest for dignity with the search for links with the old world. Two more immediate influences were a religious sect of Noble (Timothy Drew) 'Alī, the "American Moors" of the Moorish Science Temple in Newark, New Jersey. Another was the Aḥmadiyyah, a heterodox Islamic sect which emerged in India during the 19th century, one of the few groups in Islam that proselytized and established mosques in Europe and America at that period. One of the tenets of the Aḥmadiyyah identifies Christianity with the *dajjāl,* the "deceiver", that is, with the Antichrist, at the end of time. It is probably the transposition of its doctrine which produced the idea that the white man is the devil; this notion characterized the early phase of Black Muslim ideology. These various influences came together in a man called W. D. Fard who met Elijah Muḥammad (originally Elijah Poole) in Detroit in the 1930s. (The name Fard is symbolic, *see* FARḌ).

Out of the ideas of Fard (who disappeared in 1953) came the doctrine elaborated by Elijah Muḥammad of black superiority. In its original form, it contended that the white race had been derived from the black at Mecca, and that the criterion of heaven or hell was material prosperity. The Nation of Islam demanded that a separate American state be created and given to the blacks. Meanwhile, the growth of businesses sponsored by the Black Muslims helped to create economic independence for the movement.

When Malcolm X visited Mecca he saw true Islam at first hand and, adopting orthodoxy, broke away from the Nation of Islam. At the same time, other splinters from the Nation of Islam either moved over to orthodox Islam or joined pseudo-Islamic groups centered around different "Mahdīs", sometimes with apocalyptic and racist appeals.

When Elijah Muḥammad died in 1975, his son Wallace Warith Deen Muḥammad assumed the leadership. He has subsequently persuaded the movement, now known as the American Muslim Mission, to abandon its eccentricities, reconcile itself with the contributions made by Malcolm X, and adopt authentic Islam in its entirety. In its commitment to religious orthodoxy, the American Muslim Mission has sent some of its members to study at such traditional centers of Islamic learning as the al-Azhar in Cairo, and the Islamic University of Medina. Estimates of followers of the American Muslim Mission range from over one hundred and fifty thousand to almost a million; the number of those sympathetic to it, without being Muslim, is even larger.

A smaller faction under Louis Farrakhan, has retained the previous name of "Nation of Islam", and maintained its old policies. The number of followers of this continuation of the Nation of Islam is under fifty thousand. *See also* ḤANAFĪ MUSLIMS.

Black Sheep, *see* QARA QOYUNLU.

Black Stone (Ar. *al-ḥajar al-aswad*). This is a stone set in the south-east corner of the Ka'bah about one and one-half yards/meters from the ground. It is black with reddish tones and yellow particles, of ovoid shape about 11 inches/28 cm wide and 15 inches/38 cm high, set in a silver chasing. During the circumambulation of the Ka'bah the worshiper kisses the stone, or makes a gesture in its direction. A Ḥadīth of the Prophet says that it came down from heaven. The Caliph 'Umar once said during ṭawāf, or circumambulation: "I know that you are only a stone which does not have the power to do good or evil. If I had not seen the Prophet kissing you, I would not kiss you."

Tradition says that Adam placed it in the original Ka'bah. Later it was hidden in the Meccan mountain of Abū Qubays. When Abraham rebuilt the Ka'bah, the Angel Gabriel brought the stone out and gave it to him.

During the siege of Mecca in *64*/683, the Ka'bah caught fire from a flaming arrow and the heat cracked the stone into three large parts and some smaller fragments. In *317*/930 the Qarmatians raided Mecca, captured the stone, and carried it off to al-Ḥasa or Baḥrayn, where it was kept. Ransom was offered for it, which was ignored. Then in *340*/951 it was thrown, the historian Juwayni relates, into the Friday Mosque of Kufah with a note: "By command we took it, and by command we have brought it back". It was in three pieces before it was stolen; it is in seven pieces today. (*See* QARMATIANS.)

Because stone is the most durable of substances and the one that comes closest to being eternal, it offers itself readily as a symbol of eternity. The Old Testament of the Bible calls God the "Rock of Ages", and Jesus says to Simon "thou art Peter, and upon this rock I will build my church" (Matthew 16:18). Symbolically, it can also be said that undifferentiated stone hides within itself the essential and refulgent nature of gems, or precious stones.

The Black Stone, because of its color, the absence of light, lends itself especially to the symbolism of the essential spiritual virtue of poverty for God (*faqr*), that is, a *vacare deo*, an "emptiness for God", or the necessary extinction of the ego that must precede access to the center which is the heart (*qalb*).

The early Semites used unusual stones to mark places of worship and virtually every culture, ancient and modern, has recognized the inherent symbolism of stones in some hieratic usage or other. Jacob set up a pillar, and on it the stone on which he had rested his head during his dream. He anointed the stone with oil and it became an altar in the sanctuary, already sacred to Abraham, that he founded at Beth-El, near Jerusalem. Ancient British tradition identifies this stone to the "Stone of Scone" which, until recently, was kept under the royal coronation throne in Westminster Abbey). *See also* KA'BAH.

Blessing, *see* BARAKAH; PRAYERS on the PROPHET; RIḌWĀN.

Blue Men (Ar. *ar-rijāl az-zuraq*). Nomad Arab tribes, notably the Reguibat in the western Sahara, that wander over the vast desert between Mauritania and Marrakesh. They are so called because the indigo dye from their turbans and clothes (from a cloth traditionally made in Kano, Nigeria), comes off on their skin. They do not cover their faces by winding their turbans over it as do the Tuaregs, who are Berber, and with whom the Blue Men are often confused.

Bohoras (Vohoras, "traders" from Gujarati *vohorvu,* "to trade"). An ethnic group in India and Pakistan, originally a Hindu caste, most of whom are today Musta'lī Ismā'īlīs. This is a branch which split with the Nizārīs in *487*/1094 and who does not recognize the Aga Khan as its spiritual leader. Instead they are under the leadership of a *Dā'i Muṭlaq,* or "Absolute Preacher", often called the *Mulla-ji.* They were converted during the early period of Ismā'īlī propagandizing in India before the *5th*/11th century.

Most Bohoras follow that branch of Musta'lī Ismā'īlīsm known as Daudī; the Daudī Dā'i Muṭlaq is called the *Mulla-Ji* and is resident in Bombay. A minority are Sulaymānīs; their leader formerly resided in the Yemen, but in this century transferred his seat to Baroda in India, which was the seat of his Indian *Mansūb* or representative. Their population centers are Bombay and the Gujarat in India and also, through immigration, the commercial centers of East Africa. The 1931 Indian census put their numbers at 212,000. In the *9th*/15th century some Bohoras professed Sunnī Islam rather than Ismā'īlīsm, which gave rise to the Sunnī Bohoras in India and Pakistan. *See* ISMĀ'ĪLĪS.

Bokhara. City in Uzbekistan. The region around it was called Soghdiana and, by the Arabs *Ma' wara'n-nahr,* literally Transoxiana. It was traditionally a seat of learning and again today has a functioning *madrasah.* Destroyed by Jenghiz Khan in 1220 during his invasion of Khwarizm, it became a city of mysticism. It was at the end an Emirate conquered by Russia in 1868. Its muezzins are famous. *See* MAZARI-SHARIF; SAMARKAND.

Bosnia and Herzegovina. A Balkan republic with a population of over 3,000,000 made up of three ethnic groups: Bosnians, Serbs, and Croats. Formerly part of Yugoslavia. The Bosnians are Muslims of the Hanafi school of law, the Croats are Catholic and the Serbs are Serbian Orthodox. In 1992 a referendum for independence was passed and war broke out between Muslims, Serbs and Croats. In 1994 an agreement was made to create a Bosnian-Croat federation. The Dayton accords brought the war to an end but also an incertain future. Bosnia had been ruled by Croatian kings in 958 and by Hungary from 1000 to 1200. It then became autonomous and ruled Herzegovina until it disintegrated as a political entity in 1391. It was conquered by the Turks in 1463 and was a Turkish province until control passed to Austria-Hungary in 1878. It became a province of Yugoslavia in 1918. In 1946 it became a Federated republic in Yugoslavia.

The capital is Sarajevo, which in addition to its historic mosques, the Careva, Alipasa and Gazi Husref Beg Dzamijat, has a 16th-century *madrasah,* the Kurshumli. Besides the myriads of human victims, Islamic monuments throughout Bosnia were destroyed during the war.

Boujloud (lit. "father of the skins"; in standard Arabic *abū julūd*). A festival in Morocco of pagan origin. It has attached itself to the *Īd al-Kabīr,* a feast commemorating the sacrifice of Abraham. Boujloud is the name of a person who, clothed in the skins of freshly slaughtered sheep, runs through a village or encampment striking the houses or tents with a stick. This is considered to "bless" the households. The psychological meaning is clear, and parallels can be found in most cultures: a person marks himself as impure, in this case by the bloody animal skins, and "draws off impurity" – or its psychological consequences of guilt – onto himself from others, much as in Europe to see a chimney-sweep was thought to bring luck, or as gargoyles were depicted on cathedrals to discharge the tension of an awareness of one's own impurity. The *Boujloud* resembles the practice in Biblical times of sending out a scapegoat into the desert over whose head a priest had confessed the sins of the people.

It has been thought that this scapegoat was dedicated to a desert demon called Azazel; and an important aspect of *Boujloud* is its shadowy nature in that certain practices of the *Boujloud* make mockery of religion. For example, a mock Imām leads a group of people behind him in a ludicrous distortion of the canonic prayer. Taken altogether this is an example of a "carnaval-esque" festival, such as can be found in most cultures. Its equivalent is the Roman Lupercalia or, in Christian countries, the lenten carnival, or sometimes midsummer night ("the eve of Saint John"). In these events, the laws of religion are ignored for a determined period, while rebellious and shadowy human tendencies come to the surface, spend themselves, and release the tensions caused by daily conformity to social or religious ordinances.

For the sake of social equilibrium religious authorities usually have little choice, given human nature, but to ignore what amounts to a contained rebellion. It has been suggested that *Boujloud* is an echo of the pagan god Pan, doubtless because of the resemblance to the wearing of the skins of goats during the ancient Greek tragedies, where a similar cathartic function was performed by the enactment of drama. The *Boujloud* is peculiar to North Africa, but "carnevalesque" festivals are not. One of the principal gates to the walled city of Fez is named *Bāb Boujloud*. *See* SECRET SOCIETY.

Bow, prayer, *see* RAKAH.

Brotherhood of Purity (Ar. *Ikhwān aṣ-ṣafā'*). A secret society in Basra, Iraq, founded around *340*/951 and probably headed by Zayd ibn Rifāah. It served as a forum for discussion and learning, and its members probably included Abū Sulaymān Muḥammad al-Busṭī (al-Muqaddasī), Abū-l-Ḥasan 'Alī az-Zanjānī, Abū Aḥmad al-Maḥrajānī, and al-Awfī. They published fifty-one tracts known as the *Rasā'il ikhwan aṣ-ṣafā'* ("The Treatises of the Brotherhood of Purity"), which constituted an encyclopedia of knowledge in philosophy, theology, metaphysics, cosmology, and the natural sciences, including botany and zoology.

The writings of the society reveal a surprising open-minded intellectual curiosity about such civilizations as those of the ancient Greeks, the Persians, and the Indians; in fact their universalism went so far as to accept that there is truth in religions other than Islam. Their Neo-Platonic ideas, as well as the method whereby they would raise questions, but not answer them except indirectly and by implication, and their hinting at the existence of some higher authority where all could be resolved, have led them to be identified as an intellectual current flowing from the Ismā'īlīs. Their ethic of brotherhood was linked with self-knowledge and the emancipation of the soul from materialism leading to a return to God.

Despite this avowed ethic there is a curiously humanistic flavor about the Brotherhood of Purity. The 'Abbāsid al-Mustanjid, who succeeded to the Caliphate in *555*/1160, had their works burned, but the far reaching influence of the *Rasā'il* continued. It may have reached Dante through the *Fedeli d'Amore*, and had repercussions in Europe in the Middle Ages. The name *Ikhwān aṣ-Ṣafā'* comes from the animal fables of *Kalīlah wa Dimnah* by Ibn al-Muqaffa (who was himself accused of being a *zindīq*); a group of heteroclite animals are caught in a net and have to band together and combine their talents in order to escape. *See* ISMĀ'ĪLĪS.

Brunei. (State of Brunei Darussalam); Sultanate. Population 292,266. Ethnic groups: 64% Malay, Chinese 20%. Religions: Muslim: 63%, Buddhist 14%, Christian 8%. Brunei is located on the north coast of Borneo and is surrounded on the land side by the Malaysian state of Sarawak. The Capital is Bandar Seri Begawan with a population of 52,000. The head of government is Sultan Sir Muda Hassanal Bolkiah Mu'izzadin Waddaulah. The Sultanate of Brunei ruled the island of Borneo in the 16th century and dominated the Sulu Islands of the Philippines. In 1888 it was placed by treaty under the protection of Great Britain. It became sovereign in 1984. Islam of the Shāfi'ī school of law is the official religion.

Bsaṭ (*basā'iṭ*). A plural of *bast*, or "expansion". One of its meanings is "humor" as in the "four humors", and also comedy. *Bsaṭ* is the name of an old form of Arab comic folk theater.

Bū Ḥamārah. "The man with the donkey", a name for a revolutionary in Morocco, who raised a revolt against the Sultan at the turn of the 19th century, held northeast Morocco making Taza his provisional capital, and twice threatened Fez with an army of his followers. After long struggles, he was captured in 1909, brought to Fez in a cage, and shot. The theme of "the man with the donkey" is an ancient sign of the Messiah: "Rejoice greatly, O daughter of Zion; shout, O daughter of Jerusalem: behold thy King cometh unto thee: he is just, and having salvation; lowly, and riding upon an ass, and upon a colt the foal of an ass" (Zechariah 9:9). *See* DHU-l-ḤIMĀR.

al-Burāq. The miraculous steed which the Angel Gabriel brought to the Prophet for the *Mir'āj*, or Heavenly Ascent, also known as the *Isrā'*, or Night Journey. The root of the word is *baraqa*, which means "to glitter", especially of lightning. In India the *Burāq* is depicted as having the face of a woman and the tail of a peacock, but there is no basis for this in traditional accounts, in which the *Burāq* is described as a creature for riding, bigger than a donkey and smaller than a horse, of celestial origin. On the other hand, the iconography of the *Burāq* as seen through the Indian imagination, makes of it a fantastical creature, both human and animal, and thus extends its symbolism to that of being the synthesis of all creation which accompanies the Prophet to heaven.

The traditional account of the Night Journey says that the *Burāq* proceeded in flashes of speed; where its glance landed, the next bound brought it, and from this it can be seen that the *Burāq* is an embodiment of the Intellect which, when it perceives an object in Being, or a spiritual reality, can immediately recognize its nature, or knows it, without a process of analysis and reason. *See* 'AQL; NIGHT JOURNEY.

Burdah. A mantle, but especially one of the Prophet's mantles, made out of goat's hair. There are two famous poems in Arabic by this name, one by a contemporary of the Prophet named Ka'b ibn Zuhayr, and another by the *7th*/13th century poet al-Buṣīrī.

The Prophet gave away several of his cloaks, a gift which is traditionally a mark of honor; one he threw to the poet Ka'b ibn Zuhayr who had been branded as an outlaw for denouncing Islam in his poetry; when the poet repented he recited a eulogy to the Prophet in his presence in Medina by way of asking for pardon.

> Su'ad is gone, and today my heart is love-sick, in thrall to her, unrequited, bound with chains;
> And Su'ad when she came forth on the morn of departure, was but as a gazelle with bright black downcast eyes...
> Oh, what a rare mistress were she, if only she were true to her promise and would hearken to good advice!
> But hers is a love in whose blood are mingled paining and lying and faithlessness and inconstancy...
> In the evening Su'ad came to a land whither none is brought save by camels that are excellent and noble and fleet...
> One that bedews the bone behind her ear when she sweats, one
> that sets herself to cross a trackless unknown wilderness...
> I was told that the Messenger of Allāh threatened me with death, but with the Messenger of Allāh I have hope of finding pardon.
> Gently! mayst thou be guided by Him who gave thee the gift of the Koran, wherein are warning and a plain setting out of the matter.
> Do not punish me, when I have sinned, on account of what is said by the informers, even though the false sayings about me should be many.
> Ay, I stand in such a place that if an elephant stood there, seeing what I see and hearing what I hear,
> The sides of his neck would be shaken with terror – if there be no forgiveness from the Messenger of Allāh...
> Truly the Messenger is a light whence illumination is sought – a drawn Indian sword, one of the swords of Allāh,
> Amongst a band of Quraysh, whose spokesman said when they professed Islam in the valley of Mecca, 'Depart ye!'
> They departed, but no weaklings were they or shieldless in battle or without weapons and courage...
> Warriors with noses high and straight, clad for the fray in mail-coats of David's weaving.

Ka'b later treasured this mantle and would not sell it to the Caliph Mu'āwiyah for ten thousand dirhams. It became part of the national treasury after the poet's death.

Although it is sometimes said that this mantle disappeared in flames during the sack of Baghdad by the Mongols in *656*/1258, the

Ottomans claimed to possess a cloak of the Prophet (*al-khirqah ash-sharīfah*, in Turkish: *Khirqa-i-sharīf*). Possession of the Prophet's mantle – which already in 'Abbāsid times was considered to be Caliphal regalia and a symbol of the office – was used as an argument in the 19th century by the Ottomans to support their claim to the Caliphate. Today this mantle is kept in the Topkapi Museum in Istanbul.

The Burdah is also the name of another famous poem in praise of the Prophet by al-Buṣīrī (*610-695*/1213-1296), a Berber born in Cairo, a Sufi disciple of the Imām ash-Shādhilī and of his successor Abū-l-'Abbās al-Mursī. Al-Buṣīrī was suffering from paralysis when he saw the Prophet in a dream place his own mantle upon him; when he awoke he was cured of his affliction. The poem, which describes the nature of the Prophet, is held in great pious esteem. It is the custom, chiefly in countries that were once part of the Ottoman Empire, to recite this *Burdah*, or "Mantle Poem", of al-Buṣīrī's in mosques during the *Mawlid*, or anniversary of the Prophet's birth. Verse 56 of Busiri's *Burdah* is especially famous; the Prophet is:

> Like a flower in tenderness, and like the full moon in glory,
> And like the ocean in generosity, and like all Time brought into one point.

See also KHIRQAH.

Burqa. In Saudi Arabia it is women's head covering which covers her face, and may go to the ground. In Afghanistan it is the pleated head-to-foot covering women wear in public with a lattice in front of the eyes to see. In the Gulf States it is a leather face mask worn by women. *See* HIJAB; VEIL.

Buwayhids, *see* BUYIDS.

Butachaqieh. The Persian name for the ancient design that appears on the "peacock throne", which was brought to Persia from Delhi by Nadir Shah. This design was adopted from Indian motifs, and became known in the west as "Paisley", from the town in Scotland where the design was often woven.

Buyids. A dynasty which controlled Iraq and Persia from *320*/932 to *454*/1062. The Buyids (also called Buwayhids) were Daylamis, a Turkic people who had settled around the Caspian sea. By military penetration from within the armies of the Caliphate, and by conquest, they took control of the 'Abbāsid Empire while maintaining the 'Abbāsid Caliphs as figureheads. Under the title of *amīr al-'umarā'* ("Prince of Princes") the Buyid chief ruled as military overlord.

Although the Buyids are known to have been Shī'ites, the exact nature of their Shī'ism cannot be ascertained; it may well have been a kind of Zaydī Shī'ism, and it probably served to rally opposition to the Sunnī political power which they supplanted. In any case, they did not seek to depose the Sunnī Caliph but simply to use him in order to legitimize their own rule, as did later dynasties until the Mongols. The Buyids were replaced by other dynasties who divided up the areas formerly under their control; the Saljuqs ruled in the west, and eventually the Ghaznavids in the east.

C

Cadi, *see* QĀḌI.

Caesar. Among the Arabs, the term "Caesar" (Arabicised as *qayṣar*) referred above all to the Byzantine Emperor, and the word *Rūm* (Romans), in the Koran, refers to the Byzantines. In modern times the word *rūmī* has come to mean anything of European, as opposed to native, origin. *Qaysariyyah,* a fine goods market for silver, gold, cloth, incense and perfumes comes from the Arabic word for Caesar because such a market was often situated on the former Roman forum, the "place of Caesar".

Cain and Abel (Ar. *Kābil* and *Hābil*). The sons of Adam. According to tradition, each had a twin sister; Cain married the sister of Abel, and Abel married the sister of Cain. *See* IBN KHALDŪN.

Cairo (Ar. *al-Qāhirah,* "the Victorious", but also "the City of Mars", from *al-Qāhir,* "Mars"). The capital of the Fāṭimids was founded by the general Jawhar, in the name of the Fāṭimid ruler al-Mu'izz, in *358*/969. Cairo then lay between the Nile and the Muqattam hills near the site of the first Muslim capital, al-Fusṭāṭ ("the Encampment"). Nearby was the ancient city of Bābilūn, or "Babylon of Egypt", a Greco-Roman fortress, and al-Fusṭāṭ, the seat of government of 'Amr ibn al-'Āṣī who conquered Egypt for Islam. Today Cairo encloses that site as well as al-'Askar, the capital of the 'Abbāsids, and al-Iqtā'āt ("the Fiefs"), the capital under Aḥmad ibn Ṭulūn, and straddles both shores of the river.

The city was founded in accordance with astrological calculation, the Fāṭimids being avid students of this pursuit. Legend tells that when the astrologers were poised to pull on bell-ropes in order to raise a pealed signal to the workmen to turn the first clods of earth at the most propitious moment, a raven anticipated them by alighting on the rope and jingling the bells as the planet Mars (*al-Qāhir*) was rising on the horizon; hence, according to this fanciful account, the city's name of *al-Qāhirah.* In fact, Cairo was first called *al-Manṣūriyyah;* it was only when the Fāṭimid ruler entered the country four years later that it became *al-Qāhirah al-Muizziyyah* ("The Victorious [city] of [the Caliph] Mu'izz li-Dīn Allāh").

Although the Fāṭimids (*297-567*/909-1161) were the first rulers of Cairo, it is the Mamlūks (*648-1250*/922-1517) who left the most evident stamp upon the city's architecture. The great mosques are particularly celebrated: the Mosque of Ibn Ṭulūn, the Madrasah of Sultan Ḥasan, the Mausoleum of Qala'un, the Barqūqiyyah, the al-Azhar, the Ḥusayn Mosque, and many others. Notable too are the *Bāb an-Naṣr* ("The Gate of Victory"), the *Bāb al-Futūḥ* ("the Gate of the Conquests") and the Zuwaylah Gate, built by Armenians who emigrated to Egypt after the Byzantine defeat by the Saljuks at Manzikert in *463*/1071, and such picturesque and lively areas as the market of Khan al-Khalīlī.

However, it is particularly because of the prestige of the al-Azhar theological university, as well as in recognition of its leading role in Islamic history, that Cairo is recognized as one of the great cultural capitals of the Islamic world. *See* 'AMR IBN al-'ĀṢĪ; al-AZHAR; BAYBARS I; COPTS; EGYPT; FĀṬIMIDS; MAMLŪKS; MUḤAMMAD 'ALĪ.

Calendar. The Islamic calendar, called today *hijrī* or Hegirian – that is, dating from the Emigration (*Hijr*) of the Prophet to Medina – has in fact been used by the Arabs since ancient times. Like almost all Semitic calendars, it is based upon the cycles of the moon rather than upon those of the sun, on which are based the Julian and Gregorian calendars. The *actual* beginning of a month, such as the month of Ramaḍān, as opposed to its *predicted* beginning from astronomical calculations, depends upon the physical sighting of the moon. A physical sighting of the new moon, which can take place briefly only at sunset, is generally only possible one day after the astronomical new moon. (Actually, a crescent only forms when ten degrees of separation have elapsed between the conjunction positions of the sun and moon. It is therefore physically impossible to see a crescent moon less than twenty hours after astronomical conjunction.) The insistence upon the actual physical sighting reflects the sense in Islam that it is the immediate surrounding conditions, rather than theoretical ones, that reflect the Divine Will in its relation to men, and that it is these which should determine sacred acts. If the sky is overcast and the new moon is not visible within a territory, the previous month is allowed to run thirty days before the new month can begin. (Judaism had similar rules concerning the beginning of a new month.)

Although in principle a month runs from the sighting of one new moon until the next, in practice, sighting, or adjustments for sighting, are today no longer made, and calendar days run according to astronomical calculations of the moon's motion. Until recently, an exception was still made for the announcement of Ramaḍān and the month of pilgrimage, which, because of their ritual importance should, more than other days, conform to traditional principles. Now, however, with the almost universal abandonment of the traditional point of view, most countries have apparently opted to date Ramaḍān and the religious feasts simply according to astronomical calculation of the new moon without allowing for any corrections dependent upon actual sighting (*see* astronomical forming of the crescent, above). It is thus not unusual for countries to announce Ramaḍān when physical sighting of the moon would be possible in their territories only one day later, or even before a real sighting could have been made anywhere in the world. Immigrant Muslim communities often celebrate Ramaḍān not according to the country of residence, but their country of origin, which results in different ethnic groups in France or America often being out of step.

The practice of beginning the months on the basis of an astronomical calculation of the date of the new moon was in fact instituted under the Fāṭimids by the general Jawhar after the founding of Cairo in *359*/969, but was always condemned by the Sunnīs as *bid'ah*, or a false innovation. (Like modern calculations, those of the Fāṭimids were for the astronomical new moon but not for its sighting; the latter would would have been far more complex because it would have been necessary to calculate the position of the moon not only on the ecliptic, but also relative to the physical horizon.) The practice of the Ismā'īlis in using astronomical conjunction as the starting point for Ramaḍān was not, however, due to the complexity of calculating physical sighting, since that did not have to be calculated at all, it was enough to see it, but rather to their belief that their doctrines were scientific and above all to their theory that reality derived from physical existence rather than from a metaphysical Being.

The *hijrī* year consists of twelve lunar months of twenty-nine or thirty days; their lengths vary because of the need to round out a year otherwise only 354 days, 8 hours, and 48 minutes long. The annual holidays thus advance about ten days each year so that in thirty-six years, Ramaḍān, the month of fasting, moves around the entire solar year, sometimes taking place in winter, sometimes in summer. The Islamic day, like the Jewish day, runs from sunset to sunset; Thursday evening is therefore part of the Islamic sabbath Friday, which makes it a popular time for religious gatherings.

In pre-Islamic times it had become a custom to intercalate a month from time to time to align the lunar year with the solar. The Council of Mecca, the *Nidwah,* made the decision to intercalate in a given year, which was proclaimed at the fairs of 'Ukāẓ or Minā. This practice of intercalation was prohibited by the Koran in the year of the "farewell pilgrimage". The Koran legislated this change in 9:37: "The month postponed [i.e. a sacred month, *an-nasi'* – meaning here intercalation] is an increase of unbelief whereby the unbelievers go astray..." This was the only change Islam made to traditional Arab custom regarding the calendar. The intercalated days had been traditionally considered as unpropitious.

In the year 637, sixteen years after the Hijrah, or "emigration of the Prophet from Mecca to Medina", the Caliph 'Umar instituted the year of the Hijrah as the first year of the Islamic era, since it had already been the Sunnah of the Prophet to take that event as the reference point in time. Such reference points were commonly used in the past. A previous reference point for the Meccan Arabs had been the Year of the Elephant, 570 A.D., in which Dhū Nuwās attacked Mecca with an elephant, an event mentioned in the Koran, and also the traditional year for the birth of the Prophet. The cumulation of a number of events around a given year or date reflects a "rounding off" in an age when actual measure of times was of little importance. Modern scholars point out that the attack on Mecca, in fact, probably occurred earlier than 570.

The Hijrah took place in September of 622 (the exact date is not known with certainty); the first day, 1 Muḥarram, of the year in progress coincided with 16 July 622, which was thus the first day of the first year of the Hegirian calendar (since the Islamic day begins at sunset the evening of the day before was also 1 Muḥarram).

The names of the months, despite the Semitic preference for a lunar year, and thus for a lunar calendar, in fact reflect an ancient division according to the seasons of the solar year. They are as follows:

1. Muḥarram: "The sacred month"
2. Ṣafar: "The month which is void"
3. Rabīʿ al-Awwal: "The first spring"
4. Rabīʿ ath-Thāni: "The second spring"
5. Jumādā-l-Ūlā: "The first month of dryness"
6. Jumādā-th-Thāniyyah: "The second month of dryness"
7. Rajab: "The revered month"
8. Shaʿbān: "The month of division"
9. Ramaḍān: "The month of great heat"
10. Shawwal: "The month of hunting"
11. Dhū l-Qaʿdah: "The month of rest"
12. Dhū l-Ḥijjah: "The month of pilgrimage"

Five days of the week are named by the ordinal numbers beginning with the first day, *Yawm al-Aḥad*, which is Sunday. Thereafter, Friday is named "the Day of Congregation" and Saturday is "the Day of Rest", a reference to the Jewish Sabbath (of which reference most modern Muslims are unaware). They are as follows:-

Yawm al-Aḥad: Sunday
Yawm al-Ithnayn: Monday
Yawm ath-Thalāthā': Tuesday
Yawm al-Arbiʿa'or Arbaʿā': Wednesday
Yawm al-Khamīs: Thursday
Yawm al-Jumah: Friday
Yawm as-Sabt: Saturday

A solar calendar is in fact necessary for agricultural purposes, and there are several different calendars in use. Until recently, that most widely used was the Coptic calendar which is based upon the Julian calendar. This calendar is familiar in most Islamic countries but its practical use is now limited to Egypt and the Sudan, countries with Coptic populations. Another is the Turkish fiscal calendar, also a Julian calendar, adopted in the 18th century in the Ottoman empire. In the past, other solar calendars were also created by Muslim astronomers, to an admirable degree of accuracy. One such is the *Jalālī* calendar, made for the Saljuq Caliph Mālik Shāh, in the formulation of which ʿUmar Khayyam took part.

The use of a lunar calendar, and the practice of physical sighting for purposes of dating, has an interesting metaphysical moral. In classical Ptolemaic astronomy the celestial world is understood to be the way it appears to the observer on earth: the universe goes around the earth. This Ptolemaic universe corresponds to the classical theories of metaphysics and is a support for their symbolisms. The observed irregularities were mythologically explained by the perturbation caused by the fall of man. The existence of the seasons, and the variations between day and night, were explained as the result of the shifting of the cosmic axis because of man's expulsion from the garden of Eden or from a state of primordial perfection. In physical astronomy, the earth and the planets go around the sun. From the mythic point of view, it is as if the celestial consequences of the fall and the shifting of the cosmic axis have reached their utmost limit. In this system the ideal reference point, the path back to spiritual universe, seems to be completely lost; there is no metaphysics possible (except perhaps that of two opposing principles). From both points of view, Ptolemaic and modern, however, the moon goes around the earth; it remains a source of reflected light (preserving the relationship between Principle and manifestation), and whether it reflects the sun as a support of the Principle or as a source of thermonuclear power, it nevertheless reflects a psychological and metaphysical reality, in keeping with its classical alchemical symbolism as the mind or psyche of man. The moon now is what it was in the beginning, and the time it measures in the 20th century is the time it would have measured in the garden of Eden, before the fall.

In practice, the Western Gregorian calendar, usually referred to as the *Masīḥī* (the Messianic or Christian calendar), is used today as the working calendar everywhere for all purposes except for determining days of religious observance. However, Saudi Arabia, officially at least, uses the Hegirian calendar as the calendar of reference.

THE ISLAMIC HOLIDAYS:

Muḥarram
1st – *Ra's al-'Ām.* (New Year).
The first of Muḥarram, the Islamic New Year, and the first of Ramaḍān, and the first of the month of Ḥajj are calculated to fall upon the following dates in the Gregorian calendar:

Hijrī year	1st Muḥarram	1st Ramaḍān	1st Dhu-Ḥijjah
1419	iv 28,1998	xii 20,1998	iii 19,1998
1420	iv 17,1999	xii 9,1999	iii 7,2000
1421	iv 6,2000	xi 28,2000	ii 25,2000
1422	iii 26,2001	xi 17,2001	ii 14,2002
1423	iii 15,2002	xi 6,2002	ii 3,2003
1424	iii 5,2003	x 27,2003	i 24,2004
1425	ii 22,2004	x 15,2004	i 12,2005
1426	ii 10,2005	x 4,2005	i 1,2006
1427	i 31,2006	ix 24,2006	xii 22,2006
1428	i 20,2007	ix 13,2007	xii 11,2007
1429	i 20,200	ix 2,2008	xi 30,2008
1430	xii 29,2008	viii 22,2009	xi 19,2009
1431	xii 18,2009	viii 11,2010	xi 8,2010
1432	xii 8,2010	viii 1,2011	x 29,2011
1433	xi 27,2011	vii 20,2012	x 17,2012
1434	xi 15,2012	vii 9,2013	x 6,2013
1435	xi 5,2013	vi 29,2014	ix 26,2014
1436	x 25,2014	vi 18,2015	ix 15,2015
1437	x 15,2015	vi 7, 2016	ix 5,2016
1438	x 3,2016	v 27,2017	viii 24,2017
1439	ix 22,2017	v 16,201	viii 13,2018
1440	ix 12,2018	v 6,2019	viii 3,2019
1441	ix 1,2019	iv 24,2020	vii 22,2020
1442	viii 19,2020	iv 13,2021	vii 11,2021
1443	viii 10,2021	iv 3,2022	vii 1,2022
1444	vii 30,2022	iii 23,2023	vi 20,2023
1445	vii 18,2023	iii 11,2024	vi 8,2024
1446	vii 7,2024	iii 1,2025	v 29,2025
1447	vi 27,2025	ii 18,2026	v 18,2026

10th Muḥarram is *'Āshūrā',* for Sunnīs a beneficent holy day whose observance is based upon the Sunnah but which is derived almost certainly from the date of the Jewish Day of Atonement, (according to al-Bīrūnī). For the Shī'ites however, because it is coincidentally the anniversary of the slaying of Imām Ḥusayn, it is the culmination of a period of terrible mourning.

Rabī' al-Awwal
12th – *Mawlid* (or *Mīlād*) *an-Nabī* (Prophet's birthday). A festival marked by joyous celebrations, which vary according to local customs.
Rajab
27th – *Laylat al-Mi'rāj* ("The Night Journey"). Joyous celebrations according to local customs.

Sha'bān
15th – *Laylat al-Barā'ah.* This is a non-canonical holiday largely unknown in many parts of the Islamic world; it is observed in Iran and India and among those communities with cultural ties to this part of the world. The origin of this holiday, usually called by its Persian name *Shab-i Barat,* is perhaps the *Farvardin* of ancient Iran for it is connected with the memory of the dead whose souls visit their relatives this day, and with the fates of the living, a kind of All Souls Day. Hence, the Islamicised legend of the holiday says that the lote-tree of the ultimate limit (*as-sidratu al-muntaha*) is shaken that day and leaves fall with the names of those to die in the year to come.

Ramaḍān
Month of fasting. The last ten days are particularly holy; the 27th is most often presumed to be the *Laylat al-Qadr,* "the night of the descent of the Koran". A very solemn event. Secular festivities are prohibited in this month. (*See* RAMAḌĀN).

Shawwal
1st – *'Īd al-Fiṭr,* ("Feast of fast-breaking"). Three days of festivities marking the end of Ramaḍān.

Dhu l-Ḥijjah
10th – *'Īd al-Aḍḥā,* ("Feast of Sacrifice"). Commemorates the sacrifice of Abraham. It is celebrated throughout the Islamic world. (*See* 'ĪD al-AḌḤĀ). The 8th, 9th, and 10th of this month are the days of pilgrimage to Mecca. (*See* PILGRIMAGE).

18th – *'Īd al-Ghādir.* A Shī'ite festival instituted by the Buyid Muizz ad-Dawlah in *351*/962. It commemorates the event of Ghadīr Khumm, in which Shī'ites believe that the Prophet designated 'Alī as his successor. Not observed by Sunnīs.

In addition to the holidays above, Shī'ites observe many commemorations of events in the lives of the Imāms. In Iran, the celebration of the ancient Persian solar new year, the *Naw Roz*, on the spring equinox, 21st March, constitutes an important national holiday. Although secular holidays, usually of a political nature, exist in most Islamic countries, the *'ulamā'* cannot condone the addition of any holidays of a civil nature to those above.

A simple conversion formula to determine in which year New Year's day of a year of the other calendar took place, is the following:

G(regorian year) = H(egirian year) + 622 – H/33
H(egirian year) = G(regorian year) – 622 + (G-622)/32

Another method for determining the Gregorian year is to take the *hijrī* year and multiply it by 970,224. Place a decimal point counting six places from left to right (that is, divide by 1,000,000), and add 621.5774. The whole number will be the Gregorian year, and the decimal multiplied by 365 will be the day of the Gregorian year upon which the first of Muḥarram falls.

However, in order to ensure precision in determining dates, it is advisable to consult books containing tables, compiled to give the daily correspondences between the two calendars. Another calendar used in Classical Islam (in addition to Persian Calendars in Iran) was that of the Seleucid era: *Li'l-iskandar* ("The Alexandrian Calendar"). This was dated from 1 October 312 B.C.

In addition to the Islamic calendar, there is a system of Islamic time which consists in setting the watch to 12 (zero hours) at both sunset and sunrise each day. It is used, rarely, by pious people in addition to the usual time. *See* 'ĀSHŪRĀ'; BAYRAM; 'ĪD al-AḌḤĀ; 'ĪD al-FIṬR; LAYLAT al-BARĀ'AH; LAYLAT al-QADR; MAWLID an-NABĪ; MUḤARRAM; NIGHT JOURNEY; NAW ROZ; RAMAḌĀN. (*For prayer-times, see also* SALĀT).

Caliph (Ar. *khalīfah*, "successor", "substitute", "lieutenant", "viceroy"). The Koran (2:30) refers to Adam as the embodiment of the *fiṭrah*, or primordial norm, and as the Caliph, representative or vicegerent (*khalīfah*), of God on earth. Hence man, in his real nature, and not his fallen one, is cast in the role of viceroy to God. The Prophet, however, was the Caliph of God in the Adamic sense, although his successors could lay claim to the title only insofar as they were his representatives, and carried on his functions as spiritual head and temporal ruler of the Islamic state. The Prophet was at once patriarch, revealer, priest, and prince; and thus the Caliphate has been called his "shadow in history". The successors could not, of course, presume to continue the prophetic function. Nevertheless, the ultimate sense of "Caliph" always clung to the office. As the first four Caliphs, Abū Bakr, 'Umar, 'Uthmān, and 'Alī, had each a spiritual station commensurate with the function they performed, they are called *al-khulafā' ar-rāshidūn*, the "rightly guided" or the "patriarchal Caliphs". Some other Caliphs were also spiritual men, and so, perhaps, also worthy of the name in a true sense, but this term refers only to the first four. The idea of the Caliphate is, however, that of a sacred function and not merely a public office. (*See* PATRIARCHAL CALIPHS).

Originally, after the death of the Prophet the Caliph was elected, except that Abū Bakr himself appointed 'Umar. After the first four Caliphs, the office became hereditary *de facto*. Nevertheless, the procedure of legitimization was election by the recognized religious leaders or authorities, embodied after the early days of Islam in the corpus of religious scholars known as *'ulamā'*. As the supreme military leader, the Caliph, from the time of 'Umar onward, also bore the title of *amīr al-mu'minīn* – "Prince" or "Commander of the Faithful".

The first seat of the Caliphate was Medina, and then, already under 'Alī, the camp-city of Kufah. Under the Caliph Mu'āwiyah, the founder of the Umayyad dynasty, the capital moved to Damascus, and under the 'Abbāsids, to Baghdad. For some nine years 'Abd Allāh ibn az-Zubayr (d. *73*/692) claimed the Caliphate for himself in Mecca, which he held in defiance of the Umayyad Caliph 'Abd al-Malik in Damascus. The 'Abbāsid Caliphate came to an end in *656*/1258 when Hūlāgū Khān of the Mongol Horde sacked Baghdad and put the Caliph al-Mustaṣim to death. Thereafter, the title was held by the descendants of the 'Abbāsids in Mamlūk Cairo, but only with a symbolic function. The Ottomans claimed that the last 'Abbāsid ceded the title to Selim I when he conquered Cairo in *923*/1517.

It is possible that the Ottoman claim to the title of Caliph by cession from the last 'Abbāsid is a political fiction invented some time during the last three hundred years. (*See* OTTOMANS.) There are Ḥadīth which can be interpreted to mean that the *khalīfah*, or Caliph, is always to be found in the Arab tribe of the Quraysh; and the Ottomans were certainly not Qurayshīs. Nevertheless, the Ottomans in Istanbul played the role of Caliphs convincingly enough, defending orthodoxy and providing a political center for Islam. When the Ottoman Caliphate was brought to an end in 1924 through the creation of a secular Turkish state, it was Sharīf Ḥusayn of Mecca who claimed the title. Within the decade his son 'Abd Allāh, King of Transjordan, also claimed to be Caliph. They were, of course, Qurayshīs; but no-one outside their territories acknowledged their claims and no-one has claimed the title since.

Parallel to the 'Abbāsids of Baghdad, there existed rival empires which claimed the Caliphate. These were the Fāṭimid empire in Cairo from *296*/909 to *567*/1171; and the Umayyad Caliphate of Cordoba which presided over a resplendent epoch of Arabo-Islamic civilization in Spain from *159*/775 to *633*/1236. The Sultanate of Granada could lay claim to the Cordovan heritage until the fall of Granada itself in *897*/1492 to Ferdinand and Isabella, the "Catholic Kings" of Spain. *See* 'ABBĀSIDS; OTTOMANS; PATRIARCHAL CALIPHS; UMAYYADS.

Caliphs, Patriarchal, *see* PATRIARCHAL CALIPHS.

Caliphs, Rightly Guided, *see* PATRIARCHAL CALIPHS.

Call to Prayer, *see* ADHĀN.

Calligraphy. In Islam the art of calligraphy is esteemed as second only to architecture. Because figurative art is forbidden in Islam or, in practice at least, restrained, calligraphy became the foremost among the fine and decorative arts. Moreover, Islam is a civilization based upon a Book and the Word, both coming from God; thus the arts of writing assume a sacred character. Arabic calligraphy, principally of the Koran, exemplifies its hieratic nature by an extreme regularity or monotony, coupled with an extreme fluidity, or freedom; its ubiquity on architecture serves to render the Revealed Text everywhere visible and pervasive in the traditional ambience.

In the early centuries of Islamic expansion it was considered normal and obligatory that converted peoples should adopt the Arabic alphabet, the letters that give the Koran its physical substance, to write their own languages. Today, the graceful Arabic letters are used by many different languages and cultures. The present form of Arabic writing appeared quite late, shortly before the Koran itself was revealed (other styles of script had existed previously). One of the earliest Islamic styles is the Kufic which has both early and late forms, but which is inherently difficult to read at speed. Very soon, therefore, its use came to be reserved for highly decorative formal use and monumental applications, and the flowing *naskhī* was adopted for writing and communication.

The major styles in Arabic calligraphy are *naskh, talīq, thuluth, maghribī*, (which developed in the Arab West and of which an archaic form is preserved in *Timbuctu*), and the extremely fluid Turkish chancellery *diwānī* and Persian *shikaste*. The most common styles used in writing today are a modified *maghribi* used in the Arab West, and the *ruk'ah*, an Ottoman style devised originally for Turkish, which is now used as the customary written script practically everywhere in the Arab world, and which is not considered to have any hieratic character.

Hand-calligraphed Korans constitute one of the great art heritages of the Islamic world. Many rulers, ministers, and other persons of exalted station wrote out the Koran in their own hands, sometimes many times over. *See* ARABIC.

Caravanserai ("Merchants' Inn", from Persian *Kārwān*, "a company of travelers" and *sarāi* "a large inn"). Rulers often built and maintained inns on major communication routes in order to foster the cohesion of their kingdoms. Zubaydah, the wife of Hārūn ar-Rashīd, built inns, wells, and cisterns on the pilgrim route from Baghdad to Mecca, which became known after her as the *Darb Zubaydah* ("road of Zubaydah").

Privately owned inns were to be found in most towns to receive travelers and merchandise, and for this purpose they were also provided with space for storing goods. In the Middle East these inns are usually called *khāns* and, in the Arab West, *funduq* from the Greek *pandokeion* ("guest house"). They usually consisted of courtyards to stable animals, rooms for the travelers, and storage areas for their goods. Inns which have survived to the present day are often excellent historic examples of the civil architecture of their times and today evoke romantic images of a not too distant past. Some are still in use and one, in Isfahan, had been turned into a luxury hotel, the former "Shah Abbās".

"Carnevalesque Festivals", *see* BOUJLOUD.

Carmathians, *see* QARMATIANS.

Castes. In principle, Islam, more than most religions, produces a caste-less society. Yet, in Pakistan and India, there exists something like the castes of Hinduism amongst Muslims. There are the *zamindars* or land-owners, the *askeris*, or descendants of warriors, the *lohar-thrukkan* or blacksmith carpenter, the weaver, the cobbler, the entertainer-barber, and the low professions which are the equivalents of "untouchables"; some of whom use different utensils in cafeterias.

Casting of stones, *see* RAMY al-JIMĀR.

Cats. The attachment to cats of one of the Companions, Abū Ḥurayrah ("Father of the Kitten"), is proverbial. Cats, unlike dogs, are considered to be ritually clean animals and allowed to roam freely inside mosques, including the Grand Mosque in Mecca. Stories of cats that seek out persons who are praying, and of cats sensitive to the presence of grace, are common.

Chador. The black cloak worn by women covering the head and draping to the ground in various countries of the gulf and in Iran since the Islamic revolution.

Chanting of the Koran, *see* KORAN CHANTING.

Charity, *see* FIVE PILLARS; ṢADAQAH; WAQF; ZAKAH.

Children. There is a Ḥadīth which says that children are born into the world possessing the *fiṭrah*, or a primordial conformity with truth; then their parents turn them into Jews, Christians or Muslims; that is, they acquire a way of being. From this Ḥadīth one can conclude that children who die before the age of reason can be saved by virtue of their innate conformity (*fiṭrah*) with reality.

The Mu'tazilites, or "Rationalists" believed that children who died before the age of discretion went to a limbo; the theologian al-Ash'arī, in refuting the Mu'tazilite beliefs cites this Ḥadīth: "We have heard that the Prophet of God said: A fire will be kindled for all children on the Day that the Dead shall Rise; and they will be commanded: leap into that Fire! And every child who leaps into that Fire will I bring into Paradise. But every child who will not I shall cause to enter Hell."

In other words, according to this doctrine, children who die before they have had the opportunity to be responsible for their own salvation are saved if in their essential nature they are truly innocent. *See* ESCHATOLOGY.

China, *see* HUI HUI; "NEW SECT"; TĀ SHIH; T'IEN FANG; XINJIANG.

Chinguetti. A town of several thousand inhabitants in the Attar region of Mauritania. The whole country was once known by the town's Arab name *Shinqīt*; it lies on an ancient caravan route along which salt from the the Atlas mountains was transported south to be exchanged for African luxury goods, perfume, exotic wood, and gold.

The town has a small, simple, but lovely mosque that was built in the 13th century, with a sand floor, a roof of palm beams and a stone minaret. Chinguetti had a certain reputation throughout North West Africa as a holy city, not for the usual reason of its containing the tomb of a noted Saint but rather, one imagines, because of its importance as a stopping place for travelers in the ocean of the desert. Like many desert towns, Chinguetti has a private and ancestral library of ancient manuscripts and books which testifies to its past as a spiritual center.

Chishti, Muīn ad-Dīn Muḥammad (*537-633*/1142-1236). A famous Sufi of India, venerated as a great Saint and buried in Ajmir. An important *ṭarīqah* is named after him, the Chishtiyyah Order.

Chivalry, *see* FUTUWWAH.

Christianity. In theory, Islam accepts Christianity as a Divinely revealed religion. Christians in a state under Muslim rule cannot be compelled to become Muslims, their churches are not to be taken away from them, and they are entitled to civil protection. In former times non-Muslims were obliged to pay a special tax (*see* DHIMMĪ). It is legal for a Muslim man to marry a Christian woman (or a woman of any of the Divinely revealed religions).

The protection of adherents of other religions has been a legal principle in Islam from the beginning, and in most Muslim countries there have been large minorities of Christians and Jews, and lesser ones of other religions such as Hindus, Buddhists, animists, and others depending on the country.

In the Muslim view, the Christian doctrine of the Trinity and the Divine nature of Jesus, and other points of difference from Islam, are deviations from what they believe Jesus's true teachings to have been. Muslims assume that because the Koran says that Jesus was a Divine Messenger like the Prophet, his message could not have been different from the Prophet's; that is to say, that Jesus's message could not have been anything other than Islam as they know it. Despite this perspective, the historic attitude of Islam towards Christianity has been largely sympathetic. Under the Ottomans many churches received privileges which they later lost under secular Christian governments. The Koran says: "and thou wilt surely find the nearest of them in love to the believers are those who say 'We are Christians'; that, because some of them are priests and monks [those devoted entirely to God], and they wax not proud." (5:85) *See* BIBLE; JESUS; COPTS; MARONITES; NESTORIANS.

Circumcision (Ar. *khitān* or *khitānah).* Albeit strongly adhered to, this is a custom rather than a legal obligation. In South East Asia it is called simply *Sunnah,* i.e. "custom". In Muslim countries it may be performed on boys when the child is seven or older. Circumcisions are then occasions for the sacrifice of a sheep or another animal in Africa or the Middle East, and for other festivities elsewhere. However, because of the expense of such celebrations, circumcision is sometimes simply not performed among the poor. Because it is *Sunnah,* but not a requirement of the *sharī'ah,* circumcision is not obligatory upon adult converts.

"Female circumcision", even as a purely symbolic act, a light excision of skin (*khifāḍ*), is not a practice recommended by religion; but it has been apparently tolerated as custom. Such a practice, while serving no purpose except as an imitation of male circumcision, normally did not go so far as to be a mutilation; usually it was harmless. There also exist, however, practices such as clitoridectomy, and/or removal of the labia; these are a grave violence against the person and are strictly forbidden in Islam. Such practices are found in some backward milieus and are due to gross ignorance; they have absolutely no religious basis, and, like all mutilations, are not sanctioned by Islamic law and legally prohibited in the United States.

Clothing, *see* 'ABĀ'; IḤRĀM; TURBAN.

Coffin, Suspended, *see* FALLACIES and INACCURACIES about ISLAM.

Commander of the Faithful (Ar. *amīr al-mu'minīn*). A title of the Caliph (since 'Umar, the second Caliph) as military chief. It has also been used by some Kings. *See* CALIPH.

Commentaries on the Koran. Commentaries which are straightforward explanations by way of background information with some degree of interpretation are called *tafsīr;* allegorical and mystical exegesis is more strictly called *ta'wīl.* The latter as allegory (but not necessarily as mysticism) has often, rightly, been considered extremely suspect.

A standard commentary is that of 'Abd Allāh ibn Umar al-Bayḍāwī (d. *685*/1282), *Anwār at-Tanzīl wa Isrār at-Ta'wīl* ("The light of Revelation and the Secrets of Interpretation"). It was frequently used in traditional courses of study and includes some of the more dependable opinions taken from earlier commentaries. Another famous commentary, quoted by virtually all later commentators, is the *Tafsīr* of

Abū Jafar Muḥammad aṭ-Ṭabarī (d. *320*/923), entitled *Jāmi al-Bayān fī Tafsīr al-Qur'an* ("The Comprehensive Explanation of Koranic Exegesis"). This is a vast compendium of the first three centuries of Koranic exegesis. The Tafsīr al-Jalālayn, the commentaries of the "two Jalāls", Jalāl ad-Dīn as-Ṣūyūṭī, the historian (d. *299*/911) and his teacher Jalāl ad-Dīn al-Mahallī (d. *250*/864) is also highly regarded. Also important is the commentary of az-Zamakasharī (d. *538*/1144), *al-Kashshaf an Haqā'iq at-Tanzīl* ("The Unveiler of the Truths of Revelation"). This commentary is Mu'tazilite and regards the Koran as created.

All of these are based upon oral traditions of the Prophet and the Companions, and in particular upon the interpretations of the nephew of the Prophet, 'Abd Allāh ibn al-'Abbās, called the *Baḥr al-Ilm* ("Ocean of Knowledge"). Ibn al-'Abbās became somewhat of an 'oracle", and it was common to attribute mysterious, speculative, or extravagant interpretations to him as an authority of last resort.

The inimitable quality of the Koran has always been one of the arguments as proof that it is Divinely revealed. Al-Khattabi cites as one of the reasons for the inimitability, along with the internal evidence of *lafẓ* ("expression", "uttering", "vocables"), *mana* ("sense") *nuẓum* ("internal coherence"), the fact that the Koran launches a challenge to produce its like, which the Quraysh could have tried to answer in order to settle the dispute, but did not.

Many later Muslim scholars wrote commentaries on the Koran, most, if not all of them, incomplete. Some commentaries are specifically Shī'ite and others again, such as those of Ibn 'Arabī and al-Qashānī, are mystical. Fakhr ad-Dīn ar-Rāzī (d. *606*/1209) wrote a commentary called *at-Tafsīr al-Kabīr* ("The Great Commentary") which, on the one hand, is an Ash'arite answer to Mu'tazilite ideas, but which also introduced philosophical thinking into Koranic commentary. The science of Koranic study is part of the *'ilm al-uṣūl*, or "science of the 'roots', or principles, of law".

Much of Islamic Koranic commentary resembles the *midrash* of Judaism in two ways: in content because many commentaries to Biblical stories were supplied by converted Jews and are therefore called *isrā'īliyyāt*; but above all in form, because the method, which is common to all traditional civilizations, is similar. A parable or story is constructed to bring out one or another intention or possibility of the text. Such commentary by parable is usually not to be taken literally, but rather as the expression of an abstract idea. *See* KORAN; TA'WĪL.

Companions (Ar. *saḥīb*, pl. *aṣḥāb*, *sahābah*). Strictly speaking, those followers of the Prophet who were closest to him in his lifetime, kept frequent company with him, and strove to assimilate his teachings. They memorized and transmitted Ḥadīth and the Koran, before these were written down and compiled.

According to another view, anyone who had seen the Prophet during his life was a Companion, and by this definition the Companions would number tens of thousands. One middle figure which has been advanced is 12,314 of which 1,552 were women. According to this larger view there are categories or "classes" of Companions depending upon the time of their conversion and the key events in which they took part.

Concealment of Revelation (Ar. *akhfā al-waḥy*). By the device of alleging the existence of a secret teaching it is possible to introduce the exact opposite of an intended doctrine into a religion. Mahayana Buddhism, which contradicts much of Buddhism which came before it, claimed that there was a secret teaching for which the world was not ripe before Nagarjuna revealed it. It is also characteristic to sweeten the introduction of an antinomial idea by flattering the recipient as being worthy to receive a teaching which others were not capable of understanding. In the case of Buddhism, the school which does not accept the Boddhisatva idea is furthermore denigrated by being called "the little vehicle whose followers are concerned with their own salvation rather than all of humanity."

Thus in Islam, although the single most important idea is that there is no God but Allāh, very early on religious careers were made by claiming divinity for a particular person. This is still done today where one would be hard put to find a Sufi order which does not at least hint that such such and such a great teacher of its line was so united with God as to be identical with Him. It is easy to brush off objections of the orthodox by saying that the Prophet was always asking "is there a stranger among us?" meaning that certain things were reserved for the elect.

Thus in the *Ṣaḥīḥ* of Bukhāri we find 'Ā'ishah admonishing her pupil Masrūq (d. 62 or 63 A.H.) that the Prophet never kept any part of the revelation concealed: "Verily, he who tells you that the Prophet concealed a part of the divine revelation and that he has not delivered it to his people, lies." The Koran (5:70) also categorically says: "O Apostle! Deliver to the people what has been revealed to you from your Lord. If you do not do so, you will be failing in your duty to deliver His message, to those for whom they are meant."

Confederates, War of the, *see* BATTLE of the TRENCH.

"Constitution of Medina". A name sometimes given to the *Mīthaq Madina*, the agreement made between the Prophet and the Jews of Yathrib, the Arab tribes of Yathrib, and the emigrant Quraysh. Because it call these "one Ummah" and includes Muslims, Pagans, Jews, and probably Christians among the Arab tribes as well, this document been advanced as a model for Muslim in creating a multi-confessional state. It was concluded a few months after the Prophet's emigration to Medina and was concerned and prompted by questions of mutual defense.

Conversion. One enters Islam by surrendering to God. The person who thus actualizes his surrender to God first undergoes the purification of the greater ablution (*ghusl*), and then recites the two testimonies of faith in the presence of two witnesses. Following this recognition of God as the Absolute Reality, and of Muḥammad as the Messenger of God, the new Muslim is committed to keeping the Five Pillars of Islam. Converts from Judaism also bear witness that Jesus is a Messenger of God. *See* SHAHĀDAH; TAWBAH.

Copts. The most important branch of Christianity found mainly in Egypt and the Sudan. The Copts are monophysites who separated from the Christian mainstream after the Council of Chalcedon in 451. Monophysites believe that Jesus had one nature – a Divine nature only – in one person, in contrast to the dominant doctrine, enunciated at the Council of Chalcedon, that in Jesus there are two natures, human and Divine, in one person. The Copts are related to the other monophysite churches such as the Jacobites of Syria, the Ethiopian Church, and, by similarity of doctrine, to the Armenian Church. Their liturgical language is a direct descendant of the ancient tongue of the Egyptians, with the incorporation of an extensive Greek vocabulary of Christian terminology. *See also* CHRISTIANITY; JESUS; MARONITES; NESTORIANS.

Courtesy, *see* ADAB.

Creation, *see* KALĀM.

Creed (Ar. *'aqīdah*). Systematic statements of belief became necessary, from early Islam on, initally to refute heresies, and later to distinguish points of view and to present them, as the divergence of schools of theology or opinion increased. The "first" creed is the *Fiqh Akbar* which is ascribed to Abū Ḥanīfah. It is a short answer to the pressing heresies of the time. Later creeds were longer, more elaborate, and complete as being the catechisms of specific schools. Notable creeds are the *Fiqh Akbar II*, representative of al-Ash'arī, the *Fiqh Akbar III* of ash-Shāfi'ī, and the respective *'aqīdahs* of al-Ghazālī, an-Naṣafī, and al-Faḍālī.

The truly first and most fundamental creed, however, is enunciated in this Ḥadīth:

> A man dressed in white came and sat down so close to the Prophet while he was with his Companions that his knees touched the knees of the Prophet, and said: "O Messenger of God, what is Islam?" The Prophet answered, "To bear witness that there is no god but God and that I am the Messenger of God [*shahādah*]; that one should perform the prayers [*salāt*] and pay the legal alms [*zakāh*] and fast in the month of Ramaḍān [*ṣawm*] and make pilgrimage to the House [in Mecca, *ḥajj*] if that is possible for one."
>
> The visitor said "You have spoken truly. What is faith [*īmān*]?" The Prophet said "That one should believe in God and His angels, and His books, and His messengers, and in the Last Day, the resurrection from the tomb [*ba'ath man fī-l-qubūr*], and the decreeing [*qadar*] of good and evil" The visitor said "You have spoken truly. And what is virtue [*iḥsān*]?" The Prophet answered "That you should worship God as if you saw Him, for if you do not see Him, nevertheless He sees you." The

visitor said "You have spoken truly; when shall be the Last Day?" The Prophet answered "The questioned does not know more of that than the questioner." Then the visitor rose and left. The Prophet turned to his Companions and said "That was Gabriel who came to teach you your religion."

The Creed of al-Ash'arī is representative of the fully developed creeds of later Islam:

The substance of that on which the Followers of the True Way take their stand is the confession of God [Allāh], His Angels, His Script [the Revealed Books], His Apostles [the Messengers sent by God], the Revelation of God and the Tradition [Sunnah] of the trustworthy related on the authority of God's Apostle; not one of these do they reject.

God is One, Single, Eternal. There is no other god.

Muḥammad is His Servant and Apostle.

Paradise is Fact; and Hell is Fact. There is no doubt of the Coming Hour [the Day of Judgment]; and God will raise the Dead from their graves.

God's place is upon His Throne, as He has said. God has two Hands, as He has said – we do not question: in what sense? God has two Eyes, as He has said – we do not question: in what sense? God has a Face, as He has said.

It is not to be said that God's Names or Attributes are anything other than Himself. The Followers of the True Way confess that God has Knowledge as He has said. They assert the existence of His Hearing and His Sight.

They believe that there is no good and no evil on earth except by the Will of God, and that all things are by the Will of God. They confess that there is no creator save God, and that God creates the works of men, and that they are incapable of creating anything.

God gives True Believers Grace to be obedient to Him; He forsakes Unbelievers. He is well able to act for the salvation of Unbelievers; nevertheless He wills not so to act, nor so to grace them that they Believe. He rather wills them to be Unbelievers in accordance with His knowledge, forsaking and misguiding them and sealing up their hearts.

Good and evil depend on the general and particular Decrees of God. The Followers of the True Way believe in His Decrees both general and particular, in His good and His evil, His sweet and His bitter.

They believe that they are not their own masters for weal or for woe, save as God wills, for He has said so. Committing their affairs to God, they declare their dependence on Him in all circumstances, their need of Him at all times.

They believe that the Koran is God's Uncreated Eternal Word.

They believe that God will be seen with sight on the Day of the Raising of the Dead; as the moon is seen on the night of her full shall the Believers see Him; but Unbelievers shall not see Him because they will be veiled from God.

They do not brand any Muslim an Unbeliever for any grave sin he may commit, for fornication or theft or any such grave sin; but hold that such men are Believers inasmuch as they have Faith, grievous though their sins may be. Islam is the testifying that there is no god but God and that Muḥammad is God's Apostle, in accordance with Tradition; and Islam, they hold, is not the same thing as Faith [*īmān*].

They confess that God changes the hearts of men.

They confess the Intercession of God's Apostle, and believe that it is for the grave sinners of his people and against the Punishment of the Tomb. They confess that the Pool [where the Prophet will meet his Companions in the afterlife] of the Hereafter is fact, and the Bridge [over which the dead will cross] is Fact, that the Rising after death is Fact, that God's Reckoning with men is Fact, and that the Standing in the Presence of God is Fact.

They confess that Faith is both word and deed.

They discountenance argument and disputation concerning Islam. They do not inquire: in what sense? or: Why? because such inquiry is Innovation in Islam.

They believe that God does not command evil, but forbids it; that He commands good, and has no pleasure in evil, though He wills it.

They acknowledge the Elders elect of God to be
Companions of His Apostle as Fact; they cherish their virtues and eschew discrimination amongst them, giving priority to Abū Bakr, then 'Umar, then 'Uthman, then 'Alī, and believing that they are the rightly guided Caliphs, the best of all men after the Prophet.

They approve the Feast and the Friday Congregation and all gatherings for Prayer under the leadership of any Imām, be he pious or be he wicked. They believe in the precept of Holy War against polytheists. They approve Prayer for the welfare of all Imāms of the Muslims and agree that they ought not to rebel against them with the sword, nor fight in any civil commotion.

They believe in the Examining Angels Munkar and Nākir who shall visit the dead with the Punishment of the Tomb, and in the Ascension, and in visions of sleep; and they hold that Prayer for the departed Muslims, and alms in their behalf, after their departing this world, avail for them.

They believe that there is witchcraft in the world,
and that the wizard is an Unbeliever, as God says.

They approve Prayer for every Muslim departed,
be he pious or be he wicked. They confess that Paradise and Hell are created; and that he who dies, dies at his appointed term; that he who is slain is slain at his appointed term; and that Satan whispers to men and makes them doubt, then spurns them underfoot. They confess that God knows what every man will do, and has written that these things shall be. They approve patience under what God has ordained. For God's Servants they believe in serving Him, the giving of sincere counsel to brother Muslims, and the avoiding of all grave sins; of fornication, of perjury, of party spirit, of self-esteem, of condemning other men.

They approve the avoidance of every person who
calls to Innovation; they approve diligence in the Reading of the Koran and the writing of Traditions from the Companions; they approve study of the Law, pursued with humility, restraint, and good manners. They approve the abandonment of all mystification, all evil speaking, and all excessive care after food and drink. Of God alone is our grace, and He is our Sufficiency. How excellent is His Emissary! In God we seek help; in Him we trust. And to Him is our Returning.

See BILĀ KAYFA; FIQH AKBAR; ISTAWĀ'.

Crown (Ar. *tāj*). A non-Islamic concept; a Ḥadīth puts it thus: "There is no crown in Islam". However, there were, nevertheless, the equivalents of crowns in the turbans and headgears of great Muslim monarchs. The Ḥadīth cited sets itself against rulership for personal aggrandizement and hereditary Kingship which runs counter to the primordial viewpoint of Islam in which distinctions between persons spring first of all from their spiritual state. Also, the Ḥadīth sets itself against the tendency of the age which made monarchs into Divine beings.

Crusades. The expeditionary wars to conquer the Holy Land followed the call of Pope Urban II at the Council of Clermont in 1095. The Crusades were the result of a nascent expansionism in Europe as well as pressures by the Saljuks upon the Byzantine empire and the destruction of the Church of the Holy Sepulchre by the Fāṭimid Caliph al-Ḥākim in 1009. The enticements were booty, glory, territorial acquisition, and the promised remission of sins and service to God.

The Crusaders captured Jerusalem from the Fāṭimids in 1099 and created a Christian Kingdom with Godfrey of Boulogne as prince. His successor was crowned King Baldwin I. This Crusader Kingdom of Jerusalem (the Duchies of Edessa and Antioch and the others disappeared earlier) lasted until *690*/1291 when Acre fell and all of Palestine passed into the hands of the Mamlūks. Jerusalem had been captured by Saladin in *583*/1187; but from *626*/1229 to *641*/1244 it was restored to the Crusaders by a treaty made between the Muslims and Frederick II .

In Europe, the Crusades stimulated trade, increased the power of the Italian merchant city states, and finally led to the Age of Discoveries. The Knightly Orders of the Templars, the Hospitalers, and the others, which were born out of the Crusades, played a great role in European history.

Constantinople, whose protection was one of the original reasons for the Crusades, was sacked by the Christians themselves under the leadership of the Doge Dandolo of Venice during the Fourth Crusade (1204). That ancient Christian Kingdom never completely recovered its strength and could not resist the final Turkish onslaught when it came.

The effects of the Crusades upon the Islamic world, on the other hand, were negligible. In the course of the fighting Saladin consolidated his control and dethroned the Fāṭimids of Egypt, but the Crusades did not unite the Muslims against a common threat. Indeed, some Muslims allied themselves with the Franks. Although in Palestine and Syria the Crusader castles remain as traces of their passage, for Islam the Crusades were ultimately only a transient and localized episode.

Custom, *see* ADAT; 'URF.

D

Dahrī (from Ar. *ad-dahr*, "time"). A traditional term for an atheist or materialist. The term originates in the Koran (45:23-24): "Have you seen him who has taken his caprice to be his god?... They say: 'There is nothing but our present life; we die, and we live, and nothing but Time destroys us' [*ad-dahr*]". Hence also the term *ad-dahriyyah*, "atheism". *Ad-Dahr* translates the term *Aeon* (Greek: "the Age"), and *Zurvan* (or *Zervan*) meaning "time". *Zurvan* is the name of a divinity perhaps first found with the Magi of Media. *Aeon* is the Hellenist term for a related Gnostic divinity. Zurvanism was a doctrine which became dominant in Zoroastrianism under the Sassanids. In Zurvanism Ahura Mazda and Ahriman are made equal by being the twin sons of Zurvan. In orthodox Zoroastrianism Ahura Mazda is without an equal, and Ahriman appears from nowhere, as if he were the byproduct of creation.

Along with Zurvanism a female divinity became prominent, Anahita, who began to appear in Sassanid times on the rock carvings depicting the transmission of kingship to the ruler by Ahuramazda. In medieval Zoroastrianism, when Zurvanism had declined, a daily prayer remained condemning the *Dahrīs*, by the Arabic name, perhaps a legacy from a time when one could not attack the Zurvanites directly. The Arabic term *ad-dahr* is in the Koran and is a reflection of the religious forces that raged among Arabic speakers before the coming of Islam.

Dā'i (lit. a "caller", "summoner"). In the broadest sense a "missionary" or a "preacher", but specifically it means the propagandists who spread the Ismā'īlī sect. In Fāṭimid Egypt there was a hierarchy of propagandists which culminated in the *dā'i ad-du'āt* ("the missionary of missionaries"), or the *ad-dā'i 'l-muṭlaq*, meaning literally the "absolute missionary", a somewhat extreme term for the supreme propagandist. *See* ISMĀ'ĪLĪS.

ad-Dajjāl (lit. "the deceiver" or the "imposter"). A false Prophet; one who misleads people regarding religion. According to Ḥadīth there will be a number of *dajjāls* in history. The last and greatest will be *al-Masīḥ ad-Dajjāl*, the "false Messiah", or Antichrist, who will appear shortly before Jesus returns to earth at the end of time. This *dajjāl* will seek to lead people into disbelief, or to the practice of a false religion. The Ḥadīth states that many unfortunates will follow him with the excuse that they do so "only because he gives them food". In a world overtaken by chaos, the *al-Masīḥ ad-Dajjāl* will be widely believed because he will hold out the false hope of restoring equilibrium. Then Jesus will return, destroy the *Dajjāl* and his forces in a great struggle, and the Day of Judgement will follow.

In a play on words referring to the final *Dajjāl*, the word *masīh* ("Messiah"), has been changed by some traditional commentators to *masīkh*, which means "deformed", thus producing the term *ad-Dajjāl al-Masīkh*, "the deformed deceiver". This play on words is done by the addition of a single dot over the last Arabic letter, *ha'*, changing it to *kha'*, to symbolize how easy it is to deform truth into falsehood. The nature of the *dajjāl* is precisely the deformation of truth into its exact opposite, and a complete inversion, or parody, of spirituality. *See* ESCHATOLOGY.

Dalā'il al-Khayrāt (lit. "guides to good things"). The name of a book of piety which is very popular in the Maghreb, or Arab West. It is a collection of prayers and religious lore with particular emphasis upon the Ninety-Nine Names of God, compiled by Abū 'Abd Allāh Muḥammad al-Jazūlī of Marrakech (d. *870*/1465).

Dalīl (lit. a "guide"). Professional guides for pilgrims to Medina. The *dalīls* escort visitors on a circuit of mosques and tombs leading them in the pious recitations of prayers and invocations appropriate to each spot. As guides, the *dalīls* speak the principal languages of the Islamic nations and are familiar with the customs and practices of each of the *madhhabs*, or schools of law.

Their offices are to be found in the vicinity of the Prophet's mosque, and their services can be hired by the day or half-day. Use of a guide is not obligatory, but can be helpful to a visitor unfamiliar with Medina. Most *dalīls* can also provide transportation. Because the visit to Medina is called the *ziyārah*, the Medinan guides are also often called *muzawwirūn*.

Damascus (Ar. *Dimāshq*). The capital of Syria at the foot of Mount Qāsiun, Damascus ranks as one of the oldest continuously inhabited settlements in the world. It is mentioned in the cuneiform "Ebla Tablet" which dates from 3,000 B.C. Indeed, a legend recorded by 'Alī Ḥasan Ibn 'Asākir ("the historian of Damascus", d. *572*/1176) asserts that it was the first city after the Flood to erect a wall and that it was built by the Koranic Prophet Hud. Damascus owes its existence to the Barada river which flows down from mountains to the west of the city, for this river creates a vast oasis garden called al-Ghutah surrounding the city and covers 230 square miles (596 square kilometers), which produces a harvest of apples, pears and peaches and provides a green setting for a number of peaceful villages. In al-Ghutah, at Tell Aswad and Tell ar-Rimād, traces of habitation have been found dating from the Middle and New Stone Age. Although *dimashq* in Arabic means "swiftness", it is the presence of this life-giving water which probably gives the city its name, from the watered abode in an early Semitic dialect (in Arabic *ad-Dār al-Masqi*).

But other etymologies, mostly symbolic, also abound. One folk etymology takes the Arabic name and splits it into two words, *dim* and *ashq*, which it interprets to mean "blood flowed", referring to the struggle of Cain and Abel, because tradition places the tomb of Abel (in Arabic, Hābil) on a hill near the city. This spot is particularly favoured by Druzes who congregate there on Fridays to picnic and to dance. These legends emphasize that the history of Damascus is woven of the strands of religions ancient and modern. Indeed, one of its traditional gates is even called *Bāb Farādīs* ("the Gate of Paradise").

Within the precincts of today's great Umayyad Mosque, the Aramaean god Hadad was worshiped; under the Seleucids the shrine became the temple of Jupiter before giving way to the Christian Cathedral of St. John the Baptist (according to tradition his head is entombed there today) and in the reign of the Caliph al-Walīd (d. *96*/715, it became a Muslim mosque.

Paul was converted to Christianity in Damascus. Having been struck with blindness on the road to the city where he, a Pharisee Jew, was going in order to seize and persecute Christians, he regained his sight when a Jewish convert to Christianity named Ananias (whose house is today the church of St. Ananias), inspired by the Holy Spirit, put his hands upon him. The trace of the "streets called Straight" to which Ananias was guided to find Paul (Acts of the Apostles 9:11), exists today; it was one of the two cruciform avenues that were the mark of Roman cities. When Paul's former co-religionists were irate because of his conversion and preaching, he escaped out of the city by being let down the walls in a basket.

As one of the cradles of Christianity, Damascus is the home of ancient Christian communities of many filiations: Catholic, Eastern Orthodox, Uniate, Maronite and Armenian. The Christian center of the city is *Bāb Toma* (the "Gate of Thomas"). Also, a Jewish community still exists in Damascus which treasures, as part of its heritage, the 2,000 year old Jawbar Synagogue, although the one principally used today is the *al-Frange* (the "Synagogue of the Frank"), that is "of the European".

When, in *14*/635 Khālid ibn Walīd conquered Damascus from the Byzantines, the Caliph Uthmān divided Syrian territory (*ash-Shem*), into the districts of Damascus, Ḥoms (*al-Ḥims*), Jordan (*al-Urdūn*), and Palestine (*al-Filasṭīn*). Mu'āwiyah the Umayyad, the son of Abū Sufyān, on becoming governor of Damascus, was able to use it as a power-base in order to compel 'Alī, the fourth Caliph, to abandon Medina after the death of Uthmān and seek a counter-force of his own in the direction of Iraq. When the Umayyads came to power in *41*/661, Damascus became, for the next 89 years, the capital of the Islamic Empire, which now stretched from Spain to India. The Umayyads embellished the Grand Mosque in Damascus, and under the Caliph 'Abd al-Mālik (d. *86*/705) built the Dome of the Rock in Jerusalem. Although established in the midst of a sophisticated urban civilization, the nostalgia of their origins led the Umayyad rulers to build fortified pleasure palaces in the Syrian desert, such as the Qaṣr al-Khayr al-Gharbī, whose ruins remain today.

When the 'Abbāsids defeated the Umayyads at the Battle of the Zab river in *132*/750, the capital of the Empire shifted from Damascus to the newly founded city of Baghdad. From *369*/979 to *567*/1171 Damascus was ruled from Cairo by the Fāṭimids. Under later 'Abbāsid suzerainty, local dynasties ruled it. The Zengīd Atabeg Nūr ad-Dīn (d. *560*/1173) founded the Dar al-Ḥadīth in Damascus as a school for the study of Islamic sciences. Later and larger schools, which afforded a broader approach to the study of the liberal arts, are the *madrasahs* (colleges), called the Jaqmaqiyyah, 'Azīziyyah. 'Ādiliyyah and Zahīriyyah. Under the Ayyūbids (*564-658*/1169-1260), Damascus again became the capital of an Empire which now included Egypt, parts of Arabia, Palestine and northern Iraq. The tomb of the Kurdish founder of the Ayyūbids, the great Salāḥ ad-Dīn (*532-589*/1138-1193), better known in the West as Saladin, who successfully opposed the Christian Crusades, is situated by the wall of the Great Umayyad Mosque. When the Mamlūks succeeded the Ayyūbids, Syria was again ruled from Egypt.

In *658*/1260 and *700*/1300 Mongol invasions were repelled, but in *804*/1401 Damascus (and Aleppo) were plundered by Tamerlane. From *923*/1517 to the end of World War 1, Syria was under Ottoman rule from Istanbul, except for an interval from 1832-1840 when Ibrāhīm Pasha, in the name of Muḥammad 'Alī of Egypt, had conquered some parts. After World War 1, Syria was under French mandate until April 1946.

The chief of the city's monuments is, of course, the great Umayyad Mosque built under the Caliph Walīd, still magnificent although ravaged many times by invaders and by fire in 1893. But Damascus also boasts a mosque, the Sīnāniyyah, built by the great Turkish architect Sīnān (*895-996*/1488-1587), and other notable mosques; that of Dervish Pasha and the Tekiyye Sulaymāniyyah, a complex for dervishes built under Sulāyman the Magnificent. Damascus has several excellent examples of medieval caravanserais (*khāns* or *fanādiq*), notably that of Assad Pasha.

Buried in Damascus are a number of Companions of the Prophet, near one of the gates of the old city. On the outskirts is the tomb of "Sitt" (Seyyidah) Zaynab, the granddaughter of the Prophet and sister of Ḥasan and Ḥusayn, an important place of pilgrimage for Twelve-Imām Shī'ites. There is also the tomb of the mystic, Muḥyi-d-Dīn ibn 'Arabī (*560-638*/1165-1240), and that of the Mamlūk Sultan Baybars.

The National Syrian Museum houses a splendid collection of antiquities from Mari, Ugarit (Ras Shamra, where mankind's first alphabet was devised for the Canaanite language), Ebla, Doura Europos and other important archeological sites in Syria.

Dan Fodio, Usumanu, *see* SOKOTO CALIPHATE.

Dara Shikoh, *see* after DAR al-.

Dār al-Ḥadīth (lit. "house of Ḥadīth"). From the beginning of Islam until the present, religious teaching has been given in Mosques. Around the *4th*/10th century the tendency appeared for the creation of special institutions devoted to study. One of the most important of these schools, called the Dār al-Ḥadīth (also a generic name for this kind of institution) was founded in Damascus by the Atabeg Nūr ad-Dīn (d. *560*/1173). Other such schools existed in Jerusalem, Cairo, Mosul, Nayshabur, and elsewhere.

The further development of more amply endowed and broader based schools came with the Fāṭimids and Saljuqids. The Fāṭimids founded important schools for the preparation of religious propagandists. The Saljuqs countered by creating Sunnī *madrasahs. See* al-AZHAR; HOUSE of WISDOM; DĀR al-ḤIKMAH; MADRASAH.

Dār al-Ḥarb (lit. the "abode of war"). Territories where Islam does not prevail. During colonial rule in India, the *'ulamā'* decided that as long as the laws of Islam were not prohibited, or as long as the peculiar institutions of Islam existed, the country could be considered to lie within *dār al-islām* ("abode of Islam"). Symbolically, the *dār al-ḥarb* is the domain, even in an individual's life, where there is struggle against or opposition to, the Will of God.

Dār al-Ḥikmah (lit. the "abode of wisdom"). An academy founded at Cairo by the Fāṭimid Caliph al-Hakim (d. *411*/1021) in an extension of his palace. The *Dār al-Ḥikmah* was both a seat of learning and a center for the preparation of *dā'is* (propagandists) to spread the Ismā'īlī sect. An earlier academy called the *Bayt al-Ḥikmah* ("House of Wisdom") was founded near Baghdad by the 'Abbāsid Caliph al-Ma'mūn (d. *218*/833) for the translation of Greek books on sciences and philosophy and for research. Both academies included astronomical observatories. *See* HOUSE of WISDOM.

Dār al-Islām (lit. the "abode of peace"). Territories in which Islam and the Islamic religious Law (the *sharī'ah*) prevail.

Dār Nidwah. The assembly of chiefs of the various branches of the Quraysh Tribe of Mecca founded by their common ancestor Qusayy. Until the Muslim conquest, it was the ruling body of Mecca and had exercised a great influence over the Arabs of the surrounding desert. The site of the original *Dār an-Nidwah* was near the Ka'bah, within the present-day precincts of the Grand Mosque of Mecca, near the King 'Abd al-'Azīz gate. Mu'āwiyah bought the Dār an-Nidwah from the 'Abd ad-Dar for a million dirhams.

Dār as-Sulḥ (lit. the "abode of treaty"). Also called *Dār al-'Ahd*, a territory not subject to Islamic rule but having treaty relations with an Islamic state. This category is not admitted by all schools of law; the original precedent is the treaty of mutual recognition and protection entered into by the Prophet with the Christian city state of Najrān. *See* NAJRĀN.

Dara Shikoh (d.*1069*/1658). Eldest son of Shāh Jahān, the Moghul Emperor who built the Tāj Mahal. Dara Shikoh became involved in a dynastic struggle with his brothers. His brother Shujā' was a Shī'ite who seized Bengal; Mūrād, also a Shī'ite, took Gujarat.

Himself a Sufi adept, Dara Shikoh was familiar with Vedantic doctrine and Hindu paths of spiritual realization, but he aroused controversy over his universalist interpretation of the essential agreement between the various revealed religions, and by such statements as: "The science of Vedanta is the science of Sufism". He wrote a book called *Majma' al-Baḥrayn* ("The Meeting of the Two Seas" a term taken from the Koranic Surah of the Cave, 18:60, referring to the *barzakh* (the barrier) which the spritual aspirant must pass beyond to reach the end of the Path) in which he sought to reconcile two spiritual metaphysics.

Both Dara Shikoh and Mūrād were defeated and put to death by their brother Awrangzeb, a Sunnī who applied *sharī'ah* law strictly throughout his empire, and whose devoutness was such that he himself sometimes taught the *shahādah* to converts from Hinduism. He took the imperial name of 'Alamgīr ("Seizer of the World"). The brother Shujā' disappeared.

Darqāwī, Mulay-l-'Arabī (*1150-1239*/1737-1823). A Ḥadīth states that "Every hundred years God will send a restorer to the community". Mulay-l-'Arabī was the nineteenth century *mujaddid* ("renewer", or "restorer" of Islam) in the Maghreb, or Arab West. He brought about a renewal of fervor and a deepening of spiritual penetration whose effects lasted well into this century. He was considered to be the *quṭb*, the "spiritual axis", or "pole", of his age; his personal sanctity and the force of his teaching, stimulated a great outburst of vitality among the Sufi orders in Morocco.

Mulay-l-'Arabī was a Shaykh in a *ṭarīqah* (Sufi order) of the line of the Imām Shādhilī, and it is upon these orders that his influence was strongest. The *ṭuruq* which descend from him are called Darqāwī or Darqāwā after him.

He left only a few writings in the form of letters (*rasā'il*). In one of them he says:

> The soul is an immense thing; it is the whole cosmos, since it is the copy of it. Everything which is in the cosmos is to be found in the soul; equally everything in the soul is in the cosmos. Because of this fact, he who masters his soul most certainly masters the cosmos, just as he who is dominated by his soul is certainly dominated by the whole cosmos...The sickness afflicting your heart, *faqīr* [Sufi disciple], comes from the passions which pass through you; if you were to abandon them and concern yourself with what God ordains for you, your heart would not suffer as it suffers now. So listen to what I say to you and may God take you by the hand. Each time your soul attacks you, if you were to be quick to do what God orders and were to abandon your will entirely to Him, you would most certainly be saved from psychic and satanic suggestions and from all trials. But if you begin to reflect in these moments when your soul attacks you, to weigh the factors for and against, and sink into inner chatter, then psychic and satanic suggestions will flow back towards you in waves until you are overwhelmed and drowned...it is your business not to forget Him who "grasps you by the forelock." (Koran 11:56).

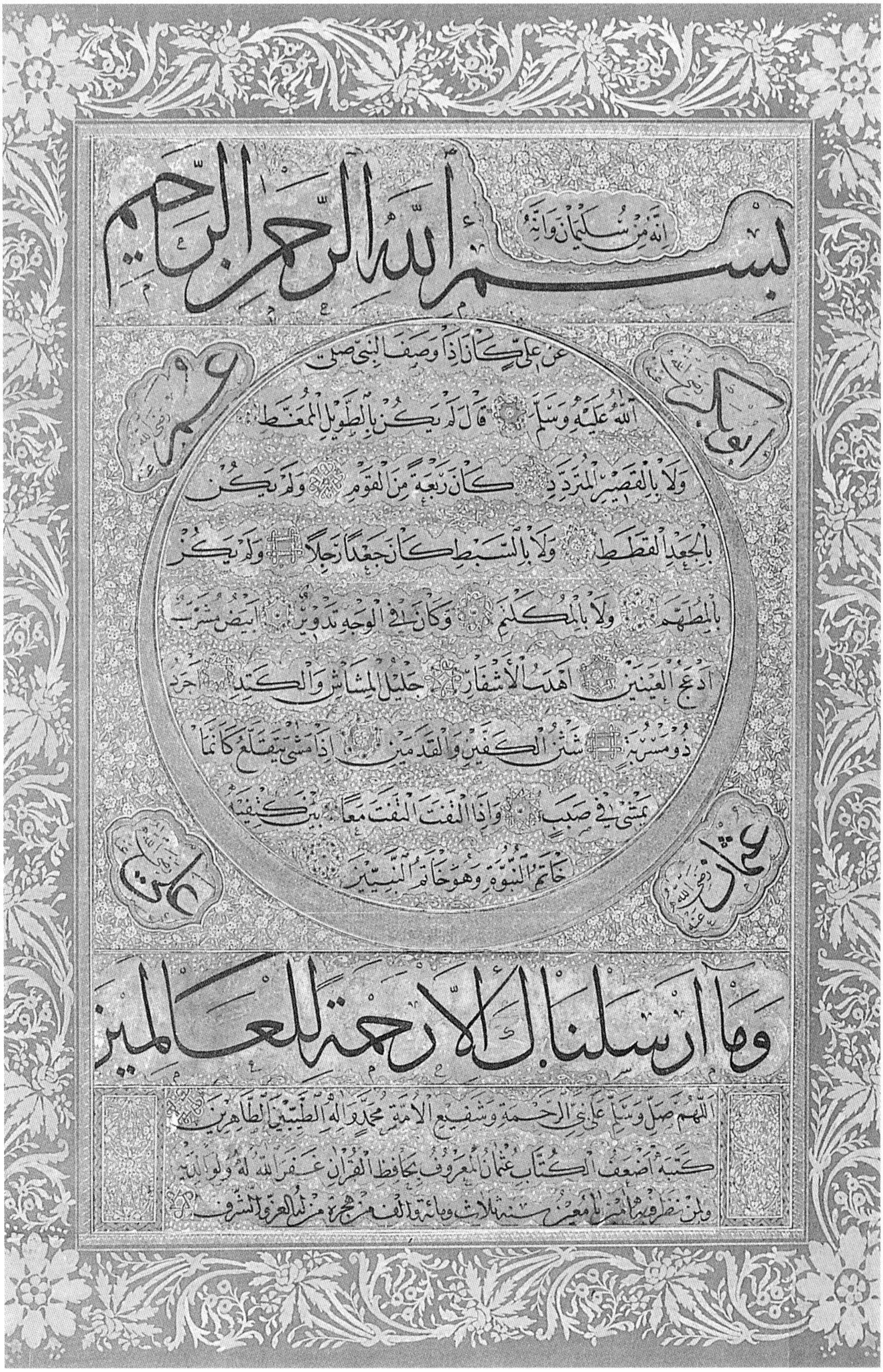

بسم الله الرحمن الرحيم
انه من سليمان وانه
عن علي كان اذا وصف النبي صلى
الله عليه وسلم قال لم يكن بالطويل الممغط
ولا بالقصير المتردد كان ربعة من القوم ولم يكن
بالجعد القطط ولا بالسبط كان جعدا رجلا ولم يكن
بالمطهم ولا بالمكلثم وكان في الوجه تدوير ابيض مشرب
ادعج العينين اهدب الاشفار جليل المشاش والكتد اجرد
ذو مسربة شثن الكفين والقدمين اذا مشى يتقلع كانما
يمشي في صبب واذا التفت التفت معا بين كتفيه
خاتم النبوة وهو خاتم النبيين
ابو بكر
عمر
عثمان
علي
وما ارسلناك الا رحمة للعالمين
اللهم صل وسلم على نبي الرحمة وشفيع الامة محمد وآله الطيبين الطاهرين
كتبه اضعف الكتاب عثمان المعروف بحافظ القرآن غفر الله له ولوالديه
ولمن نظر فيه بأمر المعز سنة ثلاث ومائة والف من هجرة من له العز والشرف

The *Hilye-i-Sharīf* ("Description of the Prophet") on the *opening page* is by the great 17th-century calligrapher Ḥāfiẓ 'Uthmān.

Opposite page: A set of calligrapher's implements included knives (*bottom right*) for cutting reed-pen nibs (*miqta'*), holders for the reed-pen while it was being cut (*bottom centre*), and burnishing tools (*bottom left*). The pen and ink holder (*beneath table*) and the low scribe's table (*centre*) inlaid with mother of pearl, ivory, ebony and tortoise-shell over goldleaf are of 17th-century Turkish origin. The panel of calligraphy (*top*) reads: "Muḥammad the Guide", and was written in the early 18th century by Sultan Aḥmad II, an accomplished calligrapher. *See* CALLIGRAPHY.

The art of calligraphy assumes a sacred character in Islam, as illustrated by the first line of the Koran to be recorded (*above*): "Read in the Name of Your Lord who Teaches with the Pen." *Bottom*: The *basmalah* ("In the Name of God, the Merciful, the Compassionate") comes from an early 15th-century Persian Koran, and is in *Muḥaqqaq* script. *See* BASMALAH.

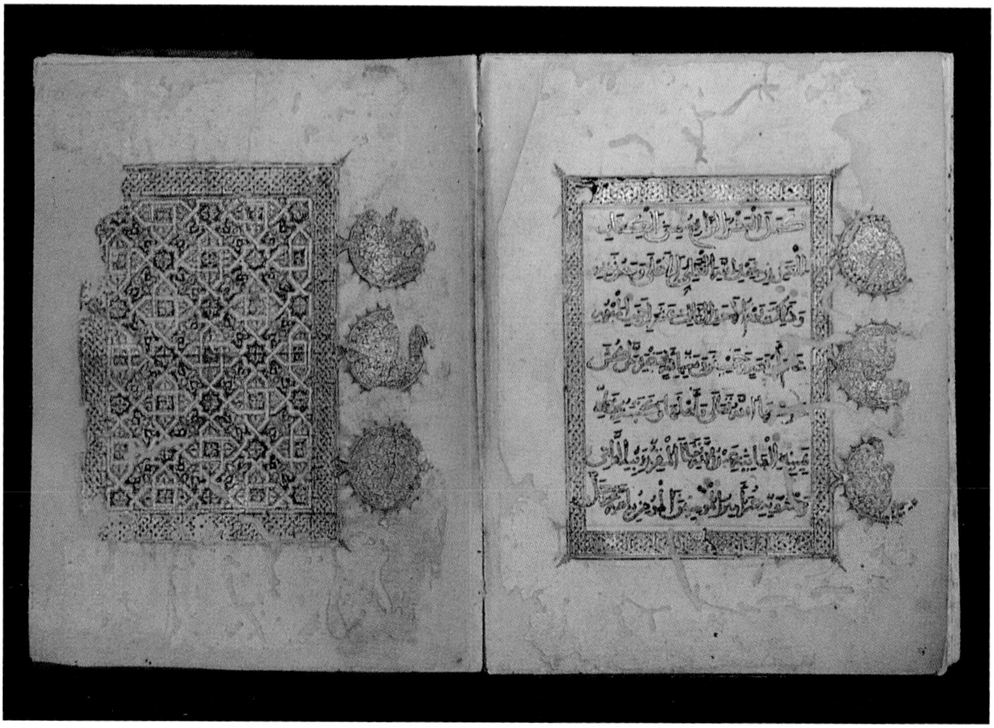

Hand-calligraphed Korans are one of the great art heritages of the Islamic world. That *above* dates from the 12th/13th century, and was executed in a typical North African calligraphy script by the Emir "el Mortada". It is now in the Musée des Oudaias in Morocco. *See* ARABIC; CALLIGRAPHY; KORAN.

Intricate calligraphic stucco decorations (*top left*) in a tiled niche off the Patio of the Myrtles (*top right*) in the Alhambra in Granada, Spain, the high point of Islamic architecture in the West. The extensive, patterned tile cladding of the mosque in Herat, Afghanistan (*left*) is characteristic of Persian mosque decoration. *See* ALHAMBRA; CALLIGRAPHY; KORAN.

Muslim astronomers built observatories, compiled tables of planetary motion and calendars, and provided much of the vocabulary of modern scientific astronomy. Such precise knowledge, together with highly skilled metalworking, lay behind astrolabes such as that (*above*) now in the Museum of the History of Science, Oxford. Used for measuring the altitude of stars, these precision instruments were a vital contribution to the voyages of the age of European exploration. *See* ASTROLOGY; ASTRONOMY; al-BĪRŪNĪ.

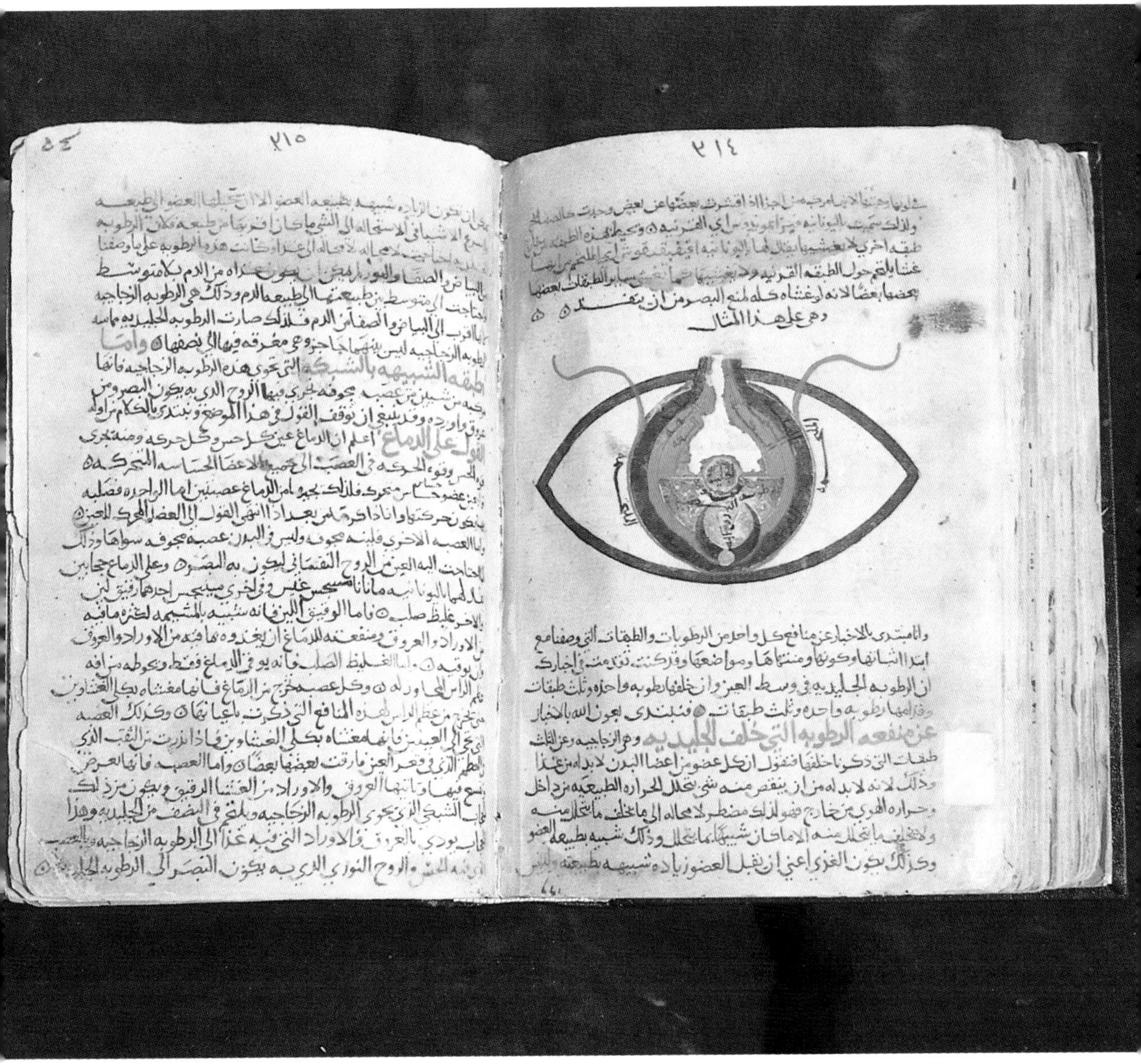

Islamic contributions to medical knowledge included a comprehensive *materia medica* and the establishment of hospitals, first in Baghdad (c. *287*/900) and then in Cairo. Considerable anatomical knowledge is implied by the 13th-century manuscript of the "Anatomy of the Eye", now in the Bibliotèque National, Paris. *See* MEDICINE.

"And thy Lord is Most Generous, who taught by the Pen, taught Man that he knew not" (Koran 96). Islam's sacred text is studied and memorized at Koran schools throughout the Muslim world, as shown here in Afghanistan (*above*), Khartoum (*below*), Mali (*right*) and China (*bottom right*). *See* KORAN; KORANIC SCHOOL.

His immediate spiritual master was the venerated 'Alī ibn 'Abd ar-Raḥmān called al-Jamal ("the Camel") whose tomb is in Fez. Mulay-l-'Arabī, a *sharīf* (descendent of the Prophet) through the Idrīssī dynasty of Morocco, is buried in Bū Berih near Fez, among a tribe called the Banū Zarwal.

Besides famous disciples such as the Shaykh Mulay Muḥammad al-Buzīdī, Shaykh Muḥammad Ḥasan Zāfir al-Madanī and Shaykh Muḥammad al-Fāsī, through whom the *barakah* ("grace", or spiritual influence) of Mulay-l-'Arabī was carried to Turkey and as far as Ceylon, several descendants of Mulay-l-'Arabī continued his work beyond his life. His son Mulay aṭ-Ṭayyib became a spiritual master as did his grandson, Mulay 'Alī ibn aṭ-Ṭayyib ad-Darqāwī, who was the Shaykh of the Darqāwī branch of the Moroccan Shādhilīs into the thirties in this century. Mulay 'Alī ibn aṭ-Ṭayyib taught theology at the Qarawiyyīn university of Fez. All over Morocco, his surviving disciples and novices taught by his *muqaddams* (representatives) celebrate his memory in the month of September. *See* QUṬB; SUFISM.

Dasong. Among Ismā'īlīs, a special tithe to the *Imām*. It is paid with extraordinary enthusiasm.

In some Ismā'īlī texts it is said that the *zakāt* is the "price for the law", which is "all that it is worth", but that the *dasong* is the price of the esoteric knowledge of the *Imām* and, by implication, that its payment brings with it a kind of absolution. The Aga Khan III was weighed against gold and diamonds at different anniversaries in his life and presented with the equivalent sums of money.

Ismā'īlī groups without Imāms, such as the Bohoras, do not indulge in such lavish occasions, but they too are punctilious about the many payments made in devotion to their leader, the Mulla-Ji.

David (Ar. *Dāwūd*). The Biblical King and Prophet who received the Divine revelation of the Psalms, called in Arabic *az-Zabūr*. In the Koran, David exemplifies the victory of God's cause against superior odds:

> ...they said, 'We have no
> power this day against Goliath and his hosts'.
> Said those who reckoned they should meet God
> 'How often a little company has overcome
> a numerous company, by God's leave! And God
> is with the patient.'
> So, when they went forth against Goliath
> and his hosts, they said, 'Our Lord, pour out
> upon us patience, and make firm our feet,
> and give us aid against the people of
> the unbelievers!'
> And they routed them, by the leave of God,
> and David slew Goliath; and God gave him
> the kingship, and Wisdom, and He taught him
> such as He willed. Had God not driven back
> the people, some by the means of others,
> the earth had surely corrupted; but God is
> bounteous
> unto all beings. (Koran 2:251-252)

In 4:163 the Koran refers to "Sabbath breakers", living by the sea. Commentaries explain that these were men who set traps to catch fish on the Sabbath and who, by this ruse, were guilty of breaking the law, albeit indirectly. David turned the Sabbath breakers into monkeys for their crime.

In Koran 38:18 two litigants break into David's palace while he is praying:

> Has the tiding of the dispute come to thee?
> When they scaled the Sanctuary,
> when they entered upon David, and he took
> fright at them; and they said, 'Fear not;
> two disputants we are - one of us has
> injured the other; so judge between us
> justly, and transgress not, and guide us
> to the right path.'
> 'Behold, this my brother has ninety-nine
> ewes, and I have one ewe. So he said,
> "Give her into my charge"; and he overcame
> me in the argument.'
> Said he, 'assuredly he has wronged thee
> in asking for thy ewe in addition to
> his sheep; and indeed many intermixers
> do injury one against the other,
> save those who believe, and do deeds of
> righteousness - and how few they are!'
> And David thought that We had only
> tried him; therefore he sought forgiveness
> of his Lord, and he fell down, bowing,
> and he repented.
> Accordingly We forgave him that,
> and he has a near place in our presence
> and a fair resort.
> 'David, behold, we have appointed thee
> a viceroy in the earth; therefore judge

between men justly, and follow not caprice,
lest it lead thee astray from the way of God.
Surely those who go stray from the way
of God - there awaits them a terrible
chastisement, for that they have forgotten
the Day of Reckoning.'(38:20-27)

Commentaries on this passage say that the litigants were two Angels who had come to reproach David for taking Bathsheba and imply, therefore, that his own conscience thus accused him; the story parallels that of Nathan's reproach to David in the Bible.

David is credited with discovering chain mail armor (21:78); the hills sing the praises of God with him:

... remember
our servant David, the man of might;
he was a penitent.
With him We subjected the mountains to give glory
at evening and sunrise,
and the birds, duly mustered, every one
to him reverting;
We strengthened his kingdom, and gave him
wisdom
and speech decisive. (38:15-19)

When the Caliph 'Umar visited Jerusalem, the Patriarch Sophronius accompanied him on the Temple Mount while he searched for the *miḥrāb Dawūd* (David's prayer-niche). Later commentaters identified this site with the "Citadel of David".

Dawah. (from Ar. *da'ā*, to "call", "invoke", "summon", to "invite".) Koranically, the word most commonly means to invoke the deity, and so to place one's faith in that deity. It also means to call to religion, and in this sense Muhammad is a *dā'ī* or caller. (Other words for caller are also used to designate a prophet.)

In the Middle Ages the term usually referred to the propaganda of such systems as the 'Abbāsid cause, or the Ismā'īlīs. Today it usually means missionary work to bring new believers to Islam, or to reinforce belief.

Dawsah. An annual ceremony performed in Cairo in which the Shaykh of the *Sadī ṭarīqah* rode a horse over his disciples who were stretched out on the ground. The disciples would be left unhurt. The ceremony took place on the *mawlid* (the Prophet's birthday). It was prohibited by the civil authorities as anti-modern in 1881.

Dawūd, *see* DAVID.

Day of Judgement, *see* YAWM AD-DĪN.

Death. "Die before ye die", the Prophet said, and: "The grave is the first stage of the journey to eternity. And the Koran states:

...Say: 'Even if
you had been in your houses, those for whom
slaying was appointed would have sallied forth
unto their last couches...' (3:148)

It is not given to any soul to die, save by the
leave of God, at an appointed time. Whoso desires
the reward of this world, We will give him of this;
and whoso desires the reward of the other world,
we will give him of that; and we will recompense
the thankful. (3:139)

Every soul shall taste of death; you shall surely
be paid in full your wages on the Day
of Resurrection. Whosoever is removed
from the Fire and admitted to Paradise, shall
win the triumph. The present life is but the
joy of delusion. (3:182).

"There are those", Ibn al-'Ārif said, "to whom death is as a draught of pure water to the thirsty. As a "last rite", the dying person recites the *shahādah*, just as, at birth, the *shahādah* is recited into the ear of the newborn. In the early days of Islam, when the opponents of the new faith were about to put a Muslim prisoner to death, the condemned man asked to be allowed to make a prayer; this was permitted him, and he prayed two *raka'at* (two bows), rather than the customary four, so it would not appear that he was trying to gain time. Thus, if one is about to be put to death, the tradition is to make a prayer of two prostrations.

Al-Ghazālī wrote:

When a man becomes familiar with *dhikr* [invocation of the Divine Name], he separates himself (inwardly) from all other things. Now, at death he is separated from all that is not God...What remains is the invocation alone. If this invocation is familiar to him, he finds his pleasure in it and rejoices that the obstacles which kept him from it have been removed, so that he finds himself alone with his Beloved.

'Alī said:

It is astonishing that anyone, seeing his familiar die, should forget death.

For the prayer for the dead, see FUNERALS.

Defterdar. Under the Ottomans, an imperial official, a treasurer in charge of accounts and disbursements. Defterdars accompanied the armies on campaigns as well as carrying on civil functions. *See* BEYLERBEY.

Delhi Sultanate (*602-962*/1206-1555). The principal Muslim kingdom in India before the Moghul conquest. Islam was first brought to India by conquering Arab armies during the early years of the Umayyad dynasty. These invaders eventually established the Multān and Manṣūrī kingdoms along the Indus, but the major Muslim incursions into India came later under Maḥmūd of Ghaznah (d. *422*/1030). A Turko-Afghan dynasty was established in Delhi by Qutb ad-Dīn Aybak in *602*/1206, a slave and general of Mu'izz ad-Dīn of the Ghurids, successors to the Ghaznavids. This displaced the previous rulers, the Hindu Rajputs.

Quṭb ad-Dīn's son Iltutmish extended the empire from Sind to Bengal. In *689*/1290 power passed into the hands of the Khaljis, and in *720*/1320 to the Tughluqids and thereafter to other short-lived dynasties until the Moghul victory by Bābūr and the definitive Muslim conquest by Humāyūn. *See* MOGHULS.

Deoband. Islamic university located some 150 kilometers north of Delhi in Uttar Pradesh, India. Popularly called the "Azhar of India," the school, *Dar al-Ulum Deoband*, was founded by Qasim Nanavtavi in *1283*/1866. Its teachers and students were prominent in the movements against British rule. The curriculum is built around traditional religious subjects. At present there are more than two thousand students, and as many as six thousand come to take entrance examinations, including a number of foreigners. The school recently added computers to its curriculum.

The faculty at Deoband takes an ambiguous stand towards mysticism; it accepts mysticism while rejecting some of the more questionable statements of the famous mystics. Thus Ibn 'Arabi is highly esteemed, while many of the things which he said are rejected as not being expressions of ideas which he professed. Indeed the school has created its own mysticism by maintaining that the exoteric teachings of Ḥadith and law which they pass on are animated by a chain of transmission from teacher to teacher not unlike that of the chain of initiation found in Sufi orders.

The *Dar al-Ulum Deoband* by producing religious school teachers throughout the subcontinent has had an increasingly strong effect on politics and some of the political parties are made up of its graduates, notably the *Jamā'at-i 'Ulamā'i Islam-i*.

Determinism, *see* KALĀM; MAKTŪB; QĀDARIYYAH.

Devil, *see* IBLĪS.

Devshirme. The conscription system used by the Ottomans. It consisted of taking male children from subject Christian populations, chiefly in the Balkans, forcibly converting them to Islam, and raising them to join the ranks of an elite military corps, the Janissaries, or to enter other branches of government service.

The boy-levy (*devshirme*) was carried out largely by force, but to be taken by it held out such promise for a brilliant future, that Ottomans sometimes tried to slip their own children into it. Many of the Viziers came from the higher levels of the pageboy training. At first every fifth boy was drafted in a levy carried out every four or five years, but later every able-bodied boy between the ages of ten and fifteen was liable to be taken in a draft carried out annually. The *devshirme* became obsolete in the seventeenth century. *See* JANISSARIES.

Dhanb, *see* SIN.

Dhāt ("Essence", "quiddity", "ipseity"). This technical term used in Taṣawwuf (Sufism) was devised from the Arabic particle *dhū*, of which it is the feminine form, to correspond to the Greek *ousia* much as the Latin *essentia* was devised for the same purpose. The particle *dhū*, meaning something like "possession of", is used to affix an attribute to a noun. The specialized use of the feminine form *dhāt* in the technical sense of "essence" etc, does not, of course, occur in the Koran. In Islamic philosophy *adh-Dhāt* refers to the nature of something in itself, as opposed to a quality (*ṣifah*) it possesses. The Divine Names are divided by the Sufis into those of the "Essence" and those of the "Qualities" (*ṣifāt*). The Sufic "Paradise of the Essence" (*jannat adh-dhāt*) refers to the Divine Reality itself.

'Al-Jīlī wrote:

> The Essence (*adh-dhāt*) denotes Absolute Being stripped of all modes, relations, and aspects. Not that they are outside of Absolute Being; on the contrary, they belong to it, but they are neither as themselves nor as aspects of it; no, they are identical with the being of the Absolute. The Absolute is the simple Essence in which no name or quality or relation is manifested...the Essence, by the law of its nature, comprehends universals, particulars, and relations, not as they are judged to exist, but as they are judged to be naughted under the might of the transcendental oneness of the Essence.

Adh-Dhāt is also called *al-māhiyyah*. See *FIVE DIVINE PRESENCES*.

Dhawq (lit. "taste"). Physical taste; but in mysticism the term means direct experience of truth. In this context, *dhawq* is similar to the word "sapience", or wisdom, derived from the Latin *sapere*, which means primarily to taste and by extension, to "discriminate", "to know". There is a famous Sufi saying: "From the first taste one knows them" [the spiritual nature of someone]. *See* SUFISM.

Dhikr (Ar. "remembrance" either silently or aloud, in which latter case "mention".) *Dhikr Allāh*, or "remembrance of God", making mention of God refers to invocation of the Divine Name, or to litanies; metaphysical "anamnesis". The Koran often speaks of *dhikr* as an act of worship: "Remember Me; I [God] will remember you" (*fa'dhkurūnī adhkurkum*) (2:152); "Invoke the Name of your Lord and devote yourself to Him with an utter devotion" (73:8); and: "Remembrance of God is greatest" (*wa ladhikru-Llāhi akbar*) (29:45).

For the Sufis, *dhikr* is a spiritual method of concentration, the invocation of a Divine Name or a sacred formula, under the direction of a spiritual master belonging to an authentic chain of transmission (*silsilah*). The spiritual master, or Shaykh, gives the practitioner the necessary "permission" (*idhn*), or mediates the pledge to God (*bayah*) that makes the method operative. It is not effectively possible, and can indeed be dangerous, to practice the *dhikr* without an assimilation of the doctrines surrounding the method and above all the revealed doctrine of discrimination between Reality and unreality, the doctrine of the nature of God Himself.

The *idhn* (or *bayah*, "pact") is an initiation in which there is a transmission of a blessing (*barakah*) whose origin goes back to the Prophet, and from him to the Angel Gabriel. The *dhikr*, or invocation, should, of course, be accompanied by the observance of all other fitting religious rituals and virtues. It cannot be practiced without adhering to the religion that vehicles and surrounds the method and the doctrine, failing which the method is as dangerous as it is ineffective.

Special forms of *dhikr* exist which include a form of dancing on a fixed spot, introduced by the chanting of religious poetry accompanied by drums, and sometimes by flutes, to create a state of devotional tension. In this dance known as the *dhikr aṣ-ṣadr*, the Divine Name Allāh is chanted; then the Name is reduced to its last syllable *Hu* (of the nominative form *Allāhu*) which corresponds to the shortened form of *Huwa*, "He", a Divine Name of the Essence. Finally, this Name and the act of invocation are reduced simply to breathing, which is, as actualized by the sacred context of the dance, both the Divine Name in its purest form, which is that of breath or of life itself, and, because of the nature of breath, also the cosmological process of creation and its opposite, the re-absorption of creation into God. (*see* ALLĀH).

This *dhikr aṣ-ṣadr*, or "invocation through the breast", symbolizes a return of essences escaping from the existential illusion of manifestation back to the Creator, a return of creatures out of the cosmos, even as the Divine Name loses its form and becomes pure breath. The *dhikr aṣ-ṣadr* is also called *'imārah*, and in the Maghreb, or Arab West, *haḍrah* ("presence").

The word *dhikr* is sometimes used loosely for all the ceremony which may surround a Sufi meeting (*majlis*) in which the *dhikr* proper is only one element, albeit the central one. Such ceremonies may include aspects which are extraneous, that is, outward elements and historical accretions peculiar to a particular tradition. Sometimes these ceremonies have been performed in public, particularly in Egypt in the last century, but their real nature is usually overlooked, obscured, and misunderstood, even in the Islamic world itself. This is all the more true in modern times, in accordance with the Ḥadīth: "Islam was born in exile, and will return to exile."

The power of *dhikr* arises from the identity of the Divine Name with Him who is invoked, the *madhkūr*, God Himself. The act of invocation, *dhikr*, is God's own Act; it is His own Self-knowledge and Self-consciousness. It is God Who invokes Himself through the invoker, the *dhākir*, as He also does through creation. If a man, while asleep and dreaming, calls out the Divine Name or the *shahādah*, he will wake without fail; the *dhikr*, by analogy, does the same for a man caught in the dream called life, for the Prophet said: "When we live, we sleep, and when we die, we wake."

"For everything", the Prophet also said, "there is a polish that takes away rust, and the polish of the heart is remembrance of God." When asked who would be highest in God's esteem on the Day of Resurrection he answered: "The men and women who invoke God much." When asked if they would rank even as those who fought in the way of God, the Prophet said: "Even though a man wielded his sword against unbelievers and idolaters until it was broken...yet would the rememberer of God have a more excellent degree..." *See* ALLĀH; FIVE DIVINE PRESENCES; SUFISM.

Dhimmī. A person belonging to the category of "protected people" (*ahl ad-dhimmah*) in the Islamic state. In classical times, these were the recognized monotheists: Jews, Christians, and "Sabians", who were granted autonomy of institutions and protection under Islam. In return they were required to pay a head tax (*jizyah*), and an exemption tax (*kharāj*).

This was usually accompanied by a number of social restrictions which could range from the remarkably oppressive to the remarkably liberal depending upon the place and the epoch. The practice no longer exists as traditional forms of government have been replaced by the modern forms of multi-confessional societies. *See* AHL al-KITĀB.

Dhirā. A unit of linear measure, the "ell" which is about one foot and a half.

Dhu-l-Ḥimār (lit. "the man on the donkey"). In the Near East, the image of "the man on a donkey", that is, someone coming from a far land and arriving in humble circumstances whose real nature is not evident from his appearance, is associated with the advent of an inspired leader. The image is mentioned in Zechariah 9:9:

> Rejoice greatly, O daughter of Zion; shout, O daughter of Jerusalem: behold, thy King cometh unto thee: he is just, and having salvation: lowly, and riding upon an ass, and upon a colt, the foal of an ass.

During the Riddah (the wars of apostasy following the death of the Prophet in 632), a short-lived messianic leader arose in the Yemen called Dhu-l-Ḥimār, who revolted against Islam and claimed revelations for himself. He was also known as al-Aswad ("the Black One") and Dhu-l-Khimār ("the man of the veil").

The "man on the donkey" attribute is also associated with the appearance of Qarmatian missionaries at the end of the *3rd*/9th century, a rebellion in Morocco which ended in 1909, and with other movements.

If it were not already a common emblem, similar to that of "the rider upon a white horse", ultimately associated with the apocalyptic appearance of the Angel Michael, the image of "the man on a donkey" became well known through the description of Jesus' entry into Jerusalem in the Gospels. Also, numerous Old Testament images, stories, and interpretations became established as a part of Islamic lore through learned Jews who were converted to Islam. Tales and parables which entered into the corpus of Koranic commentary from the Talmudic haggadah and Jewish legends are called *isrā'īliyyāt.*

It may well be the Old Testament idea of a future ruler who restores lost righteousness and glory, carried over by converted Jews, which provided the antecedents that led to the acceptance among Sunnis of the concept of the Mahdī. The Sunni idea of the Mahdī is radically different from that of the Shī'ites among whom it originated, beginning with the Kaysāniyyah movement. For the Shī'ites, the figure of the

Mahdī has an apocalyptic and Messianic significance; he is endowed with a demiurgic nature and with supernatural powers. The Sunnis later also accepted a certain notion of a kind of Mahdī, at least on a popular level, but in a more earthly sense, that of a just king. *See* al-ASWAD; BŪ ḤAMARAH; KAYSĀNIYYAH; MAHDĪ; MUSAYLAMAH; RIDDAH.

Dhu-l-Kifl. A Prophet mentioned in Koran 21:85 and 38:49. He is usually identified with Ezekiel. *See* PROPHETS.

Dhū-n-Nūn Miṣrī (*180-245*/796-859). An Egyptian Sufi who had a great knowledge of alchemy and arcane sciences. He is reputed to have been a link in the transmission of the spiritual sciences of ancient Egypt.

Among the stories the hagiographer Aṭṭār records of him there is the following:

> At nightfall he [Dhū-n-Nūn] entered a ruined building where he found a jar of gold and jewels covered by a board on which was inscribed the Name of God. His friends divided the gold and jewels, but Dhū-n-Nūn said, "Give me this board, my Beloved's Name is upon it": and he did not cease kissing it all day. Through the blessing thereof he attained to such a degree that one night he dreamed and heard a voice saying to him, "O Dhū-n-Nūn! the others were pleased with the gold and jewels, but thou wert pleased only with My Name: therefore have I opened unto thee the gate of knowledge and wisdom."

Al-Kalabādhī reported that Dhū-n-Nūn was asked: "'What is the end of the knowers?' He answered: 'When he is as he was where he was before he was.'"

Dhuwu-l-arḥam (lit. "those of the wombs"; an expression in the Koran). In Islamic law, blood relations through the mother. This relationship establishes claims of rights upon a person and, through inheritance, upon his or her estate.

Dihqān. A member of the rural, land owning gentry in Sassanid Persia, so called in Arabic, after the Muslim conquest, from the Persian for "head of the village". The Dihqans are credited with preserving orally the stories of ancient Persia which were collected by Firdawsi in the *Shah-Nameh* ("The Book of Kings").

Dikkah. A raised platform, found mainly in mosques of Turkish influence, from which the Imām can be seen by the congregation during prayers. It is also reserved for the use of the Sultan or dignitaries.

Dīn (possibly related to Ar. *dain*, lit. "debt" but more likely from Avestan *daena* (Pahl. *din*) meaning "vision", "inner consciousness", and especially "religion"). The word is employed to mean a religion together with its practices in general. Religion in the abstract is *diyānah* and a specific religion is more often called *millah* ("a way"). *Yawm ad-Dīn*, the "day of the *Dīn*" is universally taken to mean the Day of Judgement.

Divine Names. The Names by which God is known in Islam are divided first into two categories: the Names of the Essence (*adh-dhāt*), such as *Allāh* and *ar-Raḥmān*, and the Names of the Qualities (*aṣ-ṣifāt*), such as *ar-Raḥīm* and *al-Bāri'* (*'azza wa jall*). They can also be divided into the Names of Mercy, or Beauty (*jamāl*), and the Names of Rigor, or Majesty (*jalāl*). The Names altogether are called the Most Beautiful Names (*al-asmā' al-ḥusnā*): "To Him belong the most beautiful Names" (7:179).

The Names consist of those directly revealed in the Koran; others are derived indirectly from certain passages in the Koran, and others are traditional but not derived from the Koran. Not widely accepted are certain Names which are distant grammatical derivations from revealed Names.

The Name Allāh, called the Supreme Name (*al-ism al-a'zam*), stands alone. There is a Ḥadīth which says "To God belong ninety-nine Names..." Therefore, although because of variants the total of any two lists may add up to more than ninety-nine, any one list is limited to this number. The following Names are representative.

1. *al-Awwal*	The First (57:3)
2. *al-Ākhir*	The Last (57:3)
3. *al-Aḥad*	The One (112:1)
4. *al-Badī'*	The Originator (2:117)
5. *al-Bari'*	The Producer (59:24)
6. *al-Barr*	The Beneficent (52:28)
7. *al-Baṣīr*	The Seeing (57:3)
8. *al-Bāṣi*	The Expander (13:26) (a derived Name)
9. *al-Batin*	The Inner (57:3)

10. *al-Ba'ith* The Raiser (16:89)
11. *al-Bāqī* The Enduring (20:73)
12. *at-Tawwāb* The Relenting (2:37)
13. *al-Jabbār* The Irresistible (59:23)
14. *al-Jalīl* The Majestic (a derived Name)
15. *al-Jāmi'* The Gatherer (3:9)
16. *al-Ḥasīb* The Accounter (4:6)
17. *al-Ḥāfiẓ* The Guardian (11:57)
18. *al-Ḥaqq* The Truth (20:114)
19. *al-Ḥakīm* The Wise (6:18)
20. *al-Ḥakam* The Judge (40:48)
21. *al-Ḥalīm* The Kindly (2:235)
22. *al-Ḥamīd* The Praiseworthy (2:269)
23. *al-Ḥayy* The Living (20:111)
24. *al-Khabīr* The Well-Informed (6:18)
25. *al-Khāfiḍ* The Abaser (a derived Name)
26. *al-Khāli* The Creator (13:16)
27. *Dhu-l-Jalāl wa-l-Ikrām* Full of Majesty and Generosity (55:27)
28. *ar-Ra'uf* The Gentle (2:143)
29. *ar-Raḥmān* The Merciful (55:1)
30. *ar-Raḥīm* The Compassionate (2:143)
31. *ar-Razzāq* The Provider (51:57)
32. *ar-Rashīd* The Guide (a traditional Name)
33. *ar-Rāfi'* The Exalter (6:83) (a derived Name)
34. *ar-Raqīb* The Vigilant (5:117)
35. *as-Salām* The Peace (59:23)
36. *as-Samī'* The Hearer (17:1)
37. *ash-Shakūr* The Grateful (64:17)
38. *ash-Shahīd* The Witness (5:117)
39. *as-Ṣabūr* The Forbearing (a traditional Name)
40. *as-Ṣamad* The Eternal (112:2)
41. *aḍ-Ḍarr* The Afflicter (48:11) (a derived Name)
42. *aẓ-Ẓāhir* The Outer (57:3)
43. *al-'Adl* The Just (6:115)
44. *al-Azīz* The Powerful, and also the Precious (59:23)
45. *al-'Aẓīm* The Great (2:255)
46. *al-'Afuw* The Pardoner (4:99)
47. *al-'Alīm* The Knowing (2:29)
48. *al-'Alī* The High One (2:255)
49. *al-Ghafūr* The Forgiver (2:235)
50. *al-Ghaffār* The Forgiving (2:235)
51. *al-Ghānī* The Rich (2:267)
52. *al-Fattāḥ* The Opener (34:26)
53. *al-Qabiḍ* The Seizer (2:245) (a derived Name)
54. *al-Qadīr* The Capable (17:99)
55. *al-Quddūs* The Holy (62:1)
56. *al-Qahhār* The Victorious (13:16)
57. *al-Qawī* The Strong (22:40)
58. *al-Qayyūm* The Self-Subsistent (3:2)
59. *al-Kabīr* The Great (22:62)
60. *al-Karīm* The Magnanimous, the Generous, the Noble (27:40)
61. *al-Laṭīf* The Gracious (42:19)
62. *al-Muta'akhkhir* The Deferrer (14:42)
63. *al-Mu'min* The Believer (59:23)
64. *al-Mu'ta'alī* The Self Exalted (13:9)
65. *al-Mutakkabir* The Superb (59:23)
66. *al-Matīn* The Firm (51:58)
67. *al-Mubdī'* The Founder (85:13)
68. *al-Mujīb* The Responsive (11:61)
69. *al-Majīd* The Glorious (11:73)
70. *al-Muhṣi* The Counter (19:94)
71. *al-Muḥyī* The Giver of Life (30:50)
72. *al-Mudhill* The Abaser (3:26) (a derived Name)
73. *al-Muzīl* The Separator (10:28)
74 *al-Muṣawwir* The Fashioner (59:24)
75. *al-Mu'īd* The Restorer (85:13)
76. *al-Mu'izz* The Honorer (3:26) (a derived Name)
77. *al-Mu'tī* The Giver (20:50)
78. *al-Mughnī* The Enricher (9:74)
79. *al-Muqīt* The Maintainer, the Determiner, He Who brings to pass (4:85)
80. *al-Muqtadir* The Prevailer (54:42)
81. *al-Muqaddim* The Bringer Forward (50:28)
82. *al-Muqsiṭ* The Equitable (21:47)
83. *al-Malik* The King (59:23)
84. *Malik al-Mulk* Possessor of the Kingdom (3:26)
85. *al-Mumīt* The Slayer (15:23)
86. *al-Muntaqim* The Avenger (30:47)
87. *al-Muhaimin* The Vigilant, the Guardian (59:23)
88. *an-Nāfi'* The Propitious (48:11) (a derived Name)
89. *an-Nāṣir* The Helper (4:45)
90. *an-Nūr* The Light (24:35)
91. *al-Hādi* The Guide (22:54)
92. *al-Wāḥid* The Unique (74:11))
93. *al-Wadūd* The Loving (11:90)
94. *al-Wārith* The Inheritor (19:40)
95. *al-Wāsi'* The Vast (2:268)
96. *al-Wakīl* The Steward (6:102)
97. *al-Walīy* The Patron (4:45)
98. *al-Wāli* The Protector (13:11)
99. *al-Wahhāb* The Bestower (3:8).

See ALLĀH; ĀMĪN.

Divorce (Ar. *ṭalāq*). The Prophet said: "Of all things licit, the most hateful to God is divorce." Marriage in Islam is terminated a) by repudiation by the husband; b) by mutual consent; c) by judicial dissolution by a court upon the request of the wife.

In repudiation, a single statement to this effect, delivered to the wife is sufficient. It must be delivered while the wife is in a state of purity, (*ṭuhr)*, that is, not menstruating, and the husband must not have had sexual relations with her during this period of purity; furthermore, the wife must not be pregnant. The repudiation must be followed by a period of waiting for the duration of three menstrual periods, (*'iddah)*, to determine if there is a pregnancy (and implicitly to facilitate reconciliation). If the wife is pregnant, the divorce cannot take place until an allotted time after the birth of the child. During the *'iddah,* the husband must supply upkeep, lodging and food. An allowance, *muṭāh,* beyond these necessities is morally enjoined, but is not a legal requirement.

The divorce is immediately revocable by the husband at any time during the *'iddah.* Afterwards, remarriage is necessary to restore the marital state. If repudiation, or a statement of divorce, is repeated in each ensuing month or period of purity, *ṭuhr,* for a total of three repudiations (*aṭ-ṭalāq bi-th-thalāthah*), reconciliation is not possible until, and unless, the wife is married with another person and subsequently divorced. It is legally possible to pronounce three repudiations at one time but it is morally reprehensible to do so. *'Iddah* must still be observed and if pregnancy is determined, the force of the triple divorce is reduced to the conditions of a single divorce. Such triple divorce at one time is called *ṭalāq badī',* "innovative divorce". As such, it is a discouraged form of divorce, reconciliation being the desirable and sought after solution in the view of the law. In Shī'ite law, divorce is seen from a more judicial point of view, and the repudiation must be witnessed.

Divorce by mutual consent has only to be agreed upon by both parties to become effective. Divorce by judicial proceeding upon the request of the wife is obtained on varying grounds in the different schools, but these include the husband's impotence, apostasy, madness, dangerous illness, or some other defect in the marriage.

National laws in recent times have sought, within the framework of *sharī'ah* law, to give more protection to the woman against the husband's easy access to divorce. The *mahr,* or husband's wedding gift to the wife, is normally, and depending upon social status, an endowment of considerable expense; it remains with the wife after any divorce, both as a measure of compensation and also to discourage divorce in the first place. The Syrian Law of Personal Status (1953) makes the payment of maintenance to the wife obligatory for one year, which is thus a legal recourse of the wife against the husband.

The Tunisian Law of Personal Status (1957) makes repudiation by the husband invalid until it has been ratified by a court and provides for further compensation to the wife. Similar laws have been enacted elsewhere, both within an interpretive framework of traditional *sharī'ah* law, and through the operation of civil codes not based upon the *sharī'ah.* Such laws have in some cases made polygamy virtually impossible, or extremely difficult, by reason of a strict interpretation of the *sharī'ah* law which states that all wives must receive equal treatment. *See also* KHUL'; LIĀN.

Diwān (Originally a Persian word meaning a "many leaved book", and hence an account-book, record, collection of poems and, by extension, a government department containing such records. The Italian *dogana* and French *douane* are distant derivations of it. The term was taken into Arabic when Persia first became Muslim, and has since been used to describe a register of financial statistics, a cabinet or almost any kind of government office; it also means, in Arabic as well as Persian, a collection of poetry.

The first Arab *diwān* was copied from the institutions of the Persians, when the Caliph 'Umar established a registry of all members of the Islamic state in order to allot the stipends to which they were entitled from the booty of the conquests. Men, women and children were all graded according to their seniority as converts, and depending upon their being *muhājirūn* (emigrants from Mecca) or *anṣār* (native Medinan converts), their participation in the battles according to merit (Badr was in the first rank), and their family relatedness to those with such merit. According to their standing they received a share in the booty of the conquering Muslim armies.

From this booty and revenue the Caliph 'Umar also set aside a reserve for emergencies. ('Alī disagreed with the principle of such a reserve contending that it should all be distributed, doubtless upon the grounds that reliance should be placed not upon the human resource of a reserve of food, but on God alone.) The *diwān* and with it, the institution, was destroyed in civil unrest during the first century of Islam.

Diyah. The payment of compensation for inflicted injury or death; blood money. This had been part of the customary *lex talionis* of the Arabs before Islam, and came to be covered by the principle in Islamic law of *qiṣaṣ*, or retaliation. The basis of this law is Koran 5:49. The *diyah* which is best known is the compensation for the taking of a life: one hundred female camels.

This was the ransom for the life of 'Abd Allāh, the father of the Prophet. 'Abd al-Muṭṭalib, who had no sons, had prayed for children. When his prayers were answered, he promised God that in return for sons, he would sacrifice the tenth. However, when the time came for the sacrifice of 'Abd Allāh, the tenth and youngest son, 'Abd al-Muṭṭalib was grief-stricken, and consulted with a soothsayer whose oracle, after a series of unaccepted offers, confirmed that heaven would accept one hundred camels in expiation of the promise.

In countries where this provision of Islamic law is applied, the traditionally defined *diyah* is today replaced by a sum of money determined by a court of law. In recent years in Saudi Arabia the sums paid in settlement for accidental killings have been as much as sixty thousand dollars. There is a scale of damages for the various grades of bodily injury.

Dogs. These animals are considered to be ritually "unclean", and touching a dog entails a *ḥadath*, or impurity which, in the Mālikī school of law (*madhhab*), is removed by the lesser ablution (*wuḍū'*).

Hunting dogs, however, are not looked upon as unclean, and the Saluki, a kind of Arabian greyhound, is prized by the desert Arabs. It is lawful to eat game caught by a trained hunting dog if the dog is released with the pronunciation of the *basmalah*. For hunting, as for ritual slaughter, the Names of mercy are omitted from the *basmalah*, which becomes *Bismi-Llāh; Allahu akbar*, "In the name of God; God is greater".

The schools of law look upon the ordinary dog as unclean in itself; the Mālikī school, in a interesting example of legal reasoning, looks upon all living things as clean in themselves; it reconciles this with the tradition of dogs as unclean by declaring the saliva of dogs to be the polluting agent. The Islamic outlook on dogs clashed harshly with the Iranian: in ancient Iran dogs were highly esteemed and blessed animals. The Zoroastrians had a class of creatures which were considered *khafstra*, or corrupt, but these were snakes, frogs, scorpions and the like.

Dome of the Rock (Ar. *Qubbat aṣ-Ṣakhrah*). A shrine in Jerusalem often (incorrectly) called the "Mosque of 'Umar." It is more a sanctuary than a mosque and it was not built by the Caliph 'Umar but in a much later period, around *72*/691. The Dome stands over the rock on the Temple Mount from which the Prophet ascended to heaven in the Night Journey (*mi'rāj*). The place is revered by the three Semitic religions and may have been the site of the Holy of Holies in the temple of Solomon. (Both Solomon and Jesus are Prophets in Islam). Many stories extol the spiritual eminence of the Temple Mount which was, in fact, the original prayer direction (*qiblah*) of the early Muslims before the direction of Mecca placed it in the second year of the Hijrah. The Temple Mount is often referred to as the third holy place in Islam (*ḥaram*), after Mecca and Medina.

The rock itself is oblong and measures 56 feet by 42 feet (18 by 14 meters). Below it is a chamber accessible by a stairway where one can pray in a small area set aside for the purpose (this is a special oratory in addition to the large prayer area on the ground level above). A crack in the rock visible from this grotto is piously explained as having split when the Prophet ascended to heaven; the rock wished to follow. The cave is called the *Bi'r al-arwāḥ*, "the Well of Spirits".

When the Arabs conquered Jerusalem they found the Temple Mount abandoned and filled with refuse. The abandonment of the Temple site was in accordance with Jesus's prophecy that not a stone would be left standing on another. 'Umar ordered it cleaned and performed a prayer there. The sanctuary above the rock, with its golden dome that dominates the skyline of old Jerusalem, was built by the Caliph 'Abd al-Malik ibn Marwan around *72*/691. Its splendid decorative designs are noted for their Byzantine-Syrian motifs. Calligraphic decorations, characteristic of much of Islamic art, majestically dominate the Dome of the Rock. The two hundred and forty yards/meters of inscriptions, famed for their beauty, are in *Kufic* style within, and *ta'līq* on the outside. The inscriptions are all the Koranic verses about Jesus.

The Dome of the Rock's octagonal structure became the model for domed sanctuaries and Saints' tombs from Morocco to China. The octagon is a step in the mathematical series going from square, symbolizing the fixity of earthly manifestation, to circle, the natural symbol for the perfection of heaven. Traditional baptismal fonts are also octagonal in virtue of the same symbolism, baptism being an initiation which opens the door from this world to the next, or to a superior state of being. In Saints' tombs the lower part of the structure is square, or cubic; the octagon is a drum inserted as a transition between the cube of the base and the dome. In traditional Islamic architecture this configuration symbolizes the link between earth, represented by the square, and heaven, symbolized by the dome; in human terms, and according to a similar principle, the Saint is the link between man and God. In Morocco, when the King rides to Friday prayer on horseback, servants hold over him a large parasol, which corresponds to the architectural dome; this is thus a living tableau of the sacred function of man at prayer, for the monarch is also the Imām, or prayer-leader, of the nation.

In the case of the Dome of the Rock, the symbolism of its geometric forms echoes the significance of the Temple Mount as the site of the Temple of Solomon. It is the culmination of the revelations of Moses and Jesus in the restoration of the primordial Abrahamic unity which is Islam. The site of the structure is the Temple of Solomon; the calligraphic inscriptions recall the relationship between Jerusalem and Jesus, and the apocalypse to come; and the architecture, above all the octagonal form supporting a dome, is symbolic of the *mirāj*, or ascent to heaven, by the Prophet, and thus by man.

Although the Dome of the Rock was built by Syrian craftsmen trained in the Byzantine tradition, it is, nevertheless, the first major example of Islamic architecture, whose more indigenous expressions would come later. Situated on the site of the temple of Solomon, it proclaims the ascendancy of Islam. When the sanctuary was built, Mecca was being occupied by a challenger to the Caliphate, 'Abd Allāh Ibn az-Zubayr. 'Abd al-Malik therefore promulgated a decree whereby the Dome of the Rock, rather than the Ka'bah, became the goal of the *ḥajj*, or pilgrimage. This decree was annulled with the reconquest of Mecca, but it demonstrates the sanctity that Islam attaches to the place.

Only the High Priest was allowed to walk in the Holy of Holies, and since the actual position of the Holy of Holies is now unknown, Judaism forbids access to the whole area of Temple Mount; a prohibition which is observed by orthododox Jews. In all likelihood, the Holy of Holies was over the rock which is within the Dome of the Rock. Sacred history and Rabbinical decisions have closed the Temple Mount to the first of the three Semitic religions. In Christianity the veil of the Temple, which separated the Holy of Holies from the rest of the Temple, was rent in twain at the crucifixion of Jesus, to symbolize the going forth of the Shechina into the world. Islam, the third and final Semitic religion which, like Christianity, is universal, makes of the Temple Mount the place where man, as man, is joined once more to God through the restoration of Adam's relationship to God before the Fall, as expressed in the ascent to heaven of the Prophet; thus it is Islam that restores it as a sanctuary.

When the Crusaders controlled Jerusalem, the Knights Templar turned the Dome of the Rock into a church and made it the model for their chapels, or "temples". The only such chapel still extant is in the Templar Castle of Tomar, Portugal, and in the small and ancient church of the True Cross (la Iglesia de la Vera Cruz) in Segovia, Spain. The Dome was also the emblem of the seal of the Grand Master of the Order of the Knights Templar. When Saladin recaptured Jerusalem he naturally made the Dome once more into an Islamic shrine. The area around the Dome of the Rock contains a number of minor monuments which were built by the Ottomans. At the other end of the esplanade is the al-Aqsā' Mosque. *See* al-AQSĀ'; JERUSALEM; NIGHT JOURNEY; SOLOMON.

Dönmeh (Turkish: "apostate" from the Turkish root *dön,* to turn.) A sect found in Greece and

Turkey with a Muslim outer appearance, and heterodox Jewish beliefs and practices maintained in secret. There arose in Turkey a pseudo-Messiah named Sabbatai Zevi (1626-1676) from Smyrna (Izmir), a descendant of exiles from Spain after 1492. A scholar of Lurianic Kabbalah, he allowed himself to be proclaimed the Messiah in 1648 after pronouncing publicly the Divine Name in Hebrew which Jews consider to be forbidden. Zevi would enter into striking psychological states in which he acted as a man possessed and advocated the breaking of Jewish religious laws.

Zevi acquired a large following, and his reputation spread to Europe. Samuel Pepys wrote in his diary that Jews in London are speculating on a certain person now in Smyrna. Tens of thousands of Jews converged on Turkey believing he was the Messiah. Zevi, basing himself upon Christian apocalyptics, proclaimed the year 1666 as the millenium and in that year he attempted to have his followers converge upon Constantinople telling them that they would be able to dethrone the Sultan. The Turkish authorities arrested him; and upon the advice of a Jewish advisor challenged Zevi to an ordeal by poison arrows to prove that he was the Messiah. Thereupon Zevi outwardly converted to Islam, taking the name Mehmet Effendi while preserving his antinomial beliefs inwardly. At that point many Jews abandoned him, and in Italy the chronicles of the Zevi years were destroyed. Some, however, followed him into a kind of Islam and later leaders such as Jacob Josef Pilosof called "Querido" (b. 1662 in Salonika) carried on the process of further conversions.

In Europe a clandestine antinomial Sabbatian movement also arose and produced later variations of which Jacob Frank was a notable example. After various scandals Frank (1726-1791) converted to Catholicism and was made the Baron of Offenbach by Maria Theresa of Austria. Frank's antinomianism took the particular form of rampant sexuality which, like Rasputinism and other movements, was a kind of sanctification through sin. (Zevi, in the pattern of Simon Magus, had been married to Sarah, a prostitute who had been raised in a convent.) David Bakan has traced Frankist Sabbatianism down to Sigmund Freud.

The sect of the Dönmeh were found in Salonika, Edirne, Istanbul, and Izmir before the collapse of the Ottoman Empire when they were estimated as being ten to fifteen thousand. Calling themselves *ma'aminim* the sect was divided into several branches: Izmirlis (who include the Celebis, Karawajo, Cabalieros, and Kara Kashlar), the Yakubis (also called Hamdi-Beyler, a name used by Querido), and the Kuniosos, the latter being followers of Osman Baba. The Izmirlis were also sometimes called the Tarbishli, or "those who had taken the turban"; in Edirne they were also called "Sazanicos".

While professing to be Muslims and actually honoring Muhammad, fasting Ramaḍān, going on pilgrimage, they believe Zevi, and others according to the branch, to be a Messiah (or simply to be God) and perform rites in respect of this, including a paraphrasing of the *shahādah* and carry on Kabbalistic studies. They believe that the Messiah has been reincarnated some eighteen times since Adam; that Zevi's death was an appearance and that he returned as Querido, and then as Osman Baba. Some groups did not believe in Osman Baba as a reincarnation and these are called Kapanzylar; (others did not believe in Querido). Rites are held partly in Ladino (Judaeo-Spanish) and Jewish holidays and rituals are observed, in secret; there was a sacramental meal resembling the Christian agape; the followers are said to have maintained two sets of names, a Muslim public name ("for the people") and a secret Jewish name ("for paradise"); to have had houses which were interconnected, and a myriad of sectarian beliefs, practices, and particularities, such as a belief that the lamb contains within itself a secret combination of both male and female natures. Different currents among the Dönmeh would await the return of the Messiah from the north, the south, or by sea, and would go to the seashore for ritual waiting. A number of similarities can be found between them and the 'Alawi sect and Bektashi sects of the Near East.

Many Dönmeh played a important role in the 1908 revolution in Turkey as members of the the Young Turks and subsequently as laicised statesmen in the Kemalist government. *See* ANTINOMIANISM.

"Drunken Sufis", see ANTINOMIANISM; al-BISṬĀMĪ; al-ḤALLĀJ; IBN ABĪ-l-KHAYR; al-JUNAYD; al-KHAMRIYYAH; SAHL TUSTARI; TAWHID.

Druzes. A heterodox sect which developed out of Fāṭimid Ismā'īlism and the *5th*/11th century agitation of the Qarmatians. The Druzes, a kind of Ismā'īlī sub-group, call themselves the *Muwwaḥidūn*, the "Unitarians" – which is also the preferred name of the Wahhabis, and that of the Almohads, a religious movement in Morocco of the *4th*/11th century. However, the Druzes are in no way related to either of these. They are of an altogether different religion, a departure from Islam with which they have no more than an historical link through Fāṭimid Ismā'īlism. There are over 600,000 Druzes who live in Lebanon, Syria, and Israel.

The sixth Fāṭimid Caliph (and Ismā'īlī Imām) *al-Ḥākim*, who died in Cairo in *411*/1021, allowed his followers to announce that he was Divine. Two opportunists who promoted these assertions were Hamzah, a Persian, and Darazī ("the cobbler"), a Turk. The latter *dā'i* , or propagandist, left his name to the Druze sect. Darazī's publishing, at al-Ḥākim's behest, of the *bāṭinī* ("inner") doctrine of the Ismā'īlīs concerning the Imām caused an outcry and rioting in Cairo which forced al-Ḥākim to retract. In the recriminations which followed, Hamzah and Darazī quarreled; Darazī fled to Palestine or Syria where he continued propaganda concerning al-Ḥākim until his death in *410*/1020; Hamzah followed upon the heels of Darazī and had his predecessor duly anathemized, declaring himself instead, in keeping with the practices of the sect, to be the true manifester of the Divine reality of al-Ḥākim. As was the pattern with Ismā'īlī *dā'is*, Hamzah hived off what was to become the Druzes from the Fāṭimid Ismā'īlīs, attributing to al-Ḥākim a celestial function, and to himself an earthly one in the role of Imām. After his death, Baha'ad-Dīn al-Muqtana was the *Tāli'* or successor. The pastoral letters written around that epoch constitute the body of written Druze literature, the *Rasā'il al-Ḥākim*. The doctrine became established among tribes in Lebanon, Palestine and Syria. These tribes in their isolation perpetuated in secret a tradition of Gnostic beliefs going back to antiquity and were the targets of every new wave of Gnostic or Ismā'īlī missionaries, including the Qarmatians. With the propaganda concerning al-Ḥākim, a crystallization was to take place and fix the form of the dogmas; twenty years after al-Ḥākim died (or according to their beliefs went into a great occultation, the *ghaybah*) entry to the Druze religion was closed. The Druzes believe that their number remains the same since then.

Druze doctrine teaches that al-Ḥākim was a manifestation of the universal intellect, *al-'Aql al-Kullī* and that he is not dead, but mystically and secretly alive in the Unseen and that he will return as the Mahdī. Although this resembles the Twelve-Imām Shī'ite doctrine of the Hidden Imām, which is itself calqued on the Koranic description of Jesus, the two should not be confused. The Druzes believe that emanations of Divine principles are made incarnate, or act through, functionaries in the higher levels of the Druze hierarchy, the "ministers" or representatives of al-Ḥākim. Because of their Ismā'īlī origins, Druze beliefs are characteristically dualist, or Gnostic. The so-called doctrines of reincarnation which are attributed to the Druzes are probably the echoes of the Gnostic teachings of the gathering up of the illuminated souls at the end of time.

The sect is secretive. In practice there are several different degrees of initiation which, along with Druze precepts, are designed to promote obedience, group cohesiveness, and solidarity in the face of pressure from outside. The process of initiation begins at the age of eighteen. The guidance given to the Druzes is represented as being the will of al-Ḥākim expressed through his "ministers". The sectaries are divided into *'uqqāl* (sing *āqil;* "intelligent") who correpond to the "elect" or the initiates and the *juhhāl* (sing. *jahīl*; "ignorant"). The supreme chief of the Druze is the *Shaykh al-'Aql* with a *ra'īs*, or head, appointed to districts. In Lebanon there is a division into two groups, the Jumblatt and the Yazbakī, each with their own head.

It is sometimes said that the Druzes are descended from the Crusaders, but this is simply a common, catch-all mythology for many groups in the Levant. It has also been alleged that the Druzes have wives in common, but this, similarly, is the most common of slanders in the Near and Middle East, directed at any exotic group by detracting outsiders. Although these various charges are groundless, the Gnostic sects are especially vulnerable to this kind of attack because of their ambiguous attitudes towards religious law; their extreme asceticism on the one hand, and their disregard of the religious law on the other, make for an attitude of independence towards the rest of the world.

Several Druze leaders became prominent in the history of the Levant: the Emīr Fakhr ad-Dīn in the 12th century, Emīr Fakhr ad-Dīn II in the 17th, and the Emīr Bashīr Shihābī in the 19th. The Ottoman Turks found it prudent to allow the Druzes a measure of independence. The Druzes and the Maronite Christians are traditionally hostile to each other; communal warfare between the two irrupted frequently in the last century. Druzes living in Israel are accepted in the Israeli army. *See* FĀṬIMIDS; ISMĀ'ĪLĪS; LEBANON.

Du'ā' (literally a "call" or "plea"). An individual prayer, which may be spontaneous with personal petitions, or a composed individual prayer, such as the *Ṣalāt Mashīshiyyah*, or the *Ḥizb al-Baḥr*, or a special prayer for occasions of distress, the *Yā Laṭif.* The *du'ā'* is different from the ritual, or canonical prayer (*ṣalāh*), which is a non-individual prayer performed five times a day according to a traditionally established form, and which is obligatory. The *ṣalāh* is a kind of liturgy and an act of worship. What Christians usually understand by prayer, is in Islam closer to what is called the *du'ā'*.

The *ṣalāh* is normally followed by a *du'ā'*, prefaced by the recitation of certain expressions of praise and thanks to God thirty-three or more times. The *du'ā'* itself, which consists of the individual's petitions of God, is voiced inwardly and silently. The *du'ā'*, whether in a group or alone, is performed with the palms of the hands open to heaven; at the end, the words *al-Ḥamdu li-Llāh* ("praise to God") are said and the palms are drawn over the face and down, crossing over the shoulders, as if one were anointing oneself with a Divine blessing. Although there is always a (non-obligatory) *du'ā'* following the *ṣalāh*, a *du'ā'* may be made at any time. *See* FĀTIḤAH; ḤIZB al-BAḤR; IBN MASHĪSH; PRAYER; ṢALĀH; YA LAṬĪF.

Dualism (Ar. *ath-Thunā'iyyah* or *al-Ithnayniyyah*). The doctrine that there are two mutually antagonistic "principles" in the universe, good and evil, also symbolised as light and darkness. Its empirical starting point is the observation that something like evil exists concretely, like a "black light". There are numerous variants. The doctrine leads to a well-worn circle of reasoning. If the intellectual starting point is that there are two principles or two gods at war with each other, this assumption inevitably leads to the conclusion that the world is a physical mixture of these two principles. Then the world is no a "creation" but is itself a kind of material absolute, or as in the case of Bardaisan (Ibn Daisan *d.* 222), and many other Gnostics, an emanation.

If, on the other hand, the starting point is materialism (the doctrines which Muslims and Zoroastrians call *dahri*, Koran 45:23) or that a person or a thing in the world is divine, then the metaphysical conclusion is that two principles are behind the dynamics of such a world. While the mythology that covers the framework is a matter of taste, the crux of the matter is logic: if the ego or matter is not a "creation" but is itself an absolute, then the limitations which make it individual or discrete are also "absolute" or "divine". As the Taoists say, it is the absence or empty space which makes a bowl a bowl. But if the bowl is "reality" in itself and not the work of a creator, then the absence that makes the bowl a bowl is also "reality". I nothingness or "Non-Being" is itself "real" and not just a term, or, as in Aristotle, an "accident", that means it has an "essence". The essence of non-existence (were it to have an essence!) would have to be utter contradiction. This translates as the divinity of evil, as found in, say, Milton, or in Martin Luther.

Such doctrines could be called *radical* dualism and include Manicheism and such materialist ideologies as Marxism and philosophical Existentialism, as well as numerous ancient and modern sects.

A second form of dualism could be called *relative* dualism. here the world is not divine as such, but something in the world - or someone - is divine, or "somewhat" divine. "Somewhat divine" could be that "divine spark" which the Gnostics recognise in certain individuals such as those whom Paul calls "pneumatics". In Islam it is the Shiite idea that Ali and certain of his descendents possess a divine spark or element of divine light and what is called the ilm, or sacred knowledge. In this form of dualism the element of time, as Ugo Bianchi pointed out, plays an essential role. Whereas in the radical dualisms realization of final ends can come at any moment between beginning and end, in the relative dualisms there is an inexorable cosmological process which takes a pre-determined duration of time for its accomplishment. The mahdi is to come at some epiphany in the future and "establish justice in the earth".

The *relative* forms of dualism are more common - at certain times - or more widespread than the "radical" but, in time, the relative dualisms evolve or decay to become in practice indistinguishable from the radical forms, as can be seen from recent developments in Twelve Imam Shiism.

Other minor forms of dualism include Monism (such as occurs in Ibn Arabi, Christian Science, pantheism, etc.) and a dualism which is termed "Monarchic". In this latter form, the good god, say Jehovah, is slightly stronger, or has some other advantage over the evil god, Satan, and will defeat him definitively or from time to time in the cosmic drama.

Dualisms are antagonistic to each other; relative dualisms may even be more antagonistic toward a parent or a related radical dualism than to other "relative" competitors, and condemn them as being immoral, or for "going too far". (Al-Maarri was dragged out by his foot - the equivalent expression at that time and place for being "kicked out", when he expected to be welcomed with open arms by Sharif ar-Radi in Baghdad). To one extent or another, dualisms are anti-cosmic - they regard the world or the body as evil, or the world as fatally polluted, and require renunciation and asceticism from their followers - purity - unless or until the individual group is regenerated into a new and perfect entity by the accomplishment of a process or sanctified by the presnce of the holy element or person. An inevitable feature is the "external enemy", the political "Great Satan".

There is the phenomenon, of which the ancient sect of "Massalians" is the model and technical term, in which the ascetic, having denied himself, becomes a "perfectus" and everything which was forbidden to him or her becomes completely licit. This tendency, of the forbidden being permitted, of chastity becoming orgy, can be found at some point or at some time, if not in the beginning then at the "mature" stage of development, in many dualist sects. It may appear as the permission for marriages to be contracted by intention to last for one day (*see* MUT'AH). Thus the heresiarchs accused the Gnostics of orgiastic rituals, "of putting out the candles" at mixed meetings, of regressions to animal states, while their defenders point to the Gnostic's public display of strict and extreme rules of abstinence.

Islam appeared, as many religions do, when dualist doctrines were spreading inexorably throughout the classical world. One story is cited as being essence of such metaphysical error: The Koran tells how Bilqis, the Queen of Sheba (the soul), visited Solomon (the intellect), and mistook the reflection on a finely polished floor of his palace (the world) for reality:

> *It was said unto her, "Enter the pavilion". But when she saw it, she supposed it was a spreading water, and she bared her legs. He [Solomon] said, "It is a pavilion smoothed of crystal". She said, "My Lord, indeed I have wronged myself, and I surrender with Solomon to God, the Lord of all Being" (Koran 27:44-45)*

In other words, she mistook a reflection for reality, or "what is not" for a "second" or different kind of Being o anti-Being. Islam expunges the errors of dualism by the *shahadah*, the testimony of faith which attests that there is only one God, not two. *See* ISHRAQ; KHATTABIYYAH; KHURRAMIYYAH.

Duldul. The mule of the Prophet. The mule was a gift from the Byzantine Viceroy of the Copts of Egypt, the Muqawqīs as the Arabs called him.

Dungan. Chinese speaking people, some of whom are found in eastern Kyrgyztan, who are Muslim.

E

Effendi. A traditional title in Ottoman times for a religious or a civil authority. Today, in most cases it is replaced by the honorific *Bey*, also originally a Turkish term.

Egypt. Republic. Population estimated at 48,500,000 of whom 90% are Sunnī Muslims. The Malikī school is dominant in upper Egypt and the Shāfi‘ī in lower Egypt; some Egyptian Muslims are Ḥanafīs. The non-Muslim 10% are Coptic Christians, Greek Orthodox, Melkites, Jacobites, and members of smaller churches. The prestige of the al-Azhar University has often given the pronouncements of Egyptian religious leaders great weight in the Islamic world; and during the last few centuries Cairo has been the cultural capital of the Arab world. *See* ‘AMR IBN al-‘ĀṢĪ; al-AZHAR; CAIRO; FĀṬIMIDS; MAMLŪKS; MUḤAMMAD ‘ALĪ.

Eid, *see* ‘ID.

Elijah, *see* ILYĀS.

Elisha, *see* ALYASA‘.

Elkhasaios. The head of the baptising sect (*al-mughtasilah*) or the *Ṣābat al-Baṭa'ih* as Ibn Nadīm called them, to which Mani had belonged. Bell, in *Origin of Islam* says that what is said to been a secret watchword of Elkasai, "I am a witness over you on the day of judgement," is found in so many words in the Koran (22:78 and elsewhere). Mani also used the word *qerya* for the call or as a sign of recognition, along with the shaking of the hand. Among the Gnostics, the call is an important psychological reality (as it still is among some Protestant sects). In Manicheism the call (*xrustag*) is made by Adam and is answered by the Father of Greatness. The first word of the Koran is also *iqra'*. Also intriguing in this context, in which stars can be particles of light hidden in creation, is the *najmu ath-thāqiba* (86:3) the piercing star which is followed by the words "over every soul there is a watcher".

Emigration, *see* HIJRAH.

Emīr, *see* AMĪR.

Emre, *See* YUNUS EMRE.

Enoch, *see* IDRĪS.

Eritrea. Since 1993 an independent republic the size of England, formerly a part of Ethiopia. The name is from the Latin for the Red Sea, *Mare Erythraeum*. The population is three million Hanafi Muslims and Christians of the Ethiopian Church. The capital is Asmara with a population of 400,000. The Italian colony of Eritrea was created in 1890 bringing together nine different ethnic groups, including the Christian Tigrinya, the animistic Kunama, the Muslim Afars. In 1952 Eritrea was made an autonomous federated state within Ethiopia by the United Nations. In 1961 a war of independence began which led Haile Selassie to make Eritrea the 14th province of Ethiopia. The war continued under Selassie's successors. *See* ETHIOPIA.

Eschatology. The doctrines of "final ends" which refer to two things: the last days before the end of a cycle of manifestation, and the final, or posthumous, states of souls. The last days, as described in Islam, are marked by the figures of Gog and Magog (*Jūj wa Mājūj*), the Mahdī, the Antichrist (*Dajjāl*), and Jesus.

The names Gog and Magog are interpreted symbolically by Arab commentators as meaning "flaming fire" and "surging water", that is, violence, destruction, and agitation. According to the Koranic parable recounted in the Sūrah of the Cave (18:93), Gog and Magog, representing the forces of chaos, have been kept at bay, for a time, by the erection of a barrier described as being of iron and molten copper; this was erected by him "of the Two Horns" (Dhū-l-Qarnayn), generally taken to refer to Alexander the Great, who was empowered so to do by God. The barrier in the myth may be based distantly on travelers' tales of the Great Wall of China, but here it refers to the Divine Law (*Sharī‘ah*). At the end of time, chaos will break through the wall of Divinely imposed order, and the world will succumb to "outer darkness".

At the same time, it is believed, there will be a countercurrent, or a brief return to the state of spiritual lucidity and primordial integrity that obtained at the dawn of time. This is the reign of the Mahdī, the "rightly guided one". It is, however, unlikely that the doctrine of the Mahdī goes back to the Prophet himself; probably it is an invention of the early Shī'ite movements of the end of the *1st*/7th century. But a version of the Mahdī idea (different from the Shī'ite one in that it has none of the Imāmī doctrines) has been popularly accepted by Sunnī Muslims and is a feature of certain of the Sunnī creeds. It has imposed itself because an eleventh-hour sobriety, like the moment of dispassionate clarity before death, is a well-known experience. Thus, Tradition has the Prophet say: "The Mahdī will be of my stock and he will be broad of forehead and aquiline of nose." This means that he will resemble the Prophet; although the description is physical, it can be taken as a resemblance of character. Under him justice, or a sense of true proportion, and a center will be restored; law in the place of lawlessness. The Mahdī's reign of justice will mean the establishment of a spiritual Norm, of what the Far Eastern traditions call the Tao and Hinduism the *dharma*. It has often been assumed, however, that the reign of the Mahdī will be outward and wordly in its nature, with the result that many political leaders have sought power by claiming to be the Mahdī. They have come and gone; and while it is possible that the reign of the true Mahdī may be outward, it is far more likely that when it comes, at the end of time, it will be inward, in the sense of Jesus' words: "The Kingdom of God is within you".

The reign of the Mahdī will be followed by that of the Antichrist, *al-Masīḥ ad-Dajjāl* (lit. imposter messiah"). The word *Masīḥ* ("messiah") by the addition of one dot above the final Arabic letter – the minuscule discrepancy which transforms spiritual truth into falsehood – is changed to *masīkh*, "deformed", and it is by this name that some Sufi masters called the final, great, deceiver.

The deceiver will come at a time when the world is in extreme imbalance, and incapable of distinguishing authentic spirituality from false, if indeed, it does not prefer the false. The deceiver will promise – to use the terminology of Far Eastern traditions – "to stop the cosmic wheel from turning", but will himself be the very incarnation of disorder, pure disbelief, outwardness, and inversion; in short the parody of spirituality.

Better to understand the workings of the Antichrist, it is helpful to distinguish between the psychic and spiritual domains, which, from the viewpoint of the material world, are easily confounded. The psychic or subtle domain resembles the spiritual or supraformal and principial one. An Angel, for example, dwells in the spiritual realm, but to make himself manifest in the physical world, he must take on a subtle form. Magic, or the manipulation of the subtle plane, can be mistaken for miracles, which are transformations wrought in the spiritual or principial plane. This, and the confusion possible between the infra-human and the sublime (arbitrariness appearing to be freedom, lack of conscience to be self-sufficiency, and chaos to be formlessness), are the illusions by which the *Dajjāl* perpetrates his fraud; he substitutes one for the other. However, this is only possible when our ego connives to be deluded. The ego, despite being aware of its own mortality, refuses to yield to the Self which is immortal, and clings to what mirrors it. The reign of the Antichrist is the reign of the ego.

The most significant distinguishing mark foretold of the Antichrist is that he will be one-eyed. To be one-eyed is to be unable to perceive depth or space; that is, to be unable to establish the mutual relationship of objects in a field of vision and to fail to perceive the reality they manifest: to see the fact, but not its significance. Above all, it means to be unable to sense the inward depth of the sacred: the Antichrist reduces the eternal to the momentary. The reduction of consciousness to a point or an instant is not without its attractions, for it implies escape from the majesty and dread of the numinous and the utterly other, as well as from our own responsibility towards the infinite, eternal and transcendental. The Antichrist will heal the sick by making their afflictions the norm, or by making sin virtuous. He will win followers by his ability to work marvels or pseudo-miracles.

Concerning the last days the Prophet said: "A body of my people will not cease to fight for the Truth until the coming of the Antichrist" and: "Islam began in exile and will return to exile". This is also cited as prophecy of the sign of the times: "The slave-girl will give birth to her mistress [the inferior will rule and the superior will adopt the inferior as its model]; and those who were but barefoot and needy herdsman will build buildings ever higher and higher." Suddenly, however, Jesus will appear, and with him the radical correction of the world, the opening of the doors of paradise and the doors of hell, and the discrimination of spirits.

While the last times have the aspect of terrible tribulation, tradition says that when they end a new cycle begins, and with it a new golden age. Also, at the end the spiritual will be easily accessible, although few will want it. The Prophet said: "At the beginning he who omits one-tenth of the law is condemned; but at the end he who accomplishes one-tenth of the law is saved." This echoes the gospel parable of the workers in the garden where those who worked but a short time in the late afternoon were paid as much as those who worked from the early morning. Because of the increase in grace, both garnered a like amount.

With respect to individual eschatology, Islam, like all the monotheist traditions, draws a sharp distinction between the posthumous states of paradise and hell. The Prophet said: "When we live, we dream, and when we die, we wake." Whether we are true to our real selves and to the Real – this it is which determines our state after death. Identification with the Truth leads to paradise, and rejection (disbelief: *kufr*) to hell.

These, however, are not the only possible posthumous states. The Sūrah of the Heights (*al-A'rāf*) speaks of those on the heights who hear and address the people of paradise, but are not yet in paradise themselves (7:46-47). It is the sanctified who, having fulfilled the requirements of the human state, will enter paradise (*al-jannah*).

> 'O soul at peace, return unto thy Lord,
> well-pleased, well-pleasing!
> Enter thou among My servants!
> Enter thou My Paradise!'(89:27-30)

> Faces on that day jocund,
> with their striving well-pleased,
> in a sublime Garden,
> hearing there no babble;
> therein a running fountain,
> therein uplifted couches
> and goblets set forth
> and cushions arrayed
> and carpets outspread. (88:8-15)

Those who are not perfected, but are without fundamental fault, may enter into a limbo, or the kind of intermediary state without suffering to which the *al-A'rāf* refers, as they undergo final purification, a state which unfailingly opens onto the state of the blessed. (There are a number of Ḥadīth which Muslim theologians have taken to mean that children who die before the age of reason are saved, or have the posthumous possibility of salvation, because until the age of reason they embody the *fiṭrah* or primordial norm. (*See* CHILDREN.)

Purgatory, or purification with privation or suffering, is not mentioned in the Koran, at least directly, but there are Ḥadīth such as the following: "And God will say: the Angels, the Prophets and the believers have all interceded for them [the sinners] save The Most Merciful of the Merciful (*Arḥam ar-Rāḥimīn*). And He will grasp the fire in his hand and draw out a people who never did any good." This provisional passage through fire corresponds to the idea of purgatory. The Andalusian theologian Ibn Ḥazm maintained that if believers went to hell, it was necessarily for a limited time. Al-Ash'arī too admits the possibility, though perhaps less categorically. Ultimately, the Ḥadīth can also refer to an apocatastasis. The Prophet also said: "Those who have merited paradise will enter it; the damned will go to hell. God will then say; Let those leave hell whose hearts contain even the weight of a mustard seed of faith! Then they will be released, although they have already been burned to ashes, and plunged into the river of rain-water, or into the river of life; and immediately they will be revived."

There is, finally, hell itself which lasts in perpetuity – if not in eternity – until the extinction of the personality. A fifth possibility, namely of a transition through a posthumous state, whether happy or fearful to another, necessarily non-human and non-central existence, which may be better or worse than the individual's previous state, depending upon his "Karma", or "deserts", is found in some religions but does not enter into the Islamic perspective.

On the other hand, a distinction is drawn in the Koranic Sūrah of the Terror (or "the Event") (*Sūrat al-Wāqi'ah*), between two categories of those not destined to be damned as Companions of the Left (*Aṣḥāb al-mash'amah*; 56:9). These are described respectively as the "Companions of the Right" (*Aṣḥāb al-Maymanah*; 56:8) and the "Outstrippers" (or the "Foremost") (*as-Sābiqūn*), the latter being equated with those that are "brought nigh the Throne" (*al-Muqarrabūn*; 56: 10-11). There is clearly a fundamental difference of degree here, which certain of the Sufis have not hesitated to define as that between those who merely achieve salvation and those who attain to Beatitude; salvation is the reward, they say, of the exoteric religion, and Beatitude the aim of the Sufis' esoteric Path.

There is also a cyclical "ratio" of numbers of the "saved" and the "Beatified" respectively: the inevitable decline of humanity as it moves down through time ever further from the pristine norm (*al-fiṭrah*) means that those "brought nigh" will include a throng of the ancients but few of the later folk (56:13-14), whereas the Companions of the Right will consist of "A throng of the ancients and a throng of the later folk". (56: 38-39); as the end of time approaches, salvation remains open to many, but Beatitude to very few; this is not strange, since those "brought nigh" include Jesus and other Prophets and, in fact, the line of Prophets was "sealed" with the death of Muḥammad.

In any event, the Koran speaks of various paradises, each corresponding, no doubt, to different degrees of blessedness: thus there is frequent mention, in general terms, of "gardens beneath which the rivers flow", and specifically of gardens of Eden and "gardens of Firdaws" (*Firdaws* being ultimately cognate with the Greek *paradeisos*, Paradise", whilst the Sūrah *ar-Raḥmān* says: "But such as fears the Station of his Lord, for them shall be two gardens" (55:46) and "besides these shall be two (more) gardens"(55:62).

The human, or central state is distinguished from all others precisely because it is characterized by the capacity to know the Absolute. To be born human is therefore to arrive at a great crossroads. Islam simplifies the choice of direction into two main paths, because, ultimately, the consequences of being human are either that of becoming sanctified, or that of being reduced to the sub-human, whatever the modes. Damnation is the forfeit, or ultimate loss, of the human state because of revolt, disbelief, or, in the case of the "indifferent" (*ghāfilūn*), of simply abandoning the responsibilities of being God's "viceroy" (*khalīfah*) on earth. Paradise is the realization of conformity to our true nature; closeness to God because of knowledge of Him; and salvation. *See also* APOCATASTASIS; CHILDREN; HELL; al-JANNAH; TANĀSUKH; YAWM ad-DĪN.

Esop, *see* LUQMĀN.

Esoterism, *see* AARON; SUFISM; ṬARĪQAH; TAṢAWWUF.

Essence, *see* ALLĀH; BEING; DHĀT; DIVINE NAMES; FIVE DIVINE PRESENCES.

Ethnic Groups, *see* 'ALAWĪS; ARABS; AZERĪ; BAKHTIĀR; BALOCH; BERBERS; DRUZES; HUI HUI; KIRGHIZ; KURDS; LURS; MANDAEANS; PUSHTUN; QASHQAI; TUAREG; TURKS; UZBEKS.

Ethics. (Ar. *al-amr bi-al-maruf wa-an-nahy an al-munkar*, "To enjoin right conduct and prohibit indecency".) There are, besides the questions that are legislated, frequent ethical injunctions in the Koran, from:

> And whosoever earns a fault or a sin
> and then casts it upon the innocent,
> thereby has laid upon himself calumny
> and manifest sin. (4:112)

to:

> Consume not your goods between you
> in vanity; neither proffer it
> to the judges, that you may sinfully
> consume a portion of other men's goods,
> and that wittingly. (2:184)

and:

> Surely those who cast it up on women
> in wedlock that are heedless but believing
> shall be accursed in the present world
> and in the world to come. (24:23)

and:

> Woe to the stinters
> who, when they measure against the people, take full measure
> but, when they measure for them or weigh for them, do skimp.
> Do those not think that they shall be raised up
> unto a mighty day
> a day when mankind shall stand before the Lord of all Being? (83:1-6)

These may be summed up by the Koranic formula: "Ye are the best community that hath been raised up for mankind. Ye enjoin right conduct and forbid indecency; and ye believe in Allah" (3:110). The Ḥadīth express it thus: "*Iḥsān* [virtue] is to worship as if you see Him, for if you do not see Him, nevertheless He sees you"; and "God has prescribed virtue (or excellence *Iḥsān*) in all things". Other Ḥadith which deal with ethics are: "No one of you is a Muslim until you wish for your brother what you wish for yourselves", and the *Ṣaḥīḥ* Muslim related on the authority of Abū Saīd al-Khudrī: "Whosoever of you sees an evil action, let him change it with his hand; and if he is not able to do so, then let him condemn it with his tongue, and if he is not able to do so let him condemn it in his head – and that is the weakest of faith."

In practice, ethics are different in the light of different religions. Christianity makes an ideal world appear to be the reality against which actuality is measured and judges behavior according to ideals. Judaism takes it view of reality from the material world as being real as it is, and instead of the ideal places a law. Islam's view of reality mixes these two points of view seeing things and situations sometimes from the material and concrete, and sometimes from the ideal. *See* IḤSĀN; SHARI'AH.

Ethiopia. Republic. Estimated population: 25,000,000. Before Eritrea became independent some 30% of the population were Muslims of the Ḥanafī School of Law, (with some Malikīs near the Sudan); the rest are Christians of the Coptic Ethiopian Orthodox Church (which has been Monophysite since the Council of Chalcedon in 451); there remains a very small group of Falashas, or Ethiopian Jews.

By tradition, the first King of Ethiopia was Solomon's son, Menelik, by the Queen of Sheba (in Arabic she is called Bilqīs). In the 13th and 16th centuries there were wars with neighboring Muslim states, which brought increasing numbers of Muslim peoples into Ethiopia. In 1530 there was a considerable influx of Muslim Galla tribesmen from Somalia, which was repulsed by the Ethiopians with the help of the Portuguese. In 1974 the Negus, the Emperor Haile Selassie, was deposed, and a republic declared shortly thereafter. *See* ABYSSINIA; BILQĪS; CHRISTIANITY.

"Exaggerators", *see* GHULAT.

Exoterism, *see* AARON; SHARI'AH.

"Extinction", *see* FANĀ'.

"Extremists", *see* GHULAT.

Eve, *see* ADAM.

Evil, *see* IBLĪS.

Expressions, Pious, *see* PIOUS EXPRESSIONS.

Eyüp Sultan, *see* ABŪ AYYŪB.

F

Fair, *see* 'UKĀZ.

Fallacies and Inaccuracies about Islam. Victor Hugo wrote, in his book *William Shakespeare*, that in the 7th century, a certain Omar [he meant the Caliph 'Umar], "a man who drank only water and no wine", who rode a camel with a bag of dates on one side and a sack of flour on the other, came to Egypt, having laid waste 39,000 towns and villages in his conquests. This Omar, or one under his command, namely Amrou Ibn-Alas ('Amr ibn al-'Asi) destroyed the great library of Alexandria, using it as fuel for the fires of 2,000 bath-houses, which were thus supplied for six months. In actual fact, the libraries of Alexandria had undergone a depradation from the time of the Roman conquest onwards. In 391 they suffered the greatest single blow when the Byzantine Emperor Theodosius I had the pagan temples of Alexandria razed. This particular fallacy concerning the library of Alexandria, born of the mistrust of the stranger and the stranger's religion, is probably no longer current, but others are. Some of the common fallacies in the West are the following:

1. *The Suspended Coffin.* A frequently repeated tale exists that the Prophet's coffin is at Mecca, "suspended between heaven and earth". This is not an Islamic belief. Probably, it is a corruption of the idea, found in Islam, that there is a prototype in heaven of the Ka'bah called *al-bayt al-ma'mūr*, and that Angels circle this celestial center as men on earth circle the Ka' bah. The tomb of the Prophet is in Medina, in that part of the main mosque (*al-Masjid ash-Sharīf*), which was once the Prophet's house and where he died. Nearby are the tombs of the first three Caliphs and the sepulchre of Fāṭimah, although she is actually buried in *al-Baqī'* cemetery nearby.

2. *Muḥammad and the Mountain.* According to this story (proverbial in the West, but unknown in the East) the Prophet Muḥammad called a mountain to come to him and when it did not, he said: "If the mountain won't come to Muḥammad then Muḥammad will go to the mountain". There is no basis in fact for such a story which, moreover, contradicts the spirit of Islam with its emphasis on the non-miraculous and the humble. Viz. Koran 17:39: "And walk not in the earth exultantly; certainly thou wilt never tear the earth open, nor attain the mountains in height". Ṭabarī recounts that the Prophet was taunted in this way by the idolators:

> "Pray to thy Lord, Muhammad", said the men of Mecca, "that He move back the mountains that hem us in, and widen the good land for us, and thread it with rivers like the land of Syria and Iraq; or that He make our departed fathers rise from the dead, best of all that He send old Qusayy, Qilab's son, who never told a lie, so that we may ask whether what thou tellest us is true or false. If they declare thee true, we will believe in thee."

3. *Priests.* Many references to "Islamic priests" occur in Western press reports and writing on Islamic countries. This catch-all phrase covers Imāms, Mullas, *faqīhs*, *qāḍis*, and *'ulamā'*. However, the word "priests" is inappropriate, for this implies a consecration to perform a function which cannot be performed by a layman. There is, however, no distinction between priests and laymen in Islam. The dignitaries or functionaries mentioned above are distinguished from ordinary believers only by a higher degree of learning, or doctrinal expertise, but everyone is expected to perform the same religious duties. It is, for example, the ordinary believer who leads prayers, performs sacrifices and officiates; if speaking of priests, it would be more accurate to say that everyone is a priest in Islam.

The function of *Qāḍi* ("Judge") is an appointment on the basis of knowledge, and is clearly not a priestly function; that of Imām, or prayer-leader, is usually performed by someone designated for it because of age or, traditionally, knowledge of the Koran; but it can, in fact, be performed by anyone; the other functions are assumed as the result of qualifications in religious studies. There is no priesthood in Islam, nor anything corresponding to the monastic order: *lā rahbāniyyah fī-l-Islām* ("there is no monasticism in Islam") is a phrase frequently quoted which is based on the Koran's condemnation of this institution as being invented andnot prescribed by God (57:27). Every exoteric function and ritual in Islam can be accomplished by any mentally competent adult Muslim; in the absence of a competent male, a woman can perform any and every ritual on behalf of other women. In other words, every Muslim can perform all "sacerdotal" functions. Among Shī'ites not everyone can be a *mujtahid* or make independent judgements, but this also is a function of aptitude like that of a Judge among lawyers, and results from individual capacities, not consecration.

4. *Epilepsy ascribed to the Prophet.* This formally dates back to a diatribe against Islam written by a Byzantine monk called Theophanes in the 8th century A.D. Medieval European writers frequently drew upon his writings and Theophanes was the source, or the confirming authority, of other distortions which persist until today. In the 20th century some Western writers about Islam have not hesitated to explain the Koranic revelations as being the result of other kinds of non-specified morbid mental states.

In the 19th century the idea of epilepsy was a popular explanation intended to discredit religious phenomena of many kinds. It appealed to the age because it put them on a solid "scientific" footing. The Prophet's revelations were thus explained, as if the content of the Koran could possibly have been produced by epileptic seizures! St. Paul was also called an epileptic because of his conversion experience and temporary blindness. So was Julius Caesar because he had visions (some of which, as before the crossing of the Rubicon, were shared by the whole legion). There is no basis for these ideas, which are due to rationalist and atheist prejudice.

5. *Pilgrimage to Mecca as the Prophet's birthplace.* It is often said in the Western press that Muslims make pilgrimage to Mecca because it is the birthplace of the Prophet. The birthplace of the Prophet is considered to be of no importance; a library now stands on the spot which is otherwise unmarked and virtually unknown.

The pilgrimage to Mecca is ancient and antedates Islam. According to Islam, the pilgrimage was instituted by Abraham; that is, it is of primordial origin at a sanctuary dedicated to the One God since time immemorial. Thus the pilgrimage is to the sanctuary of Divine Unity and Absoluteness. Like all pilgrimages, it is to the centre of one's own being. It also commemorates the sacrifice of Abraham and pre-figures the Last Judgement. The Prophet is buried in Medina.

6. *Souls of women.* Women in Islam have souls exactly like men; the Koran is extremely clear on this. The idea that women have no souls is found in some heretical Middle Eastern sects.

Fanā' (lit. "extinction"). In Sufism one hopes "to die before one dies", that is, to die to the world and to subsist in God Alone; this latter state is called *baqā'*, subsisting or, in fact, immortality in the Real. The term *fanā'* thus corresponds exactly to the Buddhist term *Nirvānam*, which also means literally "extinction". While the word *fanā'* exists in the Koran its use by Sufism for this technical concept was probably inspired by Buddhism in Central Asia. The spiritual journey to *fanā'* involves many stages, notably the extinction of the "soul that inclines to evil" (*an-nafs al-ammārah*), and then of the "soul that accuses [itself]" (*an-nafs al-lawwāmah*), which are then replaced by the "soul at peace" (*an-nafs al-muṭma'innah*). This extinction itself is, in a sense, only penultimate; some Sufi masters speak of a *fanā' al-fanā'*, or the "extinction of the extinction". By this they mean the disappearance of *fanā'* itself before the ineffable glory of God, the state of *baqā'* being actually beyond all definition, and involving the loss of all individuality: "extinction in God" (*fanā' fī-Llāh*).

Thus, Ibn Aṭa' Allāh wrote in the *Ḥikam*:

> If you were to be united with Him only after the extinction of your vices and the effacement of your pretensions, you would never be united with Him. Instead, when He wants to unite you to Himself, He covers your attribute with His Attribute and hides your quality with His Quality. And thus He unites you to Himself by virtue of what comes from Him to you, not by virtue of what goes from you to Him.

And Niffāri:

> In the hour when I make you spectator of all existences at once in a single Vision, then at that Station I have certain forms, which if you find you know, call on Me by the forms. But if you do not know the forms, then in your agony invoke Me by the pain of that Vision.
>
> The Vision will be thus: you will be given sight of the whole Height and Depth, the whole Length and Breadth, and the All within, and all those

modes in which that Totality exists, as a thing manifest, eternal, entirely ordered, and convulsed in endless struggle. You will observe the existence of each thing...its own holy song, each directed towards Me in worship, in its own Praising, staring at Me in a Glorification...Let no fear alarm you at such a time as will come; and let no companion comfort you in the hour when I shall make you My spectator, and cause Myself to be known to you, though it may be once in your lifetime. For I will tell you in that hour, and you will know, that you are My lover, inasmuch as you will deny all things for the sake of what I have made you see, so that I shall become your Sovereign Disposer; and you will come to where I am on one side and all things on the other side. You will be attached to Me; all things else shall attach to you, and not to Me.

Such is My lover. And know this: you are to be My lover. And all your knowledge then will be knowledge of My Love...no resisting..no describing...

See SUFISM.

Faqīr (lit. "a poor man", pl. *fuqarā'*). A Sufi or initiate in a Sufi order (*ṭarīqah*: plural *ṭuruq*). The term "Sufi" is properly reserved for one who has reached the end of the spiritual path; "the Sufi is not created" (*aṣ-Ṣūfī lam yukhlaq*) according to the Ḥadīth. The origin of this use of the word *faqīr* is found in the Koran (47:38): "God is the Rich and you are the poor (*fuqarā'*)".

The word *faqīr* means to aspire to spiritual poverty or detachment (*faqr*, "poverty") which is a *vacare deo*, an emptying of the soul for God. (Cf. Matthew 5:3: "Blessed are the poor in spirit: for theirs is the kingdom of heaven.") In the Near East the Persian word *darwīsh* (dervish), with the same literal meaning, is often used in place of *faqīr*.

Al-Hujwīrī said:

It is not, however, the quantity of money that makes the moneyed man. No one who recognizes poverty as better than money is a moneyed man, though he be a king; and a man who does not believe in poverty is a moneyed man, however poor he is.

To many in the West the word in its form *fakir* has come to mean a public performer of stunts or magic, which is a deformation of its true meaning. *See* FAQR; MUTABĀRĪKŪN; SĀLIK; SUFISM.

Faqr (lit. "poverty"). Poverty, both material and spiritual. In the context of religion and especially mysticism, the idea and the word are very important. This is the virtue of spiritual poverty, detachment, and an emptiness making way for God's presence. It is the great spiritual virtue of the Prophet in relation to God. Among the mystics *faqr* is the central virtue, emblematic of all the virtues. On the one hand the Koran states: "and surely Remembrance of God is greatest" (*wa ladhikru-Llāhi akbar*); on the other, the Sufis say: "without *faqr* ("spiritual poverty") there is no *dhikr*" ("Remembrance" or "Invocation of God", the central act in the spiritual method of the Sufis).

Jesus says in Matthew 5:3: "Blessed are the poor in spirit: for theirs is the kingdom of heaven." *Faqr* is also the emptiness and removal of obstacles to theophany in the Biblical formulation in Isaiah and Matthew: "The voice of one crying in the wilderness, Prepare ye the way of the Lord, make his paths straight" (Matthew 3:3). A comparison may also be made, in another sense, to the doctrine of *kenosis* (Gr. "emptying", from *kenos*, "empty"); the emptying of self by Jesus, or the emptying of one nature in order to take on another (Phil. 2:7). *See* FAQĪR; IBN al-WAQT; IḤSĀN; SUFISM.

al-Farābī, Abū Naṣr Muḥammad ibn Tarkhān (c. *257-339*/870-950). A philosopher of the Islamic School, which integrates the doctrines of Plato and Aristotle into a single point of view. In Europe he was called al-Farabius (and also Avenasser). Among the Muslims he was called *al-mu'allim ath-thānī*, "the second teacher", after Aristotle, whose works had become available in Arabic thanks to translations made at the Academy of the Caliph al-Ma'mun in Baghdad.

Al-Farābī was of Turkish origin and was born in Turkestan; he studied in Baghdad, also traveled in Syria and Egypt, and taught in Aleppo where he carried on his studies thanks to a pension he received from the Sultan. He died in Damascus. Some of his works on Aristotle were translated into Latin in the Middle Ages; a universal thinker, he exerted a great influence on European thought. The philosopher-physician Ibn Sīnā credited al-Farābī with giving him the first keys that opened the way to his understanding Aristotle.

Al-Farābī, like al-Kindī, and virtually all

Muslim philosophers, also drew upon Neoplatonism for his metaphysics; and he developed al-Kindī's ideas further. Al-Farābī made several distinctions regarding the Intellect (the extension of Being into the center of man). He divided the Intellect into:

1. the "active Intellect" (*al-'aql al-fā'il*; "Intellectus agens"), which is the *nous* of Plotinus and the *logos* of philosophy, or the world of ideas of Plato.

2. The "potential Intellect" (*al-'aql al-hayūlānī*; "Intellectus in potentia"), the latent capacity to acquire eternal truths which subsist in the active Intellect.

3. The "acquired Intellect" (*al-'aql al-mustafād*; "Intellectus acquisitus"), learned knowledge.

Al-Farābī developed the terminology of Arab scholasticism by drawing upon the Koran, a terminology that was to be adapted into Latin and later adapted by St. Thomas Aquinas. Al-Farābī devised terms for necessary and contingent Being, act and potency, substance and accident, essence and existence, matter and form.

Al-Farābī also adapted the theories of Plato's *Republic* in his *Risālah fī Arā' Ahl al-Madīnah al-faḍīlah* and his *al-Siyyāsah al-Madaniyyah* ("Statecraft") but, naturally, as a Muslim, saw the ideal state in the past, and in *al-madinah al-faḍīlah* ("the virtuous city") he assigned to revelation the same role as Plato did to Poetry, while the perfect rule was that of the Prophet himself. He was himself a musician, a flute-player, and wrote an influential work on Music, *Kitāb al-Musīqa*, in which he drew analogies between music and mathematics. *See* BEING; al-KINDĪ; PHILOSOPHY.

Farā'iḍī Movement (often written *Farā'izī*). A political and religious reformist movement founded in Bengal at the begining of the 19th century by Sharī'at Allāh, and developed by his son Dūdhū Mīyān. It operated as a secret society of the Muslim peasantry and resisted the oppression of the *zamindars* or landowners. Its founder had lived a considerable time in Arabia and seems to have been inspired by Wahhabism. Extirpating Hindu influence from Islam in India was one of its guiding principles and it exhibited the kind of Machiavellian pragmatism and willingness to use coercion that characterized a number of movements then and since that used Islam as the vehicle for acquiring political power. The Farā'iḍī movement declined after the death of the founder's son around 1860.

Farāmūsh Khāneh. A secret society founded in Teheran in the middle of the 19th century. Because it sounds like the Persian word for forgetting, this has been called the "house of forgetfulness" but, in fact, it was a Masonic lodge (Freemasonry is *faramāsūniyyah* from the French *Franc-Maçon*) It was founded by Mirza Malkom Khān (1833-1908), a Perso-Armenian journalist, adventurer-entrepreneur, and charlatan. This lodge, unlike subsequent ones, may not have had any formal connection with any European lodge and was abolished by royal decree in 1861. The Grand Master was to be the monarch (as is the case of Freemasonry in Sweden) and the direction was to lie in the hands of Qajar princes, but Malkom Khān wanted to use the lodge for modernist reform and for his own purposes.

Masonic lodges exist throughout the Islamic world today. In Israel a Masonic lodge may include Jews, Muslims, and Christians, reminiscent of the way that Templars and Isma'ilis met in their day. The notion of the "Great Architect of the Universe" actually originated in Iran in an apocalyptical doctrine where the *Ban* or "Great Architect" prepared a grave to imprison the power of darkness after the destruction of the universe in a fire lasting 1,468 years.

Faraqlīṭ. Arabic rendering of the word "Paraclete", from John 16:7: "...And I will send you the Paraclete". This is understood by Muslims to mean the Prophet. The word "Paraclete" recalls the Arabic word *faraqa*, "to distinguish" (between truth and unreality); thus a symbolic (not an etymological) meaning of "distinguisher" has been attributed to the word *faraqlīt*. (The practice of assigning or discovering symbolic etymologies is common in all traditional thinking. It assumes that any word has meaning in its very "form" as sound, even if the word comes from a completely foreign language. Traditional thinking looks upon this form or appearance, and its resemblance to known words, not as being arbitrary, but rather as a providential expression of the word's true sense. Thus, traditional etymology does not concern itself with the history of a word, and analysis into its "causal" origins, but takes it as it appears and sees in it something like a "revelation". It seeks to recognize a resonance of thought in the immediate shape of the word. The usefulness of this kind of interpretation depends upon how much intuition and understanding is brought to it by the interpreter. The process mimics the development of language itself. In India, this kind of symbolical, sometimes mystical, "etymological" interpretation is called, in Sanskrit, *nirukta*.

There is an analogy between this sense of *Faraqlīṭ* and a name given to the Koran: the *Furqan*, which means "the Criterion", or "the Distinction" – "between truth and falsehood". *See* BIBLE.

al-Farazdaq (d. *115*/733) Poet who had satirical contests (*naqa'id*) with another poet, Jarir.

Farḍ The obligations God places upon man, such as witnessing to the truth, prayer, fasting, and so on. In most schools of law the term is synonymous with *wājib* ("duty"). However, the Ḥanafīs draw a distinction between *farḍ* and *wājib*. For them *farḍ* is a Divinely instituted obligation whose omission is sin, and *wājib* is an obligation imposed by law, thus indirectly; in this case the omission of what is *wājib* may not necessarily be sin.

A further distinction is made by the *sharī'ah* in general regarding *farḍ* itself: there is *farḍ al-'ayn*, or essential obligation which is incumbent upon all, and *farḍ al-kifāyah*, an obligation which is acquitted in the name of all, as long as it is performed by some. Obligations such as visiting the sick, returning a greeting, fighting holy war, assisting in a funeral procession, are fulfilled in regards of those confronted with the duty as long as a minimum, a specified sufficient number of respondents according to the case, fulfill them.

Fard (lit. "solitary"; pl. *afrād*). The esoteric possibility exists that a man be illumined spontaneously with a transcendent spiritual truth, without following a path or a spiritual master. Such a "solitary" (*fard*) may not even be affiliated to a particular revealed religion. If the *fard* is outside a tradition, the personal "revelation" is, so to speak, not transmissible, being individual and not destined for a collectivity.

If the *fard* is within a tradition and his illumination is the fulfillment of that tradition's possibilities of inner realization, it is nonetheless unlikely that it can be taught in its fullness to others, although the person is certainly a witness to the truth. Since the solitary has followed no specific way and used no spiritual means to obtain it, his illumination, which is often sudden, remains personal. A *fard* is the recipient of an exceptional destiny, which can only occur in extraordinary circumstances, usually where normal access to revelations and teachings is prevented.

The doctrine of the *fard* is analogous to the Catholic doctrine of spontaneous baptism, or baptism by the Holy Ghost, without human intermediary. *See* al-KHIḌR; SHAYKH.

Far(i)sī (from *Fars*, a region of Persia). Persian; the language, and the derived adjective.

Fast (Ar. *Ṣawm*). The Prophet recommended fasting as a spiritual discipline. It was taken up by the early Muslims so enthusiastically that finally the Prophet had to curtail it because excessive fasting by the Companions in Medina was making them physically weak. In addition to the fasting of the month of Ramaḍān from dawn to sunset, there are many other optional fast days in the Islamic calendar. Some occur regularly every month, and some are scattered through the year. These fast days are Sunnah, or the example set by the Prophet. The Prophet said: "He is not a good Muslim who eats his fill and leaves his neighbor hungry."

Fasting may be undertaken as a penance, for breaking an oath, and the like, and as a substitute for some other obligation. At first, fasting on the day of 'Āshūrā' was obligatory but, with the institution of Ramaḍān, it became only voluntary. *See* RAMAḌĀN.

Fatalism, *see* MAKTUB; QADRIYYAH; KISMET.

Fatawa 'Alamgīriyyah. A collection of *fatāwā* (sing. *fatwa*), or opinions and legal precedents made by jurists in the Moghul empire. It is named after the Emperor 'Alamgīr in whose reign the collection was made in the *12th*/18th century. The *Fatāwā 'Alamgīriyyah* became a fundamental source for Muslim law in India. Also called *al-Fatāwā al-Hindiyyah* ("Indian Jurisprudence").

Fātiḥah (lit. "the opening" chapter and also, by implication, "the victorious" chapter). The *Fātiḥah* is the name of the sūrah which is placed first in the Koran, although the first sūrah to be revealed was Sūrah 96, named *Iqra'* ("recite"). The *Fātiḥah* is the verse of the Koran which is recited in each standing station of the canonical prayer (*ṣalāh*). The *Fātiḥah* – along with a minimum of twelve Koranic verses, including Sūrah 112, named *al-Ikhlāṣ* ("Purity") – is the required minimum that every Muslim must memorize in Arabic. The *Fātiḥah* is often called *as-saba'ah al-mathani* (the "seven oft-repeated verses").

The *Fātiḥah* is the essence of the Koran and sums up man's relation to God.

Bismi Llāhi-r-Raḥmāni-r-Raḥīm
In the name of God, the Merciful, the Compassionate
al-Hamdu li-Llāhi Rabbi-l-'Ālamīn
Praise to God Lord of the Worlds
ar-Raḥmāni-r-Raḥīm
The Merciful, the Compassionate
Māliki yawmi-d-dīn
King of the Day of Judgement
Iyyāka na'budu wa iyyāka nastaī'n
You alone we worship, you alone we beseech
Ihdinā-ṣ-ṣirāṭa-l-mustaqīm
Lead us in the straight path
sirāṭa-lladhīna 'an'amta 'alayhim
The path of those upon whom is your grace
Ghayri-l-maghḍūbi 'alayhim
Not of those upon whom is your wrath
wa lā-d-ḍāllīn
nor the astray.
Āmīn.
Amen.

Apart from its central place in the canonical, or ritual, prayer, the *Fātiḥah* is frequently recited as part of a *du'ā'*, or individual and spontaneous prayer. It is also recited individually or in a group upon marriage, on visiting a holy place, at a funeral, or in any number of circumstances in which a *du'ā'* prayer is appropriate. The *Fātiḥah* is always concluded by saying *āmīn* ("Amen").

Fāṭimah. One of the three daughters of the Prophet, whose mother was Khadījah, the Prophet's first wife. The Prophet commended Fāṭimah's character, calling her one of the four exemplary women that he extolled in history, and she is usually referred to as *Fāṭimah az-zahrā'* ("Fāṭimah the resplendent").

She married the Prophet's cousin 'Alī ibn Abī Ṭālib, who became the fourth Caliph; and their sons Ḥasan and Ḥusayn are the ancestors of the *sharīfs*, the descendants of the Prophet. For the Shī'ites, certain descendants of 'Alī and Fāṭimah through the line of Ḥusayn are Imāms, in the special Shī'ite sense of the term, which is that of divinely empowered spiritual leaders. A third son of 'Alī and Fāṭimah, Muḥsin, died in infancy.

Fāṭimah died six months after the Prophet's death and is buried in the *al-Baqī'* cemetery in Medina. (A sepulchre called Fāṭimah's Tomb is located near the tomb of the Prophet in the Prophet's mosque. Some, notably Shī'ites, believe this sepulchre to hold her body, but that is unlikely, despite the name, and it is far more probable that the body is actually in the nearby *al-Baqī'* cemetery.) She is held in great reverence by the Sunnīs as well as by the Shī 'ites. *See* AHL al-KISĀ'; MUḤAMMAD; SHARĪF.

Fāṭimids (*297-567*/909-1171). The Ismā'īlī dynasty which founded Cairo as its capital in *358*/969, and which ruled an empire extending from Palestine to Tunisia. The Fāṭimid rulers called themselves Caliphs, thus laying claim to supreme political and spiritual authority in Islam in rivalry to the 'Abbasids of Baghdad. Their name, Fāṭimid, represents a claim to be descended from the Prophet through his daughter Fāṭimah, and her husband 'Alī, the Prophet's cousin; but this claim has been frequently questioned. Contemporaries of the Fāṭimids repudiated it by impugning the authenticity of the Fāṭimid genealogy in a manifesto formulated in Baghdad in *402*/1011 by 'Alids and jurists; historians, ancient and modern, have largely concurred in this repudiation.

The Fāṭimids were Ismā'īlīs, direct descendants of the early Shī'ites; from whom the Twelve-Imām Shī'ites are an offshoot. Other rival Shī'ite groups existed or had existed, including those who rallied around a descendant of 'Alī by another wife known as "al-Ḥanafiyyah", whose son, Muḥammad ibn al-Ḥanafiyyah became the Imām of this sect. The choice of the name "Fāṭimid" may reflect the desire to establish a clear distinction between themselves and other Shī'ites of the Ḥanafiyyah line, or more likely, an attempt to identify with Fāṭimah a female divinity from the pantheon of the Seveners such as the "Mother of the Living".

Propaganda disseminated in North Africa made much of a prophecy contained in the Ḥadīth to the effect that a time would come in which "the Sun would rise in the West". But this "Ḥadīth" and those concerning the Mahdī were clearly invented for this very purpose. Indeed, the claim was rather a challenge to the authority of Islam because the Koran says:

> Bethink thee of him who had an argument with Abraham about his Lord, because Allah had given him the kingdom; how, when Abraham had said: "My Lord is He Who giveth life and causeth death," he answered: "I give life and cause death." Abraham said: "Lo! Allah causeth the sun to rise in the East so do thou cause it to come up from the West." Thus was the disbeliever abashed. And Allah guideth not wrongdoing folk.

A singularly successful *dā'i*, or propagandist, of the Ismā'īlī organization, Abū 'Abd Allāh Ḥusayn, also called ash-Shī'ī ("the Shī'ite"), established the dynasty. He was first sent on a mission from Basra in Iraq to North Africa, where he persuaded the Ketama Berbers to accept his chief, 'Ubayd Allāh, as their religious and political leader. The Berbers of North Africa had in many instances been Christian before the recent spread of Islam; it is known that Gnostic sects were active among them, as an expression of resistance to the domination of Rome. In the *2nd*/8th century, at least one of the chiefs, the *Archegos* of the Manichean church at its seat at Madā'in (Ctesiphon-Seleucia) near Baghdad, originally came from North Africa. It is very possible that ash-Shī'ī's remarkable success in converting the Berbers to follow 'Ubayd Allāh was due to the fact that he was calling them to a contemporary version of their old beliefs, now clothed in the form of the newly dominant religion. Perhaps the link between the two was even more direct with 'Ubayd Allāh, already the leader of an existing sect in North Africa, simply returning or settling down again among his followers. Ibn Khaldun said in his history, that the Berbers to whom the missionaries addressed themselves had a *baṭini*, or esoteric religion.

Yet, there is an Ismā'īlī tradition among the Druzes, and in the *Ghāyat al-Mawālid* by al-Khaṭṭab ibn Ḥasan al-Ḥamadānī, a Yemenī *dā'i* (d.*533*/1138), quoted by Bernard Lewis, that 'Ubayd Allāh was not himself the real Imām, but *Imām mustawda'*, a trustee or representative of the real Imām; therefore, it could well be that the real leader remained in the East, whence the propagandists had come, and that the real Imām, that is, the *Imām mustaqarr* ("permanent Imām") only settled in North Africa after his representatives had paved the way for him and assured a smooth transition of the seat of power. Thus the second Fāṭimid Sultan, al-Qā'im, as *Imām mustaqarr*, would be that real leader who took over after 'Ubayd Allāh died in *322*/934, although he may have arrived in North Africa already some time before. There was a Mesopotamian institution: the "substitute king", put upon the throne when omens were exceptionally sombre as seen in the story of Irra-imitti who put a gardener, Enlil-bāni on his throne to preserve the dynasty. (Only Enlil-bāni did not relinquish the throne and instead carried on!)

According to Ibn an-Nadīm, there were scarcely five Manicheans left in Baghdad when he wrote the *Fihrist* in *377*/987. The *Archegos* had disappeared from Baghdad during the reign of the Caliph al-Muqtadir (d. *320*/932) who, like his predecessors, carried on persecutions of Manicheans.

The 'Alid declaration of *402*/1011 said that the Fāṭimids were descended from Daisan, that is, Bardesanes, a philosopher who had lived near Harran. This could not mean that they were his physical, but rather his intellectual, descendants. Now Bardesanes was a forerunner of Mani, and was recognised as such by the Arab scholars of the *5th*/11th century, as he is by scholars today. The mystery of the disappearing *Archegos* may perhaps be resolved as a case of changed identity. In any event, the Persian historian al-Juwayni (d. *682*/1283) affirmed that the Ismā'īlīs were *Mājūs*, and al-Hujwīrī (d. *469*/1077), in the *Kashf al-Maḥjūb*, said this specifically of the Fāṭimids. (For the Muslims, *Mājūs* meant not only Zoroastrianism but also the related Iranian religions and their variants.)

Ash-Shī'ī's propaganda claimed that 'Ubayd Allāh was the *Mahdī*, the Divinely guided leader for the end of time. When, however, 'Ubayd Allāh went to Tunisia from Salāmiyyah in Syria, in response to the enthusiasm of the Berbers that ash-Shī'ī had aroused, he was arrested in

292/905 by the Aghlabid rulers on behalf of the ʿAbbāsid Caliphs of Baghdad and imprisoned in Sijilmassa, in present-day Morocco. By *296*/909 ash-Shīʿī's position had become so strong that he was able to arrange the release of ʿUbayd Allāh, who then took over the leadership and soon had ash-Shīʿī put to death for his troubles.

ʿUbayd Allāh then built himself a capital called al-Mahdiyyah in Ifriqiya (Tunisia); in *358*/969 the general Jawhar conquered Egypt in the name of the Fāṭimid ruler al-Muʿizz li-Dīni-Llāh and founded Cairo (*al-Qahirah*), which became the new capital with the cryptic name "*The Victorious [city] of the Exalter of the Divine Religion*".

From here the Empire grew to include Palestine, while Ismāʿīlī propaganda was extended even further through a secret network of agitators. The reign of the Fāṭimid al-Ḥākim (d. *411*/1021) was notable for his erratic, if not actually insane, behavior. He had the church of the Holy Sepulchre in Jerusalem destroyed – one of the events which led to the Crusades – and he had himself publicly declared to be God – a claim he was obliged by the resultant uproar to retract. A similar claim, perhaps less publicly, had been made for al-Muʿizz, the seventh Fāṭimid Imām according to his alleged descent from Muḥammad ibn Ismāʿīl, the son of Jafar aṣ-Ṣādiq, and the ruler who established himself in Cairo. The Fāṭimid Caliphs were the Imāms of the Ismāʿīlīs, according to whose doctrines the Imām is a Divine hypostasis. In the case of al-Ḥākim his supporters had gone too far in making public, to his Sunnī subjects in Egypt, the deepest tenets of the sect. In the Levant, however, successful propagandizing on his behalf among remote Ismāʿīlī groups by a Turk called Darazī led to the creation of the Druzes.

In *487*/1094 a coup by the general of the armies, al-Afḍal Shāhinshāh (son of the general Badr al-Jamālī, an Armenian who came to Cairo after the Byzantine defeat at Manzikert, and who built the present walls and gates of Cairo for the Fāṭimids) put the younger heir, al-Mustaʿlī, on the throne. Badr al-Jamālī had married his daughter to al-Mustaʿlī in order to consolidate power for himself. Nizar, the eldest son, was put into prison, where he died; his followers attributed to him a son and even a grandson in order that his spiritual succession be kept alive; but as far as the Mustaʿlīs (the followers of al-Mustaʿlī) are concerned, if there were a son and grandson, these also died in prison.

This disruption of the succession went against the religious expectations of the committed Ismāʿīlīs in that the function of Imām was more or less Divine. Thus the succession of al-Mustaʿlī in *487*/1094, against the superior claims of his elder brother Nizār, confounded many Ismāʿīlīs and occasioned a schism. A Persian Ismāʿīlī named Ḥasan aṣ-Ṣabbāḥ had come to Cairo; upon his return to Persia he spread propaganda in the name of the expected Imām, Nizār. The sudden change of power in Egypt left aṣ-Ṣabbāḥ, already committed to promoting Nizār, little choice but to repudiate al-Mustaʿlī. It is through Ḥasan aṣ-Ṣabbāḥ that a Nizārī branch of Ismāʿīlīs survived and flourished. The followers of aṣ-Ṣabbāḥ took over the fortress of Alamūt in northern Persia, probably already in Ismāʿīlī hands, as the region had long been a stronghold of sects of ancient Iranian filiation.

This fortress became the Nizārī center of power. In Medieval Europe these Nizārī Ismāʿīlīs were called the Assassins, a name they had been given by the Crusaders. In the East they were known by many different names including *Taʿlīmiyyah* ("the people of the teaching"), and by this name the theologian al-Ghazālī (d. *505*/1111) disputed their religious ideas.

This split created the Nizārī and the Mustaʿlī branches of the Ismāʿīlīs. The son of al-Mustaʿlī, al-Amīr, succeeded his father as ruler in Egypt as an infant, and came first under the tutelage of al-Afḍal. Later, having had al-Afḍal put to death (*515*/1121), al-Amīr was himself assassinated (*525*/1130). This time the followers of al-Amīr claimed that he had a son who would have inherited and perpetuated the spiritual function in that line; this putative son was called aṭ-Ṭayyib, and the Mustaʿlī faction believe that there exist descendants of aṭ-Ṭayyib living in secret, or that, like the Hidden Imām of the Twelve-Imām Shīʿites, and al-Ḥākim for the Druzes, aṭ-Ṭayyib is alive in a principial state from which he will return. As far as the others were concerned, the putative son, aṭ-Ṭayyib, was assassinated along with his father. The assassination of al-Amīr was carried out by Nizārīs presumably under the orders of Ḥasan aṣ-Ṣabbāḥ in Persia.

After the death of al-Amīr, Ismāʿīlism in Egypt disintegrated. There it had been the arcane religion of the ruling class and had not been shared by the majority of subjects who were Sunnī. Smaller and smaller groups followed different Imāms in defiance of the Fāṭimid ruler's claims. By *567*/1171 the Fāṭimids had lost power, having, nevertheless, presided over an empire noted for its prosperity and cultural achievements. At their highpoint they had posed a serious ideological threat to the 'Abbāsid Empire and called forth the Sunnī reaffirmation embodied in the Saljuqs. The Fāṭimids founded the renowned al-Azhar University, today the most venerable in the Islamic world. Their successors were the Sunnī Ayyūbid dynasty founded by Saladin. Thereupon the Ismā'īlīs disappeared from Egypt, but small groups survived in Syria, Persia and Central Asia; the sect later flourished in India. *See* ASSASSINS; DRUZES; ISMĀ'ĪLĪS; MAHDĪ; QARMATIANS; SEVENERS.

Fatrah (lit. "spiritual lassitude", "a lapse"). **1.** The name given to a period of time between two Prophets, for example, the six centuries between Jesus and Muḥammad.

2. A period in the Prophet's life when no revelations descended upon him, causing him despair.

Fatwa. A published opinion or decision regarding religious doctrine or law made by a recognized authority, often called a mufti. Collections of such decisions, such as the *Fatāwā 'Alamgīriyyah*, a collection made in India under the Moghul Empire, form a code of precedents which guide Judges in the exercise of the law. *See* SHARĪ'AH.

Feddayin, *see* FIDYAH.

Festivals, *see* 'ĀSHŪRĀ'; CALENDAR; 'ĪD al-AḌḤĀ; 'ĪD al-FIṬR; 'ĪD al-GHADIR; LAYLAT al-BARA'AH; LAYLAT al-QADR, MAWLID an-NABĪ; MUḤARRAM; NAW ROZ; RAMAḌĀN.

Fez. One of the "imperial cities", or former capitals, of Morocco. The Merinid dynasty (*592-956*/1196-1549) ruled from Fez. The city was founded by Mawlay Idris II in *193*/809, and grew with influxes of emigrants from Cordova (who created the Andalusian quarter), and from Kairouan (creating the Qarawiyyīn quarter). Fez became a center of culture and learning when the Qarawiyyīn university-mosque was founded, the gift of a wealthy woman.

The old city of Fez, with its walls, gates, palaces, souks, *funduqs*, *madrasahs*, and mosques, is still largely intact, constituting an extraordinary living heritage. The narrow streets and the hilly site make motor traffic impossible in most of the old town. Although the crafts have largely disappeared or lost their authentic nature, Fez is still a singularly remarkable example of a large city which has kept the aspect of a medieval town. Until recently, the countryside began abruptly at the walls of the old city. This was the typical stamp of the ancient city, the distinction, so clear in the traditional mind, of the civilized world as only a small island surrounded by the vast natural world of God's making.

In addition to the Andalusian and Qarawiyyīn mosques (the latter is one of the largest in the world and can accommodate some 10,000 worshipers), there are several Madrasahs or schools of higher learning. These are now monuments, no longer used as schools, although they are still places of prayer. The most famous are the *'Attārīn*, the perfumers' madrasah built by that guild, and the *Abū-l-Ḥasan* built by a Sultan, who when presented with the exorbitant bill for its construction, was taken aback, thought a moment and then paraphrased an old Arabic poem: "What matters the expense as long as it is beautiful."

Fez has a rich tradition of many Saints and scholars that have walked its streets, and the tombs of Saints make Fez a city of pilgrimage. At the center of the city is the tomb of the founder, Mawlay Idris II, a mosque with a roof of green Fez tiles. This is one of the most important sanctuaries in Morocco. Near the city is the *Jabal Zalāgh* where the great Abū Madyan, as an impoverished young man, would go and pray at night. His life, and that of others who gave the city its reputation, is recounted in the collection of the lives of Saints of Fez called the *Ṣalawāt al-Anfus*.

Fidā'ī (lit. "man of sacrifice"). Someone who gives up his life for a cause; origin of the word *fidā'iyūn*. *See* FIDYAH.

Fidā'iyūn *see* FIDYAH.

Fidyah (lit. "expiation by sacrifice", "redemption"). The expiation of faults, spiritual errors, or other shortcomings by some such means as offering a sacrifice, fasting or feeding the poor (cf. Koran 2:192). Fidyah can also mean to give up one's life for a cause; the word *fidā'iyūn* ("men of sacrifice") has its root in this. *See* FIDĀ'Ī.

Fiqh. Jurisprudence. The science which deals with the observance of rituals, the principles of the Five Pillars, and social legislation. There are four schools of *fiqh*, known as the four Sunnī Schools of Law (Ar. *madhhab*, pl. *madhāhib*). In addition, the Shī'ites and the Khārijites have their own schools. Each school has its fundamental written treatises. Someone who is versed in *fiqh* is called a *faqīh*. *See* SCHOOLS of LAW; SHARĪ'AH.

al-Fiqh al-Akbar (lit. "the greatest (ie. Supreme) *Fiqh*" (ie. collection of Canonic Law)). At one time, the term (*al-Fiqh al-Akbar*) meant theology before the development of theology (*kalām*) as such. *Al-Fiqh al-Akbar* is also the name of several creeds of which the following, by Abū Ḥanīfah (d. *150*/767), is the most famous.

> **1.** We do not consider anyone to be an infidel on account of sin; nor do we deny his faith.
> **2.** We enjoin what is just and prohibit what is evil.
> **3.** What reaches you could not possibly have missed you; and what misses you could not possibly have reached you.
> **4.** We disavow none of the Companions of the Messenger of God; nor do we adhere to any of them exclusively.
> **5.** We leave the question of 'Uthmān and 'Alī to God, who knows the secret and hidden things.
> **6.** Insight in matters of religion is better than insight in matters of knowledge and law.
> **7.** Difference of opinion in the Community is a token of Divine mercy.
> **8.** Who believes all that he is bound to believe except that he says, I do not know whether Moses and Jesus (Peace be upon them) do or do not belong to the Messengers, is an infidel.
> **9.** Who says I do not know whether God is in heaven or on earth is an infidel.
> **10.** Who says I do not know about punishment in the tomb, belongs to the sect of *Jahmites* who go to perdition.

The first article above is a specific refutation of the doctrine of the Khārijites concerning sin, and other articles are responses to the assertions of various sects. The *al-Fiqh al-Akbar* is an important milestone in the development of theology. Statements one to seven succinctly give a wide definition of who is a Muslim; statements eight to ten draw a line and say, in effect, that wide as the definition may be, there is nonetheless a limit beyond which lies error.

This affirmation of a consensus marked the end of a first period of theological turmoil during which different opinions emerged as completely hostile one to another. The Khārijites set an example when they asserted the apostasy of all who did not share their opinion. In the early phase of Islam, each opinion could be taken as excluding the others to such a degree that the holders of another point of view were readily called, if not apostates, then heretics. The *al-Fiqh al-Akbar* of Abū Ḥanīfah marked a new phase in theological polemics by establishing the principle that divergences of belief, within limits, are possible and acceptable. In other words, Islam is here defined as large enough to hold a variety of views, and that rigid homogeneity is not essential to orthodoxy. *See* CREEDS; KALĀM; KHĀRIJITES.

Firāsah. Intuitions about the hidden nature of things, events, and people. The capacity for *firāsah* may be a spontaneous gift in someone, or the result of heightened awareness resulting from spiritual discipline.

Ibn 'Ata'Allāh says in his *Ḥikam*:

> Sometimes He reveals to you the invisible domain of His Realm but veils you from knowing the secrets of servants.
>
> Whoever gets to know the secrets of servants without patterning himself on the divine mercifulness (*ar-raḥmah al-ilāhiyyah*), finds his knowledge a tribulation (*fitnah*) and a cause for drawing evil (*al-wabal*) upon himself.

See KARĀMĀT.

Fir'awn, *see* PHARAOH.

Firdaws. A Koranic appellation for one of the paradises deriving either from the Greek *paradeisos* or the Middle Persian *paridaiza* meaning originally an "enclosure" and hence an "enclosed garden". *See* al-JANNAH.

Firdawsī (Abū-l-Qāsim Manṣūr) (*328-411*/940-1020). The poet, born in Ṭūṣ, who composed the Persian national epic, the "Book of Kings", (*Shahnameh*), recounting the history of the Persian people from mythic times until the Arab conquest. The poem draws upon the records of Persian history compiled in the times of Anushirvan (Chosroe I) and orally preserved by the old landed families known as *dihqans*.

Abū-l-Qāsim was called "Firdawsī" by the Sultan Maḥmūd of Ghaznah, who said the poet's compositions turned the court into an assembly of paradise (*firdaws*). Firdawsī composed the *Shahnameh*, consisting of 60,000 verses, for this ruler, and, according to tradition, spent thirty-five years on it. Disappointed with his pay, Firdawsī satirized the Sultan, and fled into exile where he composed his poem *Yūsuf and Zulaykha*. He later returned, was reconciled with the Sultan, but died before he could receive his reward: a treasure for him as full payment arrived on the backs of camels at one gate of the city of Ṭūṣ, as his corpse was brought out for burial through another.

Firmān. An Ottoman or Persian royal rescript. The term is also used for religious messages sent by the Aga Khan to his communities.

Fitfir. The name in Arabic of Potiphar, the great man of Egypt into whose household Joseph (Yūsuf) was sold as a slave. When Joseph was freed from prison after interpreting the Pharaoh's dreams, he assumed Fitfir's office. Because of a simple orthographic confusion the name is sometimes said to be Qitfir.

Fitnah (lit. "rebellion, strife"). Any sedition or rebellion against the rightful ruler is *fitnah*. Widespread *fitnah* is one of the traditional signs of the impending Day of Judgement.

Fiṭrah (lit. "primordial nature"). The primordial norm; a harmony between man, creation, and God, such as existed between God and Adam in the Garden. Islam sees itself as the restoration of the religion of Abraham (*millat Ibrāhīm*), which itself is a reconsecration and a prolongation of the religion of Adam as primordial man after his fall, and reconciliation with God. The concept of *fiṭrah*, the primordial norm, is at once the measure of truth in our actions and being, and at the same time the quality of harmony between ourselves and the cosmos. It corresponds exactly to the Hindu notion of universal *dharma*, or to the Chinese *Tao*. *See* CHILDREN.

Five Divine Presences (Ar. *al-ḥaḍarāt al-ilāhiyyah al-khams*). A metaphysical doctrine of the degrees of reality of which there are different versions. The following schema, according to the terminology of Abū Ṭālib al-Makki (d. *386*/996), is the most systematic: in descending order, the five are: *Hāhūt*, Ipseity, the Godhead, the Essence, Absolute Reality; *Lāhūt*, the Reality of Being, namely, the Divinity or Personal God; *jabarūt*, the world of Angels; *malakūt*, the subtle world; and *nāsūt*, the corporeal, or human world.

The Islamic development of the doctrine was evidently influenced by Neoplatonism. It is found in Plotinus and Dionysus the Areopagite (so-called pseudo-Dionysus); however, equivalent teachings are also found in Hinduism, Taoism, and Buddhism. As a universal metaphysical doctrine it reflects the nature of things, and is no more the creation of human thought than the rings of Saturn are the creation of Galileo.

The doctrine of the Five Divine Presences figures prominently among Sufis of the school of Ibn 'Arabī. However, it is to be found, in one form or another, wherever metaphysical considerations arise. Different versions exist, as in the *Ihyā' 'Ulūm ad-Dīn* ("the Revival of the Religious Sciences") of al-Ghazālī, or in the *al-Insān al-Kāmil* ("the Perfect Man") of 'Abd al-Karīm al-Jīlī.

The name of the first Presence, *Hāhūt*, is derived from the word *Huwa*, or "He" (a Divine Name, the Name of the Essence, *adh-Dhāt*), denoting the Ipseity. The Ipseity is That from which nothing can be taken away and nothing added. It cannot be divided; nothing is outside It; "it is not beautiful on one side and ugly on another" – It is beautiful from all sides – there is no privation in It; of which the Voice in the burning bush said: "I am That I am." Of which Sufism says: *lā ana wa lā anta: hua* "not I and not you: He." The Sūrah of Sincere Religion (112) defines Ipseity thus:

> Say: 'He is God, One,
> God, the Everlasting Refuge,
> who has not begotten, and has not been begotten,
> and equal to Him is not any one.'

This is the Absolute, to which the Name *Allāh* properly belongs. *Hāhūt* is often called "Beyond-Being". Plato, in the *Parmenides*, calls It "the One Who is One". In Vedanta It is *Parabrahman*, or *nirguáa Brahma* ("Brahma beyond Qualities"). It is All-Possibility, non-differentiated and non-determined, indivisibly One, or the Divine Name *al-Aḥad* ("The One"). Because *Hāhūt* is Absolute, and All-Possibility, It is also the Possibility, necessarily, of Its own negation or Its own "limitation". This is the invisible root of manifestation or creation, a "negation" of the Absolute. That is, the Absolute "limits" Itself as Its own Absoluteness requires and thus creates the world, which is apparently "other" than God, a "seeming negation" of the Absolute, nonetheless existing in and of the Absolute. A *ḥadīth qudsī* ("God speaking through the Prophet") puts it thus: "I was a hidden treasure; I willed to be known, therefore I created the world." The ontological bridge between manifestation (the last three presences), and *Hāhūt* is the differentiation and determination of the latter in the second Divine Presence, *Lāhūt*. The first chapter of the Tao Te Ching says: "Nameless is the origin of Heaven and Earth. The Named is the Mother of All Things ('the myriad creatures')."

Lāhūt: from the word *al-ilāh*, or "Divinity". *Lāhūt* is Being and "Personal God"; or as Plato says: "The One Who Is." In Vedanta, *Lāhūt* is *saguáa Brahma* ("Brahma Qualified"), or *Īśvara*. In relation to the Absoluteness of *Hāhūt*, this Divine Presence has been called the "relatively" Absolute. "Absolute" because seen from "below", from the point of view of existence, it is not different from the Absolute; "Relative" inasmuch as none of its distinct possibilities are absolute in themselves; they are delimited by other possibilities. Nevertheless, *Lāhūt* is Divine because everything in creation is contained within It, and Its differentiations, while not absolute, are nevertheless "perfect".

The Divine Name *ar-Raḥīm*, "the Compassionate", or the "Mercy-Giving" is a Name of the Qualities (*aṣ-ṣifāt*); it is therefore a Name of Being, or *Lāhūt*. It is act; It bestows mercy; It is event and relationship between God and creature. As one Quality among others It excludes other Names or Qualities and is different from *al-Ghafūr* ("The Forgiver"), and *al-Muntaqim* ("The Avenger"), for example. *Ar-Raḥmān* ("The Merciful One"), on the other hand, is a Name of the Essence (*Hāhūt*); It is God "Merciful in Himself". Yet *ar-Raḥmān*, like *al-Quddūs* ("The Holy One") as a Name of the Essence is inherent in all the Names, even in *al-Mumīt* ("The Slayer"). This reflects the difference between God the Absolute and God as Being. The Names of the Qualities, or of *Lāhūt*, may exclude each other but the Names of the Essence may not.

A polarization takes place within Being into pure act (determining power) and pure receptivity (and infinitude); Aristotle's *eidos* and *hyle*. The latter word has found its way into Arabic as *al-hayūlā*, with the same meaning of "substance" (also called *al-jawhar*, "the jewel"). Pure receptivity ("substance") accepts determining power (act or "bundles of qualities" – "forms" so to speak, in the abstract, the capacity to define distinct entities). From this union of power or essence (essence on a different level from that of *Hāhūt*) and substance, existence springs forth in the succeeding Presences, and possibilities become manifestation. In denoting this complementarity the Scholastics of Medieval Europe called this essence (on the level of Being) "form"; substance, they called "materia". In Vedanta this polarity is called *Puruṣa* (for the pole of power) and *Prakrti* (for the pole of receptivity). In Taoism, it is Yang (power) and Yin (receptivity-infinitude). The Koranic terms are *al-qalam al-a l'ā* (the "supreme pen") for act or power, and *al-lawḥ al-maḥfūẓ* ("the inviolate tablet") for universal substance or receptivity.

Many terms are used for this polarity, even within the same tradition, because this complementarity within the First Principle may be viewed in many perspectives. Thus the *qalam* ("power") seen from a different angle is *al-'aql al-awwal* ("first intellect"), also called *ar-ruḥ al-kullī* ("universal spirit"). The *lawḥ* ("substance") is also *at-ṭabīah al-kulliyyah* ("universal nature"), or again, *al-unsūr al-azām* ("the supreme element"). Terms multiply as the complementarity is considered in its refractions from Being down to the macrocosm, and finally to the microcosm, or man himself.

In man, the same complementarity reverberates as male and female, and is also reflected within the individual. The active pole of the individual is *al-aql al-fā'il*, the active Intellect", while the pole of receptivity is the *nafs*, or his or her soul. (*See* al-AQL; NAFS.)

The pole of receptivity, universal substance, is also reflected in the microcosm by the physical body, and, in particular, by the female body.

The structure of man mirrors superior realities. The individual himself, the content of that structure, a personality with its characteristics and its destiny, is a possibility. But while the individual is a differentiated possibility in the *Lāhūt*, it is undifferentiated in the *Hāhūt*, and thus it is possible to say that beyond the personality there is the Self; and that there is only one Self; and that all individual beings, on every plane of existence are refractions of that One Self.

Lāhūt (sometimes also called *'Alam al-Izzah*, or "World of Glory"), as the domain of the Names of the Qualities, is Creator in regard to the world, and "Personal" God, or God as "Person", God Who hears prayers, Who slays, Who gives life, Who creates, Who accepts repentance. It should be emphasised that what saves in Islam is the recognition of the Absoluteness of God, *Hāhūt*, and His incomparability; but without God as Creator the world is impossible, and without God as Revealer there is no knowledge.

In confronting the Koranic references to "God's Face", "His Hand", and so forth, which are the traces of Being conceptualized, the solution of Ash'arite theology is acceptance without further inquiry, *bilā kayfa*. Metaphysics, however, cannot be satisfied with such a theologic solution, and must enter into the domain of antinomy, whence the need to recognize that certain contraditions are only apparent in analysis but not in their synthesis, which is on a different plane altogether. *Hāhūt* and *Lāhūt* taken together are the Divinity, or in Vedanta, *Ātman*; that which is below, in the succeeding "Presences", is creation, *al-ḥijāb* (the "veil"), or in Sanksrit, *māyā*. Thus it is within *Lāhūt*, or Being, that the created and uncreated meet. There is a Ḥadīth which says:

> The first thing God created was the pen. He created the tablet and said to the pen: "Write!" And the pen answered: "What shall I write?" He said: "Write My knowledge of My creation till the Day of Resurrection."

The third Presence is the *'ālam al-jabarūt* (the World of Power"; in Vedanta: *vijñānamaya kosha*). It is also the reality which is called the "Throne" (*al-'arsh*). This is the domain of supraformal or Angelic manifestation, which surrounds and contains formal creation, just as it is itself surrounded by Being, and Being by Beyond-Being. This is already part of creation, but is not subject to the same separative conditions as the sensible world. It is the world of Angels; namely "Powers", "Exemplars", "Archetypes", "Thrones". It is also that of the Paradises of the afterlife, with the exception of the Supreme Paradise, the *jannat adh-dhāt*, or "Garden of the Essence".

The *'ālam al-jabarūt* is the level of the created Intellect, or the created Spirit (in Being the Intellect partakes of the uncreated; Meister Eckhart spoke of "something in the soul which is not created and not creatable, and this is the Intellect"). At the "center" of every Presence is a juncture which joins the Presence above it, and partakes of its nature. Without this "juncture", the world would be complete unreality and would not exist. These junctures can be thought of as a vertical axis. This vertical axis, which passes through every state and degree of existence, is symbolized, for example, by the sacred "world" trees of primordial religions, such as Yggdrasil of the Norsemen, and the (non-forbidden) "tree of life" at the center of the Garden of Eden. In the center of the *'ālam al-jabarūt*, the world of Angels, is a domain within creation which reflects the uncreated. This "reflection" seen, so to speak, from the Divine point of view, is an Angel, himself called *Rūḥ* or "Spirit" (Koran 78:38), who is so great that when the Angels stand arrayed, the *Rūḥ* takes up one row unto himself. The Angel *Rūḥ* corresponds to the Metatron of Jewish mystical metaphysics; both derive from the Spenta Mainyu of Zoroastrianism.

The *'ālam al-jabarūt* is thus the created aspect of the *rasūl* ("Messenger of God"), and the created reality of Adam, "true man" or the *al-Insān al-Kāmil*, "the universal", or "perfect man". (The subtle and material worlds correspond to the limitations of ordinary thought and ordinary imagination; the active state of the *al-insān al-Kāmil* is precisely not limited to these, nor, however, is it limited to the *'ālam al-jabarūt*, since in the Koran man is superior to the Angels – whom God instructs to bow to Adam.) (*See* ANGELS.)

The fourth Presence is the *'ālam al-malakūt*, the "World of the Dominion", the subtle, or animic, world. (In Vedanta: *sukshma sharīra*). This is the world of *jinn*, creatures who possess form like man, some of whom incarnate the *'aql* (Intellect) just as man does, and thus possess a "central state". They are therefore capable of Divine knowledge, and upon pain of damnation are compelled to integrate themselves consciously and actively with the superior Presences that confront them upon death, as is man. The revelations that have come into the human world, the *nāsūt*, have also come into the *malakūt*, and are practised there. Islamic dogma specifically holds that there are *jinn* who are Muslim, Christian, and Jewish, and therefore of other religions as well, known to this world and unknown. Man and *jinn* are addressed together in the *Surat ar-Raḥmān* as the "two having weight" (*ath-thaqalān*; Koran 55:31), that is, they possess "form". A band of *jinn*, upon hearing the Prophet recite the Koran in the desert at night on his return journey from Ṭā'if, believed, and came later to Mecca to pledge fealty to the Prophet at the spot which is now called the "Mosque of the Jinn".

> Say: 'It has been revealed to me that a
> company of the jinn gave ear, then they
> said, "We have indeed heard a Koran
> wonderful,
> guiding to rectitude. We believe in it,
> and we will not associate with our Lord
> anyone.
> He – exalted be our Lord's majesty! –
> has not taken to Himself either consort
> or a son.
> The fool among us spoke against God
> outrage,
> and we had thought that men and jinn
> would never speak against God
> a lie."' (Koran 72:1-5)

The subtle, or animic, world is the place of the lower paradises, and also of the infernal states. The Koranic metaphor for this world is the "Footstool" *al-kursī*, which is "vast...comprising the heavens and the earth" (2:257). The subtle world not only surrounds the sensory world, *nāsūt* (which is its "projection" or "solidification", just as it itself is a "projection" from the Presence "above" it), but also permeates it. Consequently, and because it is the very substance of our minds, the *malakūt* and the phenomena associated with it, psychism, magic, and so forth, are often mistaken and substituted for that which is spiritual, enabling the practice of every kind of idolatry. On the other hand, because it is a part of us – or we are a part of it – the complete denial of it, as a world, and finally as "ether", on the part of scientific and humanistic materialism, distorts and stultifies the way in which we perceive and explain the nature of our own world. (The Michelson-Morley experiment assumed that "ether" is physical, which it cannot be, otherwise it would be identical with the physical world which is the next, fifth Presence.) (*See* JINN.)

The fifth Presence is our world, the *nāsūt*, "the World of the Human" also called the *'ālam al-mulk*, "the World of the Kingdom". (In Vedanta: *sthūla sharīra*). This is the familiar sensible, or corporeal, world.

Manifestation, or existence, is the last three Presences. It is conditioned, in our experience, by what some metaphysicians reduced to five qualities: time and space – its "containers" – and form, number, and materia, or matter. Plotinus assigned to existence five conditions; Aristotle assigned to existence ten qualities, or categories (Ar. *al-ma'qūlāt*). In Aristotle, substance is itself one of the categories; as a category it is "created"; at the same time, the word was often used to mean uncreated Substance which is Being itself. Some writers substitute the concept "life", for substance and include therein some of Aristotle's other categories, such as relation. For those authors, "life" can, in a certain sense, be found in everything in this world, including inanimate objects. Whatever the categories, behind them, behind materia and the ephemeral shadows which exist in creation (*khalq*), is the real, immaterial, substance of Being. Jāmi and other Sufi poets and writers say that creatures are "foam" from the waves of the ocean, which is Substance, or Being. This is a poetical paraphrase of the explanation that Muslim philosophers, following in the steps of Aristotle, made of existence, saying that the objects of existence are "accidents" (*a'rāḍ*), which emerge from substance (*al-jawhar*).

Some of the Presences are also called by different names. The *'ālam al-malakūt* is often termed the *'ālam al-mithāl* ("World of Symbols"), and this, our world, is called the *ḥaḍrat ash-shahādah al-muṭlaqah* ("Presence of the totally Manifest"). Other nomenclatures combine two Presences together as in *'ālam al-*

ghayb al-muṭlaq ("the World of the Absolute Unseen"), which is that of the *Hāhūt* and *Lāhūt* together. Or, *ḥaḍrat al-ghayb al-muḍaf* ("the Presence of the Qualified Unseen") which is the *jabarūt* and *malakūt* together. In the vocabulary of a particular author, a name may be transposed to another Presence (especially *jabarūt* for *malakūt*, and vice-versa) which must be understood from context. Some authors introduce further divisions into the Presences. All the Five Presences taken together have been called *al-ḥaḍrah al-jāmi'ah* ("the Total Presence" or "Synthesis of Presences").

In this connection it might be mentioned that, according to the Koranic vocabulary, man is created of clay (*ṭīn*), the *jinn* of fire (*nār*), and the Angels of light (*nūr*). These terms define three modes of existence and correspond to the three *guṅas* (fundamental qualities) of Vedanta. These are tendencies that characterize everything which exists; ultimately they are modes inherent in the receptivity of substance within Being. The earth of man's creation corresponds to the downward tendency towards gross or inferior form which is, in Sanskrit, *tamas* ("gravity", "darkness" "disintegration"); fire to the expansive tendency, *rajas* ("motion", "rhythm", "multiplicity"); and light to the unitive or upward tendency to surpass form, to rejoin Being, *sattva*, ("cohesion", "light", related to the word *sat*, "being", "perfection", "positivity").

These three tendencies are also the modes of existence referred to in the *fātiḥah* as the path of those upon whom is Thy Mercy (*sattva*), not the path of whose upon whom is Thy Anger (*tamas*), nor the astray (*rajas*).

Tamas is the limitative tendency. It gives separate existence and objectifies; it is the heaviness necessary for differentiation. *Tamas* in itself is neutral and necessary. Nevertheless, it is also *tamas, which* when *it touches consciousness* ("the knowledge of good and evil"), inverts the true, the beautiful, and the good, giving birth to evil. It is the first *guṅa* to emerge in the beginning of all cosmic manifestation, and the last to disappear in the end, "On the day when We shall roll up heaven as a scroll is rolled for the writings" (21:104), and when "To Him the angels and the Spirit mount up in a day whereof the measure is fifty thousand years" (70:4).

The beginning of the Chinese *Three Character Rhymed Classic on the Ka'bah*, by an 18th century Muslim named Ma Fu-ch'u is like an introduction to the study of the Five Presences:

> Because there are Heaven and Earth
> the ten thousand creatures are born;
> because there are sun and moon
> Heaven and Earth have light;
> because there is the Sage [the Prophet]
> enlightening teachings arise.
> To hear the teaching of the Sage
> is to deepen knowledge and perception,
> to know the past,
> clearly to understand the future and the present,
> to grasp the origin of Heaven and Earth
> and the source of the myriad creatures,
> to attain to celestial principles
> and to see into the hearts of men;
> it shows us the road we have come by
> and demonstrates the return to Reality:
> it makes us aware of our heart and nature
> and enables us to penetrate ultimate mysteries;
> perpetuated by the wise men of old
> it is enshrined in scriptural classics.
> "The foundation of the Path
> is clearly to acknowledge God,
> not bounded by space
> nor limited by form,
> without end or beginning,
> not to be apprehended by the senses,
> neither near nor far,
> and Uniquely Sublime;
> not empty nothingness
> but Truth and Reality,
> mysterious and hard to fathom,
> beyond definition,
> resembling Goodness and Reason,
> yet like empty space,
> Reality, Truth and Being,
> wondrous and beyond description..."

See ALLĀH; ANGELS; al-'AQL; al-'ARSH; APOCATASTASIS; BEING; ESCHATOLOGY; DHĀT; NAFS; IBLĪS; AL-INSĀN al-KĀMIL; JINN.

Five Pillars (Ar. *arkān ad-dīn* lit. "supports, or fundaments, of the religion"). The fundamental tenets or requirements of Islam which are accepted as such unequivocally by all branches. The observance of the Five Pillars is required of all Muslims. The non-observance (but not repudiation) of four of the Five Pillars does not constitute departure from Islam, however, and in fact there are many Muslims who do not, at one or another time of their lives, observe the pillars other than the *shahādah*. The *shahādah* is essential, however, and without it no-one can consider himself a Muslim in any sense. Most would agree that the second most important pillar is *ṣalāh*, the ritual prayer, both spiritually, and legally, since there are no grounds for dispensation from the *ṣalāh*, except temporarily for menstruating women, whereas legal grounds exist for prolonged or systematic dispensation of the other three pillars.

The Five Pillars are:

1. the *shahādah* affirming that there is no god but God (Allāh) and that Muḥammad is the Messenger of God.

2. *Ṣalāh*, the five daily ritual, or canonical, prayers.

3. *Zakāh*, the giving of alms on a stipulated scale. (This is, in a sense, the equivalent of a voluntary religious tax paid directly to the poor.)

4. *Ṣawm*, the fasting of the month of Ramaḍān.

5. *Ḥajj*, the performance of the pilgrimage to Mecca once in a lifetime by those physically and financially able to do so without compromising their other responsibilities.

Jihād ("holy war") is sometimes called a "sixth" pillar. It is, however, not universally obligatory. Not all must take part in holy war even if there are valid reasons for it; it is enough that a "sufficient number" take part. Moreover, after the initial struggle for life on the part of the first Muslims in Medina against the Meccans, *jihād* was rarely declared and could even more rarely be justified.

According to a Ḥadīth related by Ṭalḥāh ibn 'Ubayy, a man came to the Prophet and asked about the religious duties of Islam. The Messenger said:

> "Five prayers by day and night." "Must I perform others?" asked the man. "No", answered the Prophet, "unless it is voluntarily". The questions were repeated and answered the same way for the other pillars upon which the man said, "By God I will not add anything to that and I will not take anything away." Whereupon the Prophet exclaimed, "He will be one of the blessed [in paradise] if he is sincere."

A Chinese Muslim, Ma Fu-ch'u, in an 18th-century treatise called *The Three Character Rhymed Classic on the Ka'bah*, describes the Five Pillars thus:

> For all lands under Heaven,
> the doctrine of the Prophet runs
> comprising Rites for human society
> and the Heavenly Path.
> To confess the Sovereign God
> is the first requirement,
> and this central ritual
> is most wondrous.
> The Heavenly Path is cultivated
> by the Five Virtuous Acts:
> the Virtuous Act of enunciating the Truth [*shahādah*]
> with the heart turned to God;
> the Virtuous Act of ritualising the Truth [*ṣalāh*]
> with the body adoring God;
> the Virtuous Act of fasting [*ṣawm*]
> to master the promptings of desire;
> the virtuous Act of heavenly charity [*zakāh*]
> to assist the orphans and the needy
> the Virtuous Act of pilgrimage [*ḥajj*]
> forsaking home and family.
> All things, deep and shallow
> reside in the heart and breast.
> The virtues of the heart
> are vehicled by the Path,
> which is therefore called
> the Vehicle of Reality.
> Now the Vehicle of the Rites
> is the foundation of all;
> the true Vehicle of the Path
> is derived from this;
> when the Rites are abandoned
> the three virtues are obscured.
> These five Virtuous Acts
> are the five norms.
> God commands men
> to conquer self
> whether they be ignorant or wise,
> saints or commoners,
> each acting in respectful obedience
> as the Rites prescribe...

See CREED; FIQH AKBAR; JIHĀD; PILGRIMAGE; RAMAḌĀN; ṢALĀH; SHAHĀDAH; ZAKĀH.

Fivers, *see* ZAYDIS.

"Flight to Medina", *see* ḤIJRAH.

Folklore, *see* MANDALAH; BOUJLOUD; BSAT; FALLACIES; GNAWAH; KHAKSAR.

Food. Like most religions, Islam makes prescriptions about food. The meat of swine is forbidden (2:167) and that of animals that have not been ritually slaughtered. The consumption of blood is forbidden, but that which remains in meat after draining upon slaughter is acceptable. Wine and inebriating drinks are forbidden (5:92), as are mind-affecting drugs, but drugs used medicinally are not prohibited. Wine mixed with various herbs was used as an anaesthetic by Muslim doctors in the Middle Ages.

In early Islam the eating habits of the Arabs were the criteria for determining what could be eaten and what not, and Ibn Hanbal, founder of a School of Law, is said never to have eaten watermelon because he never found a precedent for it in the Sunnah of the Prophet.

In general, scavenger animals are forbidden as food. Shellfish present an exception. Shellfish are scavengers (and thus eaters of carrion, which are prohibited as food themselves, Koran 2:173; 5:3; 6:145; 16:115), and are considered non-kosher in Judaism. The Sunnis, however, eat many kinds of shellfish, nevertheless. (They do, however, consider it *makrūh*, or a "discouraged practice.") Presumably, the acceptance of shellfish as food arises out of the Koranic verse: the "game of the sea and its food is made lawful for you" (Koran 5:96). It could also possibly be an example of *ijmāṭ* on the part of the Sunnis, that is, usage establishing law. Twelve-Imam Shī'ites, however, *do* prohibit the eating of shellfish, and fish without scales such as shark and eels.

Food that is acceptable is called *ḥalāl*; meat is *ḥalāl* if it consists of the flesh of acceptable animals that have been ritually slaughtered. A Muslim must consecrate the kill by saying the words *Bismi-Llāh*; *Allāhu Akbar*, and cut the throat (both windpipe and jugular vein) with one stroke. Game is *ḥalāl* if the words of consecration are spoken when it is shot, or when a trained dog is released to retrieve it. Fish are *ḥalāl* if caught when alive, but dead fish which have been gathered are not.

If ritually slaughtered meat is not available, it is admissible to consume non-*ḥalāl* meat and "the food of Jews and Christians" provided that prohibited food such as swine's flesh is avoided. When there is no alternative, in cases of necessity, even prohibited food may be eaten. During World War II, Muslim troops fighting in European armies were often obliged to eat canned ham, because other supplies were not available. (In this connection one is reminded – no parallel or conclusion is intended, it is simply a fact – of the Sepoy Mutiny a century ago which was sparked off when Muslim troops serving the British Empire in India were incited to rebel by false rumors that bullets, which they were obliged or wont to bite with their teeth, had been greased with pig fat).

In practice, all authorities would probably approve the eating of prohibited food if there were no alternative for survival, according to the legal principle that "Necessity makes prohibited things permissible." Moreover, there is an injunction in Islam to be reasonable in all things. *See* RITUAL SLAUGHTER.

"Forbidden", *see* ḤARĀM.

Forgiveness, *see* DIVINE NAMES; ISTIGHFĀR.

Formulas of piety, *see* PIOUS EXPRESSIONS.

"Four Books" (*al-kutub al-arba'ah*). The four principal collections of Ḥadīth accepted by Twelve-Imām Shī'ites. These are:

1. *Man la Yaḥḍuruhu-l-Faqīh* ("When no theologian is present") by Muḥammad Ibn Babawayh (d. *381*/991).
2. *Al-Kāfī* ("The Compendium") by Muḥammad ibn Ya'qūb Abū Ja'far al-Kulaynī (d. *329*/940).
3. *Al-Istibṣār* ("the Perspicacious") by Muḥammad aṭ-Ṭūsī (*460*/1067).
4. *Taḥdhib al-Aḥkām* ("The Confirmation of Decisions") also by Muḥammad aṭ-Ṭūsī. *See* al-KULAYNĪ; IBN BABAWAYH; ṬŪSĪ, MUḤAMMAD.

"Fourteenth Century". Although quite categorically the Prophet denied any knowledge of the future, there is a popular myth that the Prophet made a comment about each century to come and wept when he reached the fourteenth. Hence there is a very widespread idea that the world will end in the fourteenth Islamic century, which is the present one. This belief probably arises from the Manichean eschatology which says that once everyone has understood that the world was created in order to rescue the light from the attack of darkness after the Manichean big bang, no more children will be allowed to be born, and the world will come to an end, and will then burn for 1468 years, which is very close to the length of the Sothic year (1460).

Free will, *see* MAKTŪB; QADARIYYAH.

Friday Prayer (Ar. *ṣalāt al-jum'ah*). The special Friday midday prayer is performed in a congregational mosque, that is, a large mosque where worshipers come together who may well perform the other daily prayers in a smaller, local mosque. Here an Imām, or prayer leader competent to do so, delivers an exhortation (*khuṭbah*) usually lasting from fifteen minutes to a half hour.

After the *khuṭbah*, the worshipers end the assembly by performing a two-*raka'āt* prayer in place of the normal four-*raka'at Ẓuhr*, or noon prayer. Attendance at Friday prayers is insisted upon as not only meritorious but a duty. Commercial transactions between the moment the prayer is called to the time it is performed are forbidden, although business may be carried on during the rest of the day.

In Saudi Arabia where Sunday is not a holiday, Thursday and Friday are the equivalent of the two-day weekend found in the West. In other countries where European usage prevails, Saturday and Sunday are civil holidays while Friday remains the day of assembly. The observance of the special congregation takes about one hour.

Fundamentalism. The term "Fundamentalism" is Western and misleading because many Muslims are quick to claim that Islam has always been fundamentalist and that the contemporary phenomenon by this name is simply a return to Islam as such. It is not, however, an Islam that would have been familiar to al-Ghazālī or to Abū Ḥanifah, or even Ibn Taymiyyah whom many Fundamentalists regard as their model. The term used, until recently, in Arabic for the phenomenon was not Fundamentalism, but extremism (*mutaṭarifīn*). Now it has been replaced by the more politically correct *Uṣulīyyah*, a literal translation of fundamentalism. It is characterized by absolutist application of *some* ideas which constitute Islam, and the total rejection of other ideas, which are no less Islam, and no less the Koranic words of revelation. It is marked by the inability to integrate ideas into coherent and stable wholes. Fundamentalism reduces religion to rules and laws and materialism, and ignores transcendence and spirituality.

Following the modern reformer Mawdudi most Fundamentalists insist in the veiling of all women. The custom arose in some parts of the Islamic world, not in all; in 'Abbāsid Baghdad it was the reinstatement of a Persian usage. The classical Jurist Ibn Qutaybah (d. *276*/889) a leading traditionist of the *3rd*/9th century, opposed obligatory veiling saying that veiling was a special Koranic condition for the Prophet's wives only who were a focus of attention and, who unlike other women, were also not allowed to marry any one else after his death. (The "veiling" of the Prophet's wives in the Koran in all likelihood did not mean the wearing of a veil, but that audiences with them should be carried out with a separating curtain.)

Nor are apparently similar schools in the past exactly analogous to modern Fundamentalism. The rise of the Ẓahirī, or literalist school of law in the *3rd*/10th century, rather than a rigidification was in some ways actually an escape, an alternative to a hardening of legalism in the Islamic world. It was in any case an organic development rather than a reaction to forces from without. Paradoxically, this school was often adopted by extremely liberal thinkers and Sufis seeking greater freedom of thought. Similarly the acceptance by many of predestinarianism in the *2nd*/8th century was a defense against oppression (as well as the logical consequence of certain metaphysical dogmas). Politics has often disguised itself behind a religious front in the Islamic world as elsewhere. Very often ambitious leaders created their power bases around religious affiliations: the 'Abbāsids and Ṣafavids come to mind, as do the Sanūsiyyah and Tijanīyyah, and the attempt of the Emir 'Abd al-Qādir of Algeria to build support through the Qādiriyyah. A common characteristic was to label those who did not belong to movement as ungodly, or as unbelievers, in order to be able to attack them militarily, often not for conquest but simply for plunder, with a clear conscience, for war between Muslims is prohibited. This characteristic has not only continued down to present times, it has been exploited even more, down to the declaration of holy war in circumstances in which not only holy war is impossible under the legal conditions, Islam not being in danger, but any war in the first place from the religious point of view.

These earlier movements had by their nature a very high degree of religious content. The phenomenon of present day fundamentalism does not. Islam as religion, Islam as piety, has been replaced by Islam as ideology and as a kind of nationalism. Sometimes this has taken the form of grass roots democracy, but also as the rule by a class claiming religious authority. It has also taken the form of Islam seen as some kind of economic system, not readily definable, and ultimately whatever one wants it to be. It has taken root chiefly among the poor and uneducated as a utopianism without spirituality. Above all it seems to be a reaction to what are perceived as foreign systems, a reaction which has taken the form of an aggressive, sometimes totalitarian application of religious practices as blind rules. As a rejection of alien influences it can be seen as a defensive mechanism, in which, unfortunately, an awareness of the positive meaning of religion is often obscured.

What is perhaps distinctive about contemporary Islamic Fundamentalism is that it attempts to combine modernism, with its secular and materialist tendencies, with a religious conservatism in a vacuum, cut off from tradition and a matrix of organic process. Some modernist Fundamentalist movements have refused to observe Islamic laws on the grounds that they should not be expected to do so until the whole world does so! As the nature of modern Fundamentalism is contradictory, the precursors do not fall into an orderly group representing similar thinking. They in fact form a composite of the contradictory forces that make up Fundamentalism. Among them are the Indian modernist reformer Sayyid Ahmad Khan (*1232-1316*/1817-1898) who founded the Aligarh College and who saw Great Britain as a model; Jamāl ad-Dīn al-Afghānī (*1254-1314*/1838-1897) who tried to make himself the spokesman of different currents of his time for his own advancement; Muḥammad Abduh (*1265-1323*/1849-1905) who attempted to make revisions in Islamic Law to meet modern conditions, such as the *fatwah* which permitted interest on capital; ʿAlī ʿAbd ar-Razzaq in Egypt who advocated the separation of religion and state as an original historic dogma of Islam; Rashid Riḍa who advanced the notion which now is an unquestioned premise of Fundamentalist political theory, the slogan of *shura*, or consultation i.e. democracy; Ḥasan al-Bannā' in Egypt (d. *1368*/1949) the founder of the Muslim Brotherhood is another important figure. The Muslim Brotherhood has tried to overthrow what it considers un-Islamic regimes by force, including terrorism, from within; Muḥammad Iqbal (*1290-1357*/1873-1938) in Pakistan, who combined certain aspects of modern European philosophy, entirely secular and humanistic in its world view, with Islam; Sayyid Abū'-l Ala Mawdudi (*1321-1399*/1903-1979), a highly influential Pakistani thinker who advocated authoritarian conservatism with modern dynamism. Combining the militancy of the Muslim Brotherhood and the legal legitimism of Mawdudi, Sayyid Qutb denounced believing Muslims as unbelievers if they did not agree with him. Qutb was executed in *1386*/1966 in Egypt by the Nasser regime. The absolute rejection of those who disagree is in the nature of Fundamentalism, the principle of consultation being reserved for adherents of the particular school. Groups derived from Qutb have been implicated in much violence in Egypt including the assassination of President Sadat in 1981, who himself, along with Nasser when they were "Free Officers", belonged to the Muslim Brotherhood at the beginning of his career. (Sadat, as any politician, looked to various groups for possible support, including Sufis; he belonged to the Shadhilis and even as Head of State he performed pilgrimages to the tomb of Imam Shadhili by the Red Sea.)

In Iran, Dr. ʿAlī Shariʿatī (d. *1397*/1977) was extremely popular among students for what was a combination of Leftist politics, Western Existentialism, and Iranian Ishraq (the two are fundamentally very similar) served up under the label of Islam. The revolution of Ayatollah Khomeini (d. *1409*/1989) for a time provided a banner for young Muslims in many countries, who, having often been fed a diet of revolutionary rhetoric blaming the West for the under-development of the Third World, rallied around what seemed to be revolution through Islam rather than through some alien ideology. The ultimate failure of the Iranian revolution to provide any real solutions, and the disastrous Iran-Iraq war have blunted enthusiasm for the promises put forward by Islamic Government.

The heteroclitic nature of modern Fundamentalism as reaction can be seen from this description of the Muslim Brotherhood by Ḥasan al-Bannā': A Sunnī ("orthodox") Salafīyyah movement [part of a general reform restoration movement that came into being almost one hundred years ago to what was perceived as the original Islam of the "pious ancestors"], a Sufi truth (i.e. "a mysticism"), a political organization, an athletic group, a cultural and educational union, an economic company, and a social idea. From this collection of unconnected and even contradictory appeals it can be seen that the guiding principle of Fundamentalism is the attempt to acquire power, sanctified with the sauce of holy righteousness, on the part of those who do not have power today. It is also the fusion of Islam with technological modernism.

Fundamentalism is a phenomenon which has marked all religions in modern times. Materialism and literalism, the rejection of tradition, utopianism and millenarism, the dawning of the age of the dominance of the disenfranchised and oppressed are its hallmarks. In the case of Islam it is as if the magic that neutralized what were originally destructive tendencies into a beneficent synthesis has evaporated and instead of a unity or one reality which guided men's thoughts there are now two which are at war with each other and with themselves. Religions come as rectifications to a state of error and dissolution. When they age, the original forces which had to be confined behind a kind of wall, like the Gog and Magog of the Koran, burst out anew to wreak the havoc of the ancient times. *See* ḤAMĀS; HIZB ALLAH; KHOMEINI; MUSLIM BROTHERHOOD; PAHLAVI.

Funduq (lit. an "inn", from the Greek *pandokeion*). The word is often used for a modern hotel in the Arab West, but it means first of all a traditional inn, with space for the storage of merchandise, and stables for traveling and pack animals. *See* CARAVANSARAI; KHĀN.

Funerals (Ar. *janāzah* or *jināzah*). Muslims bury the dead as quickly as possible, preferably before sundown on the day of death. Cremation is not practiced in Islam. The corpse is cleaned by persons of the same sex as the deceased and given a ritual ablution, the *ghusl*, an uneven number of times, which may be followed by a *wuḍū'*. The bodily orifices are stopped with cotton wool; the body is shrouded in a winding cloth. Martyrs, however, are buried as they died, in their clothes, unwashed, for their wounds bear testimony to their martyrdom.

A funeral prayer is performed for the recently dead by the mourners and by anyone present in the mosque at the time. Funeral prayers are performed in mosques as a matter of course after the canonic daily prayers. The corpse may or may not be present. An odd number of rows of worshipers is customary for this prayer. The worshipers make an expression of *niyyah* ("intention") before this as before all ritual acts.

The opening *takbīr* ("*Allāhu Akbar*") is followed by a *du'ā'* which is a personal prayer in one's own words, in this case, pronounced silently in the standing position (*qiyām*). It is customary to use an established *du'ā'*, known as the *qunūt*, which is actually whispered beneath the breath, at this point (*see* QUNŪT). Another *takbīr* precedes a second *du'ā'*, and again, for a total of three such personal prayers. One of these prayers should be a petition for the happiness of the departed soul. After the third *du'ā'*, there is a fourth *takbīr*, and the worshipers say *as-salamu 'alaykum* to the right and to the left. In this prayer there is no *rukū*, ("bow"), or *sujūd* ("prostration").

As the mourners carry the corpse through the streets to a mosque to be prayed over or to its resting place, the *shahādah* is psalmodied. Piety calls upon those whom the procession passes to rise, join in the chanting, and help carry the bier for a short distance. The body is buried in a grave, lying on the right side with the face towards Mecca. There are no injunctions against the use of coffins, but it is more common to bury the body only in its wrappings.

Forty days after death, it is common to recite litanies in remembrance of the deceased. Other customary practices exist, which vary from community to community, and nation to nation. When a deceased person is mentioned, the words *raḥimahu* (*raḥimahā* for a woman) *Llāh*, "God be merciful to him or her", are spoken.

'Ali said: "Every day an Angel of heaven cries: 'O people there below! produce offspring to die; build to be destroyed; gather ye together to depart!'" (Attributed to 'Ali, this is also found in the poetry of Abū-l-'Atāhiyah, d. 210/825.) *See* DEATH; MOURNING; PRAYER.

Furqān (lit. "divider", in the sense of criterion or discrimination). **1.** A name for the Koran because the book is the basis for discrimination between truth and unreality.

2. The name of Sūrah 25. *See* FARAQLĪṬ.

Furū ("branch"). The branches of religious law developed from the principles or *uṣul al-fiqh. See* SHARĪ'AH.

al-Futūḥāt al-Makkiyyah (lit. "the Meccan Revelations"). A vast work of esoteric doctrine in 560 chapters by Ibn Arabī, the celebrated mystic and metaphysician of the 12th century. *See* IBN 'ARABĪ.

Futuwwah (lit. "youth", "adolescence" and, by extension, "manliness", "nobleheartedness"). The equivalent of the Western notion of "chivalry". Before Islam social responsibility was determined among the desert Arabs by blood ties alone, with little provision for the outsider apart from the prescribed rules of hospitality for guests. The Prophet in Mecca, before he received his mission, had taken part in a pact of *futuwwah* ("chivalry") to help those without succor.

The pact had come about when a visiting merchant, with no relatives in Mecca to whom he could appeal for aid, was defrauded by a Meccan merchant. The victim, a Yemeni, made a public appeal from the slopes of Abū Qubays, the hill which rises near the Ka'bah. 'Abd Allāh ibn Judān, the chief of the clan of Taym accordingly called for a pact of chivalry among the Meccans. Az-Zubayr, chief of the Hāshim clan, brought the young Muḥammad to take part in the pact. Those who took part poured water over the Black Stone, drank it, and then, with their right hands raised above their heads, made an oath to defend those in need irrespective of clan affiliation. The oath was called the *ḥilf al-fuḍūl.*

The Meccan who had wronged the Yemeni was compelled to make amends. Afterwards, the Prophet said: "I was present in the house of 'Abd Allāh ibn Judān at so excellent a pact that I would not exchange my part in it for a herd of red camels; and if now, in Islam, I were summoned unto it I would gladly respond." Abū Bakr also took part in this pact.

The idea of *futuwwah* in Islam reached its high point during the Crusades when chivalrous acts on both sides were recorded and admired. The nobility of Saladin, who was knighted by Richard the Lion Heart, became legendary in Europe and the Orient.

Under the 'Abbāsids a number of orders of *futuwwah* were created of which the Caliph was occasionally the titular head. These traditions were transferred to Cairo when the 'Abbāsids were installed as figurehead Caliphs by the Mamlūks after the Mongol conquest of Baghdad, and existed later among the Turks and the Persians.

Among the latter a trace of these orders still survive as *zurkhaneh* (Pers. "houses of strength"). Today, these are athletic clubs more than anything else, but they were the embodiment of a traditional Persian practice of the martial arts and they retain a certain sense of ceremony and dedication which recalls their origins. A *zurkhaneh* is the meeting place for a society of athletes who train together and compete as wrestlers. The *zurkhaneh* preserves vestiges of medieval Islamic chivalry, recalled by the ritualistic protocols of the assemblies, and the emphasis on virtue.

G

Gabriel (Ar. *Jabrā'īl* or *Jibrīl*, "God's Mighty One"). The Angel of Revelation and one of the Archangels. In the Bible, Gabriel is a Divine Messenger sent to Daniel, Mary, and Zacharias. In Islamic tradition Gabriel appears again and again to the Prophets, beginning with Adam, to whom he gave consolation after the Fall, taught the letters of the alphabet, and the skills of working in the world. He brought the revelations of the Koran; in Sūrah 53 (the Sūrah of the Star) he who taught the Prophet is not named, but described; the commentators unanimously accept this to have been Gabriel.

> This is naught but a revelation revealed,
> taught him by one terrible in power,
> very strong; he stood poised
> being on the higher horizon,
> then drew near and hung suspended,
> two bows'-length away, or nearer,
> then revealed to his servant that he revealed.
> His heart lies not of what he saw;
> what, will you dispute with him what he sees?
> (53:4-11)

Gabriel also took the Prophet on the Night Journey. Tradition adds that Gabriel interceded on behalf of the Prophet, giving him help on several occasions in a supernatural way.

The Jews of Medina objected that if Islam had been addressed to them, then Michael would have been the Angel of Revelation. In connection with this the verse 2:92-96 was revealed:

> Say: 'Whosoever is an enemy to Gabriel -
> he it was that brought it down upon thy heart
> by the leave of God, confirming what was before it,
> and for a guidance and good tidings to the believers.
> Whosoever is an enemy to God and His angels
> and His Messengers, and Gabriel, and Michael -
> surely God is an enemy to the unbelievers.'
> And We have sent down unto thee signs, clear signs,
> and none disbelieves in them except the ungodly.
> Why, whensoever they have made a covenant,
> does a party of them reject it?
> Nay, but the most of them are unbelievers.
> When there has come to them a Messenger from God
> confirming what was with them, a part of them
> that were given the Book reject the Book of God
> behind their backs, as though they knew not,
> and they follow what the Satans recited
> over Solomon's kingdom.

And Gabriel is mentioned again in 66:4:

> ...but if you support one
> another against him, God is his Protector,
> and Gabriel, and the righteous among the
> believers; and, after that, the angels are
> his supporters.

In Iran, Gabriel is usually referred to by his Zoroastrian name, *Sraosh*. *See* ANGELS; NIGHT JOURNEY.

Gambling. Games of chance are forbidden in the Koran (2:219 and 5:94). Nevertheless, various indigenous forms of betting, as well as lotteries, do exist, or have existed, in most Islamic countries, due to the colonial influence of European countries.

Garden (Ar. *al-jannah*). The garden is the most frequent Koranic symbol of paradise. *See* al-JANNAH.

"Garden of Death", *see* MUSAYLAMAH.

Geber, *see* JĀBIR IBN ḤAYYĀN.

Gematria, *see* ABJAD.

Genie, *see* JINN.

Ghadīr al-Khumm (lit. "the pool of Khumm"). An oasis between Mecca and Medina. Returning from the final, "Farewell Pilgrimage" shortly before his death, the Prophet stopped here with his followers. During the afternoon he called an assembly, took 'Alī's hands, raised them up, and said "Whoever has me as his master (*mawlā*) has 'Alī as his master." Then he prayed: "Be a friend to his friends, O Lord, and be an enemy to his enemies, help those who assist him and frustrate those who oppose him."

The Shī'ites (*see* SHĪ'ISM) assert that this declaration was in reality a designation of 'Alī as successor to the Prophet. The events at Ghadīr al-Khumm are advanced as one of the most important arguments for their thesis concerning 'Alī. The event is celebrated in the Shīite world by the *'Id al-Ghadīr*, or festival of Ghadīr. The observance of this as a Shī'ite festival dates to *351*/962 when it was instituted by Mu'izz ad-Dawlah, the Buyid ruler who also inaugurated the Shī'ite observance of the Āshūrā'as the commemoration of the martyrdom of Ḥusayn. At the time, the Sunnīs of Baghdad countered by making festivals of the 26th Dhū-l-Ḥijjah, the anniversary of Abū Bakr's sojourn with the Prophet in the cave, and the 18th Muḥarram, the death of Mus'ab ibn az-Zubayr who had put down the revolt of a partisan of Ḥusayn; but these observances, being quite artificial, were short-lived.

The Sunnīs deny the existence of a successor in the Shī'ite sense of an Imām in any case, and deny that this event marked the designation of 'Alī as an immediate successor. They cite as evidence the fact that Abū Bakr was unequivocally designated to lead the prayers in place of the Prophet during his final illness; this does not by itself imply that Abū Bakr was intended to succeed the Prophet, but it casts doubt on such a designation regarding 'Alī.

The Sunnī interpretation of Ghadīr al-Khumm is made in the light of the events immediately preceding it, namely that 'Alī had just been severely criticized by the army he was leading (he had not been present at the "Farewell Pilgrimage" because of a military expedition) for rescinding an order given by his deputy to distribute a ration of new clothing from the spoils of war. The Prophet's statement is seen as intended to still the criticism and justify 'Alī's actions. *See* CALENDAR; SHĪ'ISM.

Ghāfilūn, see GHAFLAH.

Ghaflah (lit. "heedlessness"). Those guilty of *ghaflah*, the *ghāfilūn*, are those who "know only a surface appearance of the life of this world, and are heedless of the hereafter" (30:7). *Ghaflah* is the sin of indifference to the reality of God. It is the "broad way" and the "wide gate". Of the indifferent, or the heedless, it is said: "because thou art lukewarm, and neither cold nor hot, I will spue thee out of my mouth" (Revelations 3:16).

Ghālib, Mirzā Asad Allah Khān. (*1212-1286*/1797-1869). Born in Agra, he spend most of his life in Delhi where he was attached to the court of the last Moghul ruler, Bahadūr Shāh Zafur. Ghālib wrote poetry in Persian and Urdu, and in a prose work, *Dastanbūy*, described the events of the time of the Sepoy Mutiny which he witnessed. With the wider publication of his works, poetry and correspondence, his fame has grown in the last one hundred years.

Ghār Hīrah, *see* HĪRAH'.

Ghassānīs. A South Arabian tribe, the Banū Ghassān, who migrated to Syria from the Yemen between the 3rd and 4th century AD and settled in the region of Damascus. Many of them became monophysite Christians. Their leaders were accorded a Phylarcate, or status of vassal kingdom, under the Byzantine Emperor Justinian (527-569). The Ghassānīs protected the southern flank of the Byzantine Empire. With the rise of Islam many of the Ghassānīs defected from Byzantine allegiance and assisted the Arabs making possible their invasion of Syria. Those Ghassānīs who did not convert to Islam at the time were accorded a special position as a people not conquered, but rather, allied to the Islamic empire.

In 272 the Roman Emperor Aurelian routed the Palmyrene army at Emesa (Ḥoms). He destroyed Palmyra (Tadmir) a great city in the Syrian desert thus ending the greatest instance, under the Queen Zenobia, of Arab political expansion up to that time. With the loss of this countervailing power against their rivals, the Persians soon thereafter installed the Lakhmids as rulers of a buffer state centered at Ḥirā' (near Kufah). The Romans followed by sponsoring the Syrian Ghassānīs between Damascus and Petra.

The Jafnid house of the Ghassānīs arose at the beginning of the sixth century when they defeated the Lakhmids. Ḥarith ibn Jabalah was recognized as ruler by the Byzantines and became phylarch. After the Muslim invasion, the Ghassānīd ruler Jabalah ibn al-Āyham accepted Islam after first fighting against it. However, he found it too democratic (he was held equal to a Beduin in an incident while on the pilgrimage), abandoned Islam and returned to Christianity. *See* LAKHMIDS; MARONITES.

Ghaybah (lit. "absence" or "being concealed").

1. A technical term of Sufism meaning "absence" from the world, that is, withdrawal from all things except the worship and awareness of God.
2. It also refers to the Shī'ite doctrine of the "occultation" or disappearance from human view – or even from the world altogether – of the Twelfth Imām of Twelve-Imām Shī'ism.

The doctrine is a calque after the example of Jesus, who, the Koran says, was not killed on the cross, but rather was raised up to a principial state, a state in Being, from which he will return at the end of the world.

Although the case of the Hidden Imām is the most prominent example, a similar belief exists among the Druzes who regard the Fāṭimid Caliph al-Ḥākim (d. *411*/1021) as having undergone *ghaybah*. Some Musta'lī Ismā'īlīs believe the same about their Imām Ṭayyib, the alleged son of al-Amīr, who would have been assassinated in *524*/1129. *See* SHĪ'ISM; HIDDEN IMĀM.

al-Ghazālī, Abū Ḥāmid Muḥammad (*450-505*/1058-1111). Philosopher, theologian, jurist, and mystic; he was known in Europe as "Algazel". He was born and died in Ṭūs, Persia. An extraordinary figure, al-Ghazālī was the architect of the latter development of Islam.

In his youth al-Ghazālī attracted the attention of his teachers because of his capacity and desire for learning. He studied at Nayshābūr with al-Juwaynī, the "Imām of the Ḥaramān", and was appointed a professor of law at the Niẓāmiyyah in Baghdad by the Vizier Niẓām al-Mulk, the great statesman, patron of learning, and a prolific founder of schools. At Baghdad, al-Ghazālī achieved renown and great success as a lawyer, but after four years experienced a crisis of faith and conscience. A temporary speech impediment, which interfered with his work, made action urgent.

Under guise of going on the pilgrimage, al-Ghazālī turned his post over to his brother (who later became a noted Sufi), and retired to Damascus. After periods of great solitude, he visited the spiritual fountainheads of Jerusalem and Hebron (the site of the tomb of Abraham), as well as Mecca and Medina. It has been said that during this period of searching he went so far as to question the senses, knowing they could deceive.

He turned his attention to the ways of knowledge one by one: philosophy, theology, and the various schools of the age. In the end he found his satisfaction in mysticism, or Sufism; or he returned to it, because it was, in fact, the intellectual climate of his family upbringing. In the light of this continuity and the certainty which he exhibits even as he describes his searching, it would seem that the crisis of his life was not one of doubt as such, but a turning inward away from the world; for al-Ghazālī says: "I arrived at Truth, not by systematic reasoning and accumulation of proofs, but by a flash of light which God sent into my soul."

He wrote his great works, the *Ihyā' 'Ulūm ad-Dīn*, ("the Revival of the Religious Sciences"), and *al-Munqidh min aḍ-Ḍalal*, ("the Savior from Error"), about his search for knowledge. In the *Tahāfut al-Falāsifah* (or "the Destruction of the Philosophers") he refutes the ability of philosophy – on the basis of its own assumptions – to reach truth and certainty, and reduces it to an ancilla of theology. His ethical works are *Kīmiyā' as-Sa'ādah*, ("the Alchemy of Felicity"), and *Yā Ayyuhā'l-Walad*, ("O Young Man"). On mysticism his most famous work is the *Mishkāt al-Anwār*, ("the Niche of Lights"). In all, he wrote about seventy books.

Al-Ghazālī was a Shāfi'ī and as such he used *qiyas* or analogy to arrive at theological decisions. Because the Malikis do not approve of the use of analogy his books were burned in one instance in Seville. He was also an Ash'arite and thus, philosophically a kind of occasionalist. Fire burns cotton, he said, not because fire is an agent, but because it is God's *sunnah*, His wont that it should appear to burn cotton and our knowledge of it burning is also this Divine wont; in miracles God changes his *sunnah* and our knowledge changes also. Al-Ghazālī talked about *dhawq*, literally "taste" but meaning "realization", and like all theologians, the need for reliable tradition with which to understand revelation. He says that as an example of mercy in the darkness of the created world there appears God's gift of knowledge. For him philosophy was irrelevant except for logic which taught one how to think correctly. Aristotle said the soul uses the body as an instrument and through it the soul employs the faculties such as sight and hearing; al-Ghazālī, in the "flying man" thought-experiment said a man is aware of his physical existence as he is aware of himself thinking.

Al-Ghazālī concluded that the mystics – the Sufis – were the heirs of the Prophet. They alone walked the path of direct knowledge and they were the decisive authorities on doctrine. At the same time, he affirmed the indispensable need for the exoteric framework, i.e. law and theology, to make that knowledge possible. He refuted in particular, after the murder of his patron the Vizier Niẓām al-Mulk, the beguiling teachings of the *Ta'līmiyyah*, or Ismāīlīs – then active as the Assassin sect – with their enticements of "secret teachings" and "hidden masters".

Towards the end of his life he returned briefly to teach at Nayshābūr and then to Ṭūs, where he lived out his days among Sufi disciples. Al-Ghazālī is a man for all seasons: for the Sufis, al-Ghazālī is a Sufi; for the theologians he is a theologian; for the legalists, he is a jurist.

"To refute" he said, "one must understand." It was clear that he had studied all the schools, had heard their case, taken all their arguments and positions into account, and had understood them. Having established a credible synthesis of philosophy, theology, law, and mysticism in his own person by working back to first principles, al-Ghazālī could put the disciplines themselves in order.

Until his time, Islam had been developing in directions that seemed to exclude each other, and yet each one claimed to be the most authentic view of Islam. With al-Ghazālī an age came to an end and a new age began. The controversies of the Mu'tazilites and Ash'arites had been played out; different sects and points of view had developed and staked their claims to truth and orthodoxy. With al-Ghazālī Islam took a second breath. After him the essential doctrines, freed from the entanglements of the groundwork, could develop their fullest expressions. If the prophetic revelation was a concave lens which diffused knowledge from the Divine world into this, al-Ghazālī was a convex lens that took the separating rays of light and refocussed them. He ushered in the second age of Islam. At the end of his *Munqidh min aḍ-dalāl*, al-Ghazālī wrote:

> We pray God Almighty that He will number us among those whom He has chosen and elected, whom He has led to the truth and guided, whom He has inspired to remember Him and not to forget Him, whom He has preserved from evil in themselves so that they not prefer aught to Him, and whom He has made His own so that they serve only Him.

After al-Ghazālī the voices of the different schools were not stilled, but a fresh measure of unity and harmony had been achieved. What had become differentiated in history from the pristine unity of the Prophet's time, became reintegrated anew upon a different plane. With it came a sense of hierarchy and a tighter re-marshalling of society's intellectual faculties to enable it to respond to the needs of a sophisticated civilization. It was as if the center had reasserted itself, and as if al-Ghazālī had looked at the pieces of a puzzle, each claiming to be the complete picture of Islam, and put them all in their proper place. There emerged the image of a new organism, a complete body with mysticism or Sufism as the heart, theology as the head, philosophy as its rationality binding the different parts together, and law as the working limbs. Islamic civilization had come to maturity. *See* PHILOSOPHY.

Ghazwah (lit. a "raid", an "attack"; pl. *ghazawāt*). In particular, the desert raid, and by extension also a battle, war, etc. Related to this is *ghāzī*, "a warrior", or "war leader", which is sometimes used as a title among the Turks. The Italian word *razzia* comes from *ghazwah*. An alternate form of the word is *ghazvat* in Turkey and Persia.

Occasionally *ghazwah* is used to mean *jihād*, or "holy war".

Ghulāt (Persian for Arabic *ghulāh* sing. *ghālī*; lit. "extremists"; "exaggerators"). A polemical name for the Shī'ite sects that endow 'Alī (or others) with Divine qualities, or simply assert that the Divinity resides in someone. Exactly who is and who is not termed *ghulāt* varies according to the school of thought. Generally, those sects that go beyond the Twelve-Imām position are *ghulāt* in almost everyone's eyes. Shahrastānī (d. *548*/1153), the historian of religions, wrote:

> The Shī'ite extremists elevate their Imāms above the rank of created beings and regard them as Divine. These anthropomorphic tendencies are derived from Incarnationists, Transmigrationists, Jews, and Christians. For the Jews liken the Creator to the creature, and the Christians liken the creature to the Creator.
>
> This anthropomorphism is primarily and characteristically Shī'ite; only at a later period was it adopted by certain sects of the Sunnīs, Followers of the True Way.

The Ghulāt were also linked to political discontent on the part of the poor. Tradition recounts that among the early leaders of the ghuluww, there was a weaver, a seller of barley, and a dealer in straw. *See* SHĪ'ISM.

Ghusl. The "greater ablution", which confers a state of purity necessary to perform ritual acts such as prayer. One must acquire the state of *ghusl* before one can enter a mosque or any area purified for prayer, and before one can touch an Arabic Koran. The impurities which occasion the need for *ghusl* are called *janābāt* (sing. *janābah* or *junub*) and are: intromission; ejaculation; menstruation; childbirth; contact with a corpse (this latter is considered by some to be *Sunnah* only, that is, recommended but not obligatory).

Ghusl is the washing of the entire body beginning with the private parts which cannot be touched again during the performance of *ghusl*. Then the *ta'awwudh* and *basmalah* are pronounced along with the formulation of the *niyyah* (intention). The right hand cups water and is passed over the head, torso and limbs in an order which gives precedence to the upper, the front, and the right side over the lower, the back, and the left. The navel is cleansed eight times. The fingers of one hand clean the interstices of the fingers of the other; the insterstices between the toes are cleaned. The mouth and nostrils are rinsed with water. At the end one pronounces the *ḥamdalah*. This is the most strict procedure, that of the Mālikī school. Other Schools of Law maintain that it is enough to immerse the body in water or simply pour water over the body, that is, to take a shower preceded by the *niyyah* and the sacred formulas above.

When it is impossible to perform *ghusl* for lack of water or reasons of health, it can be replaced with *tayammum*, or purification with earth or stone, before the performance of a ritual. An additional *tayammum* is performed before entering a mosque and a stone is placed at the doorway for this purpose. A repetition of the *tayammum* is necessary for each prayer (*ṣalāt*).

Ghusl is also performed by a convert before being formally received into Islam, after the washing of the dead, major blood letting, and before putting on *iḥrām* for pilgrimage. By way of custom and "good measure", rather than an obligation, it is performed even if not necessary, the evening before the congregational Friday prayer, and before the festivals of *'Īd al-Aḍḥā* and *'Īd al-Fiṭr*. *See* ABLUTIONS; BASMALAH; TA'AWWUDH; TAYAMMUM; WUḌŪ'.

Glorification, *see* TAMJĪD.

Gnawah. A loose association of street musicians found in Morocco, with a vaguely religious character. Originally descendants of slaves brought from Guinea, whence their name, the Gnawah practice ecstatic trance dancing, which in various forms is common to the desert and rural areas. The Gnawah are sometimes called upon to play their drums (which are beaten with curved sticks), to beat their iron clapping instruments, somewhat like large castanets, and to dance in relays for days on end in order to draw someone out of a sickness by the invigorating nature of their rhythms and music.

In some Sufi orders the mystical dance (*ḥaḍrah*) has degenerated into trance dancing; the Gnawah are the reverse: trance dancing aspiring to a higher calling by claiming to be a *ḥaḍrah*. To this end some Gnawah have claimed the famous saint 'Abd al-Qādir al-Jīlānī as the authority for their practices. Today the Gnawah are losing their ethnic identity and dying out. They often perform as professional entertainers, and for the purposes of this demand there are today many imitators, who far outnumber the authentic Gnawah.

God, *see* ALLĀH; FIVE DIVINE PRESENCES.

Gnosis, *see* MA'RIFAH.

Gnosticism, *see* MANICHEISM; SEVENERS.

Gökalp, Ziya (*1293-1343*/1876-/1924). A professor of sociology at the University of Istanbul. He promoted Turkish nationalism, or Pan-Turanianism, but his overriding aim was the secularization of Turkish society. Wishing to turn Islam into a kind of rationalist and "scientific" ethical culture, Gökalp unhesitatingly copied western models even while glorifying Turkishness. He was the precursor of Atatürk, who put Gökalp's ideas into practice with the policy of *laik*, or the laicisation of Turkish life. Until the changes imposed by Atatürk after the First World War, Turkish society was completely immersed in Islam.

Many of the ideas which set modern Turks against Islam can be traced back to Gökalp's propaganda. These blame the Arabic alphabet for the widespread illiteracy which prevailed in Turkey, as it did in all traditional countries. The introduction of the Roman script cut the Turks off from their cultural past, and the subsequent increase in literacy may more logically be ascribed to the introduction of universal and compulsory schooling. The teachings of Gökalp once moved a ministerial committee to recommend putting pews in mosques.

It is still the law in Turkey that, except for the minister of religion, one cannot wear a rimless hat, the normal headgear of Muslims, in public. (The headgear must be rimless in order to allow the touching of the forehead to the ground in prayer). Such is the extent of Gökalp's influence.

Gold. The wearing of gold ornaments by men – but not by women – is forbidden by the *sharī'ah*. Nevertheless, gold wedding rings are now commonly worn by men in Islamic countries, as well as gold watches.

The *sharī'ah's* intention behind this prohibition for men is to maintain a state of sobriety, reserve, concentration, and spiritual poverty, that is, the perfections of the center. Women, who symbolize unfolding, infinitude, manifestation, are not bound by the same constraints.

Gospel of Barnabas, *see* BARNABAS, GOSPEL of.

Grand Mosque of Mecca, *see* KA'BAH.

Greetings. The *sharī'ah* makes the offering and return of greetings obligatory. When one Muslim encounters another, the greeting is *as-salāmu 'alaykum* ("peace be upon you"), and the response is *wa 'alaykumu-s-salām* ("and upon you be peace"). In either case, one may add *wa raḥmatu-Llāhi ta'ālā wa barakātuh* ("and God's mercy and blessings"). The same greeting may be used upon parting company and at any time, day or night, although in the morning the greeting *ṣabāḥ al-khayr* ("good morning"), to which the answer *ṣabāḥ an-nūr* ("morning of light"), is more common. When two groups meet, a "sufficient number" of each group must offer and return greetings.

Because it is used all the time, it is often forgotten that *as-salāmu 'alaykum* is a religious greeting, as *pax tecum* was a greeting of Christians in the Middle Ages. Sometimes Muslims refrain from using this greeting with non-Muslims and substitute some other form of salutation.

It is the practice in letters to write *al-ḥamdu li-Llāhi waḥdah* ("praise to God alone") at the head; the *basmalah* ("In the Name of God") is properly reserved for formal documents.

Gri-Gri. In West Africa, an amulet with Koranic inscriptions sealed inside, for protection from harm. Such an amulet is called a *hajib* in North Africa.

Amulets are widely used everywhere in the Islamic world, but in some regions they are elevated to an extraordinary degree of importance, a practice which receives the disapprobation of strict and informed Muslims.

Guarded Tablet, *see* AL-LAWḤ al-MAḤFŪẒ.

Gunbad. Tombs in the form of towers, with two levels inside, used by the Saljuks, and found in the confines of their empire. The style of the *gunbad* suggests that it is the representation of a Central Asian funeral tent dressed for a great chieftain, rendered in stone.

"Guru", *see* MURSHID.

H

Ḥaḍana (lit. "care"). The right of children to receive upkeep from the father before and after a divorce.

al-Ḥaḍārāt al-ilāhiyyah al-khams, *see* FIVE DIVINE PRESENCES.

Ḥadath. The impurities which are removed by the lesser ablution (*wuḍū'*) before prayer. *See* WUḌŪ'.

Hadd (lit. "limit", "borderline", "ordinance", "statute", pl. *ḥudūd*). A legal term for the offenses and punishments which are defined in the Koran.

Hadi of Sabzawar, Mulla Haji (*1212-1295*/1797-1878) One of the foremost Persian philosophers of the 19th century, a continuator of the School of Isfahan, that is, of Mulla Sadra. Mulla Hadi had inherited means but was noted for living abstemiously and giving generously to poor students. He studied at Meshhed and at Isfahan but returned to Sabzawar to teach. He died in the course of a lecture, surrounded by students and repeating the words *Hua, Hua* (the Divine Name "He"). Among his works is the *Asraru al-Ḥikam* ("Secrets of Philosophy").

Ḥadīth (lit. "speech", "report", "account"). Specifically, Traditions relating to the deeds and utterances of the Prophet as recounted by his companions. In the time of the Prophet, Arabs in the Peninsula would greet each other by asking "what is your news (*khabar*) of the Prophet?" (*Tabarī*).

Ḥadīth are divided into two groups: *ḥadīth qudsi* ("sacred Hadith"), in which God Himself is speaking through the Prophet, and *ḥadīth sharif* ("noble Ḥadīth"), the Prophet's own utterances. Ḥadīth may enunciate doctrine or provide a commentary upon it. They deal with the contents of the Koran, social and religious life, and everyday conduct, down to the tying of sandals. They are the basis, second only to the Koran, for Islamic law (*shari'ah*).

The *Muṣannaf* are collections classified by subject: The most respected collection of all is the *Jami as-Ṣaḥiḥ* of Muhammad Ibn Ismā'īl al-Bukhārī (d. *256*/870). This has 7,397 Ḥadīth under 3,450 subject headings (*bāb, abwāb*). Next is the the *Ṣaḥiḥ* of Abū-l-Ḥusayn Muslim ibn al-Ḥajjāj (d. *261*/875); usually simply called "Muslim". These two *Ṣaḥiḥs* or *Ṣaḥiḥayn* (the Arabic dual of *Ṣaḥiḥ*) are the foremost collections. The "*Six Muṣannaf*", the principal canonic collections, (i.e. those accepted as authoritative) also known as the six books (*al-kutub as-sittah*) are the *Ṣaḥiḥayn*, and: the collection of Abū Dawūd as-Sijistanī (4,500 Hadith, d. *261*/875), Abū Isa Muhammad at-Tirmidhī (d. *279*/892 or *302*/915). The collection of at-Tirmidhī and Abū Dāwūd are *kutūb sunan*, or collections of Ḥadīth specifically relevant to the practices of the Prophet. Finally there are the collections of an-Nasa'i (d. *303*/915), and Ibn Mājā (d. *273*/886), another *kitāb sunan*. These collections include sayings of some of the Companions. Abu Hurayrah is the Companion cited as the primary source of the greatest number of Ḥadīth.

Equally famous is the *Muwattā'* of Mālik ibn Anas, the first collection ever written down. Another kind of collection is the *Musnad. Musnads* are collections grouped around the primary source. The most famous (of four well known *Musnads*) is the *Musnad* of Ibn Ḥanbal, founder of a school of law (d. *241*/855). Ibn Ḥanbal's *Musnad* contains 30,000 Hadith. That of Aṭ-Ṭayālisi (d. *202*/818) is the first *Musnad* with 2,767 *Ḥadīth* from 600 authorities.

Of later large compilations which drew upon the early collections the best known is the *Masabih as-Sunnah* by al-Baghawi (d. *510*/1116) revised as the *Mishkat al-Masabih* (over 6,000 Ḥadīth) by Wali ad-Din at-Tabrizi (d. *737*/1337). Many other Ḥadīth are found in such books as the *Ḥilyat al-Awliyā'* ("Adornment of the Saints") of Abū Nu'aym. There are are also small collections of forty significant Ḥadīth (forty as an exemplary number of Ḥadīth that everyone should know). The first is by al-Marwazi (d. *299*/912) and the most famous is the *Forty Ḥadīth of an-Nawāwī* (d. *675*/1277).

At the beginning of *Ḥadīth* literature there were important family collections of Ḥadīth, written down or maintained in memory. These came from Anas ibn Malīk (the Prophet's servant (d. *91*/710); 'Abd Allah ibn Masud (d. *32*/653); Zayd ibn Thabit (who like the Caliph 'Umar, did not wish the *Ḥadīth* to be written down, presumably so as not to rival the Koran); Ibn 'Umar (son of the Caliph d. *73*/692); Ibn 'Abbas (son of the Prophet's uncle, d. *67*/687). Listening to a recounter of prophetic Ḥadīth was an evening entertainment at the Umayyad court from the time of Mu'awiyah.

'Umar II ('Umar ibn 'Abd al-Aziz, reigned *99-101*/717-720) the pious 'Umayyad, desirous of promulgating laws in conformity with Islamic traditions, encouraged systematic gathering of Ḥadīth and commissioned Muhammad ibn Muslim ibn Shihab az-Zuhri (d. *124*/742) to make a collection. Az-Zuhri died before this was done but he is credited with establishing the standard of attaching to the Ḥadīth a full *isnad*, or chain of transmission. He had students, so Ḥadīth study was becoming a science. It could be said that all the later religious sciences were at this period subsumed under the covering notion of Ḥadīth. Even after the separate development of *fiqh* (law) and *kalam* (theology) schools of theologic study were still called *Dar al-Ḥadīth* ("House of Ḥadīth", a generic name for this kind of institution). The best known Dar al-Ḥadīth was founded in Damascus by the Atabeg Nūr ad-Din (d. *560*/1173). Other such schools existed in Jerusalem, Cairo, Mosul, Nayshabur, and elsewhere.

The *isnād* is the chain of transmission. Distinctions are made according to whether the Ḥadīth was "heard"; "reported"; "disclosed"; "found"; and other categories relating to the circumstances of transmission. The transmission is the *riwayah*; the transmitter is a *rawi*, who, it was admitted, could edit the Ḥadīth and improve upon its form and style, whence the same Ḥadīth is found reported in different degrees of amplitude. The *matn*, meaning "letters" (*mutūn*), is the actual text of the Ḥadīth.

The canonical collections grade Ḥadīth according to indices of authenticity. The highest grade is *mutawatir*, that is recurrent or reported by many different sources; then *ṣaḥiḥ* "reliable"; *ḥasan* "good"; *da'if* "weak", and *mawdua*, or "fabricated". When collections of Ḥadīth began to appear, there were also studies by scholars of what they considered to be fabricated Ḥadīth; there was a saying that there is no more reprehensible act than the fabricating of Ḥadīth, which shows awareness that many Ḥadīth were not historically authentic.

The collections of Bukhārī and Muslim were scrupulously compiled in the first two and a half centuries of Islam. Their authenticity was assured by the criterion which the people of the time found most valid, that of an authoritative *isnad*, or chain of transmission. The method was based on the assumption that it was unthinkable for God-fearing men to lie about matters which they held sacred; each human link in the chain vouchsafed the others. If in the *isnād* there were persons whose integrity could be doubted for any reason, however small, the authenticity of the Ḥadīth was to that extent weakened. Biographical study also served to establish the plausibility of the transmissions. Naturally, fabricated Ḥadīth also had fabricated *isnād*, but criticism of the *matn* would be equivalent to dogmatic discussions of Islam itself – thus analysis discussions turned around the *isnād*, but often as euphemism for a discussion of the contents. Rather than enter into a debate of verisimilitude, Ibn Khaldun remarked on the well known bad memory of the family of the principle transmitters of Mahdi Ḥadīth as a way of saying that the Mahdi Ḥadīth are false; (they do not appear in the *Ṣaḥiḥayn* and first with Abū Dawūd). But on the other hand, since there were also Ḥadīth which denied the existence of a Mahdi, it was ultimately theological consensus which determined which Ḥadīth would lead to the elaboration of doctrine, and which would not.

The Shī'ites call Ḥadīth by an another word, *khabar* ("news", pl. *akhbār*). For Shī'ites, the authenticity of a Ḥadīth is guaranteed not by an *isnād* which begins with the Companions, but by its transmission through 'Alī and the Imāms of Shī'ism. The Shī'ite collections of Ḥadīth, which were made during the Buyid period from *320-454*/932-1062, are considerably larger than the Sunnī ones, and contain references to the Imāms not found in Sunnī collections. (*See* al-KULAYNĪ; IBN BABAWAYH; aṭ-ṬŪSĪ, MUḤAMMAD.)

Western scholars have often affirmed that Ḥadīth have been invented in order to justify some legal opinion or school of thought; this is undoubtedly true and even the early compilers rejected large numbers of Ḥadīth as fabricated. However, the sceptical tendency among Western scholars at one time went so far as to reject *ipso facto* any Ḥadīth which appeared to support a particular school or tendency. One orientalist was thus led to maintain that the Sufis had invented the saying: "Remember Me [God] I will remember you", since it so evidently fitted their teachings. In fact, this is not a Ḥadīth at all, but a quotation from the Koran (2:152). Even if, from a historical point of view, a particular Ḥadīth is false, it does not necessarily follow that the opinions, practices, or doctrines linked with it are suspect. A Ḥadīth may be false in the sense that the Prophet never spoke the words, but nevertheless true in that it is wholly consistent with his message.

Islam views the actions of a Divine Messenger as providential and unlimited in their inner nature. Therefore it is with the authority of the Koran, which states: "You have a noble example in God's Messenger" (33:21), that Islam bases its Sunnah upon the Ḥadīth in addition to the Koran. If the Ḥadīth were to play such an important role in the development of an entire civilization, their scope must be vast. Throughout the centuries, as Islam evolved, it searched out the traditions of the Prophet's life to guide the faithful in situations not touched upon by the Koran. As primordial man, or as the expression of the plenitude of human possibilities, the Prophet in his life may well have manifested all the possibilities of Islam by act, thought, speech or gesture. Yet it is inconceivable that all these possibilities should be discoverable in the received canon of Ḥadīth, for they are as ultimately limitless. Thus, the legitimacy of legal decisions and intellectual developments reposes, ultimately, not upon Ḥadīth but upon their orthodoxy in relation to Islam as such; for Islam is always greater than the sum of its historical parts, and its possibilities could not possibly have been exhaustively treated in the historical Ḥadīth.

The Ḥadīth were accorded the role of basis of law in Islamic jurisprudence by the universally accepted methodology of ash-Shāfi'ī. It then became inevitable that as Islam unfolded in history, the need for the tangible support which Ḥadīth could provide for intellectual and cultural developments called forth the "missing" or "unspoken" Ḥadīth that were now required. If in the first centuries the standard by which Ḥadīth were measured was that of an impeccable *isnād*, the growing needs of an expanding Islam of later times added *de facto* another, one of verisimilitude in the eyes of a developed and sophisticated religious community.

Thus it came about that there grew up a corpus of Ḥadīth which were clearly impossible historically, and yet were repeatedly quoted and rarely questioned. To the modern Western mind this may appear an anomaly which reflects little credit on Islam's intellectual integrity, a confusion which it would be desirable to rectify. To do so would be to call into question, for example, the Sainte Chapelle, because the Crown of Thorns, which it was built to house, could be shown to be a medieval forgery. This relic, which a Byzantine Emperor in need of money sold to St. Louis (followed by the baby linen of Jesus, the lance that pierced his side, the sponge and chain of his passion, the reed of Moses, and part of the skull of John the Baptist), called forth one of the most magnificent creations of Western civilization. The resulting Chapel, rather than being a monument to gullibility, testifies to the authenticity, on the spiritual plane (which is more real than the material one), of its historical cause. Truth transcends historical niceties.

There are so-called "Ḥadīth" and "Sunnah" which are patently, or pointlessly, false, such as the common story that the Prophet went into rages upon seeing a shape resembling a cross, and shattered crosses whenever he found them. This is in such contradiction to the Prophet's nature that it is easy to see it as a zealot fable substituting human pettiness for Prophetic rigor. It is not true, nor does it add any depth or strength to what is in fact true. Then there are the polemical Ḥadīth which were invented as propaganda to support one or another party in dynastic and political struggles. There are also Ḥadīth, which have nothing objectionable in their content, but which the Prophet could not have uttered for historical reasons: "I [God] have an army in the east I call the Turks; I unleash them against any people that kindle my wrath". But there are others again which, although they appear late in history, have an authenticity of spirit about them, and have been accepted as authentic, to the extent that they were frequently repeated by Muslim scholars, and not challenged. This is a consensus of silence which amounts to acceptance. The scholars, and thence the *ummah* ("community"), have found them to be adequate expressions of the spirit of the Prophet's message. Among these are the sayings: "Who has seen me [the Prophet] has seen the Truth", and, "The first thing God created was Intellect".

When the Prophet was leading a prayer in the mosque of Medina, and had finished the words "God hears him who praises Him", a man called out from the back, "Our Lord, and to Thee praise." The Prophet said that he saw Angels rushing to record those words, which were thereafter included in the canonical prayer.

Tradition records that the ritual, or canonical, prayer was taught to the Prophet by the Angel Gabriel. Yet here, the Prophet unhesitatingly incorporated the isolated words of an ordinary person into the context of a Divine ordinance. This, in effect, is what the Islamic community has done, in accepting as authentic, Ḥadīth which clearly could not be traced back to the Prophet.

These are the expression of a transpersonal genius and the living soul of the religious manifestation, and so, for all purposes, are the utterances of the Prophet. They are *virtually* authentic because they are recognized as such by the Muslim community. Just as the Prophet could accept as part of the Divine revelation words spoken by a third party, so Islam has accepted, in effect, that some Ḥadīth are the Prophet speaking outside of time. *See* MUḤAMMAD; SUNNAH.

Haḍrah (lit. "presence").

1. Divine Presence. (*See* FIVE DIVINE PRESENCES.)

2. In later Islam a courtly reference to the Caliph.

3. A title of respect or simply of politeness to any person. In the Near East it is pronounced as *hazrat.*

4. A popular name for the sacred dance of the Sufis. *See* 'IMĀRAH.

Ḥāfiẓ (present participle of the verb *ḥafaẓa*, "to protect", "preserve" and, by extension, "to memorize"). One who has memorized the Koran. The goal of Koranic school education is to commit the entire Koran to memory, and many traditional Muslims have done so. As the Koran says of itself, it is easy to memorize; "And we have made the Koran easy for remembrance; are there then men who will be reminded?" (54:17). There are indeed *ḥuffāẓ* (pl. of *ḥāfiẓ*) who achieve this without understanding the Arabic of the sacred text, particularly in the Indian sub-continent and South-East Asia. In this case, it is the sound or the form of the revealed scripture that vehicles a supernatural, saving grace.

Ḥāfiẓ, Shams ad-Dīn Muḥammad (d. *793*/1391). A Persian poet of Shirāz, famous for his *Dīwān*, a collection of Sufic poetry. In Ḥāfiẓ there is a compression of many subjects into one *ghazāl.* The *ghazāl* has hemistichs and the rhyme is aa;ba;ca;da for 9,11,12 or exceptionally 15 lines (the epic is aa;bb;cc;dd). Ḥāfiẓ speaks of love, panegyric, wine and songs all in one, suffused by a mystical spirit, producing a multifaceted result. Because of this, in Iran Ḥāfiẓ is often opened for the purpose of oracular divination. Love in Persian poetry is often addressed to an adolescent boy who can represent the divinity (in translations made in the past, such as below by Sir William Jones, "the boy" is made into "a maid"). Translations of Ḥāfiẓ usually are one and a half times longer than the Persian original, and none has ever been able to convey the what it is that makes Ḥāfiẓ so famed.

Ḥāfiẓ was much studied by Goethe and influenced the modern school of Russian poetry. He was called the "Tongue of the Hidden".

Sweet maid, if thou would'st charm my sight,
And bid these arms thy neck enfold;
That rosy cheek, that lily hand
Would give thy poet more delight
Than all Bocara's vaunted gold,
Than all the gems of Samarcand.
Boy, let yon liquid ruby flow,
And bid thy pensive heart be glad,
Whate'er the frowning zealots say:
Tell them, their Eden cannot show
A stream so clear as Rocnabad,
A bower so sweet as Mosallay.
O! when these fair perfidious maids,
Whose eyes our secret haunts infest,
Their dear destructive charms display;
Each glance my tender breast invades,
And rob my wounded soul of rest,
As Tartars seize their destin'd prey.
In vain with love our bosoms glow:
Can all our tears, can all our sighs,
New lustre to those charms impart?
Can cheeks, where living roses blow,
Where nature spreads her richest dyes,
Require the borrow'd gloss of art?
Speak not of fate: Oh! Change the theme.
And talk of odours, talk of wine,

Talk of the flowers that round us bloom:
'Tis all a cloud, 'tis all a dream:
To love and joy, thy thoughts confine,
Nor hope to pierce the sacred gloom.
Beauty has such resistless power,
That ever the chaste Egyptian dame
Sigh'd for the blooming Hebrew boy!
For her how fatal was the hour,
When to the banks of the Nilus came
A youth so lovely and so coy!
But oh! sweet maid, my counsel hear
(Youth should attend when those advise
Whom long experience renders sage):
While music charms the ravish'd ear:
While sparkling cups delight our eyes,
Be gay: and scorn the frowns of age.
What cruel answer have I heard!
And yet, by heaven, I love thee still;
Can aught be cruel from thy lip?
Yet say, how fell that bitter word
From lips which streams of sweetness fill,
Which nought but drops of honey sip?
Go boldly forth, my simple lay,
Whose accents flow with artless ease,
Like orient pearls at random strung:
Thy notes are sweet, the damsels say;
But O! far sweeter, if they please
The nymphs for whom these notes are sung.

Ḥafsah. One of the wives of the Prophet, and a daughter of ʻUmar. She knew how to read and write and participated in the collecting of the Koran during the Caliphate of ʻUthmān. She was entrusted with the safekeeping of one of the earliest written collections of Koranic verses, a *muṣḥaf* (a copy of the Koran), which had already existed during the Caliphate of Abū Bakr. *See* WIVES of the PROPHET.

Hagar, *see* ISMĀʻĪL.

Hagiah Sophia (Gr. lit. "Divine wisdom"). The famous basilica of Constantinople, now Istanbul, and today called Aya Sofia, using the modern Greek pronunciation. Under the Ottoman Turks the architect Sīnān remodeled the church, by then a mosque, with great skill. Since the time of Atatürk it has been a museum.

When the city of Constantinople fell to the Ottoman Turks under Sultan Mehmet II on Tuesday 29 May 1453, the conqueror ordered the edifice to be converted to a mosque in time for the congregational prayer on Friday. This consisted of the erection of a wooden minaret, the construction of a *miḥrāb* (a niche to indicate the direction of Mecca), and the addition of a *minbar*, a moveable staircase which served as a pulpit.

Mehmet was to replace the wooden modifications with brick, and added arch butresses and retaining walls to the building. The three stone minarets which complete the Aya Sofia's famous outline today were added by the architect Sīnān under Selim II and Murad III. *See* SĪNĀN.

Ḥajj, *See* PILGRIMAGE.

al-Ḥajjāj ibn Yusuf (*41-95*/661-714). The leading general of the early Umayyads. On behalf of the Umayyad rulers Marwān, ʻAbd al-Malik, and al-Walīd, al-Ḥajjāj conducted a struggle against ʻAbd Allāh ibn az-Zubayr who had raised opposition to the Umayyads, declared himself Caliph, and held Mecca, finally defeating him. Then al-Ḥajjāj was sent to pacify unrest in Iraq. He succeeded by unhesitatingly applying cruelty and force, and remained Umayyad governor of Iraq for twenty years until his death.

Al-Ḥajjāj was a competent soldier and strategist, and an able administrator. Under him the Arab armies expanded into India and Central Asia. But his reputation for ruthlessness and brutality completely overshadows any good report of his qualities. It is therefore a great irony that the present building of the Kaʻbah dates in large part from his reconstruction of it after the conquest of Mecca from ʻAbd Allāh ibn az-Zubayr, and that the introduction of vowel markings into Arabic from Syriac, in order to prevent misreading of the Koran, was initiated under his direction.

Ḥākim. 1. A ruler or governor.

2. The name of a Fāṭimid Caliph who died in *411*/1021. Al-Ḥākim had the Church of the Holy Sepulchre destroyed in Jerusalem, an event which was a contributory cause to the Crusades. The ruler was noted for his erratic behaviour and was responsible for events which led to the creation of the Druze sect. He passed a series of laws which have sometimes been considered signs of madness. But these laws have also been explained as attempts to preserve a system, or rather an anti-system which was collapsing, by the rules of that anti-system. Thus Ḥākim's law against "women coming out of their houses in the day" was an attempt to remove from the system the wealth of his female relatives by not allowing them to participate in the economy, This was rather like measures put forward as the Soviet Union was collapsing, measures such as the sudden, abrupt removal of 50 and 100 ruble notes in one day from circulation which created tremendous upheaval but made sense to the Communist financial authorities. *See* DRUZES.

Ḥakīm. 1. Lit. "The Wise", *al-Ḥakīm*, a name of God.

2. In classical times a title for someone learned as a doctor. At that time medicine was part of philosophy and a *ḥakīm* was versed in both fields.

Ḥāl (lit. "a state", "condition"; pl. *aḥwāl*). A technical term in Sufism for a transitory state of illumination, as opposed to a *maqām* ("station") which, once acquired, remains a permanent station of the soul. Ibn Aṭā'Allāh says: "When He wants to show his grace to you, He creates states in you and attributes them to you."

The Persian Sufi Abū Naṣr as-Sarrāj (d. *378*/988) lists some typical states in his *Kitāb al-Lumā'*: attentiveness (*murāqabah*); the feeling of nearness to God (*qurb*); love (*maḥabbah*); hope in God (*rajā' fī-Llāh*); longing (*shawq*); familiarity (*uns*); confidence (*iṭmīn*); contemplativeness (*mushāhadah*); and certitude (*yaqīn*).

Ḥalāl (lit. "released" [from prohibition]). That which is lawful, particularly food, and meat from animals that have been ritually slaughtered. The opposite is *ḥarām*. *See* FOOD; RITUAL SLAUGHTER.

Ḥalīmah bint Abī Dhu'ayb. The Beduin foster mother of the Prophet who cared for him as a child. The name Ḥalīmah means the "mild, caring one". Customarily, the town Arabs gave a small boy to the Beduins for several years, against payment, to be brought up speaking the purer Arabic of the desert and to be tempered by the hardships of desert life. Her husband's name was Ḥarīth; they belonged to the Banū Sa'd ibn Bakr, a branch of the Ḥawāzīn. *See* RIḌĀ

al-Ḥallāj, Ḥusayn ibn Manṣūr (*244-309*/857-922). A Persian mystic born in Baida in southern Iran who was tried for heresy by the 'Abbāsid authorities in Baghdad and put to death, al-Ḥallāj was famed for his poetry which is highly appreciated to this day. He had no small number of disciples in many milieus of 'Abbāsid society, and a degree of popular acclaim. In addition to disciples he had sectarian sympathizers scattered far and wide distinguished among other things, by their vegetarianism and especially consumption of lettuce, a light bearing plant in one Iranian religion.

Miracles were ascribed to him, but so was wizardry. He seems to have been either a member of a secret organization, or even to have headed one himself. In his travels to Turkestan he was called by the title of *muqit*, which means "vegetarian provider". He may have been involved in stirring up revolt against the civil authorities, or indoctrinating people in some movement, for in the houses of al-Ḥallāj's disciples the 'Abbāsid authorities found:

> a great number of documents, written on Chinese paper, some of them in gold ink. Some were mounted on satin or silk, and bound in fine leather. Among other papers were curious files of letters from his provincial missionaries, and his instructions to them as to what they should teach, how they should lead people on from stage to stage, how different classes of people should be approached according to their level of intelligence and degree of receptiveness.

For many years he traveled widely in Persia, India and Turkestan, almost as far as the borders of China, visiting the cells of his co-religionists. From his propagandizing and religious activities he came to be called al-Ḥallāj, short for *ḥallāj al-asrār*, "the Carder (*ḥallāj*) of hearts or consciences" (to card is to disentangle, by combing, the fibers of wool, cotton, etc.). He remains enigmatic; many consider him a Saint, even a model of esoteric realization; others considered him to be too ambiguous to be a Saint; that his miracles were theatrical and staged to impress, involving the collusion of supporters or accomplices. It was reported in testimony against him that al-Ḥallāj himself, and members of his family, had encouraged veneration of him verging on worship. "God is in heaven" he said, "but He is also on earth". Even when he was young he had made claims which were startling:

"One day as I was walking with Ḥusayn ibn Manṣūr (said his master al-Makkī) in a narrow street at Mecca, I happened to be reciting from the Koran as we went along. He heard me."
"I could utter such things as that myself", said he.
"From that day on, I saw him no more."

When al-Ḥallāj had already achieved a certain notoriety, it was reported of him:

"At one time" (said Judge Muḥammad ibn 'Ubayd) "I sat as a pupil with al-Ḥallāj. He was practicing devotion in the Mosque at Baṣra in those days as a Koran teacher; it was before he made his absurd claims and got into trouble. One day my uncle was talking to him; I sat by listening. And Ḥallāj said: 'I shall leave Baṣra.'
'Why so?' my uncle inquired.
'People here talk about me too much; I am tired of it.'
'What are they saying?' my uncle asked.
'They see me do something', said Ḥallāj; 'and without staying to make any inquiry, which would have disabused them, they go about proclaiming that Ḥallāj gets answers to prayer, even that he performs evidentiary miracles. Who am I, that such things should be granted me? I will give you an example: a few days ago a man brought me some dirhams and told me to spend them for the poor. There were no poor about at the moment, so I put them under one of the Mosque mats, by a pillar, and marked the pillar. So long as I waited, no one came by; so I went home for the night. Next morning I took my place by that pillar and began to pray; and some dervishes, poor Sufis, gathered about me. So I stopped my prayer, lifted up the mat, and gave them the money. And they have set the rumor flying that I had only to touch dust for it to turn to silver!'
"He told similar stories, until my uncle rose and said good-bye to him. He never went to see Ḥallāj again. 'There's something of the deceiver about the man' he said to me. 'We shall hear more of him someday.'"

Al-Ḥallāj began as a disciple in Sufism of Sahl at-Tustarī, whom he left for al-Makkī, whom he also left. Then he attempted to enter the circle of disciples of al-Junayd al-Baghdādī, who refused him, saying: "I do not accept madmen". A well-wisher who followed the young al-Ḥallāj after this meeting tried to calm him: al-Ḥallāj answered: "I only respect [in al-Junayd] his age; the (mystical) degree is a gift and not something acquired". Al-Ḥallāj became well-known, nonetheless. He was often surprised by observers who found him in intimate conversation with God, apparently on exalted terms: "O Thou Whose Closeness girds my very skin". Despite his modest protestations that such utterings went "no further than the novice's first degree", and attempts to restrain those who heard them from proclaiming his apparent spiritual attainments, ample accounts of al-Ḥallāj's piety and nearness to God – indeed, of his Divinity – slipped out.

More than once al-Ḥallāj would cry out in the public marketplace words like these:

O men! save me from God, for he has ravished me from myself, and does not return me to myself... woe to him who finds himself bereft after such a Presence and abandoned after such a union!

This reduced the people in the market to tears. Another report of a similar public outcry says that when he saw the people begin to weep, he broke out in laughter. His ostentatious miracles often involved money: he pulled back the carpet in his house to reveal a heap of gold coins, and invited the spectators to take as much as they wanted, or he threw a purse supposedly containing a fortune into the Tigris, then later had a messenger present it intact to the remorseful giver. The purse was a reward for a cure: at a large gathering the host had implored al-Ḥallāj to heal his sick and dying son; "he's already healed" al-Ḥallāj said. The child was sent for, and brought out in good health, indeed, "looking as if he had never been ill". Reports of his cures and his divination spread far and wide.

Not everyone, of course, was convinced:

Ḥallāj converted many people to his system, and some important men among the rest. It was the Reactionaries he most hoped to win over, for he thought their belief as a good preliminary to his own; and he sent an emissary to Ibn Nawbakht, a member of that sect.

Ibn Nawbakht was a cautious, intelligent man. "Your master's miracles", he said to the disciple, "may well be conjuring tricks. I am", he went on, "what may be called a martyr to love: I enjoy the society of the ladies more than any other thing on earth. Unfortunately, however, I suffer from baldness. I have to let what hair I have grow long, and pull it over my forehead, and hold it there with

> my turban. And I have to disguise my grizzled beard with dye. Now, if Hallaj will give me a head of hair and a black beard, I will believe in whatever system he preaches; I will call him the Prophetic Vicar or the Sovereign if he likes; nay, I'll call him a Prophet, or even the Almighty!"

The clue to this account is the description of Ibn Nawbakht as a "cautious intelligent" man; that is, it was not mere incomprehension that led to his rebuffing al-Ḥallāj's advances, but the fact that he saw through him.

But al-Ḥallāj had highly placed followers in sensitive government positions, among them the Caliph al-Muqtadir's mother and his chamberlain an-Nāsir; and he preached the existence of Divinity in certain members of the 'Alid family. In *301*/913 al-Ḥallāj was placed under arrest and spent several years in detention for suspicious activities and the propagation of dubious doctrines. After a trial, he was condemned for heresy, reluctantly, by the civil and religious authorities (both exoteric and Sufis alike). The Qarmatian revolt was underway, the Fāṭimids were rising in North Africa, and the authorities were alarmed by the use of religion for political subversion. (Ḥallāj was often accused of being a Qarmati agent.) With public order at stake, religious orthodoxy, at least as regarded doctrines which cloaked organizations whose scope went far beyond spiritual contemplation, was a critical issue. In any case, al-Ḥallāj publicly proclaimed himself a heretic, saying such things as: "I have renounced faith in God, and this renunciation is obligatory for me, whereas for any Muslim it is execrable". And: "To claim to know Him is ignorance; to persist in serving Him is disrespect; to stop fighting Him is madness" etc. "To think that God can mix himself with the human", al-Ḥallāj said, "is impiety...and *shirk*" ("association"). Behind this antinomianism was his heretical interpretation of *Tawḥīd* ("Divine Unity"), which was that he, al-Ḥallāj, was God *completely* without any trace of humanity. Once in Isfahān, a preacher named 'Alī ibn Sahl was speaking about wisdom; al-Ḥallāj arrived on the scene and said: "Impudent one, you let yourself talk about wisdom while I am still alive!" – for which he was chased out of the city as a *zindiq* ("heretic" or "dualist"). Al-Ḥallāj finished his career in a public execution which drew large and sympathetic crowds; he was scourged, gibbeted, and finally decapitated. An official reported that:

> His disciples asserted that the person who had endured the scourging was not he, but some enemy of his on whom his likeness had been cast. Some of them even claimed to have seen him afterwards, and to have heard something from him to that effect, along with more nonsense not worth the trouble of transcribing.

Al-Ḥallāj is famous for having said: *Ana al-Ḥaqq* ("I am the Absolute"; or "the Real", "the Truth", as much as to say "I am God"). Aḥmad ibn Fātik said: "I heard al-Ḥallāj say 'I am the Truth; – and the truth belongs to God – clothed with His Essence, there is no difference (between us)'". This kind of declaration has earned al-Ḥallāj admiration from some; but arising in the midst of a religion whose beginning and end is the incomparable Absoluteness of God, the revelation of which in the *shahādah* is the cord of salvation, it was bound to raise questions and cause trouble. Al-Ḥallāj said *Ana al-Ḥaqq* in his poetry; according to didactic tradition he also announced it to the Sufi master al-Junayd, the mystic least likely to be impressed by such a proposition. His reply is that of orthodox Sufism: "Not so", said al-Junayd. "It is *through al-Ḥaqq* that you exist". It is not that al-Junayd denied knowledge of God without otherness (*tawḥīd*); but he defined it as the removal of obstacles between man and God. At the end of the path man remained man and God remained God, (*al-'abd yabqā-l-'abd, wa-r-Rabb yabqā-r-Rabb*) but man's realization of God was without limit, without contradiction, without reservation, without even the *shirk* ("association of another reality with God") that arises from thought and conceptualization itself. Al-Ḥallāj, and his school, claimed that there was a *personal* union; the individual was divinized, which naturally led to a cult around an individual in this world.

One Sufi described al-Ḥallāj's compositions and statements thus:

> Al-Ḥallāj wrote brilliantly, both allegories and theological and juridical formulations. All his mystical utterances are like the first visions of novices, though some are more powerful, some feebler, some more acceptable, some more improper than others. When God grants a man a Vision, and he tries afterward to put into words what he saw in the height of ecstatic power, and helped by Divine Grace, his words are apt to be

obscure, and the more so if he expresses himself hastily, and under the influence of self-admiration.

In his own time he was generally held to be a heretic, by Sufis in particular. After his death, however, a propaganda began in his favor, particularly from the region of Transoxiana, painting him as a martyr of exoteric incomprehension. Once he was long dead, with his haunting poetry surviving him, there was a partial rehabilitation of his memory. In a certain sense, the historic al-Ḥallāj was split into two persons: Ibn 'Arabī said that he saw in a vision that al-Ḥallāj was a Saint; but Ibn 'Arabī also said that he had a vision in which the Prophet accused al-Ḥallāj because al-Ḥallāj in effect had claimed to be greater than he; and so the Prophet said, it was right that al-Ḥallāj was condemned by the law. Al-Ḥallāj thus became a kind of conundrum; in virtue of which al-Ḥallāj's poetry often turns on apparent paradoxes:

God threw a man into the sea with his arms tied behind his back, and said to him: Careful! Careful! or you will get wet in the water!

Other poems deal with themes more familiar to mysticism but in a particularly dramatic fashion:

When in my thirst I stooped my face to wine, Dark in the cup I saw a shadow. Thine!

And:

I am my Love: my Love is I; two ghosts this body occupy. If you see me, He's what you see; When you see Him, you will see – me!

And:

Prophecy is the Lamp of the world's light;
But ecstasy in the same Niche has room.
The Spirit's is the breath which sighs through me;
And mine the thought which blows the Trump of Doom.
Vision said it. In my eye
Moses stood, on Sinai.

But revealing of Ḥallāj's secret are the words he spoke on the way to his execution, laughing:

"The account of Abu'l Hasan al-Hulwani who says: 'I was present that day which was the downfall of al-Ḥallāj, when he was brought bound in chains. And he walked happily under the chains, and he laughed, and I said to him: Master, whence comes this state? – This is the coquettery of the Beauty, which draws its elect to meet it.' And then he said:
'My drinking companion is beyond all suspicion,
As to his intention to betray me:
He invites, and greets me, as the host does to his guest; [He, the host, gives me to drink from the cup from which he drank himself]
But as soon the cup will go around, he calls for the mat and headsman..
This is destiny of he who drinks the wine in the month of Tammuz with the dragon.'"

Beauty is a Manichean term for the "Living Soul" or "light hidden in the world", or "the God of light". The host is Mani who, martyred, returns in the invisible to preside over a feast, which is the main ceremony of Manicheism, the Bema feast (there are other references in Ḥallāj to the Night Feast that ends the fast, and our "naw ruz"). The Host gives the same cup, that is, martyrdom, to Ḥallāj. (Several sucessors of Mani were martyred and imitation of Mani's life was the ideal.) Tammuz the month, is also the name of Tammuz-Adonis, who dies and returns to life, as did Mani, "the living", or Mani-Hayy. *See* al-JUNAYD; SAHL at-TUSTARĪ.

Ḥalqah. 1. A circle of listeners sitting in a mosque around a teacher. The term was used for those who attended the audiences of the Prophet. A *ḥalqah* also means a circle of spectators gathered on a public thoroughfare watching a performer or listening to a story teller.

2. The ruling council of elders of the 'Ibādites is called a *ḥalqah.*

Haly 'Abbās, *see* al-MĀJŪSĪ.

al-Hamaḍānī, Aḥmad ibn al-Ḥusayn called Badi az-Zamān, "the wonder of the age" (d. *399*/1008). The first writer of the stories called *Maqamat.* The narrator or *rāwī* in al-Hamaḍanī's stories is a character called Abu'l-Fatḥ al-Iskandarī, and the hero of the action Īsā ibn Hisham. The stories reflect the personalities of recognizable types from society. *See* al-ḤARĪRĪ.

Ḥamā'il, *see* AMULETS.

Ḥamālat al-Arsh (lit. "bearers of the throne"). The eight Angels whom the Koran mentions as the bearers of the throne of God.

Ḥamās (Ar. "zeal"). Ḥamās is an acronym for Islamic Resistance Movement (*Ḥarakat al-Muqāwamah al-Islāmīyah*). It grew out of the *Intifāḍah*, the Palestinian uprising against Israeli occupation in 1987. The Palestine Liberation Organization, is a secular Arab or Palestinian organization. Ḥamās arose as an Islamic militant resistance organization, following the lead of Hezbollah, a Shī'ite organization in Lebanon. Now one of its goals is to destroy the P.L.O. and it is better organized than the P.L.O. has been. Its founder, Shaikh Aḥmad Yāsīn, a crippled schoolteacher, had been a member of the Muslim Brotherhood and had run welfare and educational services in Gaza. He expanded into a military wing when the Muslim Brotherhood was being discredited for not being more active and the result was Ḥamās. His inspiration was Shaykh Izz ad-Dīn al-Qassām, a Muslim preacher in Haifa who had led revolts against British rule and Zionist settlers and who was killed in the 1930s dying in battle. The Ḥamās military wing is named after him. He was also the inspiration for the much smaller group Islamic Holy War (Islamic Jihād) dedicated solely to military struggle. Islamic Holy War's leader, Dr. Fatḥī Shiqāqī, was assassinated by Israeli agents in Malta in October 1995.

Yāsīn was arrested in 1989 and jailed in Israel. He and a number of other Hamas prisoners were released in 1997 in exchange for two Mossad agents arrested in Amman after an unsuccessful assassination attempt. He has said that Hamas would end its activities against Israel if Israel pulled out completely from the West Bank and Gaza.

In 1992, 415 Ḥamās activists were deported out of Israel and dumped on a snowy, barren hillside in Lebanon, where they remained for a long time as a reproach to Israeli policy. Ḥamās itself was the result of an Israeli policy originally to support Islamic movements in order to undermine the P.L.O. by causing religious divisions. Under Yāsīn's successor, Muḥammad Musa Abu Marzook, an American educated engineer and native of Gaza, there was a resumption of suicide bombings in protest over the Oslo accords of 1993 for limited Palestinian self-rule. He was arrested in New York in 1995 and released in 1997. Then direction passed to Emad al-Alami, an engineer from Gaza who is based in Damascus. Another leader, Maḥmud az-Zahar operated openly as the political leader in Gaza until he was arrested by Palestinians in 1996. The military wing was also run by Yahya Ayyash, known as the Engineer for his bomb making activity, until he was assassinated by a telephone bomb set by Israeli agents. He was succeeded by Muḥammad Dief.

Ḥamās is a mass movement with the support of at least a fifth of the Palestinians in the West Bank and Gaza. It has an estimated budget of seventy million dollars from the contributions of the Palestinian diaspora, supporters in the Middle East, and some governments. Thirty-five percent of the contributions originate in Europe and the United States. Most of the money goes to run charitable institutions such as schools, orphanages and clinics, and the care of families of those arrested by the Israelis, and the families of suicide bombers.

Ḥammām (lit. "bath"). The custom of Roman baths, with their "cold", "tepid" and "hot" rooms, which fulfill the requirements of the *ghusl*, or greater ablution, were adopted by the Arabs and incorporated into Islamic civilization. Baths of this type remain an amenity of Muslim towns.

Hammurabi. King of Babylonia in the 18th century B.C. A famous code of laws is attributed to him. This code of laws is an important forerunner of the laws in the Koran, as it is also a foreunner of Jewish law. After the revelation of the Koran, Roman law and Iranian Sassanid law played a great role in the shaping of Islamic law as it developed.

Hammurabi was referred to as the "king of justice" and royal decisions were *dinat sharrim*. There are 282 preserved laws in the Code of Hammurabi; it also resembles the *Sharī'ah* in that it concerns itself with economic life, morality, ethics, all in one. It is with some exception a *lex talionis*. The earlier Sumerian code of Ur-Nammu (lived 2112-2095 B.C.), King of Ur, tended more to punishment of crimes by compensation in payment. The Code of Hammurabi also made provision to protect women and children; and like Islamic law it made distinctions between compensation of damages towards victims having different degrees of social status, that is, free men and slaves.

It provided for a false witness to suffer the punishment that would have gone to the accused: "If a seignior accused another seignior and brought a charge of murder against him but has not proved it, his accuser shall be put to death." "If a seignior wished to divorce his wife who did not bear him children he shall give her money to the full amount of her marriage price and he shall also make good to her the dowry which she brought from her father's house and then he may divorce her." Some women could inherit 1/3 of their father's property or the usufruct thereof. "If a seignior struck another seignior's daughter and caused a miscarriage, he shall pay ten shekels of silver for her fetus." (Similarly in Islamic law when an abortion is caused, the father pays the woman a blood price for the fetus.)

Very similar to the Koran (83:1) are also these Sumero-Akkadian Hymns: "He who handles the scales in falsehood, he who deliberately changes the stone weights and lowers their weight will make himself lie for his profits and then lose his [bag of weights]".

Ḥamdalah. The formula *al-ḥamdu li-Llāh*, (also pronounced colloquially *ḥamdillah*), meaning "praise to God". It is uttered at the end of meals, to mark the end of an activity, and as an interjection in appropriate circumstances.

Traditionally, the phrase is a formal beginning to a speech, in which case it is followed by *wa-ṣ-ṣalātu wa-ṣ-salamu 'alā mawlānā rasūli-Llāh*, ("blessings and peace upon our Lord the Messenger of God".) The extended form *al-ḥamdu li-Llāhi waḥdah*, ("praise to God alone") is written at the head of letters. The *ḥamdalah* is used to terminate actions begun by the *basmalah*. The *ḥamdalah* is, in medieval theological and alchemical terms, the *coagula*, and the *basmalah* the *solve*.

Hamzah. One of the letters of the alphabet, an aspiration of breath, or a passage from silence to sound. The first letter of the Arabic alphabet, the *alif*, is actually a support, or *kursī*, for the hamzah. By itself the hamzah is without sound, but is the beginning of the sound of following letters, or the interval between sounds. This is highly symbolical and it should be noted that it is the first letter of the Divine Name *Allāh*.

Hamzah bin 'Abd al-Muṭṭalib. An uncle of the Prophet, an early convert to Islam and one of its more ardent champions in the battlefield. He had been a hunter and was a man of prowess. He was killed at the Battle of Uḥud by the lance of a slave called Wahshi who had been promised a rich reward for the life of Hamzah by Hind, the wife of Abū Ṣufyān, leader of the Meccan opposition. The Prophet mourned his death with particular sadness. *See* BATTLE of UḤUD.

Ḥanafī, *see* SCHOOLS of LAW.

"Ḥanafī Muslims". A Black American Muslim group which grew out of the "The Nation of Islam". Hamaas Abdul Khaalis left the "Nation of Islam" in 1958 and adopted orthodox Islam of the Ḥanafī School of Law. There are close to one hundred mosques in the U.S. which look upon Abdul Khaalis as their authority. The number of followers is not known. *See* "BLACK MUSLIMS".

"Hand of Fāṭimah" (Ar. *yadd Fāṭimah*, and *al-kaff*, "the palm"). A stylized image of the palm which is a popular decorative motif for jewellery in the Islamic world. The hand depicted in this way is a magical symbol of power, and is thus used as a talisman, for the hand is the capacity to control nature and bring order out of chaos. The symbol is ancient; it is found in many cultures, notably that of the Indians of North America. Despite its name, it has nothing to do with Fāṭimah, the daughter of the Prophet.

Handasah (supposedly derived from Persian *andāzeh* "quantity", "measure"). The science of land measurement, and then, by extension, the terracing of land and engineering in general. The Arabs built dams for irrigation in very early times. Traces of ancient dams still exist in the region of Mecca. The most famous dam of all, however, was that of Ma'rib in the Yemen, which existed before the Christian era. The collapse of this dam around 580, an event preserved in poetry and legend, sent a signal throughout the tribes as far as the Syrian desert that the epoch of the greatness of the South Arabian kingdoms had passed.

One great early work of Arab engineering was the bringing of water to Mecca from the nearby mountains. The Spanish brought a heritage of Arab engineering to the Americas, even as far north as New Mexico, in the form of irrigation techniques. *See* SĀQIYAH.

Ḥanīf. A word, of doubtful derivation, used in the Koran to describe one who adheres to pristine monotheism (pl. *hunafā'*). A descriptive name in the Koran for Abraham, and for those before Islam who by the purity and uprightness of their nature did not succumb to paganism and polytheism. The *ḥunafā'* between Abraham and the time of the Prophet were thus the faithful representatives of the Abrahamic-Ishmaelite tradition during the period called the *Jāhiliyyah* ("Age of Ignorance") which saw a descent into paganism. One of these, Umayyah ibn Abī 'ṣ-Ṣalt, was known as a great poet; another, Quss ibn Sa'īdah, was a famous orator.

Ḥaqīqah (lit. "truth" or "reality", cognate with *Ḥaqq,* "Reality", "Absolute"). The esoteric truth which transcends human and theological limitations. In this sense ḥaqīqah is the third element of the ternary *sharī'ah* ("law"), that is, exoterism; ṭarīqah ("path"), or esoterism, and ḥaqīqah, essential truth.

Ḥaqīqah is also called *lubb* ("kernel", "quintessence") related to a Koranic phrase (28:29 and elsewhere): "those who possess the kernels" (Ar. *ūlu-l-albāb*), meaning "those who have insight or grasp the essence". Hence the Sufi adage: "to get at the kernel, you have to break the shell", which means that esoterism "shatters" exoterism, just as essence "shatters" forms in the sense that it cannot be reduced to them.

In India particularly, the concept of *ḥaqīqah* was emphasized to such a degree, especially by the schools claiming *waḥdat al-wujūd* ("unity of being", or monism), that many Sufis dispensed with the practice of the religious law (*sharī'ah*). This prompted strong orthodox reactions on the part of schools which emphasized *waḥdat ash-shuhūd* ("unity of consciousness"), such as the Chishti reaction as in the words of Sayyid Muhammad Gesūdarāz:

> People keep on saying that *ḥaqīqah* is the Divine Secret; but I Muhammad Husayni say that *sharī'ah* is the Divine Secret, because I have heard talk of *ḥaqiqah* from Haidaris, Qalandaris, Mulhids [heretics], Zindiqs [Manicheans]; nay I have even heard it from the mouths of Yogis, of Brahmans, and of Gurus; but talk of *sharī'ah* I have not heard from any one's lips than the people of the true faith and beliefs [i.e. Sunnis]. From this it is evident that *sharī'ah* is the Divine Secret.

See SUFISM.

Ḥaram (lit. "restricted", "forbidden", "sacred" and, by extension, "sacred possession or place"). The sacred areas around Mecca, Medina, and the Temple Mount of Jerusalem. The first two are often referred to as the *ḥaramayn* ("the two sacred sites"), and in these it is forbidden to take life, except for the extermination of noxious or dangerous animals, along with other restrictions. Non-Muslims are not allowed into these sacred zones which extend around the cities of Mecca and Medina for a radius of several miles. Jerusalem is sometimes referred to as *thālith al-ḥaramayn* ("the third sacred site").

The Grand Mosque of Mecca is called *al-Masjid al-Ḥarām* ("The Sacred Mosque"), often referred to simply as *al-Ḥaram.*

In Arabic, that part of a house reserved for its women is called by the related word *ḥarīm* (whence "harem"). In modern Arabic, *ḥarīm* may also mean women, sing. *ḥurmah. See* also ḤARĀM below.

Ḥarām (lit. "forbidden", for revealed, i.e. sacred, reasons). That which is prohibited. In *fiqh* (jurisprudence) all actions fall into one of five categories: prohibited (*ḥarām*), discouraged (*makrūh*), neutral (*mubāḥ*), recommended (*mustaḥabb*), and obligatory (*farḍ*). *See* also ḤARAM above; FIQH.

al-Ḥaramayn *See* ḤARAM; MECCA; MEDINA; JERUSALEM.

Harem, *see* ḤARAM; ḤARĪM.

Ḥarīm (lit. "forbidden [area]"). The women's quarters in a Muslim household, whence the English word "harem". In Turkey it is called the *haramlik,* as opposed to the *salamlik,* the "place of greetings", the salon or men's quarters. *See* ḤARAM.

al-Ḥarīrī, al-Qāsim ibn Ali (*446-516*/1054-1122). Famous author of picaresque stories called *maqamāt.* The genre probably derives from Buddhist *jataka* tales. Al-Ḥarīri was from Baṣra where he was an official in the bureau of information (*Ṣāhib al-Khabar*), a sort of intelligence service of the Caliphs. His Maqamat are noted for their literary and linguistic qualities. The dramatic anecdotes center around an eloquent character called Abū Zeid of Seruj and his narrator companion Harith ibn Hammam. The choice of names, which is as non-descript as possible, is seen from this Ḥadīth "Every one of you [Arabs] is a *Harith* [one who acquires gain by trade] and everyone of you is a *Hammam* [one who is subject to cares and anxieties]. The *Maqamāt* have been translated into English as "The Assemblies of al-Hariri".

Harrān. A town called Harrān (the Roman Carrhae) in northern Mesopotamia, in what is now Altinbasak, in southern Turkey, near Urfa (Edessa). Harrān was the ancient Harranu (Biblical Haran) of Sumerian times. It lay on the safer of two roads, avoiding the deserts of the nomadic Amorites, from Ur and Babylon to the Mediterranean. Abraham came to Harran from Ur of the Chaldees. There Sin (the Semitic name of the Sumerian Nanna) the god of the moon had an important and famous temple (cf. Koran 6:76-88 which describes how Abraham first worshiped the moon, then the sun, then Allāh). Shamash the sun god (Sumerian Utu or Babar, "the resplendent") probably also had a temple. Particularly interesting from the point of view of later developments, Nusku, a god of light, the son of Sin was also venerated in Harran.

It was in Harran that Abraham's father Terah (in Arabic *Azar*) died; it was there that Abraham was commanded to go into Canaan by God in the Old Testament; it was there that Isaac married Rebekah, and Jacob labored for Laban. It was the center of the Biblical land of Padan-Aram. The land of Padan-Aram was occupied by the Amorites until 1100 B.C. and thereafter by the Arameans until they lost their national identity with their conquest by the Assyrians in 732 B.C. The adoption by the Aramaeans of the Canaanite alphabet, instead of the cuneiform script, made their language into the lingua franca of the Near East.

The philosophical development of Harran must have been strongly influenced by the proximity of the kingdom of Commagene. In what is now south east Turkey, in the former Seleucid province of Commagene, made into an independent kingdom in 162 B.C. by a governor named Ptolemy, Mithridates I an Iranian prince established himself and the kingdom became the westernmost Zoroastrian country, which unlike Zoroastrianism elsewhere depicted its divinities in the form of Hellenistic statues. The capital was Samosata. In Commagene wine was used liturgically. The rulers of Commagene were the Orontids who originally ruled in Armenia at the time of Darius. The Kingdom endured until 72 A.D. when they were wiped out by Vespasian in the course of the Jewish war.

In Islamic times, the Harranians were Hellenistic pagans whom the Christians did not succeeded in converting; nor did the Muslims. According to Ibn an-Nadīm, it was the Caliph al-Ma'mūn, who passing through the region learned of the Harranians being pagans and who informed them that unless they adopted Christianity, Judaism or Islam, they would be put to death as idolators. It was then that they hit upon the stratagem of claiming to be Sabians, a people mentioned in the Koran as People of the Book i.e., those who had received Divinely revealed religions. One of their number, Abū Iṣḥāq ibn Ḥīkal, a secretary to the Caliphs al-Muṭī and aṭ-Ṭā'i obtained a *fatwa* ("legal decision") to this effect.

Shahrastānī (d. *548*/1153), the scholar who carried out a survey of religions, and Ibn an-Nadīm (d. *385*/995), called a party of the Harranians *aṣḥāb ar-ruḥāniyyah* ("spirit worshipers"). Al-Masūdī (d. *345*/956) said that they had temples dedicated to "intellectual substances", and that the Mandaeans were a dissident sect of Harranians. There was a Manichean church in Harran (and there had been a community in nearby Edessa where Bardaisan had lived). The Harranians played an important role in transmitting the philosophic, scientific, and Hermetic knowledge of the Greeks to the civilization of Islam. Jābir ibn Ḥayyān (d. *160*/776), the famous alchemist, was of Harranian origin, as was Thābit ibn Qurrā (d. *288*/901), mathematician, physician, and philosopher, and many other men of learning. Shihāb ad-Dīn Suhrawardī founder of the school of Illuminationism (*ishrāq*) acquired some of his notions in Harran. Its proximity to Commagene doubtless made it a repository of Iranian ideas. (Al-Bīrūnī incorrectly, of course, opined that Zoroaster had belonged to the sect of Harran and had gone there with his father "to meet Elbus the philosopher and acquire knowledge from him". It had a Platonic academy. Under the Umayyads a school of medicine from Alexandria established itself in Harran and it was the capital of the last Umayyad Caliph. The city was one of several Gnostic centers destroyed by the Mongols, perhaps at the suggestion of their Shī'ite advisers eager to eliminate ideologic competitors. *See* SABIANS; SHAHRASTĀNĪ.

Harranians. *See* HARRAN.

Harratin. Populations of mixed Arab and Negro blood found in villages on the northern edge of the Sahara in Morocco.

Hārūn. The Arabic name for Aaron, the brother of Moses. (*See* AARON). In Arab folklore, Hārūn is the name of the King of the Jinn and as such is the folk word for an echo, that is, "an answer called back by a Jinn".

Hārūn ar-Rashīd (*147-194*/764-809). The fifth 'Abbāsid Caliph. Baghdad was his capital and the Caliphate reached its apogee during his reign, which declined after the crisis marked by the downfall of the Barmecides, a Persian family that had long provided the 'Abbāsids with able ministers of state. Hārūn ar-Rashīd had diplomatic relations with Charlemagne and with the Emperor of China. His sumptuous and celebrated court is associated with the present form of the tales of the *Thousand and One Nights*. *See* 'ABBĀSIDS.

Hārūt and Mārūt According to the Koran (2:96), two Angels who taught sorcery to men in Babel (Ar. *Bābil*; "Babylon" a name for Mesopotamia), and sowed division between husband and wife. However, they never misled anyone without first warning their victims of the consequences of their knowledge. The origin of the names are in Avestan *Haurvatat* ("wholeness") and *Ameretat* ("immortality"), in Pahlavi *Hordad* and *Amurdad*, two of the seven Zoroastrian divinities that are the heptad of the Amesha Spentas. Their presence in the Koran testifies to the upheaval in Semitic religious thought that began when Cyrus conquered Babylon and Mesopotamia and Zoroastrian doctrines revolutionized religious ideas in the Middle East.

When there has come to them a Messenger from God
confirming what was with them, a party of them
that were given the Book reject the Book of God
behind their backs, as though they knew not,
and they follow what the Satans recited
over Solomon's kingdom. Solomon disbelieved not,
but the Satans disbelieved, teaching
the people sorcery, and that which was sent down
upon Babylon's two angels, Harūt and Mārūt;
they taught not any man, without they said,
'We are but a temptation; do not disbelieve'.
From them they learned how they might divide
a man and his wife, yet they did not hurt
any man thereby, save by the leave of God,
and they learned what hurt them, and did not
profit them, knowing well that whoso buys it
shall have no share in the world to come;
evil then was that they sold themselves for,
if they had but known.
Yet had they believed, and been godfearing,
a recompense from God had been better,
if they had but known. (2:95-98)

Ḥasan (*3-50*/625-670). More properly al-Ḥasan, the eldest grandson of the Prophet. He succeeded his father 'Alī to become the fifth Caliph. For most Shī'ites, Ḥasan is also the second Imām. Mu'āwiyah, the Umayyad governor of Damascus, attacked Ḥasan; before a definitive battle could take place, Ḥasan himself offered to give up the Caliphate in return for remuneration and pensions for himself and his brother Ḥusayn. (Ḥasan's offer crossed with a proposal from Mu'āwiyah that the renunciation be temporary for the lifetime of Mu'āwiyah with *carte blanche* regarding the other conditions. Upon receipt of Ḥasan's offer Mu'āwiyah withdrew his own).

According to the historian aṭ-Ṭabarī, among the conditions of the abdication were that Ḥasan would retain five million dirhams then in the treasury of Kufah, that he would receive the annual revenue from the Persian district of Darabjird, and that 'Alī would not be reviled by the authorities as had been Mu'āwiyah's practice. Others say that the Caliphate was to be restored to Ḥasan upon the death of Mu'āwiyah.

Ḥasan's Caliphate lasted six months in all. He died in Medina, some eight years after his abdication. Shī'ite accounts say that he was poisoned by his wife upon the instigation of Yazīd, the son of Mu'āwiyah. But this must be taken with caution because according to Shī'ite accounts almost all the Imāms were murdered by the Sunnī rulers.

Ḥasan was famous for his many marriages

which numbered more than 130. The rapidity and frequency with which Ḥasan repudiated his wives led him to be called *al-Muṭliq* ("the Divorcer"). His father 'Alī had to warn men not to give their daughters in marriage to his son, which deterred no-one. Families favored the connection with the Prophet's family and the young women were eager to be, even if only for a short time, the wife of the grandson of the Prophet.

Ḥasan Baṣrī (*21-110*/642-728). A famous Sufi, born in Medina the son of a freed slave. He settled in Baṣra (Iraq), where he became known for his learning. During the reign of the Umayyads, when intellectual activity was at low ebb, Ḥasan of Baṣra was a lighthouse who attracted a wide circle of students.

In his school were treated all the ideas that were to grow into Islamic law, theology, and Sufism. He is a link in the transmission of many Ḥadīth, having known many Companions in Medina; most of the Sufi initiatic chains (*silsilahs*), pass through him; the Mu'tazilites started out, according to tradition, by breaking away from his school. Ḥasan, a giant of his age, left no writings, but was quoted widely by others. To judge from his influence, his scope and depth were as great as any of the later major figures whose work was more extensively recorded. Ḥasan is famous for the saying "the world is a bridge upon which you cross but upon which you should not build". (In India this is attributed to Jesus and is an inscription at Fatehpur Sikri). It is reported that he said:

> "God made fasting as a training ground for His servants, that they may run to His obedience. Some win that race and get the prize; others fail, and go away disappointed. But by my life! if the lid were off, the well-doer would be too busy about his well-doing, as the evil-doer in his evil-doing, to get him a new garment or anoint his hair."

> "The wonder is not how the lost were lost, but how the saved were ever saved.
> Fear must be stronger than hope. For where hope is stronger than fear, the heart will rot.
> My asceticism is mere lust, and my patience cowardice;
> and all my asceticism in this world is lust for the Other, the quintessence of lust. But how excellent is a man whose patience is for God's sake, not for the sake of being delivered from Hell; and his asceticism for God's sake, not for the sake of getting into Heaven. One grain of true piety is better than a thousandfold weight of fasting and prayer."

In the *Waṣiyyah* of Maḥmūd ibn 'Īsā can be found these prescriptions of Ḥasan Baṣrī's to spiritual disciples:

> One must seek to have the ten qualities of a dog: to sleep little during the night, which is a characteristic of a truly fervent soul. Not to complain of the heat or the cold, which is the virtue of patient hearts. Not to leave behind an inheritance, which is the character of true devotion.
>
> Never to be angry or envious, which is the character of the True Believer. To keep away from those who devour, which is the nature of the poor. Not to have a fixed abode, which is the quality of being a pilgrim. To be content with what we are thrown to eat, which is the virtue of moderation. To sleep where we find ourselves, which is the characteristic of a satisfied heart. Never to mistake who is our Master, and if he strikes us, to return to Him, which is the quality of hearts that are aware. To be always hungry, which is the characteristic of men of virtue... To be with the crowd dims the light of the heart.

Ḥasān ibn Thābit, see ḤASSĀN ibn THĀBIT.

Ḥasanah (pl. *ḥasanāt*). A good deed. The *ḥasanāt* are the good actions which will be placed, symbolically, upon the "scales" to determine salvation at the Day of Judgement. Ibn 'Aṭā' Allāh says:

> Do not seek recompense for a deed whose doer [the real active agent being God] was not you. It suffices you as recompense that He accepts it.

Ḥasanī **1.** An adjective for the *shurafā'* (sing. *sharīf*), or descendants of the Prophet through Ḥasan; those through Ḥusayn are called Ḥusaynī.

2. The Arab tribes of Mauritania call themselves the "Ḥasanī". They are considered to be "warrior" tribes. The Berbers of Mauritania are often called the "Ḥusaynī" tribes and are considered to be the "religious", or *zāwiyah* tribes, without, in either case, implying a descent from either Ḥasan or Ḥusayn, but rather a function or characteristic. The Arabic dialect of Mauritania is called *al-Ḥasaniyyah.*

Hāshimite. The Meccan clan – the Banū Hāshim – to which the Prophet and 'Alī belonged. The name Hāshimite is sometimes taken as a family name by descendants of the clan, as for example the royal family of Jordan, who are *shurafā',* or descendants of the Prophet. *See* MECCA; QURAYSH.

Ḥashr (lit. "assembling together"). The term used especially for the gathering together of creatures for the Day of Judgement.

Ḥassān ibn Thābit (d. 50/665). A poet of Medina who entered Islam. Ḥassān ibn Thābit composed poetry which extolled the Prophet, the faith, and such deeds of the Muslims as the victory of Badr. He recited his poetry at meetings in which Beduins came to Medina to hear of Islam. The Prophet gave Sirin – the Coptic slave-girl he had received with her sister Maryah, from the Muqawqīs of Egypt – as a gift to Ibn Thābit. *See* MUQAWQĪS; UMMĪ.

Ḥātim aṭ-Ṭā'ī. A famous figure in Arab folklore. A chieftain's son, Ḥātim aṭ-Ṭā'ī was charged with the care of sheep, or camels, by his father. As a dutiful host he slaughtered several of them in order to feast strangers who arrived at his absent father's tents. The rest of the herd he divided among the guests as a gift.

He became the honored epitome of Arab hospitality, but was also known as a warrior. His legendary exploits were to find a prominent place in Arab literature but with the spread of Islam were even more extolled in Persia, India and even Malaya.

The sister of the son of Ḥātīm aṭ-Ṭā'ī, 'Ādī ibn Ḥatīm aṭ-Ṭā'ī, had been captured by the Muslims, treated well, and released. She told her brother, a recalcitrant pagan, of her impressions of the Prophet. 'Ādī came to Medina to see for himself.

When he arrived he was received with special honor by the Prophet.

> The illustrious man's son, 'Ādī ibn Ḥātim aṭ-Ṭā'ī, announced himself: the Prophet rose to his feet (which he never did for any other unbeliever), took him by the hand, and seated him on a cushion while he himself sat on the ground. The Prophet said: "In this world God has given you all you need; lordship of your people, and a famous name that your father left you. What could you lose if God gave you the other world besides? That world will be yours if you take on the faith I speak of.' 'Ādī was silent.
>
> "By the God Who made me!" the Prophet cried, " "this faith shall one day prevail from the rising to the setting sun!" 'Ādī entered Islam and his tribe followed him.

Afterwards many from the desert tribes came to Medina to surrender themselves unto God, and that year, the 9th of the Ḥijrah, became known as the "Year of Deputations".

Ḥawārī. A term taken from the Ethiopic referring, in the Koran, to the disciples of Jesus. Also, the name of the representatives of the Prophet who were designated after the second 'Aqabah pact. *See* 'AQABAH.

al-Ḥawqalah. The name for the frequently used expression *lā ḥawla wa lā quwwata illā bi-Llāh,* "there is no power and no strength save in God". It is particularly used in moments of distress to call forth the virtue of submission. The *ḥawqalah* is also an incantation in the face of evil. *See* PIOUS EXPRESSIONS; REFUGE.

Hawwā'. ("Eve"), see ADAM.

Hayrah. In mysticism, the terrifying consternation experienced by the first consciousness when it passed from non-existence to existence.

al-Hayūlā (Arabic, derived from the Greek word *hyle,* which originally meant "wood", and later came to be used of material in general and then, as a technical term, "substance", "matter"). *Al-hayūlā* stands for substance in the metaphysical sense of *materia prima.* The Arabs adopted the word from the Greeks as philosophy developed as a branch of Islamic learning.

Another word for *materia prima,* synonymous with *al-hayūlā* but antedating it, is *al-habā'* literally "dust". Referring to the dissolution of created manifestation, the Sūrah al-Wāqiah says: "and the mountains will be shattered and become scattered dust" [*habā'an munbatha*] that is, materia disassociated from form (56:5-6). The Caliph 'Alī used the word in this sense when he said that creation is like dust in the air, only made visible when struck by light. The light in 'Alī's simile corresponds to the eidos ("form") of Aristotle, which is the other pole of *hyle. Eidos* and *hyle* are the polarizations of Being, and are the equivalents (from the static and philosophic view of Scholasticism) of the Chinese Yang and Yin.

Hyle or *hayūlā* is *materia prima* (also *natura naturans*) in Being, and *materia secunda* (also *natura naturata*, in *Arabic al-jawhar al-habā'*) in the world – but not matter-quantity, as conceived of by modern science. This latter concept of materia as matter, is *materia* seen from below and defined only by quantitative distinctions (weight, extension, and what in modern science has become the "quantums"). This special view of materia, divorced from its metaphysical reality, is what the Scholastics called *materia signata quantitate* ("materia under the sign of number"). *See* FIVE DIVINE PRESENCES.

Heaven (Ar. *as-samā' pl. as-samāwāt*). The different heavens mentioned in the Koran represent degrees of spirituality, or domains; sometimes these are symbolically assigned to different Prophets. The origin of the concept is of course the planets visible to the eye. The "seventh heaven" marks the end of supraformal creation, and, in the symbolism of the seven directions of space, is the center.

The Koran depicts the heavens as being cleft apart at the end of the world (82:1), or being rolled up like a scroll (21:24). The sky, from the point of view of man, is the place where physical reality joins metaphysical reality. The sundering of the sky or the heaven is the irruption of the Divine into the created, which is also the meaning of the apocalyptic trumpet call of primordial sound. Paradise is usually called the *al-jannah* ("garden"), or *firdaws* ("paradise"). *See* FIRDAWS; al-JANNAH; SEVENTH HEAVEN.

"Heights, the", *See* al-A'RĀF.

Hejaz (Ar. *al-Ḥijāz*, lit. "the barrier"). A region, the Red Sea coast of Arabia from the south of Mecca northward beyond Yenbo, and inland as far as Medina. Its main cities are Mecca, Medina, Jeddah, Ṭā'if, and Yenbo.

Although the Hejaz was the cradle of Islam, after the founding of the Islamic state the political center shifted from Medina to Damascus, then to Baghdad, and the Hejaz became a cultural backwater. The region came under the administration of Sharīfian families who ruled in the name of the Caliphs. In World War I, the sons of the Sharīf of Mecca were prominent in raising the Arab revolt against the Ottoman Turks. When the war ended, Sharīf Ḥusayn of Mecca declared himself King of the Hejaz. In 1924, however, the Hejaz was conquered by King 'Abd al-'Azīz of the House of Sa'ūd from the Nejd. He took the title "King of the Nejd and the Hejaz". As more regions were added by conquest, the new, united Kingdom was called Saudi Arabia. Because of the pilgrimage to Mecca, Jeddah, and with it the Hejaz, has remained the hub of commerce in Arabia.

The Hejaz has its own dialect of Arabic. It also had, until recently, a typical style of architecture. The houses had projecting wooden balconies called *rawshan*, where one could sleep at night, or sit and enjoy the evening breeze. In the north, wind towers on the roofs would catch and circulate breezes through the house. The style is also found on the island of Suakin, in the Red Sea, formerly a colony of the Hejaz. *Ḥijazī* architecture is said to be in part the result of influences introduced by Malayan craftsmen, which testifies to the cosmopolitan nature of the region thanks to the presence of the holy cities that have drawn pilgrims and trade throughout the centuries. Today, unfortunately, the examples of this splendid architecture have largely disappeared, to be replaced by modern concrete buildings.

Hell. The place of torment where the damned undergo suffering most often described as fire, a fire whose fuel is stones and men. Names of hell used in the Koran are *an-nār* ("the fire"), *jahannam* ("Gehenna"), *al-jaḥīm* ("burning"), *aṣ-ṣa'īr* ("raging flame"), *as-saqar* ("scorching fire"), *al-hāwiyah* ("abyss"), *al-ḥuṭāmah* ("crushing pressure": in Persian it is called *dozakh*).

The physical sufferings of hell are the concretization of the state of inner contradiction which ensues from the denial of God. Or as the Koran says:

> Nay, but the unbelievers still cry lies,
> and God is behind them, encompassing. (85:19-20)

Hell is the manifestation of that denial. The soul undergoing the sufferings is in fact attached to them, that is, enjoys them in a certain way, just as the cruel or self-destructive enjoy the results of their cruelty in this life; those who are or remain in hell do so because they cannot detach themselves from the errors that brought them there in the first place. If they did, they would by that very fact be liberated; but in the place of true joy they put a false one, and the habit of egocentrism that prevented them from surrendering to God in life also prevents them from recognizing the truth of their state in hell.

The consequences of this state of contradiction may be suspended in life, but are inevitable when the protective modalities, time and space, which contain the world, are removed at death. Certain limbos and intermediate states are also possible after life for the soul which is not saved, that is, the soul which is not in conformity with the superior reality beyond manifestation.

Theologians make the distinction that both hell and paradise last for perpetuity (*Khuld*) and not for eternity (*abad*), that is, that they have no limit or end, in the sense that they are indefinite temporally. This distinction is necessary, for eternity is a quality that belongs to God alone. While paradise is not co-extensive with God, it is perpetual in that the blessed finally become one with their metaphysical possibility. The distinction applies all the more so to hell, albeit in another sense, in that hell ends for the individual once the consciousness of personality disappears, which happens sooner or later for all its inhabitants, even those whom Dante placed in the lowest circle.

The Mu'tazilites believed that if one entered hell, one never came out except, so to speak, when no more consciousness of an individual substance, a *persona*, remained; since one entering hell would already possess a somewhat chaotic nature, he could be considered as already on the way to the dissolution of consciousness in this life. However, most other theologians, particularly the school of al-Ash'arī, believe that if the person who entered hell was not an idolater, a *mushrik*, one who associated another reality with God, but a believer, then God could forgive his sins or non-conformities. This could take place immediately, aided perhaps by the intercession of the Divine Messengers whom the believer followed, despite his sins. Or the forgiveness could take place after a sojourn in hell in which the non-conformities had been "burned away".

There is a Ḥadīth which refers to this: "He shall make men come out of hell after they have been burned and reduced to cinders". God can forgive any sin but one: denial of His Reality, which is most easily grasped as His essential Unity; that nothing is absolutely real, except Him.

Existence in the world, the scholastics said, in accordance with the teachings of Aristotle, is accidents in relation to Being. In Islamic philosophy, and in its mysticism, which incorporated Aristotle and Plato within the intellectual framework of esotericism, Being is called *al-jawhar* ("the Jewel"), and "accidents", or contingencies which arise out of Being in the form of existence are called *a'rāḍ*. These are due to a privation of reality, since existence is the result of the removal of qualities from plenitude, a privation of what *Is*. Whatever exists does so because of the removal of something from invisible Being.

Now according to Aristotle, the absence of a quality calls forth its opposite. The same is true of the soul, which at death, when the world's coverings of time, space, and form are removed, is called upon to face the Substance of its reality. All space and all time become one place and event. Adequacy and essential conformity to the Substance at that confrontation, which can readily be likened to the Great Judgement, is what religions call salvation. Identity with that Substance is *moksha*, or deliverance from all contingency; it corresponds to what Islam calls the state of the *'ārif bi-Llāh* ("the knower by God"). The absence of an adequate conformity to that Substance, the absence of the qualities and equilibrium of Being with which one is confronted, the absence, for example, of kindness, uprightness, dignity, (privations of the Divine Qualities of Mercy, Truth, and Majesty) calls forth their opposite. Hell is not the vengeance of a cruel God, but the consequence of the nature of reality.

> No! I swear by the Day of Resurrection;
> No! I swear by the accusing soul..
> What, does man reckon We shall not gather his bones?
> ...even though he offer his excuses..(Koran 75: 1-3; 15)

On the day when their tongues, their hands and
their feet shall testify against them touching
that they were doing.
Upon that day God will pay them in full
their just due, and they shall know that God
is the manifest Truth. (Koran 24:24)

When traditional Muslims mention hell in conversation, they set off the idea with invocations of God's protection, for themselves and for the listener, for the magic of words is such that even the thought is frightening, and its appearance in speech may be taken as a dreadful omen. *See* CHILDREN; ESCHATOLOGY.

Heraclius (Ar. *Hīrāql*). The Emperor of Byzantium who reigned from 610 to 641. In the sixth year of the Hijrah (628), Heraclius received a written invitation from the Prophet to enter Islam. Traditional stories depict the Christian Emperor as wishing to accept conversion, but being deterred by the opposition of his chief nobles; he encounters Abū Sufyān and questions him about the nature of the Prophet, recognizing in him a Divine messenger. The early Muslims also pictured Heraclius as having a prophetic dream of the triumph throughout Syria of the "Kingdom of a circumcised man", or of having seen this by reading the portents of the stars.

The story of Abū Sufyān and Heraclius is reported in the Ṣaḥīḥ of Bukhārī; it is a dialogue of the kind found in Thucydides, somewhat more idealized, and presenting the view of Muslim expectations. But it reports, doubtless accurately, the letter sent from the Prophet to the Byzantine Emperor:

'Abd Allāh ibn 'Abbās said that Abū Sufyān ibn Harb informed him: Heraclius sent for him [Abū Sufyān] with a party of the Quraysh, when they had to trade in Syria during the truce which the Messenger of God had arranged with Abū Sufyān and the unbelieving Quraysh. So they came to Heraclius when they were in Jerusalem. Heraclius invited them to his court, and around him were the gathered chiefs of the Romans. Heraclius called them and his interpreter, and said: "Who among you is nearest in relation to this man who claims to be a prophet?" Abū Sufyān said, "I am the nearest to him in relationship." Then Heraclius said, "Bring him nearer to me and keep his companions behind his back. Say to them that I am going to put some questions to this man about the one who claims to be a prophet; if what he tells me is not true, then the others will show it."

Abū Sufyān said that: "By God, if it were not the shame that they would charge me with lying, I would have lied against the Prophet." Then the first question that he put was: "What is his family standing among you?" I said: "He is a man of high birth amongst us." Heraclius said: "Did any one from among you ever advance such a claim before him?" I said: "No." He said: "Was anyone of his forefathers a king?" I said: "No." He said: "Do the men of rank and wealth follow him or the poorer ones?" I said: "Rather the poorer ones." He said: "Are they increasing or decreasing in number?" I said: "Nay, they are increasing." He said: "Does any one of them apostatize out of hatred for his religion after having embraced it?" I said: "No." He said: "Did you ever charge him with telling lies before he said what he now says?" I said: "No." He said: "Is he unfaithful to his agreements?" I said: "No, but we have made a truce with him and we do not know what he will do with it."

Abū Sufyān said: "And I got no opportunity to introduce a disparaging word into this conversation except this remark." Heraclius said: "Have you fought with him?" I said: "Yes." He said: "What was the outcome of your battles with him?" I said: "Fighting between us and him has had different turns – sometimes he causes us loss and at other times we cause him loss." He said: "What is it that he enjoins you?" He says: "Serve Allāh alone and do not set up aught with Him, and give up what your forefathers believed. He enjoins on us prayers and truthfulness and chastity and respect for the ties of relationship."

Then Heraclius said through his interpreter: "I questioned you about his lineage and you said that he was a man of high birth among you. Even thus are messengers raised from amongst the noblest of their people. And I questioned you whether any of you had ever advanced such a claim, and you said: No. I thought that if anyone had advanced such a claim before him, he could be imitating what has gone before. And I questioned you whether there was a king amongst his forefathers and you said: No. Had there been a king among his forefathers then his actions could be a wish to regain the kingdom. And I questioned you whether you had ever charged him with telling lies before he advanced the claim which he now makes, and you said: No. So I knew that it could not be that a man who abstained from telling lies about men should tell lies about God."

"And I questioned you whether men of rank and wealth follow him, or the poor, and you said that it is the poor people that follow him; such are the followers of Messengers. And I questioned you whether they are increasing or decreasing and you said that they are increasing, and such is the case of the true faith until it attains completion. And I questioned you whether any of them becomes an apostate out of hatred for his religion after having embraced it, and you said: No. Such is faith when its joy is infused into hearts. And I questioned you whether he is unfaithful to his agreements and you said: No. Even so, the Messengers are never unfaithful. And I questioned you about what he enjoins upon you, and you said that he called you to serve God and not set up anything beside Him and forbade you the worship of idols; and that he prescribed prayer and truthfulness and chastity." Heraclius went on: "If what you say is true, he shall soon be master of the place where I stand. I knew that he would appear but I never thought that he would be from among you. If I knew that I could go to him, I would have made an earnest endeavor to meet him, and if I were with him, I would indeed wash his feet."

Then he called for the letter of the Messenger of Allāh, which Dihiyah al-Kalbī had brought to the governor of Basra, and the governor of Baṣra had sent to Heraclius, and he read it:

In the Name of Allāh, the Merciful, the Compassionate. From Muḥammad, the servant of Allāh and His Messenger, to Heraclius, the Emperor of the Romans, Peace be on him who follows guidance. I invite you to the faith of Islam: surrender to God [enter Islam] and you will be in peace. Allāh will give you a twofold reward. But if you turn away, on you will be the sins of your subjects. O People of the Book, come to equitable words between us and you, that we shall not associate anything with Him and that some of us shall not take others for lords besides Allāh. But if they turn away, say, bear witness that we are the surrendered [Muslims].

Abū Sufyān said: "When he had said what he wanted to say and finished the reading of the letter, there was a great uproar in his presence and the voices became loud and we were turned out. I said to my companions, the cause of the son of Abū Kabsha [a disparaging reference to the Prophet] has become great, as the Emperor of the Romans is afraid of him; and I was certain then that he [the Prophet] would prevail, until Allāh made me embrace Islam..."

See MUQAWQĪS.

Herat. City in Afganistan, then Bactria, founded by Alexander the Great, whom Nizami described as "a figure who prepared the way for Islam". The Moghul Padishah Babur described Herat this way: "The whole habitable world had not such a town as Herat had become under Sultan Husayn Mirza...Khorasan, and Herat above all, was filled with learned and matchless men. Whatever work a man took up, he aimed and aspired to bring it to perfection."

Heresy, *see* ILḤĀD.

Hezbollah, *see* ḤIZB ALLĀH.

Hibah. In Islamic law, a gift of property.

Hidden Imām. Foreign to Sunnī Islam, the doctrine of the Hidden Imām is peculiar to Twelve-Imām Shī'ism (although several Ismā'īlī sects have developed their own variants). Twelve-Imām Shī'ites believe that the twelfth Imām, named Muḥammad and said to be born in Samarra' (*255*/869), disappeared at the age of four in the year *260*/873, upon the death of his father, Ḥasan al-'Askarī, the eleventh Imām. Some say he disappeared into the cellar (*sardib*) of the family house in Samarra', others that he disappeared in Hilla near Baghdad. He reputedly made several more or less miraculous reappearances but from that time until today he has been living supernaturally hidden from mankind. He will reveal himself at the end of time as the Mahdī.

From the time of his disappearance until the year *329*/940, when the Imām would have been about seventy years old, his will was made known through four successive representatives, or *wakīls*. The first was 'Uthmān ibn Sa'īd, the secretary of the Hidden Imām's father, Ḥasan al-'Askarī. 'Uthmān had often acted on behalf of the eleventh Imām, and he, along with the women of the household, supplied the accounts of the twelfth Imām, descriptions of his appearance, etc. The other representatives were Abū Ja'far Muḥammad, Abū-l-Qāsim ibn Rūḥ, and Abū-l-Ḥasan 'Alī ibn Muḥammad Samarrī. This period of contact with the Imām is called the "lesser occultation" (*al-ghaybah as-sughrā*). It is also called the *wukalā'*, after the representatives (*wakīls*), or the "period of emissaries" (*as-sifārah*).

On behalf of the Hidden Imām, the *wakīls* collected the *khums*, or special tithe (more literally, "fifth portion") which, among the Shī'ites, is due to the Imāms. In the Medinan community this was the share of the spoils of war, which was the special prerogative of the Prophet to distribute in the interests of religion and the state. Among the Sunnīs this tithe disappeared after the Prophet, but it was maintained by the Shī'ites in favor of the descendants of the Prophet who were Imāms.

The last *wakīl*, who died in *329*/940, declined to name a successor to his function of mediating with the Imām, saying "the matter now rests with God". Thus began the period of "the greater occultation" (*al-ghaybah al-kubrā*), which continues to this day. The Twelve-Imām Shī'ites believe that this twelfth Imām is still alive although invisible – thus there is no successor to him.

It is important to note that the eleventh Imām had no other children. If a descendant (in the event, the Hidden Imām) were not attributed to him, the line of Imāms – whose mediation in Shī'ism between man and God is necessary for salvation – would have come to an end. The theories upon which Shī'ism is based, the Imāmate (the existence of a divinely ordained and inspired intermediary of God on earth) whose principles of succession had become dogmatically and rigidly defined two hundred years previously, would have suffered a serious blow. No less important, there would have been no justification for continuing to collect the tithe of the *khums* – today received by the Mullas from their followers. According to the Shī'ite records known as the *Aqā'id ash-Shī'ah*, the eleventh Imām, who probably suffered from poor health and died at the age of twenty-eight (his father died at forty-one) had no wives; this is a very unusual case because the Sunnah insists upon marriage as "half of the religion". (The conditions which make legal marriage impossible also preclude having children).

As the eleventh Imām had no wives, the twelfth Imām is believed to have been born to a concubine, or female slave of the eleventh Imām. She was called Narjis Khatun, and is said to have been a grand-daughter of the Byzantine Emperor, who was captured (not kept for ransom), sold into slavery, and bought providentially by an agent of the tenth Imām for his son. When Narjis Khatun bore him a son, the eleventh Imām is reported to have said "bring him to me every forty days" (to birds who took the child away for safekeeping), which is to say he was not often seen, the explanation being that the child was always kept in the women's quarters (or by the birds in a secret haven).

Shī'ites call the Hidden Imām the "Lord of the Age" (*Ṣāḥib az-Zamān*), the rightful ruler of the universe, the spiritual *axis mundi*. He is also called the "Awaited Mahdī" (*al-Mahdī al-Muntaẓar*) who will return at the end of time, manifest his dominion, bring order and justice to the world and – a very characteristic point – "take vengeance on the enemies of God". (The Sunnīs have also adopted the idea of the Mahdī, but of course they do not identify him with any Shī'ite Imām. For the Sunnīs the Mahdī restores spiritual clarity at the end of time, but the aspect of "taking vengeance" is not only absent, but foreign to their conception of the matter.)

Shī'ites believe that the Hidden Imām illumines men and intercedes with God on their behalf. He hears personal prayer, and in particular it is the custom to beseech him by writing sealed letters which are left at the tombs of Imāms, and their close relatives (*Imāmzādeh*), dropped into wells, or thrown into the sea. It has been averred that, at the moment of death, he who is saved has a vision of the Hidden Imām.

It is doctrine in Islam that Jesus – in his reality – did not die upon the cross but exists in a principial state and will return to the world at the end of time. Doubtless, it is this Koranic doctrine concerning a unique prophet with an exceptional function in the world in its last days, that provides the calque, or precedent, for the unusual theory that resolves the Shī'ite predicament regarding the existence of the twelfth Imām. Following this model, other sects, including the Musta'īlī Ismā'īlīs, and also the Druzes, have "hidden" or "occulted" spiritual figures. The dogma of the twelfth Imām, however, is the most highly developed of these doctrines, and has proven to be of tremendous historical consequence for those who believe it. *See* GHAYBAH; IMĀM; ISMĀ'ĪLĪS; MAHDĪ; SHĪ'ISM; UṢŪLĪS.

Ḥijāb (lit. a "veil" or "partition"). A common meaning of *ḥijāb* today is the adherence to certain standards of modest dress for women. The usual definition of modest dress according to the legal systems does not actually require wearing a veil, but does require covering everything except the face and hands in public; this, at least, is the practice which originated in the Middle East.

Aside from its literal sense, in metaphysics *al-ḥijāb* refers to the veil which separates man or the world from God. In particular, it can mean the illusory aspect of creation, about which a Sufi proverb says that it is *khayālun fī khayālin fī khayāl*; "an illusion within an allusion within an illusion".

Ḥijāb has been used as an equivalent for the Indian concept of *māyā*, which is cosmic illusion, existential "magic" or *līlā*, creative play. Ibn 'Aṭā'Allāh says in the *Ḥikam*:

> Were the light of certitude to shine, you would *See* the Hereafter so near that you could not move towards it, and you would *See* that the eclipse of extinction had come over the beauties of the world. It is not the existence of any being alongside of Him that veils you from God, for nothing is alongside of Him. Rather, the *illusion* of a being alongside of Him is what veils you from Him. Had it not been for His manifestation in created beings eyesight would not have perceived them. Had His Qualities been manifested, His created beings would have disappeared.

The metaphysical sense of *ḥijāb* is precisely a veil which "refracts" the light of the Divine Intellect, which otherwise would be blinding. Al-Jīlī said: "The Divine Obscurity" is the primordial place where the suns of beauty set. It is the Self of God Himself. Ibn 'Aṭā'Allāh also says:

> How can it be conceived that something veils Him, since He is the One who manifests everything?
> How can it be conceived that something veils Him, since He is the One who is manifest through everything?
> How can it be conceived that something veils Him, since He is the One who is manifest in everything?
> How can it be conceived that something veils Him, since He is the Manifest to everything?
> How can it be conceived that something veils Him, since He is the Manifest before the existence of anything?
> How can it be conceived that something veils Him, since He is more manifest than anything?
> How can it be conceived that something veils Him since He is the One alongside of Whom there is nothing?
> How can it be conceived that something veils Him, since He is nearer to you than anything else?
> How can it be conceived that something veils Him, since, were it not for Him, the existence of everything would not have been manifest?
> It is a marvel how Being has been manifested in non-being and how the contingent has been established alongside of Him who possesses the attribute of Eternity.

See VEIL.

Hijrah (lit. the "migration"; often written "hegira"). The emigration of the Prophet from Mecca to Yathrib (later called *Madīnat an-Nabī*, the "City of the Prophet" or Medina) at the end of September in 622. In Mecca, persecution of Muslims had grown to the point that the Prophet's life was in danger; but in Yathrib he was offered sanctuary.

Abū Ṭālib, uncle and protector of the Prophet, had died earlier that year, and the leaders of the Quraysh decided to seize the occasion to rid themselves of the man who had caused such great dissension in Mecca. They plotted Muḥammad's murder. It was decided that a member of each of the clans would participate and thus all would share the responsibility. The Angel Gabriel warned the Prophet, who told Abū Bakr that they would flee Mecca together for Yathrib.

Muḥammad instructed his cousin 'Alī to mislead the conspirators by donning the Prophet's green cloak and sleeping in his bed. Then the Prophet, reciting the words of the Sūrah *Yā Sīn*, "we have enshrouded them so that they see not" (36:9), slipped past the enemies surrounding his house and joined Abū Bakr. The two left Mecca on camel with a flock of sheep driven behind them to cover their tracks. They hid in a cave in Mount Thawr several miles south of the town, while 'Abd Allāh, the son of Abū Bakr returned the camels. At the Prophet's house the conspirators came upon 'Alī and realized they had been tricked.

A search party arrived at the cave but never looked in it because of the sudden, miraculous growth of an acacia tree which blocked the entrance; moreover, the presence of a spider's web over the opening of the cave, and of a dove's nest with an egg in front of the cave, seemed to show that no one had entered.

After several days of hiding, the Prophet and Abū Bakr continued on camel with a Beduin guide and with food brought to them by Asmā', the daughter of Abū Bakr. During the journey of some ten or fourteen days by riding camel to Yathrib, the verse was revealed: "Verily He who has made the Koran a law for you will bring you home again". (28:85).

Some seventy Meccan Muslims emigrated to Yathrib at the same time as the Prophet. These were the original *muhājirūn* (emigrants). More followed over the course of the next few years. "This last *muhājir*" – this was the Prophet's phrase – was an uncle of the Prophet, al-'Abbās, who joined the Muslims just as they were advancing to conquer Mecca. The Hijrah took place in the year 622, at the end of September, probably on the 17th. Sixteen years later, in 637, the Caliph 'Umar formalized the Prophet's custom of dating events from the Hijrah, the moment of the establishment of the first Islamic state. Thus the year of the Hijrah became the first year of the Islamic era. *See* CALENDAR; MUḤAMMAD.

Ḥīlah (lit. "ruse", pl. *ḥiyal*). A legal stratagem to circumvent the intentions of the *sharī'ah* (canon law), without technically breaking it. Such stratagems came into use in the 'Abbāsid Caliphate chiefly among the Ḥanafīs, but were adopted to a lesser degree by the other schools when they offered solutions to otherwise difficult social problems, and were not intended merely to circumvent the law. *See* SCHOOLS of LAW; SHARĪ'AH; SLEEPING FOETUS.

Ḥilf al-Fuḍūl (lit. "oath of virtue"). The Pact of Chivalry in which the Prophet had participated some twenty years before the revelation of Islam. *See* FUTUWWAH.

Ḥillī, 'Allāmah (Mansūr Ḥasan ibn Yūsuf ibn 'Alī al-Hillī; *648-726*/1250-1325). He is also known as Ibn al-Muṭahhar. The leading Shī'ite theologian during the Il-Khanid dynasty. Hillī studied for a time with the astronomer and mathematician Naṣīr ad-Dīn aṭ-Ṭūsi, as well as with Sunnī scholars, and was the author of over seventy-five treatises on Shī'ism, such as the *Minhaj al-Karāmah fī Ma'rifat al-Imāmah* ("The Miraculous Way of Knowledge of the Imāmate").

'Allāmah Hillī established a Shī'ite methodology and terminology for the critical study of Ḥadīth literature (*dirāya*), modeled upon that of the Sunnīs, and he reorganized Shī'ite jurisprudence. He is buried in Najaf.

al-Ḥilyat al-Awliyā'. A vast compendium in ten volumes of Sufi lore, doctrine, and biography by Abū Nu'aym al-Isbahānī (d. *430*/1038).

al-Himmah (lit. "concentration", or "resolve"). The quality of perseverance or striving towards God. Its opposite is *al-ḥiss* (lit. "noise", "sensation"), distraction or inattention from concentration upon God.

Hīrah. The cave (*ghār*), or grotto, at the summit of the mountain of that name, now usually called *Jabal an-Nūr*, the Mountain of Light. The grotto is large enough for a man to perform the prayer; inside is a small opening which faces Mecca. The cave is a few miles from Mecca; the ascent to the top takes an hour or two. There the Prophet would retreat to meditate. One of his daughters would bring him food so that he could remain at the grotto the whole month. There, in the last days of Ramaḍān, on the Night of Destiny (*laylat al-Qadr*), the Koran descended into the soul of the Prophet. *See* LAYLAT al-QADR.

al-Ḥiss (lit. "sensation", "noise"). Physical sensation. Also, a technical term for the distractions which draw the soul away from contemplation of God, and the state of "distractedness". The opposite of *al-ḥiss* in this sense is *al-himmah* (spiritual concentration). Al-Hujwīrī said:

> Beware of distracting your own mind from God by trying to satisfy people whose minds are occupied with vainer things. When you meet a man of nobler mind than your own, then you may safely distract your mind to satisfy his. But otherwise, never distract yourself; "Is God not enough for His servants?" [Koran 39:36].

And Ḥaṣan of Basra said:

> Beware of this world with all wariness; for it is like to a snake, smooth to the touch, but its venom is deadly. Turn away from whatsoever delights thee in it, for the little companioning thou wilt have of it; put off from thee its cares, for that thou hast seen its

sudden chances, and knowest for sure that thou shalt be parted from it: endure firmly its hardships, for the ease that shall presently be thine. The more it please thee, the more do thou be wary of it; for the man of this world, whenever he feels secure in any pleasure thereof, the world drives him over into some unpleasantness, and whenever he attains any part of it and squats him down upon it, the world suddenly turns him upside down. And again, beware of this world, for its hopes are lies, its expectations false; its easefulness all harshness, muddied its limpidity.

And therein, thou art in peril: or bliss transient, or sudden calamity, or painful affliction, or doom decisive. Hard is the life of a man if he be prudent, dangerous if comfortable, being wary ever of catastrophe, certain of his ultimate fate. Even had the Almighty not pronounced upon the world at all, nor coined for it any similitude, nor charged men to abstain from it, yet would the world itself have awakened the slumberer, and roused the heedless; how much the more then, seeing that God has Himself sent us a warning against it, an exhortation regarding it! For this world has not with God so much as a pebble or a single clod of earth; as I am told, God has created nothing more hateful to Him, and from the day He created it He has not looked upon it, so much He hates it.

The Prophet said: "This world is under curse, and everything in it, except for the remembrance of God". The mystical abhorrence of the world, however, is heuristic, intended to lead man out of illusion, for by itself, the world is God's creation, and good as God is good. *See* DHIKR.

History, *see* IBN ĀTHIR; IBN KHALDŪN; al-MAS'ŪDĪ; RASHĪD ad-DĪN at-ṬABĪB; at-ṬABARĪ; al-WAQĪDĪ.

Ḥizb Allāh (lit. "party of God"). A term in the Koran for the Muslims, as opposed to the idolators, during the initial struggle for life.

Whoso makes God his friend, and His Messenger,
and the believers – the party of God,
they are the victors. (5:62)

and:

Thou shalt not find any people who believe
in God and the Last Day who are loving to
anyone who opposes God and His Messenger, not
though they were their fathers, or their sons,
or their brothers, or their clan. Those —
He has written faith upon their hearts, and
He has confirmed them with a Spirit from
Himself; and He shall admit them into
gardens underneath which rivers flow, therein
to dwell forever, God being well-pleased with
them, and they well-pleased with Him. Those are
God's party; why, surely God's party they are
the prosperers. (58:23)

The term has been appropriated by various movements and groups in the past as a name for their organization or viewpoint. The 1979 revolution in Iran was marked by the emergence of street vigilantes calling themselves Ḥizb Allāh and organizations called *Komiteh* who enforced the will of revolutionary factions which dispersed counter-demonstrations and closed universities. Ḥizb Allāh went on to become various militias of clerics vying for political power. They were a more irregular grouping than the *Pasdarān* or Revolutionary Guards.

In the Lebanon, in the 1970s as the Twelve-Imām Shī'ites grew more conscious of their group identity under the Iranian Mullah Imām Mūsā'ṣ-Ṣadr, the political grouping *Amal* was created in 1974. As civil unrest in Lebanon grew, this was followed, after the Iranian revolution of 1979, by the creation of *Ḥizb Allāh*, a more radical paramilitary group closely linked with Iran. Its leader, Sayyid Muḥammad Ḥusayn Faḍlallāh, a cleric, had come to Lebanon from Najaf, a center of Shī'ite teaching in Iraq. His militant following in Lebanon was reinforced by the arrival of Lebanese Shī'ite theology students expelled from Iraq in the seventies. The Iranian revolution and the Israeli invasion of Lebanon gave the impetus for Ḥizb Allāh to emerge as the leading Shī'ite military organization in Lebanon. Iranian Revolutionary Guards arrived in the Beka'a Valley in Lebanon and the goal of Ḥizb Allāh became the establishment of an Islamic state and the destruction of Israel.

Ḥizb Allāh attacked American, French and Israeli forces in Lebanon. The killing of 241 U.S. marines in their barracks in Beirut in 1983 led to U.S. and French withdrawal of their peacekeeping forces from Lebanon. Ḥizb Allāh also attacked U.S. and French embassies, carried on bombing attacks in France, hijacked airliners, and took Western hostages in Lebanon, the last of whom was released in 1992. These attacks were carried out to further their policies and in some cases the policies of Iran. The Israelis carried out bombing attacks on Shaykh Faḍlallāh, killing many but not him, on a Ḥizb Allāh leader Sayyid Abbās al-Mūsawi who was killed in 1992. Another leader, Shaykh 'Abd al-Karīm 'Ubayd was abducted in 1988. In 1989 Syria enforced an end to the civil war in Lebanon after the Ṭā'if Accord, and Ḥizb Allāh moved towards parliamentary political participation. Attacks and counterattacks continue between Ḥizb Allāh and Israeli forces in the south of Lebanon. *See* LEBANON; METAWILA.

Ḥizb al-Baḥr. "The Litany of the Sea" composed by the Imām Shādhilī using passages from the Koran (*see* SHĀDHILĪ). Its recitation has been credited with saving Damascus from conquest by an attacker. Its power resides in the ritual recitation of the litany in Arabic. The groups of letters are the mysterious "isolated letters" which stand before 29 Sūrahs. Seven consecutive Sūrahs begin with the letters *hā' mīm*, and these, along with other Sūrahs where the letters appear in combination with other letters, are called the *hāwamīm*. In such cases the isolated letters also stand for the whole Sūrah. *Tabārak* and *Yā' Sīn* are also the names of Sūrahs.

> O our God, O Most-High, O Tremendous One, O Gentle One, O All-Knowing, You are my Lord and Your knowledge suffices me. The Most Excellent Master is my Master and the Most Excellent Sufficing is my sufficiency. You help whom you will and You are the Mighty, the Compassionate. We implore security in our movements and our stillness, in words, in willing, in dangers from doubts and suppositions cloaking our hearts from contemplation of the unseen. The believers have been visited by affliction and shaken by a powerful earthquake. And the hypocrites and those with sickness in their hearts say that God and His Messenger have promised us only delusion [Koran 8:49] —Confirm us and aid us and compel for us this sea, as You compelled the sea for Moses, and compelled the fire for Abraham, and compelled the mountains and iron for David, and compelled the wind and demons and *jinn* for Solomon [cf. Koran 38:18,36]; and compel for us every sea that is Yours in the earth and the heaven, in the corporeal world (*al-mulk*) and the subtle (*al-malakūt*) and the sea of this world and the sea of the beyond; and compel for us all things, O You in Whose Hand is dominion of everything. *Kāf hā' yā' 'ayn ṣād; kāf hā' yā' 'ayn ṣād; kāf hā' yā' 'ayn ṣād.*
>
> Help us. Lo! You are the Best of Helpers, render us triumphant. Lo! You are the Best of Conquerors, and forgive us. Lo! You are the Best Forgiver, and grant us mercy. Lo! You are the most Compassionate, and provide for us. Lo! You are the Best Provider, and guide us, and rescue us from an erring folk.
>
> Accord us favorable winds as it is in Your science and spread them over us from the treasuries of Your mercy. And transport us thereby generously with peace and well-being in the religion (*dīn*) and this lower world (*dunyā*) and the beyond (*ākhirah*), for You have power over all things.
>
> Our Lord, make easy our affairs with repose for our hearts and our bodies; with peace and well-being in matters of religion and matters of the world. And be our Companion in our journeying, and Regent (*khalīfah*) with our folk and quench the faces of our enemies and confound them in their place that they may not go or come to us. "And had We willed, we verily could have fixed them in their place, making them powerless to go forward or go back." [Koran 36:66]. "Yā' Sīn, And the wise Koran, Lo! You are of those sent on a straight path. A revelation of the Mighty, the Merciful. That You may warn a folk whose fathers were not warned, so they are heedless. Already the word has come true of most of them for they believe not. Lo! We have put on their necks irons reaching to their chins, so that they are stiff-necked. And We have set a bar before them and a bar behind them, and have covered them so that they see not" [36:1-9]. Confounded be those faces. Confounded be those faces. Confounded be those faces. "And humbled be the faces before the Living, the Self-Subsisting. And already ruined is he who bears wrongdoing" [20:111].
>
> *Ṭā' sīn, hā' mīm 'ayn sīn qāf.* "He has loosed the seas, they meet. Between them is an isthmus (*barzakh*), they do not encroach upon each other" [55:19,20]. *Hā' mīm, hā' mīm, hā' mīm, hā' mīm, hā' mīm, hā' mīm, hā' mīm.* Lo! the Command is come (*humma al-amru*). And lo! the Aid. Lo! they do not look upon us. *Hā' mīm.* The Book is revealed from God, the Mighty, the Knower, Forgiving sins and accepting repentance, of

punishment far-reaching and powerful. There is no God but He. To Him is the journeying.

Bismillāhi is our door; *Tabārak* our walls, *Yā' Sīn* our roof. *Kāf hā' yā' 'ayn ṣād* is our sufficiency, *hā' mīm 'ayn sīn qāf* our protection. Allāh will be enough for them, Allāh is the Hearer, the Knower. Allāh will be enough for them, Allāh is the Hearer, the Knower. Allāh will be enough for them, Allāh is the Hearer, the Knower. The curtain of the throne is draping over us, and the eye of God is looking at us. With Allāh's strength they do not have power over us and "Allāh, all unseen, surrounds them from behind. It is a glorious Koran on a Guarded Tablet (*lawḥ maḥfūẓ*)" [85:20,21]. "For Allāh is the best of Guardians, and He is The Most Merciful of the Merciful" [12:64]. Lo! my Protector is Allāh who revealed the Book and He befriends the righteous. If they turn away, say Allāh suffices me, there is no God save Him, in Him I have put my trust, and He is the Lord of the tremendous throne. If they turn away, say Allāh suffices me, there is no God save Him, in Him I have put my trust, and He is the Lord of the tremendous throne. "If they turn away, say Allāh suffices me, there is no God save Him, in Him I have put my trust, and He is the Lord of the tremendous throne" [9:129]. In the Name of God, with which nothing in the Earth or Heaven can suffer harm. And He is the Hearer, the Knower. And He is the Hearer, the Knower. And He is the Hearer, the Knower. And there is no strength nor power except in Allāh, the Exalted, the Mighty.

See ḤURŪF al-MUQAṬṬA'ĀT; REFUGE; ash-SHĀDHILĪ.

Holy Cities, *see* JERUSALEM; MECCA; MEDINA.

Holy Days, *see* ĀSHŪRĀ'; CALENDAR; 'ĪD al-ADḤĀ; 'ĪD al-FIṬR; 'ĪD al-GHADĪR; LAYLAT al-BARĀ'AH; MAWLID an-NABĪ; MUḤARRAM; NAW ROZ; RAMAḌĀN.

Holy War, *see* JIHĀD.

Hour, the (Ar. *as-sā'ah*). In the Koran, "the Hour" is the end of the world, the Last Judgement, and the events related to it. Only God knows when it will be, but mankind knows that it will be terrible (Koran 53:50), and sudden (12:107). The Prophet said: "The Hour will not surprise the one who saith: Allāh, Allāh"

Also, those who are assembled for the Day of Judgement will believe that the time they spent on earth was but an hour, or less (10:46). *See* YAWM ad-DIN.

Houris (Ar. *ḥawrā'* or *ḥuriyyah* pl. *ḥūr*). The female companions, perpetual virgins, of the saved in Paradise. They are the symbols of spiritual states of rapture. (Koran 2:23; 3:14; 4:60). There also are in paradise eternal youths (*wildān mukhalladūn*). Western scholars of religion believe that the *houris* of Islam originate with the *Daena* of Zoroastrian eschatology. In Zoroastrianism, if the soul of the departed is saved and destined to enter paradise, it is met by its inner conscience in the form of a beautiful woman, the *Daena,* that leads the soul across the bridge into the afterlife. Zoroastrian ideas spread throughout the Near East after the conquest of Babylon by Cyrus in 539 B.C. and as far as Egypt with its conquest by Cambyses in 525 B.C. The bridge (*sirāt*) of the Zoroastrian eschatology is not mentioned anywhere in the Koran but has nevertheless become a universally accepted feature in Islamic eschatology, apparently simply taken for granted by the early theologians, many of whom, if not the majority, were Persians.

Zoroastrianism, and probably before it ancient Indo-European religion as well, believed (perhaps as a result of observing the decomposition of food set by a grave for the dead) that the soul lingers for three days before beginning a journey into the afterworld. This belief is also preserved in Islam as the idea that the dead can hear for three days. The Prophet addressed words to the bodies of those who had died at Badr, and when asked why, said: "Do you not know that the dead can hear for three days?" The three days also appears in Christianity as the lapse of time between Good Friday and Easter Sunday. The *Daena* is also the figure whom the apostles see on the Sepulchre in the cave whose stone at the mouth has been removed. *See* ZOROASTRIANISM.

House of Wisdom (Ar. *bayt al-ḥikmah*). An academy founded in *215*/830 by the Caliph al-Ma'mūn (d. *218*/833) in Baghdad for the purpose of translating Greek books on philosophy and the sciences into Arabic. The Fāṭimids later founded an academy in Egypt with a similar name, the "Abode of Wisdom"

(*Dār al-Ḥikmah*), for the propagation of Ismā'īlī doctrines. These academies had important librairies, that of the Faṭimids in Egypt being the greatest library of its time.

"Howling Dervishes". A pejorative colonial name for those Rifā'ī dervishes whose method included calling out loudly *Ya Ḥayyu, Ya Qayyūm*, "O Living One, O Self-Subsisting One".

Hubal. An idol, the God of the Moon. Centuries before Islam, 'Amr ibn Luhayy, a chief of the tribe of Jurhum who dwelt in Mecca before the coming of the Quraysh tribe, brought the idol to the city from Syria. It was set up in the Ka'bah and became the principal idol of the pagan Meccans. The ritual casting of lots and divining arrows was performed in front of it.

Hubal was pulled down and used as a doorstep when the Prophet conquered Mecca and purified the Ka'bah. *See* IDOLS; JĀHILIYYAH.

Hūd. A pre-Islamic Prophet to the Arabs mentioned in the Koran (7:63-70; 11:52-63; 26:123-139). Hūd was sent as a "warner" to the extinct tribe of 'Ād who rejected him. *See* 'ĀD; PROPHETS.

Al-Ḥudaybiyyah. A place on the road from Jeddah to Mecca just outside the *Ḥaram* (restricted precinct). Here the Prophet stopped and awaited the outcome of events when prevented from making the pilgrimage by the Meccans. A Koranic revelation (48:27) in the sixth year of the Hijrah declared the Prophet would pray at Mecca. In March of 628 he set out to perform pilgrimage at Mecca with a party of about one thousand men, unarmed and in pilgrim dress (*iḥrām*). The Quraysh stopped the party at Ḥudaybiyyah, about ten miles from Mecca.

'Uthmān, who had powerful relatives among the Quraysh, was sent to negotiate with the Meccans. When he did not return at the expected time, many thought that he had been killed or captured and that all was lost. In this moment of peril, the Prophet's followers individually made a new oath of fealty to the Prophet known as the "Pact of Felicity" (*bayāt ar-riḍwān*). The Prophet himself represented the absent 'Uthmān by proxy in this oath; one man, Jadd ibn Qays, refrained from taking it, hiding behind a camel.

Then 'Uthmān returned with some Meccans. The Quraysh agreed to a truce, the "Peace of Ḥudaybiyyah". Under the conditions of this treaty the Prophet would be allowed to make the pilgrimage, not then, but in the following year. Mecca would be emptied for three days for the Muslim pilgrims. The peace also stipulated a truce for ten years; that those who were not free but subjects or dependents of the Quraysh and who defected from the pagans to the Muslims would be returned to the Quraysh by the Muslims, whereas those who were subject to the Muslims, and who defected from the Muslims to the Quraysh, would not be returned by the Quraysh.

The Prophet performed the pilgrimage the following year. The testimony of faith declaring there is no god but Allāh, and that Muḥammad is the Messenger of God rang out in the valley of Mecca. The Quraysh, camped on the hill of Abū Qubays, heard it, a portent of the coming triumph of Islam. Other effects were equally far-reaching. The desert tribes had seen the Meccans dealing with the Prophet as an equal, and as a sovereign, and many turned to the new religion. Shortly thereafter, in the year 630, taking an incident between an allied tribe and the Meccans as a breach of the truce, the Prophet marched upon Mecca and conquered it, meeting almost no resistance. *See* MUḤAMMAD; RIḌWĀN.

Hudhud. A bird, the Hoopoe, a popular image of a kind of celestial messenger in mystical literature. The Hudhud informed Solomon about Queen Bilqīs in Sabā (Sheba), in the south of Arabia, and that her people worshiped the sun instead of God, and about the glory of her throne (Koran 27:22).

Hui Hui. A name for Chinese Muslim peoples of Turkic origin, and loosely, a colloquial and general designation for Muslims in China. It probably originated as a Chinese version of a Turkic tribal name, but was later applied more broadly to include other minorities in Central Asia, and particularly the descendants of Arab and Persian immigrants. *Hei Hui* ("Black Hui") refers to the Uigurs; *Hui Chiang* ("Hui Territory") means Turkestan.

Hui Hui Chiao ("Hui Hui Doctrine") is a colloquial Chinese designation for Islam, the formal one being Chen Ch'ing Chiao ("Doctrine of Truth and Purity"). The number of Hui Hui is estimated to be 7.2 million; the total Muslim population of China has been put at 17.6 million, but it is probably less than the true figure. See TA SHIH..

Ḥujjat al-Islām, *see* AYATOLLAH.

al-Hujwīrī, Abū-l-Ḥasan ʻAlī (d. *469*/1077). A Persian Sufi, generally known simply as al-Hujwīrī, who was born in Ghaznah and died in India at Lahore where he is known as Data Ganj Bakhsh. There is a great shrine-mosque built around his tomb. He is the author of a famous exposition of Sufism called *Kashf al-Mahjūb li-Arbāb al-Qulūb* ("The Unveiling of the Hidden for the Lords of the Heart").

Hūlāgu Khān (*614-663*/1217-1265). Grandson of Jenghiz Khan and brother of Kubilai Khan, Hulagu led part of the Mongol horde against the ʻAbbāsids and sacked their capital, Baghdad, thus ending the Arab Caliphate. Two years later he captured Damascus, but was finally checked by the Mamlūks at the battle of *ʻAyn Jalūt* in *659*/1260. Despite the Nestorian Christian influence associated with the Mongol conquests in the Islamic world (the mother and wife of Hūlāgu were Nestorians, and Nestorians advised the Mongols in their advance south), the Nestorians lost out. Hūlāgu founded the Il-Khanid dynasty in Persia, but the Mongols of the south adopted Islam with the conversions of Maḥmūd Ghazan (d. *703*/1304), and Muḥammad Khudabanda (Uljaytu; d. *717*/1304).

Although the Mongol Golden Horde on the Volga and the Il-Khanids of Persia were nominally under the authority of the Great Khan, they became in practice independent when Kubilai established his capital in China. While the Mongol invasions were disasters, spelling the end of a world amidst wholesale massacres (The historian Ibn al-Athīr called them "the greatest calamity that had befallen mankind") they were also a purge, which, sweeping away the past, ultimately vivified the countries they touched. They could not have taken place if the invaded countries had not already become decadent and stagnant. Like the pruning of trees, although a kind of death, the Mongol invasions led to a renewal on a more homogeneous footing. *See* IL-KHANIDS; JUWAYNĪ, ʻATA'MALIK; MAMLŪKS; MONGOLS; RASHĪD ad-DĪN aṭ-ṬABĪB; YASA.

Ḥulūl (Ar. "settling", "alighting", "descent" and, by extension, "incarnation"). In Islamic philosophy it refers to the settling of a superior faculty upon a support. This may be the settling of the soul in the body for example, or, again, the settling of the intellect (*ʻaql*) in the mind. Most commonly however, *ḥulūl* refers to any doctrine which upholds the idea of Divine incarnation in human form, such as that of the *avatāras* of Hinduism, the solar, Divine, or semi-Divine heroes of Indo-European religion and myth, or the Divinity of Christ in Christianity. In Islam, Jesus is a Prophet, who, although he does not have a human father, being the "Spirit of God" cast into Mary, is nevertheless not considered to be Divine.

Divine incarnation is a notion which Islam is bound to reject, in the sense that this idea, more than any other, compromises Islam's "operative effectiveness". Salvation in Islam depends upon awareness of the Absolute as Absolute and thus Unique. Therefore, it is this critical point of Divine Oneness and incomparability which is defended most strenuously. Naturally, it is also around this notion of incarnation, which challenges God's Absoluteness, that the most serious heresies have arisen. A rural preacher in Morocco once said: "In Jerusalem there is a sanctuary, divided by a wall, with two entrances; on one side the Christians go, and on the other, the Muslims. If a Christian goes in on the Muslim side, the Muslims kill him; and if a Muslim goes in on the Christian side, the Christians kill him."

There is, of course, no such place in Jerusalem, but given the common heritage between the Religions of the Book, one could say there is such a place in the soul. If the *shahādah*, the testimony of the Absoluteness of God were given to a Christian, his Christianity would receive a mortal wound. And if a Muslim were to believe: "This man is God", he would be eating of the fruit of the tree of the knowledge of good and evil, the tree which God forbade to Adam.

Praise belongs to God
who has sent down upon His servant the Book
and has not assigned unto it any
crookedness;
upright, to warn of great violence
from Him, and to give good tidings
unto the believers, who do righteous deeds,
that theirs shall be a goodly wage
therein to abide forever,

and to warn those who say, 'God has taken to
Himself a son';
they have no knowledge of it, they
nor their fathers; a monstrous word
it is, issuing out of their mouths;
they say nothing but a lie. (Koran 18:1-5)

Divine incarnation is not accepted as a doctrine in Islam and thus *ḥulūl*, the word for such incarnation, can be an accusation of doctrinal error.

Ḥurūb ar-Riddah, *see* RIDDAH.

al-Ḥurūf al-Fawātiḥ, *see* al-ḤURUF al-MUQAṬṬĀ'AT.

al-Ḥurūf al-Muqaṭṭā'at. The "isolated letters", also called *al-ḥurūf al-fawātiḥ* ("the opening letters"). These are groups of two to five letters, such as *hā' mīm*, or *alif lām rā'*, which stand before 29 Sūrahs. Some of the Sūrahs with isolated letters form blocs, such as seven consecutive Sūrahs, which begin with the letters *hā' mīm*, and which, along with other Sūrahs where the letters *hā' mīm* appear in combination with other letters, are called collectively the *hāwamīm* Sūrahs.

One explanation is that the letters are abbreviations standing for the initials of scribes. The Koranic commentator 'Abd Allāh ibn 'Abbās gave interpretations for the letters such as "I, Allāh, am One" for one set of letters. The *hā' mīm*, he said, stood for *ar-Raḥmān*, "The Merciful", a Name of God, and *alif lam mīm* for "I, God, know".

Scholars and mystics throughout history have also attempted to explain or elucidate the meaning of the letters but none have done so conclusively. Whatever the explanation behind them, the letters have taken on mystical significance as magical emblems of the Sūrahs they precede. *See* ḤIZB al-BAḤR; ILM al-ḤURŪF; KORAN.

Ḥurūfī. 1. Someone who is versed in the mystical science of letters and words called *'Ilm al-ḥurūf*, its interpretation, and divination through it. *See* 'ILM al-ḤURŪF.

2. An extremely heterodox sect, now extinct, that sprang out of Shī'ism in Iran and Turkey in the *9th*/15th century.

Ḥusayn (*5-61*/624-680) or better: al-Ḥusayn. The second son of 'Alī and Fatimah, and grandson of the Prophet. The story of Huṣayn is the central event in Twelve-Imām Shī'ite history.

When Mu'āwiyah died, his son Yazīd became Caliph in Damascus, without the usual election, since Mu'āwiyah had forced some prominent Companions in Mecca to swear fealty to Yazīd some time before. Yazīd had a reputation as a reveler. Dissensions arising from differences as to who was most suited to the dignity of the Caliphate for spiritual, political, and doctrinal reasons, not all of which were merely Shī'ite contentions, led the notables in many cities to refuse to swear allegiance to Yazīd. Among these were 'Abd Allāh ibn az-Zubayr, son of a famous Companion who later declared himself Caliph and held Mecca for a time, and Ḥusayn, the Prophet's grandson, who left Medina to take refuge in Mecca.

At Mecca, Shī'ite partisans invited Ḥusayn to go to Kufah (in Iraq) and assured him of support there. Ḥusayn sent his cousin Muslim ibn 'Aqīl ahead to prepare the way. The cousin was captured and executed by the Umayyad Governor. Ḥusayn, however, plunged ahead and decided to go to Kufah with eighteen members of his household and sixty others, of whom thirty were Companions. 'Abd Allāh, the son of the late Caliph 'Umar, advised Ḥusayn against this course of action.

Yazīd then ordered the governor of Iraq, 'Ubayd Allāh ibn Ziyād, to intercept Ḥusayn, who had now been reinforced with six hundred men. However, an army of four thousand led by 'Umar Ibn Sa'd (the son of the Companion Sa'd ibn Abī Waqqās) surrounded him at Kerbala, in Iraq, near the Euphrates river. Cut off from water for eight days, he parleyed with the Caliph's troops until at length the parties fought, at first in individual combats, as was the custom of the Arabs. Finally, Ḥusayn mounted his horse and went into battle where, weakened by thirst, he was killed. Only two of his children survived the massacre which followed. The martyrdom took place on the 10th of Muḥarram in the 61st year of the Hijrah (10th October 680 A.D.). While it had little effect upon the political situation at the time, the martyrdom of Ḥusayn was to become a symbol of capital importance for Shī'ites, first under the Buyids and then even more so after the rise of the Safavid dynasty.

For the Shī'ites, Ḥusayn is an Imām, a figure

they understand to be an intermediary between man and God. They believe this function to be hereditary, inherited from 'Alī and passed on to Ḥusayn's descendants. Among the Shī'ites there is an historical and ever-present sense of guilt surrounding the martyrdom at Kerbala. It centers on the misleading invitation made to Ḥusayn and his subsequent betrayal by the early "proto" Shī'ites of Kufah, who did not come to his aid. This, it is felt, is a repetition of the treatment of 'Ali and the pattern for the "lack of support" shown to the other Shī'ite Imāms after Ḥusayn.

The first Ṣafavids, who succeeded in conquering Persia at the beginning of the *10th*/16th century, exploited and institutionalized this guilt. Like others before them, the Ṣafavids used Shī'ism as a weapon in their struggle to seize and hold power, and as a mechanism of social control, albeit two-edged and perilous. The Ṣafavids made Shī'ism the state religion in Persia, exalting the tragedy of Kerbala to the highest degree and burning it into the national consciousness, where it is maintained by constant remembrance and insistence upon its importance, to the point that, even in taking a drink of water, it is the custom to curse Yazīd and remember how Ḥusayn was forced to thirst before his death.

The death of Ḥusayn is enacted with many gory and pitiful details in a martyrdom play (*Ta'īziyyah*) which is performed in the Shī'ite world in the days preceding the anniversary of Kerbala according to the lunar Islamic calendar.

For the Sunnīs, the event is a deplorable murder of the second closest descendant of the Prophet. But even though it is held as a terrible tragedy, it has not become a personal and national trauma. Apart from the anniversary of Kerbala, the 10th Muḥarram is a religious holiday among the Sunnīs because it was, by coincidence, a religious day of observance in the Prophet's time. It remains a beneficent holiday for the Sunnīs. For the Shī'ites the 10th Muḥarram is the terrible anniversary of the martyrdom of Ḥusayn and is the most tragic and sorrowful day of the year. At this time some Shī'ite sects work themselves up into a frenzy and beat and wound themselves in the streets. Since Ṣafavid times, Kerbala, the site of the tomb of Ḥusayn, has been the most important Twelve-Imām Shī'ite shrine. *See* IMĀM; KERBALA; RAWDAH-KHANI; SHĪ'ISM: TAĪZIYYAH.

Ḥusaynī tribes. In Mauritania, those tribes, chiefly of Berber origin who, having lost military supremacy to the *Ḥasanī* tribes, now maintain a claim to status on the basis of religious devotion. The names Ḥasan and Ḥusayn are emblematic in Mauritania of "warrior" and "sacerdotal" functions rather than any ancestral relations. The *Ḥusaynī* tribes are also called *zāwiyah* tribes.

Ḥuzn (lit. "sadness", "grief"). It means ordinary sadness, grief or melancholy, but for the Sufis it has the special meaning of a "sacred nostalgia", a longing for the Reality, beyond the veil of separation, in regard to which this world is an exile. It is this spiritual longing which motivates the birds in Aṭṭār's allegory *Mantiq aṭ-Ṭāi'r* (the "Language of the Birds") to set off to look for their missing and mysterious king, the *Simurgh.*

Tradition recounts:

> Once in Abū Bakr's time, some folk from the Yemen came to Medina. When they heard a Reader in the Mosque chanting the Koran, tears fell from their eyes.
>
> We were like that once, the Caliph said; but our hearts have grown harder since.

Hypocrites (Ar. *munāfiqūn*). A party in Medina which professed sympathy to the Prophet and Islam but whose members were actually supporters of the pagan Quraysh of Mecca. The Koran refers to them as "propped up pieces of wood" and "those in whose heart is a disease".

Their leader was 'Abd Allāh ibn Ubayy, who withdrew his three hundred horseman from the Muslim forces just before the Battle of Uḥud. He was an important figure in Medina before the Prophet arrived there; almost to the end of his life he was jealous of the Prophet and grudging in his help. It was in respect of him, and his use of some six of his female slaves, that the verse of the Koran (24:33) was revealed:

> ...And constrain not
> your slavegirls to prostitution, if they
> desire to live in chastity, that you may
> seek the chance goods of the present life.
> Whosoever contrains them, surely God
> after their being constrained, is All-forgiving,
> All-compassionate.

I

'Ibādah. A technical term in theology meaning acts of worship or ritual, from the verb *'abada* "to serve" and *'abd* "slave", "servitor".

'Ibāḍites. Also called 'Ibāḍīs, the only surviving branch of the Khārijite movement named after the moderate leader 'Abd Allāh ibn 'Ibāḍ. The Khārijites were a group in Islam (the name means the "Seceders") which established itself around the edges of the Umayyad and 'Abbāsid empires.

They hold that the Koran is created, whereas the Sunnīs hold the Koran to be uncreated, otherwise, there are today only minor differences between the 'Ibāḍites and the Sunnīs. Although they constitute their own *madhhab*, or school of law, 'Ibāḍite law resembles the Mālikī school. They are, moreover, often confused with Mālikīs because both pray with their hands at their sides (as do also the Shī'ites) whereas all the other Sunnīs clasp their hands in front of them in prayer. The 'Ibāḍites today are found in Oman (which is their historical center and where they constitute the majority), and in East Africa, Zanzibar, Libya, the island of Jerba in Tunisia, and the region of the M'zab in Algeria. *See* KHĀRIJITES.

Ibāḥah, (lit. "permissiveness", "licentiousness", "libertinism"). Libertine sects or doctrines are called *ibāḥī*. Dualist sects, particularly the Khurramiyyah and Qarmatians, the Mazdakites before them, and remnants of Gnostic sects in the Middle East today, were persistently accused of libertinism and preaching the holding of women and property in common. In the Middle East such accusations are commonly made against any sect which diverges too far from the dominant norm and is secretive. Such accusations are frequently encountered and are to be interpreted as a sociological phenomenon with one group disassociating itself from another which it does not understand.

The Gnostic sects in particular call these accusations down upon themselves because they propose that evil and good are both present in the Principle and because of their secret (*bāṭinī*) doctrines which they consistently withhold from the scrutiny of outsiders. It is not surprising, therefore, that outsiders should conclude that the sect must involve something lurid. Similar accusations were made against the Gnostic sects in the Roman Empire during their struggle with the authorities representing religious orthodoxy. However, when Manicheism spread to Rome, and became prevalent among the upper classes, many well-bred female devotees of the religion of Mani were betrayed by the pallor from their all-too zealous fasting.

The paradox, that both libertinism and asceticism could be ascribed to the same sect, is due to Dualism's conception of religious law as something negative, and even "evil". Believing that the "evil of the law" could be transcended by esoteric and secret knowledge, the Dualist sects did in some respects show contempt towards certain religious laws, but not necessarily towards all laws; they also could seek to transcend the law by extreme discipline and even mortification whereby, again, the disciple made himself independent of the law; hence the reputation for asceticism. Also, some sects prescribed a period of extreme asceticism and thereafter affirmed that the initiate was perfect, and could not sin no matter what he appeared to do. *See* KHURRAMIYAH; MAZDAK.

Iblīs (from Greek *diabolos*, "the slanderer" and hence the "devil"). A personal name of the devil, otherwise called *ash-shayṭān*, (from the Hebrew) and described in the Koran as "the adversary". Originally, he was one of the Angels, the only one who refused to bow down to Adam when so commanded by God, saying to God, "You made me of fire and him of clay". For this disobedience God cast Iblīs out of heaven, reprieving him however, from annihilation until the Day of Judgement. Iblīs tempted Adam and Eve to eat the fruit of the forbidden tree, which in the Old Testament is the tree of the knowledge of good and evil. In Islamic belief, the guilt for this sin (*ithm*), lies not with mankind as an "original sin" from which man must be redeemed, but with the devil.

Nevertheless, it is mankind that bears the sanctions and consequences of the Fall from Eden. The Fall of mankind is the result of its taking for Reality something other than God: of seeing the world as a separate reality. It is the result of perceiving the relativities of the world as absolute rather than the essences of Being. This is "associating something with God" (*shirk*), which Islam sees as the fundamental sin, the denial of the Divine Unity. It is corrected *virtually* by the *shahādah*, for thereby one becomes aware, at least theoretically, that only the Absolute is real when one testifies that there is no god but Allāh; and it is corrected *effectively* by the complete realization of the *shahādah* with the mind and the heart, whereby the relative vanishes and only the absolute remains, which was the state of Adam before the Fall.

There is a story told of the Sufi al-Junayd:

> "At one period in my life," he said, "I felt a longing to see in vision what Satan was like. And as I stood in the mosque one day, an old man came through the gateway. His face turned towards me; and at the sight of it my heart clenched with horror. He came nearer, and I cried out: 'Who are you? the look of you – the mere thought of you – I cannot bear it!'"
> 'I am him you wanted to see.'
> 'The Accursed One!' I exclaimed. 'Then answer now my question: why would you not bow down to Adam, for which God cursed you?'
> 'Junayd,' said he, 'how could you imagine that I should bow down to any except God?'
> This answer startled me. But then a secret voice inside me whispered: Say to him: 'You're lying – if you had been an obedient servant you would not have disobeyed His Command.'
> And as if he heard the whisper in my heart, the old man cried out: 'O God! You've burnt me!' And suddenly he vanished."

The devil tempts man and tries to mislead him. The *ta'awwudh* formula of taking "refuge in God from Satan the stoned one" is spoken before reciting the Koran, and before the *basmalah* or consecration through the Divine Name, "In the Name of God", when undertaking ritual action. In Islam, as in all orthodox metaphysics, evil arises within creation when the quality of limitation (in Sanskrit *tamas,* which in itself is neutral, like many of its consequences such as the property of weight, and which is the source of the differentiation between one object and another, being in fact the separativeness necessary for manifestation to take place at all) encounters consciousness. When the principle of separativeness touches consciousness, reality is inverted and the contingent and relative appear to be Cause and Absolute.

Among the traditional signs of "dark spirits" are the following: first, that they say the opposite of the truth; second, that they deny their own faults and attribute them to others, preferably to someone who is completely innocent; third, that they continually change their position in an argument, the purpose of argument being only to subvert, to turn aside from truth and goodness; fourth, that they exaggerate the evil of what is good, and the good of what is evil, that is, they define good as evil because of a shadow of imperfection, and evil as good because of a reflection of perfection; they glorify a secondary quality in order to deny an essential one, or to disguise a fundamental flaw; in short, they completely falsify true proportions and invert normal relations.

That this must be so is due to the "imperfection" of creation itself. Plato admired creation because it reflected the Absolute Good. But at the same time creation was not, and could not be, the Absolute itself. Jesus says in the Gospels, "Why callest thou me good? Only God alone is Good". The existence of creation arises from the possibility which the Absolute necessarily contains, in virtue of Absoluteness itself, of its own negation. Creation is the "illusorily real" manifestation of this possibility. It is at once nothing other than the Absolute, and at the same time an "otherness" which appears to set itself against God. It is this apparent and inescapable otherness in creation that is the introduction of evil, and that is why the Sūrah of Daybreak (Sūrah 113) speaks of the "evil of that [the world itself] which He created".

The dualist philosophies take creation as the sign of a flaw within the Absolute. They equate the possibility of self-negation with evil; and they confuse the *necessity* of the possibility of self-negation within the Absolute, the need for God to create, which is a perfection, with weakness, or see it as proof that some power outside God provoked creation. In this way, they claim that evil either exists within God or coexists with Him. Creation then becomes a drama in which God salvages Himself from the consequences of the power of evil that is His equal. It is for this reason that C.G. Jung said that the "trinity should be a quaternity" whose fourth person is the devil; a conclusion drawn from the Gnostic assumption that Satan is really an aspect of God Himself.

In order for there to be a world, there must be limitation, and limitation implies nothingness, which lies beyond the limit. When consciousness looks upon nothingness, the natural tendency is not to see nothingness – that would be enlightenment – but to see another something. The mind assigns essences to what it sees; the essence of nothing, if it were to have an essence, would be absolute contradiction, or pure evil. But in the mind that has made the error, this anti-essence then arises and makes its abode. Evil is the result of an error which then acts through the consciousness that has made the error. The struggle which results is, as Milton says, "dubious battle upon the plains of heaven", dubious because not real; the outcome is certain. When creation, or manifestation, disappears altogether in that instant between manifestations which is the *apocatastasis*, evil, the apparently "absolute" other reality that *arises only in the world*, disappears also, "shut out by the Angel Michael's sword", before Michael himself disappears and God, the Merciful is alone. See REFUGE; SHAHĀDAH; SHIRK; TA 'AWWUDH.

Ibn Abī-l-Khayr, Abū Said Faḍl Allāh (*357-440*/967-1049). One of the so-called "drunken Sufis" who were wont to claim a union with God in terms of a personal identification. Abū Yazīd (Bāyazīd) al-Bisṭāmī (d. *260*/874) was the first to be called thus, and he is remembered for his exclamation, supposedly made in a state of ecstasy, "Glory to me".

To Ibn Abī-l-Khayr is attributed the famous statement, pointing to his clothes: "there is no-one in this robe but God". This does not have the scent of ecstasy about it and seems more calculated; indeed, accounts of his life become increasingly ambiguous towards the end; he lived in an opulent and lavish style glorifying himself, suggesting that rather than a genuine Sufi, he was a false one. The Sufis are in fact careful to say, no matter what degree of union is realized, "the slave remains the slave, and the Lord remains the Lord". *See* al-JUNAYD.

Ibn Adḥam, Ibrāhīm, *see* IBRĀHĪM ibn ADḤAM.

Ibn Anas, *see* MĀLIK ibn ANAS.

Ibn 'Arabī, Abū Bakr Muḥammad Muhyī-d-Dīn (*560-638*/1165-1240). Mystic and teacher, he is considered by many as the greatest Muslim exponent of metaphysical doctrine. In recognition of this pre-eminence he was called "the greatest shaykh" (*ash-shaykh al-akbar*) and the "red sulphur" (*al-kabrit al-aḥmar*), an alchemical reference implying that Ibn 'Arabī could draw knowledge out of ignorance as sulphur "draws" gold out of lead. At the same time, there are clear ambiguities in his writings, and many a heretic could find support in him for a wide variety of extravagant beliefs. Ibn 'Arabī is often called a pantheist and, indeed, there is justification for this. What is important to bear in mind is that the school which upholds him would vehemently reject pantheism. Thus, curiously, perhaps, if there is a fundamental metaphysical error in Ibn 'Arabī, the majority of his followers, guided by their own orthodoxy, rectify it in practice and disregard the compromising elements.

Ibn 'Arabī was born in Murcia in Spain, and studied at Seville and Ceuta. He later visited Mecca and Baghdad, and settled in Damascus. Several women were great sources of mystical inspiration for him. While in Spain he had met two women Saints, then already quite old; Shams of Marchena, and Fāṭimah bint ibn al-Muthannā' of Cordova. In his biographical descriptions of Andalusian Sufis, the *Ruḥ al-Quds* ("The Spirit of Sanctity") and *ad-Durrāt al-Fākhirah* ("The Pearls of Glory"), Ibn 'Arabī describes both of them, saying he learned much from their example. In Mecca in the year *599*/1201 he met Niẓām 'Ayn ash-Shams ("the Spring of the Sun"), the young daughter of a friend, Abū Shāja Zāhir ibn Rustam. She was beautiful and young, but learned, and she participated in the intellectual gatherings in her father's home. She inspired Ibn 'Arabī to write the love poems which are contained in the *Tarjumān al-Ashwāq* ("The Interpreter of Longings"). His monumental work on mystical doctrine is the *Futūḥāt al-Makkiyyah*, ("the Meccan Revelations"). Equally famous are the *Fuṣūṣ al-Ḥikam* ("Bezels of Wisdom"). Mystical experiences confirmed for him the unity of religious forms despite their external divergences; he spoke of a *ḥāl*, or a spiritual state, in which he was joined to the nature of Jesus. In a famous passage in the *Tarjumān al-Ashwāq* Ibn 'Arabī said:

My heart is open to all forms;
 it is a pasturage for gazelles
and a monastery for Christian monks
 a temple for idols and the
Ka'bah of the pilgrim
 the tables of the Torah and
the book of the Koran.
 Mine is the religion of Love
Wherever His caravans[1]
 turn, the religion of
Love shall be my religion
 and my faith.

[1][literally "camels", a Koranic symbol for spiritual realities]

Ibn 'Arabī is particularly renowned for audacious metaphysical formulations. *Huwa* ("He"), the third person pronoun, is also a Divine Name of the Essence. Ibn 'Arabī declared that another, "inner" Name for the Divine Essence is *Hiya*, ("She"). The idea that the Divine Essence could contain a polarity is so completely heretical (it is commonly found among the Gnostics) that it lends strong support to the idea that Ibn 'Arabī compiled ideas from many sources but did not himself realize their full import.

Although Ibn 'Arabī is considered to be one of the most intellectual of Sufis, for him *maḥabbah* ("love"), and not *ma'rifah* ("knowledge"), is the summit of mysticism, for it is love which actually makes Divine union (*tawḥīd*) possible. He set down in writing the doctrine of *waḥdat al-wujūd* (the "unity of being", or monism), the counterpart within Islam of *advaita vedanta* and of the doctrine of the Tao. However, it is true that there is enough evidence to suspect an ambiguity regarding Ibn 'Arabī's own understanding of the doctrine; it is quite possible that he himself was a pantheist, as is often claimed, which is as much to say that perhaps he was a dualist. If that is so, it is nevertheless true that those who followed him understand his doctrine in a "corrected" way. In other words, the very subtlety of Ibn 'Arabī's formulation has opened him to being integrated into an orthodox mystical perspective. Thus Ibn 'Aṭā' Allāh, a great follower of Ibn 'Arabī, one generation removed, and of whose orthodoxy there is no question, says:

> Behold what shows to you His Omnipotence, (may He be exalted): it is that He hides Himself from you by what has no existence apart from Him.

And:

> How can God (*al-Ḥaqq*) be veiled by something, for He is apparent (*ẓāhir*) and has actual being (*mawjūd ḥāḍir*) in that wherewith He is veiled?

Although Ibn 'Arabī is credited with this doctrine, *waḥdat al-wujūd* is the metaphysics of Sufism as such, and Ibn 'Arabī's role was in fact that of expressing more formally, and perhaps more amply, ideas that had up until then been taught only orally. In addition to formalizing much Sufi doctrine in writing, Ibn 'Arabī was a bridge between the Sufi traditions of Spain and Morocco and the eastern Sufism of Egypt and Syria. During the great flowering of Islamic intellectuality in Atjeh in Indonesia, the names of Ibn 'Arabī and other proponents of his school of intellectual mysticism, such as Ibn 'Aṭa' Allāh, were bywords.

A famous recent disciple of Ibn 'Arabī was the Emir 'Abd al-Qādir of Algeria, a great warrior who fought French colonization in the 19th century. Also a Sufi, the Emir regarded Ibn 'Arabī, who preceded him by almost a millennium, as his foremost teacher. 'Abd al-Qādir was buried next to the Shaykh Ibn 'Arabī in his tomb in Damascus. *See* SUFISM.

Ibn 'Aṭā' Allāh, Aḥmad ibn Muḥammad (d. *709*/1309). A mystic of the order founded by the Imām ash-Shādhilī (d. *656*/1258). Ibn Atā' Allāh was originally a jurist of the Mālikī School of Law and taught at the al-Azhar school in Cairo, and at the Manṣūriyyah. His father had been a Sufi but Ibn 'Aṭā' Allāh was not only not drawn to mysticism, but was antagonistic towards it, and in particular towards Abū-l-'Abbās al-Mūrsī (d. *686*/1288) who taught Sufi disciples in Alexandria. But in *674*/1276, Ibn 'Aṭā' Allāh met al-Mūrsī, successor to the Shaykh ash-Shādhilī, and became his disciple on the spot.

Ibn 'Aṭā' Allāh wrote a celebrated book of mystical aphorisms, the *Kitāb al-Ḥikam*, which aimed at arousing spiritual awareness in the disciple. He also wrote the *Miftāḥ al-Falāḥ wa Miṣbāḥ al-Arwāḥ* ("The Key of Success and the Lamp of Spirits") on the spiritual method of invocation (*dhikr*), the *Kitāb at-Tanwīr fī Isqāṭ at-Tadbīr* ("Light on the Elimination of Self-Direction") concerning the approach of the

Shādhilī school to the practice of virtue, the *Kitāb al-Laṭā'if fī Manāqib Abī-l-'Abbās al-Mūrsī wa Shaykhihi Abī-l-Ḥasan*, about the first Masters of the Shādhiliyyah *ṭarīqah*, and other works. The intellectual mysticism of the Imām ash-Shādhilī, as well as that of Ibn 'Arabī, made a deep impression upon the Muslims of Indonesia, where the works of Ibn 'Aṭā' Allāh are well known, in particular the *Kitāb al-Ḥikam*, which has been translated into Malay.

His aphorisms include the following:

> One of the signs of relying on one's own deeds is the loss of hope when a downfall occurs.
>
> Your striving for what has already been guaranteed to you, and your remissness in what is demanded of you, are signs of the blurring of your intellect.
>
> If He opens a door for you, thereby making Himself known, pay no heed if your deeds do not measure up to this. For, in truth, He has not opened it for you but out of a desire to make Himself known to you. Do you not know that He is the one who presented the knowledge of Himself to you, whereas you are the one who presented Him with deeds? What a difference between what He brings to you and what you bring to Him.
>
> How can the heart be illumined while the forms of creatures are reflected in its mirror? Or how can it journey to God while shackled by its passions? Or how can it desire to enter the Presence of God while it has not yet purified itself of the stain of its forgetfulness? Or how can it understand the subtle points of mysteries while it has not yet repented of its offenses?
>
> How can it be conceived that something veils Him, since He is the one who manifests everything?
>
> Your postponement of deeds till the time when you are free is one of the frivolities of the ego.
>
> He who is illumined at the beginning is illumined at the end.
>
> Your being on the lookout for the vices hidden within you is better than your being on the lookout for the invisible realities veiled from you.
>
> One of the signs of delusion is sadness over the loss of obedience coupled with the absence of resolve to bring it back to life.
>
> The proof that you have not found Him is that you strive for the permanency of what is other than He, and the proof that you are not united to Him is that you feel estranged at the loss of what is other than He.
>
> Travel not from creature to creature, otherwise you will be like a donkey at the mill: roundabout he turns, his goal the same as his departure. Rather go from creatures to the Creator: "And that the final end is unto thy Lord" (53:42). Consider the Prophet's words (God bless him and grant him peace!): "Therefore, he whose flight is for God and His Messenger, then his flight is for God and His Messenger; and he whose flight is for worldly gain or marriage with a woman, then his flight is for that which he flees to." So understand his words (upon him peace!) and ponder this matter, if you can. And peace on you!

Ibn Athir. Famous as literary figures, three Kurdish brothers from northern Iraq are known by this name.

1. Majd ad-Dīn (*544-607*/1149-1210) was a lexicographer and assembler of Ḥadīth.

2. Abū-l-Ḥasan 'Izz ad-Dīn Muḥammad (*556-632*/1160-1234) wrote a history called the *Kāmil* ("The Complete").

3. Diyā' ad-Dīn (*559-637*/1163-1239) was a literary critic.

Ibn Babawayh, Muḥammad (c. *306-381*/918-991). Also known by the alternate names Ibn Bābūya, aṣ-Ṣadūq, or al-Qummī. He is one of the principal early Shī'ite theologians, the author of a large number of books of which the most famous is *Man la yaḥduruhu-l-faqīh* ("When no theologian is present"). This is one of the foundations of Shī'ite theology and one of the so-called "Four Books of Shī'ism", *al-Kutub al-Arba'ah*, the principal collections of Shī'ite Ḥadīth. The others are *al-Kāfī* ("The Compendium or the Sufficient") by Muḥammad ibn Ya'qūb Abū Ja'far al-Kulaynī (d. *329*/940), and the *Istibsar* and *Taḥdhīb al-Aḥkām* by Muḥammad aṭ-Ṭūsī (d. *460*/1067).

The father of Ibn Babawayh is said to have asked the Hidden Imām, through the third *Wakīl* ("representative"), Abū Qāsim Ḥusayn ibn Rūḥ, to pray that a son be granted him. The father received the answer "We have prayed for it", and Ibn

Babawayh would say that he was born because of the Hidden Imām's prayers. He also said that he had communicated in a dream at Mecca with the Hidden Imām who commanded him to write his book the *Kamāl ad-Dīn* ("Perfection of Religion"). Ibn Babawayh traveled widely, collected Ḥadīth and was a teacher of another important Shī'ite scholar, the Shaykh al-Mufīd. The father of Ibn Babawayh, 'Alī ibn Ḥusayn, is also called by the same name, and the two together are referred to as the as-Ṣadūqān.

Ibn Babūyā, *see* IBN BABAWAYH.

Ibn Bājjah, Abū Bakr Muḥammad (c. *500-533*/1106-1138). The philosopher known in Europe as Avempace, whose thought greatly influenced Ibn Rushd (Averroes). Ibn Bājjah was born in Saragossa, Spain, and died in Fez, having served as minister to the Emir of Murcia. He wrote a commentary on Aristotle and treatises on the physical sciences.

In one of his works, *Tadbīr al-Mutawaḥḥid*, he speaks of the "solitary", who is in the world as it is, but lives as if he were not in it at all, and adheres rather to the rule of an ideal society. The enlightened individual may attain this "perfect state or republic" inwardly, even if it is not within reach of society as a whole. For him, as for Plato, the Intellect can reach Truth by itself, even without revelation: he believed, in other words, that the capacity for revelation is inherent in the Intellect itself, and revelation is a manifestation of the Intellect. *See* PHILOSOPHY.

Ibn Baṭūṭah, Abū 'Abd Allāh Muḥammad (*704-780*/1304-1378). An explorer and traveler known as the "Arab Marco Polo". Born in Tangiers, he began traveling at the age of twenty-one when he went across North Africa to Cairo, and thence to Mecca to perform the pilgrimage. Thereafter he traveled in Syria, Mesopotamia, Persia, East Africa, Oman, Asia Minor, the Crimea, the regions along the Volga, Samarkand, Bukhara, Afghanistan, India, (where in Delhi he became a Judge), China, the Maldive Islands, Ceylon, Java and Sumatra.

His journeys were wanderings from place to place rather than a purposeful design. He frequently criss-crossed his tracks and returned to the great cultural centers of Islam. During his travels he performed the pilgrimage four times. He returned to Tangiers after twenty-four years absence but soon set out again, this time for Spain. He returned and thereafter went across the Sahara to Timbuktu and regions of the Niger.

At the end of his life he dictated a description of his travels (*Tuḥfat an-nuẓẓār fī gharā'ib al-amṣār wa-'ajā'ib al-asfār*). The narrative, known at first in fragments, but then discovered in a complete original manuscript in Algeria, is considered to be a generally accurate account of the countries seen by the most far ranging traveler of the ancient world.

Ibn al-Bayṭār, Abū Muḥammad 'Abd Allāh ibn Aḥmad Ḍiyā' ad-Dīn (d. *646*/1248). A botanist, born in Malaga, Ibn al-Bayṭār traveled widely to study plants. He entered the service of the Sultans in Egypt and died in Damascus. Ibn al-Bayṭār wrote the greatest compilation of medicinal plants made before modern times, the *Kitāb al-jāmi' fī-l-adwiyah al-mufradah.* It contains 1,400 entries including many plants never before recorded, and cites a number of Latin and Greek authors.

Ibn al-Fāriḍ (*578-632*/1182-1235). A famous Arab Sufi teacher and poet who lived in Egypt. His most famous poem is the *Khamriyyah* (the "Wine Ode"). The Sufis make wine a symbol of invocation of the Divine Name and by drunkenness describe the rapture of the knowledge of God, as in the well-known *Ruba' iyyat of 'Umar Khayyām. See* al-KHAMRIYYAH; SUFISM.

Ibn Gabirol, Solomon ben Judah (*411-463*/1020-1070). A Jewish philosopher, known in the West as Avicebron, born in Malaga. A student of Ibn Sīnā (Avicenna) and Empedocles, his famous philosophical work is *Fons Vitae* ("the Fountain of Life"). In it he explains why circles are often used to demonstrate philosophical theories by saying that they show how effects are contained in their causes. Ibn Gabirol, the first Jewish teacher of Neoplatonism in the West, emerged out of the tradition of Arab philosophy in Moorish Andalusia. He was probably the first to use the term *Qabbalah.*

He may have influenced Duns Scotus towards a material conception of the substance of manifestation (which the Scholastics called *materia signata quantitate*, "*materia* under the sign of quantity"). He was better known to the

Jews of his time as a poet than as a philosopher and, using Arab meters in Hebrew, he wrote liturgical compositions.

Ibn Ḥanbal, Aḥmad (*164-241*/780-855). The originator of the Ḥanbalī School of Law, which was established by his disciples. He studied in Baghdad and received instruction from the great legal theoretician ash-Shāfi'ī. He is the compiler of a large collection of Ḥadīth, the *Musnad.*

When the 'Abbāsid Caliph al-Ma'mūn made the Mu'tazilite doctrine of the created Koran official state dogma, Ibn Ḥanbal staunchly upheld the orthodox dogma that the Koran is uncreated. Although other figures, Judges and theologians, backed down in the face of the threat of physical punishment, Ibn Ḥanbal maintained his beliefs, for which he was at first imprisoned and then scourged. He gained a great reputation for his steadfastness in the face of persecution, and was restored to favor by the Caliph al-Mutawakkil, who put an end to the *miḥnah* (inquisition into belief), and reinstated the doctrine of the uncreated Koran.

Ibn Ḥayyan, *see* JĀBIR ibn ḤAYYĀN.

Ibn Ḥazm, 'Alī ibn Aḥmad (*384-456*/994-1064). A theologian of Arab-Persian descent born in Cordova, he was a violent opponent of the Ash'arites (*see* al-ASH'ARĪ). Literalist and singular in his approach, he was a chauvinist in regard to Islam, the Arabs, and Muslim Spain, and a noted poet. He followed the Ẓāhirī (exoterist) School of Law and so maintained that the only level of meaning in the Koran was the explicit; according to him no hidden meanings were admissible. He wrote many books on a variety of subjects including philosophy, history, and descriptions of different sects and schools of thought. For his highly polemical stands he spent the latter years of his life in a kind of internal exile, and the number of his disciples was restricted by the authorities.

Ibn Hishām, Abū Muḥammad 'Abd al-Mālik (d. *219*/834). Arab Scholar, known for his edition of Ibn Isḥāq's *Sīrat rasūl Allāh* ("Life of the Messenger of God"), the most important traditional biography of the Prophet.

Ibn Isḥāq, Ḥunayn (*194-259*/809-873). A Nestorian Christian, physician to the Caliph al-Mutawakkil, Ibn Isḥāq collected Greek manuscripts, and with his son Isḥāq, his nephew Ḥubaysh, and others, translated these manuscripts into Arabic. These included works by Galen, Hippocrates, Plato, and others. *See* NESTORIANS.

Ibn Khaldūn, 'Abd ar-Raḥmān ibn Muḥammad (*733-808*/1332-1406). Often called the "Father of Historiography", Ibn Khaldūn was born in Tunisia. His life was extremely turbulent; at one time he served the Merinid Sultan in Fez as a functionary, but was imprisoned because of court intrigue. He regained his freedom and his position, but then other troubles forced him to go to Spain. At first, Ibn Khaldūn was well received at the court of Granada, but political turmoil forced him to flee to North Africa, where he was given a post by the Sultan of Būjiya with whom he had once shared imprisonment. War and vicissitudes forced him to return to Fez, and thence to Tunis where he wrote his *Prolegomena.*

Having set out east to perform the pilgrimage, Ibn Khaldūn entered into the service of the Mamlūk Sultan of Egypt, Barqūq. In Cairo he became the Grand Qāḍi (Chief Judge) of the Mālikī rite. He was dismissed and reinstated as many as five times, this office being notorious for the fact that its holder was bound to come into conflict with the ruler's wishes. On a mission to Damascus Ibn Khaldūn was trapped inside the city by the attacking army of Timur (Tamerlane) and had to escape by letting himself down by a rope from the city walls, in the face of the conquering Timur; the latter allowed him to return to Egypt, where he died.

Ibn Khaldūn was an acute observer of human nature. He noted the tendency to admire and respect power, so that conquered people often adopt the habits and customs of the conquerors, even to the extent of adopting their dress. His observations in this domain were such that he could also be rightly called the "Father of Sociology". In studying human nature, he was led to analyze the significance of sleep and to consider the prophetic character of certain dreams according to traditional psychology. Like the *Vedanta,* Ibn Khaldūn equates dream sleep with the subtle state, and sleep without dreams to the formless or Angelic state, each with its corresponding possibilities of knowledge. (In *Vedanta* the four states are:

vaishvānara [waking], *taijasa* [dream state], *prajñā* [profound sleep], and *turiya* [the unconditioned state, which is Being]. *See* FIVE DIVINE PRESENCES.)

However, it is not his speculations on spiritual psychology, or the social sciences that constitute his greatness, but his unique contribution to the understanding of history. Ibn Khaldūn's great work, the *Muqaddimah*, or *Prolegomena*, is the introduction to his *Kitāb al-'Ibar* ("Book of Examples and the Collection of Origins of the History of the Arabs and Berbers").

The Muslim peoples considered by Ibn Khaldūn are those whose habitats alternate between deserts and settled agricultural regions. Ibn Khaldūn's theory explains a recurrent pattern in the history of these peoples: between nomads and sedentaries, who represent a primordial division of human existence in the world, he holds that there is under the best of conditions a natural state of tension. Moreover, town-dwellers inevitably tend to fall into decadence and moral corruption, from which the nomads are preserved by the arduous nature of their daily lives. Among the nomads, Ibn Khaldūn discerns a hierarchy dependent upon the intensity of their involvement with the rigors of the desert: at the summit are the camel herders who penetrate furthest into the desert; after them come the herders of sheep who stay on the fringes of the desert, and last in the hierarchy are the cattle herders, who are obliged to keep to easy pastures.

Periodically, groups of nomads conquer the towns and become the new rulers. According to Ibn Khaldūn's theory, they at first bring a new vigor, sense of justice, and spiritual acuteness to the royal function, but after three generations, the rigor and the virtue which were needed to establish their sovereignty begin to ebb away from them. The princes of the first generation know what is required of them to become rulers; those of the second generation participated in the conquest, so that they too have first hand knowledge of the requirements of kingship; the princes of the third generation, however, know of this only by hearsay; and those of the fourth believe that power and respect are no more than their due by birthright. Thus the "fourth" generation lives in a distorted, and illusory, memory of the past, and it is only a matter of time before it forfeits the right to rule. Thus, rulers and ruled alike are then laid open once more to a fresh and purifying influx of desert nomads.

Ibn Khaldūn stands apart from mere recorders of observed events; he sees effects in causes, endeavors to find the underlying reasons for historic change and explores a theory whereby future developments may be predicted. What Ibn Khaldūn drew from his observations of the rhythmic movements of history is a model that is not dissimilar to the moral of the story of Cain and Abel in the Bible.

Cain represents the farmer-sedentary who lives in time; Abel the hunter-nomad who lives in space. The farmer plants, and must wait to see the seeds grow and be transformed; he is bound to duration. The hunter stalks a prey, and successfully kills it when an instantaneous identity takes place between the hunter and the prey, as symbolized by the arrow that finds its mark. There is no duration, but a perfect moment. The art of the sedentary is pictures, for pictures represent the other dimension, space. The art of the nomad is words, or poetry, for in poetry there is succession of events, or time, the invisible dimension of the nomad's life. The two art forms are what the Hindus call *yantra*, the sacred picture, and *mantra*, the sacred word. The murder of Abel by Cain signifies the destruction of space by time. At the beginning, the world was an endless space, and time was eternity, only a rhythm, a return to the same moment. With the Fall, change enters into the world, and thence into society; eventually change begins to dominate it, and time becomes a duration. The Biblical story recapitulates the history of the world as the absorption of space by time as duration, or as Abel's death agony.

In the garden of Eden, Eve was never separated from Adam. But when the wheel becomes the means of transport, when electronic communications impose themselves as the medium, then knowledge that is direct, and recognition that is face to face recede. An inevitable gap opens up, the mirror of identity darkens. It may be only hours between continents by airplane or microseconds by telephone, but in those microseconds the separation is absolute. No matter how swift they are, communications which are born of time are never in the present, but are ghosts out of the dead past. Adam has lost Eve. Cain's sacrifices of time (rather than of himself, as symbolized by Abel's sheep), like his satellites in space, do not win God's blessing. Cain has wandered into the "Land of Nod", the world of history and change, the modern world.

When history begins, as it does with Cain and Abel, there also begins the movement away from unity, which is a movement away from the center. This movement is towards multiplicity, and towards a multitude of illusory "centers". "Perfect" or "absolute" multiplicity is an unattainable limit, but one towards which history tends and which is its ultimate goal. What Ibn Khaldūn observed in the *Prolegomena* was the dynamics of the two poles in human history, still in their traditional phase, a weaving taking place between nomads and sedentaries, before the sedentaries completely engulfed or destroyed the nomads altogether, or before Cain finished killing Abel. *See* RASHĪD ad-DĪN aṭ-ṬABĪB.

Ibn Khallikān, Abū-l-'Abbās Aḥmad (*608-681*/1211-1282) A biographer, he was born in Iraq, a descendant of the family of the Barmecides, the able viziers of Hārūn ar-Rashīd. He studied theology in Aleppo, Damascus and Cairo. The Sultan Baybars named Ibn Khallikān the head Judge of Damascus. His book, *Kitāb Wafayāt al-A'yān*, is one of the most important works of reference, along with those of al-Wāqidī, for biographical information on more than 800 of the great men up to his time. Ibn Khallikān said that chess (in Persian *satranj*) was invented by Zezeh ibn Dāher, an Indian; there is a story in the *Shahnameh* how chess was invented to show to a Queen how a son died in battle; others attribute it to Iran.

Ibn Masarrah (d. *319*/931) Spanish philosopher from the region of Cordova who was associated, in the descriptions of Islamic writers, with the doctrines of the Greek philosopher Empedocles (495 - 435 B.C.). Empedocles taught that there were two principles, Harmony and Disorder. According to him matter had a principial nature, that is, it was a self-sufficient reality, not created. He taught something like the divinity of man; he is said to have thrown himself into the crater of Mount Aetna in order that there would be no mortal remains so that it could appear that he was taken up into heaven. Ibn Massarah's ideas were apparently similar; that is, a kind of dualism and its resulting divine materialism. It is said the he believed the world to be an emanation of God.

Ibn Masarrah could also be described as a Mu'tazilite in that he subscribed to the unknowability of God; but the unknown God is fundamental to most dualist doctrines and was also taught by the Faṭīmids. At one point in his life he traveled to the Middle East establishing links with the schools he encountered on his path.

Ibn Masarrah was a continuator of pre-Islamic religious doctrines that had existed in Spain before the Arab conquest (and which existed in North Africa, the Middle East and Central Asia). Asin Palacios, who studied Ibn Masarrah, concluded that his doctrine was essentially Priscillian Manicheism. Probably, through schools that he established or led in the south of Spain, Ibn Masarrah influenced or initiated the pantheistic and Gnostic outlook of the theosophist Ibn 'Arabī and was a forerunner of the Imām ash-Shādhilī. *See* IBN 'ARABĪ.

Ibn Mashīsh, 'Abd as-Salām (d. *625*/1228). The spiritual master of Abū-l-Ḥasan ash-Shādhilī, the founder of the Shādhilī order. Ibn Mashīsh, a Berber, was the *quṭb* (spiritual axis) of his age. Although he lived as a recluse on a mountain in Morocco, the Jabal 'Ālam, today a place of great pilgrimage, his renown had spread in his lifetime throughout the Islamic world. Nothing tangible remains of him except the *ṣalāt al-Mashīshiyyah* which is recited by all the *ṭuruq* which derive from the Imām ash-Shādhilī. This is a prayer which is a spiritual portrait of the Prophet and thus of the *al-insān al-kāmil*, the "Perfect Man".

> O my God, bless him from whom derive the secrets and from whom gush forth the lights, and in whom rise up the realities, and into whom descended the sciences of Adam, so that he hath made powerless all creatures, and so that understandings are diminished in his regard, and no one amongst us, neither predecessor nor successor, can grasp him.
>
> The gardens of the spiritual world (*al-malakūt*) are adorned with the flower of his beauty, and the pools of the world of omnipotence (*al-jabarūt*) overflow with the outpouring of his lights.
>
> There exists nothing that is not linked to him, even as it was said: Were there no mediator, everything that depends on him would disappear! (Bless him, O my God), by a blessing such as returns to him through You from You, according to his due.

O my God, he is Your integral secret, that demonstrates You, and Your supreme veil, raised up before You.

O my God, join me to his posterity and justify me by Your reckoning of him. Let me know him with a knowledge that saves me from the wells of ignorance and quenches my thirst at the wells of virtue. Carry me on his way, surrounded by Your aid, towards Your presence. Strike through me at vanity, so that I may destroy it. Plunge me in the oceans of Oneness (*al-aḥadiyyah*), pull me back from the abysses of Unification (*tawḥīd*) and drown me in the pure source of the ocean of Unity (*al-waḥdah*), so that I neither see nor hear nor am conscious nor feel except through it. And make of the Supreme Veil the life of my spirit, and of his spirit the secret of my reality, and of his reality all my worlds, by the realization of the First Truth.

O First, O Last, O Outward, O Inward, hear my petition, even as You heard the petition of Your servant Zachariah; succour me through You unto You, support me through You unto You, unite me with You, and come in between me and other-than You: Allāh, Allāh, Allāh! "Verily He who imposed on you the Koran for a law, will bring you back to the promised end" (28:85).
"Our Lord, grant us mercy from Your presence, and shape for us right conduct in our plight" (18:9).

"Verily God and His Angels bless the Prophet; O you who believe, bless him and wish him peace" (33:56).

May the graces (*ṣalāwat*) of God, His peace, His salutations, His mercy and His blessings (*barakāt*) be on our Lord Muḥammad, Your servant, Your prophet, and Your Messenger, the un-lettered prophet, and on his family and his companions, graces as numerous as the even the odd and as the perfect and blessed words of our Lord.

"Glorified be your Lord, the Lord of Glory, beyond what they attribute unto Him, and peace be on the Messengers. Praise be to God, the Lord of the worlds" (37:180-182).

Ibn Mas'ūd, 'Abd Allāh (d. 33/653). A Companion of the Prophet and an early convert, he became an administrator in Kufah. He is noted for the fact that he possessed and used a version of the Koran different in some respects from that edited under the Caliph 'Uthmān. Some remnants of this variant have survived, but it was condemned by Mālik ibn Anas, who declared that prayer performed by an Imām who recited Ibn Mas'ūd's version of the Koran was invalid.

Ibn al-Muqaffa', Abū Muḥammad (d. *140*/757). A Persian, originally a Zoroastrian of possibly Manichean convictions, who was converted to Islam. He was a secretary in the Caliphal administration and renowned for an elegant style and command of Arabic. Ibn al-Muqaffa' translated into Arabic the Indian fables of Bidpai (from Pahlevi), which then became the political allegories called *Kalīlah wa Dimnah.* These stories, in which animals act out situations that arise in matters of state, are perennially popular in Arab literature.

Among the subjects of the Lion were two Jackals, named Kalīlah and Dimnah, both cunning and sagacious in the highest degree. And one day Dimnah said to Kalīlah: I wonder why the Lion keeps himself so close retired of late? I think I will solicit an audience; and if I find him in any indecision, I purpose to turn his audience to my own advantage.

You will be playing a dangerous game, Kalīlah said; for there are three things which any man will be wise to avoid, owing to the impossibility of controlling the issues of them; one, incurring the confidence of a Prince; two, trusting a woman with a secret; and three, trying the effect of poison on one's self.

If the chance of failure, Dimnah replied, were sufficient reason for never trying, you would exclude from human endeavor all conduct of human affairs, all commercial enterprise, and all military achievement.

Well, I wish you luck, said Kalīlah; and Dimnah betook himself to the Lion's court...

Ibn al-Muqaffa' was eventually executed; perhaps in the persecutions, which were beginning around that time, of the practice of clandestine Manicheism; he may have betrayed himself by suggesting that the Caliph should claim Divinity.

Ibn an-Nadīm, Muḥammad ibn Isḥāq (d. 385/995). Known as *al-Warrāq* ("the manuscriptist"). A book dealer of Baghdad, he is the author of a book called "the Catalogue" (*al-*

Fihrist) which lists books and authors of his times along with notes, commentaries, and observations on religious, spiritual, and metaphysical matters.

Ibn al-Nafīs, 'Alā' ad-Dīn Abū-l-Ḥasan (*610-687*/1213-1288). Born in Damascus, Ibn al-Nafīs was a physician who worked in Cairo at the Nasrī and the Manṣūrī hospitals and made remarkable contributions to medicine. (The institution of care for the sick at hospitals was established in the first centuries of Islamic civilization.)

Ibn Qutaybah, Abū Muḥammad 'Abd Allāh ibn Muslim (*213-276*/828-889). A philologist born at Baghdad of Persian descent, he wrote about the education necessary for a court secretary, *Adab al-Kātib*; about literature, *Kitāb ash-Shi'r wa-sh-Shu'arā'* ("The Book of Poetry and Poets"); and on moral training; *'Uyūn al-Akhbār.*

Ibn Rushd, Abū-l-Walīd Muḥammad ibn Aḥmad ibn Muḥammad (*520-595*/1126-1198). An Arab philosopher who had little influence in the East, coming, as he did, at the end of the development of philosophy in Islam, and perhaps marking its summit. Known, however, as Averroes in Europe, and translated into Latin, he became the great authority on Aristotle's philosophy, and was so celebrated that he could be referred to simply as "the Commentator". For Ibn Rushd, Aristotle was the consummate master of the Way of the mind.

In Europe, a school arose around his "Commentaries on Aristotle" which was called "Latin Averroism". Into the 15th century and beyond, he was still a vital force in European philosophy, although his thinking, abstracted from his own Muslim framework and belief, was interpreted as that of a sceptic oriented towards nominalism, or empiricism, rather than of the realist (or nowadays, idealist) that he was.

Ibn Rushd was born in Cordova, the grandson of a Judge. His friend Ibn Ṭufayl, the philosopher, introduced him to the Almohad court and he was appointed *Qāḍi* (Judge) in Seville. Because all learning was virtually one continuous science without borders in that age, he was not only a philosopher and a canon lawyer, he also served as physician to Abū Ya'qūb Yūsuf, the Almohad prince.

The Arab West is the most conservative part of all the Arab world, and is devoted to maintaining tradition; this is, in fact, the outstanding characteristic of the Mālikī School of Law. There, broad ideas often came under suspicion, and popular feelings during the rule of al-Manṣūr interpreted philosophy as heresy. For a time Ibn Rushd, who had meanwhile established himself in Morocco, was exiled back to Spain, but he was later allowed to return, and finished his life in North Africa.

In Europe, he is famous for the theory of the "Unity of the Intellect", which, corrupted into the "theory of the common soul", was called "pan-psychism". However, it is really an expression of the Neo-platonic concept that true knowledge consists in the identity of the knower with the known. The faculty of cognition, or "knowing", is the intellect, which is a projection of the metacosmic Intellect – the center of Being – into the individual knower. Creation, which is the object of knowledge, is the differentiation in the cosmos of that Intellect. Awareness of the identity between the two is knowledge; the knower knows because, in a sense, he contains what he knows. The notoriety of the doctrine arose because it was expressed as philosophy; but in Islamic mysticism it is familiar under its esoteric formulations as *waḥdat ash-shuhūd*, ("unity of consciousness"), and the essentially similar *waḥdat al-wujūd* ("unity of being"); the latter was being expounded around the same time by the metaphysician Ibn 'Arabī (d. *630*/1240) but being seen as religion, and not as philosophy, it was not read in Europe.

Ibn Rushd is also associated with what has been called the "two truths" theory; this contends that his doctrine was that there is one truth for philosophers, which is philosophy, and another for the masses, which is religion. But since for Averroes the higher truth lay in revelation and the lower in the formulations of theology, he cannot be guilty of the secret "free thinking" he was accused of in the Middle Ages. Rather, he recognized that there exists truth as such, which must needs resort to ellipses and to apparent contradictions or antinomies in order to express itself in the terms of reason rather than myth; and he recognised too that dogma, for its purposes, either simplifies the truth or expresses it only in part. Theological dogma does this in order to avoid doctrinal contradictions which cannot be resolved by ordinary reason; inevitably, however, at some point, it too is obliged to make up for what is missing from its simplifications by acknowledging certain categories as "mysteries", or by hiving off the inexplicable with the formula *bilā kayfa* ("don't ask why"), as the Ash'arites do. Ibn Rushd actually sought to harmonize the Koran and revelation with philosophy and logic. See FIVE DIVINE PRESENCES; PHILOSOPHY.

Ibn Ṣa'd (Abū 'Abd Allāh Muḥammad ibn Ṣa'd ibn Manī' az-Zuhrī, usually called Kātib al-Waqidī, the secretary of Waqidī, d. *230*/845). Biographer from Baṣra who lived in Baghdad. He wrote the *Kitāb al-Ṭabaqāt al-Kabīr*, a large biography of Companions, Helpers, and Followers, grouped as "classes" or succeeding generations.

Ibn Sa'ūd, 'Abd al-'Azīz (*1297-1372*/1880-1953). King of Saudi Arabia, known there as King 'Abd al-'Azīz Āl Sa'ūd. He was born in Riyāḍ the son of 'Abd ar-Raḥmān, Sultan of the Najd. His father had been driven out of Riyāḍ in *1309*/1891 by the adversaries of the family, the Banū Rashīd of Hā'il, and had taken refuge in Kuwait. Some ten years later, in *1319*/1901, 'Abd al-'Azīz led a raiding party of forty or so men into the Najd. In the early morning they penetrated into the city of Riyāḍ and attacked the governor on his way from the Musmak palace to perform the dawn prayer.

This daring foray succeeded; the governor was killed and Riyāḍ recaptured. With this the Sa'ūd family regained control, 'Abd al-'Azīz became King of the Najd and thereafter his Kingdom grew steadily. In *1344*/1924 he conquered the Hejaz, then the Asir and finally the rest of what is today Saudi Arabia. In *1348*/1929 the King was obliged to fight the Battle of Sibilla against dissident nomad tribe leaders. These were formerly his own supporters, who had continued carrying out raids, now against British-defended Iraq, against the King's wishes and despite the program of settlement which he initiated. The battle was fought with the King's troops mounted on Fords and Chevrolets that had been commandeered in Jeddah and driven across the desert.

In 1938 oil was discovered in Dhahran (Ẓahrān). The King signed agreements giving Standard Oil of California concessions to exploit the finds; twenty years later oil production led to an era of unprecedented prosperity.

King 'Abd al-'Azīz was by any standards a most remarkable figure. Starting out as a tribal chieftain, he became King of a new and modern nation. He had the ability to make bold political decisions in situations which were completely unfamiliar to him; he also had an immense store of good fortune. But despite his capacity to act independently of past habit and precedent, King 'Abd al-'Azīz, in the middle of the twentieth century, retained the air of a Biblical patriarch. He died in Ṭā'if of ripe old age and went to the grave with forty-two battle wounds received in his youth fighting with lance and sword. He was succeeded as King by his sons in turn, first Sa'ūd, then Fayṣāl, Khālid and Fahd.

Ibn Sīnā, Abū 'Alī Ḥusayn ibn 'Abd Allāh (*370-429*/980-1037). Physician and philosopher, and one of the renowned intellectual figures of the Middle Ages, Ibn Sīnā was born near Bukhāra, of a Turkic mother and a Persian father. A precocious student, after learning the Koran by heart at the age of ten, he studied the *Isagoge* of Porphyry and the propositions of Euclid. Logic, philosophy, and medicine were to be his calling in life. He wrote numerous treatises of which the most influential was the *Canon of Medicine*, which remained a basis for teaching medicine in Europe into the 17th century, and the *ash-Shifā'* ("Healing"), known in Europe as the *Sanatio*.

Medicine in Islam was a prolongation of the science of the Greeks, and thus Ibn Sīnā's concepts were based on those of the Greek physician Galen. His lofty reputation in Europe earned him the title of "Prince of Physicians". In the East however, where many other physicians wrote similar medical treatises, he was more renowned as an expounder of philosophy, at that time a unified study of Plato, Aristotle, and Neoplatonism. Ibn Sīnā was actually one of the prime targets of al-Ghazālī's attack on the philosophers.

Ibn Sīnā's great accomplishment was to complete the philosophy of Aristotle and elaborate an ontology of Being. Ibn Sīnā, probably despite himself, developed for the West as much as for the East, the philosophy of monotheism. Aristotle had spoken of the "First Mover" but had not described Him. This became possible only after Islam, and the revelation of the Absolute, the revelation of the nature of the "First Mover."

It was Ibn Sīnā who was to describe philosophically the relationship between the Divine Essence and Being. However, he did so "backwards"; Ibn Sīnā said, *because* God exists, therefore He has an Essence, which is Existentialism ("existence precedes essence"). Thus Ibn Sīnā thought of Being as being physical and existing. (The Ismā'īlīs say that *the soul is a projection of the body*, instead of the other way around.) In orthodox metaphysics, it is the exact opposite which must be true: namely, *because* God has an Essence, therefore He exists, or rather, has Being in the sense that Being proceeds out of the Divine Essence "by way of creation", and from Being proceeds existence. But to arrive at this, not only was Islam a necessary pre-condition as a Revelation of the Divine Essence, which is why Aristotle himself had gone no further, but it was necessary to arrive at the idea by backing into it because the Divine Essence is, in Itself, inconceivable. If nothing else, this certainly demonstrates that error teaches, that limitation brings awareness, or that good can come out of evil, even though, woe to those through whom evil comes. The fall of man must precede salvation.

Ibn Sīnā wrote that his father was an Isma'īlī and that Ismā'īlī meetings, which Ibn Sīnā attended as a child, were held in his home. Thus, although Ibn Sīnā claimed to be a Ḥanifī Sunnī, albeit with a very cavalier attitude towards religious laws for he lived the life of a medieval playboy, he came from a background in which the physical world was considered to be divine, the body of God, so to speak. He used Isma'īlī terminology such as *al-Mubdi'* for God. It was this religious formation that allowed him to follow the Koranic doctrine of the Divine Attributes or Names treated as physical, material guideposts back to their necessary center, which, understood in the human mind, would then be the Essence. An Essence that Ibn Sīnā said God had because God – or the world – "had an existence". Similarly to his idea of existence preceding essence, Ibn Sīnā postulated that if a grown man were to be suddenly created in a void, without limbs, without senses, he could nevertheless arrive at self-awareness, although how, is not clear unless one assumes that consciousness itself has differentiation, or to put it otherwise, that consciousness is material, that the soul is a thing. In keeping with this possibility, Ibn Sīnā adduced a speculative. estimative faculty which he called *wahmiyyah*, that makes a sheep run away from a wolf even if it has never seen one before.

But once the pathways running between existence-essence-God were established, even in a contrary direction, religious philosophy could forget what led to it; and God's Essence could then be recognized as existing independently of the mind of man, and independently of the world; that God was there before the creation of the world, and will be there after it is gone.

The objection that the philosophers had to the creation of the world, was that if it were not eternal, then some change had to have taken place within God which was the decision to create; and God cannot have a fluctuation within Himself, a decision to create because a change can only take place within that which is relative and mutable, which God as Absolute could not be. (This was also at the root of the problem of God knowing particulars and why the philosophers said that, as God, He can only know universals.) Thus the philosophers concluded that the world was eternal. But if the world were eternal, the theologians objected, then the world would also be God since it would have a Divine Attribute, eternity.

Although theology says the world is created, and leaves it as a dogma, this problem has never been elucidated philosophically or metaphysically because here doctrine ends; it can only be known as the object of a spiritual realization of the world and creation as an emptiness or a void. Al-Ghazālī, who attacked the philosophers, had to become a mystic in order to resolve the questions which they had raised but in doing so, al-Ghazālī became a proof that non-dualist Sufism, an orthodox Sufism was possible, despite the abundance of evidence that Sufism has usually hidden within itself precisely the doctrines from which Ibn Sīnā himself derived. Real knowledge, al-Ghazālī said, came from *dhawq* (lit. "taste") or direct intellection of reality.

Ibn Sīnā wrote prolifically, served a number of princes as physician, and had energy left over to enjoy a somewhat hedonistic lifestyle which would not have earned the approval of more moralistic observers. In seeking patrons, he was often caught in the middle of wars and rivalries and thus his life was not without adventures. At one point he was made a Vizier to the prince of

Hamadān, but mutinying soldiers demanded that he be put to death. Caught in the middle of political strife, Ibn Sīnā had to escape in disguise. He traveled widely and lived in many places in Persia, including Merv, Isfahān, Kazwin, and Hamadān, where he died, his last days spent in pious exercises and repentance, it is said. *See* PHILOSOPHY.

Ibn Tashufīn, Yūsuf (d. *500*/1106). The founder of the city of Marrakesh and leader of the Almoravids in their conquest of Morocco and Spain. *See* ALMORAVIDS; RECONQUISTA.

Ibn Taymiyyah (*661-728*/1263-1328). Born in Harran, Ibn Taymiyyah grew up in Damascus, where, following in his father's footsteps, he became a jurist of the Hanbalī School of Law. He taught first in Damascus and later in Cairo where he was imprisoned because his so-called "anthropomorphist", or more accurately, literalist interpretations of the Koran outraged scholars, particularly the Shāfi'īs. He took references to "God's Hand", and others like it, literally. He was imprisoned several times in Egypt and Syria for his religious and political opinions. Even while in prison he continued to teach religion, to his fellow inmates, and to write prolifically, so much so that his opponents were driven to deprive him of writing materials, an insult that wounded him perhaps more then prison itself.

He is famous for having said in a Friday sermon that "God comes down from Heaven to Earth [to hear prayers] just as I am now coming down [the steps of the *minbar*, or pulpit]". His literalist understanding of the Koran led him to attack many authorities in Islam including al-Ghazālī, the Sufis, and, in particular, Ibn 'Arabī. Ibn Taymiyyah stormed against what he saw to be *bid 'ah*, or innovation in religious practice. He even inveighed against the competence and authority of the Patriarchal Caliphs, 'Umar and 'Alī.

Treated as an eccentric, sometimes even as a heretic, his zeal and strong opinions nevertheless earned him the respect of many. Ironically, at his death, biographers say, his bier was followed by twenty thousand mourners, many of them women who believed that he was a Saint. Indeed, his grave became a place of pilgrimage to seek miracles, favors, and cures. This would have earned his fiercest disapproval. Ibn Taymiyyah is one of the principal figures in the fundamentalist strand of Islam, and he is an important forerunner of the Wahhābīs. *See* WAHHĀBĪS.

Ibn Ṭufayl, Abū Bakr Muḥammad ibn 'Abd al-Mālik (d. *581*/1185). An important Arab philosopher, known in the West as Abūbacer. Born near Granada in Spain, Ibn Ṭufayl was Vizier to the Almohad prince Abū Ya'qūb Yūsuf and introduced Ibn Rushd (Averroes) to the court. He wrote the famous *Ḥayy ibn Yaqẓān* ("The Living, Son of the Awake"; the "Living" is man, and the "Awake" is God). This philosophical novel describes how a youth growing up isolated on an island, through his own contemplation, arrives at the truths usually considered to be revealed – that is, through the natural faculties of the mind itself – and liberates himself from his lower soul. In his conduct on the island, the youth exemplifies the religious or ethical teachings of a number of different traditions. The relationship of the characters of the novel also implies that philosophy is necessary for the full understanding of religion.

The *Ḥayy ibn Yaqẓān* was translated into Latin by Pococke as *Philosophicus Autodidactus*, and inspired Daniel Defoe to write *Robinson Crusoe*.

Ibn Ṭufayl, along with Ibn Bājjah and Ibn Rushd, formed the *avant-garde* of Muslim philosophy, which was destined shortly to become virtually extinct, and marked the high point of its development. *See* PHILOSOPHY.

Ibn Tūmart, Abū 'Abd Allāh Muḥammad (*470-524*/1077-1130). The founder of the Almohad dynasty. *See* ALMOHADS.

Ibn al-Waqt (lit. "son of the present"). A term which refers to the state of being entirely present in the immediate moment. As one saying has it: "The Sufi is a man whose thought keeps pace with his foot" (that is, he is entirely *present*, his soul is where his body is, and his body always where his soul is). Although *ibn al-waqt* is considered to be a mystical term because it is popular with the Sufis, and akin to the precept of Hesychasm, of "keeping oneself inside the heart", or "wakefulness", it is also an interesting expression of the traditional notion of psychology. "Son of the Present" implies that one is perceiving what is really before one, and not something out of one's memory, or anticipations and wishes regarding the future; one is perceiving reality and not interposing the contents of one's psyche between oneself and the world as a filter and a dream.

> Know that the present life is but a
> sport and a diversion, an adornment
> and a cause for boasting among you,
> and a rivalry in wealth and children.
> It is as a rain whose vegetation
> pleases the unbelievers; then it
> withers, and thou seest it turning
> yellow, then it becomes broken orts.
> And in the world to come there is a
> terrible chastisement,
> and forgiveness from God and good pleasure;
> and the present life is but the joy
> of delusion. (Koran 57:19-20)

It is, above all, the reversal of the normal tendency of the psyche to be passive, to receive the impressions of the world and, rather than act, to react to them on the purely horizontal plane and in terms of a subjective, personal, dream projected onto the world. The *ibn al-Waqt* reverses this natural passivity to the world; he is present and active; if not active in a physical sense – the Prophet said: "My eye sleeps, but my heart wakes" – active in a spiritual sense, in that the physical laws of gravity are reversed in the spirit, and the soul instead of falling, rises, instead of giving in, surpasses itself.

> Have they not regarded the birds among them
> spreading their wings, and closing them?
> Naught holds them but the All-merciful. Surely
> He sees everything. (67:19).

The present that is meant in the term *ibn al-Waqt* is not an intangible instant, where future is constantly becoming past, rather it is endless; it is always there, an eternal present and also the sense of eternity.

The great Sufi of Baghdad, al-Junayd (d. *297*/910) said:

> The Saint hath no fear, because fear is the expectation either of some future calamity or of the eventual loss of some object of desire, whereas the Saint is the son of his time (*ibn waqtihi*); he has no future that he should fear anything; and as he hath no fear so he hath no hope, since hope is the expectation either of gaining an object of desire or of being relieved from a misfortune, and this belongs to the future; nor does he grieve, because grief arises from the rigor of time, and how should he feel grief who is in the radiance of satisfaction (*riḍā*) and the garden of concord (*muwāfaqāt*)?

See FAQR.

Ibn Zaidūn, Aḥmad ibn 'Abd Allāh (*395-463*/1003-1071) The most famous of the Arab poets of Spain, in Cordoba. He was in love with an Umayyad princess, Wallāda, who was also a poet.

Ibn Zuhr, Abū Marwān 'Abd al-Mālik (d. *557*/1162). One of the greatest Arab physicians, called Avenzoar in medieval Europe where his work was very influential. He was born in Seville and came from a line of physicians. Ibn Zuhr knew Ibn Rushd (Averroes) – who may have learned medicine from him – and Ibn Ṭufayl, the philosophic luminaries of the great age of Muslim Andalusia. His works on medicine, which demonstrated a good knowledge of anatomy, were translated first into Hebrew and then into Latin.

Ibrāhīm ibn Adḥam (d. *166*/783). A legendary Sufi, born a prince of Balkh. The following is recounted of him by later Sufis:

> Ibrāhīm son of Adḥam was of a princely family of Balkh. One day, he told: "I was seated on my seat of state, and a mirror was offered for my self-inspection. I looked in it. I saw only a wayfarer toward the tomb, bound for a place where there would be no friend to cheer me. I saw a long journey stretching before me, for which I had made no provision. I saw a Just Judge, and myself unprovided with any proof for my ordeal. My royalty became distasteful in that moment."

And again:

> When he was out hunting one day he followed so hard after an antelope that he left his train far behind him. And God gave the antelope voice. "Wast thou created for this?" it said to him; "who bade thee do such things?"
>
> Ibrāhīm repented of his whole way of life. Abandoning everything he entered the path of asceticism; and after this conversion never ate any food but what he earned by his own labor.

Not finding a Muslim mystic to teach him at the outset, he turned to a Christian. "My first teacher in *ma'rifah*" ("mystical knowledge") he said, "was a monk named Simeon."

> I visited him in his cell, and said to him, "Father Simeon, how long hast thou been in thy cell here?" "For seventy years", he answered. "What is thy food?" I asked. "O Ḥanīfite", he countered, "what has caused thee to ask this?" "I wanted to know", I replied. Then he said, "Every night one chickpea." I said, "What stirs thee in thy heart, so that this pea suffices thee?" He answered, "They come to me one day in every year, and adorn my cell, and process about it, so doing me reverence; and whenever my spirit wearies of worship, I remind it of that hour, and endure the labors of a year for the sake of an hour. Do thou, O Ḥanīfite, endure the labor of an hour, for the glory of eternity." *Ma'rifah* ["knowledge"] then descended into my heart.

Later, he went on to find Sufi masters. Of the path of knowledge Ibrāhīm ibn Adḥam said:

> This is the sign of the knower, that his thoughts are mostly engaged in meditation, and his words are mostly praise and glorification of God, and his deeds are mostly devotion, and his eye is mostly fixed on the subtleties of Divine action and power.

Balkh, the home of Ibrāhīm ibn Adḥam, still had remains of Greco-Buddhist civilization when the Muslims arrived; the family of the Barmecides, viziers of Hārūn ar-Rashīd, had been Buddhist priests, of a kind at any rate, in the Buddhist monastery of Nawbahar (the new *vihara*, "monastery") before converting to Islam and entering the service of 'Abbāsids. (The Sufi term "son of the moment", *ibn al-waqt*, capable of more than meaning, was shortly to come into being and may have referred to opportunistic conversion). The occasional Buddhists (called *Sumanis*) even lived in Baghdad under the 'Abbāsids.

The story of Ibrāhīm ibn Adḥam is patterned after the story of the Buddha: a young prince sees successive reminders of the transience of the world and turns to the path of enlightenment. Whether it is an edifying story simply adapted to Islam for purposes of instruction or whether a historical Ibrāhīm ibn Adḥam actually existed, one who shed a Buddhist identity in order to adopt an Islamic one, is now perhaps impossible to settle. In any case, the figure of Ibrāhīm ibn Adḥam defines a certain spiritual type, what some forms of mysticism called a *pneumatic*; and it is to these schools of mystic thought that Ibrāhīm ibn Adḥam belongs.

Another trace in Islam of contact with Buddhism is also found among the Sufis is their use of the term *fana'*, or extinction. The word is found in the Koran, but its adaptation to the technical concepts of the Sufis is probably a parallel to the Buddhist concept of *Nirvana*. *See* MAZĀR-I SHĀRIF; SUFISM.

'Īd al-Aḍḥā (lit. "the feast of the sacrifice"). Also known as the *'Īd al-Kabīr* ("the great feast") and, in Turkey, as the *kurban bayram*, this is the most important feast in the Islamic calendar. It falls on the 10th Dhū-l-Ḥijjah which is also the culmination of the pilgrimage at Mecca. For those not performing the pilgrimage, the feast is one of communal prayer followed by the sacrifice of an animal; for those who are in Mecca performing the pilgrimage, the sacrifice is the concluding rite.

The feast is a commemoration of Abrahram's sacrifice of the ram as a Divine dispensation releasing him from the intended sacrifice of his son. When Abraham had confirmed his obedience to God, the Angel Gabriel brought a ram at the last moment as a substitute for the son. This son is not named in the Koran, but it is usually accepted in Islam that the sacrifice was to be of Ishmael (Ismā'īl). For those commentators who hold that Ishmael was indeed the promised victim, Abraham's willingness to sacrifice his then only son, at an age which left no hope for another, constituted the greatness and depth of his obedience. The second son, Isaac, is precisely understood to be God's reward for Abraham's perfect submission.

In Islam the place of Abraham's sacrifice is held to be Minā, just outside Mecca. The pillars at Minā, which are stoned during the pilgrimage, symbolize the devil's tempting of Abraham, three times, to abandon the sacrifice.

On the morning of the *'Īd al-Aḍḥā* the people assemble at the communal place of prayer (*muṣallā*), usually an open field, for the *'Īd* ("feast") prayer is performed in principle, by all members of the community or city together (*see* PRAYER). In keeping with an ancient Semitic tradition, found also in Ezekiel, one returns from the *'Īd* prayer by a different route than that followed in coming to it. After the prayer, the Imām sacrifices a sheep for the nation, or the community, and then one for his family. The believers return to their homes where each head of a household sacrifices a sheep, a camel, or an ox for his family. The sacrifice is consumed over the course of several days.

The sacrifice is performed by a man, usually, but not necessarily, the head of the household. He faces Mecca, utters the appropriate ritual intention *an-niyyah* (essentially a statement of the clear nature and purpose of the act to be performed), speaks the name of the person or persons on whose account the sacrifice is being made, pronounces the words *bismi-Llāh*; *Allāhu Akbar*, and then cuts the throat of the animal, both wind-pipe and jugular, in one stroke (*see* SACRIFICE). Women who head households ask a man, a relative or the Imām of the local mosque, to perform the sacrifice for them, although a woman could perform the sacrifice herself if no suitable adult male could be found. The celebrations continue for three days and consist chiefly of family visits. The sacrifice renews a sense of consecration towards God and perpetuates a primordial sacerdotal function.

The Prophet instituted the feast in the second year of the Hijrah in Medina when he and the refugees could not fulfill the pilgrimage to Mecca. *See also* PILGRIMAGE.

'Īd al-Fiṭr (lit. "the feast of breaking fast"). After the *'Īd al-Aḍḥā*, the second most important holiday in the Islamic calendar. It follows the sighting of the new moon that signifies the end of the fast of the month of Ramaḍān. The festival is marked by the special *'Īd* prayer (*see* PRAYER) which is performed by the whole community together in an outdoor prayer ground called the *muṣallā*. In large cities the *'Īd* prayer is also performed in congregational mosques. A special alms (*zakāh*) called *zakāt al-Fiṭr*, is given at this time. The *zakāt al-fiṭr* consists of a measure of grain for every member of the household (or its equivalent in value). It is given directly to the poor. Celebrations of the *'Īd al-Fiṭr*, also called the lesser feast (*'Īd aṣ-Ṣaghīr*), normally go on for three days.

'Īd al-Ghadīr (lit. "the festival of the pool"). A purely Twelve-Imām Shī'ite festival observed on the 18th Dhū-l-Ḥijjah, which commemorates the events of Ghadīr al-Khumm, in which the Shī'ites believe that the Prophet designated 'Alī as his successor. The event became a Shī'ite celebration in *351*/962 under the Buyid ruler Mu izz ad-Dawlah. *See* GHADĪR al-KHUMM.

'Iddah (lit. "number"). The interval of time which a woman must observe after divorce or the death of a husband, before she can remarry. Its purpose is to determine the paternity of possible offspring but also, in the case of divorce which has not been pronounced three times, to provide a space of time in which a reconciliation may take place. The duration of *'iddah* is three months or three menstrual periods in the case of divorce, and four months and ten days in the case of the death of the husband.

In the case of divorce, the husband must provide lodgings and food for the woman for this period and is morally, but not legally, expected to provide upkeep (*muṭā'*) beyond the necessities. In one case in classical times when a man had provided only the legal minimum of support for his divorced wife, the Judge had no means to force him to do more; but in a later case he refused to accept his testimony as a witness because he was not morally upright.

'Idgah, see MUSALLĀ.

Idhn (lit. "permission"). Although *bay'ah* ("pact") is the more common term, *idhn* denotes initiation into the *ṭarīqah*, the path of the Sufis. The initiation is a pact sworn with God to consecrate oneself to Him and fight "in His way" for truth and against illusion with one's life and one's possessions. The pact brings with it the "permission" (*idhn*) to use the means of concentration of the Sufi order, the *dhikr*, usually a litany or an invocation, which, without the initiation and its special blessing (*barakah*), is ineffective. True initiations convey a knowledge which cannot be transmitted in any other fashion; baptism, for example, conveys the ability to see the ideal as Real, and the *bay'ah* the power to see multiplicity as the silent manifestation of the One. *Idhn* can also mean the Shaykh's permission to a disciple to teach or transmit the *ṭarīqah*. *See* BAY'AH; DHIKR; RIḌWĀN; SUFISM.

al-'Īd al-Kabīr, *see* 'ĪD al-AḌḤĀ.

Idols (Ar. sing. *wathan*, pl. *wuthun* and *awthān*; also *ṣanam* pl. *aṣnām*). Many of the idols set up in the Ka'bah in Mecca during the Age of Ignorance (*al-Jāhiliyyah*) had been brought from surrounding countries, in part, no doubt, to encourage trade with those regions. The principal gods at Mecca were Hubal (god of the moon), and the female goddesses al-'Uzzā, whose principle shrine was in the valley of Nakhlah, a day's camel ride south of Mecca; al-Lāt, who had a rich temple at Ṭā'if; Manāt whose main temple was at Quḍayḍ on the Red Sea; and Wudd, goddess of love. In addition, others were Manāf, the sungod; Quzaḥ the rainbow; Nasr, the eagle; Qa'is, the goddess of fate, and some known as little more than names such as Ba'īm, Jibt, al-Muharriq, Nuḥm, Shay al-Qawm, Ṭāghūt, Yaghūs, Ya'ūq, Zūn, and others. Apart from astral deities representing cosmic principles inherited from the Mesopotamians, many gods were Ba'ls like those of the Old Testament, and totems of particular tribes.

The cult of the idols consisted largely of pilgrimages during the months of truce, coinciding with the desert fairs, the great souks, like that of 'Ukāẓ, and Minā. The cult included processions in which a cult object was carried on the back of a camel under a pavilion called a *qubbah*. The ceremonies included singing and dancing, and circumambulations of the cult objects. Sacrifices were a very important part of the rituals.

Of the 360 idols set up in the Ka'bah, the most important was Hubal, god of the moon. Upon the conquest of Mecca the Prophet cut open some of these idols with a sword and black smoke is said to have issued forth from them, a sign of the psychic influences which had made these idols their dwelling place. The Prophet turned the idol of Hubal into a doorstep.

At the conquest of Mecca, the Prophet sent Khālid ibn Walīd to destroy the sanctuary of al-'Uzzā at Nakhlah. When Khālid returned, the Prophet asked: "Did you see anything?" to which Khālid replied: "Nothing." "Then", said the Prophet "You have not destroyed her." Khālid returned to Nakhlah and out of the ruins he saw a naked woman come, black with long, wild hair. He slew her, saying: "'Uzzā, denial is for you, not worship." When he returned he told the Prophet: "Praise be to God who has saved us from perishing! I was wont to see my father set out for al-'Uzzā with an offering of a hundred camels and sheep. He would sacrifice them to her and stay three days at her shrine, and return unto us rejoicing at what he had accomplished."

The Golden Calf which as-Samīrī brought the Israelites to worship while Moses was on Mount Sinai would produce a lowing sound, because as-Samīrī had thrown into it dust which Gabriel, whom he saw passing by on the way to the mountain, had set foot upon. The people themselves, by their frenzied attentions to the idol, contributed to its hold over them; their frenzy, as it were, rendered up to the image some of their own power over themselves. Thus the attraction the idols exerted over their devotees was not arbitrary, but the result of a projected influence; to this in return the worshiper could respond. Abū Sufyān could hope to sway in battle those of the believers whose faith was not firmly established with his war cry: "Al-'Uzzā with us – but not with you!"

In Plato's *Timaeus*, Critias speaks of Neith, a goddess of the Egyptians whom the Egyptians readily identified with Athena. Here is paganism at a stage where its adherents treat their gods as symbols of a reality that the symbol does not encompass but only indicates. The paganism of the Arabs of the *Jāhiliyyah*, however, was the end-point of religious decadence and hardening, not unlike the present hardening of the monotheisms into reductive fundamentalism. The symbols no longer pointed beyond themselves; the unique idol was itself a deity or a power. What may once have been the awareness of a spiritual reality became an enclosure for a mental influence, hellish in its heat and density.

The power of the idols, as of all illusion, depended upon the consent and the cooperation of those who gave themselves up to them. *See* al-KALBI.

Idrīs. Probably Enoch of the Bible. He is mentioned in Sūrah 21:85.

al-Idrīsī, Abū 'Abd Allāh Muḥammad (*492-576*/1099-1180). A physician born in Ceuta, and educated at Cordova, who established himself at the Arabized court of Roger II of Sicily. He is famous for his books on medicinal plants (*al-Kitāb al-jāmi' li-ṣifāt ashtāt an-nabatāt*), and geography (*Kitāb al-mamālik wa-l-masālik*).

For King Roger he wrote *al-Kitāb ar-Rūjarī*

("the Book of Roger"), a treatise on geography which became the basis of European knowledge of the subject at the time.

al-'Īd aṣ-Ṣaghīr, *see* 'ĪD al-FIṬR.

Ifāḍah (lit. "overflow", "flooding", "unfurling"). Applied to the *ḥajj*, it is a special term for the rush of pilgrims from 'Arafāt to Muzdalifah at the end of the *wuqūf* ("standing") on the Day of 'Arafāt during the pilgrimage. *See* PILGRIMAGE.

Ifrād, *see* IḤRĀM.

Ifrīqiyā (from the Roman name: Africa). The Arab name in the Middle Ages for the region which today comprises Tunisia.

'Ifrīt, *see* JINN.

Iḥrām (lit. "consecration"). **1.** The state entered into in order to perform the pilgrimage (either *ḥajj* or *'umrah*) and the name of the costume that the pilgrim wears.

2. The consecrated state required for the performance of canonical prayer (*ṣalāh*), is also called *iḥrām*. It is preceded by the purification conferred by the greater ablution (*ghusl*), and by performing the lesser ablution (*wuḍū'*). This *iḥrām* begins with the pronunciation of the words *Allāhu akbar*, that is, the *takbīr* which opens the prayer (*ṣalāh*), and ends with *as-salāmu alaykum*, the salutation that closes the prayer. *See* GHUSL; WUḌŪ'; PRAYER; ṢALĀH; TAKBĪR.

To enter into the *iḥrām* of pilgrimage, the pilgrim performs the greater ablution (*ghusl*), makes the intention (*niyyah*), indicating what kind of pilgrimage he will perform (*ifrād*, *tamattu'*, or *qirān*, *see below*), and pronounces the *ta'awwudh* and the *basmalah*.

Then the pilgrim dons the costume of *iḥrām*. (Only men put on the costume of the *iḥrām*; women enter into the consecration of *iḥrām* but do not wear special clothing; their heads are covered to conceal the hair, and the body is covered to the wrist and to the ankle; veils are not worn, but the headcovering is close to the face). The *iḥrām* garb consists of two large pieces of cloth that must be unstitched and seamless. With the legs apart to ensure that there is enough slack for walking, he wraps the lower cloth (*izār*) around the waist, tucking it in place to hold it firm, or securing it with a belt or some kind of fastening. (The belt and all worn accoutrements must not be sewn; although originally the wearing of metal was forbidden, many modern pilgrims add a safety pin or two to secure the *izār* – an innocuous innovation in an age when most pilgrims wear vinyl money belts for documents, plastic sandals, and a wrist watch).

The pilgrim drapes the upper cloth (*ridā'*), over the left shoulder, and knots it on the right side near the waist. The right shoulder is left bare, but during prayer it should be covered with the *ridā'*, although in practice this last point is often ignored. The person entering into *iḥrām* performs a two *raka'āt* prayer, and recites the *talbiyyah*: *Labbayka-Llāhumma labbayk* ("At Thy service, God! at Thy service"). From this point on the *talbiyyah* becomes the recurring invocation of the state of *iḥrām* (*see* TALBIYYAH). No other clothing is worn, but during cold weather it is permissible to cover oneself with a blanket for warmth.

Women enter into *iḥrām*, but do not put on special clothing nor do they cover their faces. The ritual ability to perform pilgrimage is not affected by menstruation, nor is it prohibited for a menstruating woman to enter the Grand Mosque of Mecca (*al-Masjid al-Ḥarām*).

Once the state of *iḥrām* is assumed one may not make sexual contact, cut the hair, pare the nails, use perfume, cut a green tree or kill an animal, with the exception of noxious insects, rodents or venomous animals such as snakes or scorpions.

Nothing must be worn which is stitched. As special sandals are not made any longer (it is permissible to walk barefoot), most people today resort in practice to plastic sandals; this is unfortunate since the purpose of the *iḥrām* costume is to reinforce the awareness of a state of primordial simplicity and purity. If clothes may not be sewn then, logically, unnatural materials like plastic should not be used either, for they are antithetical to the timelessness of the rituals. In practice pilgrims wear belts with pouches, fastened with rivets rather than sewn, or carry a shoulder bag (also unsewn) to hold their documents. The state of *iḥrām* is brought to an end by shaving the head, or much more commonly by cutting off a small, symbolic, lock of hair.

Iḥrām must be entered into at the latest before entering the perimeter of the *ḥarām* extending round the city of Mecca. There are places, today generally marked by a mosque, called *mīqāt* (pl. *mawāqīt*) which are situated on access routes to Mecca where it is traditional to enter into *iḥrām*. But *iḥrām* can also be put on at the point of departure from one's home or homeland or again, as is very usual nowadays, at the point of entry to the Kingdom of Saudi Arabia, namely, Jeddah. Everything required can be purchased there without difficulty. One should not enter into *iḥrām* for the *ḥajj* before 1st Shawwal, nor prolong *iḥrām* after the *ḥajj* is finished. In any case, it is not possible to assume *iḥrām* for the *ḥajj* after the dawn of the 10th Dhū-l-Ḥijjah. Once one has entered the consecrated state, whether for the *ḥajj* or the *'umrah*, it is obligatory to fulfill the entire rites unless, for reasons of overriding importance, one is prevented from doing so.

From the time that *iḥrām* is put on, until the end of the *'umrah*, or until the standing on ʻArafāt in the case of the *ḥajj*, the words of the *talbiyyah*, – the response of attentiveness to God's command spoken by Abraham – are constantly on the pilgrim's lips.

The intention of entering into *iḥrām* may be made for the *'umrah* alone. As for the *ḥajj*, which is always performed in combination with the rituals of the *'umrah*, there are three possibilities, one of which should be specified in the *niyyah*:

A) *Ifrād*. The pilgrim puts on the *iḥrām* with the intention of fulfilling the *ḥajj* alone on, or before, arriving at a *mīqāt*.

With the completion of the *ḥajj*, this form of *iḥrām* comes to an end. The pilgrim then assumes a fresh, second state of *iḥrām* at one of the points situated on the periphery of the Sacred Area (*ḥaram*), resorted to by the residents of Mecca when they need to change into *iḥrām*. These are the mosques of *Tanā'īm*, *'Ā'ishah*, or *Juāranah*. Then the pilgrim performs the *'umrah*. The *iḥrām* of this kind of pilgrimage, performed as two separate acts, is called a *mufrid bi-l-ḥajj* while on the *ḥajj*, and *mufrid bi-l-umrah* while performing the *'umrah*. This is also the technical term for the pilgrim.

B) *Tamattuʻ*. *Iḥrām* is put on when, or before, one arrives at a *mīqāt* intending to perform the *'umrah*. On completion of the rites, the state of *iḥrām* is foregone until the 8th Dhū-l-Ḥijjah, when the garb of *iḥrām* is donned once more in Mecca – without going to the periphery of the sacred zone – and the *ḥajj* is performed. The pilgrim is called a *mutamattiʻ*.

C) *Qirān*. The *iḥrām* is worn with the intention of performing the *ḥajj* and the *'umrah* together, and it is not put off until both are accomplished. The pilgrim performs the *'umrah* first, with only one *saʻy* to cover both *'umrah* and *ḥajj*. It is possible to change one's intention to the condition of *tamattuʻ* provided this is done before the *ṭawāf al-qudūm*, or the first circumambulation around the Kaʻbah. The pilgrim is then called a *muqrin*. *See* GHUSL; ḤAJJ; PILGRIMAGE; TALBIYYAH; ʻUMRAH.

Iḥsān (lit. "virtue", "excellence", "making beautiful"). The third element in the canonical definition of Islam as: belief (*īmān*), practice (*islām*), and virtue (*iḥsān*). *Iḥsān* is explained by the Ḥadīth: "worship God as if you saw Him, because if you do not see Him, nevertheless He sees you."

Iḥsān also refers to excellence in what we do. The Prophet said: "Allāh has prescribed *iḥsān* for everything; hence if you kill, do it well; and if you slaughter, do it well; and let each one of you sharpen his knife and let his victim die at once." *See* ĪMĀN; ISLAM.

Ijāzah. A licence or certificate. It refers to any kind of diploma, but an *ijāzat at-tabarruk* is a written testimony from a Shaykh describing what studies a disciple has undertaken and affirming his affiliation with a *ṭarīqah*.

Ijmāʻ (lit. "assembly"). One of the *uṣūl al-fiqh*, or principles of Islamic law (*sharīʻah*). Its basis is the Ḥadīth: "my community shall never be in agreement in error". *Ijmāʻ* is a consensus, expressed or tacit, on a question of law. Along with the Koran, Ḥadīth, and Sunnah, it is a basis which legitimizes law.

Ijmāʻ is above all the consensus of the religious authorities (*'ulamā'*); but popular consensus can well lead the way to this. A perfect *ijmāʻ* is always possible, but is difficult to achieve because of the divergence of religious views and the lack of an authority recognized by all parties. Thus *ijmāʻ* does not mean that there are no dissenting views, but that agreement exists among a greater or lesser majority.

Two notable dogmas established by *ijmā'*, neither of which are found in the Koran or the Sunnah, are the veneration of Saints (which is strenuously opposed by the Wahhābīs, who accept only the *ijmā'* of the Medina community of the Prophet's time) and the sinlessness of the Prophets", a notion which began among the Shī'ites. *Ijmā'* corresponds to the principle *vox populi, vox dei* ("the voice of the people is the voice of God"). *See* SHARĪ'AH; UṢŪL al-FIQH.

Ijtihād (lit. "effort"). The name comes from a Ḥadīth in which the Prophet asked one of his delegates, Mu'āz, by what criteria he would administer the regions assigned to his control. "The Koran" the man replied:

> "And then what?" the Prophet asked.
> "The Sunnah" [or example of the Prophet].
> "And then what?"
> "Then I will make a personal effort [*ijtihād*] and act
> according to that."
> And this the Prophet approved.

Ijtihād is applied to those questions which are not covered by the Koran or Sunnah, that is, by established precedent (*taqlīd*), nor by direct analogy (*qiyās*) from known laws. Those equipped with the authority to make such original judgements are called *Mujtahidūn* and in the Sunnī world the first rank of *Mujtahidūn* (after the four Patriarchal Caliphs) are the founders of the four Schools of Law, or *madhāhib* (sing. *madhhab*). Within diminishing domains of competence there are other ranks of *Mujtahidūn.* Although the possibility of a *Mujtahid* arising today is accepted in theory, the preliminary qualifications expected of him would be tantamount to perfect knowledge of all the laws expounded before him; this would surely be an insurmountable obstacle across his path. Therefore it is said that "the door of *ijtihād* is closed" as of some nine hundred years, and since then the tendency of jurisprudence (*fiqh*) has been to produce only commentaries upon commentaries and marginalia.

Nevertheless, it is also clear that *ijtihād* is always necessary and inevitable because of the need to act in situations which are new or unique, or because information is lacking or competent authorities not present. As long as an individual is responsible for himself until the Day of Judgement, every believer finds himself, at one time or another, in the position of Mu'āz, and has to fall back upon the *ijtihād* of personal decision. Within the Sunnī world, the decisions of Judges in certain domains over the years represent small increments of *ijtihād* at the levels of the Schools of Law.

In the Uṣūlī Shī'ite world, but not for the minority Akhbārī group, the situation is entirely different. *Ijtihād* is recognized as an ever present necessity and is the prerogative of the higher religious authorities. Ultimately, of course, *ijtihād* is the function of the Imām, but in his absence it is delegated to the senior authorities. Their status derives precisely from the fact that they are *Mujtahidūn*, recognized as competent to make original decisions. Moreover, every Shī'ite Muslim is expected to be under the advice and direction of a *Mujtahid.* It should be borne in mind that what Shī'ites consider *ijtihād* would not always be so considered by Sunnīs. A Shī'ite *Mujtahid* is, in fact, obliged to go through the process of *ijtihād* even when answering a question exactly analogous to one he may have answered in the past. Each act of *ijtihād* is considered unique and related to no more than the question at hand. A major decision in recent times which necessitated *ijtihād* on the part of Shī'ites – but not Sunnīs – was whether or not circumambulation of the Ka'bah was valid on the recently built second level in the Grand Mosque of Mecca. (The Shī'ite *Mujtahidūn* decided that it was.) The *ijtihād* of a particular Shī'ite *Mujtahidūn* is binding only upon his own adherents. *See* AKHBĀRĪS; SHARĪ'AH; UṢŪL al-FIQH; UṢŪLĪS.

Ikhlāṣ (lit. "sincerity", "purity"). That sincerity which is surrender to God, "with all one's heart, and all one's mind, and all one's soul". In Islam this is the affirmation of the Divine Unity. This is accomplished virtually by the first *shahādah*, seeing that there is no god but God.

The degree to which this is understood varies, of course, with human capacity. The realization of the *shahādah* is the purpose of the spiritual life. The first enunciation of the *shahādah* virtually achieves the removal of *shirk*, – the sin of "associating unreality with Reality" – in the soul. But as long as the consciousness perceives objects as independent of God, the surrender of the soul is not complete; it has not attained complete "sincerity". "There is no sin compared with the sin of your existence", said the woman Saint Rābi'ah al-'Adawiyyah.

Because the eradication of *shirk* within the soul is a life-long work, the most important Sūrah of the Koran, and after the *Fātiḥah*, the most repeated, is the 112th, the *Sūrāt al-Ikhlāṣ*. This, the "Verse of Sincerity" proclaims the unity, or absoluteness, of the Divine Essence, indicated by the word *Hua* ("He"), which is the Name of the Essence. This is amplified and deepened by the further declaration of the metaphysical truth that the Absolute cannot be the result or issue of anything other than Itself, nor, as Essence, act upon something outside of Itself:

> *Qul Huwa-Llāhu Aḥad; Allāhu-ṣ-Ṣamad; lam yalid wa lam yūlad wa lam yakun lahū kufuwan aḥad.*
>
> Say, He, God, is One. God the Everlasting. He never begot, nor was begotten, nor is there an equal to Him.

See ALLĀH; FIVE DIVINE PRESENCES; SHAHĀDAH; SHIRK.

Ikhtilāf al-fiqh (lit. "the divergences of canon law"). The Sunnī world accepts unequivocally the idea that the divergences between schools of canon law and theologians are providential and a "mercy". The concept of *ikhtilāf* is enshrined as the seventh article in *al-Fiqh al-Akbar* of Abū Ḥanīfah. Assuredly, the notion has forestalled greater rigidity, opened the door to some suppleness in interpretation and practice, and prevented conflict, as far as possible.

Ikhwān, *see* WAHHĀBĪ.

al-Ikhwān al-Muslimūn, *see* MUSLIM BROTHERHOOD.

Ikhwān aṣ-Ṣafā', *see* BROTHERHOOD of PURITY.

Ilāhīs. Turkish religious chants used by Sufis. *See* QAWWALI.

Ilḥād (lit. "deviation"). Heresy. Heretics are called *malāḥidah.* The word "religion" has been interpreted as signifying the means of binding oneself to God, which cannot be done if the apprehension of God is false or incorrect. (Thomas Aquinas also said that a "false idea of the universe will lead to a false idea of God"). There is a margin to belief and doctrine which may be broad or narrow, according to whether it touches upon the peripheral or the essential. If the deviation from a true apprehension ("right belief"; Greek: *orthodoxia*) is broad enough, the practice of religion becomes inoperative; it does not perform the goal of binding man to God. Orthodoxy is of two kinds: orthodoxy within a particular religion, and orthodoxy in the relationship of religions to God Himself.

If, to use an extreme example, a religion were based upon the cognition of space through practices built around three-sided objects, the introduction of objects of four sides would then be heretical; the process of realization through three-sided means would be impeded and perhaps even halted entirely thereby. On the other hand, if the object of realization were simply space as such, a four-sided object would not be heretical in relation to space, but only to the three-sided perspective on "religion". The great revealed religions are, in certain respects, mutually incompatible, but each is nonetheless orthodox in respect of God, who revealed it.

The mixing of religions, that is to say, syncretism (*talfīq*), and even the mixing of such aspects of religion as are seperately orthodox before God, actually produces an inoperative system which not only does not lead to God, but which increases the confusion of the adherent.

Revelations are *ipso facto* orthodox; however, because of the power of the "Divine Imagination", each can shatter the preconceptions entertained by believers of other faiths. The orthodox elaboration of Divine revelation to meet the specific circumstances of the ensuing religion depends upon a rigorous, and divinely blessed, examination of the contents of revelation (*ijtihād*), confirmed by the affirmation and consensus of the community at large (*ijmā'*). These functions were, in Christianity, carried out by the patriarchs and councils; in Islam they were performed by the founders of the Schools of Law in cooperation with the great theologians and with the grateful recognition of the *ummah* ("community"). These inspired efforts, together with the corpus of confirmed practices, customs, and teachings, constitute Tradition. *See* SUNNAH.

Ilhām. Inspiration or intuition, in principle

accessible to all, as opposed to *waḥy* ("revelation"), and *tanzīl* ("sending down") which is the inspiration of the Word of God into the nature of a prophet. *See* REVELATION.

Il-Khanids. A Mongol dynasty which ruled Persia (*654-754*/1256-1353). It was founded by Hūlāgū Khān, brother of Kubilai, and descendant of Jenghiz Khān. Hūlāgū sacked Baghdad in *656*/1258 putting the 'Abbāsid Caliph al-Mustasim to death. The Mongols were stopped in their westward advance by the Mamlūks at the Battle of 'Ayn Jalūt ("the Well of Goliath") in Syria in *658*/1260.

The Il-Khanids ruled in Persia in the name of the Great Khān of Mongolia and China, but when Kubilai moved his capital to Khanbalig, and especially after his death in *693*/1294, their rule became, in practice, independent. Maḥmūd Ghazan (d. *703*/1304), who instructed Rashīd ad-Dīn aṭ-Ṭabīb (d. *717*/1317) to write his universal history, and Uljaytu (Muḥammad Khudabanda; d. *717*/1317) were converted to Islam. Shī'ism at this time was making important advances in Persia; the Shī'ites, who had in fact supported the Mongol invasions against the 'Abbāsids, made strenuous efforts to turn the Il-Khanids to Shī'ite Islam.

Under Maḥmūd Ghazan, and the able Vizier Rashīd ad-Dīn, there was agricultural and fiscal reform, the establishment and revision of tax registers, and an energetic program of building which included caravansarais, bridges, and whole towns. The Il-Khanid capital was Tabrīz, which became a center of East-West trade. However, within a hundred years of the Mongol conquest, their domains in Persia disintegrated into small kingdoms, ruled by dynasties such as the Muzaffirids and the Jalayrids; and this state of affairs persisted until the rise of Timur. *See* HŪLĀGŪ; MONGOLS; RASHĪD ad-DĪN aṭ-ṬABĪB; TIMURIDS.

"Illiterate Prophet", *see* UMMĪ.

'Ilm (lit. "science", "knowledge"). There is a Ḥadīth which says: "seek science" [*'ilm*], even unto China. In the sense of *'ilm* as "revealed knowledge", the Koran itself had provided the essentials to metaphysical knowledge and to an understanding of the relationship between man and God. A repeated theme of the Koran is that revealed knowledge alone avails man in relation to God, and that speculative thought (*aẓ-ẓann*) is invalid. "They engage only in speculation, and speculation is of no avail with the Real" (53:28). As regards *'ilm* in the meaning of "science", the Arabs at the time of the revelation were not well endowed with it. In the wars of the conquest one desert Arab warrior demanded a ransom of one thousand dinars for a very important hostage. When asked by others why he had demanded so little, the Beduin said "I didn't know there was a number higher than a thousand."

At the height of the 'Abbāsid dynasty in Baghdad, Islamic civilization acquired great sophistication by absorbing the intellectual heritage of other peoples, including that of India and China. Because of the dual implication of the word *'ilm* in Arabic, some minds have constantly confused principial, or metaphysical, knowledge with empirical knowledge. Thus it is frequently claimed nowadays that Western scientific knowledge somehow originated in the Islamic revelation, the *'ilm* of modern science being perceived as deriving from the *'ilm* of the Koran. This is to ignore the role of peoples such as the Greeks in the development of modern thought, and to fail to see that words change their meanings. special usage of the word *'ilm* in Shī'ism refers to the esoteric knowledge possessed only by the Imām.

The Prophet said: "One of the signs of the Hour is that knowledge [*'ilm*] will be taken away and ignorance reign supreme."

'Ilm al-Ḥurūf (lit. "the science of letters"). A mystical procedure which consists of adding up the numerical *abjad* values of letters in one word and constructing other words with the same numerical value as part of the mystical interpretation of the Koran. This numerical value is then treated as a kind of archetype which may reflect in another word or words a related aspect of it, yet a different one. When used for divination, usually a magic square is also constructed. Those who use this science are known as *ḥurūfīs*. The science is also known as *al-jafr*.

This is the Arabic counterpart of the Hebrew *Gematria* of the Ka'bbalists. A well known example of *'ilm al-ḥurūf* is that *Ādām wa Hawwā'* (Adam and Eve) is contained in the Divine Name Allāh because the numerical value of the letters of the Name and the phrase are both 66. Another is *al-ḥikmah al-ilāhiyyah* ("Divine

Wisdom") which is the same sum as *taṣawwuf* ("Sufism").

Ibn 'Arabī, the great exponent of mystical doctrine, tells of the following example of divination by *ḥurūf*: a "man of God", of the city of Fez told him, in a discussion of the prospects of the Almohad armies which had crossed the straits into Spain, that "God promised his Apostle – peace and blessings of God upon him – a victory this year; He revealed it in His book in the words: 'Indeed We have given you a clear victory.' The glad tidings are contained in the words 'clear victory' (*fatḥan mubīnan*) ...consider the sum of the numerical value of the letters."

The numerical value of *fatḥan mubīnan* comes to *591* which is the Hijrī year of the victory over the Christians by the Almohad Ya'qūb al-Manṣūr at Alarcos in *591*/1194.

The historian al-Juwaynī describes how the Assassins took the name of their principle fortress, Alamūt (which comes from *aluh*, "eagle"), and by analyzing the name into Aluh Amut, found in it by *abjad* the year in which they captured it. As letters, the analyzed name is ALH AMWT; which is 1+30+5+1+40+6+400 = 483, a Hijrī year which corresponds to 1090. *See* ABJAD.

Ilyās. The Prophet Elijah, from the Greek form of the name, Elias. He is one of the Prophets mentioned in the Koran:

> Elias too was one of the Envoys;
> when he said to his people, 'Will you
> not be godfearing?
> Do you call on Baal, and abandon the
> Best of creators?
> God, your Lord, and the Lord of your
> fathers, the ancients?'
> But they cried him lies; so they will be
> among the arraigned,
> except for God's sincere servants;
> and We left for him among the later folk
> 'Peace be upon Elias!'
> Even so We recompense the good-doers;
> he was among Our believing servants. (37:123-132)

Ilyās is also mentioned in the Koran 6:85.

Ilyasā', *see* ALYASĀ'.

Images. On the basis of Ḥadīth, the making of images is prohibited in Islam; those who make them will, on the Day of Judgement, be told "to breathe life into what they have created" and, failing to do so, will be punished. The degree to which the religious authorities censure images differs, however, according to whether the images are of a living thing – an important distinction is made between depictions of vegetable and animal life – whether they are on a flat surface, or representations which "have a shadow", that is, statues.

In fact, images of plants have been used as decorative motifs on mosques, in addition to abstract motifs (such as circles, jagged lines and spirals, all legacies of architectural traditions going back as far as Sumeria), at least since the Dome of the Rock was built at the end of the *1st*/7th century by Syrian Byzantine craftsman for Umayyad patrons, and doubtless even before. The use of floral designs interwoven with Koranic calligraphy on manuscript or carved into wood or plaster is very common. One of the most famous works of art in the Alhambra is the fountain with stylized *statues* of lions. Turkish and Persian miniatures represent not only secular scenes but the popular illustrations of the Prophet's ascent to heaven, the *Mi'rāj-nāmeh*. The Prophet's face is customarily veiled in these books. The representation of his face is a line which, for many reasons, is clearly an unbroachable limit.

Despite initial resistance to the taking of photographs on the popular level, no modern political figure, regardless of how vehemently religious strictness is proclaimed, has foregone the use of photographs. Today it would be hard to find objections to them voiced anywhere in the Muslim world. What can be said then, with certainty, is that the setting of an image in a place of prayer, would be reproved for drawing the attention away to a form instead of letting it seek the formless – although nowadays one can find religio-political posters even in mosques. It can also be said that the use of realistic paintings or realistic statues such as one finds in Europe or in Muslim cities which have undergone modern European influence, is alien to the spirit of Islam. By contrast, *stylized* representations which do not seek to create an illusion, or a *pretense of reality*, are acceptable, or are at least tolerated, outside of places of prayer.

The prohibition of images would seem on the one hand to be intended to avoid the concretization or "solidification" of forms in the mind. Such a concretization is an obstacle to the emptying of the mind in order to apprehend the supraformal. A further intention is doubtless to prevent the creation of counterfeits of reality – idols – to which the beholder would lend life out of his own soul or substance.

To counter the natural tendency of desert peoples to "condense" ideas and their figurative representations into psychological "hardenings" (the Koran speaks of the "hardening" and the "melting" of hearts), Islamic art has, in addition to not using realistic images, cultivated means which actively produce the opposite effect. That is, Islamic art often seeks to dissolve psychic knots by the rhythmic repetition of design motifs, particularly of geometric designs and arabesques, in order to bring the beholder a taste of infinity, and by abstraction, to restore a sense of space as a means of escape from imprisonment within forms.

Imām (lit. "model", "exemplar"). **1.** An Imām is the leader of prayer, for a particular occasion or as a regular function. He leads by standing in front of the rows of worshipers; if only two persons are praying, he stands to the left, and slightly in front, of the other. The basis for the dignity is knowledge, particularly of the Koran, age or social leadership. In groups of equals, the function may simply be performed by each in turn. Every mosque has one or more Imāms who lead prayers, in whose absence any suitable male may be Imām. A woman may lead the prayer for female members of her household.

2. A title, perhaps in addition to other titles, of the head of a community or group. The founders of the schools of law (*madhāhib*, sing. *madhhab*), in particular, are called Imāms, as are the heads of the Khārijite or 'Ibādite communities. Imām is also an honorific, as in Imām al-Ghazālī or Imām ash-Shādhilī.

3. Among the Shī'ites the word has the special significance of an intercessor, unique and predestined to the age, who must be recognized and followed in order to be saved. Imām is the title and spiritual function of 'Alī and his descendants through Fāṭimah (although for one group of Shī'ites, who no longer exist, the function belonged to a descendant of 'Alī by another wife). Most Shī'ite groups believe there can only be one Imām at a time, and disagreement about the identity of the Imām and the nature of his function has caused the Shī'ites to split into sects with divergent dogmas.

In general, the Imām, whose function is called the Imāmate, is credited with supernatural knowledge and authority, and with a station of merit which, as it were, is an extension of, and virtually equal with, that of the Prophet. For the Twelve-Imām Shī'ites, also called "Imāmīs", the Imām is an intermediary between man and God. In addition to his spiritual authority, the Imām has an absolute right to civil authority, and one who prevents the Imām from exercising temporal power is an usurper. The Imām is the summit of sanctity for Twelve-Imām Shī'ites, who hold to the doctrine of the "cycle of sanctity" (*dā'irat al-wilāyah*) which follows the closing of the "cycle of prophecy" by Muḥammad, who is the Seal of the Prophets (*khatam al-anbiyā'*) for all Muslims. The sects of Shī'ites known as the *Ghulāt*, or extremists, even consider their Imām to be Divine. *See* SHĪ'ISM.

Immanence, *see* TASHBĪH.

Imām al-Ḥaramayn ("the Imām of the two Sanctuaries"). A title for the theologian al-Juwaynī. *See* al-JUWAYNĪ.

Imām, the Hidden, *see* HIDDEN IMĀM.

Imāmī. An appelation of the Shī'ites (the "Imāmīs"), and an adjective describing their doctrine. It is in particular applied to the Twelve-Imām Shī'ites (*ithna'ashariyyah*). The Imāmīs are those who believe that there is a figure called an Imām, who, being an intermediary between man and God, has supreme spiritual and temporal authority. *See* SHĪ'ISM.

Imāmzādeh. In Iran, a term for a prominent descendant of one of the Imāms, or the tomb of such a descendant. The most important such tomb is in Qumm, that of Fāṭimah al-Ma'sūmah, the sister of the Imām 'Alī ar-Riḍā'. *See* IMĀM; SHĪ'ISM.

Īmān (lit. "faith"). This is faith in itself and a term designating those articles of belief which are part of Islam. *Īmān* is defined as faith in God, His Angels, His books (revelations), His Prophets, and the Day of Judgement. Islam as religion is divided into a ternary of which *Īmān* is one aspect along with *Islām* (in a second sense, as an aspect of the religion, that is, the rites and the law), and *iḥsān*, or virtue. It is faith which saves because God is beyond comprehension by the mind; therefore to know Him one must believe; it is faith which brings knowledge of God.

The Prophet said: "Faith [*īmān*] is a confession with the tongue, a verification with the heart, and an act with the members." *See* IḤSĀN; ISLAM.

'Imārah. The name used in North Africa for the Sufi dance, which is a spiritual means, known also as a *ḥaḍrah*, ("Presence", "Remembrance in the Breast") and technically as the *dhikr aṣ-ṣadr*. *See* DHIKR.

'Imrān. The father of the Prophets Moses and Aaron; in Islam also the name of the father of Mary.

> God chose Adam and Noah
> and the House of Abraham
> and the House of 'Imrān
> above all beings, the seed of one another;
> God hears, and knows. (Koran 3:30)

Also:

> And Mary, 'Imrān's daughter,
> who guarded her virginity,
> so We breathed into her of
> Our Spirit... (Koran 66:14)

'Imru' al-Qays. One of the most famous poets of the *Jāhiliyyah*, the pagan "Age of Ignorance". He is the author of one of the celebrated poems – odes written in gold – which were acclaimed at the yearly fair of 'Ukāz and perhaps hung in honor in the Ka'bah, for which reason they were called *mu'allaqāt* ("hung") and collected under that title.

> "Here halt and weep, for one long-remembered love, for an old
> Camp at the edge of the sands that stretch from the Brakes to Floodhead,
> From Clearward to the Heights. The marks are not gone yet,
> For all that's blown and blown back over them, northward, southward.
> Look at the white-deer's droppings scattered in the old yards
> And penfolds of the place, like black pepperseeds.
> The two who ride with me rein closer to my side:
> What! take thy death of grieving, man? Bear what's to bear!
>
> I tell ye both, I'll be the better for these tears –
> Where is the place among these crumbling walls to weep it out?
> The same old tale as ever – the same as with that other
> Before her – the same again with her at the Whettingstead.
> When women rose and stood, the scent of them was sweet
> As the dawn breeze through a clove tree.
> I suffered so for love, so fast the tears ran down
> Over my breast, the sword-belt there was soaked with weeping.
> And yet – the happy days..."

Incarnation, *see* ḤULŪL.

Incense, *see* ALOES.

India. Population 918,570,000, of which 11% are Muslims. Muslim expansion into India began with the first Arab conquests in Sindh under Muḥammad ibn Qāsim in *93*/712. Islam was carried deeper by the Ghaznavid invasions, especially under Maḥmūd of Ghaznah (d. *422*/1030), and firmly established in the Punjab and Kashmir. Under the Delhi Sultanate (*602-962*/1206-1555), and under the Moghuls (*932-1274*/1526-1858), Islamic rule in India reached its height. *See* ALIGARH; CHISHTI; DELHI SULTANATE; KHĀN, SIR SAYYID; MOGHULS; QUṬUB-I MINAR; SHĀH WALĪ ALLĀH.

Indifference, *see* GHAFLAH.

Indonesia. The country with the largest Muslim population in the world. There are 192,217,000 Indonesians of whom 80-90% are Muslims of the Shāfi'ī school; the rest of the population are Hindu, Buddhist, Dutch Protestant, and Catholic, with some animist religions. The Islamization of Indonesia is not well documented but it is known that the Sufi *ṭurūq* played a very important role in the process as did expansion through peaceful trade. Unlike Islam in the Middle East and India, no military conquest was involved. Today, the various *ṭurūq* remain influential, and various branches of the Shādhiliyyah,

Qādiriyyah, Khālwatiyyah, and other *ṭurūq* are widespread. At the beginning of the *11th*/17th century, the Kingdom of Atjeh in the north of Sumatra marked a golden age of Islam in Indonesia, especially in the reign of the Sultan Iskandar Muda. Indonesian Islam is a remarkable blending of many cultural influences. The Indonesians are noted for the fervor with which they undertake the pilgrimage to Mecca. *See* ADAT; ATJEH; MENANGKABAU; MUḤAMMADIYYAH; SLAMETAN; SULŪK.

Infidel, *see* KUFR.

Inheritance (Ar. *mīrāth*, "inheritance", or *farā'iḍ*, "allotments"). The Koran prescribes the distribution of an estate amongst certain relatives and fixes the proportion of the estate allotted to each (4:11-13). Before Islam, inheritance among the Arabs had always passed to the adult male relatives of the deceased in the interests of consolidating wealth among the powerful in order to strengthen the clan. Thus the Prophet, as a posthumous orphan, received no inheritance from his father and was raised as the poor ward of his grandfather.

The Koran decrees a radical redistribution of inheritance rights entitling nine categories of relative who previously had no share in inheritance. Six of these are women, including the wife, daughter, and sisters of the deceased.

Since not all categories or possibilities are expressly legislated for in the Koran, a complex science of inheritance has arisen as a special branch of law to determine priorities when different relatives compete with one another for an estate.

The amount of a willed legacy (following precedents in Roman law) is limited to no more than one-third of the estate after all debts are paid, the remainder to be distributed according to the schedules established by the Koran. If a legacy is made in favor of an inheritor who also inherits according to the Koranic schedules, with the result that his inheritance is greater than the share provided by law, the other inheritors must agree to this, otherwise only the schedule can apply. Shī'ite law provides greater latitude for legacies, possibly as an historical reaction to the harsh treatment that Fāṭimah received at the hands of the Caliph Abū Bakr, who denied her the small property of Fadak because of a very strict interpretation of the Prophet's words that a Prophet leaves nothing behind him in this world.

The distribution according to the schedules of inheritance may be modified, if complications arise, by means of legal decisions for the resolution of conflicting claims. To avoid the distribution of property according to these schedules, the person may give away or distribute his property during his lifetime, without legal limit, restriction, or constraint.

Koranic law among the Sunnīs is practically always superimposed upon the customary law that has traditionally prevailed locally. Thus, traditional inheritors according to the national custom of the people, continue to inherit, *after* those entitled by the Koran, or even, if there are no surviving relatives as defined by the Koran, to replace them altogether.

Among the Shī'ites, Arab customary inheritance is excluded, and descendants are favored over other relatives. This results, with historical implications in support of the Shī'ite point of view, in greater legitimacy being accorded to the claims of the Prophet's descendants through Fāṭimah, than to claims through the descendants of the Prophet's uncle al-'Abbās, who would be favored by Arab customary law. The Shī'ite law of inheritance would thus have favored the legitimacy of the 'Alid claims over those of the 'Abbāsids.

Inheritors can be divided into two categories: those who *share* with other inheritors, and residuaries who receive if there are no sharers. A person can be both a sharer and a residuary. The sharers participate in proportions of 1/2, 1/4, 1/8, 2/3, 1/3, and 1/6 according to their priority. The shares may be all reduced proportionately, if there are many inheritors, in order to divide the estate between competing inheritors in a particular category. A fundamental rule is that male relatives receive twice as much as female relatives of the same category. (Islamic law assumes that women have a place in a household headed by a male, and encourages this at every turn.) The nearer degrees exclude the more remote. In practice, the Koranic laws of inheritance have been somewhat modified by statute laws in some countries.

Initiation, *see* BAY'AH; IDHN; RIḌWĀN.

Injīl, *see* BIBLE.

Innovation, *see* BID'AH.

al-Insān al-Kāmil (lit. "perfect, or complete, man"; hence "universal man"). A doctrine of Sufism (found also in other traditions) described most fully by 'Abd al-Karīm al-Jīlī (d. *820*/1417) in his treatise *al-Insān al-Kāmil*. The basis for this doctrine in Islam is the Ḥadīth, reported by Ibn Ḥanbal, that "God created Adam in His image [*'alā ṣūratih*]", and certain other Ḥadīth of the Prophet such as: "I have a time when only my Lord is great enough to hold me", and "I am an *'Arab* without the *'ayn*, I am Aḥmad without the *mīm*; he who has seen me has seen the Truth (*al-Ḥaqq*)". *'Ayn* is the name of a letter of the alphabet, but it is also a word with the meanings of "source", "fountain", "eye"; and abstractly it means "origin" or "differentiation". Without the *'ayn*, and the separation it symbolizes, the word *'Arab* becomes *rabb* ("Lord"). The letter *mīm*, in the symbolism of Arabic letters, stands for death. If the *mīm* of mortality is removed from Aḥmad – name of the Prophet meaning the most praised – it becomes *Aḥad* ("One"), a Name of God.

The doctrine of the perfect man (*al-insān al-kamīl*), is akin to the hermetic doctrine of the Emerald Tablet: "As above, so below; the universe [*macrocosm*, in Arabic: *al-kawn al-kabīr*] is a big man, man [*microcosm*, in Arabic: *al-kawn as-saghīr*] is a little universe." This doctrine is first found written in Arabic in a text by Jābir ibn Ḥayyān, the alchemist, in the *2nd*/8th century: "Thus the little world is created according to the prototype of the great world. The little world is man when he has realized his original nature, which was made in the image of God."

The Perfect Man or Universal Man is also to be found in the Qabbalah as "Adam Kadmon" (primordial man), and is related to the medieval theory of the "Great Chain of Being". It asserts that there is a hierarchy of existence which includes all that is in creation, and that man is the synthesis of all creation by his nature. Man contains all the manifested possibilities as potentialities within his own being, or more precisely, within the created and uncreated intellect, or *'aql*, itself the projection into the individual of supra-cosmic, ontological Being, or uncreated Intellect. The center of the supra-cosmic Being is also called *ar-Rūḥ* ("Spirit"), among other names. Al-Ghazālī wrote:

> Before the creation, God loved himself in absolute Unity and through love revealed Himself to Himself alone. Then, desiring to behold that love in aloneness, that love without otherness and duality, as an external object, He brought forth from non-manifestation an image of Himself, endowed with His attributes and His Names. The Divine image is Adam.

Many others voiced similar ideas, Ibn 'Arabī among them. The doorway to the state of the *al-insān al-kāmil* is revelation. The means are the revealed doctrine of discrimination between the Real and the unreal, and concentration upon the Real through the perfection of the virtues both human and supernatural. If it be within his destiny, a man can reach the center of his being, and be man essentially and not "accidentally". Here his every act is in accordance with the Divine Will, with which it is in fact identical; he is in perfect activity but "motionless", because he is identified with the First Cause but not with effects. This is the state of "Ancient Man" (*Adam Kadmon*) or primordial man who is in harmony with the *fiṭrah* ("cosmic norm"). This the Chinese Tradition calls true man (*chen-jen*). If it is the Divine will, man can, by virtue of his theomorphic nature, effectively assimilate all the other states of existence, which are like planes, each being a degree of the vertical axis that passes through the center of each state of existence. One of the most common symbols of that "world axis" is the tree, especially the tree of paradise, the tree of life in the center of Eden.

When man has realized all the states of being, he contains the whole universe and has effectively returned to the state of Adam as he was before the Fall: his will and knowledge are in no way contradictory to God's, he is the master of the garden, the perfect "slave" (*'abd*) of God, and thus the "perfect man" (*al-insān al-kāmil*).

Al-Jīlī said:

> As a mirror in which a person sees the form of himself and cannot see it without the mirror, such is the relation of God to the Perfect Man, who cannot possibly see his own form but in the mirror of the Name Allāh; and he is also a mirror to God, for God laid upon Himself the necessity that His Names and attributes should not be seen save in the Perfect Man.

A Chinese treatise called *The Three Character*

Rhymed Classic on the Ka'bah, by an 18th-century Muslim named Ma Fu-ch'u speaks of the *al-insān al-kāmil* thus:

Now Man
is the Essence of Heaven and earth:
among the ten thousand transformations
his is a special creation;
the quintessence of Heaven
is Man's heart;
the glory of earth
is his body;
the ten thousand intelligent principles
are Man's essential Nature.
Man's descent into the world
marked a great transformation;
when the first ancestor,
whom we call P'an ku [Cosmic and Primordial
Man, here meaning
Adam, and also Abraham],
first entered manifestation,
he dwelt in a country of the West,
the land of the Ka'bah...

...the servitor
has no person of his own,
no desires of his own,
no heart of his own,
but fearing the command of God
he cultivates his person assiduously,
makes his intentions sincere
and rectifies his heart.
The ancient name for this
is Purity and Truth [a Chinese name for Islam]
to be able to conquer self
can be called Purity,
and to return to the Rites determined by Heaven
can be called Truth;
neither to conquer self
nor to return to the Truth
can only be called hypocrisy [Ar. *nifāq*].
A man has a body
and he has also a heart; when the body meets
objects emotion and desire are joined;
the heart in relation to human nature
is like the spirit of Heaven [Ar. *rūḥ*];
if the promptings of desire prevail
a man rejoins the birds and beasts;
but if reason masters desire
he becomes a True Man. [Chinese *Chen-jen*; Ar. *al-insān al-kāmil*]
A man who cultivates goodness
must endeavor to be sincere, [Ar. *mukhliṣ*]
to realize himself in the way of the Prophet
and constantly live the Truth..

See also BEING; FIVE DIVINE PRESENCES.

In shā'a-Llāh (lit. "if God wills"). The Koran 18:24-25 says: "And do not say, regarding anything, 'I am going to do that tomorrow,' but only, 'If God will.'" These words are used to express the conditionality and dependence of human will upon God's will, and are used in all references to futurity and possibility in the future. *See* PIOUS EXPRESSIONS.

Inspiration, *see* ILHĀM; REVELATION.

Intellect, *see* 'AQL; FIVE DIVINE PRESENCES.

Intention (Ar. *niyyah*). A legally necessary step in the performance of all rituals, prayer, pilgrimage, ablution, sacrifice, recitations of the *Yā Laṭīf* prayer, etc. The believer makes the intention out loud or inwardly to perform the ritual in question.

In Islamic law the basis of judging someone's actions is his intention. The Ḥadīth which defines it is: *innamā-l-a'māla bi-n-niyyah, wa innamā li-kulli imri'in ma nawā*... "Actions are according to their intentions, and to each man there pertains that which he intended..." This Ḥadīth opens the canonical collections of Muslim and Bukhārī.

Interest, *see* ISLAMIC BANKING; RIBĀ.

Intifada (Ar. lit. "shaking off"). The Palestinian Arab uprising which began in December of 1987 after twenty years of Israeli occupation of the West Bank and Gaza. The occupation after the 1967 war led to various forms of oppression of Palestinians: collective punishment, demolition of Arab homes, confiscation of land and the allocation of much of the West Bank to Israeli settlers, imprisonment without trial, torture of prisoners, deportation of Palestinians, etc. The Intifada was characterized by civil unrest, political agitation, and attacks by Palestinian youths and children throwing stones at Israeli soldiers. It led to the growth of increasingly more militant organizations among the Palestinians such as Ḥamās and numerous violent incidents. The Intifada came to an end with the Oslo accords and the beginnings of Palestinian autonomy, after several thousand Palestinians and scores of Israelis were killed. The peace process itself broke down in 1997 with the rise of Jewish fundamentalists and hardliners after the assassination of Yitzhak Rabin, and the uprising resumed in the form of suicide bombings inside Israel.

Intoxicants, *see* WINE.

Invocation, *see* DHIKR.

Iqbal, Sir Muḥammad (*1290-1357*/1873-1938). Indian philosopher, poet, and politician. Sir Muḥammad studied at Government College, Lahore, at Cambridge University, and the University of Munich. He practiced law and was a president of the Muslim League. He wrote poetry in Urdu and is the author of many works on religious reform and self-advancement. He was strongly affected by nineteenth century secular European humanism, writing, for example: "the Qur'anic legend of the Fall has nothing to do with the first appearance of man on this planet."

In his *Reconstruction of Religious Thought In Islam*, Iqbal tried to combine the ideas of modern Western philosophers such as Bergson and Nietzsche with the Koran.

Iqṭa' (lit. "allotment", "parcel"). The granting of fiefs to their Turkish army chiefs by the 'Abbāsids. The revenue from the fiefs provided income for the support of such chiefs, and it was an alternative to direct taxation by the state. In the case of Iraq, where agriculture depended upon the maintenance of a complex system of irrigation, the effect of the *iqṭa'* system was harmful in the extreme, for the fief holders sought to extract as much income as they could without returning adequate investment for the maintenance of irrigation. *See* MANṢAB.

Irade (from Ar. *īrādah*, "will"). The term describing a decree issued by the Ottoman Sultan.

Iran. Islamic Republic. Est. population: 59,275,000 of whom 98% are Muslim. Of the Muslims 8% are Sunnī and 92% are Twelve-Imām Shī'ites (of the Uṣūlī school; there are some Akhbārīs in Khuzistan). Armenian and Assyrian/Chaldean Christians are estimated to be 1% of the population. A small number of Jews remains in Iran. There are also 30,000 Zoroastrians, 50,000 Bahā'īs, and small numbers of 'Alī Ilāhīs, Shaykhīs, Bābīs, and Ismā'īlīs. Ethnic Persians are the majority (63%), but 26% of the population speak Turkic languages (Azeris, Balochis, Qashqai, Turkomans, and others). There are over two million Kurds in Iran, and there is an Arab minority in Khuzistan (called Arabistan by the Iraqis). *See* AFSHARIDS; AKHBĀRĪS; 'ALĪ ILĀHĪS; AQ QOYUNLU; AYATOLLAH; BĀBĪS; BAHĀ'ĪS; BAKHTĪAR; BIHBAHĀNĪ; DIHQĀNS; IL-KHANIDS; IMĀMZĀDEH; 'IRFĀN; ISHRĀQĪ; KHOMEINI; LUR; MAZDAK; MANICHEANS; MULLA SADRA; NI'MATU'LLĀH; NURBAKSH; PAHLAVI; QAJARS; QANĀTS; QARA QOYUNLU; QIZĪL BASH; QUMM; RAWḌA KHĀNĪ; ṢAFFARIDS; SAMANIDS; ṢAFAVIDS; SHAYKHĪS; SHĪ'ISM; ṬĀHIRIDS; TADJIKS; UṢŪLĪS.

Iraq. Republic of Iraq. Population: 21,422,292, of whom 95% are Muslim and 4% are Christian. Approximately 55% of the Muslims are Twelve-Imām Shī'ites (and many of these are Persians or Arabs of Persian descent). In southern Iraq, centered in Baṣra, the legal school of the Twelve-Imām Shī'ites is Akhbārī (which was driven out of Iran by the Uṣūlīs in the 18th century), whereas the northern Twelve-Imām Shī'ites are largely of the Uṣūlī school. The Sunnīs are mostly of the Ḥanafī rite. Yazīdīs comprise 0.31% of the population; and there are about 20,000 Mandaeans. An estimated 77.8% of the population are Arabs; 17.9% are Kurds; 1.2% are Persian (but many of those considered to be Arab are also of Persian descent). 1.2% of the population are Turkmen. Assyrian Christians make up 0.5% of the population; Jacobite Christians make up 0.26%; Chaldeans and Jacobite Uniates (Churches in communion with Rome) are 2.21%. *See* AKHBĀRĪS; 'ABBĀSIDS; BAGHDAD; BIHBAHĀNĪ; MANDAEANS; NESTORIANS; QARMATIANS; SHĪ'ISM; YAZĪDĪS; UṢŪLĪS; ZANJ.

'Irfān. Gnosis or esoteric knowledge. The word is used mostly in Shī'ism, and actually corresponds to the general ideas of Sufism removed from the operative context of disciple and master (*ṭarīqah*), and formal transmission through an intiatic chain (*silsilah*).

The Shīʻite authorities have always been rather jealous of Sufism because it tends to displace the role of the Imām. Thus Mullas such as Bihbahānī and Majlisī wrote diatribes against it, seeing in it a dangerous competitor. Hence the schools of *ʻirfān* and *ishrāq* are a philosophical Sufism, removed from its operative framework and its method, which is the *dhikr*; since they do not engage the individual totally they can all the more easily be accommodated to Shīʻism. Sufi *ṭuruq* do exist in Persia, but they are a relatively small number, and from Ṣafavid times they were forced to subordinate themselves to the exoteric and doctrinal exigencies of Shīʻism. Before he was exiled from Iran in 1963, Ayatollah Khomeini was an exponent of *ʻirfān* in the city of Qumm. *See* NIʻMAT ALLĀH.

Irtidād, *see* APOSTASY.

ʻĪsā, *see* JESUS.

Isfahān. City in Iran, capital under the Ṣafavid dynasty. It is in the centre of the country and sits on the river Zayndeh Rūd (formerly Zindeh Rūd) "the life-giving" river. Shāh Abbās I (1587-1629) built palaces and mosques, the Hasht Behest ("eight paradises" palace) and the Masjid-i Shāh (today Masjid-i Emam), a famous mosque on the plaza or maydān, which also fronts the Sheykh Lutf Allāh Mosque. In the time of Shāh Abbās, the population of the city was 600,000 and the saying appeared *Isfahān nesf-é jahān*, "Isfahān is half the world".

A city has been on the site for five thousand years from the time of a legendary king of the Iranians, Jam, whose fortress there was mentioned in Zoroastrian writings. Isfahān was also the site of an Archaemenid capital and was called Anshan and Gabae. It is also associated with the legendary blacksmith Kavi, who chained Azhi Dahhaka in Mount Demavend. At the time of the Arab invasion in 640, it was called Jaī. The name Isfahān is derived from *Aspadana,* "army camp". The present day city was the result of a consolidation of several towns, Sheheristan and the Jewish town of Yehudieh, which was made by the Buyid ruler Rukn ad-Dīn in the 10th century. Isfahān was the capital of the Saljūqs. The city was not destroyed by the Mongols, but Timur made a mountain of skulls there to warn others not to resist him.

Ishan (lit. Persian, "they"). A name for Sufi spiritual masters used in some areas of Central Asia. Elsewhere the term *Pir* is used, and amongst Arabs, Shaykh. *See* SHAYKH.

Ishmael, *See* ISMĀʻĪL.

Ishrāqī (lit. "illuminationist"). A school of philosophy of characteristically Iranian inspiration founded by Shihāb ad-Dīn Suhrawardī (*549-587*/1154-1191), which combined elements of Sufism and Shīʻism with Hellenistic and Orphic philosophy, Hermetics, and Zoroastrian Angelology. The Ishrāqī school, more of a mystical intellectualism than a mysticism, insisted upon an aspect of "wisdom" in philosophy or suprarational realization. It exerted an important influence in Iran up to the 18th century.

Jurjāni in his *Tarifāt* calls the Ishrāqis philosophers whose master was Plato while al-Qashanī called them followers of Seth. As Suhrawardī lived in northern Mesopotamia he must have had contact with the religion of Harrān. He said that in the cosmos were four cardinal points, one of which was pure light and the other pure darkness. At the other two points darkness was mixed with some light (as if darkness were itself something positive that exists independently of light!) and where "light was mixed with some darkness."

The Ishrāqī philosophy was refined by Mīr Dāmād and Mulla Ṣadra in Isfahān in the *11th*/17th century; it also exerted a strong influence on the Shaykhī sect in Iran. Intellectually it is very similar to Western Existentialism. *See* ʻIRFĀN; MULLA ṢADRA; SUHRAWARDĪ.

Islam (lit. "surrender", "reconciliation", from the word *salām*, "peace" or "salvation"). The religion revealed to the Prophet Muḥammad between 610 and 632 A.D. It is the last of all the Divine revelations before the end of the world. The name of the religion was instituted by the Koran (5:5) during the farewell pilgrimage: "Today I have perfected your religion for you, and I have completed My blessing upon you, and I have approved Islam for your religion."

Besides designating the religion, the word has a further technical meaning in the triad *islām, īmān, iḥsān*, the three fundamental aspects of the religion, of which *islām* is here the equivalent of *'ibādah*, that is, acts of worship, the Five Pillars, and the *sharī'ah*. (*See* FIVE PILLARS; ĪMĀN; IḤSĀN.)

Islam is the last of the universal religions and today numbers some 800 million followers. While some countries which are the original home of Islam are almost 100% Muslim, today every country has at least a small Muslim minority. In recent years it has shown itself to be not only the most widespread religion in the world, but also the most dynamic, attracting converts at a faster rate than at any time in the last few centuries.

Islam is the third major Semitic religion and has an intimate relationship with the other two; it accepts all the Prophets of Judaism as Prophets of Islam; moreover it also accepts Jesus, not as the Divine manifestation he is to Christians, but as a Prophet, albeit of an extraordinary kind since in Islam also, he does not have a human father but is rather the "Spirit of God" cast into Mary. Judaism takes God and "nationalizes" Him as the God of a "peculiar" people; Christianity universalizes Him making Him the God of the Gentile as well as of the Jew through the person of the Divine Jesus; Islam, as the third revelation, returns to the unity of the point of departure of the first Semitic revelations before conceptions of tribe and nation had emerged and before the apotheoses of men-gods. Islam restores the primordial relationship between creature and Creator as it existed in the Garden of Eden. In Islam, as in Eden, man in his essence is perfect and unfallen; in his Intellect he is capable of perceiving and recognizing God in the Unseen. God in Islam is known under the aspect of eternity, without commitments in history, neither "repenting" nor sending down "a son", always returning to His Absoluteness, and seen from the abstract of metaphysics rather than as a participant in a religious drama shared with his creation.

Al-Jīlī said:

> All other revelations are only a reflection of the sky of this supreme revelation, or a drop of its ocean; while being real, they are nonetheless annihilated under the power of this essential revelation, which is exclusively of God by virtue of His knowledge of Himself, whereas the other revelations are of God by virtue of the knowledge of other persons.

See FIVE PILLARS; SHAHĀDAH.

Islamic Banking. The Koran prohibits usury, or interest on loans (*ribā*). This has been interpreted as meaning that money can be used as a means of exchange, but cannot be treated as a commodity. Since money *qua* commodity is inextricably bound up with modern economics, the general practice in modern times has been to accept the requirements of economic necessity, and disregard the question of interest. Banks in most Muslim countries have long given interest on deposits and taken interest on loans. This is not without legal basis: it is an accepted principle among the schools of law that "Necessity makes prohibited things permissible".

Already in early Islam, the question of interest posed problems because it was implied in certain commonplace economic exchanges. The custom of bartering unripe dates on the tree for ripened dates was a type of such a transaction because it involved the selling of an article today, against expectations of its future price. A pure futures market in the army camp of Kufah arose out of a speculative buying and selling of army pay tenders that were redeemable for grain, in anticipation of the future cost of the commodity. The reaction of the lawyers to this futures market was that it was usurious, and tenders could not be sold without the owner taking receipt of the grain. In the case of the dates however, Mālik ibn Anas made an exception on the basis of social necessity and established practice.

In the past, various legal devices were used to circumvent the prohibition against interest. In modern times, the prohibition has most often been simply disregarded. Even Ottoman banks, for example, charged and paid interest. However, there have always been those, who, on religious grounds, have refrained from placing their money in banks. For many, the custom of holding the family money in women's jewellery of silver and gold has been the traditional savings system.

A common means of circumventing the whole problem of interest has been to call interest by a different name: commission. Recently, however, renewed attempts have been made to provide banking without interest. These revolve around the classical devices: the *murābaḥah*, whereby a commodity is sold, with a contract to buy the commodity back with a price differential equal to the agreed interest; and *mushārakah*, whereby the depositor is a partner and, setting aside a remuneration for management, shares in the profits, but can also share in the losses; and the *muḍārabah*, the "sleeping partnership", putting up financial backing for operations entrusted to someone else, and profit sharing in the profits of these operations. Several banks promoting these approaches have grown up with various degrees of success and endorsement from religious authorities. *See* MUḌĀRABAH.

"Islamic Jihād" *see* ḤAMĀS.

Ism (lit. "name"; pl. *asmā'*). As well as meaning "name" in the everyday sense, it also designates the Divine Name, Allāh, the Supreme Name (*al-ism al-aẓam*). The Divine Names taken together are called "The Comely Names" (*al-asmā' al ḥusnā*), and are divided into the Names of majesty or rigor (*jalāl*), such as the "Slayer", the "Mighty", the "Victorious", and the Names of Mercy (*raḥmah*), the "Merciful", the "Restorer", the "Nourisher". The number of Divine Names mentioned in any one list is ninety-nine. *See* ALLĀH; DIVINE NAMES; KUNYAH; LAQAB; NAMES.

'Ismah. The doctrine of sinlessness, which originated among the Shī'ites in regard to the Imāms, and then entered Sunnī Islam. The Sunnīs attribute this to Prophets, and the Shī'ites to Prophets and Shī'ite Imāms. This does not render the Prophets free from error; the Koran clearly cites errors on the part of David and Solomon (38:24-26 and 35) as does also the Old Testament, not to mention the Fall of Adam. These errors, however, do not engage their substance; they are "faults" (*dhunūb*, sing. *dhanb*) but not "transgression" (*ithm*). For such faults the Prophets suffer sanctions in this life but not punishments in the afterlife. *See* SIN.

Ismā'īl (Ishmael) 1. The eldest son of Abraham by Hagar, Ismā'īl being the Arabic form of Ishmael; he is the immediate patriarch of the North Arabians just as Isaac (Ar. *Isḥāq*) is of the Jews.

The Koran does not name the son who was to be sacrificed by Abraham, but it does say that for his obedience Abraham was rewarded, and it is understood by most Muslim commentators that the reward precisely, was a second son: Isaac, born to Abraham and Sarah in their great old age. This, and other arguments, have generally meant that in Islam, Ishmael is considered to be the son Abraham was about to sacrifice, although great commentators who hold the opinion that it was Isaac can also be found.

After the birth of Isaac, Hagar and Ishmael were then cast by Abraham into the desert because of the jealousy of Sarah. There are provisions in the code of Hammurabi to protect the sons of the first wife against those of the slave girl or concubine and guarantee the children's rights against undeserved disinheritance. Sarah did not have the Code of Hammurabi to call upon, so the fate of Hagar was to be abandoned with Ishmael in the desert. When the water in the goatskin given by Abraham was spent, Hagar feared for the life of her son and rushed between two hills in anguish. The Bible says:

> And God heard the voice of the lad [Ishmael means "God hears"]... for I will make of him a great nation. And God opened her eyes and she saw a well of water; and she went, and filled the bottle with water, and gave the lad drink. And God was with the lad; and he grew and dwelt in the wilderness, and became an archer... and his mother took him a wife out of the land of Egypt. (Genesis 21: 17-21)

These events are identified with Mecca. The hills Ṣafā and Marwah are a hundred yards from the Ka'bah; running between the two is a rite of the pilgrimage; between Ṣafā and the Ka'bah is the well of Zamzam which sprang from beneath the foot of Ishmael. According to tradition both Hagar and Ishmael are buried in the *hijr Ismā'īl* ("Ishmael's enclosure") which is an enclosed area next to the Ka'bah. The place of sacrifice of Ishmael, for whom the angel Gabriel substituted a ram at the last moment, is situated by Islamic tradition at the foot of a hill in Minā, a few kilometers outside Mecca.

Islamic tradition relates that Abraham later visited Ishmael and that together they built the Ka'bah, replacing a temple first erected by Adam. Ishmael married a woman of the tribe of Jurhum, and his descendants are the North Arabians, including the Prophet himself. Ishmael is a Prophet (*rasūl*) with a major revelation, as are Abraham and Muḥammad. *See* ABRAHAM; KA'BAH; PROPHETS.

2. The eldest son of Ja'far aṣ-Ṣādiq, whom the Shī'ites consider the sixth Imām. According to the Shī'ites, Ismā'īl was designated to succeed Ja'far as Imām. However, the designation was revoked and another son, Mūsā-'l-Kāẓim became Imām (after his older brother 'Abd Allāh died without children), at least in the view of Twelve-Imām Shī'ites.

The question of succession arose because Ismā'īl died (*145*/762) before his father. One group, the Seveners, held that the Imāmate passed through Ismā'īl to his son Muḥammad, and either ended there, according to some groups, or continued through his descendants, according to the Ismā'īlīs. Out of this controversy, and more importantly out of the ideological reasons behind it, issued several branches of Shī'ites. *See* ISMĀ'ĪLĪS; SEVENERS; SHĪ'ISM.

Ismā'īlīs. A sect which is usually considered to be a Shī'ite branch of Islam. This classification, however, can be misleading. Ismā'īlism's Shī'ite affinities do not constitute its essential element. Rather, it is the metaphysics of Ismā'īlism which is its singular characteristic. The sect is a manifestation within Islam of ancient Persian religious systems. Islam gives them an outer clothing, a form, and a vocabulary, but the central core of Ismā'īlism is far more ancient. Ismā'īlism is the Islamic parallel to Gnosticism (the alternative Dualist form of Christianity), and is related to Hellenistic pagan Gnosticism, and Manicheism. A further parallel to the appearance of Ismā'īlism in Islam is the emergence of Manicheism among the religions of China as the result of influences transmitted through the Uighur Turks of Central Asia; this produced the *Ming Chiao* ("religions of light"), which are Dualistic forms of Buddhism ("the Buddha of Light") and Taoism.

Around its Dualist core beliefs Ismā'īlism adapts the doctrines and practices of exoteric Islam to the sect's own needs. Sometimes exoteric Islam is practiced fully, sometimes partially, sometimes not at all; in the history of Ismā'īlism all these variants can be found at different times and in different places. However, even when outward Islam is observed, it is modified to accommodate the inner and essential doctrines of Ismā'īlism which are by their nature secret (*bāṭinī*).

The starting point of the Gnostic-Dualist philosophy is to attribute substance, or an essence, to evil. The solution which Gnostic-Dualism offers for the problem of the existence of evil is to say that it must exist within God, the Principle, whereas the theodicy of orthodox theologies sees evil as the absence of good – an "accident" without essence which appears on the plane of existence, but which has no origin in Reality since it disappears when existence is reintegrated back into Being.

If both evil and good were *absolute*, but necessarily in irreducible mutual opposition, then the Principle in which they originate would be inconceivable because of its inherent internal contradiction. It is for this reason that the God of the various Gnosticisms has to be affirmed as being completely unknowable. Classical Ismā'īlism called the Absolute *Ghayb Ta'ālā* ("Supreme Unseen", "Supreme Void" or "This Great Absence", later called *al-Mubdi'*, "originator", "principle"). This corresponds to the "Abyss" (*Bythos*) of Hellenistic Gnosticism. What Ismā'īlism calls Allāh (which, for Sunnīs, is the Name of God both as Being and as Abolute) is for them no more than *the first emanation* or hypostasis (*maẓhar*) of the "unknowable" and nameless God. For this reason Ismā'īlī theologians were able to say that the Name Allāh is derived from the word *walaha* ("to lament"), because this "first intelligence" (*al-'aql al-awwal*) "knows something" of the otherwise unknowable Abyss and "laments" its exile from the Abyss, as in Hellenist Gnosticism Sophia (the Aeon or emanation of wisdom) laments the same exile. Of course, such an interpretation and etymology are untenable and unacceptable from the point of view of orthodox Islam. (Ibn 'Arabī also professed this etymology which belies the Priscillanist nature of his teachers.)

Although especially associated with Valentinian Gnosticism, it is common to all the Gnostic philosophies to propose that the world is the result of a conflict between the polarization of the two forces of good and evil within the world of emanation, a metacosm called the *pleroma.* As a result of this conflict, they say, the emanation known as the *Demiurge* creates the world. (The Manicheans see creation as a kind of defensive tactic whereby the emanation of the "good" aspect of God takes refuge from attack by the "evil" one. Once hidden in creation in the form of light, they say, God is then "liberated" by the realization and acts of the Gnostics, or "Knowers", who, moreover, expedite the process by the sacramental eating of vegetables which liberates the light particles trapped in them.)

The *pleroma* (Gr. "fullness", "plenitude") is called by some Ismā'īlī writers the "abode of origination" (*dār al-ibda*); one of the emanations, called the Demiurge, then becomes creator of the world itself. The world is called the *kenoma* ("the emptied sphere", from Gr. *kenos*, "empty"). In the Hellenistic mythological formulation, in this world there are fragments of the emanation known as *Sophia*, the *Aeon* who personifies "Wisdom"; *Sophia* knowing something of the unknowable God from which she emanated, tried to return to this God in a "hopeless leap" whose course was shattered by *Horos*, another Aeon who personifies limitation. The fragments of wisdom thus shattered reside in men – the Gnostics, the Knowers – who hear the *call* that tells them they "are the son of a King" and "gold that has fallen into the world's mud". It calls them to throw off the impure "clothing" of forms, and false, external knowledge, and to realize their "nature of light". It is this metacosmic confrontation, they say, which was a kind of war among the Angels, whence arises the story of Lucifer, the "fallen" Angel, whose revolt caused, or arose out of, the creation of the world and the mixing together of light and darkness. (*See* NOAH.)

The world, however, like the unknowable "God" who contains within Himself the two principles in mysterious and unfathomable union, also contains the two principles, but in conflict with each other. Thus, in a certain sense the physical world, too, is "divine" or "absolute" or an "autonomous" reality, in the sense that existentialists say that "existence precedes essence". Thus Gnostic psychologies often say that the mind is "a projection of the body" (rather than the other way around, as in orthodox cosmologies). This is a possibility expressed in the arresting literary idea of shadows suddenly declaring their independence of the objects or persons that cast them. In the "realized" consciousness, however, the two principles can coexist, just as they do in the unknown God; and that "realized" consciousness is considered by the Gnostics to be itself an hypostasis of the Divinity; or simply Divine. This does not prevent it from manifesting contradiction, as indeed it must; but that very contradiction, inscrutable and inexplicable, is taken to be proof of its unquestionable "Divinity".

The awakening call is an essential element in Gnostic mythology; hence the name of "caller" (*dā'ī*) given to Ismā'īlī propagandists. On hearing the call, the Gnostics form communities; their salvation lies in the recognition of the Divinity hidden in the world in the form of the Gnostic teacher; it awaits the end of the world (in the terms of the "New Preaching" of Alamūt in Persia, the *qiyāmat al-qiyāmah*, "the resurrection of the resurrection"), when the world and evil disappear and there remain, along with the Abyss, the principles of light and darkness, which when unmixed are neither good nor evil. However, their reward for waiting is salvation, which is nothing less than Deification.

In Ismā'īlism, the Gnostic doctrine of syzygies (or "alter egos") emerges as the doctrine of dual prophetic functions, or the notion that every Prophet has his counterpart: one Prophet, the *nāṭiq* ("the speaker"), makes manifest what the other Prophet, the *sāmit* ("the silent one") knows secretly. Thus, in most forms of Ismā'īlism, Muḥammad is the speaking counterpart to the "ineffable" knowledge of 'Alī. In the early forms of Ismā'īlism (as in the *2nd*/8th century book called the *Umm al-Kitāb*), rather than 'Alī it is Salmān al-Farsī, the manumitted Persian who is the hidden manifestation of Divine knowledge. Literal interpretation of scripture, and strange interpretations, often opposite to the face meaning of those accepted by orthodox authorities, the raising of obscure problems, are characteristic of Gnosis. Regarding this technique of a startling unveiling of "hidden truth", compare Irenaeus' explanation of Ptolemaeus' Gnostic exegesis of Matthew 8:9: when the centurion tells Jesus: "I have soldiers and slaves under my authority, and whatever I command, they do"; according to the Gnostics, the commanding Centurion is in reality the Demiurge learning from Jesus that of which he, the creator of the world, was ignorant. According to this view, Muḥammad reveals only a part of the knowledge which 'Alī knows *in toto* as the *asās* ("foundation").

For the purpose of indoctrination, a *dā'ī*, or propagandist, could claim that the doctrine of the Prophet's being no more than a spokesman for a higher authority, namely, 'Alī or Salmān al-Farsī, is taken in fact from the Koran. Through the science of allegorical interpretation and the elucidation of secret meanings, a *dā'ī* could, for example, throw a light on the following Koran quotation that would reveal an unsuspected doctrine such as to startle an ordinary believer:

> Say: 'I am only mortal
> the like of you; it is revealed to me
> that your God
> is One God.
> So let him, who hopes for
> the encounter with his Lord,
> work righteousness, and not associate with his
> Lord's service
> anyone'. (Koran 18:110)

Interpreted as a hidden teaching, the word "Lord" could be revealed as actually referring to 'Alī. It is of this Gnostic 'Alī that Naṣīr ad-Dīn aṭ-Ṭūsī wrote in the *Tasawwurāt*:

> 'Abd Allāh ibn 'Abbās says: "No women could give birth to a man like 'Alī Ibn Abī Ṭālib! Verily by God, I saw him in the Battle of the Camel", without armor, riding between the arrayed armies of the warriors, and saying: 'I am the Face of God who has been appointed by Him. I am the side of [pointing towards] God, towards which you have been instructed to turn, whether one is praying for forgiveness, or repenting his sins. I am the lord of the Great Throne [*'arsh-i aẓam*], and the mystery of God, I am the face of God, and His hand, and His side, of which God says that you have sinned with regard to it. Who is he who repents? I accept his repentence. Who prays for forgiveness? I may forgive him.'"

An 'Alī so described is no less startling to Sunnī Muslims than the belittling notion of the Prophet given above; Orthodox Islam, needless to say, must reject both definitions.

According to Ismā'īlism, Prophets come in cycles which comprise a great week of seven thousand years. Each cycle is presided over by one of the Prophets whom the Koran calls *Ulū 'l-'Azm* ("Possessors of Steadfastness") as its outward Prophet (Adam, Noah, Abraham, Moses, Jesus, Muḥammad), as well as by an "intermediary" (*wāṣī*), (Seth, Shem, Ishmael (Ismā'īl), Aaron, Peter, 'Alī), and a "permanent Imām" (*Imām-Qa'im*), (namely Mālik Shulim, Mālik Yazdaq, Mālik as-Salīm – all different names for Melchizedek – Maadd, the ancestor of the North Arabians, and, again, 'Alī). The symbolic number seven, the sum of the six directions of space and the center, represents the completion of a cycle of manifestation. Similarly, the counterpoise of light and darkness, and of speaking and silence among the Prophets, is repeated in the relationship between the living Imām and his spokesman, the *Ḥujjah* ("proof"), who discloses part of the knowledge that the Imām possesses. Since it would be invidious for the Imām to declare his own Divinity, it is declared for him by his "alter ego", the *Ḥujjah*. Salvation, in both Ismā'īlism and in Gnosticism, depends upon the secret knowledge which is recognized by the "spark of light" in the gnostic. In those Ismā'īlī systems which possess or emphasize a doctrine of Imāms, this knowledge is embodied in the Imām himself. In Ismā'īlism, the Imām, finally, is one of the hypostases of the Abyss, whence the equation which is frequently drawn between the Ismā'īlī Imām and God. In Gnostic-Dualism any leader of note claimed as much; Valentinus readily affirmed that he was the Logos, as did others. Ḥasan aṣ-Ṣabbāḥ, the founder of the "New Preaching" at Alamūt, wrote: "If I assert the *ta 'līm* [the Gnostic teaching], and there is none who takes the *ta'līm* position except myself, then the designation of the Imām rests with me."

Thus in Indian Ismā'īlism, the Angels Munkar and Nākir, who interrogate men upon death, ask only: "Did you recognize who was the Imām?". This is, for them, the meaning of the *shahādah*; it is this recognition which saves; not to have recognized the Imām leads the soul back into the world to be reincarnated for an interminable length of painful existence until the opportunity arises again to recognize the Imām of the age. (*See* TANĀSUKH). Abū Muḥammad al-Irāqī, who scrutinized the Ismā'īlīs after al-Ghazālī, complained that they made the Prophet superfluous since obviously the Imām as conceived by the Ismā'īlīs was superior. Both al-Ghazālī and Shahrastānī took issue with the fact that the Imām had only his own being to present as the saving doctrine.

Historically, Ismā'īlism seemingly began as an offshoot from what was later to crystallize as Twelve-Imām Shī'ism. However, it is also possible to view Twelve-Imām Shī'ism as an offshoot of Ismā'īlism, or rather as the result of blending political Shī'ism, which sought someone to champion political justice who should be of the line of 'Alī, with doctrine that had overflowed from Near Eastern Dualism, whose purer form is precisely Ismā'īlism. The Shī'ites believe certain successive descendants of 'Alī to be intermediaries between man and God. There is a considerable difference between the Twelve-Imām Shīʿite and the Ismāʿīlī notions of the Imām, reflecting their divergent theological viewpoints, whereas Sunnīs do not, of course, accept it at all; for them, the word refers only to a prayer-leader.

The first dynasty of Islam, the Umayyads, encountered political resistance on the part of those to whom the Umayyad policy of Arab supremacy was intolerable. The resistance often looked to the descendants of ʿAlī and Fāṭimah for leadership, precisely because they were of the family of the Prophet. So it was that Jaʿfar aṣ-Ṣadīq (d. *148*/765) was widely looked upon as the most suitable leader of a resistance both political and religious in nature. For the Shīʿites, Jaʿfar was the sixth Imām; and the sixth holder of the spiritual and religious authority inherited from ʿAlī. Jaʿfar, however, was a scholar who showed no inclination to lead a movement. His eldest son, Ismāʿīl, would have inherited Jafar's authority had he not died in *145*/762, before his father, leaving the group around him (the early Ismāʿīlis who had hoped to gain influence with his succession) without a figurehead. At this point the main body of Shīʿites looked first to ʿAbd Allāh, the next son of Jaʿfar, and when he, too, died without a son, to the third oldest son, Mūsā al-Kāzim, as the legitimate successor. The followers of Ismāʿīl, whose conception of the Imām was more absolute than that of the other Shīʿites in that for them the Imām was no mere intermediary but Divinity itself, maintained on the contrary that the next Imām should be Ismāʿīl's son.

These followers of Ismāʿīl came to be called Seveners (*sabʿiyyah*) because they declared that Ismāʿīl was the seventh Imām, and that, with the number seven, a cycle had now been completed, heralding a new beginning and a fresh doctrine. The identity of the seventh was actually open to argument and interpretation, depending upon the requirements of each doctrine and group; the son, or some other successor, of Ismāʿīl could be made the seventh Imām by not counting Ḥasan, usually considered to be the second Imām; Ḥasan could be considered the representative, or *Imām Mustawda*, of his brother Ḥusayn, usually considered to be the third Imām but now to be seen as the second. The Sevener movement produced many splinters, in keeping with the subtle and fluid nature of its doctrines. The schools were to split and branch out again and again. Some factions maintained a loyalty to certain descendants of Jaʿfar through Ismāʿīl, others to leaders whom they themselves threw up; and others, notably the Qarmatians, dropped the need to believe in a supreme spiritual authority altogether (although it cannot be excluded that Hamdān Qarmat may have played for them the very role that the Fāṭimid Caliph played for the others). The various Sevener movements were, in fact, to become a secret insurrection, an underground with branches all over the Muslim empire, seeking to overthrow the ʿAbbāsids, the dynasty which followed the Umayyads.

One of these Sevener, or Ismāʿīlī, groups succeeded in conquering Egypt, and became the Fāṭimid dynasty. Another, the Qarmatians, succeeded in seizing East Arabia and Baḥrayn, and at one point also seized Mecca. The Qarmatians were to disappear, leaving behind such remnant groups as the ʿAlawīs of Syria and the ʿAlī Ilāhīs of Iraq and Iran, and possibly the Yazīdīs.

In *487*/1094 a *coup d'état* took place in Fāṭimid Egypt. The leader of the armies, Badr al-Jamālī (an Armenian general who had fought for the Byzantines at the Battle of Manzikert) had married his daughter to al-Mustaʿlī, the younger son of the Fāṭimid Caliph. When the moment came for succession, Badr al-Jamālī's son al-Afḍal Shāhinshāh deposed the elder son, Nizār, put him in prison, where he died, and made al-Mustaʿlī Caliph and Imām instead. This caused a schism between the Egyptian Ismāʿīlīs, who followed al-Mustalī, and the eastern Ismāʿīlīs, who remained loyal to Nizār. A Persian *dāʿī*, or propagandist, named Ḥasan aṣ-Ṣabbāḥ, who had captured the fortress of Alamūt in north Persia, became the leader of the Nizārīs, and created his own organization which forged political terror into a deadly weapon. His followers were to be called the Assassins (a European name given them by the Crusaders; the name most commonly used in the Islamic world was the *Taʿlīmiyyah*, the "people of the teaching", i.e. "gnostics"). Alamūt thereafter became the principle center of Ismāʿīlism.

In *524*/1130 the Nizārīs assassinated al-Amīr, the son of al-Mustaʿlī, and the belief developed among his followers that al-Amīr had had a son named aṭ-Ṭayyib who had gone into hiding or "concealment" on the death of his father. Thus some of the Mustaʿlī Ismāʿīlīs believe that a descendant of aṭ-Ṭayyib subsists somewhere in secret and fulfils the function of Imām. Others believe that, as with the *ghaybah* of the Hidden Imām for the Twelvers, and al-Ḥakīm for the Druzes, this concealment is supernatural and the function is still held by aṭ-Ṭayyib himself in the invisible world, and that he will show himself again at the end of time. In Egypt, after the assassination of al-Amīr, Ismā'īlī allegiance to the last Fāṭimid Caliphs became ever more fragmented, with sometimes more than one claimant to the function of Imām. Shortly thereafter, in *567*/1171, Ṣalāḥ ad-Dīn al-Ayyūbī (Saladin) conquered Egypt and put an end to the Fāṭimids altogether. Ismā'īlism in Egypt, which was in any case the doctrine of the ruling class rather than of the general population, disappeared from Egypt and took refuge in the Yemen, where the chief of the Ismā'īlīs for a time after the death of al-Amīr was a woman, as-Sayyidah Ḥurra (d. *532*/1138).

Not long before the fall of the Fāṭimids of Egypt the function of Imām reappeared among the Nizārīs at the Assassin stronghold of Alamūt in northern Persia. Ḥasan 'Alā Dhikrihi-s-Salām ("Ḥasan, on whose memory peace"), the grandson of Ḥasan aṣ-Ṣabbāḥ's successor, Kiya Buzurg Umud, claimed that he was the Imām. According to other accounts, he claimed to be the *Ḥujjah*, or "witness", to the knowledge of the Imām; there is nothing, however, to stop him from having claimed both at different times. The history of Ismā'īlism is the stripping away of one secret to reveal another known only to the inner circle; nowhere is the labyrinth so complex as when it comes to the multiple and fugitive identities of the Imāms where one person is a mask for another. By various explanations, such as the migration of a pregnant concubine of Nizār's (or his putative son al-Hādī) from Egypt to Alamūt, and the substitution of children at the appropriate time, Ḥasan's followers made him into a descendant of Nizār for those who believed that physical descent was an essential condition of the Ismā'īlī Imāmate.

In *559*/1164, Ḥasan 'Alā Dhikrihi-s-Salām, by a ritual repudiation of Islamic law which ceremonially put an end to the fast of Ramaḍān, proclaimed the *'Īd al-Qiyāmah* ("the Feast of the Resurrection"), ushering in a new age in which there was no longer any need to cover the Assassin religion with the appearance of Islam and its religious law, which latter was, moreover, likened to the flood of Noah. In Ismā'īli *ta'wīl* (allegorical interpretation) the flood is compared both to the *sharī'ah* ("religious law") and to its opposite, the *da'wah* (the Gnostic call).

In the Alamūt *Qiyāmah*, the "veiling of the truth" by the Islamic law was lifted, and the law superseded by the "inner" and secret "truth" of the Gnostic doctrine. The end of the law expresses the Gnostic doctrine of the falling away of all beliefs "like clothes" when the secret truth is understood and the great awakening comes. However, a successor to Ḥasan, Jalāl ad-Dīn (also called Ḥasan III), drew the outward covering of Islam over matters again and professed to be a Sunnī Muslim. His conversion was readily accepted by the Caliph an-Nāṣir and other Princes, and Jalāl ad-Dīn was known as the *naw musalman* ("the new Muslim"). This policy of Jalāl ad-Dīn actually bought time for the power of Alamūt; it was accompanied by the building of mosques and bathhouses in Ismā'īlī villages, signifying the acquisition of the status of a civilized state; Sunnī legists were even invited to instruct the villagers in the use of the new mosques. The outward resumption of Islam which followed the *Qiyāmah* was called the *Satr* ("veiling"), and resembled the *Satr* which had preceded it, except that the Divinity of the Imām, in his public aspect of *Qā'im*, having been more or less openly so declared, remained thereafter a more accessible doctrine.

In *654*/1256 the Assassin stronghold of Alamūt fell to the Mongols and shortly thereafter the last Grand Master, Rukn ad-Dīn, was put to death. Ismā'īlism survived in communities scattered through Persia, Central Asia, the Yemen and Syria. Before the Mamlūks stamped out Ismā'īlī power in Syria, the Ismā'īlīs there had offered to ally themselves with the Crusaders and to become Christians. The offer was enthusiastically received by the Christian King of Jerusalem and his court, but nullified by the Knights Templar, who put the Ismā'īlī envoys to death.

Despite the sharp decline of the fortunes of the Ismā'īlīs in Syria and Persia, another great expansion of Ismā'īlism was yet to come, in India. Ismā'īlī propagandists had been active and successful in gaining converts in Sindh since the early days of the Seveners, presumably amongst existing followers of pre-Ismā'īlī Gnostic-Dualisms in India. According to tradition, Ḥasan 'Alā Dhikrihi-s-Salām (himself assassinated in *561*/1166) sent a Nizārī missionary to Sindh named Nūr ad-Dīn, also called Nūr Satagur; others put the date of Nūr ad-Dīn somewhat later, *575-640*/1179-1242. The most successful of the Nizārī leaders in Sindh was Pir Ṣadr ad-Dīn (*9th*/15th century), also known by Hindu names such as Sahadev. Ṣadr ad-Dīn converted a Hindu caste called the Lohanas to Ismā'īlism and gave them the name of Khojas, derived from the Persian word *Khwājah* ("Lord"). He is associated with an important Ismā'īlī book called *Das Avatār* ("the Tenth Incarnation"), and the local name he gave to Ismā'īlism was the *Satpanth* ("Way of Truth"). It should be noted that there is a Dualist school of metaphysics in Hinduism too. All the Ismā'īlī missionaries in India freely adapted Hinduism to Ismā'īlism, and vice versa. Indeed, it is in the nature of Gnosticism-Dualism to take any religious form as its starting point and then to lead the novice through it to the hidden and secret knowledge. As part of his approach, Pir Ṣadr ad-Dīn taught that the tenth *avatāra* ("incarnation") of Vishnu was none other than the Caliph 'Alī.

Similarly, Musta'lī Ismā'īlīs from Egypt, and later from the Yemen, sent missionaries to India, especially to the Gujarat. Musta'lī missionaries succeeded in converting another originally Hindu caste, who became known as the Bohoras (or Vohoras, "the traders"). The head of the Musta'lī community in the Yemen was called *al-Dā'i-l-Muṭlaq*. With the growth of the community in India, the *Dā'i* moved there from the Yemen in *946*/1539. Not long afterwards, on the death of the 26th *dā'i*, a split occurred, with most of the Indians favoring a *dā'i* called Dāwūd Burhān ad-Dīn (d. *1021*/1612) in India, and the Yemenis a *dā'i* in the Yemen called Sulaymān ibn Ḥasan (d. *1005*/1597). The two groups, and remnants of other fissions, exist today. In 1936 the Sulaymānī *al-Dā'i-l-Muṭlaq* also moved to Bombay from the Yemen. The leaders of both groups are now in India and are each called the Mulla-Ji.

Splits also occurred among the Nizārīs because any charismatic leader could, and did, claim to be the Imām. Thus the historic lists of Imāms vary considerably, the two major groupings being known as Muḥammad Shāhīs and Qāsim-Shāhīs. But the older factions among the Nizārīs are disappearing, to be replaced by a new self-awareness and assertiveness, as if Ismā'īlism in this century were awakening after a long period of dormancy. In general, the Bohora Ismā'īlīs (some Bohoras and some Khojas are Sunnīs) resemble Sunnī Islam somewhat more than the Nizārīs do, who more readily treat the ritual principles of orthodox Islam in a symbolic or allegorical fashion. The doctrine in any case is a prerogative of the Imām and can be changed at any time. The Ismā'īlīs, particularly the Nizārīs, practiced *taqiyyah* (dissimulation of one's real religion to avoid persecution) to a high degree. This was also very much the position of the Manicheans *vis-à-vis* the early Christians. In Persia, the Ismā'īlīs were often obliged to pass themselves off as Twelve-Imām Shī'ites, and in this guise a number of Ismā'īlīs played an important role in the Ni'matu'llāhī Sufi order (*ṭarīqah*).

Today's Ismā'īlīs are found mainly in India and Pakistan (both Nizārī and Mustalī branches), with smaller groups in the Yemen (chiefly Sulaymānī-Musta'lī), Syria (chiefly Nizārī), Central Asia (Nizārī), and Iran (Nizārī). Large numbers of Ismā'īlīs have emigrated from the Indian sub-continent to various East African countries. Others have emigrated to Europe and America, particularly since the expulsion of Asians from Uganda. The Indian census of 1931 put the number of Musta'lī Ismā'īlī Bohoras (of whom the majority are Dāwūdī-Musta'lī) at 212,000, and the number of Nizārī Ismā'īlī Khojas at slightly more than that. Nizārī Khojas added to other Indian Nizārī groups such as the Guptis, the Shamsis, the Burusho of Hunza (in Kashmir), and others, were estimated at that time to amount to 250,000 Nizārīs in India. To this can be added a few thousand Ismā'īlīs in other countries for a total estimate, in the 1930s, of all Ismā'īlīs, both Nizārī and Musta'lī, to be 500,000. Today they probably number more than one million. Not all Khojas and Bohoras are Ismā'īlīs; some are Sunnīs and others are Twelve-Imām Shī'ites. The present Imām of the Nizārīs is the Aga Khān IV who resides near Paris.

Among the important books of the Ismā'īlīs is the *Da'ā'im al-Islām* of Qāḍi Nu'mān ibn Muḥammad at-Tamīmī (d. *873*/974), a Fāṭimid work of the *4th*/10th century. It is an expression of Ismā'īlī jurisprudence (*fiqh*), in a period when the outward aspect of Ismā'īlism was at its closest to orthodox Islam. Thus, in many ways, the book is indistinguishable from ordinary exoterism except for its allusions to the Imāmate. Works of a more doctrinal kind in which the *bāṭin* ("inner doctrines") or *ḥaqā'iq* ("ultimate realities") came far more to the forefront, culminating in the *Qiyāmah* doctrine, were written by the *dā'i* Abū Ya'qūb Sijistānī (d. *4th*/10th century), Ḥamīd ad-Dīn al-Kīrmānī (d. *411*/1021), Naṣīr-i Khusraw (d. *452*/1060), who is still highly venerated by the Ismā'īlīs of Central Asia, and Naṣīr ad-Dīn aṭ-Ṭūsi (d. *673*/1274). The book *Kalām-i Pīr* is ascribed to both Abū Isḥāq and Naṣīr-i Khusraw. The *Umm al-Kitāb*, a book from the *2nd*/8th century, from the very origins of the Seveners, is influential among the Ismā'īlīs of Central Asia and Badakshān in Afghanistan, and is representative of the first, early attempts to integrate the Gnostic doctrine into an Islamic framework. In this sense it is not completely successful; its alien origins are apparent despite the masterly choice of name. (The word *Umm al-Kitāb*, "the mother of the book", is an allusion to the name of the celestial prototype of the Koran among the Sunnīs.) The *Umm al-Kitāb* transposes formulations into Islam which had been developed by Gnosticism in order to infiltrate Christianity; hence a somewhat "trinitarian" approach (perpetuated by the 'Alawīs) and an echo of the demiurge idea. But in the end, especially after Alamūt, the formulations became so refined that they were transparent to orthodox Islam, and orthodox Islam became transparent to them. Islam became truly married to Gnosticism and its outer garment: the *shahādah* became recognition or knowledge of the Imām; prayer (*ṣalāh*) came to be directed to the Imām; *zakāh* came to be given for the Imām; fasting meant keeping his secret; *ḥajj*, visiting the Imām, and so on. The Alamūt period represents the culmination of a perfected Ismā'īlism in which Gnosticism was so closely adapted to Islam (admittedly a Shī'ite Islam), that they fit together like hand and glove.

During the period of their ascendancy, when they ruled Egypt and threatened to topple the 'Abbāsid Empire with the power of the syllogism, the Ismā'īlīs had a profound influence upon the development of Islam. They were the leaven which by intellectual fermentation brought forth a developed mysticism out of inchoate possibilities. Dualism had performed the same function in regard to Judaism from the first contact of the Jews with the Parthians, during the Babylonian Captivity, thereby producing the first school of mysticism in Judaism, in the shape of the *Merkava*. A later Dualist permeation of Judaism, at the time of the Qumrān sect, called forth the response of Christianity. Again, at a still later time, the Ismā'īlī *Rasā'il Ikhwān aṣ-Ṣafā'* ("The Epistle of the Brotherhood of Purity") stimulated Jewish rationalists at Baghdad and influenced their interpretation of the 3rd-6th century A.D. *Sefer Yetsira* ("The Book of Creation", which described creation as the result of thirty-two means – ten numbers and the twenty-two Hebrew letters) and so, perhaps, stimulated the flowering of the Qabbalah. (This, it may be noted, appeared in Provence not far from the irruption of the Christian Gnostic sect of the Cathars, or Albigensians.)

In Islam (as in Judaism), mysticism, or the doctrine of recognition of, and identity with, the Real was inherent in the revelation itself. The service that Dualism performed was a challenge to orthodoxy that brought forth a complete development of its possibilities; much as the fragrance of the Eagle Wood tree, aloes (*al-'Ūd al-Qimārī*), much beloved of the Sufis, is a resin which is secreted by those trees to counter an alien organism.

Because the metaphysics of Gnosticism-Dualism tend to interpret the cosmos as the "shadow" of Reality, the Ismā'īlīs pursued the study of science vigorously. Regarding themselves as heirs to the inward and secret truth of all religions, the Ismā'īlīs demonstrated a great curiosity about other faiths and examined them in greater depth than most Sunnīs, who were largely content to view other religions from afar, and to interpret them almost entirely from Islamic reference points. The Ismā'īlīs were especially well-informed about Christianity, which, with its doctrine of the incarnation, and of a spiritual truth which goes beyond appearances, provided many parallels to Ismā'īlism – as well as vital differences. The facts account for the great success the Ismā'īlīs and other strands of Gnostic-Dualism enjoyed in penetrating other religions. Certain Ismā'īlī formulations proved useful to Sunnī Islam and were used by many thinkers, some of whom never stopped to wonder where certain ideas, such as the *Nūr Muḥammadī* ("the Muḥammadan Light") and Sahl at-Tustarī's *'umūd an-nūr* ("pillars of light") actually originated. By being open to ideas from all sources, as evidenced by the writings of the

Brotherhood of Purity (*Ikhwān aṣ-Ṣafā'*), a group founded around *340*/951 in Baṣra, the Ismā'īlīs facilitated the assimilation and adaptation of Hellenistic thought within Islam. *See* also AGA KHĀN; 'ALAWĪS; ASSASSINS; BOHORAS; BROTHERHOOD of PURITY; DRUZES; FĀṬIMIDS; JAMAT KHĀNAH; KHOJAS; QARMATIANS; MŪKHĪ; NŪR MUḤAMMADĪ; SEVENERS; SHĪ'ISM; TA'WĪL.

Isnād. The chain of transmission supporting a Ḥadīth. The authority, and character, including moral probity, of every member of a chain in the transmission of a given Ḥadīth, and the existence of alternate chains of transmission for a saying, were fundamental criteria for accepting Ḥadīth as authentic. *See* ḤADĪTH.

Isrā', *see* NIGHT JOURNEY.

Istanbul. The capital of the Ottoman Empire was originally called Constantinople, the extension built beginning in 328 A.D. by the Roman Emperor Constantine to the original city of Byzantium. The name Stamboul at first designated the central quarter of the city. The word presumably comes from the Greek *eis tēn polin* ("into the city"), and was already in use before the Turks. The Turks usually called the city Kustantiniyya and did not officially adopt the name Istanbul until 1930.

Istanbul stands at the southern extremity of the Bosporus, a channel where the the waters of the Black Sea, on their way to the Mediterranean, rush into the sea of Marmora. The channel, now bridged, narrowly separates Europe and Asia. The city is a promontory with the Sea of Marmora on the south, and a bay of the Bosphorus called the Golden Horn on the north (in Turkish, *Halice*, from Arabic *khalij*, a "bay").

The city of Byzantium was founded by the Greeks under Byzas in 657 B.C. It had a tumultuous history under the Greeks and Macedonians. When the Roman Empire became dissociated from the city of Rome, its natural center of gravity moved east. The Roman empire had been failing; Valerian had been captured by the Persians (A.D. 260); the frontiers of the empire could not be defended. Aurelian (A.D. 270-275) and Diocletian (284-305) had held back decline. Diocletian, who abdicated, travelled incessantly to hold the empire together; he made his capital Nicomedia in Asia Minor; he created the Tetrarchy; when that failed Constantine became the victorious ruler. Constantine, recognizing the strategic advantages of the fine harbor and commanding site defended by natural barriers made Byzantium, which like Rome also has seven hills, his capital. The city of Constantinople was founded on 8 November, 324. By tradition, the Emperor was protected by Apollo; Constantine did not immediately stop deification of the Emperor as a result of his conversion, but the founding of the city was the changing point of the empire from a pagan empire to a Christian one.

At first thought to be too large, the New Rome grew such that in 413, Theodosius II, not yet emperor, had to enlarge it again leaving his stamp on Christian Constantinople. With extensions to its ancient walls, the city acquired its classical limits in 439.

These walls were a wise investment, for from then on attempts to conquer the city were frequent until Mehmet Nasir invested the city in 1453. By then the city had been attacked by Huns, Avars, Slavs, Bulgarians, and repeatedly by Arabs, who dreamed of its conquest from the beginning of Islam. But Constantinople was most weakened not by Arabs but by the Fourth Crusade which under the Doge Dandolo sacked the city in 1204 and reduced its population to a quarter of its former size. The city was so depopulated that when the Turks captured the city they sent servants to all the lands, to say: "Whoever wishes let him come, and let him become owner of houses, vineyards and gardens in Istanbul."

Under the Christians the city was the seat of Eastern Christianity; it was full of churches, the chief of which was the Cathedral of the Hagia Sophia, the Holy Wisdom built by Justinian the Great (A.D. 527-565) who brought to fruition the work begin by Constantine. The city lived out its theology attempting to fulfill the expectations of the heavenly Jerusalem; because the streets of the heavenly Jerusalem were paved with gold, Constantinople collected gold with a religious zeal; because the heavenly Jerusalem was populated with Angels, Constantinople was full of an earthly approximation: eunichs. Because the heavenly Jerusalem was the fulfillment of Divine Law, heavenly measures with absolute punishments were applied to trade. A loaf of bread had to be baked to a strict weight as if it were the the projection of a Platonic ideal into the world. If the ideal weight was off, the punishment was drastic, as if the weights and measures were in the hands of the Angels at the Day of Judgement. The coinage was also, at first, extremely reliable, and assured Constantinople a dominant position in international trade. But the passions of theology were to be surpassed by the passions of chariot racing and the city rivalries of the Blues, the Reds, and other teams. The Hippodrome stands, showing its later importance, in front of the Cathedral, now the mosque of Aya Sofia and next to the Mosque of Sultan Aḥmet.

Ottoman Constantinople continued the cosmopolitan tradition of the city. By the time of Suleyman, the population of Istanbul was at least half a million, and in 1593 an English traveler, John Sanderson, cites the population as 1,231,207. At the end of the 19th century, Muslims were in the minority in the city, surpassed by Greeks, Armenians, and foreigners. The reign of Sulaymān (1520-66) was the high water mark of the Ottoman empire, and the period of Istanbul's greatest splendor. The architect Sinan built the Sulaymāniyyah Mosque, one of the great examples of world architecture, and embellished the city with other buildings. Much of Constantinople had been rebuilt by the pious Sultan Bayazid II (1481-1512) called the *Veli* "the Saint". At the time of Sulaymān the administration was such that it was considered the paragon of the world. The custom of the ruler to sit by the gate of the city to dispense justice and receive petitions associated the word gate and government throughout the Middle East. In Istanbul the palace of the Grand Vizier was the effective seat of government and was called the *Bab-i* 'Alī, High Gate, whence the Turkish government was called "the Sublime Porte."

In the 17th century a poet named Nabī described Istanbul as:

> "There is no place where knowledge and learning
> Find so ready a welcome as Istanbul.
> No city has eaten the fruits of the garden of art
> So richly as the city of Istanbul.
> May God cause Istanbul to flourish
> For it is the home of all great affairs.
> Birthplace and school of famous men,
> The nursery of many nations,
> Whatever men of merit there may be
> All win their renown in Istanbul."

See OTTOMANS; TURKEY; TURKS.

Istawā (from *istawā 'ala'l-'arsh*, lit. "He (God) mounted on the throne", 32:4 and *passim*). One of several Koranic passages which "anthropomorphize" God, or speak of Him as having human attributes. It should be borne in mind that what has often been called "anthropomorphism" in debates around this question is really nothing more than a *conceptual* tendency. References occur to God's Face, His Hands, and His footstool (*al-kursī*). The school of Ibn Ḥanbal insisted that these references be accepted literally, without drawing any conclusions, but without question (*bilā kayfā*). The Ash'arites did the same, but in addition to the literal aspect, also saw a symbolic allusion to God's assumption of majesty towards His creation. Nevertheless, in modern times these passages are generally understood symbolically. Al-Asha'rī wrote in *al-Ibānah 'an Uṣūl ad-Dīyānah* ("The Elucidation of the Foundations of Religion"):

> Certain Rationalists [Mu'tazilites] have maintained that God's words "the Merciful is seated on the throne" mean merely that He has dominion, reigns, exercises power. God, they say, is everywhere; and this denies that He is on the Throne. They hold that His being seated is merely an expression referring to His Power. If they were right, the distinction between the Throne and the earth would be lost, for the Power of God extends over the earth and all worldly things.. so that He would be seated on the Throne, and on earth, and on heaven...and on everything. But since no True Believer regards it as right to say God is seated..it necessarily follows from this consensus of Believers that being seated in this passage has a meaning particular to the Throne and does not refer to anything else. Be God exalted above their thought.

See BILĀ KAYFĀ.

Istibrā'. Washing the private parts after passing water as a preparation for the ablution. *See* ISTINJĀ'; WUḌŪ.

Istidrāj (lit. "a baiting by degrees", "a lure to destruction"). A fall from grace from what may even appear to be an exalted state as a consequence of a hidden chain of harmful causes and effects in a person's being which has not in fact been rooted out or effectively neutralized.

Ibn al-'Ārif says in the *Maḥāsin al-Majālis* ("Beauties of Spiritual Sessions"):

> It was said: "Do not be deceived by good times, because in them lurk the secrets of calamities". In how many springs have the flowers and trees bloomed, and people thought highly of it all, only to be soon inflicted with a heavenly disaster! God says: "Our scourge comes down upon [the crop], by night or in broad day, laying it waste, even though it was in bloom only yesterday" (10:24). How many disciples have shone with the splendor of their will to serve God and felt the intense effects of spiritual joy; they became renowned, were put above everything, and were supposed to be the chosen friends of God. But how often has the serenity of such a man changed into grief, and his spiritual illumination into depravation! So it is that the Sufis recite the following verses:
>
> "You made your thoughts pleasant like the days,
> Not fearing the disaster which fate was bringing."
>
> "The nights soothed you, and you were deceived by them; But when nights are serene, troubles follow."

But as Ibn 'Aṭā' Allāh says:

> Sometimes darknesses come over you in order that He make you aware of the value of His blessings upon you.

Istighfār (lit. "asking for forgiveness"). Seeking the forgiveness of God through the words *astaghfiru-Llāh,* ("and ask for God's forgiveness"). One is in effect asking that the evil incurred in created existence through the breaking of Divine Law should be covered or neutralized by what transcends existence and its evils. When one turns to God for forgiveness in sincere repentence, with the intention of not repeating the offense, God forgives unconditionally, for He is *al-ghafūr,* ("the All-Forgiving", the One who covers over").

The Prophet recited the *istighfār* one hundred times, or alternately seventy times, each day. There is a famous Ḥadīth: "My heart is clouded until I have asked God's forgiveness seventy times during the day and the night".

Istiḥsān (lit. "seeking the good", "aiming at the best", "improvement"). A legal principle, akin to the *istislāh* of Mālik ibn Anas, whereby laws are established on the guidelines and injunctions furnished by the Koran and Sunnah. This is the working principle used by Abū Ḥanīfah, founder of the Ḥanafī School of Law. It is, in effect, simply the expression of the idea that it is equity and justice as defined by God that must determine both the formulation and the interpretation of laws. Today the principle of the morality of law seems self-evident, and in most non-totalitarian countries is to be taken for granted. However, the origin of human law cannot be other than Divine law. In this sense, the ideal enshrined in *istiḥsān* and *istislāh* remains timelessly valid.

Istikhārah (lit. "asking for the best choice", "seeking goodness"). A practice, based upon the Sunnah, of asking God for guidance when faced with important decisions or perplexing situations. *Istikhārah* consists of praying a two *raka'āt* prayer immediately before retiring to sleep along with a *du'ā'* (personal prayer) in which one presents the problem to God and asks for guidance: a response may come in the form of a dream, a sign, or a sudden certitude. Alternatively, one may seek the answer in the Koran, using the same procedure: after a *two raka'āt* prayer and a *du'ā'* to put the problem to God, the Koran is opened and the hand placed upon the page. The verse under the hand, or above or below, may shed light upon the question. Such use of the Koran is frowned upon by many Sunnī authorities, as is – *a fortiori* – the not uncommon use of the Mathnawī of Jalāl ad-Dīn Rūmī in Shī'ite lands. *See* MATHNAWĪ.

Istilāḥāt. Technical vocabularies. One of the first signs of the formalization of Sufism was the appearance of detailed technical vocabularies such as those by al-Ḥakīm at-Tirmidhī (*3rd*/9th century), and later by many others, such as al-Hujwīrī.

Istinjā'. The practice of washing the orifices to clean the body after calls of nature. If water is not available, sand or earth is used. For some Schools of Law *istinjā'* is obligatory in the preparation for assuming the state of *wuḍū* for prayers, while other schools only recommend it. As Western style toilets are not equipped, as are toilets in the East, with running water in the cabinets, this practice is not always possible. *See* ISTIBRĀ'; WUḌŪ.

Istiṣlāḥ (lit. "Seeking what is correct, wholesome"). A principle invoked by the jurist Mālik ibn Anas, to the effect that public and individual good must be the criterion for the development of the law. The basis of law is Divine injunctions as found in the Koran and Sunnah. These canonic sources however, make implicit only the framework of Islamic law; the rest being elaborated by such guiding principles as *istiṣlāḥ* or *istiḥsān*. *See* ISTIḤSĀN.

Istisqā'. A two *raka'āt* prayer to ask for rain. It is performed by the entire community, in a *musallā* (communal prayerground), in the morning. *See* PRAYER.

Istithnā', *see* PIOUS EXPRESSIONS.

Ithm. One category of sin. *See* SIN.

Ithnā'ashariyyah (lit. "Twelvers" from *ithnā 'ashar*, "twelve"). The most important division of the Shī'ites, the Twelve-Imām branch, so-called because they hold that there were twelve Imāms, the last of whom is still mysteriously alive since his occultation in the *3rd*/9th century, and will return as the Mahdī. The Twelvers are the dominant religious group in Iran, constitute the majority in Iraq, and are found in Syria, Lebanon, Pakistan, some of the Gulf states, and in several other countries, including the Eastern Province of Saudi Arabia. *See* HIDDEN IMĀM; SHĪ'ISM.

Ithnayniyyah, *see* MANICHEISM; SEVENERS.

Īwān. A feature of Persian architecture which spread to other parts of the Islamic world, notably India, it consists of a semi-circular vault open on one side – which frequently faces onto a courtyard – and closed on the other three. The brick ribbing which supports the vault is concealed, and the outer arch may well be pointed.

Izār (lit. "a wrap", "a cloth sheet"). The lower of the two unsecured cloths which constitute the consecrated pilgrims' garb, or *iḥrām*. It is fastened around the waist and falls below the knees.The upper cloth which is draped over the shoulders is called a *rida'*. *See* IḤRĀM; PILGRIMAGE.

'Izrā'īl. One of the *qarībiyyūn*, or Archangels. 'Izrā'īl is the Angel of death. Although mentioned by name in non-Koranic mythology, in which his description is of a being of cosmic dimensions with innumerable eyes and feet, he is not named in the Koran. The Sūrah as-Sajdah says: "Say thou: the Angel of death that is encharged with you will bring you to your end, and then to your Lord ye will be returned" (32:11). *See* ANGELS.

J

Jabarī or Jabrī (from Ar. *Jabr*, "compulsion"). This designates a member of the Jabariyyah school of early Muslim theoreticians who maintained determinism as opposed to free will. Freedom of the human will was the thesis of the Qadariyyah school. *See* KALĀM; MAKTŪB; QADARIYYAH.

Jābir ibn Ḥayyān (*103-160*/721-776). A celebrated alchemist, not a Muslim, but a Harranian from the community of the Harranian "Sabians" of North Syria. He may not be a historical figure, but a symbol for a collective process of adaptation into Arabic of Hermetic sciences by Bardesanians of Edessa/Harran. By tradition Jābir went on to Baghdad. The name became the foremost in medieval science, known and studied in Europe as Geber. The Jābir writings on alchemy and chemistry were still being read in the 16th century.

As an alchemist, Jābir was first of all concerned with the purification of the soul. He is cited in the medieval texts:

> All Metallick Bodies are compounded of Argentvive and Sulphur, pure or impure, by accident, and not innate in their first Nature; therefore, by convenient Preparation, 'tis possible to take away such impurity...It is called by Philosophers, one Stone, although it is extracted from many Bodies or Things.

The importance of the Arab/Islamic contribution to chemistry can be seen in the word "chemistry" itself: it comes ultimately from the Arabic *al-kīmiyā'* ("alchemy") which means "the science of *Khem*", an ancient name for Egypt, which referred to that country's "black earth" together with a symbolic allusion to the color black standing for the metaphysical void, or Beyond-Being, or perhaps to the alchemists' *materia prima.* Likewise, the word alembic comes from the Arabic *al-inbīq*, elixir from *al-iksīr*, alkali from *al-qilī* ("potash"), alcohol from *al-kuḥl* ("antimony powder"); athanor from *at-tannūr* ("an oven"), and so on.

Jacob, *see* YA'QŪB.

Jadhb (lit. "attraction"). A term in mysticism for the "Divine attraction" which certain souls experience. It refers especially to states of violent, sudden cognizance of a superior reality, disturbing everyday human equilibrium. One who is subject to such states, the consequence of which may be temporary or permanent, and resemble a benign madness, is called *majdhūb,* "one attracted [to God]" and corresponds to one who would be called in the West "God's fool" or a "holy fool".

Ja'farī. An adjective derived from *Ja'far* "to qualify" the body of religious law of the the Twelve-Imām Shī'ites, whence the expression Ja'farī Shī'ites. *See* JA'FAR AṢ-ṢĀDIQ; SHARĪ'AH; SHĪ'ISM.

Ja'far aṣ-Ṣādiq (*80-148*/699-765). A descendant of the Prophet. A renowned scholar of the religious sciences, including mysticism, he is also traditionally considered to be a master of such cosmological and arcane sciences as alchemy. He had a circle of students in Medina, and two founders of Sunnī Schools of Law, Mālik ibn Anas and Abū Ḥanīfah, studied with him. The Twelve-Imām Shī'ites consider him to be the founder of their School of Law, which is called *Ja'farī* after him.

Twelve-Imām Shī'ites hold that the Prophet had successors to his function, in the form of intermediaries between man and God. These successor-intermediaries, known as Imāms, were descendants of 'Alī ibn Abī Ṭālib. According to the Shī'ites, Ja'far was the sixth Imām. The doctrine of the Imāmate came to hold that the function was passed on by designation (*naṣṣ*). Thus Ja'far aṣ-Ṣādiq is said to have first named his eldest son Ismā'īl as Imām to succeed him; then, it is said, he revoked this designation in favor of his third son, Mūsā Kāzim after 'Abd Allāh, the second son, had died without children. Those who chose even so to follow Ismā'īl and his son became the Seven-Imām Shī'ites ("Seveners" or *sab'iyyah*), who survive as present day Ismā'īlīs. Those who followed Mūsā Kāzim became the Twelve-Imām Shī'ites ("Twelvers" or *ithnā'ashariyyah*).

Ja'far is a pivotal figure in the development of Shī'ism. Before him, the movement had had a distinctly political nature with the Imāms acting rather as rallying points for resistance to the Umayyads and as the focus of rival aspirations. After him, it became transformed by the development of new religious currents of which he was the spokesman and authoritative founder. This coincided with the penetration of the, in fact, heterodox doctrines of the Seveners into Islam as what later became known as Ismā'īlism.

In keeping with the tradition that he is a well-spring of esoteric doctrines second only to 'Alī himself, the Shī'ites claim that Ja'far possessed a book of secret knowledge (*Kitāb al-Jafr*; *jafr* meaning "vellum", not the name Ja'far), known only to the family of the Prophet.

Without the least acquiesence in, or acceptance of, the role Ja'far is alleged to have played in Shī'ism, he is nonetheless considered to be a great Sufi by the Sunnī mystics, and appears in the more prominent *silsilahs*, or initiatic chains, of the Sufi orders. *See* 'ABD ALLĀH ibn MAYMŪN; ISMĀ'ĪLISM; KITĀB al-JAFR; NAṢṢ; NŪR MUḤAMMADĪ; SEVENERS; SHĪ'ISM.

al-Jafr A name for the "science of letters". *See* 'ILM al-ḤURŪF; KITĀB al-JAFR.

al-Jāhiliyyah (from *jāhil,* "ignorant", "untaught"). The time of ignorance or period of Arab paganism preceding the revelation of Islam. Since Islam restores the Abrahamic, or primordial, religion the *Jāhiliyyah* is considered to be that epoch which came immediately before the Islamic revelation like darkness before the dawn. During the *Jāhiliyyah,* the pristine monotheism of Abraham declined and gave way to an opaque and oppressive paganism, and general decadence.

Many of the idol cults, and the idols themselves, were brought to Mecca from other parts of the Middle East. Indeed not all the Arabs were by any means pagan, many tribes being Christian or Jewish. Moreover, there were always certain spiritually gifted individuals called *ḥunafā'*, (singular *ḥanīf*), who remained unattached to these two religions and who continued to hold to the original monotheism of Abraham.

Typical of the period were the great fairs, such as those of Minā and 'Ukāẓ, and the months of truce that made them possible. These great gatherings of pagan times, the *sūq al-A'rab*, were replaced under Islam by the *ḥajj* ("pilgrimage") alone. Before Islam, several sites in Arabia with sanctuaries similar to the Ka'bah (the church of Najran was called a Ka'bah) had attempted to rival its attractions as a centre of pilgrimage, but none was as successful as Mecca in either religion or trade. *See* IDOLS; al-KALBI.

al-Jāḥiẓ (*160-254*/777-868) Abū 'Uthmān Amr ibn Bahr, called "the goggle-eyed", Arab litterateur. Grandson of a Negro slave, al-Jāḥiẓ wrote theological tracts, a large work on rhetoric (*Kitāb al-Bayān wa-t-Tabyīn*), forty treatises, and a collection of essays called "The Book of Animals" (*Kitāb al-Ḥayawān*), "The Book of Misers" (*Kitāb al-Buḥalā*), "Excellences of the Turks", "The Superiority in Glory of the Blacks over the Whites" and other essays called *rasā'il.* He lived in Baṣra and was favored by Ibn az-Zaiyāt, the vizier of the Caliph Wāthiq and so spent time at the court in Baghdad and in Sāmarrā'. He admired Greek civilization, had wide-ranging and eclectic interests, and was a Mu'tazilite, giving his name to a sect called the Jāhiẓiyyah. He is considered a master of the Arabic language and is noted for his humor. "Ideas," he said "run about the street. It's how you express them that matters."

Jahm, *see* JAHMITES.

Jahmites. The followers of Jahm ibn Ṣafwān Abū Muḥriẓ (d. *128*/745), a radical heretic who taught that God had no attributes, i.e. a God beyond any comprehension and apprehension, but who also followed to an extreme the opinions of the determinists, and apparently held that man had no free-will. This implied that salvation was pre-determined and that man, in effect, could not work either for, or against, his salvation. The Jahmites were condemned by Abū Ḥanīfah in his *Fiqh Akbar. See* FIQH AKBAR; MAKTŪB.

Jalāl ad-Dīn ar-Rūmī (*605-672*/1207-1273). One of the greatest mystics of Islam. There are, nevertheless, salient elements of heterodoxy in his teaching; he believed in metempsychosis, which is a belief that orthodox doctrine must reject or reduce to a metaphor; and his universalism went far enough to be questionable. However, the effect of tradition has been to disregard these and integrate him into the mainstream. He was of Persian origin from Balkh, but left at an early age with his father Bahā' ad-Dīn Walad, a scholar who had had a disagreement with the rulers. After several years of wandering, the family was invited by the Saljuq Sultan of Rūm to settle in Iconium, now Konya, Turkey. To show his respect for Bahā' ad-Dīn, the Sultan advanced out of the town to meet the scholar as he approached Konya, dismounted from his horse, and led Bahā' ad-Dīn's mount by the hand into the city. Because of the Byzantine past of the region it retained the name *Rūm* ("Rome") among the Turks; and it is from this that Jalāl ad-Dīn came to be known as ar-Rūmī, "the man of Rome [Byzantium]".

It is said that while in Damascus in *618*/1221 Jalāl ad-Dīn had been seen walking behind his father by Ibn 'Arabī, the great exponent of Sufi doctrine, who had exclaimed: "Praise be to God, an ocean is following a lake!" In Konya, ar-Rūmī became a religious teacher, and he was already a Sufi when, at the age of thirty-nine, he met Shams ad-Dīn at-Ṭabrīzī (d. *645*/1247), a mysterious figure, who was to exert the most powerful effect upon the poet and to vivify, like a veritable sun, the growth of his latent spiritual and literary genius. Ar-Rūmī later wrote of him: "Sun of Tabriz...the absolute light...the sun [Ar. *shams*] and the ray of the lights of Divine Truth."

Shams ad-Dīn of Ṭabrīz, considered to be one of the spiritual poles (*aqṭāb*) of his age, transformed ar-Rūmī, and brought him to taste direct knowledge. The *Mathnawī*, a vast six-volume work of spiritual teaching and Sufi lore in the form of stories and lyric poetry of excellent quality, was one of the outward results of ar-Rūmī's discipleship to Shams ad-Dīn at Ṭabrīzī, to whom he dedicated much of his work. The *Mathnawī* stands as one of the treasures of the Persian-speaking world, known to all speakers of the language and memorized in part by every literate member of Persian society. The inward realization which Shams ad-Dīn called forth gave Jalāl ad-Dīn ar-Rūmī the force which lives in the dervish order of the Mevlevi (Ar. *Mawlawī*) which he founded and whose center is in Konya.

At one point, it is related, Shams ad-Dīn disappeared from Konya and Jalāl ad-Dīn sent men to look for him. Two years later, he was either found or simply reappeared in Konya; after a further sojourn in the home of Jalāl ad-Dīn he was murdered by persons jealous of him. By that time, however, his disappearances and mysterious re-appearances, and his strange nature may well have been blended into an allegory created by ar-Rūmī to symbolize the dawning or unveiling of the spirit, the reflection of Being within the soul.

The Mevlevi order whom Jalāl ad-Dīn ar-Rūmī founded are known as the "Whirling Dervishes" for their dancing and music (*samā'*), both of which are supports for their spiritual method. Apart from the dancing and music of the Mevlevi order, ar-Rūmī is associated with music in other ways, for the singing of the *Mathnawī* has become an art form in itself.

Jalāl ad-Dīn ar-Rūmī came to be a powerful spiritual influence not only in the Persian-speaking world, including Afghanistan and Central Asia, but also among the Turks, and in India. Sage and poet, his tomb in Konya is a place of pilgrimage for the pious and the questing. For eight centuries he has been a living presence for his followers, many of whom experience his *barakah* ("grace") directly as if he were still with them.

Among the many famous quotations from ar-Rūmī is this:

> Every form you see has its archetype in the Divine world, beyond space; if the form perishes what matter, since its heavenly model is indestructible? Every beautiful form you have seen, every meaningful word you have heard – be not sorrowful because all this must be lost; such is not really the case. The Divine Source is immortal and its outflowing gives water without cease; since neither the one nor the other can be stopped, wherefore do you lament?... From the moment that you came into the world a ladder was put before you that you could escape. First you were a mineral; then you became a plant; then you became an animal. Did you not know that? Then you were made man, given consciousness, knowledge and faith. Think on this body made from dust – what perfection it has! When you have transcended the condition of man you will doubtless become an angel. Then you will have finished with the earth: your home will be heaven. Go beyond the angelic state; go into that ocean so that your drop of water will become one with the sea.

And also:

> Appear as you are, be as you appear. You are not this body, but a spiritual eye – what the eye of man contemplates it becomes...

And the famous:

> Tell me Muslims, what should be done? I don't know how to identify myself. I am neither Christian nor Jewish, neither Pagan nor Muslim. I don't hail from the East or from the West, I am neither from land nor sea. I am not a creature of this world...

See MEVLEVI; QUṬB; SUFISM.

Jamā'at-i Islāmi. Political party founded in 1941 by Sayyid Abū al-A'la Mawdūdī along with several other intellectuals. The party has branches in India and Bangladesh. They call their program *iqamat-i-deen*, the establishment of religion and subordination of all activities to religion and the establishment of an Islamic state, the abolition of bank interest, introduction of *zakāt* and Islamic law. They believe in the use of democratic means although they do support guerrilla movments in Kashmir.

The party is distinguished by an extremely disciplined organization and stringent selection of cadres, admitting less than 2% of its supporters to full membership. *Jamā'at-i Islāmi* views Islam, however, as an ideology, and virtually as a political activity in this world rather than a spiritual way directed at the posthumous state of the believer. The aim of restoring the conditions of the first Four Rightly Guided Caliphs, which is the goal of all Fundamentalist Islamic groups, can only be called Utopian. It should be noted that the constitution of Pakistan prohibits the passage of laws which contradict Islam, which along with other institutions, has led some scholars to say that Pakistan is in fact as much an Islamic government as is practically possible. Despite its excellent organization, *Jamā'at-i Islāmi* has been relatively unsuccessful in winning political representation in parliament and has recently boycotted elections in Pakistan protesting that the other candidates, contrary to rules, could not be considered as people of "good character". In India, where Muslims are in a minority, the party is dedicated to preserving Islamic values.

The *Jamā'at-i Islāmi* is headed by an emir, or president, who is elected for five years who is assisted by a Majlis-i Shoora, an elected consultative council. *See* MAWDŪDĪ.

Jam'at Khānah. An Ismā'īlī meeting place.

Jāmī, Nūr ad-Dīn 'Abd ar-Raḥmān (*817-898*/1414-1492). A famous Persian Sufi poet. His most famous works are the *Lawā'iḥ*, ("flashes of light"), "Salmān and Absal", "Yūsuf and Zulaykhah", and the *Bahāristān* ("Abode of Spring").

Jāmī wrote:

> Being's a sea in constant billows rolled,
> 'Tis but these billows that we men behold;
> Sped from within, they rest upon the sea,
> And like a veil its actual form enfold.
> Being's the essence of the Lord of all,
> All things exist in Him and He in all;
> This is the meaning of the Knower's phrase,
> "All things are comprehended in the All".

Janābah. A state of impurity which invalidates the performance of ritual acts such as, for example, the canonical prayers. Its causes include intromission, sexual intercourse or emission, giving birth, menstruation, or contact with a corpse. The state of impurity thus occasioned is removed by the greater ablution (*ghusl*). Other, minor, impurities called *ḥadath* are removed by the lesser ablution (*wuḍū'*). *See* ABLUTIONS.

Janāzah. The funeral process, the procession, and the coffin with the corpse. *See* FUNERALS.

Janissary (from Turkish *yeni cheri*, "new troops"). An elite military corps within the Ottoman Empire selected out of the *devshirme*, the boy-levy of Christian children from the Balkans who were compelled to enter Islam and then raised and trained to be soldiers or officials according to their aptitudes. The beginnings of the Janissaries may date back as early as *731*/1330. They and the system of *devshirme* underwent further development under the Sultan Mūrād II (d. *855*/1451), and both reached the stage of being fully organized in the reign of Selim I (d. *926*/1520). The Janissary corps were put down and disbanded after they rose in rebellion in *1242*/1826 against the Sultan Mehmet II.

The Janissaries were created to meet the need

for an infantry corps during the struggle against the Byzantines. The Turks fought normally as mounted horsemen, but warfare against fortresses called for different kinds of military skills, and an infantry had to be formed. To insure their loyalty, the Janissaries were converted to Islam in their youth, and for this reason remained more reliable than other troops created later from adult converts.

The Janissaries rarely numbered over fifteen thousand, until wars with Persia swelled their ranks to several times that number. After they were given permission to marry in *989*/1581, membership of the corps naturally tended to become hereditary, and the subsequent decline in their military effectiveness was perhaps inevitable, since their selection was based less and less upon military ability. As the core of the army, the Janissaries exerted great influence in the sphere of politics, their power being such that they could sometimes dictate a change of Viziers – or even demand his head – and exact enormous bribes before they allowed a new Sultan to accede to the throne.

In *1242*/1826 the Janissaries rose up in opposition to the creation of a new regular corps called the *Muallem Eshkinji* ("drilled guard"). The Sultan reacted vigorously and induced the religious authorities to issue a malediction against the Janissaries, after which their barracks were surrounded by loyal troops, banners proclaiming holy war were unfurled and, in the attack upon them, most of the Janissaries were killed; their flags and traditional headgear were then publicly dragged through the mud to signify their disgrace. The Bektashi religious confraternity which was peculiar to the Janissaries was outlawed. *See* DEVSHIRME.

al-Jannah (lit. "the garden"). The garden is the most frequent Koranic symbol of paradise. The word suggests that which is veiled, covered or surrounded; hence an "enclosed garden" luxuriant with foliage of tall, shadowing trees and sheltered from storm or tempest. A further significance pointed out by the commentators is that the delights prepared therein for the blessed are concealed and hardly imaginable in man's present state of existence; fruits of obedience to God ripen unseen.

...and the Outstrippers: the Outstrippers [i.e. the Foremost]
those are they brought nigh [the Throne,]
in the Gardens of Delight
(a throng of the ancients
and how few of the later folk)... (56:10-14).

The Companions of the Right (O Companions of the Right!)
mid thornless lote-trees and serried acacias,
and spreading shade and outpoured waters,
and fruits abounding
unfailing, unforbidden,
and upraised couches...
...for the Companions of the Right.
A throng of the ancients
and a throng of the later folk. (56:27-39).

In the Koran, *al-jannah* also refers to the Garden of Eden where Adam dwelt with Eve before the Fall.

The desert is dead, sterile and odorless. To come out of the desert into an oasis, is to be overwhelmed by the perfumes of plants and flowers, and the sudden proliferation of life; it is also to be blest with coolness, repose after journeying and water after thirst. To a desert people more than to any other, the planted garden with shade and running water is the most powerfully concrete example by which their imagination may grasp the nature of another, supernatural world.

The Koran often speaks of "Gardens [of paradise] underneath which rivers run". Deep in the Arabian peninsula are aquifers which carry water under pressure, drop by drop, through porous rock from the mountains of the Red Sea to the Gulf on the other side. There (and in spots across the deserts, as well as on the sea floor of the Gulf itself) these aquifers well up as springs, sometimes warm springs, which create the vast oasis of al-Ḥāsa. The movement of the life-giving water from one end of the peninsula to the other takes as long as ten thousand years, a mysterious, secret presence hidden in the earth.

This is the similitude of Paradise
which the godfearing have been promised:
therein are rivers of water unstaling,
rivers of milk unchanging in flavour
and rivers of wine – a delight
to the drinkers,
rivers, too, of honey purified;
and therein for them is every fruit,
and forgiveness from their Lord – (Koran 47:15)

Give thou good tidings to those who believe
and do deeds of righteousness, that for them
await gardens underneath which rivers flow;
whensoever they are provided with fruits therefrom
they shall say, 'This is that wherewithal
we were provided before'; that they shall begiven in
perfect semblance; and there
for them shall be spouses purified; therein
they shall dwell forever. (Koran 2:23)

We shall strip away all rancour that is
in their breasts;
as brothers they shall be upon couches
set face to face;
no fatigue shall smite them, neither
shall they ever be driven forth from there. (Koran
15:47-48)

Surely the pious shall drink of a cup
whose mixture is camphor,
a fountain whereat drink the servants of God,
making it to gush forth plenteously.
They fulfil their vows, and fear a day whose evil is
upon the wing;
they give food, for the love of Him, to the needy,
the orphan, the captive...

...So God has guarded them from the evil of
that day, and has procured them radiancy
and gladness,
and recompensed them for their patience
with a Garden, and silk;
therein they shall recline upon couches,
therein they shall see neither sun nor
bitter cold;
near them shall be its shades, and its clusters hung
meekly down,
and there shall be passed around them vessels of
silver, and goblets of crystal,
crystal of silver that they have measured
very exactly.
And therein they shall be given to drink a cup
whose mixture is ginger,
therein a fountain whose name is called Salsabil.
Immortal youths shall go about them;
when thou seest them, thou supposest them
scattered pearls,
when thou seest them then thou seest bliss
and a great kingdom.
Upon them shall be green garments of silk
and brocade; they are adorned with
bracelets of silver, and their Lord shall
give them to drink a pure draught.
Behold, this is a recompense for you, and
your striving is thanked. (Koran 76:5-22)
...and wide-eyed houris
as the likeness of hidden pearls,
a recompense for that they laboured. (Koran
56:22-24)

Perfectly We formed them, perfect,
and We made them spotless virgins,
chastely amorous, like of age
for the Companions of the Right. (Koran 56:35-
38)

Gardens of Eden that the All-merciful
promised His servants in the Unseen; His
promise is ever performed. (Koran 19:61)

Therein they shall hear no idle talk, no cause of sin,
only the saying Peace, Peace!' (Koran 56:24-25)

See ESCHATOLOGY.

Jāpa-yōga, *see* DHIKR.

Jarraḥiyyah, *see* KHALWATIYYAH.

Jazīrat al-'Arab (lit. "the island of the Arabs"). The Arabian peninsula.

Jeddah. A city on the Red Sea, Jeddah is the main port of Mecca and Saudi Arabia. (In antiquity the port of Mecca was Shu'aybiyyah, now a beach area.) The name "Jeddah" has been variously interpreted as meaning simply "port", or "new city" (cf. *jadīd*, "new"). However, the traditional view is that it means "grandmother", normally spelled *jiddah*, that is, Eve, the grandmother of all mankind whose "sepulchre" of prodigious length once lay in a cemetery which is today covered over in the centre of the city.

Jeddah is one of the largest and busiest cities in Saudi Arabia, the Kingdom's center of commerce and the major port of entry for pilgrims coming by sea and by air. The vast King 'Abd al-'Azīz Airport was opened in 1981. Its centerpiece is the striking open-air mass transit terminal designed as a gigantic tent city to handle the millions of pilgrims who converge on the city at the time of the *ḥajj*. *See* PILGRIMAGE.

Jerusalem (Ar. *al-Quds*, "the Holy", probably

originally so called from *al-bayt al-muqaddas*, "the Holy House", that is, the Temple of Solomon). The holiest place in Islam after Mecca and Medina, Jerusalem is sometimes referred to as "the third *ḥaram*". Its holiness for Muslims derives, in the first place, from its association with the Old Testament Prophets, who are also Prophets in Islam. The association with Jesus is no less important, and Jerusalem figures in popular accounts of apocalyptic events as seen by Islam.

However, the sacred nature of Jerusalem is confirmed for Muslims above all by the Night Journey, in which the Prophet Muḥammad was brought by the angel Gabriel to the Dome of the Rock on the Temple Mount. From here they ascended together into the heavens (Koran 17:1). The Koran refers to Jerusalem as the *al-Masjid al-Aqṣā*, or "the Furthest Mosque" (that is, the Temple of Solomon) "whose precincts We [God] have blessed" (Koran 17:1). The Dome of the Rock sanctuary now stands over the rock, and nearby is the mosque today called *al-Masjid al-Aqṣā*. The Temple Mount is called *al-Ḥaram ash-Sharīf* ("the Noble Sanctuary").

Other Islamic monuments in Jerusalem include the Ashrafiyyah, Jawliyyah, As'ardiyah, Mālikiyyah, Tankiziyyah, and 'Uthmāniyyah *madrasahs*, the 'Umarī and al-Ḥamrā' mosques, fountains (those of Qa'it Bey, Bāb an-Nadhīr), *khāns* or hospices (of Muḥammad Ibn Zamīn), and gates, palaces, and mausoleums.

Jerusalem's importance is such that when 'Abd Allāh ibn az-Zubayr was elected Caliph in defiance of the Umayyads and seized Mecca in *64*/683, the Umayyads could proclaim that the pilgrimage was to be performed to Jerusalem, which they controlled, instead of Mecca.

The city first came under Muslim rule in *17*/638 when the patriarch Sophronius surrendered it to the troops of Caliph 'Umar. The Caliph visited the city after the conquest and Sophronius accompanied him to the Temple mount to search for the *miḥrāb* (prayer niche) of David, of which 'Umar had heard the Prophet speak. The Temple mount had fallen into great disorder through neglect, and was covered with refuse. The Caliph ordered it cleaned and had a place of prayer built nearby.

The Turkish Caliphs paid a great deal of attention to the city, adding more edifices to its ancient heritage. The present walls were built by Sulaymān the Magnificent. *See* al-AQṢĀ'; DOME of the ROCK; NIGHT JOURNEY; SOLOMON.

Jesus, Son of Mary (Ar. *'Īsā ibn Maryam*). He holds a singularly exalted place in Islam. The Koran says that Jesus was born of a virgin (3:45-47); that he is a "Spirit from God" (*rūḥun mina' Llāh*), and the "Word of God" (*kalimatu-Llāh*) (4:171). He is usually called "Jesus son of Mary" (*'Īsā ibn Maryam*), and his titles include Messiah (*masīḥ*), Prophet (*ǻabī*), Messenger of God (*rasūl*) and "one of those brought nigh [to God]". According to the Koran he performed various symbolic miracles; he raised the dead, brought the revealed book of the Gospel (*Injīl*), and called down as a sign from heaven a table laden with sustenance (5:112-114), which symbolizes the communion host of Christianity.

In Islam, on the authority of the Koran, Jesus has a mission as a *rasūl*, a Prophet of the highest degree who brings a restatement of God's religion (3:46-60). It is said, too, that he did not die upon the cross: "They slew him not but it appeared so to them" (4:157). A crucifixion took place, but Jesus is alive in a principial state, outside the world and time: "But God took him up to Himself. God is ever Mighty, Wise" (4:158).

It is in fact the common belief among Muslims that the crucifixion was an illusion, or that someone else was substituted for Jesus. Although this bears a resemblance to the Docetist teachings regarding the event, the reasons for the idea are quite different. While popular belief cannot be held to account, the crucifixion as a pointless charade can hardly be meet to God's purpose, and two thousand years have not shown what God could have meant by such sleight of hand. Nor does the Koran warrant such a view. Rather, it is that the crucifixion of Jesus does not play a role in the Islamic perspective any more than does his superhuman origin, for salvation in Islam results from the recognition of the Absoluteness of God and not from a sacrificial mystery. Since Islam believes that Jesus will return at the end of time, his death was no more than apparent and did not, as in Christian belief, involve a resurrection after the event. In Islam it is the absolute, or higher, reality that takes precedence in the Koran over the appearances of this world, be they of life or of death. It is this verse about the state of martyrs which holds the key to understanding "They slew him not": "Say not of those who are slain in God's way that they are dead; they are living but you perceive not" (2:154). Or: "Think not of those who are slain in the way of God that they are dead. Nay! they are living. With their Lord they have provision" (3:169).

According to various Ḥadīth, Jesus will return before the Day of Judgement, and destroy the Anti-Christ (*ad-dajjāl*) who, towards the end of time, presents an inverted version of spirituality, misleading mankind in a final and fatal delusion. Then Jesus, it is said, will bring the cycle of Adamic manifestation to an end, and inaugurate another, in what is, in effect, the Second Coming.

There are certain Ḥadīth which say that Jesus and Mary did not cry out when they were born; all other children do because, according to the symbolic interpretation, they are touched by the devil in coming into this world. In the words of the Prophet Muḥammad, Jesus and Mary were the only beings in history to be born in such a state of sinlessness.

Although the position of Jesus in Islam is extraordinary in a number of ways, even for a Prophet, that Islam should concede any idea of his divinity or admit that he is the Son of God is entirely precluded. This, or any trinitarian idea of God, or any suggestion that Jesus is somehow an hypostasis of God, is rejected by Islam.

Many Muslims think that the Christian trinity includes Mary, and certain Christian sects in ancient Arabia actually held such a belief. However, the trinitarian concept, in any form, is necessarily alien to Islam, because the principle which saves in Islam is precisely the recognition of the Divine *Unity*, the all-embracing Reality of the Absolute.

Because the Koran says that all God's Prophets have brought only the one religion of Islam, it is impossible for most Muslims to conceive that the religion brought by Jesus could, in reality, have been anything other than the Islam of the Muslim believer, the Islam of the "Five Pillars". That there is an Islam beyond form which is the religion of each Divine messenger as he faces God, or that a formless Islam is the essence of each religion, are necessarily esoteric concepts. That Christianity as it exists is based upon the doctrine that Jesus is a Divine incarnation, and that his crucifixion and resurrection have redeemed the sins of mankind and saved those who believe in him, can only be explained in the mind of the Muslim as some extraordinary historical error of interpretation or understanding.

It would perhaps seem therefore that Jesus as he is viewed in Islam, and despite the extraordinary attributes credited to him by the Koran, would actually have a role and a nature that could be interpreted into the Islamic universe only with great difficulty. Such, however, is not the case, because Christianity, like Judaism, is specifically mentioned as a revealed religion and Islamic legislation gives it a protected status. It is the nature of Jesus as a Prophet among the other Prophets of the Old Testament which is decisive for Muslims, and the disturbing elements of Christianity as it actually exists are simply set aside, placed outside of Islam, and in practice pose no great enigma, being seen as a kind of archaic survival which God in the Koran has chosen to tolerate. If this seems puzzling to Christians, they must remember that their rejection of the Prophethood of Muḥammad is an equally incredible act for Muslims. Ultimately, it is perhaps only with the fulfillment of the role that God has assigned in prophecy to Jesus at the end of time, when the world and history are swallowed up by the purely miraculous, that the different cadences of the great religions will resolve themselves into one. *See* BIBLE; DAJJĀL; MARY.

Jihād (from Ar. *jahd*, "effort"). "Holy war", a Divine institution of warfare to extend Islam into the *dar al-ḥarb* (the non-Islamic territories which are described as the "abode of struggle", or of disbelief) or to defend Islam from danger. Adult males must participate if the need arises, but not all of them, provided that a "sufficient number" (*farḍ al-kifāyah*) take it up.

An important precondition of *jihād* is a reasonable prospect of success, failing which a *jihād* should not be undertaken. According to the Sunnah, a *jihād* is not lawful unless it involves the summoning of unbelievers to belief, and the *jihād* must end when order is restored, that is, when the unbelievers have accepted either Islam or a protected status within Islam, or when Islam is no longer under threat. It is impossible to undertake a *jihād* against Muslims.

In colonial times, when many Islamic countries were under non-Muslim domination – an anomalous condition from the point of Islamic law – it was concluded that, provided Islam was not prohibited, and indeed as long as certain of the institutions peculiar to it were allowed to continue, holy war could not be justified.

Although the essential elements of a mosque remain constant, the architectural style may vary greatly. The *Masjid-i-Shaykh Luṭfullāh* in Isfahan (*above*) is perhaps the finest and most important work of the Ṣafavid period (1501-1732). Built on the *Maydān-i-Shāh,* the great polo ground laid out under the direction of Shāh 'Abbās (1587-1628) when the capital of Persia was transferred from Qazvīn to Isfahan in 1598, it has the ornate tiled façade and dome typical of Persian mosques of the period. *See* MOSQUE.

The mosque of Sultan Aḥmad in Istanbul (*below*) completed in 1616, is known as the "Blue Mosque" because of its blue tilework. Both are expansive and ample-domed buildings based on Byzantine models. The Dome of the Rock in Jerusalem (*below right*) was founded by the Caliph 'Abd al-Malik in 687 (completed in 691), from which the *mi 'rāj* ("Night Journey") of the Prophet began. *Opposite bottom left* is the Badshahi Mosque in Lahore, Pakistan; *opposite bottom right* is the resplendent courtyard of the *madrasah* Ben Youssef in Marrakesh, Morocco. The Great Mosque of Cordova is the world's third largest mosque. A Christian church since the 15th century, it was begun in the 8th century, and frequently added to, notably in the 10th century. The hexafoil arches in two tiers (*far right*), whose nineteen aisles form the sanctuary, represent an important departure in Islamic architecture, in the Hispano-Mauresque style. The central dome (*right*) in front of the *miḥrāb* was completed by al-Ḥakam II (961-76) and is supported by a series of intersecting ribs. *See* al-AQṢĀ'; DOME OF THE ROCK; MADRASAH; MIḤRĀB; MOSQUE; NIGHT JOURNEY.

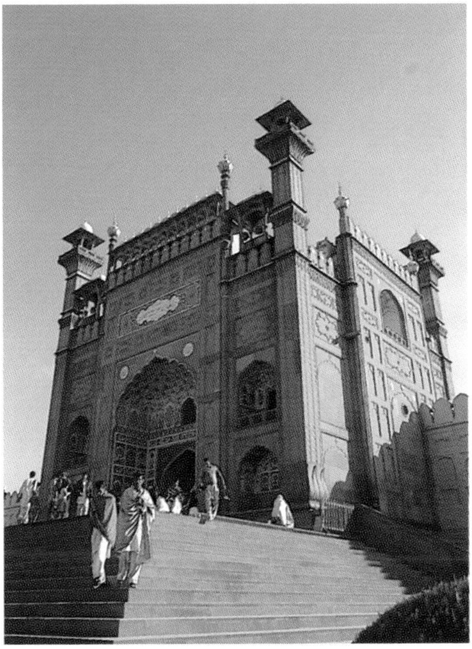

The Djenna mosque in Mali (*left*), made of clay and earth rammed together, is a fine example of the indigenous mosque architecture which developed in countries bordering the Sahara. The spiral minaret of the *Malwiyyah* at Samarra', Iraq (*below*) is thought to have been based upon the form of pre-Islamic ziggurats. The largest ancient mosque still extant, it was begun by al-Mutawakkil in 847/1443. But the largest mosque in the world is now the Shah Alam Mosque in Selangor, Malaysia (*below left*). The *madrasah* school in the Great Mosque complex in Samarkand (*opposite*), where Tamerlane is buried, features the lobed dome and extensive external tiling characteristic of 15th- and 16th-century Persian mosque architecture. The band of ornamental Kufic on the minaret reads "Eternity is for God" (*al-Baqa' li-Llāh). See* MADRASAH; MINARET; MOSQUE; TIMURIDS.

The interior of the al-Aqṣā' Mosque in Jerusalem (*opposite*) with the carved wooden *mimbar* and the *miḥrāb* which indicates the *qiblah,* the direction of Mecca. The Ardabil carpet (*left*) was woven for the Ismail Shah Mosque, Tabrīz, in *918*/1512. Almost certainly the largest ever woven in Persia, its fine decoration includes traceries of flowers, Koranic inscriptions and hanging mosque lamps. The 13th-century incense burner (*below*) exemplifies the achievements of Islamic metalwork in a variety of materials, including copper, brass and bronze. *See* al-AQṢĀ'; DOME OF THE ROCK; MIḤRĀB; MINBAR; QIBLAH.

Although some branches of Islam prohibit the veneration of tombs, there is, nevertheless, an important heritage of funerary architecture, the most famous example being the Taj Mahal (*above*) near Agra, built by Shah Jahan (1628-1658) in memory of his wife Mumtaz Mahal, and completed in 1648. The mosque of the shrine of 'Ali, the *Mazār-i-sharīf* (*below*), is in Afghanistan. *See* MAZĀR-i SHARĪF.

Although opportunistic calls to *jihād* have been made sporadically when the interests of particular political leaders could be advanced by such warfare, they have never received general support from the religious authorities (*'ulamā'*).

Those who die in a genuine *jihād* – and the laws determining this are complex – are considered to be martyrs (*shuhadā'*), who, as such, have special merit, and enter paradise directly. The Khārijites made *jihād* a sixth pillar of the religion, and it is still so among their modern descendants, the 'Ibādites. On the other hand, the *jihād* is legally impossible for the Twelve-Imām Shī'ites until the return of the Hidden Imām. A genuine *jihād*, as opposed to merely political warfare, has rarely been invoked since Islam's original struggle for survival against the Meccans.

A *4th*/10th century sermon by a preacher named Ibn Nubata exhorts thus to *jihād*:

> How long, ye men, will ye hear warning and heed not?
> And how long will ye abide the whipping and stir not?
> Your ears shake off the Preacher's words. Or are your hearts too haughty to hear? The Fiend has roused up those others to fight for his lies, and they rise up and follow,
> While the Omnipotent summons you to His Truth, and you ignore His Call.
> Beasts fight for mate and cub; birds will die for their nests; yet Prophet and Revelation have they none. But you, who understand, and have the Law and wisdom, scatter away like startled camels before their foes.
> God claims your faith and steadfastness; God promises His Help and Victory again.
> Do you not really trust Him?
> Do you doubt His Justice or His Goodness?
> Give your soul, man, wholly up to Him unto Whom it doth belong. Put no trust in prudence: your prudence will not put off your appointed term to die.
> War! War! ye men of heart!
> Victory! Sure Victory! ye resolute!
> Paradise! Paradise for you who march on!
> And Hell! Hell for you who fly!
> Victory's reward in this world, and the martyr's in the Next; and of these two how much the sweeter is the last!
> Then stand by God; for Him who helpeth God, will God most surely help. (22:40)

And the Koran says:

> Leave is given to those who fight because
> they were wronged – surely God is able
> to help them –
> who were expelled from their habitations
> without right, except that they say
> 'Our Lord is God.' Had God not driven back
> the people, some by means of others,
> there had been destroyed cloisters and churches,
> oratories and mosques, wherein God's Name
> is much mentioned. Assuredly God will
> help him who helps Him – surely God is
> All-strong, All-mighty... (22:40-42)

It is said popularly, that *jihād* was once the eradication of polytheism and false belief and the spread of Islam. Then it became defense of Islam; but it is also removing evil with the tongue or by an act, or when that is not possible, by condemning it in the heart. *See* FIVE PILLARS; MARTYRS.

al-Jīlānī, 'Abd al-Qādir, *see* 'ABD al-QĀDIR al-JĪLĀNĪ.

al-Jīlī, 'Abd al-Karīm (*767-820*/1365-1417). A famous mystic, born in Jīl near Baghdad. He was a Sufi of the school of Ibn 'Arabī and wrote the book *al-Insān al-Kāmil* ("the Perfect Man"). This is a treatise on the doctrine of realization of the true self. *See* al-INSĀN al-KĀMIL.

Jinn (from which the English word *genie*). The inhabitants of the subtle and immaterial – or subtly material – world, the *'ālam al-malakūt* into which the material and physical world is plunged, as if into a liquid. If we picture a room in our mind, the "medium" in which that imagined room exists supports form, but is itself subtle; it is the *'ālam al-malakūt*. In traditional cosmology, the physical world is a "crystallization", or projection, out of the subtle world, the "ether"; the "ether" is a projection out of the surrounding formless, or Angelic, world; and the Angelic world is projected out of Being (*see* FIVE DIVINE PRESENCES).

Jinn are the inhabitants of the subtle world, some of whom are "non-central" beings like the non-human creatures of this world, whilst others are central beings, like men, *jinn* with free will, endowed with the Intellect and capable of grasping Reality, and thus capable of being saved. The *jinn* who occupy this central state have therefore religions and revelations, and some of their religions correspond to the religions of the world of men.

During the Prophet's journey to Ṭā'if he recited the Koran at night in the desert and a party of the *jinn* came, listened, and believed. Later their chiefs came to the Prophet and made a *bay'ah*, or an allegiance, with him on the spot which is today the "Mosque of the *Jinn*" in Mecca.

Satan, considered to be a *jinn* who was originally an Angel, forfeited his Angelic nature by disobeying God. Angels, who belong to the formless world, the *'ālam al-jabarūt*, and are formless as the odors of perfumes have to take on a subtle nature in order to appear to men. In other words, they take on a substance of the subtle world, which is formal (in that what exists in that world has "form") and then they assume a visible "form". For example, magnetic fields are only visible when they work upon a substance that responds to them, and if Angels appear, they must do so in an "ethereal" form.

The Koran says that the *jinn* were created of "smokeless fire" (55:15) whereas man was created of clay, as by a potter; the Angels are created of light. Some *jinn* are friendly to mankind, and others hostile; some are beautiful, and others, the *'ifrīt* and *ghūl* (from which the word *ghoul* derives), are hideous. Solomon is famed for his power to command the *jinn* to his bidding, in building the temple, and in the working of prodigies (38:37-41). Islamic lore says, moreover, that the lives of certain *jinn* are incomparably longer than human lifetimes, and that there are *jinn* alive today in the subtle world who were alive in the time of the Prophet.

Sometimes the Koran addresses men and *jinn* together, as in the Sūrat ar-Raḥmān which is directed throughout to that duality. It says: "O ye two having weight" (*thaqalān*), meaning the two species of creation having *form* (55:31): and "O company of *jinn* and men, if ye are able to pass beyond the regions of the heavens and the earth, then pass beyond! Ye shall not pass, except by authority. Which then, of the favors of your Lord, do the two of you deny?" (55:33-34). *See also* ANGELS.

Jinnah, Muḥammad 'Alī (*1293-1367*/1876-1948). The first president of Pakistan. Born in Karachi, he studied law in Britain and entered into politics in India in 1910. From 1913 he played an active role in the Muslim League, whose president he became in 1916. He was a Niẓārī Ismaīlī.

At first he took part in efforts by the Muslim League and the Congress Party of India to promote Hindu-Muslim cooperation in the political sphere. He withdrew from the Congress in 1930 to pursue a policy which led to the partition of India at independence, and the birth of Pakistan as a nation in August 1947.

Jizyah. A tax formerly levied on such non-Muslim adult males as were able to pay it, provided that they belonged to a religion recognized as Divinely revealed, that is, were "People of the Book" (*Ahl al-Kitāb*). Pagans conquered and brought into the Islamic state had, in theory, either to accept Islam or death; however, this provision was rarely, if ever, applied; the Harranians, who were Hellenist Pagans, eventually obtained the status of people with a revelation and were called "Sabians". The infirm and poor were excluded from paying the tax.

The basis of the *jizyah* is the Koran (9:29):

> Fight those who believe not in God and the Last Day
> and do not forbid what God and His Messenger
> have forbidden – such men as practise not the
> religion of truth, being of those who have been given
> the Book – until they pay the tribute out of hand
> and have been humbled.

It was normally understood to be a tax for civil protection and the upkeep of the army, but it did in practice sometimes take on the aspect of a tribute. The minimum *jizyah* was one dinar. The *kharāj*, another and later tax on non-Muslims, and one not indicated in the Koran, was based on the yield from land. *See* AHL al-KITĀB.

Jñāna Marga, *see* MA'RIFAH.

Job, *see* AYYŪB.

John the Baptist, *see* YAḤYĀ.

Jonah, *see* **YŪNUS.**

Jordan. Hashemite Kingdom of Jordan.

Population 5,198,000. 92% Muslim, 8% Christian. Most of Jordan is desert and the only port is Aqaba, on the Red Sea. In Arabic the country is called Urdunn, and was, in Ummayad times a "military district" called a *jund*. The present Kingdom sprang from the Emirate of Transjordan which was created from the disintegration of the Ottoman Empire. The first ruler was the Emir 'Abd Allāh, later King, son of the Sherif of Mecca, ruler of the Hejaz who had aided the British during the First World War. He took the title of King when the country became independent of the British mandate in 1946. Jordan came into being when East Jerusalem and the West bank were annexed in 1948 after the creation of Israel and the war which followed. In the Arab Israeli war of 1967 both were lost to Israel, and in 1988 King Hussein renounced them which led to the peace treaty with Israel of 1994. Jordan is a constitutional monarchy since 1952.

Joseph, *see* YŪSUF.

Journey, Night, *see* NIGHT JOURNEY.

Judaism, *see* BANŪ ISRĀ'ĪL; DÖNMEH.

Judge, *see* QĀḌI.

Judgement, Day of, *see* YAWM ad-DĪN.

al-Junayd, Abū-l-Qāsim ibn Muḥammad (d. *297*/910). One of the most famous of the early Sufis, who taught in Baghdad, he was a disciple of the Sufi Sarī aṣ-Ṣaqaṭī. An important figure in the development of Sufi doctrine, like Ḥasan of Basra before him and Imām ash-Shādhilī after him, al-Junayd was widely respected and quoted by other Sufis, to the point of being known as the Sultan or Sayyid ("lord") of the *'ārifīn* ("knowers of God").

He wrote no books, but his teachings are reported in the *Kitāb al-Lumā'* of as-Sarrāj (d. *378*/788), in the letters which he wrote, and in the writings of other Sufis. The doctrine as formulated by him is systematic and sober; he advocated the integration of mysticism into ordinary life, commending that Sufis live as householders and not as wandering mendicants. His approach is characterized by an attitude in which Divine knowledge is stabilized within the soul in this world. This the Sufis call *ṣawḥ* ("sobriety"), as opposed to *sukr* ("inebriation" or "ecstasy").

In the first centuries of the Hijrah, Islam was exposed to many influences in the course of its expansion. Converts from Iranian religions in particular brought with them a tendency to deify the major exponents of religious realization, whether Saints or charismatic leaders. This gave rise to the emergence of so-called "drunken Sufis", such as Bāyazīd al-Bisṭāmī, al-Ḥallāj and Ibn Abī-l-Khayr, with their intriguing implications of a "personal" union with God. Al-Junayd became the spokesman of rigor and the defender of a Sufism firmly planted in exoteric orthodoxy. A Sufi reported:

> *Intoxication* is a mystic term denoting ecstatic love for God; *Sobriety* proposes the attainment of some end. Bāyazīd and his disciples, who think Intoxication the higher way, maintain that Sobriety stabilizes human attributes which are the greatest of all Veils between God and man. But my own Shaykh, following al-Junayd, used to say that Intoxication is a playground for children, and Sobriety a mortal battleground for men.

Al-Junayd was a merchant and he kept a shop in Baghdad. He rejected al-Ḥallāj from his circle saying "I do not accept madmen". To al-Ḥallāj's assertion that "I am the Reality" (*Ana al-Ḥaqq*), tradition has al-Junayd respond: "No. It is *through* Reality that you exist."

In his approach to *ma'rifah*, or gnosis, al-Junayd emphasized the aspect of witness and consciousness (*shuhūd*), rather than that of Being (*wujūd*), and the aphorism, "everything that you see is the Act of One" is the very essence of his approach. Of *tawḥīd*, or union with God, al-Junayd said: "It is the removing of the temporal from the eternal." The opposition of the *shuhūd* ("consciousness") school to *wujūd* ("being") turns precisely on the danger of *wujūd* leading to an identification of the world with God. *See* al-BISṬĀMĪ; al-ḤALLĀJ; SUFISM; TAWḤĪD.

Jundishāpūr (also called Gandisapora, Gundishahpur, etc.). An academy founded in the third century near Ahvāz, in the region of modern Sānābād in Khuzistān, when Persia was ruled by the Sassanids. The academy was founded by oriental Christians who became Nestorians after the council of Nicea. It was a center which transmitted the study of Hellenistic learning and philosophy to the Muslims.

Translations were made here from Greek to Syriac, and later to Arabic. In 'Abbāsid times it was also an important school of medicine teaching the methods of Hippocrates and Galen.

A number of famous medical figures were associated with it, notably the Bakhtishishu family and Ḥunayn ibn Isḥāq, all of whom were Nestorians.

Juvaini, 'Alā ad-Dīn 'Aṭā' Mālik, *see* JUWAYNĪ, 'ALĀ ad-DĪN 'ATĀ' MĀLIK.

al-Juwaynī, 'Abd al-Mālik (d. *478*/1085). A Persian Ash'arite theologian who fled persecution under Tughril Beg and took refuge in the Hejaz, teaching at Mecca and Medina. Because of this he acquired the epithet *Imām al-Ḥaramayn*, "the Imām of the two Sanctuaries".

The initial hostility shown by the Saljūqs towards Ash'arism receded and finally vanished as awareness of the ideological threat represented by the Fāṭimids brought them to realize that Ash'arite doctrine, being clear, vigorous, and unambiguous, provided a defensive weapon. As a result, al-Juwaynī became a protégé of the Vizier Niẓām al-Mulk, who founded the Niẓāmiyyah school at Nayshābūr for him. Al-Juwaynī was one of the teachers of al-Ghazālī and also of al-Anṣārī.

Al-Juwaynī wrote, among a vast number of works, the *Ghiyāth al-Umam* ("the Saviour of Nations") which argued that the Caliphate, by tradition a prerogative of the Quraysh, could be held if necessary by whoever could assure just government; it is likely that, in writing it, he had Niẓām al-Mulk in mind.

al-Juwaynī, 'Alā ad-Dīn 'Aṭā' Mālik (*623-682*/1226-1283). A Persian historian, of a distinguished Khorasan family, his grandfather and father were in the service of the Khwārizm-Shāhīs. When the Mongols drove the Khwārizm-Shāhī Sultan Muḥammad and his son Jalāl ad-Dīn out of the region, Juwaynī's father Baha' ad-Dīn entered the service of the Mongols, administering the conquered territories and frequently visited Qaraqorum.

Al-Juwaynī succeeded his father and accompanied Hūlāgū Khān on his invasions of Persia. He was present at the conquest of Alamūt and inspected the famous library of the Assassins, rescuing what he called "choice books" and burning others which he considered heretical. Al-Juwaynī, a Twelve-Imām Shī'ite, became the governor for the Mongol Il-Khanids of the territories which had been directly ruled by the 'Abbāsids and so took up residence in Baghdad. He acquired great wealth and authority, but several times was accused before the Mongols, by rivals eager to unseat him, of conspiring with the Mamlūks or of embezzling fortunes. These accusations led to swings in his position with the Mongols towards the end of his life. He died of grief, and was buried in Ṭabrīz.

In *658*/1260 al-Juwaynī wrote an erudite history of the Mongols in a highly sophisticated Persian style. It is called *Tarīkh-i Jahān Kūshā* ("The History of the World Conqueror"), and included a detailed history of the Fāṭimids and the Assassins ("a sect of people...in whose hearts was rooted a fellow-feeling with the Magians"). *See* MONGOLS.

K

Ka'bah (lit. "cube"). The large cubic stone structure, covered with a black cloth, which stands in the center of the Grand Mosque of Mecca. In one corner, the Ka'bah contains the Black Stone. Neither the stone nor the Ka'bah are objects of worship, but they represent a sanctuary consecrated to God since time immemorial, and it is towards the Ka'bah that Muslims orient themselves in prayer; thus the Ka'bah is a spiritual center, a support for the concentration of consciousness upon the Divine Presence. (If one makes the ritual prayer inside the Ka'bah, it can be made in any direction; this is also true at the antipodes of Mecca in the South Pacific Ocean.) The Ka'bah is also called the "holy house" (*al-bayt al-ḥarām*) and the "Ancient house" (*al-bayt al-'atīq*). The Black Stone (*al-ḥajar al-aswad*) is in the southeast corner, set one and one-half meters from the ground. In the opposite corner, set somewhat lower, is another stone of a reddish color called the "stone of felicity" (*ḥajar as-sa'ādah*). It is the center of the Ka'bah which marks the direction of the *qiblah*, the focal point of ritual prayer. Overhanging the roof on one side is the *mith'āb* or rainspout. The foundation at the base of the Ka'bah is called the *shadrawān*. The space between the Black Stone and the door is the *al-multazam*, "the place to hold on to". Around the Ka'bah is a restricted precinct called the *ḥaram* of Mecca; this, in fact, surrounds the city on all sides, in some directions as far as twelve miles or twenty kilometers. In this precinct the taking of any kind of life (except that of noxious or dangerous creatures) is not allowed, and only Muslims are allowed to enter.

The Ka'bah was originally founded, tradition says, by Adam, and after his death rebuilt by his son Seth. When the time came, it was rebuilt by Abraham and his son Ishmael. This Ka'bah was built without a roof but with doors at ground level on the east and the west sides. When it was finished, Abraham was commanded by God to go to Mount Thābir nearby and call mankind to pilgrimage to "the ancient house" (*al-bayt al-'atīq*).

Afterwards, the Ka'bah was rebuilt by the clan of the Amālikah, descendents of Noah, and then by the Banū Jurhum, who also descended from Noah through Qaḥṭān, the Joktan of the Bible. Several hundred years before the revelation of the Koran, the Ka'bah was rebuilt again by Qusayy ibn Qilab, who had led the Quraysh tribe to Mecca. At that time, according to the historian Azraqī, the Ka'bah, without a roof, was 4.5 meters high, and there were venerated stones in all four corners.

Eighteen years before the Hijrah it was rebuilt again. A Byzantine ship which had been wrecked in Mecca's port of Shu'aybiyyah provided the wood for the Ka'bah, which was built in alternate layers of teakwood and stone by a Coptic carpenter called Baqūm. When the time came to replace the Black Stone, strife broke out between various persons demanding the honor of putting it back, leading to so serious a dispute that bloodshed was threatened. A solution to the dispute being asked of Muḥammad, then known as the "Trustworthy" (*al-Amīn*), and not yet called to his prophetic mission, who, as if it were a sign from God, had appeared among the disputers at a crucial moment, he invited the leaders of the clans to carry the stone by holding a cloth onto which it had been placed; he then lifted up the stone himself and set it in the corner of the wall.

After the establishment of Islam, Caliphs 'Umar and 'Uthmān both felt the need to enlarge the Mosque (*al-Masjid al-Ḥarām*) around the Ka'bah. They compensated the owners of the surrounding houses which had to be demolished in order to increase the circumambulation area (*al-maṭāf*), and 'Umar was the first to build an enclosure around the Ka'bah, less than the height of a man, with gates and lamps. 'Uthmān introduced covered porticos for prayers.

When in *64*/684 Mecca, then under occupation by the insurgent 'Abd Allāh ibn az-Zubayr, was besieged by the army of Yazīd, the Umayyad, a flaming arrow from one of the besiegers set fire to the Ka'bah, which was destroyed. The heat cracked the Black Stone into three pieces. On examining the original foundation of the now demolished Ka'bah, Ibn az-Zubayr concluded that the Ka'bah had previously included the enclosure to one side (*al-ḥijr*) containing the graves of Ishmael and Hagar. He therefore rebuilt it on a larger scale, increasing its greatest length to 26 cubits from the previous 18. He also made it higher, raising it from 18 to 27 cubits, and built it of stone, with two doors. The Black Stone was repaired and held together by a silver band around the three pieces. He brought mosaics and columns from a church in the Yemen (originally built by Abrahah who had wished his church to rival the religious attraction of Mecca), using the mosaics for decoration and setting three polychrome marble columns inside. In the tradition of the Caliph Mu'āwiyah, Ibn az-Zubayr covered the Ka'bah with black silk.

'Abd Allāh ibn az-Zubayr, who had declared himself Caliph in opposition to the Umayyads, was slain by the troops of the Caliph 'Abd al-Mālik ibn Marwān led by al-Ḥajjāj ibn Yūsuf, in *73*/692. Al-Ḥajjāj, for his part, disliked the changes which had been made and reduced the Ka'bah to its former size, leaving a semicircular wall surrounding the *ḥijr*, and the *ḥijr* itself, outside the Ka'bah. Further building was done by the Caliphs Mahdī, Mu'tamid, and Mu'tadid. Mahdī extended the *maṭāf*, and added three rows of colonnades, himself participating in the work. By *167*/782, the Ka'bah had much the appearance it has today.

In *979*/1571 the famous architect Sīnān, who had already built many resplendent mosques in Istanbul and Turkey, began rebuilding the Mosque around the Ka'bah, the previous mosque having been demolished the year before on the orders of the Ottoman Sultan Selim II. For the sacred mosque, *al-Masjid al-Ḥarām*, Sīnān created a colonnade of 892 columns of marble and stone over which were set 500 arches and cupolas. The interior decoration of gold designs and calligraphy was the work of 'Abd Allāh al-Muftī. The whole was completed by *994*/1586; it had seven minarets and nineteen entrances, and there was prayer space for 12,000 in the covered part of the mosque; another 24,000 could pray in the open courtyard. In *1030*/1620 floods swept away the Station of Abraham (*Maqām Ibrāhīm*), the lamps, and part of the walls of the Ka'bah. Sultan Mūrād ordered extensive repairs which did not, however, involve any restructuring.

However, from *1375*/1955 a massive program of enlargement and rebuilding of the mosque was initiated and carried out in the reign of King Fayṣal of Saudi Arabia. In *1377*/1957 cracks were found in the Ka'bah and repaired – the first work on the structure since *1039*/1629. In this rebuilding the mosque was considerably enlarged. It has since then perhaps held several hundreds of thousands of worshipers at a time. The *sa'y* course, which until then had been outside the mosque, was roofed over and is now within the precincts of the mosque, which was rebuilt on two levels on both of which the ritual circumambulation (*ṭawāf*) is now performed.

The architects had originally recommended that the mosque of Sīnān be torn down, to be replaced by an entirely new structure. King Fayṣal thereupon called a conference of architects to discuss the question, who proceeded to make the same recommendation. To his very great credit, King Fayṣal insisted that the rebuilding and expansion of the mosque conserve as much as possible of the mosque of Sīnān; this was done, thereby saving this magnificent monument from demolition.

The dimensions of the present day Ka'bah are: the north-east wall 12.63 meters, the eastern wall 11.22 meters, the western wall 13.10 meters, and the northwest wall 11.03 meters (it is not completely regular). Its height is 13 meters. The door on the northern side is 2 meters from the ground and is 1.7 meters wide.

A new *kiswah* (cover or cladding) is made for the Ka'bah each year; it is a black cloth with black calligraphic patterns woven into it, and a band of Koranic calligraphy in gold thread around the top portion. The old *kiswah* is removed and cut up after the annual pilgrimage and the pieces are distributed to pilgrims. The Ka'bah is then covered with a new *kiswah*; while it is being replaced a temporary white covering is placed upon the Kabah.

The 12th century Sufi Ibn 'Arabī said that the Ka'bah represents Being. As the Adamic temple, it is the first temple of mankind; and as the temple of the last religion, it is the final temple of mankind, the once forgotten sanctuary, the keystone. In Christianity, the end of the cycle of Adamic creation is marked by the symbolism of the perfect city, the descent of the new Jerusalem from heaven. The perfect city is a crystalline, geometric symbol from the mineral world, in complementary opposition to the organic symbolism of the beginning of the cycle, which is the garden, vegetation, and, above all, the tree of the knowledge of good and evil at its centre. Islam shares the symbol of the garden of the beginning with Judaism and Christianity, but its symbol of the center at the end of time is not that of the city, the abstract, man-made habitat that replaces nature, but of the geometric essence of the city, reduced to its simplest form. This is nothing more than a cube, the abstraction of a crystal, the cube of the Ka'bah. Thus the eschatological paradigm of the symbolic "squaring of the circle" is completed, or transposed; the sphere is made cube, the perfect potentiality of the beginning reduced to the perfect completion and stability of the end. The juxtaposition of the organic and the crystalline is also prominent in the decorative calligraphy that is so striking a feature of Islamic architecture: here, the words of the Koran, the crystallization of Divine speech, intertwine with floral motifs; the Intellect intertwines with existence.

One should add that the Ka'bah represents the "ultimate enclosure" for the Divine Presence that the Old Testament calls the Shekhinah (also "Schechina"). After the covenant with Abraham the Shekhinah "dwelt" in the Ark until, when the Jews ceased to be nomads and Solomon built the Temple, the Shekhinah dwelt in the Holy of Holies. The New Testament says that when Jesus' body was pierced with the lance, the veil of the Temple was rent in twain and the Shekhinah went out of the Holy of Holies into the world. Thus the Ka'bah is both the Ark of the Covenant and the Holy of Holies, not in the sense of enclosing the Divine Presence but, rather, as the center of a Holy of Holies that stretches out in all directions; thus the whole earth becomes the locus of prayer for every Muslim, who each day fulfills the role that the Jewish high priest performed only on the Day of Atonement. Since Islam is the return to the primordiality of Adam, the whole earth is once more symbolically the paradisal garden, from any point of which, man, like Adam, may talk in sacred speech with God. *See also* BLACK STONE; ḤIJR; TAWĀF.

Kābil and Hābil, *see* CAIN and ABEL; IBN KHALDŪN.

al-Kaff, *see* "HAND OF FĀṬIMAH".

Kāfir (lit. "he who conceals by covering", plur. *kafirūn, kuffār, kafarah, kifār*). The *kāfir* is "one who refuses to see the truth; an infidel" who rejects the evidence of Divine Revelation through the mission of the Prophet Muḥammad or the Divine messengers before him, and who is thus ungrateful to God, and an atheist. One can sometimes hear Muslims refer to Christians as *kafirūn*; but this is loose usage and incorrect according to Islamic law; the People of the Book (and those who believe in God) are *not kafirūn*. Such a misusage once caused a scandal in an Egyptian court of law. *See* KUFR; SHIRK.

Kāhin (a priest, wizard, or soothsayer, akin to the Hebrew *kohen*. Feminine: *kāhinah*). In pre-Islamic Arabia, soothsayers were often the guardians of sanctuaries considered to be holy places, some of which were on heights, and often in groves of trees, that is, places where there was underground water. It was believed that the *kāhins* had supernatural powers; they could confer blessings or cast curses; and remove curses cast by others. They were consulted by those seeking solutions to problems, to find lost animals, and to settle disputes. The *kāhin* would speak with his "familiar spirit" (perhaps his own psychic projection), look into people's souls, and read the future. Sometimes in a consultation the *kāhin* would go into a trance and make pronouncements in rythmical prose called *saj'*.

The Prophet's grandfather, 'Abd al-Muṭṭalib, consulted such a soothsayer when he sought to find an alternative to fulfilling a vow to sacrifice his youngest son 'Abd Allāh, who became the father of Muḥammad. The Meccans also used special sacred divining arrows (*azlam*) without points, which were kept at the Ka'bah, to make supernatural inquiries about courses of action. This practice was forbidden by the Koran: "...partition by the divining arrows, that is ungodliness..." (5:3) and also: "...idols and divining arrows are an abomination..."(5:90).

After the death of the Prophet, revolts to Islam (*ḥurūb ar-ridda*) arose in Arabia which were often led by soothsayers. One was a woman, called the *Kāhinah*; another was the revolt of Musaylamah, and another that of al-Aswad.

Mukhtar (d. *67*/687), who led the revolt of the Kaysaniyyah which attempted to push Muḥammad ibn Ḥanafiyyah (the son of 'Alī by the Ḥanifite woman) to power, came to Iraq, claimed to be inspired by the Angel Gabriel, and preached in a trance-like state in *saj'* prose, in the style of the *kāhins*, that Muḥammad ibn Ḥanifiyyah was the Mahdī. *See* 'ABD al-MUṬṬALIB; KAYSANIYYAH; MANDALAH; MUSAYLAMAH.

Kairouan (*Qayrawān*). A city in Tunisia with a population of over 100,000, famous for its Grand Mosque, the *Zaytūnah* and the Islamic university of the same name. The city was founded by 'Uqba ibn Nafi in *50*/670 and became the capital (*184-297*/800-909) of the Aghlabids and later, the first capital of the Fāṭimids (*297-309*/909-921).

al-Kalabādhī, Abū Bakr (d. circa *390*/1000) A Sufi, author of a compendium of Sufism entitled *Kitāb al-Ta'arruf li madhhab ahl at-Taṣawwuf* (translated as "The Doctrine of the Sufis").

Kalām (lit. "speech", or "dialectic"; applied to theology which is the "study of Divine Speech. This use of the word probably follows Greek usage in philosophy as in *logos*, "word" for "logic"). Islamic scholastic theology. Theologians were called *ahl al-kalām* ("the people of *kalām*") or *mutakallimūn*. After the death of the Prophet, the Muslim community tried to carry on applying established precedents in regards to legal decisions and beliefs. The people who preserved the corpus of doctrine, law, and custom, were called *ahl al-ḥadīth*, the traditionalists. As new circumstances arose with the expansion of the empire, there was a need for unprecedented decisions, and guidelines for the future. This gave rise to the Schools of Law, who constituted the Sunnīs, namely, those who follow tradition. At the same time, however, the community was confronted with certain new issues, which, naturally, evoked different responses and opinions. One of them concerned the question of the fitness to rule of a ruler who committed sins. This produced the Khārijites, with their declared opinion that the commission of sin was an absolute disqualification even to be called a Muslim. This in its turn called forth the Murji'ites who maintained that the question of sin should be left to the Divine Mercy, to be determined after death. Thereupon the question of responsibility for sin led to the school of the Qadariyyah, who held man to be absolutely free, the creator of his acts, and completely responsible for them. The reaction to this was the emergence of the Jabariyyah, who held that man's actions were completely predetermined.

These schools came about essentially in response to isolated questions, and none of them attempted a systematic interpretation of revelation. In addition, moreover, to these movements or schools, *ad hoc* responses to problematic situations and cases were made by individuals with greater or lesser influence such as the Companions, mystics such as Ḥasan of Basra, and political leaders.

Theology was originally considered to be part of canon law (*fiqh*), although it was known as the "greater" canon law, *al-fiqh al-akbar*, and it was the Mu'tazilites who constituted the first real school of theology, insofar as they sought to apply reason to a broad range of questions and to make use of the methods of argument, reason and dialectic. With these methods they generated a set of answers which they held to be dogma. Although briefly in vogue, Mu'tazilite solutions were in some ways not orthodox, that is, they did not appear to reflect an adequate understanding of spiritual reality, and this led to vigorous objections on the part of religious thinkers; by the middle of the *4th*/10th century the Mu'tazilites had run their course.

Al-Ash'arī (d. *324*/944) was originally a Mu'tazilite, but abandoned them at the same time as adapting certain of their rational methods into Sunnīsm. He thus became the real founder of theology along with his follower, al-Baqillāni (d. *403*/1012), the independent al-Māturīdī (d. *333*/944), and aṭ-Ṭahāwī (d. *321*/933). In fact, al-Ash'arī's ideas changed with time, and do not in every case coincide with those of the school which bears his name. At first, Ash'arism, which was not a perfect solution, ran into strong opposition, and Ash'arites such as al-Juwaynī had at one time to flee persecution. But in the *5th*/11th century the Sunnī Islam of the Saljūqs came under attack from the doctrines of the Fāṭimids, and the only viable counter-weapon was the broad response to religious questions which the Ash'arites had built up. They were therefore rehabilitated, to become the foremost defenders of Sunnī theology. They, and the school of al-Māturīdī, who was intuitional and less concerned with rational exposition, but in practice quite similar, have remained the standard theology of Islam ever since. (*For the Creed of al-Ash'arī, see* CREED.)

Ash'arite theology in its day presented certain problems, and still does if accepted at its face value. But it was a viable attempt to combine revelation and reason to the minimum requirements of causality. Those whose needs for causality went beyond the minimum, naturally went beyond Ash'arism. Muslim philosophers in many cases provided extremely intelligent answers to intellectual problems, but never succeeded in integrating answers based on logic, Pythagoras, Plato, Aristotle, and Neoplatonism, with a religious expression accessible to ordinary believers. It is for this reason that certain critics – who actually misunderstood them – claimed that they were propagating a double doctrine: intellectual arguments for the elite, and blind belief for the masses. The mystics produced their explanations, which depended even more upon the integration of philosophic intelligence with faith; but these explanations were at the same time highly intuitional, and could be grasped only by those with an aspiration to a spiritual path. Nevertheless since, in later Islam, half – or more than half – of the populations of whole countries belonged to Sufi orders, there is no doubt that the Sufis did produce an exceptionally rich theology which has not been fully assessed or appreciated because much of it was, and still is, restricted to oral teachings.

It was al-Ghazālī who took large measures of philosophy, theology, and mysticism and put them together in a synthesis broad enough to serve the needs of the community at large, and indeed, the whole civilization. His synthesis remains functional to this day, and in making it he performed for Islam, in his person and his intellect, a function analogous to that which Paul and the Church Councils realised for Christianity. (Interestingly, Shahrastānī, the Persian historian of religions, says that Paul brought philosophy to the "religion of Peter").

Kalām is dominated by the school of al-Ash'arī. Although certain aspects of Ash'arism seem harsh, it must be remembered that Al-Ash'arī was concerned to combat certain Rationalist complacencies and was zealous in insisting on God's transcendence. God deals with man in accordance with his acts; he does not send the pious to hell, but for al-Ash'arī the transcendence of God means that He might do so. Such Ash'arite dogmatisms have in practice been mitigated by attitudes borrowed from the school of al-Māturīdī. The latter prevailed chiefly in Asia and more readily accepted antinomial formulations ("antinomial" here referring to the metaphysical paradigm and having nothing to do with the sects of that name).

For the Ash'arites, the Koran is uncreated in its essence, but created in its sounds and letters; that is, created in its written form and when recited, while inwardly it is the Word of God and Divine. (Al-Ash'arī himself seems to have inclined in the end to the Ḥanbalī belief that the Koran is uncreated even in its written letters and pronounced sounds. Shī'ites, following the Mu'tazilite theology in many respects, believe the Koran to be created.) The Ash'arites hold that God's Attributes are eternal and distinct from His Essence; that God is not All-Powerful because He possesses the attribute of being All-Powerful, as the Mu'tazilites would have it, but that the Attribute proceeds from God because He is All-Powerful; and that the Attributes are not the Essence, nor are they different from the Essence.

The Ash'arites uphold that the Koranic references to God's Face, His Hand, His Throne mean that He has a Face, a Hand, and a Throne, but that these cannot be likened to human hands, or a human face; anthropomorphic qualities may not be imputed to God. These Koranic descriptions must be accepted as they are, they say, without asking how. Nevertheless, the Ash'arites, while not admitting that these descriptions are *symbolic*, assert that they must be understood literally *and* spiritually at the same time. Ultimately, therefore, on this question as on many others, the Ash'arites insert several steps into a process that turns out to be an antinomy, whereby a contradiction on one plane is resolved on another. The difference between the Ash'arites and the school of al-Māturīdī is that the Māturīdites admit antinomial formulations more readily.

The Divine Reality is intuited by the human spirit as Real; but It surpasses analysis by the mind. Antinomy is the recognition that this is so. It does not mean that God cannot be known; but it means that God must be known through a means. One can grasp immediately what a triangle is by apprehending that it has three sides. A figure with 943 sides cannot be grasped in the same way as a triangle, but it can be known through a name. It is because God cannot be grasped directly, that man is saved through faith. And it is because God has a revealed Name, that man can know Him.

The Ash'arites deal with the problems of free-will and causality by their theory of atoms. To explain how the creature, lacking the positive and absolute qualities of God, could exercise will and action, the Ash'arites said that the action itself was created by God and then "acquired" (*kasb*, *iktisāb*) by the creature. Their most notable formulation, from the point of view of intellectual history, is their theory that atoms are simultaneously atoms of both space and time – instants in space, but without extension. This is essentially an attempt to explain phenomena – the world being apparently detached from God – by making the physical universe into an infinite collection of mirrors which reflect and refract an invisible Divine Reality into experience. It is a traditional forerunner of the modern and material theories of atoms. The Ash'arite idea precedes Descartes's theory of vortices, and modern science's atomism, which has now become the theory of "super-strings". All of these are also "little mirrors", from which the Divine Reality has been removed; little mirrors which, not reflecting God, create reality out of nothing.

The position of the Ash'arites on free-will is not entirely satisfactory; it holds back from openly admitting that there is great enigma in the question. God knows what will happen from eternity; yet we must still be free in order to be responsible for our acts, whose consequences may result in damnation or salvation. Do we then possess free will? There is one respect in which unquestionably we do: at any moment, we are free to choose or accept God as Reality. We may not be free in respect of our actions towards the world, wherein we undergo a variety of compulsion and a chain of cause and effect. But we are absolutely free and responsible in our rejection or acceptance of Absolute Reality, an act which takes place in consciousness; in that we are as free as God; the rest is cause and effect. (*See* HELL; IBLĪS; MAKTŪB; SHAHĀDAH.)

Apart from the *mutakallimūn*, and without establishing an atomistic theory, many Islamic thinkers say, basing themselves on the Koran, that creation is a continuous process, each instant being a new act of creation. ("Every day He is in act" 55:29). It is thus, for example, that Ibn 'Arabī explains the Koranic story of how the throne of the Queen of Sheba was brought instantly to Solomon by a *jinn*. The *jinn* did not physically bring the throne, but *transposed* on the subtle plane – "redirected", one could say – its *place* of continuous creation. The throne was created in Sheba one moment; the next its continuous creation took place in Jerusalem instead. Creation thus envisaged is not a process, but an instantaneous act; and the changes which natural and human history imply are the successive revelations of that act in time, which, along with extension, number, and the other conditions of existence, exist for man, but not for God. The links between apparently "successive" creation may appear to be cause and effect on the "horizontal" human plane, giving rise to the theory of evolution, for example; but not *in divinis*. On the earth night becomes day, continents form, mammals appear, empires rise and fall, Alexander conquers as far as the Indus, Napoleon retreats from Moscow. These are events over millennia; for God they are all in the eternal present, along with Adam's fall and the end of the world.

By the *7th*/13th century the development of *kalām* had run its course, although commentaries continued to be written even into modern times. *See* AKHBĀRĪS; al-ASH'ARĪ; BILĀ KAYFĀ; CREED; FIQH AKBAR; FIVE DIVINE PRESENCES; al-GHAZĀLĪ; HELL; IBLĪS; IBN 'ARABĪ; ISTAWĀ'; al-MĀTURĪDĪ; MU'TAZILITES; PHILOSOPHY; UṢŪLĪS.

al-Kalbi, Abū-l-Mundhir Ḥishām ibn Muḥammad (d. *206*/821-822). He was a member of a family of scholars from Kufah; he addressed himself to the study of Ḥadīth and history. According to an-Nadīm, al-Kalbi wrote 118 works, while Ya'qut makes it 121. Among those which have survived is the *Kitāb al-Aṣnām*, "the Book of Idols" which is a source on the idolatry of the *Jāhiliyah*, or "Age of Ignorance". (It was a principle in Medieval Islam that to report on heresy was not itself heresy.)

He relates that the poet king 'Imru' al-Qays consulted the divining arrows of the idol Dhū-al-Khalaṣah (a piece of cut quartz crystal) in Tabālah before setting out to attack the Banu Asad. The arrows were called the "enjoiner" (*al-āmir*) the "forbidder" (*al-nāhi*) and the "vigilant" (*al-mutarabbiṣ*). He drew three times the forbidder; Thereupon he broke the arrows and hurled them at the idol exclaiming; "Go bite your father's penis! Had it been thy father who was murdered, thou wouldst not have forbidden me avenging him." He then raided the Banu Asad and defeated them. Thus he was the first to denounce this idol.

Ibn al-Kalbi relates that there was a Ka'bah of Sindād in the region between al-Kufah and al-Baṣrah; but he says it was not a place of worship but a celebrated edifice. And another, the Ka'bah of Najran, is mentioned by al-A'sha in one of this odes. This too, al-Kalbi says was not claimed as a place of worship but merely a hall. However, in the *Diwan*, al-A'sha says "to visit the Ka'bah of Najrān is an ordinance incumbent upon you."

Jarīr ibn 'Abdallah who entered Islam at the conquest of Mecca or in the last six months of the Prophet's life was sent to destroy Dhū al-Khalaṣah which was located six days south of Mecca in the direction of San'a'. He had to kill three hundred custodians and others who defended it. Dhū al-Khalaṣah was a white quartz crystal; it was turned into the doorstep of the mosque of Tabālah which is the site of the idol. Al-Kalbi cites a Ḥadīth which says: "This world shall not pass away until the buttocks of the women of Daws wiggle [again] around Dhū-al-Khalaṣah and they worship it as they were wont to do [before Islam]." (Bukhārī: *Fitan*: 24). *See* IDOLS; JAHILIYYAH.

Kalimah (lit. "the word"). A name sometimes used for the testimony of the faith (*shahādah*). In the terminology of Christian Arabs the word *kalimah* means the Logos, or Christ. *See* SHAHĀDAH.

Kalmuck. A Mongolian people found in the Russian Federation, the Oyrat, who are Lamaist Buddhists. They number some 100,000 in Russia. They are related to another larger, Mongol Buddhist group in Russia, the Buryat. One of Lenin's grandfathers was a Kalmuck. Their spiritual leader is the Khambo Lama whose central lamasary (*daitsan*) is in Ulan Ude.

Kano. A city in northern Nigeria of approximately half a million inhabitants, with a history going back more than a millennium. One of the most important Hausa city-states, with a highly developed economic base and craft industry, Kano had trade links throughout West Africa and even with Europe, where its leather products were known as Moroccan leather. It is still the center for many crafts, including the manufacture of the indigo dyed cloth worn by the Tuaregs and Blue Men of the Sahara. In the 16th century Islam was adopted in Kano and scholars came from Morocco, the best known being one called al-Magīlī, to put religion on a firm footing. Kano was ruled by an Amīr assisted by several chamberlains, who shared power with a Hausa aristocracy.

Kapudanpasha. Under the Ottomans, the Beylerbey of the sea, or admiral in command of the naval forces. In 1531 Selim appointed the pirate Khayr ad-Dīn Barabarossa as Kapudanpasha in order to prosecute a sea war against the Spanish. *See* BEYLERBEY.

Karāmāt (lit. "acts of generosity"; sing. *karāmah*). Gifts or powers of a spiritual or psychic nature acquired by a Saint, short of miracle working. The term is not used for the psychic powers that could be possessed by a sorcerer, and is equivalent to the Sanskrit *siddhi* in the elevated sense of "spiritual attainment".

Karma Marga, *see* MAKHĀFAH.

Kashkul. A vessel carried by some wandering dervishes and beggars in Iran and India. It was made from large nuts called "*coco de mer*", 20 to 30 cm long. The black colored, double-sided nuts wash up, mysteriously, on the shores of Iran and India. They fall into the Indian Ocean from palm trees on the Seychelle Islands (Praslin in the Vallée de Mai). The cocos can weigh 30-40 kilos; once germinated the seeds take nine months to flower; every seven years the palm lets the nuts drop to the ground. The nuts were split into two down the central seam and were hollowed out creating a left hand and a right hand vessel which could be used as a multi-purpose bowl which was carried slung over the shoulder.

After Ṣafavid times the *kashkul*, copying the shape of the original, natural *coco de mer*, was also made by craftsman out of metal, particularly brass, and ornamented (as were natural ones). A folklore developed around the size, and left or right-handedness of the *kashkul*, and mendicant groups could be identified by their bowls. Another emblem of wandering dervishes in Iran, India, and Central Asia, along with the bowl, was an axe, which in addition to being a weapon, was meant to be the equivalent of the sword as a symbol of spiritual discrimination.

Kashmir. Strategic state in the northwest of India next to Pakistan, bordering on China. The population of Jammu and Kashmir at the time of partition in 1947 was close to 80% Muslim but the Maharajah was Hindu and refused to give a decision over which country he would join. The Maharajah did begin massacres of Muslims which were then but the latest of a long pattern of oppression of the Muslims of the region. The massacres led to an intervention on the part of Pakistan, in the face of which the Maharajah joined India in October 1948. India promised a referendum which has never taken place. The part seized by Pakistan in the course of the war which followed is called Azad ("Free") Kashmir. Although one Muslim faction in Kashmir had favored union with India, there has been a continuous opposition to Indian rule which in 1987 became widespread unrest and resistance leading to Indian military occupation. This has now become guerrilla warfare. The unresolved question of Kashmir has been the stumbling block to the improvement of relations between India and Pakistan.

Kaysānīs, *see* KAYSĀNIYYAH.

Kaysāniyyah. A Shī'ite group, who maintained that the Imām, or rightful leader, after the death of Ḥusayn, was not a descendant of Ḥusayn, but a half-brother, Muḥammad ibn al-Ḥanafiyyah (d. *81*/700). This was a son of 'Alī by a woman of the Ḥanafī tribe, who was thus called the Ḥanafite (*al-Ḥanafiyyah*). This branch of Shī'ism was in fact some form of indigenous Iranian religion seeping into Islam. It lingered on as a distinct sect after the death of the Imām. Although some members of the sect briefly gave allegiance to a descendant of Muḥammad ibn al-Ḥanafiyyah, others declined, saying that the Imām was concealed and would return to the world.

The term *Kaysāniyyah* may come from a name for the leader of the original sect in Kufah, or from a name for Mukhṭār, the actual leader who promoted revolt against the Umayyads using Muḥammad ibn Ḥanafiyyah as the figurehead (for this reason the Kaysānīs are sometimes called the *Mukhṭāriyyah*). Mukhṭār was the nephew of 'Alī's governor in Madā'in. After taking part in 'Abd Allāh ibn az-Zubayr's struggle against the Umayyads, Mukhṭār appeared in Iraq claiming to be inspired by the Angel Gabriel and, in verse imitative of the Koran, preached about the appearance of the Mahdī who would eliminate injustice in the earth; Muḥammad ibn al-Ḥanafiyyah, he said, was this very Mahdī. Raising a force of discontented Aramaic and Persian clients (*mawālī*) of the occupying Arabs, Mukhṭār put them under the command of Ibrāhīm ibn al-Mālik al-Ash'tar, the son of one of 'Alī's generals. The forces of Mukhṭār won several victories in Iraq and defeated a Syrian army led by 'Ubayd Allāh ibn Ziyād, the Umayyad governor who had sent troops against Ḥusayn at Kerbala. ' Ubayd Allāh ibn Ziyād was killed and Mukhṭār celebrated the victory by a ceremony in front of an empty throne, held by some to be a chair belonging to 'Alī, which he took to represent the presence of God. This ceremony of the empty chair, resembling the "Bema Ceremony", may link the Kaysāniyyah to the Manicheans.

Mukhṭār originated the concept of *bada*, not accepted by Sunnī Islam, of the possibility of changes in the Divine Will. Before one battle he told his followers that God had informed him of their coming victory; when in fact they were defeated, Mukhṭār explained that "God's will had changed". Mukhṭār himself was killed in *67*/687. *See* IMĀM; MAHDĪ; SHĪ'ISM.

Kazakhstan. Independent in 1991 from the former Soviet Union, population 17,376,000. Over 7,000,000 are Kazakhs, the rest are Russians, Ukrainians, and Germans. The capital is Almaty. The Kazakhs are an amalgam of Turko-Mongolian peoples who emerged as a distinct people in the 15th or 16th century. The dominant strain among them are the ancient Qipchaqs. Before the 1917 revolution the Kazakhs were called the Kirghiz, (or Kighiz-Kazak) while the present day Kirghiz were called Kara-Kirghiz. They are Sunnī Muslims islamicised in the 18th century by missionaries from the Tatars. The tra
ditional way of life was sheepherding. Besides the Kazakhs in Kazakhstan another 800,000 live in the Sinkiang region of China, and some 63,000 in western Mongolia.

Kebatinan. (Indonesian abstract noun formed from the Arabic *bāṭin*, "esoteric"). Esoteric organizations in Indonesia. These include a wide variety of groups from animist and Hindu based movements in Java, to regularly constituted Sufi orders in Atjeh.

Kemal, Muṣṭāfā (1881-1938). The first president of Turkey from 1923 until his death in 1938. He was called *Atatürk* ("Father of the Turks") by his supporters known as the "Kemalists". Kemal made *laik* ("laicisation") an important, if not the main, aspect of his political program. The substitution of the Latin alphabet for the Arabic one (the adoption of the Arabic alphabet by any people had historically been part of its adoption of Islam) under the pretended aim of increasing literacy, served to cut the Turks off from their past by making most of them unable to read their literature. The subsequent "Turkification" of Turkish – the attempted removal of as many words as possible of Arabic origin – could only be partly successful, but even so it raised further barriers to communication with other Islamic countries, and even, it has been said, between generations of Turks themselves.

By turning the Aya Sofia Mosque into a museum, and making compulsory the wearing of the European hat, which has a rim and thus impedes the prostration which is intrinsic to Muslim prayer, Mustafa Kemal caused as much controversy in the Islamic world of the time, as he did by the outright ban against wearing turbans in public.

Kemal was a model to be emulated by other modernizing leaders of Islamic countries, most notably Reza Shāh, founder of the short-lived Pahlavi dynasty of Iran, Enver Hodja of Albania, and others.

Kerbala. The place in Iraq where Ḥusayn, grandson of the Prophet Muḥammad, was martyred in *61*/680. It is now a city. The tomb, *Mashhad Ḥusayn*, is the holiest shrine of the Twelve-Imām Shī'ites. The first edifice was built there in *369*/979 by the Buwayhids (also called Buyids), although an enclosed area (*hā'ir*) existed much earlier. The tomb and shrine were destroyed several times by Sunnī rulers to remove this focus of Shī'ite agitation. Today, there is a domed shrine over the tomb of Ḥusayn, and the tomb of 'Abbās, his half brother, is nearby.

Clay from Kerbala, sanctified by the "blood of martyrdom", is stamped into little cakes onto which Twelve-Imām Shī'ites rest the forehead during the prostration in the prayer. The clay is also considered to have curative powers. The body of Ḥusayn rests in Kerbala, but the head, which was brought to the Umayyad Caliph Yazīd, reposes in the Ḥusayn Mosque in Cairo. In the Grand Umayyad Mosque of Damascus, where the head once lay, a sanctuary remains; both places are points of pilgrimage for Shī'ites, and to a certain degree Sunnīs as well. *See* ḤUSAYN; SHĪ'ISM.

Khadījah. First wife of the Prophet, and, during her lifetime, the only one. The Prophet was twenty-five years old at the time of their marriage, and she, a wealthy widow, forty; she died at the age of sixty-five in the year 619, before the Hijrah.

The Prophet had been master of her caravans before they married. They had two sons, Qāsim and 'Abd Allāh (who both died in infancy), and four daughters, Zaynab, Ruqayyah, Fāṭimah, and Umm Kulthūm. Khadījah is buried in the al-Malā' cemetery in Mecca.

Khaksars. 1. Also called *Ḥaydaris*, these are one of the more numerous of the *darvishi* groups in Iran. *Darvishis* (from *darvish*, Persian for *faqīr*, the technical term for a Sufī) are irregular semi-secret organizations common in Iran and among Kurds in Turkey and Iraq. They are Sufi-like but the basis of the associations is not clearly around a doctrine and method firmly based upon Islam as is the case with more authentic Sufis.

The origins of the *darvishi* associations are obscure and markedly pre-Islamic as can be seen from a characteristic stance found in *darvishi* rituals. This is a stance called *qapi* with the right big toe placed over the left big toe, and with the arms folded over the chest. This is related to a ritual position found in Zoroastrianism (in which the priest's hands are crossed but not folded under the arms; rather the Zoroastrian priest holds his earlobes). Ivanow said the position was also found in Mithraism, and in other ancient Iranian religions. This ritual position is also used by many Turkish Sufi orders such as the Jarrahiyah and the Mevlevis, but amongst them Islamic elements are more prominent.

2. A modern political movement in northern India founded in 1931 by 'Inayat Allāh Khān al-Mashriqī (d. 1963), a mathematician working as a government functionary. He had been educated in Germany. The Khaksārs were modeled on the Nazi S.A. They wore brown uniforms and a badge of brotherhood (*ukhuwwa)* on the upper right arm and carried out community and social services. Their name means "earth" and "head" and they strove to be as "humble as dust" but also drilled in a military fashion carrying spades. They interpreted the Koran "scientifically" and it was their aim to make Islam dominant over the globe. In 1941 the movement had more than a million adherents but became divided during the war, and now has almost disappeared.

Khālid ibn al-Walīd (d. *22*/642). A famous warrior in the war between Mecca and Medina, and during the early conquests of Islam. A Qurayshī and at first an opponent of Islam, he was converted a year before the conquest of Mecca. The first Caliph, Abū Bakr, made him the leading general of the Muslim armies. He defeated the imposter Musaylimah at the "Garden of Death" during the Wars of Apostasy (*ḥurūb ar-riddah*), and in the campaign to conquer Syria he defeated the Byzantines near Damascus. He was called the "Sword of Islam" (*Sayfu-l-Islām*) by the Prophet. *See* SWORD of ISLAM.

Khalīfah, *see* CALIPH.

Khalīl ibn Aḥmad (d. *175*/791). The Grammarian from Oman. He worked out complex metrical theories about Arab poetry (inspired it is said by listening to the rhythms of the coppersmiths beating plates in the market) and compiled the first dictionary (*Kitāb al-'Ayn*) using a phonetic scheme according to the origins of sound of use to poets and possibly influenced by Indian ideas. *See* SĪBAWAIH.

Khalwatiyyah (from Ar. *khalwah*, a "spiritual retreat"; Turkish: *Halvetiyye*). A widespread Sufi order that was founded by Shaykh 'Umar al-Khalwatī (d. *800*/1397) who is called its first *pīr* ("master"). It is also said that the name originated with Shaykh 'Umar's master, Muḥammad ibn Nūr al-Bālisī who was called al-Khalwatī because of his frequent retreats. The second *pīr* of the order was Shaykh Yaḥyā l-Shirwānī (d. *869*/1464), the author of a litany called *Wird as-Sattār*, recitation of which is among the obligations imposed upon the members of most branches.

The foundations of this order are considered to be voluntary hunger, silence, vigil, seclusion, *dhikr* ("invocation"), meditation, maintaining a state of permanent ritual purity and binding one's heart to the spiritual master.

The Khalwatiyyah spread in the Caucasus, Anatolia, and Azerbaijan from the late *8th*/14th to the end of the *11th*/17th century. In the *10th*/16th century it spread to Egypt and Muslim Africa. The order is a branch of the Suhrawardiyyah, and has many branches among which are the Jarraḥiyyah, Sha'bāniyyah, Sunbuliyyah, Sīnāniyyah and Tījāniyyah. The late Shaykh Muzaffar of the Jarraḥī branch, whose center is Istanbul, established the order in Europe and North America.

al-Khamriyyah. The "wine ode", a mystical poem by Ibn al-Fāriḍ (*577-633*/1181-1235), the most famous of Arab Sufi poets. For the Sufis, wine is a common symbol of Divine knowledge and invocation (*dhikr*). The full moon is the amplitude of the Divine revealer, or the spiritual master; the crescent, the aspirant to Divine knowledge; the army, the warriors engaged in the "greater holy war", against one's own soul...

> We quaffed upon the remembrance of the Beloved a wine wherewith we were drunken, before ever the vine was created.
> The moon at the full its cup was; itself was a sun, that a crescent moon passeth round; how many a star gleams forth, when that wine is mingled!
> And but for its fragrance, never had I been guided unto its tavern; and but for its radiance, never had the mind's imagination pictured it.
> And Time hath not left aught of it save a last gasp; as if its being vanished were a concealment in the breasts of human reasons;
> Though if it be but mentioned among the tribe, the people of the tribe become intoxicated, yet guilty of no disgrace or crime.
> From the very bowels of the vats it has mounted up, and naught remains of it in truth but a name:
> Yet if on a day it cometh into the thought of a man, great joy will dwell in him and all sorrow will depart.
> And had the boon-companions beheld no more than the impress of the seal upon its vessel, that impress would surely have made them drunken, without the wine itself;
> And had they sprinkled therewith the dust of a dead man's tomb, the spirit would surely have returned unto him, and his body been quickened.
> And had they but cast, in the shade of the wall where groweth its vine a sick man, and he nigh to death, his sickness would have departed from him;
> And had they brought nigh to its tavern one paralyzed, he would have walked; yea, and the dumb would have spoken upon the mention of its flavor;

And had the breaths of its perfume been wafted through the East, and in the West were one whose nostrils were stopped, the sense of smell would have returned to him...

...And had an enchanter drawn its name on the forehead of one afflicted with madness, the letters drawn would have cured his sickness;

And had its name been inscribed above the banner of an army, surely that superscription would have inebriated all beneath the banner...

...More ancient than all existing things was the tale of it told in eternity, when neither was shape nor trace to be seen;

And there did all things subsist through it for a purpose wise, whereby it was veiled from all that had not an understanding mind. And my spirit was distraught with love for it, in such a manner that the twain were mingled together in unification, and not as body is permeated by another:

'Tis a soul and no wine there, when Adam is reckoned my father, but a wine and no soul there, when the vine thereof is reckoned my mother.

Now the subtility of the vessels is really consequential upon the subtility of the inward truths, and the inward truths augment by means of the vessels.

And the division truly has taken place, while yet the whole is one: our spirits being the wine, and our corporeal shapes the vine...

...Then let him weep for himself, whose life is all wasted, and he not in all his days of the Wine taken part or portion.

See DHIKR; IBN al-FĀRIḌ; SUFISM.

Khamsa. A parasol carried over the 'Abbāsid Caliph when he appeared outside in public; the custom probably originated in India. It is still preserved in Morocco where a parasol is carried over the King as he rides to Friday Prayer on horseback.

Khān. 1. An inn and warehouse for traveling merchants (*see* CARAVANSARAI).

2. A Turkic word for chief or prince, used as a title for rulers and incorporated by the Turks as one of the titles of the Caliph.

Khān, Sir Sayyid Aḥmad (*1232-1316*/1817-1898). An Indian reformer and modernist who advocated that India adopt Western ideas. Sir Sayyid founded the Muḥammadan Anglo-Indian Oriental Aligarh College in 1875; in 1920 the school became a university. Aligarh gave its name to a modernizing movement in India.

Sir Sayyid served in the East India Company and was a local magistrate at the time of the Sepoy Mutiny; he was noted for his actions in saving Europeans during the disturbances. Although Sir Sayyid was pro-British, he also wished to see an independent India where the religions could exist peacefully side by side.

Khānaqah. The Persian name for a meeting place of dervishes, or Sufis (*see* SUFISM). In the Arabic-speaking world the term used is *zāwiyah* (lit: "corner"). Before many Khāniqahī in Iran were meeting places for Sufis, they had already been meeting places for members of other Persian religions,

Khandaq, *see* BATTLE of the TRENCH.

Kharāj (lit. "produce"). A tax on kind, amounting to a land tax, from non-Muslims within the Islamic state. It was imposed later, and in addition to, the *jizyah*, or poll-tax. *See* JIZYAH.

Khārijites (Ar. *khawārij*, sing. *khārijī*, lit. the "seceders"). A sect that arose in opposition to both 'Alī and Mu'āwiyah upon the occasion of the arbitration that followed the Battle of Ṣiffīn (*37*/657). The Khārijites had been part of 'Alī's army, but when it was announced that the question of the successsion to the Caliphate was to be decided by negotiation, they left; hence the name "seceders". The Khārijites felt that such a matter could not be resolved by compromise; their cry was "Decision is God's alone".

Their starting point was puritanism, a nostalgia for the Islam of the Caliphate of 'Umar; they could be called "old believers" (many of the Khārijites had been *qurrā'*, public reciters of the Koran). Their doctrine of sin, which became the most characteristic aspect (logically so, since they considered the upheavals which befell the Muslim polity a fall from a state of perfection), appeared within a Khārijite sect called the Azraqīs around *74*/693.

The Khārijites were a populist group in revolt against the evident hardening of the Caliphate into an Arab Kingdom. Arab supremacy was expressed in the practice of adopting non-Arab converts into an Arab tribe but at the same time imposing upon each one a "protector"; in order to achieve a status within the community, each convert was made a "client" (*mawlā*, plural *mawālī*) of an Arab, although 'Alī himself was a notable exception to this policy, treating all converts as equals. However, this general relegation of non-Arabs to inferior status naturally provoked resentment and caused new converts to rally around movements that promised redress of wrongs.

'Alī at first ignored the Khārijites, being preoccupied with Mu'awiyah; but he finally turned, and attacked them at the Battle of Nahrawān *38*/658. Most of the Khārijites were killed, but a few escaped and perpetuated the movement. 'Alī himself was later assassinated in the mosque of Kufah by Ibn Muljam, a Khārijite either seeking revenge for the death of his family, or else induced to it by a woman who demanded the assassination of 'Alī as her bride-price.

For hundreds of years the Khārijites were a source of insurrection against the Caliphate. They survive today in one of the more moderate forms of Khārijism, namely the 'Ibāḍites. 'Ibāḍī Khārijism is the Islam of Oman, but minority 'Ibāḍī communities also exist in Tunisia (the island of Jerba), Algeria (the M'zab), Libya, and in Tanzania (Zanzibar was once an Omani colony).

According to the Khārijites, anyone can be the leader of the community if he is morally irreproachable. Their leader is accordingly called an "Imām", and is elected, whereas for the Shī'ites their Imām must be a descendant of 'Alī and an intermediary between man and God; and for the Sunnīs, the supreme leader of the Islamic state had to be, at the beginning at least, a member of the tribe of Quraysh of Mecca.

The Khārijites hold that there is an obligation to revolt against an Imām that has sinned. Indeed, in their doctrine, major sins forfeit salvation and the condition of believer, making a sinner *de facto* an apostate, without remedy. For them, faith without works does not save, whereas for the Sunnīs there is no despairing of the mercy of God. For the Ash'arites, God in His Mercy may even draw a sinning Muslim out of Hell.

This absolute doctrine of sin may well have been a reaction on the part of the Khārijites against the tendency of the desert Arabs to accept external adhesion to Islam as adequate, without any corresponding inward conversion and commitment. It was also an ideological reinforcement in their struggle against non-Khārijites.

The Khārijites considered the fact of being a Muslim absolute in itself and equivalent to salvation; Islam represented a perfect state of soul and to be a Muslim was already to be saved. Sin was therefore a contradiction which nullified the state of believer, or demonstrated that the sinner had turned against Islam. If a person sinned, he could not possess a perfect state of soul and therefore was not really a Muslim. His sin proved inward apostasy, and for it he could be put to death. Non-Khārijites could also be considered apostates, and they and their families put to death. This doctrine of sin was one of the important points repudiated by the book *al-Fiqh al-Akbar* of Abū Ḥanīfah. Likewise this extreme Khārijite attitude led to the Murji'ite reaction, a pietist philosophy which said that to profess Islam with the tongue made one a Muslim, and that the question of one's inner conversion was deferred to the Day of Judgement. The profound controversy which raged around this question led Abū Ḥanīfah to declare categorically in *al-Fiqh al-Akbar*: "no one is to be considered an infidel on account of sin".

The Khārijites did not accept the authority of the Caliphate after 'Alī's decision to turn to arbitration (nor, did they accept retrospectively the whole of 'Uthmān's Caliphate). They went so far as to consider all but themselves unbelievers and traitors to Islam, and finally believed it impossible even to live among them. The 'Ibāḍites are a moderating branch in this respect and have survived, whereas the more rigid groups have disappeared. Despite its categorical attitude towards other Muslims, the Khārijites view other religions differently, notably conceding that, provided that the non-Muslim "People of the Book" (*Ahl al-Kitāb*) acknowledge the Divine mission of the Prophet, they need not automatically abandon their own religion.

A Khārijite sermon of the 2nd century of the Hijrah gives a taste of their point of view:

> Know this, ye men: we did not leave our homes and goods out of a vain restlessness, nor in quest of pleasure, nor to claim old right, nor to win empire. But when we saw the lamps of justice all put out, then indeed the earth, vast as it is, was straitened [Koran 9:118]) upon us. We heard as it were a Herald call us to obedience unto the Merciful, and

> to the Judgement of the Book of God.
>
> We met your warriors. We called them to obey the Merciful and abide by the Judgement of the Book; they called us to obey Satan and abide by the judgement of the children of Marwān. Then they came at us, galloping, clamoring, and riotous, for Satan laughed among them, and their blood seethed with his fires. And the wheel turned; and we went up and they went down, for such a smiting there befell as made the ungodly totter.
>
> When 'Uthmān reigned, he walked six years in the ways of Abū Bakr and of 'Umar; and then worked innovation in Islam. And the bond of unity was loosed; and every man wanted Caliphate for himself. Then reigned 'Alī, who wandered from the path of truth and proved himself no beacon for the guidance of men. Then reigned Mu'āwiyah son of Abū Sufyān, that accursed son of an accursed father, whom God's Prophet himself did curse, who spilt innocent blood as it were water and made God's Servants his own slaves, a man who grasped the moneys of God into his own hands, a traitor to the Faith and a ravisher of women, who did the bidding of his lusts until he died.
>
> And after him came his son Yazīd, Yazīd the drunkard, Yazīd the huntsman, the tender of hawks and leopards and apes, who consulted not the Book but soothsayers, and followed his lusts to his death, God curse and punish him!
>
> Then came Marwān, that excommunicate and accursed son of a father whom God's Prophet cursed, who drowned in the filth of his vices, God curse him and his fathers all! And then sat Marwān's sons upon the throne, children of that accursed House, who have devoured the moneys of God and mocked at his Religion and made His Servants their own slaves. And this wickedness has gone on and on. And O Muḥammad's People, how have ye been unhappy and forsaken!

See AHL al-KITĀB; 'ALĪ; FIQH AKBAR; 'IBAḌITES; MURJI'AH; SIN.

Khāṭi'ah. A category of sin. *See* SIN.

Khatm al-Anbiya', *see* SEAL of PROPHECY.

Khatm an-Nubuwwah, *see* SEAL of PROPHECY.

Khatm al-Wilāyah, *see* SEAL of SANCTITY.

Khaṭṭābiyyah. A Sevener dualist Manichean sect in Iraq in the *2nd*/8th century whose leader, Abū-l-Khaṭṭāb Muḥammad, asserted that Ja'far aṣ-Ṣādiq was Divine, and later that he himself was likewise Divine, a spiritual descendant of Ja'far by adoption. The Sect was attacked by the 'Abbāsid authorities in Iraq and the leader killed. Some of his followers affirmed that his death was only an illusion; there were numerous splinter groups and many eventually joined other Manichean sects. *See* MANICHEANS; QARMATIANS; SEVENERS.

al-Khayyām, 'Umar see 'UMAR KHAYYĀM.

Khidhlān (Ar. "abandonment"). According to theologians, an attitude of God when he leaves someone to his own devices and thus inevitably prey to his weaknesses. It corresponds to the Christian idea of "fall from grace" and is remedied in the same way, by prayer and seeking out blessing.

Ibn 'Aṭā' Allāh said in his *Ḥikam*:

> Sometimes He makes you learn in the night of contraction (*layl al-qabḍ)* what you have not learned in the radiance of the day of expansion (*fī ishrāq nahar al-basṭ*). You do not know which of them is nearer to you in benefit. (4:11)

See ISTIDRĀJ.

al-Khiḍr (lit. "the green one"; also, and perhaps originally, *al-khaḍir*). A spiritual *persona* identified with the figure in the Koran 18:64: "One of Our servants, unto whom We [God] had given mercy from Us, and had taught him knowledge proceeding from Us." He is not, of course, mentioned by name in the Koran.

When Moses and his servant, as is recounted in the Sūrah of the Cave (Koran 18:61-83), go looking for the union of the two seas, that is, the sea of this world and the sea of the next, or manifestation and Being, Moses is distracted. The fish which they are carrying to eat comes to life and slips away, showing them that they have passed – seeing, but not observing – their goal. In retracing their steps they encounter the figure described above. Moses wishes to follow al-Khiḍr but is told that he will not be able to bear with that mysterious figure. Therefore, Moses promises to ask no questions, but simply to obey. The two, Moses and al-Khiḍr, (the servant of the previous episode is not mentioned further) now encounter three situations in which al-Khiḍr performs apparent outrages, sinking a ship, killing a lad, and repairing a wall for unworthy folk. Moses each time, and despite his promise, expresses dismay at the actions and is finally abandoned by al-Khiḍr, who explains upon parting the hidden reasons behind his acts, which were intended to bring a greater good out of an apparent evil, and which were done at the command of God.

According to the most usual, but not exclusive, Sufi commentary, Moses represents exoterism with its limitations, grasping at the external and apparent, whereas al-Khiḍr represents the inner dimension, esoterism, which transcends form. He appears to men in those moments when their own soul bears witness to an awareness of that dimension. In that rare case when there is a spontaneous realization of spiritual truth on the part of a *fard*, a "solitary" or someone who is by destiny cut off from revelation or from normal channels of spiritual instruction, it is al-Khiḍr who is the teacher as in the saying "when the disciple is ready, the master appears". The Sufis, upon entering an empty room, greet the void, because al-Khiḍr is there, and also say *as-salāmu 'alaykum* whenever he is mentioned, because at his mention his presence is called forth.

Al-Khiḍr is known everywhere throughout the Islamic world. He is a personification of the revealing function of the metaphysical Intellect, the "prophetic soul", the projection into the soul of the center of Being. The Sufi Ibrāhīm ibn Adham said: "In that wilderness I lived for four years. God gave me my eating without any toil of mine. Khiḍr the Green Ancient was my companion during that time – he taught me the Great Name of God." Philologists are no less intrigued by him, and connect him with Elijah or Utnapishtim of the Gilgamesh epic. *See* FIVE DIVINE PRESENCES; SUFISM; UWAYS al-QARANĪ.

Khilāfat Movement. A movement of Muslims in India from 1918 to 1924 to influence British policy towards Turkey after World War I and to preserve the Caliphate as a uniting institution for Islam. The Khilāfat Movement came into full existence with the creation of the All-India Khilāfat committee in 1918. The Turks themselves, however, abolished the Caliphate in 1924. The Movement then split into those who supported an Ottoman Candidate and those who supported a Hashemite. It disappeared not long after that. The Khilāfat Movement had grown out of tendencies gathering at the end of the 19th century. The Khilāfat movement had benefited from Hindu-Muslim nationalist cooperation against British rule that had begun during the war, and was supported by Gandhi after it. Eventually, however, the Islamic nature of the Khilāfat Movement led to an increase in differences in the goals of Hindu and Muslim political groups and led to nationalist aspirations along religious lines.

Khil'ah. An ornately made "robe of honour", often accompanied by other gifts, given by the ruler as a reward or mark of distinction. Such gifts were also made to other rulers. The giving of the robes was a hallmark of the court style of the 'Abbāsids of Baghdad. The Arabic word *khil'ah* has come through Italian into European languages as *gala*.

Khirqah (lit. "a rag", "a tatter"). A cloak worn by some orders of dervishes. Patched continually as it wears out, the *khirqah* is a sign of poverty and renunciation of the world. In some orders the initiation is transmitted by the Shaykh's laying of a cloak over the disciple. According to the circumstance the act may also represent only a blessing. The patched cloak is also called a *muraqqa'ah*. *See* BURDAH; MURAQQA'AH; SUFISM.

Khirqa-i-sharīf, *see* BURDAH; KHIRQAH.

Khiva. City in what is Uzbekistan today, it was the capital of Khwarizm, near the Amu Darya, or Oxus, and near lake Aral. Once a satrapy of the Achaemenids, it became the seat of the Khwarizm Shāhis until they were destroyed by Jenghiz Khān in 1219. It was a Khānate at the time of the Russian conquest in 1873. It has today a relatively well preserved old city.

Khojas. An ethnic group, in India and Pakistan, formerly a Hindu caste (which still preserves a strong group identity), most of whom today are Nizārī Ismā'īlīs. Most Khoja Ismā'īlīs, but not all, recognize the Aga Khān as their spiritual leader, the Imām.

The *dā'i* (lit. "caller", "propagandizer") Pīr Ṣadr ad-Dīn (also called by the Hindu name

Sahadev) converted the Khojas to Ismā'īlism from Hinduism during early Ismā'īlī propagandizing in India in the *9th*/15th century. The sect was also spread in a Hindu form as the *Satpanth* ("true path"). The name Khoja was given to the followers by their missionary leader and means "lord" (*khwajah*) in Persian. Population centers of the Khojas are Bombay and the Gujarat in India and, through emigration, East Africa. Some Khojas have also emigrated to Europe and America, particularly after the expulsion of Asians from Uganda, and the decolonization of Mozambique.

In 1866 some of the Khojas sued the Aga Khān I in the Bombay courts to recover property from his control. The Khojas who are not followers of the present day Aga Khān derive from this split and are mostly Twelve-Imām Shī'ites. Other Khojas are Twelve-Imām Shī'ites going back a much longer time. Until the middle of the last century the Ismā'īlī Khoja self-awareness as a distinctive group was not highly developed; it has since then increased considerably, causing the Ismā'īlī Khojas to distance themselves from Twelve-Imām Khojas. Among Khojas in East Africa, this development did not take place until this century, and caused some social dislocations. Some Khojas are Sunnī Muslims, while others are Hindus. The Indian census of 1931 put their numbers at somewhat over 200,000. Today it would be considerably more, especially taking into account Khojas in Africa.

Khomeini, Ruhollah Musavi (1902-1989). Of a Persian family which had returned to Iran after several generations in Kashmir, Khomeini was born in the village of Khomein. He carried out his higher theological studies with Ayatollah Hā'eri, one of the most noted Mujtahids of his time. 'Abd al-Karīm Hā'eri from Yazd had taught at Najaf and Kerbela; Khomeini studied with him in the Iranian city of Arak and in 1921 accompanied him to Qum. At that time nationalism was on the rise in Iran and Iranians wished to have a center of theological learning to rival those in Iraq: this Iranian center was to be Qum.

The Faiziyeh madrasah in Qum had been founded by Fath 'Alī Shāh, the second Qajar; Khomeini was to study there and later teach theology and Islamic law. In the early 1960s he had enough followers to be considered one of the rare teachers called Ayatollahs.

In 1962 administrative procedures for local councils were instituted in Iran which allowed councilors to swear when taking office by the holy book (rather than the Koran specifically). The Mullahs took this to be an open door for non-Muslims and in particular Bahā'īs to take control of the seats of government. In January of 1963 a land reform law was passed which included lands of religious endowments which the Mullahs had wished exempted. The land reform law was popular although the results actually proved counterproductive for agriculture later; it was passed over the opposition of the Mullahs. In February the Shāh gave women the right to vote, an act which the Mullahs opposed. Tensions between the government and the religious teaching establishment led to government raids upon the Faiziyeh in March of 1963 in which a student was killed. Khomeini made a series of inflammatory sermons which climaxed on the sensitive anniversary of Ḥusayn's death at Kerbela. The themes of his sermons decried what he perceived to be insults to men of religion and berated enemies of Islam, which included Israel and opressive anti-Islamic governments. (The government of the Shāh was friendly towards Israel and supplied it with Iranian oil while Israel provided the Shāh with support and technical advisors).

On 5 June 1963 Khomeini was imprisoned. Rioting broke out in several cities. After several months in prison he then spent eight months under house arrest. Not long after being liberated, he made a speech in November of 1964 opposing a law being considered by the Iranian parliament which would have given American military forces in Iran diplomatic immunity, making them subject only to American courts and American laws. The embarrassing law passed by a very narrow margin, and was followed by a loan from the American government to Iran. In a characteristic style that absolutized relative points (he once said in a sermon at Qum that in killing Ḥusayn at Kerbela the Umayyad Caliph Yazid wished to exterminate all the descendants of the Prophet), Khomeini called the new law of diplomatic immunity the enslavement of Iran which acknowledged that Iran is a colony; "it has given America a document attesting that the nation of Muslims is barbarous...if the Shāh should run over an American dog, he would be called to account, but if an American cook should run over the Shāh, no one has any claims against him... It is America that considers the Koran and Islam to be harmful to itself and wishes to remove them from its way; it is America that considers Muslim men of religion a thorn in its path."

The sermon was clandestinely printed and distributed on tape cassettes. Several days later Khomeini was exiled to Turkey, but Khomeini's ideas had struck a chord with the mass of Iranians and when he went by invitation in 1965 to Najaf in Iraq to teach theology he had become one of the most prominent Shī'ite religious authorities.

In January of 1978 a wave of demonstrations broke out in Iran; Khomeini had to leave Iraq and went to Paris. The BBC Persian service carried a speech by Ayatollah Shariatmadari, until then cautious, blaming the government. The demonstrations in Iran led to shootings by the army. Every forty days thereafter, on the occasions of mourning for the dead of the previous demonstrations, new demonstrations and new shootings took place. The bazars at Qum were closed and remained closed except for forty days until the next year. On August 19 a cinema burned and four hundred people died; the government blaimed provocation by religious conservatives; the religious opposition blamed SAVAK. Violence continued until the Shāh left Iran on January 16, 1979. On the first of February Khomeini returned.

In 1971 Khomeini had published the *Vilayat-i Faqih*, "The Government of the Jurisprudent" which proposed that in the absence of the Hidden Imām competent Jurists are mandated by the Hidden Imām to govern in his place. In theory, this resolved the tension of Shī'ite political practice which otherwise assumes all government other than that of the Hidden Imām to be illegitimate. In actual fact, the need for legitimate government in the absence of the Imām had already called for its theoretical legitimization. Very early in the development of Shī'ism, serving in the government had become perceived as betraying the Imām; therefore Murtaza 'Alam al-Hudā (d. *436*/1044) formulated the Shī'ite principle that "if the person accepting a government office knew or considered it likely on the basis of clear indications that he would be able, through his tenure of office, to support a right or to reject a false claim or to enjoin the good or forbid evil, and that nothing of this would be accomplished but for his holding office, it was obligatory for him to accept office."

What was new in Khomeini was that the political authority who could govern in the place of the Imām was to be a jurisprudent. This grew out of the movement of the Shī'ite *Uṣūlī* school of law, and such milestones as the Mullah Naraqi. In 1829 a Persian Mullah, Aḥmad Naraqi (*1185-1245*//1771-1829), collected historical materials and Ḥadith regarding political authority in a document called the *Awa'īd al-Ayyam*. He quoted what he believed to be an inspired tradition which concluded that "while the kings have authority over the people, the religious scholars have authority over the kings."

In the new government system adopted in Iran following Khomeini's lead, the highest authority must specifically be filled by a Jurisprudent. The constitution also provides that there be a *rahbar*, also a Jurisprudent, who may impeach the head of government if he deviates from religious principles.

Khomeini was called the *Naib-i Imām* or the representative of the Imām, a term often shortened to Imām implying that he was the returned Hidden Imām, something which Khomeini did not claim to be but a practice which he did not stop. He had three daughters and two sons. The eldest, Mustafa, had died in Iraq in 1977. He wrote stylized *irfani* ("mystical") poetry, a custom among Shī'ite religious teachers, under the the pseudonym "the Indian". Many Mullahs cultivate characteristics and idiosyncracies which fascinate their publics and focus attention; Khomeini always spoke in an even tone of voice, never raised it, and his students could set their watches by his regular appearance at prayers and the Friday sermon.

Khomeini could set into motion drastic acts in the name of a merciful God without revealing in himself any apparent trace of self-contradiction. He did this with a kind of totality or ipseity. Having thus combined diametric opposites within himself, having become what his particular theology calls a place between two places, he could exercise a profound fascination over those who came into his presence. This is how an American journalist, Robin Carlsen, described its effect: "A hurricane he was, yet immediately one could see that there was a point of absolute stillness inside that hurricane; while fierce and commanding, he was yet serene and receptive... This was no ordinary human being...none possessed quite the electrifying presence of Khomeini...Imām Khomeini broke into my heart and my brain with a current of emotion that I can only describe as extreme positivity, what I prefer to call 'love.' Yes, despite his call for Islamic executions (and in his very speech that day he called for a pardoning of thousands of prisoners who were amenable to change allegiance) his unwavering sternness of mien, his invulnerability to individual feeling, he was charged with a love that actually seemed to purify my heart, to fill it with a bliss that I had not known before...imagine for a moment the pushing of the body of oneself out of one's mother's womb, or the moment when one might awaken to the fact that one was being created inside a foetal body, or the moment when one was conscious of dying...Khomeini was that powerful, Khomeini was that strong; Khomeini was that egoless and invincible. In a moment I saw all the impulses of the revolution, the whole history of the overthrow of the Shāh, the rhythms of martyrdom...all of this contained in the presence of this man..." (*The Imām and His Islamic Revolution.*) *See* HIDDEN IMĀM; IRAN; PAHLAVI; UṢŪLĪS.

Khul' (lit. "release"). A form of divorce based upon mutual consent in which the wife is obliged to return the bride-price. *See* DIVORCE.

Khuṭbah, *see* SERMON.

Khums (lit. a "fifth part"). The portion of the spoils of war that the Prophet reserved for himself and for the use of the community. Among the Sunnīs the institution lapsed with the death of the Prophet, but among the Shī'ites it is preserved as a special religious tithe collected by the *Mujtahids* from their followers on behalf of the Hidden Imām.

Khurramiyyah (also called "Khurramdinids"). An Iranian dualist sect of pre-Islamic origin in the *3rd*/9th century centered around Badh in north Persia, near Azerbaijan. After the Muslim conquest, many followers of such sects outwardly professed Islam, while secretly keeping their own beliefs. In the time of the Caliph al-Ma'mūn (d. *218*/833) the Khurramiyyah were led by a figure called Jawīdān and caused civil unrest. After the death of Jawīdān, the Khurramiyyah were led by a successor called Babak, who acquired a great notoriety in the 'Abbāsid Empire.

The Khurramiyyah were held in abhorrence by the Muslims of the age because they were believed to be libertines in the tradition of the Mazdakites, a Manichean sect which arose within Zoroastrianism at the beginning of the 6th century A.D. who practiced vegetarianism and – or such is the usual accusation – held women and property in common. The Mazdakite sect flourished for a short time under the Shāh Kobad (d. 531 A.D.) and was then put down with a massacre. The story of the Mazdakites was cited by the Vizier Niẓām al-Mulk (d. *485*/1092) in his "Book of Government" (*Siyāsat-Nāmeh*) as a warning to the Saljūq princes and the 'Abbāsids regarding the Assassin sect of his age.

In the reign of the Caliph al-Mu'taṣim (d. *227*/842), at a time of civil unrest caused by famine, the Khurramiyyah rose in revolt; Babak, however, was captured by Afshin, a Persian prince and general of the Caliph, and was put to death in Samarrā' in the year *223*/838. Afshin was greatly honored and richly rewarded for putting down the revolt. Ibrāhīm ibn Mahdī, an uncle of the Caliph, said in a sermon from the pulpit: "Prince of True Believers, Glory, Glory to God! Thy warfare is accomplished; God is thy Warrior, let God's good slave Afshin take luck for his reward; the blow he struck has fastened a radiance on his face."

After the death of Babak, the Khurramiyyah persisted under this name for some time thereafter, all the while being progessively Islamicised, at least outwardly.

Afshin himself, shortly after the execution of Babak, was accused by Mazyar, another rebel, a chieftain of Tabaristān, of instigating the revolt for which Mazyar was himself captured. According to Mazyar and other captured rebel chiefs from Soghdiana, they were all of them, including Afshin, secretly members of a Magian religion. Afshin, on being tried by the 'Abbāsid authorities, professed himself a dutiful Muslim who had only permitted peoples under his control in Soghdiana (a stronghold of Manicheism) to retain their old religions for the sake of civil tranquility. However, one of his accusers, a Soghdian warlord, said that Afshin received letters addressing him as "God of gods", a title his family had possessed in their old religion as Princes of Surushna. From the revelations against him, and his own admissions, Afshin was found guilty of treason and put to death, as were his accusers and rebelling co-religionists.

Khusraw, Nāṣir-i see NĀṢIR-I KHUSRAW.

Khwārizm Shāhīs (Islamic rulers from the *2nd*/8th century until *628*/1231). Rulers of a Persian kingdom, Khwārizm, situated around the Oxus (Amu Darya) river south of the Aral Sea, and extending in the direction of the Syr Darya (Jaxartes) river. The region had been ruled by Persian dynasties from the 4th century A.D. on. A slave-vassal of the Saljūqs, Anushtigin, founded the last dynasty around *470*/1077. For a while the Khwārizm Shāhīs filled the power vacuum after the Saljūqs and controlled regions far to the south of Khwārizm until the Mongols arrived on the scene in *617*/1220. Later the region was known as the Khānate of Khiva.

al-Khwārizmī, Muḥammad ibn Mūsā (d. *226*/840). The mathematician, born in Khwārizm, Persia, after whom the *algorithm* is named. The word *algebra* is derived from his use of the word *al-jabr* ("coercion", "restoration"), which first appeared in his book on mathematics *al-Maqālah fī ḥisāb al-jabr wa-l-muqābilah.* It was the Latin translation of this work that introduced the algebraic concept into Europe.

His works on mathematics established the use of the Indian system of counting which became known as Arabic numerals, and the use of the zero. He also made astronomical calculations and did work on geography, sundials, and astrolabes.

al-Kindī, Abū Yūsuf Ya'qūb ibn Isḥāq (d. *256*/870). The first important philosopher in Islam, and a student of the sciences and medicine. Born in Kufah, al-Kindī was known in Europe as the "Philosopher of the Arabs"; some of his works were translated into Latin but many of the three hundred Arabic treatises attributed to him are lost; around seventy survive. Al-Kindī, a calligrapher at the Caliphal court at Baghdad, was the forerunner of the tradition of Islamic philosophy which studied Plato and Aristotle as complements to each other.

Al-Kindī made contributions in mathematics, astronomy, chemistry and the theory of music. He defined philosophy as "the knowledge of the realities of things according to human capacity" and said there was a universal and supreme Truth (accessible to reason, which in religion and revelation, is taken to be self-evident).

He was one of the first to confront the problem of creation, which according to Aristotelian philosophy is eternal whereas, according to revelation, it is an act of God out of nothingness, *ex nihilo.* Al-Kindī's solution was to turn to Pythagoreanism and Neoplatonism, and to propose that creation is an emanation from an ultimate sphere, and that the ultimate sphere is created by God and can be "uncreated" by Him. It can be said that al-Kindī affirmed emanation and creation side by side in a solution resembling the apocatastasis of the Stoic philosophers and the early Church Fathers. Al-Kindī's approach developed in a climate when Mu'tazilite rationalism dominated religious thinking, and when it was important to establish harmony between reason and revelation.

Al-Kindī proposed allegorical interpretation of the Koran, or *ta'wīl*, as the solution to a typical problem such as the following: when the Koran affirms that "God says to a thing: 'Be!' and it is"(Koran 2;117; 3:47; 6:73; 16:42; 19:36; 40:70), God addresses something as existing *before* its existence. Allegorical interpretation here resolves the apparent logical contradiction; but what is important is that al-Kindī recognized that antinomy is inherent in metaphysics, antinomy being the recognition that contradictions irreducible on one plane (as opposed to paradoxes, which are a different matter), may be resolved – or cease to exist – on another. If such apparent contradictions and non-contradictions exist, they do so because the mind, in order to conceive reality analytically, is forced to reduce its formulations to one or another plane. It is thought itself which creates the kind of problem antinomy resolves. *See* APOCATASTASIS; BEING; FIVE DIVINE PRESENCES; KALĀM; MU'TAZILITES; PHILOSOPHY.

Kirām al-Kātibīn (lit. "noble scribes"). The recording Angels are conceived of, in popular Islam, as working in pairs, one to the right and one to the left of each person, inscribing respectively the individual's good and evil deeds (82:11). It is further believed popularly that the salutation of peace to the right and then to the left is directed to these recording Angels.

Kirghiz. A pastoral Muslim people found in the former Soviet Republic of Kyrgyzstan, in China, and Afghanistan. The Kirghiz are *yurt* nomads rather than *tent* nomads. Most of the Afghan Kirghiz have now fled to Pakistan.

The Kirghiz are Turkic-speaking, but of mixed Turkic and Mongol descent who lived in the Minusinsk Steppe on the upper branches of the Yenesei river in southern Siberia. They migrated to the Tien Shan where they merged with Mongols. They belonged to the "White Horde" fraction of the "Golden Horde" of Hūlāgū Khān and separated from the suzerainty of the Uzbeks in the fifteenth century. They came under the control of Uzbek Khānate of Kokand in the 19th century and were conquered into the Russian empire in 1876. Before the 1917 revolution they were called Kara-Kirghiz whereas the people now called Kazakhs were called the Kirghiz. They were Islamicised in the 18th century. There are 2,480,000 Kirghiz in Kyrgyzstan and another 100,000 in Sinkiang in China. There were over 25,000 Kirghiz in Afghanistan, most of whom fled to Pakistan during the Afghan war. They have a national epic called the Manas which is 250,000 lines long and is recited from memory by *shamans*. *See* KYRGYZSTAN; MONGOLS.

Kismet (from Ar. *qismah*, "part", "portion", "lot"). This word for fate made its way into European languages from Arabicized Persian through Turkish.

Kiswah. The black cloth which covers the Ka'bah, it is woven of a mixture of silk and cotton and is embroidered with calligraphic inscriptions from the Koran in gold thread in bands around the top. The whole cloth also has the Divine Name Allāh patterned in black on black throughout.

Tradition (probably to exalt the family of the 'Abbāsids) says that the mother of 'Abbās was the first to drape the Ka'bah with a *kiswah*. Originally the *kiswah* was woven by the Hārīthiya in Najran, a center of weaving; later at the imperial Dār al-Tīraz in Tustar in Iran. In modern times the *kiswah* was woven and embroidered in Cairo from generation to generation by a family called as-Sa'di; now the workshop has been moved to Mecca. The *kiswah* is changed each year; the old *kiswah* is cut up and distributed to pilgrims. During the changing, the Ka'bah is covered for several days with a white *kiswah*, and is popularly said to be "putting on *iḥrām*" ("consecration") as would a pilgrim. The color black has a sacred meaning (as in the ancient name of Egypt, *Khem*, the "Black Country") because it can symbolize the non-manifestation of Beyond-Being, or the Absolute.

Kitāb al-Jafr (lit. the "Book of Vellum" from *jafr*, a lamb, the book being written on vellum). An alleged book of secret teaching which the Shī'ites believe was compiled by 'Alī for the use of his descendants.

First specific mention of such a book is associated with Ja'far aṣ-Ṣādiq, the sixth Imām. That 'Alī kept a notebook (*ṣaḥīfah*), which may have contained his interpretations of Koranic verses and other thoughts is likely; that it contained anything substantial which he did not transmit to those who came to him for guidance is another matter, and indeed, the Sufis hold that 'Alī was one among others, who transmitted esoteric doctrine; that the notebook contained great secrets is a belief of those who believe there are great secrets. Allusions to such a book have filtered into Sunnī folklore where it is called the "Book of Hidden Things" (*Kitāb al-mughaybāt*), and it has become common to ascribe various predictions, typically of apocalyptic events, to such a book. In modern Arabic the term *'ilm al-jafr* ("the science [of the Book] of Vellum") has come to signify divination and fortune-telling.

Koran (Ar. *al-qur'ān*, lit. the "reading", or the "recitation"). The holy book of Islam, the Koran is commonly also called the *muṣḥaf* ("collection of pages", "scripture"), *al-furqān* (lit. the "discrimination – between truth and unreality"), *al-Kitāb* ("the book"), *adh-dhikr* ("the Remembrance") and many other names. In formal speech it is called *al-qur'an al-karīm* ("the Noble Koran"), or *al-qur'ān al-majīd* ("the Glorious Koran").

The Koran was revealed by God in a form of Arabic closely corresponding to the refined usage of the Meccan aristocracy of the Quraysh, but readily accessible to the speakers of other tribal dialects. However, although the language of the Koran is related to what had already become the poetical *koine* of the Arabs, it cannot be equated with it, for in every respect the Koran is subject to no rule, to no measure, to no standard; it is itself its own law. Its language became the basis of formal or classical Arabic, both literary and spoken, but while unquestionably the standard, its style is nevertheless inimitable. The Koran could be called poetry, or poetic prose, though much is of a striking austerity. The earlier, Meccan passages are frequently reminiscent of the pre-Islamic style called *saj'*, which stands between poetry and prose, with assonances, rhymes and near-rhymes, and line-lengths and meters which frequently shift. The following example, the Sūrah 81, gives some idea of this style, necessarily remote in translation:

In the Name of God, the Merciful, the
Compassionate
When the sun shall be darkened,
when the stars shall be thrown down,
when the mountains shall be set moving,
when the pregnant camels shall be neglected,
when the savage beasts shall be mustered,
when the seas shall be set boiling,
when the souls shall be coupled,
when the buried infant shall be asked for what sin
she was slain,when the scrolls shall be unrolled,
when Heaven shall be stripped off,
when Hell shall be set blazing,
when Paradise shall be brought nigh,
then shall a soul know what it has produced.

No! I swear by the slinkers,
the runners, the sinkers,
by the night swarming,
by the dawn sighing,
truly this is the word of a noble Messenger
having power, with the Lord of the Throne secure,
obeyed, moreover trusty.

Your companion is not possessed;
he truly saw him on the clear horizon;
he is not niggardly of the Unseen.

And is not the word of an accursed Satan;
where then are you going?

It is naught but a Reminder
unto all beings,
for whosoever of you who would go straight;
but will you shall not, unless God wills,
the Lord of all Being.

The revelation of the Koran began about the year 610; the Prophet was engaged, that year as others, in meditation in the cave of Ḥirā' (*ghār Ḥirā*), near the very summit of the mountain Jabal Nūr, during the holy month of Ramaḍān. In one of the last nights of the month (*see* LAYLAT al-QADR) the Angel Gabriel appeared to him with the first revelation, the beginning of Sūrah 96:

Read out! [*'iqra*, from which *qur'an*, "reading"], in
the Name of thy Lord who creates,
who creates man from
a blood-clot. Read out!
for thy Lord is the Most Munificent
who teaches by the pen, teaches
man that which he knew not.

The revelation continued sporadically, reflecting the events attendant on the birth of Islam, and directing the actions and responses of the Prophet as circumstances required. The Koran contains laws for society and warnings of the end of the world, descriptions of judgement, of Heaven and of Hell. There are stories of Biblical figures, but often in a form surprisingly different from that of the Hebrew Scriptures, as if the same events were being witnessed from a different point of view. It also contains stories of figures unknown to the Bible, and passages which are metaphysical and non-descriptive. Sacred history is a secondary preoccupation; the subject of the Koran is above all the Divine Nature and the means of salvation.

Many stories in the Koran resemble those of the Jewish *midrash*, popular and didactic versions of Biblical events which act as commentaries on the Scriptures. Here God is speaking, as it were, in terms of the lore inherited by the Arabs as descendants of Abraham and Ishmael, such as the accounts of creation, of Adam, and of Noah, the legends of Moses and Solomon, and events from the Arabs' own history, such as the stories of the Prophets Hūd and Ṣālih. These were well-known to the men of the Prophet's day, and indeed to the Prophet, who incarnated the spiritual heritage of the Arabs.

In order to grasp the phenomenon of the Koran, what needs to be borne in mind is that Divine revelation is destined by God not simply for scholars, historians and those who have knowledge of comparative religion, but for the commonalty of men living at a particular place at a particular time, to whom the revelation is needful in order to encompass the truths of God and immortality. It is addressed, more immediately, to such men of that time and place as God has chosen to lay the foundations of a new society, to establish and consolidate in the world a religion that will endure beyond their time and spread beyond their land. To this end, God addresses men in a language they know, in concepts that are in part familiar (and in part amazingly new), against a background of received common knowledge, hearsay, mythology, and even prejudice. It is not surprising, therefore, that certain of the Koranic narratives or accounts of the creeds of Christianity and Judaism do not correspond to those religions' understanding of their own legends and beliefs.

What is certain, however, is that these Koranic expositions were – and are – appropriate to the knowledge, mentality and emotions of those whom God wished to be Muslims; they necessarily reflected a corpus of truths as perceived in the world of that time from which God could lay down a "Straight Path" leading to His absolute Truth to which, for them, no other faith was possible: "Praise belongs to God, who guided us unto this; had God not guided us, we had surely never been guided" (7:43); to use allegory, analogy, repetition and multiple reflection of the innumerable facets of myth and doctrine is part of the Divine contriving whereby men are saved: "God has sent down the most excellent of records, a book allegorical and many-layered..."(39:23). And "now We have coined for men, in this Koran, every kind of parable, that perchance they may bethink themselves, a Koran in Arabic, with nothing crooked in it, that perchance they may learn piety" (39:27-28).

The extent to which God has adapted His Message to men's knowledge and questioning – both inevitably relative and inadequate from the perspective of God's absolute and total (and to us unimaginable) knowledge –is indicated by the frequency of such introductory phrases as the following: "They [will] ask: when is the Judgement Day?" (51:12); "They will ask thee: when [will] the Hour fall?" (59:42); "They [will] ask thee about the Spirit" (17:85); "They [will] ask thee about him of the two horns [*dhū-l-qarnayn*, Alexander the Great as mentioned in legend]; say thou: I shall recite to you an account of him" (18:83). Here, as everywhere in the Koran, God is addressing the Prophet; referring to men's questions, God gives the answer to men, through the inspiration vouchsafed to His Prophet.

And because the legends were well known, the Koran's recounting of the myths is frequently so concise, and even elliptical, that an acquaintance with the store of popular oral literature current in the Prophet's day is needed to fill out the details, but not to fill out what the Koran is expounding by them. In practice, these legends remain familiar today; most Muslims know that the name of the Queen of Sheba was Bilqīs, and that the mysterious guide of Moses in the Sūrah of the Cave was al-Khiḍr, although neither name occurs in the text of the Koran.

However, in the concise re-telling of traditional tales and the purveying of understanding about other "religions of the Book", the essential and specifically Islamic doctrines of the Oneness of God, and the duties of men in the face of this re-asserted Oneness, are expounded with an eloquence and profundity that have left Muslims over the centuries in no doubt that the Koran is the direct and saving Word of God. And the miracle of it is that, out of this material that was very much of its age and place, there has come forth a Message that is timeless and universal. The Koran was the sole miracle, of any kind, which the Prophet admitted during his entire ministry of prophethood.

Western writers who, for reasons of the defence of Christianity and Judaism, or for reasons of their disbelief (*kufr*) in any Divine Revelation, have been wont to disparage the Koran as regards factual, historical accuracy, or have spoken of Muḥammad's confused knowledge of history or of his imperfect or deficient knowledge of Judaism are, in every respect, wide of the mark. To begin with, such observations presume the Prophet's participation in the composition of the Koran, which is in no way admissible. The accusation is not new; it was made in the Prophet's day and refuted frequently in the Koran itself, as in, for example, the Sūrah of the Star:

> By the Star when it plunges,
> your comrade is not astray, neither errs,
> nor speaks he out of caprice.
> This is naught but a revelation revealed,
> taught him by one terrible in power...
> ...then revealed to his servant that he revealed.
> His heart lies not of what he saw;

what, will you dispute with him what he sees?
(53:1-5, 10-11)

Al-Jurjānī (Ash'arite theologian, d. *816*/1413) asked what it was that made the Koran different from human literature, for the stories could be imitated, and so could the style. The difference, he concluded, was a spiritual presence in the Koran, a force, a blessing, a *barakah*. Although the stories in the Koran have their historical origins, they undergo a transformation which lifts them out of their former context into a retelling which is not that of a human tongue. For example, the story of Dhū-l-Qarnayn and his building of a great wall (18:95), possibly reflects legends the Arabs had heard about the Great Wall of China, or the great wall built at Derbent near the Caspian by the Sassanid king Chosroes (Anushirvan) against the Huns. Divine revelation then took this material and used it for its own purposes; the origins of the story become irrelevant, and it serves instead as a support to mirror heaven's sense, a *mathal*, or similitude. The once Chinese wall becomes the partition of Divine Law erected by God's viceroy between His creation and chaos, which will be breached in the apocalypse. Folklore stripped to its essence becomes pure symbol; God coins similitudes [*amthāl*] for men, and God has knowledge of everything (24:36). And: God is not ashamed to strike a similitude even of a gnat (2:24).

The Trinity as seen in the Koran, is not the trinity of the Apostles' Creed, nor the Nicene Creed, but a Trinity empty of all exegesis, a Trinity compared only to the evidentness and Absoluteness of the Divine Unity. Similarly, the Docetist doctrines concerning the crucifixion of Jesus as appearance were known among the Arabs. The description of the crucifixion in the Koran as an illusion (4:156), however, is not touched by any Docetist origins and purposes, for these are as alien to Islam as they are to Christianity. Instead, God recasts a cosmic event which, in Christianity, is seen providentially from the human point of view, into God's vision of it in Islam. The event seen by God becomes a restatement of the *shahādah*: *lā ilāha illa-Llāh*: there is no god but God."

The revelation of the Koran was the ordering of the Prophet's very soul into the form of sacred words according to the Divine Command, to God's disposition of things. This occurred in the "Night of Destiny or of Power", the *Laylat al-Qadr*, the night of revelation. This sacred night, according to 'Ā'ishah, the Prophet's favourite wife, was the very soul of the Prophet.

Behold, We sent it down on the Night of Power;
And what shall teach thee what is the Night of Power?
The Night of Power is better than a thousand months;
in it the angels and the Spirit descend,
by the leave of their Lord, upon every command.
Peace it is, till the rising of the dawn. (97)

The words were then brought out of the being of the Prophet into the day, as Sūrahs, and *āyāt*, called forth in many cases by the immediate circumstances as events unfolded for years to come.

The revelations ended with these words: "Today have I perfected your religion for you, and I have completed My blessing upon you, and I have approved Islam [*al-Islām*] for your religion" (5:5). This was part of the sermon to the multitudes delivered during the farewell pilgrimage in March 632 (A.H. *10*), a few months before the Prophet's death on 8 June 632 (A.H. *11*). Abū Bakr wept when he heard these words because he understood then that this was the end of the revelations. The camel upon which the Prophet was mounted during the sermon buckled under the numinous weight which often came over the Prophet when the Spirit settled upon him.

The Koran was written down in part during its revelation, but above all it was committed to memory, as is the custom of traditional and largely pre-literate cultures. Until the most recent times the first phase of primary education in the Muslim world was the memorizing of the Koran. In many countries, even today, thousands upon thousands know the entire Koran by memory. According to tradition, a definitive editing of the Koran was carried out in the Caliphate of 'Uthmān in order to avoid complications caused by variant texts. Earlier collections may have been made in the Caliphates of Abū Bakr and 'Umar, but 'Uthmān's definitive text was determined by a commission headed by a secretary of the Prophet, Zayd ibn Thābit, along with 'Abd Allāh ibn az-Zubayr, Sa'īd ibn al-'Ās, and 'Abd ar-Raḥmān ibn al-Ḥārith. The Koran was collected from the chance surfaces on which it had been inscribed: "from pieces of papyrus, flat stones, palm leaves, shoulder blades and ribs of animals, pieces of leather, wooden boards, and the hearts of men."

The Koran is the foundation and primary source of doctrine of Islam. In this, it is followed by the Ḥadīth (traditions of the Prophet) and Sunnah (the Prophet's example). The Koran is recited as a blessing to both reciter and hearer, and studied as the key to the knowledge of God. Islamic law prohibits the touching of the physical Arabic Koran (and formal, but not casual, recitation) unless the person is in a state of purity which corresponds to the greater ablution, or *ghusl* (*lā yamassuhū illa-l-muṭahharūn*). It is a prescription that every Muslim must commit at least twelve verses or lines of the Koran to memory.

The Koran is divided into 114 chapters each of which is called a Sūrah (a "row" pl. *sūrāt*). The Sūrahs are composed of verses each of which is called an *āyah* (lit. a "sign"; pl. *āyāt*). Today the Koran is arranged in such a way that all the longer Sūrahs precede the shorter; and the whole is divided into thirty approximately equal lengths called *ajzā'* (sing. *juz'*), for the purposes of regular reading. One *juz'* is allotted for each day of reading in a month. Each *juz'* is divided into two *aḥzāb* (sing. *ḥizb*), one to be read in the mosque with the *salāt aṣ-ṣubḥ* ("morning prayer") and another with the *salāt al-maghrib* ("evening prayer"). This and other divisions are customarily marked in the margins.

The revelations are identified as having been revealed either at Mecca, or at Medina. The earlier, Meccan revelations have a more poetic and enthusiastic character, throwing forth powerful images of the world's end and existence's reabsorption into the Divine uncreatedness. The Medinan revelations are, on the other hand, like the calm after a storm, and deal mainly with the giving of laws. However, in the canonic recension of the Caliph 'Uthmān, some Meccan chapters contain verses revealed at Medina and vice versa, so that the text's disjointed and irregular character has tempted Western scholars to try to rearrange it in a more apparent order.

These attempts are ill-advised, however, for the Koran's sudden shifts in meaning, points of view, and depth are in the very nature of the text. The Koran is heaven's sense compressed or refracted into human intelligibility, and it is inevitable that the vicissitudes the Koran has undergone in the world, namely, its first limitation into human language, memory, understanding, and dialect, and then its historic assembly into a written text, reflect the disparity between the human order as it is – not in an ideal world – and the Divine order. Jalāl ad-Dīn ar-Rūmī suggested that it is this very nature, outwardly chaotic, that is a "ruse" of the Koran to approximate the chaotic nature of the human soul, in order then to catch it, as a net catches a fish, and to bring it back to absorption in the Divine from which the soul has wandered. The impression the Koran can make when it is read is like a progression in a labyrinth which suddenly opens out into a secret and transcendent center. Its stories are those of the past, but they are also stories of the present and the future. They multiply themselves into an infinity of reflections, and then without motion bring the subject face to face with the Unity of God.

Fundamental to Islam and self-evident beyond any question to the believer is the fact that the Koran is Divinely revealed, that its author is God Himself. That He sometimes speaks in the first person singular, sometimes in the plural, sometimes in the third person, has never troubled Muslims, and has never been a stumbling block to belief. These shifts confront one with a space or consciousness different from our own, beyond our human limitations, and total, compared to which the human sense of logic is clearly small and fragmentary, incommensurate, and almost irrelevant. Faith is conviction through direct experience, and not the result of a process of reason.

The substance of the Koran is completely wedded to its Arabic form. Because the Koran is what is called in Sanskrit *shruti* ("primary revelation" or God Himself speaking) – unlike much of the New Testament which is *smriti* ("secondary revelation") – and because of the nature of Arabic as a sacred language, a language capable of transmitting *shruti*, it is completely impossible to translate the Koran in its *reality* into another language. Translations are therefore unusable for ritual and liturgical purposes. The sound itself, of inimitable sonority and rhythmic power, is numinous and sacramental.

It is a fundamental doctrine of Islam that the Koran, as the speech of God, is eternal and uncreated in its essence and sense, created in its letters and sounds (*ḥarf wa jarḥ*). It has been asserted that the doctrine of the uncreated Koran was the result of exposure to the Christian dogma of the Logos; that, as the Christians defined Jesus as the Word of God and as having two natures, one human and one Divine in one person, so the Muslims transposed this doctrine by analogy to the Koran as the Word of God made book. The Muslims were indeed aware of the Christian doctrine; the Caliph al-Ma'mūn (d. *218*/833), who supported the Mu'tazilite theory that the Koran *was* created, wrote to one of his governors that belief in the uncreatedness of the Koran resembled the Christians when they claim that Jesus was not created because he was the "Word of God". During the brief Mu'tazilite ascendancy which began in the Caliphate of al-Ma'mūn, belief in the uncreated Koran was temporarily suspended arousing fierce opposition. The Koran was declared to be created, and those opposed to this view were persecuted during an inquisition called the *miḥnah* (*218-232*/833-847) into the beliefs of the religious authorities. Yet lawyers and Judges staunchly upheld the dogma of the uncreated Koran, and nurtured it when necessary in secret. Ibn Ḥanbal went further, and declared that the Koran was uncreated from "cover to cover", that is, also in its letters and its sounds. In this he was certainly not intending to imitate the Monophysites, but he was flogged for his beliefs. When the *miḥnah* came to an end, the doctrine of the uncreatedness was restored, and has not been challenged since, in the Sunnī world. The Khārijites differ from the Sunnīs on this point, and in their dogmas the Koran is entirely created, which is also true for the Shī'ites, both Twelve-Imām and Zaydi, whose theology in many ways is an extension of that of the Mu 'tazilites. *See also* al-ḤURŪF al-MUQATTA'ĀT; LAYLAT al-QADR; MUḤAMMAD; PROPHETS; QIRĀ'ĀT; REVELATION; UMMĪ.

Koran, Chanting. The recital (*tilāwah* or *qirā'ah*) of the Koran is governed by the science of *tajwīd* (lit. "adornment", making beautiful or "striving for excellence") which determines the full, smooth and balanced pronunciation, in context, of each letter and syllable. On this basis, which is fundamental as being the necessary and minimum according of respect to the revealed Word of God, there are three "*tempi*" of recitation: slow and measured (*tartīl*); moderate (*tadwīr*); and rapid, as for swift narration (*ḥadr*). One whose mastery of *tajwīd* and psalmody qualifies him for regular chanting in public is known as a reciter (*qāri'*, pl. *qurrā*).

Only the canonical Arabic text, as collected and compiled under the Caliph 'Uthmān with the consensus of the Companions (*ijmā' aṣ-ṣahābah*) may be recited, in one of the seven acceptable versions of punctuation and vocalization (*al-qirā'āt as-sab'ah*). These, though fixed only in the fourth century of the Hijrah, are taken to correspond to the seven *aḥruf* ("letters", versions or, possibly, "dialects") of the Koran which, according to a Ḥadīth, the Prophet referred to as all having divine authority. In practice, only two of the seven readings have become customary: in Egypt, for example, the "reading" of Hafṣ according to the scholar Abū Bakr 'Āṣim; and in the rest of Africa that of Nāfi'.

The punctuation laid down by these *qirā'āt* is important because single verses may well contain more than one sentence, and the punctuation will then indicate the pause that should be made at the end of the sentence, or sentences. Or, on the contrary, a single sentence may run across more than one verse, in which case it would break the sense to pause at the end of a verse. Korans are therefore marked to help the reader to determine where stops and pauses are possible, and where they should not be made. If the meaning of the words is understood, this is usually clear from the text, but many Koran chanters, even those of Arabic mother tongue, do not always fully understand the sense of the words, and there are instances, notably passages which are "embracing" (*mu'āniqah*), where one sense is possible if a stop is made, and another if it is not. In such passages tradition determines how they are to be read. Some Korans have a *mim* and *'ayn* symbol, which stands for *mu 'āniqah*, indicating that a line or a word can be understood as referring to either the passage preceding or following; these are then marked with three dots (cf. *fīhi* in Koran 2:2, which can either end the previous phrase, or begin the following; tradition indicates no stop to be made here).

The rules of *tajwīd*, which seem complex considered separately, are essentially the application of phonetic principles inherent in the

Arabic language, and can be summarized under three headings: 1. Assimilation of certain consonants (cf. Sanskrit *sandhi*); 2. Modification of vowels; 3. Pausal abbreviations.

1. Consonants with the same point of articulation "blend" in Arabic, cf. the so-called "solar" consonants following the *al* of the definite article: as *al-nūr* is pronounced *an-nūr*, conversely *in-lā* becomes *illā*; the final nasal (*tanwīn*) of, say, *Muḥammadan rasūl* becomes *Muḥammadar-rasūl* (although the nasal remains gently audible); *mīn-bad* is pronounced *mim-bad*; *an-yabud* is pronounced *ay-yabud*; *qad tabayyan* is pronounced *qat-tabayyan* etc.

2. The quality of the three fundamental vowels (*a i u*) is affected by an adjacent, and in particular by a preceding, consonant. For example, the gutturals and palatal hard consonants make for an "open" *a*, in contrast to the tendency for this letter to undergo "umlaut" (*imālah* meaning "learning" [towards *i*]) after soft consonants. The open long *ā* in the Divine Name *Allāh* is particularly important and characteristic, for in this word alone in the entire language the consonant *l* is hard and palatal; however, if the Divine Name is prefixed by the preposition *li*, making the compound *li-Llāh*, then under the influence of the vowel *i*, the double *l* is softened and the following long *ā* is subject to *imālah*.

Long vowels before double consonants or two consonants together are shortened: e.g. *fī s-samāwāt* is read *fissamāwāt*, the long *i* of *fī* being shortened by the *ss*; and *mā'ktasabat* is pronounced *maktasabat*. In an apparent exception to this, a long vowel before a double consonant which is historically single is lengthened in compensation, and for the sake of clarity: eg. *ḍāllīn* from an underlying *ḍālilīn*. Similarly a long vowel followed by the glottal stop called *hamza* is lengthened by the degree of 3-1 if it occurs within a word, and by the degree of 2-1 if it occurs between two words.

3. In pausal forms, i.e. in words at the end of phrases or sentences, the final element – be it *tanwīn* (nasal), declensional or conjugational vowel (*i'rāb*) or dotted *h* (pronounced *t*) – is dropped: thus, for *waḥdahu*, *waḥdah*; for *khayran*, *khayra*; for *yu'minūna*, *yu'minūn*; for *jannatun*, *jannah* (because two rules, as it were, come conjointly into play).

Other rules of *tajwīd* aimed at clarity and comprehensibility include an emphatic pronunciation of all doubled consonants (*tashdīd*) and particularly of the double *n*, as in *innā*; and, in the not uncommon occurence of final *m*, the compressing of the lips until after the voicing ceases.

Adherence to these phonetic rules over the centuries has been successful in conserving a smooth, "classical" pronunciation of great beauty, power and sonority; it has also saved the sound of the Koran from being corrupted by the many phonetic reductions that have impinged upon the various Arabic vernaculars.

There are passages in the Koran (cf. 41:37; 96:19 and others) which when read or heard, oblige the hearer, if possible, to make a bow (*rukū'*), or a prostration (*sajdah*). Some such *sajdahs*, in 48:25, are prescribed by some schools, in this case Abū Ḥanīfah and Ibn Mālik, but not by the other schools. If the reader or hearer of a passage called for a *sajdah* or *rukū'* is seated, he should rise up and perform a *rukū'* if it is called for, but a *sajdah* can be performed directly from a sitting position and the reading then continues. If these occur in the recitation portion of a ritual prayer (*ṣalāt*), a *sajdah* or a *rukū'* is performed at that time and the prayer resumes from the point at which the bow or the prostration occurred. In most Korans these passages are marked with the words *rukū'* or *sajdah* in the margin or between the lines. Not every *sajdah* so marked is obligatory for all schools of law. *See* QIRA'AH.

Koran, Translation of . It is sometimes said that the Koran cannot be translated, in the sense that translation is prohibited by religious law. The Koran has in fact been translated from the very beginning when there were variant readings because of variations in Arabic dialects. Partial translations always existed for the use of non-Arabic speakers, and complete translations were made, for example, by Sadi Shirāzī and Shaykh Walī Allāh into Persian, and by the sons of Walī Allāh into Urdu. Printed Arabic Korans with interlinear Persian and Urdu translations have existed for some time. However, a translation of the Koran cannot be used ritually, for prayer, for invocation, or for serious study; for these only the Arabic Koran can be used. (In Asia, exeptionally, there are some Muslims who use the Koran in translation for certain ritual applications.) It is inevitable that translations of the Koran imply some point of view. For example, the very popular translation by A.

Yūsuf ʻAlī into English is translated from the Bohora Ismāʻīli point of view and contains their doctrinal notions, and that of Maulana Muḥammad ʻAlī, from the Aḥmadiyyah. For Sunnīs, one of the translations with the least number of objections is the Muḥammad Marmaduke Pickthall rendering.

Koranic School. Traditionally, the first schooling a child receives in Islamic societies. The Koranic school is being replaced by modern systems of education but is still found in many places. Colloquially, these schools are often called *kuttāb* or *m'seyyid*, and here children from four or five years of age learn to read and write, and are sometimes taught arithmetic. The full course of such a school culminates in the complete memorization of the Koran. The voices of a chorus of children reciting the Koran is one of the most characteristic neighborhood sounds of a traditional Islamic town. When the Koran is memorized in its entirety, the student's education is finished unless he goes on to the *madrasah* ("upper school"). As modern systems of education have today replaced the traditional one, the Koranic school has become a largely pre-school institution or an educative parallel for young children.

Traditionally, the teacher is paid at intervals as the student learns more of the Koran. The learning of the fifty-fifth chapter, the Sūrah *ar-Raḥmān*, marks an important step; the teacher is paid a bonus, often a certain number of sheep. (The payments are made for portions of the Koran actually memorized. In Arab pre-Islamic and Islamic custom the basis of remuneration is for accomplishment, not for effort or time). In addition, a sheep is sacrificed and a celebration called the *nafas ar-Raḥmān* ("the infusion of the breath of the Merciful One") is held for the child.

In Koranic schools the writing is traditionally done on wooden tablets called *lawḥ* which are painted over with a lime mixture to provide a clean smooth surface and to erase the previous lesson. The ink is a mixture made primarily from burnt wool to which water is added; the pen is a sharpened reed with the point cut at an angle on the left to produce the characteristic thick and thin of Arabic letters. A pupil's tablet may be very beautifully decorated by the calligraphy of the teacher to be brought home to the parents as a sign that some particular stage of Koranic study has been reached.

"Kosher", *see* ḤALĀL.

Kubrā, Najm ad-Dīn ibn ʻUmar (d. *618*/1221). A Khwarazmian Sufi, a disciple of Ismāʻīl al-Qaṣri at Dezful and Ammar ibn Yāsir Badlisi of the school of Abū Najib Suhrawardi, but also influenced by and related to the school of *ishrāq* of Shihāb ad-Dīn Suhrawardī (d. *587*/1191). He died at Khiva during the Mongol invasions. Kubrā was the founder of the Kubrāwiyyah order which was particularly influential in Central Asia. This Central Asian School of Sufism, related to Rūzbehān Baqlī of Shiraz (d. *606*/1209), evolved a complicated, Gnostic system of symbolism of light and colors as alchemical signs and visions experienced by the adept on his path of transformation. Henry Corbin, who brought this school to the attention of scholars, called this doctrine of colors photisms.

Najm ad-Dīn Rāzi (*573-654*/1177-1256), the successor of Kūbra, and Shams ad-Dīn Muḥammad Jīlānī Lāhījī (d. *912*/1506) said that black light (in Persian *nūr-e siyāh*) constituted the highest spiritual stage. (Semnānī said, however, that the "black light precedes an outburst of perception of green light or the emerald vision"). Black light is a construct for evil divinized. Metaphysically, evil is a lack of good or an error made by a consciousness in treating nothingness as if it were a substance and therefore as if it were derived from a Principle or from God. The Central Asian School is a form of radical Dualism because it treats evil positively and makes it equal to God or makes God into the source of evil. (*Lāhījī* was a Shaykh of the Nūrbakhshīyyah, closely related to the Kūbrawiyyah, and wrote a commentary of the *Gulshan-i Rāz*, "The Rose Garden of Mystery" of Mahmūd Shabistarī, d. *720*/1320.)

This radical Dualism of the Central Asian school parallels the doctrines of *ishrāq* for Shihāb ad-Dīn Suhrawardī also spoke of darkness as having a positive existence and created a cosmology in which there are points at which light is mixed with darkness, as if darkness existed without light. Both of these schools of thought, and other related ones, are late extensions in Islamic times and within an Islamic framework of heterodox Zoroastrian offshoots and consequently are repositories of Persian legend and metaphysical speculation.

Bahā' ad-Dīn Walad of Balkh (*540-629*/1145-

1231), father of Jalāl ad-Dīn ar-Rumī, is also considered to have been a disciple of Kūbra, although Balkh was itself an ancient home of this type of theosophy, and Bahā' ad-Dīn probably belonged to a collateral branch of the school, as did Rumī himself. A later well known figure of this school was 'Alā'ad-Dawlah Semnānī (*659-736*/1261-1336). The school had a great influence upon certain branches of Sufism in India through some, but not all, of the Naqshanbiyyah. Later branches of the Kūbrawiyyah are the Dhahabiyyah (for *silsilah dhahabiyyah*, the "school of the golden initiatic chain") in Shiraz, the Firdawsiyyah (in Bihar, India), the Rukniyyah, Ashrafiyyah (in India), Ya'qubūbiyyah (in India), Ightishāashiyyah, Hamadāniyyah, Nūrbakhshiyyah, and Lahjāniyyah. *See* ISHRĀQĪ.

al-Kufr (lit. "covering", "hiding" and, by extension, "disbelief"). Unbelief in God, the state of being an infidel, blasphemy. The word has more shocking and dreadful associations in the mind even of a Muslim of today than does the word "unbelief" for a Western believer. Unlike the idea of mere unbelief, which implies passivity, *kufr* clearly implies an active striving to block out God's evidentness, a will to oppose Him, a lack of gratitude for life and revelation. It is a denial of God, the *only* sin which God cannot forgive, because it refuses Him and His Mercy. The adjective is *kāfir*, an atheist, and the plural is *kāfirūn*, *kuffār*, *kafarah*, and *kifār*.

> Say: O unbelievers,
> I serve not what you serve
> and you are not serving what I serve,
> nor am I serving what you have served,
> neither are you serving what I serve.
>
> To you, your religion, and to me, my religion! (109)

See KĀFIR; SHIRK.

al-Kulaynī, Muḥammad Ibn Ya'qūb (d. *328*/939). Shī'ite theologian, author of the "Compendium of the Science of Religion" (*al-Kāfī fī 'Ilm ad-Dīn*). The book has two parts, the *Uṣūl al-Kāfī* ("Foundations of the Compendium"), and the *Furū' 'al-Kāfī* ("Branches of the Compendium"), and contains sixteen thousand Ḥadīth, or traditions, including those particular to Shī'ism. His work is one of the most important to Shī'ites among whom he is called the *Thiqat al-Islām* ("The Trust of Islam"). He died in Baghdad and is buried in Kufah. *See* SHĪ'ISM.

Kumūn. In Mu'tazilite philosophy the hiding of an effect within the cause, as in the idea, alluded to in the Koran, that fire is hidden in wood: "Have ye observed the fire which ye strike out; Was it ye who made the tree thereof to grow, or were We the grower?" (Koran 56:71-72). The idea was prominent with Nazzām; with this the world could be hidden in matter, only a different balance of qualities allowed one or another aspect to emerge in a particular manifestation at any one time. In this way, matter would be the source of reality as it is in modern physics. *Kumūn* is also an implicit assumption in theories of evolution, which were advanced by all the Gnostic schools who believed that souls transmigrated into higher states of life. Opposed to *kumūn* in Islamic philosophies are the occasionalists such as the Ash'arites and the *ashab al-arād*, "accidentalists", or Aristotelians.

Kun. The word "Be!". The Divine command which God gives to possibilities to manifest themselves, or be created. "When He decrees a thing, He but says to it: 'Be!'" (2:111): and "His command, when He desires a thing, is to say to it 'Be', and it is." (36:81) *Kun* is better translated as "exist!", for what is involved in this Divine command is a bringing into existence out of Being; God speaks to what already has being but what has not yet undergone the reduction that is manifested existence. It is for this reason that the verbal noun corresponding to *Kun* is *Kawn* which means the manifested "world", "cosmos", "universe"; and the corresponding causative noun *mukawwin* means "maker", "creator". In the terminology of the Sufis this distinction is made explicit by the use of the word *wujūd* for Being, as in Ibn 'Arabī's *waḥdat al-wujūd* (the "Unity of Being"). *See* al-KINDĪ.

Kunyah. An honorific name of paternity or maternity, as Abū Bakr, the "father of the virgin" or Umm Khulthūm, mother of Khulthūm. Often a man will be called by the name Abū, "father of" followed by the name of his first-born son. A mother may be called Umm, "mother of" followed also by the name of her eldest son. Such names arise from the idea that calling someone directly by their given name is impolite while a more oblique form of address is more honorable. (In Japan the socially polite word for "I" regularly changes as a particular elliptic form, such as "*boku*" which literally means "your servant" becomes too literally an affirmation of self and becomes itself impolite.)

But such a name can also stand on its own and be given to a child, especially as it is expected that a son will name his own son after the name of his father. Thus a young boy may often be called Abū Muḥammad if his father's name is Muḥammad. In some countries, particularly Egypt and Morocco, the Abū names are considered rustic. But in Iraq the use of kunyahs has become particularly elaborate. Everyone whose given name is Muḥammad may be referred to Abū 'l-Qasim because this was a *kunyah* of the Prophet Muḥammad. Everyone whose given name is 'Alī may be called Abū 'l-Ḥusayn because 'Alī was the father of Ḥusayn, and thus with other names that are associated with historical figures. The name Abū may also be used to createa name out of an outstanding characteristic. The Companion Abū Hurayrah was known as "father of the kitten" because of his affection for cats; the explorer Richard Burton was nicknamed the "father of the mustachios", Abū Shuwarib, when he performed the pilgrimage in disguise, for his appearance. *See* ISM; NAME; LAQAB; NISBAH.

Kurds. An Indo-European people, not Semitic or Turkic, who live mainly in a region referred to as Kurdistan, which includes parts of northern Iraq, western Iran, eastern Turkey, and northeastern Syria. Within this region there are about sixteen million Kurds who are nationals of the countries above. There are also some Kurds in Lebanon and the Soviet Union (where they are a recognized nationality).

The Kurds believe that they are descended from the ancient Medes. Although most Kurds are considered Sunnī, some in Iran are Twelve-Imām Shi'ites. A large number belong to such minority sects as the Yazīdīs and the 'Ahl-i Haqq (also called 'Alī Ilāhīs and 'Alawīs). Amongst those who are considered Sunnīs there exist many *darvishī* or "folk" mystical affiliations which are strongly heterodox. Besides the deeply ingrained folk practices within Kurdish Islam, the established Sufi organizations, the Naqshabandiyyah, and particularly the Qādiriyyah also teach secret beliefs which further augment a climate of sectarianism apparent on the surface and deeply engrained beneath it. Before Islam the Kurds were Zoroastrians and many traces of Magian religions are preserved among them. Saladin (Salāh ad-Dīn) was a famous Kurd who fought the Crusaders and founded the Ayyūbid dynasty.

Kurds have their own Iranian language which is broken into two main dialects and further sub-dialects. The Kurds were a tribal people; today only about 15% are herders, most are farmers. Under the Ottoman empire the Kurds had a measure of autonomy and were governed by tribal leaders and princes of tribal confederations. The rise of nationalism and the distintegration of the Ottoman empire left the Kurds divided between several countries in each of which they are a minority.

In this century, failing to achieve self-determination at the end of World War I, although the promise was held out by the Treaty of Sévres, the Kurds have fought lasting rebellions in attempts to gain independence, or at least greater autonomy. Between 1960 and 1975 in particular, because the Shāh of Iran gave Iraqi Kurds under General Mustafa Barzani support in uprisings against the Baghdad government, the Kurds fought long and hard. Their struggles, however, were without success for the Shāh's support was withdrawn once his own goals towards Iraq had been achieved.

In 1958 the regime of Colonel Kassim attempted to reach an accord with the Kurds of Iraq. General Barzani was allowed to return from exile in the Soviet Union and in 1959 Barzani assisted the government in putting down a revolt. By 1961 when Kurdish expectations had not been met, a revolt broke out. Reactions of the Baghdad government to Kurdish uprisings have been particularly sharp because of the economic importance of oil fields located in or near Kurdish areas. In 1964 talks were opened between the government and the Kurds. Agreements were announced in 1970; Kurdish was to be recognized as a national language along with Arabic; certain political concessions were promised. In 1974 an autonomy law was passed against a background of continuing armed struggle in which Iran and Syria provided staging areas for the Kurds, Israel supplied arms, and the United States economic support while the Soviet Union aided Iraq. Throughout the struggles the policy of the Baghdad government was to divide Kurds among themselves, offering one faction concessions while severely repressing another. There have also been sharp divisions among the Kurds themselves.

Promises were frequently made and broken. Tensions increased between Iran and Iraq until an agreement was made in March 1975 in Algiers on frontiers between the two countries, particularly the status of the Shatt al-Arab waterway. Iranian support for the Kurds was immediately withdrawn. The Iranian revolution led to Kurdish revolts in Iran and the Iran-Iraq war also involved Kurds on both sides.

Kursī (lit. "stool"). The "footstool" of God's "throne", (*al-'arsh*). It is also held that *kursī* is synonymous with *'arsh* and thus means "throne" as well. There is a famous Koranic verse known as the *ayat al-kursī*, or "verse of the throne".

One of the symbolic interpretations is that *al-'arsh* is Being, and *al-kursī* is non-formal manifestation, or the Angelic world. *See* ĀYAT al-KURSĪ; FIVE DIVINE PRESENCES.

Kuwait. State on the Arabian coast of the Persian Gulf, bordering on Saudi Arabia and Iraq. Population: 1,576,000 The majority are Sunnīs.

Kyrgyzstan. Independent in 1991, formerly part of the Soviet Union. Population 4,769,000, of whom 52% are Kirghiz and the rest Russians and Uzbeks. Capital Bishkek. *See* KIRGHIZ

L

Lailat.., *see* LAYLAT.

La'nah (lit. "cursing"). An ancient, but rare ritual of mutual imprecation which can be used to resolve certain disputes. *See* LI'ĀN; AHL al-KISĀ'.

Lahore (lit. "iron fort"). First mentioned by Baladhuri (d. *279*/892) as al-Āhvāar, and by the *Hudūd al-Ālam*, it is the most important city in the Punjab in Pakistan. Probably founded around the 2nd century A.D., this was a capital of the Ghaznavid empire, and after 1187 that of the Ghurids before being set aside in favor of Delhi. The Mongols sacked it in 1241, but under the Moghuls after its reconquest by Humāyūn in 1555 it became a great city again. It was the residence of Jahāngīr, Shāh Jahān, and Aurangzeb. After being fought over by Mahrattas, Persians, Afghans and Sikhs, it was made the capital of Ranjīt Singh who was declared Mahārājāh of the Punjab in 1802. In 1849 it came under British control.

Lahore has an excellent museum, the Shālimar gardens, the Bādshāhi mosque, and the tombs of Muḥammad Iqbal, al-Ḥujwīri (Dātā Ganj Bakhsh), Miān Mīr of the Qādiriyyah, and Jahāngīr.

Lakhmids. An Arab dynasty which ruled a pre-Islamic kingdom in present day Iraq. Its capital was Ḥirā'. The Lakhmid kingdom extended down to the Persian Gulf. The Lakhmids depended upon the Sassanids for their political existence, forming a buffer on the western edge of the Persian empire. The Lakhmids maintained for the Persians a series of strategic trenches used to discourage Arab attacks. When the Arab invasion of Iran came, many of the tribes making up the Lakhmid kingdom, some of whom were Nestorian Christians, joined with the Muslims in the onslaught upon the Persians, helping to bring about the Persian defeat at Qādisiyyah.

After the battle of Qādisiyyah in 636 or 637 the city of Ḥirā' went into decline and was displaced by the newly founded garrison city of Kufah some fifty kilometers away. Ḥirā' had been founded near Babylon in the 2nd century B.C. The Lakhmids arose at the end of the 3rd century A.D. and lasted until 602. Tabarī names twenty of their kings. The Lakhmids had been installed as kings of Ḥirā' by the Persians around 272. In 298, after the defeat of the Persians by the Romans in the reign of Diocletian, the Lakhmids under Imru' al-Qays I went over to the Romans and overran North and Central Arabia even laying siege to Najran, then held by Shammar Yuharish III of Ḥimyar. Soon after they returned to alliance with the Persians, however, and they reached the height of their rule c. 504-554 with Mundhir III under the Persian suzerainty of Kabad and Chosroes I.

Among their rivals were the tribe of the Kinda to the south who had founded a kingdom in the Yammamah of Arabia with cities whose excavation reveals an hitherto unsuspected degree of Hellenist influence. Around 525, Harith of Kinda, grandfather of the poet Imru' al-Qays, was killed along with 48 other members of the tribe by Mundhir III the Lahkmid king. In the turmoil following, some members of the Kinda rejoined the Yemen branch of the Kinda tribe. The father of Imru' al-Qays, the Amīr over the Kinda clan of the Asad, was assassinated. Imru' al-Qays unsuccessfully tried to avenge his father's death; destiny drove him into exile guarding five coats of mail armor and his family. He was called by the Byzantine Emperor to Constantinople; on his way back he died at Ankara, perhaps poisoned by the Byzantines after having been appointed by them as head of the Arab armies of the Ghassānīs under the Ghassānīd King Ḥārith ibn Jabalah.

But Ḥirā' had played an important role in the expansion of Islam. In 293, Amr ibn 'Adi, Lakhmid king of Ḥirā', became a protector of Manicheism and under him a center of Arab Manicheism developed. In order to spread Manicheism clandestinely, Mani had pioneered the use of small books which could easily be concealed even on the body, rather than ponderous scrolls which could not. Since books and writing were critical to the spread of the new Persian religion which had become established at Ḥirā' (and was persecuted by both Romans and Persians), a system of writing Arabic also developed there. This system of writing Arabic was shortly to benefit the spread of Islam by facilitating the writing of the Koran.

Ibn Rustah, in the *Kitāb al-Alaq an-Nafisa* reported that Manicheans had come to Mecca from Ḥirā' before Islam. Ḥirā' was also on the route from Mecca to Mada'in, the Persian capital. Thus trading Arabs from Mecca passing through Ḥirā' could have observed the Bema ceremony, the central rite of Manicheism which commemorates the return of the martyred Mani as an invisible presence seated upon an apparently empty chair before which is spread a feast. A knowledge and image of the Bema feast reported by traveling Meccans, among whom the Prophet could easily have been one, is perhaps mirrored in this picture in the Koran: "Think not of those, who are slain in the way of Allāh, as dead. Nay, they are living. With their Lord they have provision". (*inda Rabbihim razzaquna*) (Koran: 2:154 and 3:169).

The universalist and Manichean notion of many religions with one and the same message expressed by messengers sent to different nations may also have come from Ḥirā' to Mecca where revelation transformed it into positive religion; the term Seal of Prophets originally used for Mani but found in the Koran for the Prophet must also have been used in Ḥirā'; this and other Gnostic terminology from Aramaic and Persian would have been adapted to Arabic in that region and put at the disposal of other Arabs and thus found its way into the theological speculation of the desert Arabs.

As Arab speakers acquainted with Persian ideas, the Lakhmids were important transmitters of these ideas to the Arabs further south, a process which had begun with the conquest of Babylon by Cyrus in 539 B.C. Among those originally Zoroastrian ideas were the conviction that the world will come to an apocalyptic end, a resurrection of the dead, a universal judgement, an afterlife in a paradise or a hell. After Islam appeared on the scene the Lakhmid Arabs were swept up with the new revelation coming out of the desert both in religious and political terms but their heritage continued to manifest itself through the urban center of Kufah in contributions to theology, scholarship and art, notably Kufic calligraphy, but also in attempts to re-establish their once leading role through such revolts as the Kaysaniyyah and later through the Qarmatians.

Laqab. Honorific names such as those adopted by Caliphs or Sultans.

Laṭā'if (the plural of *luṭf*, "subtlety"). Subtle centers in the body mentioned by some, but not all, schools of mysticism. These are similar to the *chakras* of Hindu Tantrism, but their theory is neither so diverse nor so developed.

They vary according to school, but include as most important the forehead as seat of consciousness and the perception of forms; the breast as the focus of breath, or life; and the heart – but not the physical heart – as the junction of the individual with Being, or with what is supra-individual and beyond form. *See* NAQSHBANDIYYAH; SIRR.

Law, *see* SHARĪ'AH.

Lawāmiḥ (lit. "flashes"). Intuitions and understandings of a spiritual order which suddenly settle upon the soul. Also the title of several books by Sufis.

Ibn 'Aṭā' Allāh says:

> Rarely come the Divine intuitions except on a sudden, lest the slaves should claim them as a result of their preparations.

al-Lawḥ al-Maḥfūẓ, (lit. the "guarded tablet"). The Koran says of itself that "it is written on the guarded tablet" (85:21-22). This has become the term for metaphysical substance (Aristotle's *hyle* or Sanskrit *prakriti*). The corresponding Islamic term for metaphysical form (the Greek *eidos* or the Sanskrit *purusha*) is the Pen (*al-qalam*) which writes upon the *lawḥ al-maḥfūẓ*. The tablet is also the repository of destiny (*al-qadr*), giving rise to the expression it is written (*maktūb*), for something fated. *See* BEING; FIVE DIVINE PRESENCES.

Laylah... *see* LAYLAT...

Laylat al-Barā'ah. On the night of the 15th Sha'bān, religious observances are held in many places in the Islamic world in the belief that destinies for the coming year are fixed that night. (It is the night before the day of the 15th which is the holy night since the Islamic day runs from sunset to sunset.) In Arabic it is called the *Laylat al-Barā'ah* ("night of forgiveness"). In Iran and India it is called *Shab-i Barat.* The origin of this holiday is perhaps the *Farvardin* of ancient Iran for it is connected with the memory of the dead whose souls visit their relatives this day, and with the fates of the living, a kind of All Souls Day. Hence, the Islamicised legend of the holiday says that the lote-tree of the ultimate limit (*as-sidratu al-muntaha*) is shaken that day and leaves fall with the names of those to die in the year to come. *See* CALENDAR.

Laylat al-Isrā' wa-l-Mi'rāj, *see* NIGHT JOURNEY.

Laylat al-Qadr (lit. "night of power" or "destiny"). The night in the year 610 A.D. in which the Koran descended, in its entirety, into the soul of the Prophet. It is one of the last ten nights of the month of Ramaḍān. For this reason the last ten days of Ramaḍān are taken to be particularly holy. In that night the Angel Gabriel first spoke to the Prophet, the Koran was revealed, and the Divine mission began.

The Sūrah 97 describes the Night of Power as "better than a thousand months... peace until the rising of the dawn." It is related that 'Ā'ishah, the Prophet's favourite wife, explained that the *Laylat al-Qadr* is the "soul of the Prophet". That is to say, since the Prophet is also all of creation in the form of a man, that night corresponded to his soul. This also implies that the true nature of the human soul is a receptacle for God's revelation.

There is a widespread belief that the Night of Power is the 27th of Ramaḍān. It is certain that this common belief originates in Manicheism where the 27th day of the month of fasting is the celebrated anniversary of the death of Mani, for there are no Islamic sources for such an idea. *See* CALENDAR; KORAN.

Lebanon. Population estimated at over 3,575,000. There have been significant demographic changes, or changes in representation in the last twenty years; the population balance has shifted towards the Muslims. It is now estimated that 48% of the population are Muslim; 40% are Christian; 10% are Druze; 2% are 'Alāwīs and Ismā'īlīs. Of the Muslims, it is estimated that 68% may be Twelve-Imām Shī'ites while the Sunnīs are 32% (formerly Sunnīs were in the majority or thought to be in the majority). Of the Christians, 60% are Maronites, and the rest are Greek Orthodox, Melkites, and a number of smaller Christian churches. (There are more than 600,000 Druzes distributed throughout the countries of the Levant including Syria and Israel; since the 1970s, the 'Alāwī sect has been in power in Syria. The various Shī'ites of Lebanon are called *Metawila* inside the country. *See* 'ALAWĪS; AMAL; DRUZES; ḤIZB ALLĀH; METAWILA; SHĪ'ISM; SUNNĪ.

Legacies (Ar. *waṣāyā*; sing. *waṣiyyah*). Bequests made through the will of a testator can amount to only one third of his inheritable property under Islamic law (a condition which is taken from Roman law). As regards the other two-thirds, or indeed the whole estate if no bequest has been made, a complex law of inheritance exists which divides the estate among inheritors according to established schedules. Wills may be oral, but oral or written, they must be attested by two witnesses. A bequest to an inheritor, above the portion due to him by the law of inheritance, must be approved by the other inheritors. The law of a third also limits the property which may be given to endowments for pious works, "the Dead Hand" (*waqf*). No limit is placed on the portion of one's estate which may be disposed of as gift before one's death. *See* INHERITANCE; WAQF.

Leilat... *see* LAYLAT...

"Letters, Isolated", *see* al-ḤURŪF al-MUQAṬṬA'ĀT.

Letters, Science of the *see* 'ILM al-ḤURŪF.

Lex Talionis, *see* QIṢĀṢ.

Li'ān (lit. "imprecation"). An uncommon form of divorce which is nonetheless possible in Islamic law, based upon the husband's accusing his wife of infidelity. He supports the accusation by taking an oath four times (instead of the requirement, otherwise, for the infidelity to have been seen by four witnesses) and by calling imprecations upon himself in case of falsehood on his part.

The wife then denies the accusation by taking four oaths, and calls imprecations upon herself in case of falsehood on her part. The marriage is thereby dissolved, and the two can never be remarried to each other again. The wife keeps the dowry. *See* DIVORCE.

LIBYA — LŪṬFĪ

Libya. (Libyan Arab Republic. Instead of the usual word *jumhūriyyah* for "republic", the word *jamāhīriyyah,* based, no doubt symbolically, on the collective plural, is used). The estimated population in 1994 was 4,899,000. The country is 98% Muslim, of whom some forty thousand are 'Ibāḍī Khārijites. The Sunnīs are largely of the Mālikī rite. One third of the population is affiliated with the Sanūsī order (which, outside Libya, now only has followers in the Sudan). *See* 'IBĀDITES; SANŪSĪYYAH.

Limbo, *see* A'RĀF; ESCHATOLOGY.

Lord, *see* RABB; SAYYID.

Lot, *see* LŪṬ.

Luqmān. A figure mentioned in the Koran in Sūrah 31:11, as a man having wisdom. He was known in Arab legend as a sage, and later tradition attached to his name a corpus of proverbs and moral tales reminiscent of those attributed to Aesop in Western Europe. Luqman was identified by Darmsteter as the homologue of Balaam the son of Beor. The meaning of Beor in Hebrew is to swallow, as Luqman means to swallow in Arabic. Originally the figure was doubtless common to all the Semitic peoples. The tales of Aesop are probably also of Mesopotamian origin.

Lur. A people in Iran, most of whom are of Indo-European origin. They speak a language which is close to ancient Persian or Pahlavi. The Lurs number over 500,000 of whom the majority are Shī'ite. Many are nomadic and graze their flocks in the region of the Zagros Mountains of southwest Iran.

Lūṭ. The Prophet Lot. He is mentioned in the Koran (6:88); (7:78); (11.77); (15:59); (21:71); (22:44); (26:161); (27:55); (29:31); (37:133); (54:33). He is described as a warner of his people, the inhabitants of the "overwhelmed cities" (*al-Mu'tafikah*), of God's impending punishement for their indecency and sodomy, but is rejected. His household are saved except for his wife who lingered.

Lūṭfī. A member of a chivalrous brotherhood. From time to time, and particularly in the 19th century, these turned to brigandage, and the term became synonymous with bandits.

M

al-Ma'arrī, Abū-l-'Alā' (*363-449*/973-1057). One of the most famous of Arab poets, al-Ma'arrī was born and died in Ma'arrat al-Nu'mān in Syria. Blind from childhood, he lived to a ripe old age withdrawn from the world but widely celebrated for his powerful verses.

He achieved originality and urbane elegance while still breathing an air of desert freedom reminiscent of the poets of the pre-Islamic "Age of Ignorance" (*Jāhiliyyah*). Somewhat like the author of Ecclesiastes, al-Ma'arrī described the world from an aloof, aristocratic and slightly scornful point of view.

Paradise, Hell: the sweet, the lurid Light
Both feed on Darkness; so we flit from state
To state like marsh-fire through the one long Night.

The wailing funeral was not long gone
Before a wedding pomp followed upon.
The Wheel groaned. Both went on into the dark:
The sob, the shouting sounded soon as one.

Al-Ma'arrī had been a vegetarian; he was well acquainted with the Qarmatian *dā'i* of Syria, Mu'ayyad Salmani of Shiraz, possibly a teacher of Ma'arī, who wrote works called the *Majalis* which are very similar to his. Ma'arrī had once been dragged by his foot out of the house of Sharīf ar-Rāḍi of Baghdad. Ibn al-Jawzi accused him of being a *zindīq*: "As for Abū-l-'Alā', his poems make no secret of their heresy; he went to all lengths in his hatred of the prophets but floundered about in his attempts to mislead, being afraid of execution, till he died in his destitution. There has been no period without successors to these two parties [Bāṭinīs and Khārijites], only thank God, the fuel of the more audacious has been extinguished." Al-Ma'arrī had written:

They all err – Moslem, Christian, Jew, and Magian;
Two make Humanity's universal sect;
One man intelligent without religion,
And one religious without intellect.

In his *Risalat al-Ghufrān*, al-Ma'arri describes a visit to the afterworld which may have served as a model for Dante's *Divine Comedy*. This theme is derived from the 4th century Pahlavi book of *Arda Virāz* ("Book of the Holy Virāz"); the story is actually older than the 4th century for Plutarch relates a similar vision of Aridaeus who was said to be a man of Soli in Asia Minor. In it, a wise man, chosen by an assembly of wise men, reaches the afterlife in a hashish inspired dream, returns after seven days and relates the punishments and rewards of heaven and hell.

Madhhab (lit. a "direction"; pl. *madhāhib*). A system of thought, an intellectual approach. Specifically, the term *madhhab* is used to refer to each of the schools of law. *See* SCHOOLS of LAW; SHARĪ'AH.

Madinah, *see* MEDINA.

"The Mad Mullah", *see* MUḤAMMAD IBN 'ABD ALLĀH ḤASAN.

Madrasah (lit. a "place of study"; pl. *madāris*). A traditional school of higher study, in the sense that students entering a madrasah were presumed to have already committed the entire Koran to memory. The course of studies corresponded to the *trivium* of the liberal arts (grammar, logic and rhetoric) and included law (*fiqh*), traditional systems of mathematics (*abjad*), literature, history, higher grammar, the calculation of prayer times, Koranic exegesis and chanting, and so forth. Medicine and agronomy were sometimes also taught.

The madrasah was actually more a residence than a place of study, since instruction was given in the mosque itself with students sitting around the teacher (although a small mosque was an indispensable part of the madrasah). Some madrasahs, such as the Abū-l-Ḥasan Madrasah in Fez, were built by princes who then provided a small pension for the students. Others were built by merchant and craft guilds, for example the *'Aṭṭarīn* or perfumer's madrasah in Fez. Many madrasahs that still exist are architectural masterpieces, particularly those in India and Morocco. Usually the madrasah had a central courtyard, a prayer hall, and small rooms where the students lived. It was the custom for the teacher to give the student a certificate (*ijāzah*) at the end of a course of study which could last for several years.

The Fāṭimids spurred the development of schools throughout the Islamic world. On the one hand they founded the al-Azhar university in Cairo as well as schools of the type called *dār al-'ilm* ("house of knowledge") in order to train propagandists for their sect. On the other hand, Sunnīs responded by opening their own schools of theology to meet the threat. Niẓām al-Mulk and the celebrated Saladin, for example, established many madrasahs with the avowed aim of countering the theological subversion of the Fāṭimids. But madrasahs had existed from earlier times; and among the most famous institutions were the *Bayt al-Ḥikmah* founded by the Caliph al-Ma'mūn in Baghdad in the *3rd*/9th century, the *Niẓāmiyyah* founded by the Vizier Niẓām al-Mulk in the *5th*/11th century, and the *Mustanṣiriyyah* founded by the Caliph al-Mustanṣir in *631*/1234. The madrasahs of Bukhāra were said to hold thousands of students, and some important cities had dozens at one time.

The Muslim madrasahs provided the model for the European university. From the madrasahs came such traditions as the wearing of collegiate black gowns (worn at learned disputations in Fāṭimid Egypt), the division into undergraduate and graduate faculties, and much more besides. In Java, in addition to newer schools of Islamic study called madrasahs, an older form of Islamic school still exists called the *pesantren*. *See* ABJAD; DĀR al-ḤADĪTH; FIQH; KORANIC SCHOOL.

Maennerbund. *See* SECRET SOCIETY.

Mafrūḍ (from *farḍ*, "that which is obligatory"). A religious obligation. *See* FARḌ.

al-Maghrib (lit. the "place of sunset", the "west"). **1.** An abbreviation of the term *ṣalāt al-Maghrib*, the evening prayer, which may be performed a few minutes after the sun has set, and until the red glow fades from the western sky. (*see* PRAYER.)

2. *Al-Maghrib al-'Arabī*, The Arab West, the "Maghreb" is the region comprising Morocco, Mauritania, Algeria, Tunisia, and Libya. The classical Arabic name of Morocco is *al-Maghrib al-Aqṣā'* ("the farthest west"). Morocco, a European name, is derived from the city of Marrakesh.

Magic (Ar. *as-siḥr*). Although the distinction is made between *as-siḥr al-abyaḍ* ("white magic") and *as-siḥr al-aswad* ("black magic"), magic as such is condemned in Islam, and its practice forbidden. Nevertheless, it is widely practiced. The term *as-siḥr* connotes specifically sorcery; *ad-da'wah* means incantation and exorcism; and *kahānah* or *kihānah* is divination. The verses of the Koran known as the *āyāt al-ḥifẓ* ("verses of protection", or "safeguard") are used as talismans against magic as well as for the avoidance of, or escape from, adversity.

The Prophet himself was the victim of a type of sorcery which involved spells cast by breathing on knots. In a vision he saw two Angels who informed him that the spell affecting him was on a rope that had been thrown into a well. The revelation of Sūrahs 113 and 114 dissolved the spell, each of the eleven verses undoing the effect of one of the eleven enchanted knots of the rope. These two verses are called the *al-mu'awwidhatān* ("the two of taking refuge"):

> Say: 'I take refuge with the Lord of the Daybreak
>   from the evil of what he has created
> from the evil of darkness when it gathers,
> from the evil of the women who blow on knots,
> from the evil of an envier when he envies'.
>
> Say: 'I take refuge with the Lord of men.
>   the King of men,
>   the God of men,
> from the evil of the slinking whisperer
> who whispers in the breasts of men
>   of jinn and men.'

A very common form of magic still found today uses the diagram of the manḍalah. *See* MANḌALAH; REFUGE.

Maḥabbah (lit. "love"). In spiritual psychology the meaning corresponds to the Greek *agape*, the Hindu *bhakti* and the Mahāyānist *Karuṇā.* It is the attitude of soul which implies devotion, "sacrifice" of self (i.e. transcending the ego), and "love of God". *Maḥabbah* is also the expansive aspect of the spiritual path, the fulfillment of the primordial norm called the *fiṭrah*, and the imitation of the example of the

Divine Messenger, the Sunnah.

Maḥabbah may predominate as an operational attitude, but it is always associated with *makhāfah* ("fear of God", but also purification and "contraction") and with *ma'rifah* (gnosis or "knowledge of God"). Any of the three may constitute the principal spiritual methodology, but all three also are necessary elements of any spiritual development. *Makhāfah,* as purification, precedes *maḥabbah* as expansion. *Ma'rifah,* as union, is the culmination.

In the *Maḥāsin al-Majālis*, Aḥmad Ibn al-'Ārif says that "*maḥabbah* is the beginning of the valleys of extinction (*al-fanā'*) and the hill from which there is a descent towards the stages of self-naughting (*al-māḥū*); it is the last of the stages where the advance guard of the mass of believers meets the rear guard of the elect." See FIṬRAH; MAKHĀFAH; MA'RIFAH.

al-Mahdī (lit. "the guided one"). A figure many Muslims believe will appear at the end of time to restore righteousness briefly – over the span of a few years – before the end of the world, the Day of Judgement (*yawm ad-dīn*). The doctrine, and the early Ḥadīth literature associated with it, probably originated with the Kaysāniyyah, who were followers of Muḥammad ibn al-Ḥanafiyyah, a descendant of 'Alī by a woman of the Ḥanafī tribe. Muḥammad ibn al-Ḥanafiyyah tried unsuccessfully to resist Umayyad tyranny. His followers maintained after his death that he had disappeared into hiding at Mount Raḍwā in northwest Arabia, in the region of Yenbo and Medina, and that he would return to bring righteousness into the world.

If the Mahdī Ḥadīth do in fact date from this movement, as is likely, the later development of the doctrine of the Mahdī took hold because of the immediate political and religious aspirations of the Twelve-Imām Shī'ites. At the same time, both Shī'ite and Sunnī theologians believed it plausible that a reflection of the "Golden Age" of Islam would take place in history before the end of time, just as, by analogy, the sunset mimes the colors of the dawn. Or perhaps they saw in the rule of the Mahdī a kind of foreshadowing of the Second Coming of Jesus as announced in the Koran. Thus, at the time of the saintly Umayyad Caliph 'Umar ibn 'Abd al-'Azīz (d. *101*/720) the early historians record that: "A man once asked the Traditionist Ṭāūs: Is 'Umar the Mahdī?' 'He is a Mahdī', replied Ṭāūs, but not *the* Mahdī'".

The various Ḥadīth about the Mahdī appear to be inventions to support political causes. There are no Mahdī Ḥadīth in Bukhāri and Muslim; they appear much later in Tirmidhī and Abū Dāwūd. They state that he will be a descendant of the Prophet and have the same name, Muḥammad, possibly in one of its other forms, such as Aḥmad. Another Ḥadīth, however, in all appearance an invention to counter pro-Mahdī Ḥadīth, proclaims that there is no Mahdī but Jesus, son of Mary.

Despite this, some non-Shī'ite Muslims believe that the Mahdī will come in addition to the Second Coming of Jesus, and that the Mahdī is a respite in the darkening of the cosmic cycle. In this anticipation it is held that the reign of the Mahdī will reflect, towards the end of time, the pristine purity of the Prophet's rule and thus unite the schools of law and all the sects; the reign of the Mahdī will be finished before the Antichrist (*al-masīḥ ad-dajjāl*) appears to play his role; and once the Antichrist has led away his followers, Jesus will then come to destroy the Antichrist in the closing moments of the cosmic drama.

Belief in the Mahdī has been rejected by noted Sunnī authorities as being a Messianism incompatible with a religion in which salvation does not depend upon intercession, especially intercession at a particular point in time, making all of time dependent upon that event. The Twelve-Imām Shī'ites identify the Mahdī with the Twelfth Imām, called the *muntaẓar* ("the awaited"), who is the "Hidden Imām". Other small Shī'ite groups have their own special interpretations of the Mahdī.

Predictions and lore concerning the Mahdī abound; the places where he will manifest himself are cited many times, and the signs of his coming are enumerated. While his reign is often understood as being an inward or spiritual one, it has also been interpreted as being outward and temporal, a new universal Caliphate. A number of political leaders have exploited these expectations for their own ends and claimed to be the Mahdī. Ibn Tūmart (*470-525*/1077-1130) of the Almohads, and the Mahdī of the Sudan, Muḥammad Aḥmad ibn 'Abd Allāh (*1259-1303*/1843-1885), are historical examples, but contemporary ones are not lacking. See DAJJĀL; HIDDEN IMĀM; JESUS.

al-Mahdiyyah. A city in Tunisia, founded by the Fāṭimids as their capital in *300*/912. It was so named because the founder of the dynasty claimed to be the Mahdī. See FĀṬIMIDS.

Maḥmal (lit. "litter"). A richly decorated camel litter, of the kind which would normally carry an important personage, it accompanied the yearly pilgrim caravan to Mecca from Cairo, and later from Damascus as well. The *maḥmal* was an emblem of state and rulers. Princes sent it as a token to represent them at the "standing" on the Day of 'Arafāt during the pilgrimage. (See PILGRIMAGE.)

The custom began in the times of the Mamlūks or the Ayyūbids, perhaps initiated by the widow of the last Ayyūbid who one year went on the pilgrimage and the next year sent her empty litter. The Egyptian *maḥmal* was often the most lavish, decorated with silk, gold, silver, and precious stones, but empty except for a Koran; the camel which bore it was led and not ridden. The Egyptian caravan also brought the kiswah, or covering of the Kabah, which is renewed each year. The practice of the *maḥmal* was discontinued when the Wahhābīs conquered Mecca in 1924.

Maḥmūd of Ghaznah (*360-422*/971-1030). Founder of the Ghaznavid dynasty and ruler of Afganistan and Khorasan, Maḥmūd was the son of Sabuktagin, a Turkic slave of the governor of Khorasan, himself a vassal of the Sāmānid rulers of Bokhara. Sabuktagin was a noted successful military leader who bequeathed a kingdom to his son Ismā'īl. When Maḥmūd asked his brother to divide the domains with him, Ismā'īl refused, whereupon Maḥmūd attacked and conquered the whole kingdom. As a vigorous military leader, he made a number of successful expeditions into India, did not retain captured territory for his rule, with the exception of Lahore, but brought back great spoils. No less vigorous was his advancement of Islam, persecuting Shī'ites and others with whom he did not agree. The 'Abbāsid Caliph al-Qādir invested Maḥmūd with a *khil'ah* ("robe of honor") and titles of sovereignty ending Maḥmūd's titular vassalage to the Sāmānids. Maḥmūd of Ghaznah was one of the first rulers to use the title of Sultan (from Arabic *sulṭān*, "authority").

The court of Ghaznah, on a trade route in Afghanistan between Kabul and Kandahar, was a haven to many scholars, including the great scientist and thinker al-Bīrūnī. The presence of many learned men, riches brought from India, and Maḥmūd's own architectural creations including the great mosque called the "Celestial Bride", made the ancient walled city influential in many ways. Maḥmūd was himself greatly interested in literature and theology, and was an active participant in the intellectual life of his court. Al-Bīrūnī accompanied Maḥmūd on his campaigns in India and used these as opportunities to learn Sanskrit, to study the intellectual treasures of that nation, and to translate such classics as the *Patanjali Yoga* into Arabic. See al-BĪRŪNĪ.

Mahr. The bridal gift which the groom pays to the bride, and which remains her property. She keeps all of it in the case of divorce, and half of it if the marriage is dissolved before consummation. The Arabs gave a bride-price before Islam and the Koran authorized the practice (4:4).

For the poor, no dowry is too small – the Prophet said to one poor man an iron ring would do. In modern times the expectation of large dowries, amounting to fortunes, has created social problems.

Majallah. A uniform codification of the laws of contract and obligation, based upon Ḥanafī law, promulgated in Turkey between *1286*/1869 and *1293*/1876 for use in the new secular courts, the Niẓāmiyyah. The Majallah was in force throughout the Ottoman Empire. It was replaced in Turkey by the adoption of the Swiss Civil Code in 1927 and elsewhere by other national laws; it is still in use in Jordan.

Majdhūb (lit. "attracted", from *jadhaba,* "to pull", "attract"). One whose sense has been deranged in a benign way, presumably from an overpowering perception of Divine Reality. A *majdhūb* is a "holy fool", one who is in some way mad, or seemingly mad, but possesses an aura of sanctity. The state may be temporary or permanent. One such figure, famous in Morocco for his aphoristic utterances and poetry, was 'Abd ar-Raḥmān Majdhūb, who lived in the *12th*/18th century.

Al-Hujwīrī said of such a one:

> It is related that one day when ash-Shiblī (a famous

> Sufi of Baghdad) came into the bazaar, the people said 'This is a madman.' He replied: 'You think I am mad, and I think you are sensible: may God increase my madness and your sense!'

And 'Abd Allāh ibn As'ad al-Yāfi'ī (d. *770*/1367) said:

> They say: 'Thou art become mad with love for thy beloved'. I reply: 'The savor of life is for madmen'.

And also:

> 'Alī ibn 'Abdān knew a madman who wandered about in the daytime and passed the night in prayer. 'How long,' he asked him, 'hast thou been mad?' 'Ever since I *knew.*'

Majlis (lit. "a sitting", "a session"). A gathering of notables in a Beduin tent, the audience of a Shaykh, an assembly, a ruling council, a parliament. It is also a Sufi gathering for the purpose of reading instructive texts, invocation, and singing – corresponding to what in Hinduism is called *satsang.* In Turkey the word *durgah* is similarly used, and in India, *durbar.*

al-Majlisī, Muḥammad Bāqir ibn Muḥammad at-Tāqī (*1038-1111*/1628-1699). A Shī'ite theologian, author of the *Biḥār al-Anwār* ("Oceans of Light") concerning the Imāms, *al-Ḥaqq al-Yaqīn* ("The Confirmed Truth"), and other books which are classics of Shī'ism, including several written in Persian. The foremost Shī'ite scholar of his time, al-Majlisī was also a popular Shī'ite polemicist and a violent opponent of philosophy. Towards Sufism, in which he saw a rival and competitor to Shī'ism, he was implacably hostile and was able, with the approval of the Shāh, to have it banned and ousted from Isfahan, where al-Majlisī was born and died. He was a student of the father of Vahid Bihbahānī.

al-Majūsī, 'Alī ibn al-'Abbās (d. *384*/994). Known in Europe as "Haly 'Abbās", al-Majūsī, a Persian, was court physician to the Saljūq Sultan, 'Aḍud ad-Dawlah. "The Royal Notebook" (*al-Kunnāsh al-Malikī*), his book on medicine, was translated into Latin and called the *Liber Regius* (later known as "The Complete Art of Medicine").

Makhāfah (lit. "fear"). The state or emotion of fear and reverence towards God. *Makhāfah* implies purification; it is the beginning of awareness as in the Solomonic proverb: *ra'as al-ḥikmati makhāfatu-Llāh* ("the beginning of wisdom is the fear of God"). It is a spiritual attitude towards God that must be sustained permanently being a kind of reflection of, or response to, God's rigor and majesty; it also constitutes a phase, one of the threefold aspects, of the spiritual path. From this point of view it precedes *maḥabbah* ("love") which is sacrifice and expansion into the mold of the *fiṭrah,* or primordial norm. The third and final aspect of the path is realization, *ma'rifah* – gnosis or union. See FIṬRAH; MAḤABBAH; MA'RIFAH.

Makkah, *see* MECCA.

Makrūh. (lit. "disliked" from *karaha,* "to dislike"). The category of actions which are discouraged by the Sunnah. The other categories are *farḍ,* or *wājib,* which are the obligatory acts of prayer, fasting, etc.; *mustaḥabb,* or *mandūb,* actions which are recommended, *mubāḥ,* actions which are permitted or neutral, and *ḥarām,* actions and things which are forbidden. See FARḌ; ḤARĀM; SHARĪ'AH.

Maktūb (lit. "written", "ordained"). In the sense of "it is written", it is an expression pronounced frequently in resignation to God's Providence. It refers to the Divine decrees written on *al-lawḥ al-maḥfūẓ* ("the guarded tablet"), and to such Koranic statements as: "There befalls not any happening in the earth or in your souls except it is in a book [*kitāb*] before We [God] manifest it." (57:22). Ibn 'Aṭā' Allāh says in the Ḥikam:

> Antecedent intentions [*sawābiq al-himam*] cannot pierce the walls of predestined Decrees [*aṣwār al-aqdir*].

While Islam views man's life as predestined in the sense that nothing can finally oppose the Will of God, man nonetheless has the gift of free will in that he does make choices and decisions. Resignation to the Will of God is a concomitant to striving in the Path of God. Above all, man is completely free in what is essential, that is, he can accept the Absolute and surrender himself to It, or reject God and pay the price. In this he has absolute free will. The Talmud also says: "Everything is in the Hands of God, except the Fear of God." *See* LAWḤ al-MAḤFŪẒ; KALAM.

Malāḥida, *see* ILḤĀD.

Malak, *see* ANGELS.

Malā'ikah, *see* ANGELS.

Malakūt, *see* FIVE DIVINE PRESENCES.

Malāmatiyyah (lit. "men of blame"). The *malāmatiyyah* is often referred to as if it were a Sufi order (*ṭarīqah*). Rather than being an order, it is the designation of a tendency, or of a psychological category, of people who attract blame to themselves despite their being innocent. This may be due simply to maladjustment, but it can also be a measure of self-defence in order to hide a spiritual aptitude until a time of ripeness or, as a deliberate self-humiliation, to purify and loosen a positive quality from the grip of the lower soul (*an-nafs*). This is a very subtle spiritual operation which could well assume a morbid character, but it has, even so, been recognized as a legitimate possibility in Sufi lore. Al-Hujwīrī wrote:

> In the Path there is no taint or Veil more difficult to remove then self-esteem. And popularity does more than any other single thing to deter human nature from seeking to come to God.
>
> The Contemptuary, or votary of Contempt, is careful
> never to resent whatever is said of him; and for the sake of his own salvation he must commit some act which is legally neither a deadly sin, nor a trivial sin, but which will ensure his being generally disapproved.
>
> I once saw enough of a certain Transoxiana Contemptuary to feel at home with him. 'Brother', I asked him on one occasion, 'why do you personally do these things?'
>
> 'To make other people's opinions unreal to me', he
> answered.
>
> Others follow the discipline of Contempt from an ascetic motive: they wish to be generally despised for the sake of mortification of the self. To find themselves wretchedly humiliated is their intense joy...I saw...why the elders always suffered fools.

Malaysia. Federation. Population 20,103,000; Islam is the official state religion and the 55% of the population that is of indigenous Malay stock is Muslim of the Shāfi'ī School of Law (some elements of the population are Ḥanafīs). The rest consisting of ethnic Chinese, Indian, etc, are Buddhist, Taoist, Christian, Sikh, and animist. Islam came to Malaysia with merchants from the Hadramaut beginning at the end of the 7th century. Sufi *ṭuruq* include the Qādiriyyah, Shādhiliyyah, and Naqshbandiyyah.

Mālik (from the root *malaka,* to "possess"). A King. In Islam the more usual title for the ruler of a state, after Saljūq times, was Sultan (from the Arabic *sulṭān,* "authority"), for reason of the associations of the word *malik*: as it stands it is a Divine Name (*al-Mālik*), which could be construed as impious if used to designate a human office; moreover, when Kings are mentioned in the Koran the references are not always flattering, for example: "...as for kings (*mulūkan*), when they enter a city they despoil it..." (27:34).

Mālik ibn Anas, Abū 'Abd Allāh (*94-179*/716-795). Founder of the Mālikī School of Law. He was born and died in Medina, and received traditions from Sahl ibn Sa'd, one of the last surviving Companions. Mālik ibn Anas studied with Ja'far aṣ-Ṣādiq, the great scholar and descendant of the Prophet. He knew Abū Ḥanīfah, who had also studied in Medina, then the cultural center of Islam. Mālik's approach to canon law relied heavily on the customary usages (*a'māl*) of Medina and used *ijmā'* ("consensus") and *ra'y* ("opinion") secondarily.

His book, the *Muwaṭṭa'* ("The Path made Smooth"), is the earliest collection of Ḥadīth and the first book of law. The Mālikī School of Law which derives from him is dominant in the Arab West and is also found in southern Egypt. *See* SCHOOLS of LAW.

Mamlūks (from the Ar. *mamlūk,* "one owned [by another]", a "bondsman", a "slave"). A military corps made up of slaves originally from beyond the Islamic domains and non-Muslims who were converted as youths. Most came from the steppes and were Circassians, Turkomans, or Mongols. They were raised to be soldiers with loyalty to a single chief.

The Fāṭimid dynasty from the *4th*/10th century on, and the Ayyūbids after them, depended upon them as the backbone of the army. In *652*/1254 this military corps revolted against the last Ayyūbid and put one of their own number, Aybak, in control by marrying him to the step-mother of the murdered Sultan, thus establishing themselves as the power that ruled until the Turks conquered Cairo in 923/1517. The Mamlūks remained, however, an influential military and landowning class until Muḥammad 'Alī Pasha crushed them decisively in *1226*/1811.

With few exceptions, Mamlūk Sultans ruled for a very short time, their power being dependent upon the whims of the military class that supported them. One chieftain, Quṭuz, defeated the Mongols of Hūlāgū Khān at 'Ayn Jalūt in *659*/1260, thus checking the Mongol advance, but he was soon replaced by his lieutenant Baybars (d. *676*/1277), one of the most celebrated Mamlūk Sultans. It was Baybars who made the descendants of the 'Abbāsids, who had been deposed in Baghdad by the Mongols, into figurehead Caliphs in Cairo in order to legitimize his own Sultanate. He was the first Sultan to maintain all four schools of law on an equal footing in his domains, a practice later scrupulously adhered to by the Turks.

After Baybars, there began a decline in the line of the *Baḥrī* Mamlūks ("Sea Mamlūks"), so-called because their headquarters were situated on an island in the Nile at Cairo. In their place rose the *Burjī* Mamlūks ("Mamlūks of the citadel"), a line headed by the Sultan al-Manṣūr Sayf ad-Dīn Qalā'ūn (d. *689*/1290), and firmly established with az-Zāhir Sayf ad-Dīn Barqūq (d. *802*/1399).

Struggles against the Crusaders, the Mongols, the Timurids and the Turks marked the Mamlūk period, as did also the far-reaching diplomatic relations established by them. An enduring stamp of architectural accomplishment rested upon Cairo and the other territories under Mamlūk dominion. The Ottoman Sultan Selim I conquered Cairo in *923*/1517 and incorporated Egypt into the Ottoman Empire, his victory being due in part to the Mamlūks' neglect of cannons and firearms as being beneath them, with the result that they were no match for the Ottomans, whose skill in such weapons was highly developed.

The Mamlūks, transformed into a landholding aristocracy, were only eliminated as a political factor by Muḥammad 'Alī, the viceroy of Egypt, in *1226*/1811; inviting three hundred leading members of the Mamlūk community to dine in the Citadel, he had them massacred.

al-Ma'mūn, Abū-l-'Abbās 'Abd Allāh (*167-218*/783-833). An 'Abbāsid Caliph, the son of Hārūn ar-Rashīd, he promoted scientific study and the translation of works of Greek learning into Arabic. He also founded an academy in Baghdad called the *Bayt al-Ḥikmah* ("House of Wisdom"), which included an observatory, for the advancement of science; Greek manuscripts were sought in Constantinople to enrich its library and to be translated into Arabic. A medical school was also founded in his reign.

When his brother al-Amīn was Caliph, Al-Ma'mūn had been governor of Merv, important by reason of its location and its trade links to distant lands. Buddhists, Shamanists, Muslims, Turks, Arabs and Persians rubbed shoulders in its markets; art flourished. It was there that al-Ma'mūn was exposed to the many stimuli which made him one of the great intellectuals among the Caliphs. Because his mother was a Persian, the daughter of a Khorasani revolutionary Ustad Sis, al-Ma'mūn was familiar with Persian civilization, and popular with his Persian subjects.

When his father died, al-Ma'mūn became involved in a power struggle with his elder brother. The orthodox party in Baghdad opposed al-Ma'mūn because he was under the influence of an astrologer from Balkh who had been introduced by Yaḥya Barmak and converted to Islam. Al-Ma'mūn's troops conquered Baghdad, but various rebellions marked his reign, initiated by members of his own family and also by Shī'ites who supported 'Alid factions. Towards the end of his life he engaged in military campaigns against the Byzantines.

Al-Ma'mūn declared the Imām of the Shī'ites, 'Alī ibn Mūsā ar-Riḍā, to be his successor to the Caliphate. The Imām died before him however, and was buried next to the tomb of al-Ma'mūn's father, Hārūn ar-Rashīd, on a site now considered holy by Shī'ites and called Mashhad. After the Imām's death, the Caliph inclined towards the doctrines of the rationalist Mu'tazilites, and in *212*/827 their dogma of the created Koran was declared official, the obligation to accept this doctrine being enforced in *218*/833 by an inquisition (*miḥnah*), into the beliefs of Judges and religious leaders. (The orthodox doctrine, now everywhere accepted, is that the Koran is uncreated in its essence.) Aḥmad Ibn Ḥanbal became famous for being flogged for maintaining that the Koran was not uncreated only in its essence but from "cover to cover". After al-Ma'mūn, the *miḥnah* was abolished and the heyday of the Mu'tazilites came to an end.

Al-Ma'mūn was a pivotal figure in the history of the 'Abbāsid dynasty. It was in his reign that a coalition with the Persian factions of Khorasan that had brought the 'Abbāsids to power began to unravel and al-Ma'mūn, more than any other 'Abbāsid, was keenly aware of the theological tiger on which the 'Abbāsids had ridden to power.

In the course of the early political struggles of Islam, the descendants of 'Abbās seemingly retired from the stage to a remote place by the Dead Sea. However, their retreat lay on the route between Medina and Damascus and here they could discreetly observe the political scene and tap into the line of communications. The recently conquered Persians were seeking ways of politically reasserting themselves. After unsuccessfully attempting to use Ḥusayn, the nephew of the Prophet, and later Muḥammad ibn Hanafiyyah, both of them prestigious Arabs, to lead an insurgency against the Umayyads, the leaders of the Kaysaniyyah from the region of Kufah, and their allied Persian factions from Khurasan, turned to the 'Abbāsids. The Arabs were in power in the Islamic empire, and a succesful political movement, especially a non-Arab Iranian one, needed to have Arabs as figureheads if it was to succeed.

This gave rise to the coalition of the 'Abbāsids with Abū Muslim and Khorasan. Propaganda played a very strong role in the revolution and a pseudo-Ḥadīth was launched (the Prophet denied knowing the future) which was even put into the mouth of Mu'āwiyah, the founder of the Umayyads, and said: "When al-Ḥakam's offspring reach the number of thirty males, they will make God's money a source of exploitation amongst themselves, they will turn God's religion into one of deceitfulness, and they will turn God's servants into slaves." Many of the Persians in the movement deliberately used Arab names to further make it appear that this was an Arab revolt; nevertheless, al-Bīrūnī and others afterwards referred to the 'Abbāsids as a foreign Khorasani dynasty (*dawlah ajamiyyah khurasaniyyah*). The 'Abbāsids rallied the Arab elements while the Persians provided a power base, a base which 'Alī was already seeking against Mu'awiyah when he turned towards Kufah before being assassinated.

The Kaysaniyyah and Khurasanis had attempted to use the 'Alīds to come to power; when this had failed they tried to use the 'Abbāsids. The 'Abbāsids, however, turned the tables and used them instead. Once the revolution was successful, they put to death the Khorasani architect of the revolt, Abū Muslim who had begun to assume power for himself. Thereafter, however, the 'Abbāsids were a hostage to the two forces they had united. If they gave too many concessions to the Persian ideologies left behind by the Sassanids, and particularly the radical ones of Khorasan and Kufah, the Arabs representing conservative Islam would withdraw their support; but so would the Persians if they did not get what they wanted. Early into the 'Abbāsid era a group called the Rawandiyyah came to the palace of al-Manṣūr and asked him to make known his divinity as they apparently had been promised he would. This was more than an embarrassment to al-Manṣūr; it was dangerous *vis-a-vis* the essential Arab bloc and he unceremoniously had the Rawandis, several hundred of them, put to death before further damage was done to his position. (An Iranian historian has surmised that al-Manṣūr had actually converted to a secret sect in order to cement the bonds with the Khorasanis: "*Paris vaut une messe.*")

Hārūn ar-Rashīd, for his part, catered to the nascent Shī'ism of Iraq and Iran (which had been created by the Kaysaniyyah in the first place) by having a vision in which his cousin 'Alī revealed to him his grave, which had been forgotten and unknown. In this way Najaf became the shrine of 'Alī. Then, toward the end of his reign, Hārūn ar-Rashīd suddenly turned on the family of his viziers, the Barmecides from Balkh (who represented the new leadership within the Persian bloc), and had them put to death, probably because they were hollowing out a Khorasani empire within that of the Arabs. The sudden elimination of the Barmecides by Hārūn ar-Rashīd is reminiscent of Philippe le Bel's elimination of the Knights Templar for similar reasons.

Al-Ma'mūn had been born at Merv, then the economic and intellectual center of Persian

Khorasan (and also a center of Nestorianism); his accession to power was through a civil war with his half-brother who represented the Arab bloc while al-Ma'mūn represented the Persian. Al-Ma'mūn's victory put him even further into the Persian debt. Al-Ma'mūn named the 'Alid figure, 'Alī ar-Riḍā, the 8th Shī'ite Imām as his successor. In *203*/818 'Alī ar-Riḍā suddenly died in Nagaun near Tus, presumably poisoned, and was buried next to Hārūn ar-Rashīd, the father of al-Ma'mūn. This double burial place, probably intended to merge loyalties into one symbolic shrine, became Mashhed, after the Ṣafavids come to power. It survives only as a Shī'ite memorial: Hārūn ar-Rashīd is today forgotten and even despised; few who visit Mashhed even know that he is also buried there.

The pro-Shī'ite gestures of the 'Abbāsids, such as they were, did not give anything to the non-Shī'ite elements that had actually created Shī'ism and inspired it, and which at the time were the more critical and politically dangerous segment of the Persian religious spectrum. Mu'tazilitism, however, perfectly suited the indigenous Iranian theologies that had become powerful both religiously and politically – the two being inseparable in Iran – under the Sassanids. Al-Ma'mun's imposition of Mu'tazilitism as the official state dogma gave the Khorasanis and these indigenous factions religious carte blanche for their beliefs. At the same time, rival ideologies were suppressed; Al-Ma'mūn (perhaps also as a counterbalancing gesture towards Arabs) took measures against the Harranians. In imposing Mu'tazilitism al-Ma'mūn was paying back the family political debt as the price for the Caliphate; it did not necessarily reflect any belief on his part but was simply "Realpolitik".

The founder of Mu'tazilitism, Waṣīl ibn 'Aṭā' (d. *131*/748) was a mysterious figure. A *mawla*, or Iranian client convert to Islam, he was apparently the head of a secret organization, for Jaḥiz, the famous Arab writer, said of him: "Beyond the Pass of China, on every frontier to far distant Sus and beyond the Berbers, he has preachers. A tyrant's jest, an intriguer's craft does not break their determination. If he says 'Go' in winter, they obey; in summer they fear not the month of burning heat" (Jahiz, Bayan I, 37). And at this time there arose a saying armored as a Ḥadīth: "The Mu'tazila are the Majus [adherents of Iranian religion]; do not follow one in prayer, nor join in carrying his bier when he is dead." It was these factions, under the leadership of the Persian Abū Muslim, that had provided the 'Abbāsids with the critical support they needed to come to power.

The imposition of Mu'tazilitism by al-Ma'mūn in *212*/827 aroused Arab resistance and had to be accompanied with a religious inquisition beginning in *218*/833. The use of force led to a stony intransigeance on the part of the Arabs and the orthodox. Al-Ma'mūn's successor was obliged to lift the miḥnah within ten years and to renounce Mu'tazilitism. But he was also obliged to turn to mercenary Turks to protect himself and Turkish slaves replaced the Iranian element in the army; soon he had to leave Baghdad and live in the military garrison city of Samarra'. The Kufans and Khorasanis for their part, their aspirations, indeed their plan to acquire power for themselves, ultimately not satisfied by the coalition with the 'Abbāsids, withdrew their support.

Feeling betrayed by those whom they themselves were using, they began to work to subvert and destabilize the regime: first they encouraged the Black slaves to revolt in the Zanj uprising (*257-269*/870-882). Then, in *269*/882, the Governor of Kufah, Aḥmad ibn Muḥammad aṭ-Ṭā'ī, informed the authorities in Baghdad that a people were grouping in southern Iraq who had a non-Islamic religion; and they were prepared to fight the Community of Muḥammad "with the sword and impose their own religion"; but no-one listened to him until the Qarmatians began seizing control of whole regions. Further, in the reign of the Caliph al-Muqtadīr (began *295*/908) the head of the Manichean religion, the Archegos, left Baghdad, rumors had it for Samarkand, where he never appeared, while a man heralded as the Mahdī came to Tunisia, founded a new dynasty and proclaimed himself the true Caliph and rightful ruler of the Islamic world. The 'Abbāsids had become prisoners of forces they could no longer control; by the time they began to reassert themselves history had passed them by, and the Mongols were about to bring this phase of Islamic history to a close. See 'ABBĀSIDS; MU'TAZILITES.

Man, the Perfect, *see* al-INSĀN al-KĀMIL.

Manāqib (lit. "virtues", "glorious deeds"). Hagiographical literature, such as the *Salwat al-*

Anfus ("The Solace of Souls"), or the *Tadhkīrāt al-Awliyā'* ("Memorials of the Saints"), which are lives, records, and anecdotes of the Saints and the pious.

Manāsik al-Ḥajj. The rites of pilgrimage. *See* PILGRIMAGE.

Mandaeans (from Aramaic *Mandā d'Haiyē*, "the Knowledge of Life"). A small sect which probably migrated originally from Palestine to their present home in the marshlands of Iraq, they now number less than 15,000, with some living in Iran. They have their own quarter in Baghdad, and many are silversmiths. Their religious writings are in a dialect of Aramaic. The principle book of the Mandaeans is the *Ginza* ("the Treasure", also called the "Great Book"), along with the "Book of John", and the "One Thousand and Twelve Questions". It appears that they were originally a heretical sect of Judaism, and their beliefs are a mixture of elements from all the Semitic religions, but the essence of their religion is Gnostic-dualism. The "Knowledge of Life" after which they are named is a celestial "emanation", and represents the Gnostic call to recognise one's true nature. Their beliefs include certain elements of Babylonian "astral" religion, evidenced by such things as turning towards the north star for worship, and metaphysical formulations which are heavily influenced by astrology.

The principal rite of the Mandaeans is repeated sacramental lustrations in fresh running water. They venerate John the Baptist, for which, by a misunderstanding of one of their names, *Nāsoreans* or "the observers" (of John, *Yohāna*), they became known in Europe as "St John's Christians". They no longer call themselves *Nāsoreans*, but that is still the name of the priestly class (also called *tarmidē*), their followers being known as *Mandāyē*. This division, typical of all Gnostic sects, resembles the division into *electi* ("the chosen"), and *auditores* ("hearers") of the Manicheans. It may be that there is a filiation with the followers of John the Baptist, but the Mandaeans have no real affinity with Christianity, and are in fact antagonistic towards it, calling Jesus the "prophet of lies". They are also hostile towards Judaism (because Gnosticism considers the religious law to be compromised and evil), and call Moses the prophet of the evil spirit *Rūhā*, whilst Adonai they say is a false god. Despite their Gnostic doctrines they were once identified as the *sabi'ah*, or "Sabians", of the Koran, a people cited as having a revealed religion and thus belonging to the "People of the Book" (*Ahl al-Kitāb*). Other groups have also been identified as Sabians, notably a people of Harrān in Syria.

Because of the many resemblances, it is possible that the Mandaeans are related to the Qumran sect and to the Essenes, who had similar beliefs and also practiced sacramental lustrations. Some scholars identify the Mandaeans with the *Mughtasilah*, the "washing sect" spoken of by Ibn an-Nadīm (d. *385*/995), whom he also calls the *Sabat al-Baṭā'iḥ* ("the Sabians of the Lowlands") in the *Fihrist* published in Baghdad in *378*/988. If this is so – and some scholars dispute it – the Mandaeans, or their forerunners, would be the baptising sect of the Elchasaites, to which Mani (216-276 A.D.) belonged with his father Patik (Ar. Futtuq) until the age of 24, when he went off to create his own gnostic religion, Manicheism. See AHL al-KITĀB; MANICHEANS; SABIANS; ZINDĪQ.

Mandalah. A magical operation based on a diagram resembling the Hindu *maāḍalah*, which was once very common and widespread and which may still be encountered in Africa and the East. It involves drawing a design consisting of an inkspot surrounded by several Koranic verses on the palm of the hand of a young boy. One of these verses is always 50:22: "Lo! we have removed your veil and today your sight is piercing." Incantations are then made which are believed to cause him to see visions inside the inkspot in answer to questions put to him concerning things and acts unknown, in the past, or at a distance. In Morocco it is known as inducing the *ḥarakah* ("movement"). Although the *mandalah* uses Koranic verses, its origin is clearly not Islamic, for Islam does not condone magic. *See* MAGIC.

Mandūb, *see* MUSTAḤABB.

Manicheism. Mani is an intriguing figure in the history of religion. Born in 215 or 216 A.D. in a region which lies between Persian and Arab territories, he died in imprisonment in 276 A.D. His father Patik (known later to the Arabs as Futtuq) had been converted to a Dualist sect which practiced sacramental ablutions (*see*

MANDAEANS), and which must have believed, as all Dualists do, that God is made up of two contrary and absolute forces, good and evil, light and dark, etc. Mani was raised in this sect and dedicated to it, but in his early twenties he showed a genius for organization, and created his own religion. This was propagated with great success owing to its simple, comprehensive, and explicit system, and above all, to the fact that Mani presented it as being the inner, secret, truth of *all* religions, and thus as a kind of "universal", "pure" esoterism. He did not hesitate to adapt his religion to the outward form of any other, or to simply disguise it as another religion. These host religions included Christianity, Zoroastrianism, Hellenist paganism, Hinduism, Taoism, and Buddhism. This ingenious formulation meant that the propagandists of Manicheism were able to take advantage of the organization of existing religions.

The sophistication and pragmatism of his approach evokes a comparison with modern business theories; he was able, by means of packaging, organization, and positioning, to gain an immediate "market share" where established religions had worked long and hard; and Mani's scope was international and trans-religious. He himself traveled widely to oversee his missionaries in the field, in the Near East, India, Transoxiana, and even on the frontiers of China. His missionaries were highly dedicated because the incentives were high: the organisation of the religion was such that a missionary who established his territory was bound to receive an ample livelihood from his novices; it is generally a characteristic of Gnostic sects that salvation is a commodity dispensed by the sect's founder in return for recognition of his "real", divine, nature; this power is delegated to his representatives, who, in many cases, make themselves organisationally independent, and establish their own network; secret knowledge (and with it salvation) is sold to the initiated on a deferred payment plan. Care for the priestly élite, the *electi,* in return for the precious knowledge the followers believed was being imparted to them, was one of the important duties of the *auditores* ("the hearers"); the latter, who were still trapped in the "snares of ignorance", had to keep the preachers supplied with good vegetarian food from which the elect, by eating it, "liberated the light" supposedly entrapped in it. The division into the "knowers" and "ignorant", "divine" and "profane", is characteristic of virtually all Gnostic sects, as for example, in the Qumran sect between the "Sons of Light" and the "Sons of Darkness" or in the Druze religion between the *uqqāl* ("the knowers", the initiates) and the *juhhāl* ("the ignorant", the uninitiated). This doctrine is taken so far in the esoteric interpretations of certain sects, that outsiders are not even thought of as being real", but as being of illusory or "demonic" substance; this was true of the *Qiyāmah* doctrine of the Assassins of Alamūt, and it is also found in the *Qabbalah.*

In keeping with the nature of his religion, Mani cultivated the hermetic sciences and his image of guru by dressing in the yellow-green flowing robes of a Mithraic priest, but they were not his strong point; records of a system of astrology which bears his name have survived. His achievement and innovation lay in his ability to address pagans and Christians, Zoroastrians and Buddhists, convincingly in their own terms: in bold mythologizing, in imitating the Church fathers by producing exegetical variations on sacramental mysteries, and in creating dramatic rituals.

In Mani's lifetime, his cult was established throughout the Middle East, and the Persian and Roman Empires. After his death, in North Africa in particular, Manicheism became even more entrenched as Christianity gained power, because it became identified with resistance to the political hegemony of Rome. Thus, in the middle of the *2nd*/8th century, the head of the Manichean Church, the Arch-Egos, known by that time as the Imām, whose seat was in Madā'in (Ctesiphon-Seleucia, twenty miles from Baghdad), was a North African named Abū Hilāl ad-Dayhūrī. Manicheism spread to Rome itself and eastward among the Turkic tribes as far as China. In Turkestan a Manichean state existed in the 9-10th century. Naturally, the established religions resented it; inevitably there were persecutions, public disputations, scandals, and punishment; both Rome and Byzantium had their hands full for centuries rooting out Manicheans and their Gnostic familiars, who were constantly infiltrating the Christian churches. Europe followed suit when the Cathars sprang up in the Middle Ages from Bulgaria to Germany, Italy and France.

The organizational hierarchy of the Manichean church was as follows: The Arch-Egos, followed by 12 Apostles (*Hamozag*) or magistrates; 72

Bishops (*Espasag*); 360 Priests (*Mahistag*); the Elect (Ardavan, in Arabic *Siddiqun*); the Hearers (*Niyashagan* in Arabic *Sammāūn*). This is mirrored by the Fāṭimid *dā'i* hierarchy, and by what the early Sufis believed was the hierarchy of their leaders or their saints, starting from the *qutb* or pole.

Propaganda was the Manichee's strength. They developed an artistic calligraphy with minuscule script which became their hallmark, together with the elaborate illumination of manuscripts, and the making of elegant scrolls and beautiful books. Mani's followers believed that his art was divinely inspired; his use of gold paint may have had an influence on the Christian art of the icon as it certainly did that of the Persian miniature. In Arabic, almost a thousand years later, the verb *qarmaṭa* (from the Aramaic *qarmat*, a "man with red eyes", meaning a "teacher of secret doctrines"), meant to write a text in very small letters with a very fine hand. Manicheans unhesitatingly used hyperbole to extol themselves: thus crucifixion was the Manichean term for any kind of suffering or privation on the part of one of them. Mani himself, however, was crucified, flayed alive, and his skin stuffed with straw when the Sassanid authorities turned against him.

By the 6th century A.D., despite persecution by the Christians, Manicheism (sometimes said to mean *Mani Ḥayy*, "Mani Lives") was widespread as the religion of the educated classes in Iraq, Persia and parts of North Africa, but was also found elsewhere, particularly in Syria, Central Asia and Sindh. With a cell-structured network, it was so highly organised that it has been said they possessed their own system of communication consisting of post houses where couriers could change horses while carrying official messages. (Perhaps this system was the imperial Sassanid post which they had parasitized for their own purposes.) The irruption of Islam out of the desert of the Arabs posed a special problem for the Manichees. Mani the lame, but "a healer from the land of Babel", as he introduced himself to the King of Persia, had claimed unequivocally to be the last prophet; yet suddenly, in the first third of the 6th century, Islam appeared, a new religion of the first magnitude, a new revelation which was sweeping the world. As Mani called himself the "Apostle of Jesus" (and the Buddha), the obvious solution, after several false starts, such as those in the book *Umm al-Kitāb*, was to turn the Prophet into *the apostle of Mani.*

The following is an attempt to sketch out the complex and highly secretive steps taken by the Manicheans, after several tentative and unsuccessful attempts, in order to establish their own school within Islam, as they had done within Christianity, Buddhism and Taoism. Around 685-687, in the revolt of the Kaysāniyyah, we find the first appearance of the Ḥadīth concerning the Mahdī, and we see the revolt's instigator, Mukhtar, after a successful battle with the Umayyads, performing a ceremony which has every appearance of being that of the Manichean "Bema"; this ceremony involves the empty chair of Mani, which Mukhtar, however, here calls the "throne of 'Alī". It is thus that Mani's posthumous metamorphosis begins. These events took place around Kufah which replaced the city of Ḥirā' and became a center of Shī'ite activity. They later were to shift to Khorasan whose centers were Merv and Balkh.

Shahrastānī said that Abū Muslim, the leader of the 'Abbāsid revolt was a Kaysani. He took on Islam in Kufah and then went to Khorasan where the 'Abbāsid revolt was declared towards the end of the month of fasting of Ramaḍān in 747 outside of Merv. Certainly the Khorasan movement had the marks of a widespread clandestine religious base, whose members assumed Islam and Arab names for the purpose of their cause. One can surmise that the Manicheans having failed against the Umayyads on their own in the early Shī'ite revolts, and unable to find enough support in order to use Ḥusayn and other 'Alīds to rally followers to their cause, turned to the 'Abbāsids. The 'Abbāsids had remained aloof from the early power struggles and had taken up a strategic position near the Dead Sea, where, although apparently in the middle of nowhere, they could tap into the communications between Medina and Damascus. With the offer of a Khorasani army claiming to be Muslims in order to stage a just revolt against the purported tyranny of the Umayyads, the 'Abbāsids made their uneasy coalition and could rally orthodox Arabs to their revolt. The Iranian scholar Zabih Behzad believed that al-Mansur had secretly become a Manichean in order to seal the cooperation. (Al-Mansur was a name with Messianic significance in the Yemen and was later used by avowed

Dualists as well as hidden ones.) This would explain the curious incident of the Rawandis, reported by Tabari, who came to the provisional capital of Hashimiyyah and claimed that they knew that al-Mansur was divine asking him to give them food and drink (which could mean the Bema). For their troubles al-Mansur had hundreds of them killed for such scandal would have been very troubling to true Muslims supporters of the ʻAbbāsids.

Abū Muslim, once the revolt had succeeded, lost no time in declaring his own divinity and in moving to double-cross the ʻAbbāsids who proved to be more Manichean than the Manicheans and had Abū Muslim killed first. But the Manicheans did receive concessions: the choice of Baghdad as seat of the new dynasty brought the capital back to the vicinity of Ctesiphon, and again made the residence of the Archegos the center of the world. And Manicheans played a leading role in the government of the ʻAbbāsids, at least in the beginning.

We next see, sometime after 765, the doctrine of the *Nūr Muḥammadī* ("the Muḥammadan Light") being attributed to the sixth generation descendant of ʻAlī, Jaʻfar aṣ-Ṣadīq; thereupon follows a shower of sparks which is the appearance of the "Seveners" who are, in fact, various Gnostic groups within Islam. The confusions surrounding which of the children of Ismāʻīl was the Imām is the reflection of the difficulties that the Manicheans experienced in controlling their followers who were being manipulated and believed they were following an Islamic program of belief. Shortly thereafter there begins the rise of mystics in Islam who are in reality crypto-Manicheans. Notable among these are the "drunken Sufis". To this day many Turkish Sufis leave an empty lambskin at their meetings for their deceased founder to sit upon, the most famous of which is the red lambskin for Shamsi Tabrizi, the martyred teacher of Rumi who is simply re-made version of Mani. These groups also preserve a ritual position of the feet with one toe over the other. The Mevlevis call it *niyaz* and the others *ayak muhulemek* sealing the feet. This ritual position is found in Zoroastrianism but also in the derivative religions of Persia.

But the coalition of the ʻAbbāsids and Khorasanis proved troubled. The Barmakids, who had been Buddhist priests in Balkh, became the ministers of state of the ʻAbbāsids. But since they moved inevitably to create an empire within an empire, as Ibn Khaldūn surmised, Hārūn ar-Rashīd had the Barmakids killed and imprisoned, displaying the ʻAbbāsid survivor instinct, much as Philip le Bel was to do with the Templars on a different stage later. Al-Ma'mūn tried to continue riding the Manichean Tiger, which was in any case his necessary support in the initial war against his brother, by instituting Muʻtazilitism as the official theology, a policy which proved unpopular. (The Muʻtazilites, to the extent that they were Muslims were themselves critical of Manicheism, but their theology represented a giant concession to Dualist theology.) The objection of the conservative Muslims forced the repeal of Muʻtazilitism as the state theology. This marked the final rupture between the ʻAbbāsids and their Khorasan supporters. Thereafter, the ʻAbbāsid dynasty turned to Turkish slaves for their military support and became virtual prisoners within Samarra'.

Throughout the 9th century, there were persecutions of Manicheans by the Muslim authorities in Syria and Iraq. There were also various revolts against Islam in Khorasan and the revolt of the Zanj which Massignon says was supported and stimulated by Manicheans. North African Manicheism is now seen to have assumed a more dominating role towards its original center in the Near East. Around 895, a missionary arrived in North Africa with a fabricated Ḥadīth to the effect that soon now "the sun will rise in the West" and proclaimed that the Mahdī would come to North Africa from the East. His astounding success among the Berbers is easier to understand in light of the fact that Ibn Khaldūn says that the Berbers of Ketama belonged to a secret (Bāṭinī) religion, and the region was the center of the most important Manichean colony outside the Middle East, the one to which Augustine had most likely belonged.

Around the same time, a split which had already taken place centuries earlier in Manicheism emerged as a separate movement opposed to Islamic political institutions: the Qarmatians. They founded a centre in southern Iraq which they called the "House of Refuge" (Dār al-Hijrah). They then spread down the coast to al-Ḥasa, where they founded Mu'miniyyah ("the City of the Believer"), present day Hofuf, and to Baḥrayn. (The word *qarmaṭa,* originally an Aramaic term referring to the teaching of secret doctrines, afterwards took on in Arabic the meaning "to write in a minuscule handwriting", which is characteristic of Manichean books.) The Qarmatians favored world revolution as necessary to bring about the Millennium; that is, Manicheism had to be instituted everywhere, whereas the other branch believed that a Manichean Millennium could begin within the confines of one state before overtaking the world. The Qarmatians had a ceremony, the Night of the Imām which this hypothesis affirms is the Bema.

In 909 the Fāṭimid dynasty, of obscure origin but claiming descent from 'Alī and Fāṭimah (a claim later refuted by the 'Ālīds of Baghdad) was established in North Africa, their first capital being Mahdiyyah ("the City of the Mahdī"). Around this time the head of the Manichean Church, the Archegos (in Arabic *Imām*), had disappeared from Baghdad, (or more precisely, nearby Mada'in, or Ctesiphon-Seleucia, the ancient seat of the Manichean religion in "the land of Babel"). Rumours were put out that he had gone to Samarkand, where we note, however, that he did *not* reappear. Later, a second ruler of the Fāṭimids in North Africa, bearing the title of the "Permanent" or the "Perennial" (*al-Qā'im*) assumed command and took over the Imāmate from his predecessor, the "Trustee" (*al-Mustawdah'*). This hypothesis affirms that the Archegos, the head of Manicheism, moved from Baghdad to North Africa in two phases; the first was the emigration of a stand-in for the Archegos, who if captured, as apparently happened (Ubayd Allāh was supposedly rescued from imprisonment in Sijilmassa), could be denied. And then, once a transition had been executed successfully the secret emigration of the true Arch-Egos could take place. (The Assassins were once surrounded in a fortress by a Sunnī army, they negotiated a retreat in which the first half of the garrison would leave the fortress, and once they were allowed to depart safely, the second half would leave. The first half left; and the Sunnīs waited for the second half to leave. And waited.)

In 930, the Qarmatians raided Mecca and stole the Black Stone from the Ka'bah, Public outcry followed the abduction of the Black Stone and unsuccessful attempts were made to ransom it. Muslim historians of the day linked its disappearance with the Fāṭimids, for they said that the earth refused to receive the body of the first Fāṭimid for burial so long as the stone remained stolen. But the Manicheans had studied the religious writings of other religions and knew the saying: "Thou art Peter (Greek *petrus,* "rock") upon this rock, I will build my Church..." And in Aramaic, one of the principal languages of Manicheism, "that which surrounds a rock" is a word meaning "church". The Manicheans were keenly aware that the relationship between Jesus and Peter was that between a kind of esoterism and a kind of exoterism, for it was they who had brought the very notion into Islam, transposing it into the relationship between 'Alī and Muḥammad. According to their formula, Muḥammad was the exoteric manifester (*nāṭiq,* "spokesman") of the knowledge of 'Alī, who thus became esoteric and "silent" (*samīt*). 'Alī, as esoterism incarnate, according to their interpretation of esoterism as a "universal and perennial truth" independent of outward forms and even, ultimately, opposed to them, could be identified as Mani himself, and as literally Divine.

In 951, the Black Stone was suddenly and mysteriously returned; it was thrown, wrapped in a sack, into the Friday Mosque at Kufah, with the note: "By Command we took it, by Command we return it." No ransom had ever been asked for nor accepted. At the reconstruction of the Ka'bah in the year 692, the stone was in three pieces; today it is in seven (according to the Report of the Engineer rebuilding the Grand Mosque of Mecca in the reign of King Faysal). This fracturing of the stone dates from the abduction and thus marks the completion of one cycle of history and the beginning of a new age, according to Sevener ideology. (Only a few historians at the time alluded to the stone's fracturing; the 'Abbāsids had every reason to keep this portentous event secret as revolutions swirled around them.) The stone was now broken like the "seven lands", or regions of space, broken like the original unity of the Manichean church, now divided into disparate communities extending from North Africa to China and India, separated by the domains of exoteric Islam.

In 969 Egypt was conquered, and Cairo, the new Fāṭimid capital was founded (next to cities founded by previous conquerors) with the name: "The Victorious City of the Exalter of God's

Religion", This was the title-name of the ruler, *al-Mu'izz li-Dīn-Llāh,* himself considered to be the seventh Imām of the Seveners after their first appearance. The conquering Fāṭimid general al-Jawhar (who was from Sicily) also founded the al-Azhar College ("the Resplendent") to train missionaries (daīs), who often operated under cover when infiltrating Sunnī and Twelve-Imām Shī'ite domains in order to spread Fāṭimid doctrine. Fāṭimid Egypt then maintained regular and fervid communications with Persia, Turkestan and Sindh through the sending of rescripts (*sijill*) and missionaries (*da'īs*). Many postulants from these regions, such as Nāṣir-i Khusraw, and Ḥasan aṣ-Ṣabbāh came to Cairo for training. This spread of Ismā'īlī propaganda also forced the Sunnīs to found universities in order to counter the ideological onslaught. (The emphasis on Fāṭimah may be a transmutation of the Manichean divinity called the "Mother of the Living.")

Ibn an-Nadīm, writing in 988 in the *Fihrīst,* noted the mysterious disappearance of the Arch-Egos some sixty years earlier, as well as the fact that in his time, for some reason, there seemed to be no more than a handful of Manicheans left in Baghdad, formerly plentiful in the historic center. But later, the Spanish theologian Ibn Ḥazm (d. *456*/1064) remarked of the Fāṭimids: "I can see that Mazdak has become a Shī'ite." In Baghdad the religious authorities issued declarations stating the Fāṭimids were not descended from 'Alīds but from Marcion and Bardaisan, the forerunners of Mani.

In 1094 a schism took place among the Fāṭimids in Cairo; the Imāmate thereafter disappeared. But in 1164, in the schismatic Assassin fortress of Alamūt in northern Persia, we observe that the Imāmate reappeared and the "Festival of Resurrection" (*'Īd al-Qiyāmah*) was declared, which entailed the dropping of outward Islamic religious forms (*sharī'ah*). However, shortly thereafter, in the face of threat from the surrounding 'Abbāsid Empire, still largely Sunnī, the outer forms were again resumed with a great vigor, and the epoch was designated as the renewed "drawing over of the curtain" (*satr*).

In 1256, the Mongols of Hūlāgū Khān, on their way to sack Baghdad, destroyed Alamūt. In Syria, the Mamlūks, who took over Egypt after the Ayyūbids restored the country to Sunnī control, rooted out the defenders of the last Assassin castles, and with this collapse on two fronts, the sect virtually disappeared from history, leaving only flickers and embers in remote and far-flung places. In this violent way, it was the Mongols and the Turks who brought to an end the process of transmutation which had begun when Islam and Manicheism first came into contact. From the very first the two recoiled and there ensued a titanic struggle between the most adamantine non-dualism, which is Islam, and the most radical dualism, which is Manicheism, a true star wars fought in the shadows, and in men's minds. The process certainly enriched Islam and drew out its latent spiritual treasures in the form of fully developed doctrines and methods, theology and mysticism. But if the process of transformation had gone on indefinitely, even if it could never have completely co-opted Islam, it would have melted the outward form of the religion, which is indispensable to salvation, and introduced a fatally misconceived notion of the nature of the Divine Absolute. Thus, violent and painful though they were, as they laid waste whole cities and uprooted the civilization of millennia, the Mongols were nevertheless a providential catharsis.

In some cases a direct link can be established between a Gnosticism of antiquity, and one of its later or even modern developments. But sometimes, again, no apparent connection can be drawn other than that a certain thought entered someone's mind, the question where evil arises, a chance idea about "another woman" – Lilith – in the Garden of Eden, or a query as to why God in Genesis is spoken of in the plural (in Hebrew: *Elohim*). Or, as the parable teaches (Matthew 13:24), the event may appear to be spontaneous, from seeds that had traveled a great distance in time and space and suddenly sprouted out of nowhere, as if, while men slept, someone came, sowed tares among the wheat and went his way. See 'ALĪ ILĀHĪS; DUALISM; ELKHASAIOS; FIVE DIVINE PRESENCES; IBLĪS; KAY-SĀNIYYAH; KHAṬṬĀBIYYAH; KHURRAMIYYAH; MANDAEANS; MAZAR-I SHARIF; MAZDAK; NŪR MUḤAMMADĪ; QARMATIANS; SEVENERS; UMM al-KITĀB; YAZĪDĪS.

Manṣab. A military title of the Moghuls, created by the Emperor Akbar (d. *1014*/1605). The title brought with it a fief for the livelihood of its holder, in return for which concession the landholder, the *manṣabdārī*, provided horse soldiers to make up an army for the Emperor upon demand. The numbers could be from 10 to 10,000 horse in accordance with his grant. *See* IQṬĀʻ.

Maqām (lit. "a standpoint", "a station"). A spiritual station such as a virtue or an attitude which becomes the dominant complexion of the soul. A *maqām* may be an aspect of Divine knowledge which is profoundly realized and permanently acquired by the soul, as opposed to a transitory spiritual state (*ḥāl*). A particular *maqām* may be characteristic of a particular Saint or Prophet.

Al-Ḥujwīrī says:

> A station is a man's standing in the Way (*ṭarīqah*). It denotes his perseverance in fulfilling what is at that period of his life obligatory on him. He may not pass on from that *maqām* without accomplishing all he is bound to do there. The first station, for instance, is Penitence, the next Conversion, then Renunciation, then Trust, and so on. A man may not pretend to Conversion without complete Penitence, nor to Trust without complete Renunciation.
>
> A *ḥāl* on the other hand, is something that comes down from God into man's heart quite independently... it is a grace. Junayd says: *ḥāls* are like flashes of lightning... Everyone who longs for God has some particular station, which is his clue at the beginning of his quest. Whatever good he derives from other stations through which he may pass, he will finally rest in one, since one station and its own quest include and call for complex combination and design, not merely conduct and practice.
>
> Adam's *maqām*, for example, was Penitence, Noah's was Renunciation, and Abraham's Resignation. Contrition was Moses' station, and Sorrow David's. The station of Jesus was Hope, that of John the Baptist Fear. Our Prophet's was Praise. Whatever these men drew from other wells by which they dwelt a while, each man returned at last to his original station.

The Persian Sufi al-Qushayrī (d. *465*/1072) lists some typical *maqāmāt*: repentance (*tawbah*; the beginning of the way); withdrawal (*wara*ʻ); renunciation (*zuhd*); silence (*samt*); fear of God (*khawf*); hope (*raja*ʼ); sadness (*ḥuzn*); poverty (*faqr*); patience (*ṣabr*); trust (*tawakkul*); and contentment (*riḍā*ʼ). Lists by Sufis go on to as many as forty five different stations, some of which can if transitory also be listed simply as "states" (*ḥāl*; pl. *aḥwāl*).

The term also has technical meanings in poetry and music. In music, the *maqām* is the opening passages which establish the mode and style of the piece.

Maqām Ibrāhīm (lit. "the standing place of Abraham"). At a spot a few meters from the Black Stone corner of the Kaʻbah, there is a small kiosk which contains a stone with a figurative indentation of a footprint. By tradition this is the footprint of Abraham impressed into rock during the building of the Kaʻbah by Abraham and Ishmael. In the vicinity of the *Maqām Ibrāhīm* a prayer of two *rakaʻāt* is performed during the rites of pilgrimage. *See* ABRAHAM.

al-Maqdisī. The name of a famous Jerusalem family (*Bayt al-Maqdis*) which produced a number of scholars and jurists. The most famous of them is Muwaffaq ad-Dīn ibn Qudāmah al-Maqdisī (d. *620*/1223), the author of the *Kitāb al-Mughnī* on Ḥanbalī law.

al-Maqrīzī, Taqī ad-Dīn Aḥmad (*767-846*/1364-1442). An historian and biographer. Born in Cairo, al-Maqrīzī was a *muḥtasib*, or inspector of markets, who later wrote a book on weights and measures. He became a *khaṭīb* ("preacher") in a mosque and a religious teacher. He wrote histories of the Fāṭimid, Ayyūbid, and Mamlūk dynasties.

Maqṣūrah. An area of a mosque set aside for use by important personages, it is usually surrounded by an enclosure of lattice work or some kind of screen. The first *maqṣūrah* may well have been built by the Caliph ʻUthmān in the mosque in Medina as a protection against attack.

Marabout (a French word derived from the Ar. *marbūṭ*, "attached", in the sense of being bound to God). A term used in North and West Africa for a Saint, or a venerated descendant of a Saint. Although Saints are revered to some extent throughout the Islamic world, in the Arab West and West Africa the respect paid to Saints is a very important dimension of spiritual practice. Only in countries where Wahhābī doctrine prevails have all traces of veneration previously accorded to Saints been expunged.

The Saint is considered to exercise a spiritual influence, grace or blessing (*barakah*), which after his death may remain at his tomb indefinitely and bless those who visit it. The intercession of Saints is often called upon in prayers; indeed, saintly *barakah* may also be recurrent in a family, bursting forth from generation to generation in the descendant of a great Saint as a special piety or sanctity, rather as certain healing powers were attributed to the British royal family, and to the French Kings.

In the Arab West, Saints' tombs with their characteristic domes dot the landscapes and Saints' festivals (*mawsim*, *moussem* in French), adorn the year, being occasions for gatherings, sometimes of many thousands of visitors, and for fairs, powderplay (the execution of fighting manoeuvers on horseback and the firing of matchlock rifles), and other festivities.

"Marabout" is a term used more often in French than in Arabic, and is peculiar to those areas of North and West Africa that were once part of the French colonial empire. In French the word maraboutism was invented to describe this veneration of saints.

Ma'rib Dam (Ar. *sadd al-ma'rib*). In South Arabia there were a number of simple earthen dams built for irrigation purposes. Some dated from the 6th century B.C. and were the pride of the South Arabians, the most famous being that of Ma'rib. When it burst about 580 A.D. after a long period of neglect, the event had a profound effect upon the Arabs of the south as marking the end of an epoch, and closing the period of their greatness which stretched back into the legendary times of the Queen of Sheba (Saba').

The Koran may refer to the destruction of the Ma'rib Dam in 34:14-17:

> For Sheba also there was a sign in
> their dwelling-place – two gardens,
> one on the right and one on the left:
> 'Eat of your Lord's provision, and give thanks
> to Him; a good land, and a Lord
> All-forgiving.'
> But they turned away; so We loosed on
> them the Flood of Arim, and We gave them,
> in exchange for their two gardens,
> two gardens bearing bitter produce
> and tamarisk-bushes, and here and there
> a few lote-trees.
> Thus We recompensed them for their unbelief;
> and do We ever recompense any but
> the unbeliever?

Dams which were built much later, but reminiscent of the style of Ma'rib, can be found today still intact not far from Mecca. See SABA'.

Ma'rifah (lit. "knowledge"). Knowledge in general, especially in modern Arabic usage, but in religious literature specifically gnosis, that is, esoteric, or mystical knowledge of God. It corresponds to *jñāña* in Sanskrit. In Sufism, *ma'rifah* is part of a triad that includes *makhāfah*, "fear" (of God), and *maḥabbah*, "love". The three are attitudes any one of which can determine a spiritual way, but they are also phases in every spiritual path. *Makhāfah* is a necessary phase of purification, *maḥabbah* the expansion to "fill the mold" of a Divine messenger, and finally *ma'rifah*, which is wisdom and realization of truth: union. These correspond in some respects to the three "paths" (*margas*) in Hinduism, of deeds (*karma*), devotion (*bhakti*), and gnosis (*jñāña*). See MAKHĀFAH; MAḤABBAH; SUFISM.

Maristān. A traditional infirmary, usually for the insane. A *maristān* was often attached to a Saint's tomb where it was hoped that the blessing of the Saint, and the supportive ambiance which prevails in such places, would help recovery. See MEDICINE.

Marja' at-Taqlīd (lit. "reference point of emulation"). In the Uṣūlī school of Shī'ism, a Mujtahid, that is, a religious authority of the first rank whose competence is such that he can arrive at original, unprecedented decisions in theology and religious law. Everyone who is not himself a *marja' at-taqlīd* is obliged to be a *muqallid*, that is, an emulator, or follower of a living Mujtahid (it is forbidden to be a follower of a dead Mujtahid). See AYATOLLAH; UṢŪLĪS.

Maronites. A Christian Uniate sect in the Lebanon (with some members in Syria, Israel, Cyprus, and Egypt, and through emigration, in the United States and South America), named after an eponymous St. Maron of the 5th century. Since the Crusades, and the year 1182, the Maronites have accepted the supremacy of the Pope and are today in communion with the Catholic church. But the origins of the Maronites lie in the divergence of opinion regarding the nature of Jesus which led to the Council of Nicea.

Originally the Maronites were probably Monophysites who held that Jesus was entirely Divine, one person with one nature. (The Orthodox belief is that Jesus is one person with two natures, human and Divine.) At the beginning of the Muslim invasions, the Ghassānī Arabs of Syria, who were Monophysite, and at odds with the Orthodox Melkites of Syria, allied themselves with the Muslims and turned against Byzantium. The Byzantines, seeking to win back the support of the Ghassānīs, offered the religious compromise of the *Ecthesis* in 638, to bring about greater religious harmony between themselves and the Syrians. This compromise was that of Monotheletism, a doctrine that the will of Jesus was one with the Divine Will, a concession to Monophysitism that does not go as far as to posit a continuity between God and creation which is Monophysitism. The Maronites, who were Monotheletists, are apparently the historical result of that compromise between the Byzantines and the Syrian Monophysite Christians.

In 1182, a Maronite Patriarch of Antioch, Amaury, convinced other Maronite Bishops to ally themselves with Rome. Communion with Rome was ratified at the Council of Florence in 1445. Many Maronite practices, however, remained at variance, such as mixed convents of monks and nuns, and in 1736 the Maronite Church received a constitution from Rome which was intended to bring about greater conformity. A married priesthood is still allowed, although not marriage after ordination, and, like the Orthodox, two kinds of clergy exist, married and celibate. French protection of the Maronites began with Louis XIV, permitted by a decree of the Ottoman Sultan. This led to intervention in the 19th century because of massacres of Maronites at the hands of the Druzes. After clashes between the two in 1860, the Sultan established the province or *sanjak* of Lebanon with an Ottoman Christian governor. Representation in the council, or *majlis* of the province was distributed among the religious groups including Orthodox, Druzes, and Shī'ites.

After 1860 a great migration began out of Lebanon while the process of identifying with French institutions continued. After World War I France assumed administration of both Lebanon and Syria, later subdivided into autonomous states. To justify continued outside intervention, a region was created with a Christian majority in the original Ottoman province but now with an added substantial Muslim minority: to Mount Lebanon, the Christian heartland, was added the then predominantly Muslim city of Beirut, Tripoli, Sidon and Shī'ite south Lebanon. Under the terms of the mandate a constitution was adopted in 1926. There began an unwritten tradition that Lebanon's president was a Maronite, the Prime Minister a Sunnī, and the President of the Chamber of Deputies a Shī'ite. Defense was usually headed by a Druze. A new constitution was promulgated from Paris in 1934.

A first free election for the Syrian and Lebanese parliaments in 1943 resulted in a defeat for French-supported candidates; the governments demanded control of administration for themselves. The French commander Catroux responded by arresting the Presidents and the cabinets. In Lebanon, the pro-French, Emile Edde was appointed head of state, but he did not succeed in forming an effective cabinet. After the war ended in Europe, fighting broke out in Damascus; with the help of the United Nations, both Lebanon and Syria became independent.

During this period Sunnīs favored a union with Syria; the Maronites looked upon Lebanon as a part of Europe, and promulgated a nationalism called Phoenicianism that held the Lebanese to be a distinct group from the other nations of the Levant. The Greek Orthodox, however, favored a secular identity as Arabs first (over that of Christians). Reaction to Arab nationalism led to the development of Pierre Jemayel's Maronite-dominated (80%) Phalangist movement, with its motto "Lebanon above all".

Three of Lebanon's ethnic-religious groups, Maronites, Shī'ites, and Druzes (in Syria one can also add the 'Alawīs) have in common doctrines which absolutize something in creation. In the case of the Christians with a Monophysite and Monotheletist tradition, the physical person of Jesus, in the case of the Shī'ites, the Imām, in the case of the Druzes, al-Ḥākim. Theologically very similar, they are very antithetical on the plane of their outside forms because of the absolute within, the absolute hidden on the material plane. These have co-existed in the past under a hegemony of outside powers, that of the Muslim empires, then the Ottomans, and the French. In this century those hegemonies have disappeared. To the south, another absolutism has appeared in the form of the state of Israel which has resulted in the displacement of large numbers of Palestinians into Lebanon; at the same time a demographic shift has taken place in which the Muslims now outnumber the Christians in Lebanon, along with a sharp increase of population within the Shī'ite community, now outnumbering the Sunnīs, who have particularly suffered as a result of the Israeli invasion of Lebanon which attempted to oust the refugee Palestinians but succeeded in radicalizing the Shī'ites. A new equilibrium has yet to emerge. *See* GHASSĀNĪS.

Marriage (Ar. *an-nikah*). In Islam, marriage is accomplished through a contract which is confirmed by the bride's reception of a dowry (*mahr*) and by the witnessing of the bride's consent to the marriage. If she is silent, her silence is also taken as acceptance; the Mālikīs and Shāfi'īs insist if the bride is a virgin, that she be represented by a male guardian (*walī*), usually a relative, who accepts the terms on her behalf. A woman cannot be forced to marry against her will.

When agreement to the marriage is expressed and witnessed, those present recite the *fātiḥah* (the opening chapter of the Koran). Normally, marriages are not contracted in mosques but in private homes or at the offices of a Judge (*Qāḍi*). It is often the national or tribal customs that determine the type of ceremony, if there is one, and the celebrations which accompany it (*'urs*). In some parts of the Islamic world these may include processions in which the bride gift is put on display, receptions where the bride is seen adorned in elaborate costumes and jewelry, and ceremonial installation of the bride in the new house to which she may be carried in a litter. The groom may ride through the streets on a horse followed by his friends and well-wishers, and there is always a feast called the *walīmah*.

In religious law it is legal for a Muslim man to marry a Christian woman, or a woman of any of the Divinely revealed religions. It is not legal however, for a Muslim woman to marry outside her religion. In the past, non-Muslims marrying Muslim women have entered Islam in order to satisfy this aspect of Islamic law where it is in force. It now happens more and more frequently that Muslim women marry non-Muslim men who remain outside Islam. Such marriages, when and where they do not offend against the civil law, meet with varying degrees of social acceptance, depending upon the milieu. *See* WOMEN.

Martyrs (Ar. *shahīd*, pl. *shuhadā'*). Believers who die for the faith, in defense of it, or persecuted for it, are assured of Heaven. They are buried as they died, unwashed and in the same clothes, the bloodstains testifying to their state.

Moreover, the Koran (3:169) says: "count not those who are slain in the way of God as dead; nay, they are living; with their lord they have provision." (It has been suggested that this elucidates Koran 4:157-158 which states that Jesus was not killed but raised up to God). Assimilated to martyrdom are those whose death has been tragic; their burials, however, follow the normal course of ablution and change of linen, before interment.

Mary (Ar. *Maryam*). The mother of Jesus. In Islam she is mentioned with her honorific *sayyidatunā* ("our lady"), as the Prophets are titled *sayyidunā* ("our lord"). In the Koran she is the daughter of 'Imrān and Hannah. She was raised by Zakariyya; it was her custom to retreat in the *miḥrāb*, the prayer niche in a holy place, and whenever Zakariyya went into the *miḥrāb* where she was, he found that she had food. "He said: 'O Mary! Whence cometh this unto thee?' She answered: 'It is from God; God giveth without stint to whom he will'" (3:37). This is almost always the verse which is written on prayer niches when they are decorated with calligraphy.

> And mention in the Book Mary
> when she withdrew from her people
> to an eastern place,
> and she took a veil apart from them;
> then We sent unto her Our Spirit
> that presented himself to her
> a man without fault.
> She said, 'I take refuge in
> the All-merciful from thee!

If thou fearest God.'
He said, 'I am but a messenger
come from thy Lord, to give thee
a boy most pure.'
She said, 'How shall I have a son
whom no mortal has touched, neither
have I been unchaste?'
He said, 'Even so thy Lord has said:
"Easy is that for Me; and that We
may appoint him a sign unto men
and a mercy from Us; it is
a thing decreed."'
So she conceived him, and withdrew with him
to a distant place.
And the birthpangs surprised her by
the trunk of the palm-tree. She said,
'Would I had died ere this, and become
a thing forgotten!'
But the one that was below her
called to her, 'Nay, do not sorrow;
see, thy Lord has set below thee
a rivulet.
Shake also to thee the palm-trunk,
and there shall come tumbling upon thee
dates fresh and ripe.
Eat therefore, and drink, and be
comforted; and if thou shouldst see
any mortal,
say, "I have vowed to the All-merciful
a fast, and today I will not speak
to any man."'
Then she brought the child to her folk
carrying him; and they said,
'Mary, thou hast surely committed
a monstrous thing!
Sister of Aaron, thy father was not
a wicked man, nor was thy mother
a woman unchaste.'
Mary pointed to the child then;
but they said, 'How shall we speak
to one who is still in the cradle,
a little child?'
He said, 'Lo, I am God's servant;
God has given me the Book, and
made me a Prophet.
Blessed He has made me, wherever
I may be; and He has enjoined me
to pray, and to give the alms, so
long as I live,
and likewise to cherish my mother;
He has not made me arrogant,
unprosperous.
Peace be upon me, the day I was born,
and the day I die, and the day I am
raised up alive!'
That is Jesus, son of Mary... (19:16-34)

In Koran 19:28 she is called "Sister of Aaron". This is often understood to mean Aaron, the brother of Moses, on the ground that Mary's relationship to the revelation of Jesus was analogous to that of Aaron in regard to Moses. Like Aaron, she has an inward function rather than an outward one in respect of revelation. On the Prophet's journey to Ṭā'if a Christian slave asked him how he knew of Jonah. The Prophet replied: "He is my brother; he was a Prophet, and I am a Prophet." In other words, brotherhood can be a kinship on a spiritual plane, and the Prophet's point of view specifically included this possibility. Joseph, the husband of Mary in the Gospels, does not appear in the Koranic accounts.

When the Muslims conquered Mecca, the Ka'bah was cleansed of the many stone and wood idols it contained. Inside the Ka'bah, on the walls, were several paintings, among them a picture of Abraham and an icon of the Virgin and Child. The Prophet covered the icon with his hands, instructing that everything else should be painted over. *See also* AARON; JESUS.

Mas'ā. The walkway between the two hills Ṣafā and Marwah, which is today within the precincts of the rebuilt and extended Grand Mosque of Mecca. This space, which is 1,247 feet/394 meters, is walked seven times in the performance of the rite of the *'umrah.* The ritual walking is called the *sa'y,* and it commemorates the running back and forth of Hagar, when she cast about looking for water for her son Ishmael. *See* KA'BAH; PILGRIMAGE.

Masaḥ 'ala-l-Khuffayn (lit. "wiping the inner shoes"). The *khuffayn* are a kind of footwear, a soft shoe worn inside a boot, which modern practice has assimilated to stockings. If they have no holes and are put on while the person is in a state of ablution (*wuḍū'*), then, in renewing the ablution, it is enough to wipe them with moist hands without removing them and wiping the bare feet. This Sunnī practice is not accepted by the Zaydīs. The Mālikī school of law accepts the principle of *masaḥ 'ala-l-khuffayn* but insists that it applies only in the case of actual *khuffayn,* which exist today as a kind of soft leather under slipper worn in Turkey. Many individual Mālikīs, however, do not make this distinction. However, whereas as many Ḥanafīs only touch the socks with a moist hand, the Mālikīs who assimilate socks to inner shoes actually wipe the foot with a moist hand as if it were bare. *See* ZAYDĪS.

Masallā, *see* MUṢALLĀ.

Maslamah, *see* MUSAYLAMAH.

Mash'ar. A place where it is traditional to perform a ritual action, as in the two prayer sites in the pilgrimage, *al-mash'ar al-ḥarām*, and *al-mash'ar al-ḥalāl. Al-mash'ar al-ḥarām* is in Muzdalifah, within the restricted precinct, the *ḥarām,* and *al-mash'ar al-ḥalāl* is in 'Arafāt, just outside the precinct. *See* PILGRIMAGE.

Mashhad (lit. "the place of martyrdom"). The term used by the Shī'ites for the tombs of their Imāms, such as the *mashhad Ḥusayn* at Kerbala. *Mashhad* without further qualification usually refers to the tomb of the eighth Shī'ite Imām 'Alī ibn Musā 'r-Riḍā (or 'Alī Reẓā) (d. *203*/818) and the town, also sometimes spelled Meshed, which has grown up around it, is the capital of Khorasan province in northeast Iran. Its population today is close to 500,000. The shrine of the Imām is one of the most important in Twelve-Imām Shī'ism, as it is the only tomb of an Imām in Iran itself, and the most important after Kerbala and Najaf (the burial place of 'Alī). The Caliph Hārūn ar-Rashīd is also buried there, having died in the place on a journey ten years before the death of the Imām.

The Shī'ites advance in testimony of the sanctity of Mashhad the following Ḥadīth: "A part of my [the Prophet's] body is to be buried in Khorasan, and whoever goes there on pilgrimage, God will surely destine to paradise, and his body will be forbidden to the flames of hell; and whoever goes there with sorrow, God will take his sorrow away."

Al-Ma'mūn, the son of Hārūn ar-Rashīd, ordered a tomb to be built there for his father, who died in the place before 'Alī ar-Riḍā. This tomb was successively expanded, particularly by Shāh Abbās, not because of Hārūn ar-Rashīd, but because of the tomb's other occupant, the Shī'ite Imām. It has since become one of the most lavish shrines in Islam. (As Hārūn ar-Rashīd was not a Shī'ite, and is considered rather as an enemy of Shī'ism, his tomb is not honored and its place in the shrine is coincidental unless, of course, al-Ma'mun had the Imām poisoned, as is claimed.)

In 1911 the city was occupied by rebels, and the Persian government, lacking forces, permitted the Russians, who had military units stationed in Khorasan, to take action. This they did by bombarding the city; the golden dome of the shrine was damaged, and a wave of opprobrium against the Russians swept through Persia.

Masīḥī (from *al-masih,* "messiah"). The proper name for Christians, pl. *masīḥiyyūn.* This use of the word was first established by Christian missionaries, in preference to the term *Naṣārā* ("Nazarenes").

Masjid, *see* MOSQUE

.

al-Masjid al-Ḥarām, *see* KA'BAH.

Masjid an-Nabī ash-Sharīf, *see* MOSQUE of the PROPHET.

al-Mas'ūdī, Abū-l-Ḥasan 'Alī ibn al-Ḥusayn ibn 'Alī (d. *345*/956). An historian, geographer, philosopher and natural scientist, he was a descendant of the Prophet's Companion 'Abd Allāh ibn Mas'ūd. A Shī'ite born in Baghdad of a Kufan family, al-Mas'ūdī had an excellent education. He knew the great men of Baghdad of his time, and his many teachers included Sīnān ibn Thābit ibn Qurra (d. *331*/943), the Mu'tazilite theologian al-Jubba'ī (who was the teacher of al-Ash'arī), and he knew al-Ash'arī himself (d. *324*/935), the founder of Sunnī *Kalām* ("theology"). He debated with the physician, philosopher, and alchemist Abū Bakr Muḥammad ibn Zakariyya ar-Rāzī (d. 320/923). Al-Mas'ūdī traveled extensively in the East, including India. He also went to Egypt but, strangely, not to North Africa or Spain. He described the places he visited, and chronicled the events of his times in his book *Murūj adh-Dhahab wa Ma'ādin al-Jawhar* ("the Meadows of Gold and Quarries of Jewels"), and his *Murūj az-Zamān* ("Meadows of Time"). He wrote thirty-four works, most of which are lost.

"The Meadows of Gold" is actually an encyclopedia of medieval Islamic knowledge. It rambles over every imaginable kind of subject: geography, historical notices including the history of the Prophets, the ancient Arabs, the Romans, the Persian Kings, the Islamic dynasties, the French Kings, the peoples of the ancient world together with their customs, religions, curiosities, temples, monuments, commerce, medicine, astronomy, astrology, science, the nature of the soul, psychology and legends.

Of India, Mas'ūdī says that in the ancient past "it was there that order and wisdom reigned". He makes many interesting observations, among other things, on Indian theories of the cycles of time and history. At the beginning of a cycle, al-Mas'ūdī says, the circumference which contains all the principles to be manifested in it is greater, and there is more freedom to act. At the end of a cycle, it draws tighter and there is compression; the quality of time itself changes: in the beginning of a particular cycle of manifestation time can contain more events, and at the end, less, which gives the impression of rapid succession, speed, and havoc. "Meadows of Gold and Quarries of Jewels" contains an apt and accurate description of this.

Matn. In the analysis of Ḥadīth, the *matn* is the body, or content, of the Ḥadīth; the *isnād* the chain of transmission. In another sense, *matn* may denote the actual text of an author, which may be published with a commentary, the *sharḥ*. *Matn* means letters (*mutūn*) as quoted by Goldziher from a poem by Labid: *wajalā s-sulūlu 'ani 't-ṭullūli ka'annahā Zubrun tujiddi mutūnahā aqlāmuhā* : "the torrents make the traces of the camps reappear as if they were letters restored by the strokes of a reed pen." *See* ḤADĪTH.

Matter, *see* HAYŪLĀ.

al-Māturīdī, Abū Manṣūr Muḥammad (d. *333*/944). A theologian (*mutakallim*), born near Samarkand. Together with al-Ash'arī and others, he is one of the founders of *Kalām* (Islamic theology). Little is known about the man himself, for his school became established as the result of the writings of his disciples, in particular an-Naṣafī. Traditionally, the doctrinal differences between the school of al-Māturīdī and that of al-Ash'arī are numbered at thirteen, seven of them being only a difference in the way matters are expressed.

The most important difference is that al-Māturīdī accords human free will the logic of its consequences, that is, that the just are saved on that account, whereas with al-Ash'arī God's will is unfathomable: God may send the just to hell. Al-Māturīdī recognizes that God's reward or punishment is in relation to man's actions and this view has largely been tacitly accepted, in practice even by Ash'arites. In general, the school of al-Māturīdī has not hesitated to enunciate dogmatic antinomies, (man has free will, but is predestined; the speech of God is both created and uncreated) which has won more adherents than the Ash'arites have in Central Asia and the Far East. It should be noted, even so, that the school of al-Māturīdī, whilst enunciating these doctrines, has largely avoided explaining them, and left that enlargement to the mystics. *See al-*ASH'ARĪ; KALĀM; SUFISM.

al-Ma'ūdah. In the Arab desert society that predated Islam, the *ma'ūdah* was an unwanted female child that was buried alive. The practice was forbidden by Islam. ("On the Day of Judgement the victim will be asked for what sin she was slain" (Koran 81:8).)

The practice probably originated because of the conditions of perpetual famine in which the desert Arabs lived; infanticide reflected the struggle for survival.

Mauritania. Islamic Republic. Population: 2,211,000 of whom half are Arab and Berber whites, and half are members of various black tribal groups, Sarakoll, Fulānī and Wolof, who are also found in Senegal. Besides Arabic, of the dialect called Ḥasaniyyah, French is the dominant language, especially among the blacks, for whom, with fourteen native languages, it is the common medium. 99% of Mauritanians are Muslims of the Mālikī School of Law. Mauritania was Islamicised by the Almoravids, whose center was near the city of Aṭṭār, from *442*/1050 on. Many Mauritanians are loosely affiliated with the Qādiriyyah *ṭarīqah*, and the Tijāniyyah is influential in the south of the country. The white tribes are divided into "Ḥasanis", or Arabs, and "Ḥusaynis", or Berbers. The Berber tribes are also called the *zāwiyah* tribes.

There is a caste structure to society: the nomads, Arabs and Berbers, who call themselves the "bones", undisputedly consider themselves the nobles, while the others, who are town dwellers, include musician castes, craft and artisan castes, fisherman castes, and other small groups, each with a distinct place on the social ladder. These are called the "flesh" (*laḥm*). The traditional name of Mauritania is *Bilād al-Bīḍān* ("The Country of the Whites"), and in North Africa the country was known as *Shinqīt,* after the holy town of (in French) Chinguetti. Although there is a republican form of government, in the desert, the chiefs, the Emirs, are the ruling force. *See* CHINGUETTI; ḤASANĪ.

al-Māwardi, 'Alī Muḥammad (d. *450*/1058). A Judge in Baghdad and a figure at court, al-Māwardi wrote one of the important books of political science entitled *Kitāb al-Aḥkam as-Sultaniyyah* ("The Book of Rules of Government"). It is in the genre of a mirror for princes, (*nasihahatu-l-muluk*). Al-Māwardi discusses the *bilād ad-dīn,* a state ruled by religion; *bilād al-quwwah,* rule by power (in respect of the rise in the 10th century of the sultanate state based on force), and *bilād ath-thawra*, anarchy. In this al-Māwardi followed Ibn Muqaffa' who said that there were three forms of government, those based on justice and truth, on injustice and political realism, and those of meddling and squander. Before Ibn Khaldūn addressed the question, al-Māwardi discussed the reasons why rulers lost power.

Al-Māwardi mentions that the Sassanid state was based upon *maslaḥah,* welfare, and not *sharī'ah,* religious law. The principles of Sassanid rule, however, in the *Ahd Ardashir* ("The Testament of Ardashir I", the founder of the dynasty), said that kingship and religion are twin brothers, no one of which can be maintained without the other. For religion is the foundation of kingship and kingship is the guardian of religion. Kingship cannot subsist without its foundation and religion cannot subsist without its guardian. "For that which has no guardian is lost, and that which has no foundation crumbles."

Mawdūdī (or *Maudūdi*), Sayyid Abū al-A'la (*1321-1399*/1903-1979). A highly influential Muslim revivalist and politician. Born in Aurangabad, India, he spent much of his life in Hyderabad and later in Lahore, where he is buried after having died in America while on a journey. He came from a family which had been displaced as a result of colonialism and the subsequent loss of political power on the part of the Muslims in India. He was involved in the Khilafat movement and the early Congress party, but turned towards Muslim nationalism and then Islamic utopianism. Mawdūdī had received the diploma of an *'alim* or religious authority, a fact which he did not disclose at a time when he was wrongly criticised for not being an 'alim.

In 1941, along with other intellectuals, Mawdūdī founded a political party, the *Jamā'ati Islāmi,* which became divided with the partition of India into several branches. This party is an embodiment of his views which treats Islam itself as an ideology and a political activity, setting aside its spiritual aspect. He viewed the Islamic state as a sixth pillar of the religion. In his state social ills can be overcome by the literal meaning of the Koran; a non-Muslim cannot be a member of parliament or hold a high government post. Social evolution, Utopianism, and struggle with non-Islamic forces characterized his outlook.

Much of his life Mawdūdī was a journalist, starting as editor of an Urdu weekly magazine Madina at the age of sixteen. He was the editor of daily newspaper *Taj* and later, *Jam'īat,* which was the newspaper of *Jam'īat-i 'Ulamā-i-Hind,* a political party in Delhi. From 1933 to 1979 he was the editor of *Tarjuman al Qur'an,* a monthly which was the forum for the expression of his ideas. His major works amongst many which he wrote as a journalist are *Jihād in Islam* (which attracted Muḥammed Iqbal who invited Mawdūdī to come to Lahore), *Towards Understanding Islam,* and his *magnum opus,* a translation of the Koran and commentary in Urdu, *Tafhīm al-Qur'an,* which is widely read in Pakistan and has appeared in English. As *emir* or leader of his party Mawdūdī was imprisoned several times after the creation of Pakistan.

Mawlā (pl. *mawālī*). During the first century of Arab expansion following the revelation of Islam, converts to Islam outside Arabia were adopted into Arab tribes. This "adoption" was made by the convert becoming a client (*mawlā*) of an Arab who was the protector. This status was a kind of second class citizenship in the Islamic state and was resented, particularly by the Persians. It is said that this system was not practiced by 'Alī, who treated all converts among the conquered people as equals of the Arabs.

The *mawālī* system declined and was abolished by the Umayyad Caliph 'Umar ibn 'Abd al-'Azīz (d. *101*/720), but it had by then contributed to the growth of political Shī'ism which hoped to find greater equity through the overthrow of the Umayyads and the promotion of one of the 'Alīds to the Caliphate. The word *mawlā*, in its sense of "master" or "patron", or simply as an expression of respect, has come into modern English as Mulla ("religious authority"). *See* UMAYYADS.

Mawlānā Jalāl ad-Dīn ar-Rūmī, *see* JALĀL ad-DĪN ar-RŪMĪ.

Mawlawī, *see* MEVLEVI.

Mawlay (lit. "my master" from *mawlā*). A title used in Morocco for *sharīfs*, descendants of the Prophet. It is often encountered in its French form, *Moulay*.

Mawlid an-Nabī. The birthday of the Prophet, the 12th of Rabī' al-Awwal. The observance of the *mawlid* as a public holiday began around the *6th*/12th century. In *690*/1291 the Merinid Sultan Abū Ya'qūb introduced *mawlid* celebrations into Morocco; and in Mamlūk Egypt a century later the fervor of the celebrations reached great heights.

The manner of observing the *mawlid* is a matter of local custom. Most typical is the recitation of various litanies in mosques. In countries that were once part of the Ottoman Empire, it is the custom upon the *mawlid* to recite the *Burdah* ("The Mantle"), a poem by al-Buṣīrī whose theme is praise of the Prophet.

In some countries there are street processions, such as the procession of wax displays in Salé, Morocco, perhaps inspired by Spanish Saints' processionals. See BURDAH.

Mawlūd, *see* MAWLID an-NABĪ.

Mawsim, *see* MOUSSEM.

Māyā, *see* ḤIJĀB.

Mazār (from Arabic *mazhar*, "appearance", "manifestation"). A term used in Iran and Central Asia for the tomb of a Saint, or a place associated with his life.

Mazār-i Sharīf. A town with a population of less than 50,000 near what was once Balkh in north Afghanistan, near Uzbekistan. It is famed for its splendid shrine which is held to be the tomb of 'Alī (his actual tomb is in Iraq, most probably in Najaf). Still piety has insisted that 'Alī's presence graces Mazār-i Sharīf as well. An inscription at Mazār-i Sharīf in Persian declares: "It is said that Murtada 'Alī is in Najaf. Come to Balkh and see how beautiful it is. Sa'dī said that 'Alī is in the land of the two rivers and between the mountains [a description of the situation of both Iraq and Balkh]. There is only one sun, but its light shines everywhere."

In the time of Sultan Sanjar, who reigned in the first half of the 12th century, a report reached Balkh from Sind (today Pakistan) that the grave of 'Alī was nearby. A Mullah of the place at first denied it but then 'Alī appeared to him in a dream and confirmed the report. A shrine was erected by Sultan Sanjar which was finished in 1136. It was destroyed by Jenghiz Khān in 1220 when he sacked Balkh. Not long afterwards Marco Polo could still call it a great and noble city. In 1481 the tomb was replaced by Hussein Baikara. Thenceforth it became a place of pilgrimage. Mazār-i Sharīf overtook Balkh (which was 23 kilometers from the shrine) as Mashhed had overtaken Tus.

Whoever is actually buried in Mazār-i Sharif antedates Islam. By identifying him with 'Alī, his partisans thus assured that his tomb became protected and honored by the Islamic establishment. At this point it will be impossible to positively identify the personage so protected, but the circumstances connecting Sind, 'Alī, and Balkh lead to the guess that it is Mani's Iranian missionary Mar Ammo.

Mar Ammo had come to Afghanistan where a goddess named Bagard (Lakhshmi) stopped him. He said that he brought a new religion to which she answered that they had enough religions. Mar Ammo stopped and prayed for two days; the spirit of Mani appeared to him and told him a list of books to read to the goddess whereupon she allowed him to continue.

Balkh was the origin of many astrologers, and center for Ismā'ilism, which is still found in Badakshan and the Pamir. Rumī and his father were expelled from Balkh and went to Konya when orthodox reaction became too strong, like Nāṣir-i Khusraw before them. Khusraw, railing against the development of orthodox control wrote:

As for the province of Khorasan, once the Abode of Learning,
It has become a cavern of sordid and effeminate demons.
Balkh! The House of Wisdom! and now fit for the axe, its fortune turned topsy-turvey on its head.
Khorasan, once the Kingdom of Solomon – How has it become the domain of Satan.

The town of Balkh is ancient; the Iranians said it was founded by Gayomart, the first man, and called it "mother of cities". By legend Zoroaster had lived there and begun his mission there and even died there. In Alexander's time it was called Alexandria-Bactra or Zainaspa, and it was the capital of Bactria, which, at times, included Soghdiana, Merv, part of Khorasan and Ferghana, not including Khwarizm, and saw Greek settlements. Gold from Siberia flowed through it, and later Indian and Chinese trade. After the Seleucids, Bactria was captured by the nomad Yueh-Chi Kushans and became Tocharistan. It later was a center of Buddhism, and in Central Asia Buddhism was influenced by Zurvanism and the cult of Amitābha grew.

The Chinese Buddhist pilgrim Hsuan Tsang visited Balkh around the year 630 and reported that in addition to about one hundred Hinayana monasteries, with about three thousand devotees, there were at some distance from them, what he called *Nava Sangharama*, recognizable as *Naw Bahar* or *Nava Vihara*, from Soghdian Buddhist texts. It was from these new, perhaps Mahayana monasteries created as a vehicle for Manicheism that the Barmakids, then abbots of a Buddhist monastery, were called to Baghdad to become ministers for the 'Abbāsids. Hsuan Tsang said that Buddhism was brought to Central Asia by Trapuṣa and Bhallika (referring to Balkh) two merchants who were the first to offer food to the Buddha after his "Enlightenment" and who became his first lay followers. Buddhism existed side by side with Islam in Central until around the year 1000 when its decline was observed by al-Bīrūnī. Buddhist monasteries may have influenced the architecture of the *madrasah*. *See* IBRĀHĪM ibn ADHAM; KHUSRAW, NAṢIR-I; KUBRĀ; JALĀL ad-DĪN ar-RŪMI,

Mazdak (early 6th century A.D.). A Magian priest in Persia who became the leader of a cult within Zoroastrian Mazdaeism. He preached the holding of women and property in common, and advocated Dualism (Ar. *thanawiyyah*), a system of belief in which evil is equal to good and possesses essence and substance. The Persian Shāh Kobad (488-531) became a follower of the cult, but was finally convinced of its unorthodoxy. Mazdak was put to death, as were thousands of his followers; the succeeding Shāh, Chosroes I (Anushirvan, "Great Soul"), embodied a revival of Zoroastrianism in Persia.

Ibn Muqaffa' translated the *Book of Mazdak* into Arabic. The Persian Vizier of the Saljūqs, Niẓām al-Mulk (d. *485*/1092), wrote about Mazdakism in his *Siyaset-Nāmeh* ("Book of Government") as a warning to the rulers of his age, which was also beset by irruptions of Dualist sects. The Mazdak epoch was remembered with anguish in Iran as the time when children did not know their fathers. The system was, as exactly as possible in a pre-Industrial age, a form of Communism with good and evil playing the role of what in Marxism is thesis and anthesis. After the restoration under Chosroe, many Mazdakites were expulsed from Iran to the Yemen and to the region of Hira, where, four centuries later, Mazdakism reappeared as Qarmatianism. *See* QARMATIANISM; MANICHEISM.

Mecca (*Makkah al-Mukarramah*; lit. "Mecca the Blessed"). For thousands of years Mecca has been a spiritual center. Ptolemy, the second century Greek geographer, mentioned Mecca, calling it "Makoraba". Some have interpreted this to mean temple (from *maqribah* in South Arabian) but it may also mean "Mecca of the Arabs". The Dravidian Purāās also speak of an ancient holy place there dedicated to the god of wisdom. Originally, Mecca was called Bakkah ("narrow"), a description of the site between the mountains that press upon the city and valley of the Holy Places. The Koran says: "The first sanctuary appointed for mankind was that at Bakkah, a blessed place, a guidance for the peoples" (3:96).

Of visible monuments that date back to ancient times there exists today only the Ka'bah, Abraham's temple to God, towards which Muslims throughout the world turn to pray, and which has been rebuilt several times. The landscape surrounding the city is of a striking aridity, as if of immeasurable age. It is nature reduced to its bare foundations, evoking the limitless and the invisible. The Koran calls Mecca the "uncultivated" or "seedless" valley; and, indeed, its inhabitants have always depended upon commerce for their livelihood. The Quraysh of the Kinānah tribe, who descended from an ancestor called Fihr, had inhabited Mecca for several centuries before the revelation of Islam, entering into commercial agreements with surrounding countries and financing caravans to carry trade-goods. The Koran mentions the "Winter and the Summer Caravan" which sometimes numbered thousands of camels; the great incense trade of the Yemen was routed through Mecca.

Two trees grow in the Yemen, one of which produced myrrh and the other frankincense. In the ancient world, these were used in cosmetics, religious ceremonies, and embalming. Since Mecca is at the crossroads of Africa, the Mediterranean, and the East, the location called forth an entrepreneurial spirit. The demand for myrrh and frankincense was high – the state funeral of a Roman Emperor's wife once exhausted a full year's production. The materials were light and precious, their transport profitable, and as a result, many Meccans were always exceedingly rich.

Before Islam, there were as many as six cities in ancient Arabia with temples similar to the Ka'bah. Yet the prestige of Mecca was greater than them all; this, and the wealth that trade brought, made the Quraysh the aristocrats of the Peninsula. After the patriarchal dominance of Qusayy, a council of the chiefs of the important families governed Mecca. The notables (*al-mala'*) met at the general council called the *Dār an-Nidwah* when any important decisions had to be made. The first *Dār an-Nidwah* was built by Qusayy ibn Qilāb himself, the chief of the Quraysh who had established the tribe in Mecca several generations before the Prophet. Qusayy also rebuilt the Ka'bah. This temple, a center of pilgrimage for the Arabs from ancient times, lies in the hollow of the valley. Because it was a matter of pride to live near the Ka'bah, the most important families were called the Quraysh *al-Biṭāḥ*, the "Quraysh of the Hollow". The houses of the Prophet, Abū Bakr, 'Umar, and 'Uthmān, were all located in the area around the present Grand Mosque; the house of Arqam and the building of the *Dār an-Nidwah*, were within what are now the precincts of the Mosque itself.

Because this valley is the lowest part of the city and its environs, it is subject to flooding. When the mountain rains are heavy, as can happen every few years, the water drains quickly and suddenly towards Mecca, unchecked by any vegetation. Flooding then occurs around the Ka'bah to the depth of several meters. On such occasions it has not been unknown for the circumambulation of the Kabah (*aṭ-ṭawāf*) to be performed swimming.

The Caliphs 'Umar and 'Uthmān attempted to control these floods by building dikes, but their efforts were no more successful than those of later Caliphs. At the present time there is a storm water project underway to remedy this ancient inconvenience.

During the *Jāhiliyyah*, ("the Age of Ignorance" before Islam), there were several important yearly fairs (*aswāq*) near Mecca in the truce of the holy months which suspended the perennial fighting and desert feuds. At Ukāẓ, desert poets declaimed their compositions, and the most acclaimed was written in gold letters and hung in the Kabah, such poems being known as *mu'allaqāt* ("the hung ones"). A number have survived to the present day. Another fair was held at Minā; the *suq al-A'rāb*. Both of these fairs were used as occasions to announce intercalations of extra months every few years in order to bring the lunar calendar into line with the solar, until these intercalations were forbidden by the Koran. Before the Hijrah, the Prophet had preached Islam at Minā and here such opponents as Abū Lahab attacked him with abuse, and hired poets insulted him in verse.

After Islam was established and Medina became the seat of government, many important Meccan families migrated there. This, and the opening of other trade routes through the expansion of Islam, led to the decline of Mecca as a trading center, although the increase in pilgrimage traffic compensated somewhat for the loss. A number of the descendants of the Companions continued to live there, and it became for a time a place of culture and learning. In general, however, Mecca underwent a period of comparative neglect as political activity shifted to Medina, Kufah, Damascus, and finally Baghdad. As a result, there were frequent disorders in Mecca. At one time 'Abd Allāh ibn az-Zubayr seized the town and held it against the Umayyad Caliph, claiming the Caliphate for himself. At another, it was captured by a Khārijite leader, and in *317*/930, the Qarmatians of East Arabia and Baḥrayn raided Mecca and carried off the Black Stone from the Ka'bah, keeping it in al-Ḥāsa, or perhaps Baḥrayn, for a number of years before returning it in *338*/956.

Thereafter, control of Mecca fell to the hands of *Sharīfs* (descendants of the Prophet), who ruled it from *350*/966 down to recent times, under the suzerainty of the Caliphs. In Ottoman times, the Hejaz (the western region of Arabia) was administered by a Sharīfian dynasty in the name of the Sultan in Istanbul, while Turkish troops were garrisoned in its cities.

In World War I, the Sharīf of Mecca, Ḥusayn, encouraged by the British, revolted against the Turks. His sons Fayṣal, 'Alī, and 'Abd Allāh led Arab forces in the fighting. After the war, Ḥusayn declared himself King of the Hejaz; 'Abd Allāh went on to become King of Transjordan, and Fayṣal, King of Iraq. 'Alī would have succeeded his father Ḥusayn but in *1344*/1924 Mecca, and later the rest of the Hejaz, were conquered by King 'Abd al-'Azīz al Sa'ūd of the Najd. It was at first administered as a separate Kingdom, and then integrated into the Kingdom of Saudi Arabia.

Mecca today, except for the presence of the Ka'bah, is in outward appearance an ordinary Middle Eastern city. It is unusual only in that the population, in addition to the descendants of the Quraysh and the indigenous Arabs, has communities made up of immigrants from all parts of the Islamic world, as does Medina. Virtually nothing remains of the characteristic and charming Hejazi style of architecture, with its projecting, latticed *rawshān* windows. Upon the site of Abū Bakr's house, which in his time he had already turned into a Mosque, there stands today a Mosque named after him. Upon the site of the Prophet's house is a library, and on that of 'Alī's, a school. Two Sharīfian palaces survive as administrative buildings. A contemporary mosque called the "Mosque of the *Jinn*" stands upon the site of an oratory where the *Jinn*, or people of the subtle world, were said to have come and pledged fealty to the Prophet. At the top of the hill known as Abū Qubays, which looks down upon the Ka'bah and over the city, stands a mosque called the Masjid Ibrāhīm, popularly known as the Mosque of Bilāl. In Minā, at the pass of 'Aqabah, where the Medinans made their two oaths of fealty, is a graceful mosque of a simple but authentic Arabian style, which, together with what remains of the Mosque of Sīnān within the Grand Mosque, is the only relic of traditional architecture.

Immediately adjacent to the city lie the pilgrimage places of Minā, Muzdalifah, and 'Arafāt, and also *Jabal Nūr*, the "Mountain of Light" where in a cave at the top (*Ghār Ḥirā'*) the revelation of the Koran began. Also not far away is the *Jabal Thawr*, another cave where the Prophet hid with Abū Bakr on their escape to Medina.

Mecca has a number of other names of which *Umm al-Qurā*, or "Mother of Cities" is the most frequently used. It is surrounded on all sides by a restricted holy area, called the *ḥarām* of Mecca, where the taking of life, except of harmful or dangerous creatures, is forbidden, and where only Muslims are allowed to enter. *See also* 'AQABAH; 'ARAFĀT; BLACK STONE; KA'BAH; MINĀ; MUZDALIFAH; PILGRIMAGE; QURAYSH; ZAMZAM.

Medicine (Ar. *aṭ-ṭibb*). In classical times the study of medicine was part of philosophy, and all physicians were also philosophers. Medical studies among the Muslims derived from the Nestorian Christians of Jundishāpūr, a city which was located near present day Ahvāz in Iran. Jundishāpūr was a school founded by the Nestorians in the third century under the Persian Sassanid dynasty. This school which transmitted both the philosophy of the Greeks and the medical science of Hippocrates and Galen, and produced physicians who practiced throughout the Islamic Near East, among them such influential figures as the Nestorian Gabriel Bakhtishishu, physician to the Caliph Hārūn ar-Rashīd, and Ḥunayn Ibn Iṣḥāq, physician to the Caliph al-Mutawakkil. The "Sabians" of Harran (Carrhae) in Syria, a pagan religious and ethnic group, also transmitted Greek and Babylonian learning to the Muslims.

Hospitals were founded in Baghdad around the year *287*/900, and later in Cairo and elsewhere. With the spread of such institutions, medicine developed to an advanced state. The scientific heritage of the Greeks, Egyptians, Babylonians, Persians, and later of India, was fused into the corpus known as Islamic science. The Muslims established, moreover, a comprehensive *materia medica* based upon the study and classification of medicinal plants by Dioscorides and other Greek scientists.

The most famous figures in the Islamic science of medicine are ar-Rāzī (Rhazes), Ibn Sīnā (Avicenna), Ibn Baytār, al-Bīrūnī, and Ibn Zuhr. *See* MARISTAN.

Medina. The epithet *al-Munawwarah*, "the radiant", is usually added to the name of this city. Originally it was called Yathrib, a name with pagan connotations, and became known as *madīnat an-nabī*, the "city of the Prophet" after the Hijrah. At the time of the revelation there were two Arab tribes that inhabited Medina, the Aws and the Khazraj, both of South Arabian origin, and several Jewish tribes, the Banū Naḍīr, the Banū Qaynuqā', and the Banū Qurayẓah.

Medina was an oasis famed for the dates from its palm groves. It is situated in the midst of volcanic hills around a small plain called the *manakhah* (from *nikh*, the command to make a camel kneel) where caravans to the city would stop and camp.

The two Arab tribes, aided by the Jewish tribes allied with them, had been in an intermittent state of civil war immediately before Islam appeared to call the Medinans to a new way of life. In 620, six men of Medina of the tribe of Khazraj, on pilgrimage to Mecca, entered Islam by the hand of the Prophet at the pass of 'Aqabah. The first man of Medina to become a Muslim was named Iyas. In the following two years, the first Muslims returned to Mecca and brought others with them. In 622 seventy-three men and two women took an oath of fealty to the Prophet which, for the men, also included the duty of protecting him. In September of that year the Prophet emigrated to Medina and was joined by seventy emigrant Meccans called the *Muhājirūn*, whilst the native Medinan Muslims were known as the *Anṣār*, "helpers". The creation of an Islamic state led inevitably to war against the Meccans and their Beduin allies which ended in victory for the Prophet and the Muslims in *8*/630. The Prophet remained in Medina for the rest of his life, and Medina was the capital of the Islamic empire until the Caliph 'Alī moved his headquarters to the military camp-city of Kufah. Medina was a center of intellectual activity for some time, but after *63*/683, when it was sacked by troops of the Umayyads because of unrest and rebellion, the city went into decline and much of the population migrated to Spain.

Almost everyone who makes the pilgrimage to Mecca also visits Medina to pay homage at the the tomb of the Prophet. Next to the Prophet in the Prophet's mosque are also buried the Caliphs Abū Bakr, 'Umar, and 'Uthmān. Not far from the Prophet's mosque is the al-Bāqī cemetery where many Companions are buried, as well as other great figures in the history of Islam. At Qubā', in the suburbs of Medina, stands the first mosque of Islam, the *Masjid at-Taqwā*. Other famous mosques in the city are the *Ghamāmah* (*Musallā 'n-Nabī*) where the Prophet prayed for rain, the *Sabaq* mosque which was the site of the original festival prayers, the *Jum'ah* mosque, and several small mosques near the *Jabal Salā'*. Just outside the city is the *Jabal Uḥud*, where the famous battle took place. *See* 'AQABAH; MOSQUE of the PROPHET; MUḤAMMAD.

Meditation, *see* DHIKR; TAFAKKUR.

Mehmet II (*833-886*/1429-1481). An Ottoman Sultan, Mehmet II was known as "the Conqueror" (*an-Nāṣir*) for his conquest of Constantinople in *857*/1453. He also conquered the Balkans, adding vast territories to the empire. Mehmet is credited with the design of the cannons, the largest yet built, needed to bombard Constantinople during its fifty day siege. The Sultan devised much of the strategy and joined in the fighting himself. At one point, overcome with excitement, he drew his sword and rode his horse into the Bosphorus, swimming among the ships and rallying the sailors during a sea battle.

It was his bold decision to carry ships overland, around the chain barriers impeding entrance to the channel of the Golden Horn, which proved to be the decisive maneuver that led to the Turkish victory. Seventy-two light Turkish ships were dragged from the Bosphorus over the isthmus of Pera to the Golden Horn. Thousands of workmen prepared slipways greased with oil, tallow, and fat, working overnight and in secret, for if the Byzantines had realized what was happening, they could have destroyed much of the Turkish fleet. Once inside the Golden Horn, an attempt by the Venetians in Constantinople to sink the intruding Turkish fleet was betrayed by their commercial rivals the Genoese, and failed.

The Turks then built a pontoon bridge of barrels to bring another army over to besiege the city, and attempted tunnelling beneath the walls; they had reached a distance of one-quarter mile inside the city walls before a Byzantine engineer succeeded in heading them off with a counter-tunnel, which connected with the Turkish one, to foil the sappers. The Turks also made a breach in the walls with a siege tower which the Byzantines succeeded, at great sacrifice, in filling. After more tunnels and more siege towers, the Turks offered favorable terms to the Byzantine Emperor but he, even though he had learned that help was not going to come from his Venetian allies, refused, saying "it is not in my power nor in the power of anyone here to surrender this city. We are ready to die and we shall leave this world without regret."

Even so, by 27 May 1453, the Turks were on the point of withdrawal when a military leader named Zagan Pasha, made an impassioned appeal against it; a referendum was put to the army and it was decided to venture another assault. The final attack was amphibious. Two waves of Turks, (the attacking army was over one hundred thousand strong, the defenders only a few thousand) were beaten back. A third was almost repelled. Then confusion developed amongst the defenders, signals were misunderstood, consternation grew, and a Janissary force breached the outer wall and came upon a secret gate, through which the Byzantines were receiving supplies. This gate had not been locked, and suddenly the Turks found an open door through which to enter the city. The Emperor threw off his regalia, joined in the hand to hand fighting and was killed. On 29 May 1453, Constantinople fell.

As a Sultan, Mehmet II was fairly liberal towards the populations he conquered, extending protection to the Christian churches and monasteries that fell under his sway. In fact, in the end, the Ottomans became virtually the protectors of the Orthodox church. Mehmet II knew Persian, Arabic and Turkish, as well as some Latin and Greek. He wrote poetry in Persian and was a patron of the arts. *See* HAGIA SOPHIA; OTTOMANS.

Menangkabau. The central region of the island of Sumatra in Indonesia, and its ethnic group, which is matriarchal. This region was one of the first to be Islamicised in Indonesia, starting in the *5th*/11th century, undergoing influences from Atjeh in the north.

Menstruation (Ar. *mahā'id*, *hā'id*). Considered a state of ritual impurity, it excludes a woman from performing *ṣalāh* (ritual prayers, which do not then have to be made up), from touching the Koran, sexual intercourse; entering a mosque (but not the Grand Mosque of Mecca, which can be entered since *al-Masjid al-Ḥarām* is an exception to many ordinary rules, as are certain other sanctuaries which are open to anyone in any state. Menstruation does not preclude making *du'ā'* (personal prayer).

At the end of a period of menstruation, a woman performs the greater ablution (*ghusl*) to restore ritual purity. The state of menstruation does not affect the performance of pilgrimage, either *ḥajj* or *'umrah*; these can be performed, as well as the circumambulation (*ṭawāf*) of the Ka'bah, but the canonical prayers (*ṣalāh*) are omitted. The *du'ā'*, however, are performed. According to legal decisions based on Ḥadīth concerning special circumstances, a menstrual flow which never ceases, or chronic discharge, is disregarded from the point of view of ritual. In such a case, rituals are performed as if the person were in a state of normal ritual purity except that the *wuḍū'*, or *tayyamum*, is performed before every prayer. *See* ABLUTIONS; GHUSL; TAYAMMUM; WUḌŪ'.

Metaphysics, *see* FIVE DIVINE PRESENCES.

Metawila (also romanized as "Metalwi", from Arabic *mutawālin*, pl. *matāwilah*, "successor"). A colloquial designation in Lebanon and Syria for Twelve-Imām Shī'ites, but also applied by extension to the sects of the Ismā'īlīs, 'Alawīs, and Druzes.

The Twelve-Imām Shī'ites of Lebanon have been amongst its poorest and most backward people. In 1959 an Iranian Mulla named Mūsā-ṣ-Ṣadr came to Lebanon, and from that point there began a marked growth in the community's self-awareness. Until that time the community had been dominated by important local Shī'ite families such as the al-As'ad and the Ḥamada. Under Mūsā-ṣ-Ṣadr's leadership, representative organs of political expression were created. In December 1967 the Shī'ite Supreme National Council was set up by act of parliament, and in 1969 Mūsā-ṣ-Ṣadr was elected its president.

In 1974, Mūsā-ṣ-Ṣadr created *Amal* as a political organization to mobilize the Shī'ites in the Baqā valley and in southern Lebanon. Like other political groupings in Lebanon, *Amal* acquired a militia. Shortly thereafter, other Shī' ite groups of a more expressly military nature came into being, as a result of continued political upheaval in Lebanon, notably *Jihād*, and later *Ḥizb Allāh*, a radical military organization directly linked with revolutionary Iran and associated with a leader called Shaykh Muḥammad Ḥusayn Faḍlallāh.

Imām Mūsā-ṣ-Ṣadr was mysteriously abducted on a visit to Libya in 1978, and is now presumed dead, a fact which his followers in Lebanon continued to refuse to accept. *See* LEBANON; SHĪ'ISM.

Mevlevi (Arabic *Mawlawī*). A Sufi order in Turkey founded by Mevlana (Mawlānā, "our lord") Jalāl ad-Dīn ār-Rūmī (d. *672*/1273). The members of this order are sometimes called "Whirling Dervishes" in the West because part of their method of spiritual realization consists of dancing in which they revolve to the music of flutes, drums, and the chants of *ilāhīs* (Turkish Sufi songs). The training of a Mevlevi dervish includes exercises for the dance in which the first two toes of the right foot grasp a nail on the floor while the dervish pivots around it. The dervishes' turning requires a great deal of practice to master, but is extremely graceful when performed in a ritual meeting. The presence of the founder, Jalāl ad-Dīn ar-Rūmī, is strongly manifested in the order, and many dervishes experience intense personal relationships with him.

The dancing became a formal part of the Mevlevi method with ar-Rūmī's successor, his son Sultan Veled. During a Mevlevi dancing session (*samā'*), a red sheepskin is placed upon the floor, symbolizing the presence of Shams-i Ṭabrīz, the mysterious figure who inflamed Jalāl ad-Dīn ar-Rūmī with Divine awareness. The dancing lasts about an hour, in four movements called *salams*; at the end, the *pīr*, or spiritual master, makes his appearance among the dancers. The *ney*, or reed flute, figures prominently in the symbolism of the dervishes. The trembling of the reed as the breath – or spirit – gives it life and its cry recalls the nostalgia of its separation from the rushes where it grew, from its origin, as ar-Rūmī's poetry declares. And the reed crying for return to the Principle is the Spiritual Master, or ar-Rūmī himself.

Hearken to this Reed forlorn,
Breathing, ever since 'twas torn
From its rushy bed, a strain
Of impassioned love and pain.

The secret of my song, though near,
None can see and none can hear.
Oh, for a friend to know the sign
And mingle all his soul with mine!

'Tis the flame of Love that fired me,
'Tis the wine of Love inspired me.
Wouldst thou learn how lovers bleed,
Hearken, hearken to the Reed!

The dance is called *muqābalah* ("encounter") and is an expression of the doctrine of the Mevlevis whereby the soul encounters, and awakes to Reality; it is universal in its sentiments, and almost Hindu in spirit. Each dancer sees his own face in that of the others, who are like mirrors to him; but although it is his own face, through the repetition of the reflection in others, his individuality becomes unreal and the other becomes oneself. The dancing moves in a semi-circle. This is creation, the arc of descent proceeding away from God (*qaws-i-nuzūl*). While creation descends, however, creatures within creation ascend. As the dancing progresses, the Shaykh enters and the culmination of the furthest point of the first arc brings the dancers face to face with the Spiritual Master. This is the moment when night changes into dawn (*al-fajr*), the sun rises, and the arc of ascent (*qaws-i-'urūj*) begins which leads to realization. The dancers whirl to the other side, completing in dance one whole cycle of creation and return to the One.

It should be mentioned, at the risk of disturbing what is a compelling metaphor, that this rather powerful imagery of souls passing through different stages of existence in the world is not found in orthodox theology. While it may be useful in evoking a recognition and a desire to return to the source, it also implies a permanence of the substance of the soul, a kind of divinity of created substance. For this reason metempsychosis is not accepted by orthodox Islam or by any monotheism. Islam holds that man is created directly into the human state.

The Mevlevi order was forbidden in Turkey, as were all other Sufi orders, during the initial secularization of the country in 1925, but it has since been allowed to return to the surface of Turkish life. Some Mevlevis have presented performances of their music and dancing in the West.

A contemporary Mevlevi *Pīr*, Shaykh Sulaymān Loras has said:

> If we do not strive for inner perfection, we will remain what we are now – talking animals. The world has never been without teachers. Each age has its teachers. Jesus, Buddha, and Muḥammad were some of the great ones, but there are always *aqṭāb* [plural of *quṭb*, "someone who fulfills the role of spiritual axis"], special beings who take care of the world. The perfect man, the complete man, lies within each one of us.

Mevlevis are also found in Syria, Egypt, and other countries which were once part of the Ottoman Empire; however, at the present time only the branches in Konya and in Istanbul are active. Ar-Rūmī said: "Come, come, whoever you are, unbeliever or fire-worshiper, come. Our convent is not of desperation. Even if you have broken your vows a hundred times, Come, come again." *See* JALĀL ad-DĪN ar-RŪMĪ.

Miḥrāb. A niche in the wall of a mosque to indicate the *qiblah*, the direction of Mecca, towards which all Muslims turn in prayer. It also provides a reflecting surface so that the voice of the Imām is clearly heard by those behind him. The *miḥrāb* was introduced around *90*/709; in the Mosque of Qubā', a stone was used in the time of the Prophet. As an architectural device, the *miḥrāb*-type niche appears in the Hellenist synagogue of Doura Europos. The *miḥrāb* also has its antecedents in the *cella*, a small room or niche in a temple where a statue of the god or goddess was kept, and to which access was sometimes restricted to priests.

The earliest surviving *miḥrāb* may be that in Jerusalem, in the chamber beneath the rock in the Dome of the Rock (*Qubbat aṣ-Ṣakhrah*). However, the most famous and splendid *miḥrāb* is unquestionably that of the mosque of Cordova. Decorated with multicolored mosaics of melted glass and gold that were a gift from the Byzantine Emperor Nicephoras to the Caliph Hakim II, the niche is carved alabaster and marble, and the ceiling is a single piece of marble in the shape of a seashell, creating remarkable acoustics: a mere whisper is reflected audibly a great distance.

The *miḥrāb* embodies the symbolism of the cave, the hidden place, the cavity within a mountain. The cave is a universal token of inwardness, initiation and profound worship amongst all peoples, from the *kivas* of the Hopi to the cave of the thousand Buddhas. In the cave, the sky cannot be seen, and yet it is within it that heavenly reality must be found, just as it is through faith that man is saved. The cave is taken to be the heart, and the mountain which surrounds it is the physical world, or body, which imprisons the spirit. It is within the heart that one encounters the truth.

> Or dost thou think the Men of the Cave
> and Er-Rakeem were among Our signs a
> wonder?
> When the youths took refuge in the Cave
> saying, 'Our Lord, give us mercy from Thee,
> and furnish us with rectitude in our
> affair.'
> Then We smote their ears many years in
> the Cave...
> And we strengthened their hearts, when
> they stood up and said, 'Our Lord is
> the Lord of the heavens and earth;
> we will not call upon any god, apart
> from Him, or then we had spoken
> outrage.
> These our people have taken to them
> other gods, apart from Him. Ah, if only
> they would bring some clear authority
> regarding them! But who does greater
> evil than he who forges against God
> a lie?
> So, when you have gone apart from them
> and that they serve, excepting God,
> take refuge in the cave, and your Lord
> will unfold to you of His Mercy, and will
> furnish you with a gentle issue of your
> affair.'
> And thou mightest have seen the sun,
> when it rose, inclining from their Cave
> towards the right, and, when it set,
> passing them by on the left, while they
> were in a broad fissure of the Cave.
> That was one of God's signs; whomsoever
> God guides, he is rightly guided,
> and whomsoever He leads astray, thou
> wilt not find for him a protector... (18:9-11,
> 14-17)

Mīlād, *see* MAWLID an-NABĪ.

Millah. A religion, creed, faith, sect or spiritual community, as opposed to *dīn*, which denotes religion in particular and Islam specifically. *Millah* is often used in the compound "the religion of Abraham" (*millat Ibrāhīm*). The Turkish form *Millet* was used in Ottoman Turkey as a name for the religions within the Empire; but the word is more usually used in both Turkish and Persian to mean "nation", "people" or "state".

Mimbar, *see* MINBAR.

Minā. Islamic tradition proclaims it the site of Abraham's sacrifice of the ram in place of his son Ishmael; the spot is on the eastern side of the rocky valley and is known as the *majār al-kabsh* ("the place of the bleating of the ram"). The small town of Minā, five kilometers/three miles, from Mecca, only comes to life at pilgrimage time.

Not far from the town of Minā is a rise known as the *'Aqabah* ("the incline") where the first groups of Medinans swore fealty to the Prophet; here a mosque called the *Masjid al-Bay'ah* ("the Mosque of the Covenant") stands today, a noble – and rare – example of the traditional Hejazi mosque style remarkably preserved amidst rampant modernization.

The valley is called the *sūq al-A'rāb* ("fair of the Arabs"), for Minā, along with 'Ukāẓ, was one of the great yearly fairs of pre-Islamic Arabia. In the center of this area – now enclosed by gigantic pedestrian ramps so that the thousands of pilgrims can approach on two levels – are the three *jamarāt*, or pillars, which are stoned as one of the rites of pilgrimage. They represent three occasions on the way to the fateful sacrifice when Satan appeared to Ishmael to warn him of Abraham's intention to sacrifice him, and was three times stoned by Ishmael.

The Khayf mosque stands in Minā; here pilgrims pray during the pilgrimage. Throughout the valley are sites now forgotten, where mosques once stood marking the places where Koranic verses were revealed. *See* MECCA; PILGRIMAGE.

Minaret (from Ar. *manārah*, "a lighthouse"). Towers from which the Muezzin (*mu'adhdhin*) makes the call to prayers (*adhān*). The first minarets were built towards the end of the first Hijrah century. *See* MOSQUE.

Minbar (also written and pronounced *mimbar*). A pulpit in a mosque used by the Imām for preaching the Friday sermon (*khuṭbah*). It is actually a movable staircase. The first *minbar* was that used by the Prophet and it had three steps. When Abū Bakr used it as Caliph he only mounted to the second step; 'Umar to the first; but 'Uthmān to the second, and that is what Imāms normally do today, although *minbars* are usually built with many more steps. A speaker's podium has come into use in some places instead of the *minbar*.

Minorities. When Islamic law was in force (today it has largely been replaced by civil law in most countries), recognised non-Muslim minorities were allowed to retain their own legal systems, at least for their internal affairs. (This recognition would exclude idolators, although in practice non-monotheist religions or other non-conforming religions were assimilated to the status of "People of the Book" (*Ahl al-Kitāb*), sometimes by being considered Sabians.) Thus, while wine is forbidden for Muslims, Christians and Jews were not forbidden to make, sell and drink it.

In Morocco, for example, Rabbinic law is still recognized as applicable within the Jewish community. In medieval Baghdad, the ancient head of the Jewish community, the Resh Galuta, was given a wide latitude of authority, which in some periods went so far as to allow him to judge disputes involving Muslims and Jews (and not simply those between Jews). Tribal law, and local customary law (*adat*) exist side by side with Islamic law and civil law in many places. *See* AHL al-KITĀB.

Mīqāt (lit. "appointed time", "date" and by extension, "place and time of meeting"). On the traditional overland approaches to Mecca, and situated in some cases a considerable distance away, are the points each called *mīqāt*, at which pilgrims on their way to perform the greater pilgrimage (*ḥajj*) assume *iḥrām*, that is, consecration and the ritual dress, that marks it. Pilgrims approaching Mecca by way of the Red Sea would, at the latest, put on *iḥrām* when the ship passes the latitude of one of the *mīqāt*. Today pilgrims coming to Jeddah by air often put on *iḥrām* at the point of embarkation.

Some of the *mawāqīt* (pl. of *mīqāt*) are: Dhāt Irq, 80 kms to the northeast of Mecca; Dhāt

Ḥulayfah 250 kms north of Mecca and 9 kms away from Medina; Juhfah, to the northwest of Mecca 180 kms distant; Qarn al-Manāzil 50 kilometers to the city's east; and Yalamlam, sixty kilometres to the southeast.

Mīr. A title of respect used in the Indo-Persian world for descendants of the Prophet, it is a contraction of the Arabic *amīr*, "prince", "commander".

Miracles (Ar. *mujizāt*). Some minor traditions attribute a number of miracles to the Prophet but there is nothing conclusive about their nature; they play no role in Islamic theology, nor do they embody any essential element in the life of the Prophet. One event which is thought to be miracle is called "the splitting of the moon". This is deduced from the beginning of Sūrah 54:

> The Hour has drawn nigh; the moon is split.
> Yet if they see a sign they turn away, and they say 'A continuous sorcery!'
> They have cried lies, and followed their caprices; but every matter is settled.
> And there have come to them such tidings as contain a deterrent –
> a Wisdom far-reaching; yet warnings do not avail.

The notion that this passage refers to an event called forth by the Prophet in Mecca before the Hijrah appears to be only the result of late Koranic interpretation, and thus conjecture, and is not supported by any contemporary references. It has become a part of Islamic folklore, but the Koranic passage should rather be taken to refer to a coming apocalyptic event, or possibly an allusion to the dissolution of the world at one's own death.

Thus it can be said that while Islam does not deny miracles, neither does it accord them any role of significance. If there is a miracle which is often pointed to, it is the Koran itself. And the Koran says (17:37): "And walk not in the earth exultant. Lo! thou canst not rend the earth, nor canst thou stretch to the height of the hills." Then there are writers who have also dismissed miracles:

> If thou canst walk on water
> thou art no better than a straw.
> If thou canst fly in the air
> Thou art no better than a fly.
> Conquer thy heart
> That thou mayest become somebody. (Anṣārī)

And, the Persian Bāyazīd al-Biṣṭāmī (d. *261*/875) said:

> Even if you see a man endowed with miraculous powers to the point of rising in the air, do not let yourself be deluded, but investigate whether he observes the Divine precepts and prohibitions, whether he stays within the limits of religion and whether he accomplishes the duties this imposes upon him.

But this is misleading because al-Biṣṭāmī is really saying that miracles are possible, just not very important. In other words, he is saying "do not pay attention to any miraculous powers that I may have (in magic what is termed 'a hook and load' to created the desired belief)." It was in fact the school of the Drunken Sufis, and especially al-Ḥallāj that used stories of miracles systematically to influence the gullible. Al-Ḥallāj's many miracles, which Massignon called "harmless legerdemain", can be explained as stage magic. One famous miracle is the following:

> Ḥallāj wished to convert a certain Ibn Hārūn, a man who used to hold salons where the better-known Baghdad shaykhs engaged in discussion. When all the guests were seated on one of these occasions, Ḥallāj opened the conversation with this riddle: have you no time to recognize me? Then recognize my verity! My first is softer than my fourth, my fifth is longer than my third, My second commonest of all The thrice three threes. What is the word? Divine; and you shall see me stand upright Where Moses stood, on Sinai, wrapped in light. Everyone was baffled.
>
> It happened that Ibn Hārūn's little son was sick at that time, and sinking fast. And the host presently said to Ḥallāj: 'My boy is sick; I wish you would pray for him.'
>
> 'He is already healed,' said Ḥallāj; 'don't worry any more.'
>
> It was only a few minutes later that the child was brought in, looking as if he had never been ill. Everyone present was dumbfounded; Ibn Hārūn pulled out a sealed purse and offered it to Ḥallāj.
>
> 'Shaykh,' said he, 'use this as you will.'
>
> Now the saloon where they were sitting opened on the Tigris bank. Ḥallāj, taking the purse, which contained three thousand dinars, threw it into the river.

'You had some questions to ask me, I think,' he said,
addressing the company of shaykhs; 'but what questions could *you* ask of *me*? for I see only too well how right you are, and how wrong I am.'
And with these words he went away.
Next day, Ibn Hārūn paid visits to the various shaykhs who had been present with Ḥallāj, and showed them the very purse which Ḥallāj had tossed into the stream. 'Yesterday,' said he, 'I could not stop thinking about the present I had offered him: and I began to wish he had not thrown it into the river. Scarcely an hour after that thought came into mind, a poor disciple of his came to my gate to say: "The shaykh greets you and bids me say to you: Make an end of regret and take this purse; to one who obeys Him God gives power, even over earth and water." And he put my own purse in my hand.'

In other versions, the messenger appears with the purse dripping wet while a new company of visitors is present listening as the miracle cure of the previous evening is being recounted; the purse is opened in front of the listeners, and the gold is inside. The explanation will be familiar to stage magicians. The riddle is intended to distract the audience's attention ("misdirection"). No one sees the child sick ("the load"), it is only the word of the accomplice, Ibn Hārūn, and the child is too young to be questioned; a healthy child is brought out; an empty purse is thrown into the river, and a similar purse, wet as if miraculously retrieved from the river is shown to the audience, with the gold.

Explaining al-Ḥallāj's other miracles was a popular pastime in the Middle Ages. *See also* KARĀMĀT.

Mir'āj, *see* NIGHT JOURNEY.

Mīr Dāmād (d. *1041*/1631). A Persian scholar and philosopher, the teacher of Mulla Sadra. Mīr Dāmād's full name was Muḥammad Baqīr ibn ad-Dāmād. He combined the *Ishraqī* ("illuminationist") philosophy of Suhrawardī with theology and mysticism. This kind of synthesis became characteristic of Shī'ite thinking. His most famous work is *aṣ-Ṣirāṭ al-Mustaqīm* ("The Straight Path").

Mīr Fendereski (d. *1050*/1640). Shī'ite theologian.

Mirzā. An Indo-Persian title of respect.

Miskīn (lit. "poor"). In addition to its meaning of someone who is poor in material terms, it is used to mean, in a very laudatory sense, someone who is meek, or "poor in spirit", and thus worthy of sympathy. As such it is a very frequently heard expression.

Miswāk (from the word *sāka*, to "brush", to "polish"). A toothstick, often mistakenly translated as toothpick. It is a method of cleaning the teeth, highly recommended by tradition, using a suitable twig with the bark cut and the fibers loosened by some preliminary chewing. The end fibers become a convenient brush for scrubbing the teeth after eating. Because it is hallowed by the Sunnah, many pious people use the *miswāk* in addition to the modern toothbrush.

Miyan. A title of respect in the Indo-Persian world.

Mīzān (lit. "the balance scale"). The Koran's symbol of harmony in creation and of cosmic equilibrium, and also of eschatological justice and retribution for deeds in this life. (The scales are also an important symbol in Zoroastrianism.)

The sun and the moon to a reckoning,
and the stars and the trees bow themselves;
and heaven – He raised it up, and set
the Balance.
(Transgress not in the Balance,
and weigh with justice, and skimp not in the
Balance.) (55:5-9)

The scales of this balance weigh one's works of good and evil down to an atom's weight.

When earth is shaken with a mighty shaking
and earth brings forth her burdens,
and Man says, 'What ails her?'
upon that day she shall tell her tidings
for that her Lord has inspired her.

Upon that day men shall issue in scatterings to
see their works,
and whoso has done an atom's weight of good
shall see it,
and whoso has done an atom's weight of evil shall
see it. (99)

Some of the early literalist interpreters in Islam took the *mīzān*, along with God's throne (*'arsh*), footstool (*al-kursī*), the pen (*al-qalam*), the guarded tablet (*al-lawḥ al-maḥfūẓ*), to be actual celestial entities rather than symbols. The term is also used for a "ground design" in architecture, and as a technical term for musical patterns and rhythmic modes. *See* ISTAWĀ.

Modernization, *see* ALIGARH; 'ABDUH; KEMAL, MUSṬAFĀ; SALAFIYYAH; TANẒĪMĀT.

Moghuls. The celebrated Muslim dynasty of India, noted for the cultural refinements of its rule which, by blending elements from Persia and India, created one of the most sophisticated civilizations known to history. Its achievements were outstanding in the spheres of architecture, music, literature, and in all the arts of living, not least cuisine.

The Moghul Empire was founded by Bābur (*888-937*/1483-1530), a descendant of Timur on his father's side, and of Jenghiz Khān on his mother's. The name "Moghul" is simply "Mongol" in a phonetic form adapted to the Persian language and the Arabic script. Bābur became a ruler at the age of eleven in Ferghana in Transoxiana, and conquered Samarkand at the age of fourteen. Then he lost both, and went off to Afghanistan, seized Kabul and then Qandahar. At the Battle of Panipat (*932*/1526) he defeated the Sultan of Delhi and established his own capital there and at Agra. His son Hūmāyūn (*912-963*/1506-1556) warred for years with his brothers over the succession, and only reigned effectively for the last six months of his life. He introduced the art of Persian miniature painting into the court.

Hūmāyūn's son Akbar (*949-1014*/1542-1605), called the Great, ruled over the greatest extension of the Moghul Empire, comprising most of northern India and Afghanistan. He devised a syncretist religion called *din-i-ilāhī* ("religion of God") an amalgam of several religions that Akbar was acquainted with in India, including Christianity. This syncretist mixture, of which he made himself the head, was only practiced at court. In the Moghul Empire of Akbar's time, Hindus played an important role in the government. He created the class of officials called Manṣabdārs (*see* MANṢAB). Akbar built Fatehpur Sikri near Agra to be his capital, but had to abandon it before occupation for lack of water supply.

The next Emperor, Jahangīr (*977-1037*/1569-1627) built palaces at Lahore, as well as the Shalimar gardens in Kashmir. Shāh Jahān (*1001-1077*/1592-1666) built the Tāj Mahal, as well as the Red Fort in Delhi and the Great Mosque. The Red Fort has a famous inscription in Persian: "If there is a paradise on earth, it is here, it is here, it is here." Shāh Jahān's successor Aurangzeb (*1028-1118*/1618-1707), also called 'Alamgīr, was the most zealous Muslim of all the Moghul Emperors. He enforced Islamic rules in a court that was more famed for omitting them, and thereby earned the enmity of his Hindu subjects and officials in a way that had not occurred under his predecessors. It was doubtless this action on Aurangzeb's part that accelerated, if it did not indeed initiate, the decline of Moghul power; disaffection by Hindus and attempts to seize central and local power by Muslim princes and princelings, together with the armies of Afghanistan and Persia, then weakened the dynasty further.

Aurangzeb was the last of the Emperors known as the "Great Moghuls". Although he actually extended Moghul rule into the Deccan, the decline otherwise in Moghul authority was met with renewed vigor on the part of Hindus, and expansion by the British. In *1274*/1858 the last Moghul, who no longer had any real power, was deposed by the British for alleged complicity in the Sepoy Mutiny.

Monasticism. Islam expressly forbids the institution of monks or priests. Christian monks were known in pre-Islamic Arabia and may even have been a familiar phenomenon; but as Islam spreads a net of salvation for every man, in his daily social life, it precludes the setting aside of a class of men in a category different from society as a whole. Nevertheless, numerous men have lived as religious recluses, including such celebrated saints as Ibn Mashīsh. There was even an institution of those called *al-Murābiṭūn* ("the bound ones"), who dedicated some years of their lives to live in isolation in remote outposts called *rubuṭ* (sing. *ribāṭ*) in order to defend the frontiers of *Dār al-Islām* ("Abode of Islam"). *See also* PRIESTS.

Mongols. The Mongols were a people of the Siberian forests who came from the North into the steppes of Mongolia. Calling themselves "the children of the blue-grey fox and the fallow deer", and mimicking the life of totem animals, they were Shamanists; that is, as in Shintoism and the religion of the Indians of North America, they saw God as a Spirit whose Presence is active in nature. The greatest manifestation of this Great Spirit was "the Eternal Blue Heaven"; but, like the Japanese *Kami*, It also appeared in distinct manifestations called *Tengri*. The Mongols followed as leaders those who, through visions and theurgic power, such as calling forth a "storm of darkness" to confound the enemy, showed that the Spirit moved in them. Even after they became Buddhists, visions and a magical sense of the universe continued to dominate their religious understanding. The Mongol Empire, carved out at the expense of the Ch'in dynasty in North China and the Sung in South China, was founded by Temujin (1162-1227), a great-grandson of Qabul Khān; his family having fallen on hard times, Temujin assumed the power-name of Jenghiz Khān ("Oceanic", or universal ruler, perhaps "Ruler between the Seas"). His former name of Temujin means "Blacksmith".

The orphaned son of a Khān, whose mother fought like a wolf for the survival of her children, Temujin had himself to regain his stolen bride Borte, and fight his way back to power, making alliances with his blood brothers, and resorting to mutual oath-taking whereby a follower would abandon his tribal identity to attach himself to Temujin alone. He united the Mongol tribes and was declared paramount Khān of the Mongols by a assembly (*quriltai*) of Mongol chiefs in 1206 at Qaraqorum. Through a Uighur scholar named Tatatonga employed by Jenghiz Khān, the Mongols adopted the Uighur script which is derived from Aramaic through Soghdian, and in 1240 the first Mongol book was written down: the *Altan Daptīr* ("the Golden Book") of which the Persian historian Rashīd ad-Dīn aṭ-Ṭabīb was given some accounts by the Il-Khanid Maḥmūd Ghazan. He was not shown the book for, in the belief of the Mongols, such a Chronicle represented a fearful magical power that could be turned against them. It was probably this book, or one similar to it, that was taken to China and transcribed into Chinese after the Mongols had lost power, as the *Yuan Ch'ao Pi Shih* ("The Secret History of the Mongols"). The Mongol legends speak of a dream that Temujin saw in a cave, in which a spirit, later identified with a Bodhisattva, commanded him to restore the earth to the primordial condition it had known before civilization hid the face of nature. When Temujin awoke from the prophetic dream, he found on his hand a ring that confirmed his mission. In the subsequent Mongol invasions, it was indeed as if some pent-up force had suddenly exploded with primeval power.

Beginning with campaigns in 1205, 1207 and 1209, Jenghiz Khān led the Mongols and their allied Turkic tribes to destroy the kingdom of the Western Hsia, and drive the Ch'in to the Yellow River. In *615*/1218, after a Khwarazmian governor massacred one hundred Mongol envoys at the Otrar river, calling them – no doubt correctly – spies, the Mongols began invading the Muslim realms. At Jenghiz Khān's death in *624*/1227, the Empire was divided between a grandson and three sons. Batu, son of Juchi, received as his territory the Qipchaq steppe in Russia, in Jenghiz' words: "as far as the Mongol horses had trodden"; Chagatai received territories from Transoxiana to Chinese Turkestan, the former Kara-Khitai empire. Ogedei received outer Mongolia; and Tului, eastern Mongolia and northern China. Ogedei was elected Great Khān; after his death in 1241 (which recalled the Mongol Sabotai from an invasion of Hungary), Ogedei's widow Turakina was regent until Ogedei was suceeded by his son Guyuk in 1249. An envoy of Pope Innocent IV, Plano Carpini, was present at the election. But after him the leadership passed to sons of Tului, Mongka and Kubilai.

Mongka (Khān 1251-1259), the son of a Nestorian woman, told the friar William of Rubruk, envoy of Louis IX of France, that religions are numbered like the fingers of one hand; he himself favored Buddhism. He had certain Taoist books burned after public disputation in 1255. His brother Kubilai, who suceeded Mongka, followed his example regarding Taoist books in 1258. Kubilai (1214-1294; declared Khān by his armies in 1260) founded the Yuan dynasty in China (1260-1368); Kubilai's brother Hulagu invaded the 'Abbāsid Empire, sacked Baghdad, took Damascus, and founded the Il-Khanid dynasty.

The military superiority of the Mongols lay in their tribal unity, their extremely strict discipline and ability to endure hardship, and their strategic use of spies, terrorism, and superior siege equipment manned by Chinese engineers. Despite their heavy armaments, the Mongol nomad armies were very mobile, overtaking enemy armies that fled before them. Where they went, accounts of cruelty and barbarism multiplied. The more conservative of the Mongol chiefs, who preserved the *Yasa*, or sacred law of the Mongols, believed that they must not settle among the peoples they conquered, but only collect tribute from them. Others argued for going amongst the vassals and governing. These succumbed to civilization, and lost their power.

After the conquest of China, the Mongol capital became, in 1264, the newly founded Khanbaliq (Peking). The Mongols had been Shamanists, and as such were naively open to other religions, treating their rites as so much magic which could be used in conjunction with each other. Even before their conquest of China, they were influenced by elements of Buddhism, and even by Nestorian Christianity and doctrines current among the Uighur Turks, which they easily blended into their original spirit beliefs. After the conquest of China, the eastern Mongols more formally adopted Buddhism, as they adopted civilization, with Lamaist Buddhism eventually gaining the central and Western Mongol territories. (The title of Dalai Lama means, like Jenghiz, the "Oceanic" Lama, and is Mongol in origin. The Chinese, fearing a new irruption of the Mongols, prohibited successors of great Lamas from being sought among Jenghiz Khān's descendents.)

The Golden Horde of the Volga (in which the Ghuzz/Oghuz Turkic elements soon submerged the Mongols) and the Il-Khanids in Persia became Muslims, followed somewhat later by the Mongols in Transoxiana. Although they were nominally under the authority of the Great Khān, once the center of rule shifted to China they became in practice independent. *See* HŪLĀGŪ KHĀN; IL-KHANIDS; JUWAYNI, 'ALĀ-ad-DĪN; RASHĪD ad-DĪN aṭ-ṬABĪB; YASA; YURT.

Months, *see* CALENDAR.

Moon (Ar. *al-qamar*). The Arabic term for the crescent moon is *al-hilāl*; the full moon is *al-badr*. Their waxing and waning are a symbol of time's cycles and rhythms, and of existence, which is subject to birth and death, as opposed to being, which is beyond mutability. "And the moon, We have measured it out in stations, until it becomes again like a shrivelled date-stone" (36:39). The moon measures out not only the months of the year but the passing of the years too, for the Islamic calendar is lunar and the pre-Islamic intercalation to align it with the solar year was abolished by the Koran. When the Prophet saw the new moon he would say: "O crescent of good and of guidance, my faith is in Him who created thee." The crescent and star feature in the flags of many Islamic countries which were formerly part of the Ottoman Empire. Thus, in the language of conventional symbols, the crescent and star have become the symbols of Islam as much as the cross is the symbol of Christianity. However, this use of the crescent as a symbol for Islam was introduced late and did not originate with the Arabs.

The crescent and star appear on Mesopotamiam monuments where the star is the planet Venus or one of the female divinities who represent Venus. In the 5th century the crescent and star appear on a Sassanid coin. The Manicheans used the crescent to symbolize the moon-boat which in that religion carried the star representing particles of light dispersed in creation back to its reconstituted origin. In the Islamic world they appear on the Fāṭimid Caliph's robes, and were used by the Ottoman Turks who made the symbols universal ones after they conquered Constantinople in *857*/1453 1452.

A crescent on the cupolas of mosques is used to indicate the *qiblah* (direction of Mecca). Often three golden balls are placed below the crescent; traditionally they stand for the material, subtle, and Angelic worlds (*see* FIVE DIVINE PRESENCES) and the crescent then symbolizes the world of Being.

Sūrah 54 of the Koran speaks of "the splitting of the moon". It is sometimes understood to be a prodigious sign worked by the Prophet. According to this interpretation, the Prophet stood on the hill called Abū Qubays which overlooks the Ka'bah, and made the moon appear to split into two parts which then moved around the Ka'bah. The unbelieving Meccans are supposed to have seen this, but to have replied that the event was only sorcery. The spot where the Prophet supposedly stood, near the later "mosque of Bilāl", is called popularly *shaqq al-qamar* ("the splitting of the moon"). But while this is the opinion of the commentator al-Bayḍāwī and others, the story appears to be only the result of interpretation of the words of the Koran after the times of the Prophet. There are no contemporary accounts of such an event. It is far more likely that the Koran is speaking allegorically of a sign of the Last Day, rather than of a miracle. *See* MIRACLES.

Moon god, *see* HUBAL.

Moors (from the Latin *maurus*, which is derived from the Greek *mauros*, "dark complexioned"). The classical name in Europe of the people of North Africa, who, since the Arab invasions, have been made up of a mixture of Arabs (approx. 40%) and Berbers (approx. 60%). Morocco and Algeria, and, to a lesser degree, Tunisia and Mauritania, correspond to the lands of the Moors. In Spain, Arabs are still called *Moros*, and the Arabs who remained in Spain, outwardly accepting Christianity after the Reconquest, were called *Moriscos*. Starting with the period of European colonial expansion, the term "Moor" came to be synonymous with Muslim in many contexts. The Muslims of south India and Sri Lanka are frequently called "Moors", just as the Muslim minorities in the Philippines are known as *Moros*.

Moriscos. Muslims who remained in Spain after the fall of Granada in 1492. Many accepted Christianity outwardly in the course of years and because of persecution, but continued to practice Islam in secret. A large number of them were expelled from Spain in 1619.

Some of those who remained in Spain maintained threads of a hidden Islam, sometimes into the 20th century. Before the expulsions, a large number of Moriscos emigrated to North Africa, particularly after the failure of their last attempt to regain Granada in the Alpujarra uprising in 1571. They used a language called *Aljamiado* which was a mixture of Spanish and Arabic, written in Arabic script.

Morocco. Kingdom. Population: 26,590,000 (1984 est.). 98% of the population is Muslim of the Mālikī School of Law. There are now fewer than 150,000 Europeans in Morocco and a small Jewish population. 60% of native Moroccans are Berbers and 40% are Arab. The legal system is mixed. The civil law is based upon French codes, and Mālikī *sharī'ah* law. Jewish Rabbinic law is recognized. Many branches of the Shādhilī *ṭuruq*, such as the Darqawiyyah, Ketaniyyah, 'Isawiyyah, Ouezzaniyyah, are active. Other Sufi orders include the Qādiriyyah (usually known as the Jalālah), and the Tījāniyyah.

Moses (Ar. *Mūsā*; to whose name is sometimes added the epithet: "God spoke to him" (*Kallamahu'-Llāh*), i.e. out of the burning bush). In Islam he is a *rasūl*, a Divine Messenger who brings a new revelation (Judaism and the Mosaic Law), rather than only a *nabī*, who prophecies within the limits of an existing revelation.

The story of Moses in the Koran is told extensively and is very similar in its manifold details to that in the Old Testament. One of the signs associated with him in Islam is the "white hand": during his appearance before Pharoah, "He drew his hand from his bosom and it was white" (7:108) to signify that his activity in the world had been made sacred. He is also depicted as having a speech impediment which he asks God to remove so that his words may be understood.

Many popular stories of Moses make him representative of the exoteric point of view, the *sharī'ah*, or outer law. This is exemplified in the Koran by the account of his encounter with al-Khiḍr (18:61-83), a personification of transcendant knowledge and realization. But Moses could not, as one to whom God spoke, be simply a symbol of the outward; a Sufi interpretation of this same legend makes Moses outwardly the noble and spiritual aspirant, and inwardly the Heart seeking the guidance of the Spirit that "moves where it will".

As a precursor of Muḥammad, the Prophet of Islam, Moses is linked to Abraham, the patriarchal founder of Semitic monotheism; and the Koran describes itself as confirming the teachings revealed to Abraham and Moses as, for example, at the end of Sūrat al-'Al'ā: "This indeed was in the first scrolls [revelations], the scrolls of Abraham and Moses" (87:18-19).

Moses' story is told in the following verses: (2:51ff.); (5:20ff.); (7:102ff.); (7:138ff.); (7:150ff.); (9:51); (10:76ff.); (14:5ff.); (17:101ff.); (18:61ff.); (20:9-80, 92ff.); (27:7ff.); (28:3f. 114ff.); (21:48); (40:23 ff.); (42:13); (43:43ff.); (44:17ff.); (51:38); (61:5); (79:15 ff.). *See* AARON; al-KHIḌR.

Mosque (from Ar. *masjid*, "a place of prostrations" through French *mosquée* based on Egyptian dialect *masqid*). In pre-Islamic times the area around the Ka'bah was called the *masjid*. Abū Bakr built a place of prayer next to his house in Mecca before the Hijrah, and a mosque stands on the spot to this day. But the prototype of the first mosque is that of Qubā' in Medina, which the Prophet built upon his arrival there from Mecca.

The style of mosques varies greatly, but the elements are constant. The fundamental requirement is for a consecrated space, either open or covered or both, upon which the worshipers, ranked in rows behind the prayer-leader (*imām*), perform the actions of canonical prayer, standing, bowing and kneeling. No-one should set foot in this space except in a state of ritual purity. To indicate the direction of Mecca (*qiblah*) which all face in prayer, there is generally a closed arch, of varying degrees of adornment and elaboration, called the *miḥrāb*. In very large mosques there may well be more than one *miḥrāb*. To the right of the *miḥrāb* in larger mosques stands the pulpit (*minbar*), from which the Friday exhortation, or sermon, (*Khuṭbah*) is delivered.

It is customary for the sacred space to be bright and uncluttered; indirect sunlight may well stream down from openings surrounding a covering dome, as if symbolizing the grace of Heaven descending upon the faithful. Open courtyards supplement the covered space, in which fountains are often placed; it is essential, in any case, that mosques should provide facilities for the ritual ablution preceding all prayers. Another striking feature of the larger mosques in particular, is the illumination, traditionally provided by mosque-lamps that were outstanding examples of the art of the metal-worker and which were able to flood the interior of the mosque with light, particularly during the night-time ceremonies of Ramaḍān.

The typical Arab mosque is a flat building with arches imitating the original palm trunks which, cut at the top, were the support pillars of the first mosques. At first there were elevated platforms attained by steps to call the prayer. These were to be found in the early mosques in Medina and in the mosque of 'Amr ibn al-'Āsī in Fuṣṭāṭ (Cairo). These platforms evolved into minarets of which, in later times, the most characteristic were the slender cylindrical minarets of the Turks, which contrast with the expansive and ample-domed mosques built after the style of Byzantine churches. The minarets with elaborate bulbous structures around the muezzin's platform identify a Mamlūk mosque (and similar features are found on some of the Shī'ite mosques of Iraq and Iran). The square towers, originally imitations of the square fire towers of the Zoroastrians, identify the minarets of the Arab West. Exceptional styles are the gigantic spiral minaret of the *Malwiyyah* mosque in Samarra', built in imitation of Babylonian ziggurats, and wooden towers found in the Far East. The word minaret itself derives from *manārah*, a "lighthouse".

Almohad art put a characteristic stamp on mosque design, and today some of its features can be found almost everywhere. Mosques in the Sahara are often no more than a half circle of stones. The simple and venerable 13th century mosque of Chinguetti in Mauritania, with a feeling as ancient as the Biblical desert city of Daumat al-Jandal, has fine sand for its floor. The more elaborate mosques of the Saharan cities and sub-Saharan Africa are dried mud buildings that seem to have the ponderous strength of the earth itself, and indeed seem to be part of it. Many of these African mosques, with their tendency towards pure geometry, are exquisite examples of vernacular architecture.

Mosques in Iran and India are famed for the delicacy and profusion of surface decoration, and the most sophisticated of formal styles. In China, mosques are typically built in the styles of Chinese temple architecture, although examples which are strongly Arab in style can be found as far away as Canton, at the end of the sea-route.

In Malay countries traditional mosques are frequently open structures, the walls not fortress-like as in the Middle East. Others, of ancient design, have curved, swallow-tail triple roofs, sometimes surmounted by lotuses, showing the influence of pre-Islamic symbolism, notably the *Triloka*, "Heaven, earth and the underworld", esoterically signifying formlessness, form and desire. Others are characterized by whitewashed courtyards with tall minarets like lighthouses, a style brought by Arabs from East Africa and the Hadramaut. One of the characteristic architectural traits of all mosques is that in the use of space there is conveyed "an absence of tension between heaven and earth", unlike, for example, a Gothic Christian cathedral which, soaring upwards, seems to call for a spiritual heroism. The architectonics of a mosque express the equilibrium between man and God which is in the nature of Islam. *See also* KA'BAH, MIḤRĀB; MINBAR; MINARET.

Mosque of the Prophet (Ar. *Masjid an-Nabī* also called *al-Masjid ash-Sharīf*, and *al-Masjid an-Nabawī ash-Sharīf*). This mosque in Medina is the second most venerable mosque in Islam, after the *al-Masjid al-Ḥarām*, or Grand Mosque of Mecca. The first mosque on the site of today's structure was supported by the trunks of standing palm trees that had grown there, and the Prophet himself worked on its construction. A stone originally indicated the direction of prayer (at first Jerusalem, and later Mecca). In its time, the mosque of Medina was the principal mosque in Islam, where the Prophet spent much of his time with the Companions.

The mosque was enlarged first by the Prophet, and then by the Caliphs Abū Bakr, 'Umar, 'Uthmān, al-Walīd (the Byzantine Emperor sent gifts on this occasion), and al-Mahdī. The present mosque was built by the Mamlūks, in particular by the Sultans Baybars and Qa'it Bey, and the Ottomans, with additions made in this century by King 'Abd al-'Azīz Al Sa'ūd. The enormous number of visitors to the mosque at pilgrimage time make further expansion inevitable.

Within the mosque today is the tomb of the Prophet whose house was adjacent. In accordance with the Ḥadīth that "Prophets are buried where they die", the tomb stands on the spot which was 'Ā'ishah's room in the *hujrah*, or women's apartments. Next to the Prophet's tomb are those of Abū Bakr and 'Umar whose burial was admitted in the Prophet's house by 'Ā'ishah. Next to these is a sepulchre which is called that of the Prophet's daughter Fāṭimah, although it is more than likely that she is buried in the *Baqī'* cemetery nearby.

Between the Prophet's tomb and a free standing *miḥrāb* a short distance away (this *miḥrāb* is much sought after as a place of prayer of exceptional potency) is a space called the *rawḍah* ("garden"). It is so named because the Prophet said: "Between my house and my pulpit is a garden of the gardens of paradise."

Elaborate ceremonies have grown up surrounding visits to the tomb of the Prophet. The program of a formal visit (*ziyārah*) has specific stations within the mosque which are accompanied by pious recitations. The visitation of the Prophet's mosque is non-canonical, and even frowned upon by fundamentalist circles who insist on a Ḥadīth that advises against the visiting of tombs. Nevertheless, most Muslims aspire to visit the tomb of the Prophet, a visit which is usually combined with the *ḥajj* or the *'umrah*.

Mosque of Qubā'. This Medinan mosque is also known as the "Mosque of Reverence" (*Masjid at-Taqwā*). Although Abū Bakr turned his house into a mosque while still in Mecca, and prayers were also performed at the house of Arqam, the Mosque of Qubā' is considered to be the first mosque in Islam. A mosque still stands upon the spot today.

Qubā' is about 5 kilometres/3 miles from Medina. Nearby is the *Mabrak an-Nāqah* ("kneeling place of the she-camel"). Upon his arrival in Medina the Prophet loosed his camel Qaswā' to wander and choose where he would stay. Here the camel knelt. The Prophet himself settled nearby, then moved when the larger mosque was built in Medina.

The name *Masjid at-Taqwā* is a reference to the Koran (9:108): "A place of worship which was founded upon reverence from the first day... wherein are men who love to purify themselves. Allāh loves the purifiers."

Mosque of the Two Qiblahs (Ar. *Masjid al-Qiblatayn*). A mosque in Medina where the Prophet suddenly turned towards Mecca during the prayer. Until then he had always prayed facing Jerusalem. The congregation followed suit and a revelation of the Koran later confirmed the establishment of Mecca as the new *qiblah* (prayer direction). *See* QIBLAH.

"Mother of cities", *see* UMM al-QURĀ.

Moulay, *see* MAWLAY.

Mouloud, *see* MAWLID an-NABĪ.

Mourning. Widows are required to observe a period of mourning marked by various abstentions for four months and ten days. *See* FUNERALS.

Moussem (the French form of the Ar. *mawsim*, "term", "season"). A Saint's festival in Morocco, which is the occasion for large fairs. A tent city springs up and, in the case of great festivals such as those of Mawlay 'Abd Allāh near Agadir, or Mawlay Idrīs Zerhun, pilgrims come from distant places. Displays called *tabarrud* ("powderplay") are given, charging on horseback, firing rifles and turning about in the classic Arab cavalry maneuver. At a *moussem*, musicians, story tellers, and street performers congregate, and on some occasions processions take place of which the most famous is that of the *'Isawiyyah* religious fraternity in Meknes.

Some *moussems* may have a different focus. The Imilchil *moussem* is a marriage fair for spouse seekers with no time to waste. Little, or no bride gift is expected, and, apart from a brief stop at the magistrate's booth for registration of the marriage, there is no ceremonial. Other *moussems* are private, albeit large, gatherings of disciples to celebrate an anniversary in the life of a Saint or a spiritual master.

The Arabic word *mawsim* has entered European languages through Portuguese as the season of rains, *monsoon*.

Mozarab (Sp. "*mozarabe*" from Ar. *musta'rib*, "one who is Arabized"). Christians living under Arab rule in Moorish Spain and having adopted Arab life-styles. Today Mozarab denotes the style of their handicrafts and decorative arts, which persisted long after the Arabs had been first subjugated and then in large part expelled from Spain, their style being characteristic of a whole facet of Spanish art.

Muallaqāt (lit. "the hung ones"). The poems that were acclaimed at the yearly fairs such as Minā and 'Ukāẓ, written in gold letters and said to have been hung in honour in the Ka'bah. A small number of such odes have come down to modern times, the most famous being those of 'Imru'-l-Qays, 'Antarah, and Labid.

The sequential nature of poetry recreates the dimension of time, and thus is the supreme art of the herding and hunting nomad, whose life unfolds in space. (Similarly, image-making, which recreates space, is the art of the sedentary, who is bound to the agricultural seasons, and lives in time. It is for this reason also that geometry arose among the Greeks, a sedentary people, and algebra, the mathematics of changing relationships, among the Arabs and Persians.) To this day the high point of royal and shaykhly gatherings in Arabia is the recitation of poetry, sometimes in contest. A royal poet may greet guests to a state feast in verse.

The *mu'allaqāt* are *qasidahs* or odes. The classical ones always have the description of the old Beduin camp and the erotic prelude called the *nasib*; the description of a journey on swift-footed camels called the *rakhil*, and the praise of the host or the tribe. The poet is called the *maḍiḥ*.

Mu'allim. Any kind of teacher, or master of a trade or craft.

Mujahid (pl. *mujāhidīn*). Someone who takes part in a *jihad* or holy war. The word became known in the West during the PLO struggles with Israel and has now taken on the meaning of an Islamic guerrilla fighter.

Mujizah, *see* MIRACLES.

Mu'ānaqah (lit. "embracing"). Phrases of the Koran which in Arabic can be considered as referring to either the preceding or following word, e.g. *fihi* ("therein") in 2:2 which can refer to the word *rayba* ("doubt") before it as: "This book, there is no doubt therein", or to *hudan* ("guidance"), the word after: "therein is guidance for those who strive for piety." As an editorial aid in some Korans the phrase is marked by three dots before and after, and the letters *mim-'ayn* are written in the margin.

Mu'āwiyah (d. *60*/680). One of the sons of Abū Sufyān who led Meccan opposition to the Prophet, Mu'āwiyah became the sixth Caliph and founder of the Umayyad dynasty, having forced Ḥasan, the son of 'Alī, to abdicate. When Caliph, Mu'āwiyah also compelled the leading sons of the Companions to acknowledge his own son Yazīd as successor to the Caliphate, thereby making this originally elective office hereditary *de facto*.

Taking decisive and ruthless action when it was required to achieve his ends, Mu'āwiyah at other times was extremely forbearing. And he understood the style of his people. When a certain Arab said to him:

> "By God! thou hadst better do right by us,

> Mu'āwiyah, or we'll correct thee, be assured of that!" the Caliph simply asked:
> "How will you do that?"
> "With a stick!" said the man.
> "Very well", Mu'āwiyah replied, "I will do right."

"This is the Arab Caesar", the Caliph 'Umar used to say when he saw Mu'āwiyah. Mu'āwiyah was of the family of 'Uthmān, and used revenge for the assassination of 'Uthmān (Mu'āwiyah was at the time governor of Syria) as the pretext virtually to seize the Caliphate out of the hands of 'Alī, who could neither marshal consensus behind him, nor take decisive action to hold onto political power. 'Alī's son Ḥasan, who became Caliph after the death of 'Alī, gave up all authority to Mu'āwiyah without a fight.

> "I do not use my sword when my whip will do," was one of his sayings; "nor my whip when my tongue will do. Let a single hair still bind me to my people, and I'll not let it snap; when they slack, then I pull; but when they pull, then I slack."
> "What's approved today was reproved once, he said; even so things now abominated will someday be embraced."
> "Abū Bakr sought not the world, nor did it seek him. The world sought 'Umar for all that he sought it not. But ourselves are sunk in it, to our middles."
> "I," said he, "am the first King [in Islam]."

See UMAYYADS.

al-Mu'awwidhatān, *see* MAGIC; REFUGE.

Mubāḥ (lit. "permitted"). The category of actions which are permitted and neutral. The other categories are: *farḍ* or *wājib* for that which is obligatory; *mustaḥabb* or *mandūb* for that which is recommended; *makrūh* for that which is discouraged; and *ḥarām* for that which is forbidden. In *fiqh*, or jurisprudence, all actions fall into one of these categories. *See* FARḌ; ḤARĀM.

Muḍārabah. A business partnership where one partner puts up the capital and the other the labor; a sleeping partnership. This device, known and used in the past, has now been applied by some Middle East banking enterprises to an arrangement whereby the *muḍārabah* is a deposit of money making the depositor a limited partner in the ventures of the bank, thus earning a return on investment. As interest is forbidden in Islam (but nevertheless often paid by banking institutions either openly or by a different name), the *muḍārabah* is an expedient that has been endorsed by a number of religious authorities as a legal device to authorize earnings on deposited capital. *See* ISLAMIC BANKING.

Mudejar. The Spanish name for Arabs who remained in Spain after the Reconquest. It is also the name of the art style, inspired by Islam, which dominated southern Christian Spain afterwards and remains an influence today. *See* MOZARAB.

al-Mudhākarah (lit. "negotiation", "deliberation", "learning", "memorization"). A spiritual discourse or exposition as might be given during a meeting (*majlis*) of Sufis.

Muezzin (Ar. *Mu'adhdhin*). One who makes the call to prayer (*adhān*) from a minaret or the door of a mosque. During the prayer, the muezzin usually performs the function of respondent to the Imām. Customarily the muezzin chants the Koran from the minarets at night while awaiting the moment to call morning prayer.

al-Mufīd, Shaykh (Abū 'Abd Allāh Muḥammad al-Ḥārithī al-Baghdādī, *338-413*/950-1022). A Shī'ite scholar and author of the *Kitāb al-Irshād* ("Book of Instruction"), a description of the Twelve Imāms.

Shaykh al-Mufīd was called Ibn Mu'allim ("Son of the Teacher"). He lived when the Buyids controlled the Caliphate, and the pro-Shī'ite climate promoted an expansion in Shī'ite scholarship. Shaykh al-Mufīd's teachers were Ibn Qulawayh, and Ibn Babawayh. He is a bridge between the tradition oriented Shī'ism which preceded him, and the theologically speculative kind of Shī'ite scholarship which developed later. Among his own students were ash-Sharīf ar-Raḍī (d. *406*/1015) who compiled the *Nahj al-Balāghah* ("the sayings of 'Alī"), and his brother Sayyid al-Murtada (d. *436*/1044). *See* AKHBĀRĪS; BIHBAHĀNĪ.

Mufrad (lit. "singular", "unique"). A particular consecration for the performance of pilgrimage. *See* IḤRĀM.

Muftī. A legal functionary who may be an

assistant to a *Qāḍi* (Judge) or a *Qāḍi* himself, empowered to make decisions of general religious import, called *fatāwā* (sing. *fatwā*). *See* FATWĀ; QĀḌI.

Muhājirūn (from Ar. *hijrah*, the "migration", sing. *muhājir*). That group in Medina who had fled from persecution in Mecca for being Muslims. Those who were originally of Medina were called the *Anṣār* (the "helpers").

Muḥammad, the Messenger of God. The name of the Prophet of Islam. It means "the Praised one" or "he who is glorified", and the name Aḥmad, by which the Prophet is also known, is a superlative form meaning "the most laudable": both from the verb *ḥamada* ("to praise, laud, glorify"). Traditionally, every mention of the Prophet by name or by title is followed by the invocation *salla-Llāhu 'alayhi wa-sallam* ("God bless him and give him peace") or by *'alayhi-ṣ-ṣalātu wa-s-salām* ("upon him be blessings and peace"), a practice also observed following the mention of Jesus, son of Mary, and after the other prophets and the Archangel Gabriel. It is also sufficient to say *'alayhi-s-salām* ("Peace be upon him").

Tradition assigns two hundred names to Muḥammad, including: *Ḥabīb Allāh* ("Beloved of God"), *an-Nabī* ("the Prophet"), *ar-Rasūl* ("the Messenger"), *Abū-l-Qāsim* ("Father of Qāsim", a son who died in infancy), *Tā' Hā'*, *Yā' Sīn* (names of Sūrahs of the Koran), *Dhikru-Llāh* ("Remembrance of God"), *Miftāh ar-Raḥmah* (the "Key of Mercy"), *Miftāh al-Jannah* (the "Key of Paradise"), *Sayyid al-Kawnayn* ("Lord of the Two Worlds"), *Rūḥ al-Ḥaqq* (the Spirit of Truth"), *Khātim al-Anbiyā'* ("Seal of the Prophets"), *Khātim ar-Rusul* ("Seal of the Messengers"), *Ṣāḥib al-Mi'rāj* ("He of the Night Ascent"), *Sa'd Allāh* ("Joy of God"), *Sa'd al-Khalq* ("Joy of Creation"), *'Ayn an-Na'īm* ("Fount of Beneficence"), *Sayf Allāh* ("Sword of God"), *Al-Amīn* ("The Trusty") and so forth. The Bible also gives him a name: Shiloh. In Genesis 49:1-10 it says: "And Jacob called unto his sons and said, Gather yourselves together, that I may tell you that which shall befall you in the last days... The sceptre shall not depart from Judah, nor a lawgiver from between his feet, until Shiloh come; and unto him shall the gathering of the people be." Since Jesus is of the house of David, and thus of Judah, the prophecy – and the name – must concern a Prophet coming after him, who is Muḥammad. And Deuteronomy (18:15/18) "I will raise them up a Prophet from among their brethren, like unto thee, and will put my words in his mouth; and he shall speak unto them all that I shall command him."

Muḥammad was born, according to tradition, in 570 A.D., the "Year of the Elephant", when Mecca was attacked by the army of Abrahah, an Abyssinian ruler of the Yemen.

The father of Muḥammad was 'Abd Allāh, son of 'Abd al-Muṭṭalib, and grandson of Hishām, the founder of the Hāshimite clan of the Quraysh. The patriarch of the Quraysh, two generations before Hishām, was named Fihr of the Kinānah tribe, and it is from his epithet of Quraysh (diminutive of *qirsh*, "shark") that his descendants take their name. Since Fihr was able to trace his lineage from Ishmael, Muḥammad is a descendant of Ishmael and Abraham, and heir to God's promise to Hagar: "Arise, lift up the lad, and hold him in thine hand, for I will make him a great nation" (Genesis 21:18).

Muḥammad was born after the death of his father and, as a minor, unable by pre-Islamic Arab tribal law to inherit from his father, he became the poor ward of his grandfather 'Abd al-Muṭṭalib. In keeping with the custom of the settled Arabs, the infant was entrusted to a Beduin foster mother to be raised in the desert. She was Ḥalīmah of the Banū Sa'd ibn Bakr, a clan of the Hawāzin. While the child was with them, the Beduin family experienced many unaccustomed blessings, but one event frightened them, for, as it was reported by a son of Ḥalīmah: "Two men came dressed in white and opened Muḥammad's breast and stirred their hands inside." In later years the Prophet explained that the visitors were Angels who had washed a dark spot from his heart with snow; he also said that "Satan touches every son of Adam when he is born, except Mary and her son."

Not long afterwards, Muḥammad returned to Mecca. When he was eight 'Abd al-Muṭṭalib died, and an uncle, Abū Ṭālib, became his guardian, his mother having died two years before. As a youth, the Prophet went on caravans and came to take charge of others' trade abroad, being known for his honesty as "al-Amīn" (the "Trustworthy"). It was on one such journey he met a Christian monk in Syria called Bahīrah who recognized in him the signs of his coming prophethood.

At the age of twenty-five, he married Khadījah, a wealthy widow forty years of age, whose caravans Muḥammad had had in his charge. Khadījah bore the Prophet two sons who died in infancy, and four daughters. At the age of forty, or around 610, the Prophet, who had already experienced visions which he described as "the breaking of the light of dawn", received the first revelation of the Koran while on retreat near Mecca during the holy month of Ramaḍān. In a mountain-top cave called Ḥirā', the Angel Gabriel came to him with the beginning of the Divine message. (*See* KORAN, REVELATION.)

The Meccans were for the most part idolaters worshiping a miscellany of gods and goddesses, and propitiating them with sacrifices. (*See* IDOLS.) But among the idolatrous Meccans there lived also a certain number of Christians from the oasis of Najrān in the south of Arabia, which was an important Christian center whose bishops came to the great Arab fairs to preach. (*See* NAJRĀN; WARAQAH.) Jewish tribes lived in and near Medina (then called Yathrib); and some Arabs were *ḥunafā'* ("upright ones", sing. *ḥanīf*), still practicing, as individuals, the monotheism which was the legacy of Abraham. Muḥammad had been a *ḥanīf*, and had sought in his retreats to bring himself closer to the one God, the God of Abraham. (*See* ALLĀH.) Now, through the Prophet, began the restoration or renewal of the primordial religion of Abraham, and of Adam, in which man faced God as the Absolute with the same immediacy and simplicity as he did on the first day of creation.

Khadījah was the first to believe that the Prophet had indeed been charged with a Divine mission, followed by 'Alī, his cousin, and Zayd, his servant. The first convert from outside the family circle was Abū Bakr, a respected merchant and Muḥammad's friend. The Prophet began the public preaching of his message by warning his own clan, the Hāshimites, of the danger of punishment for those who did not worship the one God.

However, as followers of the new religion (*al-muslimūn*, "they that surrender to God"), increased, so did the opposition of the pagan Quraysh, who, quite apart from their attachment to their idols, feared for the prosperity of Mecca. The city was a center of pilgrimage because of the Ka'bah, a sanctuary founded by Abraham, sacred indeed to Allāh, but at that time crowded with the idols of neighboring tribes and nations. The Quraysh saw a threat in this new religion which condemned idolatry, fearing that it would deprive them of the respect they enjoyed as guardians of the Ka'bah and diminish the benefits they reaped from the yearly pilgrimage. Although there were several cubic stone sanctuaries like the Ka'bah in Arabia, all of them objects of veneration, it was the Ka'bah of Mecca that was held in the highest esteem. It drew great numbers of desert Arabs who came at the appointed season as pilgrims to worship.

With time, resistance to Islam became virulent. After the Prophet had refused all compromises and even an offer to make him King of the Quraysh, a ban was put upon his clan, the Hāshimites, prohibiting commerce with them. To escape persecution in Mecca, some of the Muslims emigrated to Abyssinia. Eventually the ban was lifted, but soon after, Abū Ṭālib, the Prophet's uncle, died. This uncle, while not a believer in Islam, as head of the clan had protected the Prophet against the animosity of his opponents. Abū Lahab, another uncle, but a fierce enemy of the religion, now became head of the Hāshimites, and let the Quraysh know that Muḥammad no longer enjoyed the clan's protection.

At the same time, some six men of the tribe of Khazraj of Yathrib (Medina) entered Islam during the pilgrimage to Mecca in the year 620; the next year five of them returned, bringing with them seven others, two of whom were members of the Aws, the other important Yathrib tribe. This time they took an oath pledging fealty to the Prophet. This was the so-called First Pledge of 'Aqabah, named after the 'Aqabah pass, or incline, at Minā, near Mecca, where the event occurred. The next year, seventy-three men and two women took the oath during the pilgrimage, namely, the so-called Second 'Aqabah, whereby the men pledged to protect the Prophet from his enemies.

From this point it became customary for Muslims fleeing persecution at the hands of the Quraysh to emigrate to Yathrib, and shortly afterwards, the Prophet, his life now in danger, left the city with Abū Bakr by stealth and under cover of darkness, evading search parties by hiding in a cave in the Thawr mountain near Mecca. This celebrated journey was the Hijrah ("emigration"). On the 17 September 622 the Prophet entered Yathrib; the year which, according to the Arab and the later Islamic calendar began on 15 July (sometimes said to be the 16th because the Muslim day begins on the previous evening), was afterwards designated by the Caliph 'Umar as the first year of the Islamic era, because the Prophet's arrival in Yathrib marked the beginning of the first Islamic state. Thereafter the city became known as *Madīnat an-Nabī*, "the city of the Prophet", Medina. (*See* HIJRAH.)

The Prophet was soon joined by some seventy fellow emigrants (*Muhājirūn*) from Mecca, and also by his wife Sawdah, a widow he had married after the death of Khādijah. In Medina, his third wife, 'Ā'ishah, the daughter of Abū Bakr, entered his household; they had been married in Mecca, but the consummation of the marriage was put off until after the emigration because of her tender years. 'Ā'ishah was to be his favorite wife, although the Prophet always retained the highest regard for Khādijah. Thereafter the Prophet was to make other marriages, some of them important as political alliances, others to widows without means, and some for reason of personal affinities. (*See* WIVES of the PROPHET.)

He was of robust health, rarely suffering from anything more than a headache on long campaigns. Of medium height, he had a beautiful face. His long black hair reached his shoulders and he sometimes twisted it in two plaits, sometimes four. Between his shoulders, at the bottom of his back he had a mark, "big as a silver dirham", with hair growing around it. This was the "Seal of Prophecy", the mark of the last Divine Messenger to the world.

> Such force of life was in his walk that a man might think him pulling his feet loose from stone; and yet so light it was that he seemed to be stepping ever downhill. And he had such a sweetness in his face that when a man was in his company it was hard to go away.
>
> People used to ask 'Ā'ishah how the Prophet lived at home. Like an ordinary man, she answered. He would sweep the house, stitch his own clothes, mend his own sandals; water the camels, milk the goats, help the servants at their work, and eat his meals with them; and he would go to fetch a thing we needed from the market.
>
> He would visit any sick; he would walk as a mourner after any bier he met in the street; and if a slave bade him to dinner, he would go dine with him.

He was a man; it was said, "a man, but not like other men, rather like a jewel among stones".

When he laughed, he would throw his head back and one could see his teeth. But he never laughed uproariously, and said that "this world is under curse, and accursed all things in it save the remembrance of God, and such things as help us to remember." And he said: "Be in this world as a stranger or as a passer-by"; but also: "do for this world as if to live forever, and for the next, as if to die on the morrow."

He was fond of milk, honey, and the use of a toothstick (*miswāk*), a kind of brush made of threadwood, with the bark peeled away, still used today in the traditional world, which, when rubbed on the teeth, cleans them. He said that dearest to him were "prayer, perfumes, and women", all that in this world is fragrant of paradise.

A first mosque was built at Qubā', a village near Medina. Others followed as more and more people of Yathrib joined Islam. Among these were, however, a group the Koran was to call the "Hypocrites" (*al-munāfiqūn*) who in the councils were "like propped-up pieces of wood" (63:4) because their allegiance to Islam was lukewarm and external, and their willingness to do battle for it wavering.

When it became apparent that the Muslims would have to fight for Islam the Koran exempted from their enmity only the adherents of the revealed religions, the Christians, the Jews, the Magians (Zoroastrians) and the Sabians. (A number of religions which the Muslims of the times deemed to be Divinely inspired, were identified as Sabians. (*See* AHL al-KITĀB.) But idolaters (*mushrikūn*), and unbelievers (*kāfirūn*), who denied the transcendent Divine Reality, could make no claim upon God's indulgence, and had no "right" to peace.

After a skirmish with a Meccan caravan, a small army of three hundred Muslims defeated a force of one thousand Meccans at Badr in March 624. (*See* BATTLE of BADR.) The next year a Meccan force of three thousand defeated about one thousand Muslims at Uḥud, because of the disobedience of a small group of Medinan soldiers. (*See* BATTLE of UḤUD.)

Two years later, in April 627, a massed army of Quraysh, accompanied by the desert tribes of the Ghaṭafān and some Jews from the tribe of the Banū Naḍīr who had been expelled from Medina, attacked Medina, where they were unexpectedly confronted by a hastily built defensive trench (*See* BATTLE of the TRENCH.) After a completely unsuccessful siege, known as the "War of the Confederates" (*al-Aḥzāb*), they abandoned their campaign, and thereafter hostilities between Medina and Mecca all but ceased, although expeditions were sent from Medina against other tribes.

Tradition relates that during the building of the Trench the Prophet was called to help to remove a large stone. The Prophet split the stone with three blows and three flashes of light emerged, the first of which illuminated for the Prophet the castles of the Yemen, the second the castles of Syria, and the third the palace of Kisra (Chosroe) at Māda'in (Ctesiphon-Seleucia). This he understood to be a sign that God was opening up the lands to the South, the West, and the East of Arabia to conquest by the armies of Islam. Following this, the Prophet sent out messengers to eight kings, among them Heraclius, Emperor of Byzantium, the Muqawqīs (Coptic ruler of Egypt) Chosroes of Persia and the rulers of the Yemen, bidding them enter Islam before they were conquered and subjugated. The Muqawqīs sent gifts by way of return; the Persian Shāh Siroes who had succeeded Chosroes in the meantime tore up the letter. Badhān (*Qā'il* or "ruler") of the Yemen, whose emissaries were in Medina, seeing that certain prophecies made by the Prophet regarding the death of Chosroe in Persia had already been fulfilled, rebelled against the Persian suzerainty, and entered Islam.

In the following year, a revelation promised the Prophet that he would shortly pray at the sacred mosque of Mecca, at the Ka'bah. In March 628, therefore, he set out with about 1,000 men as pilgrims, not armed for battle, and with seventy camels consecrated for sacrifice. At Ḥudaybiyyah, some twelve miles from Mecca, the Prophet's pilgrimage came to a halt while tense negotiations were conducted with the Quraysh. During a moment of great danger and uncertainty, when the defenseless Muslims could have been annihilated, the Prophet, in a state of rapture like that of his revelations, called everyone to come and take an oath to him; this oath became known as the Pact of Felicity (*Bay 'at ar-Riḍwān*).

God was well pleased with the believers
when they were swearing fealty to thee
under the tree, and He knew what was
in their hearts, so He sent down the
Shechina upon them, and rewarded them with
a nigh victory
and many spoils to take; and God is ever
All-mighty, All-wise. (48:18-19)

(*See* ḤUDAYBIYYAH).

The Muslims reached an agreement with the Quraysh by which they stopped short of Mecca that year. The Prophet, however, sacrificed his camels at Ḥudaybiyyah and cut his hair as if the pilgrimage had been accomplished. The agreement stipulated that next year the Muslims would be allowed to reach their goal and that Mecca would be evacuated for them for three days. A ten-year treaty of peace was concluded between the Quraysh and the Prophet.

The Koran called this a "clear victory":

Surely We have given thee
a manifest victory,
that God may forgive thee thy former and thy
latter sins,
and complete His blessing upon thee, and guide
thee
on a straight path,
and that God may help thee
with mighty help.

It is He who sent down the Shechina
into the hearts of the believers, that
they might add faith to their faith –
to God belong the hosts of the heavens and the
earth
God is All-knowing, All-wise... (48:1-5)

The next year the Quraysh, who were watching the proceedings from the hill of Abū Qubays, saw and heard Bilāl, the muezzin of the Prophet, proclaim from the roof of the Ka'bah: "there is no god but Allāh", and "Muḥammad is the Messenger of God". Thereafter, having seen the Quraysh treat with the Prophet and acknowledge him as a sovereign, a rising tide of converts flowed towards Medina from all quarters of Arabia.

The Quraysh had not anticipated this turn of events: in effect they had given up their struggle without knowing it. The treaty, moreover, freed the Prophet to deal with others, and in the expeditions which followed, the Muslims conquered the redoubtable citadels of the Jews of Khaybar, giving the Jews the choice of entering Islam or paying tribute, thereby bringing riches to Medina and impressing their neighbors and the Arabs of the peninsula with the growing strength of the Islamic state.

It was on this campaign that the Prophet received by terms of surrender the oasis of Fadak as his personal property; after the Prophet's death his daughter Fāṭimah requested Fadak as her inheritance, but the Caliph Abū Bakr, who, to Fāṭimah's chagrin, refused, retained the oasis for the state, basing this judgement upon a Ḥadīth to the effect that a Prophet leaves no property behind him in this world. It was also on this campaign that the widowed wife of Sallām ibn Mishkam, one of the Jews of Khaybar, attempted to assassinate the Prophet by poisoning a roast lamb. The Prophet took a bite of the shoulder of the lamb but spat it out, warning those with him to stop eating, as the shoulder had told him it was poisoned. However, one of his Companions, Bishr ibn Barā', had also taken a bite which he had already swallowed, so that he soon turned pale and died. The Prophet pardoned the woman who confessed to the deed as revenge for the death of her family; but the Prophet said that a trace of that poison remained with him to the end, making him share in a martyr's death with the others who had been killed outright in the way of God.

But also of the Jews of Khaybar was a woman named Ṣafiyyah, the daughter of one who had counseled the Jews still remaining in Medina, the Banū Qurayzah, to break their treaty with the Prophet during the War of the Confederates. This bad counsel and breach led to their demise. Ṣafiyyah had dreamed of a brilliant moon hanging over Medina, a dream for which she had been rebuked by her family. After the conquest of Khaybar she was among the captives; the Prophet, learning of her dream, offered to set her free to return to her people, but she accepted Islam, and married him on the return to Medina.

A fight between Beduins, in which the Quraysh took sides against a group allied to the Muslims, was taken by the Prophet as a breach of the ten-year treaty of Ḥudaybiyyah. In January 630, therefore, at the head of an army of 10,000, he invaded Mecca, meeting almost no resistance. The Ka'bah was purified of idols (a painting inside of the Virgin and Child was expressly allowed by the Prophet to remain) and in the course of the following weeks, almost to a man, the Meccans accepted Islam.

The conquest of Mecca was followed by the Battle of Ḥunayn against the Beduin Hawāzin, who were defeated but took refuge with their allies of the city of Ṭā'if, only to surrender later and enter Islam. The Arabs could plainly see that the Prophet's pagan adversaries, if they surrendered to God in Islam, were accepted without rancor, and that Christians and Jews, if they were conquered, could keep all they had by entering Islam, or could accept protection with the new state through payment of tribute. Resistance melted away.

A great expedition of thirty thousand was then sent to Tabūk in the north of Arabia. It returned having encountered no resistance, marking the beginning of Islam's expansion towards Syria and Persia. Upon his return from Tabūk, the Prophet found that some of the lukewarm Muslims of Medina had founded a separate mosque at Qubā', the "mosque of dissension"; a revelation of the Koran, the Sūrah of Repentance, categorically told the Prophet not to acknowledge it, and the mosque, which may have been the hiding place of an opponent of the Prophet, Abū 'Amīr ar-Raḥīb, was pulled down at night:

> And those who have taken a mosque in opposition
> and unbelief, and to divide the believers,
> and as a place of ambush for those who fought
> God and His Messenger aforetime – they will swear
> 'We desired nothing but good'; and God testifies
> they are truly liars.
> Stand there never. A mosque that was founded
> upon godfearing from the first day is worthier
> for thee to stand in; therein are men who love
> to cleanse themselves; and God loves those
> who cleanse themselves.
> Why, is he better who founded his building upon
> the fear of God and His good pleasure, or he
> who founded his building upon the brink of a
> crumbling bank that has tumbled with him into the
> fire of Gehenna? And God guides not the
> people
> of the evildoers. (9:107-111)

The ninth year of the Hijrah is known as the "Year of Deputations" when delegates came from all over Arabia to accept Islam from the Prophet. The pilgrimage was closed to non-Muslims, and in the following year, in March 632, the Prophet led a pilgrimage caravan from Medina of thirty thousand men and women. In this, "the farewell pilgrimage", the new law was established: "Verily God has made inviolable for you each other's blood and each other's property, until you meet your Lord, even as he has made inviolable this, your day, in this your land, in this your month." During the sermon of 'Arafāt the last passage of the Koran was revealed:

> Today the unbelievers have despaired of
> your religion; therefore fear them not,
> but fear you Me.
> Today I have perfected your religion
> for you, and I have completed my Blessing
> upon you, and I have approved Islam for
> your religion. (5:4-5).

The Prophet looked up and cried: "My Lord! Have I delivered aright the Message I was charged with and fulfilled my calling?" And the multitude answered shouting "Ay, by God you have!"

On 8 June 632, the Prophet died, and was buried, in accordance with his wishes, in his house. As leader of the community he was succeeded by Abū Bakr with the title of *khalīfah* ("he who is left behind", deputy, successor, or Caliph). The expansion of Islam continued. Within a hundred years its realm extended from Spain to India. Today it is found in every corner of the world, and over 800,000,000 people are counted as Muslims, who recite, as the foundation of their faith, the words: "There is no god but God, Muḥammad is the Messenger of God."

> God has indeed fulfilled the vision He
> vouchsafed to His Messenger truly...
> ...Thou seest them
> bowing, prostrating, seeking bounty
> from God and good pleasure. Their
> mark is on their faces, the trace of
> prostration. That is their likeness
> in the Torah, and their likeness
> in the Gospel: as a seed that puts
> forth its shoot, and strengthens it,
> and it grows stout and rises straight
> upon its stalk, pleasing the sowers... (48:27,29)

See 'ABD al-MUṬṬALIB; AHL KISĀ'; 'Ā'ISHAH; 'AQABAH; BATTLE of BADR; BATTLE of ḤUNAYN; BATTLE of the TRENCH; BATTLE of UḤUD; HERACLIUS; HIJRAH; ḤUDAYBIYYAH; KORAN; MECCA; MEDINA; MUQAWQĪS; NAMES of the PROPHET; NIGHT JOURNEY; PROPHETS; QURAYSH; RIḌĀ'; UMMĪ; WIVES of the PROPHET.

Muḥammad II, *see* MEHMET II.

Muḥammad ibn 'Abd Allāh Ḥasan, *see after* MUḤAMMAD ALĪ.

Muḥammad Aḥmad ibn Sayyid 'Abd Allāh (*1260-1303*/1844-1885). The "Mahdī of the Sudan". A charismatic religious leader, founder of his own dervish order, in *1298*/1881 he declared himself to be the *mahdī*, the Divinely guided leader predicted by Ḥadīth. He declared a holy war, and his followers fought against Anglo-Egyptian control of the Sudan. He succeeded in restoring his own rule in the country but died soon afterwards. In *1316*/1898 the Mahdīsts were completely defeated by Lord Kitchener, and the Sudan came once more under Anglo-Egyptian control. When the tomb of the Mahdī in Omdurman had become a place of pilgrimage, in order to prevent the site from being used to stir popular unrest, the body was burned and thrown into the Nile.

Muḥammad 'Alī (*1193-1265*/1769-1849). First a pasha, then hereditary viceroy of Egypt, who founded the Khedival dynasty, Muḥammad 'Alī was an Albanian Turk who enlisted as a Bashi-Bazouk, or common soldier, and rose through the ranks to become a commander in the Turkish army. The Napoleonic wars brought him to Egypt. To the end of his life he was illiterate, but when he had wrested control of Egypt from the Turks, he modernized both his army and the government along European lines, and conducted a number of highly successful military campaigns aided by skillful diplomatic maneuvering between the European powers and Turkey.

In *1226*/1811 the massacre of the traditional Egyptian ruling class of the Mamlūks brought Muḥammad 'Alī undisputed control of Egypt. In *1233*/1818 his son Ibrāhīm Pāsha crushed the growing strength of the Wahhābīs in Arabia by besieging and destroying their home town of Dir'iyyah in the Najd. In *1238*/1823 Muḥammad 'Alī conquered the Sudan and laid the foundations of Khartoum.

Muḥammad 'Alī fought for the Ottomans in the Greek campaign which ended in 1827 with the Turkish-Egyptian naval defeat at Navarino. He fought against the Ottomans to secure his independent rule and to acquire Syria, even letting Ibrāhīm Pāsha carry the campaign into Anatolia. He was finally forced to back down in the face of European support for the Turks, but made his control of Egypt hereditary; the dynasty of the Khedives lasted until the overthrow of King Faruq in 1952.

"Muḥammadan Light", *see* NŪR MUḤAMMADĪ.

Muḥammad ibn 'Abd Allāh Ḥasan (d. *1339*/1920). A Somalian political and religious leader. After performing the pilgrimage in 1895 he became a disciple of Ibrāhīm ar-Rashīdī, founder of a group called the Ṣāliḥiyyah. Inspired by ar-Rashīdī and the example of the Mahdī of the Sudan, Muḥammad ibn 'Abd Allāh sought to unite around himself his tribe, the Oqaden, and others in Somalia, on the basis of religion and military expansion. In 1899 he declared himself to be the Mahdī.

He fought against British and Italian troops sporadically until he was disowned by his religous precepter ar-Rashīdī and denounced by the Qādiriyyah *ṭuruq* (religious orders) in Somalia. In 1920 he fled from advancing British troops and died among his tribesmen. In the British press he had meanwhile acquired the sobriquet "the Mad Mulla".

Muḥammadiyyah. An Islamic modernizing and nationalist reform movement founded in Indonesia in 1923 under the impetus of colonization. Like most such movements, it reflected an ambition to imitate the colonizer under the guise of self-expression. It had a separate women's branch, the 'Ā'ishiyyah, and included a Boy Scout organization under the name *Ḥizb al-Waṭan* ("party of the nation"). The Muḥammadiyyah also copied Western missionary techniques and organization, and trained missionary-preachers under the name of *muballigh.* During World War II it was eclipsed by religious organizations sponsored by the Japanese occupation (notably Masjumi), and made only a small comeback afterwards. *See* INDONESIA.

Muḥarram. The first month of the Islamic calendar, the first ten days of which are a period of mourning by the Shī'ites for the death of Ḥusayn. The culmination of this period, the 10th Muḥarram, is the anniversary of his martyrdom. During this time the *ta'ziyyah,* or passion-play representing the martyrdom, is performed, and there are those who wander the streets whipping or wounding themselves in penance. This is part of the Shī'ite syndrome of guilt on the recurrent theme of abandoning and betraying the Imāms in their time of need and peril.

The 10th Muḥarram is completely different in the Sunnī world; the events of Ḥusayn's death are not associated with it. It is instead celebrated according to the Sunnah as a benefic day of blessing corresponding to similar holy days in the Jewish calendar. The first day of Muḥarram is the Muslim new year (*ra's al-'ām*). Traditionally it is noted as a day of piety but without special observances, although presence at the mosque for dawn prayer is highly recommended.

al-Muḥāsibī, Abū 'Abd Allāh Ḥārith ibn Asad (d. *243*/857). A Sufi born in Baṣra. The sobriquet "al-Muḥāsibī" means "He who has rendered account [of his conscience]". He inclined first towards the Mu'tazilites and their rationalism, but left them, turning instead to Sufism, which he laced with philosophy and theology. Al-Muḥāsibī, a spiritual master of al-Junayd, was an intellectual, and thus a forerunner of the school of the Imām Shādhilī. Al-Muḥāsibī wrote the *Ri'āyah li-Huqūq Allāh,* a practical manual of the spiritual life. *See* SUFISM.

Muḥrim. A person who has put on the clothing and state of *iḥrām* ("consecration") for the performance of pilgrimage to Mecca, whether *hajj* or *'umrah. See* IḤRĀM.

Muḥtasib. A public functionary whose task, as it has existed since 'Abbāsid times, has been that of supervising the merchants' quality and prices. The *muḥtasib* checks and verifies weights and measures and the use of materials in crafts. He gives expert appraisal of the values of cloth, rugs, woven articles, brass and copper utensils.

These estimates are not binding as a price between buyer and seller, but are indicative of the fair market price. The *muḥtasib* is still to be found in some traditional markets.

Mujaddid (lit. "renewer"). A timely renewer of the faith. There is a well known Ḥadīth: "At the beginning of every hundred years God will send a renewer for my community." Ash-Shāfi'ī, al-Ghazālī, Abū Madyān, and others have all been considered as the renewers of their age, bringing a drowsing people back to the fountainhead of revelation and faith.

Mujtahid (lit. "one who strives"; pl. *mujtahidūn*). An authority who makes original decisions of canon law, rather than applying precedents already established. For Sunnīs, the door of personal effort is now "closed" according to general opinion. The *Mujtahidūn* were the founders of the schools of law and their principal exponents.

For the Shī'ites of the Uṣūlī school the situation is radically different. Not only is *ijtihād* (the making of original decisions) possible, it is also necessary, even when a case is clearly a repetition of a previous decision. Those who make these decisions are the highest religious authorities, originally few, but since the last century, expanding in numbers and very influential because they have vast personal followings, as every Uṣūlī Shī'ite is expected to adhere to one or another *Mujtahid*. They also collect a special tithe called the *khums*, which does not exist among the Sunnīs, and so some *Mujtahidūn* dispose of financial means as well. *See* AKHBĀRĪS; AYATOLLAH; IJTIHĀD; MARJA' at-TAQLĪD; UṢŪLĪS.

Mukhī. An Ismā'īlī religious dignitary and teacher. He is aided in his functions by an auxiliary called a *Kamadia*. In Western literature the *Mukhī* is sometimes referred to as "the Treasurer", and the Kamadia is called "the Accountant".

Mulay, *see* MAWLAY.

Mulla (from Ar. *mawla*, "master"). In Iran and Central Asia it is a title accorded to religious scholars and dignitaries. It corresponds roughly to the term *faqīh* in the Middle East and North Africa. The use of the term Mulla in Iran and north and east of it for someone learned in religion apparently arose from the fact that the early converts to Islam were adopted into Arab tribes as the clients (*mawla*) of a patron (also *mawla*). Thus for instruction about Islam one would turn to an established convert, or a *mawla*; this with time became Mulla.

Mulla Naṣruddīn. A humorous folk-story character, something like an Islamic Till Eulenspiegel, he appears in folk tales from Morocco to India. He is also known as Jūha and Naṣruddīn Khoja; he is always imposing his comical interpretation of the world on his wife, his neighbors, and the *Qāḍi* (Judge). The character is also linked to Abū Nuwāṣ, a poet and jester-like figure at the court of Hārūn ar-Rashīd in Baghdad.

Mulla Ṣadra (*979-1050*/1571-1640). A Persian scholar and teacher of the school of Isfahan. His real name was Muḥammad ibn Ibrāhīm Ṣadr ad-Dīn ash-Shīrāzī; he was a pupil of Mīr Dāmād and one of the most important Shī'ite philosophers. His thought characteristically combined mysticism, philosophy, and theology. Mulla Ṣadra achieved an original intellectual synthesis of Aristotle, Avicenna, Suhrawardī, and Shī'ite Islam. He is the foremost exponent of what has been called the School of Isfahan and is a remarkable example of a flowering of philosophy long after it had become dormant in the Sunnī world. In the last decades in Iran interest in Mulla Sadra has renewed and he is still a motivating force in Shī'ite thinking today. The School of Isfahan is essentially *Ishraq*, or illuminationism (a form of radical Gnosticism) recast in a more dialectical mode.

One of his most prominent formulations was the idea of the "gradations of Being", namely that Being exists in different degrees in different creatures, strong in some, attenuated in others. Although Mulla Ṣadra thereby implies that everything contains Being, albeit in different intensities, and although this appears to accord with traditional metaphysical formulations, it stands, nevertheless, in direct contrast to the predominant and universal mystical conception that, while creatures are outwardly themselves, their inward being is indistinguishable from Being itself. The essence of operative notions of non-duality is, one might say, that the reflection of the sun is nothing other than the sun itself.

Now although Mulla Ṣadra's formulation appears to be simply a different way of putting it, the element of essential identity is lacking or weakened; it remains a theory, and an inoperative one so long as the recognition of identity, which is essential for realization, is absent. (Moreover, Aristotle stated as "the supreme law of thought", or reality, that there is no intermediary between Being and non-Being; namely, that something either is, or is not, but is not both at the same time. Mulla Ṣadra's theory is similar to the premise of Arianism or Western Gnosticism in general. In modern times it has led to the assertion in Iran that if two Mujtahids contradict each other, they are both nevertheless right, but to different degrees!

In the *al-Asfar al-Arba'ah* ("The Four Journeys"), Mulla Ṣadra described the spiritual path as being at first a journey in which a man detaches himself from the physical world and the carnal self, reaching extinction in the Divine. In the second journey he reaches the degree of the Divine Names and Attributes, which is the station of Sainthood, he hears and sees and acts through God. The third journey is the end of extinction (*fanā*), and a transformed remainder of the individual (*baqā'*) subsides in this world. In the fourth journey, the Saint returns to the world (in what the Sufis call *jalwah*) and brings guidance to others.

Mulla Ṣadra's philosophy is extolled by himself as the "sublime wisdom" (*al-ḥikmah al-muta'aliyyah*), the title of one of his writings, which cannot but recall the title of of the Mahāyānist Sutra, "the perfection of wisdom" (Prajña Pāramitā). Another of his most influential writings is *Shāhid ar-Rubūbiyyah* ("The Witness of Lordship"). *See* 'IRFĀN.

al-Multazam (lit. "that which is held onto"). The space between the Black Stone (*al-ḥajar al-aswad*) and the door of the Ka'bah. Praying before this area (or from any part of the Mosque facing this spot) consitutes one of the stations of the pilgrimage. *See* KA'BAH; PILGRIMAGE.

Mulūk aṭ-Ṭawā'if, *see* TAIFAS, REYES de las.

Mūlud an-Nabī, *see* MAWLID an-NABĪ.

al-Mumkināt (lit. "possibilities", fem. pl. of *mumkin*, "possible"). In the metaphysics of Sufism according to Ibn 'Arabī, among others, possibilities are contained principially in Being in a differentiated state; and in Beyond-Being, that is, in the Absolute, in a non-differentiated state. At some point, and in some world, all possibilities, everything which is possible, must become manifest and existent.

While still in Being the possibilities are said to be in a state of "contraction" (*karb*). When they are "released", or made manifest, they become subject to "dilation" (*tanfīs*), or to "being breathed out" into existence. It is by the Divine command (*al-amr*) that the possibilities become manifest. This Divine command as given in the Koran is the word *Kun*, literally, "Exist!"

Ibn 'Arabī said: "In truth all possibilities resolve principially into non-existence." *See* al-AMR; NAFAS ar-RAḤMĀN.

Munāfiqūn, see HYPOCRITES.

Munkar and Nakīr. Two Angels who question the departed in the tomb. They correspond to the Zoroastrian angel Rasht who presides over the eighteenth day of the Zoroastrian month. The Koran describes some punishment in the tomb (6:93; 8:52) but the names of the Angels and further elaboration comes from tradition; sometimes in tradition one Angel is named and sometimes two. On the fourth day after death these Angels come and interrogate the deceased regarding their belief. The unbelievers are beaten until the day of Judgement and even the righteous suffer some anguish here. *See* ANGELS.

Muqaddam (lit. "one who is promoted"). A title used for a representative of the civil authorities on the level of a neighborhood, a kind of ward keeper.

While it can mean any kind of representative, it means, in particular, the representative of a Shaykh, or spiritual master, who is authorized to give instruction and initiate disciples in certain Sufi orders.

al-Muqanna' (lit. "he who is veiled or masked"). The sobriquet of Hāshim, a Persian from Merv, who was a follower of the propandist of the 'Abbāsids, Abū Muslim; after Abū Muslim was put to death, al-Muqanna' raised a revolt in *161*/778 and seized the Persian province of Khorasān. He claimed to be an incarnation of the Divinity and wore a veil to cover his "refulgence" from the eyes of the profane. In *164*/780 after several military defeats, he shut himself up in his fortress with his family, and burned it down.

Muqarnas. Characteristic decorative devices of Persian origin, used in Arab-Islamic architecture in corners where walls meet ceilings, or as an ornamental articulation of the transition from cubic structures to domes. The *muqarnas* consists of numerous carved pieces of wood wedged together, or of plaster moldings grouped vertically to round out a corner, giving the appearance of a wasp's nest, or, more typically, of stalactites. This beautiful and characteristic geometrical device is found in windows, doors, *miḥrābs*, domes, etc.

Muqawqīs. The title, Arabicized, of the Byzantine viceroy of Egypt to whom the Prophet addressed an invitation to enter Islam in the sixth year of the Hijrah. A traditional account says that in the building of the trench around Medina to hold up an attack by the Confederates, the Prophet struck a stone three times which shattered, sending out flashes of light to north, south and east. After this omen, letters were sent to various contemporary rulers, inviting them to submission in Islam. That sent to the Muqawqīs and his reply are preserved in Muslim tradition; he declined politely, but sent gifts and two female slaves, one of whom, Mary the Copt, became a concubine of the Prophet and the mother of his son Ibrāhīm, who died in infancy.

The letter to the Muqawqīs read:

> In the Name of God the Merciful the Compassionate.
> From the Apostle of God to the Muqawqīs, chief of the Copts: Peace be upon him who followeth the guidance.
> To proceed: I summon thee with the Call of Islam; make Submission to God as a Muslim and thou shalt live secure; and God shall double thy reward. But if thou wilt not, then on thy head will lie the guilt of all the Copts.
> O ye people of Scripture, come to a fair covenant between us and you, that we serve God alone, associating no peer with Him, and no more take our fellow men as Lords beside God. But if ye will not, then bear witness: we are the ones who are the Muslims.

The Governor sent reply:

> I am aware that there is a Prophet yet to arise; but I am of the opinion that he is to appear in Syria. For the rest, thy envoy hath been received with due honor; and I send for thine acceptance two virgins such as are highly esteemed among the Copts, and a robe of honor and a riding mule.

See HERACLIUS, MUḤAMMAD.

Muqtaḍi (lit. "one who is appointed or called upon"). He who stands behind the Imām (prayer leader) and calls out the *iqāmah* (the call to prayer made immediately before praying in the mosque), and repeats the *takbīr* (the phrase "*Allāhu Akbar*") in a loud voice so that it is heard in the furthest ranks, and thus initiates the responses within the prayer. In a very large mosque, the *muqtaḍi's* function can be carried out by a number of people. In this way, through a series of men who repeat instructions by calling them out to others who then repeat them in their turn, a congegration of thousands can pray in unison, or a speaker address a vast multitude. The *muqtaḍi's* function is usually performed by the Muezzin, the official caller to prayer. *See* MUEZZIN.

al-Murābiṭūn (lit: "those who are stationed, lined up, in position"). Men who, in religious-military organizations, defended the frontiers of the Islamic world (*Dār al-Islām*), often in remote outposts called *rubuṭ* (sing. *ribāṭ*). The institution goes back to the Islamic state under the Caliph 'Umar when, briefly, the Arabs were not allowed to own land in the conquered territories, the intention being to create a permanent mobile class for the expansion of Islam. This code was modified under the successor Caliph 'Uthmān, but the status of *murābiṭūn* reflects this early historical phase. One *murābiṭūn* movement led to an empire in the Arab West, more familiar under the Spanish version of its name, the Almoravids. *See* ALMORAVID.

Murāqabah (lit. "vigilance", "recollectedness"). An aspect of meditation (*tafakkur*), a waiting upon a spiritual presence, a permanent state of awareness. The Prophet said: "My eye sleeps but my heart wakes." It also means an examination of conscience, which in some spiritual methods is performed daily. The methods of Islamic mysticism make meditation a background for invocation (*dhikr*), which is the principal means of spiritual realization, in accordance with the injunction found frequently in the Koran: "And the remembrance of God is greatest" (*wa la dhikru Llāhi akbar*).

Al-Hujwīrī said:

> When self-will vanishes in this world, contemplation is attained, and when contemplation is firmly established, there is no difference between this world and the next.

See DHIKR.

Muraqqa'ah. A patched garment worn by some Sufi orders in the past as a discipline of poverty. (It is still seen today, albeit extremely rarely.) Some Sufis, who also lived from alms, wore such threadbare frocks that were repeatedly patched rather than replaced, until the whole garment was nothing but patches on patches.

Al-Hujwīrī said:

> A right patch is a patch that is stitched because one is poor, and not for show: if it is stitched for poverty it is stitched right, even if it is stitched badly". And also: "It is not, however, the quantity of money that makes the moneyed man. No one who recognizes poverty as better than money is a moneyed man, though he be a king; and a man who does not believe in poverty is a moneyed man, however poor he is.

It was a characteristic of the Shādhilī order of Sufism not to wear such garments. Imām Shādhilī himself sometimes wore rich garments because he taught that poverty (*faqr*) is above all something inward, that it is not riches which create an obstacle to spirituality, but attachment to them. A cloak in general, as well as the patched cloak, is also called *khirqah*. *See* KHIRQAH.

Murīd (lit. "one who is desirous [of spiritual realization]"). A disciple in a Sufi order. A more commonly used name is *faqīr* or *dervish*. *See* FAQĪR.

Muridism. A modern Sufi movement which has become widespread in Senegal. It was founded by Amadou [Aḥmad] Bamba (1852-1927) who has had five successors called *khalifahs* (caliphs), the fourth of whom died in 1990. The present, the fifth, is named Serigne Saliou Mback.

Bamba came from a family of religious teachers; he originally led a religious school. Following a familiar pattern, he announced one day to his students that his personal teachings superseded acquired doctrine and that adherence to himself was essential to spiritual progress. Some of the students left him at that point, while those who remained became the core of the new movement. As his influence grew, Amadou Bamba was exiled by the colonial authorities to Gabon in 1895 and later to the Congo. He returned to Senegal in 1902 but was later again exiled to Mauritania for five years in Boutilimit. These events were to give him the aura of a political anti-colonial hero. To his claim for spiritual authority were added accounts of miracles.

The figure of Bamba thus combines the prestige of a champion of the poor and oppressed in a political struggle against a colonizing power (and thereby against the dominance of the West in general) along with miraculous powers and hopes of salvation. This Messianic image has drawn to itself the dispossessed of modern times in West Africa and in particular those Senegalese who have had to face the trials of immigration abroad.

Murji'ah (from Ar. *irjā'*, "postponement", "deferment"). A sect of early Islam that may be termed "quietists". They believed that serious sins are offset by faith, and that punishment for them is not everlasting. Therefore, they withheld judgement and condemnation of sinners in this world. This led to attitudes of political uninvolvement. One of their doctrines, that prayer led by an Imām of doubtful character is, nevertheless, valid, became an accepted principle of Sunnī Islam (but not of Shī'ite Islam).

The Murji'ites appear to have emerged in reaction to the Khārijites, who attribute to sin a quasi-absolute and definitive nature; it is against the Khārijites rather than against the mainstream that the Murji'iah stand out in contrast. Much like St John's "sins unto death", and sins which are "not unto death", the notion of major (*kabā'ir*) and minor (*saghā'ir*) sins is due to the Murji'iah, although the Koran adumbrates it in such passages as: "...surely thy Lord knows best who is straying from His path, and He knows best who it is that is truly guided. For to God belong the Heavens and the earth, that He may reward them that do evil according to what they have done and reward them that do well according to the best; who avoid major sins [*Kabā'ira-l-ithm*] and enormities, only falling into minor faults: surely thy Lord's forgiveness is broad..."(53:30-32).

Some of Abū Ḥanīfah's attitudes derive from the Murji'ite reaction to the extremism of the Khārijites. The Murji'ite doctrine, however, of accepting the outward profession of Islam with the tongue as adequate, would inevitably have led to decadence; it was cognizance of this danger that brought about their final extirpation. *See* KHĀRIJITES.

Murshid (lit "guide", "instructor"). An instructor in any field, but in particular a spiritual master, that is, with the ability and a heavenly mandate, in addition to the necessary knowledge, to guide souls. Conversely, no guide (*murshid*) will be accessible to him whom God allows to go astray: "For him whom God sends astray, thou wilt find no guiding pattern [*waliyyan murshida*]" (18:17). A *murshid* is also called a Shaykh and, from Turkey to India, a *Pīr*. *See* PĪR; SHAYKH; SUFISM.

al-Murtaḍa, Sayyid (also called ash-Sharīf, and ash-Shaykh Murtaḍa d. *436*/1044). A Shī'ite scholar, student of the Shaykh al-Mufīd, and leader of the Shī'ite community of Baghdad. He was an *Imāmzādeh*, a relative of a Shī'ite Imām, being the great-great-grandson of Mūsā Kāzīm. He is also known as *'Alam al-Hudā* ("the Banner of Guidance").

Murtadd. *see* APOSTASY.

Muṣallā. A place of prayer, and more specifically the public praying field where, for the festival prayers of the *'Īd al-fitr*, *'Īd al-adhā*, and prayers for rain, the whole population of a city may well meet for communal worship. In Iran the *muṣallā* is called an *'idgah*. The original *muṣallā* was in Medina, at the site of the present Sabaq mosque.

Musalmān. The Persian and Turkish variant form of the Arabic *muslim* ("one who has surrendered [to God]"), as "Moslem" is the common English form. It is from the Persian that the French acquired *musulmane* for Muslim, usually written Mussulman in English.

Musaylamah. The foremost of a number of false prophets who appeared in Arabia towards the end of the life of the Prophet and during the Caliphate of Abū Bakr. Musaylamah claimed to have received divine revelations, and spoke of himself as the "Raḥmān [which is a Name of God] of the Yamāmah" (the east-central region of Arabia). The name Musaylamah, by which the Muslims called him, was a contemptuous diminutive of his real name, Maslamah. He was slain in battle by Waḥshī, the slave who had killed Ḥamzah at Uḥud. The Muslim army was led by Khālid ibn Walīd.

The battle at 'Aqrabah in the Yamāmah between the Muslim forces and those of Musaylamah was the most bloody that Arabia had ever seen. The followers of Musaylamah had already defeated one Muslim force led by 'Ikrimah. At 'Aqrabah, Khālid ibn Walīd divided his army into Beduins, Anṣār (Medinans) and Muhājirūn (Meccan emigrants) to spur competition among them to fight to the utmost. When the Muslims appeared to be losing the struggle, the Anṣār were roused by insults from the rebels and turned the tide. The rebels retreated into a fortified orchard where Musaylamah sat, but then were pursued by the Muslims and there slaughtered. In this battle seven hundred of the Companions were killed, among them some of the oldest, and seven thousand of the followers of Musaylamah. The orchard came to be called "the Garden of Death".

Although more rebellions had yet to be put down in Oman and the Yemen, this battle announced the imminent end of the period of strife which broke out among the desert Arabs after the Prophet's death. During this period, a number of imitators of the Prophet appeared; the *Kahīnah* ("Prophetess") in the north among the Tamīm; Dhū-l-Ḥimār in the Yemen, and others. It is called the *Riddah* (the "period of apostasy").

Mūsā Shākir, the Sons of. Three brothers, Aḥmad, Ḥasan, and Muḥammad, who acquired renown as scientists at the court of Baghdad in the *3rd*/9th century. They were mathematicians, astronomers, and engineers who designed the mechanical creations of the time. Known as the

Banū Mūsā, they participated in the labor of translating Hellenistic writings into Arabic at the *Bayt al-Ḥikmah*, the academy founded by the Caliph al-Ma'mūn (d. *218*/833). A work of theirs on geometry was translated into Latin as the *Liber Trium Fratrum* ("the Book of Three Brothers").

Mushrabiyyah. (Also *mashrabiyyah* and *mashrabah*). Lattices made of turned dowels, they are typical features of Islamic architecture throughout the Middle East, North Africa, Persia and India. The carved wooden lattice, which forms a pleasing contrast to the often unadorned exteriors of buildings, keep out the hot sun whilst allowing the air to pass.

Mushrikūn (lit. "those who associate"). Idolators. *See* SHIRK.

Muslim (lit. "one who has surrendered to God", from Ar. *aslama*, "to surrender, to seek peace").

1. A Moslem, an adherent of Islam. The word implies complete surrender, submission, and resignation to God's Will. The Muslim is submitted; ideally, therefore, it is not the Muslim who acts, but God, and the actions of the Muslim are an appearance due to his swift and spontaneous obedience to the decrees of fate. This is why the Sufis say that one must be like "a body in the hands of the washers of the dead", moving without resistance to the Divine Will. In this there is peace – "*salām*", "surrender", "wholeness", "security". The word *islām* ("surrender", "submission") is the verbal noun corresponding to the adjective *muslim* ("surrendered", "submitted"). It is, incidentally, important to pronounce the *s* of *Muslim* sharply as in the English word "slim"; the voiced pronunciation with the *s* as in "chisel" or "nose", produces a word which means – or sounds somewhat like a word that means – "benighted", cruel", and which is therefore offensive.

2. Abū-l-Ḥusayn Muslim (*210-261*/816-873), born at Nayshābūr, the great compiler of Ḥadīth. His *Ṣaḥīḥ al-Muslim* and the *Ṣaḥīḥ al-Bukhārī* rank as the two most authentic collections.

Muslims, Black, *see* BLACK MUSLIMS.

Muslim Brotherhood (Ar. *al-Ikhwān al-Muslimūn*). A religious organization founded in Egypt in 1929 by Ḥasan al-Bannā', it opposed the tendency towards secular regimes in Muslim countries.

Ḥasan al-Bannā' was assassinated in 1949, and in 1954 the movement was banned in Egypt. It has existed since as a clandestine opposition movement in Egypt, Syria, Sudan, and other countries in the Middle East. Its goal, which is that of the establishment of "Islamic states", is pursued by assassination and terrorism. In Syria, the first priority of the movement is opposition to domination by the 'Alawīs. The Muslim Brotherhood is held responsible for perhaps more than its share of underground political opposition.

They should not be confused with the *ikhwān* ("brothers"), the desert warriors who helped King 'Abd al-'Azīz in the conquest of Arabia. The name *ikhwān* was also used for Beduin settlement projects in Arabia such as at al-Artawiyyah.

Musnad. The collection of 30,000 Ḥadīth made by Ibn Ḥanbal (d. *241*/855). *See* ḤADĪTH; IBN ḤANBAL.

Mustaḍ'afūn (lit: "the downtrodden"). A term made current by the Ayatollah Khomeini in the course of the Iranian revolution. Like the "*sans culottes*" of the French Revolution, or the "*descamisados*" of Juan Peron, it refers to the disadvantaged whose interest the Iranian revolution claimed to serve. In Iran it is pronounced *mostazafun*. The Pahlavi Foundation was renamed the Mustaḍ'afūn Foundation.

Shī'ism has always been the movement of radical popular causes and has claimed to be the champion of the oppressed; at the same time the main beneficiaries have been the leadership, the party, the "vanguard" and nouveau riche that emerged as a result of political upheaval.

Mustaḥabb. The category of actions which, whilst not being obligatory in canon law, are recommended. This is also called *mandūb*. The other categories are *farḍ*, or *wājib*, that is, obligatory; *mubāḥ*, permitted or neutral; *makrūh*, disliked and thus discouraged; and *ḥarām*, forbidden. All actions fall into one of these categories, under Islamic law. *See* FARḌ; ḤARĀM.

Mutabārikūn (lit. "those who would participate

in blessing"). Those who enter a Sufi *ṭarīqah*, or "fraternity" (lit. "path"), to seek a blessing in addition to the blessings accorded by adherence to the *sharī'ah* ("the outward Divine Law"). The *mutabārikūn* are thus passive members of a *ṭarīqah*. The active members are those who enter the path because they see in it a way to union with God. The latter are called the *sālikūn*, or "travelers".

The *mutabārikūn* recognize the *ṭarīqah* as a means of grace but do not grasp its possibility as a means of realization. As there are *ṭuruq* ("fraternities") that number hundreds of thousands of adherents, and in the North African desert often include whole communities and towns, it must be assumed that the vast majority are *mutabārikūn*.

al-Mu'tafikah (lit. "the overwhelmed ones"). In the Koran, the fated cities of the plain Sodom and Gomorrah, associated with the Prophet Lot (Ar. *Lūṭ*), which were destroyed.

Mut'ah. A marriage stipulated to be temporary, sometimes called a "marriage of pleasure". The marriage is automatically terminated at the end of the agreed period. *Mut'ah* is allowed by the Twelve-Imām Shī'ites, but forbidden by the Sunnīs.

al-Mutanabbī (d. *303-354*/915-965). One of the most famous of Arab poets. The name *Mutanabbī* means the "would-be Prophet", an allusion to the claim, attributed to him, that he was able to write poetry comparable to the language of the Koran. He had, in fact, in his youth been involved in various Shī'ite conspiracies, according to certain of his biographers, and had actually claimed prophethood and the receipt of revelation. His real name was Abū-t-Ṭayyib Aḥmad ibn al-Ḥusayn al-Ju'fī. He was a court panegyrist, and one who could change his allegiance, and was noted also for his impassioned yet pessimistic view of life. He often extolled Beduin *mores* in his poetry. His quixotic independence, arrogance, boasting and generosity have endeared him to generations of Arabs, who feel an affinity with him; and he was a master of the Arabic language. His most famous line is: "The horseman, night and the desert know me; and the sword and the lance, paper and the pen."

The measure of the resolute is seen in their resolves.
As generous deeds display the worth of noble souls.
Honor the man of noble soul, he becomes your slave, but the mean-souled man when honored grows insolent.
Naught will suffice for the understanding of men
When the light of day itself stands in need of proof.
Whoso desires the ocean makes light of streams.
Men bury and are buried and our feet trample the skulls of those who went before.

Mutaṭāwi'ah (lit. "those who enforce obedience"). A peculiar institution of vigilantes who enforce the performance of prayer and may even inflict beatings for moral laxity. They are found only in some fundamentalist milieus. The practice of the public enforcement of morality by such means is not common in Islam as a whole because of the Koran's insistence that "There is no compulsion in religion" (2:258).

Strict public enforcement of morality, not unlike that of the *mutaṭāwiah*, was prominent in theocratic republics such as that founded by 'Abd al-Karīm in the Rīf in the 1920s, and in the communities in the Caucasus under Imām Shāmil.

Mutawalli. The administrator of a religious establishment; a term encountered mainly in Iran and India.

Mutawila, *see* METAWILA.

Muṭawwif (from Ar. *ṭāfa*, "to circumambulate", from which comes *ṭawāf*, "circumambulation of the Ka'bah"). One who guides pilgrims in the performance of the rites of pilgrimage, whether *ḥajj* or *'umrah*. The *muṭawwifūn* are residents of Mecca, many of them Qurayshīs. They were a guild in classical times, and the right to be a *muṭawwif* is handed down in the family, but today requires a royal patent.

While it is not necessary to hire a *muṭawwif* in order to perform the *'umrah*, regulations require that pilgrims arriving for *ḥajj* be assigned to a *muṭawwif*, either one of their own choice or one designated by the authorities. The *muṭawwif* works through representatives and handles thousands of pilgrims at *ḥajj* time, providing lodging and transportation, and sometimes food as well. *Muṭawwifs* guide pilgrims according to their respective *madhāhib*, or schools of law.

There are published fees covering various aspects of the *ḥajj* services which are fixed by the Saudi government. Arrangements can be made with a *muṭawwif* in advance of the actual pilgrimage, and it was once the practice for *muṭawwifs* to travel in Islamic countries in order to prospect for clients.

For the *'umrah*, *muṭawwifs* can be found in the Grand Mosque (*al-Masjid al-Ḥarām*), sometimes at the gates, near the Maqām Ibrāhīm, or near Ṣafā and Marwah. Usually they collect several pilgrims together to perform the rites as a group. *See* ḤAJJ.

Mu'tazilites (from Ar. *a'tazala*, "to take one's distance", "to remove oneself", "to withdraw"). A school of thought that was born out of, or inserted itself into, the controversies of the civil war between 'Alī ibn Abī Ṭalīb and the Companions az-Zubayr and Ṭalḥāh, and the absolute black-and-white condemnatory views of the Khārijites. Faced with a conflict between opposing parties, none of whom could reasonably be considered absolutely reprehensible, the need arose for dogmatic nuances. One response was formulated as: *manzilah bayna-l-manzilatayn* ("a position between the two positions"). This was the answer to a question treated in the circle of Ḥasan al-Baṣrī as to whether a Muslim who had committed a grave sin was a believer or not, in which the Khārijite position was that one who had committed a grave sin was no longer a believer, and therefore could be put to death. Ḥasan al-Baṣrī's answer was that such a one was a believer but a hypocrite; that of Waṣīl ibn 'Atā' (d. *131*/748) was that he was neither a believer nor an infidel, but somewhere between the two, and this marked the beginning of the Mu'tazilite school, those who "had taken their distance" from Ḥasan al-Baṣrī, as the great teacher reportedly had said.

This position between two positions is what is known in Christianity as the Arian heresy; philosophically it is a violation of Aristotle's law of non-contradiction; which is to say it is a violation of objective reality, and opens the door to total subjectivism and solipsism. Which is also why the Chalcedonian answer is theologically another version of Aristotle's law and a fundamental statement about the nature of reality. Formulations like the position between two positions appear constantly in different disguises and are infinitely tempting for they are the illusory having it both ways.

The other prominent figures of the new school were 'Amr ibn 'Ubayd (d. *145*/762), and later Abū Ḥudhayl (d. *235*/849) and an-Naẓẓām (d. *225*/840), who was the most important formulator of the Mu'tazilite teachings. The school took stock of the philosophic tools of Hellenistic antiquity, and applied reason to the solution of philosophical problems, leading thereby to the birth of *kalām*, Islamic theology itself. Mu'tazilitism catered to certain ideologies in Persia, and through its historical position between the point of view of the Umayyads and the Shī'ites, it lent itself easily for a time to being the dominant philosophy of the 'Abbāsids. Its doctrine of free will, moreover, could be used as an arm against the Umayyads, who defended their regime with arguments of Divine predestination propounded by the traditionalists (*ahl al-ḥadīth*).

Although the theology may have been invented in order to move Islam onto dualist tracks, the Mu'tazilites themselves, like antibodies created after vaccination, became opponents of dualism.

The Mu'tazilites held, as rationalists (and materialists), that the Koran is created. (The orthodox dogma is that the Koran is uncreated in its essence.) This was proclaimed official doctrine by the Caliph al-Ma'mūn in *212*/827 and enforced by a *miḥnah*, a scrutiny of the beliefs held by the various religious authorities, which was a virtual inquisition. Ibn Ḥanbal, founder of one of the schools of law, was scourged for publicly maintaining the uncreatedness of the Koran (in a particularly categorical fashion: he said the Koran is "uncreated from cover to cover"; this could also be taken as an anti-materialist stance). But shortly thereafter, when, under the Caliph Mutawakkil, this doctrine was suppressed, the Mu'tazilites went into a sharp decline and fell out of favor, until it reappeared as the theology of Twelve Imām Shī'ism. Today, the outlook which results from Mu'tazilitism is also evident in modern movements among Sunnīs.

Nevertheless, the influence exerted by the school was considerable: it established the widespread use of rational arguments in the subsequent development of theology, and many of its original conclusions were adopted by the mainstream, although the school as a whole was attacked as heretical.

The Mu'tazilites called themselves *ahl al-'adl wa-l-tawḥīd* (the "People of Justice and [Divine] Unity"), and their school was based upon the following five principles:

1. *tawḥīd* ("unity");
2. *'adl* ("justice");
3. *al-wa'd wa-l-wa'īd* ("the promise and the threat");
4. *al-manzilah bayn al-manzilatayn* ("a position between two positions");
5. *al-amr bi-l-ma'rūf wa-n-nahy 'an al-munkar* ("commanding the good and prohibiting evil").

By *tawḥīd* they meant a paradoxical doctrine; Sunnīs say that some of the divine attributes ("Names") are of the Essence and some are of Being. By the Mu'tazilite *tawḥīd,* the essence is unknowable, and none of the attributes are of the Essence; these attributes or Names are reduced to a kind of demiurgic level, to being some kind of created energies.

This unknowability of God led the Mu'tazilites to deny the generally accepted idea that those whom salvation brings into paradise have a vision of God, arguing that such seeing of God would place Him within space. The Ash'arite and Sunnī position is that God is knowable; that some Divine Names are names of the Essence and not some created energy. This became symbolized by the vision in Paradise. (*See* BEATIFIC VISION.) The Prophet is credited with saying that the inhabitants of paradise would see God. When asked how, he said "as people see the full moon"; i.e. by reflection as the moon reflects the light of the sun.

It is these problems which al-Ash'arī, emerging out of Mu'tazilitism, addressed with his theory of atoms of time and space which are "mirrors" of the One Reality, and his theory of will as the "acquiring of Divine action on the part of the creature" (*iktisāb*).

In the orthodox idea, according to which God is both Absolute and Being (*Hāhūt* and *Lāhūt*), there is a continuity of identity between the Attributes and the Absolute. The Attributes are not the Essence, neither are they anything other than the Essence; an inescapable and necessary antinomy. It is this vertical identity, "with God and One with God", which is true non-duality, in virtue of which the Divine Attributes are not other Divinities. (*See* BEING; FIVE DIVINE PRESENCES.) The Mu'tazilite *tawḥīd,* like that of some modern philosophers such as Martin Buber, is a unity in name only; the question of how the supposed unity can contain differentiated contraries is simply ignored.

By *'adl* ("justice") they affirmed that man has free will, which is necessary because of Divine justice. (The early Shī'ites believed that God created and determined Men's acts; present day Shī'ites believe in free will). The Mu'tazilites also asserted that God does what is best (*ṣalāḥ* or *aṣlaḥ*) for the world he has created; that God compensates the saved for sufferings they endured in life. What makes this idea of Divine justice scandalous, however, is that it means that what a man does obliges God; it puts God on an equal plane with man; if a man does a good act, God must react accordingly, if a man does an evil act God must react accordingly. What the Mu'tazilite Divine justice means, therefore, is *reciprocity* between man and God. The absurdity of this was not lost on the detractors; but because of the psychology which results from a position between two positions neither did it faze the supporters, contradictions were not a problem. It was one thing to make God observe the necessity of his Own Nature, as did Aristotle; it was another to make Him dependent upon something created.

The Ash'arites claimed, not without reason, that Mu'tazilitism made God into a servant of man, because it made him respond to human acts and made God, as they put it, into the impregnator of women. The idea of *ṣalāḥ* became the point on which al-Ash'arī revolted against the Mu'tazilites, neatly showing its weakness, (but not, however, disproving the idea that necessity is an aspect of perfection). (*See* al-ASH'ARĪ; CHILDREN.)

By the third principle they meant heaven and hell. They believed that if someone went to hell, he would not leave by reason of Divine Mercy or intercession. (Reciprocity, above, limits God's ability to act; the Ash'arites, on the contrary, believe that sins may be pardoned even in hell, or that a believer may be withdrawn from hell once his sins are expiated.) Present day Shī'ites generally accept that a sinner can be saved from hell because, ironically, of the power of the Imāms.

The fourth principle, "a position between two positions" was, on the one hand, their philosophical method, but also their political outlook in the historic controversies. This was a middle position between the Sunnīs and the Shī' ites (of the *3rd*/9th century who were more *ghulat* than the Twelvers have been until recently, although this is again changing), which made the creed of the Mu'tazilites the chosen theology of the early 'Abbāsids, and the decisive theological influence upon the Shī'ites. (It would perhaps be more accurate to say that Mu 'tazilitism was the doctrine of those who brought the 'Abbāsids to power, and therefore they were obliged to accept it until power shifted.)

In present day Shī'ism this idea of "the position between two positions", in so far as it relates to the idea of a sinner being between belief and unbelief, has been abandoned. The Shī'ites, apart from the doctrine of the Imāms, developed their theology much later, under the Buyids. By that time Mu'tazilite thinking had already formed the base of Twelve-Imām theology, through the Nawbakhti family of Baghdad, and, being established, was not further modified, while the doctrine of the Imāmate continued to undergo development.

There is in Mu'tazilitism a strong flavour of a metaphysical outlook alien to Islam. This was recognised even before al-Ash'arī, for the following Ḥadīth (evidently invented but showing the reaction of an affronted orthodoxy) gained wide circulation: "The Mu'tazilites are the Mājūs [an all-embracing name for the religions of Persia]; do not follow one of them as a prayer leader, and do not attend their funerals." The fifth principle, the establishment of order in society, was not different from the view of the Sunnīs. *See* al-ASH'ARĪ; "BEATIFIC VISION"; CHILDREN; CREED; ḤASAN BAṢRĪ; ISTAWĀ; KALĀM; KHĀRIJITES; KUMŪN; al-MA'MŪN; MĀTURĪDĪ; MIHNAH; PHILOSOPHY.

al-Muwaḥḥidūn (lit. "the unitarians"). The name by which the Wahhābīs prefer to call themselves, and also the Druzes, and the Arabic name of the Almohad movement. Despite the name, however, there is no connection whatsoever between the three groups. *See* ALMOHADS; DRUZES; WAHHĀBĪS.

Muwaqqatah (from Ar. *waqt*, "time"). The establishment of the correct times for the daily prayers. Because the prayer times change with the position of the sun, this must be done each day. The need to know exact time encouraged the study of astronomy, and up until this century muezzins often learned to use astrolabes. In 1900 the last man in Fez still skilled in the use of the astrolabe was over 100 years old and had no more disciples.

For a simple means of determining prayer times, *see* ṢALĀH *and also* PRAYER.

Muwaṭṭa' (lit. "The Way made Smooth"). This is the name of the first compilation of Ḥadīth. It was made by Mālik ibn Anas (*94-179*/716-795) of Medina, the founder of the Mālikī School of Law. It is not as systematic as the *ṣaḥīḥān* of Muslim and Bukhari, but it laid the foundation for Ḥadīth studies. *See* MĀLIK IBN ANAS.

Muzawwir (from *ziyārah*, "a visit"). A guide who leads visitors through the steps of a formal visit to the Prophet's mosque in Medina and the environs. Also called simply a guide, *dalīl*. *See* ZIYĀRAH.

Muzdalifah. A place between 'Arafāt, 8 km/3.5 miles away, and Minā, 3.5 km/2 miles distant from Mecca. Here pilgrims spend the night after the "standing of the Day of 'Arafāt" during the *ḥajj*. They pray at *al-Mash'ar al-Ḥarām* monument and gather pebbles for the ceremony of the stoning of the *jamarāt*, the stone pillars which represent the devil, in Minā. *See* PILGRIMAGE.

Mysticism, *see* SUFISM.

N

Nabī. A Prophet, one who prophesies within an existing revelation, as opposed to a *rasūl* ("messenger"), who brings a new revelation. *See* PROPHET.

Naḍīr Shāh, *see* AFSHARIDS.

Nafas ar-Raḥmān (lit. "the breath of the Merciful"). A term in Sufi metaphysics for the manifestation of possibilities, and thus for the creation of the world, based upon the symbolism of the breath. The world is created by God figuratively "breathing out". Creation, and man, receives the breath and with it the means – life – to return to the Creator. The "breathing in" by God is a reabsorption of creation, an extinction of manifested possibilities in Being, and, in the apocatastasis, the disappearance of Being, *Lāhūt*, "the Personal God".

Speech in man, which is vehicled by the breath, is an analogous function. In speaking man makes manifest or objective that which is subjective and hidden within him. The hearer receives the speech and understands it or integrates it into his subjectivity, or consciousness. Breath, – *prāṇa* – *spiritus* – which is life itself, is thus the sacred medium in which creation takes place.

The Koran says that God is Creator at every instant (55:29); this eternal creation is sometimes referred to as the "overflowing" (*fayḍ*) of Being, or the "renewing of creation at each instant" or "each breath" (*tajdīd al-khalq bi-l-anfas*). In the *Fuṣūṣ al-Ḥikam*, the chapter on Solomon, Ibn 'Arabī wrote that man does not "spontaneously realize that with each breath he is not, and then again is" (*lam yakun thumma kān*), because the moment of annihilation coincides with the moment of manifestation, and because the act of creation is instantaneous. In history there are progressions of events and change, but metaphysically, the process of creation is continuous and instantaneous, the world being made anew at every instant, differently, reflecting the flux and progression within it.

An incidental meaning of the term *nafas ar-Raḥmān* is a celebration which is held when a pupil in a traditional Koranic school has memorized the Koran from the beginning, the Sūrah *al-Baqarah*, up to the 55th Sūrah called *ar-Raḥmān* ("the Merciful"). *See* ARABIC; KALĀM; SOLOMON.

Nāfilah (pl. *nawāfil*). The voluntary prayers consisting of one, two, or four *raka'āts* which the pious add before and after canonical prayers (*ṣalāh*). *Nawāfil* are not performed, however, after the performance of the dawn prayer (*ṣubḥ*) until the sun has risen, and after the mid-afternoon prayer (*'aṣr*) has been performed until the evening prayer (*maghrib*).

The *nawāfil* provide a means for the increased exercise of zeal and devotion on the exoteric plane. In addition to the *nawāfil* which accompany the canonical prayers, there are additional prayers which can be performed at certain times: for example, the *ishrāq*, a supplementary prayer in the morning after sunrise; the *ḍuḥā*, performed before noon; and the *tahajjud*, at night. There are also special prayers such as the *istikhārah*, or "asking for help in choosing the good". Religious teachers recommend that, if one does perform the supplementary prayers, they should occasionally be omitted to underline their optional character.

Nafs. The soul. The Arabic *nafs* corresponds to the Latin *anima* and the Greek *psyche*. It is the individual substance, and corresponds to the receptive pole of Being. It exists alongside *rūḥ* ("spirit"), corresponding to Latin *spiritus* and Greek *pneuma*, which is non-individual and represents the active pole of Being in man, also called the *'aql* ("Intellect"). (*See* 'AQL.)

Often the term *nafs* is used in a pejorative sense, because in its fallen, unregenerate state, admixed with passion and ignorance, it is *an-nafs al-ammārah bi-s-sū'* ("the soul which incites to evil", 12:53). Passing through the stage of *an-nafs al-lawwāmah* ("the reproachful soul", 75:2), which corresponds in some sort to conscience, advocating conversion, it can become purified and reconciled to the source of its reality as *an-nafs al-muṭma'innah* ("soul at peace") assured of paradise:

> O soul at peace, return unto thy Lord,
> well-pleased, well-pleasing!
> Enter thou among My servants!
> Enter thou My paradise!' (89:27).

See FIVE DIVINE PRESENCES; RŪḤ.

Nafy (lit. "negation"). The first part of the *shahādah* ("testimony of the faith") is *lā ilāha* ("there is no god"). This is the *nafy*, the negation of unreality, which precedes the *ithbāt* ("affirmation") *illā' Llāh* ("except Allāh"). *See* SHAHĀDAH.

Nahj al-Balāghah (lit. "the way of eloquence"). A collection of sermons, sayings, and speeches attributed to 'Alī ibn Abī Ṭālib. It was compiled by ash-Sharīf ar-Rāḍi (d. *406*/1015), a Shī'ite scholar, the brother of Sayyid al-Murtaḍa (d. *436*/1044), and a disciple of the Shaykh al-Mufīd (d. *413*/1022).

The book is a model for classical Arabic style, as Cicero is for Latin.

Nahr. The sacrificial slaughter of a camel. *See* SACRIFICE.

Nā'ib. A deputy of a civil authority; also, in certain Sufi orders, the representative of a Sufi Shaykh, superior to a *muqaddam* ("representative").

Najaf. The site in Iraq of the tomb of 'Alī ibn Abī Ṭālib, the fourth Caliph. The actual place of burial is not known; 'Alī was assassinated at Kufah and some say that he was buried there in the courtyard of the Mosque. The Shī'ites, however, explain that the dead body, according to 'Alī's wish, was placed upon a camel and the place where it knelt became the burial place, Najaf being four miles from Kufah. Tradition relates that intuition led the Caliph Hārūn ar-Rashīd (d. *194*/809) to recognize the place as the site while hunting, and to build a shrine there. From *366*/977 an important tomb built by the Buyid chief Adūd ad-Dawlah stood there; it was destroyed and rebuilt a number of times.

The shrine of 'Alī is known among Shī'ites as the *Mashhad Gharwah* ("the wondrous place of martyrdom"). Mazār-i Sharīf in Afghanistan also claims to be the tomb of 'Alī. This is impossible, in fact, but it is not impossible that the blessing of 'Alī should be found in both places.

Najd (lit. "the highlands"). The central plain of Arabia where Riyāḍ, the capital of Saudi Arabia, is located.

Najrān. A city and region in southern Arabia near the Yemen, before Islam, it was an oasis, with a Christian population and the seat of a bishopric. A Himyarite king called Dhū Nuwās ("he of the curls", his actual name was Yusūf As'ar), a convert to Judaism, called upon the people of Najrān to abandon Christianity for his own Jewish religion. When they refused, he had them slaughtered and thrown into burning ditches. When the Emperor of Byzantium, Justin I, heard of the massacre, as protector of Christianity he called upon the Negus of Abyssinia, Ella Aṣbeḥa, another Christian king, to punish Dhū Nuwās. The Negus sent an army in 525 A.D. and Dhū Nuwās was killed. The martyrs of Najrān are remembered in the Christian calendars and are mentioned in the Koran 85:4-8:

> ...slain were the Men of the Pit,
> the fire abounding in fuel,
> when they were seated over it
> and were themselves witnesses of what they did with the believers.
> They took revenge on them only because they believed in God
> the All-mighty, the All-laudable...

The traces of the original Najrān can still be seen in the desert. The bishops of Najrān, who were probably Nestorians, came to the great fairs of Minā and 'Ukāẓ, and preached Christianity, each seated on a camel as in a pulpit.

In the tenth year of the Hijrah a delegation of sixty Christians from Najrān came to Medina to make a treaty with the Prophet, and were permitted by him to pray in his mosque. Najrān was a center of cloth making and originally the *kiswah* or covering of the Ka'bah was made there. The church of Najrān was called the Ka'bah Najrān. (Several other shrines in Arabia were also called Ka'bah). *See* AHL al-KISĀ'; CHRISTIANITY; NESTORIANS.

Nāmāz (Pers. "prayer"). This Persian word replaces the Arabic word *ṣalāh* as the name for the canonic prayer from Turkey to India.

Name (Ar. *al-ism*). Muslim names are made up of a proper name followed by a *naṣab*, a name referring to an ancestor in the form of *ibn* ("son") or *bint* ("daughter") and the name of the father, then the grandfather, and so on for as many generations as one has patience. A person could also be called by a *kunyah*, an indirect honorific name whose form was that of "father of" (*Abū*), or "mother of" (*Umm*). *Kunyahs* could become proper names in themselves, without the person actually being the "father of 'Abbās" (Abū-l-'Abbās), and be combined with an *ism* ("name"), a *naṣab*, and so forth. To the name by usage could also be added a *nisbah* (an "association"), which could be the place of birth, such as ar-Rūmī, ("from Rum", that is, Byzantine Konya) or ar-Rāzī ("from the town of Rayy"), or the name of a profession such as al-Khayyām ("tentmaker") or al-Ḥāsib ("accountant or mathematician"), or a clan or tribal name such as al-Hāshimī ("of the Hashimites"), or a distinction, such as al-Anṣārī, one descended from the original Muslim converts of Medina. Then one could have an honorific formal name, which replaced the given name in ceremonial usage, a *laqab*. Such names were adopted by the later 'Abbāsids when they became Caliph, such as al-Manṣūr ("the Victor") and were given out, in very ostentatious forms, to the Buyid princes such as *'Imād ad-Dawlah* ("Pillar of the State").

When the Prophet accepted converts to Islam, many of them had distinctly pagan names, such as Slave of the goddess 'Uzzā. These he changed for Muslim names; when a person already had an acceptable name, the Prophet sometimes left it as it was, adding a Muslim name to it. Since then, when one enters Islam, he is given or chooses a Muslim name. As a name has a great and mysterious resonance upon the soul, giving it a sacred identity and a dignity towards which it must grow, or, if a profane name, a weight of triviality or profanity which drags the soul down, the choice of a name which transmits a presence of nobility and piety is a matter of gravity. Therefore, it is common to consult the Koran when the choice of a name comes up, and nothing otherwise directly suggests itself.

Names define the object or person named; thus the more important, sacred, or profound an object or a person is, the more names there are to describe it. For example, there are many names for the Koran, and for the cities of Mecca and Medina. The Names of God are limited by those which have been revealed, but the Prophet is identified by two hundred names (of which, however, only a handful would be commonly recognized). *See* DIVINE NAMES; ISM; KUNYAH; LAQAB; NAṢAB; NISBAH.

Name, Divine *see* ALLĀH; DIVINE NAMES; ISM;

Names of the Prophet. The *Dalā'il al-Khayrāt* ("Guides to Good Works") of al-Jazūlī lists two hundred names of the Prophet; others list even more. This is a selection of the traditional names:

'Abd Allāh	The Servant of God
Abū-l-Qāsim	Father of Qasim
Abū Ibrāhīm	Father of Ibrahim
Aḥmad	The Most-Praised
Ajmal Khalq Allāh	The Most Beautiful of God's Creation
'Alam al-Hudā	The Banner of Guidance
al-Amīn	The Faithful
'Ayn an-Naīm	The Fount of Blessings
Bāligh	The Proclaimer
al-Bashīr	The Bringer of Good Tidings
al-Burhān	The Proof
Dalīl al-Khayrāt	The Guide to Good Deeds
Dār al-Ḥikmah	The Abode of Wisdom
Dhikr Allāh	The Remembrance of God
al-Fātiḥ	The Opener
al-Ghawth	The Redeemer
Habīb Allāh	The Beloved of God
al-Ḥāshir	The Gatherer on the Day of Judgement
al-'Ilm al-Yaqīn	The Knowledge that is Certitude
Imām al-Muttaqīn	The Model Leader of the God-Fearing
al-Kāmil	The Perfect
Kāshif al-Karb	The Effacer of Grief
Khalīl ar-Raḥmān	The Friend of the All-Compassionate
Khātim al-Anbiyā'	The Seal of the Prophets
Khātim ar-Rusul	The Seal of the Messengers
Madīnat al-'Ilm	The City of Knowledge
al-Mahdī	The Rightly-Guided
al-Mas'ūm	The Infallible
Miftāḥ al-Jannah	The Key of Paradise
Miftāḥ ar-Raḥmah	The Key of Mercifulness
al-Miṣbāḥ	The Niche of Lights

Muḥammad	The Praised
al-Muḥyī	The Reviver
al-Munīr	The Illuminator
al-Muṣṭāfā	The Chosen
an-Nabī	The Prophet
an-Nadhīr	The Warner
an-Najm ath-Thāqib	The Piercing Star
an-Nūr	The Light
al-Qamar	The Moon
Rāfī' ar-Ruṭab	The Exalter of Ranks
Raḥmah li'l-'Ālamīn	A Mercy to the Universe
Rahmaṭ Allāh	The Mercifulness of God
ar-Rasūl	The Messenger
Rūḥ al-Ḥaqq	The Spirit of Truth
Rūḥ al-Quddūs	The Holy Spirit
aṣ-Ṣādiq	The Truthful
Ṣāḥib al-Bayyān	Master of the Clarification
Ṣāḥib ad-Darajah ar-Rafī'	Lord of the Exalted Degree
Ṣāḥib al-Mi'rāj	The Possessor of Ascension
as-Sayyid	The Liege Lord
Sayyid al-Kawnayn	Liege Lord of the Two Worlds
Sayyid al-Mursalīn	Liege Lord of the Messengers
Shāfi' al-Mudhnibīn	The Intercessor for Sinners
ash-Shāhid	The Witness
ash-Shams	The Sun
ash-Shāri'	The Legislator
aṣ-Ṣirāṭ al-Mustaqīm	The Straight Path
Ṭā' Hā'	(Sūrah of the Koran)
aṭ-Ṭāhir	The Pure
aṭ-Ṭayyib	The Good
Walī Allāh	The Friend of God (The Saint)
al-Wakīl	The Advocate
al-Wāṣil	The Joiner
Yā 'Sīn	(Sūrah of the Koran)

See MUḤAMMAD.

Nāmūs (from Greek *nomos*, "law"). An archaic term, borrowed from the Christians, for Being, or the personal God. It was personified as an Angel who imparted knowledge or brought revelations. This was the Angel, one could say, of *intellection*, or knowledge obtained through the universal contents of the mind being brought to consciousness in the lightning flash of recognition, a "natural" revelation. "As often as it [lightning] flasheth forth for them they walk therein and when it darkeneth against them they stand still." (2:20).

Waraqah Ibn Nawfal, a cousin of Khadījah, the Prophet's wife, identified the Angel bringing revelations to the Prophet as the *Nāmūs*. *See* WARAQAH IBN NAWFAL.

Naqshbandiyyah. A prominent Sufi order founded by Muḥammad ibn Muḥammad Bahā' ad-Dīn Naqshband (*717-791*/1317-1389) of Bukhara. Silence as a method of recollectedness and concentration is characteristic of the order, which is particularly widespread in the Caucasus and Central Asia. (Imām Shāmil was a Naqshbandī.) One of the special Naqshbandī prayers is called the *khatm al-Khawājagān* ("the seal of the masters") and is recited after some of the canonic prayers. (Most Sufi orders have something similar, which is invocation of its initiatic chain, in effect a belief that the past masters can help the disciple.) The principal spiritual method of the Naqhshbandīs is *dhikr* ("invocation") with the heart. The Divine Name is invoked not with the tongue, but with the consciousness centered on the spiritual heart, the subtle symbolical center of the person, which may or may not coincide with the awareness of the physical heart. It is this spiritual center which calls upon the Name in an existential rather than mental invocation. The method bears some resemblance to the Hesychast prayer of the heart, but is not identical with it. *See* KUBRA: LAṬĀ'IF.

Nasab (lit. "lineage", "descent", "derivation"). Generally used of a name which refers to a parent, as Ibn Sa'ūd, the "Son of Sa'ūd", or Bint Jaḥsh, "the daughter of Jaḥsh". The *nasab* may be employed serially to indicate a line of descent from grandfather, great-grandfather and so on. The *nasab* may be used in addition to other given names indicating profession, ancestral home, etc. *See* NAME.

Naṣārā (lit. "Nazarene", sing. *naṣrānī*). An Arabic name for Christians. Today the formal name is *Masīḥī*, from *Masīḥ* ("Messiah"), a usage established by Christian missionaries.

Naskh (Lit. "deletion", "abrogation" or "copying", "transcription"). The principle by which certain verses of the Koran abrogate (or modify) others, which are then called *mansūkh* ("revoked"). What is generally at issue is the modification of a universal meaning by a more specific one, a modification caused by an historic change of circumstance. It is also a question of the "style" natural to a Divine revelation, which cannot speak with clauses, exceptions and qualifications in the manner of a legal document, but must be direct and absolute. One set of such direct and absolute statements may condition another set of direct and absolute statements which are thereby rendered *mansūkh*, or conditional; the original statement is not untrue, but is subordinated to another which is more immediately relevant. In this way, by *naskh*, or self-limitation, the "absoluteness" of the Koran accommodates itself to the relativities of the human situation. The Koran itself speaks of the principle in 2:106 and 16:101.

Naskhī. One of the most common styles of Arabic writing. *See* CALLIGRAPHY.

Nāṣir-ī Khusraw, (*394-452*/1003-1060). A Persian poet, born in Qubadian near Merv. He says he visited the court of Maḥmud of Ghaznah. Khusraw was a magistrate in Merv and perhaps a court poet who eulogized kings but later destroyed these poems when he underwent a mystical experience at the age of forty-one. In the experience someone appeared to him and rebuked him for drinking wine; this led him to go on pilgrimage to Mecca. Mecca may have been incidental to Fāṭimid Cairo as his real destination, for he went there first, stayed for six years and became invested as an Ismā'īlī *dā'i* ("propagandist") of high rank, the Ḥujjat of the Jazirah of Khorasan by the Fāṭmid Caliph al-Mustanṣir. He also met Abū-l-'Alā' al-Ma'arrī, the freethinking poet.

From Mecca he visited the Qarmatians in al-Aḥsa. On his return to Persia, he carried on Ismā'īlī agitation in Balkh until the Saljūq authorities forced him to flee. His opponents incited a mob to attack his house and his life was threatened. He fled to Mazandārān, and eventually to the valley of Yamgan ruled by the Emir of Badakshān in Afghanistan, where there was a Gnostic community dating back to pre-Islamic times. There he called himself "the prisoner of Yamgan" and there he is buried, venerated as the founder of a mystic order.

Khusraw expressed his religious ideas and philosophy in poetry, and his main works are the *Dīwān*, the *Safar-Nāmeh* ("The Book of Travels"), and the *Rawshanāī Nāmeh* ("Book of Light") probably written in *444*/1053. This is about Ismā'īlī concepts of Divine Unity, Logos, Universal Soul, the Human Soul and its Becoming, the necessity for a Spiritual Guide, and reward and punishment in the hereafter. It is 582 lines and is known as the *Shish Faṣl* ("The Six Chapters"). Also, he wrote the *Wajh-i Dīn* ("The Face of Religion"), *Gushāyish va Rahāyish* ("Release and Deliverance"), *Khwān al-Ikhwān* ("Feast of the Brethren"; here the author draws on many Ismā'īlī works which are no longer extant), the *Zād al-Musāfirīn* ("Provision for the Road") and the *Jāmi' al-Ḥikmatayn* ("Harmonization of the Two Wisdoms"), his attempt to harmonise Greek philosophy with the tenets of Islam and particularly Ismā'īlism, written at the request of the Emir of Badakshan. *See* MAZAR-I SHARIF; ISMĀ'ĪLĪS.

Nasoreans, *see* MANDAEANS.

Naṣṣ (lit. "designation", "appointment", "stipulation"). The designation of a successor. The Shī'ites contend that the succession to the Prophet, that is to say, the Caliphate, could not possibly be a matter for election, although, in the event, election is what happened, following the customs of the desert Arabs regarding their chiefs. For the Sunnīs the succession was largely, although not entirely, the temporal matter of selecting a leader from several possible candidates to oversee the worldly continuation of the Islamic community. For the Shī'ites the succession concerned the eminent and indispensable, spiritual functions of the Imāmate, which could only be filled first by 'Alī, and then by his descendants. For them, the statements the Prophet made at Ghadīr Khumm amounted to the designation or appointment (*naṣṣ*) of 'Alī, although the Shī'ites would say that the matter was determined in heaven at the time of creation itself. An early appellation for the Shī'ites was *Ahl an-Naṣṣ wa-t-Tayīn* ("People of Designation and Appointment").

The question of who was the true successor arose again later, and reached a head with the sons of Ja'far aṣ-Ṣādiq, the sixth Shī'ite Imām. The eldest son, Ismā'īl, who would normally have inherited the office, died before his father, thereby throwing the various partisans into confusion. *Naṣṣ* is Twelve-Imām Shī'ism's answer to the problem of this succession and the discrepancies of fate. The Twelvers explain that Ja'far withdrew the *naṣṣ* from Ismā'īl and gave it to the next oldest brother, Mūsā Qāzim. For good measure, and as a reason for the revocation, the partisans of Mūsā revile Ismā'īl as a drunkard; this accusation is also a symbolic rejection of the Sevener's theology and their attitude towards Islamic law. The Seveners, however, countered by maintaining that *naṣṣ* exists, but once given is irrevocable, and hence that Ismā'īl, pre-deceasing his father, had inherited the Imāmate even so, and passed it on to his son.

The development of the doctrine of *naṣṣ* affected the adherents of another branch of Shī'ism, the Zaydīs, causing them eventually to take a stand on the issue when it arose. For the Twelve-Imām Shī'ites the line of Imāms passed through Muḥammad al-Bāqir upon the death of 'Alī Zayn al-'Ābidīn, Shī'ism's fourth Imām. For them, it is thus Muḥammad al-Bāqir who received the *naṣṣ*. Yet it was Zayd, the brother of Muḥammad al-Bāqir, who actually headed resistance to the Umayyad Caliphate. The descendants of Zayd were politically successful in the Yemen, and thus Zaydism, or "Five Imām Shī'ism" came into being. The refutation of the doctrine of *naṣṣ* is therefore as fundamental to Zaydī Shī'ism as is its affirmation to the Twelvers. *See* GHADĪR KHUMM; IMĀM; SHĪ'ISM; ZAYDĪS.

Nāsūt. A technical term of Sufism describing the sphere of what is human and mortal, as contrasted with *lāhūt*, the sphere of the Divine nature. The Sufis make a pun on the word *nās* ("men", "Mankind"), purporting to derive it from the verb *nasiya* ("to forget"), thus equating human nature with forgetfulness of God.

The root of *al-insān* ("man") with its collective plural *nās* is actually *anisa* ("to experience", "to perceive", "to be sociable or intimate"). From it is derived the noun *uns* ("Intimacy"), another technical term of Sufism related to love for God. *See* FIVE DIVINE PRESENCES.

"Nation of Islam". The former name of the sect popularly known as the "Black Muslims" of America. The original Nation of Islam underwent great changes after the death of its founder Elijah Muḥammad in 1975 the majority being led by stages to orthodox Islam by Elijah Muḥammad's son Wallace, now named Warith Deen Muḥammad. This orthodox branch, centered in Chicago, took the name "American Muslim Mission". A dissident faction, led by Brother Louis Farrakhan, retains the name Nation of Islam as well as the sect's original anti-white and separatist doctrines. *See* "BLACK MUSLIMS".

Naw roz (Pers. originally meaning "new light" [*roz* being cognate with Latin *lux*], later coming to mean "new day"). It is the name of the festival of the new year, according to the Persian solar calendar, after the spring equinox on 21 March. It is a holiday celebrated in Iran, as are so many Islamic holidays, by family visiting.

Naw'ī. A pair of planets or stars, one of which is rising on the east horizon while the other is sinking on the west horizon at any moment, but particularly at sunrise and sunset. These pairs of planets play an important role in Arab astrology, more so than the descendant and ascendant in European astrology. *See* ASTROLOGY.

Neoplatonism, *see* PHILOSOPHY.

Nestorians. A branch of Christianity which separated from the mother church after the stormy Council of Ephesus, called in 431 to decide the controversy raised by the opposition of St. Cyril, Patriarch of Alexandria (supported by Pope Celestine I and representing the views of the majority of Christendom) to the views of Nestorius of Constantinople. Nestorius (d. 451), who had been named Patriarch of Constantinople in 428 by the Emperor Theodosius II, taught that Jesus possessed two natures, one human and one Divine. In that, he was in agreement with the general view, but he differed from it insofar as he taught that in Jesus there were also *two persons* (in the majority opinion there is *one* person), and that Jesus was at one time the Divine person and at others the human one.

The Council of Ephesus, after great struggles between the opposing factions, affirmed that in accordance with the Nicene Creed, Mary could be called "Mother of God" and that the Divine and human natures in Jesus were so coherent that they could not be separated into two persons; this was confirmed by the Council of Chalcedon of 451. Nestorius was then deposed by the

Council and sent into exile at Antioch, where many of his sympathizers were to be found. From there he went to Arabia and finally to Egypt. Nestorius' doctrine has been called *dyophysite*.

The sect which followed his teachings flourished, and Edessa (modern-day Urfa in Turkey) became its center. It adopted Syriac as its liturgical language in place of Greek. The Sassanid Persians welcomed the Nestorians as a Christian group inimical to the Byzantines, and thus it is that the Nestorians maintained a shool of philosophy and medicine founded in the 3rd century A.D. at Jundishāpūr, near Ahvāz, modern Sānābād, in Khuzistan. Together with Syriac-speaking Christian schools in Syria, the school of Jundishāpūr played an important role in transmitting Hellenistic learning to Islamic civilization. The Nestorian Bishopric of Urmia, in Western Persia, was, and still is, one of the ancient seats of this branch of Christianity. Nestorianism also spread throughout the Yemen and was probably the form of Christianity practiced in Najrān, in southern Arabia. Cooperation between the Nestorians and the Persians helped to lead to the Sassanid conquest of the Yemen at the end of the 6th century A.D. Nestorian Churches used to keep a copy of the agreement concluded between the Prophet and the Christians of Najrān, giving them the protection of the Islamic state (*see* NAJRĀN.)

Nestorian influence was at its height from the 7th century to the 12th, during the whole of which period the sect was very active, with scholar missionaries establishing churches in Persia, Central Asia, India, China, and among the Mongols. In 735 A.D. a group of Nestorian missionaries, whose leader was called in Chinese transcription A-lo-pen, received permission from the T'ang Emperor T'ai Tsung to found a church in Ch'ang An, then the capital of China. The Nestorians in China carved an intricate stone tablet which retold Old and New Testament versions of world history in Chinese and Syriac, and described their mission. At the beginning of the 9th century the tablet was buried as a result of persecutions of the Nestorians in China, and remained hidden until 1625 when it was unearthed in the course of excavations for buildings. It is today one of the great relics of religious history.

The Nestorians developed close relations with the 'Abbāsid dynasty and supplied the Muslims with many teachers, advisors, scholars, and physicians. The physician of Hārūn ar-Rashīd was Jibrā'īl Bakhtishishu, from a Nestorian family of seven generations of physicians.

The Nestorians, however, were also closely linked to the Mongols of Hūlāgū Khān whose horde destroyed Baghdad in 1258, for both the mother and the wife of Hūlāgū were Nestorian Christians, and perhaps the Nestorians had hoped to convert the as yet shamanist Mongols to Christianity, and to succeed where they had failed with the Muslims. They were, therefore, together with the Shī'ites, prominent advisors to the Mongols during their invasions of the Near East. In the end, however, it was Sunnī Islam that gained the conversion of the Mongols.

The Nestorians accord a great veneration to the Cross (which may account for the ancient and erroneous notion held by many Muslims that Christians worship the cross); they believe that their special altar bread is a "holy leaven" derived from the leaven of the bread at the Last Supper.

In Iraq the Nestorians and their Kurdish allies fought unsuccessfully against the Turks at the turn of the last century and again during World War I. During the mandate in Iraq, many Nestorians served in the British forces keeping order in the country. When the British left, the Nestorians found themselves again vulnerable, so that after harsh persecutions in the 19th and 20th centuries, many emigrated to America. Among the emigrants was the head of the church, the Catholikos, also called the "Patriarch of the East". The function of Catholikos is hereditary from uncle to nephew, as is that of Bishop.

The Nestorians are now frequently known as "Assyrian Christians", and groups are found in Syria, Iraq, Iran and the Malabar coast of India. Beginning centuries ago, a large group of the Assyrians have entered into communion with Rome and are called "Chaldean Catholics". *See* AHL al-KISĀ'Ī; CHRISTIANITY; JESUS; NAJRĀN.

"New Sect". A militant movement among Chinese Muslims directed against the Manchus. It was inspired by a Naqshabandī leader called Ma (Muḥammad) Ming-hsin (d. *1195*/1781). The "New Sect" was opposed to the acquiesence in the rule of non-Muslims that had become customary among Chinese Muslims, an attitude which was thereafter called the "Old Sect". The emergence of the New Sect led to rebellions, and for a short time in the 19th century, to an independent Muslim state.

New Year, *see* CALENDAR; NAW ROZ; MUḤARRAM.

an-Niffarī, Muḥammad ibn 'Abd al-Jabbār ibn al-Ḥasan (d. *354*/965). A Sufi, probably born in Iraq. Very little is known about his life, but his mystical writings, the *Kitāb al-Mawāqif* ("Book of Spiritual Stations") and the *Mukhāṭabāt* ("Discourses") are famous for their compelling vigor and enigma. *See* FANĀ'.

Nigeria. Federal Republic. Population: 108,476,000 of whom 50% are Muslim of the Mālikī School of Law with a large number of Aḥmadiyyah. 35% are Christian, and the others are animists. The Islamicisation of Nigeria began in the *8th*/14th century and received great impetus during the Hausa-Fulbe struggles at the beginning of the 19th century which led to the Sokoto Caliphate. The Tijāniyyah, Qādiriyyah, and Shādhilī *ṭuruq* are important Sufi orders in Nigeria. Recent years have seen the rise of small heretical groups such as the Yan Tatsine, which are the result of social dislocation. *See* BALEWA, Sir ABUBAKAR TAFAWA; DAN FODIO; KANO; SOKOTO CALIPHATE; YAN TATSINE.

Night Journey (Ar. *isrā'* and *mi'rāj*). Some time before the Hijrah, the Prophet experienced that which came later to be called the Night Journey (*al-Isrā'*), or the Ascent (*al-Mi'rāj*). The original account of the event is extremely terse; it is tradition which has supplied the details. One night he was sleeping in the sanctuary (*hijr*) next to the Ka'bah, when the Angel Gabriel woke him and led him to a beast called the *Burāq*, "smaller than a mule but larger than an ass", according to Bukhārī, and winged.

Mounted on *Burāq* with Gabriel alongside, the Prophet was borne through the sky to Jerusalem where, with the Prophets, Abraham, Moses, Jesus, and others, he prayed at the site of the Temple of Solomon. This Temple had once been the meeting place between Man and God, but in the 7th century it lay in ruins after its destruction by the Romans, for it had been left as it was, in keeping with Jesus' prophecy that not a stone would be left standing.

Two vessels were there offered to the Prophet to drink, one of wine and one of milk. The Prophet chose milk, whereupon Gabriel said that he had chosen the primordial path for himself and his people. Carried by Gabriel, the Prophet rose to heaven from the rock of the temple mount, doubtless the site of the Holy of Holies of the Temple, which the Koran calls the "Farthest Mosque" (*al-masjid al-aqṣā'*). The Dome of the Rock sanctuary stands there today, and close by is the al-Aqṣā' mosque which is named after the Koranic name for the whole Temple Mount.

The Prophet ascended to the Divine Presence through the "seven heavens", which symbolize the degrees separating non-manifestation from manifestation. As he did so, the Archangel assumed his celestial and spiritual form, as did the Prophets with whom he had prayed but whom he now encountered on the ascension as spiritual realities, each in his heavenly sphere. (Of himself the Prophet had said: "I was a Prophet while Adam was yet between water and clay.")

At the summation of the ascent was the "Lote Tree of the Uttermost Limit" (*sidrat al-muntahā*), the limit of Being before the Absolute. The Koran says: "When there enshrouded the Lote Tree that which enshrouds, the eye wavered not, nor did it rebel. Indeed he beheld of the signs of his Lord, the greatest" (53:16-18).

There the Prophet received the command from God that men should perform the prayer fifty times each day; when the Prophet descended, Moses advised him to return in order to ask that the number be reduced to one more within men's capabilities; it was finally reduced to five.

As he was returning from Jerusalem to Mecca, the Prophet saw caravans making their way across the desert. In the morning he made it known that he had visited Jerusalem during the night; the Quraysh mocked him and told Abū Bakr of this, who retorted: "If he says so, then it is true", which earned him the title *aṣ-Ṣiddīq* ("the truth-witnessing"). To the Quraysh the Prophet said nothing of his ascent to heaven, speaking of it only to his Companions. Later the caravans which he had described seeing during his return journey arrived in Mecca, confirming his statement.

The journey from Mecca to Jerusalem is called

the *isrā'*, and the ascent from Jerusalem to heaven, the *mi'rāj*. Together they are known as the Night Journey, which has often been pictured in books of Persian miniatures called the *Mi'rāj-Nameh*. Although the date of the *mi'rāj* is not known, the event called "the night of the journey and the ascension" (*laylat al-isrā' wa-l-mi'rāj*) is often celebrated as the 27th Rajab. The event is referred to at the beginning of the *Sūrat Banī Isrā'īl*:

> Glory be to Him, who carried His servant by night
> from the Holy Mosque to the Further Mosque
> the precincts of which We have blessed,
> that We might show him some of Our signs.
> He is the All-hearing, the All-seeing. (17:1-2)

See BURĀQ; DOME of the ROCK; HEAVEN; SEVENTH HEAVEN.

Night of Power, *see* LAYLAT al-QADR.

Ni'mat Allāh, Shāh Walī (d. *834*/1431). The founder of the Ni'matu'llāhī Sufi order, he settled at the court of Timur in Herāt and died near Kirmān. Some of his successors moved to Hyderabad in India, whilst those who remained in Persia became Shī'ites under the Ṣafavids. With its branches, the Kawthar 'Alī Shāhī, Gunābādī, Dhū-r-Riyasatāni, Ṣāfi 'Alī Shāhi, and the Shams Urafa', the Ni'matu'llāhī is the most important and widespread Shī'ite Sufi order, and is itself a branch, along with the Dhahabī, of the Kubrawiyyah. Shī'ite Sufi orders refer to their Shaykh as the *nāib* ("representative") of the Hidden Imām.

Nisbah. That part of a name which indicates a profession either of the holder or his forebears, such as Khayyām ("tent-maker"), or place of origin, such as ar-Rūmī ("the Roman", Byzantine). Such a name may be used in addition to other given names. See KUNYAH; LAQAB; NAME; NASAB.

Niyyah, *see* INTENTION.

Niẓām ad-Dīn Awliya (*636-725*/1238-1324). Sufi Saint buried in Delhi in a complex where he is surrounded by tombs of his disciples, including the poet Amir Khusraw. Niẓām ad-Dīn was a member of the Chishti line. He was born in Badaun in India the only son of Aḥmad Bukhari and Zulaykha. His parents had fled Bukhara from the Mongols. His father died when Niẓām ad-Dīn was five years old. When he grew up, Niẓām ad-Dīn came first to Delhi and then became the disciple of Baba Farid at Ajodhan. After he had succeeded his teacher, he founded his own *khanaqah* in the village of Ghiyaspur on the banks of the Jumna river. This is now the Durgah within Delhi which is focus of Muslim spiritual life in the capital.

Niẓām al-Mulk (d. *485*/1092). An intriguing figure in the history of the Caliphate, when the Saljuq Turks established their Sultanate in the name of the Caliphs of Baghdad, Niẓām al-Mulk was their Vizier or first minister, serving first the Sultan Alp Arslan, son of Toghrul Beg, the founder of the dynasty, and later his son Mālik Shāh.

The reins of empire were held firmly in the hands of Niẓām al-Mulk; the Sultan himself exercized little authority and the Caliph in Baghdad even less. It was Turks who held military control, but it was Niẓām al-Mulk, a Persian, who directed policy; as the Vizier he established schools, built roads, diminished taxes and presided over a period of prosperity.

Niẓām al-Mulk was a patron of the arts and sciences who had himself studied Islamic law at Nayshābūr under Hibat Allāh al-Muwaffaq. In his time the Fāṭimids of Egypt and allied Ismā'īlī sects throughout the 'Abbāsid Empire posed a political and ideological threat. This danger led Niẓām al-Mulk to turn to the Ash'arites, a Sunnī school of speculative theology previously held in opprobrium by the Saljuqs, for a line of doctrinal defense. To uphold religious orthodoxy against the propaganda of the Shī'ite sects, particularly the Ismā'īlīs, he founded the *Niẓāmiyyah* university in Baghdad. Students lived and studied at the expense of the Sultan, and the *madrasah* set the model for all other schools of higher education. Niẓām al-Mulk also founded a less renowned *Niẓāmiyyah* at Nayshābūr, and others elswhere.

He appointed the Ash'arite theologian al-Juwaynī, known as the "Imām of the Ḥaramayn" and a teacher of al-Ghazālī, to teach at Nayshābūr. Al-Juwaynī wrote his *Ghiyath al-Umam* ("The Savior of Nations") with Niẓām al-Mulk in mind, in order to promote the notion that political rule, or the Caliphate, belonged to the leader who could best advance the interests and stability of the Islamic polity, irrespective of dynasty and the traditional criteria of legitimacy to the Caliphate. Later Niẓām al-Mulk appointed al-Ghazālī to teach in the *Niẓāmiyyah* of Baghdad. Al-Ghazālī also taught in Nayshābūr at the end of his life.

An intriguing, but possibly apocryphal, story is recorded by the Persian historian Rashīd ad-Dīn aṭ-Ṭabīb, to the effect that Niẓām al-Mulk, 'Umar Khayyām, and Ḥasan aṣ-Ṣabbāḥ studied together at Nayshābūr, and vowed that he who succeeded in life would help the others. When Niẓām al-Mulk became Vizier, Ḥasan aṣ-Ṣabbāḥ came to him and was given a post. However, he embroiled himself in intrigue, and was obliged to leave, going first to Fāṭimid Egypt and then back to Persia, where he organised his followers into the Assassin sect. 'Umar Khayyām was given a post as astronomer and scholar, and took part in the creation of the Jalālī calendar for the Sultan Mālik Shāh. A romantic story of fate; what is true is that 'Umar Khayyām made his calculations to reform the solar calendar during the Vizierate of Niẓām al-Mulk in *467*/1074, and that Niẓām al-Mulk fell victim to an Ismā'īlī assassin despatched from Alamūt. The Ismā'īlīs feared him not only because he opposed them on religious grounds, but also because his strong rule was a threat to their political designs of terrorism and fragmentation. Niẓām al-Mulk wrote a treatise on politics called the *Siyāsat-Nāmeh* ("The Book of Government").

Niẓāmī (Abū Yūsuf Muḥammad Ilyās ibn Yūsuf Niẓām ad-Dīn) (*535-598*/1141-1202). A Persian poet and mystic, he was born in Ganja in Azerbaijan. His most famous works are a rendition of a tragic Arab love story, "Laylah and Majnūn", and the "Seven Princesses", an allegory about illusion and paradise. These, together with other writings, make up a collection called the *Khamsah* ("the Five").

Noah (Ar. *Nūḥ*). In Islam, Noah is considered to be a *rasūl* ("Messenger") although he does not have a revealed book. The story of how he built the Ark and filled it with two of every species to save the righteous from the Deluge (*tufan*) is very popular and has received much embellishment in tradition. The origin of the holy day of the *'āshūrā'* is made by tradition the commemoration of the day the Ark came to rest on Mount Jūdī. The Deluge is the great traditional divider between the primordial cycles of time and those at the dawn of history, that is, between pre-history and history.

Al-Mas'ūdī says that the Angel Gabriel brought Noah a sarcophagus containing the bones of Adam, to put into the Ark; that on the Ark were forty men and forty women; and that when, after five months, the Ark came to rest on land, they founded a city called *Thamānīn* ("The Eighty") at the foot of Mount Jūdī. Forty is the letter *mim*, a circle, which represents death; hence the symbol of the forty days in the desert, etc. The flood is a myth reflecting universal human experience. Before it, there prevailed the Adamic consciousness of the Divine Unity, first as the Sole Reality in the Garden, and then as a fading memory for mankind. In the individual experience this is the state of childhood; Islam says that every child is born innately a Muslim, that is, aware of Divine Transcendence. The flood symbolizes the submerging of the awareness of God as God by the overpowering experience of the *world* as God. In the progress of mankind, the stone age and before, consciousness of the Divine Reality is submerged (the Flood) by an awareness of a Divine Multiplicity in which God and the world are merged; the lightening flash is perceived as Divine, the seasons are perceived as divine, the heat, the cold, the moist, the dry, the subtle, the hard, the fluid, the transforming, are perceived as divine. In other words, existence and experience dominate the sense of Reality. Consciousness is mixed with creation. When the "Flood was over" – the dawn of history – and the waters gone down, awareness of the Divine Unity – preserved in the Ark, the "conscience", the "inner observer" – re-emerged.

In the Flood, God and the world merged. As the "waters" (this confusion of self and the world around us which is, for the individual, the experience of adolescence, the emergence of the sexual power of creation into the mind) receded, they left behind in the mind, gods and goddesses, of which the divinized heavenly bodies, as the most abstract, were the last to lose their power.

The Ark came to rest on solid ground; the adolescence of mankind was over. In Abraham the separation of consciousness from creation was complete; Abraham renounced the stars, moon, and sun, as God (which his forefathers had taken to worshiping) and recognized the

God of Adam again as God, Who is unlike anything in Creation, and Master of it. Monotheism returned, and in Abraham a reconsecration took place of the primordial religion.

The universal symbol of the Flood is the projected metaphor for this experience of adolescence on the part of the individual and on the part of mankind as a whole. In the individual it is the transition from the innocence of childhood to the knowledge of adulthood which brings in its wake knowledge of the world. For mankind it is the passage from an age of pre-history to history, and brings with it knowledge of cosmology and the sciences, crafts, and arts.

The Canaanite myth of "God's struggle with the sea monster" (*Chaoskampf*) is not really God struggling with the world, but the world struggling with the idea of Divinity in the mind of man, attempting to retain its hold over man at the moment when it is being superseded by the new awareness of God from the point of view of man's maturity and the cycle of prophetic revelation.

The story of Noah is told in the Koran in the following verses: 3:33; 4:163; 6:85; 7:59; 10:72; 11:25; 14:9; 17:3; 21:76; 22:42; 23:23; 26:106; 29:14; 33:7; 37:75; 42:13.

Nūr Muḥammadī (Persian, lit. "Muḥammadan light" or "light of Muḥammad"; a reduction of the Arabic form *an-Nūr al-Muḥammadiyyah*). The essence of the Prophet, also called *al-ḥaqīqah al-Muḥammadiyyah* ("Muḥammadan Reality" or "the Reality that is Muḥammad"), was created before the creation of the world, when "God took a handful of light and commanded it to be Muḥammad". From it the world itself was created. Much emphasis is placed upon this idea by the Shīʻites, who find this light eminently manifest in their Imāms, but the term is also encountered, mainly in the context of mysticism, among the Sunnīs, as a doctrine not unlike that of the *logos*.

Its origin is a corpus of sayings attributed to Jaʻfar aṣ-Ṣādiq, and repeated among Shīʻite theologians. In one form it is reported by Masʻ ūdī in his *Murūj adh-Dhahab* ("Meadows of Gold"), in which the following words are attributed to ʻAlī ibn Abī Ṭālib:

> When God wished to establish creation, the atoms of creatures, and the beginning of all created things, he first made what he created in the form of small particles. This was before He stretched out the earth or raised the heavens... He cast forth a ray of light, a flame from his splendor, and it was radiant. He scattered this light in the midst of invisible atoms, which he then united in the form of our Prophet. God the Most High then declared to him: "You are the first of those who shall speak, the one with the power of choice and the one chosen. To you I have trusted my light and the treasure of my guidance... For your sake I will appoint the people of your household for guidance. I will bestow upon them the secrets of my knowledge: no truth will be hidden from them and no mystery concealed. I will designate them as my proof to mankind, as those who shall admonish men of my Power and remind them of my Unity..." He had chosen Muḥammad and his family...

Jaʻfar aṣ-Ṣādiq is also reported to have said:

> The light descended upon our most noble men, and shone through our Imāms, so that we are the lights of heaven and earth. To us is heaven committed and from us are the secrets of science derived, for we are the destination that all strive to reach... the Mahdī will be the final Proof, the seal of the Imāms... we are the most noble of mankind, the most exalted of all creatures, the Proofs of the Lord of the Worlds, and those who cling to our friendship will be favored in this life and in death they will have our support...

This concept of the "man of light" appealed to Shīʻites as one more item of perfection in their Imāms, and it thus became an important constituent of their doctrine of the Imāmate. But it brought in its wake the overtones of emanationism ("a flame from His splendor"), illuminationism, and arcane knowledge.

It appealed to Sunnīs in a different way, as underpinning the concept that the *rasūl* ("the Divine Messenger") is the manifestation of Being; this is the Intellect in the Platonic sense.

However, the real origin of this doctrine, as put into the mouth of Jaʻfar aṣ-Ṣādiq, is the Manichean myth of creation, according to which the Creator, under assault from the principle of evil (which Dualism assumes to be as absolute as God Himself), created the world and made Himself into particles of light which he cast into creation, in order to "take refuge" from evil, the "other side" of the Absolute. In Manicheism, this light is God

Himself who is liberated and restored through the Elect, the Gnostics, who free the light imprisoned in nature and in themselves against a final universal salvation of the "knowers" at the end of time. It is for the Dualists that the concept of this light has the widest and deepest and, indeed, the original meaning; it came into Islam when Dualism assumed its Islamic form as the Sevener movement. *See* ʻABD ALLĀH ibn MAYMŪN al-QADDĀH; JAʻFAR aṣ-ṢĀDIQ; MANICHEANS; SEVENERS; SHĪʻISM.

Nūḥ, *see* NOAH.

Nūrbaksh, Muḥammad. (Muḥammad ibn ʻAbd Allāh; *795-869*/1393-1465). A Sufi, a descendant of the Prophet, born in Persia of a family from eastern Arabia. A charismatic figure, he was given the name Nūrbaksh ("gift of light") by his spiritual master, Isḥāq al-Khutlānī, a Shaykh in the spiritual line (*silsilah*) of the Sufi ʻAlī al-Ḥamadhānī. Nūrbaksh declared himself to be the Mahdī and, taking the title of Caliph, tried several times unsuccessfully to lead popular revolts and seize power in Persia. He was captured and pardoned. A Sufi *ṭarīqah*, the Nūrbakshiyyah, descends from him; this order became Shīʻite in Ṣafavid times. One of his followers, Shams ad-Dīn ʻIrāqī from Jīlān also propagated the order in Srinagar in India.

Nusayris, *see* ʻALAWĪS.

O

Occultation, *see* GHAYBAH.

Occulted Imām, *see* HIDDEN IMĀM.

Oman. Sultanate. Population: 2,186,548. The great majority are 'Ibādite Muslims, 25% are Sunnīs, and a smaller minority are Twelve-Imām Shī'ites. 'Ibādite *sharī'ah* law is largely in force.

Omar, *see* 'UMAR.

Omar Khayyām, *see* 'UMAR al-KHAYYĀM.

Omar, Mosque of, *see* DOME of the ROCK.

Orthodoxy, *see* FIVE PILLARS; ILḤĀD; SUNNAH.

Osman, *see* 'UTHMĀN.

Osmanlis, *see* OTTOMANS.

Ossetians. An Iranian people of the North Caucasus. According to the census of 1979 they numbered 542,000, of whom 365,000 live in Ossetia, the south part of which was the South Ossetian Autonomous Oblast of the Georgian republic, and the north was the North Ossetian ASSR. Since the break up of the Soviet Union they are divided between the Russian Federation and the Republic of Georgia. The language of the Ossetians is an Iranian language; the majority are Russian Orthodox although some are Sunnī Muslims.

Othman, *see* 'UTHMĀN.

Ottomans (*7th*/13th century-*1342*/1924). Also called Osmanlis, they were a clan of the Ghuzz (Oghuz) branch of Turks, descended from a chieftain of the *7th*/13th century called Ertoghrul, whose son 'Uthmān (alternate spellings are Othman, Osman, and Usman) founded a principality in Asia Minor. The clan controlled Western Anatolia, and in *758*/1357 began a series of conquests which brought Macedonia, Serbia, and Bulgaria under their control; regions which the Turks called "Rumelia", from *Rūm*, the Byzantine ("Roman") Empire. Bāyazīd I, called *Yildirim* ("the lightning bolt") acquired the title of "Sultan" from the 'Abbāsid Caliph in Cairo. The ascent of the Ottomans was temporarily checked when the same Bāyazīd was captured in Battle by Timur (Tamerlane) in *804*/1402.

Constantinople had been the great prize since the Prophet's time, and Muslim armies had made many unsuccessful attempts to conquer it. Ironically, the blow from which it never recovered was delivered by Christians, when in 1204, Doge Dandolo of Venice led the Fourth Crusade against Constantinople, which was taken and sacked. The Turks, and others before them, had been nibbling at the Byzantine Empire, so that by the mid-*9th*/15th century, only a small remnant of territory surrounding the city remained in Christian hands. In *857*/1453 the Ottoman Turks led by Mehmet II Nāṣir ("the Victor") conquered it and renamed it Istanbul.

The city was besieged for fifty-four days by a Turkish force of 150,000, whilst defense depended upon an army of only 8,000 led by some 400 Venetian mercenaries. The Turks attacked not only by land, and by tunneling, but by sea as well. Because entry into the Bosphorus was impeded by a chain, the Turks were compelled to carry their ships overland by way of Pera, a narrow isthmus, in order to bring their small navy to bear upon the city. At one point the Sultan Mehmet, a man of fiery temperament, rode his horse into the Bosphorus and swam among the ships, shouting orders to the brandishing of his sword. He was not only daring, but also ingenious; he designed some of the special high trajectory cannons which bombarded the city.

With the conquest of Constantinople the great age of the Ottomans began. In *923*/1517 Selim I *Yavuz* ("the Grim") conquered Egypt, thus marking the end of the 'Abbāsids who had lived in Cairo under the Mamlūks as figurehead Caliphs since the conquest of Baghdad by the Mongols in *656*/1238. The Ottomans later claimed that the last 'Abbāsid in Cairo, al-Mutawakkil III, had relinquished the Caliphate to them; certainly no 'Abbāsid after him claimed the title. According to modern scholars, however, Selim I had neither the political foresight nor the desire for titles that would have suggested the obvious step of acquiring a useful and not inglorious claim to legitimacy by adding the name of Caliph to those of Sultan and Khān.

Instead, it now seems to be accepted among European scholars that the title to the Caliphate "disappeared"; its transference to the Ottomans was a fiction invented in the 18th century when the idea of a Turkish Caliphate became a useful strategem to bolster waning military power. According to this view, the Turkish claim to the Caliphate was inspired by the treaty of Kuchuk Kaynarja of 1774, when the Russian Tsar acquired the right to protect the Orthodox Christian Church in the Turkish Empire, and the Russians were induced in turn to acknowledge the Turkish ruler's religious authority over Muslims in the Russian Empire. By virtue of this, the Ottomans did not demand travel documents of Muslims coming from outside their empire because they wished to demonstrate that they were all spiritually subject to the Ottoman Caliph. This was essentially to imitate those European policies of "protection" that frequently foreshadowed open colonization. The Treaty of Kuchuk Kaynarja, and such political "fictions" as it embodied, were a mirror held up to European designs.

As time passed, the Turks certainly exploited the idea of the Caliphate further to support their imperial claims; their holding the regalia of the Caliphate, the mantle of the Prophet, in Istanbul, was made much of in token of their legitimacy; even if their claims were invented, they were taken seriously by the Europeans; the British in particular saw the Turkish Caliphate as a threat to the stability of the Muslim areas within the British Empire. They therefore attacked the notion of the Ottoman Caliphate on religious grounds, declaring that the 'Abbāsids had no right to relinquish the title, or alternately, that the 'Abbāsids would have been within their rights to do so, were it not for the technical irregularity raised by the Ḥadīth which said that rule belongs to Arab Quraysh so long as there are two Qurayshis left, one to rule and one to be subject.

Given that it had not occurred to most Muslims to contest the validity of a Turkish Caliphate, this disparagement of Turkish claims was somewhat as if the Mufti of Cairo had advised the British Monarchy that, on technical grounds, they could not be "defenders of the faith".

In the end, the Ottomans fulfilled *de facto* the role of Caliphate; in the absence of ruling Qurayshis, they provided Islam with a clear political center, if not in the persons of the Caliphs themselves (who, as individuals, after Sulaymān the Magnificent sank so abysmally low that it has been suggested they could not have been genuine descendants of their predecessors), then certainly in the institution of the Caliphate. It defended Islamic orthodoxy, and in so doing reflected the religious fervor of the Turkish people, who thought of themselves as Muslims first and Turks second. In any case, Ottoman rulers had used the title of Caliph before the conquest of Egypt, as early as Mūrād I (d. *761*/1360). Indeed, they had used the title even before Bāyazīd acquired the title of Sultan from the 'Abbāsids. Ultimately, the authenticity of their claim depended upon its credibility, and this was accepted by the Islamic world. (*See* CALIPH.)

The Ottoman Empire reached its height under Sulaymān the Magnificent (d. *974*/1566), known as *al-Qānūnī* ("the lawgiver"). He controlled Asia Minor, Syria, Iraq, Egypt, North Africa, the coastal regions of Arabia, Azerbaijan, the Balkans, Hungary, and vassal states in the Volga region and the southern steppes of Russia. Apart from military prowess, this period also saw great Turkish achievements in administration, social institutions, architecture and public works. Istanbul became, again, one of the great cities of the world.

In *943*/1536 Turkish military power was everywhere unmatched but, by *979*/1571, in the sea battle at Lepanto, the Turks lost control of the Western Mediterranean, although the European powers did not then exploit their victory fully. The Portuguese had meanwhile already wrested supremacy from the Turks in the Indian Ocean, and the Russians had begun making inroads against the Turks' Tartar vassals from the time of Ivan the Terrible; they continued to pursue their dream of conquering Constantinople into the 20th century. Although the Ottomans besieged Vienna for a second time in *1094*/1683, where they were narrowly routed by Jan Sobiesky, King of Poland, they were by this time in rapid decline.

Before decline turned to stagnation, however, there ensued the 19th-century reforms (*tanẓīmāt*) whereby Turkey began the process of

Westernization. This led to the stirrings of Turkish nationalism which finally displaced the Turks' first and foremost identity as Muslims, culminating in the creation of a completely secular Turkish state under Mustāfā Kemal Atatürk, once the empire had been completely lost in World War I.

The Ottoman Sultanate was abolished in 1922 with the establishment of a republic, and the Caliphate was abolished in *1342*/1924. *See* BEYLERBEY; DEFTERDAR; DEVSHIRME; JANISSARIES; ISTANBUL; KAPUDAN-PASHA; MEHMET II; QĀḌI 'ASKER; SHAYKH al-ISLĀM; SĪNĀN; SUBLIME PORTE; SULAYMĀN the MAGNIFICENT; TANẒĪMĀT; TURKEY; TURKS.

"Ovliad" (from *awlad*, "Arabic children"). A tribe in Turkmenistan claiming apocryphal descent from the first four Caliphs. Such claims are more correctly understood as implying an Arab origin or strong Arab influx within the group at some point in the past, rather than literal descent from a particular figure.

P

Padishāh. A Persian title for the ruler, also used among the Turks.

Pahlavi. A dynasty in Persia from *1343-1399*/1924-1979. The first Shah of this dynasty was Reza Pahlavi, originally the leader of an Army Cossack Brigade. Like Atatürk in Turkey, Reza I sought to modernize Persia, and took a hostile stand towards the representatives of religion, the Mullas. He set the tone for a nationalistic policy laying claim to territories which were at that time outside Persian control.

In *1351*/1934 the name of Persia was changed to Iran. At the beginning of World War II, Iranian territory was occupied by Allied troops, and the Shah, obliged to abdicate, went into exile. His son Muḥammad Reza replaced him on the throne (although his coronation did not take place until over thirty years later).

The first ten years of Muḥammad Reza's reign were marked by political turbulence of every kind, made much worse by the foundation of the *Tudeh* Communist party in *1361*/1943. The question of oil revenues and the Anglo-Iranian Oil Company, the subsequent attempt at nationalization and the assumption of dictatorial powers by the Prime Minister Dr. Mossadegh together with the outbreak of popular disaffection, led the Shah to leave the country on 16 August 1953. Following brief hostilities in Teheran and its seizure by General Zahedī, there was a turnabout of public opinion and the Shah returned on the 21st to the acclaim of the populace.

The period before and after the departure of the Shah was marked by the volatile influence of *Bāzārī*, elements in the traditional economic sector, agitation by the Communist Party, and initiatives on the part of religious leaders, the Mullas. A member of the *Majlis* ("parliament"), Ayatollah Qashānī, spoke publicly about the will of the Hidden Imām and was implicated, through the confession of a Persian Fedayyin assassin, in the direction of political terrorism.

Nevertheless, the oil revenues of the sixties and seventies, brought a climate of growing prosperity, offset only by unexpectedly severe failures in agriculture as a result of inept agricultural innovations. The 1970s saw an ever more insistent acerbation of the profound tensions inherent in Shī'ite political theory. The victory in the *12th*/18th century of the Uṣūlī school over the Akhbārī had cleared the way for a startling growth in the influence and power of the Mullas, comparable to the resurgence of priestly power under Mazdeism in ancient Persia. The Mullas moreover controlled vast sums of money acquired through the religious taxes of *zakāt* and *khums* (which do not exist among the Sunnīs) and were closely linked by family with the conservative and rich *Bāzārī* merchant class.

The Shah's regime was becoming ever more irksome to the religious authorities who, ever since Shī'ism became the state religion at the beginning of the *10th*/16th century, and during the last two hundred years in particular, had been formulating doctrine which accorded greater power and competence to themselves. This was no more than the perpetration of Persia's original pre-Islamic religious ethos, of which Shī'ism was itself an irruption within Islam. Although the Shah attempted by such means as his lavish coronation held in Persepolis to assert himself as the legitimate heir to ancient Persian sovereignty, it was the Mullas who incarnated a more telling claim, and one which had been alive in Persia ever since the Arabs first invaded and introduced Islam.

The Shah stood for modernism; even if he had stood for religion, by the very definition of political legitimacy as deriving from the Hidden Imām, he could not have claimed that legitimacy; but the Mullas could. Therefore the rule of the Shah became synonymous with foreign influence and centuries of foreign domination; in the revolutionary code words, his government was referred to as the Umayyads, and himself as Yazīd, the Arab persecutor of Ḥusayn. Combined with the social dislocations of modernism, the continuing affirmation of the ethos of ancient Iran brought about a revolution which overthrew the Shah in 1978. The Safavid Ismā'īl I had come to power by exploiting a desire for revenge in the name of the Imāms who had been denied their right, as they saw it, to rule; the force he had unleashed now turned against his successors. *See* AYATOLLAH;

HIDDEN IMĀM; SAFAVIDS; SHĪ'ISM; UṢŪLĪS.

Paighambar (Persian: "prophet"; in Turkish: *peygamber*). A Persian word which generally replaces both *nabī* and *rasūl* in the Indo-Persian world.

Pakistan. Islamic Republic. Population: 129,275,660 of whom 97% are Muslim, 1.2% Christian. There are small minorities of Hindus, Parsis, and others. 20% of the Muslims are Twelve-Imām Shī'ites and perhaps a million are Ismā'īlīs; the rest are Sunnīs of the Ḥanafī school of law. The Suhrawardi, Chishti, and Qādiriyyah *ṭuruq* are the most important Sufi orders. *See* IQBAL, SIR MUḤAMMAD.

Palestine. (*Ar. Filasṭīn*). "Land of the Philistines," inhabited from 3,000 BC by the Canaanites and Egyptians and later by Hyksos, Hittites, and Philistines, conquered by the Jews around 1020 BC, and ruled by them until 587 BC and then again, partially, from 164 BC until Roman rule in 63 BC. It was also conquered and ruled by the Assyrians and Persians, the Byzantines, and from AD 635 by the Muslims who called it a *jund*, a military administrative district, like that of Jordan. Under the Crusaders it was a Frankish kingdom. Under the Ottomans it was divided into several administrative areas. In 1923, the region corresponding to the Roman province of Palestine became a British Mandate. In 1947 the United Nations divided Palestine, making part of it the Jewish State of Israel. A war ensued after which Jordan annexed the Arab part of Palestine and held it until it was conquered by Israel in the 1967 war. Jordan has since renounced its claims in favor of an independent Palestine. Since the 1993 Washington accords, parts of the West Bank have become autonomous, starting with Jericho.

The population of Palestine at the turn of the century was extremely heteroclitic and included many groups such as Armenians, Greeks, Bosnians, Circassians, groups of Persian descent, Kurds, as well as descendents of ancient populations, such as Canaanites, Arabs, Jews and Samaritans. After the Jewish diaspora, a small Jewish population remained in Palestine throughout the Middle Ages. From 1870, with the growth of Zionism, this Jewish population grew by immigration from Europe, and in 1939 totaled 400,000.

In 1910, it was estimated that the population of Palestine was 650,000, of whom two-thirds were Muslims and the rest Christians of many sects, and about 60,000 Jews, or about 11% of the total. At the present time, the population of Israel is 5,916,700 of whom 80.5% are Jewish, 14.6% are Muslim, 3.2% are Christian, and 1.7% Druze, including Israeli citizens in the West Bank and Gaza strip. Population of Gaza: 924,000; population of the West Bank: 1,428,000.

Pan-Turanianism. Pan-Turkish nationalism. The word *Tūrān*, designating the nomadic homeland of peoples speaking cognate non-Indo-European languages, was employed by the Persian poet Firdawsi who, in his *Shāhnāmeh* ("Book of Kings", *c.* A.D. 1000) wrote: "The whole part of the earth which is comprised between the Jihūn and the frontiers of Rūm [Byzantium] and which extends from there in a continuous line to China and Khotan became ... the empire of the people of Tūrān." The term is an ancient one, which occurs repeatedly in the Zoroastrian *Avesta*, and appears to designate the Altai mountains and the dry, steppe region in Central Asia including the Amu Darya and the Syr Darya rivers, and the Kara Kum and Kizl Kum deserts, all occupied by Turkic peoples. The Pan-Turanian movement began in Turkey in the 19th century as Muslim awareness began to yield to that of ethnic identity under the impact of Western ideas. Its aim was to unite the peoples of Turkic origin in the Middle East, Russia, Persia, Afghanistan and Central Asia into a potent political bloc, most of whom were Muslims. Its broader aim was to embrace all the related Finno-Ugric and Magyar nations; in this it failed. However, Pan-Turanianism still exists as a latent force between the Turkic peoples of, for example, the Crimea, Azerbaijan, Central Asia and so forth.

Paradise, *see* al-JANNAH.

Pasha. A Turkish military and civil title of high rank. It is still used in Arab countries to designate a civil authority such as a regional ruler or mayor.

Pathans, *see* PUSHTUN.

Patriarchal Caliphs (Ar. *al-khulafā' ar-rāshidūn*). The so-called "rightly guided Caliphs" were the first four Caliphs, Abū Bakr, 'Umar, 'Uthmān, and 'Alī, whose spiritual stations were commensurate with the dignity of being successors to the Prophet; all having been his close Companions during his prophethood. In the hands of later Caliphs, although there were some men of true sanctity, the office became one of political authority alone, although it carried the prestige of its religious connotations.

The Shī'ites recognize as legitimate only the Caliphate of 'Alī and the brief Caliphate of his son Ḥasan who succeeded him. They consider the first three Caliphs to be usurpers. The Khārijites (today's 'Ibādites) do not recognize all of 'Uthmān's Caliphate as being legitimate, nor 'Alī's after the Battle of Ṣiffīn.

The Sunnīs, on the other hand, who comprise at least 90% of the Islamic world, greatly respect and venerate the first four Caliphs.

The reigns of the Patriarchal Caliphs are:

Abū Bakr	*11-13*/632-634
'Umar ibn al-Khattāb	*13-23*/634-644
'Uthmān ibn 'Affān	*23-35*/644-656
'Alī ibn Abī Ṭālib	*35-40*/656-661

This was followed by the short-lived Caliphate of Ḥasan, the son of 'Alī, in *40*/661. Thereafter followed the dynasty of the Umayyads of the family of those who had opposed the Prophet during his lifetime. *See* 'ABBĀSIDS; CALIPH; ḤASAN; UMAYYADS.

People of the Bench, *see* AṢḤĀB aṣ-ṢUFFĀH.

People of the Book, *see* AHL al-KITĀB.

People of the Cloak, *see* AHL al-KISĀĪ.

People of the House, *see* AHL al-BAYT.

People of the Scripture, *see* AHL al-KITĀB.

Perfect man, *see* al-INSĀN al-KĀMIL.

"Permitted", *see* MUBĀḤ.

Persia, see IRĀN.

Pharaoh (Ar. *fir'awn*). The title of the rulers of Egypt in ancient times. The Pharaoh with whom Aaron and Moses dealt is depicted in Islam as the epitome of evil; the Koranic account sees him overwhelmed in the Red Sea, in pursuit of the Children of Israel, but saved alive by his repentance:

> And We brought the Children of Israel
> over the sea; and Pharaoh and his hosts
> followed them insolently and impetuously
> till, when the drowning overtook him, he said
> 'I believe that there is no god but He in whom
> the Children of Israel believe; I am of those that
> surrender.'
> 'Now? And before thou didst rebel, being of those
> that did corruption.
> So today We shall deliver thee with thy
> body, that thou mayest be a sign to those
> after thee.' (10:90-92)

The sin of Pharaoh was, above all, pride; he rejected guidance and a Divine Message and, by asserting his own "Lordship", as it were challenged God:

> ...So he showed him the great
> sign, but he cried lies, and rebelled,
> then he turned away hastily, then he
> mustered and proclaimed, and he said,
> I am your Lord, the Most High!'...(79:20-25)

The Koranic accounts are, as is usual, amplified in their detail and trends by contemporary tradition which declares, in illustration of the Pharaoh's pride, that he built a tower which darkened the sun and from its summit shot an arrow into the sky at the God of Moses which, by God's contriving, returned bloodied; Pharaoh's pride was thereby heightened and his doom made more certain; a tradition which echoes a legend of the Jews about the Tower of Babel. Where the Koran differs from the popular traditions of the age of the Prophet is in the significant theme of Pharaoh's repentance and forgiveness. It is frequently forgotten that each Sūrah of the Koran but one begins with a reference to God's mercy. Perhaps not unrelated to this theme is the fact that the wife of the Pharaoh who pitted himself against Moses is, in the Koran, described as a believer, and is considered in tradition also to have been of an exalted spiritual station. Her name, according to Islamic tradition, was Asiyah:

> God has struck a similitude
> for the believers – the wife of
> Pharaoh, when she said, 'My
> Lord, build for me a house in

Paradise, in Thy presence, and
deliver me from Pharaoh
and his work, and do Thou
deliver me from the people
of the evildoers.'

Philosophy (Ar. *falsafah*). Islam came into the world without philosophy; it was God reaching down to man rather than man, through his own efforts, discovering the ways of God.

For its first century, Islam had no philosophy as such; although it is possible to speak of Islamic epistemology or ethics even at this early period, there was no conscious method or system. However, as it expanded in the direction of Persia, Islam was exposed to the philosophies of antiquity. Wherever Islam spread, Alexander the Great had gone before, leaving behind the legacy of Hellenistic learning which the Eastern churches put to use. Thus the Nestorians had maintained a school of philosophy in Jundishāpūr (or Gandisapora) near Ahvāz in Persia from the 3rd century A.D. on.

The Mu'tazilites, or rationalists, were the first to embody the influence of Hellenistic philosophy within Islam. In the long run their efforts were perceived by the orthodox as an intrusion, alien in spirit and dangerous to the faith, for too often doctrine was diminished to fit the measures of reason.

After *212*/827 the Mu'tazilites succeeded in exerting the dominant influence on official doctrine during the Caliphate of al-Ma'mūn (*198-218*/813-833). The movement then declined and was so severely denounced by the theologian al-Ash'arī (d. *324*/935), himself a former Mu'tazilite, as to lose all hope of regaining its former prominence. In later days its name merely served to disguise the freethinker or the agnostic. But al-Ash'arī himself, it should be noted, was a thinker in the Greek philosophical tradition and incorporated the dialectical methods of the Mu'tazilites into Islamic theology.

In the early Christian world, and beyond its confines even as far as India, Neoplatonism had flourished. Greek wisdom had permeated the soil that Islam conquered, and Hellenistic thought did not fail to find adherents among the thinkers in Islam, as well as in the various heterodox sects, of whom the Seveners are the most remarkable example; in the event it was the Dualist Seveners who became the channel whereby the arcane and Gnostic teachings of late classicism entered Islam. The most important flowering of this hidden tradition (which also produced writings that alarmed theologians and rulers alike) was the Brotherhood of Purity (*Ikhwān aṣ-Ṣafā'*) around *350*/961, who elaborated an encyclopedia of universal knowledge.

When Baghdad (founded in *145*/762) became the 'Abbāsid capital, the intellectual dominance of Islam by Persians was in the ascendent. The second 'Abbāsid Caliph, al-Manṣūr (d. *136*/754), had encouraged Greek learning, but Aristotle was not translated into Arabic until the reign of al-Ma'mūn (d. *218*/833). Then there began the momentous study of the Greek philosopher which came to an abrupt end in the Islamic world some centuries later, first in the East and then in Arab Spain, but not before being transmited thence to Christian Europe. In Europe this took the form of Latin "Averroism", named after Ibn Rushd, or "Averroes" as he was known to Europe, an Aristotelian school of thought which lasted well up into the 17th century.

The Muslims have been accused of combining Plato and Aristotle into one philosophy. This had already been done to some extent by the Neoplatonists and the Syriac and Nestorian Christians. The synthesis was carried further in the works of al-Kindī (*2nd*/9th century) and al-Fārābī (c. *257-339*/870-950). (*See* al-KINDĪ; al-FĀRĀBĪ.) In one sense, however, the Muslim philosophers did not create a synthesis; rather, they simply found no conflict between the two great philosophers and looked upon Aristotle as the primary commentator on Plato. Questions of authorship, authenticity, or historical sequence concerned them little. Even less were they inclined to separate out the Neoplatonism that colored their perceptions of Greek thought. Whether Aristotle was truly the author of all the works attributed to him was of little importance; the ideas were what counted.

In Plato they found the analogical view which absorbed all discontinuities, the vertical dimension which united all levels of reality; in Aristotle, the study of the horizontal and apparently separate levels. Between the two they found a complementarity, and moreover, a system of thought that was compatible with the Islamic revelation. Or at least they made it so; Aristotle's concept of the Prime Mover evidently had to yield to the Islamic revelation of the Absoluteness of God and His nature in the Koran, and existence must permanently depend upon Him.

Above all, the Muslim philosophers were Realists, never Nominalists. They believed in one, higher reality, a realm of essences, more real than the realm of things; and that the world is the manifestation of that reality. They believed that universals exist before things (*ante res*). This line of thought is more evident in Plato and his world of ideas than in Aristotle, but the Muslim philosophers did not find Aristotle opposed to it; indeed, he is not.

Nominalism is the tendency to assert that universals are mere "names" which exist after things (*post res*) or that reality is a function of physical existence and that universals exist "only in the mind". Today, this tendency has gone so far in certain quarters as to declare that behavior is a function of biology, that atoms alone constitute reality. A kind of Nominalism may have been voiced as early as Porphyry (d. 304) but was not taken seriously until after William of Ockham (d. 1349).

The attribution of Nominalism to Aristotle is the result of interpretation or emphasis; above all, the idea that Aristotle is a Nominalist is the result of the banishment of God from philosophical thought, which never happened among the Muslim philosophers; it finds its justification in the idea that Aristotle allowed universals a place in things (*in rebus*), that is, within existence itself. Aristotle is quoted as having said: "I love Plato; I love truth; but I love truth more." Aristotle attributed a substance to individuals; in Plato's formulation, the world is pure illusion; Aristotle, in enunciating the principle of non-contradiction, namely that something cannot be and not be at the same time, found it logical to say that while the world is not real in the same sense as its Principle, it is nevertheless real on its own plane. This he expressed by attributing a substance to individuals. But he was not a Nominalist in that substance is not merely a name or an appearance; the individual substance, or the world, is real; but its reality and existence derives from the removal of the qualities of absoluteness from Reality itself. Its reality is like that of a particular color (manifestation), which is the result of the removal of the other colors from "white" light (the Principle in regard to light and colors), which itself is colorless but contains all the colors. According to Plato, the world can be reduced to God if its illusion is removed; according to Aristotle there is no illusion; but the world is always less than God. He perfectly well recognized the absolutely transcendent nature of the First Mover, beyond the "sublunary sphere" of change, and it is therefore no surprise that the Muslim philosophers found in him the means by which the mind extends its field of knowledge, without denying the supremacy of the Ideal, or supra-Real.

Unlike doubt-ridden modern philosophy, the classical philosophy of the Muslims was based upon the certainty of God and revelation. For Plato and Aristotle, revelation was a function of the intellect itself. Not a few Muslim philosophers came to this conclusion themselves, notably Ibn Ṭufayl (d. *581*/1185). This view never led them to deny Koranic revelation, but, nevertheless, horrified the theologians. Al-Ghazālī (d. *505*/111) was harsh towards those who held that the world was eternal, that God's knowledge being universal did not extend to particular events, and that there was a resurrection of the soul but not of the body. Like al-Ash'arī, he upheld transcendence and revelation against reason. Al-Ghazālī was obliged, in the name of religious orthodoxy, to denounce the philosophers by writing his *Tahāfut al-Falāsafah* ("Refutation of the Philosophers") in order to forestall a neo-pagan renaissance within Islam. In Europe a similar suspicion arose concerning some of the philosophers; the great commentator of Aristotle, Ibn Rushd or "Averroes", was strongly associated with humanism in the European reading of him, but religious scepticism was certainly not the view of the *qāḍi* of Seville himself; it is sometimes forgotten that Ibn Rushd was, after all, a judge (*qāḍi*) according to the religious law of Islam. It was the Western philosophers, and not the Muslims, who took the further step beyond the edge and looked at the world purely empirically.

The Muslim philosophers, then, were realists in their understanding of Aristotle and, necessarily, of Plato. They were predominantly Aristotelian insofar as he is the dialectical means of understanding the Ideal, or the Real. For the Muslim philosophers, Aristotle, the student of Plato, was also his greatest commentator, building an intellectual infrastructure out of the Ideal world up to the edge of the manifested world, or world of things. Al-Fārābī and others fashioned a vocabulary for Aristotelian philosophy in Arabic, drawing upon the Koran. Being or substance they called *jawhar* ("jewel");

"accidents" (or contingencies within Being which are existence) they called *'araḍ* (pl. *a'rāḍ*), which arise out of the "privation" of Being (*'adam*), the categories they called *ma'qūlāt*.

In the classical mold, the Muslim thinkers were never exclusively philosophers in the modern sense, but natural scientists, physicians, and often poets too. Thus Ibn Sīnā, or "Avicenna" (d. *429*/1037), was still published in Europe as a physician into the 17th century, long after his influence as a philosopher and a logician – the most famous of philosophers in Europe and the Orient – had waned. Ibn Bājjah, or "Avempace" (d. *533*/1138) was famous as a philosopher, and the precursor of Ibn Rushd's theory of the "One Intellect", but he also influenced Galileo (through Averroes) by equating the speed of a moving object to the force which set it into motion, minus the factor of friction, and by affirming an identity between the force which moves physical objects on the earth and that which moves the planets. For him, however, this force was not merely a physical phenomenon but had its origin in the spiritual sphere and in the Divine.

The most Aristotelian of all the Muslim philosophers was Ibn Rushd, or "Averroes" (d. *595*/1198). Yet he was responsible for the most Platonic of notions, that of the "One Intellect". (*See* FIVE DIVINE PRESENCES.) The idea is a variant on the fundamental metaphysical notion that the principle of knowledge and cognition, the intellect (*al-'aql al-fā'il*) at man's center, is the same as the principle of creation at the center of Being (*al-'aql al-awwal*, or what Christians would call the *logos*, and Hindus *buddhi*), and that the objective world is Being differentiated, woven into existence. Hinduism expresses the same idea in its concept of Brahma and Ātmā. Sufism already had an aphorism to this effect: "Everything that you see is the Act of One". The mystic Ibn Arabī (d. *638*/1240) was to develop this further in a more complete and esoteric form in the theory of *waḥdat al-wujūd* ("the unity of Being") in the time immediately following Ibn Rushd. The idea had also been taken up by Ibn Tufayl (d. *581*/1185) in his *Ḥayy ibn Yaqẓān*, an allegory in which natural philosophy and thought lead to insights which parallel those of revelation and mysticism. Through Averroism in Europe, the idea of the "One Intellect" spread quickly, but in the absence of a developed philosophic framework became corrupted into a "theory of one soul" common to all mankind, called "panpsychism".

It was this capacity of philosophy to intoxicate its votaries and ultimately to become independent of religion that led al-Ghazālī to write his "Refutation of the Philosophers", which accomplished just that. He attacked them, with Ibn Sīnā in mind, for, among other things, maintaining the "eternity of the world" and for ascribing knowledge to means other than revelation. Al-Ghazālī specifically denounced twenty theses; three he said were *kufr*, or disbelief: the eternity of the world; the idea that God does not know particulars; the denial of bodily resurrection. The other points he called *bid'ah*, or "objectionable innovation". He only argued with philosophers who were *ilahiyyun*, or those who professed to believe in God, and did not bother with the atheist materialists nor the naturalists (by whom he meant Galen). What he sought was to establish the limits of philosophy: to have it be "the handmaiden of theology" and no more; and if not that, then nothing. Philosophy had created various means of studying and analyzing the world and thought itself, but for al-Ghazālī a dangerous frontier had been reached. The development of philosophy was leading away from the light of revelation and ideas *into* the darkness of Plato's cave, by virtue of a purely empirical view of a material world. Beyond it lay the abyss into which Christian Europe was to fall: Renaissance humanism, which led fatally to a dehumanizing materialism. It was the fall into this abyss that al-Ghazālī wished to avert: providentially so, for he had no means of foreseeing its full consequence, which is the modern world.

To the philosopher's quest to know reality with the mind or thought alone, al-Ghazālī opposed Divine transcendence. Theologically he was an Ash'arite and played towards the philosophers the role that al-Ash'arī had played towards the Mu'tazilites. But remarkably, he was also a mystic who strove to redirect the energies of the thinkers towards the mystic path. His success indicates that the pruning of the philosophical tree made it grow higher and attain to a different world altogether, for after al-Ghazālī there was a tremendous flowering of mysticism.

Philosophy in Baghdad had seen its day. But in Spain the books of al-Ghazālī were burned by the Almoravids in disagreement with certain of the views expressed in the *Iḥyā' 'Ulūm ad-Dīn* ("The

Revitalization of the Religious Sciences"), specifically the use of *qiyas* or analogy in law which was a hallmark of Shāfi'īs of whom al Ghazālī was one. In the brief reprieve thus afforded, Ibn Rushd and other Spanish thinkers completed their work. Ibn Rushd answered al-Ghazālī by writing his work *Tahāfut at-Tahāfut* ("Refuting of the Refutation"). Indeed, he could easily argue that the "eternity of the world" was implied in the immutability of God, that as God is always Creator, and He never undergoes change, therefore creation is permanent; hence the philosophers conclude that the world is eternal. At the same time theologians see this as a threat to the notion of the Absolute itself; Plato himself calls creation a "second god". The resolution of the apparent contradiction between these two views (of, on the one hand, theology denying the eternity of creation, and on the other, philosophy affirming it), lies in the metaphysical idea of the apocatastasis, or the Hindu *mahāpralaya*, the "moment between creations" when the Absolute is without the *ḥijāb*, the "veil" of manifestation.

At the apocatastasis all manifestation comes to an end; there is God Alone: "My play is ended", says the Śrīmad Bhagavatam. Then, because God is the Absolute, and the perfection of the Absolute includes the possibility of the negation of the Absolute, God creates anew. This metaphysical idea receives little attention in religion because it undermines all notions of striving for salvation, reducing them to a "joy of return", since the damned are released from hell, and the saved from paradise; it also resolves, however, the question of the "eternity of the world"; the world is "eternal" as a permanent possibility of the Absolute, an "inner dimension".

Similarly, the Philosophers also raised another problem, that of the omniscience of God, concluding that God's knowledge embraced all universals, but did not extend to particulars. The Theologians, naturally, maintained that God's omniscience had no limit.

Philosophy was eclipsed as an active force in Islamic thought after Ibn Rushd, who represents the summit and terminus of Aristotelian thought in Islam. For Europe too, he was a figure of such importance that Dante called him the author of the "great commentary", and placed him, along with Avicenna (that is, Ibn Sīnā) in the first circle of his *Inferno*, with the other great philosophers who await the harrowing for their salvation; upon the single figure of Averroes a whole school of European philosophy was founded.

The great period in which the works of Muslim philosophers were translated into Latin began with the conquest of Toledo by the Christians (*478*/1085). Archbishop Raimundo patronized this task until his death in 1151, and others, including Frederick II of Germany, carried on after him. To emulate the intellectual sparkle of Arab courts, Spanish kings too commissioned translators, often converted Spanish Jews, to put Arab books into Latin. It was by way of this that the Greek classics came again to the attention of Europe.

Islamic thought did not disappear after Ibn Rushd. Rather, it was swallowed up in a tremendous flood of mysticism which broke out from Moorish Andalusia in the *7th*/13th century and spread to the East. This effusion of mysticism attracted and nourished, from then on, the greatest minds in Islam and affected all levels of intellectual activity. Even in its decline, this trend marked many Islamic countries right up to the colonial period and the advent of modernism. Nor was the contribution of philosophy lost; it provided the groundwork for the great metaphysical formulations which followed. That philosophy was indeed integrated into esoterism can be seen from the fact that the greatest exponent of metaphysical Sufism, or mysticism, Ibn Arabī, could be called *Ibn Aflaṭūn*, or the "son of Plato". *See* ALEXANDER; APOCATASTASIS; al-ASH'ARĪ; BEING; BROTHERHOOD of PURITY; al-FARĀBĪ; FIVE DIVINE PRESENCES; al-GHAZĀLĪ; KALĀM; al-KINDĪ; KUMŪN; IBN 'ARABĪ; IBN BAJJAH; IBN RUSHD; IBN SĪNĀ; IBN ṬUFAYL; MU'TAZILITES; RŪḤ; SEVENERS; SUFISM.

Pictures, *see* IMAGES.

Pietists, *see* MURJI'AH.

Pilgrimage. The idea of pilgrimage is expressed by three ideas and words, namely, *al-Ḥajj*, *al-'Umrah* and *az-Ziyarāh*.

Al-Ḥajj ("the greater pilgrimage"), the canonical pilgrimage, one of the "five pillars" of Islam (*see* FIVE PILLARS), is an elaborate series of rites, requiring several days for their accomplishment, performed at the Grand Mosque of Mecca and in the immediate environs of the city, at a particular moment of the Islamic year, which, because of the lunar calendar, advances some ten days each each year.

The *Ḥajj* is obligatory upon those who can "make their way" (3:97) to Mecca. That is to say that the requirement is not absolute, but incumbent upon those whose health and means permit it, and who, in doing so, do not compromise their responsibilities towards their families. Those who have made the pilgrimage are entitled to prefix their names with the appellation "Pilgrim" (*al-Ḥajj*).

In this century the number of people performing the *ḥajj* in one year could be as few as 10,000, before World War II, and may well exceed a million today. Air transport has in one way made the *ḥajj* easier, but now that over a million pilgrims participate together, it has become far more arduous because at certain moments all the pilgrims are performing the same rites in the same place. Thus, by force of numbers, the circumambulation of the Ka'bah, for example, can overflow outside the Grand Mosque, and be very difficult to perform.

Al-'Umrah ("the lesser pilgrimage", or "visitation"), an abbreviated version of the *ḥajj* – and also one of its constituent elements – can be performed at any time. Its rites can be accomplished in one and one-half hours, and they now take place entirely within the reconstructed and extended Grand Mosque in Mecca. The *'umrah,* which consists essentially of seven circumambulations of the Ka'bah and seven courses, partly walked and partly run, between Ṣafā and Marwah, may be performed at any time of the year except during the "greater pilgrimage" (when it is combined with the *ḥajj*), and at any time of day or night. It is possible to perform the *'umrah* for another by proxy, making an intention to that effect. *'Umrah* does not fulfill the requirement of ḥajj, but those who perform the *'umrah* are called, loosely, *ḥajjī* while accomplishing it. (The proper term for one performing *'umrah* is *mu'tamir.*)

Az-Ziyārah ("visit"), a non-canonical custom – not a rite (it even contradicts a Ḥadīth expressly forbidding it), of visiting the tomb of the Prophet in Medina. By extension, the word *az-ziyārah* is sometimes applied to the visiting of any holy place. Such visits are often carried out according to a traditional program, but do not in fact have ritual elements, although the *Fātiḥah,* the fundamental prayer (*see* FĀTIḤAH), is always recited in connection with a visit of this kind, and canonical prayers may be performed.

Pilgrimage to the Ka'bah antedates Islam. The Koran says that the pilgrimage of the Arabs of pagan times had become so degenerate that "their worship at the House is nothing but a whistling and a handclapping" (8:35). Taking elements of the pilgrimage as it then existed, the Prophet gave a new model based upon his two pilgrimages after the founding of the Islamic community; the pilgrimage of the year 7 of the Hijrah (March 629), after the treaty of Ḥudaybiyyah, and the "farewell" pilgrimage of the year 10 (March 632). The latter was the more important from the point of view of exemplary situations.

However, the Koran says that the founder of the rite of pilgrimage is Abraham:

> And when We settled for Abraham the place
> of the House: 'Thou shall not associate
> with Me anything. And do thou purify
> My House for those that shall go about it
> and those that stand, for those that bow
> and prostrate themselves;
> and proclaim among men the Pilgrimage,
> and they shall come unto thee on foot
> and upon every lean beast, they shall come from
> every deep ravine
> that they may witness things profitable to them
> and mention God's Name on days well-known
> over such beasts of the flocks as He has
> provided them: "So eat thereof, and feed
> the wretched poor."
> Let them then finish with their self-neglect
> and let them fulfil their vows, and go about
> the Ancient House'. (22:26-30)

The *ḥajj* is performed at the Grand Mosque (*al-masjid al-ḥarām*), and in Minā, Muzdalifah, and Arafāt, which are places directly adjacent to Mecca and contiguous one to the other. 'Arafāt is the farthest from Mecca, being an extensive plain, part of which lies beyond the sacred environs (*ḥaram*) of Mecca; on one side of it rises a small hill called the Mount of Mercy (*jabal raḥmah*). The whole plain is suitable for the rite of the "standing" (*wuqūf*) at 'Arafāt. Minā, which is closest to Mecca, is hemmed in by mountains, and here the pillars are located which are stoned during the *ḥajj.* Mu'zdalifah lies between Minā and Arafāt. But the *ḥajj* and/or the *'umrah* begin, as do all rites, with the stating of intent (*an-niyyah*), and this is bound up with the putting on of *iḥrām* (*see* IḤRĀM), the state of consecration, and the primordial costume which goes with it of two seamless – unsewn – pieces of cloth.

The *'umrah* consists of the following: before setting foot in the sacred area around Mecca, the pilgrim intending to perform the *'umrah* dons the *iḥrām*. Those who are already in Mecca go to certain mosques on the boundary of the sacred area, such as the Ju'ranah mosque, in order to do this. Most visitors from abroad put it on in Jeddah, although it is possible to assume it even in one's country of departure.

1. Upon arriving at the Ka'bah the pilgrim performs seven circumambulations of the Ka' bah.

2. This is followed by a personal prayer (*du'ā'*) whilst pressing oneself to the wall of the Ka'bah at the spot called *al-multazam* between the Black Stone and the door. Since it is difficult because of the number of pilgrims at any time actually to perform this at that precise point, in practice, the pilgrim usually recites his prayer facing the Ka'bah at a point some distance away, near the Station of Abraham (*maqām Ibrāhīm*).

3. The pilgrim then performs a two-*raka'āt* prayer at the Station of Abraham, a small kiosk which contains an imprint, said to be of Abraham's foot, in stone.

4. The pilgrim drinks of the water of Zamzam which is found at the watering place, reached by a flight of steps, where the spring in the courtyard of the Great Mosque has been channeled, or from the drinking fountains set up throughout the Mosque.

5. He then proceeds to the ritual walking (*sa'y*) between the two hills Ṣafā and Marwah, seven times. (Ṣafā to Marwah is one course, Marwah to Ṣafā another.) This is begun at Ṣafā and ends at Marwah, at the far end of the Mosque, where a lock of hair is cut from the pilgrim's head signifying the end of the rite and of the state of *iḥrām*.

Commonly, a new pilgrim hires a professional guide, called a *muṭawwif*, to lead him in the rites of *'umrah*. There are recitations traditionally associated with each step of the rites, but these have no binding character and may be replaced by simple spoken prayer.

The *ḥajj* is a more extensive ritual lasting several days. *Iḥrām* is assumed at a greater distance from Mecca than that of *'umrah*, at one of the "boundaries", each known as *as-miqāt* (*see* MIQĀT). Many pilgrims put on *iḥrām* as they leave their own countries, particularly those arriving by air.

The intention (*niyyah*) formulated for the *ḥajj* varies according to how the '*umrah* is combined with it. There are three possibilities:

1. *Ifrād;* the *ḥajj* alone; a second intention for the *'umrah* is then formulated at Mecca as the starting point. The second *iḥrām* is put on at the boundary for the Meccan *ḥaram*.

2. *Tamattu;* an interrupted pilgrimage; *iḥrām* is put on for the *'umrah* which is performed sometime before the pilgrimage; the state of *iḥrām* is then terminated, to be resumed when the moment comes for the greater pilgrimage.

3. *Qirān*, the combining of *'umrah* and *ḥajj* without interruption of the consecrated state of *iḥrām*. (*See* IḤRĀM.)

The daily stages of the greater pilgrimage are as follows:

The First Day: 8th *Dhū-l-Ḥijjah*

The name of this day is the *yawm at-tarwiyah* ("the day of deliberation or reflection"). The pilgrim must have entered into *iḥrām* outside Mecca at one of the *mawāqīt* (sing. *mīqāt*) before arriving in Mecca. If he is performing an interrupted pilgrimage according to *tamattu'* (*see* IḤRĀM) and has put off his *iḥrām*, he should resume it early in the morning after cutting his hair and nails, performing the ritual ablution, and pronouncing the *talbiyah* invocation: *labbayka-Llāhumma labbayk* ("At Thy service, My God, at Thy service!").

1. If the pilgrim has not yet performed the *ṭawāf al-qudūm* ("the circumambulation of arrival") he must now do so; one walks seven times around the Ka'bah. (*See* ṬAWĀF). The circumambulation at this point in the pilgrimage is optional, but the Mālikī School of Law considers it obligatory (*farḍ*). Because of the number of people, it is difficult to approach the Black Stone to kiss it; therefore a gesture towards the Stone as one walks past, without actually touching it, suffices.

2. After the seventh round is completed, the pilgrim makes a personal prayer, at the area between the Black Stone and the door of the Ka'bah, or at a spot facing this area.

3. The pilgrim then goes to the Station of Abraham (*maqām Ibrāhīm*), or any place near it, and performs a prayer of two *raka'āt*.

4. The pilgrim drinks the water of Zamzam. Thus far, the rites have been exactly the same as those of the *'umrah*, which is a component of the *ḥajj*; but from this point they can diverge. If one is performing pilgrimage in conjunction with the *'umrah* (*qirān*) (*see* IḤRĀM) (the pilgrim is then called a *muqrin*) one should now perform the "running" (*sa'y*) which will count for both *'umrah* and *ḥajj;* alternatively it may also be postponed until the second ambulation (*ṭawāf al-ifāḍah*). Those performing the *ḥajj* alone (*ifrād*) or separate from the umrah (*tamattu*) will perform the *sa'y* after the *ṭawāf al-ifāḍah* (also called the *ṭawāf az-ziyārah*). After the rites performed in the Grand Mosque, the pilgrims leave for Minā to spend the night until the dawn prayer. For Ḥanafīs and Mālikīs this stay at Minā is obligatory, whereas for others it is recommended. Therefore some pilgrims stay at Minā while others go directly to 'Arafāt from Mecca.

The Second Day: 9th *Dhū-l-Ḥijjah*

This day is called the the *yawm al-wuqūf* ("the day of standing"), and also *yawm 'Arafāt* ("the Day of 'Arafāt"). Those who are not already at 'Arafāt go there after the dawn prayer at Minā. At 'Arafāt the afternoon and late afternoon prayers are combined, under the leadership of the Imām, and also shortened. One *adhan* (general call to prayer) is performed with two *iqāmahs* (call to the assembled worshipers immediately before the prayer).

The *wuqūf* ("standing"; it is not necessary actually to stand) is an essential element (*rukn*) of the *ḥajj*. Usually the pilgrims stay at 'Arafāt from noon until after sunset, that is, some part of the day and some part of the night. This is the opinion of the Mālikī, Ḥanafī and Shāfi'ī schools. Ḥanbalis stay there all day from morning. Some insist on staying at 'Arafāt until sunrise on the 10th, but it is sometimes pointed out that in accordance with one Ḥadīth, *any time* spent at 'Arafāt fulfills the requirement of presence or "standing", as long as this is accomplished *before* the sunrise of the 10th. After sunrise the time for this requirement has definitely lapsed, and without the standing at 'Arafāt there is no *ḥajj*.

During the "Day of 'Arafāt", the pilgrim should recite the *talbiyah* frequently. (*See* TALBIYAH.) This is indeed the central invocatory prayer of the pilgrimage. The symbolism of this day which is one of solemnity, invocation of God, and the examination of conscience, has been interpreted as a foretaste of the Day of Judgement.

It is not necessary to climb the hill the Mount of Mercy (*jabal raḥmah*) at 'Arafāt, and indeed because of the number of people, it is safer not to do so. Any spot at 'Arafāt is suitable for the performance of the rite. One must not wear anything on the head, but one may carry a parasol, which is in fact advisable. After sunset most pilgrims leave for Muzdalifah in what is called the *ifāḍah* ("overflowing") or the *nafrah* ("rush"). The invocation of the *talbiyah* comes to an end. At Muzdalifah the pilgrims perform the sunset and night prayers combined together and pray these at the time of the night prayer (*'ishā'*). The pilgrims pass the night at Muzdalifah.

The Third Day: 10th *Dhū-l-Ḥijjah*

This day is called the *yawm an-nahr* ("the day of sacrifice"). The dawn prayer is performed at Muzdalifah and the monument called *al-mash'ar al-ḥarām*, an open area, is visited. The pilgrim gathers 49 pebbles if he is going to stay at Minā for two days, and 70 if he will stay three. These pebbles should be approximately the size of a chickpea and they will be used to stone the symbolic pillars (*al-jamarāt*) during the following days.

On the way to Minā the pilgrim passes though a depression called *Wādi Muḥaṣṣar* (also called *Wādi Nār*). This is the place where the Army of the Elephant was turned away and, as it is "a tormented place", the pilgrim hurries through without lingering.

Upon reaching Minā, the pilgrim casts seven stones at the *jamarat al-'aqabah*, the largest pillar, which represents the temptations of Satan. The casting of stones on this day is obligatory.

After casting the seven stones, the pilgrim may perform the sacrifice at any time until the end of the 13th. (There is a rush for sacrifice on the 10th; the well advised pilgrim puts off the sacrifice until a following day.) The sacrifice may be a camel, an ox, or a ram. Actual blood sacrifice may be replaced by fasting three days during the pilgrimage and seven days at a later time for a total of ten days. For followers of the Shāfiī school the blood sacrifice is irreplaceable.

At this point the hair of the pilgrim is clipped. Woman cut only a symbolical lock of hair, but many men have the head completely shaved. Cutting a lock, however, is acceptable for men as well. The state of *iḥrām* is terminated, that one may resume normal dress. However, the conditions of abstinence associated with *iḥrām* continue until the pilgrim has definitively left Minā.

Now the pilgrim goes to Mecca and performs the *ṭawāf al-ifāḍah* (also called *ṭawāf az-ziyārah*). However, this, and the "running" (*sa'y*), if not performed earlier, may be performed until sunset on the 13th.

The Final Days: 11th, 12th and 13th *Dhū-l-Ḥijjah.*

During these days, called the *ayyām at-tashrīq* ("days of drying meat"), the pilgrim stays at Minā and each day throws seven stones (*ramī-l-jimār*) at each of the three *jamarāt*, first pelting the small *jamarah* closest to 'Arafāt, then the middle *jamarah*, and ending with the large *jamarah*. These pillars stand in a row in the valley of Minā, now accessible by ramps on two levels. Stoning may not be carried out between sunset and sunrise, and it is Sunnah to do it before noon on the first day, and after noon on the other days. It is permissible to end the pilgrimage by leaving on the 12th, as long as one departs before sunset, or has effectively made preparations for departure by sunset. If not, one must remain for the third day. If one needs more pebbles for stoning, they may be gathered in Minā. Upon leaving Mecca one usually performs the *ṭawāf al-wadā'* ("circumambulation of farewell"), which is not obligatory, but commended.

It has been said: "the pilgrimage is a journey to the heart". The yearly flood of pilgrims from the remotest places of Islam has been a remarkable means of spiritual renewal for distant communities which are thus brought closer to the manifest center of Islam.

Historically, the pilgrimage has been a means of knitting together the many races and nations that make up the Muslim community, and there is no other event on earth that can compare with it. Besides its contribution to social cohesiveness, it has, in the past, been a journey for learning and for the interchange of ideas. For many scholars the journey to Mecca has been the turning point of their intellectual careers because of the encounters it provided with other minds. The Almoravid movement was set into motion as a result of the pilgrimage of one man, and other events no less momentous can be traced to the sacred journey.

In the days when travel was done by land or sea, people unable to hire transport could well go on foot to Mecca from, say, West Africa. There are many alive today for whom the pilgrimage was such a journey, when, typically, it took two years in one direction and two years back, because pilgrims would sojourn along the way. Many remained in the Middle East, and in Mecca and Medina especially, where there are communities of Indians, Malays, Indonesians, and Africans, erstwhile pilgrims who settled there. Similarly, Cairo, Damascus, and Baghdad were great stages of the journey, catering to the yearly flood of pilgrims who today travel by air instead.

The caravans which assembled in these cities for the last stage of the journey to Mecca disappeared only towards the middle of this century. In a way, these caravan routes are still viable; pilgrims now come by automobile from neighboring countries. The economic importance of the pilgrimage has increased with the number of pilgrims, and dominates the economic life of Mecca and Medina, and to some extent, Jeddah. But the pilgrimage is no less important to the economies of Pakistan, Turkey, Nigeria, and Indonesia, whose nationals continue to take part in the pilgrimage in very large numbers to this day. *See* 'ARAFĀT; FĀTIḤAH; FIVE PILLARS; ḤARĀM; IḤRĀM; KA'BAH; MAQĀM IBRĀHĪM; MĪQĀT; MINĀ; MULTAZAM; MUZDALIFAH; RAMY al-JIMĀR; ṢALĀH; ṢAFĀ and MARWAH; TALBIYAH; ṬAWĀF.

Pious Expressions. Koranic formulas are used in every day expressions. The most important is the *basmalah*, or *Bismi 'Llāhi 'r-Raḥmāni -r-Raḥīm* ("In the Name of God the Merciful, the Compassionate") which can begin any lawful, positive activity and must be spoken at the beginning of all rituals.

The *ḥamdalah* or *al-ḥamdu li-Llāh* ("praise to God") marks an end to an action expressing thanks and acceptance, wonder and reverence, as do likewise *subḥān Allāh* ("God be praised!") and *Allāhu Akbar* ("God is Greater or Greatest"), or *Lā hawla wa lā quwwata illā bi-Llāh* ("there is no power nor strength save in God"). The *istithnā'*, or *In shā'a-Llāh* ("if God wills") is used in reference to any action or state in the future. *Innā li-Llāhi wa innā ilayhi rāji'ūn* ("we belong to God and to Him we return") is said when in distress or upon hearing of a death. *Ṣabrun jamīlun wa-Llāhu karīm* ("Patience is an adornment and God is gracious") is another expression in moments of trial. *Al-mu'minūna fī kulli ḥālin bi-khayr* ("believers are blest in all circumstances"). *Tawakkal 'ala-Llāhi wa huwa ni'ma-l-wakīl* ("trust in God, for what a Guardian is He!"). These expressions echo daily in a Muslim's life and, at their most heart-felt, are the support of an unflinching reliance upon God; one may, in the nature of things, fall, but with faith one will "fall upward", and be held by *ar-Raḥmān* ("the Merciful") as he supports the dove in flight. Similar expressions, such as *in nomine Deo, Deo gratia, laus Deo,* were used in the same way in Christian Europe in the Middle Ages. *See* BASMALAH; ḤAMDALAH; al-ḤAWQALAH; REFUGE; TAHLĪL; TALBIYYAH; TAMJĪD; TA'AWWUDH.

Pīr. A spiritual master, a teacher (*murshid*). From Turkey to India this title is used in preference to the Arabic word *shaykh.*

Pish-Namāz. In Iran, the term for the leader of the prayer, to avoid confusion with the Shī'ite meaning of Imām, which is the term among Sunnīs. *See* IMĀM.

Pole, spiritual, *see* QUṬB.

Polygamy. *see* POLYGYNY; WOMEN; WIVES of the PROPHET.

Polytheism, *see* SHIRK; IDOLS; JĀHILIYYAH.

The Pool (Ar. *al-ḥawḍ*). This is part of the symbolical "topology" of the afterlife. The pool is a lake fed by the spring of Kawthar at the entrance to paradise, attained by crossing over the "bridge" of death and Judgement. The believers who enter paradise will drink from the spring of Kawthar; it was by the Pool that the Prophet promised to meet his Companions. The spring of Kawthar is the inexhaustible plenitude of God; the word contains the root *kathara,* indicating abundance amplified by the letter *waw* (w) which stands, according to Sufi interpretations, for *al-Wāḥid* (the "Single", the "One"; a name of God). The price demanded by God for this plenitude is prayer and sacrifice:

> Surely We have given thee abundance;
> so pray unto thy Lord and sacrifice.
> Surely he that hates thee he is the one cut off.
> (106)

Postal System, *see* BARĪD.

Power, Night of, *see* LAYLAT al-QADR.

Prayer. This English word serves to translate three different concepts in Islam, namely *du'ā', ṣalāh* and *dhikr.*

Du'ā' (lit. "calling") is an "individual" or spontaneous prayer in which the worshiper expresses his personal sentiments and petitions God. A special form of *du'ā'* is the *Yā Laṭīf* prayer which is used in moments of distress, or in cases of grave illness.

Ṣalāh (lit. "worship", from an Aramaic word whose root meaning is "to hallow") is the canonical or "ritual" prayer which must be performed at five appointed times each day. The basic unit is the *rak'ah* (a round of ritual actions and sacred phrases), so that each canonical prayer consists of a prescribed number of *raka'āt* (pl. of *rak'ah*). Superogatory *raka'āt* are permitted and, indeed, encouraged. Conversely, if for any valid reason it is not possible to pray the canonical prayers at the appointed time, they are to be made up afterwards. The form and contents of the *ṣalāh* are fixed by the Sunnah, the Prophet's example, and by the traditions of the schools of law. *Ṣalāh* is an act of worship, a religious service, special forms of which are prescribed for the occasions of death, religious festivals, and solar eclipses, or to ask for guidance in particular circumstances (*istikhārah*), or to pray God for rain (*istisqā'*).

The third category of prayer is the inward prayer of remembrance of God, invocation, *dhikr. For further descriptions see* DHIKR; DU'Ā'; FUNERALS; ṢALĀH; YĀ LAṬĪF.

Prayer for the Dead, *see* FUNERALS.

Prayer of Ibn Mashīsh, *see* IBN MASHĪSH.

Prayer Niche, *see* MIḤRĀB.

Prayers on the Prophet (Ar. *aṣ-ṣalāh 'ala-n-Nabī.* The word *ṣalāh,* which denotes the ritual prayer of Islam, and its verb *sallā* "to praise", "to bless", often translated as to pray upon", appears to originate from Aramaic, the root meaning being "to hallow"). The Koran says: "Verily, God and his Angels send blessings upon the Prophet. You who believe, call blessings upon him and peace." (33:56). Muslims use a number of such invocatory prayers in various rituals and ceremonies. The *du'ā'* (petitioning prayer), which follows the *ṣalāh* (ritual, or canonic prayer), is always introduced with a prayer on the Prophet. This is one version used in North Africa:

> *Aṣ-ṣalātu wa-s-salāmu 'alayka yā Nabiyya 'Llāh, aṣ-ṣalātu wa-s-salāmu 'alayka ya Ḥabība-Llāh, aṣ-ṣalātu wa-s-salāmu 'alayka ya Rasūla-Llāh; alfu ṣalātin waalfu salāmin 'alayka wa alā ālik wa-r-riḍā'u 'an aṣḥābika, yā khayra mani 'khtāra 'Llāh.*

> Blessing and peace be upon you, O Prophet of God; Blessing and peace be upon you O intimate of God; Blessing and peace be upon upon you O Messenger of God. Thousandfold blessing and thousandfold peace upon you and upon your people, and God's felicity upon your Companions, O best of the chosen of God.

Or:

> *Allāhumma ṣalli 'alā Sayyidinā Muḥammadin 'adada khalqika wa riḍa'i nafsika wa madadi kalimatika. Subḥāna-Llāhi 'ammā yaṣifūn, wa salāmun 'alā-l-mursalīn, wa-l-ḥamduli-Llāhi Rabbi-l-ālamīn.*

> Our Lord, bless our master Muḥammad as much as the number of your creations, the felicity of your essence, and the ink necessary to write your words. Magnified be God above what is attributed to Him, and peace upon the Messengers, and Praise to God, the Lord of the worlds.

When a believer mentions the Prophet – and he is rarely mentioned by name, but rather by the title Prophet (*Nabi*), or Messenger of God (*Rasūlu -Llāh*) – it is customary to add: *ṣalla-Llāhu 'alayhi wa sallam* ("May God bless him and give him peace"). The blessings (*ṣalāh*) refer to "vertical" graces descending into the soul, and "peace" (*salām*) to a "horizontal" grace of inward dilation which receives and stabilizes those blessings. *See also* QUNŪT.

Presences, Five Divine, *see* FIVE DIVINE PRESENCES.

Priests (In Arabic, *rāhib*, pl. *ruhbān*, referring only to Christian anchorites or monks). "There are no priests in Islam" is a Ḥadīth which states the position simply enough. Therefore, the term Islamic Priests sometimes used in the Western press to mean a functionary such as an Imām, a *faqīh*, or a *mulla*, is misleading and alien to Muslim understanding.

Whereas the Christian sacerdotal function implies a special consecration of the person and the power to carry out rituals which a layman cannot perform, there is no ritual in Islam which cannot be performed by any believer of sound mind, either a man, or a woman if no man is present. Some functions, such as that of prayer leader (Imām), may fall to a particular person because of knowledge (particularly of the Koran), respectable repute or age, but could be performed by anyone. Most public functions such as Imām, *qāḍi* ("Judge"), *'ālim* (a doctor of religious science) are based upon knowledge and scholarship (one might say skill), but do not require a consecration that sets the performer of the function apart from other believers. This is consistent with Islam's claim to restore the religion of Abraham, or the "primordial religion"; it could be said that Islam needs no priests because every Muslim is a priest. *See also* MONASTICISM.

Primordial Norm, *see* FIṬRAH.

Prophets (Ar. sing. *nabī*, pl. *anbiyā'*). The Prophets are divided into two classes according to their missions:

1. *Rasūl* (lit. "Messenger", "Envoy", pl. *rusul*; the Koran, moreover, frequently refers to *al-mursalūn*, "those who are sent"). A Prophet who brings a new religion or a major new revelation. This category include Adam, Seth, Noah, Abraham, Ishmael, Moses, Lot, Ṣāliḥ, Hūd, Shu'ayb, Jesus, Muḥammad. The Koran calls some of the *mursalūn* the possessors of constancy (Ar. *'ūlū-l-'azm*; 46:35); the Koran does not name them, but commentators have proposed their candidates.

2. *Nabī* (lit. "Prophet"). A Prophet whose mission lies within the framework of an existing religion. A Prophet is also called *bashīr* ("he who brings glad tidings") and *nadhīr* ("a warner") according to the nature of the message they bear; but most are both bringers of glad tidings as well as warners, since the Mercy and the Rigor of God, which these categories respectively reflect, are complementary, as are Beauty and Majesty.

The Koran says that there is no people to whom a Prophet has not been sent (10:48) and Ḥadīth literature puts the number, symbolically, at one hundred and twenty-four thousand, that is, a number so large that humanity cannot claim it was not adequately warned of the universal Judgement. (The Prophets in their inner nature are one: "We make no distinction between any of His Messengers" (2:135-140 and 2:285) and: "And those who believe in God and His Messengers and make no division between any of them, those We shall surely give them their wages" (4:152).)

The Koran mentions four Arab Prophets, or Prophets sent specifically to the Arabs: Ṣāliḥ, Hūd, Shu'ayb, and Muḥammad. In addition, Abraham is equally the patriarch of both Arabs and Jews.

In the *Nihāyat al-Iqdām fī-'Ilm al-Kalām* ("Limits to Prowess in Theology") Shahrastani says: "By my life, the Prophet's soul and temperament must possess all natural perfections, excellent character, truthfulness and honesty in speech and deed before his appointment to the office, because it is by virtue of these that he has deserved Prophetic mission and has come into contact with Angels, and received revelation."

The following are the Prophets mentioned by name in the Koran: Adam, Alyasa' (Elisha), Ayyūb (Job), Dā'ūd (David); Dhū-l-Kifl (Ezekiel), Hūd, Ibrāhīm (Abraham), Idrīs (Enoch), Ilyās (Elijah, Elias), 'Īsā (Jesus), Isḥāq (Isaac), Ismā'īl (Ishmael), Luqmān (Aesop?), Lūṭ (Lot), Muḥammad, Mūsā (Moses), Nūḥ (Noah), Ṣāliḥ, Shu'ayb (Jethro), Sulaymān (Solomon), Yūnus (Jonah), 'Uzair (Ezra), Yaḥyā (John the Baptist), Ya'qūb (Jacob), Yūsuf (Joseph). There are also possible references to others, such as Isaiah. Also mentioned by name are Azar (father of Abraham, Terah in the Old Testament, a transformation through the form Athar), Dhu-l-Qarnayn (Alexander the Great), Hārūn (Aaron), Maryam (Mary), Zakariyyā (Zacharias, father of John the Baptist), and others. *See* ABRAHAM; ADAM; HŪD; ILYĀS; ALYASA'; JESUS; LUQMĀN; MARY; MOSES, MUḤAMMAD; NOAH; REVELATION; ṢĀLIḤ; SHU'AYB; YAḤYĀ; YŪNUS.

Psalms, see ZABŪR.

Purdah. In Afghanistan and India, the covering of the face and body by women in public, and their general seclusion. *Ḥijāb* ("veil") is becoming the modern term for such observance in Western Islam.

Purgatory, *see* A'RĀF; ESCHATOLOGY.

Purification. A ritual which consecrates a place for prayer, it does not normally precede prayer in the open air, but is used for interiors such as a mosque, a room in a house, or office, or simply a carpet.

The believer cleans the space or carpet to be purified, often with a brush, and then sprinkles water over it after having pronounced the *ta 'awwudh* and the *basmalah.* It is recorded that when the Prophet held babies in his arms which were incontinent, he would remove the impurity from his clothes by sprinking water and pronouncing the *basmalah.*

A mosque or place of prayer is normally purified by cleaning with water and pronouncing the *basmalah;* if a person in the state of major impurity, which requires the greater ablution (*ghusl*) should enter, the purification of the place is deemed to have been lost, and it is necessary to re-purify it. For this reason non-Muslims are not, strictly speaking, allowed into mosques which are actually used for prayer. In some countries this condition is observed; in others, special slippers are provided for non-Muslims to wear when they enter mosques, or else the ground is covered to provide walking areas. In others again, the condition is simply ignored. *See* ABLUTIONS.

Purity, Sūrah of, *see* IKHLĀṢ.

Pushtun. (better *Pashtūn*, pl. of *Pashtāna*). The Pashto-speaking tribesman who live in Afghanistan, where they are one of the main ethnic groups, and in Pakistan, where they are generally called by the variant term Pathan (Hindi and Urdu). The majority are nomads and live in black goat's hair tents. They are Sunnī Muslims and number over fourteen million.

Q

Qabḍ (lit. "contraction", "spasm"). A term in Sufism meaning a contraction, or straitness of soul. The rhythms of life and particularly of the spiritual life, inevitably call forth periods in which the soul experiences its limitations as distress. The opposite is "expansion" (*basṭ*). Spiritually, however, it is contraction which is beneficial, for it is by trials that one is purified; al-Hujwīrī says:

> *qabḍ*... is the contraction of the heart in the state of being veiled... *basṭ* the heart's expansion in the illumined state... both are the result of the same spiritual effusion from God upon man, which either stimulates the heart and depresses the soul, causing *basṭ*, or enlargement, or depresses the heart and stimulates the soul, in *qabḍ*, or straitness.

Ibn 'Aṭā' Allāh says in the *Ḥikam*:

> He expanded you so as not to keep you in contraction and contracted so as not to keep you in expansion, and He took you out of both so that you not belong to anything apart from Him.

And:

> Whoever worships Him for something he hopes from Him, or in order to stave off the arrival of chastisement, has not concerned himself with the real nature of His Attributes.

And:

> When He gives, He shows you His kindness; when He deprives, He shows you His power. And in all that, He is making Himself known to you and coming to you with His gentleness.

See BASṬ.

al-Qadam ash-Sharīf (lit. "the noble footprint"). The footprint is often used in Islam as the symbol of the immaterial "trace" of the Divine Messenger. The stylized "footprint" of Abraham is enshrined in a kiosk near the Ka'bah.

The image of a footprint in which are written the praises of the Prophet is a popular decorative motif. The poet Jalāl ad-Dīn ar-Rūmī said: "If you do not know the way, seek where his footprints are."

Qadaris, *see* QADARIYYAH.

Qadariyyah (from Ar. *qadar*, "power", "will"). Those who upheld the notion of free will against the advocates of predestination (the *Jabarīs* or *Jabariyyah*) in Islam's early theological debates. A solution to the problem of free will and determinism was sketched out by the Ash'arites in their theory of man's acquisition of acts which originate with God. Later, the mystics proposed an antinomial solution to the problem which suggested that the individual does indeed possess free will, and is thus responsible for his decisions, but that these decisions – which are seen in time – nevertheless ultimately fulfill a destiny determined outside time. In other words, they contended that although Divine Will has determined all things, the freedom of human will lies in its capacity to choose, or to deny, the Absolute. In any case, the word *qadar* means "capacity" and implies limitation, and thus destiny; that is, the word for will and destiny is in fact one and the same. For this reason, at other times *Qadari* has had an opposite meaning, that of determinist.

Ibn 'Aṭā' Allah said:

> To soften for you the suffering of affliction, He has taught you that He is the One who causes trials to come upon you. For the one who confronts you with His decrees of Fate is the same Who has accustomed you to His good choice.

And Jalāl ad-Dīn ar-Rūmī said:

> If we let fly an arrow, that action is not from us: we are only the bow, and the shooter of the arrow is God.

See KALĀM; MAKTŪB.

Qāḍi (pl. *quḍāh*). A judge, appointed by a ruler or a government on the basis of his superior knowledge of Islamic law. This Arabic word is sometimes rendered as "cadi" in English, and produced the Spanish *alcalde* for "mayor". The

Qāḍi's decisions are binding and final. In the Sunnī world, the "door of *ijtihād*", or decisions made on one's personal assessment, has been "closed", and judges are thus expected to apply only the precedents of the past in making their decisions. In practice, however, judges have applied new solutions (*ijtihād nisbī*, "relative *ijtihād*") to legal problems, at least by small increments, finally producing a new corpus of legal decisions; this could be called *ijtihād* by degrees. In the Shī'ite world, on the contrary, a decision is made only by a *mujtahid*, a high religious authority, and is a new "unique" decision, even if an identical precedent exists.

The *qāḍi* must be free of business interests which could compromise his impartiality. Because *qāḍis* are subject to great pressures from political authorities, the office has sometimes been turned down by men of repute to avoid the stigma of complicity with the political power.

Although a *qāḍi* is a necessary functionary for a community, many disputes are decided by civil authorities such as Shaykhs and Governors, since legal power and political authority are inseparable in traditional Islam. In West Africa the term *qāḍi* has a broader meaning, being sometimes used to designate any man who is well-informed on religious matters but has no official position; such a one would be called a *faqīh* in North Africa. *See* SHARĪ'AH.

Qāḍi 'Asker ("Army Judge"). An important office among the Ottomans. The Army judges followed the armies on their campaigns.

Qādiriyyah. A famous Sufi order founded by 'Abd al-Qādir al-Jīlānī (d. *561*/1166) in Baghdad. He is one of the great Saints of Islam, and veneration of his memory is a hallmark of the Qādiriyyah. The Qādiriyyah was the first *ṭarīqah* as such to emerge in Sufism; until then the path had been relatively undifferentiated, although groupings had formed around particular spiritual masters called *ṭawā'if* (sing. *tā'ifah*) groups, bands or factions. With 'Abd al-Qādir the tradition begins in Sufism of looking back to a particular teacher and considering him as a watershed in method and doctrine; until then Sufis had looked directly to the Prophet as the founder, and considered their own spiritual masters as his representatives; they still do so, in principle, but with an awareness that has, in the individual case, to be actualized.

'Abd al-Qādir's tomb is in Baghdad. He is credited with saying that if someone in spiritual distress calls upon him, "he will come riding on a charger" to bring him help.

The Qādiriyyah is widespread from India to Morocco. In the Arab West the order is called the *Jilālah* and its practices are marked by an intrusion of "folk" Sufism, resulting in the degeneration of the *ḥaḍrah* (sacred dance) into trance dancing, and an emphasis on unusual states of mind and prodigious feats to the detriment of a coherent doctrine of spiritual development. Like the *Hamidsha* and *'Isawiyyah*, their ecstatic dancing to an accompaniment of characteristic flute and drum music is often performed in public. *See* 'ABD al-QĀDIR al-JĪLĀNĪ.

al-Qāhirah, *see* CAIRO.

Qajars. A dynasty in Persia from *1209-1343*/1794-1924, they were the leaders of a Turkmen tribe, one of the original tribes of the *Qizīl Bash*. The first Qajar, Aga Muḥammad, fought his way to power. It was under the Qajars that Teheran, a small town, became the capital of Persia and the country became more involved in world affairs. In *1343*/1924 the Qajars were deposed by Riḍā Pahlavi, who founded a new dynasty. *See* PAHLAVIS; QIZĪL BASH.

Qalam (Ar. "reed", pen from Greek *kalamos* of the same meaning). The Koran says several times that God teaches men by the pen, that is, by the revelation of scripture. The *qalam* is also symbolically the instrument of creation, inscribing existence onto the cosmic tablet (*lawḥ*). The *qalam* corresponds to Aristotle's *eidos* ("form"), the Sanskrit *purusha*, while the tablet corresponds to *hyle* ("substance"), or *prakriti*.

The *qalam* also symbolizes the "writing" of individual destinies onto the "tablet of fate". The concrete nature of this and similar images in the Koran was a stumbling block to some early theologians. Ibn Ḥanbal and al-Ash'arī insisted that these images be taken literally without further elaboration and without questioning, *bila kayfa* ("without asking how").

Qalandar. Used in the East, chiefly Iran and India, for wandering "dervishes" who lived on alms, the word became popular because of its frequent occurence in the *Thousand and One Nights*. Obscurity surrounding Qalandar beliefs, and stories that their founder was expelled by the Bektashis (themselves a heretical syncretism) suggest that rather than an order of mystics whose rule required perpetual wandering and poverty, it was really a catch-all term for beggars whose ornate bowl was a mere pretension of spirituality.

In this context a supposed distinction is made between so-called Sufi orders which are *ba-shar'*, or formal ("within the *sharī'ah* or law"), and those which are *be-shar'* ("without the *sharī ah* or law"); this is no more than a fiction or euphemism, for the so-called *be-shar'* are in reality a class of social outcasts, pariahs, and the mentally incompetent, who would more accurately be called unbelievers (*kāfirūn*). *See* GNAWAH.

Qanāt. Water irrigation channels in Iran, which run underground in order to minimise loss from evaporation, with openings to the surface at regular intervals to give access for maintenance. They are sometimes as long as twelve miles. The word today can mean any kind of channel.

Qānūn (from the Greek, *canon*, "a rod", "a carpenter's rule"). A civil law (as opposed to *sharī'ah*, or religious law). A related term is a *ẓāhir*, or decree made by a ruler. A Divine decree however, is *qaḍā'*. *See* SHARĪ'AH.

Qarāmiṭa, *see* QARMATIANS.

Qara Qoyunlu. "The Black Sheep", a Turkmen horde of the Steppes which arose as a political confederation in Anatolia, Iraq, and West Persia, whose name came from the black sheep on their standards. They were a branch of the Ghuzz/Oghuz, once part of the Golden Horde. Qara Yusuf, who conquered Tabrīz in *791*/1389, founded the dynasty. The dominion of the Qara Qoyunlu, who were Shī'ites, was supplanted by that of their Sunnī rivals, the Aq Qoyunlu, the "White Sheep", after *873*/1468.

Qāri' (lit. "a reader", pl. *qurrā'*). **1.** A reciter in public of the Koran by reason of his skill in *tajwīd*.

2. In the early days of Islam when few people could read, so that those who could were of great importance in spreading the faith, sometimes it would happen that a tribe newly entered into Islam had to rely even upon a child to lead their prayers, if he was the only one who could read. To be a "reader" was, therefore, the equivalent of being an authority in religion, and these "readers" formed a political block, representing the first conservatives within the religion. For a time they were the main supporters of 'Alī ibn Abī Ṭalīb in his struggle with Mu'āwiyah. Later, many of them left him, dismayed by his willingness to negotiate the question of succession to the Caliphate which the readers believed was a matter Divinely ordained. These seceders became the Khārijites.

3. *Qāri'* also denotes the authorities whose reading of the Koran originally set the model for vocalization, punctuation and so forth. They are known as the "seven readers" (*al-Qurrā' as-Sab'ah*). *See* QIRĀ'AH.

Qarmatians (Ar. *al-Qarāmiṭah*, also called Carmathians). An early offshoot of the Seveners, the resurgent Gnosticism which emerged in Islamic guise after the death of Ismā'īl, the son of Ja'far aṣ-Ṣādiq, in *145*/762. The Qarmatians appeared around *277*/890 and are named after Ḥamdān Qarmaṭ, a peasant who was their founding propagandist (*dā'ī*). (The name *Qarmaṭ* means, in Aramaic, "he of the two red eyes", perhaps signifying "a teacher of secret doctrines"; interestingly, in Arabic, the verb *qarmaṭa* also means "to write in extremely fine letters", a noted characteristic of Manichean books of antiquity.) The Qarmatians combined secret religious doctrines with revolution and a program of social justice and redistribution of wealth. Ḥamdān's brother-in-law Abdān wrote a treatise on what was originally seven degrees of initiation.

The Qarmatians emerged from the region of Wāsiṭ in Iraq as a conspiratorial insurrection against the Caliphate referring to their base as *Dār al-Hijrah* ("the House of Emigration"). One of the leaders, Abū Sa'īd Ḥasan ibn Bahrām al-Jannābī, established a state in eastern Arabia, with the help of the Beduin tribe of the 'Abd al-Qays, around the vast oasis of al-Aḥṣā (or al-Ḥāṣa). They named their capital *al-Mu'miniyyah* (from *Mu'min*, "believer"), present day Hofūf in the Eastern Province of Saudi Arabia. The Qarmatians had branches in Syria among the Banū 'Ulays (under Dhikrawaih ibn Mihrawaih al-Dindānī, d. *293*/906;), Iraq, and Khorasan. In the beginning, the chiefs of the Qarmatians were called, among other titles, "Lords of Purity", and one of them, Abū 'Abd Allāh Muḥammad, proclaimed himself Caliph but died shortly afterwards in *288*/901. His brother, Abū 'Abd Allāh Aḥmad, took the title, but was captured and executed in Baghdad two years later, in *291*/903. (There had been a Manichean sect called "The pure ones" or "Denawars", in Arabic *Dīnāwarīyyah* beyond the Oxus. For a time the sect reunited with the Archegos leadership in Ctesiphon at the end of the 7th century. The division, which probably dated in one way or another from the 4th century, reappeared as the Mihriyyah, who collaborated with outside rulers [Mihr, an Archegos, had received the gift of a mule from the Governor of Iraq] and the Miqlasiyyah, who were more "pur et dur". Miqlas had succeeded Zad Hormus as Archegos who had succeeded Mihr.)

The Qarmatians represented an uprising by the peasantry and the dispossessed, who passionately hurled their heretical religion back at the orthodox establishment and attempted to seize its considerable wealth by conspiracy, rebellion, and terrorism. A movement of peasants and laborers, they bear a remarkable resemblance to modern "liberation armies". Casting far and wide for every dissenting thought they could find to fashion their own system, they brought about a ferment of ideas by using Greek, Persian, and Indian sources without reservation to build complicated and speculative doctrines of cosmology and metaphysics.

The most puzzling sects in the Islamic world, such as the 'Alī Ilāhīs and the 'Alawīs, may well be remnants of Qarmatian propagandizing. The Qarmatian social philosophy was a kind of communistic egalitarianism. A ritual "love-feast" (*agape*) with the consumption of the "bread of paradise" is attributed to the Qarmatians. In al-Ḥāsa they had a secret ceremony called the "Night of the Imām". This Imām however, was not 'Alī, or at any rate, not the historical 'Alī, for in an account by a captive, the Qarmati captor who was drunk one evening revealed what he thought about the first four Caliphs, He declared that 'Umar had been a brute, had an equally low opinion of 'Uthman, but unexpectedly declared with contempt that 'Alī was an old woman. The Prophet, however, was respected as someone who was forceful and knew how to command men and rule a state.

It may be that the trade guilds which took on an importance in medieval Islamic society as well as in Europe, (and still exist today, in Fez, for example), were a restoration by the Qarmatians of ancient initiatic orders based on crafts. The ideology of the Qarmatians, like that of the Ismā'īlīs, was a Gnostic Dualism, which sees evil as having a reality and substance of its own, as the good has. The vital point on which they differed from the Fāṭimid Ismā'īlīs, with whom they otherwise had great sympathies, is that they rejected allegiance to the Fāṭimid Imām. Naṣir-i Khusraw from Balkh in Khorasan, was given an official function by the Faṭimids in Cairo, and stopped off in al-Ḥāsa on his way back home, perhaps on a mission.

The communistic tendencies of the Qarmatians suggest that their filiation was ultimately from the Mazdakite branch of Manicheism. In any case, Manicheism divided into two branches early on: one advocated the achievement of their eschatological goals by Manicheism dominating the world by a kind of world revolution, and the other, by Manicheism first becoming dominant in one country. This corresponds to the different approaches of the Qarmatians and Ismā'īlīs, who otherwise seem to be kindred spirits, and demonstrates that similar philosophies evolve in uncannily similar ways, for the Communist movement in our times split into Communism as world revolution (Trotsky) and Communism first in one country (Stalin). The subsequent effect that the Fāṭimid state had upon the 'Abbāsids and its eventual collapse bear other remarkable resemblences to the life cycle demonstrated by the Soviet Union.

In *317*/930 the Qarmatians raided Mecca and carried away the Black Stone, keeping it in al-Ḥāsa, or perhaps Baḥrayn, before returning it in *340*/951. According to the historian al-Juwaynī, the stone was thrown into the Friday Mosque at Kufah with a declaration saying: "By command we took it, and by command we returned it." The Qarmatians had not accepted offers of ransom; in other words, they used the incident as a powerful means of propaganda. When the Qarmatians stole the Black Stone it was in three pieces and smaller fragments; it is now in seven. Did they deliberately break it to bring the number of pieces in line with the new age marked by the seven Imāms?

Opinion of the times linked the Fāṭimids to the

Qarmatians; it was said that the Fāṭimids prevailed upon them to return the Black Stone. Indeed, both the Fāṭimids and Qarmatians were the same philosophy under different guises. The story was told that the earth refused to accept the burial of the Fāṭimid ruler 'Ubayd Allāh until the Stone was returned, and that this was done at the order, or urging, of the third Fāṭimid Caliph, al-Manṣūr.

The Qarmatians disappeared not long afterwards, or rather were absorbed into the Nizari Ismaīlīs under the leadership of 'Alamut. While they existed their revolutionary presence was dreaded within the 'Abbasid Empire, and the influence they exerted on a number of heterodox sects which survive to this day was considerable. Travellers frequently report that Qarmati villages still exist in Oman and in Yemen. *See* FĀṬIMIDS; ISMĀ'ĪLĪS; al-MA'MUN; MANICHEISM; SEVENERS.

al-Qāshānī, 'Abd ar-Razzaq Kamāl ad-Dīn. (d. *730*/1329). Commentator on the *Fusūs al-Ḥikam* of Ibn Arabi. Al-Qāshānī also wrote a treatise on Sufi vocabulary, but he is especially known for his "Esoteric Commentary on the Koran" (*Ta'wīlāt al-Qur'ān*). The latter is very reminiscent of Jakob Boehme's commentary on the book of Genesis, where the operative principle is poetic substitution. Words having one meaning are purported to really mean something else. For example, if the Koran says that glass beakers are passed among the blessed in Paradise, al-Qāshānī says this means certain kinds of deeds which they performed in life, when it says they sit on cushions this means other deeds and so on.

Qashqai. A Turkic people, pastoral nomads of the Zagros Mountains of southwest Iran, numbering over 400,000, the Qashqai are divided into many tribes. They profess Twelve-Imām Shī'ism, with some latitude. The average man may be fervent, but as is the case with many nomads, his grasp of formal dogma is loose. The simplicity of Islam is precisely one of its great advantages: its fundamentals fit easily into a nomad's packs.

Qaswā'. The Prophet's camel, which he rode into Medina when he left Mecca. Upon arrival in the outskirts of the city, the camel was set loose to find the place where the Prophet would stay. The spot where the camel stopped is called the *mabrak an-nāqah* ("the kneeling of the she-camel"). The Prophet's riding mule was called Duldul, a gift from the Byzantine viceroy of Egypt. The Prophet's horse was called Sakb.

Qaṭar. A Shaykhdom on the Arabian coast of the Persian Gulf. The population is 547,761 and most are Wahhābīs, with a minority of Twelve-Imām Shī'ites.

Qawwali. A form of Sufi singing in Urdu, but also in Persian, found in India, Pakistan, Afghanistan, and neighboring regions. It resembles the Sufi liturgical singing heard in other parts of the Islamic world, such as the *ilāhīs* in Turkey, and the mystical *qasīdahs* in Arabic, but can be distinguished by its particularly ardent and effusive style. A *qawwal* begins with praises on the Prophet, proceeds to poetry of love directed at God or the Prophet, passes through a phase exemplifying extinction in God called *fanā'*, then through subsistence in God (*baqā'*), and finishes by a return to sobriety (*sawh*). *See* FANĀ'; MAJLIS; SUFISM.

Qayrawān, *see* KAIROUAN.

Qayṣariyyah. A market for fine goods such as cloth, jewelry, perfumes, and gold. In dialects this is often rendered as *qīṣariyyah*. The word comes from *qaysar* ("Caesar") in Arabic because usually such markets were established upon the sites of forums – the place of Caesar – in cities formerly Roman.

Qiblah. The direction the Muslims face when performing the *ṣalāh* ("ritual prayer") toward the Ka'bah in Mecca. The *qiblah* was originally orientated on the Temple in Jerusalem, but was changed to the direction of Mecca in the 2nd year of the Hijrah. One day, when the Prophet was leading the mid-day prayer in the mosque of the Banū Salīmah in Medina, after the first two *raka'āt* ("prayer rounds"), he was suddenly inspired to turn towards Mecca to complete the following two *raka'āt*. The congregation naturally followed his example. Henceforth the mosque was called *Masjid al-Qiblatayn* ("the Mosque of the two *qiblahs*").

The *qiblah* is usually marked in mosques by the *miḥrāb* ("prayer niche"). Originally, it was often indicated simply by a stone. To help orient those praying outside the mosque, the *qiblah* may be indicated by a decorative device which can be seen from a distance, for example, the figure of a crescent moon on the top of a minaret spire; the center of the circle forming the crescent indicates the direction of Mecca.

It was established in certain mosques by means of accurate measurement long after they were built that the building's orientation was imperfect; in some cases it is the custom to make the necesary correction towards the true *qiblah* by having each worshiper in the prayer line turn slightly to the side, while the row faces in the original orientation of the building. This is the practice in the Qarāwiyyīn Mosque in Fez. But in other mosques in the same situation, with a less exalted reputation to maintain, it has not been considered necessary to insist upon the precise, mathematical, accuracy of the *qiblah*, the general opinion being that the *approximate* direction of Mecca is adequate. When it is impossible or impractical to determine the *qiblah*, the prayer is performed in any direction, all ultimately being valid. ("To God belong the East and West and wheresoever ye turn, there is the face of God", 2:115).

Qipchaq. A Turkic steppe people, who progressively invaded the Islamic world before the coming of the Mongols, they were related to the Saljuqs. The Russians called them Polovsti and Cumans. They were shamanists before being converted to Islam. They dominated the regions north and south of the Caspian and the lower Volga. The Mongols, after their invasions, were for the most part absorbed into the Qipchaq peoples, and the fusion of the two produced many kingdoms, among them the Khanate of the Qipchaq Steppe.

Qirā'ah (lit. "reading", pl. *qirā'āt*). A Ḥadīth declares that the Koran was revealed (*unzila*, "sent down") in seven scripts (*aḥruf*, "letters", plural of *ḥarf*), each of which is valid. The meaning of the word *aḥruf* has occasioned debate, and has been taken by some to refer to the seven principle dialects spoken by the tribes of Arabia. However, the Arabic of the Koran is, of all Arabic, the most elegant, copious and pure, by the common consent of Muslims and Arabs alike, and corresponds in its forms – with minor exceptions – to the morphology and best usages of the dialect of the Quraysh, the aristocrats of Mecca; there is no question of its being, in any literal sense, a blend of differing dialects. The Sufis take *aḥruf* to mean rather "modes" or "levels"; that is to say, they accept that there are seven levels of meaning from the most outward and concrete to the most inward and hidden, corresponding to the seven layers of the Heavens and presenting, therefore, ascending degrees of understanding and approach to the Truth, the Real.

Historically speaking, after the definitive recension of the Koran made at the command of the Caliph 'Uthmān, certain variant readings existed and, indeed, persisted and increased as the Companions who had memorized the text died, and because the inchoate Arabic script, lacking vowel signs and even the necessary diacriticals to distinguish between certain consonants, was inadequate; in practice, the authority of oral transmissions and reciters was an essential complement to the recorded, written text. As Islam became diffused among peoples whose Arabic fell far short of the Quraysh standard, or for whom Arabic was not even a mother tongue, it became a matter of urgency to remedy the deficiencies of the script, formalize grammar and preserve the integrity of the revealed text and of Arabic, the sacred language. The rapid vulgarization of Arabic that ensued in the first centuries of Islam when the language, no longer protected by its isolation, became the *lingua franca* of a vast realm, was a phenomenon noted and deplored by the scholars of the age.

In the 4th Islamic century, it was decided to have recourse to "readings" (*qirā'āt*) handed down from seven authoritative "readers" (*qurrā'*); in order, moreover, to ensure accuracy of transmission, two "transmitters" (*rāwī*, pl. *ruwāh*) were accorded to each. There resulted from this the seven basic texts (*al-qirā'āt as-sab'*, "the Seven readings"), each having two transmitted versions (*rwāyatān*) with only minor variations in phrasing, but all containing meticulous vowel-points and other necessary diacritical marks. These "Seven Readings" have, in the course of time, come to be associated with the seven *aḥruf* of the Ḥadīth.

The authoritative "readers" are: Nāfi (from Medina; d. *169*/785); Ibn Kathīr (from Mecca; d. *119*/737); Abū 'Amr al-'Alā' (from Damascus; d. *153*/770); Ibn 'Āmir (from Baṣra; d. *118*/736); Ḥamzah (from Kufah; d. *156*/772); al-Qisā'ī (from Kufah; d. *189*/804); and Abū Bakr 'Āṣim (from Kufah; d. *158*/778).

The predominant reading today, spread by Egyptian Koran readers, is that of 'Āsim in the transmission (*riwāyah*) of Ḥafs (d. *190*/805). In Morocco, however, the reading is that of Nāfi' in the *riwāyah* of Warsh (d. *197*/812) and Maghrebin Korans are written accordingly.

Qirān. One of the forms and intentions of consecration for the pilgrimage, whereby the *ḥajj* and the *'umrah* are performed in conjunction. *See* IḤRAM.

Qiṣāṣ. The principle, introduced by the Koran, of retaliation for harm inflicted. Where a life is lost and the victim and perpetrator are of equal status, the death of the perpetrator is an expiation for the death of the victim. In harm short of the taking of life, a similar harm to the perpetrator is an expiation. Along with the establishment of these principles, which are those of the *lex talionis* of the Mosaic Law, Islam explicitly recommends the substitution of compensation on another plane, i.e., pardon for the guilty person (an act which expiates sins for the pardoner), or material compensation for the harm suffered (5:45).

In actual practice, the Prophet inclined to the milder punishments or to the minimum prescribed penalty for the crimes brought before him. Nevertheless, he judged according to the intrinsic nature of the case, once ordering the execution of a man who had murdered a woman. In the circumstances of that case he put the nature of the crime (murder) before the question of the relative status of the two parties.

In the case of manslaughter, or accidental killing, retaliation cannot be exacted; only compensation may be claimed. The compensation for death is called a *diyah*, and was once fixed by law at one hundred camels, and today by statutory sums.

The principle of *qiṣāṣ* effected a profound modification in the Arab sense of justice. Previously, Arab tribal law had called for revenge for harm suffered; in the case of personal injury this was *tha'r*, or blood revenge, and it could be taken upon any member of the clan of the perpetrator. *Qiṣāṣ* made the actual perpetrator alone guilty, and alone liable to punishment; moreover, the punishment must be the exact equivalent of the crime. This, the reestablishment of social, or indeed, cosmic, equilibrium after it has been disturbed by an infraction, could also be transposed onto a different plane by a material or spiritual compensation. Thus, *qiṣāṣ* is the very essence of justice, the recognition that consequences are contained in acts, or that effect is contained in the cause. In Islam, as in Judaism, *qiṣāṣ* objectified was made the principle of law. This replaced the older, subjective, and thus non-differentiated, tribal sense of revenge.

Qitfir, *see* FITFIR.

Qitmir. The name, according to tradition, of the dog of the Seven Sleepers of Ephesus. The name is used in mysticism or magic to invoke a protection for one's interests or some object. *See* SEVEN SLEEPERS.

Qiyās (lit. "measure", "scale" or "exemplar" and hence "analogy"). The principle by which the laws of the Koran and Sunnah are applied to situations not explicitly covered by these two sources of religious legislation. Ash-Shāfi'ī (d. *204*/820) was one of the foremost developers of the use of *qiyās*. *See* SHARĪ'AH.

Qizil Bash (Turkish, lit. "red heads"). The name of seven Turkic tribes who supported Ismā'īl, the first Safavid, in his struggle for power. The Qizil Bash wore red caps with twelve black tassels, standing for the twelve Shī'ite Imāms. Their relationship to the Safavids was loyalty with a religious flavor, since Ismā'īl was seen as a descendant of the seventh Shī'ite Imām, Mūsā-l-Kāẓim. Later, two of these tribes in turn, the Afsharids and the Qajars, became the power bases of short-lived dynasties.

A Shī'ite may still be called Qizil Bash in Afghanistan. *See* SAFAVIDS.

Qubā'. A village immediately outside Medina where the Prophet first arrived after his emigration (*al-hijrah*), from Mecca, and where he built the first mosque, later known as *Masjid at-Taqwā* (the "Mosque of Reverence"). *See* MOSQUE of QUBĀ'.

Qubbat aṣ-Ṣakhrah, *see* DOME of the ROCK.

al-Quds (lit. "The Sanctuary"). The usual Arabic name for Jerusalem, referring to *al-bayt al-muqaddas* ("the holy house"), the Temple of

Solomon. By extension, the name is sometimes applied to the whole of Palestine. *See* JERUSALEM.

Queen of Sheba, *see* BILQĪS.

Quietism, *see* MURJI'AH

Qumm. A small city in central Iran which contains an important shrine of the Twelve-Imām Shī'ites. It is the tomb of the sister of the eighth Imām 'Alī ar-Riḍā, called Fāṭimah al-Ma ṣūmah, or Fāṭimah "the sinless". As it is one of the few tombs of the immediate relatives of the Imāms within Iran, it is much revered.

Qumm is a desert city lying on the crossroads between Isfahan and Rayy. It had undergone cultural influences coming from the city of Kufah, home of political and religious radicalism under the Umayyads. Refugees from Kufah, the Yemeni dynasty of Āl Sa'd ibn Mālik of the tribe of 'Ashar, as *marzbāns*, or rulers, gave asylum to a number of heretics and Shī'ite jurists between *125*/742 and *278*/891. Afterwards Qumm was ruled by a *wālī*, or governor, appointed by Baghdad, but by then Qumm was already a Shī'ite center.

Qumm, however, did not have an important madrasah until Fath 'Ali Shah, the second Qajar, founded the Faiziyeh madrasah to rival centers of Shi'ite learning in Iraq. Since the last century Qumm has become the main center of Shī'ite religious studies in Iran.

Qunawī, Ṣadr ad-Dīn (d. *729*/1329). A Persian Sufi in the tradition of Khorasan.

Qunūt. A prayer, or supplication (*du'ā'*) occasionally inserted in the canonical prayer (*ṣalāh*), a practice based upon the Sunnah. The Prophet would sometimes utter requests of God at some point in the *ṣalāh*. Different supplications are called *qunūt*, although what is most commonly meant is a calling of blessings upon the Prophet. This is recited in the "sitting" position (*julūs*), after the "greetings" (*taḥiyyāt*) and before the ending of the prayer.

A frequently used *qunūt* is:

Allāhumma ṣalli 'alā sayyidina Muḥammadin wa 'alā āli sayyidinā Muḥammadin kamā ṣalayta 'ala sayyidinā Ibrāhīma wa 'alā āli sayyidinā Ibrāhīma, wa bārik alā sayyidinā Muḥammadin wa 'alā āli sayyidinā Muḥammadin kamā bārakta 'alā sayyidinā Ibrāhīma wa 'alā āli sayyidinā Ibrāhīma, innaka anta-l-ḥamīdu-l-majīd.

Our God bless our Lord Muḥammad and the people of our Lord Muḥammad, as you blessed our Lord Abraham and the people of our Lord Abraham, and prosper our Lord Muḥammad and the people of our Lord Muḥammad, as you prospered our Lord Abraham and the people of our Lord Abraham for you are the Praised, the Magnified.

See PRAYER.

Qur'ān, *see* KORAN.

Quraysh. The tribe of Mecca. The name comes from the root to "bite" (*qarasha*), whence also the word for the shark, "the biting fish" (*qirsh*), sometimes thought to be the "totem" of the tribe. Possibly Quraysh, which is a diminutive form, "little shark", was the nick-name of Fihr, the ancestor of the tribe, whose other name was *an-Naḍr*. The tribe was settled in Mecca by an ancestor of renown called Qusayy who displaced the previous inhabitants, the Khuzā'ah. The clans who lived in the immediate vicinity of the Ka'bah, in the lowest part (*al-Baṭhā'*) of Mecca, were known as *Abṭaḥī* or *Biṭahī*, or as *Quraysh al-Biṭāḥ* (the "Quraysh of the Hollow"). Less illustrious families, who lived further out, were known as *Quraysh aẓ-Ẓawāhir* (the "Quraysh of the Outskirts").

The location of Mecca on important caravan routes across the peninsula, and the prestige of the Ka'bah in the Age of Ignorance (*jāhiliyyah*), gave it a considerable advantage as a trading city, with the result that the Quraysh became one of the richest and most powerful tribes. This, together with their descent from the Kinānah and Ishmael, gave them claims to an aristocratic pre-eminence.

The Prophet Muḥammad was of the Banū Hāshim clan of the Quraysh: and all of the Arab Caliphs were of the Quraysh. Indeed there is even a Ḥadīth which has been taken to mean that rulership and the Caliphate is a prerogative of this tribe alone. (*See* MECCA; MUḤAMMAD).

The Quraysh are mentioned by name in the Koran:

For the composing of Koraish,
their composing for the winter and summer

> caravan!
> So let them serve the Lord of this House
> who has fed them against hunger,
> and secured them from fear. (106)

According to a Sufi interpretation, this refers also to the soul's vicissitudes and to the protection afforded by God to the noblest elements in the soul in its spiritual economy.

Qurayẓah. A Jewish tribe of Medina that betrayed the Muslims during the Battle of the Trench (*see* BATTLE of the TRENCH). When the Quraysh abandoned the siege of the city, Gabriel commanded the Prophet not to lay down arms until the Qurayẓah were subdued. Their hands freed by the departure of the Quraysh and their confederates, the Muslims turned upon the Banū Qurayẓah and besieged their defensive towers for twenty-five days.

When the Banū Qurayẓah surrendered, they were judged, as a concession, by Sa'd ibn Mu'ādh, a chief of their former allies, the Aws; lying on his deathbed, in pain from a wound inflicted during the fighting with the Quraysh, he passed a rigorous judgement: the adult men should be put to death and the women and children sold into slavery.

> And He brought down those of the People of the Book who supported them from their fortresses and cast terror in their hearts; some you slew, some you made captive. (33: 25-27)

In books written in the West, this episode has been the occasion for criticism as an example of extreme cruelty. But it was not an unusual event; similar punishment was meted out elsewhere, as in the destruction of the Albigensians in France, for example, and for much the same reason. It is a case of the final judgement overtaking a people while still in this world. In the Bible there are numerous comparable cases. Jewish law itself prescribes such treatment for the conquest of a city as a matter of course, even when betrayal is not in question: "When the Lord thy God hath delivered it unto thy hands, thou shalt smite every male therein with the edge of the sword: but the women, and the little ones, and the cattle, and all that is in the city, even all the spoil thereof, shalt thou take unto thyself" (Deuteronomy 20:12). This is perhaps why Sa'd ibn Mu'ādh gave the Qurayẓah this sentence; that their own law should be used on them. *See* BATTLE of the TRENCH.

Qurb (lit. "nearness"). The grace of the nearness of God. Those most exalted in paradise are those who are "brought nigh" (*al-muqarrabun*).

Qurbān (from *qarraba*, "to bring near"). Any practice that brings one closer to God. In particular, it means sacrifice, and especially the animals sacrificed in the *'Īd al-Aḍḥā* ("Feast of Sacrifice"), which in Turkey is called *Kurban Bayram*. Among Arab Christians, the word *qurbān* refers to the eucharist.

Qurrā', *see* QĀRI'; QIRĀ'AH.

al-Qushayrī, Abū-l-Qāsim (d.*465*/1072). A Persian Sufi, author of a highly respected treatise on the doctrine of Sufism called the *Risālah*. He also wrote a mystical commentary on the Koran.

Qusṭā ibn Lūqā (d. *311*/923). A Christian philosopher and scientist born in Baalbek. He wrote treatises, and translated Aristotle and other Greek works into Arabic.

Quṭb (lit. "axis", "pole"). The center which contains the periphery, or is present in it, is a primordial spiritual symbol. The idea of the *quṭb* is the recognition that the function of "spiritual center" can reside in a human being, or be associated with a human being. The *quṭb* is at the same time a celestial reality, and when actualized as the delegation of authority upon earth, it implies a sanctity of the highest order.

Quṭb has been given as an honorific title to great Saints, but it is rather a *function* which manifests itself, not in a continuous manner but from time to time, through a person, or indeed through some other support in the world. A story is told of the famous Moroccan Shaykh Aḥmad ad-Darqāwī of the 19th century, who when he was walking in the Resīf market of Fez crossed shoulder to shoulder with an otherworldly figure dressed in white. As they crossed, the person – an Angel, it is understood – said: "*al-Quṭb*", without indicating whether he meant himself, ad-Darqāwī, something else, or even the moment itself. The nature of the quṭb or the spiritual axis, which can work through a person, is thus an elusive reality.

The first four Caliphs, because their personal station was commensurate with the function they fulfilled, are thought of as being each the *quṭb* of his age. They were not so at all times, but only in those moments when they transcended their individual limitations while acting on those around them as heaven's true vicegerents. The spiritual center then manifested itself through them. The function of *quṭb*, or celestial axis, can also manifest itself through more than one person at a time. Ibn Khaldūn, the historian, says that the Sufis got the idea of the *quṭb* from the extreme Shī'ites. *See* SUFISM.

Qutb, Sayyid (1906-1966) Egyptian of Indian origin, member of the Muslim Brotherhood, he was executed by the government of Egypt on charges of sedition and terrorism. When he travelled to Europe and North America, he was repelled by contact with an alien view of reality, and became an opponent of the West. He became a propagandist for an absolutist view of Islam, although he found the basis for Islamic democracy in the Koran and in the idea of shūrā. His ideological influence was vast, especially during the Iranian revolution.

Qutub-i Minar (lit. "the axis minaret"). A minaret in New Delhi, India, famous for its height (240 ft/73 m), built by the Sultan Shams ad-Dīn Iltutmish (d. *633*/1236) around *627*/1230. His tomb is next to the Quwwat al-Islām mosque, which was begun by Quṭb ad-Dīn Aybak (d. *607*/1210).

Originally a victory column, the minaret is almost 50ft/14m around its base and 9ft/3m around the top. It is decorated with calligraphic inscriptions in stone. The minaret was restored in *770*/1368, and again in *1245*/1829 after being damaged in an earthquake in *1218*/1803.

R

Ra'āyā (plural from Ar. *ra'iyyah*, "flock", "common folk"). A name given to the non-Muslim populations, subject to poll-tax (the Muslims paid only poor-tax, *zakāh*), in the domains of Muslim rulers. This was a metaphor used in this sense in Mesopotamia from ancient times.

ar-Rabb (lit. "the Lord"; "He who, like a parent, watches, guides and sustains the growth of what is in His care"; "the Sustainer"). A Divine Name of the qualities (*ṣifāt*) but not of the essence (*dhāt*). The most common forms of this Name are the phrases: *Rabb al-'Alamīn* ("the Lord of the Worlds") and *Rabb al-'Izzah* ("the Lord of Might"). In other combinations, however, it may simply mean "owner" without being a name calling upon God. *See* DIVINE NAMES.

Rābi'ah al-Adawiyyah (*95-185*/713-801). One of the most famous Saints in Islam, she extolled the way of *maḥabbah* ("Divine love") and *uns* ("Intimacy with God"). Her mystical sayings are noted for their pith and clarity; some have become proverbs throughout the Islamic world.

In reply to one who claimed not to have sinned for a long time she declared: "Your existence is a sin to which no other sin can be compared." That is, the affirmation that we exist is itself a sin (*dhanb*) because in reality only God Is. To remove the idea that we are an independent reality is to remove the origin and possibility of sin.

Rābi'ah also said: "I am going to light a fire in paradise and pour water in hell so that both veils may completely disappear from the pilgrims and their purpose may be sure. Thus the servants of God may see Him, without any object of hope or motive of fear."

She was born, lived and died in Baṣra. Originally from a poor family, she was stolen as a child and sold into slavery. Freed, by reason of her evident sanctity, she gathered a circle of disciples around her and lived a life of extreme asceticism. The Sufis who came after her acknowledge their doctrinal debt to her, and she is mentioned in most biographies of the saints.

ar-Rābiṭah al-Islāmiyyah. The Islamic Association, often referred to as the *rābiṭah*, an organization for the promotion of Islam sponsored by the Saudi government. Its headquarters are in Mecca.

Rāfiḍīs (lit. "repudiators"; in Arabic generally *ar-Rāfiḍah* or *al-Rawāfiḍ*). A general name, abusive in tone, given by the Sunnīs to the Shī'ites because they repudiate the validity of the Caliphs who preceded 'Alī. These Caliphs, Abū Bakr, 'Umar, and 'Uthmān, along with 'Alī, are considered to be "the rightly guided" Caliphs by the Sunnīs. Shī'ites believe that only 'Alī and his descendants had the right to the Caliphate, and so consider the first three to be usurpers.

ar-Raḥīm (from the root *raḥima*, "to show mercy", "be merciful"). This Divine Name, which is often translated as "the Compassionate", refers to God's Mercy under the aspect of action reaching into the world, and leading beyond the world back to God. The Divine Name *ar-Raḥmān* means "Merciful by His very Nature", and is a Name of the Essence (*dhāt*). *Ar-Raḥīm* is one of the Names that describe the Divine Qualities (*ṣifāt*). It is most habitually used in the combination *ar-Raḥmān, ar-Raḥīm* ("the Merciful, the Mercy-Giving"). Another combination, characteristic of Arabic rhetorical construction, is *Arḥam ar-Rāḥimīn* ("the Most Merciful of Those Who give Mercy"). *See* DIVINE NAMES; ar-RAḤMĀN.

Raḥmah (lit. "mercy" from the root *raḥima*, "to be merciful", "to show mercy"). This is an attribute of God which the Koran emphasizes over and over again, in keeping with its nature as the last revelation. At the end of time, man's weakness and confusion is greater than ever, but God's mercy is also nearer.

Al-Ghazālī said: "The Divine Mercy is perfect, in the sense that it answers every need. It is universal, in the sense that it spreads alike over those who merit it and those who do not merit it."

ar-Raḥmān (lit. "the Merciful One"). A Divine Name of the Essence, (*ism min asmā' adh-dhāt*). After the Name Allāh, *ar-Raḥmān* is the most frequently cited Name of God, and is used very often in the Koran almost as the equivalent of Allāh. "Say: call upon Allāh or call upon ar-Raḥmān; whatever ye call Him, His are the Most Beautiful Names" (17:110). This Name is most often used in the combination *ar-Raḥmān ar-Raḥīm* ("the Merciful in Himself, the Mercy-Giving"). The Quraysh refused to recognize this Name in the treaty that was made with the Prophet at Ḥudaybiyyah. From this (and other evidence) it appears that this Divine Name was revealed along with Islam, and was unknown to the Arabs, unlike the Name Allāh. *See* ALLĀH; DIVINE NAMES; NAFAS ar-RAḤMĀN; ar-RAḤĪM.

Rainbow (Ar. *qaws Allāh*, "the bow of God", doubtless so called after the sign God gave Noah, but also known by many popular names). A symbol associated with Noah and the flood, signifying the end of one cycle and the beginning of another.

Rajā' Hope.

Raj'ah (lit. "return", "restitution"). The dogma found in several Shī'ite and related sects regarding the return to the world of their spiritual leader, the Imām. In particular, the return of the Twelfth Imām in Twelve-Imām Shī'ism. *See* SHĪ'ISM, HIDDEN IMĀM.

Rajm. Lapidation, or stoning to death. The term *ar-rajīm* ("the stoned one") is applied to Satan. *See also* RAMĪ-i-JIMĀR.

Rak'ah (lit. "a bowing", from the verb *raka'a*, "to bow"). One complete cycle of sacred words and gestures during the ritual prayer (*ṣalāh*). It includes standing, bowing, prostration, and sitting. Each prayer is made up of several such cycles, or *raka'āt*. *See* ṢALĀH.

Ramaḍān. The ninth month of the Arab and Islamic calendar. The word *Ramaḍān* meant originally "great heat", a description which originates in the pre-Islamic solar calendar. This month was holy in Arab tradition before Islam and was one of the months of truce. Fasting during the month is one of the Five Pillars of Islam (*ṣawm Ramaḍān*).

> ...the month of Ramaḍān, wherein the Koran
> was sent down to be a guidance
> to the people, and as clear signs
> of the Guidance and the Salvation
> So let those of you, who are present
> at the month, fast it; and if any of you
> be sick, or if he be on a journey,
> then a number of other days; God desires
> ease for you, and desires not hardship
> for you; and that you fulfil the number, and
> magnify God that He has guided you, and haply
> you will be thankful. (2:182)

The month of fasting begins with the physical sighting of the new moon. (A new moon cannot be seen with the naked eye until at least twenty hours after the astronomic new moon, or conjunction of moon and sun.) If the new moon is not sighted on the twenty-eighth day of the previous month, this may be lengthened to twenty-nine or thirty days so that the beginning of fasting may correspond with the beginning of the month of Ramaḍān. Following Turkish custom, many countries signal the beginning of the month of Ramaḍān to the population by the repeated firing of cannon on the eve of the first day. (In the Islamic calendar a day runs from sunset to sunset.) Cannon are also used to signal the beginning and end of each fast day.

During Ramaḍān a Muslim does not eat or drink from daybreak, when a thread of light may be seen on the horizon, until the sun has set. After the evening prayer (*maghrib*), a breakfast is eaten. Somewhat later in the night a larger meal is taken. It is common to take a meal, sometimes called *suhūr*, in the early morning before the fast begins. Musicians and criers walk through towns at night to wake the people to take this meal; the criers often do this as a pious act.

The daily fast is begun by formulating the intention to perform the fast as a rite. Children begin fasting gradually, first half a day, then several days, until they grow old enough to fast without injuring their health. No one is required to fast if his health is not up to it, and if a fast threatens health it should be stopped. Pregnant and nursing women are exempted from fasting. Menstruating women are also exempted but must make up the lost fast days afterwards during the course of the year.

Travelers are exempted from fasting (but not forbidden to fast), if the distance traveled is great, or if they are on a journey which continues for more than three days. Fast days which are lost for reasons of health or travel must be made up during the year. Exemption from the entire period of fasting is theoretically allowed if one feeds thirty poor people *each* day of the fast, as is partial exemption on the same terms, but it is, in fact, frowned upon and never resorted to by people of means. It is clear from experience that there is a great blessing in ritual fasting; Ramaḍān itself is a blessed month, a moment in the year when God's graces seem closer and more easily accessible.

During the daytime fast, not only must the believer not eat or drink, but he must also abstain from sexual enjoyment, listening to music, and as far as possible from all pleasures of the senses. During the night, pleasures of the senses are again licit, although extraordinary events of enjoyment, such as celebrations, should not be held during Ramaḍān.

The principle of fasting is related to that of limitation. Without limitation, knowledge is impossible, for it is when we come to the end or limit of a thing that its true nature becomes evident. Ramaḍān's marking the end to indulgence, or imposing a clear limit to it day after day for a month, offers an unmistakable spiritual lesson. It also consitutes a purification and a kind of sacrifice, which, like the pruning of trees, leads to renewal and fresh strength. On the moral plane it also brings a direct understanding of the suffering of the hungry.

Ramaḍān, which moves through the year because of the lunar calendar, sometimes takes place in the winter months, when it is easier, and sometimes in the summer months, when the sacrifice is greater. Despite its solemn nature, it has a joyous atmosphere about it, even one of festival, although festivities during the month are forbidden.

The Koran was revealed in one of the last ten nights of Ramaḍān, the *Laylat al-Qadr*, the holiest night in the Islamic calendar. During the month of Ramaḍān supplementary prayers called *tarāwīḥ*, numbering twenty or thirty-two *raka'āt* each, are performed during the small hours before the dawn prayer (*ṣubḥ*), and also before the night prayer (*īshā'*). The month is the occasion for intensive reading of the Koran. *See* FAST; FIVE PILLARS; LAYLAT al-QADR.

Ramī-l-Jimār. One of the rites of the pilgrimage, the throwing of stones at three columns in Mina on the 10th, 11th, and 12th day of Dhū-l-Ḥijjah. The pebbles, called *jimār*, are gathered at Muzdalifah the night before, where the pilgrims stop on the way from 'Arafāt.

As are the other rites of pilgrimage, the throwing of the stones is linked to Abraham. As Abraham proceeded to Minā to carry out God's command to sacrifice his son Ishmael (Ismā'īl), the devil appeared three times to tempt his son, who was lagging behind his father, to run away. On each occasion Ishmael pelted Satan with stones at the spot marked by the three columns or pillars (*al-jamarāt*) representing the apparitions of Satan.

The three pillars, aligned in a row in the flat valley of Minā, are today accessible from ground level and from above by way of an overhead ramp constructed to accommodate the millions that now come to perform the pilgrimage. The first pillar from Muzdalifah is called *al-jamrah as-sughrā*, or *al-jamrah al-ūlā* ("the small", or "first pillar"); the second is *al-jamrah al-wuṣṭā* ("the middle pillar"); and the third is the *al-jamrah al-kubrā*, or *jamrat al-aqabah*, ("the large pillar or the Aqabah pillar").

On the 10th of Dhū-l-Ḥijjah the pilgrims throw seven pebbles, one after the other, at the large pillar, repeating the words *Allāhu Akbar, lā ilāha illā Llāh* ("God is Greatest, there is no god but God"). On the 11th, the actions are repeated at the first, middle and large pillars, and again on the 12th. This completes the usual lapidation of the pillars, for which 49 pebbles are gathered at Muzdalifah. If one stays for another day, the 13th, then 70 pebbles are gathered. A pilgrim remaining past this time will continue stoning the pillars on following days, and he will have gathered more stones at Muzdalifah accordingly. This rite is a means, in a palpable, easily understandable way, of purification, or of taking a distance between oneself and evil in all its forms, not just temptation.

Failure to perform this rite during the pilgrimage may be expiated by fasting or sacrifice. The repetition of the essential *talbiyah* invocation comes to an end with the final stoning of the pillars, although some say the *talbiyah* ends just before the lapidation begins. *See* PILGRIMAGE; TALBIYAH.

ar-Rāqid, *see* SLEEPING FOETUS.

Rashīd ad-Dīn Sīnān (d. *589*/1193). The leader of the Syrian Ismā'īlīs who was known to the Crusaders as the "old man of the mountain" (*shaykh al-jabal*). He was born in Baṣra and educated in Persia; presumably he was appointed to his place as the chief of the castle of Masyāf by the master of the order at 'Alamūt in Persia. Rashīd ad-Dīn fought both the Crusaders, and then Salāḥ ad-Dīn al-Ayyūbī (Saladin). After Rashīd ad-Dīn, the Nizārī Ismā'īlī power in Syria declined and was brought to end when the Mamlūks captured their castles. A community of Ismā'īlīs exists near Masyāf to this day.

Rashīd ad-Dīn aṭ-Ṭabīb, Faḍl Allāh *645-717*/1247-1318). A Persian, son of an apothecary, Rashīd ad-Dīn was converted to Islam from Judaism at the age of thirty. He was born in Ḥamadān, belonged to the Shāfi'ī school of law, and was a physician. He became Vizier, or minister, of the Mongol Khan Abaqa of the Il-Khanid dynasty. As Vizier, Rashīd ad-Dīn was a noted builder of mosques, *madrasahs*, and public works in the various cities which the Mongols used as their capitals in Persia. He built complete neighborhoods in Tabriz and Sulṭāniyyah.

At the bidding of the Mongol Khān Ghāzān, Rashīd ad-Dīn wrote a monumental history of the world in Persian, *Kitāb Jāmi' at-Tawārīkh* ("The Universal History" also known as the *Ta'rīkh-i Mubārak-i Ghāzān-i*). It encompasses Adam and the Patriarchs, the Prophets, the history of the Persian Kings and the Muslim dynasties, and gives accounts, together with geneologies of the ruling houses, of the Jews, Arabs, Persians, Turks, Mongols, Chinese, Indians, and Buddhists, and it even includes material on the Franks, about whom Rashīd ad-Dīn was remarkably well-informed, describing the Popes and Emperors. One of its most valuable sections was that describing the history of the Mongols, for Rashīd ad-Dīn learned this from Ghazan himself, and from Balad Ching-Sang, the Mongol representative in Persia of the Great Khans.

Perhaps knowing that the history of the Mongols, preserved only in the memory of the people he met and in a secret book which he was not allowed to see, was likely to be lost for ever now that they had abandoned their nomadic life on the steppes for a sedentary existence, Rashīd ad-Dīn made great efforts to see that many copies of his history were made and widely distributed.

Rashīd ad-Dīn also wrote other works in Arabic: *Kitāb al-Aḥyā wa-l-Āthār* ("The Book of Animals and Monuments", on botany, agriculture, and architecture) which has not survived, and a collection of smaller works, *al-Majmūāt ar-Rashīdiyyah*, on metaphysics and mysticism, religious disputations, and correspondence on political and financial matters. He also wrote a commentary on the Koran called *Miftāḥ al-Tafsīr* ("The Key to Commentary").

After the death of the Khan Uljaytu in *717*/1317, who had entered Islam as Muḥammad Khudabanda, Rashīd ad-Dīn was pursued, as he had been before, by political enemies who accused him of poisoning the Khan. This time they succeeded and Rashīd ad-Dīn was executed. *See* al-JUWAYNĪ; MONGOLS.

Rashīd Riḍā, Muḥammad (1865-1935). An early Islamic reformer born in what was then Syria and today is Lebanon. He worked with Muḥammad 'Abduh and believed that Islam could be combined with modernism. His legacy is a coherent body of thought and especially an idea of democracy based upon Islamic precedents, namely that of the *shūrā* or consultative assembly.

Rasūl, *see* PROPHETS.

Rationalists, *see* MU'TAZILITES.

Rawdah Khānī. (also: *rawzah khāneh*). In Iran, the ritual recitation of the sufferings of the Shī'ite Imāms, in particular of Ḥusayn ibn 'Alī. These are frequently carried out in homes and mosques by preachers who specialize in playing upon the emotivity of the occasion by recalling the sufferings of the Shī'ite martyrs and moving their listeners to expressions of grief. On the 10th day of the month of Muḥarram, the anniversary of the death of Ḥusayn (which for different reasons going back to early Islam is also a Sunnī holiday) these *rawda khānī* lead to public frenzies in which some devout Shī'ites cut themselves with swords and knives, and beat themselves with chains in paroxysms of guilt towards the Imāms, and in joyous expiatory self-punishment.

Martyr plays are also put on in Iran for the same reason, perpetuating deep complexes of guilt, inferiority, resentment, and desire for vengeance which, for centuries, the religious, and sometimes the political, authorities have not hesitated to cultivate, control, and exploit.

The *Rawdah khānī* is so called from a book, "The Garden (*rawdah*) of the Martyrs", an account of the sufferings of the Imāms. There is an imitation called the "Deluge of Weeping" and the "Mysteries of Martyrdom". The *Rawdah khanī* reciters are given access to private quarter of homes, the *andarunis* which no other group in society has. *See* SHĪ'ISM; TA'ZIYAH.

ar-Rawḍah (lit. "the garden"). The area in the Mosque of the Prophet (*al-Masjid ash-Sharīf*) in Medina, between a free-standing prayer niche (*miḥrāb*), and the tomb of the Prophet. It is thus called because of the Ḥadīth: "Between my house and my pulpit is a garden [*rawḍah*] of the gardens of paradise." The Prophet's tomb is on the spot where he died, in what was his house, which was adjacent to the mosque.

Ra'y (lit. "opinion"). A legal principle, that of the personal opinion of the jurist, which is the last resort after the Koran, Sunnah, and precedents have been exhausted in resolving a legal issue.

Ray'ah, *see* RA'ĀYĀ.

ar-Rāzī, Abū Bakr Muḥammed ibn Zakariyyā (*236-313*/850-925). Better known in the West under his Latinized name of Rhazes, he was a Persian physician. His Arabic works which were current in Europe were later translated into Latin and Greek, and finally into modern European languages. Throughout the Middle Ages in Europe he exercised a strong influence upon medicine. His most famous books are the *Liber Pestilentia* (in which he distinguished measles from smallpox), the compendium *Almansor* (*al-Kitāb al-Manṣūrī*), and the Encyclopedic *Liber Continens* (*al-Ḥāwi*). This first became available as a manuscript translated by a Jewish physician in Sicily and was later one of the first books to be printed. Ar-Rāzī recognized the role that psychosomatic medicine or autosuggestion plays in healing and wrote a treatise explaining why untrained practitioners, quacks, laymen, and "old-wives' remedies" often have greater success in healing patients than trained doctors.

In the great tradition of the Middle Ages ar-Rāzī was a universal thinker and pursued all the sciences including theology, astronomy, and music. It was, however, as an alchemist that his other great contribution to European science was made, and his descriptions of the alchemical processes were put into practice by European alchemists such as Nicholas Flamel and Paracelsus.

Ḥujwīrī called Rāzī a disciple of Hallaj which is to say, of the same ideology; he was known for his freethinking.

ar-Rāzī, Fakhr ad-Dīn (*544-606*/1149-1209). Philosopher, historian (he wrote the "History of the Dynasties"), and theologian, he belonged to the Shāfi'ī school of law and was a defender of orthodox views in his book, *Kitāb al-Muḥaṣṣal*. His commentary on the Koran is called the *Mafātīḥ al-Ghayb* ("The Keys of the Unseen"), itself a quotation from the Koran (6:59: "With Him are the Keys of the Unseen"). He was born south of Teheran and he died in Herat.

Readings of the Koran, *see* QIRĀ'AH.

Reconquista ("reconquest"). The reconquest of the Iberian peninsula by the Christians. The first serious setback to the Moorish invasion of Spain which began in *93*/711 was their defeat at the battle of Covadonga around *102*/720 at the hands of the Asturian chief Pelayo. This was followed by their being decisively checked and defeated at the battle of Tours (*114*/732) by Charles Martel.

Visigoths driven out by the Arab-Berber invasion flocked to Pelayo the Asturian, naming him their King, and the province of Asturias maintained its sovereignty throughout the whole Muslim domination of Spain. From that area and, on the east, from the Spanish March (*Marca Hispanica*), that is to say, border, created by the Franks, began the resistance to the Moorish rulers which eventually developed into the reconquest.

Spreading out from the Asturias there grew a line of fortification which expanded, eventually centering upon Burgos. The area enclosed by the fortification was called "Castilla", the land of castles. A rallying point of the reconquest was the legend of Santiago Matamor, St. James the Apostle, "Killer of Moors", who had appeared to the Christian defenders at the battle of Tours. His tomb had been discovered in Galicia at the end of the *1st*/8th century, and he was believed to help the Christians in their battles.

The development of the Christian kingdoms in the *4th*/11th century corresponded to a weakening of the Caliphate of Cordova. This took place after the reigns of 'Abd ar-Raḥmān III and al-Manṣūr Bi-Llāh, and the Caliphate then disintegrated into the small principalities called *ṭawā'if* (sing. *ṭā'ifah*). The rivalry between the *ṭawā'if*, their willingness to ally themselves with the Christians against their co-religionists, as well as their inability to create stable institutions and thus ensure continuity from ruler to ruler, led to their downfall. The reconquest, until then a series of back and forth skirmishes over the same territory, now entered a new and more important phase. In *428*/1037 Ferdinand I of Castile, claiming to represent "the Spains", captured Leon and led an increasingly united offensive against the Moors.

The fall of Toledo in *478*/1085, long protected by its strategic position and spared by Alfonso of Castile for reasons of friendship with the Emir, made the rulers of the other *ṭawā'if* realize that their situation was perilous and look to North Africa for help. It was a dangerous step because it meant calling in powers foreign to Spain. But as al-Mu'tamid the 'Abbāsid prince of Seville said: "I do not want to be held responsible for handing Andalusia over to the Christians...I do not want to be vilified from the pulpits of Islam. If I had to choose, I would rather tend camels for the Almoravids, than pasture swine under the Christians."

Help for the Muslim princes of Spain came from the Almoravid ruler of North Africa, Yusūf ibn Tashfīn, and reinforced and combined Muslim forces delivered a setback to the Christian armies at az-Zallaqah (Sagrajas near Badajoz) in *479*/1086. This was followed, however, shortly afterwards, by the formation of the knightly orders of Calatrava, Santiago, and Alcantara, and the added impetus of the Crusades. In Portugal, the first King, Alfonso Enriquez, completed the reconquest of his country by *543*/1148 with the assistance of English, French and German Crusaders, who had actually been driven onto his coasts by a providential storm. In Spain, during a period of pronounced French influence, the adoption by the Church of the Roman rite in place of the Visigothic, signified that the country was now a salient of Europe, and no longer an "island" on its own.

Against the Almohads, who succeeded the Almoravids, the Spanish kingdoms rallied a united force from Castile, Aragon, and Navarre, reinforced with Portuguese knights. They defeated the Almohads at the battle of Las Navas de Tolosa in *609*/1212, the single most important battle of the reconquest, which led, eventually, to the fall of Cordova in *634*/1236 and of Seville in *646*/1248; the remaining kingdoms of Granada, its dependency Malaga, and Cadiz, were reduced to the status of tributary states. The battle standard of the Muslims, captured at the battle of Las Navas, now hangs in the convent of Las Huelgas Reales in Burgos.

With the union of Spain under the "Catholic Kings", Ferdinand and Isabella, the moment had arrived for the balance to swing completely to one side. It came then as a great surprise when a massed assault by a vast Christian army against Granada was successfully contained. At the siege camp of Santa Fe, Isabella swore she would not remove her shirt until Granada fell, an oath she surely came to regret because Granada held out for two more years and then collapsed only because of internal dissension. In 1492, Granada, the last sovereign Moorish kingdom in Spain surrendered. The morning after, the prince "Boabdil" or Abū 'Abd Allāh, halted for a moment in a pass of the Sierra Nevada on his way to exile in Morocco, looked back on the Alhambra resplendent in the dawn sun, and wept. The spot is now called *el ultimo sospiro del moro*, ("the last sigh of the Moor").

Nevertheless, there remained a large Moorish population in Spain for some time thereafter. In the middle of the 16th century the Spanish Moors rebelled in a final, unsuccessful, attempt to retake Granada. In 1619, the *Moriscos*, or Moors superficially converted to Christianity, were expelled. Some remained, practicing Islam in secret, perhaps up to recent times. Today, ethnic groups such as the Maragatos of Astorga in Leon, are the descendants of Moorish groups left behind in the reconquest of Spain. *See* ALMOHAD; ALMORAVID.

Reforms, *see* ALIGARH; 'ABDUH, MUḤAMMAD; MUḤAMMADIYYAH; ṢALAFIYYAH; TANẒĪMĀT.

Refuge. Many passages in the Koran are incantations in which the believer can take refuge from evil. The foremost is the so-called "taking of refuge" (*ta'awwudh*): *a'ūdhu bi-Llāhi* *min ash-shayṭāni-r-rajīm* ("I take refuge in God from Satan the stoned one"). Then the last two Sūrahs (113 and 114) of the Koran are called the "two Sūrahs of refuge" (*al-mu'awwadhatān*) about which it is related that a spell was cast upon the Prophet by an Arabian form of magic which consisted of tying knots in a rope and blowing upon them while making incantations, to which verse 114:4 refers. Angels informed the Prophet of what had been done and the location of the well where the rope had been thrown. The revelation of the two Sūrahs undid the spell, each verse dissolving one of the enchanted knots. For the Sufis the "knots" are also psychic knots or entanglements and the "women that blow on knots" are uncontrolled emotivity, anger, rancor, resentment, jealousy, desire, lust and so forth. (*See* MAGIC.)

> By the afternoon!
> Surely Man is in the way of loss,
> save those who believe, and do righteous deeds,
> and counsel each other unto the truth,
> and counsel each other to be steadfast. (113)

> Woe unto every backbiter, slanderer,
> who has gathered riches and counted them over
> thinking his riches have made him immortal!
> No indeed; he shall be thrust into the Crusher;
> and what shall teach thee what is the Crusher?
> The Fire of God kindled
> roaring over the hearts
> covered down upon them,
> in columns outstretched. (114)

Some of the verses of refuge (*āyāt al-ḥifẓ*) are: 12:64 ("God is the best protector, and He is the Most Merciful of those who show mercy"); 13:11 ("Nor have they a defender beside Him"); 15:17 ("And we have guarded it from every outcast devil"); 37:7 ("With security from every froward devil"); and (4:81); (33:3); 33:48 ("Put your trust in God; God suffices as a guardian"); 39:62 ("He is Guardian over all things"); and the most famous, the verse of the throne", *āyat al-kursī*, 2:256 (*see* ĀYAT al-KURSĪ) and the *āyat al-'arsh* (also meaning verse of the throne"), 9:130 ("Now, if they turn away (O Muḥammad) say: Allah suffices me. There is no God save Him. In Him have I put my trust, and He is Lord of the Tremendous Throne"). The efficacy of these verses resides in their invocation in Arabic.

In many countries, Saints' tombs and places of worship have been places of political refuge where the ruler's agents would not seize anyone fleeing from his authority. In Islam, mosques everywhere have been used as sanctuaries inviolable to pursuit. In the Mawlay Idris Mosque in Fez there is a room accessible from a narrow passageway which has been used as a haven by fugitives.

In Persian, the taking of refuge and the place of refuge is called *bast*. Great Shī'ite asylums are the 'Abd al-Azīm mosque a few kilometers outside of Teheran at Rayy, where Jamāl ad-Dīn Afghānī took refuge from the Shah. Mosques within the city of Qumm, but also the the royal stables of the Shah and foreign legations were used as places of refuge. When the telegraph was built between India and Europe across Iran and inaugurated in 1865, the popular belief arose in Iran that the telegraph wires ended at the foot of the Persian throne. Telegraph offices became places where one could claim refuge from the authorities. In 1893, 2,000 people, following bread riots, marched on the telegraph office in Shiraz insisting that a message be sent to the Shah. The crowd swelled to 10,000 and held the staff prisoner until an answer was received from Teheran. *See* AMULETS; ĀYAT al-KURSĪ; ḤIZB al-BAḤR; MAGIC; RUQYAH; TA'AWWUDH.

Reincarnation, *see* TANĀSUKH.

Resignation (Ar. *Islām*, "peace through surrender", or *ṣabr*, "patience", or "endurance"; also *idh'ān* and *ruḍūkh*, "humble compliance"). This is one of the chief virtues and fundamental attitudes in Islam. The joyful is accepted with the words *al-ḥamdu li-Llāh* ("praise be to God"), and the sorrowful with equanimity, and therefore with the same words "praise be to God", perhaps amplified with *'alā kulli shay'* ("in all things"). An oft-uttered saying in this context is: *mā shā'a-Llāh* ("whatever God has willed"); likewise, as regards the outcome of events in the future one qualifies every hope or purpose with the words *in shā'a-Llāh* ("if God wills"). *Innā li-Llāhi wa innā ilayhi rāji'ūn* ("we belong to God and to God we return") expresses a resignation that goes beyond the vicissitudes of this life. There is a famous Ḥadīth which says that "half of Islam is enduring" (*ṣabr*).

Resurrection (Ar. *ba'th*, *nushūr*). The doctrine of

the resurrection of the bodies from the graves, and their reuniting with souls to face the great Judgement is a fundamental dogma of Islam. It is much insisted upon in the Koran, and is present in numerous creeds apart from Islam. The Koran says:

They say, 'What, when we are bones
and broken bits, shall we really
be raised up again in a new
creation?'
Say: 'Let you be stones, or iron,
or some creation yet more monstrous
in your minds!' Then they will say,
'Who will bring us back?' say: 'He
who originated you the first time.'
They will shake their heads at thee,
and they will say, When will it be?'
Say: 'It is possible that it may
be nigh, on the day when He will call you, and
you will answer praising Him, and
you will think you have but tarried
a little.' (17:51-54)

What, does man reckon We shall not gather his bones?
Yes indeed; We are able to shape again his fingers.
(75:3-4)

Again, the Koran compares the resurrection to the revivification of the parched earth by rain:

God is He that looses the winds, that stir up cloud,
then We drive it to a dead land
and therewith revive the earth, after it is dead.
Even so is the Uprising. (35:10)

The Rabbinic explanation of the apocalyptic reconstruction of the bodies of the dead from the "indestructible" bone at the bottom of the spine (*luzz*) was known to Muslim thinkers in the Middle Ages. (Islamic doctrine does not specify how the body is resurrected.) When Indian doctrines were encountered through the Persians, the *luzz* was easily identified with the *piáḍa* of Indian yoga and cosmology. This is the microcosmic reflection, within the person, of the macrocosmic *hiraáyagarbha* ("world egg"), designated in Persian *majmā-i anāsīr hasti* ("the totality of elements of existence"), or what the Koran (97:4) calls the *kulli amr* ("all decrees").

The Christian doctrine of the resurrection of Jesus does not exist in Islam. It is understood that the crucifixion was an appearance only; that Jesus did not die on the cross but instead passed into a principial state; that he is in this state alive in the invisible and will return from it again in the Second Coming which will mark the end of the cycle, or the end of the world. *See* JESUS.

Retaliation, *see* QIṢĀṢ.

Revelation. In Arabic this is denoted by two words: *waḥy* and *tanzīl*. *Waḥy*, from a root meaning "to inspire", implies a Divine source that is beyond the world and beyond the recipient; *tanzīl* ("sending down") is used particularly for the revelation of the Koran or other *direct* revelation as the descent of a form from heaven. *Waḥy* and *tanzīl* are thus complementary, and may be called direct revelation from God, corresponding to what is called *shruti* ("what has been heard") in Sanskrit. *Ilhām* ("inspiration or intuition") is the source of a secondary or indirect revelation, arising within the individual, or reflected within him. This corresponds to the Sanskrit *smriti* ("what has been recommended, or held in the mind"), secondary revelation. The difference between the two is shown by the Apostle Paul's distinction between that which came from the Spirit and that which came from himself.

The Ḥadīth which are called *ḥadīth qudsī* ("holy Ḥadīth"), are the utterances of God through the Prophet, and come thus from *waḥy*, whereas the *ḥadīth sharīf* ("noble Ḥadīth") may be inspired utterances of the Prophet himself and, if so, come through *ilhām*.

The Koran speaks of Jesus as having received *tanzīl* from God. The Gospels, without pretence to the contrary, are for the most part, except for the words of Jesus, secondary inspiration, being a description of events by his disciples, and not *tanzīl*. Muslim commentators were surprised to find doctrinal divergences between the Gospels and the Koran, and this has given rise to the historic accusations on the part of Muslim theologians that the Gospels have been changed (*takhrīf*). Rarely has it been suggested that the *tanzīl* of Christianity is in the person of Jesus himself as the Messenger of God and His Word (*Kalimatuh*) (4:17).

The theory of the revelation of the Koran is particularly complex. The Koran was revealed, or descended, in its entirety in one night, the "Night of Destiny" (*Laylat al-Qadr*), into the soul of the Prophet, *which itself is that night*. Thereupon it became manifest through him, in segments, sometimes entire Sūrahs, as particular circumstances and requirements in the world and the Prophet's life called them forth. The Prophet said that this manifestation of the Koran came in two ways: "Sometimes Gabriel reveals to me as one man to another, and that is easy; but at other times it is like the ringing of a bell penetrating my very heart, rending me, and that way is the most painful." *See also* BIBLE; FARAQLĪT; KORAN; MUḤAMMAD.

Rhazes, *see* RĀZĪ, ABŪ BAKR.

Ribā (from the root *rabā*: "to grow, increase, exceed"). Usury or profit – interest – from the loan of money or goods, which is prohibited in any degree. Today the prohibition is hardly observed in any Islamic country. Either it is simply disregarded – the Egyptian Mufti Muḥammad 'Abduh once declared "moderate interest" lawful – or else it is referred to by some such euphemism as "commission". To stay within the letter of the religious law and soothe consciences, some banks offer the solution of *muḍārabah* (sleeping partnership): this defines the placing of capital as a co-investment, which naturally brings a return to both parties. *See* ISLAMIC BANKING.

Ribāṭ (pl. *ribāṭāt* and *rubuṭ* from the verb *rabaṭa*, "to bind"; "a post", "a hospice", "a fort"). A fort on the frontier of Islam, the origin of the word is perhaps associated with "tethering a horse in enemy territory". The performance of garrison duty at the frontiers of *dār al-Islām* ("the abode of faith") was viewed as a pious duty from the time of 'Umar, when it was accepted that the Arab armies would advance without laying down their arms until Islam was established on the edges of the world.

Those who performed this duty of vigilance and defence in later Islam were called *al-murābiṭun* (the "ones bound [to religious duty]"). This became the name of the movement of the Almoravid (the Spanish name of the dynasty derived from the term *al-Murābiṭ*). The most famous of their forts was the *Ribāṭ al-Fatḥ* ("the camp of victory") from which the Almoravids set out on the conquest of southern Spain and North Africa. The *Ribāṭ al-Fatḥ* has given Morocco the name of its present capital, Rabāṭ. The institution of the *ribāṭ* mingled military service with religious observance and some *ribāṭat* became with time the meeting places of Sufis, that is, *khānaqahs* or *zāwiyahs*. *See* ALMORAVIDS.

Ridā'. The cloth which constitutes the covering of the upper body over the shoulders in the consecrated pilgrim's garb, the *iḥrām*. *See* IḤRĀM.

Riḍā'. The act of suckling a baby which establishes a foster-kinship, which, in certain degrees and under certain conditions, is an impediment to marriage.

After the conquest of Mecca the clans of the Beduin tribe of Hawāzin gathered to attack the army of the Prophet. The battle took place in a defile called Ḥunayn; eventually the Hawāzin were routed. To increase the valor of the Hawāzin men, their families had accompanied them, and so it came about that the women and children of the Hawāzin were captured. When one of these captives, an old women of seventy years, claimed to be the sister of the Prophet, she was brought before him. Asked for proof of her claim, she showed him the scar of a bite he had inflicted on her when she carried him as a child, for she was the daughter of Ḥalīmah and Ḥārith, two Beduin of a Hawāzin clan, to whom for a time the Prophet had been entrusted as a child, in order to be raised and strengthened in the desert, according to the custom of the Arab city dwellers. The Prophet recognized that the old woman, Shaymā', was indeed his foster sister; he offered to bring her back to Medina with him, but she preferred to remain with her desert clan of the Banū Sa'd ibn Bakr. She was therefore set free with gifts. Thereupon the Hawāzin all claimed to be related to the Prophet as cousins, a claim which he, however, did not countenance.

Riḍa, Muḥammad Rashīd (1865-1935). Muslim reformer, born in Syria, associated with Muḥammad Abduh, published a magazine called *al-Manār* ("the Lighthouse") in Cairo. He was concerned with the decline of the Islamic world, looked upon the Arabs as its champions, believed in the existence of a Caliphate for the sake of unity and promoted democratic consultation on the part of the government which he called *shūrā*.

Riddah. Apostasy from Islam. An apostate is called *murtadd*. The word is also applied to the period of insurgency and the rise of false prophets among the desert tribes which followed the death of the Prophet. *See* APOSTASY; al-ASWAD; DHŪ-l-ḤIMĀR; MUSAYLAMAH.

Riḍwān (lit. "felicity"). The word is used to mean "God's good pleasure" as in Mark 1:11, and has the same meaning as the Greek *eudokia*. The verb from which it is derived is used to call blessings upon the Companions of the Prophet: *raḍiya-Llāhu 'anhu* ("may God be well-pleased with him"). This formula is said when the name of a Companion or acknowledged saint is mentioned. The pact which the Prophet made at Ḥudaybiyyah with his followers, which is the model for the ritual of initiation in Sufism, is called the "pact of felicity", or *bay'at ar-riḍwān* ("God was well pleased with the Believers... 48:18).

In Sūrah 9:74, *riḍwān* means something higher again, the removal of the veil of separation from God which exists even in paradise:

> God has promised the believers, men and women, gardens underneath which rivers flow, forever therein to dwell, and goodly dwelling-places in the
> Gardens of Eden; and greater, God's good pleasure
> [*riḍwān*]; that is the mighty triumph.

Or again as this Ḥadīth clarifies:

> God will say to the people of Paradise: 'Are you well pleased?' and they will say: 'How should we not be well pleased, O Lord, inasmuch as You have given us that which You have not given to any of your creatures else?' Then will He say: 'Shall I not give you better than that?' and they will say: 'What thing, O Lord, is better?' and He will say: 'I will let down upon you My *riḍwān*'.

In other words, *riḍwān* in its ultimate sense is the final and absolute acceptance of a soul by God:

> 'O soul at peace, return unto thy Lord,
> well-pleased, well-pleasing!
> Enter thou among My servants!
> Enter thou My Paradise!' (89:27-30)

See also ḤUDAYBIYYAH.

Rightly guided Caliphs, *see* PATRIARCHAL CALIPHS.

ar-Rijāl, Abū-l-Ḥasan 'Alī (d. *432*/1040). Spanish mathematician, astronomer and astrologer known in the West as Abenragel.

Risālah (from *arsala*, "to send", "a missive", "message" or "epistle"; pl. *rasā'il*). **1.** The mission or "ministry" of a Divine Messenger (*rasūl*). **2.** *Risālah* also means a treatise, such as the *Risālah* of al-Qayrawānī on Mālikī law, the *Risālat al-Aḥadiyyah* ("Treatise on Unity") by Ibn 'Arabī, or *Rasā'il*, a collection of "belles lettres", etc. *See* PROPHETS.

Rizq (lit. "sustenance"). The "Sustainer" is a Divine Name: *ar-Razzāq*. The Shaykh al-'Arabī ad-Darqāwī wrote in his *Rasā'il* ("collected letters"):

> Nothing makes us so vulnerable to psychic and satanic attacks as concern for our sustenance. And yet our Lord (be He exalted) vowed to us by Himself: "Your sustenance and all ye have been promised is in Heaven; by the Lord of Heaven and earth, this is as true as it is true that ye have speech" (51:21-22). And He also said: "Prescribe prayer for thy people and be constant therein. We ask thee not to provide sustenance; We will provide for thee and it is piety that will gain the issue" (20:132). The same meaning is to be found in many other passages from the Koran as also in the many sayings of the Prophet (may God bless him and give him peace). There is also the saying of the Saint Abū Yazīd al-Bisṭāmī (may God be well pleased with him): "My part is to worship Him, as He commanded me, and His part is to feed me as He promised me", and so forth. I mention all this only because I am afraid you may lapse into the misfortune that afflicts most men. For I see them busy with many activities, religious as well as worldly, and fearing nothing so much as poverty. If they knew what riches are to be had from being occupied with God, they would forsake their worldly activities entirely and busy themselves with Him alone, that is, with His commandments. But in their ignorance they keep on increasing their worldly and religious activities while remaining uneasy from fear of poverty or from fear of creatures, which is serious forgetfulness and a deplorable state; and this is the state in which the

majority of people – almost all – exist; may God preserve us from it! Therefore be on guard, my brother, and devote yourself entirely to God; then you will see marvels.

God's sustenance is given to men both here and in the hereafter, and is essentially the same in all states of existence; the Blessed who are given the fruits of paradise as sustenance recognize that they were given the like on earth.

> Give thou good tidings to those who believe
> and do deeds of righteousness, that for them
> await gardens underneath which rivers flow;
> whensoever they are provided with fruits
> therefrom
> they shall say, 'This is that wherewithal
> we were provided before'; that they shall be
> given in perfect semblance... (2:23)

Rites (Ar. *mansik*, pl. *manāsik*, also *nusuk*). The rites of Islam are few: the pronunciation of the *shahādah* into the ears of a newborn child, the sacrifice of the *'Īd al-Kabīr*, the prayers for special purposes, and the recitation of the Koran, are virtually all the rites which exist in addition to the Five Pillars. The most intricate of all the rites are those of the *ḥajj* ("the greater pilgrimage"). *See* FIVE PILLARS.

Ritual Slaughter. Animals, with the exception of game, must be ritually slaughtered to be legally acceptable (*ḥalāl*) as food. After formulating the intention (*niyyah*) of performing ritual slaughter, the Divine Name is pronounced over the animal, which consecrates its death, the formula for this being *bismi-Llāh*; *Allāhu akbar* ("In the Name of God; God is Most Great"). Before such an act as slaughter, the Names of Mercy (*ar-Raḥmān ar-Raḥīm*) are *not* pronounced. The throat of the animal is cut, severing both the windpipe and the jugular vein in one stroke. The slaughter must be performed by a Muslim. If the animal is sacrificed for a purpose such as the *'Īd al-Aḍḥā*, the sacrificial feast of the "greater pilgrimage", this fact and the names of those for whom the sacrifice is being made are mentioned as part of the formulation of intention. Game can be used for food. If hunting is carried out, it must be done with the intention of consecrating the kill; for example, while loosing a hunting dog or firing a shot, the formula of consecration used in slaughter should be recited either aloud or mentally.

The blood of the slaughtered animal must be drained as completely as possible. Blood is forbidden as food in Islam, as in Judaism, because it is considered to be the substance which joins the physical body and the psyche in the individual, and can therefore transmit psychic elements from one creature to another.

When *ḥalāl* meat from ritually slaughtered animals is not available, it is permissible for Muslims to resort to meat slaughtered by Christians or Jews in accordance with the Koranic principle that necessity creates exceptions. *See* FOOD.

Riwāyah. Oral transmission or tradition; in particular the traditions of the ways of reciting the Koran. *See* QIRĀ'AH.

Rock, Dome of, *see* DOME of the ROCK.

Rosary (*Subḥah*, pl. *subuḥāt*; or *misbaḥah*, pl. *masābiḥ*). The rosary in Islam is made up of 99 beads, the number of the Names of God. The Name Allāh is represented by the *alif*, or the piece in which the two threads of the rosary are joined together. The most common subdivision is into three sections, each of 33 beads, but other subdivisions exist depending upon the litanies (*awrād*, sing. *wird*) which are to be recited. Such litanies are used particularly in Sufi orders, although some are in general use. Various formulas including the *shahādah* ("There is no God but God"), the *hamdalah* ("Praise be to God"), the *tasbīḥ* (*subḥāna' Llāh*; "God be Glorified"), or phrases from the Koran, form the recitation of the rosary which is essentially a means of concentration. The systematic repetition of the same words fixes them, or their idea, in a moment outside the flow of time, reinforcing concentration.

Because the Prophet himself used his fingers to keep count of recitations, moving the thumb across the finger-joints of one or both hands, typically to count out formulas recited 33 times after the end of the prayer (*ṣalāt*), the Wahhābīs opposed the use of the rosary as an innovation, even though it had been used for a long time in Islam. Its use is so deeply established, however, that opposition is rarely heard today.

The members of some Sufi orders wear a large rosary around their necks as a sign of their commitment. The widespread habit of the Turks, and some other Islamic peoples, of carrying a rosary in the hand at all times, ostensibly as a mnemonic device to encourage constant remembrance of God, was taken up in the Balkans as a profane custom of busying the fingers to pass the time which led to the unfortunate expression "worry beads". *See* WIRD.

Rozah. The Persian term for the Arabic *ṣawm*, or fast. *See* FAST; RAMADĀN.

Rubā'iyyāt, the (from sing. *rubā'iyyah*, or quatrain). Any poem written in quatrains, but above all a collection of verses in Persian attributed to the mathematician and astronomer 'Umar Khayyām (d. *517*/1123).

The free translation by Edward Fitzgerald (1809-1883) became justly world famous and is much more remarkable, both as poetry and substance, than the original. Fitzgerald's poem is made up of variations on themes found in Khayyām's poems, and is a distillation of Platonism in Sufi guise. Few of Fitzgerald's verses exist as such in the Persian; yet all, or almost all of them, echo something from the Persian originals. What Khayyām himself wrote cannot be known with certainty, for his Rubā'iyyat exist only in manuscripts which date centuries after his death; more than 1,500 quatrains are attributed to him, and many of these are also attributed to other poets. Moreover, the popularity of Fitzgerald's work inspired the creation of a number of forged manuscripts in this century which added more corridors to the Khayyām labyrinth; in many ways, Khayyām in Persian has become the reflection of Khayyām in Fitzgerald's English.

The Fitzgerald translation is an extremely intelligent compilation of Sufi (and anti-Sufi) ideas so successfully disguised as hedonism that it is often, perhaps even usually, thought to be praise of the pursuit of pleasure. Which it is, but in its antinomianism it is sometimes also the exact opposite: the tavern is the *khānaqah*, or meeting place of dervishes, wine the remembrance of God, and the Beloved, God Himself. Being two opposite tendencies at the same time, it draws the mind into itself all the better. Fitzgerald himself professed to take its disguise at face value; yet as the real creator of the "Rubaiyat of Omar Khayyam", he crammed it as full of Sufi lore as only a 19th-century Victorian orientalist could. But he was not the only one to do so: in 1853, Captain Sir Richard Burton (1821-1890) wrote the "Kasīdah of Hājī 'Abdū el-Yezdi" (translated and annoted by His friend and Pupil F.B.) The "F.B." (Francis Baker, his middle and his mother's name) is Richard Burton himself. This rubā'iyyat becomes philosophical in the manner of Fitzgerald, quotes Ḥafiz and Khayyām and deals with the same themes, almost as successfully as Fitzgerald, who published his in 1861. *See* UMAR KHAYYĀM.

Rūdakī, Farid ad-Din. (d. *343*/954). The first great modern Persian poet. He was born in Transoxiana and was the court poet of the Sāmanīd ruler al-Amīr as-Sa'īd Naṣr II ibn Aḥmad (d. *331*/943). Only a small number of the vast opus attributed to him has survived, but he had a decisive influence on every genre of Persian literature. Hedonist and unconventional, legend has it that his eyes were put out at the orders of his royal patron for being an Isma'ili Qarmatian. More likely he went blind naturally rather than for his beliefs since such metaphysics were not unusual in Central Asia at the time; it is later commentators who felt it necessary to assure posterity for the sake of morality that Rūdakī's freethinking had not gone unpunished.

Rūḥ (lit. "spirit"). The word is used in all the possible meanings of "spirit", but in particular means the non-individual aspect of the soul, the intellect or *nous*, in Arabic *al-'aql al-fa'āl* (or *fā'il*) ("active intellect"), as opposed to the lower individual soul, the *psyche*, in Arabic *an-nafs*.

The spirit (*al-rūḥ*) in the individual is continuous with Being itself, *al-wujūd*, or *al-'aql al-awwal* ("first intellect"), and is the dignity which exalts man above animals, and even above Angels. This is signified by the ability of Adam in the garden to name the objects of existence, which the Angels could not do and by which they recognized Adam's superiority over them, except of course Iblīs, the devil, who saw in Adam only clay – and not spirit – and so revolted against God.

Within the individual, *al-rūḥ* is also referred to as *al-ḥaqīqah* ("reality") or *as-sirr* ("the secret"). The center of Being, which is the point of transition to creation, is symbolized by an Angel (also called *ar-Rūḥ*), who is so great that, whereas the other Angels can form rows, *ar-Rūḥ* occupies a whole row by himself. This Angel corresponds to the *Metatron* in Hebrew or to *buddhi* in certain contexts in Sanskrit. The origin is the *Spenta Mainyu* or "Holy Spirit of God" in Zoroastrianism.

Rūḥ Allāh (the "Spirit of God"), is a special name of Jesus (4:169) in the Koran (and also of Adam, but it is not used as his epithet: 15:29). *See* FIVE DIVINE PRESENCES.

Rukhkh. The Arabic name of the phoenix, but *rukhkh* has also been used for other mythical and gigantic birds such as the Hindu *Garuḍa*. The name is presumably derived originally from the Hebrew *ruakh* ("spirit"), corresponding to the Arabic *rūḥ*. The phoenix is, in fact, the spirit; more exactly, it symbolizes the vertical intervention of the spirit in the processes of transformation, "rebirth" from ashes, new life emerging out of the corruption of death, and the transmission of the seeds from one cycle of manifestation to the other. It is an important symbol in alchemy and in cosmology, and mirrors both the immortality of the soul in its victory over death, and also the transcendence of the Intellect in relation to the soul. The Arabic *rukhkh* comes into English as "rook", the alternative word for the castle in chess, *rukhkh* alone being used in the game as played in Persia and the Middle East.

ar-Rukn al-yamanī (lit. "the southern" or "Yemeni corner"). The corner of the Ka'bah which contains the Black Stone. *See* BLACK STONE; KA'BAH.

Rukū' (Ar. "a bow"). The name of the bow in the canonical prayer (*ṣalāh*). There are certain passages in the Koran where it is clear from the sense of the words, and also from there being some symbol or the word *rukū'* in the margin, that the reader and his listeners should bow in the direction of Mecca. This is done even if the passage occurs during the recitations within the prayer (*ṣalāh*); after the bow the prayer continues normally.

A *rukū'* is also the name of a section of a Sūrah of the Koran often marked in texts by a *hamzah* or an *'ayn* in the margin. *See* RAKAH; ṢALĀH.

ar-Rūm (lit. "the Romans"). The name the Koran and the Arabs gave to both the Byzantines and the Romans of the western empire as well. To this day in dialectical Arabic, the adjective *rūmī* refers to that which is western or non-indigenous.

Rumelia. Lands of the Ottoman Empire in Europe. The word is derived from *Rūm* ("Rome"), a term used by Muslims to designate Byzantium, and the whole of Christian Asia Minor before its conquest by Islam.

ar-Rūmī, Jalāl ad-Dīn, *see* JALĀL ad-DĪN ar-RŪMĪ.

Ruqayyah. One of the daughters of the Prophet and his first wife Khadījah. She emigrated to Abyssinia with her husband 'Uthmān ibn 'Affān. After the Hijrah they both went to Medina. She died in Medina while the Battle of Badr was taking place.

Russia. Russian Federation; population 149,909,089; Russians are 82%; the largest ethnic group of Muslim origin are the Tatars who are 4%. Other ethnic groups who are of Muslim origin are: Abazi, Adygei, Aguls, Azeris, Balkars, Bashkirs, Chechens, Cherkess, Crimean Tatars, Dargins, Dungan, Gypsies (Central Asian Gypsies are Muslim; in other regions they are mostly Russian Orthodox); Ingush, Iranians, Kabardians, Karachai, Karakalpaks, Kazakhs, Kirghiz, Kumyks, Kurds, Laks, Lezgins, Nogai, Ossetians, Rutuls, Tabasarans, Tadjiks, Talysh; Tats, Tsakhurs, Turkmen, Turks, Uighurs, Uzbeks. Many individuals of Muslim origin have a very tenous understanding of Islam. Most of these groups are Turkic (with the exception of the Tadjiks, the Ossetians, the Iranians, the Kabardians, the Balkars, and some others, notably the Daghestani groups). Some ethnics groups have their own republics within the Russian Federation and outside of it. The Tatars are centered around the Volga and Kazan, and are scattered throughout European Russia (and are found in Poland, as well); in the Crimea (now part of the Ukraine) there are large Muslim populations, and the Caucasus are almost entirely peoples of Muslim affiliation. A geat deal of inter-marriage has taken place within the former Soviet Union.

Ruqyah (lit. "incantation"; pl. *ruqā*). These are incantations, sometimes in unrecognizable sounds, which are used to ward off evil or harm. Many have existed since pre-Islamic times. The Arabs presented the incantations they knew to the Prophet who, one by one, accepted some as lawful and rejected others. Some were ascribed to anterior Prophets. Most surviving incantations today are based on the Koran. *See* AMULETS; ĀYAT al-KURSĪ; ḤIZB al-BAḤR; REFUGE.

Ru'yā (lit. "vision"). The word is often used metaphysically for intellectual understanding or, again, psychic visions or intuitions. It may refer to a prophetic dream, as when the prophet dreamed before the treaty of Ḥudaybiyyah, that he and his people had entered the Sacred Mosque at Mecca without hindrance, in order to perform the rites: "God has already fulfilled in truth the dream [vision, *ar-ru'yā*] for His Prophet..."(48:27).

S

Sabā'. One of the kingdoms of ancient South Arabia, the capital of which was Ma'rib, near a famous dam that collapsed around 580 A.D., an event which sent a wave of lamentation through the desert tribes. For the Arabs this was one of the few markers in an otherwise timeless world; an age had passed.

In the Bible this kingdom is called Sheba, and it reached the heights of its development in the 6th century B.C., having colonized Abyssinia four centuries previously. The Queen of Sabā', known in Islam as Bilqīs, is accorded a prominent place in Islamic lore as the consort of King Solomon. *See* BILQĪS; MA'RIB DAM.

As-Sab' al-Mathānī (lit. "the seven repeated [lines]"). A popular name for the Fātiḥah, or opening Sūrah of the Koran. The Fātiḥah is recited several times in every ritual prayer (*ṣalāh*), and on numerous occasions as a universal prayer.

Sabians (Ar. *Ṣābi'*, pl. *Ṣābi'ūn* or, collectively, *aṣ-Ṣābi'ah*). A people named in the Koran (2:59; 22:17), along with Christians, Jews, and Magians (the Zoroastrians), as having a religion revealed by God. Many religious groups, including various Christian branches, and various groups in India, have at one time or another been identified as Sabians.

An ethnic group in Harran in northern Mesopotamia (today Altinbasak in Southern Turkey near Urfa), who were more or less Hellenistic pagans with roots in ancient Babylonian religions, once claimed to be the Sabians as a means of escaping persecution for their non-Islamic beliefs. A number of famous scholars, particularly mathematicians, originated among these people, including the astrologer and scientist Thābit ibn Qurrā and the alchemist Jābir ibn Ḥayyān. Sometimes the Mandaeans or Nasoreans of Iraq have been identified with the Sabians. However, it is not known with certainty who the Sabians of the Koran really are or were.

The very fact that many different groups were assimilated to the name and that it is impossible to fix the Koranic term definitively to any one of them, suggests that the concept of the Sabians was an open door for toleration to any religion which upon examination appeared to be an authentic way of worshiping God. The word "Sabians" may derive from the Egyptian *sb*, which means both "wisdom" and "stars". This Egyptian word may be also the origin of the Greek word *sophia* ("wisdom") and perhaps – rather more dubiously – of the Arabic word *ṣūfī* ("mystic"). *See* HARRANIANS; MANDAEANS.

Sabīl Allāh (lit. "way of God"). The general name, used in the Koran, for all those acts which are pleasing to God.

Sacrifice. The Arabic words *aḍḥā*, *dhabaḥa* and *naḥara* all mean primarily "to slaughter an animal", "to immolate"; the noun "*qurbān*" implies a sacrifice with or without slaughter, and is derived from the verb *qaruba* ("to draw near"), related to the Hebrew *qorbān*, of the same significance. *Al-'Īd al-Kabīr*, or the *'Id al-Aḍḥā*, which commemorates Abraham's sacrifice of the ram in the place of his son, is the most prominent sacrificial rite, and takes place on the 10th of Dhu-l-Ḥijjah. The 10th, 11th, and 12th are possible days for the sacrifice which may be any of the acceptable animals: a sheep, a camel, a cow, or a goat. The sacrifice is performed according to the rules of ritual slaughter with the words *Bismi-Llāh*; *Allāhu akbar* (instead of *Bismi-Llāhi-r-Raḥmāni-r-Raḥīm*), the blood is drained and the meat used for food. It is not lawful to sell the animal for gain after sacrifice.

Sacrifice may be performed at any time with the intention of coming closer to God. It is the custom to perform the sacrifice called *al-'aqīqah* when a child is born. *See* RITUAL SLAUGHTER.

de Sacy, Baron Silvestre (1758-1838). The most distinguished Orientalist of his time and the founder of the modern school of Arabic scholarship in Europe. The son of a notary, de Sacy was born in Paris. Educated for the civil service, he studied jurisprudence and in 1781 obtained a government post which he held until 1791.

An indefatigable worker, he had little need of rest; in the course of his work and studies he learned the principle Semitic languages and published studies on the Bible. He began the decipherment of Sassanid Pahlavi inscriptions. During the French revolution he retired from the civil service and lived in seclusion until 1795 when he was called to be professor of Arabic in the newly founded Ecole Spéciale des Langues Orientales Vivantes.

This was the occasion of furthering his already vast knowledge of Oriental languages. He wrote *La Grammaire Arabe* and *La Chrestomatie Arabe*. He was deeply familiar with Arabic literature. Among his works are a translation of the *Maqamat* of Hariri; he prepared an edition of *Kalilah wa Dimnah*, and the *Alfiyyah* of Ibn Malik. Many subsequent Arabists were his students: Freytag, Fluegel, Fleischer, Ahlwardt, Tornberg, Rosegarten, De Slane, Quatremère and Reinaud. Several chairs of Oriental studies were created in French universities upon his recommendation, as also in Prussia and Russia. He was a founder of the Société Asiatique in whose publication his own work reached the public; he was peer of the realm of France, a grand officer of the Legion of Honor, and the holder of many foreign titles.

Sa'd ibn Abī Waqqāṣ (d. *55*/674). One of the most famous Companions and earliest converts to Islam, also a veteran of all the Battles. He is one of the "Ten well-betided ones" who were told by the Prophet that they were assured a place in paradise.

Under the Caliph 'Umar, Sa'd ibn Abī Waqqāṣ led the armies in the battle of Qādisiyyah against the Persians in *16*/637 and was the first governor of Kufah, which he founded. He was one of the electors of the third Caliph, 'Uthmān. *See* COMPANIONS.

Sa'd ibn Mu'ādh (d. *5*/626). The chief of the tribe of Aws and one of the early converts from Medina. Upon his deathbed, after being wounded in the Battle of the Trench, Sa'd passed the judgement which sealed the fate of the Jews of the Banū Qurayẓah. *See* QURAYZAH.

Ṣadaqah (lit. "righteousness", from the root *ṣadaqa*, "to speak truth", "to be true"). The voluntary giving of alms (as opposed to *zakāh* which is obligatory) to the needy. In the Koran the word is used very frequently in the plural *ṣadaqāt* ("deeds of kindness and generosity").

God will efface usurious increase [*ar-ribā*] but will increase [profit] from deeds of charity [*aṣ-ṣadaqāt*] and God has no love for any disbeliever or sinner. (2:276) A particular form of *ṣadaqah* is the distribution to the poor of a quantity of grain at least equal to about two quarts, or its monetary equivalent, for every member of the household upon the *'Īd al-Fiṭr* at the end of Ramaḍān.

Sa'dī, Muṣlaḥ ad-Dīn (*580-692*/1184-1292). A famous poet of Shiraz in Persia, and a didactic moralist. His major works are the *Bustān*, ("The Fruit Garden"), the *Gūlistān* ("The Rose Garden"), and his *Dīwān*. He studied at the Niẓāmiyyah of Baghdad and took the name Sa'dī from his protector Sa'd ibn Zengī, the Atabeg of Fars.

Sa'dī was a Sufi, having been the disciple of Shihāb ad-Dīn Suhrawardī. Much of Sa'dī's life was spent in travel. He visited the Gujarat and Delhi (where he learned Hindustani), the Yemen, and North Africa.

Near Jerusalem he was captured by the Franks and worked at hard labor until ransomed. In Syria he was appointed prayer-leader (*Imām*) and preacher (*khatīb*) at a Friday congregational mosque. He died in Shiraz where he returned after the age of 70.

Ṣadr ad-Dīn Shirāzī, *see* MULLA ṢADRĀ.

Ṣadr-i azam. In Ottoman Turkey and Iran, the chief "minister", or what in Arab lands was called "the Wazir".

aṣ-Ṣādūq, *see* IBN BABAWAYH.

Ṣafā and Marwah. Two small hills, one now partly removed to make a roadway, near the Ka'bah in Mecca. What remains of both hills is enclosed within the Grand Mosque (*al-Masjid al-Ḥarām*). The two hills are separated by a distance of 394m/1247ft. Between their bases is a course which is called the *masā*. This distance (293m/927ft) is walked, and in part run, seven times by those performing the *ḥajj* or *'umrah*. This ritual going back and forth between the two hills is called the *sa'y* (the "run", "course" or "endeavour"). The names of both hills are different words for rock or stone, and the origin of the rite of the *sa'y* is the casting to and fro of Hagar looking for water for her son. *See* HAGAR; ISHMAEL; PILGRIMAGE; SA'Y.

Safavids. A dynasty which ruled Persia from *907-1145*/1501-1732. The first Safavid, Ismā'īl, used Shī'ism as a power base to rally support and to deny the legitimacy of those he was supplanting. The Safavids made Twelve-Imām Shī'ism the state religion, thereby establishing the basis for internal unity, but tending also to isolate Persia from its Sunnī neighbors, as well as laying it open to the tensions inherent in Shī'ism.

As a descendant of the family of the Imāms, Ismā'īl claimed to represent the Twelfth, or "Hidden" Imām, and, in order to intensify political passions he introduced the cursing of the first three Caliphs. In the long run, however, his emphasizing the claims of the Hidden Imām made all rulers theoretically illegitimate substitutes, thus introducing the seeds of political instability (*See* HIDDEN IMĀM.) Moreover, since the efficacy of the religion also depended upon the Hidden Imām, the door was open to others who could claim to represent him; in the 19th century this led to the birth of dissident sects, one after the other: the Shaykhīs, the Bābīs, the Bahā'īs.

The Safavid dynasty originates from Shaykh Isḥāq Safī ad-Dīn (d. *735*/1334) who lived in Ardabil in Azerbaijan. He was the head of a Sufi order called, after the Shaykh, the Ṣafavī Order; this name was adopted to designate the dynasty. (In Europe it became confused with Sufism, so that the Shah was sometimes called the "Grand Sophi".) The order was associated with Shī'ism and its adherents were seven Turkic tribes called the *Qizil-Bash*, or "red caps", after the caps they wore, which had tassels standing for each of the twelve Imāms. Legend said that some of the followers were descended from captives freed by Timur to honor Shaykh Ṣafī ad-Dīn, who was given control of the region. The Safavids later claimed that Shaykh Ṣafī ad-Dīn was descended from the seventh Shī''ite Imām, Mūsā-l-Kāẓim.

A descendant of this Shaykh, Junayd, married the sister of Uzun Ḥasan, one of the last Aq Qoyunlu rulers. The son of this union, Haydar, was married by Uzun Ḥasan to his daughter. The son of Haydar, Ismā'īl, turned against the Aq Qoyunlu ruler, however, and with the *Qizil-Bash*, using Shī'ism as a political and ideological base, began expanding his power. He took the title of Shah and became the first Safavid king.

At first the Ottomans were the greatest threat to Safavid rule but, when they became increasingly preoccupied with expansion into Europe, Shah 'Abbās I ("the Great") took the opportunity to make peace with them, and was thus able to turn his attention to repressing the Uzbek tribes that perennially raided into Persia. Shah 'Abbās moved his capital from Qazvin to Isfahan. His reign marked the peak of the Safavid dynasty's achievements in art, diplomacy, and commerce. It was probably around this time that the court, which originally spoke a Turkic language, began to use Persian.

Following the example of the Safavids, and with military help and propaganda from Persia, other Twelve-Imām Shī'ite regimes were established in various parts of India: Yūsuf 'Ādil Shāh in *908*/1503 made Shī'ism the state religion of Bījāpūr in the Bahmānī kingdom; Sultan Qūlī founded a Shī'ite dynasty, the Quṭb Shāhī, in Golconda in Hyderabad. Shams ad-Dīn 'Irāqī from Gīlān, a follower of Muḥammad Nurbaksh, propagated Sufism of a Shī'ite inspiration in Srinagar, and Bābūr the Great, the Moghul Emperor, was helped by Ismā'īl I, and his troops wore the *Qizil Bash* cap for a time.

In Persia, the Safavid dynasty was followed by that of the Afsharids. *See* AFSHARIDS.

Ṣaffārids (*253-900*/867-1495). A dynasty in Sistān, in eastern Persia. The founder, Ya'qūb ibn Layḥ, whose dynastic name came from the profession of coppersmith (*ṣaffār*), raised an army about him at a time of unrest and instability in which the Khārijites who had fled from the west played a role. Although the Ṣaffārids were laid low first by the Sāmānids of Transoxiana, and later by the Ghaznavids, they frequently returned to power as local rulers or governors.

Ṣaḥābat an-Nabī, *see* COMPANIONS.

Ṣāḥib az-Zamān (lit. "the Lord of the Age"). A title given by the Shī'ites to the twelfth Imām whom they believe to be the Mahdī. *See* HIDDEN IMĀM.

Ṣaḥīfah (lit. "a portion of writing", pl. *ṣuḥuf*). **1.** Any of the books revealed to the Divine Messengers who came before the Prophet.

2. The name of a notebook that may have been kept by 'Alī ibn Abī Ṭālib, which gave rise to the legend of a book of secret prophecies, supposedly known only to the descendants of the Prophet and called the *Kitāb al-Jafr*; Shī'ites maintain that this was retained in the hands of those descendants of 'Alī who were considered to be Imāms. *See* KITĀB al-JAFR.

aṣ-Ṣaḥīḥ (lit. "the sure", "the authentic"). The name of two different collections of Ḥadīth, one by Muslim, and the other by Bukhari. Both are highly authoritative. Together, the collections are called *aṣ-Ṣaḥīḥān*. *See* ḤADĪTH.

Sahl at-Tustarī (*203-283*/818-896). An early mystic who was born in Tustar, Persia and died in Baṣra, he is credited with many fundamental Sufi intellectual formulations of doctrine and an analysis of the steps in the movement of *metanoia*, repentance or turning to God (*tawbah*), and devotion.

Highly unorthodox, he was one of the teachers of al-Ḥallāj. Sahl at-Tustarī explained the famous Sufi saying ascribed to the Prophet: "I am He and He is I, save that I am I, and He is He" (*ana huwa, wa huwa ana, ghayra an ana ana, wa huwa huwa*) as a mystery of union or realization at the center of the Saint's personality, called the *sirr* ("the secret"), or the heart, where existence joins Being. Sahl at-Tustarī said: "God is [only] known by the union of contraries attributed to Him".

He said that he was the disciple of "ancient masters" (thus, presumably pre-Islamic ones) and spoke of the essence of Muḥammad as a "column of light *[amud an-nur]* which had *emanated* from God Himself and which had bowed down before Him a million years before the Adamic Covenant, and which has been disseminated in particles of uncreated certitude (*yaqin*) in a certain number of hearts, those of the intimate elect... In his pristine perfection man exists in the form of a particle of light as an atom (*darr*). Tustari claimed to have met 'One thousand five hundred righteous ones (*siddiqin*, among them forty substitutes (*budala'*) and seven pegs (*awtad*),' and said: Their path (*tariqah*) and their way (*madhab*) is the same as mine.'"

At-Tustarī compiled, along with a group that he led, a commentary on the Koran, called simply *Tafsīr al-Qur'ān*. He said that the Koran contained several levels of meaning. These could be reduced to the outer (*ẓāhir*), accessible to the common man (*āmm*), and the inner (*bātin*), accessible only to the elect (*ḥāṣṣ*). (In addition there were, he said, a limit, *ḥadd*, and a *maṭlā*, "point of transcendence.") By this device of splitting doctrine into inner and outer, at-Tustarī and his colleagues adapted such philosophy of Persian inspiration into the inner meaning as would have normally been rejected by Islamic doctrine had it been taken at its face value. Tustarī treated time as three moments: Man's existence in this world is suspended between the Day of Covenant and the Day of Resurrection. On his course from pre-existential infinity (*ibtida'*) to post-existential infinity (*intiha'*) man passes through his phenomenal existence, marked by the moment of his creation and the instant of his death. He created a construct of individual pre-existence in the form of a Day of Covenant (*yawm al-mithāq*), in which, he said, individuals had already existed in the form of light particles. Something like this can be found in the Koran as the eternal acknowledgement by Adam's *descendants* that God is the Absolute. In the Koran, however, there is no question of light particles, nor the meaning which the event takes on in at-Tustarī's overall schema.

Then he took the Day of Resurrection (*yawm al-Qiyamah*), which of course also exists in the Koran, but in a different sense, as a post-existence leading to reintegration of the individual into the Principle after the drama of manifestation. These two, pre-existence and post-existence, together with the present time (which becomes a kind of duration without qualitative evolution), are recognizably the Zurvanite doctrine of the three moments which in this way was Islamicised, (as, by a similar process, it was also introduced into some forms of Chinese Buddhism through the *Sutra of the Two Principles and Three Moments*). With this doctrine, creation is no longer *ex nihilo*, but is instead a transformation or exile of a divine Substance into matter which will ultimately return to itself as principle or God. An equation is thus drawn between matter and God. In fact, the whole idea of creation is turned upside down; rather than the world being created out of nothing, it is instead created out of God.

At-Tustarī was one of the early "drunken" Sufis who ascribed divinity to himself and made *shatahāt*, or so-called "ecstatic utterances" to this effect. He also used the idea of the *nūr Muḥammadi*, or "Muhammadan Light" which has since become common to many Sufis. Much more strikingly, from the point of view of

Iranian comparative religion, he tried to introduce into Islam the idea of columns of light (*umūd an-nūr*); this latter did not find much acceptance outside of some Central Asian and Iranian Sufi groups.

What did leave a big trace was the notion, apparently first introduced by at-Tustarī, that Satan was really the strictest believer, the most perfect monotheist, and the most faithful and unwavering servant of God. This rehabilitation of Satan amounts to the introduction into Islam of a second Absolute in the form of evil or as the the other side of God. This extremely heretical idea was taken up by some other Sufis (although, of course, not all), notably by al-Hallāj (the most prominent pupil of at-Tustarī's school), and by Ibn Arabī, Aṭṭār, and 'Abd al-Karīm Jilī. An important consequence of this makes God the creator of evil as well as of good, which, though less dramatic than Satan being actually turned into God, is no less far-reaching. Radical as at-Tustarī was, his formulations were so innocuous on the surface that he escaped serious censure during his own lifetime. However, those like his disciple al-Hallāj (d. *309*/922), 'Ayn al-Quḍāt Hamadānī (d. *525*/1131), a disciple of Abū Ḥamīd Muḥammad al-Ghazalī's black sheep brother Aḥmad, Shihāb ad-Dīn Yaḥyā Suhrawardī (d. *587*/1191), and Muḥammad Nūrbakhsh (d. *864*/1465) who enthusiastically presented the same ideas to the public rather than to private circles, aroused the authorities sufficiently to be all put to death. *See* ANTINOMIANISM; al-ḤALLĀJ.

Sahm-i Imam ("the share of the Imam"). Monies sent to the Shī'ite holy places for their upkeep, the support of the '*ulama*, and for distribution at their discretion.

Saḥūr (or *suḥūr*). A light meal taken before the dawn and the beginning of the day's fasting in the month of Ramaḍān. In cities and towns many people make rounds in the street at night, calling out or beating drums and playing flutes, as a pious duty to wake the dwellers to partake of the meal.

Sai. *See* SA'Y.

Saints (Ar. *awliyā'*, sing. *walī*, from *walī Allāh*, "friend of God"). The term *walī Allāh* ("saint") comes from the Koran (10:63): "Lo, the friends of God, there is no fear upon them, neither do they grieve." There is a widespread cult of Saints throughout the Islamic world, and there are various degrees of sanctity; below the degree of *walī* there is that of *ṭāhir*, or one who is "purified", which could well correspond to the Catholic degree of one who is "blessed".

According to popular belief, above the *walī* there is an invisible hierarchy of Saints who are necessary to cosmological equilibrium. These are the four *awtād* ("the pegs"), the forty *siddīqūn* ("the truthful ones", who correspond to the Jewish idea of *tsadeqs*), and so on.

The doctrine of sanctification is defined by a famous Ḥadīth:

> My servant does not cease to approach Me (God) with acts of personal devotion, until I love him; and when I love him I become the Hearing with which he hears, the Sight with which he sees, the Hand with which he grasps, the Foot with which he walks.

Another Ḥadīth says:

> The Heavens and earth cannot contain me (God) but the heart of my believing servant can contain me.

The highest degree of sanctity in this life is the *'ārif bi-Llāh*, ("the knower through God"), which is the supreme state of realization. This state is the equivalent of *mukti* ("liberation", "realisation"), the *'ārif bi-Llāh* corresponding in Sanskrit exactly to the Hindu *jīvan mukta* ("the liberated in life").

Saints' tombs dot the countryside in the Islamic world. Commonly the tomb has a dome (whose sphere symbolizes heaven) which rests upon an octagonal drum (the number eight here represents transformation from one state to another. Eight is the first number in a mathematical progression from four – the stable, material world – to the sphere, heavenly perfection). The octagonal drum rests in turn upon a cubic structure which symbolizes the earth. Thus, symbolically, the tomb resumes the Saint's role as a bridge between heaven and earth.

Many countries have a Saint who is virtually the national patron, or one of several national patrons, for example Mulay Idrīs I in Morocco, and Abū Madyān in Algeria. The French created the name "Maraboutism" from the Arabic *marbūṭ* (one "who is bound [to God]") for the cult of Saints in North and West Africa.

The Wahhābis categorically deny the idea of Saints on the grounds that it infringes *tawḥīd.* This word means "acknowledging or asserting the Oneness or Uniqueness of God", but the Wahhābis take it to mean the exclusion of the Divine or sacred from anything in creation. Paradoxically, *tawḥīd* is used by others for the idea of union with God", it is the verbal noun of the verb *waḥḥada* ("to make one", "to unite" "to consider, or admit, as one").

Ibn 'Aṭa' Allāh said in his *Ḥikam*:

> Glory be to Him who has not made any sign leading to His saints save as a sign leading to Himself, and who has joined no one to them except him whom God wants to join to Himself.

See QUṬB.

Sajdah (lit. "a prostration"). The touching of the forehead to the ground during the prayer (*ṣalāh*). There are, moreover, many places in the Koran where the sense of the words advises the performance of a prostration. When one of these passages is read (for example 84:21 or 19:60) readers and listeners perform a brief prostration, either directly from the sitting position, if one is sitting, or from the standing position if, for example, the passage is uttered during the prayer; the prayer is then resumed in the normal order and fashion.

The sense of a Koranic text calling for a prostration is sometimes amplified by printing a line above the determinative words, and the word *sajdah* is then inscribed in the margin. In some cases a *sajdah* during a particular passage of the Koran is a custom of one school of law, but not of the others, and this may also be indicated in the margin of the Koran.

A small prayer rug is called a *sajjādah*, and the word also is the root for *masjid*, a mosque, a place of prostration. *See* PRAYER; ṢALĀH.

Sakb. The Prophet's stallion, which he rode to the Battle of Uḥud. One of the Prophet's camels was called Qaswā', and his mule, Duldul.

aṣ-Ṣakhrah, Qubbat, *see* DOME of the ROCK.

Sakīnah (lit. "tranquility", "peace", "calm", from the root *sakana*, "to be quiet", "to abate", "to be still", "to dwell"). In Islam the word designates a special peace, the Peace of God which settles upon the heart. "He it is Who sent down the *Sakīnah* into the hearts of the believers, that they might add fresh faith to their faith..." (48:4). Although the word is clearly related to the Hebrew *Shekhinah*, and is used in the Koran to refer to the Ark of the Covenant (2:248), it does not go so far as to mean the indwelling of the Divine Presence. (9:26; 9:40; 48:4; 48:18; 48:26).

Saladin, *see* ṢALĀḤ ad-DĪN al-AYYŪBĪ.

Salaf (lit. "predecessors", "ancestors"). The first generations of Muslims, considered by later generations to be the most authoritative source for Islamic practice and guidance. The comments of these first Muslims are used to elucidate questions whose solutions are not explicit in the Koran and in the Sunnah. The *salaf* cover three generations: that of the Companions of the Prophet, that of the *Tābiūn* ("the successors") who knew the Companions, and that of the *Taba' at-Tābiīn* ("the successors of the successors"). Each successive generation's testimony is less authoritative.

The Wahhābīs do not accord a special validity to the opinions and practices of any authority after the *Tābiūn*, and regard all practices introduced after that generation to be unwarranted innovation, at least in theory; in practice this original severity of view has now been much softened. *See* TĀBI'ŪN.

Salafiyyah. A movement, begun at the turn of the century, whose name derives from the phrase *salaf aṣ-ṣāliḥīn* ("the pious ancestors"), it was founded by Jamāl ad-Dīn al-Afghānī and Muḥammad 'Abduh while they were in exile in Paris. Its influence was centered in Egypt, and increased when Abduh became Mufti. Through Egypt, it had a profound influence on the other Arab countries, and similar movements sprang up in other parts of the Islamic world, such as the Aligarh in India and the Muḥammadiyah in Indonesia.

Contrary to the implication of its name and to its claim to be a restoration of the original Islam, it was rather a movement of modernization. Although it denounced lukewarm devotion, its exhortation to piety clothed a call to humanism and "progress". The *Salafiyyah* sought to accommodate Islam to the ideas of secular materialism, and did not hesitate to declare that, where there was conflict between millennial Islam and modern needs, Islamic law could be changed. As Mufti, Muḥammad Abduh declared that "moderate" interest on deposited capital was legal; he called for the dissolution of the four schools of law, which he saw as an archaism, and for the establishment of a unified law which, in the reshuffling, would incorporate modifications to comply with the demands of modern times. The movement emulated Christian missionary endeavor, and sponsored the training of Islamic propagandists to spread a religion presented as *rational* ("the fast of Ramaḍān is healthy and good for the stomach"), *progressive*, and *better* than Christianity or Judaism. The *Salafiyyah* encompassed the first feminist movements in Islam. By declaring itself disposed to accept the theory of evolution, the movement took modern science as a higher authority than the Koran. The publication *al-Manār* in Egypt was for many years the principal mouthpiece of the *Salafiyyah*.

The movement has now run its course, but its influence has been considerable. Many Muslims with a modern education tend to feel that their beliefs are more surely supported by scientific evidence and rational arguments, than by appeals to the authority of revelation. They find, somehow, that the atomic bomb is mentioned in the Koran and this is, apparently, a solid argument for faith. On the other hand, the curious notion that the totality of modern knowledge is due to Islam alone can also be traced to the *Salafiyyah*. If the idea of making Islam submit to the dictates of the modern world has not found general acceptance, the principles of the *Salafiyyah* have, nonetheless, succeeded to the extent that, in the face of any embarrassing or inconvenient contradiction, Islam has often been simply ignored in favor of the imperatives of the times. In recent times the ideology of the *Salafiyyah* has been overshadowed by a fundamentalist reaction. The name *Salafiyyah* today is actually used for such Fundamentalist and non-compromising movements as the Ahl-i Ḥadīth. The term today is applied not to thinking which seeks accommodation with rationalism, but to groups which are literalist and categorical appliers of Islamic law rather than adaptors as was 'Abduh.

Ṣalāḥ ad-Dīn al-Ayyūbī (*532-589*/1138-1193). The son of Ayyūb, a Kurdish general in the army of the Sultan of Mosul, Saladin, as the Crusaders called him, began his career as a lieutenant to his uncle who led the Sultan's armies against the Fāṭimids of Egypt. The Christians of the Latin kingdom of Jerusalem intervened because the Fāṭimids were not an active and outright enemy and, in fact, sometimes allied themselves with the Crusaders. Saladin's uncle was killed in the campaign; Saladin replaced him as commander, and went on to become Vizier, or minister. In *566*/1171 Saladin supplanted the Fāṭimids in the name of Nūr ad-Dīn, Sultan of Mosul.

From Egypt, Saladin began the conquest of Syria and attacked the Christians. By *571*/1175 he had taken Damascus and declared himself an independent sovereign, recognized by the 'Abbāsid Caliphs. Thereafter he consolidated his empire which extended into Konya in Anatolia, and pressed hard upon the Crusader states by creating a unified kingdom around them. In *583*/1187 he defeated the Crusaders at the Horn of Hattin above Tiberias and conquered Jerusalem, but did not succeed in taking the last Christian stronghold of Tyre.

From Tyre the Crusaders received reinforcements, and in *589*/1191 Richard the Lionheart arrived and took Acre. Thereupon began the period of Crusader warfare which made Saladin a famous figure in the West, the match of Richard in knighthood and the epitome of chivalry. He was acknowledged as a warrior remarkable for his sense of justice and goodwill towards the weak and defenseless.

Saladin died in Damascus, leaving the control of Syria, Palestine, and Egypt divided among his descendants, having founded the Ayyubid dynasty.

Ṣalāh (lit. "prayer", "worship", pl. *ṣalawāt.* The verb from which it derives is *ṣallā* ("to hallow"); as an act of God it is translated as to bless"; as an act of men it is translated as "to pray". It is possible, since the word is used only in its so-called second mode, that it is not originally an Arabic word, but one derived from Aramaic.) *Ṣalāh* is the canonical, or ritual, prayer, as opposed to the spontaneous petitioning of God which is called *du'ā'*. It consists of a series of movements and recitations, and is thus a ritual, more of a liturgy, or an act of worship, than the supplication usually associated with the word "prayer" in the West. As an act of worship, the *ṣalāh* is a *yoga* which models the body, mind, and soul – the latter in the form of speech – to the invisible prototype of awakened consciousness, or of the individual aware of God. The performance of the *ṣalāh* five prescribed times daily is obligatory (*farḍ*), beginning at the age of reason, which is deemed to be seven years. The performance of additional *ṣalāh* prayers is possible but not obligatory. These voluntary prayers are called *nawāfil* (sing. *nāfilah*). The obligatory *ṣalāh* is, however, one of the Five Pillars, and is clearly the most important after the *shahādah*.

The *ṣalāh* is composed of a series of movements repeated several times. Each series, or cycle of sacred speech and movement, is called a *rak'ah* (pl. *raka'āt*), a "bowing". Some prayers are "silent" in whole or in part; that is to say, the *fātiḥah* and the chosen passage of the Koran are then not pronounced out loud. Others prayers are spoken aloud throughout, and others again are mixed, two cycles being voiced and the rest silent. Prayers which are performed aloud at their correct time are performed in silence when they are made later.

The obligatory prayers, and a simple method of determining their time (*mīqāt*), are the following:

1. *Ṣalāt aṣ-Ṣubḥ*, or morning prayer; two *raka'āt*, out loud. Its time is between the moment of dawning when "a thread" of light appears on the horizon, until the actual rising of the sun (*ash-shurūq*). This period of time is called *al-fajr*, this is also the name for a voluntary, silent prayer of two *raka 'āt* which can be performed at this time. The same word, *al-fajr*, is loosely sometimes applied to the canonical morning prayer itself. The *ṣalāt aṣ-ṣubḥ* is commonly performed as a "missed" prayer, that is to say, it is performed upon waking, and in silence.

2. *Ṣalāt aẓ-Ẓuhr*, the noonday prayer; four *raka'āt*, silent. It is performed after the moment when the shadow of a stick set vertically in the ground has reached its shortest length at noon and has begun to lengthen as the sun passes its zenith, until the time of *al-'asr*.

3. *Ṣalāt al-'Aṣr*, the late afternoon prayer; four *raka'āt*, silent. It is performed from the moment when the shadow of a vertical stick is equal to the length of the stick *and* the minimum shadow of the stick at noon, at the sun's zenith (from about 3:30 pm), until the setting of the sun. According to Ḥadīth, once the *'asr* prayer is performed, no other prayer can be performed until after the sunset prayer is completed.

4. *Ṣalāt al-Maghrib*, or sunset prayer; three *raka'āt*, the first two *raka'āt* are out loud, the third silent. The prayer may be performed any time during the period of approximately twenty minutes starting four minutes after the sinking of the sun below the horizon until the last red glow (*shifāq*) in the sky.

5. *Ṣalāt al-'Ishā'*, or night prayer; four *raka'āt*, the first two out loud, the last two silent. It is performed after the onset of night until the dawn, but is preferably accomplished before midnight. In congregational prayer it is accomplished within one and one-half hours after the sunset prayer.

In polar regions, where special conditions prevail, the prayer times must be determined by some agreed convention such as, for example, choosing the intervals that would occur at Mecca. Such has been the decision of councils which have considered such special situations.

The *farḍ* prayer may be performed alone, or in groups led by an Imām. A call, the *adhān*, is made at the beginning of the prayer period to summon people to the mosque for prayer. Sometimes this call is repeated twice. It is preferable (*mustaḥabb*) in each case to perform the prayer early in its allotted time period, with the exception of the *ẓuhr*, which may be delayed to avoid the hottest part of the day. For the convenience of the congregants, the *ẓuhr* and the *'aṣr* may be performed together, one after the other, at either the time of the *ẓuhr* or the time of the *'aṣr*. The call for the second prayer in combination is reduced to the *iqāmah*, the secondary call for assembly and rising, which is made inside the mosque immediately before the prayer. The *maghrib* and *'ishā'* prayers may be similarly combined when it is difficult or impossible for the congregation to assemble many times during the day; it is also admissible when praying alone, at the individual's discretion.

There are moments when *ṣalāh* is forbidden: at the rising of the sun; when the sun is overhead at the zenith; and at the actual moment when the sun is setting. A prayer should not be begun at these moments, but may be continued through these if begun before. On Fridays the *ẓuhr* prayer is replaced by the congregational prayer (*ṣalāt al-jum'ah*) for those present in the congregational mosque; it consists of two *raka ʻāt* prayed silently under the leadership of an Imām. On a journey (in the days of camelback travel the minimum distance of such a journey was the equivalent of forty-five to sixty miles, or seventy-five to one hundred kilometers) in which the traveler spends the night away from home, or spends less than three nights in one place, prayers of four *rakaʻāt* may be prayed in the shortened form (*bi-t-taqsīr*) of two *rakaʻāt*. From the fourth night spent in one place the normal prayer length is resumed.

To perform the prayer, the person must be in the state of ritual purity conferred by the greater ablution (*ghusl*) and the lesser ablution (*wuḍūʼ*). The prayer must be performed in a clean place (not, therefore in a bath house, cemetery, slaughterhouse, and so forth) facing the *qiblah* (direction of Mecca), if this can be determined. If it cannot be determined, prayer can be performed in any direction (as it is done when one is *inside* the Kaʻbah).

A man's body must be covered from the navel to the knees; a woman's from the neck to below the elbow and to the ankles. The shoes are removed in a place of prayer. (Some Imāms wear slippers or sandals which they wear only inside a mosque.) If there is coming and going, the space in front should be symbolically delimited by some object placed in front of the worshiper (*sutrah*). For this reason, those praying a solitary prayer choose for preference to stand before the wall or a pillar. The worshiper must formulate the intention of the prayer to be performed by naming it (*niyyah*).

The motions of the prayer are as follows:

1. Standing with the feet only slightly apart, the worshiper raises his arms to the level of his ears, palms open forward, and declares out loud the *takbīr al-iḥrām* ("the consecratory magnificat"): *Allāhu akbar*. (This raising of the hands to the level of the head occurs only at this first *takbīr*. Some schools, and in practice, some individuals of all schools, raise the hands partway up at every pronunciation of a *takbīr*.) This opens the prayer. Then the hands are placed at the sides in the Malīkī rite (as also among the Khārijites), or clasped right over left at the waist above the navel in the Ḥanafī rite, (which was the traditional position of a worshipper in the presence of divinity in ancient Babylonia) or clasped at the center of the chest in the Hanbali rite, or above the heart in the Shāfiʻī rite. (All of these have precedents in the Sunnah of the Prophet; each rite has opted for one possibility without excluding the others, and all are acceptable.) In this standing position, which is called the *qiyām*, the worshiper pronounces the *fātiḥah* (which may or may not be preceded by the *Basmalah*). At the end of the *fātiḥah*, the worshiper says: "*āmīn*". If there is an Imām, and the *fātiḥah* has been said out loud, this *āmīn* is pronounced as a response by the congregation. In the first two *rakaʻāt* of the prayer (but not in subsequent *rakaʻāt*), after the *fātiḥah*, some verses from the Koran are recited, as for example, the *sūrat al-Ikhlāṣ* (112). This recitation is called the *qirāʼah*. Among the Sunnīs, the verses recited at this point are the choice of the person praying or leading the prayer. Among the Shīʻites, the verse is almost always the *sūrat al-Ikhlāṣ*. This ended, the worshiper says: *Allāhu akbar* (the *takbīr* are always said aloud), and bows, placing his hands upon the knees.

2. In this position, which is called the bow (*rukū*), he says silently: *subḥāna-Llāhi-l-ʻAẓīm* ("Glory to God the Mighty") three times, or a similar formula.

3. Rising now to the standing position called *wuqūf*, the worshiper says out loud *samiʻa-Llāhu liman ḥamidah* ("God listens to him who praises Him"). Then he, or the congregration following an Imām, says as response: *Rabbanā wa laka-l-ḥamd* ("Our Lord, and to Thee belongs praise").

4. Saying: *Allāhu akbar* out loud while still standing upright, the worshiper then prostrates himself, touching the forehead to the ground and with both palms on the ground. In this position, which is called the *sujūd* or the *sajdah*, he says silently: *subhāna Rabbiya-l-ʻAlā* ("Glory to my Lord the Most High"), or a similar formula, three times.

5. He raises himself to a seated position and says: *Allāhu akbar*. In this seated position, called *jalsah* or *julūs*, the Mālikīs say nothing, but the Ḥanafīs add a formula such as: *Rabbī-ghfir-lī*, ("Lord, cover my transgressions"). The correct posture for this seated position involves placing the outside of the left foot underneath oneself with the right foot crouched and the big toe of the right foot hooked on the ground. As hooking the toe on the ground is very difficult, and even painful if not practiced from childhood, no insistence is placed upon this precise position, and all sitting positions with the knees upon the ground can be seen.

6. After having marked a momentary halt seated thus, the worshiper pronounces again: *Allāhu akbar*, and makes a second prostration (*sajdah*) exactly as the first. This completes one cycle (*rak'ah*). If this is the first *rak'ah* of any prayer (except the single *rak'ah* of the voluntary night prayer, the *witr*), the worshiper stands up, pronounces: *Allāhu akbar*, and repeats the cycle again as the second *rak'ah*. At the end of the second and fourth (and final) *rak'ah* of all prayers, and the third (final) *rak'ah* of the sunset prayer, before rising from the sitting position (*jalsah*), or before ending the prayer, while in this sitting position, the worshiper utters a formula known as *at-taḥiyyāt*, or the *at-tashahhud*:

> *At-taḥiyyātu li-Llāhi wa-s-ṣalawātu wa-ṭ-ṭayyibātu, as-salāmu 'alayka ayyuha-n-nabiyyu wa raḥmatu-Llāhi wa barakātuh, wa-s-salāmu 'alaynā wa 'alā' 'ibādi-Llāhi-ṣ-ṣālihin. Ashhadu an la ilāha illā-Llāh, wa ashhadu anna Muḥammadan 'abduhū wa rasūluh.*

> Salutations, prayers, and good works are all for God. Peace on thee, O Prophet, and God's Mercy, and His blessings. Peace be on us and on all God's righteous servants. I testify that there is no god but God; and I testify that Muḥammad is His servant and His Messenger.

There are in practice minor variations to this formula, as to all others used during the prayer. While reciting these words, the Mālikīs, and sometimes the other schools, move the forefinger of the right hand in a counterclockwise circle, while the hand rests on the knee. During the saying of the *shahādah*, it is the custom to stop the circling movement and to point the finger upwards. If this is the end of the prayer (the second *rak'āt* of the *ṣubḥ*, the third of the *maghrib*, or the fourth of all other prayers), it is the non-obligatory custom to recite at this point a formula called the *qunūt* (*see* QUNŪT). Thereupon the worshiper seals the prayer by turning his head to the right and saying: *as-salāmu 'alaykum*, and then repeating these words to the left. The salutation of closing is called the *taslīm*. Alternately, it can be said once with the head turned right for the beginning of the greeting, and left for the end.

In the Shāfi'ī rite, when the *fātiḥah* is said out loud, the Imām utters the *fātiḥah* first and then pauses to allow those following him to recite the *fātiḥah* silently themselves. At each uttering of the *Allāhu Akbar* (and not only for the opening *takbīr*), the Shāfi'īs raise their hands upwards, as all the schools do for the opening *takbīr*. (For these subsequent *takbīrs*, the Shāfi'īs do not raise their hands upwards as high as for the first.)

It is usual, after the public prayer, to remain seated in order to recite one or more formulas repeated thirty-three times, counting on the fingers. This is an introduction to a *du'ā'*, an individual supplication, which is made with the hands upraised slightly, the palms open upwards. At the end, marked by the words: *al-ḥamdu li-Llāh* ("praise be to God"), the open hands are drawn across the face as if a blessing had fallen into them. Then the worshipers rise and greet those next to them with the words: *as-salāmu 'alaykum*. Some then perform individual, voluntary prayers, except after the *'aṣr*. These are usually of two *raka'āt*.

In addition to these voluntary, or Sunnah prayers performed before or after the main prayers, there are additional voluntary and optional prayers at specific times: *ishrāq* after sunrise, *ḍuḥā* before noon, and *tahajjud* at late night along with the *witr*. The Prophet certainly performed all of these at one time or another, but not necessarily all of them all the time. Piety makes numerousness of prayers the preferred expression of zeal. This said, it should perhaps be repeated that the number of obligatory prayers is *five* daily. Multiplicity being the easiest way to express quality or profundity, it was related of the great teacher al-Junayd of Baghdad that he performed three hundred *raka 'āt* each day at his shop in the market and four hundred at his house each night, in addition to reciting certain formula thirty thousand times each day. The eloquence of the Arabs has failed here to find a better way than big numbers of saying that al-Junayd was not forgetful of God!

The Friday congregational (*jum'ah*) prayer of two *raka'āt*, replaces the normal noonday prayer and is preceded by a sermon (*khuṭbah*). The Friday prayer is performed in a large congregational mosque which can accommodate a greater number of worshipers than can a neighborhood mosque. It also has a preacher in addition to an Imām, or a preaching Imām; to preach requires in principle greater knowledge than does leading the prayers, which is the minimum that everyone must know. The Friday prayer brings together a larger number of people from different neighborhoods, thus increasing a sense of community. Other exceptional prayers are those of the festivals. On the morning of the festivals of the *'Īd al-Aḍḥā* and the *'Īd al-Fiṭr*, there is a special prayer of two *raka'āt* for which, in principle, the whole community, or even the whole city, gathers together in a special prayer ground called the *muṣallā* (also called *'idgah*). The peculiarity of the *'Īd* prayer is that it is opened with eight *takbīr*, pronounced slowly one after the other, before the first *fātiḥah*. Six *takbīr* are pronounced before the second *fātiḥah*.

A *ṣalāh* is considered to have been interrupted, and to need repeating from the beginning, by the following actions: talking to others, yawning, laughing (but not suppressing a smile or a yawn), and breaking wind. Chronic conditions such as incontinence and bodily discharge, however, are disregarded as far as effect upon the prayer is concerned; the prayer is performed as if these conditions did not exist.

It is best not to interrupt a prayer except for reasons of *force majeur*, but a prayer which is interrupted is simply said again. Different procedures exist for "repairing" an error made in a prayer, such as losing count of the number of *raka'āt*; the lower number of *raka'āt* is assumed, and the worshiper continues until the end of the prayer. After the closing salutation, he immediately performs two prostrations (*sujūd*) from the sitting position, called the prostrations of *ṣaḥw* ("attentiveness"). They are finished by the greetings (*taḥiyyāt*) and *as-salāmu 'alaykum* just as if it were the final two *sujūd* of a prayer. If there are other defects, for example of errors added to a prayer, it is customary to add two extra prostrations (*sujūd*) before the closing of the prayer, and then the two *sujūd* described above.

Prayers which are missed at the correct time should be made up afterwards. These are called *qaḍā'* and are prayed silently. Menstruating women do not pray and do not make up missed prayers. With this exception, despite popular opinion to the contrary, the obligation of *ṣalāh* for women is no less than for men.

If one is prevented by illness or infirmity from praying, it is possible to reduce the motions of the prayer to gestures, or even to intentions of gestures, as it is also possible to pray with gestures on camelback, or horseback, and therefore on any means of conveyance when so obliged.

Special prayers, with some modifications, are also recited upon solar and lunar eclipses, to ask for rain (*istisqā'*), to ask for guidance (*istikhārah*), and for funerals (*janāzah*).

Three people in prayer, one leading and two following, constitute a congregation. If two persons pray together, they pray in one row, and the one who acts as Imām stands on the left and slightly forward. If there are three persons, the two following form a row to the back of the leader, and to one side. Three followers form a row behind the Imām. If a row is complete and can hold no more, a new arrival draws a person from the end of a row – not the middle since this would leave an empty space – to join him to form a new row, and he can do this even if the prayer has begun, during the standing for the *fātiḥah* and *qirā'ah*, even though normally one cannot move oneself once the prayer has begun. Joining others for prayer is recommended rather than praying alone, when possible.

If one comes late to a prayer which has already begun, one joins immediately by saying the *takbīr* of consecration, while the congregation is in the standing position (*qiyām*) or in the bow (*rukū'*). Once they have risen from the *rukū'* and the words: *sami'a-Llāhu* have been spoken, joining in that cycle of prayer is not possible, and one must wait for another *qiyām*. Having joined, one continues individually after the congregation has stopped, to complete on one's own the total number of *raka'āt* which make up the prayer at hand. If prayer is joined during the *rukū'*, the worshiper pronounces two *takbīr*, one for entering the prayer and one for moving to the bow.

The form of the *ṣalāh* is a creation of the Sunnah. The inspired nature of the *ṣalāh* is indicated by the tradition that Gabriel came and performed it five times at the right moments of the day and night; the Prophet joined in prayer with the Angel, having learned it from him.

In the *ṣalāh* it is not the individual who prays, but rather it is man as such, a representative of the species or all mankind recognizing his relationship to the Absolute. Or again it is creation, with the voice of man as a universal patriarch, praying to the Creator. The *takbīr*, or *Allāhu akbar* – "God is greater [than anything]" – which opens it, is the door into the Divine Presence, and the subsequent *takbīr* are the

The Ḥajj is the great annual pilgrimage which now brings together as many as 2 million worshipers. The Rites of Pilgrimage are performed in the Grand Mosque of Mecca (*left*) and in the desert environs of the city. The Ka'bah (*above*), the stone structure at the centre of the Grand Mosque, contains the Black Stone, and is the sanctuary towards which Muslims turn in prayer. *See* BLACK STONE; HAJJ; KA'BAH; MECCA; PILGRIMAGE.

'Bilāl's Mosque", or the *Masjid Ibrāhīm* (*above*), overlooks the Grand Mosque from Abū Qubays hill. Pilgrims in the costume of *iḥrām* (*left*) pray before the Ka'bah; (*opposite*), they circle the Ka'bah, shown with its door to the right, with its covering of black cloth, the *kiswah*, inscribed with gold thread (*below*). *See* IḤRĀM.

The *sa'y* of "walking" between the hills of Ṣafā and Marwah, is performed (*above*) immediately after the circumambulation of the Ka'bah. In the plain of 'Arafāt, 12 miles/20 km southwest of Mecca, the pilgrims assemble around the Mount of Mercy (*opposite top*) for the "standing" (*wuqūf*), said to be an occasion which foreshadows the Day of Judgement. The pilgrims proceed *en masse* along gigantic pedestrian ramps to Minā (*opposite bottom*), where they stone the three *jamarāt,* or pillars (*below*). *See* 'ARAFĀT; MINĀ; ṢAFĀ AND MARWAH; SA'Y; WUQŪF.

Ṣalāh, the canonical prayer, is performed five times each day; here it is being led by an Imām in the Nin Jie Mosque, Peking (*opposite top*) and (*opposite bottom right*), during Ramaḍān, in the Regent's Park Mosque, London. Worshipers celebrate the end of Ramaḍān (*opposite bottom left*) with dawn prayers in Yogyakarta, Java, Indonesia. A Touareg in a desert *muṣallā* (prayer-ground) in Algeria (*above*) faces Mecca to perform the *ṣalāh*. *See* IMĀM; MUṢALLĀ; RAMAḌĀN; ṢALĀH; TUAREG.

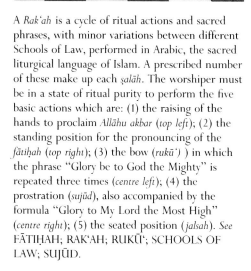

A *Rak'ah* is a cycle of ritual actions and sacred phrases, with minor variations between different Schools of Law, performed in Arabic, the sacred liturgical language of Islam. A prescribed number of these make up each *ṣalāh*. The worshiper must be in a state of ritual purity to perform the five basic actions which are: (1) the raising of the hands to proclaim *Allāhu akbar* (*top left*); (2) the standing position for the pronouncing of the *fātiḥah* (*top right*); (3) the bow (*rukū'*)) in which the phrase "Glory be to God the Mighty" is repeated three times (*centre left*); (4) the prostration (*sujūd*), also accompanied by the formula "Glory to My Lord the Most High" (*centre right*); (5) the seated position (*jalsah*). *See* FĀTIḤAH; RAK'AH; RUKŪ'; SCHOOLS OF LAW; SUJŪD.

acknowledgment that all activity, that all power, is God's alone.

The prayer must be performed in Arabic, which is at once a sacred and a liturgical language, that is, a language which has preserved in its forms and sounds a close correspondence – an analogy – to the metaphysical prototype of the reality it designates, and not merely a convention which subsists after a process of phonetic and linguistic decay. In all prayer, and in the *ṣalāh* in particular, it is *reintegration* into the uncreated which is at issue. The *ṣalāh* vehicles this by its nature, and by its symbolism: the individual is diminished in the bow (*rukū'*), and is extinguished in the protestation (*sujūd*), which takes the shape of the letter *mim*, the letter of death. The first *sajdah* is the *fanā'*, or the extinction of what is created, leaving, in the symbolism of the sitting, the *baqā'* or "that which persists", which is the immortal soul. In the second prostration, the *fanā' al-fanā'* ("the extinction of the extinction"), all remnants of the contradiction or disequilibrium that creation illusorily poses in the face of the Divine Reality symbolically disappear. The Arabic words, which are sacred words in a sacred language, are an essential aspect of the efficacy of the rite.

Ibn 'Aṭā' Allāh says in his *Ḥikam*:

> Ritual prayer is the place of intimate discourses and a mine of reciprocal acts of purity wherein the domains of the innermost being are expanded and the rising gleams of light ray out. He knew of the existence of weakness in you, so He made the number of ritual prayers small; and he knew of your need of His grace, so he multiplied their fruitful results.

And:

> Ritual prayer is a purification for hearts and an opening up of the door of the invisible domains.

See ABLUTIONS; ADHĀN; ARABIC: DHIKR; ĪD al-AḌḤĀ; 'ĪD al-FIṬR; ISTISQĀ'; ISTIKHĀRAH; KHUṬBAH; PRAYER.

Salamlik. 1. In traditional Turkish homes the *salamlik* is the reception area for visitors and, in a general sense, is the part of the house open to men, as opposed to the *haramlik*, the area for women.

2. It was also the name of the ceremonial visits made by the Ottoman Sultan to the royal mosques in Istanbul to take part in Friday prayers.

Ṣalāt *see* ṢALĀH.

Ṣalāt al-Ḥājjah (lit. "prayer of necessity"). A prayer of four to twelve *raka'āt* recited at night to seek Divine remedy from distress.

Ṣalāt al-Jum'ah. The congregational Friday prayer of two *raka'āt* performed in place of the normal noon prayer (*ẓuhr*). It can only be performed in a group and normally follows the *khuṭbah* (sermon).

Ṣalāt al-Khawf (lit. "The Prayer of Fear"). A special form of the canonical prayer used, theoretically, by soldiers in times of imminent danger. The prayer is performed in four *raka'āt*; part of the group prays the first two *raka'āt* and ends its prayer while the Imām stands paused; the other part of the group then prays the next two *raka'āt* behind the Imām while the first resumes guard. It could not have been very practical as a method of worship but could certainly unnerve an unbelieving enemy if performed in the middle of a battle, as it was by Khālid ibn al-Walīd.

Aṣ-Ṣalāh al-Mashīshiyyah, *see* IBN MASHĪ'SH.

Ṣalāt at-Tarāwīḥ (lit. "prayer of rest"). A voluntary prayer consisting of twenty, thirty-two, or forty *raka'āt* recited at the end of the night before the canonical morning prayer (*ṣubḥ*), and in the evening after the evening prayer (*ishā'*), only during the month of Ramaḍān. Contrary to the practice of normal prayers, the Imām chooses long Koranic passages for recitation aloud. A pause is made every four *raka'āt* for personal prayer (*du'ā'*).

Because of the long recitations, those behind the Imām who are tired are permitted to remain sitting after the previous *rak'ah* for most of the Imām's standing recitation of the Koran, and to rise just before the first bow (*rukū'*) of the *rak'ah*. The name of the prayer, *Tarāwīḥ* ("rest"), is a euphemism for one of the most strenuous exercises designed to tap religious fervor, when Imāms often have to pray in relays, one taking over for another as his voice or energies fail.

Ṣāliḥ. A Prophet with the rank of Divine Messenger (*rasūl*) mentioned in the Koran as having been sent to the tribe of Thamūd. The symbol of the essence of his message, or *ḥaqīqah*, was a she-camel which his people hamstrung, rather than giving the camel water, as they had been asked. The camel lends itself readily as a symbol of humble endurance and submission to God and of a gift from God to be cherished. Indeed, the Koran makes many references to the camel and to caravans, the support of life. Ibn 'Arabi spoke in a poem of the essences of different religions as camels.

God's punishment came down upon the people of Thamūd in the form of an earthquake (7:73-79). Because the people of Thamūd hewed their homes from rock (7:74), the city has been identified as the Nabatean ruins of Madā'īn Ṣāliḥ (lit. "the cities of Salih") in North Arabia.

Sālik (lit. "a traveler"; pl. *sālikūn*). A member of a Sufi order whose intention is actively to seek the realization of God. This distinction is made because in fact most members of Sufi orders are *mutabārikūn* (sing. *mutabārik*), "those seeking to share in blessings", that is, members whose understanding of spiritual possibilities is limited and whose vocation is above all to seek an increase in blessing for themselves. The *mutabārikūn*, seek more of the viaticum as provided by the exoteric religion, rather than seeking to broach the different dimension to which esoterism is the door.

At one time, the *sālikūn* were travelers not only in a spiritual sense, but also in the sense of going from place to place seeking teachings from different masters. The Prophet said: "Be in the world like a traveler, or like a passer by, and reckon yourself as of the dead."

Saljūqs. A Turkic people from the Steppes, a branch of the Ghuzz/Oghuz, who entered military service within the 'Abbāsid Empire and succeeded in seizing control for themselves under their leader Toghril Beg. Toghril Beg assumed the title of Sultan, which had never been used before, and this was stamped on his coinage. The dynasty which he founded began in *429*/1038 and lasted until *582*/1194. An offshoot, the Saljūqs of Rūm in Anatolia, existed as a power until shortly before *707*/1307.

Without abolishing either the Caliphate or the 'Abbāsids, the Sunnī Saljūqs in *447*/1055 entered Baghdad and displaced the Shī'ite Buyids who had preceded them as the effective masters of most of the eastern part of the 'Abbāsid Empire. Saljūq expansion to the west, encroaching upon the Byzantine Empire, was one of the causes of the Crusades. The second and third Saljūq Sultans, Alp Arslan and Jalāl ad-Dawlah Mālik Shāh, benefited from the services of their Persian Vizier Niẓām al-Mulk, who achieved fame as one of the most able political figures in Islamic history.

After Mālik Shāh, the Saljūq Empire underwent progressive fragmentation, giving way to other dynasties such as the Khwarizm-Shāhīs, originally governors for the Saljūqs, and finally to the invading Mongols. The period of the Great Saljuq Sultanate did, however, provide a stability and political unity to a degree rarely achieved afterwards. It marked a broad Sunnī restoration in the Empire after the expansion of Shī'ism under the Buyids. Although at first the Saljūqs were opposed to Ash'arite theology, and theologians like al-Juwaynī were obliged to go into exile, when their great Vizier Niẓām al-Mulk saw the need to counter the religious propaganda of the Fāṭimids, the Ash'arites were rehabilitated and made the theological spokesmen of the dynasty. The Saljūq invasions changed the demographic configuration of the Middle East; Isfahan was their capital. *See* al-ASH'ARĪ; NIẒĀM al-MULK.

Salmān the Persian (*Salmān al-Fārisī*). A Companion who was so close to the Prophet as to be called by him a member of the family (*ahl al-bayt*). Salmān was a Persian who, after becoming a Christian, followed various teachers to Syria. Learning from one of them of the imminent advent of a Prophet in Arabia, he went there. After being betrayed, he was sold into slavery and brought to Yathrib, the town destined to become *Madīnat an-Nabī* ("the city of the Prophet"). When the Prophet arrived, Salmān recognized him as the one foretold.

Among the signs of which Salmān had heard was that this Prophet would have a large lump at the bottom of his back, a symbol of the Seal of Prophecy. One day when Salmān was close to the Prophet and filled with thoughts about this sign, the Prophet, who was facing the other way, nonetheless sensed what was preoccupying Salmān, and he let his cloak drop from his shoulders. When Salmān saw the sign he leaped forward and kissed it.

With the Prophet's help he bought his freedom from slavery and went on to become one of the most important figures of early Islam, ending his life as a governor in the newly conquered regions of Iraq during the Caliphate of ʻUmar or ʻUthmān. Salmān is a link in many initiatic chains (*salāsil*, sing. *silsilah*), of the Sufis. He is credited with the idea of defending Medina from the attack of the clans allied with the Quraysh, or the *Aḥzāb*, by building a trench around the city. Referred to by its Persian name *khandaq*, this stratagem was unknown to the Arabs, and it confounded the attacking army. After the death of the Prophet and the events of the Saqifa of Medina in which Abu Bakr is elected Caliph the Shiʻite traditions say that Salmān said the cryptic words: *kardīd o nakardīd*: "you have done and you have not done."

Because he is pictured as one who offered the Prophet crucial, and one might even say, arcane advice, certain Dualist sects on the fringe of Islam have attributed some curious identities to Salmān al-Fārisī. Some have said that he was the Angel Gabriel in disguise; the ʻAlawīs make of him one, and perhaps the highest, of three aspects of Divine theophany along with the Prophet and ʻAlī ibn Abī Ṭālib; others have seen in him a secret Divine emanation. As a foreigner in Medina, Salman has been assigned the role of *Allogenes* ("he who is born elsewhere") by those sects who are inspired by Hermetic tradition.

The significance of Salmān's being providentially very close to the Prophet in his lifetime has been interpreted as more convincingly foreshadowing the great role that the Persian genius was to play in Islam. Salmān represented the very spirit of the nation that provided so many of the great thinkers, theologians, doctors, philosophers, and scientists who brought the power of their synthesizing imagination and inspiration to shape the historical development of Islam. He is, in all likelihood, not a historical figure, but an allegory. Massignon saw in him a literary projection of the Iranian primordial man, Khormuzta, into events that were to affect the Iranian world so profoundly from the outside. As an allegory he plays no historical role after the death of the Prophet as do actual Companions and his burial place is symbolically the Taq, the ruined Sassanid palace of Ctesiphon, outside of Baghdad.

Samāʻ (lit. "listening"). The use of music by most Sufis as a means of inspiration or as an aid to contemplation. Music is forbidden in Islam, because it can bear the soul away, but is, nevertheless, practiced everywhere. It is now tolerated even by the Wahhābīs who, when taking Mecca in 1924, were aroused to religious fury by the sound of military trumpets sounding reveille.

Despite the legal prohibition on music, it was, even from early times, and still is today, a common practice among many Sufi *ṭuruq* to use music together with religious poetry to call forth a contemplative attitude in the soul. In particular, music is used to create the appropriate state of mind for the performance of the *ḥaḍrah*, or sacred dance. It is because of this esoteric aspect of music that it was admitted by the Sufis even while being prohibited by exoterism.

Al-Ḥujwīrī says:

> Theologians agree that listening to instrumental music is permissible so long as it is not merely for amusement, and does not induce sinful thought. But the merely permissible is proper for a beast alone. A man ought to seek spiritual good in everything he does.
>
> Right listening consists in hearing everything as it is. Men are seduced, and their passions stimulated, by instrumental music because they hear unreally. Music is a presentment of Reality, which rouses the heart to long for God; those who listen with what is real in themselves participate in Reality; those who listen in selfish soulfulness participate in Hell. And ash-Shibli describes music as an outward temptation and an inward premonition: if you know the password you will safely hear the premonition, but if you do not, by inviting temptation you are courting disaster. Another Shaykh puts it thus: Music makes the heart aware of what keeps it in exile, so that its effect is the heart's turning to God.

Sāmānids (*204-395*/819-1005). A Muslim Persian dynasty founded by Sāmān-Khudā, who originated from the region of Balkh, a member of the old Persian aristocracy, the Dihqans. The Sāmānids ruled in Khorasan and Transoxiana as vassals of the ʻAbbāsids. Until the conversion to

Islam of the Turkic peoples of the steppes, the Sāmānid domains amounted to a buffer state. But when the Turks became Muslims, Sāmānid rule, in part eroded by internal instability, declined in the face of Turkish penetration into the 'Abbāsid Empire. The Sāmānids were replaced by the Turkic dynasties of the Ghaznavids and Qarakhanids.

As one of the first purely Persian dynasties (following the Ṭāhirids) to return to power after the Arab conquest, the courts of the Sāmānids in Samarkand and Bukhara were the focal points of continuity of old Persian culture and the staging place for the renewal of Persian literature.

Samarkand. Today a city in Uzbekistan, a country which was called Soghdiana in the Middle Ages. It was once the capital of Tamerlane who brought artisans from the four corners to beautify it. His tomb called the Gur-Amir stands there today. The center of Samarkand boasts one of the greatest architectural monuments in the world, the Reghistan. This square is bounded by the *madrasahs* of Ulug Beg, Shir-Dar, and Tilla-Kari. Nearby is the madrasah of Bibikhanum erected in 1388 by a Chinese wife of Tamerlane. The summer palace of Tamerlane, called the Hazrat Shah Zindeh, is near the tomb of Qasim ibn Abbās, which is a shrine.

Outside the city lie the ruins of the original town of Maracanda called Afrasiab after an Iranian hero, and near them is the observatory of Uleg Beg. The city of Maracanda was destroyed by Alexander the Great in 329 B.C. The Arabs under Qutaiba ibn Muslim conquered it in 711 and called it Samarkand. It was the capital of the Samanids (*204-395*/819-1005). It was destroyed again by Jenghiz Khan in 1221.

A poet described it and its sister city thus:

Samarkand saikal-i rowi zamin hast
Bukhara quwwat-i Islami din hast

Samarkand is resplendent upon the face of the earth,
Bukhara is the strength of Islam.

Samarkand was a center of Manichaeism. Maqdisi speaks of the existence in the villages of Transoxiana of the people in white raiment whose rites resemble those of the Zindiqs. The white clothes were also the distinctive sign of the party of Abu Muslim, the *sāpid-jāmagān* ("the wearers of white raiment", in Arabic *al-Mubayyiḍa).* Into the middle ages many of the mystics in the region were still vegetarians.

as-Sāmirī. The name which the Koran gives to the tempter who beguiled the Jews to the worship of the golden calf while Moses was on the mountain (20:85). As-Sāmirī gave the calf the power to make a lowing sound by casting into it dust from the footprints of Gabriel who had brought revelations to Moses. As-Sāmirī's punishment was to warn men not to touch him, a reference to the implied connection between him and the Samaritans, a people held by the Jews to be impure.

Sanūsīyyah ("the Sanūsīs"). A political-religious organization, with at one time a somewhat military outlook, found in Libya, where a third of the population is affiliated to it, and to some degree also in the Sudan. The Sanūsīs were founded by an Algerian named Sayyid Muḥammad 'Alī as-Sanūsī (*1206-1276*/1791-1859), who studied first in Fez and later went to Mecca, where he became imbued with Wahhābī ideas. It was in Mecca that he founded the first lodge of his organization, the Sanūsīyyah. Calling himself the "Great Sanūsī", the ideals he propagated were a curious mixture of Wahhābī puritanical fundamentalism with a dash of Sufi teachings eclectically adapted from several different orders. The legal basis of his organization was Mālikī *fiqh*, but his claims to *ijtihād* were soundly denounced by the religious authorities of Cairo. Essentially, the Sanūsīyyah preached a return to exoteric puritanical religion and, much in the style of the Wahhābī movement, and even more like the Tijāniyyah, used this preaching to establish a power-base.

From Arabia, as-Sanūsī moved to Jabal Akhḍar in Cyrenaica, Libya. After his death, the work of expanding the organization was carried on by his sons, and the chief among them, Sayyid Muḥammad al-Mahdī (d. *1320*/1902), established hundreds of lodges, or *zāwiyahs.* His son became King Muḥammad Idrīs of Libya, first under Italian tutelage, and later as the monarch of an independant kingdom in *1370*/1951. In *1389*/1969 the King was overthrown in a *coup* led by Colonel Muammar al-Qaḍḍāfī.

Saqīfah. The name of the assembly of the Medinans. After the death of the Prophet the *Anṣār* met at the *Saqīfah* to decide the critical question of leadership. The Medinans proposed choosing one leader from the *Anṣār* (natives of Medina), and another from the *Muhājirūn* (Meccans who had emigrated). To head off a split, 'Umar proposed that Abū Bakr should be the sole leader. The "affair (*amr*) of the Saqīfah" figures retrospectively as an important event in the history of Shī'ism because 'Alī ibn Abī Ṭālib was absent from the meeting attending to the funeral preparations. Still young at the time, being in his thirties, he was not, in fact, a prominent candidate for political leadership in a society which favored age. Nonetheless, the Shī'ites allege, in the light of their theory that a Divine function subsists within the family of 'Alī, that the election of Abū Bakr to succeed the Prophet was in effect a conspiracy to deprive 'Alī of his right as the only legitimate and providential successor. *See* SHĪ'ISM.

Sāqiyah (or *siqāyah*; "irrigation", "water-supply"). The Arabs inherited the science of irrigation from the civilizations of Mesopotamia. The very name of Iraq, which derives from a verbal root describing the spread of water, appears to refer to these ancient irrigation systems. The Arabs themselves devised sophisticated irrigation systems for crops. Some of these in the Sahara involved placing sea shells along a water channel so that the wind would blow away deposited sand and thus keep the channel from silting.

Water wheels, sometimes of the giant size that are still in use in Syria, were a common feature of such irrigation systems. In Persia and elsewhere, irrigating channels called *qanāt* were sometimes run underground for great distances to cool water and keep it from evaporating. *Qanāt* had openings at the surface to provide access for maintenance.

The Spanish word *acequia* ("watering ditch") is derived from the Arabic *sāqiyah.* The *Acequia Madre* irrigation systems used by the Spanish in South America and the American southwest are ultimately contributions of Arab science to the New World. *See* HANDASAH.

Sardar. A Persian title meaning a prince with a military command. The title was adopted by the Turks, and by the Indians into Urdu.

Sarts. A group in Central Asia, especially in the cities of Uzbekistan, who are a mixture of Turks and Tadjiks, predominantly with Tadjik culture.

Satan, *see* IBLĪS.

"Satanic Verses". Within the first three centuries of Islam an assertion was made, recorded by Tabarī, that during the revelation of the surat 53, "The Star", the devil succeeded in inserting some words after line 20, where the Koran says: "Have ye thought upon al-Lat and al-'Uzza and Manat, the third, the other?" These were pagan female divinities. The assertion is that the Devil inserted the words: *tilka'l-Gharāniq al-'ulā minhā shafā'a turtajā* into the revelation: "These are sublime swans whose intercession may be sought."

The assertion was cemented by an appeal to plausibility that the Prophet was seeking to win support of the Meccans and was disposed to compromise. The assertion said the verses were allowed to stand a little while before being repudiated. The story of the Satanic Verses was denied by al-Bayḍāwī and by others. Indeed, there is no contemporary record of such a perturbation in the revelation taking place and the nature of the event, the import of the verses, is in complete contradiction to the nature of the Prophet. It is this very contradiction which is a clue to the origin of the story of the Satanic Verses.

In 895 a missionary in North Africa, preparing the way for 'Ubayd Allāh the first Faṭimid, spread a fabricated Ḥadith which said that in the third century of the Hijrah, the sun will rise in the West. This is a retort, as exactly opposite as possible, to the Koran 2:258: "Bethink thee of him who had an argument with Abraham about his Lord, because Allah had given him the kingdom; how, when Abraham said: 'My Lord is He who giveth life, and causeth death,' he answered: 'I give life and cause death.' Abraham answered: 'Lo! Allah causeth the sun to rise in the East, so do thou cause it to come up from the West.' Thus was the disbeliever abashed. And Allah guideth not wrong-doing folk."

The central mechanism of the Ḥadith about the sun rising in the West is the strategic establishment of an antinomial idea, here an equality of a second Principle, proposed in such a direct head on way that denial seems even more improbable than the original assertion. The

Koran affirmed that God made the sun rise in the East, and challenged an opponent to make it rise in the West. In saying the sun would rise in the West a rival was being raised to God Himself. In a Muslim climate such a defiance is so unthinkable that even denial of such a saying is thereby curtailed. (In a similar free-thinking vein, also ascribed to 'Ubayd Allāh is the epistle of *The Three Imposters*.)

The Satanic Verses follow a similar pattern. Line three of the surah in question says "By the Star when it setteth, Your comrade erreth not, nor is deceived; nor doth he speak of his own desire. It is naught save an inspiration that is inspired, which one of mighty powers taught him" (50:1-5). Thus in the midst of the Koran's own affirmation that something could not be inserted into the Koran, the most unlikely place to attempt to insert a contradiction, in fact such an attempt was made, as if to affirm the power, again, of a rival to God. The audacity of the imposture of the Satanic Verses at that particular point in the Koran made them almost plausible by their very improbability. For example, the story of the Satanic Verses has often been defended as a story so unlikely it could not be invented. Yet this is what an inventor seeks, that human psychology itself work in favor of his invention.

A similar case is the creation of a book around *100*/750 with doctrines completely antithetical to Islam deliberately entitled *Umm al-Kitāb* (lit. "Mother of the Book"). The Koran says "He it is Who hath revealed unto thee the Scripture wherein are clear revelations – they are the "Essence of the Book" [*Umm al-Kitāb*] – and others are allegorical (5:7). In these cases the words of the Koran are used as points of departure for doing precisely that which the Koran says cannot or should not be done; this is the signature of antinomial movements which arise in all religions and mirror backwards the tenets of that religion. (For similar reasons the Sufi Bisṭāmī was accused of practising a backwards prayer (*ṣalāt maqlubah*). There were several religious currents within Islam that introduced female divinities such as Kuni as intermediaries between God and the world. The Satanic Verses story probably reflects an attempt to introduce a support for these new female divinities as a kind of lost or secret revelation. What probably followed was the subsequent neutralization of this intervention on the part of defenders of orthodoxy as being verses the devil had once produced and which the Prophet had already repudiated in his time.

With the perspective of time, however, it is clear that the idea expressed in the Satanic Verses is so completely against the spirit of the Islamic message that it is impossible to believe that the Prophet could have actually entertained them as authentic even for a moment. After the point at which the verses were supposed to have arisen the Koran goes on: "They are but names which ye have named, ye and your fathers, for which Allah hath revealed no warrant." (53:23). The pseudo *Ḥadith* about the sun rising in the West still circulates as an esoteric teaching. *See* ANTINOMIANISM; DUALISM; UMM al-KITĀB.

Saudi Arabia. Kingdom. Estimated population: 19,409,058. Except for foreign nationals employed in Saudi Arabia, the population is 100% Muslim. There is a small Twelve-Imām Shī'ite minority in the Eastern Province. Many Yemenis are permanent residents in Saudi Arabia, and many of these are Zaydī; there are also many Zaydīs in the southern province of 'Asīr. The populations of Mecca and Medina include peoples from virtually all Muslim countries, and thus every form of Islam is represented. The cradle of Wahhābism is the Najd and there it is strongest, although it is also the dominant school of thought throughout Saudi Arabia. *See* IBN SA'ŪD; MECCA; MEDINA; WAHHĀBISM.

Sawdā' bint Zam'ah. After the death of Khadijah, the second wife of the Prophet. She was the widow of one of the emigrants to Abyssinia and had returned to Arabia upon the death of her first husband. *See* WIVES of the PROPHET.

Ṣawm, *see* FAST.

Sa'y, The walking back and forth seven times between the hills Ṣafā and Marwah in Mecca. This is one of the rites of pilgrimage, both *'umrah* and *ḥajj*, and is performed immediately after the circumambulation of the Ka'bah is completed by the prayer at the Station of Abraham (*Maqām Ibrāhīm*) and the drinking of Zamzam water. At each hill there are recitations which are made standing, and which begin with the words: "Ṣafā and Marwah are among the signs of God..."

The *sa'y* is performed walking except for a portion in the middle, today marked by green lights, where the pace is quickened. The fast pace, for a distance of some twenty meters/yards, is described by the verb *harwala* ("to hurry, make haste"). The covered course of the *sa'y* is called the *mas'ā* and is today paved and enclosed within the precincts of the Grand Mosque; its length is 293m/927ft. Before the present mosque was built in the 1950s, the *sa'y* took place, as it always had, in the area adjacent to the market, the *Sūq al-Layl*, where the human traffic of the town mingled with the pilgrims walking back and forth between the hills.

The completion of the *sa'y* marks the completion of the rites of the *'umrah* and at the Marwah gate the pilgrim's hair is clipped, or even shaved completely, to signify the end of the state of consecration (*iḥrām*). Near *Ṣafā* it is possible to hire wheelchairs and litter bearers to assist the infirm in the performance of the *sa'y*.

The origin of the rite goes back to Hagar who, despairing for the life of Ishmael when the water in the goatskin that Abraham had given them was spent, ran back and forth between the two hills. Then suddenly the water gushed forth from the well of Zamzam. The *sa'y* may therefore represent the casting to and fro in this world from illusion to illusion until true guidance and true life come. *See* HAGAR; PILGRIMAGE; ZAMZAM.

Sayyid (lit. "liege lord"). A title of respect used for the descendants of the Prophet through his daughter Fāṭimah and 'Alī ibn Abī Ṭālib. These are the *shurafā'* (sing. *sharīf*). In the Arab West they are more often referred to as *mawlay* (*mulay*, and in French-speaking countries written *moulay*), since *sayyid* (or *seyyid*) is also a general title of address like sir, monsieur, or mister. It can also be a proper name.

Sayyid Ahmad Khan, Sir, *see* KHAN, Sir SAYYID.

Sayyid al-Murtada, *see* al-MURTADA.

Schechina, *see* SAKINAH.

Schools of Law (Ar. *madhhab*, pl. *madhāhib*; lit. "movement", "orientation", "trend", "direction"). There are four schools of law among the Sunnīs: the Ḥanafī; Ḥanbalī; Mālikī and Shāfi'ī. These schools are sometimes, in the context of religious practices, referred to as "rites". Each school, or "rite" is a legal system developed out of the so-called "foundations of sacred law" (*uṣūl al-fiqh*). The founders of the schools are Mālik ibn Anas (d. *179*/795); Abū Ḥanīfah (d. *150*/767) Muhammad ibn Idrīs ash-Shāfi'ī (d. *205*/820); and Aḥmad Ḥanbal (d. *241*/855). The Mālikī school is dominant in the Arab West and West Africa; the Ḥanafī school is dominant in most countries that were formerly part of the Turkish Empire and in India. The Ḥanbalī school is only observed in Saudi Arabia and in Qatar. Technically, the Wahhābīs consider themselves to be "non-imitators" or "not attached to tradition" (*ghayr muqallidūn*), and therefore answerable to no school of law at all, observing instead what they would call the practice of early Islam. However, to do so does correspond to the ideal aimed at by Ibn Ḥanbal, and thus they can be said to be of his "school". The Shāfi'ī school is dominant in Indonesia, Malaya and the Philippines; it is also important in Egypt, where the Ḥanafī and Mālikī schools are also represented, in some parts of Central Asia and the Caucasus.

In addition, there are also several Shī'ite schools. The most prominent is the Ja'farī school of the Twelve-Imām Shī'ites and the school of the Zaydīs. The Khārijites ('Ibādites), have their own school.

Among the Sunnīs, each school regards the others as orthodox, but a Muslim is expected to adhere to one school. The mixing of precedents and applications between schools is called *talfīq*, and is frowned upon. *See* SHARĪ'AH.

Science, *see* ASTRONOMY; al-BĪRŪNĪ; BROTHERHOOD of PURITY; DĀR al-ḤIKMAH; HANDASAH; JĀBIR IBN ḤAYYĀN; HOUSE of WISDOM; al-KHWĀRIZMĪ; MEDICINE; at-ṬUṢĪ, NĀSIR ad-DĪN.

"Science of the letters", *see* ABJAD; 'ILM al-ḤURŪF.

Seal of Prophecy (Ar. *khatm an-nubuwwah*, and also *khatm al-anbiyā'*). **1.** A title of the Prophet because he is the last Prophet, and the last Divine Messenger (*rasūl*) before the end of time and the Day of Judgement. That there will be no new revealed religion between his message and the end of the world is an important point of Islamic doctrine.

2. It is also the name given to a large lump of flesh "the size of a pigeon's egg" in the small of the back of the Prophet, which was taken as a physical sign of the "Seal of Prophecy". Analogously, Jesus is sometimes referred to as being the ""Seal of Sanctity" (*khatm al-wilāyah*), in virtue of being the Prophet who externalized his inner sanctity to the highest degree.

Seal of Sanctity (Ar. *khatm al-wilāyah*). A title given to Jesus, as the prophet whose sanctity manifested itself outwardly to the highest degree. The Prophet Muḥammad is called the "Seal of Prophecy", as the final Messenger to mankind.

Seceders, *see* KHĀRIJITES.

"Secret society". The technical term, in the science of religions, is *Maennerbund.* A Maennerbund is a secret society whose members undergo an initiation in which they take on, as far as possible, the personality of different animals. The origin of the Maennerbuende lies with the dawn of time; stone age man, in order to hunt successfully, imitated one or more of the salient hunting animals around him as a model. It was a form of sympathetic magic in which the instincts of hunter animal as well as those of the prey were learned or acquired by man by identifying with the animal. This began with an initiation in a cave under the direction of a shaman, probably as a puberty rite, and probably with the aid of mind affecting plants such as the *amanita muscaria* mushroom, still used in Siberia, and other plants, *ephedra* sometimes thought to be the *haoma* of the Iranians, for example. These plants varied according to what could be found locally in different regions. It was a method of teaching what society had learned as techniques of survival. These simulations were part of religious rites. Usually the hunter model was the wolf, which was especially suitable for man since wolves hunt in packs, and humans could act in concert. The members in traditional settings are usually men or women (the Amazons of antiquity and the *Maenads* of Euripides), mixed groups being exceptional. Initiation is practiced in three steps: **1.** Seclusion from everyday life (*rites de séparation)*; **2.** Living at the margin of society (*rites de marge*); **3.** Initiation proper (*rites d'agrégation*) (A. van Gennep).

During the ice age, when men often had to share caves with bears, the bear, and in particular the now extinct cave bear (*Ursus Spelaeus*) was also an animal of imitation and hunt. Cave bear worship cults in the Alps have given us one of the oldest altars of sacrifice found thus far, and traces of primitive man's relationship with bears exist abundantly in language and myth. One of the best known Maennerbuende was that of the Viking "berserkers", literally bear-skin-men. Most words for bear are euphemisms for the real word (bear in English means "brown one"; *medved* in Russian means the "honey lover") in order to avoid calling up the actual presence of the feared animal through the magic of names. In other areas of the world animals such as jaguars and tigers provided the instinctual training model. The werewolf is now a strange, seemingly distant phenomenon, but even the foundation of the city of Rome is tied up with it as seen from the myth of Romulus and Remus being suckled and raised by a wolf. Secret societies have continued to play the role of founding nations into the twentieth century.

The Maennerbuende were superseded by other forms of religious expression but persisted in some areas of the world into classical and even modern times. Maennerbuende were particularly influential in the region around the south Caspian which was called Hyrcania (the Greek form of Iranian *Varkana* "land of the wolf"). It was noted for the presence of two-legged wolves (*varka bisagra*) among the early Iranians and Firdawsi said in the *Shahnameh* that Mazandaran was a region of demons. Around the southern Caspian the antinomialism of the Maennerbuende tradition later fueled the radical Shī'ism of the Assassins, the *Qizil Bash* ("the Red Hats") supporters of Shah Isma'il, and the Shaykhis. The red hat, probably the forerunner of the Fez, had a tassel, probably representing the tail of an animal, although the interpretation later was that the strands stood for the twelve Imāms. Hats symbolizing animals were very common; the dog ear cap of Nigeria even gives the wearer the "look of a wolf."

In ancient Greek mystery rites the wolf was the usual animal of transformation for men, and the mare for women. It is thought that the wearing of goatskins by the acolytes of rites in which cathartic dramas were performed is at the origin of the word "tragedy" (from *tragos* for goat). Even in modern times there are records of Maennerbund activity in Europe such as a werewolf trial in Latvia in 1691 recorded in the *Geheimbuender der Germanen*, published in 1928. Today traces still appear, in the Tongs of China, the lodges of the American Indians, or as folklore, for example in the men's societies of the Alpine countries in which men emerge at the dawn of Mardi Gras costumed as animals and take mild liberties with any women who are found on the street, reminiscent of the Roman Lupercalia. These practices, hidden throughout the year, are permitted to show themselves at the moment when everyone wears a mask, echoes of what were once ancient rites that culminated in the fertility festivals of Easter and May.

Similar practices were found in Russia at the eve of Saint John, or Midsummer's eve, which commemorates Maennerbund religious holidays. In some places in Iran, a practice which has now disappeared since the turn of the century, the populace would work themselves into in a frenzy during the *'Id al-Ghadir* and tear with the teeth into honey filled cakes representing the first three Caliphs (who in later Shī'ism became despised).

The transformation into an animal is a widespread taboo. The Bible and other religious legislation forbids the eating of blood because the psychic nature of the animal was believed to be in the blood. It is probably because red is the color of blood that it was associated with the Qarmatians, a related secret organization in pre-Ming China called the "Red Scarf", the *Qizil Bash*, the "Red Hats", and other Gnostic societies. The leader of the Qarmatians was described as mounted on a camel and wrapped in a red cloak. The red robe is also associated with Jesus. In the case of Jesus it is his own blood which becomes a viaticum, at once forbidden and sacred, in a rite of multiple transformations, wine into blood, blood into a sacrament.

The positive contributions of the Maennerbunde to religions are two central and crucial ideas. One is initiation into an unknown reality, which in Christianity has become baptism, and in Islam a pact made with God. While transformation into an animal today has only negative and regressive connotations, it still has something liberating about it, being a surpassing of one's state. Thus the transformation into something entirely alien, initially into an animal, also introduced the idea of self-transcendence, a possibility in an upward rather than a downward direction. In the mind of the primitive hunter, when animals escape they do so into lairs which were perceived as "holes in the universe", three such "escape holes" to which the animal bolts took on special and almost universal cosmological symbolism in all cultures. The first is the *cave*. This readily takes on the symbol of the "heart" or center of the being and there secret and initiatic rites were often held. Another is the "bottom of the sea". Here Gilgamesh looked for the plant of immortal life, a story which appears in the Koran as the search for immortality at the invisible "meeting of the seas" as described the Surat 18 (which is called *The Cave*). And the third "hole" is the sun, the supreme spiritual escape out of the cosmos through the center of creation. What Spanish city does not have it *Puerta del Sol*, the principal gate? In Hinduism it is the way which the soul goes to attain *moksha* or "deliverance".

But the Maennerbund's essential characteristic lies in making licit in secret that which society forbids outwardly. Secrecy and antinomialism, or the practice of what is forbidden under guise of transcendence or esoterism, are bound up in the Maennerbund phenomenon, not always with positive results. Historically they are bound up with Gnostic movements.

Mircea Eliade correctly identified the Aissawa in Morocco as being a Maennerbund disguised as a Sufi order; the founder of the Aissawa was supposed to have given his followers permission to eat scorpions and snakes, and other animals, alive – as animals do – while they were obliged to cross a desert. This is, however, an innocuous explanation for the fact that the Aissawa take on animal states in which they eat small animals as if they themselves were wolves. Lycanthropy is still very common in Africa today, as reported by Albert Schweitzer, and by others. In Senegal it is simply called "loup". Besides the Aissawa, a number of other North African pseudo-Sufi orders such as the Hamidsha are in reality Maennerbuende and the phenomenon known as the Boujloud, "the father of the skins", during which the antinomianism emerges as a deliberate breaking of religious laws, is also of Maennerbund origin.

As well as pseudo-Sufi orders which are entirely Maennerbuende, other Sufi orders have undergone strong Maennerbund influence, in particular, the Qādiriyyah. Others, especially in Turkey, have preserved a particularly shamanistic role for the Shaykh. Even those Sufi orders which are close to religious orthodoxy nevertheless have some Maennerbund characteristics. Almost all have hidden somewhere what is most radically antinomial for Islam: the notion that men are or can become God. This is rarely explicit and is sometimes submerged for generations, but because of the nature of secret beliefs, the idea reforms itself and surfaces even after having been denounced and its proponents subjected to persecution.

A common Sufi story in Iran and Turkey tells of a disciple who, at the wave of the master's hand, or because he disobeyed him in some small instance, sees the other disciples, or even people on the street, take on the appearance of animals. Maennerbund manifestations can emerge spontaneously when certain conditions are present; secrecy, authorization to perform what society forbids, secret knowledge. These then call forth a primordial identification with animals. The *oprichnina* or secret police of Ivan the Terrible carried a wolf's head, the Nazi SS imitated Roman legions in carrying animal skins and had a special affinity for leather. Other examples, innocent and sinister abound in all societies.

In summary, the Maennerbund has, sociologically, a strong hierarchic order; entails separation from everyday life; promotes measures which prevent weakening the links of the member with the group and prevent his re-solidarization with society at large; a tendency to absolutize the group's aims and put them beyond all other moral considerations. In other words the group beliefs, or practices, or goals are morally exempt; in fact, the use of what others would call evil can be justified to achieve the group's wishes. Psychologically this exalts the individual and makes him feel part of an elite, if not in this world then in the next and makes the old personality fall apart because of the segregation from one's past life and from society. Reason is deemed to be inadequate to understand the teaching. Will is similarly broken down and replaced by obedience and passivity. Myths of a sacred horde play a useful role in this process, with the death of the individual and his rebirth into the new life of the sacred group. Predestinarian ideas are also useful in creating the state of mind propitious to the process of indoctrination. These tendencies can easily be seen in many modern political groupings especially radical and terrorist groups and in such sociological manifestations as "Wilding" in the big cities of America. See ANTINOMIANISM; BOUJLOUD; QIZIL BASH.

Seeking Guidance, *see* ISTIKHĀRAH.

Senegal. Population 9,092,749. The Islamicisation of Senegal began with the Almoravid movement, around *442*/1050. Islam experienced a second period of substantial growth this century, with the result that 86% of the population is now Muslim and adheres to the Mālikī school of law. Some 4% are animists and the rest consist of various Christian groups of which the Catholics are the most numerous. Although the importance of Islam is overwhelming, Senegal is not a theocratic state, and civil law is based upon French models, with certain allowances made in the direction of religion. Religious tolerance is the rule. The Tijāniyyah Sufi order (*ṭarīqah*) is very widespread, with the Qādiriyyah represented as well.

Sepahi (A Turkish word meaning a mounted soldier). The name of several new clandestine organizations in Pakistan made up of vigilante militants. The Sepahi Ṣaḥaba are Sunni vigilantes who attack and assassinate Shi'ites. The Sepahi Muḥammad are Shi'ites who attack and assassinate Sunnis. The *Sepahi Masih* is a Christian militant defense organization. An attempt to bring the Muslim vigilantes to discussion is the *Mille Yakjahti* or National Solidarity Council in Karachi organized by Shah Ahmad Nawrani.

Sermon (Ar. *khuṭbah*). The exhortation made on a Friday in a congregational mosque before the special prayer (*ṣalāt al-jum'ah*) is called a *khuṭbah.* The custom goes back to the practice of the Prophet in Medina, who first delivered his sermons standing, and then later, sitting, on a small series of steps, the *minbar*, which was built as a pulpit. It is from such a pulpit, or in some countries a speaker's podium, that the sermon is delivered.

The Schools of Law prescribe that a *khuṭbah* must contain certain elements: it must open with the *ḥamdalah* ("Praise be to God"); then blessings are called down upon the Prophet, the two witnessings of faith (*ash-shahadatān*) are uttered and the unity of God is proclaimed. These are followed by an exhortation or spiritual message, at the close of which blessings are called upon the believers and supplication is made for those in distress. By custom, blessings are also called upon the ruler of the country and divine aid invoked for him. The *khuṭbah* thus became the occasion for a declaration of sovereignty. In addition, the name mentioned in the *khuṭbah* was an indication, in areas of doubt, of the political allegiance of the region. The calling of blessings upon the ruler is still practiced where there are traditional rulers today, and it is reported that the practice in some places in East Africa is to call down the blessings on the last Turkish Caliph, like the persistence of a habit whose cause have long been forgotten. (The Turkish Caliphate disappeared in 1924.)

Once during the sermon the Prophet's grandson Ḥasan came up to him with a toy. The Prophet interrupted the sermon to attend to the child, an example of how the Sunnah is multifaceted. In this case the Prophet taught by concrete example that no matter how busy an adult is, he must not ignore a child's needs. *See* ḤAMDALAH; PRAYERS upon the PROPHET.

Seveners (Ar. *sab'iyyah*). Ismā'īl died in *145*/762 before his father Ja'far aṣ-Ṣādiq, the sixth Shī'ite Imām. This led to a radical realignment among the various Shī'ite factions, for the death of Ismā'īl, their heir apparent, left the succession in doubt, and the opportunities thus created were eagerly seized upon by the contending parties, each leader seeking in the climate of confusion to advance his own cause. One would declare that the line of 'Alid Imāms had come to an end in accordance with imputed principles of cyclic manifestation; another that he himself was the successor, through "spiritual filiation", if need be, of Ismā'īl; whilst others committed themselves to follow, or perhaps control, the fortunes of Ismā'īl's infant son. The mainstream of Shī'ites – in all, a very small number – recognized the next eldest son of Ja 'far, 'Abd Allāh, as Imām. He, however, died without an heir, and so the leadership devolved to yet another son, Mūsā al-Kāẓim, whose followers were to become the Twelve-Imām Shī'ites. That others pinned their hopes on other, younger sons, suggests that the doctrine of *naṣṣ*, or designation of the succeeding Imām by his predecessor, became established precisely as the aftermath of this situation, and in response to the problems it raised.

One explanation advanced by these sects to account for the anomaly in the succession, and its results, was the theory that the number seven, always symbolic because it is the sum of the directions of space (right, left, forward, backward, above, below, and the center which resumes the others), signified the completion of a cycle. Those who took this opportunity to divest themselves of the idea of Imāms altogether or, at any rate, of 'Alid Imāms, arranged the count so that their last Imām, called *at-tamm* ("the final") was the seventh, who closed the cycle, terminated the conditions which ruled it, and perhaps opened another. A Fāṭimid ruler, Mu'izz li-dīni-Llāh, wrote an esoteric prayer which referred to the son of Ismā'īl, Muḥammad, as the "Seventh *nāṭiq*" ("speaking messenger") and the "founder of a new *sharī'ah*" ("religious law"). Mu'izz was himself, according to Fāṭimid claims, the Imām seven times removed from Muḥammad ibn Ismā'īl, and thus the culmination and beginning of another cycle. By calling Muḥammad ibn Ismā'īl the *nāṭiq*, Mu'izz left open for himself the far higher role of the *sāmit*, or "silent" manifestation, of which the "speaker" is merely the mouthpiece.

In the power struggle after the death of Ja'far, those who did not follow Mūsā al-Kāẓim chose the number seven as symbolic of their new point of departure, the beginning of a new cycle. A number of Sevener groups came into existence in this way, but their adherents were certainly very few, at least in the beginning.

Two of these groups became prominent: the Fāṭimids, whose rulers were the Imāms of the sect, and, under Hamdān Qarmaṭ, the Imām-less Qarmatians. (It is not clear whether Hamdān Qarmaṭ, or one of the other leaders, was their Imām, whether they considered the Fāṭimid rulers their Imāms, or whether the Qarmatians were a school of "everyman his own Imām".) The Qarmatians followed a populist ideology of collectivism and pursued a program of political insurrection, while yet maintaining a certain sympathy with the Fāṭimids. These, and many other groups, constituted the Seveners. They were called *bāṭinīs* (the "inner" or "secret ones") because they professed to have secret teachings. Indeed, they had not only secret teachings, but an altogether secret religion, differing from orthodox Islam radically on several vital points. Not only an alternate religion, the Seveners were also an alternate political allegiance which threatened the 'Abbāsid Empire for centuries, all of which made them into an inevitably clandestine movement.

Their teachings were imparted through indoctrination which sought to break down the certainties of the ordinary believer and to replace them with submission to the authority of a chief or master, more often than not a hidden figure. Perhaps the nominal chief was sometimes imaginary, as a mythical leader can be more awe-inspiring than one of flesh and blood. The abandonment of outward religious practice was encouraged, for it represents a compelling step towards the acceptance of some other authority. The step could be justified by claiming that the presence of a divinely guided leader (or, rather, in Gnostic terms, of a divine leader), made the religious law (*sharī'ah*) superfluous. Since the presence of the Prophet had not made the *sharī'ah* superfluous in his time, this naturally suggested that here before one's eyes or yonder in the shadows there was an even higher authority; this objection was strenuously voiced by al-Ghazālī, Shahrastānī and others. This tendency took its most explicit form in the abolition of the *sharīah* by the doctrine of the *qiyāmah* ("resurrection") declared by Ḥasan, called "'Alā Dhikrihī-s-Salām", the fourth master of Alamūt. (*See* ASSASSINS.)

The intimation of alternate or allegorical meanings to accepted religious truths was another Sevener technique. The postulant was led by degrees to a "realization" of the "hidden" meaning of the Koran as, for example, when it says: "Serve thy Lord until the irrefutable [*al-yaqīn*, "the certain"] comes to you" (15:99). The "irrefutable" in the Koran means "death", but was used by the Seveners to open onto another, unsuspected, world, and in allusion to the acquisition of a superior knowledge supplied by the sect. The Koran 43:84: "And He Who is God in heaven and God on earth" could be used to spring the idea that there were *two* (or more) "Gods" or, again, that someone on earth is God. This higher knowledge could suggest that God had two natures, or that He Himself had his own "God", or that He was not completely all-powerful and had to cede in some respects to another principle, etc. In other words, it was the fateful knowledge of Dualism. (*See* DUALISM.)

It is understandable, then, that Sevener doctrines are only rarely to be discovered in any full or explicit form; mystery had value both as a defense and as an allurement. A cryptic hint would serve to start a potential recruit on the path into a parallel system of belief, virtually into a different world from that of orthodox Islam.

Historically, the Seveners played a fascinating role. In the nascent moments of their entry into Islam, they exercised a definitive influence upon Shī'ism, which began more as a political than a religious movement. They infused into Shī'ism the ideas which made possible, as if by catalysis, the subsequent development of Shī'ite speculative theology and the doctrine of the supernatural nature of the Imāms, a development of which Ja'far aṣ-Ṣādiq is portrayed as the watershed. Although it happened that orthodox theology sometimes stumbled into the Sevener labyrinths and came out intoxicated, it is through them that much Hellenistic learning flowed into Islam. The Seveners were aware of the buried treasure of pre-Islamic thought beneath their feet and they provided a channel for tapping the intellectual power of Neoplatonism, Hermetic sciences, and Hellenist philosophy to stimulate intellectual development within orthodox Islam. For their own purposes, the Seveners found great use for these neglected wisdoms before the mainstream of Islamic thought did.

It could be said that the Seveners came upon the syllogism and discovered in it a force to destabilize the 'Abbāsid Empire. In effect, they precipitated a struggle which wrested control of whole kingdoms from Baghdad's grasp. The movement manifested itself as a flurry of small sects but also as major uprisings: the Khaṭṭābiyyah, the Khurrāmiyyah, the Qarmatians, and others, some of which have been called "'Alid revolts".

Saladin was obliged to take measures to protect himself from them, when as the sect of Assassins, they used political assassination as a means for furthering their power. Not only did

Saladin have to defend his life from them, he had to compete with them politically and militarily to preserve his own power and his Sunnī dynasty, the Ayyūbids. Even when the Fāṭimids in Egypt had fallen, Saladin felt compelled to found *madrasahs*, or schools of theology, to counteract Fāṭimid propaganda. Similarly, the Saljūqs had found themselves obliged to turn to the Ash'arites in order to create a doctrinal bulwark and founded many schools to offset the *da'wah* ("preaching") coming out of Fāṭimid Egypt. Al-Ghazālī saw in them, under the name of *Ta'līmiyyah* ("the people of teaching"), a most serious threat to orthodox religion which he fought polemically. Numerous sects that exist today, the Druzes, the 'Alawīs, the 'Alī Ilāhīs (the Ahl-i Haqq), are the remnant of the heyday of the Seveners, preserving fragments of their ideology and perpetuating their methods of obedience.

The accusations of libertinism which have often been made against Sevener sects – for the most part a simple expression of abhorrence at their utilitarian view of exoterism – may at first appear to contradict the pronounced asceticism of the Manicheans in the time of Augustine. But both attitudes are different sides of the same coin; they reflect the conviction of the gnostic's independence of revealed laws, which they look upon as being "evil", and the conviction of the superiority of the knowledge they believe to possess through Dualism. The fragmentary and unstable nature of the Seveners and their offshoots bears witness to the normalizing function of the *sharī'ah*, the sacred law; when it is present a coherence is maintained even in the face of powerfully subtle doctrines, and when it is absent, the providential discrimination of form disappears, and with it, intellectual order. Al-Ḥujwīrī (d. *469*/1077) remarked in the *Kashf al-Maḥjūb*: "At the present day the Shī'ites of Egypt, who are a remnant of these Magians, make the same assertions... that everything stated by the Moslems has an esoteric interpretation, which destroys its external sense." *See also* ASSASSINS; DUALISM; FĀṬIMIDS; ISMĀ'ĪLĪS; KHAṬṬĀBIYYAH; KHURRĀMIYYAH; MANDAEANS; MANICHEISM; NŪR MUḤAMMADĪ; QARMATIANS; TA'WĪL.

Seven Salams. Seven instances in the Koran where the word *salam* ("peace") is used in the sense of blessing either upon the blessed or upon the Prophet: 36:57; 37:79; 37:109; 37:120; 37:130; 37:181; 97:5. (There are also many instances of its use in different senses.) These verses are recited in times of distress or upon auspicious occasions. Other series of phrases or references in the Koran are also deemed to have special power; those Sūrahs recited together which have the opening letters *hā' mīm*, for example.

Seven Sleepers of Ephesus. Story in the Koran (18:9-22) of some young men who were persecuted for believing in one God, in a time before Islam. They took refuge in a cave, and slept there for many years, in an act of grace from God. The pious legend story was known. The Quraysh went to Jewish Rabbis of Yathrib and consulted with them on how to determine if the Prophet was really sent by God. The Rabbis advised the Quraysh to put three questions to the Prophet, one of which was how long the sleepers had slept.

The question was put to the Prophet, in order to trap him, and test his Prophetic knowledge. The Prophet said that he would give the answer on the morrow, but a number of days went by. When the answer did come, it was in the form of the Surah of the Cave (18), and having recounted the legend then said that the time they slept was known only to God, and laid down the rule: "do not say that you will do something on the morrow, without saying If God Wills." The incident shows the Prophet's sincerity in believing that God was sending him revelations. There is a Church in Turkey, near Ephesus, dedicated to the Seven Sleepers.

Seven Speeches (or "Seven Scripts", Ar. *sab'at aḥruf*). A Ḥadīth says that the Koran is revealed in "seven speeches", "readings", "scripts" or "versions"; the meaning of *aḥruf*, which is a plural of *ḥarf* ("a letter", "a written character"), is problematical, and the best interpretation is almost certainly that of seven levels of meaning. There have, on the contrary, also been schools of thought which declare anything but the literal meaning to be heresy; for example, Ibn Hazm said that there could be no "inner" meanings (*bāṭin*). The interpretation which refers the seven readings to the dialects of seven Arab tribes: the Quraysh, Tayyi', Hawāzin, Yamānī, Thaqīf, Ḥuzayl, and Tamīm, is dubious. *See also* QIRĀ'AH.

Seventh Heaven. The degrees of Being which separate creation from the Absolute are spoken of in the Koran symbolically as the seven spheres, "skies", or heavens, the seventh being furthest from the material world and nearest to Beyond-Being. The final gulf between the two is marked by "the lote tree of the uttermost limit" (*sidrat al-muntahā*, 53:14), the limit of Being itself, which in some traditional accounts, together with the throne, the shade of paradise and the words of revelation, will not disappear when all of manifestation is withdrawn, when, as the Koran says, "the sun will be folded up". This is as much to say that these are not created. (The question of defining the relationship between created and uncreated was one of the great problems debated between philosophy and theology. The Koran and the Divine command *Kun*! ("Be!") were focuses of the debate; *see* al-KINDĪ.)

The notion of seven heavens appear prominently in early Jewish pre-Qabbalah mysticism, the Merkava ("chariot"; i.e. the chariots of Ezekiel) or Heikhalōt ("the Divine Palaces") school. In the Heikhalōt, the mystic in his search for God in the Divine "palace" ascends to the seventh heaven. At each heaven he is opposed and must struggle to gain entry with the use of Divine Names and secret signs, that is, with the knowledge of God. The origin of the idea of seven heavens appears to be Babylonian, or perhaps Persian, the seven heavens being the spheres of the planets visible to the eye, beyond which lies the sphere of fixed stars, which in symbolic astronomy corresponds to Being. *See* HEAVEN; NIGHT JOURNEY.

Sex. In Islam, sexual relations are not considered to be only a step in procreation, tolerated because of the need to continue the species. The pleasure of sexual relations does not have a negative connotation; rather it is considered to be a Divine Mercy – even sacramental – and thus completely legitimate within social rules.

> Mankind, fear your Lord, who created you
> of a single soul, and from it created
> its mate, and from the pair of them scattered
> abroad many men and women; and fear God
> by whom you demand one of another,
> and the wombs; surely God ever
> watches over you. (4:1)

Men and women complete each other; a Ḥadīth says: "the world is a possession and the best possession is a virtuous woman." There is no obstacle in Islam towards admitting a tantric perspective and the Prophet himself, as well as many Sufis, gave evidence of drawing spiritual inspiration from earthly love. Literary sources affirm that when the Prophet saw Zaynab, with whom he fell in love, he said: *Yā Muqallib al-qulūb, thabbitnī qalbī* ("O Overturner of Hearts, make mine steadfast").

As can be seen from the literature of Islam, sexual union readily prefigures the felicity of paradise, and eroticism within marriage is condoned. One author could say: "When a man looks at his wife and she looks at him, God looks upon them both with mercy. When the husband takes his wife's hand and she takes his hand, their sins vanish between their fingers... Pleasure and desire have the beauty of mountains. When the wife is with child, her reward is that of fasting, prayer, *jihād*." Celibacy or continence in marriage was not encouraged by the Prophet; against excess of asceticism al-Bukhārī records this Ḥadīth: "I fast, and I break the fast, I pray, I sleep, I go in unto women; beware! Whosoever deviates from my *sunnah* is not among my followers." Nevertheless, some infrequent example of celibacy as part of a spiritual renunciation of the world can be found among the stories of the Sufis.

Al-Ḥujwīrī says:

> God said: "Women are a garment for ye, and ye for them" [Koran 2:187].
> Marriage is permissible to all, both men and women. It is obligatory on all who otherwise cannot abstain from sin. And Satan, who is with the solitary, adorns lust and presents it beautified to the mind.
> No human Companionship compares with marriage in quality of reverence and saving power where husband and wife are well suited. But no pain or care is a worse evil than an uncongenial wife. Therefore the dervish must consider well what he is about, weighing in his imagination the evils of marriage against the evils of celibacy, so that he may choose that state whose evils he personally can more easily master. Neither marriage nor celibacy are disastrous in themselves: the mischief lies in self-assertion, and in surrender to desires. The root of the matter is the difference between Retirement and

> Companionship as modes of life. Those who choose Companionship are right to marry; but to those who would retire from human affairs celibacy is an ornament.

But if there are some grounds for celibacy in the world, from the description of paradise in the Koran, it is hard to imagine celibacy there. Legally a marriage must be consummated and forty days are allowed for this, failing which the marriage contract is void.

A Ḥadīth says: "Marriage is half of the faith; the other half is patience." Its esoteric meaning is clearly tantric; not only is pleasure of union sanctioned, but marriage is a means of reintegration of man and woman into their metaphysical prototypes within Being; a return to the Principle. The female becomes infinitude in face of the Absolute, the male is absorbed and disappears into the infinitude of the female, each becoming one's real Self.

Islam tolerates polygamy but does not encourage it. The number of wives is fixed at four. The existence of polygamy in Islam is a recognition of the universal social conditions of the times and corresponds to a view of man in which the male reflects the unity of the metaphysical principle, and the female its infinity, and thus the multiplicity of the *ḥijāb*, or Divine power of manifestation.

Fornication and adultery are condemned. Intercourse during menstruation is prohibited, as is anal intercourse, and also violence and force against a partner's will. But these are the only restrictions; the Koran says "Your women are your fields; go to your fields as you wish" (2:224). From very early times various methods of birth control have been practiced in Islam and legal opinion generally admits the use of contraceptive devices if the partners agree. *Qāḍis* ("Judges") are known to admonish husbands whose wives complain that they have not carried out their duties towards them, and *vice versa*.

Ibn ʻArabī said: "The most intense and perfect contemplation of God is through women, and the most intense union [in the world] is the conjugal act." And Jalāl ad-Dīn ar-Rūmī said: "I do not wear a shirt when I sleep with the Adored One."

Shab-i-Barat, *see* LAYLAT al-BARA'AH.

ash-Shādhilī, Abū-l-Ḥasan ʻAlī ibn ʻAbd Allāh (*593-656*/1196-1258). Usually called "Imām ash-Shādhilī", he is the founder of the *Shadhiliyyah*, one of the most important Sufi brotherhoods; it is named after him, and includes the *Darqawiyyah*, the *ʻAlawiyyah*, and many other orders.

Born in Ghumara, Tunisia, his first master was Muḥammad Abū ʻAbd Allāh ibn Ḥarazin (d. *633*/1236), himself a spiritual descendant of the famous Abū Madyān. He also followed for a time a Shaykh called Abū-l-Fatḥ al-Wāsiṭī, but desired to find the *quṭb* ("spiritual axis") of his age, and upon the advice of Abū-l-Fatḥ went to seek him in Morocco.

There he found ʻAbd as-Salām ibn Mashīsh of Fez, who lived in retreat in the Rif on the Jabal ʻĀlam. This was to be ash-Shādhilī's definitive teacher who, at their first meeting told him to perform the *ghusl*, or greater ablution. When ash-Shādhilī did so, Ibn Mashīsh told him to perform the *ghusl* again. The third time ash-Shādhilī understood, and said: "I wash myself of all previous knowledge and learning", removing from himself the obstacle of provisional knowledge before accepting the spiritual illumination of the Saint.

After he left Ibn Mashīsh, ash-Shādhilī made Egypt the center of his activity and teaching, and was well received there. His teaching insisted upon the inward nature of the spiritual path, thus his disciples did not wear the patched cloak (*khirqah*) that was frequently worn as an outward badge of asceticism by many Sufis, nor did they abandon their livelihood to undertake mendicant wandering, or renounce property and material comfort, or even hesitate to wear fine clothes. For ash-Shādhilī, detachment from worldly things did not mean to despise beauty or to need to mortify the flesh. Above all, the emphasis of the Shādhilī perspective is upon *maʻrifah*, discernment and the intellectual penetration of reality. This is no mere intellectualism, but corresponds to the initiatic process of finding the center through the maze of existence, as exemplified in the myth of Theseus and the labyrinth, or of Aeneas' arrival at the city of Dido where he traverses, mentally, a maze drawn on the city walls. Symbolizing the intellectual process and the spiritual journey, there is a maze drawn in stone on the floor, between the entrance and the altar, of the Cathedral of Chartres. A postulant who traverses this maze seeking its center will find himself approaching it and receding from it, from time to time lost, and obliged to retrace his steps, before he can attain to it. It is a game of hide and seek, of losing and finding, played with God.

Imām ash-Shādhilī had a vision in which he saw the names of his disciples written in the "inviolate tablet" where God's decrees are inscribed (*al-lawḥ al-maḥfūẓ*), and understood this to be a promise from heaven that those of his spiritual descendants who held to his precepts and the precepts of his successors would be spared the fire of Hell. A provisional or temporary entering into the fire for those who will ultimately achieve a paradisal state corresponds to the notion of "purgatory"; to achieve paradise directly is, however, considered to be an exceptional possibility, and ash-Shādhilī's vision is understood to be a dispensation in which, if further purification after death were necessary, the soul would undergo it as a temporary deferring of paradise, in a state which is neither hell nor yet paradise, whereby the soul would be purified in a beneficent way rather than through expiatory suffering.

Imām Shādhilī is buried in Humaithra, a village near the Red Sea, where he died while returning from the pilgrimage.

He left no writings except for a half-dozen litanies such as *Ḥizb al-Barr* ("the Litany of the Earth"), and *Ḥizb an-Naṣr* ("the Litany of Help"), all of which he claimed were inspired. The most famous is the powerful litany known as the *Ḥizb al-Baḥr* ("the Litany of the Sea"). The essence of his teaching is masterfully contained in the writings of Ibn Aṭā' Allāh al-Iskandarī (d. *709*/1309), the *Kitāb al-Ḥikam* ("Book of Aphorisms") which has been frequently translated and commented upon. Ibn 'Aṭā' Allāh was himself a disciple of Abū-l-'Abbās Aḥmad al-Mursī (*616-686*/1219-1287), an Andalusian from the circle of ash-Shādhilī in Alexandria who played an important role in perpetuating and establishing ash-Shādhilī's teachings. It was said of ash-Shādhilī that it was enough that a disciple spend a few days with him for an opening (*fatḥ*) to be made in the soul that would begin to dissolve the existential illusion and start him on the way to realization. *See* DARQĀWĪ; ḤIZB al-BAḤR; IBN 'AṬĀ' ALLĀH; SILSILAH; SUFISM.

ash-Shāfi'ī, Muḥammad ibn Idrīs (*150-205*/767-820). The architect of systematic Islamic law, he was born in Palestine and raised in Mecca. He was a Qurayshi who had lived in contact with Beduin tribes, thereby deepening his knowledge of Arabic and poetry. He studied law in Medina with Mālik ibn Anas, and also pursued studies in Baghdad, to which he returned several times, thus becoming intimately acquainted with Ḥanafī law.

As against the customary usages (Sunnah), of the Medina community upon which Mālik ibn Anas drew to amplify the law, and against the deductions and speculations of the Ḥanafī school, ash-Shāfi'ī promoted the Ḥadīth and Sunnah of the Prophet as being the primary authority for the interpretation of Koranic injunctions. These, he said, were more important than *qiyās* ("analogy"), and were followed in degree of importance by *ijmā'* ("consensus") as the legitimizing basis of law. Koran, Ḥadīth and Sunnah, *qiyas* and *ijma'* thus became jointly *uṣūl al-fiqh* (the "roots of jurisprudence"), that is, the systematic basis of law.

Ash-Shāfi'ī did not himself found a school of law; this was done by his disciples. His methodology was universally adopted by the other schools. Ash-Shāfi'ī is buried in Cairo. *See* SHARĪ'AH.

Shah of Iran, *see* PAHLAVI.

Shah Walī Allāh (*1115-1175*/1703-1762). A religious leader who promoted a reformed, active, and more militant Islam in India. His writings drew upon all fields of Islamic study – jurisprudence, theology, and mysticism – synthesized in accordance with his own original approach and intuitions.

Shahādah (from the verb *shahida*, "to observe", to "witness", "to testify"; "a perceiving", "a testimony"). The affirmation and creed that is fundamental to Islam; the first and most important of the "Five Pillars of Islam". The Prophet said: "I have brought nothing more important than the *shahādah*." When it is accepted sincerely – or "seen" – the consequence is surrender (*islām*) to God, Allāh, and becoming *muslim*. It is made up of two statements, the "two testifications" (*ash-shahādatān*); the dual of *shahādah*. In this context it should be noted that the word *shahida* (and hence the noun *shahādah*) has double significance typical of the genius of the Arabic language: it embraces the acts of seeing or perceiving and then of declaring that one has seen or perceived. The key to this is the link between act and speech which, in the Arabic soul, is so swift and spontaneous that many words bear a double significance reflecting it. For example, *dhikr* ("memory") is also "mention", that is, the verbalization of memory. It is for this reason that the first meaning of "observe", "see", "perceive" passes on to the complementary meanings of "bear witness", "testify", "live out the truth that has been perceived and, even, "die for that truth": the word *shahīd* means "martyr". The Arabic *shahādatān* are *Ashhadu an lā*[1] *ilāha illā-Llāh, wa ashhadu anna Muḥammadan rasūlu-Llāh* ("I perceive (and bear witness) that there is no god except Allāh and I perceive (and bear witness) that Muḥammad is the Messenger of God.")

[1]The rules of euphony in Arabic elide the *nun* into the following *lam* and *ra'*; thus this is correctly pronounced *Ashhadu al-lā ilāha illā-Llāh* and *Muḥammadar-rasūlu-Llāh.*).

It is the Arabic alone that vehicles the ritually effective and sacramental force of the words. Ultimately, the one condition of salvation is the complete acceptance of the *shahādah*. The *shahādah* expunges the error of Adam – symbolized by the eating of the forbidden fruit – of seeing objects as reality, in place of God. The sense of the *shahādah* is that one sees that only the Absolute, only Allāh, is Reality. The second *shahādah*, in defining the Prophet Muḥammad, also defines through him the relationship of manifestation or creation as a message or revelation from God.

It is sometimes held that a single uttering of the *shahādah* is sufficient in order to be saved. But while the encounter of the *shahādah* is a unique event out of time, man lives in time and multiplicity; the depth of his affirmation and the extent to which he is transformed by it cannot be conclusively demonstrated from one utterance. Therefore the *shahādah* must be repeated and lived until the implicit realization has penetrated to the center of his being, until through concentration upon the truth, and virtue, the individual substance is transformed and made itself adequate to the truth.

The Bedouins say, 'We believe.'
Say: 'You do not believe; rather
say, "We surrender"; for belief
has not yet entered your hearts...
The believers are those who believe
in God and His Messenger, then have
not doubted, and have struggled
with their possessions and their selves
in the way of God; those – they are
the truthful ones.' (49:14-15)

The primary *shahādah* is made up of two elements: the first is the *nafy* ("negation"): *lā ilāha*, ("there is no god"). The second is called the *ithbāt* ("affirmation"): *Allāh*. Between them is a bridge, *illā*, which is a word made up of a conditional (*in*, "if") and a negation (*lā*, "not"). The conditional "side" of the bridge *illā* faces the negating *nafy*, and the negation "side" of the *illā* faces the affirming of the *ithbāt*. Thus it says that "there is no reality if it is not the Absolute Reality, God"; its juxtaposition of "if" and two negatives is a kind of magical or miraculous pathway out of the world towards that which can never be negated, *Allāh*.

The first *shahādah* casts man into an endless ocean, that of the Eternal, the Tremendous. The second, *Muḥammadun rasūlu-Llāh*, in which Muḥammad is at once Prophet, revelation and creation, is a vessel coming from the unique Reality, and thereby existing through It, which saves man from drowning in the infinite depths of the Absolute. *See* FIVE DIVINE PRESENCES; FIVE PILLARS.

Shahīd (lit. "witness", pl. *shuhadā'*). A martyr, first of all he who dies fighting, bearing witness to the faith. Such are assured a place in paradise and are buried in the clothes they wore in battle. At the resurrection their bloodstains will testify to their merit. Assimilated to martyrdom are those whose death has been tragic or arousing compassion. *See* MARTYRS; SHAHĀDAH.

Shahrastānī, Abū-l-Fatḥ Muḥammad ibn 'Abd al-Karīm (*469-548*/1076-1153). Historian and student of religions, he was a Persian born in Shahrastān, in Khorasan. Shahrastānī was a Sunnī, an Ash'arite, who studied jurisprudence with Abū-l-Muzaffar Aḥmad al-Khawāfī and Abū Naṣr ibn al-Qushayrī, and theology in Nayshābūr with al-Anṣarī, a student of al-Juwaynī. Shahrastānī wrote a book on theology called *Nihāyat al-Iqdām fiilm al-Kalām* ("The Limits of Prowess in Theology"), and a circumscription of philosophic competence in *Muṣana'āt al-Falāsifah* ("The Productions of the Philosophers").

It is because of the remarkable survey of the religions of his time, *Kitāb al-Milal wa'l-Niḥal* ("The Book of Religions and Systems of Thought") that he is highly regarded, for he was an observer who saw to the heart of the matter in regard to religious doctrines and beliefs.

Placing Islam at the center, Shahrastānī studied other religions and graded them according to their proximity to Islam. It is interesting to note that, although this appears at first sight to be a purely ethnocentric approach, it is a classification that would make little sense around any other religion, for example Buddhism; but it is in fact a natural way to proceed in the case of Islam, since it is the religion of the Absolute revealed as such. Shahrastānī showed his sense of objectivity by freely admitting that some of the practices of Islam were against reason (though not false for all that).

Shahrastānī analyzed the divergences among Shī'ite sects, treated of Christianity and Judaism, the Philosophers, Hellenists, the Gnostic sects such as the late Valentinians, or Bardesanians, and the Buddhists. In the Hindus, Shahrastānī recognized in their esoterism the same theories as in Pythagoras, who, as an Indo-European, was indeed kindred to the Hindus, Greek Paganism being in certain ways an attenuated form of elements in Hinduism. Of the link between Pythagoreans and Hindus, Shahrastānī said that a student of Pythagoras named Qalanus went to India and taught a disciple called Brahmanan who became ruler of the country; which can perhaps be thought of as a very condensed account of the Aryan invasions of India. Shahrastānī provided precious information on Zurvanism, a heretical form of Zoroastrianism, and on other long vanished religions.

Shahrastānī classified religions according to four categories:

1. Those who possess a revealed book: Muslims, Jews, Christians.
2. Those who possess something like a revealed book: Magians and Manicheans.
3. Those who subscribe to laws and binding judgements without benefit of a revealed book: Sabians (Hellenist Pagans).
4. Those who have neither a book nor fixed laws: worshipers of stars and idols.

He was very sympathetic towards the Sabians, by which he meant the Hellenist Pagans of Harran, calling a group of them *aṣḥāb ruḥāniyyah* ("people of the Spirit", or non-Muslim peoples with an apprehension of revelation). He recognized their origins as coming from a primordial Prophetic tradition which he called that of the *Adhimun*. In particular, Shahrastānī thought that their Prophet was Hermes (who is often identified with the Prophet Idrīs, or Enoch, in Islam).

Shahrastānī presented the beliefs of the Sabians in the form of a discussion between them and the *hunafā'*, the pre-Islamic Abrahamic Monotheists. Of Christianity, he recognized "that Paul had introduced philosophy into the religion of Peter". In reporting strange mythologies, he spoke of the legend of the Pheonix, *al-'anqā' al-khurāfiyyah* ("the legendary griffon") a bird consumed by fire within itself, and then reborn, which the Muslims held to be one of the mythological marvels of India. *See* AHL al-KITĀB; GHULAT; HARRAN; RUKHKH; SABIANS; TA'LĪMIYYAH.

Shah Walī Allāh, *see before* SHAHĀDAH.

Shāmil, Imām (*1212-1288*/1797-1871). The courageous and tenacious leader of the Muslim tribes of Daghestan in the Caucasus, who led his people in the war against Russian conquest from 1834 until his capture in 1859. During the time he was the chief of the Lezghian tribe, Daghestan was organized as a theocracy, run strictly according to the *sharī'ah.*

The discipline imposed by Shāmil, who was of the Naqshbandī order of Sufis, inspired a desperate resistance against increasing odds. When he was captured and Daghestan annexed to the Russian Empire, Shāmil was received with honor by the Tsar, and albeit in exile, lived on a pension with his family in St. Petersburg. He was allowed to go on the pilgrimage, in the course of which he died. He is buried in the *Baqī'* cemetery in Medina.

ash-Sharānī, 'Abd al-Wahhāb (*898-973*/1493-1565). Egyptian Sufi author.

Sharī'ah (from the root *shara'a*, "to introduce", "enact", "prescribe", "revealed religious law"; also *shar'* and *shir'ah*). The canonical law of Islam as put forth in the Koran and the Sunnah and elaborated by the analytical principles of the four orthodox schools (*madhhab*, pl. *madhāhib*), the Shāfi'ī, Ḥanbalī, Ḥanafī, and Mālikī, together with that of the Shī'ites, the Ja'farī. The Zaydī Shī'ites also have their own school of law as do the 'Ibādīs, or Khārijites.

The *uṣūl al-fiqh* (lit. "roots of jurisprudence") are the basis of Islamic law among the Sunnīs: Koran, Ḥadīth and Sunnah (acts and statements of the Prophet), *qiyās* ("analogy"), and *ijmā'* (popular consensus of the community, or *ummah*). Another principle, *ijtihād* ("effort"), is the extrapolation from these principles to specific cases. In the Sunnī world, and among *Akhbarī* Shī'ites, the age of *ijtihād* is considered to be passed in the sense of having been the prerogative of the period in which the systems of law themselves were established. At least this is the official, or doctrinal, position, for, in fact, a certain degree of *ijtihād* is always inevitable and has always gone on. Among the *Uṣūlī* Twelve-Imām Shī'ites in Iran, the situation is the opposite; *ijtihād* has not only continued officially, but since the victory of the *Uṣūlī* school in Persia over the *Akhbarīs* two hundred years ago, it has been continuously intensified, and modern developments are carrying the Shī'ites into completely uncharted territory.

The Wahhābīs and Ḥanbalīs limit *ijmā'* to the generation of the Companions and their immediate followers, the *tābi'ūn*; Khārijites limit *ijmā'* to their own community; Twelve-Imām Shī'ites add the teachings of their Imāms to the Sunnah, and *Uṣūlīs* admit the *ijtihād* of qualified contemporary Shī'ite religious authorities.

According to Islamic law, every act fits into one of the following categories: *farḍ*, obligatory under law, such as the performance of prayer; (to this is added *wājib*, obligatory through legal extrapolation but not expressly mentioned in the primary sources of law so that its omission is no sin); *mustaḥabb* or *mandūb*, not obligatory but recommended; *mubāḥ*, neutral or permitted; *makrūh*, not forbidden but discouraged; and *ḥarām*, forbidden. The principle of retaliation for an offense, which corresponds to the Mosaic law, is called *qiṣāṣ*. In place of the revenge embodied in the tribal custom which preceded it, *qiṣāṣ* introduces the principle that the consequences of an act are contained in the act itself. Intention (*niyyah*) is the critical factor in determining the nature of every act, in accordance with the Ḥadīth: "Actions are according to their intention..."

Islam makes no distinction between religion and life, nothing being excluded from religion, or outside it and "secular". Islamic law covers not only ritual but every aspect of life. It is often said that in practice today Islamic law is limited in many Muslim countries to questions of family and religious practice, whereas civil administration and commerce are covered by separate legal systems. In fact, a similar situation prevailed from early times; the parallel system of law was the civil law of the prince, which, being also of indigenous origin, did not raise the kinds of objections which are being raised today by traditionalists against the modern legal systems which represent modern times and are therefore borrowed from European models. Because Islamic law is extremely idealistic in its approach, assuming a natural desire to conform to the truth, and the existence of a "holy" society disposed to religious conformity, there has always existed a parallel system of justice administered by the state.

It is not possible to incriminate someone in *sharī'ah* law upon circumstantial evidence; there must be witnesses, or the confession of the accused. This makes the prosecution of criminal cases difficult, if not impossible, in practice. Thus the justice carried out by the political authorities was always a necessary complement to the *sharī'ah*; and the ruling prince could administer punishment and hand down rulings which superseded those of the religious courts. This exercise of judicial authority by the civil authorities, the prince and his delegates down to the local level, was called *siyāsah shar'iyyah* and accounted for as much administration of justice as did the religious courts. The Prince also promulgated *qānūn*, or civil law (from the Greek, *kanon*, "canon"), and published edicts (*aẓ-ẓahīr*), prerogatives which are taken over by modern governments and legislatures.

In addition, *sharī'ah* law is in practice traditionally limited by the customary laws of people who adopted Islam. Among the Arabs this has meant that the customary rules of Medina and Kufah were integrated into *sharī'ah* as such, but for peoples who came upon the scene later, such as the Berbers or the Qashqai, for example, this meant that as long as the community maintained its tribal or group identity, the traditional customs of the tribe were interpreted into the community's legal usages. In many cases these tribal customs (*'ādāt*) supersede *sharī'ah* law. This situation is particularly marked in the Malay countries, and above all in Indonesia where the customary law, called *adat*, plays a very prominent role.

Nowhere today, with the exception of Saudi Arabia and some Gulf states, is *sharī'ah* law the dominant legal system. In some countries it has been replaced entirely by legal systems copied from European countries; in others it has been relegated to deciding cases of family law; and in others it exists side by side with European legal systems adopted in the 19th century and first applied to commercial transactions. The Code Napoleon was established in Egypt by Muḥammad 'Alī; in Turkey during the *Tanẓīmāt*, the period of reforms in the last century, a synthesis was made from European legal systems; Jordan still uses the 19th century Ottoman legal system, while Turkey itself, since the abolition of the Sultanate, has adopted codes drawn up even more closely upon European models. Countries that underwent European colonialism adopted in large part the legal codes of the colonial power, and the creation of modern constitutions has led to further adoption of European law.

The desire to return to a more religious society, or to rediscover expressions of political life though indigenous forms rather than borrowed ones, and the rise of modern fundamentalism and new nationalisms as a way of "protest" and revolution, have obliged many governments to make gestures of "a return to Islamic law". These have taken the form of superficial, symbolic, and sporadic applications of the more rigorous aspects of such punishments as public flogging in order to play up to popular sentiments. However, to return to *sharī'ah* law would symbolize the return to an age of faith, and that is entirely beyond the capacities of modern peoples as a whole, and still less of their governments which, even despite themselves, have accepted the premises of materialism and so crossed a point of no-return.

The application of *sharī'ah* law exclusively and in its totality is not possible today without compromising admixtures of modern ideas (as exemplified by the reformers who adopt modern rationalism as axiomatic), or through stultifying simplification; it cannot be, unless the world itself were to return to another age. And this is not feasible for whole societies without changes of cosmic proportions which are out of human hands, whatever may be possible for individuals. This was foreseen by prophecy, for there is a saying attributed to the Prophet that: "In the beginning, if one omits a tenth of the law, one will be punished, but at the end of time, if one accomplishes a tenth of the law, one will be saved." *See also* ABŪ ḤANĪFAH; AḤKĀM; AKHBARĪS; CREED; DIVORCE; FARḌ; FATWĀ; FIQH; al-FIQH al-AKBAR: FIVE PILLARS; ḤADĪTH; ḤARĀM; IBN ḤANBAL; IJTIHĀD; IKHTILĀF; INHERITANCE; INTENTION; ISTIḤSĀN; ISTIṢLĀḤ; KORAN; LEGACIES; MADHHAB; MĀLIK IBN ANAS; MUWATTA'; QĀḌI; QIṢĀṢ; SCHOOLS of LAW; ash-SHĀFI'Ī; SUNNAH; TALFĪQ; TANẒĪMĀT; THEFT; UṢŪLĪS; WĀJIB; WAQF; ẒĀHIRĪ.

Sharīatī, 'Alī (1933-1977). Modernist Iranian political thinker and activist. Although he was Iranian, he died in Damascus and is buried there. He was noted for his eclectic ideas and his opposition to the West and to capitalism, to which he thought the answer lay in his understanding of Islam, an understanding which appears to have been fashioned by a kind of Existentialism drawn paradoxically from Western sources rather than from Iranian ones. He was popular with university students.

Sharīf (lit. "noble", pl. *Shurafa'*). The descendants of the Prophet through his daughter Fāṭimah and 'Alī ibn Abī Ṭālib. The Prophet had other daughters, but upon the marriage of Fāṭimah the Prophet called a special blessing. Each *Sharīf* draws his line of descent from one of the two grandsons of the Prophet, Ḥasan and Ḥusayn.

Today there are many thousands of *Shurafā'* in Islamic communities. They are treated with respect and addressed in traditional societies by a particular title: Sidi, Sayyid, Mawlay etc. In some countries special registers exist to inscribe those who are entitled to be called *Shurafā'*. Two ruling families today are Sharīfian, those of Morocco and Jordan.

Shaykh (lit. "old man", "elder"). The title of the head of a village, or of a whole tribe, usually elected. It is also the title of one who has authority, whether spiritual or political, and in particular of a savant or a learned, or otherwise venerable, person.

A special meaning of the word is that of a spiritual master, a *guru*, the head of a Sufi order, which in Arabic is also *murshid* ("guide"). In this sense, its equivalent in Iran and India is *Pīr*, which is used in place of Shaykh.

Distinctions are made regarding the function: a *Shaykh al-barakah* (or *Shaykh at-tabarruk*) is one who gives initiation into a Sufi order. One who gives, in addition, doctrinal or spiritual teaching is a *Shaykh as-sālikīn*; one who has achieved a knowledge not through an application of doctrine and method, but through ecstatic exaltation, is a *Shaykh al-jadhb*. Such a one, who may possess something of a spiritual state because of his experience, has little means of conveying a useful teaching for the edification of others.

The Shādhilīs make the following three distinctions: a *Shaykh at-ta'līm*, one who knows doctrine, what the Hindus would call a *paṇḍit*; a *Shaykh at-tarbiyah*, or master who can give effective instruction in the spiritual path; and a *Shaykh at-taraqqī*, a "Master of ascension" who possesses a degree of spiritual realization of the truth, and can bring others to his degree of direct knowledge. *See* SUFISM.

Shaykh al-Islām (lit. "the Elder of Islam"). A title which came into use at the time of the Buyids, a period in which very extravagant names and titles were popular, it was applied occasionally as an honorific to religious leaders of high standing.

The title acquired an increasingly specific function during the Ottoman Caliphate, and finally became the office of Mufti of Istanbul. The Shaykh al-Islām was appointed by the Caliph. Towards the end of the Caliphate, the office had become a sizable institution with a secretariat to carry on its duties, but was abolished in 1924 along with the Caliphate itself.

Shaykhis. A Persian Shī'ite sect founded by Aḥmad ibn Zayn ad-Dīn al-Aḥsā'ī (*1166-1241*/1753-1826). After the disappearance of the twelfth, or "Hidden Imām" in *260*/873, four successive persons claimed to represent him until *329*/940, when there began the "greater occultation" (*al-ghaybah al-kubrā*). During this period, which continues today, contact with the Hidden Imām, except for several legendary occasions, has been broken off.

Eight hundred years later, Aḥmad al-Aḥsā'ī, calling each of the four original *wakīls*, or representatives of the Hidden Imām, the *bāb* ("door"), believed himself to be under a special guidance from the Imām and gathered followers. He evolved a neo-Sevener doctrine which was branded as heretical by the Shī'ite authorities. Its speculative theory that earthly bodies are a mixture of material and subtle natures, and that there exists an intermediate spiritual world, which he called the *hurqalya* (something very like the *pleroma* of Gnosticism), posed no threat to Shī'ite essentials and was common enough; but the new doctrine exalted the Imāms and their role in creation beyond the claims of ordinary Shī'ism to the point of polytheism.

The successor to al-Aḥsā'ī was Sayyid Karīm Reshti (d. *1259*/1843), who claimed to be guided by the Hidden Imām in dreams. By this time the sect was already regarded with great suspicion by the authorities, and grounds for their concern were to grow when, after Sayyid Karim died, some of the Shaykhis found a new leader in the person of Mirzā 'Alī Muḥammad ash-Shirāzī. The year *1260*/1844 was believed to be the year in which the Twelfth Imām would return to the world; Mirza went so far as to claim publicly to be the *Bāb* ("door") – a more direct link than before – to the Hidden Imām. He was brought before the courts – such a claim having serious religious *and* political implications in Persia – and spent much of his career imprisoned. In 1848 he claimed to be the Twelfth Imām. He was shot by a firing squad at the age of thirty in Tabriz in *1267*/1850, after his followers had caused riots.

In addition to claiming to be the spokesman, the *Bāb* ("door"), to the Hidden Imām, and the Imām himself, Mirzā 'Alī had in his brief career gone on to found a new religion. This incorporated modernist elements such as the equality of women and abrogation of the Koran, advocated the removal of the Ka'bah and the tomb of the Prophet, and proposed a bizarre set of pseudo-mystical practices centering on the numbers 19 (the lunar metonic cycle) and 28 (another lunar cycle). The number 19 is also the numeric value of the Divine Name *al-Waḥad*

("The One"). The claims of the *Bāb* expanded into prophethood and beyond. He also predicted a "promised one" who would fulfil his teachings.

The proselytizing of his followers led to civil disturbances, insurrection, and his own demise. The writings of the *Bāb* are the *Bayān*, or "Explanation", and his followers, called *Bābīs*, exist to this day in Iran in small numbers.

The question of his succession, in the characteristically unstable fashion of such doctrines, led to further developments. Some followed the *Bāb's* original teachings, but a new group arose which was shortly to split into two new sects. The new group was led first by a figure called by the cult name of Ṣubḥī Azal ("Eternal Dawn"); and a schism occurred with the emergence of another leader called Bahā' Allāh ("the Radiance of God"), thus creating two sects, the *Azalīs* and the *Bahā'īs*.

Not all the original Shaykhīs had adhered to the *Bāb*, and those who had not now proceeded, under the leadership of one Muḥammad Karīm, a descendant of the imperial Qajars, to form the "new" Shaykhīs, of whom thousands still exist in Iran today, along with the "Old Shaykhis", survivors of the *Bābīs*, and the Bahā'īs.

Al-Aḥṣā'ī had changed the Twelve-Imām Shī'ite doctrine of "Five Supports" (Divine Unity, Prophecy, Resurrection of the Body, Imāmate, and Justice) to four, combining some supports and eliminating others; the fourth he made the principle of the "perfect Shī'ite" who is in communication with the Hidden Imām. At the present time, although the Shaykhīs possess two of their own schools of theology, many, if not most of them, have beliefs and a conception of Shī'ism indistinguishable from that of the Twelve-Iman Shī'ites of Iran.

Nevertheless, this series of fissiparous sects is clearly a reaction to the tension created in Twelve-Imām Shī'ism by the doctrine of the Hidden Imām. The absolute importance of the Imām in the perspective of Shī'ism on the one hand, and the absence of anyone for a thousand years to fulfill the role – were it possible to do so – has caused innumerable convulsions of this kind in Persian history, and continues to do so today. *See* BĀBĪS; BAHĀ'ĪS; HIDDEN IMĀM; SHĪ'ISM.

Shī'ah (lit. the "factions", "party", from *shī'at 'Alī*, "the party of 'Alī"). Those who supported the claim to the Caliphate of 'Alī ibn Abī Ṭālib are called the *shī'ah*. They did so because they alleged that 'Alī had a Divine right to the Caliphate, or successorship, and that he had received a special mandate from the Prophet; and because of their presuming a unique, spiritual authority in 'Alī, which was passed on to certain of his descendants. *See* SHĪ'ISM.

Shī'ism. A branch of Islam comprising 10% or less of the total of all Muslims, with doctrines significantly different from those of the orthodox Sunnī majority. Shī'ites themselves are divided into three principal groups:

The largest division by far, Twelve-Imām Shī'ism, also called "Twelvers" (*ithnā 'ashariyyah*), has been the official religion of Persia since the Safavid dynasty came to power in *907*/1501. Twelve-Imām Shī'ites make up 60% of the population in Iraq and Lebanon, and Twelve-Imām Shī'ite minorities are also present in Afghanistan, Pakistan and Syria, as well as in the Eastern Province of Saudi Arabia and some Gulf States.

The Zaydīs, also called "Five-Imām Shī'ites" or "Fivers", are found in the Yemen, where they make up about 40% of the population.

The third largest group, altogether a million or more, the Ismā'īlīs, who are "Seven-Imām Shī'ites", are concentrated in India, and scattered across Central Asia, Iran, Syria, and East Africa.

These groups each contain further subdivisions, and in some case have given rise to offshoots, such as the Shaykhīs, whilst certain sects on the fringes of Islam have been influenced by ideas of a dominantly Shī'ite – and often Ismā'īlī – stamp.

The name Shī'ite or *Shī'ah* means "a partisan" and comes from *shī'at 'Alī* (the "party of 'Alī"). The latter comprised a small circle, originally fewer than than a dozen men, who advocated the candidacy of 'Alī ibn Abī Ṭālib for the Caliphate, or successorship to the Prophet. 'Alī was a cousin of the Prophet as well as his son-in-law, having married the Prophet's daughter Fāṭimah. He was, moreover, one of the first converts to Islam and later gained fame as a warrior.

Historically, the roots of Shī'ism reach to the time immediately following the Prophet's death, when Abū Bakr was elected as Caliph (*khalīfah*, "lieutenant" or "successor" to the Prophet) at the popular assembly (*saqīfah*) in Medina. The election was carried out in haste as the worsening rivalry between the *Anṣār* (native Medinans) and the *Muhājirūn* (Meccan immigrants) threatened to split the Islamic community. 'Alī was not present, since he had stayed at the Prophet's deathbed. He was then just thirty years old; Arab respect for age naturally favored claimants of riper years, although historical exceptions to such a rule did exist, but 'Alī's partisans, a handful at the time, felt that his claims had been unjustly passed over. This has always been the Shī'ite contention.

'Umar, designated by Abū Bakr as his successor, became the second Caliph. When, upon 'Umar's death 'Alī was offered the Caliphate on condition that he abide by the precedents set by Abū Bakr and 'Umar, he refused to be bound, or expressed himself inconclusively, and the function was instead awarded by an arbiter to 'Uthmān. When 'Uthmān was assassinated during an insurrection in Medina, in a climate of growing dissension within the Empire because of the depotism of the Umayyad clan, 'Alī was elected as the fourth Caliph in *35*/656. He immediately had to face an insurrection on the part of two Companions, Ṭalḥāḥ and Zubayr, who were joined by 'Ā'ishah, a widow of the Prophet. The three were defeated by 'Alī at the Battle of the Camel. But 'Alī also encountered opposition from Mu 'āwiyah, a relative of 'Uthmān and governor of Syria, which led to the prolonged and inconclusive Battle of Ṣiffīn in *36*/657, and to the secession of the Khārijites, or "Separatists", from 'Alī's army. In *40*/661, 'Alī was assassinated by the Khārijite Ibn Muljam. His son Ḥasan was elected Caliph, but under threat of attack from Mu'āwiyah ceded the Caliphate to him.

After the death of Ḥasan, his brother Ḥusayn, the only other son of 'Alī and Fāṭimah (there was also a sister, Zaynab, a daughter of Fāṭimah, and sons of 'Alī by other wives, who, not being born of Fāṭimah were not descendants of the Prophet) led a revolt against the Umayyad Caliph Yazid ibn Mu'āwiyah, counting on support promised by the people of Kufah, which was not forthcoming. Ḥusayn's tragic death at the hands of Mu'āwiyah's forces at Kerbala in *61*/680, is the central event of Persian-inspired Twelve-Imām Shī'ism, comparable to Christ's crucifixion in the powerful emotions it evokes. It became the focus of profound themes of guilt for betrayal, of the expectation of vengeance and justification, and, with messianic overtones quite alien to Sunnī Islam, of the chosen one's death as a sacrifice in expiation for the sins of others. The anniversary of the event, the 10th of Muḥarram, which coincides with an auspicious holiday observed in the Sunnī calendar since the Prophet's time, is for Twelve-Imām Shī'ites the culmination of a turbulent ten-day period of mourning. At this time some Shī'ites scourge themselves publicly in atonement for their ancestors' abandonment of Ḥusayn to Caliph Yazīd's army, and for the perceived betrayal of subsequent Imāms, or descendants of 'Alī who inherited his spiritual mandate. According to Shī'ite accounts, the Imāms, almost to a man and even in harmless old age, were poisoned by the Caliphs, perpetuating a theme of persecution of monumental proportions closely bound up with the Shī'ite ethos. (Dualist doctrines often require that there be an external enemy who is held to threaten a mortal danger.)

The fate of 'Alī and his sons, then, is of the highest import in the Shī'ite scheme of history. The Sunnīs, too, assign 'Alī a high place since, for them, he is the great champion of Islam in its early fight to survive, and the venerable fourth Caliph, one of *al-khulafā' ar-rāshidūn*, the "rightly guided" or Patriarchal Caliphs. For the Sufis, moreover, who dominated much of Sunnī theology from the *7th*/12th century on, 'Alī is the fountainhead of esoteric knowledge and, along with Abū Bakr, figures in most of the initiatory chains, or *silsilahs*. 'Alī is also credited with laying down the first rules of Arabic grammar. His descendants through Fāṭimah are also descendants of the Prophet, beginning with Ḥasan and Ḥusayn.

The Shī'ites, however, hold that 'Alī had a special spiritual function alongside that of the Prophet which, according to them, gave him pre-eminent sanctity that entailed the absolute right to spiritual leadership, known as the Imāmate. This function was passed on by designation to his descendants, who, together with 'Alī, are the Imāms. This meaning of the word is peculiar to Shī'ism: for the Sunnīs an Imām is simply a prayer leader; the first significance, from which the others devolve, is "exemplar" or "model". The differences among the various Shī'ite groups hinge in part upon the identity of the Imāms, that is, which of 'Alī's descendants inherited his authority, and also upon the question of the extent and nature of this authority. At one end of the spectrum are the *ghūlāh* (from *ghuluw*, "exaggeration"), the most extreme of whom are outside Islam altogether and make 'Alī into nothing less than Divine. They are sometimes called "ultra-Shī'ites", but sects like the 'Alī Ilāhīs ("'Alī-Divines") are really "*trans*-Shī'ites", beyond Shī'ism altogether. At the other end of the spectrum is a sect like the Zaydīs who see in the Imāmate a function which may or may not be exercised at a particular time by a descendant of the Prophet, and which does not necessarily include a claim to sanctity. Midway between these points of view, the Twelve-Imām Shī'ites assert that the Imām holds a spiritual and political pre-eminence and possesses special graces, miraculous powers, secret knowledge (*'ilm*) and favor which God has bestowed on no-one else. The Imāms channel a Divine light (the *Nūr Muḥammadī*) and are also considered to be "sinless". The Imām is necessary both for creation to be sustained, and for the believer to win salvation. A saying is attributed to Ja'far aṣ-Ṣādiq, the sixth Imām: "Who dies without knowing the Imām of his time dies an unbeliever." In other words, Twelve-Imām Shī'ites make the Imām into an intermediary between man and God.

This clearly resembles the idea of the *Logos*; the Imāms are envisaged as half-human and half-Divine means of salvation, and this is an idea which the rest of Islam precisely avoids in favor of salvation by direct surrender to God without intermediaries. Moreover, such a conception of 'Alī and the Imāms necessarily implies a profound ambiguity regarding the Prophet himself. No such claims are made for the Prophet in Shī'ism and this inevitably gives the Prophet a lesser role, in fact if not in name, as compared to 'Alī. It is this which creates the real divergence with orthodox Sunnī Islam. H.A.R. Gibb made the observation that all the Gnostic doctrines of the Middle East had flowed into Shī'ism. This in itself created a tension with orthodox Islam which was a reaction to such tendencies in the first place and in Shī'ism the ideological resistance joined hands with political resistance.

The *Shī'ite* doctrine of the Imāms can be summarized by certain details which are found in Twelve-Imām versions of the *mir'āj* (the Prophet's ascent to heaven): the ancient Prophets whom the Prophet encounters affirm that their missions were in part intended to prepare the way for him *and for the Imāmate of 'Alī*; God instructs the Prophet to look out from heaven into the empyrean, and he sees the twelve Imāms performing the prayer in seas of light; God says of them: "These are my proofs, vicegerents, and friends, and the last of them will take vengeance on my enemies."

Whereas no reference at all to 'Alī and his descendants is made in the Sunnī account of the *mi'rāj*, Shī'ite understanding makes the Prophet *share* his spiritual station and function with 'Alī and eleven descendants, emphasizes the miraculous and outwardly avataric nature of their role, and, in the case of the last Imām, prescribes revenge and vindication for itself. This capital variation in the Islamic doctrine was the source of great upheaval for the Shī'ites.

According to Twelve-Imām Shī'ism the Imāms are:

1. ***'Alī ibn Abī Ṭālib*** (d. *41*/661) buried in Najaf, Iraq, one of the most important shrines.

2. *Ḥasan ibn 'Alī* (d. *49*/669) buried in Medina. (Some Ismā'īlīs considered Ḥasan a "viceroy" of Ḥusayn, and not an Imām in his own right.)

3. *Ḥusayn ibn 'Alī* (d. *61*/680) buried in Kerbala, Iraq, perhaps the most important Shī'ite shrine of all.

4. ***'Alī*** *Zayn al-Ābidīn* (d. *94*/712) buried in Medina. Shī'ites believe that his mother was a daughter of the last Persian King of the Sassanid dynasty. Thus his descendants, the subsequent Imāms, would perpetuate the royal blood of the Persian pre-Islamic dynasties. (This is, however, in all likelihood a legend, This putative daughter of Yazdagird, "Shahrbanu", has been identified by Mary Boyce as a cultic name for Anahid, or Anahita, a Zoroastrian divinity of particular importance under the Sassanids who represents an incorporation into Zoroastrianism of the Babylonian goddess Ishtar. Such legendary geneologies were common among the Persian royal houses as virtually obligatory supports for claims to legitimacy.)

5. *Muḥammad al-Bāqir* (d. *113*/731) buried in Medina. A faction recognized his more active brother Zayd as Imām, giving rise to another branch of Shī'ites, the Zaydīs, known as "Fivers".

6. *Ja'far aṣ-Ṣādiq* (d. *148*/765) buried in Medina. Famous as a scholar, teacher of religion, and fountainhead of hermetic sciences, he is credited with originating the Shī'ite school of law, and many sayings which shape Shī'ite doctrine are attributed to him. Some Shī'ites believe that he designated his eldest son Ismā'īl to succeed him as Imām, then revoked the designation in favor of Mūsā-l-Kāẓim, another son. The adherents of Ismā'īl (who predeceased his father) asserted that the Imāmate rested with Ismā'īl's son Muḥammad. From this schism derive the Ismā'īlīs, another Shī'ite sect who are one of a number of groups comprising the historical "Seveners", and who gave rise to the Fāṭimids and the Assassins. This divergence went deeper than the question of the identity of the Imāms, however; its roots lie in the radically different religious doctrine at the center of Ismā'īlīsm.

7. *Mūsā-l-Kāẓim* (d. *203*/818) buried at the great shrine of the *Kāẓimayn* in Baghdad.

8. *'Alī ar-Riḍā* (also called *'Alī Reza*; d. *203*/818). The 'Abbāsid Caliph al-Ma'mūn named him as his successor to the Caliphate, but the Imām died, while traveling, in the village of Nagaun near Ṭūṣ in Iran, and was buried near the tomb of the famous Caliph Hārūn ar-Rashīd, father of al-Ma'mūn. The town is now called "Mashhad" (which means "place of martyrdom" and is technically the name of all the shrines of the Imāms, all being considered "martyrs", or indeed a kind of sacrificial victim who purifies the people). This, the only tomb of an Imām within the borders of modern Iran, is perhaps second only to Kerbala and Najaf as a Shī'ite holy place.

9. *Muḥammad at-Taqī* ("the Pious") *al-Jawād* (d. *220*/835) buried at the *Kazimayn* in Baghdad.

10. *'Alī an-Naqī* ("the Pure"; d. *254*/868 at the age of forty-one), buried in Samarra', Iraq, a garrison city where he was kept under surveillance by the Caliphs. *'Askarī* ("of the army") is one of his epithets.

11. *Ḥasan al-'Askarī* (d. *260*/873 at the age of twenty-eight) also buried in Samarra', where, like his father, he was kept under surveillance. According to the *'Aqā'id ash-Shī'ah*, he had no legal wife but, according to Shī'ite tradition, he had a son by a concubine named Narjis Khatun, whom Shī'ite tradition calls granddaughter of a Byzantine Emperor. She was captured while on a journey, sold into slavery, and destined for the household of the Imām.

12. *Muḥammad*, called *al-Mahdī-l-Muntaẓar* ("the awaited Mahdī"), and *al-Qā'im* (the permanent Imām until the end of time) said to be born, according to Shaykh al-Mufīd, on the 15th of Sha'bān, a festival known as the "night of forgiveness" (which exists independently of this event) in *255*/869. He is said to have disappeared from the world in what is called the "lesser occultation" (*al-ghaybah as-sughrā*), upon his father's death in *260*/873. During the "lesser occultation" the wishes of this Imām were represented in the world by four representatives. In 329/940, at the death of the fourth representative, who did not name a successor, the "greater occultation" (*al-ghaybah al-kubrā*) began, during which no one has been in communion with the Imām. He is considered to be alive in the unseen, the "*Hidden Imām*" who is expected to return as the *Mahdī*.

This twelfth Imām is called the "Master of the Age" (*ṣāḥib az-zamān*). Shī'ites believe that at the age of four, when his father died (*260*/873), he disappeared into the cellar (*sardib*) of the family house in Samarra'. Until *329*/940 he was represented in the world by four consecutive intermediaries called *wakils*. The first was 'Uthmān ibn Sa'īd, the secretary of the father, Ḥasan al-'Askari, who had often taken charge of the affairs of the eleventh Imām (who was probably of poor health and died at the age of twenty-eight). Together with the women of the household, this representative supplied information about the twelfth Imām, describing his appearance, etc. The fourth and last *wakīl* declined to name a successor, but said on his deathbed: "The matter now rests with God".

Adherents, however, continued to believe in the existence of a successor to the eleventh Imām, and thus the period of the "lesser occultation" ushered in the period of "greater occultation" which continues today. The twelfth Imām is considered to be alive, and will return (the *raj'ah*) as the *Mahdī*, and so is called the "awaited *Mahdī*" (*al-Mahdī-l-muntaẓar*). (The appearance of a leader called the *Mahdī*, or "Guided One", before the end of the world is mentioned in Ḥadīth, but *not* in the canonical collections, and historically the idea appears to be of Shī'ite origin. Nevertheless, many Sunnī Muslims today share this idea; it is the identification of the *Mahdī* as the twelfth Imām which is Shī'ite.) Shī'ites believe that the twelfth, or Hidden Imām", hears prayers and intercedes in the affairs of this world. (*See* HIDDEN IMĀM; MAHDĪ.)

Originally, Shī'ism was largely a political movement. The Umayyad dynasty imposed a system of Arab dominance in which conquered peoples, in accepting Islam, were adopted into Arab tribes as inferior clients (*mawlā*, plural *mawālī*) dependent upon an Arab protector. This was put to an end by the Caliph 'Umar ibn 'Abd al-'Azīz (d. *101*/720), who also ended the execration of 'Alī from the pulpits which had been common since the time of Mu'āwiyah. But this, and Umayyad oppression, had sparked continuous insurrection. Revolts among the Christian populations of Syria were rare, but frequent among converted populations in Iraq and Persia. Rebellions seeking redress against Umayyad oppression made descendants of 'Alī, among them also Muḥammad ibn Ḥanafiyyah, a son of 'Alī by another wife, popular rallying points. Although all political movements, in this climate of expectation of imminent reform and millenial fulfillment, had something religious about them, early Shī'ism amounted broadly to political resistance, as is shown by the Shī'ism of the Buyids (Buwayhids), Daylami or Azeri Turks, and by the surviving Shī'ism of the Zaydīs. It was the emergence of the Seveners – a contemporary variant of ancient dualism that penetrated Islam in the middle of the second *Hijri* century in order to escape persecution and to gain ascendancy – that introduced the notion of "Divine leaders" into the body of Islam. It could well be that this, coinciding with the political Shī'ism of the time, produced a hybrid which became Twelve-Imām Shī'ism. Certainly, it is Ja'far aṣ-Ṣādiq, head of the Alid clan, eminent scholar and religious authority, who is made to be the spokesman of the doctrine of the Imāmate, and it is in his time that the Seveners broke upon the scene. (*See* SEVENERS.)

After Ja'far aṣ-Ṣādiq, these aspirations and expectations took an increasingly supernatural turn. Personal salvation became a matter of "knowing the Imām of the age" and the Imāms became quasi-messianic redeemers, destined by God to be His indispensable instruments in the world. This phase coincides with the rise of the Sevener movement. Thereafter, there are the "pre-Sevener" Zaydīs, who stuck to their conception of the Imām as being, above all, a political leader; the Seveners, for whom the Imām is absolutized as a Divine hypostasis; and the "post-Sevener" Twelve-Imām Shī'ites, who lie somewhere between the two.

The next phase in Twelve-Imām Shī'ism was the development of speculative theology during the rule of the Buyids from *320*/932-*454*/1062 which codified the doctrine of the Imāmate. These pro-Shī'ite Daylamīs controlled the 'Abbāsid Caliphs and the Empire and permitted the open expression of Shī'ite thought and literature, which proliferated. It was also under the Buyid Mu'izz ad-Dawlah in *351*/962 that the Shī'ite celebration of the 'Īd al-Ghadīr and the formal public mourning for the death of Ḥusayn on the 10th of Muḥarram were instituted. Imāmate doctrine was thus complete.

The final phase took place when the Safavid dynasty came to power in Persia at the beginning of the 10th/16th century, claiming to be related to the Imāms. They exploited the Shī'ite complex of persecution, of being surrounded by "enemies", that is to say, by Sunnīs, on all sides, and they turned the anger generated by the displacement of the rightful ruler, the Imām, to the furthering of their dynastic interests. After gaining political control, they promoted Shī'ism from a minority sect to being the state religion in Persia.

The doctrines of Shī'ism are not the same for all Shī'ite groups, not even within the groups themselves. Twelve-Imām Shī'ism, having been the state religion in Persia for five hundred years, has developed the greatest homogeneity and the largest corpus of established dogma. Nevertheless, a wide variety of beliefs and interpretations of the accepted doctrine exists among the various social and intellectual levels of Shī'ism. Even between *Mujtahids*, or religious leaders within Twelve-Imām Shī'ism, there are considerable divergences. Moreover, all the doctrines have been greatly modified over the years, although an appearance of uniformity has been contrived through the retroactive realignment and adjustment of Shī'ite theory. In the last two hundred years, with the victory in Iran of the Uṣūlī school, which not only allows the leading authorities to exercise original judgements in theology and law, but makes it necessary that someone should do so, a process of accelerated change in Shī'ite doctrine has been set in motion. This process is still active, and recent changes in depth that have overtaken Iranian Shī'ism, are today widening the gap with Sunnī Islam; in the early part of this century, this gap had seemed to be disappearing. (*See* AKHBARĪS; USŪLĪS.)

Shī'ite theology includes a doctrine known as the five supports: these are Divine Unity (*tawḥīd*), prophecy (*nubuwwah*), resurrection of the soul and body at the Judgment (*ma'ād*), the Imāmate (*imāmah*), and justice (*'adl*). The first three are found in Sunnī Islam, albeit with some differences of emphasis and meaning; the Imāmate, however, is the essence of Shī'ism, and the last, justice, is an inheritance from the Mu'tazilites, or rationalists, whose system is in many ways perpetuated in Shī'ite theology, its brittle and reductive aspects being compensated for by the mystical doctrine of the Imām. By the term justice, what is meant is a reciprocity between man and God; God is *obliged* to react in certain ways to man's acts. What it means in effect is that man's actions are also absolute or, in effect, divine. This caused the greatest objection on the part of the Sunnis, who said in response that God does what he wants, and does not carry out the bidding of man; God does not depend upon man, as many Gnostics hold.

As regards rituals, the differences between Zaydīs, Twelve-Imām Shī'ites, and Sunnīs are slight in practice when it comes to such matters as the prayers. All Shī'ite sects naturally have their own schools of law; the Twelve-Imām school is called the *Ja'farī* after Ja'far aṣ-Ṣādiq. (It is interesting to note that both Mālik Ibn Anas and Abū Ḥanīfah studied with Ja'far aṣ-Ṣādiq, but came away without any trace of Shī'ite doctrine: both went on to found two of the four Sunnī schools of law.)

Twelve-Imām Shī'ite practice differs from the Sunnī in such small points as adding a few lines to the call to prayer (*adhān*), notably *'Aliyyu waliy yu-Llāh* ("'Alī is the friend [that is, Saint] of God") added under the Safavids. They also add extra utterances of *Allāhu Akbar* to the funeral prayer. During the pilgrimage they use only open-roofed buses especially made for them, whereas Sunnīs use vehicles which can be either open or closed. Shī'ites systematically combine the two afternoon prayers and two evening prayers together as the Sunnīs also do, but only occasionally. They do not accept, as do the Sunnīs, that it suffices to wipe over the covering of the feet (*masaḥ 'alā khuffayn*) during the ablution. They permit the consumption of meat not slaughtered by Muslims, which Sunnīs admit only under reserve of necessity. More important differences are that the Shī'ites, unlike the Sunnīs, accept temporary marriage (*mut'ah*), and the doctrine that God changes his decisions (*badā'*); this was put to use by certain early Shī'ite sects, and it survives in greatly attenuated and transposed form in Twelve-Imām Shī'ism. Shī'ites deny the efficacy of prayers led by a morally unworthy prayer leader, whereas Sunnīs make a distinction between the function and the person, and accept a prayer as valid regardless of the character of the prayer leader, provided that the prayer is technically in order. Shī'ites also entertain the doctrine of a "cycle of sanctity", a series of saints which begins with 'Alī and runs to the Day of Judgement; the Sunnīs too have Saints (except for such groups as Wahhābīs), but no such doctrine, which is clearly a reflection of the cycle of prophecy. For both Sunnīs and Shī'ites the "cycle of prophecy" has been closed by the Prophet, who is the "Seal of Prophets". Because Shī'ite theology is in many ways a prolongation of Mu'tazilite rationalism, the Shī'ites deny both the uncreatedness of the Koran and the "beatific vision". (*See* BEATIFIC VISION.)

The greatest single difference, however, between the two resides in the emotional, messianic climate of Shī'ism. Sunnīs find Shī'ism's vilification of the greatly venerated first three Caliphs repellant; and, indeed, the political theories resulting from the conception of the Imāmate as the source of all temporal and spiritual authority, and of the Imām as a kind of "priest-king", have not found sympathy in the Muslim world at large.

For centuries, Umayyad and 'Abbāsid rulers were hostile to the Shī'ite minority, who posed a permanent political threat. It was to protect themselves from this hostility that Shī'ites resorted to the deliberate dissimulation (a characteristic of Dualisms) called *taqiyyah*, and pretended to be Sunnī, which, by force of practice, many became.

From the Sunnī point of view, Shī'ites are Muslims because their doctrines coincide for the most part with orthodox Islam; the Shī'ite belief in the mystic role of the Imāms, while deplorable, does not put them beyond the pale. For most of the 20th century, therefore, differences between Sunnī and Shī'ite were tending to be overlooked, and, in fact, forgotten; but this tendency has now been reversed with the growth of Islamic militancy.

For centuries the absence of the Imām caused tension in Shī'ism, since he is indispensable in all domains; for example, some held that the Friday prayers must be suspended until his return. This tension ultimately produced such movements as the Shaykhīs and the Babīs, who claimed to represent the Hidden Imām. The absence of the Imām continues to perturb Iranian society even now, for it is understood – and from Safavid times this has been official, and even written into recent constitutions – that the only legitimate ruler is the twelfth Imām, whose return is awaited. It was for this reason that the Shah paid a symbolic rent for his palaces, which he was considered to be holding in trust until the return of the Imām. Anyone who rules in the climate of Shī'ism is necessarily held to be a usurper. In the Sunnī world the religious authorities have often been controlled by the political; but in Iran the Mullas have usually maintained a sharply independent, not to say occasionally hostile, attitude towards the throne.

In the 1920s the Shah Reza Pahlevi tried to put down the power of the religious leaders, thus ending the centuries-old policy of previous dynasties which had sought warily to maintain a cordial relationship with them. In the past, this had been done as if the religious authorities were a sovereign entity, so that marriages had even been arranged to cement or create bonds between the royal and religious spheres.

Unlike the Sunnī world, where no allegiance to a religious authority is required other than accepting the procedures of a school of law, Shī'ites must in principle adhere personally to a superior authority called a *Mujtahid.* The *Mujtahids*, the most important of whom are called *Ayatollahs*, not only decide religious matters for their followers, but also control considerable sums of money, because they collect a special tax called the *khums* (a "fifth"), which was, during the Prophet's life, his share of the spoils of war, held by him in effect for the public treasury. The *Mujtahids* collect this tax from their followers on behalf of the Hidden Imām. By their unique authority to make religious decisions, their control of sometimes vast sums of money, and their influence on the *bāzārī* sector of the economy, the traditional, small, shopkeepers, the *Mujtahids* or eminent Mullas wield a power that the Sunnī *'ulamā'* normally never have. (*See* AYATOLLAH.)

The question of religious authority and Dualism/Non-Dualism is at the root of Shī'ism. The custom of the Arabs of the North Arabian desert to simply elect a successor to the Prophet, was unthinkable even to many Arabs of South Arabian origin; and it was, above all, unthinkable to the Persians, with their traditions of priest-kings. Such a matter could not be left to human choice but had to be determined by a Divine decision; moreover, the Divinely designated leader could not be other than Divinely empowered. To this the martyrdom of Ḥusayn added the aspect of a passion. This drama of suffering and injustice appealed irresistibly to the Persians, a proud people with an ancient culture vastly superior to that of the Arabs, yet humiliated by defeat at their hands. Not only were they conquered and compelled to undergo centuries of foreign domination; but their national religion was replaced, by conquest as much as by conversion, and by a revelation from outside their traditional past. It was above all this nostalgia for the Gnostic religions, centered upon God in human form and upon the principle of sacrifice, that led them to exalt the person of 'Alī, whom they called the *haydar* (the "lion") and *shāh-i wilāyat* (the "King of Sanctity"). In 'Alī and his descendants, through the doctrine of the Imāms, they recreated the Divine, redeeming, solar heroes that the austere religion of the desert denied them. *See also*: AFSHARIDS; AKHBARĪS; AHL al-BAYT; 'ALĪ IBN ABĪ ṬALIB; 'ĀSHŪRĀ'; AYATOLLAH; BĀB; BIHBAHĀNĪ; GHADĪR KHUMM; ḤASAN; ḤILLĪ, 'ALLAMĀ; ḤUSAYN; HIDDEN IMĀM; IBN BABAWAYH; 'ĪD al-GHADĪR; IMĀM; IMĀMZĀDAH; IRAN; ISMĀ'ĪLĪS; al-KULAYNĪ; MAHDĪ; MAJLISĪ; MASHHAD; METAWILA; MĪR DĀMĀD; MĪR FENDERESKĪ; al-MUFĪD, MULLĀ; MULLĀ ṢADRĀ; MUJTAHID; MARJĀ at-TAQLĪD; MUTĀH; NAṢṢ; NAW ROZ; NŪR MUḤAMMADĪ; PAHLAVI; PAIGHAMBAR; QUMM; RAWḌA KHĀNĪ; SAQĪFAH; SEVENERS; SHAYKHĪS; TAQIYYAH; at-ṬŪSĪ, MUḤAMMAD; UṢŪLĪS; ZAYNAB bint 'ALĪ; ZAYDĪS.

Shirk (lit. "association"). This is the fundamental error at the root of all sin or transgression. It is the "association" of something with God, other than God Himself. God is the Absolute. This means that He is Complete, He is Totality, He is Reality. Nothing can be added to Him, and nothing can be taken away. He is All-Possibility. He is One and Indivisible.

To set anything alongside God as Reality is to commit the sin – the error that engages our consciousness and our being – of "association", which is the *only* sin that God cannot forgive, because it denies Himself, and prevents forgiveness:

> God forgives not that aught should be with Him
> associated; less than that He forgives
> to whomsoever he will. Whoso associates
> with God anything, has gone astray
> into far error. (4:116)

The sin of *shirk* ("association") is a name for paganism; pagans are called "the associators" (*mushrikūn*). But *shirk* is the fundamental state of being in revolt against God, irrespective of any professed belief in other gods. It is also atheism, or the putting of nothingness in the place of God. *Shirk* is the opposite of surrender to God, which is acceptance and recognition of His Reality: knowledge, or Islam. Because Islam is knowledge, it is initiated by the act of recognition: the *shahādah*. The *shahādah* is perceiving and declaring that "there is no god but God". *See* KUFR; SHAHĀDAH.

Shu'ayb. One of the Prophets mentioned in the Koran whose mission took place in the interval between Abraham and the Prophet. He was sent to the people of Midyan, and he has sometimes been thought to be Jethro, the father-in-law of Moses. (7:83-91). *See* PROPHETS.

Shuhūd (verbal noun of the verb *shahida*, "to witness", "be witness", "observe", "experience"). This can mean simply consciousness or refer to the transpersonal Self that is ultimately the only Doer and the only Witness. This corresponds exactly to the Hindu notion of God as *kartr* ("doer") and *bhoktr* ("witnesser" or "enjoyer"). It is particularly in this sense that the word was developed by the Sufi al-Junayd (d. *298*/910) in his theory of the one actor: "everything that you see is the Act of One". The Koran says: "And God sufficeth as Witness (48:28). *Shuhūd* is thus a complement to *wujūd* ("being").

Shu'ūbiyyah. (Nationalism, ethnocentricity). From the early Islamic Empire onward, converted peoples, resenting the policy of Arab supremacy, have tended to engage in forms of national and separative self-expression, politically and in the arts, especially literature. In no case, however, has *Shu'ūbiyyah* involved apostasy from Islam.

Shūrā consultation. A consultative assembly elected the third Caliph Uthman. The term now refers to representative democratic institutions rooted in Islamic tradition. The concept was much promoted by Muḥammad Rashīd Riḍā (d. 1935).

Sībawaih, 'Amr ibn 'Uthman (d. *177*/793). A Persian philologist, called "the little apple" a student of Khalil ibn Aḥmad, one of the earliest authorities. He is the author of "The Book" (*al-Kitāb*) which determined the principles of Arabic grammar and remains the most authoritative book on the language. Sībawaih died young, perhaps at 33.

Ṣifah (from the verb *waṣafa*, "to describe", "an attribute" pl. *ṣifāt*). An attribute of objects in the philosophic sense, but also an Attribute of God as distinct from His Essence. In Islamic theology, seven particular Attributes of God are posited thus: Knowledge, Life, Power, Will, Hearing, Seeing, and Speech. Other Divine Attributes are often expressed as a Divine Name, such as the "Magnanimous" (*al-Karīm*); the "Compassionate" (*ar-Raḥīm*); and so forth. Some of the Names are not attributes, but Names of the Essence (*adh-dhāt*). *See* DIVINE NAMES.

Sihr, *see* MAGIC.

Silsilah (from *salsala*, "to concatenate", "interlink"; "a chain", "series"). In Sufism, the initiatic chain of transmission of a Divine *barakah* ("blessing") is called a *silsilah*, *barakah* being a grace or a Divine influence which comes from God alone. A *barakah* was transmitted by the Angel Gabriel to the Prophet, and from him to his Companions. *Silsilahs* consist, therefore, of persons who have subsequently received that pristine *barakah* and from whom it has been passed on. Most recorded *silsilahs* come back to the Prophet through Abū Bakr, 'Umar, and 'Alī jointly, bringing together many collateral strands, particularly in the early stages of each *silsilah*. These chains originate in pacts of allegiance made with the Prophet on three occasions: the pacts of the first and second 'Aqabah and in particular, the "Pact of Felicity" (*Bayat ar-Riḍwān*) which was made in a moment of extreme danger at Ḥudaybiyyah just outside Mecca.

Completeness and authenticity of the initiatic chain is indispensable to the legitimacy of anyone claiming to be a Sufi Shaykh. Ibn Jawzī (d. *597*/1200), the theologian, preacher, and universal scholar who wrote *Talbīs Iblīs* or the *Devil's Delusions*, denounced many deviant practices and notions. Among them he easily demonstrated that several Sufi *silsilahs* were historically impossible; that the persons who were supposed to have passed on the chains could never have met. In answer to this common defect some Sufis claimed that the historically impossible connections were *Uwaysian* links, that is, transmissions across time and space when physical reality interposed itself. (*See* UWAYS al-QARĀNĪ). A more serious deviation than the occasional corruption to which religious organizations are prone, is the fairly common practice which had arisen from early times among many Sufis which was that of systematically reciting *silsilah* prayers. Even when they are presented as merely a pious remembrance of the past masters, these become a regular, weekly ritual invocation of the human beings themselves, something which the Koran categorically prohibits, saying call upon none other than God: "Say: Can ye see yourselves, if the punishment of Allah come upon you or the Hour comes upon you, (calling upon other than Allah?) Do ye then call (for help) to any other than Allah? (Answer that) if ye are truthful." (6:40 and 6:71; 7:37; 10:66; 10:106; 13:14; 17:67; 31:30; 43:86; 72:18). On the other hand, what is often called canonic prayer among the Ismā'īlīs is actually a recitation of the names of the Imāms, or a case of a *silsilah* prayer carried to its limit.

There are two singular *silsilahs* in Sufism, namely that of the Tijāniyyah Order, whose founder, Sidi Aḥmad at-Tijānī, in the last century claimed to have received his initiation directly from the Prophet in a vision, and that of the Khāḍiriyyah order which claims to have its transmission, not from the Prophet, but independently from al-Khiḍr, a figure who represents the incarnation of the universal Intellect. Such a prodigy is hard to justify historically because of the ubiquitous presence of normal chains in the Islamic world; nevertheless, it cannot be dismissed out of hand. Religions recognize such possibilities as valid, and Catholic canon law, for example, admits the efficacy of baptisms received in visions or dreams.

An example of a typical *silsilah* is the following:

Gabriel
Muḥammad
'Alī ibn Abī Ṭālib
al-Ḥasan
Abū Muḥammad Jābir
Sa'īd al-Ghazāwī
Fatḥ as-Su'ūd
Sa'd
Abū Muḥammad Sa'īd
Aḥmad al-Marwānī
Ibrāhīm Baṣrī
Zayn ad-Dīn al-Qazwīnī
Muḥammad Shams ad-Dīn
Muḥammad Tāj ad-Dīn
Nūr ad-Dīn Abū-l-Ḥasan 'Alī
Fakhr ad-Dīn
Tuqay ad-Dīn al-Fuqayyir
'Abd ar-Raḥmān al-'Attār az-Zayyāt
'Abd as-Salām ibn Mashīsh
Abū-l-Ḥasan ash-Shādhilī
Abū-l-'Abbās al-Mursī
Aḥmad ibn 'Aṭā'illāh
Dāwūd al-Bakhīlī
Muḥammad Wafā'
'Alī ibn Wafā'
Yaḥyā al-Qādirī
Aḥmad ibn 'Uqbā-l-Haḍramī
Aḥmad Zarrūq
Ibrāhīm Afahham
'Alī as-Sanhājī ad-Dawwār
'Abd ar-Raḥmān al-Fāsī
Muḥammad ibn 'Abd Allāh
Qāsim al-Khaṣṣāṣī
Aḥmad ibn 'Abd Allāh
al-'Arabī ibn Aḥmad ibn 'Abd Allāh
'Alī al-Jamāl
al-'Arabī ibn Aḥmad ad-Darqāwī
Muḥammad ibn 'Abd al-Qādir
Muḥammad ibn Qaddūr al-Wakīlī
Muḥammad ibn Habīb al-Buzīdī
Aḥmad ibn Muṣṭafā-l-'Alawī (*1286-1353*/1869-1934)

See ḤUDAYBIYYAH; al-KHIḌR; RIḌWĀN; SUFISM.

Sīma. A dark spot on the forehead which develops from touching the head against the ground in prayer. The Koran mentions it: "Their mark is on their faces, the trace of prostration." (48:29). In North Africa it is colloquially called a *sfiha*; in Egypt as *zbībah aṣ-ṣalāt*.

Sin (Ar. *dhanb*, pl. *dhunūb*; or *khaṭi'ah*, pl. *khaṭāyā*; or *ithm*, pl. *athmām*). In Islam sin is divided into two categories. The first is that of *dhanb*, which is a fault or shortcoming, a limitation, an inadvertence, the consequence of which is a sanction rather than a punishment. Sin as *dhanb* is distinguished from wilful transgression (*ithm*), which is more serious and clearly incurs punishment rather than sanction. Moreover, since *ithm* engages will and intention to the highest degree, it necessarily contains the aspect of *dhanb* as well, whereas *dhanb* by itself can exclude *ithm*. The term *khaṭi'ah* is used in practice indiscriminately for both concepts of sin.

The concept of original sin does not exist in Islam. There is a Fall, the expulsion from Paradise of Adam, but not an inherent guilt which entails punishment or requires redemption. Indeed, the responsibility for the Fall is not Adam's; rather, it is Satan's. Adam's part in it is *dhanb* ("fault"), and its consequence is the earthly exile of Adam and his descendants, but not an infirmity which condemns them to a state of "original sin". The restoration of the damage of the Fall is anticipated by the acceptance of the *shahādah*, and accomplished by its complete realization.

The Islamic doctrine of the "sinlessness (*iṣmah*) of the Prophets" excludes the possibility that sin as *ithm* should have existed in the acts of Adam, although *dhanb* was possible, and occurred. It follows that, in Islam, sin as transgression did not enter the world until Cain killed Abel. The Shī'ites have a similar doctrine which they apply to their Imāms.

The remedy for *dhanb* is to remove it, and for *ithm* to repent and seek God's forgiveness. The interpretation of the meaning of sin in early Islam was the principal doctrinal point which occasioned the schism of the Khārijites; and it was reactions within Islam to this schism, in particular that of the "Pietists" (Murji'ites), which gave impetus to the development of orthodox theology. The problem led to the enunciation of *al-Fiqh al-Akbar* by Abū Ḥanīfah, which says: "We do not consider anyone to be an infidel on account of sin; nor do we deny his faith." The Murji'ites developed the concept of "small" (*saghā'ir*) and "great" (*kabā'ir*) sins which found its place in theology. This is similar to the Christian division into "sins unto death" and sins not unto death.

The creed of al-Ash'arī says:

> They [Muslims] do not brand any Muslim an Unbeliever for any grave sin he may commit, for fornication or theft or any such grave sin; but hold that such men are Believers inasmuch as they have Faith, grievous though their sins may be. Islam is testifying that there is no god but God and that Muḥammad is God's Apostle, in accordance with Tradition [Sunnah]; and Islam, they hold, is not the same thing as Faith.
> They confess that God changes the hearts of men. They confess the intercession of God's Apostle, and believe that it is for the grave sinners of his people and against the Punishment of the Tomb.

Sinful thoughts do not constitute sin if they are not put into action, and God can forgive any sin except *kufr* (disbelief and ingratitude), for which there is nevertheless the remedy of *tawbah* (turning to the Truth of God). It says in the *Ḥikam* of Ibn 'Aṭa' Allāh:

> Sometimes He opens the door of obedience for you but not the door of acceptance; or sometimes He condemns you to sin, and it turns out to be a cause of arriving at Him. There is no minor sin when His justice confronts you; there is no major sin when His grace confronts you.

And the Prophet said of God (in a *Ḥadīth Qudsī*):

> So long as you call upon Me and hope in Me, I forgive you all that originates from you: and I will not heed, O son of man, should your sins reach the horizon of the heavens, and then you asked My pardon and I would pardon you.

Sīnān (*895-996*/1488-1587). The renowned Turkish architect who built some of the most famous mosques in Istanbul and Turkey. Among these, one of the most successful is the Selimiye Mosque of Edirne which, like other Turkish mosques, takes the Hagiah Sofia as its model, with a central dome and surrounding smaller ones. Sīnān, however, makes of the model a more perfectly geometric form, less redolent of religious mystery, but more reposed. In addition to mosques in Istanbul, he also rebuilt the Grand Mosque of Mecca. (This mosque was again rebuilt in the 1960s when, most fortunately, King Faysal ordered that Sīnān's structure be preserved and the new mosque built around it.)

Sīnān was of Christian origin, one of the *devshirme* (Balkan "boy-levy") who had been converted to Islam and inducted into the Janissary corps. As a soldier he took part in the campaigns of Belgrade, Rhodes, and Mohacs, and in the siege of Vienna he was chief of the Corps of Engineers. He then went to Baghdad, and when he returned to Istanbul, he entered the service of the palace as chief architect.

His output was enormous: seventy-five large and forty-nine small mosques, forty-nine madrasahs, seven Koranic schools, seventeen public kitchens, three hospitals, seven viaducts, seven bridges, twenty-seven palaces, eighteen caravanserais, five treasure houses, thirty-one baths, and eighteen burial chapels. After building the Suleymaniyye Mosque, Sinan said to the Sultan: "I have built for thee, O Emperor, a mosque which will remain on the face of the earth till the day of judgement: and when Hallaj Mansur comes, and rends Mount Demavend from its foundation, he will play at tennis with it and with the cupola of this mosque..."

Sincerity, *see* IKHLĀṢ.

Sinf. A tradesman's guild.

Sinkiang, *see* XINJIANG.

Sinlessness, *see* 'IṢMAH.

al-Sirhindī, Aḥmad al-Farūqī (d. *1034*/1625). Indian religious scholar, known as *Mujaddid al-Alf ath-Thānī* ("The Renewer of the Second Millenium"). Sirhindī was very critical of the mystical school known as *wahdat al-wujūd.* He said "the mental condition of these so-called Sufis of the last type... is artificially produced (*maj'ul ast*), they cannot be regarded as possessed of a spiritual state (*ḥal*); they do not even know what 'the station of the heart' (*maqam-i-qalb*) is...nor do they possess reasoned knowledge (*'ilm*). It is these who misinterpret the genuine experiences of the real sufis (*tawḥid-i shuhūd*) into a popular form of the unity of Being (*tawhid-i wujūdi*) and lead people away from the Sharī'ah that is, the moral law into licentious perfidy (*ilhad-i zandaqah*)."

"Since the great Shaykh Muhy al-Din has overlooked the real evil, badness and corruption of the Essences of the contingents, he has regarded them as 'Ideas of the Mind of God the Exalted'. These ideas for him, have cast a reflection in the mirror of the Being of God – besides Whom, according to the Shaykh, nothing exists externally – and have acquired an external shadow being (*namūd*). And (since) he does not consider these Ideas to be anything except the Names and Attributes of the Necessary Being, he inevitably declares the doctrine of the Unity of Being, and affirms the identity of the contingent with the Necessary Being. Holding that evil and badness are relative, and denying that there is an absolute evil or pure badness and says that there is nothing evil in itself."
See IBN ARABĪ.

as-Sirr (lit. "secret"). The spiritual center of one's being, the *'aql* ("intellect"), whose symbolic location is the heart. It is in this center that the mystics speak of there being a "union" (*ittiḥād*) with God.

Slametan (from Ar. *salāmah*, "well-being", "security", "integrity"). A religious ceremony of Islam as practiced in Indonesia. It represents an adaptation of Islam to the national religious ethos.

A feast is prepared to greet the ancestors; the word *salāmah* becomes in the Indonesian languages *selamat* ("greetings!"). The *shahādah* is recited in the course of the ceremony, as is the *fatihah.* Afterwards, the meal is eaten by those present. The ceremony is carried out at home at regular intervals, as often as once a week. This practice is Indonesian in origin and central to religious practice in that country. The *slametan* is observed even by those Muslims who do not regularly attend prayers in a mosque.

Slavery. This is an institution which, as elsewhere in the ancient world, Islam took for granted both at the time of the Koran's revelation and subsequently. However, Islam mitigated slavery by recommending kindness and the freeing of slaves as acts of great merit, and declaring that their mistreatment would cause damnation, at the same time as insisting that pagan slaves be taught Islam, and stipulating that free Muslims or protected populations could not be pressed into slavery. Legally, slaves could only be obtained as captives of war or as the progeny of existing slaves.

In the early years of the Prophet's mission in Mecca, Abū Bakr spent his wealth in ransoming slaves who had accepted Islam and were persecuted for it by their masters. The acceptance of Islam by a slave does not, however, entitle him to freedom. Freedom can be bought through agreement with the master. The child born of a slave and a master is free (and the slave mother is free after the death of the master). Many rulers in the Islamic world were sons of such unions.

The corps of slave bodyguards such as the Mamlūks and Janissaries often used their position to seize power. The slaves who were not a military force were usually treated as members of the household and sometimes given a measure of autonomy. It even happened that slaves were given a position at court, and slaves in notable households frequently had more status than they might have had as free men. Sometimes rulers of one country were the slave vassals of another ruler.

At the present time slavery has been prohibited in most countries. In Saudi Arabia, where the maintenance of *sharī'ah* law in its totality militates against the prohibition of an institution recognized in the Koran as legal, the statute of slavery was eliminated by King Faysal, who purchased and freed the existing slaves and prohibited the importation of new ones.

"Sleeping Foetus" (Ar. *ar-rāqid*). The idea that the period of human gestation may extend for a maximum of two years in the Ḥanafī school of law, and five, or even seven, years in the Mālikī. The "sleeping foetus" is a legal fiction designed to avoid the application of punishments which the illegitimacy of a child would entail. In some countries this has become a folk belief taken as literally true.

Similarly, if a case is brought to court of an unwed mother who has never been married, and thus cannot plead the "sleeping foetus", the legal stratagem which has become the acceptable solution is to determine that the woman had visited a public bath around the time of conception. As public baths normally alternate between women's days and men's days, upon learning that the woman visited the bath right after the men's hours, the Judge concludes that accidentally she came in contact with the sperm of conception by sitting on a bench where a man had sat only a short time before. *See* ḤĪLAH.

Sokoto Caliphate. A kingdom founded in northern Nigeria around *1225*/1809 by Usumanu dan Fodio. In *1217*/1802, Usumanu dan Fodio (Fodio means *faqīh*, "religious teacher") went on pilgrimage to Mecca. He returned inspired by Wahhābī ideas and began preaching among his people, the Fulanis (also called Fulbe and Peulh). He declared holy war on the pagan Hausa, and succeeded in conquering a growing territory reaching to Niger and Chad. Upon his death in *1232*/1816 he was succeeded as ruler by his sons Muḥammadu Bello and 'Abd Allāh. The Sokoto state grew weaker with time, diminished by opposition to its unpopular stringent moral reforms regarding music and dancing, and suffered attrition at the hands of diverse groups including the Saharan Tuareg. In *1322*/1904 the British occupied Sokoto.

Solomon (Ar. *Sulaymān*). A Prophet held in Islam, and its sister religions, to be the paragon of wisdom, the author of the saying: "the beginning of wisdom is the fear of God" (*ra's al-ḥikmah makhāfat Allāh*). His wisdom is also knowledge of the unseen, and the traditional sciences of cosmology. He could speak the "language of the birds" (*manṭiq aṭ-ṭā'ir*), and had powers over the subtle world. He is traditionally associated with stories of the marvelous.

Solomon is also the epitome of the mystical love of women, as in the Old Testament's "Song of Songs". In Islam, this mystical love is expressed in the story of Bilqīs, Queen of Sabā' (Sheba) who was converted from paganism through being brought to see the difference between illusion and the One Reality, as in the *shahādah*: "there is no God but God", and thus became his consort. When she entered the palace she had taken the polished floor to be water, and lifted her skirt; then realizing her error, and opting, as it were, for reality, she "surrendered to God". In traditional accounts, her father is a *jinn* ("genie"), which is a way of indicating that she incarnated a supernatural nature and was, so to speak, an expression of cosmic infinitude which complemented Solomon, as Wisdom or Self, in the same way that Māyā complements Ātmā.

The chronicles of Solomon tell of prodigies: he could command the *jinn* who, when he set them to build the Temple for him, went on toiling even after his death, tricked because they saw his petrified body, or a statue, standing in the courtyard and seemingly alive. Then the staff on which the body was propped up collapsed because a worm had eaten through it, giving away Solomon's last ruse. At the command of Solomon the throne of Bilqīs was brought miraculously and instantly from the Yemen and placed in his palace in Jerusalem. Ibn 'Arabī explains this in the *Fuṣūṣ al-Ḥikam* by reference to the traditional theory of creation as an instantaneous and continuous act, not a process. At one moment the throne was being created in Bilqīs' palace in Sabā', and the next its creation was continued in Solomon's; the Jinn who brought the throne had done no more than move the site of its creation, but not the object itself.

For a month Solomon lost the graces of heaven, his kingdom and his powers – signified in the loss of his signet ring – because of idolatry in his palace: one of his wives had returned to the worship of her old idols. As a sanction, a "mere body" (one of Solomon's servants) was set upon his throne, while Solomon himself was forced to wander unknown in Jerusalem and to beg for his bread. In the Koranic account, the fault of his wife was "unknown" to him, that is, the fault did not incur his substance and responsibility, but he had committed a *dhanb* ("fault", *see* SIN), for which he underwent a sanction. When Solomon realized what had happened, he sought forgiveness; his signet ring was miraculously restored to him and with it his sovereignty and his dominion over the spirit world (38:35-36).

The "Seal of Solomon", the six pointed star, has been a frequent motif used on coins in the Islamic world, and as decoration.

Somalia. Republic. Population: 9,639,151. The country is almost completely Muslim. Some of the Muslims are Zaydī Shī'ites, mostly Arabs from the Yemen. Otherwise the Somalis are Sunnīs of the Shafi'ī school of law. Islam was established in Somalia from the first century of the Hijrah through trade contacts. Almost all Somalis belong to a Sufi brotherhood (*tariqah*). The major *ṭuruq* are the Qādiriyyah, Ṣāliḥiyyah, and Rifā'iyyah. Somalia is noted for possessing an oral literary tradition, memorized and not recorded, of great richness.

"Son of the Moment", *see* IBN al-WAQT.

Soul, *see* NAFS; RŪḤ.

Spiritual axis, *see* QUṬB.

Station, *see* MAQĀM.

Subḥah, *see* ROSARY.

Sublime Porte (a French rendering of the name *Bāb-i Alī*, "the high gate"). The designation of the Grand Vizierate of the Ottoman Turkish Government and hence of the Turkish government as a whole.

Subud. A sect founded originally in Java by an Indonesian named Muhammad (called Bapak, or "father") Subuh, but fostered in the West by followers of Gurdjieff in Britain and American where the sect has adherents. The name Subud is said to be a composite word from three Sanskrit terms: *Sulisa* ("right living"), *Bodhi* ("enlightenment"), and *Dharma* ("the cosmic norm"). Its central ritual is a psychic experience called *latihan* (Malay for "an exercise" or "training") which manifests itself outwardly as moans, crying, laughter, dancing and various involuntary body movements. The *latihan* is experienced in groups at regular meetings.

Subud has nothing to do with Islam although it is often associated with it because of its origin in a Muslim country where it has some practitioners, the fact that adherents in the west sometimes took Muslim names, and that some Muslims were attracted to it, thinking it was an offshoot of Sufism.

In fact, the founder claimed to have attained to a spiritual realization without following any master, Sufi or otherwise, and affirmed that various masters had told him so, naming in particular a Naqshbandi Shaikh 'Abd ar-Raḥman. Subuh was born in 1901; in 1925 he had the experience of a ball of light descending upon him; by 1933 he was proselytizing in Java. In 1956 he was invited to the Gurdjieffian center at Coombe Springs in England, which had been founded by J.G. Bennett, in the hope and expectation on the part of certain Gurdjieffians that he represented the fulfillment of a prediction by Gurdjieff concerning the future of his school.

In the course of his visit, over four hundred people in one month underwent the experience of *latihan*, (or, in Subud terms "were opened"), one of them being so affected by it that he died on the spot. Many who leave the sect find themselves afflicted by various mental and psychological ailments.

Sudan. Population 31,065,229. 70% of the population are Muslims of the Mālikī rite, although the legal system is very much influenced by Ḥanafī law; the rest are largely Christians of various denominations. There is a Muslim theological university at Ummdurman. Important Sufi *ṭuruq* are the Qādiriyyah, the Anṣār (who are "Mahdists", or the continuation of the Mahdī movement in the Sudan), and a number of Shādhilī *ṭuruq*. The Sanusiyyah Order of Libya also has a following in the Sudan.

aṣ-Ṣuffah, Aṣḥāb, *see* AṢḤAB aṣ-ṢUFFAH.

Sufi, *see* FAQĪR; SUFISM.

Sufism (Ar. *at-taṣawwuf*). The mysticism or esoterism of Islam. The word is commonly thought to come from the Arabic word *ṣūf* ("wool"): rough woolen clothing characterized the early ascetics, who preferred its symbolic simplicity to richer and more sophisticated materials. It could also come from the Greek *sophistēs*, or sophist.

Sufism's doctrines and methods are derived from the Koran and Islamic revelation but their development was influenced by other, ubiquitous mystical teachings. Like exoteric Islam, Sufism freely makes use of paradigms and concepts derived from Greek and even from Hindu sources, and it is not at all strange that the most recent of the great revealed religions should take account of the intellectual developments which preceded it. It is true that philosophies of antiquity, in particular certain Persian schools of thought, played the role of catalyst or "leaven", forcing Muslims to develop the potentials of Islam, and here and there a trace of these foreign influences remain, like the blows of a hammer upon a sword. That it resembles other esoteric doctrines is certainly not accidental, for God is One and man universally aspires to knowledge of God. Sufism is found everywhere in the Islamic world; it is the inner dimension of Islam, from which the efficacy and force of Islam as a religion flow.

The character of Sufism remained the same in the later period, when Sufis spoke the intellectual language of Plato and Aristotle, as it was in the age of its inception, before philosophy was integrated into Islam. As the Koran 2:20 says: "The lightning [revelation, or intellection] well nigh snatches away their sight; whensoever it gives them light, they walk in it, and when the darkness is over them, they halt." The spiritual development of a Ḥasan of Basra (d. *110*/728), at a time when the conceptual structures of Islamic thought were still rudimentary, could be likened to a series of flashes of intuition and realization. Yet if he had somehow encountered a philosophically adept Sufi of later times, such as Ibn 'Arabī (d. *638*/1240), whose dialectic made use of many intellectual bridges, Ḥasan of Basra would have had no difficulty in recognizing in him the very doctrines that had already been enunciated in monolithic and religiously didactic terms.

In the early days, Sufism was not recognized as the inner dimension of Islam, as it is now, but was identified with Islam as such. Indeed, to disparage the weakening of human aspiration after Islam's first efflorescence, Sufis have said: "In the beginning Sufism was a reality without a name, today it is a name without a reality." For the Sufis the great Master, the true Master, is none other than the Prophet himself, who taught the essential doctrines of esoteric Islam to his Companions, who in turn passed them on to succeeding generations. It is from this source that the Sufis trace their inspiration and their teachings. The Companions also transmitted the grace, blessing, or spiritual influence (*barakah*) which the Prophet received from God at the beginning of his mission and which he thereafter conveyed to his disciples through the *bay'at ar-riḍwān* (the "Pact of Felicity"), made at Ḥudaybiyyah (Koran 48:10). The chain of transmission whereby the original pact made with the Prophet is passed on from Shaykh to Shaykh is called a *silsilah*, an initiatic chain. All authentic Sufi orders are linked into one of these chains.

Historically, the Sufis have been grouped into organizations called *ṭawā'if* (sing. *ṭā'ifah*), or *ṭuruq* (sing. *ṭarīqah*, "path"), the latter word being used more commonly in the later period, from the time of the Qādiriyyah order. *Ṭarīqah* is now also a technical term for esoterism itself. *Ṭuruq* are congregations formed around a master, meeting for spiritual sessions (*majālis*), in *zāwiyahs*, *khānaqahs*, or *tekke*, as the meeting places are called in different countries. These spiritual meetings are described in the words attributed to the Prophet: "Whenever men gather together to invoke Allāh, they are surrounded by Angels, the Divine Favor envelopes them, Peace (*as-sakīnah*) descends upon them, and Allāh remembers them in His assembly."

In the beginning of Islamic history all the *silsilahs* that go back to either Abū Bakr or 'Alī are actually intertwined; many of the early Sufis (not yet, of course, so named) made pacts with several of the original Companions, including Anas ibn Mālik, Salmān al-Fārisī and others. In the 2nd century of the Hijrah these chains diverged outwards with the geographic expansion of Islam, and later, the names that succeeded one another, such as Ibn Mashish in Morocco and Imām ash-Shādhilī in Egypt, reflect journeys undertaken across the earth in search of masters whose reputation bespoke their spiritual realization.

'Alī is the great early link in these chains; independently of his role in Shī'ism, he is held by Sufis everywhere to be the fountainhead of esoteric knowledge. Another is Ḥasan of Basra who, lacking the philosophical tools available to later generations, left no corpus of written teaching, although he was widely quoted by others; the universal respect he was accorded and the wide circle of his disciples testify to his having possessed wisdom of a very profound order.

Certain Sufis of the later period such as al-Junayd (d. *297*/910), 'Abd al-Qādir al-Jīlānī (d. *561*/1166), Abū Madyān (d. *594*/1198), and Imām ash-Shādhilī (d. *656*/1258) were all famed throughout the Islamic world during their lifetimes. Imām Shādhilī is noted for an approach to Sufism which is especially intellectual. Some of these Sufis left writings as well as oral teachings, and Sufi doctrines have been described in great depth and detail in the works of Ibn 'Arabī, Jalāl ad-Dīn ar-Rūmī, al-Jīlī, al-Ghazālī, Ibn 'Aṭā' Allāh and many others. A number of Sufis likewise wrote allegories; of which an outstanding example is the *Language of the Birds* (*Mantiq at-Ṭā'ir*) by Farīd ad-Dīn 'Attār, in which the birds (souls) set out on a journey to find their king (God). Above all, it has been characteristic of Sufis to express their spiritual insight in great poetry; Ibn al-Fārid's "Ode to Wine", which likens the imbibing of Divine knowledge to drunken ecstasy, is one example of this.

Sufism is an "inward" path of union, which complements the *sharī'ah*, or "outward" law, namely, exoterism, the formal "clothing" of religion. Sufism is esoterism, the perception of the supraformal essence which is "seen" by the "eye of the heart" (*'ayn al-qalb*). All true belief has the "taste" of Sufism in it, for without it belief would be theoretical knowledge which committed one to nothing and engaged one in nothing. Sufism takes the Islam, and the testimony of faith (*shahādah*), and removes limitations from the understanding of its meaning until the dividing line between "world" (manifestation), and Reality (God), has been "pushed back" to the very limit and nothing but God remains. The Koran calls those who know the essence of things the "possessors of the kernels" (*ūlū-l-albāb*); in turn, the Sufis liken esoteric knowledge to a "kernel" (*lubb*), hidden within a shell. This kernel is the "essence" or "intrinsic truth" (*ḥaqīqah*), which resides at the center of the circle of knowledge and, at the same time, contains the circle itself. Leading to this center from the circumference, which is exoterism, is the radius, the Sufic spiritual path (*ṭarīqah*).

The Persian Sufi Bāyazīd al-Biṣṭāmī said: "This thing we tell of can never be found by seeking, yet only seekers find it." Contrary to notions sometimes encountered in the West, to embark upon the path of Sufism it is absolutely necessary to be a Muslim, for Sufism's methods are inoperative without this religious affiliation, and may even prove destructive to the individual who lacks the protective and normative consecration of the religion of Islam, which is its vehicle. While exoterism is incumbent upon all, for all are called to salvation and to conformity with Divine law, esoterism is a matter of individual vocation. Initiation (*al-bay'ah* or *al-idhn*) is the necessary point of entry from the exoteric, for this transmits a spiritual influence (*barakah*), a grace conveyed by the Angel Gabriel to the Prophet at the time of revelation; initiation plants a seed in the soul; like baptism, it is the beginning of a new life, for the initiation bestowed by a spiritual master (*shaykh*) has a lineage that goes back, through the entire series of spiritual masters, to the Prophet. The master, who is always an orthodox Muslim, must incarnate the truth of the doctrine of which he is the living example; only he who has achieved a realization – in some degree at least – of the Divine Truth can "put in motion the wheel of the doctrine" for an individual seeker. Ultimately, as al-Kalabādhī said: "The Sufis are agreed that the only guide to God is God Himself."

Sufism takes many forms, but it always contains two poles: doctrine and method. Doctrine can be summarized as intellectual discrimination between the Real and the unreal, the basis for this being found essentially in the *shahādah*: "there is no god but God" or "there is no reality but the Reality". Method can be summarized as concentration upon the Real by the "remembrance of God" (*dhikr Allāh*), the invocation of the Divine Name (*dhikr* means "remembrance", "mention", "invocation"). Both doctrine and method must, however, be complemented by perfect surrender to God and the maintenance of an equilibrium through the spiritual regime, which is Islam. Invocation, called in Sanskrit *japa-yoga*, and exemplified in Christianity by the "Jesus Prayer", is the quintessential means of actualizing the Divine Presence and passing from intellectual theory to experience and realization. In Scholastic terms this is a movement from potency to act – in effect to "union" with God (*ittiḥād*) or the realization of the Oneness of God (*tawḥīd*), which is the goal of Sufism. The Koran often underlines the importance of invocation in words such as these: "Remember God standing and sitting" (3:191); "...Those who believe and do good works, and remember God much..." (26:227); and "Surely the Remembrance of God is greatest" (*wa la-dhikru-Llāhi akbar*) (29:45). The principle of reciprocity between God and man is expressed by God's revealed words: "Therefore remember Me; I will remember you" (*fādhkurūnī adhkurkum*) (2:152).

All spiritual method also necessarily involves the practice of the virtues, summarized in the concept of *iḥsān*, the surpassing of self, which a Sacred Ḥadīth defines thus: "Worship God as if you saw Him, for if you do not see him, nevertheless, He sees you." To this, the Sufis add: "And if there were no *you*, you would see", and make the summation of mystical virtue the quality of "spiritual poverty" (*faqr*). By *faqr* they mean emptying the soul of the ego's false "reality" in order to make way for what God wills for the soul. They seek to transform the soul's natural passivity into re-collected wakefulness in the present, mysteriously active as symbolized by the transformation of Moses' hand (*see* IBN al-WAQT). Humility and love of one's neighbor cut at the root of the illusion of the ego and remove those faults within the soul that are obstacles to the Divine Presence. "You will not enter paradise", the Prophet said, "until you love one another." The disciple should live in surroundings and in an ambience that are aesthetically and morally compatible with spiritual interiorization, in the sense that "The Kingdom of God is within you". The need of such supports for the spiritual life can be summed up in the Ḥadīth: "God is beautiful and He loves beauty". Ibn 'Aṭā' Allāh wrote:

> Amongst the attributes of your human nature, draw away from every one that is incompatible with your servanthood, so that you may be responsive to the call of God and near His Presence.

As he also points out, the path is the surpassing of self:

> The source of every disobedience, indifference, and passion is self-satisfaction. The source of every obedience, vigilance, and virtue is dissatisfaction with one's self. It is better for you to keep company with an ignorant man dissatisfied with himself than to keep company with a learned man satisfied with himself. For what knowledge is there in a self-satisfied scholar? And what ignorance is there in an unlearned man dissatisfied with himself?

Sufis divide the path into three movements: *makhāfah* ("the way of fear", or "purification"); *maḥabbah* ("the way of love", or "sacrifice and conformity"); and *ma'rifah* ("the way of knowledge"). Here knowledge is not mere mental knowledge, but identity between the knower and the object of knowing. This is why the Sufi in the highest or final degree is called the "Knower by God" (*'Ārif bi-Llāh*). This supreme degree is beyond temporary spiritual states of soul (sing. *ḥāl*, pl. *aḥwāl*), and even beyond permanent stages of realization (sing. *maqām*, pl. *maqāmāt*). He has reached the end of the path, and is "perfected", or completely divested of ignorance; this corresponds exactly to the Vedantine notion of the *jīvan-mukta*, or one who is "delivered in life", from all duality, alteration, and becoming.

Ma'rifah ("knowledge") is also frequently

translated by the word "gnosis", which is cognate with Sanskrit *jñāna*. An aspect of *ma'rifah* is self-knowledge in the sense of the Ḥadīth: "He who knows his soul, knows his Lord". Besides direct metaphysical knowledge, *ma'rifah* can also encompass spiritual psychology (knowledge of the microcosm), and cosmology (knowledge of the macrocosm); this does not mean empirical science, but the intuitive, traditional science which discerns clearly the supernatural Cause in all effects, and the trace of the Absolute everywhere.

Alchemy, for example, combines an awareness of ultimate causes with a study of effects. The purification of souls and their union with their center is viewed as a cosmological process carried out by analogy on metals. Speaking of this, Jābir ibn Ḥayyān (known in the West as "Geber" (d. *160*/776) said: "It is called by Philosophers, one Stone, although it is extracted from many Bodies or Things." And: "These imperfect Bodies are not reducible to Sanity [purified from chaos] and Perfection, unless the contrary be operated in them; that is, the Manifest be made Occult, and the Occult be made Manifest." These statements echo the Sufi saying: "Our bodies have become our Spirits, and our Spirits have become our bodies", or that, in reality, according to another saying: "trees have their roots in the sky."

In a similar vein, Abū-l-Qāsim al-Irāqī, an alchemist of the 7th/13th century, wrote:

> At the beginning of the operation it [the metal to be transformed, or, analogously, the soul] is a mixture of various things. Then it is placed in coction in a light fire and putrifies; and changes; and goes from state to state until it becomes finally *one nature*.

This is a symbolical view of physical processes, and its purpose, like that of mysticism, is to lead to becoming *one nature*, that is, to union. Thus alchemy, unlike a purely empirical science such as chemistry, was a symbolical science and in reality constituted a spiritual way, parallel to Sufism and sometimes blended with it.

To a greater or lesser degree, all traditional sciences, whatever the civilization, look upon natural phenomena as not merely material, but above all symbolical. Thus the traditional four elements, air, earth, fire, water, are not the physical elements, but *modalities* of existence, modified by the *qualities* of cold, warm, dry, and moist, and themselves contained in the quintessence. When it is understood that traditional science views physical reality as of secondary importance and as being dependent upon a higher and principial reality, it cannot be considered "primitive", for it stands in a category which makes great use of symbolism and is altogether different from modern and material science.

The threefold division of the path into *makhāfah*, *maḥabbah*, and *ma'rifah*, is the equivalent of the Vedantine ternary *karma* ("action"), *bhakti* ("devotion"), and *jñāna* ("knowledge"). And while these are different ways", they are also each phases of the Path present in differing degrees in each of the ways. Moreover, the three ways offer us an insight into the character of the three Semitic religions: Judaism is the way of fear or obedience, Christianity the way of love and sacrifice, and Islam is the way of knowledge, predominantly, although each necessarily contains the other elements.

The Sufi doctrine has been likened to Neoplatonism, to Vedanta, to the mystical theology of Eastern Christianity, and even to Taoism, all of which it clearly resembles. Jahāngīr, the Moghul Emperor, took instruction from a Hindu teacher called Jadrup and said: "His Vedanta is the same as our *taṣawwuf*" ("Sufism"). The famous Sufi Ibrāhīm Ibn Adhām said: "My Master in Spiritual Knowledge was a [Christian] monk called Father Simeon."

The most celebrated expression of Sufi doctrine is "the unity of being" (*waḥdat al-wujūd*), which asserts that everything which exists can only exist because it is an aspect of Divine Reality, hence an aspect of the Divine Unity Itself. This doctrine has erroneously been called "pantheism". In fact it is nothing other than the intellectual consequence of the Koran's declaration that "Everywhere you turn, there is the Face of God" (2:115). *Waḥdat al-wujūd* does see God everywhere, but does *not* reduce God to everything. God remains supremely transcendent; even though everything which arises out of substance, everything which exists resembles Him (*tashbīh*), He resembles nothing but Himself (*tanzīh*).

In recent times more than ever, especially as Islamic modernists make Sufism the scapegoat for the technological and industrial backwardness of the Muslim nations, Sufism has been accused of "unorthodoxy". These accusations arise out of a lack of understanding, for Sufism, as the inner dimension of the religion which carries it, is necessarily completely orthodox; it could not be otherwise, and Sufis are the most fervent of Muslims. This does not mean that there are not, or never have been, deviant manifestations, for that is inevitable; but in itself, Sufism is necessarily orthodox because it exists within and depends upon the framework of exoterism, although it ultimately surpasses it; as such, it is not always understood by purely theological thinkers. But the charges of unorthodoxy were in fact laid to rest by al-Ghazālī (d. *505*/1111), who was at once jurist, theologian, and Sufi. In his person and his writings he bridged the gap between the outer and the inner, for those for whom such a gap had appeared to exist. As Duncan Black MacDonald has written, al-Ghazālī saw that "the light in which they [the Sufis] walk is essentially the same as the light of prophecy." Of his own turning to Sufism al-Ghazālī speaks in *al-Munqidh min aḍ-Ḍalāl*:

> Then I turned my attention to the Way of the Sufis. I knew that it could not be traversed to the end without both doctrine and practice, and that the gist of the doctrine lies in overcoming the appetites of the flesh and getting rid of its evil dispositions and vile qualities, so that the heart may be cleared of all but God; and the means of clearing it is *dhikr Allāh* and concentration of every thought upon Him. Now, the doctrine was easier to me than the practice, so I began by learning their doctrine from the books and sayings of their Shaykhs, until I acquired as much of their Way as it is possible to acquire by learning and hearing, and saw plainly that what is most peculiar to them cannot be learned, but can only be reached by immediate experience and ecstasy and inward transformation.
>
> I became convinced that I had now acquired all the knowledge of Sufism that could possibly be obtained by means of study; as for the rest, there was no way of coming to it except by leading the mystical life. I looked at myself as then I was. Worldly interests encompassed me on every side. Even my work as a teacher – the best thing I was engaged in – seemed unimportant and useless in view of the life hereafter. When I considered the intention of my teaching, I perceived that instead of doing it for God's sake alone I had no motive but the desire for glory and reputation. I realized that I stood on the edge of a precipice and would fall into Hellfire unless I set about to mend my ways... Conscious of my helplessness and having surrendered my will entirely, I took refuge with God as a man in sore trouble who has no resource left. God answered my prayer and made it easy for me to turn my back on reputation and wealth and wife and children and friends.

In any case, after al-Ghazālī, most of the religious authorities in Islam at all levels have been at least nominal Sufis; even Muḥammad ibn 'Abd al-Wahhāb (d. *1201*/1787), the founder of Wahhābism, could not in his time avoid being affiliated at one point with Sufi *ṭuruq*.

Nevertheless, any esoterism, including Sufism, will always be "suspect" in the eyes of exoterism, just as Christianity could not be other than "suspect" in the eyes of Judaism. The *raison d'être* of esoterism is precisely the knowledge of Reality as such. This is a realization which exoterism can only point towards but cannot attain, since it means shattering forms, and with them, exoterism's necessarily dogmatic formulations. Ibn 'Aṭā' Allāh said, quoting the Koran 27:34 (the Queen of Sheba alluding to King Solomon): "Surely, when Kings enter a town, they destroy it", just as the oak tree destroys the acorn from which it grew. The Sufis say: "To get the kernel, one has to break the shell."

"Metaphysical" Sufism, as taught by the great spiritual masters, is different from "folk" Sufism. In some countries hundreds of thousands of disciples have at times been attached to a single master, more than could possibly have had a true vocation for an integral spiritual path. A kind of Sufism has evolved which reflects a popular idea of spirituality. As happens in every civilization, this popular spirituality confuses piety (augmented by great zeal and a multiplication of ritual practices) with pure spiritual intuition and lustral, transcendent knowledge. Needless to say, folklore hawked as the "wisdom of idiots" may be exactly that, but it has nothing to do with Sufism of *any* kind, nor is it a "self-development" divorced from its religious framework.

An offshoot of popular devotional Sufism seeks reassurance above all in psychic phenomena, communication with spirits, or *jinn*, trance dancing, magic, prodigies such as eating glass, piercing the body with knives, and so forth. In psychic powers and extraordinary mental states it finds proofs of spiritual attainment. It has given rise to the European use of the word *fakir* (which comes from the word for an authentic Sufi disciple, a dervish, or *faqīr*, literally "a poor one") to mean a market-place magician or performer, and has attained notoriety not only among Western observers, but also in Islamic societies.

Metaphysical, or true, Sufism is a spiritual way at the heart of Islam. Its starting point is discrimination between the Real and the unreal, its method is concentration upon the Real, and its goal is the Real. In the words of a Sacred Ḥadīth: "My servant does not cease to approach Me with acts of devotion, until I become the foot with which he walks, the hand with which he grasps, and the eye with which he sees." Bāyazīd al-Bisṭāmī said: "For thirty years I went in search of God, and when I opened my eyes at the end of this time, I discovered that it was really He who sought me." *See also*: AARON; 'ABD al-QĀDIR al-JĪLĀNĪ; al-'ALAWĪ, ABŪ-L-'ABBĀS AḤMAD ibn MUṢṬAFĀ; ABŪ SA'ĪD AḤMAD ibn 'ISĀ al-KHARRĀZ; 'ĀRIF; BARAKAH; BASṬ; BEGGING; al-BIṢṬĀMĪ; CHISHTĪ; DARQĀWĪ; DHIKR; FANĀ'; FAQĪR; FAQR; FIVE DIVINE PRESENCES; al-GHAZĀLĪ; ḤĀL; al-ḤALLĀJ; ḤAQĪQAH; ḤASAN BASRĪ; ḤIJĀB; al-ḤISS; ḤIZB al-BAḤR; ḤUDAYBIYYAH; IBN ABĪ-L-KHAYR; IBN 'ARABĪ; IBN 'AṬĀ' ALLĀH; IBN MASHĪSH; IBN al-WAQT; IBRĀHĪM ibn ADHĀM; al-INSĀN al-KAMĪL; ISTIDRĀJ; JALĀL ad-DĪN ar-RŪMĪ; al-JUNAYD; KHALWATIYYAH; al-KHAMRIYYAH; al-KHIḌR; KASHKUL; MAQĀM; MALĀMATIYYAH; MEVLEVI; MURIDISM; MUTABĀRIKŪN; NAQSHBANDI; PĪR; QABḌ; QĀDIRIYYAH; QUṬB; SAINTS; SĀLIK; SHĀDHILĪ; SHAHĀDAH; SHAYKH; SHIRK; SILSILAH; SULŪK; ṬARĪQAH; TAWḤĪD; WAḤDAT al-WUJŪD; ZĀWIYAH; ZUHD.

Suhayb. Companion of the Prophet; the first Byzantine Greek to be converted to Islam.

Suhrawardī, Shihāb ad-Dīn Yaḥyā (*549-587*/1154-1191). The founder of the *ishrāqī* ("illuminationist") school of philosophy which exerted a powerful influence on thought in Iran. Suhrawardī's most influential work was the *Kitāb Ḥikmat al-Ishrāq* ("the Book of Illuminationist Wisdom"). Suhrawardī was born in Persia, but later established himself in Aleppo; there he was imprisoned by the authorities of Saladin under suspicion of seditious heresy, and put to death. Thus he is often called *al-Shaykh al-Maqtūl* ("the murdered master"), or Suhrawardī Maqtūl to distinguish him from other famous members of his family: 'Abd al-Qāhir ibn 'Abd Allāh Suhrawardī (*491-564*/1097-1168), a Sufi and a scholar; and Abū Hafs 'Umar Suhrawardī (*540-632*/1145-1234), also a Sufi and a statesman. *See* ISHRĀQĪ.

Sujūd (lit. "prostration"). The phase of the prayer (*ṣalāh*) which consists of the act of touching the ground with the forehead. *See* ṢALĀH.

Sulaymān the Magnificent (*900-974*/1494-1566). The Ottoman Caliph under whose reign the Empire reached its high point, Sulaymān conducted successful military campaigns in Europe, besieging Vienna and annexing Hungary, advancing through Persia, and along the Arabian coast, and gaining control of the Hejaz. He was an able administrator and lawmaker (in the Islamic East he is called *al-qānūnī*, "the lawgiver").

In *937*/1530 he handed down the *Kānūnnāmeh*, a corpus of laws which sought, among other things, to remedy abuses in the administration of the military fiefs. He withdrew from the Beylerbeys ("governors") the right to bestow fiefs, requiring them to submit a request called the *tezkere* to the Bāb-i 'Alī, the office of the grand Vizier. Sulaymān was also a patron of the arts, and great builder of public works, including many important constructions in Jerusalem, among them the present city walls. The famous architect Sīnān worked for Sulaymān.

Sulaymān was very attached to one of his wives, Roxelana, a Russian slave whom he prefered to the mother of the heir, and raised to a unique position of power from which she intrigued to have one of her favorites, Rustem, made Grand Vizier, and eventually contrived to have her son Selim, a dissolute drunkard, succeed to the throne. The elder son Muṣṭafā (by another mother), who was popular with the army and had the qualities of a leader, found death at his father's command, and Bāyezīd, a younger but more capable brother of Selim, was eliminated through an unsuccesful bid for power. From then on the harem had an increasing hold over the rulers in Ottoman Turkey, and the Sultans who followed exhibited few qualities as either statesmen or warriors. *See* SĪNĀN.

Sulūk (lit. "journeying" – to God). The Sufis' state of soul or activity seen as "journeying" to God. The term also denotes a quasi-magical and spiritualist ceremony, of local inspiration, performed in Indonesia, known as the *suluk ceremony*. In this ceremony the aspirant seeks to obtain psychic or magical powers by withstanding terrifying assaults from the spirit world during a night in which he symbolically dies. *See* SĀLIKŪN.

Sumayyah bint Khubbāṭ A woman whose name is highly honored as the very first martyr in Islam, killed by the Meccan Abū Jahl for her belief. She was the mother of the Companion 'Ammār ibn Yasar.

Sunnah (lit. "custom", "wont", "usage", pl. *sunan*). A general term that can be applied to the usages and customs of nations, the predominant meaning of Sunnah is that of the spoken and acted example of the Prophet. It includes what he approved, allowed, or condoned when under prevailing circumstances, he might well have taken issue with others' actions, decisions or practices; and what he himself refrained from and disapproved of.

The Sunnah is the crucial complement to the Koran; so much so, that there are in fact isolated instances where, in fact, the Sunnah appears to prevail over the Koran as, for example, when the Koran refers to three daily prayers (24:58 and 11:116), but the Sunnah sets five. On the other hand, there are cases from the earliest days of Islam of universal practices which appear to contradict express Sunnah.

Moreover, the Koran does not make explicit all of its commands; not even all those which are fundamental. Thus it enjoins prayer, but not how it is to be performed: the form of canonical prayer (*ṣalāh*) is based entirely on Sunnah.

The importance of the Sunnah arises from the function of the Prophet as the founder of the religion, and hence the inspired and provident nature of his acts, and the Koran's injunction to pattern oneself after him: "You have a good example in God's Messenger" (33:21). The Prophet himself was aware of his acts as establishing custom and precedent, although he may not have known that such details as the way he tied his sandals would be a matter of record.

The Sunnah falls into several categories: *as-sunnah al-mu'akkadah*, that which is "confirmed", by being demonstrably repeated in the Prophet's lifetime, so that it has assumed an almost obligatory character, sometimes legally binding when it concurs with clearly essential aspects of ritual and law; and the *as-sunnah al-zā'idah*, the supplementary or elective Sunnah in matters less essential. Whilst emulation of the Sunnah is clearly commendable, there are some aspects that can apply only to the Prophet himself, but are not "legal" for all believers, such as the number of the Prophet's wives, for example.

The applicable aspects of the Sunnah form an element of the *uṣūl al-fiqh* ("basis of law"), after the Koran, and along with *qiyās* ("analogy"), and *ijmā'*("consensus"), which determine the religious law of Islam. A remarkable example of how strictly some Muslims have sought to emulate the Sunnah, and the literal way it which it has been interpreted, is the case of Ibn Ḥanbal: in his life he never ate a watermelon because he could not find an example of the Prophet's having done so. *See* MUḤAMMAD.

Sunnī (the adjective from Ar. *sunnah*, "custom [of the Prophet]"). The largest group of Muslims are the Sunnīs, often known as "the orthodox", who recognize the first four Caliphs, attribute no special religious or political function to the descendants of the Prophet's son-in-law 'Alī, and adhere to one of the four Sunnī schools of law.

Those who are not Sunnī include the Shī'ites (*see* SHĪ'ISM), the minority sects of the Khārijites, or 'Ibādites (*see* KHĀRIJITES), and other small groups such as the Aḥmadiyyah (*see* AḤMADIYYAH). These non-Sunnīs make up less than 15% of Muslims. The full name of the Sunnīs is *ahl as-sunnah wa-l-ijmā*, "the People of the Sunnah" [the custom of the Prophet] and the Consensus. *See* CREED; SCHOOLS of LAW.

Sūq al-'Arab *see* UKĀẒ.

Sūrah (lit. "a row", pl. *sūrāt*). A chapter of the Koran of which there are 114. The names of the *sūrāt* frequently derive from some notable word mentioned in them, such as "the Cow", "the Heights", "the Emissaries", etc. Others are named after the mysterious Arabic letters that appear at the head of certain *sūrahs*, such as *Yā' Sīn* and *Tā' Hā'*. *See* KORAN.

Sūrat al-Ikhlāṣ, *see* IKHLĀṢ.

as-Sūryāniyyah, al-Lughah (lit. "The Syriatic language"). The name given to the universal language supposedly spoken by mankind before the Flood (*ṭūfān*), a language common to mankind before the "Tower of Babel", the dispensation of races and the evolution of different tongues. It would have been the language spoken by Adam in paradise although some writers say, illogically, that Adam spoke Arabic in paradise, and *Sūryāniyyah* after the Fall).

It is said that there are traces of *Sūryāniyyah* in Arabic, in the words implied by the isolated letters before certain Koranic Sūrahs, in mysterious utterances and exclamations of Prophets and Saints, and in the speech of children before they learn conventional language.

Sutrah (lit. "covering"). A symbolic barrier established by an object, often a rosary, placed in front of one when the canonical prayers are being performed (*salāh*) in order to demarcate the space needed, particularly that which is touched by the forehead in the prostration. If this area is encroached or trodden on by another person during the prayer, the prayer is considered – by some authorities, but not all – "interrupted" and must be repeated. Without the *sutrah*, an indefinite area in front of the person praying could be considered as the precinct of the prayer and thus violable.

For this reason, a solitary worshiper in a mosque usually chooses to pray, when possible, immediately in front of a wall or pillar. In practice, and in the absence of a *sutrah*, a prayer is only considered interrupted if someone walks upon the space where the head would touch during the performance of the prayer. A different opinion also exists, to the effect that the prayer is not in fact interrupted, but that he who violates the space incurs blame. In sum, the establishment of a *sutrah* in such situations is desirable *adāb* ("courtesy"), but not an absolute requirement.

Sword of God. (Ar. *sayf Allāh*). A name by which the Prophet once addressed his general Khālid Ibn al-Walīd, which then became his honorary title.

In the seventh year of the Hijrah, the Prophet had sent messages to various rulers, calling upon them to enter Islam. The second messenger to the governor of Bostrah in Syria had been put to death by the Ghassanids, Christian Arab allies of the Byzantines, and a party of fifteen delegates sent to Arab tribes in Syria had also been attacked, and fourteen of them killed. To avenge these deaths, an army of three thousand was sent from Medina under the leadership of Zayd, the adopted son of the Prophet. They learned on route that a far superior force of Ghassanids and Byzantines was gathering to confront them, but in a council of war the Muslims decided to continue. At Mu'tah the two forces met.

In a vision, the Prophet saw Zayd fall wounded and, as he lay dying, pass the white standard to Ja far, his second in command; thence it was handed to 'Abd Allāh ibn Rawāḥah, and then to Thābit ibn Arqam, who finally handed it to Khālid ibn Walīd, the famous warrior who, not long before, had abandoned the cause of the Meccans and entered Islam. Khālid collected the forces and led them in a retreat to safety. Of his vision the Prophet said to his Companions: "...One of God's swords took the standard, and God opened up the way for them"; thus Khālid came to be called the "Sword of God". *See* HERACLIUS.

Sword of Islam (Ar. *sayf al-Islām*). A stylized wooden sword held or presented by the Imām during the Friday sermon (*khuṭbah*). The sword was symbolic of the Prophet's words after a battle: "we have returned from the lesser holy war (*al-jihād as-aṣghar*), to the greater holy war (*al-jihād al-akbar*)", by which he meant that the greatest holy war is to overcome the weakness of one's own soul and to rescue it from vice, ignorance, and disbelief. The use of this ceremonial sword disappeared during the last century.

Syria. (Syrian Arab Republic). Population 15,608,648, of whom 11% are Christians, 6% are 'Alawīs, 1.2% are Druzes, and some 30,000 are Ismā'īlīs. The rest are Muslims with a small minority of Twelve-Imām Shī'ites. 88% of the population is considered Arab; 6% are Kurds and there are also ethnic Turks, Armenians, and other groups. *See* 'ALAWĪ; DRUZES; ISMĀ'ĪLĪS.

T

Ta'awwudh. The expression: *a'ūdhu bi-Llāhi mina-sh-shayṭāni-r-rajīm* ("I take refuge in God from Satan the stoned one"), often shortened to *a'ūdhu bi-Llāh* ("I take refuge in God"). It precedes the *basmalah* before ritual actions and the recitation of the Koran.

> If a provocation
> from Satan should provoke thee,
> seek refuge in God;
> He is All-hearing, All-seeing.
> The godfearing,
> when a visitation of Satan
> troubles them,
> remember, and then see clearly. (7:199-200)

See also ĀYAT al-KURSĪ; REFUGE.

aṭ-Ṭabarī, Abū Ja'far Muḥammad ibn Jarīr (*225-310*/839-923). A scholar born in Tabaristan in northern Iran, aṭ-Ṭabarī was a prolific writer on the subjects of theology, literature, and history. Two of his works became definitive reference-works in their fields: the commentary on the Koran called the *Jāmi' al-Bayān fī Tafsīr al-Qur'ān* ("The Full Exposition of Koranic Commentary"), and the universal history of the world from creation until his own times, the *Tarīkh ar-Rusul wa-l-Mulūk* ("History of Prophets and Kings").

aṭ-Ṭabīah (lit. "nature"). As used in *tabi'at al-kull* it means "universal nature", that is, *materia*, or substance, from which the world is created. *See* FIVE DIVINE PRESENCES.

Tābiūn (from *tabaa*, "to follow", "followers", "successors"; sing. *tābi*). The generation which followed that of the Companions of the Prophet, and thus received his teachings at second hand. Those who succeeded them are the *tābi'ū-t-Tābi'īn* (the "followers of the followers"). Together they constitute the *salaf* (the "first generations"), whose authority in religious opinions is superior to that of succeeding generations, proximity to Prophetic times being taken as a index of orthodoxy. The Wahhābīs regard the *tābi'ūn* as the limit of authority, and exclude the *tābi'ū-t-tābi'īn* from the qualification of exemplary orthodoxy.

This is in accordance with a Ḥadīth: "The best of my people are those of my generation; then those who follow them; then those who follow them." This is the opposite of the idea of progress, and is instead the point of view of tradition, that the height of inward perfection is that which is closest to the moment of revelation, the beginning. From the beginning, from the moment of revelation which is origin and center, the immutable law of manifestation is that of decay, even though there may be outward signs of development as seminal possibilities which are inward become externalized.

But in this externalization, as when the Temple replaced the Ark of the Covenant, there is nevertheless a loss. Appearances may argue a new richness, but it is a wealth due to a "devaluation", so to speak, caused by slipping from a higher to a lower state of equilibrium. Despite this, there are necessarily moments of restoration as a cycle unfolds, and its final moments, when the traditional norm is forgotten altogether, presages a sudden, cataclysmic reversal, when the Center once again irrupts into the world.

Speaking to his people of the inevitable law of decadence, the Prophet said: "You will follow in the ways of those who came before you [the Jews and the Christians], and even if they were to descend into a snake's lair, you will follow them."

Tablīghī Jam'āat. The Society for Teaching and Propagation founded by Maulānā Muḥammad Ilyās (1885-1944) in India for the propagation of Islam. It is now an international revivalist movement directed by a *shura* council and holds an annual convention in Raiwind, Pakistan, and in North America.

The conference in Raiwind, which is some thirty kilometers from Lahore, is attended for three days by 700,000 people. Tablīghī Jam'āat sends missionaries to hundreds of countries in groups of eight to twelve persons under the leadership of one member who is called the *emir*. They pay their own way and subsist on a bare minimum. They do not seek to convert non-Muslims but to strengthen the religious resolve of believers. They scrupulously avoid all politics and controversy. The missionaries spend four months at Raiwind discussing their methods and witnessing to each other much like evangelicals do in America. They critique their successes and failures. At any one time up to seven thousand people are undergoing seminars at Raiwind.

The Tablīghī have a six point program which is made up of **1.** the testimony of faith; **2.** performance of parayer with concentration and devotion; **3.** 'ilm and dhikr, knowledge and invocation; **4.** nobility of character which includes wishing well of unbelievers; **5.** sincerity and the examination of conscience so that their intentions are only to serve God; **6.** going out on mission in the path of Allah. The ambience of the Tablīghī is suffused with mysticism without actually practicing any form of mysticism.

The *amir*, or president. of the Tablīghī Jam'āat in 1989, Maulan Inamul Hasan, said to a conference: "Go and take the eternal message of Islam to the four corners of the globe. Remind your brethren of their religious duties; remind them of the day of Judgement; and call them to the remembrance of Almighty Allah, to submission to His Will, and obedience to Prophet Muhammad, peace be upon him."

Tābūt. The elevated sepulcher, or tomb, usually draped with cloth, in which persons of rank, Saints, and Prophets, are buried. A special meaning of the word is the Ark of the Covenant (*tābūt al-'ahd*). The word *ḍarīḥ* refers to a mausoleum as a whole. Tabarī says that the Kaysāniyyah revolt of 685-687 carried a *tābūt* with them, even into battle.

Tadjiks, *see* TAJIKS.

Tafakkur (a verbal noun from *tafakkara*, "to ponder", "contemplate", "meditate"). A word often used to describe contemplation or meditation, it should not be confused with *dhikr*, which is invocation or "remembrance". *See* DHIKR.

Tafsīr (a verbal noun from *fassara*; "to explain", "elucidate"). Any kind of explanation, but especially a commentary on the Koran, *tafsīr* designates opinions, elucidation, background information and commentary on the Koran. *Ta'wīl* is another kind of commentary, an exegesis of the inner meaning of the Koran or other text, most often of a mystical nature. The first commentator on the Koran was 'Abd Allāh ibn al-'Abbās, son of the Prophet's uncle, al-'Abbās, who drew heavily on the *Haggadah* for inspiration, of which he learned from Jewish converts to Islam. *See* COMMENTARIES; TA'WĪL.

Tahajjud. The practice of keeping vigils at night. It was widely observed by the Companions in Medina during the first years of the Hijrah, but to such a drastic degree that their strength began to suffer, so that it had to be curtailed.

Night vigils are still commonly practiced today, particularly during the early morning when the Koran says figuratively that "God descends close to the earth to hear prayers".

The voluntary prayers performed after the *ishā'* are often also called *tahajjud*.

Taḥannuth (lit. "pious practice"). Seeking after God by shunning the world and distraction in the soul. The Koran says: "Say Allāh, then leave them to their pointless disputation" (6:91); "disputation" (*khawḍ*) implies involvement in things, argument, haste; "pointless" (*yalabūn*), lit. "they play", i.e. are not committed to any serious purpose; hence it is clear that the Koran is contrasting the single-minded purposiveness of the *dhikr*, "say Allāh", with distraction and dissipation either in the world or in the soul.

Tahārah (lit. "purification"). The act of purification, spiritual and physical. Its implications can be extended to cover all forms of ablution and is sometimes applied to circumcision as well.

aṭ-Ṭaḥāwi, Abu Ja'far Ahmad ibn Muḥammad (*229-321*/843-933). Theologian, born in Ṭaḥā and died in Egypt. He first studied Shāfi'i law with his maternal uncle Abu Ibrahim al-Muzani, a celebrated student of Imām Shāfi'ī and then changed to study Ḥanāfī law with Abu Ja'far Aḥmad ibn Abu Imrān, who was to become the chief Qadi of Egypt. Among his many written works is the *Bayān as-Sunnah wa aj-Jamā'ah* known as the *Aqīdah aṭ-Ṭahawīyyah* ("The Tahawi Creed"). His theology is a continuation of Imam Shāfi'ī and Abu Hanifah (*Aṣḥāb ar-ā'i wa al-qiyās*).

Ṭāhir (lit. "the purified one"; feminine: *ṭāhirah*).

A degree of sainthood, below that of *walī* ("Saint"), comparable to the station of "Venerable", or "Blessed" in Catholicism. *See* SAINTS.

Ṭāhirids (*205-259*/821-873). A Persian dynasty in Khorasan founded by Ṭāhir ibn al-Ḥusayn, from a family of clients (*mawālī*) of the conquering Arabs. First serving the Caliph al-Ma'mūn, Ṭāhir soon made himself virtually independent, but he and his descendants, beginning with his son Ṭalḥāḥ, continued to send tribute to the 'Abbāsids. The court at Nayshābūr became the first focal point of the renascent Persian cultural consciousness after the Arab conquest. The Ṭāhirids were replaced by the Sāmānids and Saffārids.

Tahlīl (lit. "making lawful"). The uttering of the *shahādah*: *lā ilāha illā-Llāh* ("there is no god but God").

Taḥmīd. The uttering of the *ḥamdalah*: *al-hamdu-li-Llāh* ("praise be to God").

Taḥrīf (lit. "corruption"). The charge made by Muslim theologians against the Christians, of having modified, and falsified, the Gospel (*al-injīl*) to suppress predictions of the Prophet. In the *Radd al-Jamil* al-Ghazālī expresses the opinion that it is not the text of the Bible what has been altered, but rather the interpretation. *See* BIBLE.

Ṭā'if. A city near Mecca, built on a high plateau, it is considerably cooler than Mecca or Jeddah in the summertime. It was famous for its grapes, and many notables of Mecca owned vines there. The Prophet went to Ṭā'if to preach during his Meccan years, before the migration to Medina, but was driven out. On the return journey from Ṭā'if he recited the Koran in the night and the Jinn gathered around to listen to him in the desert.

After the conquest of Mecca the Prophet besieged the town unsuccessfully. Shortly thereafter, seeing the mild treatment accorded to those who accepted Islam, the town and its allies surrendered.

Taifas, Reyes de (Sp. "Kings of the factions", Ar. *mulūk al-ṭawā'if*). The epoch of four centuries of Muslim rule in Spain which followed the disintegration of the Caliphate of Cordoba after *422*/1031. The epoch of factions lasted, in effect, until the defeat of the Naṣrids of Granada in *897*/1492.

During this time the Muslim Empire of Spain was ruled by local princes, including the early Zīrids of Granada, the Banū Ḥammūd of Malaga and Algeciras, the Banū 'Abbūd of Seville, the Banū Ḥūd of Saragossa, and others.

Tajalli (lit. "a coming forth into the light", "an effulgence", "a revealing"). A term in mysticism meaning an epiphany, a manifestation of the numinous, an emanation of inward light, an unveiling of Divine secrets, and enlightening of the heart of the devotee. The related word *jalwah* has been devised by the Sufis to echo the word *khalwah* ("withdrawal", "emptiness") and to describe the complement of emptiness for God, namely, "being filled by God's revealing peace".

Tajikistan. Population 5,900,000. Independent in 1991. Former republic of the Soviet Union, with Uzbek, Russian and other minorities. 80% of the population is Sunni Muslim. Capital Dushanbe. *See* TAJIKS.

Tajiks. An agricultural people who are Sunni Muslims of Persian stock and language. There are three million in Tajikistan, which borders Afghanistan, including the groups which exist in all the bordering ex-Soviet republics and especially in such cities as Samarkand and Bukhara. Another four to ten million million live in Afghanistan speaking Dari-Tajik. The mountain Tajiks of Badakshan are Isma'ilis, as are those of Northern Afghanistan, and for this reason are sometimes considered as a completely alien people by other Tajiks. Among the Pamir peoples the Shchugnantsi and Rumantsi have preserved early Indian and Iranian beliefs and customs.

The first mention of Tajiks is in the *Tarikh-i Masud* by Bayhaqi in 1041; they had their own language, West Iranian close to contemporary Farsi and to the Dari of Afghanistan. Originally they had come from West Iran to Central Asia where they had been forced by Soghdian Bactrians and Khwarezmians.

Early Tajik took on East Iranian words especially from Soghdian in the 10th century by which time they already had a literature whose outstanding figure is Farid ad-Din Rudaki, the

Sultan of Persian poets. This literature could be called "Tajiko-Persian" and besides Rudaki, includes Firdawsi. The first dynasty which restored Persians to rule after the the Islamic invasions, the Samanids, were Tajiks. Bukhara was their center but their domain was greater than Central Asia for it also included Afghanistan. The Tajiks are Europoid, they are Brachycephalic (Iranians are Dolocephalic.) Other Iranian peoples in the former Soviet Union are the Ossetians, Novo-Sogdians in the hills of Zarafshan who have now moved to the plains; these are East Iranians.

Tajwīd, *see* KORAN CHANTING.

Takbīr (the verbal noun from the verb *kabbara*, "to declare greatness", "to magnify"). The expression *Allāhu akbar* ("God is greatest") is described by the word *takbīr* ("magnificat", "declaring (God's) greatness"). In Arabic the same form is used for the comparative and the superlative forms of the adjective. *Akbar* thus means "greater" than anything else or than anything conceivable, and hence also "greatest". The *takbīr* punctuates the canonical prayer (*salāh*) and is used constantly in daily life as a pious exclamation.

Takfir (from *kufr*, "disbelief"). A practice in Shī'ite Islam, but relatively unknown amongst the Sunnis of declaring someone an unbeliever. (An rare example among Sunnis was Ibn 'Arabi who was declared an unbeliever). It reached its height in the 19th century in Iran, when a mujtahid, or several mujtahids, would declare someone an unbeliever for one or another of his tenets. This was done to Shaikh Ahsa'i, the founder of the Shaikhis (for denying the ressurection of the body), to the Bab, to Jamal ad-Din al-Afghani, and to any of a number of religious or political enemies. The device has now appeared amongst Sunni Fundamentalists.

Takiyyah. A place of religious retreat, a sanctuary, a meeting place of dervishes, or a pilgrim inn. In Turkey the Turkish form of the word is used: *tekke*, together with another word, *durgah*. As a meeting place for dervishes, two other terms are common: in Persia, *khānaqah*, and in the Arab West, *zāwiyah*.

Talbiyah. The words which the Koran attributes to Abraham when he called mankind to the pilgrimage to Mecca:

Labbayka-Llāhumma labbayk
labbayka-Llāhumma labbayk
lā sharīka laka, labbayk
inna-l-ḥamda wa-n-ni'mata laka wa-l-mulk
la sharīka laka, labbayka-Llāhumma labbayk
Here am I, God! here am I!
Here am I, God! here am I!
and associate none with Thee; here am I!
Surely Praise and Blessing are Thine, and dominion!
and associate none with Thee, here am I, God! Here am I!

This is the central, ritual recitation of the greater pilgrimage (*ḥajj*) to Mecca, recited from the moment of taking the consecration and donning the pilgrim's garb (*iḥrām*), until the end of the Day of 'Arafāt. It is also repeated during the lesser pilgrimage (*'umrah*). It expresses the state of awareness of God's presence by a "readiness" and "watchfulness" of the heart and mind. The *talbiyah* recalls Isaiah 6:8:

> Also I heard the voice of the Lord, saying, Whom shall I send, and who will go for us? Then said I, Here am I; send me.

See PILGRIMAGE.

Talfīq (lit. "invention", "concoction", "patching together"). The mixing of elements of the four schools of law. In some respects, the rituals differ according to each school (*madhhab*), and legal methods and conclusions differ also. The mixing of the approaches or practices of the different schools is frowned upon; a practitioner and a lawyer are expected to remain within the guidelines of one school. In modern times, however, precedents have increasingly been set for using decisions made in the other schools.

Talḥāḥ ibn 'Ubayd Allāh (d. *64*/683). A Companion, one of the "Ten Well-betided Ones" who were assured of paradise by the Prophet. He took part in the insurrection against 'Alī ibn 'Abī Ṭālib, the fourth Caliph, and was killed in the Battle of the Camel.

Ṭālib (lit. "an asker", "a seeker"). A student, formerly only a student of Divinity. In some countries *ṭālib* is also used to mean a disciple of a spiritual master.

Taliban (Lit. "students"). The political movement which arose among the children who grew up in refugee camps during the Soviet invasion of Afghanistan. With only rudimentary education, spurred on by fundamentalist teachers who provided meager religious instruction and much jihad theology, they have become an army which captured Kabul and imposed a harsh and primitive form of religious dictatorship in that part of Afghanistan which they control. The breakdown of traditional society through war and the loss of traditional Islamic values have played a major role in creating the Taliban. In Afghanistan this loss of traditional values has been through war but in other Islamic societies this loss of traditonal values is also taking place because of drastic population growth.

Many of the Taliban came from camps which were in the region of Quetta in Pakistan, and they were taught by teachers from the Dar al-'Ulum Deoband. A great number of the Taliban are war orphans. Their financial support has come from the Jama'at-i 'Ulama-i Islam-i, a political party in Pakistan associated with the Deoband school in India. The source of the funds has been from Saudi Arabia and from the Gulf states, many claim with the encouragement of the United States. Anti-Taliban forces, such as the Tajik General Massoud, have been supported by Iran and Russia. Uzbekistan has supported General Dostum, an Uzbek, against the Taliban. The rise of the Taliban began in 1994 when the Taliban captured a munitions depot in Afghanistan at Spinbaldak near the Pakistan border, bringing the Taliban 800 truckloads of arms and ammunition that had been stored in caves since the Soviet occupation, and making them the best supplied group of all. Units of the army and other guerrilla units came over to their side. The Taliban also gained the support of Nasirullah Babar, Pakistan's Interior Minister at the time. After they took control of Kandahar he saw them as the means to an economic alliance with the states of Central Asia who have sought a way to the sea. The project of building a gas pipeline from Turkmenistan to Karachi, over Afghanistan instead of Iran, has played an economic role in the strategic reasoning. The potential of the Taliban in destabilizing the Northwest Frontier Province and Baluchistan was however to give Pakistan second thoughts.

Since the Taliban are themselves Pathan (Pushtun), Kandahar, a Pathan area, became their center and from there they began to expand their control over Afghanistan. Their leader has been a figure called Mullah 'Umar. Their program is the "promotion of virtue and the prohibition of vice.". This has not stopped them from using traffic in narcotics for their revenue as other guerrilla groups have done before them. They are very centralized and hierarchical as concerns decision making. They have a *shura* or consultative council in Kabul. However, in carrying out their program in the streets they have been extremely idiosyncratic, individually making up the rules as they go along.

In September 1996 the Taliban captured Kabul. The government of Burhannudin Rabbani and his troops fled northward. The Taliban hanged Muhammad Najibullah who had headed the Soviet backed government during the Afghan war and his brother Shahpur Ahmadzai and later two more such leaders, Turkhi and Jafzar. When they came to Kabul they encountered a society which to them was shocking. Kabul was a relatively cosmopolitan city and, as a result of Communist rule, the status of women was fairly emancipated. The Taliban program has since fallen upon women most heavily. Women were prohibited from going about without the head to ground covering, the *burqa'*, from working, from being "provocative" which could simply mean walking with their shoes making a tapping sound. In the name of Fundamentalism the Taliban prohibited woman physicians from practicing medicine and made children caught foraging for food stand in the street with their faces smeared with ordure as a punishment for theft short of amputation because they are minors. The Taliban has also prohibited showing all pictures of living things and ordered that men grow beards of a certain length. By their literalist interpretation of religious rules they show a similarity and a sympathy with the ideology of the groups known as Ahl-i Ḥadith, which are growing in Pakistan.

A backlash ensued against the Taliban, and the Tajik General Massoud's troops made the Pathan Taliban retreat from positions north of Kabul. Fortunes continued to shift during the late 1990s. Shah 'Abbas Stanakzai, representing various ministries, has been one of the main spokesmen of the movement.

Talīmites, *see* TALĪMIYYAH.

Talīmiyyah (lit. "people of the teaching"). A name for the Ismā'īlīs, around the *6th*/12th century, because their propaganda promised secret, gnostic, teachings. It is under this name, and that of "Bāṭiniyyah", that al-Ghazālī attacked the Assassins in his writings, particularly in the *Faḍā'iḥ al-Bāṭiniyyah*. Al-Ghazālī concentrated on the problems he knew were raised by the exoteric and outer aspects of their doctrine. Abū Muḥammad al-'Irāqī, who scrutinized the Ismā'īlīs after al-Ghazālī, complained that they made the Prophet superfluous since obviously the Imām as conceived by the Ismā'īlīs was superior. Both al-Ghazālī and Shahrastānī took issue with the fact that the Imām had only his own being to teach as the saving doctrine. *See* ASSASSINS; al-GHAZĀLĪ; GHŪLĀT; ISMĀ'ĪLĪS; SHAHRASTĀNĪ.

Talqīn (verbal noun of *laqqana*, "to instruct", "inspire", "insinuate"). **1.** Spiritual teaching or instruction.

2. The suborning of witnesses (a term used in Islamic Law, *sharī'ah*).

Tamattu' The combining of the greater and the lesser pilgrimages (*ḥajj* and *'umrah*) by taking a single consecration (*iḥrām*) to cover both. *See* PILGRIMAGE.

Tamjīd (verbal noun of *majjada*, "to glorify"). The frequently used expression *subḥāna-Llāh* ("may God be glorified"). Some authors also use the word *tamjīd* to refer to the so-called *ḥawqalah*, the expression: "There is no power and no strength save in God." *See* ḤAWQALAH; PIOUS EXPRESSIONS; REFUGE.

Tanāsukh (from *nasakha*, "to abrogate", "to copy"). This single word is used to mean, according to context, any of the following: transmigration (the passing of a soul from one state of existence to another, starting from the lower degrees to the higher until the arrival in the human state); metempsychosis (the transmission after death of psychic *elements*, such as memories or aspects of personality, from one person to another as in the Tibetan doctrine of spiritual teachers known as *tulkus* who succeed each other from generation to generation); and, finally, reincarnation (rebirth in a human state of the integral soul of one who has existed already in the human state). Although they are important to the Druzes and other heretical sects such as the 'Alī Ilāhīs, who say: "Men! Do not fear death! The death of men is like the dive the duck makes", such doctrines play virtually no role in Islam. The metaphysical objection to them is that they imply that that which transmigrates is real; that it has a substance or a sufficient cause unto itself. This would be as if it were a "piece of God"; which is unthinkable.

Islam emphatically denies "reincarnation" after human life, defining human life as the point of ultimate decision, of definitive meeting with the Absolute. From the Islamic point of view, because God is Absolute, and because the human state exists precisely in order that the creature may know God, and through that knowledge proceed to a posthumous state in paradise, a human birth carries with it a responsibility which is unique to that lifetime and not repeatable. Otherwise, it would not truly be a human life. However, because humans are capable of rejecting God and thus of leading lives below their nature, it is not only paradise that is a possible consequence of human life, but hell too.

In one lifetime, only a few of the possibilities of the individual in regard to the world can be manifested; the number of combinations of the relative with the relative may be innumerable; but it is not the labyrinthine encounter of the individual with the world which constitutes the reason for creation and thus for life, but the encounter with God. In this regard, one lifetime is unbounded. A Ḥadīth says:

> I [God] was Hidden Treasure; I desired to be known; therefore I created the world.

Because of the nature of the confrontation of the limited individual with God the Unlimited, even a single, unique, lifetime is enough to determine one's destiny for eternity. Indeed, life is precisely that unfolding of the contents of the soul. Once unfolded and spread out there is hardly any reason to pack it up to repeat the process in a different order.

When heaven is split open,
when the stars are scattered,
when the seas swarm over,
when the tombs are overthrown,
then a soul shall know its works, the former and the latter.

O Man! What deceived thee as to thy generous Lord
who created thee and shaped thee and wrought thee in symmetry
and composed thee after what form He would?

No indeed; but you cry lies to the Doom;
yet there are over you watchers
noble, writers
who know whatever you do.
Surely the pious shall be in bliss,
and the libertines shall be in the fiery furnace
roasting therein on the Day of Doom,
nor shall they ever be absent from it.

And what shall teach thee what is the Day of Doom?
Again, what shall teach thee what is the Day of Doom?
A day when no soul shall possess aught to succour another soul;
that day Command shall belong unto God.
(82:1-16)

In this encounter there is one decisive element, the recognition and acceptance of the Divine Reality on the part of the "central" creature whose awareness is capable of knowing God. We are that central creature in this world, for our subjective sense, our awareness of ourselves, is not different from God's own "subjectivity" save that as "fallen" man we are born with the desire to see a "fallen" world, the world of limitation and contingency that replaced the Garden of Eden. Divine revelation makes it possible to "see", through the means of salvation which God offers, what Adam saw before he fell, or, to repair the defective will which chooses the "fallen" state as normal, or simply to obey a sacred law which brings with it that state of conformity of one's individual substance to supra-individual substance, which is essential in order to enter into a beatific state after death. In any case, revelation and providence provide a sufficient glimpse of the Truth to give birth to a faith in the soul that will save it, and then nourish that faith. In Islam this recognition is the *shahādah*, the testification that one sees that only God is Real. The moment that it takes for faith to enter the soul, the moment that it takes to formulate the *shahādah* with the tongue and heart constitutes all, finally, what matters in life. By its nature, this encounter with God, which is human life, cannot be made into a "rehearsal" whose consequences are merely provisional.

Till, when death comes to one of them, he says,
'My Lord, return me;
haply I shall do righteousness in that
I forsook.' Nay, it is but a word
he speaks; and there, behind them,
is a barrier until the day that they
shall be raised up. (23:101-104)

From the human state, because of man's capacity to understand the Absolute, and his free will in respect of either choosing the Absolute – surrender to God (Islām), or rejecting the Absolute – disbelief (*kufr*, or also *kidhb*, "refusal" or "lying"), the path divides at the judgement after death to lead either to heaven or to hell but not back into the world. Limbo, or some other solution is evidently a possibility in the case of infants who have died, and souls that otherwise have not reached maturity or responsibility, but those capable of desiring heaven are thereby also competent to take the one step of faith which leads to it, or suffer the consequences.

Gardens of Eden they shall enter; therein
they shall be adorned with bracelets of gold
and with pearls, and their apparel there
shall be of silk.
And they shall say, 'Praise belongs to God
who has put away all sorrow from us. Surely
ur Lord is All-forgiving, All-thankful...
...As for the unbelievers, theirs shall be the fire of Gehenna;
they shall neither be done with and die, nor shall its chastisement
be lightened for them. Even so We recompense every ungrateful one.'
Therein they shall shout, 'Our Lord, bring us forth, and we will do righteousness, other than what we have done.'
What, did We not give you long life, enough to remember in for him who would remember? To you the warner came;

so taste you now! The evildoer shall have
no helper.' (35:30-34)

In one passage through life the soul plays out its drama on many planes, given that intentions also amount to acts, and that what is done also implies what is not done in any given situation. On more than one plane a full range of choices is also presented to a soul which acts or reacts accordingly; one life is thus, in fact, already "many lives". A reincarnation would be a mere repetition in different modes. This redundancy, like that of a game, would take away the importance and significance of human life, whose superiority over that of animals, its majesty, lies precisely in its definitive aspect, its absoluteness.

The pre-existence of souls (which is denied by Avicenna on Aristotelian grounds) is another matter. The Koran pictures all the descendants of Adam being called forth at the beginning of the world to testify that there is no God but Allāh. Thus they come into this world knowing the truth of the nature of things, a knowledge to which religion only recalls man. In al-Ghazālī's *Mishkāt al-Anwār* ("The Niche of Lights"), 'Ā'ishah relates that the Prophet said: "Souls before they became united with bodies were like assembled armies, and afterwards they were dispersed and sent into bodies of mankind." *See* ESCHATOLOGY.

Tanzīh (the "elimination [of blemishes or of anthropomorphic traits]"; and hence, the "assertion of [God's] incomparability"). This is a technical term which describes the viewing of God in the light of those aspects which are transcendent and incomparable. The Koran constantly affirms that God has no equal and that nothing is like God. The complement of this (or the opposite) is *tashbīh* ("immanence"), or what is analogous. See TASHBĪH.

Tanzīl (a "sending down [from Heaven]"). A major revelation, such as that of the Koran, having an uncreated, celestial source. *See* INSPIRATION; KORAN; REVELATION.

Tanzimat. The period of government reforms in Turkey which began in *1255*/1839 with the reign of Abdulmecid I, the first reform being the edict known as the *Hatt-i Sharif* of Gülhane; this latter word was the name of a particular pavilion in the palace which lies on the sea of Marmara outside Istanbul, to which dignitaries of the Sublime Porte, foreign ambassadors, and representatives of the Ottoman and subject populations were summoned for the edict's proclamation. It promised all subjects in the Empire, regardless of nationality and religion, security of life, honor, and property; regular military service for Muslims; the lifting of oppressive monopolies; the abolition of confiscations; the end to the leasing of the right to taxation of the provinces to the highest bidder. It made the death penalty dependent upon judicial verdicts following systematic investigation. A series of other laws followed.

The period came to an end when the *Qanun-i Asasi*, proposed by the Vizier Midhat Pasha in *1293*/1876, which would have created a constitution and parliament, was rejected by Abdulhamid II in *1298*/1880, marking a return to absolutist rule. This came as a reaction to Turkish military defeats at the hands of European powers.

This constitution was finally put into effect in *1326*/1908. By that time the upheavals of the Second World War were imminent; in its aftermath the Sultanate was abolished in *1339*/1920 and in *1342*/1923 the Turkish republic declared. In March of *1342*/1924, the office of the Caliphate, filled by Abdulmecid II, brother of the last Sultan (Abdulmecid had succeeded to the Caliphate but not the Sultanate), was abolished. *See* OTTOMANS.

Taqiyyah (from the root *waqā*, "to safeguard"; "self-protection" and hence "dissimulation [in order to protect oneself]"). The principle of dissimulation of one's religious beliefs in order to avoid persecution or imminent harm, where no useful purpose would be served by publicly affirming them. It is contained in the Koran 16:106:

Whoso disbelieves in God, after
he has believed – excepting him
who has been compelled, and his heart
is still at rest in his belief –
but whosoever's breast is expanded
in unbelief, upon them shall rest
anger from God, and there awaits them
a mighty chastisement...

A Prophet, however, cannot dissimulate the

truth. Otherwise, recourse to this refuge is universally accepted in Islam. It is, however, associated most closely with the Shī'ites who practiced *taqiyyah* systematically and widely during periods of Sunnī domination to hide their beliefs from Sunnī Muslims. The Ismā'īlīs have also practiced it in regard to Twelve-Imām Shī'ites.

Taqlīd (lit. "to hang around the neck"). Originally it meant a practice, now extinct, of designating an animal destined for sacrifice by hanging a marker around its neck so that it would not be used for any purpose that could render it ritually unsuitable. A related meaning was to appoint persons to a public duty by hanging a badge or chain of office around their necks; from this there evolved the now more general meaning of "public acceptance", "tradition", or the received way of doing things in human affairs, from crafts to religion. In religious matters it is the opposite of *ijtihād*, the pursuit of original solutions to questions; in law it is the reliance upon the decisions and precedents set in the past. In many modernizing Islamic societies today, the word has become pejorative, implying what is old-fashioned and retrogressive.

Taqwā. The piety which comes from the awe of God.

Tarḍiyah. The expression *raḍiya Llāhu 'anhū* or *'anhā* ("May God be pleased with him" or "her"), a formula inserted into speech or writing immediately following the name of a deceased figure of note, such as a Companion of the Prophet or a Saint. For the recently deceased the formula is *raḥimahū* or *raḥimahā Llāh* ("May God have mercy on him" or "her").

Ṭarīqah (lit. "path", pl. *ṭuruq*). A generic term referring to the doctrines and methods of mystic union, and rightly synonomous, therefore, with the terms esoterism and mysticism (*taṣawwuf*, or Sufism); it refers also to a "school" or "brotherhood" of mystics, of which there are very many, all ultimately linked to a single source.

The names of the *ṭuruq* are rather loosely applied, and if a teacher becomes renowned, his branch may be called after him from that moment on. Thus the apparent number of *ṭuruq* has grown to hundreds. They are, however, ramifications which may be brought back to several main "lineages" descending from the great masters.

All *ṭuruq* trace their authority through a "chain of transmission" (*silsilah*) back to the Prophet himself through his Companions. The time of the Prophet witnessed mysticism, or esoterism, as the pure, inner dimension of Islam in which all the Companions shared. Later Sufi masters, in response to different circumstances or to clarify certain nuances, chose different formulations for making explicit what had been implicit only. At the same time Islam became partitioned to a growing extent between the exoteric (the *sharī'ah*, "the wide road") and the esoteric (the *ṭarīqah*, "the path"), just as the souls of men became a dark forest following the progessive spiritual darkening of the age. This accounts for the development and diversity one finds in Sufism today.

The first *ṭarīqah* to emerge was the *Qādiriyyah*. One *ṭarīqah*, the *Tijāniyyah* claims that its origin is from the Prophet, in a vision made directly to its founder in the last century, without an historical chain, and another, the *Khāḍiriyyah*, claims to have originated in a direct initiation of its founder by al-Khiḍr. *See* AARON; 'ABD al-QĀDIR al-JĪLĀNĪ; BEKTĀSHĪ'; FAQĪR; KHALWATIYYAH; al-KHIḌR; MEVLEVIS; NAQSHBANDĪ; QĀDIRIYYAH; QALANDĀR; SĀLIK; SILSILAH; SUFISM; ZĀWIYAH.

Tartīl, *see* KORAN CHANTING.

Tarwiyah (lit. "watering"). The name, coming from pre-Islamic times, which is given to the eighth day of *Dhū-l-Ḥijjah*, one of the days of the greater pilgrimage. On this day the pilgrims set out from Mecca to be present at 'Arafāt on the ninth. The Ḥanafīs make a night stopover at Minā obligatory at this time. Whereas other schools of law regard this stopover as recommended but not obligatory, so that many go straight on to 'Arafāt. *See* PILGRIMAGE.

Taṣawwuf. Esoterism, Islamic mysticism, or Sufism. The word apparently originates from *ṣūf* ("wool"), the preferred fabric, because of its simplicity, for the garments of the early ascetics. It is often noted that through *abjad* (the science of the relationship between the numeric values of letters and their meaning) *taṣawwuf* corresponds to the value of the words *al-ḥikmah al-ilāhiyyah* ("Divine Wisdom"). *See* SUFISM; TARĪQAH.

Tasbīḥ. The expression *subḥāna-Llāh* ("glory to God"). This is often used in everyday speech to express marvel.

Tashahhud (lit. "testifying"). A station within the *ṣalāh* (ritual prayer), in which the *shahādah* (testimony of faith) is pronounced.

Tashbīh (lit. "the making of comparisons or likenesses"). That there is in the nature of God, an aspect – or aspects – to which analogy can be made is the metaphysical point of view expressed by this term. That which admits, or stresses, God's incomparability is *tanzīh*, for the Koran says that "God is not like anything". There is also the well-known Ḥadīth, reported by Ibn Ḥanbal, that "Adam was created in God's image" (*'alā ṣūratih*). Thus controversy has raged in history as to what is comparable and what is not, and is complicated by the numerous "anthropomorphic" references in the Koran to God as sitting on a throne, speaking, seeing, hearing, having a hand, and so forth. Beyond the historical controversies, however, it can be said that *tashbīh* finally refers to immanence, while *tanzīh* refers to transcendence.

The comparability arises out of the fact that the world reflects the Divine Names which are its archetypes; the mystic Ibn 'Aṭā' Allāh described that matter as follows:

> By the existence of His created things (*āthār*), He points to the existence of His Names (*asmā'*), and by the existence of His Names, He points to the immutability of His Qualities (*awṣāf*), and by the existence of His Qualities, He points to the reality of His Essence (*dhāt*), since it is impossible for a quality to be self-subsistent. He reveals the perfection of His Essence to the possessors of attraction (*arbabu'l-jadhb*); then He turns them back to the contemplation of His Qualities; then He turns them back to dependence (*at-ta'alluq*) on His Names; and then He turns them back to the contemplation of His created things. The contrary is the case for those who are progressing (*as-sālikūn*): the end for those progressing (*nihāyatu 's-sālikīn*) is the beginning for the ecstatics (*bidāyatu 'l-majdhūbīn*), and the beginning for those progressing is the end for the ecstatics. But this is not to be taken literally, since both might meet in the Path (*aṭ-ṭarīq*), one in his descending (*fī tadallīh*), the other in his ascending (*fī taraqqīh*).

The durability of stone reflects the Divine Name *al-Bāqī* ("The Enduring") and the fire's power of reducing forms to nothing reflects the Divine Name al-Jalīl ("The Majestic"). Thus creation resembles God. But God resembles nothing. *See* ISTAWĀ; TANZĪH.

Ta Shih. An ancient Chinese name for the land of the Arabs. Accounts which reached the Chinese from the lands of the various Western barbarians were necessarily garbled and the realities somewhat entangled with fantasy. Arabs were frequently confused with Persians, then as now.

A T'ang dynasty writer described Ta Shih as follows;

> *Ta Shih* comprises a territory which formerly belonged to Persia. The men have large noses and black beards. They carry a silver knife on a silver girdle. They drink no wine and know no music. The women are white and veil the face when they leave the house. There are great temples. Every seventh day the king addresses his subjects from a lofty throne in the temple in the following words: "Those who have died by the hand of the enemy will rise again to heaven; those who have defeated the enemy will be happy". They pray five times a day to the Heavenly Spirit...
>
> At the time of the Sui dynasty, a man from Persia [Arabia] was feeding his cattle on the western mountains of Motina [Medina]. A lion said to him: "On the western side of the mountains are many holes. In one of these is a sword, and close to it a black stone with the inscription in white, 'Whoever possesses me becomes ruler'. The man proclaimed himself king on the western frontier and overcame all who withstood him."

See HUI HUI.

Tashrīq (lit. "drying of meat"). The name of the 11th, 12th, and 13th days of *Dhū-l-Ḥijjah* (the "days of drying meat") *ayyām at-tashrīq*, so called because the pilgrim will then have made the animal sacrifice bringing the pilgrimage to a close.

Taslīm. The saying of *as-salāmu alaykum*

("Peace be upon you") as a greeting, and in particular at the close to the ritual prayer (*ṣalāh*).

Tatars, *see* RUSSIA,

Ṭawāf. The ritual circumambulation of the Ka'bah. This is done counterclockwise with the Ka'bah on the left hand side, seven times. Because there are large numbers of worshipers constantly performing the *ṭawāf* day and night, with the exception of actual prayer times, it is difficult to reach the Black Stone (*al-ḥajar al-aswad*) to kiss or touch it on each round as the Sunnah prescribes. It suffices, therefore, to make a gesture reaching out towards the stone when one passes by it.

The lesser pilgrimage (*'umrah*) begins with the circumambulation (*ṭawāf*) as does the greater pilgrimage (*ḥajj*), during which it is performed several times. The opening circumambulation of the *ḥajj* is called *ṭawāf al-qudum* ("the circumambulation of arrival"). The first three turns are done with the quickened step known as the *harwalah*, as was done by the Prophet on his pilgrimage in the year *8*/629 to indicate to the Meccans that he and his Companions were not tired after the journey. The last four turns are walked at a leisurely pace called *ta'ammul*. Each turn is called a "round" (*ṭawfah*, pl. *ṭawaf*), or a "course" (*shawṭ*, pl. *ashwāṭ*). One complete cycle of seven turns is an *usbū'* (a "sept"). In performing the circumambulation, men who are wearing the consecrated garb of two seamless cloths (*iḥrām*) – for it is only in the *umrah* and certain circumambulations of the *ḥajj* that it has necessarily to be worn – leave the right shoulder uncovered during the first three rounds but cover it for the remainder to avoid sunburn.

Apart from the circumambulation of the Ka'bah carried out at certain prescribed moments of the pilgrimage, it is also possible to perform them at any time, when they are referred to as *ṭawāf sunnah* ("customary circumambulations") and the state of purity conferred by the greater ablution (*ghusl*) is not obligatory for them.

Traditionally, certain recitations are made during the ritual which are inscribed in manuals of pilgrimage, but these are not obligatory apart from the opening *basmalah* and the closing *ḥamdalah*. It is permissible to go round the Ka'bah ritually mounted on a camel, pushed in a wheelchair, or carried in a litter.

Circumambulation is an ancient rite which appears in all the Semitic religions. It is found in the Jewish marriage ceremony, and in archaic magical ceremonies preserved amongst Sephardic Jews. Its origin lies in Mesopotamian astral religions for it imitates the apparent motion due to the rotation of the earth of the stars and planets around the polar star. The symbolism and meaning of the rite is to establish an identity between the circumambulator and what is circumambulated. In the pilgrimage, the pilgrim is of course not identifying with the K'abah but with the center of his being, and through the symbol of the number of completion, the totality of directions of space which is seven, does this in terms of his final ends or destiny. *See* PILGRIMAGE.

Tawakkul. The virtue of trust, or reliance on God, expressed in numerous Koranic sayings such as: "Whosoever puts his trust in God, He shall suffice him" (65:3); "And therefore upon God let them that trust put all their trust" (14:13). Trust must also be joined to adequate human action and precaution where possible, for the Prophet said: "Trust in God but tie your camel".

Tawbah (lit. "turning"). Conversion to the truth, *metanoia*, change of heart, and also repentance. As the Old Testament speaks of God "repenting", that is, relenting or manifesting a different attitude, the Koran also uses the word *tawbah* as a figure of speech, for God's willingness to "turn" towards those who "turn" towards Him.

Tawḥīd (the verbal noun of *waḥḥada*, "to make one" or "to declare or acknowledge oneness"). The acknowledging of the Unity of God, the indivisible, Absolute, and the sole Real. This doctrine is central to Islam and, indeed, it is the basis of salvation, but is understood within Islam in two diametrically opposed ways, as it were, that of exclusivity and that of inclusivity.

One, a comparatively modern view represented most clearly today by the Wahhābīs, intends by *tawḥīd* the utter exclusion of any analogy, similarity, or quality in creation that reflects or transmits God. This admirably strict and upright definition also removes the possibility of all holiness or sacredness from the world. An exception is the Koran, which doctrinally is conceded to be uncreated, and, according to the Ḥanbalīs, uncreated not only in its essence, on which all Sunnīs agree, but even in its letters and sounds.

This Wahhābī idea of *tawḥīd* is not carried so far as to say the world does not exist, however, and makes a *de facto* assumption of the world's materiality in a sense very much like that of modern science (that is, in complete separation from a transcendent principle) without drawing any conclusions as regards the consequence, which is namely, to leave unanswered the question: whence does the apparent reality of the world derive? This view of *tawḥīd* is based upon the negation (*nafy*), within the *shahādah*, the testimony of faith ("There *is no god* except Allāh").

The other understanding of *tawḥīd* is all-inclusive, that nothing is outside God. It is based upon the affirmation (*ithbāt*), within the *shahādah* ("There is no god *except Allāh*"). It is perhaps this latter view of *tawḥīd* which predominates outside of fundamentalist milieus today, and which certainly dominated Islam in the past.

For the Sufis, the realization of *tawḥīd* is union with God; by this they mean the removal of the consciousness of all that is not God, in the sense that "what is it that could possibly veil the reality of God?". The fundamentalist understanding of *tawḥīd* considers the Sufi view as unthinkable. It is important to bear in mind that as regards *tawḥīd* as "unification" with God, the Sufis were very careful to emphasize that: "The Lord remains the Lord, and the servant remains the servant" (*ar-Rabb yabqa' ar-Rabb, wa-l-'abd yabqa' al-'abd*). Al-Hujwīrī declared:

> Unification disproves what human knowledge affirms about things. Ignorance merely contradicts knowledge; and ignorance is *not* Unification, which can only be attained by realizing the falsity of that appropriation of ideas to oneself in which both knowledge and ignorance alike consist. Unification is this, says Junayd again: that one should merely be a *persona* wielded by God, over which His decrees pass, dead to both the appeal of mankind and one's answer to it, lost to sense and action alike by God's fulfilling in onself what He has willed, namely that one's last state shall become one's first state, and that man shall be what he was before he existed.

The most celebrated expressions of the metaphysical understanding of *tawḥīd* are found in Ibn 'Arabī's *Risālat al-Aḥadiyyah* ("Treatise on Oneness") and in the doctrine of "The Unity of Being" (*Waḥdat al-Wujūd*), which pervades his writings and those of his followers. The fundamentalist point of view is best preserved in Muḥammad Ibn 'Abd al-Wahhāb's treatise, *Tawhid. See* SHAHĀDAH; WAḤDAT al-WUJŪD; WAHHĀBĪS.

Ta'wīl (lit. "reducing to its beginning"; hence: "interpretation"). Allegorical or symbolic interpretation of the Koran, especially with a view to elucidating its most profound, inward doctrine. This is a complement to, and part of, *tafsīr*, which is also commentary, but which can be of a more outward and circumstantial nature. Some schools in Islam insist upon a literal interpretation of the Koran only; others, theologians, philosophers, and mystics, turn to symbolic interpretations when circumstances demand it. (*See* al-KINDĪ.)

Ta'wīl especially means allegorical intepretation. The Ismā'īlīs took this to its utmost possibilities and applied this to the Koran extensively and in a special, and abusive fashion, for the purposes of their doctrine. The Ismā'īlīs also extend, when circumstances allow, allegorical interpretation of aspects of the *sharī 'ah*. For them, the *shahādah* (the testification of faith) can become the formal recognition of the Imām, the *Fast* keeping his secret, and so on.

That this transgresses the orthodox bounds of *tawīl* is made clear in the statement of al-Hujwīrī above: an allegorical interpretation may never contradict the apparent and exoteric sense, and may not replace it; for this, obviously, is the prerogative of God, and His revelation. This has always been understood by authentic Sufis. *See* ISMĀ'ĪLĪS; KORAN; SEVENERS.

al-Tawrāt. The Torah or Books of Moses, which are accepted as Divine revelations by Islam. *See* BIBLE.

Tayammum. The purification by sand or stone, instead of water, replacing the customary ritual ablution (*wuḍū'*), or, if necessary, the greater ablution (*ghusl*) as well. The substitution is made if water is not available or if, for health reasons, one cannot use water.

The *tayammum* is performed by formulating

the intention of purification, pronouncing the *ta'awwudh* and the *basmalah* together, as is done before all ritual actions, rubbing the hands over a natural stone, uncut and not worked by man (not, therefore, over concrete blocks, or the walls of houses as is thought allowable in some popular belief), then rubbing the hands together, touching the stone again and rubbing the face and neck. The stone or sand is touched again and the left hand is passed over the right hand and arm up to the elbow, then the right hand is passed over the left hand and arm up to the elbow both arms being bared to the elbow. This completes the *tayammum*.

It is performed immediately before the prayer, after the "call" (*iqāmah*) which directly preceeds the act of praying has been made. If earth or sand is used in place of a stone, it is only touched with the palms and then shaken off. The hands are passed over the face and arms but the earth is not rubbed in; the purpose is contact and not a "cleaning" by spreading earth on the skin. It is necessary to perform a separate *tayammum* for each prayer, even if the prayers are performed one after the other.

The principle which is invoked here resides in the primordial nature of earth and stone, and its capacity – given the mysterious efficacy of rituals consecrated by revelation – to symbolize purity and convey purification, as water obviously does. The rites *wuḍū'* and *tayammum* give water and earth the power to purify and renew, in the way that metaphysical substance can re-absorb its own creations and renew them, removing psychic pollution and imbalance. It is because of this that worked stone or manufactured materials, even if made from earth and stone, are unacceptable for *tayammum*; only that which God has fashioned, and not man, opens us to this power of nature.

Because one cannot enter a mosque in the state of sexual impurity (*janābah*) which necessitates the greater ablution (*ghusl*), a stone is often placed at the door of the mosque so that *tayammum* to replace *ghusl* may be performed there by those not able for any valid reason, to use water. This is a special use of *tayammum* which is often ignored, or unknown.

It is admissible to use the *tayammum* when the time needed to perform *wuḍū'* with water would cause the person to miss an irreplaceable prayer such as that of a festival, *'īd*, or a funeral prayer; but this dispensation does not apply to ordinary prayers which can be made up individually.

Pronouncements made in the 19th century by religious leaders in Nigeria have resulted in the *tayammum's* being frequently accepted there as a normal substitute for *wuḍū'* even when water is available; but this practice has not been sanctioned by the consensus (*ijma'*) of the Islamic community.

Ta'zīr. Punishments or sanctions for offenses at the discretion of the Judge (*qāḍī*), ranging from admonishment to public shaming or whipping. Limits are imposed on the extent of such punishments. As opposed to *ta'zīr*, certain offences incur a punishment defined by the Koran, and are not subject, therefore, to the Judge's discretion.

Ta'ziyah (lit. "solace" "condolence"). **1.** A representation of the tomb of Ḥusayn carried by Shī'ites at mourning ceremonies at the anniversary of his martyrdom at Kerbala, the 10th of Muḥarram.

2. It is also the name of a "passion play" performed in Iran at that time which recreates the martyrdom with details designed to arouse frenzied pity for Ḥusayn on the part of observers. These rites may have their origin in the rites for the Persian hero Siyavosh.

Tazkiyah (lit. "purification"). **1.** A technical term of Islamic law (*sharī'ah*) referring to the testification of the integrity of a witnesses.

2. Purification in general or in a moral sense, through the virtues of giving and generosity. *See also* ZAKĀH.

Testimony of the Faith, *see* SHAHĀDAH.

Tenth Day of Muḥarram, *see* 'ĀSHŪRĀH'.

"Ten well-betided ones", *see* 'ASHARAH MUBĀSHARAH.

Thābit ibn Qurra (*221-288*/836-288). Mathematician, astronomer and physician. Through Muḥammad ibn Mūsā ibn Shākir, one of the "Three Brothers" known as the "Banū Mūsā" who were noted scientists, he was associated to the scientific academy founded in Baghdad by the Caliph al-Ma'mūn. Thabit ibn Qurra was not a Muslim, but a member of the Hellenist sect of Harran, where he originated.

(Harran is today called Altinbasak, and is in Turkey, near Urfa.) He was instrumental in gaining his co-religionists the status of *Ṣābians* which, by making them "People of the Book" (*Ahl al-Kitāb*), or a people with a divinely revealed religion, protected them from the bout of religious scrutiny begun under the Caliph al-Ma'mun and exempted them from forced conversion to Islam.

Thamūd. A people mentioned in ancient records as well as in the Koran, according to which a Divine revelation was sent to them through the Prophet Ṣāliḥ. His message was symbolized by a camel which the people killed; for the rejection of the revelation they were destroyed by an earthquake and a thunderbolt. They have usually been identified as the Nabateans, whose capital was Petra in Jordan, and who had a colony in Arabia. The ruins of this Nabatean city, northeast of Medina near al-'Ulā, are called *Madā'in Ṣāliḥ*, or the "cities of Salih" by the Arabs, and their civilization has, for this reason been called "Thamūdic". *See* ṢĀLIḤ.

Theft (Ar. *sariqah*). The conditions of theft are minutely detailed by Islamic law and precedent. For theft to be established, the stolen goods must have been in custody, namely, in a location belonging to someone, such as a home or a shop, or under watch. The punishment for theft prescribed in the Koran (5:42) is the cutting off of the right hand, and this sanction can be applied for the theft of articles of an established minimum value, for example ten dirhams, but not to articles of insignificant value.

In practice, as in the case of other harsh punishments found in Islamic law, this punishment is rarely applied, but plays the role of a deterrent. There must be either confession by the thief or the testimony of two witnesses; and in that event, the Judge would normally seek mitigating evidence or testimony to throw doubt upon the act and reduce its seriousness. Moreover, punishment can be avoided if the thief provides restitution and is forgiven by the injured party, which, in the eyes of the law, is the desirable outcome which the Judge would encourage.

> But whoso repents, after his evildoing,
> and makes amends, God will turn towards him;
> God is All-forgiving, All-compassionate. (5:43)

Actually, since early times, the punishment for theft has in practice been imprisonment. The sporadic application of amputation for theft in the modern world is not normative; it goes against the current of legal precedent and is, more than anything else, a byproduct of cultural and political upheaval. *See* SHARĪ'AH.

Theodicy, *see* IBLĪS.

Theology, *see* KALĀM.

Thousand and One Nights, (Ar. *alf laylah wa laylah*). A collection of oriental stories, many of them erotic, some simply entertaining, and others with a profound symbolic and spiritual meaning. The framework is the story of King Shahryār, who, betrayed by women, marries one after the other and puts each to death before she can cuckold him. Then he marries Shahrazād, the daughter of his Vizier, who entrances him with story after story, for a thousand and one nights, in the process giving him three children. In the end he is cured of his wickedness and anguish, and Shahrazād, the image of *māyā*, creating reality out of the void, puts an end to this mistreatment of womankind.

Most of the stories originated in India, either in the *Jātaka* tales of the Buddhists or in the collection of Hindu moral tales called the *Hitopadesha*. They passed into Persian where they were known as the "Thousand Tales", and it was around the *3rd*/9th century that they were translated into Arabic, at the height of the 'Abbāsid Caliphate in Baghdad, the city with which they became associated. They were also popular, later, in Mamlūk Egypt where they took on their final Arabic and Islamic form. The *Thousand and One Nights* first became known in Europe in the French translation of J. A. Galland in the beginning of the 18th century and gained in popularity. Well into the 20th century they usually appeared in European editions which were often expurgated; the parts considered obscene were either omitted or put into Latin, for the benefit of deserving men of reasonable education.

Many stories describe the journey of the soul through life; the treasures which are sought are realizations of reality, and the magicians who are vanquished are the different kinds of illusions which the ego throws up to keep its hold over the immortal self which must be freed from the imprisonment of the earthly condition. Along with these sometimes profound and mysterious elements, the *Thousand and One Nights* were the Hollywood of their age, perfected by storytellers and still alive right up until the moment when television wiped away the traditional spoken arts.

"Throne verse", *see* ĀYAT al-KURSĪ.

T'ien Fang, (Chinese: "cube of heaven"). The Chinese Muslim name for the Ka'bah. *See* HUI HUI.

Tijāniyyah. A *ṭarīqah*, or religious brotherhood, widespread in Morocco, Algeria, and sub-Saharan Africa. It was founded by Abū-l-'Abbās Aḥmad at-Tijānī (*1150-1231*/1737-1815) who is buried in Fez. He studied the religious sciences in Tlemcen, Cairo, Mecca, and Fez, and joined several other *ṭuruq* before founding his own. He claimed to have received the command to found a *ṭarīqah*, and an initiation directly from the Prophet in a vision. To emphasize the objectivity of this vision, the Tijānis insist that it took place in daylight.

Thus, despite the founder's previous affiliation with at least three other religious fraternities (*ṭuruq*), the Tijānīs claim that the line of descent (*silsilah*) of their blessing (*barakah*) runs directly from the Prophet to Aḥmad at-Tijānī rather than through the links from generation to generation as with other *ṭuruq*. They also claim that only at-Tijānī is to be honored and obeyed and only his *ṭarīqah* recognized as authentic. This is alien to the spirit of most, if not all, the other *ṭuruq* who generally accept that the esoteric viewpoint has at any one time different representatives; acknowledge each other; and respect the sanctity of great spiritual masters even of other lines. This customary universality is replaced in the Tijāniyyah by an adherence to at-Tijānī to the exclusion of all other spiritual teachers before or since. To further loyalty to himself, at-Tijānī made the claim to a special privilege that no other Saint possessed, that is, to admit to paradise a follower who had committed major sins. At-Tijānī also claimed to be the "Seal of Sanctity" (*khatm al-wilāyah*) and the "Pole of Poles" (*quṭb al-aqṭāb*).

The general tone of the Tijāniyyah is exoteric, that of adding a greater degree of zeal to one's religious life. Two special *du'a'* prayers are used by the Tijānīs: the "Prayer of Victory" (*Ṣalāt al-fatḥ*) and the "Jewels of Perfection" (*Jawharat al-kamāl*). The Tijānīs believe that the Prophet taught the latter to the founder. After an initial period of unsuccessful struggle with civil adversaries for political and military supremacy, the Tijāniyyah adopted a policy of accommodation with rulers, particularly with the French in North Africa. This policy was successful and the sect became widespread in French West Africa, through the efforts of traveling merchants. In this region it is one of the most prominent religious organizations today, particularly among the poor. In many ways it bears a certain resemblance to the Sanusiyyah, another politically inspired religious organization, as well as to the Wahhābīs. The tomb of Aḥmad at-Tijānī is in the heart of Fez, near the Qarāwiyyīn Mosque. The artistic style of this sanctuary, the most important Tijānī mosque, bears the marks of European influence.

Tilāwah. Recitation of the Koran. *See* KORAN CHANTING.

Timurids. A dynasty (*771-906*/1370-1500) founded by Timur, also called Timur-i-Leng, or Tamerlane (*737-807*/1336-1405), a Turkoman prince of Samarkand in Transoxiana. His tomb bears his claim to be a descendant of Jenghiz Khan (which he was not). Tamerlane's armies ranged over the northern steppes down to Persia and India, his name becoming a synonym for terror, and recalling the image of heaps of skulls piled up outside the cities he conquered.

His descendants were not so bloodthirsty. Shah Rukh (*780-850*/1378-1447) "desired not so much to extend but to repair the ravages caused by his father". His wife Jawhar is credited with the building of her mosque at Mashhad and the mausoleum complex at Herat, including an educational institution (*madrasah*). A grandson of Timur, Ulug Beg, built an observatory, now destroyed, outside the walls of Samarkand, made astronomical calculations himself, and helped to recalculate the calendar. There was a Timurid Renaissance in the fifteenth century. After the destructions of the Mongols, the Timurids led the way to a new consolidation of faith; the Turks lost contact with Chinese materialism and now, after having already accepted Islam as a religion, made it the basis of their social institutions.

Afterwards, however, the Timurids fell to fighting amongst themselves and so lost their sovereignty; but from them is descended the dynasty of the Moghuls. *See* MOGHULS.

at-Tīrmidhī, Abū 'Īsā Muḥammad (*209-279*/824-892). The author of one of the six canonical collections of Ḥadīth, called *as-Ṣaḥīḥ* ("the Authentic"), or *al-Jāmi* ("the Collected"). *See* ḤADĪTH.

Tombs. The use of funerary monuments was forbidden by the Prophet in keeping with the primordial nature of Islam and its view of life as a temporary exile. Nevertheless, Islam as a civilization could not avoid marking its history, and it became the custom to erect tombs for Saints and rulers. Thus, despite the prohibition, a very rich funerary architecture flourished whose high point is, of course, the Taj Mahal.

An exception to it today are the Wahhābīs who prohibit the custom of visiting family graves on Fridays, and keep their own graves as inconspicuous as possible. The site of the grave of King 'Abd al-'Azīz, for example, is unknown outside the family, despite the fact that he is the founder of modern Saudi Arabia. When the Wahhābīs conquered Mecca and Medina they removed the multitudes of grave markers and mausoleums from the major cemeteries, including the most renowned resting place in Islam, the *Baqī'* cemetery in Medina. They were even going to raze the domed mausoleum over the Prophet's tomb when international outcry prevailed upon the King, and this tomb was spared.

Trench, Battle of, *see* BATTLE of TRENCH.

Transcendence, *see* TANZĪH.

Translation of the Koran. It is sometimes said that the Koran cannot be translated, in the sense that translation is prohibited by religious law. The Koran has in fact been translated from the very beginning when there were variant readings because of variations in Arabic dialects. Partial translations always existed for the use of non-Arabic speakers, and complete translations were made, for example, by Sadi Shirāzī and Shaykh Walī Allāh into Persian, and by the sons of Walī Allāh into Urdu. Printed Arabic Korans with interlinear Persian and Urdu translations have existed for some time. However, a translation of the Koran cannot be used ritually, for prayer, for invocation, or for serious study; for these only the Arabic Koran can be used. (In Asia, exeptionally, there are some Muslims who use the Koran in translation for certain ritual applications.) It is inevitable that translations of the Koran imply some point of view. For example, the very popular translation by A. Yusuf 'Ali into English is translated from the Bohora Ismā'īli point of view and contains their doctrinal notions, and that of Maulana Muḥammad Ali, from the Aḥmadiyyah. For Sunnis, one of the translations with the least number of objections is the Muhammad Marmaduke Pickthall rendering. *See* KORAN.

Tuareg (spelled "Touareg" in French). A Berber people of the Sahara, their language, Targui, is written in its own script. Formerly they were herding nomads and famed as fierce warriors whose resistance to the French continued into the 1920s, when the use of motor vehicles in the desert made the nomads too vulnerable.

Their society is matriarchal and they are noted because the men, for an unknown reason, cover their faces at all times with the cloth of their enormous blue turbans. These are often more than ten yards/meters long.

The Tuareg are often confused with the "Blue Men", certain tribes of the western Sahara who are Arabs, notably the Riguebat tribe. The Blue Men do not cover their faces, but both wear a costume called a *durrā'ah* or, in West Africa, a *bubu.* This is of blue cloth formerly made with indigo dye from Kano, Nigeria. The dye comes off on the skin, giving them the name of "Blue Men".

Tubba'. The title of the ruler of some of the South Arabian, or Himyaritic, kingdoms in pre-Islamic times. *See* ARABS.

Ṭūfān, *see* NOAH.

Tughrah. Elaborate calligraphic seals used by the Ottoman Sultans for offical documents.

aṭ-Ṭūl (lit. "length" or "height"). A mystical term for spiritual exaltation, or a state of spiritual development, the highest degree of which is of course that of the Prophet. It has a complement in the concept of *'umq* ("depth", in a spiritual sense).

Tunisia. Republic. Population 9,019,687. 99% are Muslims of the Mālikī School of Law. A small minority, under 50,000, are 'Ibādites who lived on the island of Jerba. This community has become somewhat dispersed in recent years. Although the constitution requires that the president be a Muslim, there is considerable secularization of Tunisian institutions, and the fast of Ramaḍān has been formally discouraged. The principle *ṭuruq*, the Shādhilī branches, the Qādiriyyah, and the Tijāniyyah, have also lost their influence under the onslaught of modernism.

Tunku, 'Abd ar-Raḥmān (1903-1973). The son of the Sultan of Kedah, Malaya, he was the first Prime Minister of Malaya from 1957 until his retirement in 1970. He studied law at Cambridge and held posts in the civil service. During World War II he was active in clandestine resistance to the Japanese. In 1961 he put forth a plan for the Federation of Malaysia which was approved in 1963.

Turan, *see* PAN-TURANIANISM.

Turbah. A cake of baked clay-like earth, the size of a bar of soap, from Kerbala, the place where Ḥusayn was killed and is buried. It is placed by the Shī'ites on the ground before them in the prayer so that the forehead touches it during the prostration.

Also called *muhr*, these earth cakes are sold in the Shī'ite holy places in Iraq and also in Iran.

Turban (Ar. *'imāmah*, pl. *'amā'im*). The characteristic headdress, elegant in its simplicity, used by Muslims and some other peoples in Asia, as well as oriental Christians and Jews. The experienced observer can distinguish nationalities and tribes simply from the style of wrapping the turban which can vary in length from only one meter, to more than ten meters. In some societies the elaboration and size of the turban became a badge of social standing, and the excesses to which notables in Turkey carried the practice of wearing giant, impractical turbans, led to the adoption of the Fez (*tarbush*) as official head covering by the government in the 19th century.

Since then, other variants on headgear have been introduced in attempts to appear modern. The use of the western hat in Turkey, whose rim is an obstacle to the prostration (*sujūd*) in the prayer, as opposed to the traditional headgear which is naturally compatible with praying, was viewed both in Turkey and abroad as distinctly anti-Islamic. Its inclusion as a point in the Kemalist program of laicization raised great controversy at the time.

The importance of the turban lies in the fact that the head is the seat of the sovereign function of consciousness – that in man which recognizes and most directly mirrors God. To cover the head during prayers is part of traditional custom (Sunnah), and to cover the head, even inside the house or on the street, has been regarded as befitting the theomorphic dignity of man. The skull cap, which is worn by itself or under the turban, is called a *taqiyyah* ("piety") because of the traditional rule that the head should be covered. Up until recent times it would have been completely unthinkable to show oneself in public with the head uncovered, and this is still the case in Beduin societies. Other forms of Islamic headgear include the headwindings called *kavuk* in Turkey, the high crowned caps worn by dervishes in Turkey and Persia, the *kulah*, the *qalansuwa* and, in Central Asia, the cap called the *kalpak*.

Türbe. The Turkish word for a funerary monument, referring both to the enclosing structure (Ar. *ḍarīḥ*), and to the sepulchre (Ar. *tābūt*). It is also the name given to the characteristic Turkish headstone of a grave, with a turban carved in stone at the top; a familiar sight in the cemeteries of the lands of the former Ottoman Empire.

Turkey. Population 62,484,478. 98% are Sunnī Muslims although, as a result of the policy of laicisation carried out this century, many are consciously non-practicing. Two million of the population are Kurds and there are some ethnic Arabs in the south, as well as Christian minorities, notably the Armenians. There is a heterodox group called Alevis, related to the 'Alawis of Syria, and another called Yezīdīs, found among the Kurds. Since the development of a more liberal attitude towards religion in Turkey in recent years, the estimations of the number of Alevis has risen into the millions. *See* BEYLERBEY; DEFTERDAR; DEVSHIRME; GÖKALP, ZIYA; ISTANBUL; JANISSARIES, KAPUDANPASHA; KEMAL, MUSTAFA;

MEHMET II; OTTOMANS; PAN-TURANIANISM; QĀḌI 'ASKER; SUBLIME PORTE; SHAYKH al-ISLĀM; SĪNĀN; SULAYMĀN the MAGNIFICENT; TANẒĪMĀT; TURKS.

Turkmenistan Former republic of the Soviet Union, independent in 1991. Population: 4,075,316, of whom 73% are Turkmen, and the rest Russian and Uzbek. The capital is Ashkhabad. The Karakum desert covers 80% of the country. The Turkmen or Turkoman are Sunnis with small divergent religious groups like the Qizil Bash. The location of the extinct city of Marv (or Merv), once a major city of Iranian civilization is in Turkmenistan.

Turkomans. A nomadic people related to the Turks, found in Central Asia and Sinkiang. *See* TURKMENISTAN.

Turks. A people whose original homeland appears to have been in the Altai mountains of the Tien Shan range in China from which they had migrated to many areas of Central Asia, and at one time controlled the steppes and regions far north into Russia. Others came West with the horde of Jenghiz Khan. Before their conversion to Islam they were shamanists.

Many dynasties ruling in the name of the 'Abbāsids were of Turkic origin; the Daylamites or Buyids, the Ghaznavids, the Saljūqs. Most of the kingdoms to the north of the 'Abbāsid Empire were Turkic, such as the Qipchaq Khanate. So were a number of Persian dynasties including the Safavis, Afsharids, and Qajars. The greatest of the Turkish empires was of course that of the Ottomans, so named after their original tribal leader Osman (or 'Uthmān). Such was the importance of the Turkic peoples that a Sacred Ḥadīth (*ḥadīth qudsi*) is attributed to the Prophet, in which God says: "I have an army in the East which I call the Turks; I unleash them against any people that kindle my wrath".

Peoples related to the Turks inhabit the regions from Turkey to Sinkiang and include Tartars, Turkomans, Uzbeks, Kirghiz, and others. Most are Sunnī Muslims. *See* AZERBAIJAN; AZERI; KIRGHIZ; TURKEY; TURKOMAN; UZBEKS.

Ṭuruq, *see* ṬARĪQAH.

aṭ-Ṭūsī, Muḥammad ibn Ḥasan (*385-460*/995-1067). Shī'ite theologian, author of one of the so-called "four books", the principal Shī'ite collections of Ḥadīth, the *Istibṣār* ("Examination"). He also wrote the *Fihrist* ("Index") of Shī'ite works, and the *Taḥdhīb al-Aḥkām* ("Correcting of Judgements"), as well as many other works. Aṭ-Ṭūsī was also known as the Shaykh at-Ṭā'ifah; he was a student of the Shaykh al-Mufīd and Sayyid Murtada.

aṭ-Ṭūsī, Naṣīr ad-Dīn (*598-673*/1201-1274). An astronomer, mathematician, and astrologer born in Ṭūs, Persia. For some time he stayed at the Assassin stronghold of Alamūt, and at Maimundiz, and is known to have written Ismā'īlī treatises. After the destruction of Alamūt by the Mongols under Hūlāgū Khān, he joined the Mongols in the capacity of astrologer, professing to be a Twelve-Imām Shī'ite, and was teacher to the important Twelve-Imām Shī'ite theologian 'Allamā al-Ḥillī, and the mystic Qutb ad-Din Shirazi.

As an astronomer at the observatory of Maragha in Western Persia he compiled the astronomical tables known as the *Zīj Il-Khānī* for the Mongol Khans, as well as writing many other treatises on scientific subjects. He proposed a model for the study of planetary motion, the "Ṭūsī couple", which has been named after him, and also authored numerous treatises on theosophical and theological subjects including the *Tajrīd al-Itiqādāt* ("Definition of the Articles of Faith") and *al-Akhlaq an-Nāṣiriyyah* ("The Nasirean Ethics").

Ṭuwā. The sacred valley where Moses saw a fire, approached it and was addressed: "Surely I, even I, am thy Lord; therefore take off thy shoes for this is the sacred valley of Ṭuwā; and I have chosen thee. Hearken, therefore, to what shall be inspired (in thee)" (20:12-13). This is also the name of a well and its surrounding district in the city of Mecca, where the Prophet halted during his triumphal entry.

Twelve-Imām Shī'ites, *see* ITHNĀ'ASHARIYYAH; SHĪ'ISM.

Twelvers. *See* ITHNĀ'ASHARIYYAH; SHĪ'ISM.

U

Ubūdiyyah (from *'abada*: "to save" (as a servitor) or "to worship"). Literally meaning both "slavehood" and "adoration" or "worship", the term defines the normal human relationship of man to God, who is the Perfect Master. It implies complete obedience and resignation, but also expresses elliptically, and transposed into human terms of a human relationship, the nature of Being to Beyond Being, that is, of *wujūd* to Allāh (or in technical terms *Lāhūt* to *Hāhūt*; *see* FIVE DIVINE PRESENCES).

The highest example of the relationship of man to God is the Prophet's service and ministry, for he represents the prototype of *'Abd Allāh* ("Slave of God"). *'Abd* is one of his titles, along with "Messenger "(*rasūl*), Prophet (*nabī*), and "Intimate of God" (*ḥabīb*).

'Ūd al-Qimārī, *see* ALOES, FRAGRANT.

Udu, *see* WUDU'.

Uḥud, *see* BATTLE of UḤUD.

Uighurs, *see* XINJIANG.

'Ukāẓ (also transcribed as *Okadh* and *Ukadh*). A site in the Hejaz in the region of Ṭā'if southeast of Mecca at which, once a year in the "Age of Ignorance" (*Jāhiliyyah*) before Islam, a fair was held beginning on the first day of the month Dhu-l-Qadah. It was here that the desert poets recited their odes (*qasīdahs*), describing the great deeds of times past, the so-called "Days of the Arabs" (*ayyām al-'Arab*). It is probable that it was the most acclaimed of the poems recited at 'Ukāz, that were written in gold letters and hung in the Ka'bah, thence to be known as the hung ones (*al-mu'allaqāt*), of which a mere handful of some ten have survived, the most famous being that of Imru'-al-Qays.

The fair lasted for weeks and was one of the great occasions when the scattered inhabitants of the Arabian peninsula came together. Not only poets came, but also religious preachers, among them the Bishops of Najrān, which was then a flourishing Christian oasis in the south. But as the fair was predominantly a pagan institution, it was abolished by the Prophet. *See* 'IMRU'al-QAYS.

'Ulamā' (pl. of *'alīm*, "learned", "savant"). Those who are recognized as scholars or authorities of the religious sciences, namely the Imāms of important mosques, Judges, teachers in the religious faculties of universities and, in general, the body of learned persons competent to decide upon religious matters. Normally, even in hereditary monarchies, the sovereign is officially "elected" by the *'ulamā'*, who thus confirm his authority to rule. The *'ulamā'* have always represented legitimacy in state and religion, and been a confirmatory thread from regime to regime which survived the fall of sultans and dynasties. Among the Twelve-Imām Shī'ites the *'ulamā'* are the superior *Mullas*, the *Mujtahids* whose leading members are called *Hojjatalislam* (*Ḥujjat al-Islām*), and *Ayatollah* (*Āyat Allāh*).

Because in the Shī'ite world these leaders have a personal following, and have the prerogative of making legal descisions (*ijtihād*), they are a more direct and independent political force than the *ulamā'* of the Sunnī world. *See* AYATOLLAH.

'Umar ibn al-Khaṭṭāb (d. *23*/644). The second Caliph and the second of the Four Patriarchal Caliphs, one of the most notable figures in Islam, he was famed for his strong will and direct, impetuous, and unambiguous character. Before he became Caliph, 'Umar was known to be uncompromising and even violent. When the responsibility of the Caliphate was given him he became more even-tempered, but still forceful. Under his rule the Islamic Empire expanded with almost miraculous speed, and it is fair to say that it was 'Umar who, after the Prophet, was most influential in molding the Islamic state, and in determining its nature.

He had, at first, been a fierce enemy of Islam, the circumstances of whose conversion four years before the Hijrah are famous: he had set out to kill the Prophet, when he learned that his sister Fāṭimah and her husband Sa'īd ibn Zayd were converts to the new religion; coming to admonish them, he let them recite verses of the Koran to him and was converted on the spot. Once converted, he became the most steadfast of the Companions, and on his deathbed said: "It would have gone badly with me, if I had not been a Muslim."

In the indecision which followed upon the death of the Prophet, 'Umar thrust the leadership onto Abū Bakr, and was the first to swear fealty to him in order to forestall a split in the community between Meccan immigrants, the *Muhājirūn*, and the Medinans, the *Anṣār*. 'Umar himself being later designated Caliph by Abū Bakr on his deathbed, he was the first to assume the title *Amīr al-Mu'minīn*, generally translated as the "Commander of the Faithful". It was he who determined that the year of the Hijrah should be the first year of the Islamic era, and organized the administration of the newly conquered territories. He instituted scourging as punishment for certain crimes. In his reign Syria and Jerusalem were conquered; also Egypt, Libya and Iraq; the Persians were defeated at Qādisiyyah. The wealth which poured in was distributed among the Arab Muslims according to a register called the *dīwān*, which included a proportionate stipend for all, according to merit and station, down to slaves and children.

> Am I a king now? Or a Caliph? 'Umar once asked Salmān the Persian.
>
> If thou tax the land of Believers in money, either little or much, and put the money to any use the Law doth not allow, then thou art a king, and no Caliph of God's Apostle.
>
> By God! said 'Umar, I know not whether I am a Caliph or a king. And If I am a king, it is a fearful thing.

> I went to a festival outside Medina once, said a Believer from Iraq, and I saw 'Umar: tall and bald and grey; he walked barefoot, drawing a red-broidered cloth about his body with both hands; and he towered above the people as though he were on horseback.

During 'Umar's Caliphate, the Arabs were prohibited from owning land in order to be, instead, a permanent fighting force carrying Islam to the ends of the earth. His era, marked by his powerfully simple and puritan character, came to be looked upon as a golden age, particularly by the Khārijites, who recoiled from the increasingly complex political and theological questions that arose afterwards. All later movements that attempted the restoration of a "pure Islamic state" looked back to the Caliphate of 'Umar as the ideal model, with the exception of Twelve-Imām Shī'ites, for whom all rulers not of the family of 'Alī are usurpers, especially the first three Caliphs.

'Umar was assassinated in *23*/644 by a certain Abū Lu'lu'ah Firōz, a Persian slave of the governor of Basra, Mughīrah ibn Shubah. The slave had made complaints to the Caliph about his duties, but had been dismissed, in revenge for which he stabbed 'Umar as he was marshalling worshipers in the mosque for the daybreak prayer. On his deathbed 'Umar appointed a council, the *Shūrā*, to elect a new Caliph, consisting of 'Alī, 'Uthmān, 'Abd ar-Raḥmān ibn 'Awf, Zubayr, and Sa'd ibn Abī Waqqāṣ. Talḥāḥ would also have been a member had he not been absent from Medina.

'Umar al-Khayyām (*439-525*/1048-1131). A mathematician and astronomer, who is most famous as a poet. The name Khayyām means tent maker. His collection of poetry in four-line stanzas called *rubā'iyyāt* ("quatrains"), has been translated into many languages. Khayyām's fame in the West is due to a powerful 19th-century English translation by Edward Fitzgerald. It is curious that his fame in the East, even in Persian, is also largely due to this translation, without which Khayyām would not have reached the level of acclaim he enjoys today.

More than one thousand quatrains are attributed to him, many of which are also attributed to others; as the extant manuscripts of Khayyām's poems date from two centuries after his death, it is difficult to say which he actually wrote, if, indeed, any. It is his reputation as a clear thinker that has resulted in the attribution to him of the most sapient and perceptive of the quatrains. In recent years, manuscripts in Arabic and Persian attributed to Khayyām, which are straightforward treatises on metaphysics and Sufism, as well as works on mathematics, have been discovered and published in Iran.

The historian Rashīd ad-Dīn aṭ-Ṭabīb recounts in a legendary story known as the *Sar-Guzasht-i-Sayyidnā* ("The tale of the Three Schoolfellows"), that 'Umar Khayyām, Niẓām al-Mulk, and Ḥasan aṣ-Ṣabbāḥ were schoolfellows together in Nayshābūr. The three swore that if one succeeded in life he would help the others. Niẓām al-Mulk became Minister to the Saljūqs; Ḥasan aṣ-Ṣabbāḥ came to him and acquired an important post. Then, because of intrigue, aṣ-Ṣabbāḥ was forced to flee, went to Fāṭimid Egypt, and returned as the chief of the Assassin sect in the fortress of Alamūt in northern Persia. Niẓām al-Mulk fell as a victim of an assassin sent from Alamūt.

What is certain about the rather enigmatic 'Umar Khayyām is that under the Vizier Niẓām al-Mulk, Khayyām worked with a group of mathematicians to reform the Persian solar calendar. The result was the *Jalālī* calendar of *467*/1079, named after the Saljūq Sultan Jalāl ad-Dawlah Malik Shāh. This calendar was not put into use, but its astronomical basis is more accurate than the Gregorian calendar with a discrepancy, it is said, of only one day in 3,770 years. To this end Khayyām compiled astronomical tables called the *Zīj Malik Shāh*. Khayyām was the first to solve cubic equations, of which he distinguished thirteen kinds, providing both algebraical and geometric solutions. *See* RUBĀ'IYYĀT.

'Umar, Mosque of, *see* DOME of the ROCK.

Umayyad (Ar. *ad-dawlah al-umawiyyah*). The first dynasty of Islam which began with the reign of Mu'āwiyah in *41*/661 and ended with that of Marwān II in *132*/750. The Umayyad capital was established in Damascus by the son of Abū Sufyān, Mu'āwiyah, who had been governor of Syria under the third Caliph 'Uthmān, his relative. The family name is that of a clan descended from Umayyah of the Quraysh.

The dynasty became notorious for running the Empire for its own benefit as though it were its personal fief, and it was the worldly and tyrannical nature of the Umayyads, more characteristic of the pagan age than of Islam, which led to their downfall. Typical of their tyranny is their association with al-Ḥajjāj ibn Yūsuf, a figure notorious for his cruelty, who crushed dissent in Iraq and the revolt of 'Abd Allāh ibn az-Zubayr in Mecca. An exception, however, to the run of the Umayyads was the saintly and abstemious Caliph 'Umar ibn 'Abd al-'Azīz. It was noted that Abū Bakr, 'Umar, and 'Alī had been bald, and so was 'Umar ibn 'Abd al-'Azīz; but after him, there were no more bald Caliphs.

In Arabia, the practice had always been to regard individuals as no more important than their tribe or clan. Despite Islam, this attitude was carried beyond Arabia by the Umayyads; the people of newly conquered territories, who had no tribal affiliation to protect them, were regarded as lacking status entirely unless, as was necessary, they each acquired an Arab protector. This ubiquitous client dependancy in the Empire naturally caused great resentment and was emblematic of the oppressiveness of Umayyad rule, occasioning unrest, rebellion and finally the overthrow of the dynasty. The system was brought to an end by 'Umar ibn 'Abd al-'Azīz but it had by then already done its damage. It played no small role in the development of Shī'ism, the 'Alids representing, in the eyes of the oppressed minorities, the hope of a more just government. The 'Abbāsids, who were also related to the Prophet, used these Shī'ite aspirations to rally popular support to themselves.

Revolution broke out in Khorasan, incited by an 'Abbāsid agitator named Abū Muslim. After the defeat of the Umayyads at the battle of the Zab river in *132*/750, the 'Abbāsid forces hunted down all the Umayyads they could find, but one of them, 'Abd ar-Raḥmān ibn Mu'āwiyah, called later *ad-Dākhil* ("the Incomer"), escaped the destruction of his house at the hands of Abū-l-'Abbās ("the Spiller"), the first 'Abbāsid ruler. In *138*/756 'Abd ar-Raḥmān founded an Umayyad kingdom in Spain at Cordoba and, when the Fāṭimids of Egypt declared themselves to be a Caliphate, the Umayyad 'Abd ar-Raḥmān III an-Nāṣir of Cordoba did the same.

The Umayyads in Spain, however, turned out to be vastly different from the tyrants in Damascus. They ruled from *138*/756 until *422*/1031, when Moorish Spain disintegrated into the small kingdoms called factions (*aṭ-ṭawā'if*); but, at the height of Umayyad rule, the Islamic realm in Spain attained an unprecedented prosperity and cultivation. The arts and sciences flourished, particularly philosophy. Under 'Abd ar-Raḥmān III (d. *300*/912) the court and the capital of Cordoba were the most brilliant in Europe.

Of the founder of the Umayyad kingdom of Spain, al-Mansūr, the second 'Abbāsid ruler, who had Abū Muslim put to death, said once to his courtiers: "Who deserves to be called the Falcon of the Quraysh?" "Yourself, surely" the courtiers answered. "No, the Falcon of the Quraysh is 'Abd ar-Raḥmān, who wandered alone through the deserts of Asia and Africa, and had the great heart to seek his destiny, with no troop at his back, over the sea in an unknown land."

Between the Patriarchal Caliphates and the Umayyads, there was the short-lived Caliphate of Ḥasan, the son of 'Alī ibn Abī Ṭālib, in the year *41*/661. Then followed the Umayyad dynasty. The Umayyad Caliphs are:

Mu'āwiyah ibn Abī Sufyān	*41-60*/661-680
Yazīd I ibn Mu'āwiyah	*60-64*/680-683
Mu'āwiyah II	*64*/683
Marwān ibn al-Ḥakam (I)	*64-65*/684-685
'Abd al-Malik	*65-86*/685-705
al-Walīd I ibn 'Abd al-Malik	*86-96*/705-715
Sulaymān	*96-99*/715-717
'Umar ibn 'Abd al-'Azīz	*99-101*/717-720
Hishām	*105-125*/724-743
al-Walīd II	*125-126*/743-744
Yazīd II	*126*/744
Ibrāhīm	*126*/744
Marwān II al-Ḥimār[1]	*127-132*/744-750

[1]His nickname, "the Wild Ass of Mesopotamia" was meant in admiration, the wild ass, or onager, being an animal of the hunt. He received it because his reign was spent in constant warfare in defense of his kingdom.

Thereafter the Caliphate continued under the 'Abbāsids in Baghdad. A separate branch of Umayyads was established in Cordoba and became the "Western Caliphate". *See* 'ABBĀSIDS; CALIPH; PATRIARCHAL CALIPHS.

Ummah. A people, a community; or a nation, in particular the "nation" of Islam which transcends ethnic or political definition, at least traditionally and before the days of modern, Western-style nationalism. Among the Sunnīs the consensus (*ijmā'*) of the *ummah* is a legitimizing principle in the interpretation and application of the *sharī 'ah* (Islamic law).

Umm al-, *see* after UMMĪ.

Ummī (lit. "unlettered"). An epithet of the Prophet. Although *ummī* is understood by Muslims to refer to the fact that the Prophet was unlettered, the etymology of the word is disputed by some Western scholars who have claimed that it means "gentile", by connecting *ummī* with *ummah* ("nation") because, they say, the Prophet preached an Abrahamic revelation to the gentiles or non-Jews. However, *ummah* does not mean a "nation" in the sense of the Hebrew *goy*, and Islam is not a religion coming out of Judaism, as Christianity is; St. Paul's distinction of: "first to the Jew, then to the Gentile" is not meaningful to Islam. Nor is the Muslim understanding of the word *ummī*, as yet other Orientalists have also maintained, a polemical support to argue the miraculous quality of the Koran. The Koran is miraculous, were the Prophet literate or not.

The Medinan poet Ḥasan ibn Thābit, a contemporary, devoted himself after his conversion to composing verses praising the Prophet. He once characterized the Prophet's mission in these words: "revelation written on a smooth page". The "smooth page" is the soul of the Prophet, which is unlettered because God's writing could not be inscribed where human writing had gone before. That the Prophet should be considered symbolically, or, in fact, unlettered is linked with the mystery whereby Revelation made him the inviolate instrument of the Koran, for *no other writing* had touched him. The first meaning of *ummī* is "maternal", from *umm*, "mother". The uncreated prototype in Heaven of the Koran is called the "Mother of the Book" (*Umm al-Kitāb*). It is, therefore, in evocation of the mystery and glory of revelation that the Prophet is referred to as *an-Nabī al-Ummī* (the "unlettered prophet"). *See* MUḤAMMAD.

Umm al-Kitāb (lit. "the Mother of the Book"). **1.** The Koran is said to have a prototype in heaven. This prototypal Koran is inscribed symbolically on the guarded tablet (*al-lawḥ al-maḥfūẓ*), the pole of substance within Being. (*See* BEING; FIVE DIVINE PRESENCES.)

2. *Umm al-Kitāb* is also the name of a book of proto-Ismā'īlī teachings in which the Dualist doctrine of this sect is most openly expounded. It dates from the *2nd*/8th century. As the premises of this book are alien to Islam, and its use of Islamic concepts crude and wide of the mark, it is clearly an early attempt to enter into Islamic terminology and structure, rather than a case of Islam's acknowledging Ismā'īlī tenets. As the penetration of Islam by the various Dualist sects of antiquity continued, their propaganda became more sophisticated and more difficult to distinguish from orthodox doctrine.

Umm Kulthūm. The youngest daughter of the Prophet and his first wife Khadījah. Umm

Kulthūm was married to a son of Abū Lahab, the uncle of the Prophet who became an implacable and vicious enemy of Islam. This marriage was dissolved and later she became the wife of 'Uthmān, the third Caliph.

Umm al-Mu'minīn (lit. "Mother of the Believers"). A title given to each of the wives of the Prophet, but used in particular of 'Ā'ishah. *See* WIVES of the PROPHET.

Umm al-Qurā (lit. "Mother of Cities"). A name for Mecca (42:7) which, because of the sanctuary of the Ka'bah, is symbolically the center of the world.

Umm Salmah. One of the wives of the Prophet, the widow of Abū Salmah who was killed at the battle of Uḥud. *See* WIVES of the PROPHET.

Umm al-Walad (lit. "mother of the child"). As concubinage is allowed between a female slave and her master, the status of "mother of the child" is conferred upon a slave who gives birth to a child of the master. The child thus born is free and legitimate. The mother cannot be sold, and automatically becomes free upon the death of the master, if she is not freed before. In the case of royal children who became heir to the throne, the status of the mother increased accordingly. In Turkish she is called the *valide*.

'Umrah. The "lesser pilgrimage", or visit to Mecca, which can be performed at any time; its ceremonies take place entirely within the precincts of the Grand Mosque of Mecca and require a little over an hour to accomplish.

The *'umrah* is also a part of the "greater pilgrimage" (*al-ḥajj*) a rite that requires several days to accomplish and can only be performed at a fixed date of the Islamic year.

The *'umrah* is composed of the seven circumambulations of the Ka'bah (*ṭawāf*), followed by a prayer of two *raka'āt* facing the space between the Black Stone and the door of the Ka' bah known as *al-multazam*, the drinking of the water of Zamzam, and finally the ritual walking between the hills of Ṣafā and Marwah, seven times (*as-say*).

The consecrated garb for the *'umrah*, consisting of two pieces of unseamed white cloth (*iḥrām*), is usually put on in Jeddah or at one of the mosques around the perimeter of the Ḥarām of Mecca. The state of consecration is ended at the seventh passage between Ṣafā and Marwah by the cutting of a lock of hair or even by shaving the head. The *'umrah* may be performed by proxy on behalf of one who is absent simply by formulating the intention of performing the *'umrah* on behalf of another, the rest of the rites then being performed normally. *For a more detailed description, see* PILGRIMAGE. *Also see* IḤRĀM; SA'Y; ṬAWĀF.

Unbeliever, *see* KĀFIR.

United Arab Emirates. A federation of small states on the Arabian coast of the Persian Gulf. The states are: Abū Dhābī, Ajmān, Dubai, Fujairah, Rā's al-Khaimah, Sharjah (Shariqah), Umm al-Qaywayn. The total population of the UAE is over 200,000. Most of the population is Sunnī with small Shī'ite minorities. The schools of law practiced are Ḥanafī, Ḥanbalī, and Mālikī. Formerly the states were known as the Trucial States.

Unity, Divine, *see* ALLĀH; FIVE DIVINE PRESENCES; IKHLĀṢ; TAWḤĪD.

'Urf. Local customs or laws which may exist alongside Islamic laws. *See* ADAT.

'Ushr (lit. "a tenth part"). Sometimes confused with the *zakāh*, the *ushr* is a tithe on property owned by Muslims, as opposed to *kharāj*, a tax on property owned by non-Muslims. Since the tax on property (*kharāj* or *ushr*) persisted even if the property changed hands from non-Muslim to Muslim, the distinction between them became blurred, particularly when, as a concession, the Caliph 'Umar permitted the Christian Arab Ghassanids, who had voluntarily allied themselves with the Muslims to the West of Syria from the Byzantines, to pay their tax under the name of *ushr*, that is, as an unconquered people with the same status as Muslims.

Uṣūl al-Fiqh (lit. "roots of jurisprudence"). The bases of Islamic law. Among the Sunnīs these are: the Koran, the Sunnah (acts and statements of the Prophet), *qiyās* ("analogy"), and *ijmā'* (popular consensus or agreement). *Ijtihād* ("effort") is the extrapolation from these principles to specific cases.

The Wahhābīs and Ḥanbalīs limit *ijmā'* to the

generation of the Companions, that is, to the generation of the Prophet, and their immediate followers, the *tābi‘ūn*. The Khārijites limit *ijmā’* to their own community. The Twelve-Imām Shī‘ites add the teachings of their Imāms to the Sunnah and admit the *ijtihād* or decisions of qualified contemporary religious authorities. *See* SHARĪ‘AH.

Uṣūlīs. The dominant school of Shī‘ite theology consisting of those who favor speculation and extrapolation on the basis of principles (*uṣūl*). They exist in distinction to the *Akhbārīs*, or traditionalists, now in the minority and found only in India, Baḥrayn, and southern Iraq. The victory over the Akhbārīs of the Uṣūlī Mullā Vahid Bihbahānī (d. *1207*/1792) led to a very great expansion in the power of the Shī‘ite religious authorities.

The Uṣūlīs maintain that competence to arrive at original decisions and interpretations of the religious law resides in living authorities entitled the *marja‘ at-taqlīd* (“exemplars for emulation”), or Mujtahids. Every Uṣūlī Shī‘ite who is not himself a *marja‘ at-taqlīd* is an “emulator” (*muqallid*), who must adhere to a Mujtahid – it is considered obligatory – to whom he pays *zakāh* (religious tax), and the *khums*, a special revenue originally due to the Prophet from the spoils of war which has lapsed in Sunnī Islam but still exists in Shī‘ism. To follow a Mujtahid brings a heavenly reward, even if the Mujtahid’s views are in fact erroneous. It is forbidden to follow a dead Mujtahid.

The “exemplar for emulation” (*marja‘ at-taqlīd*) is considered to be a general representative (*nā’ib ’amm*), of the Hidden Imām. There is no one Mujtahid who is a unique representative (*nā'ib khaṣṣ*) of the Hidden Imām, not, at least as yet, for the development of the Uṣūlī tendency has not run to the limit; attempts to establish one unique representative of the Hidden Imām and thereby, by implication, of God, were made notably by the Shaykhīs and the Bābīs last century. The decisions of the Mujtahid are taken to have the agreement of the Hidden Imām; if two Mujtahids differ, and the Hidden Imām does not manifest his approval or disapproval by what would be an act of God, then it is considered that the Imām is in agreement with both, at least to some degree. (*For the doctrine of the presence of Being in relative degrees, see* MULLĀ SADRĀ.)

Since every Uṣūlī Shī‘ite is obliged to be a follower of a Mujtahid, the numbers of Mujtahids have grown from modest numbers at the beginning of the last century to hundreds now. The leading Mujtahids have moreover adopted titles of ever increasing grandeur, calling themselves first *Ḥajjatalislam* (*Ḥujjat al-Islām*, “Proof of Islam”), and, in the beginning of the 20th century, *Ayatollah* (*Āyat-Allāh*, “Sign of God”). The distinction between the *marja‘ at-taqlīd* and the ordinary believer, has led to the establishment of a priestly class, or more precisely, of a caste with the unique prerogative of interpreting God’s Will. This is a further step towards the affirmation of the principles including caste, pervading the ancient and indigenous religions of Iran before Islam. At the same time, it affirms Iranian nationalism, repudiates foreign domination, of which the persecution of the Imāms is made a mythic theme, and assays the re-establishment of Persian influence as it was before the rise of the Islamic Empire. (*For the differences between Akhbārīs and Uṣūlīs, see* AKHBĀRĪS.) *See also* AYATOLLAH; HIDDEN IMĀM; PAHLAVI; SHĪ‘ISM.

Usury, *see* RIBĀ.

‘Uthmān ibn ‘Affān (d. *35*/656). The third of the Four Patriarchal Caliphs (*al-khulafā‘ ar-rāshidūn*), ‘Uthmān was elected by a council called the *shūrā*, which had been appointed by ‘Umar as he was dying of the wounds inflicted by a disaffected slave. ‘Uthmān’s reign was marred by nepotism in favour of his clan, the Umayyads. Dissatisfaction with the tyranny of Umayyad governors and the Umayyad conspiracy (in which ‘Uthmān was probably not involved) against the son of Abū Bakr, who had impugned Umayyad usurpation of power, led the latter to stage a revolt against the Caliph and murder him after twelve years of rule.

The first half of ‘Uthmān’s Caliphate had been peaceful; the troubles began, legend says, when ‘Uthmān lost the seal-ring of the Prophet which he dropped accidently into a well on the outskirts of Medina; assiduous search failed to recover it. Afterwards, revolts began in Iraq and Egypt, civil wars arose between the Companions and, with the hostility that ensued between Mu‘awiyah and the ‘Alids, the unity of the Prophet’s time was shattered.

It was ‘Uthmān who ordered the compilation of

the Koran from the memories of the Companions and such written records as existed, after which it was then edited and a definitive recension which bears his name, was copied and sent to the four corners of the Islamic Empire.

'Uthmān was called *Dhū-l-Nūrayn* ("he of the two lights") because he had, at different times, married two daughters of the Prophet, Umm Kulthūm, and Ruqayyah.

One of the earliest converts to Islam, one night in the desert when he was returning from Syria with a caravan, 'Uthmān had been awakened by a voice crying: "Sleepers, awake! for Aḥmad hath come forth in Mecca" (Aḥmad is a form of the name Muḥammad); he then consulted Abū Bakr (who was known to the Quraysh as an interpreter of signs), who brought him to the Prophet to accept the testimony of the faith (*shahādah*).

Despite the troubles of his Caliphate, 'Uthmān is held innocent of them, and the Creed of al-Ash'arī says: "his murderers killed him out of wickedness and enmity."

Uways al-Qarānī. A legendary figure, described as a contemporary of the Prophet and already a mystic before the coming of Islam, it is said of him that he lived in the Yemen and, although he had not met the Prophet, knew of him, as the Prophet knew of Uways, and that Uways communicated with the Prophet in dreams and visions. Uways is the prototype of the *fard*, the exceptional person in whom spiritual realization is spontaneous. The legend goes on to say that Uways came to Medina after the death of the Prophet and received a mantle that the Prophet had left for him. The term Uwaysian transmission means to lay claim to a link with some spiritual figure with whom contact would have been clearly impossible. A form of pious or impious deceit, according to the case, some Sufis have asserted an Uwaysian transmission of authority, that is, across space and time without the two persons actually meeting. *See* FARD; al-KHIḌR.

Uyghuristan, *see* XINJIANG.

'Uzair. This name is often identified as being that of the Biblical Ezra, especially in Muslim folklore. It is mentioned once in the Koran 9:30: "And the Jews say: Ezra is the son of Allah, and the Christians say: the Messiah is the son of Allah." The reference to Ezra as "son of God" is obscure, and cannot be explained by anything in the Bible or from other sources. Rather than Ezra, the Hebrew scribe, prophet and religious reformer of the 5th century B.C. the name in the Koran may actually be that of a fallen Angel in some Gnostic sect which has disappeared.

Uzbekistan. Population: 23,089,261 of whom 71% are Uzbek. Independent in 1991, formerly part of the Soviet Union. The capital is Tashkent. Uzbekistan contains the cities of Bukhara and Samarkand which were once major centers of Islamic civilization. *See* UZBEKS,

Uzbeks. A Turkic speaking people of Central Asia living today in Uzbekistan with minorities in other Soviet republics such as Kazakhstan, Tajikistan, as well as in Afghanistan and China. They number over sixteen million, making them the largest single non-European ethnic group in the USSR.

The Uzbeks, who are a remnant of the Turkic Ghuzz/Oghuz tribes of the Golden Horde of the Mongols, take their name from their leader Uzbeg Khan (d. *741*/1340). In the *9th*/15th century they settled between the Syr and Amu Darya rivers. At the height of their power, they ruled an empire that extended into Persia, Afghanistan and China. They have been much influenced by Persian culture, and some Uzbek dialects have been much affected by Persian, but they are nevertheless Sunnīs of the Ḥanafī School of Law. Today Uzbek is more often written in the Cyrillic script than in the Arabic, which is customary for Muslim peoples.

The Naqshbandī *ṭarīqah* is the most widespread Sufi order among the Uzbeks, and in Central Asia in general. The most important cities of the Uzbeks are Samarkand, Bukhara, and Tashkent. Their national costume is a sleeved gown called the *chapan*, worn with a black and white cap whose rim is squared off. *See* MONGOLS.

al-'Uzzā. One of the more important idols of the pagan Arabs, closely associated with al-Lat and al-Manāt. All three were considered to be females. It is known that human sacrifice had been made to them on occasion. The other principal idol of the Meccans was Hubal, god of the Moon. *See* IDOLS.

V

Valide, *see* UMM al-WALAD.

Veil (Ar. *hijāb*, "cover", "drape", "partition"; *khimār*, "veil covering the head and face"; *lithām*, "veil covering lower face up to the eyes"). The covering of the face by women is usually referred to by the general term *ḥijab* in the present day; it is called *purdah* in the Indo-Persian countries, and Iran has furnished the use of the word *chador* for the tent-like black cloak and veil worn by many women in the Middle East. The Koran advises the Prophet's wives to go veiled (33:59).

Koran 24:31 speaks of covering women's adornments from strangers outside the family. In traditional Arab societies, even up into the present day, women at home dressed in surprising contrast to their covered appearance in the street. This latter verse of the Koran is the institution of a new public modesty rather than veiling the face; when the pre-Islamic Arabs went to battle, Arab women seeing the men off to war would bare their breasts to encourage them to fight; or they would do so at the battle itself, as in the case of the Meccan women led by Hind at the Battle of Uḥud.

This changed with Islam, but the general use of the veil to cover the face did not appear until 'Abbāsid times. Nor was it entirely unknown in Europe, for the veil permitted women the freedom of anonymity. None of the legal systems actually prescribe that women must wear a veil, although they do prescribe covering the body in public. The prescription that a woman's body must be covered in public to the neck, the ankles, and below the elbow is not in the Koran, which, for its part, enjoins modesty. Covering to the neck, wrist, etc. is simply the interpretation of one particular society in the Middle Ages as to what modesty is. In many Muslim societies, for example in traditional South East Asia, or in Beduin lands a face veil for women is either rare or non-existent; paradoxically, modern fundamentalism is introducing it. In others, the veil may be used at one time and European dress another. While modesty is a religious prescription, the wearing of a veil is not a religious requirement of Islam, but a matter of cultural milieu.

In India the introduction of the use of the veil among Muslims, which happened comparatively recently, amounted to a great liberation. *Purdah*, the separation of women from men, meant that women of the classes that could afford to practice *purdah* could not leave their homes. The introduction of the veil amounted to a portable purdah and allowed women a mobility they had not previously enjoyed. This aspect of mobility granted by the use of the veil, a freedom to come and go, is an unsuspected advantage in those societies; there are some Muslim societies where women go sometimes veiled and sometimes unveiled according to their desire to be seen or unnoticed, as the case may be. *See* ḤIJĀB; WOMEN.

"Verse of the throne", *see* ĀYAT al-KURSĪ.

Vilayat-i al-Faqih, *see* WILĀYAT al-FAQĪH.

Vizier, *see* WAZĪR.

W

Waḥdat al-Wujūd (lit. "unity of being"). The doctrine of the unity of being, associated with Ibn 'Arabī and his school, corresponds to the Hindu doctrine of non-duality known as Advaita Vedanta and states that there is only one Self which is refracted by manifestation into the multiplicity of beings, persons, creatures, and objects in existence; and that this Divine Self, *Allāh*, God, the Real, the Absolute, is the hidden identity of all that is; "the more He reveals Himself" (by the limitless variety of His creatures) the more He conceals Himself is a well-known saying of the Sufis. Individual natures are two-fold; on the one hand they are masks that partly reveal the one Self, and on the other, they are illusions caused by ignorance, which hide it. The ego is at once a reflection of the Self which thus conveys an idea of what the Self is, but it is also its own impediment to union with the Self when, through delusion and pride, it refuses to admit its own provisional nature and give up its claims to self-sufficiency (*istighnā'*).

The creature in existence appears to be separate from the Principle, or the Self, although God tells man that He is closer to him than his jugular vein, and indeed it is through revelation, and only through revelation, that creatures are re-united to God, because only a way opened up by God Himself could lead back to Him. Reintegration requires purification, conformity to the Divine norm (*fiṭrah*), and recognition of the Principle within manifestation. What is involved is the dispelling of the illusion of separateness and of a multiplicity apart from God, and this is made possible by two inseparable and indispensable means: doctrine and method. Doctrine renders Reality intelligible and teaches discrimination between the Real and the unreal; method, concentration upon the Real, leads to union with the Real.

The Persian Sufi Bāyazīd al-Bisṭāmī said:

> Dost thou hear how there comes a voice from the brooks of running water? But when they reach the sea, they are quiet, and the sea is neither augmented by their in-coming nor diminished by their out-going.

And al-Jīlī said:

> Unity has in all the cosmos no place of manifestation more perfect than thyself, when thou plungest thyself into thy own essence in forgetting all relationship, and when thou seizest thyself with thyself, stripped of thy appearances, so that thou art thyself in thyself and none of the Divine Qualities or created attributes (which normally pertain to thee) any longer refer to thee. It is this state of man which is the most perfect place of manifestation for Unity in all existence.

Although the doctrine of the unity of being (*waḥdat al-wujūd*) is ascribed to Ibn 'Arabī, it is in fact the fundamental and central doctrine of all Sufism. What he did was to respond to the needs of his age by writing down and making explicit that which before him had been taught orally and in synthesis with a method which englobes a whole style of life. However, the "Unity of Being" could also be misinterpreted as meaning a continuity or identity of substance between the world and God, that the world is God in disguise or a "dismembered serpent" which has to be reconstituted. Against this everpresent danger or abuse which rages more fiercely in one age than another, there arose the school of "Unity of Consciousness" (*waḥdat ash-shuhūd*) which put awareness in the place of existence. The great Sufi Junayd of Baghdad (d. *297*/910) was one of its exponents. *See* FIVE DIVINE PRESENCES; IBN 'ARABĪ; SUFISM.

Wahhābīs. A sect dominant in Saudi Arabia and Qaṭār, at the beginning of the 19th century it gained footholds in India, Africa, and elsewhere. Adherents of this sect named after its founder Muḥammad ibn 'Abd al-Wahhāb (*1115-1201*/1703-1787), prefer to call themselves *Muwaḥḥidūn* ("Unitarians"). However, this name is not often used, and is associated with other completely different sects extant and defunct.

Wahhābism is a steadfastly fundamentalist interpretation of Islam in the tradition of Ibn Ḥanbal, founder of the Ḥanbalī School of Law, and the theologian Ibn Taymiyyah. The Wahhābīs are often said to "belong" to the Ḥanbalī School of Law (*madhhab*), but strictly speaking, like the *Ahl al-Ḥadīth* ("the People of

Tradition") they are *ghayr muqallidūn* ("non-adherents"), and do not see themselves as belonging to any school, any more than the first Muslim generations did. Wahhābism is noted for its policy of compelling its own followers and other Muslims strictly to observe the religious duties of Islam, such as the five prayers, under pain of flogging at one time, and for the enforcement of public morals to a degree not found elsewhere.

The founder, Ibn 'Abd al-Wahhāb, was born in 'Uyaynah in Arabia, into the Tamim branch of the Banū Sīnān tribe. After studying in Medina he traveled in Iraq and Iran. On his return to Arabia he first preached his austere doctrines in his native town but encountered resistance there. He cast about until he came to the village of Dir'iyyah in the Najd desert, near present day Riyāḍ, where his dogmas were well received by the Emir, Muḥammad ibn Sa'ūd.

Ibn 'Abd al-Wahhāb branded all who disagreed with him as heretics and apostates, thereby justifying the use of force in imposing his doctrine, and political suzerainty with it, on neighboring tribes. It allowed him to declare holy war *(jihād)*, otherwise legally impossible, against other Muslims. To this end, Ibn 'Abd al-Wahhāb also taught the use of firearms in place of the sword and the lance, the traditional weapons of the desert.

The alliance of Ibn 'Abd al-Wahhāb, as religious or ideological head, with Muḥammad Ibn Sa'ūd, as political and military chief, was sealed by the marriage of the daughter of Muḥammad ibn Sa'ūd to the preacher; this marked the beginning of a military expansion, which proceeded rapidly under the leadership of 'Abd al-'Azīz, son of Muḥammad ibn Sa'ūd, eventually encroaching upon the Ottoman Empire. In 1802 the Wahhābīs captured Kerbala, the site of Ḥusayn's tomb in Iraq, and in 1803 they seized Mecca, putting a red *kiswah* ("covering"), on the Ka'bah.

By now the Turks were becoming alarmed. Muḥammad 'Alī of Egypt and his son Ibrāhīm Pasha suppressed the first Wahhābī state on behalf of the Ottomans by the reconquest of the Hejaz in 1813. But the Wahhābīs were not crushed; only in 1818 did Ibrāhīm Pasha finally devastate Dir'iyyah after a very long siege and bombardment with canon brought laboriously across the desert.

However, the Sa'ūd clan succeeded in recouping its control over the Najd under the leader Turkī, making nearby Riyāḍ the new capital. Then a fresh challenge to the Sa'ūd dynasty came from a cousin who seized control of the Jabal Shammār in the north, establishing a dynasty of his own clan, the Rashīd of Ḥā'il who did not espouse the Wahhābī cause and, moreover, driving the Saūds out of Riyāḍ in *1309*/1891.

In *1319*/1901 the young 'Abd al-'Azīz Āl Sa'ūd (*see* IBN SA'ŪD) dramatically recaptured Riyāḍ with a handful of companions in a daring raid, and from there his new kingdom grew with astonishing success: in *1332*/1913 he captured al-Ḥasā from the Turks, in *1343*/1924 the Hejaz, and thereafter the 'Asīr.

After the conquest of the Hejaz, an attempt was made to settle the Wahhābī Beduin raiders, called *Ikhwān* ("brothers"), in agricultural communities, the first of which was named Irtawiyyah. The policy of settlement at first failed, and certain tribal groups attempted to continue the Wahhābī holy war (*jihād*), with raids into Iraq. The firearms introduced earlier led to the use of machine guns in the 20th century, thus threatening wholesale extermination of the Beduins in the course of the traditional desert raids, which had been far less destructive when fought with swords and individual combat. The new weapons were one more reason to turn warriors into settled farmers.

The Beduin revolt was, however, doomed from the outset, for the *Ikhwān*, attacking across the border, would have been no match for the airplanes of the R.A.F. which defended Iraq. Moreover, King 'Abd al-'Azīz reacted decisively to this threat to his authority by immediately raising a force which set out from Jeddah and defeated the insurgents at the Battle of Sibilla in 1929. This was fought in the desert; the fighters on the King's side were mounted on camelback and also in automobiles, Mercedes, Chevrolets, and Fords, which had been driven across the desert from Jeddah to bring warriors loyal to the King to put down the revolting Beduins.

This internal struggle with the Beduins was the only serious obstacle to the growth of the Kingdom of Saudi Arabia after the reconquest of Riyāḍ. Wahhābī doctrines and practices were imposed by the conquests although in a progressively gentler form as more urban areas passed into Saūdi control. This was particularly true of the Hejaz, with its more cosmopolitan traditions and the traffic of pilgrims which the new rulers could not afford to alienate. Thus, although the sound of a trumpet calling reveille in Mecca when it was newly conquered was enough to cause a riot among the Wahhābī soldiers – music was forbidden – such that only energetic intervention on the part of the young Prince Faysal, later King, prevented a massacre, today music flows freely over the radio and television.

The creed of Wahhābism centered upon the principle called *tawḥīd*, the assertion of Divine Oneness. Ibn 'Abd al-Wahhāb had written a book by this name upon his return to Arabia from his theological studies and travel abroad. But what he actually understood by *Tawḥīd* was the exclusiveness of the Divine Reality, and not the Oneness that encompasses everything, which is the usual meaning of the term in Islamic metaphysics. Moreover, Wahhābīs do not take into doctrinal consideration any opinions other than those expressed by the generation of the Prophet and his Companions and those of the generation immediately following. Therefore Wahhābism precludes the principle of *ijmā'* ("consensus") as a basis of *sharī'ah* ("Islamic law"). The legal approach of Wahhābism is in many respects unique, but it coincides most closely with the school of Ibn Ḥanbal, and may be considered a kind of Ḥanbalism, although the Wahhābīs would deny this, or any other, affiliation. The sign of changing times in Saudi Arabia is that the exigencies of the modern world and pragmatism have opened the door to accepting the legal precedents of the other schools.

The Wahhābīs consider, or previously considered, many of the practices of the generations which succeeded the Companions as *bid'ah* ("objectionable innovation"); these included the building of minarets (today accepted) and the use of funeral markers. The cemeteries of Mecca and, above all, Medina, were once filled with colorful sepulchral markers which were all removed at the Wahhābī conquest, leaving bare fields. Even the tomb of the Prophet was almost destroyed by Wahhābī zealots; it was left untouched through the forbearance of King 'Abd al-'Azīz, protests by the diplomatic representatives of various Islamic countries, and the bad aim of Beduin gunners. When Medina was conquered, the – perhaps groundless – rumor spread rapidly to the effect that the desert tribesmen had turned Turkish cannons captured in Medina on the Prophet's tomb, its presence being a scandal in their eyes because of the Prophet's saying: "Do not make of my grave a place of pilgrimage as the Christians make of theirs."

Wahhābism vigorously denies all esoterism or mysticism, and rejects the idea of Saints, including the visiting of Saint's tombs or any tomb or grave, exception being made only to the pressure of universal custom as regards visiting the tomb of the Prophet.

To call upon Saints for aid or protection, and even to entertain the notion of *barakah* ("blessing") rouses indignation in Wahhābī breasts as being nothing less than polytheism (*shirk*). They also reject all notions of the holiness or sacredness of objects or places as detracting from the exclusive holiness of God and as infringing Divine Unity. This attitude would actually be more comprehensible if it were defending God's *Absoluteness*, which fundamentalists feel is threatened when secondary causes are admitted. Compared to traditional Islam, the Wahhābī view is extremely "dry" and tends to reduce religion to a set of rules.

Typical of Wahhābī Islam are the *muṭawwi'ūn* ("enforcers of obedience"), who are, in effect, religious police. While in some countries for a Muslim to eat in public during Ramaḍān is legally public scandal or disorderly conduct, among the Wahābbīs *private* nonobservance too can be a matter for sanction. In Saudi Arabia the *muṭawwi'ūn* patrol the streets to punish those who do not perform the prayer or to enforce prompt closing of shops at prayer time. They keep a close eye on what elsewhere would be matters of private conscience and not public morality. In old Riyāḍ, if the enforcers of public morality smelled tobacco, they did not hesitate to enter a private house to beat the offender; today the *shisha* cafe, where water pipes are smoked, is found almost everywhere.

Wahhābī Islam has now become much milder than it was on the day that it sprang out of the Najd desert. Attitudes prevalent in other Muslim countries have crept in, so that the stringent denunciations made by the founder, Ibn 'Abd al-Wahhāb, are now explained as having been a reaction to an improbable lapse into idolatry on the part of some tribes in Arabia two centuries ago. Ibn 'Abd al-Wahhāb's descendants are today known as the ash-Shaykh family. Their fortunes naturally followed those of the Sa'ūd half of the original "alliance" made in Dir'iyyah at the end of the 18th century between Ibn 'Abd al-Wahhāb and Muḥammad ibn Sa'ūd. *See* TAWḤĪD.

al-Wahm. Illusion, fantasies arising out of the mind which are substituted for reality, as distinguished from the cosmic illusion, shared by everyone, due to the "veil" (*ḥijāb*) drawn across Being. The term is used in mystical as well as ordinary psychology.

al-Waḥy. Inspiration from God, and also revelation. *See* REVELATION.

Wajd (lit. "ecstasy"). A mystical term referring to states of ecstasy produced by the Divine Presence.

'Abd al-Qādir al-Jīlānī said:

> Rapture [*wajd*] is the blessed plenitude of spirit provoked by the exercise of invocation, and the blessed plenitude of soul, in communion with the spirit.
> Allāh then gratifies His friend with a cup filled with wine that has no equal, and which intoxicates him with a spiritual drunkenness. His heart then seems endowed with wings, which raise him to the gardens of sanctity. At this moment the enraptured one, submerged by this indescribable magnificence, swoons away losing all consciousness.

Al-Junayd said: "When Truth cometh, ecstasy itself is dispossessed." *See* BASṬ.

Wājib. That which is "obligatory", specifically religious duties. All actions fall into one of the following categories according to the religious law (*sharī'ah*): *wājib*, obligatory; *ḥarām*, prohibited; *mubāḥ*, permitted; *mustaḥabb* or *mandūb*, recommended; and *makrūh*, discouraged. *Farḍ*, which also means obligatory, is that which has been made obligatory by Divine institution. *See* SHARĪ'AH.

Walī (pl. *awliya'*). Saint; more properly *Walī-Allāh* ("friend of God"). *See next and* SAINTS.

Wāli A governor. A province is a *wilāyah*. *Wāli al-ahd* is the heir apparent to a ruler. *See also above.*

Walīmah. A feast accompanying a wedding. *See* MARRIAGE.

Waqf (lit. "standing", "stopping", hence a "perpetuity"; pl. *awqāf*). The giving of property by will or by gift in perpetuity to the Islamic state for pious works or for the public good. It is then managed by a ministry, or *Awqāf*; in North Africa the term *ḥabs*, *ḥubus*, pl. *aḥbās* is more usual. The proceeds pay for the upkeep of mosques and charities. Property given over to the *waqf* cannot normally be regained by the original owners, its distinguishing feature being precisely that it is given in perpetuity.

In the time of the 'Abbāsids when the government simply confiscated the wealth of the rich in order to make up its deficits, *waqf* trusts were set up to be proof against government expropriation; the donor continued to manage the trust and the right was inherited by the eldest son. The Caliph al-Qāhir (d. *332*/934), when in need of money had a number of such trusts prised away from the mother of his half-brother al-Muqtadir, by a court order which declared them void.

In modern times the accumulation of *waqf* property administered by the state has amounted to a considerable proportion of the land of the whole nation, and this has posed economic problems. Legal devices have sometimes been found to return such properties to private ownership so that land may be used more efficiently. *See* INHERITANCE.

al-Wāqidī, Abū Muḥammad ibn 'Umar (*130-207*/747-822). One of the most important early historians, born in Medina and attached to the court of Hārūn ar-Rashīd in Baghdad. Author of the *Kitāb al-Maghāzī* ("Book of Campaigns"), sources for the early history of Islam and biography of the Prophet. *See* IBN SA'D.

Waraqah ibn Nawfal ibn Asad. A cousin of Khadījah, the first wife of the Prophet. He is considered to have been a "*ḥanīf*", one who practiced the Abrahamic monotheism inherited by the Arabs which, however, had in general lapsed, except for a few individuals, during the period preceding Islam. Khadījah told him of the Prophet's revelation and Waraqah said that the revealing Angel was the *Nāmūs* (Greek, *nomos*), the Angel who had spoken to Moses: Waraqah thus declared that he recognised the mission of the Prophet. He knew the Christian scriptures and told the Prophet that Jesus had prophesied his coming. See NĀMŪS.

Wāṣi (lit. "inheritor"). A title which Shī'ites give to 'Alī ibn Abī Ṭālib, who, they claim, was the designated inheritor of the Prophet's functions as spiritual and political head of the Islamic nation. See SHĪ'ISM.

Wasm (Ar. "mark"). A totemic mark or symbol by which a tribe or person marked property, including cattle. It is also the symbol on carpets identifying the tribal designs or the weaver.

Waṣīl ibn 'Aṭa', (d. *131*/748). The founder of Mu'tazilitism. He was a convert to Islam, a *mawla* who lived in Basra and at one time frequented the circle of Ḥasan al-Baṣrī whom he quit when he, Waṣil ibn 'Aṭa', put forth Mu'tazilitism. He was said to have an amazing ingenuity for although he could not pronounce the letter "r" (which may not have been literally true but would mean he could not pronounce the second half of the *Shahāda* which says that Muḥammad is the Messenger of God, or part of the *basmalah*, for example) he could say anything he wished in beautiful Arabic. The writer Jāhiz said of him: "Beyond the Pass of China, on every frontier to far distant Sus and beyond the Berbers, he has preachers. A tyrant's jest, an intriguer's craft does not break their determination. If he says 'Go' in winter, they obey; in summer they fear not the month of burning heat" (*Bayan* I 37). He was a friend of Bashshar ibn Burd, a Iranian poet known as a *zindiq*, or "Dualist", and the first major poet in Arabic of non-Arab origin, and he was related by marriage to 'Amr ibn 'Ubayd Abu 'Uthman, the number two Mu'tazilite.

Wazīr (from *wazara*, "to carry a burden"). A Vizier, or minister of government or, in Caliphal times, close advisors to the Caliph; under the Safavids and Ottomans, *Wazīr* was a name for governor. The most famous *wazīrs* are the Barmecides, a family that served the 'Abbāsids until Hārūn ar-Rashīd wiped them out to a man, for reasons that are not clear. The most celebrated *wazīr* of all, however, was Niẓām al-Mulk, the minister who completely ran the government under the early Saljuqs. Among the Druzes the term is used for certain important religious figures who are considered to be the "ministers", or representatives, of the Fāṭimid Caliph al-Ḥakīm, who for them, exists in the unseen world.

"Weeping Sufis". Sufis who sought, by constant weeping, to draw closer to God (as Thomas À Kempis advised the spiritual postulant "to seek the gift of tears"). The Prophet wept sometimes during the ritual prayer (*ṣalāh*). The Koran 17:107-109 says:

> Say: 'Believe in it, or believe not;
> those who were given the knowledge before it
> when it is recited to them, fall down
> upon their faces prostrating, and say,
> "Glory be to our Lord! Our Lord's promise is
> performed."
> And they fall down upon their faces
> weeping; and it increases them in
> humility'. (17:107-109)

Apart from those who sought occasion to weep intensely and "methodically", most Sufis have passed through phases of weeping as a sign of the "melting of the heart" or the melting of existential knots.

> In Abū Bakr's time, some folk from Yaman came to Medina. When they heard a Reader in the Mosque chanting the Koran, tears fell from their eyes.
> We were like that once, the Caliph said; but our hearts have grown harder since.

Whistling. This is forbidden in Islam, doubtless because of its association with sorcery and the casting of spells in pre-Islamic times, for which reason it is still considered popularly to be communication with the Jinn. It also has connotations of mindlessness or vulgarity.

Whirling Dervishes, *see* MEVLEVI.

White Sheep, *see* AQ QOYUNLU.

Widows. A widow must observe a period of waiting called *'iddah*, of four months and ten days before remarrying. If the widow finds herself with child from the deceased husband she must refrain from marriage until the pregnancy is brought to term.

Wilāyat al-Faqīh. (lit: "guardianship or

government of the Jurisprudent"; in Iran: *Vilayat-i al-Faqih.*) The Shi'ite theologian al-Muḥaqqiq al-Hillī (d. *728*/1326) asserted that religious leaders, the *'ulamā'*, had a function in exercising "guardianship" *(wala' al-imāmah)* over the Imamate of the Hidden Imām. In 1829, following the establishment of the Uṣūlī school of Shī'ism in Iran, an Iranian Mullah, Ahmad Naraqi (*1185-1245*/1771-1829), collected historical materials and Ḥadith regarding political authority in a document called the 'Awa'id al-Ayyam. He quoted what he believed to be an inspired tradition which concluded that while "The kings have authority over the people, the religious scholars have authority over the kings."

In 1971 Khomeini published *The Government of the Jurisprudent* which proposed, in an argument similar to that once used by Ḥasan Ṣabbāh to assume authority, that in the absence of the Hidden Imām competent Jurists are mandated by the Hidden Imām to govern in his place. In theory, this resolved the tension of Shī'ite political practice which otherwise assumes all government other than that of the Hidden Imām to be illegitimate. In actual fact, the need for legitimate government in the absence of the Imām had already called for its theoretical legitimization. Very early in the development of Shī'ism, serving in the government had become perceived as betraying the I476

; therefore Murtaza 'Alam al-Hudā (d. *436*/1044) formulated the Shī'ite principle that "if the person accepting a government office knew or considered it likely on the basis of clear indications that he would be able, through his tenure of office, to support a right or to reject a false claim or to enjoin the good or forbid evil, and that nothing of this would be accomplished but for his holding office, it was obligatory for him to accept office."

What was new in Khomeini was that the political authority who could govern in the place of the Imam was to be necessarily a Jurisprudent *(faqīh)* instead of an emir or a prince, or other secular figure who was not a religious scholar.

In the new government system adopted in Iran following Khomeini's lead, the highest authority must specifically be filled by a Jurisprudent, or Mullah. The constitution also provides that there be a *rahbar*, also a Jurisprudent, who may impeach the head of government if he deviates from religious principles. Practical problems in implementation and even theory emerged from the start and are still in flux. See HIDDEN IMAM; KHOMEINI; IRAN; SHĪ'ISM; UṢŪLĪS

Wine (Ar. *al-khamr*). This is forbidden in Islam, as are all intoxicating drinks and drugs which affect consciousness (2:219; 5:92). Wine, however, is not a substance without spiritually redeeming qualities; thus the Koran says that in paradise there are rivers of wine (47:16); it is on earth that the negative effects of wine are felt, and these outweigh its benefits.

Nevertheless, in many Islamic countries, there are now, as there generally have been in the past, those who consume alcohol (and drugs) despite social disapprobation which may be mild or severe according to the milieu. In some otherwise Islamic countries, the use of alcohol is officially admitted by civil laws which regulate and license its sale.

Clearly, the use of psychotropic drugs for medical purposes, such as anesthesia, is legal from every point of view. Medieval Muslim physicians used wine mixed with herbs as an anaesthetic. It might be mentioned that wine is forbidden because in a sense it is too elevated for man to enjoy without a loss of equilibrium; there is wine in paradise, where it is licit and does not cloud the understanding, and which flows in celestial fountains along with pure water and milk.

Among the Sufis, or Mystics, wine is a popular symbol of mystical knowledge. *See* al-KHAMRIYYAH.

"Wiping of the inner boots", *see* MASḤ 'ALĀ KHUFFAYN.

Wird (pl. *awrād*). A series of Koranic formulas, each recited usually a hundred or more times, which constitute a daily religious exercise of concentration, at morning and evening. These are used by the Sufi congregations (*ṭuruq*), and by others as well. The style and formulae of the *awrād* vary greatly but often include an asking for forgiveness (*istighfār*), a prayer on the Prophet, and the *shahādah.* Sometimes other Koranic excerpts are used such as *a-lā bi-dhikri-'Llāhi taṭma'innu-l-qulūb* ("Is it not in the remembrance of God that hearts find rest?"; 13:28).

There is a famous Ḥadīth: "My heart is clouded until I have asked God's forgiveness seventy times during the day and the night."

Ibn 'Aṭā' Allāh wrote:

> Only the ignorant man scorns the recitation of litany (*al-wird*). Inspiration (*al-wārid*) is to be found in the Hereafter, while the litany vanishes with the vanishing of this world. But it is more fitting to be occupied with something for which there is no substitute. The litany is what He seeks from you, the inspiration is what you seek from Him. But what comparison is there between what He seeks from you and what you seek from Him?

Witr (lit. "odd number"). A prayer of an odd number of prayer-rounds (*raka'āt*) performed after the night-prayer (*'isha'*), and before the dawn prayer (*subḥ*). It is a voluntary prayer except in the Ḥanafī School where it is a duty (*wājib*), but not one that is imposed by Divine institution (*fard*).

Wives of the Prophet. Like the great figures of the Bible, including David and Solomon, the Prophet had more than one wife. Few of his marriages were contracted because of personal affinity; some of his wives were widows who had no-one to turn to, and other marriages were political, for the purposes of creating allies. Polygamy was normal to those times; Islam codified the practice by requiring that each wife be treated equally. In the early part of his life the Prophet had one wife only, Khadījah, who was forty years old and twice a widow when, at the age of twenty-five, he married her around the year 595. She was the first to believe in his mission, and he always revered her memory. She was, moreover, the only wife to bear him children; two, some say three, sons, (who all died in infancy) and four daughters, Umm Kulthūm, Ruqayyah, Zaynab, and Fāṭimah. All the daughters married, but died before the Prophet, except for Zaynab and Fāṭimah. Khadījah died in the year 619, before the Hijrah.

Thereupon the Prophet married Sawdah, aged thirty-five, the widow of a Companion named Sakran. Soon afterwards, he also married the daughter of Abū Bakr, 'Ā'ishah, who was six years old when they were married in Mecca; the marriage was not consummated until she came of age, after the Hijrah. She was to be the Prophet's favorite wife, and a presence that kindled his intuition and sense of spiritual immanence.

In February of 625 in Medina, after the Battle of Badr, the Prophet married Ḥafsah, the eighteen-year-old daughter of 'Umar. She was the widow of Khunays, and had returned from the first emigration to Abyssinia. One year after Badr, the Prophet married Zaynab bint Khuzaymah, a widow of 'Ubaydah, who had died at Badr. She was known as the *Umm al-Masākīn* ("the mother of the poor") for her generosity. She died not long after the marriage.

Umm Salāmah, the widow of Abū Salāmah who died at Uḥud, became another wife. The Prophet married Zaynab bint Jaḥsh, the divorced wife of his adopted son Zayd. She became a fifth wife at the time. A revelation of the Koran authorized more than four wives for the Prophet (Islam limits marriage to four wives at one time). Revelation also authorized marriage to a wife formerly married to a son by adoption, adoption having had for the Arabs the same quality as blood relationship until that time. This was the occasion by which the Koran denied the validity of such a view of adoption. Zaynab was forty years old then, and the Prophet was sixty. Unlike some of the marriages which were political alliances, the marriage to Zaynab was one of personal affinity.

After the Battle of the Trench and a campaign against the Banū Mustalīq, the Prophet married Juwayriyyah bint Ḥārith, daughter of the chief of the Banū Mustalīq, who thus became allied to the Prophet. Umm Ḥabībah, the daughter of Abū Sufyān, the leader of the Meccans fighting Islam, and widow of 'Ubayd (who had been converted to Christianity in Abbysinia, where he died) became the next wife. She was married to the Prophet by proxy by the Negus of Abyssinia while still in Abyssinia. Thus Abū Sufyān became the father-in-law of the Prophet.

Ṣafiyyah, the eighth wife and the tenth marriage, was the seventeen-year-old widow of Kinanah, chief of the Jews of Khaybar who had been conquered. She became a Muslim and married the Prophet on the return journey to Medina. Maymunah, the eleventh and last marriage – after the pilgrimage to Mecca – was the sister of 'Abbās, and a widow.

In addition, the Prophet had at least two concubines, Rayhanah, captured from the Banu Qurayẓah, who was originally Jewish, and Maryah, a Christian slave who was a gift from the Muqawqīs, the Byzantine viceroy ruling the Copts in Egypt. She bore the Prophet a son, Ibrāhīm, who died before his second year.

Women. In discussing the status of women in Islamic societies it is important to bear in mind that Islam cannot be equated to the norms or the style of a particular society. In some Muslim societies, that of the Berbers, for example, women are very free; in others they are not; these differences are due to cultural factors rather than to Islam. In ancient Arab society, the coming of Islam brought women rights where they had none, or few, before. "You have rights over your women", says a Ḥadīth, "and your women have rights over you." These rights were conferred as an integral part of Divine legislation without being demanded; that is to say, there is no evidence that they were the result of any struggle on the part of Arab women. A spirit of freedom which women had under early Islam may in fact have been curtailed later, under the 'Abbāsids. In the last hundred years, modern societies, Arab as well as European, have given women greater freedom as the natural outcome of new forces at play in the modern world. Such freedoms are not necessarily incompatible with Islam.

It is essential that the traditional Islamic viewpoint concerning the respective roles of man and woman be understood in its own terms, setting aside modern polemics. The traditional perspective cannot be fully grasped without taking into account its metaphysical dimension. Islam views man as a soul encountering God in this life in order to know, love, and obey Him, thereby gaining entrance to paradise and immortality; consequently, Islam views men and women as equal before God. Indeed it views them as identical in this respect, and the Koran says that man and woman were "created of a single soul" (4:1; 39:6 and elsewhere).

Biologically and psychologically, however, men and women are different, male and female corresponding to different prototypes in the metacosm or in Being. Consequently, Islam views it as entirely in the nature of things that man and women should play different roles in society.

From the point of view of salvation men and women are according to Islam identical, and are so treated. However, the concept of equality, implying some sort of quantifiable measure to ascertain it, is alien to Islam, which does not view man as a material entity, either as a "social animal", or as a unit of production.

That men and women are not held to be socially equal by Islam (which does not mean one is inferior to the other) may appear unjust; yet it arises from their inherent differences and is in the nature of things. "Male and female created He them": this corresponds to the polarity within Being of *eidos* and *hyle*, potency and receptivity (in Sanskrit *Purusha* and *Prakriti*; *see* FIVE DIVINE PRESENCES). It is the pure receptivity of substance in the principial state that foreshadows the qualified receptivity of the feminine pole in the world. *By its receptive perfection*, it yields precedence to the qualified power of the masculine pole, the reflection of pure act in Being. One may object that this is no more than an abstraction and an ideal, but for traditional societies the ideal *is* real, and the norm around which it seeks its equilibrium. In the world, it is normal for men and women each to contain both male and female poles. But in each person a different pole predominates and is expressed through different modalities, particularly as regards the psychic and the physical natures.

In pure Being, the relationship is perfectly harmonious, as symbolized by the Far Eastern depiction of Yin and Yang. In the world, the perfect harmony of Being encounters the margin of imperfection inherent in manifestation. Human relationships exist in the shadow of this imperfection; doctrinaire egalitarianism, while professing to correct injustice, makes the margin of imperfection the criterion. On the plane of the world, Islam must make prescriptions which translate the difference between masculine and feminine from the traditional point of view into the complexities of social legislation. This plane can never be ideal; it is, at best, a balance between the greater good and the lesser evil. Certain social inequalities are inevitable; the testimony of women in court is less than that of men, because their life of the home does not force them to objectify themselves as the world forces men to do; women are not socially independent in Islam, but legally need a man to act on their behalf; their share of inherited property is less, and so on. However, women have rights that men do not, such as the right to be supported and to a certain inviolability which is respected even by the most rude and warlike Beduins.

On the other hand, the identity between man and woman is affirmed by the capacity of woman to perform all rites; the sacerdotal function in Islam is as much woman's as it is man's (with precedence given to men as concerns the communal performance of rites, leading the public prayer, performing the sacrifice and similar functions).

How the Koranic framework is carried out in practice is largely determined by cultural factors and differs from society to society. While the spirit of Islam is clearly patriarchal, some Islamic cultures, notably those in the Sahara, certain parts of Africa, and regions of South-East Asia are matriarchal. Among Berbers, or the Kirghiz, women have a great deal of social liberty, while in neighboring, or even surrounding, Muslim cultures they may be crushingly restricted. It would be incorrect to attribute abuses that undoubtedly exist within the Islamic world to Islam itself rather than to human nature.

As the spirit of Islam is vast enough to embrace peoples of such diverse human types as Africans and Chinese, the range of social relationships possible within it must be equally vast. The Middle Eastern norm for relationships between the sexes is by no means the only one possible for Islamic societies everywhere, nor is it appropriate for all cultures. It does not exhaust the possibilities allowed within the framework of the Koran and Sunnah, and is neither feasible nor desirable as a model for Europe or North America. European societies possess perfectly adequate models for marriage, the family, and relations between the sexes which are by no means out of harmony with the Koran and the Sunnah. This is borne out by the fact that within certain broad limits Islamic societies themselves differ enormously in this respect.

The existence of polygamy within Islam reflects the cultural norms of ancient Semitic society. It was perpetuated on the one hand because it corresponds to metaphysical possibility, wherein the man represents the oneness of the Principle, and woman the multiplicity of Divine Infinitude, and on the other because desert societies always had a surplus of women, the men being killed off in continual warfare:

> Marry the spouseless among you, and your
> slaves and handmaidens that are righteous;
> if they are poor, God will enrich them
> of His bounty; God is All-embracing,
> All-knowing. (24:32)

Polygamy thus fulfilled a social need, giving women security when independent life was virtually impossible outside marriage, the household and the family. As it says in Isaiah 4:1: "And in that day seven women shall take hold of one man saying, We will eat our own bread, and wear our own apparel: only let us be called by thy name, to take away our reproach. "The limitation of four wives comes from Judaism where it is a Talmudic injunction.

Because the legal statute of polygamy requires fair treatment and equal support of all the wives, it is in practice becoming rare today for economic reasons, as well as for reasons of the social stigma of being looked upon as un-modern. Using the Koranic requirement of equitable treatment as a justification, and the injunction that "the door to abuses should be closed", some countries like Syria have actually prohibited polygamy. In most of the Islamic world where it is still practiced, only 1 to 3% of marriages are polygamous.

> Men and women who have surrendered,
> believing men and believing women,
> obedient men and obedient women,
> truthful men and truthful women,
> enduring men and enduring women,
> humble men and humble women,
> men and women who give in charity,
> men who fast and women who fast,
> men and women who guard their private parts,
> men and women who remember God oft –
> for them God has prepared forgiveness
> and a mighty wage. (33:35)

See VEIL.

Wuḍū'. The "lesser ablution", commonly called in Persian *abdast.* This is performed, when the conditions of the "greater ablution" (*ghusl*) have been fulfilled, in order to be in the correct state to perform the canonical prayer, the *ṣalāh.* Once the purification of *wuḍū'* is acquired it is valid until lost by the following impurities termed *aḥdāth*: calls of nature, breaking wind, loss of consciousness, deep sleep, light bleeding (but not a "flow" of blood from insect bites or the like), for a man, touching his private parts, or any of the circumstances which necessitate *ghusl.* A chronic condition such as incontinence of urine is disregarded for the purposes of ablution, and the person performs a *wuḍū'* before each prayer. In effect, the conditions of the state of purity are of a subtle nature and the legal definitions are indicative rather than absolute.

The *wuḍū'* consists of the following actions:

1. Formulating the intention.
2. Pronouncing the *basmalah.*
3. Running water over the right hand and then the left and washing the hands by rubbing one over the other three times. (Rubbing between the fingers, which is a part of *ghusl,* is sometimes added also to *wuḍū'* and considered a requirement, as well as moving a finger-ring, if possible, to allow water to penetrate around it.)
4. Cupping water in the right hand and rinsing the mouth three times (*maḍmaḍa*).
5. Raising water in the cupped right hand to the nostrils (*istinshaq*) and squeezing it out with the left (*istinsar*), three times .
6. Washing the face three times with both hands.
7. Washing the right arm up to the elbow three times with the left hand, and then the left arm up to the elbow three times with the right.
8. Passing the wetted right hand over the head, first back and then forward using the left hand to raise the turban or headgear, once. If both hands are free for this operation, then both wetted hands are passed over the head. It is not necessary in the *wuḍū'* to use much water. The head is only lightly wiped. At this point the *shahādah* is recited.
9. Putting the wetted forefingers in the ears, and with the thumbs behind the lobes, moving both fingers upwards following the conformation of the outer ear, and then from the top of the ear down along the outer ridge, thus wiping the entrance to the ear, and the outer ear.
10. Washing the right foot with the left hand by wiping the outside of the foot with the fingers, palm against the sole, starting at the heel and moving to the toes; from the toes back with the palm against the inside of the foot, fingers along the sole, and then up to the ankle. Similarly the left foot is wiped by the right hand, palm against the inside, fingers against the sole starting from the toe down to the heel, then upwards palm against the sole, the fingers around the foot wiping the outside, and then up to the ankle. (Wiping between the toes is a condition of *ghusl,* but popularly is believed to be a requirement of *wuḍū'.*)

The ablution is completed with the pronunciation of the *ḥamdalah.* It is Sunnah to perform each gesture of the *wuḍū'* three times, but legally once is sufficient. Under certain conditions *wuḍū'* with water may be replaced by a variant, shorter purification with sand, earth, or stone, called the *tayammum.*

It is an assumption of the *wuḍū'* that water or earth has been used to cleanse the bodily orifices after calls of nature (*istibrā'* and *istinjā'*). In Islamic countries, privies are provided with running water for this purpose. As toilet-paper generally replaces water in the West, this practice becomes difficult if not impossible, but not all schools insist upon the *istibrā'* and the *instinjā'* as indispensable for *wuḍū'.*

Normally, water for *wuḍū'* must be running water, or water poured from a container from a source which can be considered clean. If it is necessary to use water which is not running, but nevertheless clean and thus suitable for ablution, a special problem is posed if there is no utensil with which to pour it. It is usually believed that dipping a hand into still water before that hand has itself been washed, ritually, compromises the water for ablution. If there is no way to raise the water to pour, the popular expedient is to scoop water from the surface with a rapid motion of the left hand until the right hand is wetted and can then be dipped in to continue the ablution. Although there are certainly situations more trying, this is perhaps a small example of the firmly established principle: "Necessity makes prohibited things permissible."

Usually, mosques have fountains in the entrance courtyard or other sources where water for ablution can be obtained. If an area of skin is covered with bandages, such that water does not reach it, it does not affect the validity of the ablution.

It was the Sunnah to use a very small amount of water for *wuḍū',* showing that its primary nature is not a physical cleaning, since that is already presumed, but a purification – the reestablishment of an existential equilibrium, through the symbolism of water as primordial substance, made possible by the ritual. It is *because* it is a ritual, a series of acts established by heaven, or consecrated by Divine "approval", that the symbolic nature of water can effect a spiritual purpose. *See* ABLUTIONS; GHUSL; ISTIBRĀ'; ISTINJĀ'; TAYAMMUM.

Wuqūf ("standing"). One of the rites of the

greater pilgrimage *(ḥajj)* is that of the "standing" (it is not physically necessary to stand) on the plain of 'Arafāt on the 9th day of *Dhū-l-Ḥijjah.* While some schools of law prescribe the presence of the pilgrim for the whole day, and others from noon onwards at least, it is admitted on the basis of Ḥadīth that even a momentary presence there before sundown fulfills the requirement of *wuqūf.* Failing that, however, the pilgrimage is incomplete.

An Imām delivers the sermon (*khuṭbah*) at 'Arafāt at the time of the noon prayer. The "standing" is the time when the invocation of the *talbiyah* is at its height. Altogether, the rite, which today brings millions of worshipers from around the world to one sacred place, is a foretaste of the Day of Judgement. At sundown the pilgrims proceed in a ritual "hastening" (*ifāḍah*) to nearby Muzdalifah which lies in the direction of Mecca. *See* PILGRIMAGE.

X

Xinjiang (Sinkiang: Chinese: "New Frontier" or "New Territory"). Formerly called Chinese Turkestan (*Hui Chiang*: Uighur territory), this western province comprises many cities of the "Silk Road": Kashgar, Urumchi, Yarkand, Khotan and the sites of Turfan (Qocho) and Dun Huang. It is also home to the Chinese nuclear test center of Lop Nor. It contains the Taklamakan desert and the Tarim river basin. The northwestern province of China, Xinjiang borders on Afghanistan, Pakistan and Kashmir and the Central Asian republics of Kazakhstan, Kyrgyztan and Tajikistan. Xinjiang is inhabited largely by Uighurs (in Chinese *Hei Hui*, "Black Hui"), a Turkic people from the Altai who are Muslim.

Xinjiang covers one-sixth of China and the Uighurs and other Muslim groups living there have been involved in a centuries' long struggle with the Chinese. Official Chinese figures put the Uighur and other Muslim nationalities' population in China at 17.6 million. This includes the Uighurs and the Hui, and others. The Hui, although the word is derived from the word "Uighur", denotes a people who are more Han than Turkic and most of whom do not live in Xinjiang. In Xinjiang the percentage of the population who are Muslims is 48% and Han Chinese 38%. Uighur groups outside China put the total figure of Uighurs higher, at 25 million, and say that almost all the Han Chinese settled in Xinjiang in the last forty eight years, raising the percentage to its present figure from an original proportion of 4%. There are also Uighurs in neighboring Kazakhstan and Kyrgyztan and Uzbekistan as well.

In 762 a Uighur army liberated the T'ang Chinese eastern captial of Lo-yang, on the Yellow River, south of Peking. Among those who greeted the victors were Soghdian Manichean priests, and the Uighur leader, the Khagan Mo-yu (Bogu Qan) was converted to Manicheism in an event which is recorded in a tri-lingual inscription in Karabalghasun on the river Orkhon in Mongolia. The Uighur ruler became a protector of Manicheism in Central Asia, including that area which was under Muslim control, because he threatened to slaughter the Muslims in his territory if Manicheans were harmed in Khorasan. In 840 the Uighur kingdom collapsed in the face of an attack by the Kirghiz, a related people, and Manicheism which had been allowed temples in the Yang-Tse basin in China was again proscribed by the Chinese rulers from 843 onward. Manichean priests were even massacred and dressed to look like Buddhists in death to remove traces of the religion. This came at a time of weakness of the T'ang dynasty, when Taoism gained over Buddhism while foreign ideas in art, science and religion penetrated China.

With the fall of the first Uighur Empire, the Uighurs moved south to Turfan from their former power base near lake Baikal. The second Uighur Empire flourished at Qocho (Kao-chang) which is modern Turfan, also as a Manichean kingdom at least as far as the ruling elite was concerned. The ruler of Qocho, the Idiqut, was visited by the Sufi al-Hallaj in the early 10th century. In the mid-13th century the Tarim basin was conquered by the Mongols under whom, later, Islam was to replace Buddhism and Manicheism in the region ever since.

After seventy years of struggles with the Dzungar Mongols, in 1759 Eastern Turkestan was conquered by the Qing dynasty but the local populations continued to resist the conquerors on and off. Under the Manchus there were a number of Muslim revolts in China and wars against them in 1820-28 (Lanchu), 1830 (Che Kanio), 1847 (Xianjiang), 1857 (Yunan), 1861 (Shansi). Led by Yaqub Beg, Turkestan became independent from 1867 to 1877. In 1884 the region was renamed Xinjiang and declared China's 19th province. After the republic of Sun Yat Sen in 1912, Turkestan rose in the Qumul rebellion which led to an independent Turkestan republic in 1933, and from 1944 to 1949.

In the last few years there have been many incidents in the province indicating resistance to the policy of imposing Chinese language and cultural dominance. These include Baren in 1990, Khoten in 1995 and Ghulje (Yining) in 1997. They include alleged arrests of over 57,000 ethnic Uighurs, masssacres, and summary executions of hundreds because of anti-Han chinese demonstrations or activities. *See* HUI HUI.

Y

Yaḥyā. John the Baptist, an important figure in Islam as a prophet mentioned in the Koran. The prayer of his father Zakariyyā (21:89) for a child in his old age is often cited as a model of a petition answered by God. He is also mentioned in the Koran 6:85; and 19:14-15:

> 'O John, take the Book forcefully';
> and We gave him judgement, yet a
> little child, and a tenderness from Us,
> and purity; and he was
> godfearing, and cherishing
> his parents, not arrogant, rebellious.
> 'Peace be upon him, the day
> he was born, and the day he
> dies, and the day he is raised
> up alive!'

Yalamlam. One of the stations on the approaches to Mecca known as *mawāqīt* (sing. *mīgāt*) where pilgrims must put on consecrated garb (*iḥrām*) if they have not already done so. Yalamlam is the *mīqāt* for pilgrims from the Yemen.

Yā Laṭīf. A supplementary prayer *(du'ā')* invoking the Divine Name al-Laṭī ("the Subtle", "the Gracious"), which can be recited in situations of distress, particularly serious illness, when Divine remedy is sought. It is very often performed by several persons on behalf of one who is afflicted and probably absent. Its form and order are as follows:

1. Formulation of the intention (*niyyah*) of the Yā Laṭīf prayer.
2. The *ta'awwudh* ("I take refuge in God from Satan the stoned one") is pronounced.
3. The *basmalah* ("In the name of God the Merciful, the Compassionate") and the *Sūrat al-Ikhlāṣ* (the Chapter of "Sincerity", Koran 92) is recited three times.
4. Then the following Koranic verse (42:19) is said: *Allāhu laṭīfun bi'ibādihī yarzuqu man yashā'u wa huwa-l-Qawiyyu-l-Azīz* ("God is gracious to His servants; He succors whom He will and He is the Strong, the Mighty").
5. A personal petition is silently made.
6. A prayer on the Prophet (*ṣalāh 'ala-n-nabī*) is said. For example:

> aṣ-ṣalātu wa-s-salāmu 'alayka yā sayyidī yā ḥabība-Llāh; aṣ-ṣalātu wa-s-salāmu 'alayka yā sayyidī yā nabiyya-Llāh; aṣ-ṣalātu wa-s-salāmu 'alayka yā sayyidī yā rasula-Llāh; alfu ṣalātin wa alfu salāmin 'alayk; wa ṣalla-Llāhu 'alayka wa 'alā 'ālika wa raḍiya 'an aṣḥābika, yā khayra mani ikhtāra-Llāh.
>
> Blessings and peace be upon you O Intimate of God; blessings and peace be upon you O Prophet of God; blessings and peace be upon you O Messenger of God. Thousandfold blessing and thousandfold peace, God bless You and Your people, and may His Grace be upon Your Companions, O best of them that God has chosen!

7. The petitioner says *Yā Laṭīfu* turning the head to the right, and *Yā Laṭīf* turning to the left, for a total of 129, or 300, or 500 or 1,000 times.
8. Then the petitioner repeats (6) the *ṣalāh 'alā n-nabī.*
9. A personal petition is made.
10. The prayer is closed by saying *al-ḥamdu li-Llāh* ("Praise to God").

See BASMALAH; al-IKHLĀṢ, SŪRAH; TA'AWWUDH.

Yan Tatsine. A heretical movement centered around Kano, Nigeria. Its members rose in rebellion against the civil authorities in December 1980 and were put down by the Nigerian Army in bloody fighting at the end of that month. The leader of the movement, Mallam Muhammadu Marwa, of Camerounian origin, was dubbed Mallam Maitatsine for his habit of calling God's curse (tatsine) on "anyone who doesn't agree with me".

Although the movement claimed to teach the Koran, it regarded the Prophet with derision, while the Mallam took the prophetic function to himself. The movement appealed to the disposessed young who had lost their roots in social upheavals of recent years. The Mallam was killed on December 29 1980, and police inquiries put the total number of dead at over 4,000. Since then, similar movements have arisen in Nigeria among the poor, as a result of social and economic dislocations, although not on such a scale.

Yaqūb. The Jacob of the Bible; he is mentioned

several times in Sūrah 12 of the Koran and also in 2:132-140.

Yasa. The tribal and religious law of the Mongols, who were shamanists. On several points the Yasa distinctly clashed with the prescriptions of the *sharī'ah.* The *Yasa* prescribed the slaughter of animals by a blow to the head; the Muslims slaughter animals ritually by cutting the throat and draining the blood. The *Yasa* looked upon water as a magical substance not to be used for washing (a Mongol was only washed after birth, and after death; in life he was only washed by the rain). The Mongols feared that the Muslim ablutions would bring down catastrophe through lightning and that the ablutions were in reality a magical ceremony. An additional point of antipathy as far as Muslims were concerned was that the Mongols were heavy drinkers, even the women regularly drinking themselves into a stupor.

The Mongol overlords inflicted punishment on their Muslim subjects because of the tensions between the *Yasa* and the *sharī'ah* until they were themselves converted to Islam. This was particularly true in Transoxiana, the *ulus,* or territory, of Chagatai (d. 639/1241), a son of Jenghiz Khan.

Eventually, the southern Mongols were converted to Islam. The law of Jenghiz Khan says:

> When there is no war raging against the enemy, there shall be hunting; the young shall be taught how to kill wild animals so that they become accustomed to fighting and acquire strength and endurance and will subsequently fight without sparing themselves against an enemy as though against wild animals.

In 1222, returning from the first Mongol incursion into the Muslim world, Jenghiz Khan stopped in Bukhara and expressed an interest in Islam, which was explained to him. He approved its principles and said that Allāh was not other than the Supreme Deity of the Mongols, the "Eternal Blue Sky" (*Tengri*). But he thought the pilgrimage was unnecessary since the *Tengri* is everywhere. *See* HŪLĀGŪ KHĀN; IL-KHANIDS; MONGOLS; RASHĪD ad-DĪN at-ṬABĪB.

Ya' Sin. The name of the thirty-sixth Sūrah ("chapter") of the Koran, so called after two letters of the Arabic alphabet with which the Sūrah begins. There is no unanimity about their interpretation; according to Ibn 'Arabī they stand for two Divine Names: al-Wāqi ("the Protector") and aṣ-Ṣalām ("Peace"). This Sūrah was called by the Prophet *qalb al-qur'ān* (the "heart of the Koran"). Dealing with the mysteries of revelation; immortality; life, death, Judgement, Heaven and Hell; the great cycles of time and the movements of the heavenly bodies; the mystery of the "pairs" (the dualities in manifestation); resurrection; creation, and so forth in passages of surpassing power and beauty, it is believed to contain all the essentials of the revelation. It is particularly recited for the dead (and recalls Matthew 25:21), and also to aid the recovery of the sick.

> And a sign for them is the night; We strip it of the
> day and lo, they are in darkness.
> And the sun – it runs to a fixed resting-place;
> that is the ordaining of the All-mighty, the All-knowing.
> And the moon – We have determined it by stations,
> till it returns like an aged palm-bough.
> It behoves not the sun to overtake the moon, neither
> does the night outstrip the day,
> each swimming in a sky.
> And a sign for them is that We carried their seed
> in the laden ship,
> and We have created for them the like of it
> whereon they ride;
> and if We will, We drown them,
> then none have they to cry to,
> neither are they delivered,
> save as a mercy from Us, and enjoyment
> for a while. (36:36-44)

It contains a famous parable introduced by the words: "And coin a parable for them, of the people of the city when the Messengers came to it" (36:13). This has been interpreted, as is possible with parables, in many ways; but within the context of this Sūrah's message about the Islamic revelation and the role of the Prophet as one of those that have been sent by God: "*Yā' Sīn,*; by the Generous Koran, verily Thou art one of them that have been sent, upon a straight path, in a sending down [revelation] by the Almighty, the Compassionate..." (36:1-5), the parable appears to refer to the Semitic monotheisms; the first two messengers are Abraham and Moses, the third Jesus and the fourth and last, the Prophet Muḥammad.

In virtue of this, *Yā' Sin* is one of the two hundred names of the Prophet.

> Strike for them a similitude –
> the inhabitants of the city, when
> the Envoys came to it;
> when We sent unto them two men,
> but they cried them lies, so We
> sent a third as reinforcement.
> They said, 'We are assuredly
> Envoys unto you.'
> They said, 'You are naught but
> mortals like us; the All-merciful
> has not sent down anything. You
> are speaking only lies.'
> They said, 'Our Lord knows we are
> Envoys unto you;
> and it is only for us to deliver
> the Manifest Message.'
> They said, 'We augur ill of you. If
> you give not over, we will stone you
> and there shall visit you from us
> a painful chastisement.'
> They said, 'Your augury is with you:
> if you are reminded? But you are a
> prodigal people.'
> Then came a man from the furthest parts of
> the city, running; he said, 'My people,
> follow the Envoys!
> Follow such as ask no wage of you,
> that are right-guided.
> And why should I not serve Him who
> originated me, and unto whom
> you shall be returned?
> What, shall I take, apart from Him, gods
> whose intercession, if the All-merciful
> desires affliction for me, shall not
> avail me anything, and who will
> now deliver me?
> Surely in that case I should be in
> manifest error.
> Behold, I believe in your Lord;
> therefore hear me!'
> It was said, 'Enter Paradise!'
> He said, 'Ah, would that my people
> had knowledge
> that my Lord has forgiven me
> and that He has placed me
> among the honored.'
> And We sent not down upon his
> people, after him, any host
> out of heaven; neither would We
> send any down.
> It was only one Cry and lo, they were
> silent and still.
> Ah, woe for those servants! Never
> comes unto them a Messenger, but
> they mock at him.
> What, have they not seen how many
> generations We have destroyed
> before them,
> and that it is not unto them
> that they return?
> they shall every one of them be arraigned
> before Us. (36:14-33)

In the *Kitāb Jawāhīr al-Qur'an* al-Ghazali explains that the surah *Yā' Sīn* is the heart of the Koran because it speaks of the entry of the saved one into paradise, and this is an awakening of the individual himself; the opening of one's own eyes is superior to the knowledge through the eyes of others.

Yathrib. The original name of Medina. The latter name of the city comes from *madīnat an-nabī* ("city of the Prophet"). *See* MEDINA.

Yawm ad-Dīn (lit. "the day of the religion" or "of the Judgement"), also called the "day of resurrection" (*yawm al-qiyāmah*), and the "hour" (*as-sā'ah*), and many other names. On that day the world is rolled up like a scroll, and the dead issue from their graves and are reunited with their bodies; the limbs testify to reveal the owner's good or evil deeds. On the scales of God's judgement nothing is overlooked: an atom's weight of good is manifest, and an atom's weight of evil. According to their deeds, and their belief, men are judged and their real nature revealed. Those who clove to the truth enter Paradise, and those who did not, enter Hell. The Koran as the last revelation looks forward to the end; many passages speak of the final day, when the trumpet is blown and the world struck down. The trumpet is blown again and the dead rise up. The blowing of the trumpet symbolizes the destruction of forms by pure sound or transcendence, or again, the separation of forms and their contents. The Koran speaks thus of that day:

...'When shall be the Day of Resurrection?'

But when the sight is dazed
and the moon is eclipsed,
and the sun and the moon are brought together,
upon that day man shall say,Whither to flee?'
No indeed; not a refuge! (75:6-12)

Upon that day faces shall be radiant,
gazing upon their Lord;
and upon that day faces shall be scowling,
thou mightest think the Calamity has been
wreaked on them.

No indeed; when it reaches the clavicles
and it is said, Who is an enchanter?'
and he thinks that it is the parting
and leg is intertwined with leg,
upon that day unto thy Lord shall be the driving.
(75:22-30)

When earth is shaken with a mighty shaking
and earth brings forth her burdens,
and Man says, What ails her?'
upon that day she shall tell her tidings
for that her Lord has inspired her.

Upon that day men shall issue in scatterings to
see their works, and whoso has done an atom's
weight of good shall see it, and whoso has done
an atom's weight of evil shall see it. (99)

.

...upon the day when the earth and the
mountains shall quake
and the mountains become a slipping heap of
sand.
(73:14)

If therefore you disbelieve, how will you
guard yourselves against a day that shall make
the children grey-headed?
Whereby heaven shall be split, and its promise
shall be performed. (73:17-18)

So be thou patient with a sweet patience;
behold, they see it as if far off, but We
see it is nigh.

Upon the day when heaven shall be as molten
copper and the mountains shall be as plucked
wool-tufts,
no loyal friend shall question loyal friend, as
they are given sight of them. The sinner will wish
that he might ransom himself from the chastisement
of that day even by his sons, his companion wife,
his brother, his kin who sheltered him, and
whosoever is in the earth, all together, so that then
it might deliver him.

Nay, verily it is a furnace
snatching away the scalp,
calling him who drew back
and turned away,
who amassed and hoarded.

Surely man was created fretful,
when evil visits him, impatient,
when good visits him, grudging,
save those that pray
and continue at their prayers,
those in whose wealth is a right known
for the beggar and the outcast,
who confirm the Day of Doom
and go in fear of the chastisement of their Lord
(from their Lord's chastisement none feels
secure) and guard their private parts
save from their wives and what their right hands
own, then not being blameworthy
(but whoso seeks after more than that,
they are the transgressors),
and who preserve their trusts
and their covenant,
and perform their witnessings,
and who observe their prayers.
Those shall be in Gardens, high-honoured.
What ails the unbelievers, running with
outstretched necks towards thee
on the right hand and on the left hand in knots?
What, is every man of them eager to be admitted
to a Garden of Bliss?
Not so; for We have created them
of what they know.

No! I swear by the Lord of the Easts and the
Wests, surely We are able
to substitute a better than they; We shall
not be outstripped.

Then leave them alone to plunge and play
until they encounter that day of theirs
which they are promised,
the day they shall come forth from the
tombs hastily, as if they were hurrying
unto a waymark,
humbled their eyes, overspreading
them abasement. That is the day

which they were promised. (70:5-44)

God is He that looses the winds, that stir up cloud,
then We drive it to a dead land
and therewith revive the earth, after it is dead.
Even so is the Uprising. (35:10)

And what shall teach thee what is the Day of Doom?
Again, what shall teach thee what is the Day of Doom?
A day when no soul shall possess aught to succour
another soul; that day the Command shall belong unto God. (82:17-19)

See ESCHATOLOGY; al-JANNAH.

Yasawiyyah. A *tariqah* found in Central Asian named after Ahmad ibn Ibrahim Ibn 'Alī of Yasi from Turkestan (d. 562/1166). Yasavi belonged to the tradition of Yusuf Hamadani; originally his *tariqah* was one of wanderers. It is not as large today in Central Asia as the Naqshbandiyyah, but it is related to it very closely as Yasawi was a spiritual predecessor of Baha'u ad-Dīn Naqshband. The Yasawis are also closely related to the Kubrawiyyah, all three being really branches of one original group. *See* SUFISM; KUBRAWIYYAH.

Yazdagird (d. 31/651). The last Sassanid ruler of Persia whose armies, led by the general Rustum, were defeated at the battle of Qādisiyyah in Iraq in 14/635. After the definitive Persian defeat at the Battle of Nihawand in 22/642, Yazdagird fled into Khorasan to seek help from his satraps, but found none; one by one his followers abandoned him. Finally, near Merv, he took refuge with a peasant, a miller, who, in a traditional account, asked him: "Who art thou?"

A Persian and a fugitive, said the King.

If thou canst content thee with barley bread, and the poor cresses that grow by the banks of the brook, I offer it to thee freely, said the miller, for that is all I have.

Content, said he, but get me some holy barsom twigs for my ritual besides.

So the poor miller went out to borrow barsom. But those he met with took him before the traitor Mahwi, the King's enemy; and Mahwi said to the wretched drudge; For whom does the like of thee seek barsom? The miller told his tale; and Mahwi knew it must be Yazdagird. Go back, said he; and cut off his head straightway; if not, thine own shall fall.

The poor man heard the word; but little he knew the reach of the deed. It was night whe he got home, and came into the presence of the King. Shame and fear in his heart, dry at the lips, he drew softly near, as he would whisper in his ear; then struck a dagger in his breast. And death was in the stroke. One sob the King gave; then his diademed head tumbled on the ground beside a barley loaf he had before him.

The world's soul is a mindless void; and witless is the turning Heaven. A mystery is its hatred or its grace. 'Tis wisest not to care – to watch changes without anger, and without love.

Then came in two cruel-hearted serving men, and dragged out the King's body bleeding. They heaved it into the whirling eddies of the Zark; and there the corpse of Yazdagird drifted, face up for a while, and then face under.

There is a Shī'ite legend that one of the daughters of Yazdagird was married by 'Alī to his son Ḥusayn, thereby bringing the blood of the Sassanid dynasty into the 'Alid line, which Twelve-Imām Shī'ites were to venerate. This is unlikely, and the name of the putative daughter, Shahrbanu ("Lady of the Land"), appears to be a particular cult name for the goddess Anahid (or Anahita), a Zoroastrian adoption of the Babylonian goddess Ishtar. Anahid was particularly important to the Sassanids who promoted a Zurvanite and heretical form of Zoroastrianism. Every Persian dynasty has claimed relation to the dynasties of the past.

Yazīdīs. An obscure dualist sect found among some Kurds in northern Iraq and also in Syria, Turkey and Iran. They may number a hundred thousand or more. Much religious practice is centered on the tomb of a certain Shaykh 'Ādī ibn Musāfīr in Lalish in the district of Mosul, who was probably an Ismā'īlī preacher. Nestorian Christians considered the tomb, notable for its depiction of a serpent at the entrance, to be that of a Christian. Various dates are given for his death: *557*/1162, *695*/1296, and also *133*/750. He is considered to be the author of a book called the *Kitab al-Jalwah* ("The Book of the Emergence"). Another canonic book is the *Mishaf Resh* or "Black Book" by Shaykh Ḥasan ibn Ādī.

The Yazīdīs' own name for themselves is *Dawasin* or *Dasnayye* (Yazīdī, implying a connection with the Umayyad Caliph Yazid at whose orders Ḥusayn was killed, probably originated as a name of abuse given them by Twelve-Imām Shī'ites; or perhaps the word comes Persian *yazata* or *yazdan* meaning "divinities"). They are often called scornfully "devil worshipers". The "Peacock Angel" (*Malak Ṭā'ūs*) is their euphemism for evil, or the devil, which they fear and seek to appease, and do not call by the customary term in Arabic, *Shaytan*. They believe that evil is part of the Divinity, along with good. The Yazīdīs make representations of this Peacock Angel which they carry in festivals. The Yazidis believe that evil is to be found in lettuce, or as their traditions put it "the devil once hid in a lettuce patch". This belief is ridiculed by their neighbors; it probably goes back to the Manichean practice of vegetarianism, for the Manicheans believed that the Divine light was contained in plants in a greater proportion than any other substance in this world; but lettuce poses a special problem; the evil of the lettuce may be nothing more than a folk warning of the ancient vegetarian cults regarding a plant which any well-informed modern traveller in the East also avoids religiously, just as he or she drinks tea rather than unboiled water.

The Yazīdīs' more important heterodoxies have cost them innumerable persecutions and struggles. They are closely related to similar Gnostic sects like the Ahl-i Ḥaqq. *See* AHL-I ḤAQQ; MANICHEISM.

Yemen (from an Arabic root meaning "felicity"). The region in the south of the Arabian peninsula, which was called Arabia Felix by the Romans, was divided into two separate countries: the Republic of Yemen with its capital at Sana'a', and the People's Democratic Republic of Yemen with its capital at Aden. In 1990 the two countries were formally united as the Republic of Yemen. The population is now 13,483,178. The Yemen receives the monsoon rains from the Indian Ocean, is fertile and agriculturally very rich. It was the seat of numerous civilizations in pre-Islamic times, notably the Sabaean, Minaean and Himyaritic.

Until the time of Constantine the Great, when cremation in the Roman Empire was replaced by the practice of burial, the economic basis of the Yemen was the export of frankincense used as incense, and myrrh used for cosmetics, both from indigenous trees. Many religions in turn played an important role in the Yemen: Judaism was the religion of one of the kings in the Yemen named Dhū Nuwāṣ, who was overthrown by the Christian Negus of Ethiopia acting on behalf of the Byzantine Emperor who had called for the punishment of Dhū Nuwāṣ because of the destruction of the Christian community of Najrān (523 A.D.) in South Arabia.

Christianity spread widely in the Yemen as a result of Abyssinian suzerainty, until, when the Yemen became a Persian satrapy (around 575 A.D.), Zoroastrianism was introduced.

In the first century of the Hijrah, the Yemen was converted to Islam. Today, 40% of the population of the Republic of Yemen, mostly tribesmen in the mountains, are Zaydī Shī'ites. (The most recent Imām of these Shī'ites died in exile in London after the declaration of the republic.) The rest are Sunnīs of the Shāfi'ī School of Law. There are also small minorities of different branches of Ismā'īlism, remnants of once larger communities.

Yemenis from the Hadramaut were noted seafarers in the age of the dhows, and in the age of steamships they became stokers famed for their ability to withstand great heat. They have migrated near and far, to India and particularly to Indonesia where there is a large community of Indonesians of Yemeni descent.

Yezidis, *see* YAZIDIS.

Yemen, Breath of the. It was a saying of the Prophet that "there is a wind which comes from the Yemen which brings me comfort". The saying is also well-known in India as: "There is a wind from India ."

Yunus. The Jonah of the Bible. He is also called Dhū-n-Nūn ("he of the fish"). Yunus was a Divine Messenger (*rasūl*), who was swallowed by a fish, praised God nevertheless, and was delivered. The Arabic letter *nūn* (with the ancient meaning of fish) is a semi-circle, open at the top, with a point in its center. It symbolizes a vessel, or ark, which carries the point, the germ of future manifestations, across the gulf that separates one cycle from another. This transition between worlds must be made in darkness and the preservation of the immortal soul or, macrocosmically speaking, the continuity between cycles, is symbolized by Yunus' trials. His message is salvation through complete resignation to God.

Yunus Emre (d. *725*/1325?). An Anatolian Turkish poet who composed Gnostic poetry in the vernacular. He is very popular with Turkish Sufis and his poetry has often been set to mystic songs. It is very likely that he is an apocryphal figure, a name around which a genre and a popular corpus of anonymous poetry has collected. Humanism is one of his themes:

> Here or in India or in Africa
> All things resemble each other.
> We feel the same love for grains.
> Before death we tremble together.
> I am Job: I have found all his patience
> I am St. George: I died a thousand times."

The sentiments are very close to Rumi:

> Whoever has one drop of love
> Possesses God's existence.

and he is essentially Gnostic, the ideas resembling those of al-Hallaj, who was also very popular in Turkey:

> If you don't identify Man as God,
> All your learning is of no use at all.
> The universe is the oneness of Deity
> The true man is he who knows this unity.
> You better seek Him in yourself
> you and He aren't apart – you're one.
> The image of the Godhead is a mirror:
> The man who looks sees his own face in there.
> Death should give you no fear at all
> Fear not, your life is eternal.
> He is God Himself – human are His images.
> See for yourself: God is man, that is what He is.

Yurt. A round dwelling, made of wood and felt, used by Mongolian and Turkic nomads in the regions around Central Asia. This style of nomad dwelling is completely different from the famous "black tents" of the Arabs, made of twisted goat's hair. Yurt, as well as meaning the home, also means a home territory. The yurt and the tent are respectively symbols of the two great nomadic cultures each with a different origin and filiation in the dim past. See MONGOLS; YASA.

Yūsuf. The Joseph of the Bible, his story is told with concise beauty in the Sūrah *Yūsuf* (the "Chapter of Joseph") of the Koran. The favorite son of Jacob (*Ya'qūb*), he was sold into slavery by his jealous brothers, and taken to Egypt; there he was taken as a slave into the household of Fitfir (Potiphar; also misread as "Qitfir" in some manuscripts), a great man of the country. He was so handsome that when the women of Egypt saw him, in their distraction, they cut their hands with their serving knives. This proverbial beauty is said to be one of the rewards of paradise, where all men are as beautiful as Yūsuf.

The wife of Fitfir made advances to Yūsuf. He resisted them and tried to escape, and his innocence was proved by the fact that his shirt was torn at the back. He was, nevertheless, put into prison, and released only after many years for correctly interpreting Pharaoh's dreams. His brothers came to him to ask for food in time of famine. His shirt sent to his father restored the sight Ya'qub had lost from weeping for the loss of Yūsuf.

Z

Zabūr. The Arabic name of the Psalms of David (*Dāwūd*). The word echoes the Hebrew *Zamīr* ("song") and *Mizmōr* ("melody"), both of which are used to designate the Psalms of David. The *Zabūr* is described in the Koran as having been given to David by God: "and to David We gave the Psalms (*Zabūr*)" (4:163). This means that the Psalms are accepted in Islam as being revealed scripture, along with the Pentateuch and the Gospels. *See* BIBLE.

Zāhid (from *zahida*, "to abstain", and cognate with *zuhd*, "abstinence"). An ascetic. *See* ZUHD.

Ẓāhir (lit. "outward"). *Aẓ-Ẓāhir* is a Divine Name ("The Outward"), which is complementary to *al-Bāṭin* ("The Inward"). To these are joined in the Koran the Divine Names *al-Awwal* ("The First") and *al-Ākhir* ("The Last"). "He is the First and the Last, the Outward and the Inward, and He is All-knowing of all things" (57:3).

The words *ẓāhir* and *bāṭin* are also used to mean "exoteric" and "esoteric". The theologians and legal scholars representing an exoteric point of view are sometimes termed the *'ulamā' aẓ-ẓāhir* ("the savants of the exterior") by the mystics who are called the *'ulamā' al-bāṭin*. The Koran makes the statement quoted above in the context of verses relating to manifested creation; the First and the Last refer to time and the Outward and the Inward to space; quite clearly any scholarly perspective that attempts to exclude the outward in favor of the inward, or vice versa, is partial. The true Sufis have never failed to make this point clear and to aim at a realization of the Totality.

Ẓāhirī. A school of law which never gained a significant acceptance and is now extinct. It was begun by disciples of Dāwūd ibn Khalaf al-Isfahānī, called *aẓ-Ẓāhirī* ("the literalist"; *204-241*/819-855 or *297*/910).

He had been himself a disciple of ash-Shāfi'ī but he rejected completely the doctrine of analogy (*qiyās*), and the opinions of any but the closest of the Companions, and insisted upon a strictly literal interpretation of the Koran and Sunnah. The objection to analogy went so far as even to forbid *searching* for the reasons for a religious law.

Ibn Ḥazm in Spain was a Ẓāhirī, as were a number of Sufis including Ibn 'Arabī. This surprising fact leads one to conclude that the literalism of the Ẓāhirīs was not simply a desire for simple solutions. Their literalism did not stop at the letter, but rather took it as a point of departure, as an intensification of the apprehension of the Divine Reality. It is Dāwūd ibn Khalaf who reports the Ḥadīth: "he who loves with unrequited love and remains chaste, dies a martyr". This ambiance of heroic lyricism seems an aspect of the absoluteness of the Ẓāhirī stand. It breathes the same kind of certainty which comes from the Koran itself for, in the words of the Ẓāhirīs: "We describe God as He describes Himself."

Zā'ir (lit. "visitor"). A name for a person visiting the tomb of the Prophet. Such visits are called *ziyārah*; the term is transposed for visits in search of blessing made to Saint's tombs. In some countries the visiting of Saint's tombs is a very important part of religious life, despite the fact that there are Ḥadīth which discourage this.

Zakāh (Taken to mean "purification" from the verb *zakā* which signifies "to thrive", "to be wholesome", "to be pure"). The giving up of a portion of the wealth one may possess, in excess of what is needed for sustenance, to purify or legitimize what one retains. *Zakāh* is one of the Five Pillars and is in effect a tax on one's possessions. It may be paid directly to the poor as alms, or to travelers, or to the state. *Zakāh* may be used for the upkeep of the poor, for those who own less than that prescribed for the paying of *zakāh* and who have no earning capacity; for the destitute; Muslims in debt through pressing circumstances; travelers in need; those serving the cause of Islam, and fighting in the way of God (*al-muqātilūn fī sabīl Allāh*); for slaves to buy themselves out of bondage; for benevolent works. Those who collect tax on behalf of the state for disbursement are also allowed to take the needs of their livelihood from it.

The amount due varies according to different

kinds of properties. A contribution in kind, whose minimum schedule is called a *nisbah*, is specified on numbers of livestock according to species but only on those which are freely pastured and not used for the immediate needs of the household or as work animals. On land it is the *'ushr*, or tenth, of its produce, although further refinements exist in regard to different grains, irrigated and non-irrigated lands, etc. On gold and silver, that is, liquid assets, to which are also assimilated merchandise, financial instruments, stocks and bonds, beyond an untaxed franchise of "200 dinars", the *nisbah* is 2.5% of that value which has been held for one year. On the other hand, alms need not be limited to the legal minimums; what is paid over the legal minimum is *sadaqah*; while benevolent, it is also recommended as a pious and expiatory act.

The classical rates of *zakāh* assumed that wealth was held in the form of cattle and land rather than financial instruments or paper. The rates of *zakāh* on cattle and land production are much higher than those on monetary possessions. Therefore, some modern Muslim scholars are studying ways on how rates of *zakāh* may be equitably adjusted to contemporary modes of wealth, so that the religious tax falls between 5-10% of income in excess of essential need.

The person liable for *zakāh* must be Muslim and not indebted to the value of the worth upon which the tax is due. Tithe is not due upon personal dwellings. It is also not assessed on basic necessities, personal possessions, furniture, tools and instruments, riding and draft animals etc.

The *zakāh al-fiṭr*, more commonly known as *fitrah*, is considered by most to be non-obligatory alms, but almost always paid by the pious, roughly equivalent to a quart of grain per person in a household, paid directly to the needy at the end of Ramaḍān. *See* FIVE PILLARS; KHARĀJ; SADAQAH; 'USHR.

Zakariyyā. The father of Yaḥyā (John the Baptist), in the Koran he was a guardian of the Blessed Virgin who kept vigil in a *miḥrāb* (prayer niche), which is symbolically assimilated to the Holy of Holies. When Zakariyyā came to see her he found that she received sustenance directly from God and required no food (3:37). Zakariyyā in his old age had petitioned God for a son and was granted Yaḥyā (3:38). As a sign of God's favor Zakariyyā was struck dumb for three days.

Zakāt, *see* ZAKĀH

Zamakhsharī, Abū-l-Qāsim Maḥmūd ibn 'Umar (*467-538*/1075-1144). A Persian who was a great authority on the Arabic language, he wrote studies of grammar and literature (*Asās al-Balāghah*, "Foundations of Rhetoric"), but is best known for his commentary on the Koran, *al-Kashshāf an Ḥaqā'iq at-Tanzīl* ("The Unveiler of the Truths of Revelation"). While this book maintains the Mu'tazilite, or "rationalist", point of view, and affirms the createdness of the Koran, it was much studied because it extols the literary beauty of the text.

Zamzam. The name of the well near the Ka'bah. It is located 20m/60ft southeast of the Black Stone corner of the Ka'bah, near the Station of Abraham (*Maqām Ibrāhīm*), within the Grand Mosque of Mecca. The spring of Zamzam appeared when Hagar and her son Ishmael, abandoned in the desert, had exhausted the water in the goatskin given them by Abraham. Then Hagar cast herself to and fro in desperation, but God heard Ishmael (*Ismā'īl*; the name means "God hears") and the water gushed forth, making the sound *zam, zam*.

The site of the well was later forgotten for a time, for it had been filled up with stones and treasure trove by the Jurhumites who inhabited Mecca before the Quraysh. Its site was rediscovered by the uncle of the Prophet, 'Abd al-Muṭṭalib.

To drink the water of Zamzam is a rite of both the lesser and the greater pilgrimages. Today the well is not open at the surface; instead the water is led off to underground galleries reached by a flight of steps where numerous faucets supply the water to scores of people a time.

The well itself is 31m/100ft deep and is lined by masonry stones to approximately a third of its depth. The circumference of the opening is approximately 1.80m/5ft. Today the water is passed under ultraviolet lights for bacterial control. The water supply is extremely copious, enough for thousands of people daily. The well is fed by several springs, the largest of which enters the well at a third of the distance from the surface. Contrary to descriptions once current in the West, the taste of Zamzam is agreeable and refreshing, and it can be drunk in vast quantities.

The water is carried by pilgrims back to all parts of the Islamic world where it is drunk as water filled with blessing and given to the sick. The well of Zamzam is mentioned in Psalm 84: "How amiable are thy tabernacles, O Lord of hosts! Blessed are they that dwell in Thy house... who passing through the valley of Baca [Bakkah is the ancient name of Mecca] make it a well..." *See* MECCA; KA'BAH.

Zanānah. The name of the women's quarters in a Indian Muslim household, equivalent to the Turkish *haramlik.*

Zands. A short-lived (*1163-1209*/1750-1794) series of monarchs in Persia who seized power during the lengthy period of instability after the reign of Nādir Shāh (*see* AFSHARIDS). The most able of the Zands was Muḥammad Karīm who ruled as the representative (*awkil*) of a nominal Safavid Shah, Ismā'īl III. The Zands were supplanted by the Qajars.

Zanj. The name given by the Arabs to the black tribes inhabiting the coastal regions of East Africa (whence "Zanzibar"), which were a source of slaves for the Muslim Empire. In the decade around *257*/870 a group of Iraqi farm slaves rose in rebellion ("the revolt of the Zanj") against the 'Abbāsids, and maintained control over much of the Shaṭṭ al-Arab. They sacked Basra before they were finally put down by the Caliph's troops.

Zayd ibn al-Ḥārith (d. *8*/630). A slave given to the Prophet by Khadījah, the Prophet's first wife; when Zayd's father found him and tried to free him, Zayd refused to leave the Prophet, who himself freed him and made him an adopted son.

The Prophet once entered the house of Zayd and, looking upon his wife Zaynab, was enchanted by her beauty; there was some embarrassment, after which Zayd divorced Zaynab and the Prophet married her. A revelation later treated of the legality of marrying the wife of an adopted son (33:37). Zayd was a noted warrior and died in battle.

Zaydīs (Ar. *Zaydiyyah*). A branch of Shī'ism, also called "Fivers", found in the Yemen. Upon the death in *95*/713 of the fourth Shī'ite Imām Alī Zayn al-'Ābidīn, the Zaydīs diverged from the other Shī'ites (who went on to become the Twelve-Imām majority) in that they chose to follow Zayd (d. *122*/740) as Imām, rather than his brother Muḥammad al-Baqīr. They rallied to Zayd's more vigorous resistance to the Umayyads.

Today the Zaydīs are the most moderate of all Shī'ite groups and the closest to the Sunnīs, although they have their own school of law (*madhhab*). Their Shī'ism is derived from a political preference for the rule and authority of 'Alī and his descendants, and it has little or none of the ascription of supernatural powers, supernal knowledge and the function of intermediary between man and God that is found among the Twelve-Imām Shī'ites. Because of their affinity with other Shī'ites, however, the Yemen has historically been a place of refuge for Shī'ite exiles, notably various splinter groups of the Ismā'īlīs. A Zaydī state also existed near the Caspian Sea among the Daylamites from *250*/864, with interruptions, until *520*/1126.

From the beginning of the *4th*/10th century the Zaydīs have been established in the Yemen, first at Sa'ādah and later at Sanā'a' and today comprise about 40% of the population of the Yemen Arab Republic. The rest of the Yemenis are Sunnīs of the Shāfi'ī School of Law. In the Zaydī theory of the Imāmate any descendant of 'Alī can be Imām; there can be more than one, or indeed, none at all. The claim is established by a demonstrated capacity for rule – that is, by taking power – and confirmed by learning. But there are no overtones of supernatural knowledge, miraculous powers, and prerogatives that hedge the concept of the Imāmate among the the Twelvers. The Zaydīs accept the Caliphates of Abū Bakr and 'Umar, and are split over 'Uthmān, some accepting his Caliphate as being legitimate only for the first years. The Zaydīs do not admit *mut'ah* (temporary marriages), as do the Twelve-Imām Shī'ites. They were historically much influenced by the Mu'tazilites, or rationalists.

The Zaydī kingdom of the Rassī dynasty was founded by Yaḥyā ibn Ḥusayn ar-Rassī. The dynasty ruled in Sanā'a', with many wars and interruptions, from the *4th*/10th century until 1962, when it was overthrown by Colonel 'Abd Allāh as-Sallāl. Internal fighting between Republicans and Royalists continued until 1972, but the Imām had gone into exile in London before that and has since died.

Zaynab bint 'Alī. A daughter of 'Alī and Fāṭimah.

Zaynab bint Jaḥsh. A wife of the Prophet. She had been the wife of his adopted son Zayd. Zayd divorced her so that the Prophet could marry her. *See* WIVES of the PROPHET.

Zaynab bint Khuzaymah. A wife of the Prophet and a widow of 'Ubayd, a Muslim slain at Badr. She died not long after her marriage to the Prophet. For her kind nature she was called the "mother of the poor", *Umm al-masākīn. See* WIVES of the PROPHET.

Zaynab bint Muḥammad. A daughter of the Prophet and Khadījah. Her husband Abu-l-'Āṣ was an unbeliever; she left him to join her father in Medina. Abu-l-'Āṣ was taken prisoner by the Muslims at the Battle of Badr and ransomed by Zaynab. He returned to Mecca and was later taken prisoner again and freed by Zaynab a second time before he finally entered Islam.

Zāwiyah (lit. "a corner"). In North Africa the word means an oratory or small mosque, a place of religious retreat, or in particular, a meeting place of Sufis for prayer and the invocation of the Name of God (*dhikr*). A *zāwiyah* may be small or large, even a mausoleum of a Saint associated with a religious order. It is the equivalent of what is called a *khānaqah* in the East, or a *tekke* or *durgah* in Turkey. It can also be that part of a home that is set aside for prayer.

Zikr, *see* DHIKR.

"Zikrism." A modern Soviet name for the Qadiriyyah Sufi *tariqah.* The term is inexact since all Sufi orders practice some form of invocation or *dhikr* ("*zikr*"). See DHIKR.

Zīnah. Fornication or sexual relations which are illicit in Islamic law, a sin and socially considered a crime, for which the Koran mentions different degrees of punishment, from mild to severe. Stoning, however, is not one of them; this existed among the Jews (see Deuteronomy 22:21-24). Zealous stories to the contrary do exist which intend to show that stoning was a punishment in Islam, but they carry the marks of apocrypha.

Conviction for *zīnah* in a court of law requires four eye witnesses (thus apocryphal stories typically have the guilty spontaneously confessing). The witnesses can themselves be liable for equal punishment for false accusation, and since even confessions need to be made four separate times and can be retracted, it is in practice something which Islamic law has put beyond the scope of society's punishment.

Islam's approach to the problem of applying some of its harsher laws is analagous to the situation prevailing in Judaism which, in the case of similar laws, has imposed so many conditions to their being carried out, that extreme sentences are never imposed for moral crimes. In the past Islamic courts have been so reluctant to impose sanctions in such cases that even a child out of wedlock need not be taken to be a proof. For this there came into existence the strategem of the Sleeping Foetus. (As one Muslim Judge in the Gulf recently said "What would we have to have done with the Virgin Mary?") *See* SLEEPING FOETUS.

Zindīq (from Persian *zand*, "free interpretation" meaning "heresy"). A freethinker, atheist, or heretic. Originally *zindīq* meant dualist; thus one could speak of a Christian zindīq. In the West the term was sometimes translated as materialist because dualists make matter equivalent to God, or rather, two gods. If matter is considered to exist independently of a higher principle then limitation is also an absolute, and an anti-god which means a god of evil, is an inevitable consequence. This can be seen in physics which, when it concludes that matter (rather than a principle of God is reality), also concludes that creation begins with matter and anti-matter. If matter is divine or reality itself, then so is the individual, hence dualist and freethinker are associated concepts.

Zindīq was a term used in Persia in the reign of Bahram I (Varahran 273-276) when the Sassanids tried to expel from their empire all "Ahrimanic" beliefs and practices, notably the Manicheans. It is in this sense that zindīq was also used by the Muslims. Manicheans were present in great numbers among the clerks employed by the 'Abbāsids in Iraq and Persia, among them Ibn al-Muqaffā', the author of *Kalīlah wa Dimnah* (or such at least was the accusation made against him, for he was nominally a convert to Islam from a Persian religion).

For a time Manicheism threatened to become the dominant religion of the educated classes, but from *162*/779 to *169*/786 there was a wave of persecution of Manicheans in the 'Abbāsid Empire. The Caliph al-Mahdī had Manicheans crucified in Aleppo, and in the last two years of his reign a systematic attack was begun which sought to extirpate them. They were sought out, brought before an officer called the *Arīf* ("expert"), and punished. A history of the time says:

> 'Tolerance is laudable', the Spiller [the Caliph Abu-l-Abbās] had once said, 'except in matters dangerous to religious belief, or to the Sovereign's dignity.'
>
> Mahdī [d. *169*/785] persecuted Freethinkers, and executed them in large numbers. He was the first Caliph to order the composition of polemical works in refutation of Freethinkers and other heretics; and for years he tried to exterminate them absolutely, hunting them down throughout all provinces and putting accused persons to death on mere suspicion.
>
> "Hast thou any doubt at all in thy mind", runs a catechism of these times, "that the Koran was brought down to the Prophet of God by the faithful spirit Gabriel; that in that Book God has declared what is lawful and what is unlawful, and ordained His rules, and established His observances; and has expounded the history of what has been and what is to be to the end of time?"
>
> "I have no doubt", the catechumen shall reply.
>
> "Hast thou any doubt at all in thy mind that..."
>
> "I have no doubt."

This continued under al-Hādī, and Hārūn ar-Rashīd, and into the Caliphate of al-Ma'mūn (d. *218*/833), but by this time most Manicheans had gone underground, disguising themselves as Muslims, and many were to metamorphose into the Seveners. In his *Fihrist*, Ibn an-Nadim (d. *385*/955) gives several lists of theologians and writers whom he says were really Dualists in disguise. Others were being uncovered at the time. Manicheism is now called *al-Manawiyyah* in Arabic. (*See* SEVENERS.)

After the early period, with some notable exceptions, the practice in Islam in regard to atheism or various forms of heresy, has been more and more one of tolerance as long as it is a private matter. However, heresy and atheism expressed in public may well be considered a scandal and a menace to society; in some societies they are punishable, at least to the extent that the perpetrator is silenced. In particular, blasphemy against God and insulting the Prophet are major crimes. There is a document called the Letter of the Three Imposters which was the most scandalous free-thinking treatise of its time which is attributed to Ubayd Allāh the Fāṭimid and which found its way into Europe. *See* ANTINOMIANISM; MANICHEISM.

Ziryāb (*173-243*/789-857). A famous singer and musician in Baghdad, a pupil of Ibrāhīm al-Mawṣilī, or his son Isḥāq, Ziryāb left Iraq and came to Cordova where he was well received by the Umayyad ruler 'Abd ar-Raḥmān II (d. *237*/852). Ziryāb's real name was Abu-l-Ḥasan 'Alī ibn Nāfi'. He brought to Spain a new musical form from Baghdad of which he was the master; he also improved the instrument *al'ūd* ("lute") by adding a fifth string. The resulting new style flourished in Spain and became classical "Andalusian" music which is still played today, particularly by the Arab orchestras of Morocco. Ziryāb became the arbiter of fashion at Cordova and introduced other cultural refinements of the East of his day, including fine cooking, another tradition which has survived in Morocco.

Ziyārah (lit. "visit"). A visit to the tomb of the Prophet and to the holy places of Medina in general. Traditions have grown up about the order in which various stations in the Prophet's Mosque (*al-Masjid ash-sharīf*) are to be visited, and what recitations should be made in each place. The program of visits also includes other mosques in Medina, the battlefield of Uhud, and the al-Baqī' cemetery.

The word is also used for the visits to the tombs of Saints or Shī'ite Imāms. The practice is in fact forbidden in Islam by Ḥadīth, but the *ijmā'* ("consensus") of the Islamic community has made it otherwise. The interdiction is upheld by the Wahhābīs, who have nevertheless been obliged to tolerate the visiting of the tomb of the Prophet.

It was, and still is, a common Sufi practice to visit the tombs of Saints as places appropriate for meditation and seeking God's grace. There are innumerable such pilgrimage Saint's tombs from Morocco to Indonesia, and many renowned as great gathering places of Sufis, particularly at times of festive commemoration. Some are renowned in different ways; the Shaykh al-Būzīdī advised the seeker who could not find a true spiritual master to go and pray at the tomb of Abū Madyān in Algeria.

The visiting of tombs of Shī'ite Imāms and their relatives is an important religious activity for Twelve-Iman Shī'ites. Such places include Medina, Mashhad, Kerbala, Najaf, Kāzimayn, and Qumm. Shī'ite manuals of pious visitations are called *ziyarat-nama*. *See* MOSQUE of the PROPHET.

Zoroastrianism. A renewal of the original Indo-European tradition as transmitted to the Iranian peoples. The Koran calls the Zoroastrians *Mājūs*. Muslim authorities, going back to the Caliph 'Umar, accept Zoroastrians as a "People of the Scripture", with a revealed religion, and thus qualified for the protection of the Islamic state. Known in Iran as *Zardushtis*, Zoroastrians had the status of *dhimmis*, who could not be compelled to enter Islam. See AHL al-KITĀB.

Zoroastrianism is extremely ancient; its Prophet, Zoroaster lived some time between 1400 and 1200 B.C. or even earlier, and was the first to proclaim that salvation is possible for all, the humble of mankind as well as the heroes of legend. He composed hymns called *Gāthās* to glorify the Creator, to which were later added the writings known as *Avesta*. Among his teachings are doctrines of a resurrection after death as the assembly of the bones and their reunion with a heavenly body, the existence of the soul (*urvan*), the existence of heaven and hell, (and an intermediate state, or limbo between the two), the end of time and the world (*frasho-kereti* the perfection of time or *frashegird*) after a struggle between the forces of good and evil (sometimes defined as that between the Saoshyant, the world saviour, and Azhi Dahhaka, a kind of demon, not destroyed by an early mythic hero and chained inside in Mount Demavend), and a universal Last Judgement. These concepts, of course, reappear in Christianity and Islam. Zoroastrian metaphysics provides the prototype for the doctrine of the Logos (the *Amesha Spenta*) and that of the Angels. Michael and Satan in particular, are considered by many scholars of religion as the transformed assimilation into Semitic religions of the figures of Ahura Mazda (later called Ohrmazd) and Angra Maiynu (later called Ahriman). Thus, many of the teachings of Zoroaster are found in post-exile Judaism.

The conquest of Babylon by Cyrus in 539 B.C. and thereafter Egypt by his son Cambyses in 529 B.C. brought Zoroastrian doctrines to all the classical world. The Indo-European peoples have demonstrated an intellectual propensity to think metaphorically, to idealize, to take the concrete and turn it into the abstract. The Semitic peoples have a marked propensity to concretize. When these two dynamics of consciousness came in contact with each during the Iranian expansion into the Semitic world, being diametrically opposed to each other, a reaction took place which could be termed alchemical, a reaction which is still going on to this day. Semitic religious elements combined with Zoroastrian ones to produce new religions. Notably numerous Gnosticisms, and then Christianity and Islam appeared on the Semitic side of the equation. These appeared not only through Judaism, but through the action of Zoroastrianism directly upon the Abrahamic monotheism of the Arabs, and on other religious traditions of Mesopotamia. Zoroastrianism also felt the effect of Semitic consciousness, and this produced Mithraism (evidently strongly influenced by Hellenism as well), but especially Zurvanism, and Manicheism on the Iranian side of the equation. In religious terms, the collision of worlds formed the spiritual, intellectual, and psychological ambience for the revelation of Christianity and Islam.

Zoroaster taught the coming of a world saviour (*Saoshyant*), and Zoroastrian myth recounts, moreover, that the seed of Zoroaster was preserved in a lake and that a virgin bathing in that lake would conceive the saviour. The story of the Magi, or Zoroastrian priests, bringing gifts and following a star (perhaps the astra of Zoroaster, as it was once interpreted) is the mythic element used to confirm to the intended audience which at the time of the New Testament was familiar with Zoroastrian prophecies, that here indeed, was the prophesied Saoshyant or world saviour. (Probably also influencing the Magi story was the journey of a Zoroastrian King Tiridates of Armenia, a vassal, who came to Rome to swear fealty to Nero). In Christianity, besides the Zoroastrian elements which are the bedrock, the Canaanite myth of Tammuz, the vegetation god who dies and returns to life, obviously provides the other critical element.

Besides the great metaphysical and eschatological context that Zoroastrianism contributes to Islam (it is worthy to note that the Arabic word for Paradise, *firdaws*, is originally from Persian *pardes* through the Greek, revealing the origin of the concept), one can point to the five daily prayers, also found among the Zoroastrians, the use of water for sacralization before prayer and as a great purification (ablutions and *barashnom*), and an emphasis on ritual purity. (In Zoroastrianism water has the power to return the priest to the state of unfallen man for the performance of rituals; this becomes ritual ablution among the Essenes and the Mandaeans, Baptism for the Christians, and ritual ablution in Islam.)

The importance of intention in Islam, in Arabic *niyyah*, would seem to derive from the Zoroastrian "good thought". Besides Iranian influences upon the Arabs for many centuries before Islam, afterwards there followed many centuries where innumerable Muslim theologians of Persian origin brought their cultural background into their religion. Many other originally Zoroastrian details have been incorporated into Muslim doctrine and practice such as the idea, familiar to most Muslims, of the soul crossing the bridge after death (this is the Zoroastrian *chinvat*; no reference to a bridge exists in the Koran), and the widespread injunction among Muslims, attributed to Ḥadīth, of not breathing into fire as, for example, in not blowing out a candle with the breath. (Zoroastrians regard fire as sacred, and the maintenance of perpetual flames, some today which have existed without interruption for two thousand years, is a central element of ritual worship.) The Muslim belief that the dead can hear for three days probably originates with the Zoroastrian idea that the dead soul lingers for three days before departing for the other world. (Whence also the three days interval between Good Friday and the Sunday) The dialogue between between God and Satan as found in the Koran (and also in Goethe's *Faust*), is prefigured by a similar exchange between Ahura Mazda and Ahriman in Yasna 30/40 (*Zand Akasih*) and in the *Bundahishn*. The assembly of the bones, found in Ezekiel, and in the Koran as part of the resurrection of dead, is in the Zoroastrian *Zodsperad*. In Zoroastrianism there is a primordial tree in the first world whose leaves contained the cure for all the diseases that entered the world after it was attacked by Ahriman. There is a widely repeated saying in Islam, usually presented as a Ḥadith, that "for every illness there is a cure."

Despite appearance, Zoroastrianism is fundamentally non-dualist in that the principle of evil, Angra Mainyu, while "uncreated" (but rather a byproduct of creation), is not symmetrical with the Creator and the principle of good, Ahura Mazda. Angra Maiynu cannot attack Ahura Mazda Himself (unlike Manicheism where the principle of evil attacks the principle of good). Angra Maiynu attacks instead the creation of Ahura Mazda after a period of thousands of years. Nor can Angra Maiynu even corrupt *all* of the creation of Ahura Mazda. He can only corrupt the lowest part of the creation, the *getik*, or material plane which is vulnerable to the principle of evil, while the creation in itself is thoroughly good. (In Manicheism the physical world itself is a mixture of the two principles.) Nor can Angra Maiynu corrupt the world forever; there comes a time when it is restored to its original state. Indeed, in virtue of this non-dualism Zoroastrianism calls itself *behdin*, the "Good Religion".

Cosmic history is divided into three "times". The first is that of primordial integrity (*bundahishn*), before manifestation is corrupted by the principle of evil. In the first world there is no death or disease, the seas are not salt, and fire has no smoke. The middle time is the mixture of good and evil, (*gumeshisn*) on the lower material planes of creation. Angra Maiynu swoops upon the world, rather the way he does in *Paradise Lost*, bringing death and disease, and plunges into the oceans making them salty. This middle time is familiar to us all. But then after the end of the world, after the eschatological separation, there is a third new world (*wizarishn*) which is again good, like the first.

The fall of man idea derives from this Zoroastrian idea of the corruption of the original perfect world. The story in Genesis of the garden of Eden is of Iranian origin. But the descent of the heavenly Jerusalem in the New Testament, or restoration of a perfect world in the *Apocatastatis*, is the restoration which

Zoroastrianism called the third time. Because Zoroastrianism was the first religion to speak of the end of the world, apocalyptic ideas appeared in the Biblical world after the conquest of Babylon by Cyrus. They were met with incredulity ("we are only destroyed by time") and so they were at first transmitted as secret doctrines to the initiated. The first mysticism or esoterism are these Zoroastrian apocalyptic doctrines which were openly expounded within Zoroastrianism, but which became mysterious secrets when they reached new peoples. Thus when the the Book of Revelation speaks of the chaining of Satan for a thousand years, Persian folklore tells that he is Azhi Dahakka chained inside Mount Demavend near Teheran, put there by the holy blacksmith Kavi, founder of the legendary dynasty, the Kavianeh, whose legendary leather apron studded with precious stones, the *Drafhsi Kavianeh*, pops up in history and was used by the Persians as a battle flag, captured by the Arabs at the Battle of Qadisiyah. But at the end of time the chains which hold Azhi Dahhaka also break loose, along with chaos. (The bottomless pit of Revelations was also known among the pre-Islamic Arabs, and is probably the mysterious term *hawiyah* of Koran 101:9.)

Zoroastrianism, therefore, accords with Islam in that Satan is given the latitude to corrupt creation, but not the heavens. Satan himself disappears into non-existence when the world disappears, or even when the consciousness capable of conceiving nothingness refuses to fall into the metaphysical error of attributing a substance to nothingness, for Satan's "existence", or power to subvert the believer, depends upon the believer's free will and responsibility.

However, after the late 5th century B.C., that is, after the Iranians swept the Middle East, there appeared the consequences within Zoroastrianism of the effect of contact with the diametrically opposing world view of the Semitic peoples. This reaction emerged as a powerful heresy among the Parthians known as Zurvanism. In Zurvanism Ahura Mazda as Ohrmazd and Ahriman (Angra Mainya) became the "twin suns" of a higher principle called Zurvan ("Time"), who thus included both within himself. In this way the development of monotheism which begins with Zoroastrianism took a detour. The principles of good and evil were brought into a symmetry which is dualist where original (and subsequent) Zoroastrianism was not. Zurvanism became the dominant state doctrine under the Sassanids who ruled Persia at the time of the revelation of Islam. As Zurvanism became dominant it was accompanied by the emergence of other radically dualistic doctrines in Persia. Interestingly, along with Zurvanism (which was to disappear from Zoroastrianism proper with the Islamic conquest) the Sassanids also raised to prominence a Persian form of the Babylonian goddess Ishtar, who as Anahid (or Anahita), became the patron of the dynasty. But this detour which Monotheism took in Zurvanism also led to Manicheism, in which Zurvan, Ohrmazd and Ahriman, became simply two abstract principles, virtually devoid of personality, defined only by their opposition to each other; and this abstraction of two principles mathematically opposed to each other triggered the rectification brought by Islam which presented mankind with a dramatically more transcendent understanding of Reality in a single God beyond personality: Allah.

For the Arabs, the term *Mājūs* covered all the Iranian religions, dualist and non-dualist according to case. It is perhaps for this reason that the Koran is ambiguous in its inclusion of the *Mājūs* among the "People of the Book", rather than categorical, as it is in regards to Christians and Jews. The inclusion of the Zoroastrians was decided as a matter of interpretation; in its ambiguity the Koran left the matter open to be determined at the proper time when direct experience shed the necessary light for adequate discernment, and when the Muslims were in a position to discriminate between the different currents that actually made up the Iranian religions.

There are today some 30,000 Zoroastrians left in Iran, mostly in Teheran and Yazd, where they have a distinguished reputation for honesty and uprightness, and a population of some 130,000 in India, in Bombay and the Gujerat, where they are known as Parsees.

The Greeks had much contact with the Persians. Heraclitus' doctrines were doubtless influenced by them, and in Plato's *Symposium* the discussion of love being spheres looking for their lost halves is Zoroastrian in origin. One of Plato's students was a Persian and a Chaldean (a Magi) who was a house guest played a flute with soothing mystical melodies while Plato was dying in order to calm his fever while a Thracian sang. *See* AHL al-KITĀB.

Zubayr ibn al-'Awwām (d. *36*/656). A famous Companion, one of the Ten Well-Betided Ones who were assured of paradise by the Prophet, and the fifth convert to Islam, having adopted Islam while still a child. He was a grandson of 'Abd al-Muṭṭalib on his mother's side and so a cousin to the Prophet, who called him *al-ḥawārī* (the disciple") the word used by the Koran for the disciples of Jesus), because of his military services and personal services to him. He was married to Asmā', a daughter of Abū Bakr.

Zubayr was given dispensation to wear silk clothes because of illness (garments made *wholly* of silk are forbidden to men, but not garments partly of silk, that is with stripes of alternating materials).

During the Caliphate of 'Alī, Zubayr joined the rebellion of Ṭalḥāḥ and 'Ā'ishah and was killed in the Battle of the Camel fighting against 'Alī's army. One of his sons, 'Abd Allāh ibn Zubayr, revolted against the Umayyads, declared himself Caliph, and seized control of Mecca for a time before being finally defeated.

Zubaydah. The favorite wife of Hārūn ar-Rashīd, she built a road for the use of pilgrims from Baghdad to Mecca. Cisterns to provide water supply still stand along the way which is called the *Darb Zubaydah* ("Zubaydah's Road"). She was known for her generosity, keeping a lavish court, and for the building of mosques.

Zuhd (lit. "asceticism"). The renunciation of ease and comfort in the name of religious discipline in order to detach the soul from the world. An ascetic is called a *zāhid.* This is, above all, a mystical attitude which finds its example in the Prophet himself, who practiced frequent fasts and long hours of application in prayer in the middle of the night. But it is not an indispensable aspect of mysticism, at least insofar as hardship is concerned. The widespread school of Imām ash-Shādhilī, for example, prescribed a detachment which is inward rather than outward, without of course admitting indulgence, or love of creature comfort, but also without pursuing mortification for itself.

Ibn al-'Arīf said:

> Asceticism is for the common run of people, since it consists in making the concupiscent appetite abstain from pleasures, in renouncing the temptation to return again to that from which one is separated, in dropping the search for what one has lost, in depriving oneself of superfluous desires, in thwarting the goad of the passions, in neglecting all which does not concern the soul. But this is an imperfection as regards the path of the elect, for it presupposes an importance attached to the things of this world, an abstention from their use, an outward mortification in depriving oneself of things here, while inwardly an attachment is felt for them.
>
> To make an issue of the world amounts to turning thyself toward thyself: it is to pass thy time struggling with thyself; it is to take account of thy feelings and to remain with thyself against thy concupiscence...
>
> In all truth, asceticism is the ardent aspiration of the heart towards Him alone; it is to place in Him the aspiration and desires of the soul; to be preoccupied uniquely with Him, without any preoccupation, in order that He (to Whom be praise!) may remove from thee the mass of these causes.

Or, as al-Ḥujwīrī said: "The poor man is not he whose hand is empty of provisions, but he whose nature is empty of desires."

Zurkhāneh, *see* FUTUWWAH.

Wa'Llāhu a'lam
And God knows best.

الحَمدُ لِلّهِ

THANKS BE TO GOD

HISTORICAL SYNOPSIS OF THE ISLAMIC WORLD

This map and its companion *overleaf* provide a synopsis of many of the places that have played a significant part in Islam's history. Place names from different periods of history are therefore found alongside one another.

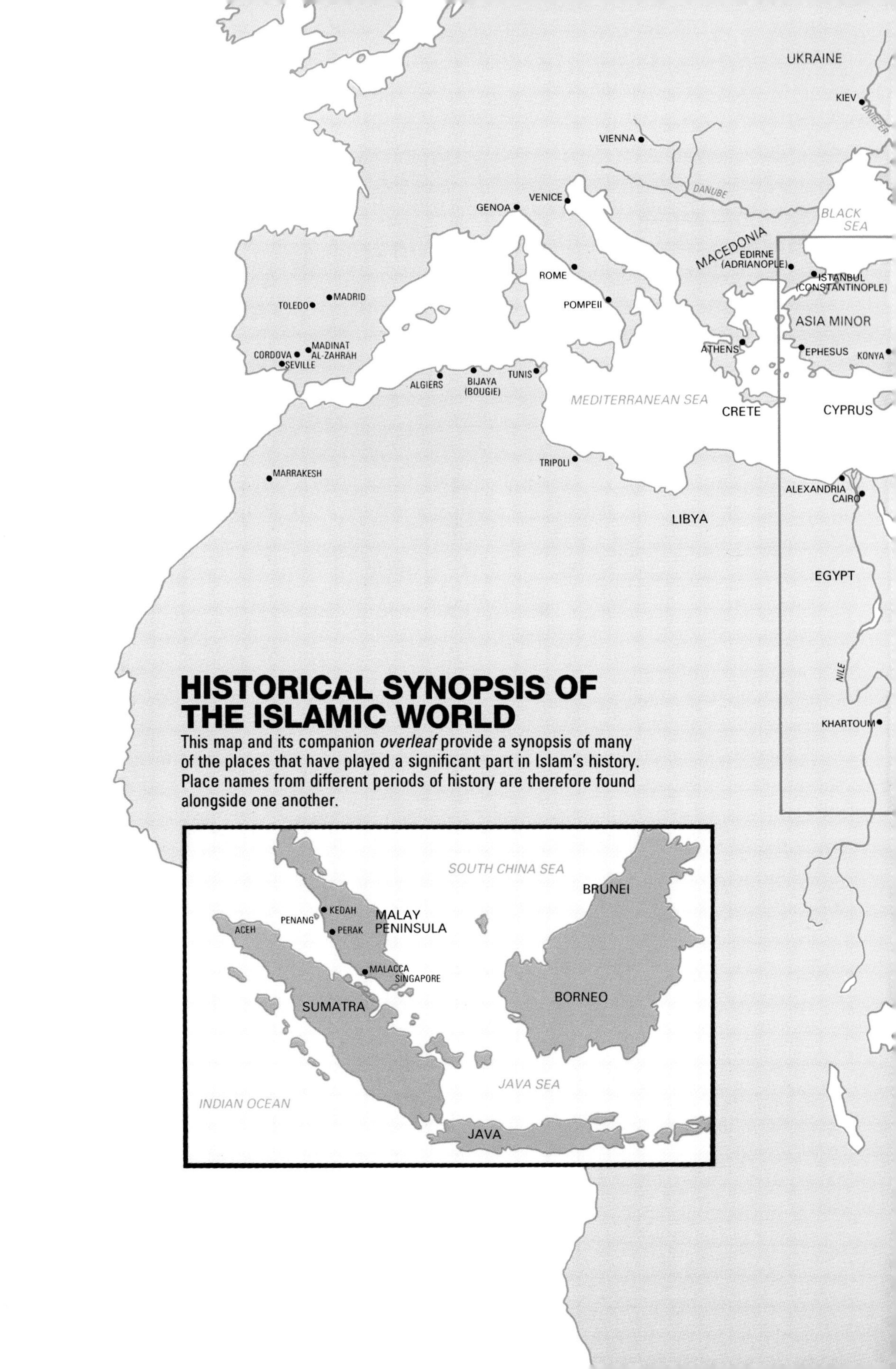

NOVGOROD
KAZAN
RUSSIA
MONGOLIA
KARAKORUM
SARATOV
VOLGA
DON
SARAI
URAL
KIRGIZ STEPPE
UIGHURS
ASTRAKHAN
TURKESTAN
LAKE BALKASH
SOLDAIA (SUDAK)
ARAL SEA
SYR-DARYA (JAXARTES)
GOBI DESERT
CAUCASUS MTS
DAGHESTAN
CASPIAN SEA
SOGDIANA
HAMI
TURFAN
TOMAK
KHARASHAHR
KHWARIZM
TRANSOXIANA
KUCHA
TUN-HUANG
KHIVA
URGANJ
ARMENIA
TAKLA MAKAN
BUKHARA
SAMARKAND
BADAKHSHAN
YARKAND
CHERCHEN
URFA (EDESSA)
AZERBAIJAN
TABRIZ
ARDABIL
AMU-DARYA (OXUS)
NIYA
SINKIANG
QAZVIN
MAZAR-I SHARIF
KHOTAN
DAYLAM
MESHED (MASHHAD)
ANTIOCH
ALEPPO
TEHRAN
BIG ZAB
PARTHIA
DASHT-E KAVIR (SALT DESERT)
BACTRIA
KHORASAN
LITTLE ZAB
KABUL
BEIRUT
DAMASCUS
IRAQ
BAGHDAD
PERSIA (IRAN)
QUHISTAN
HERAT
GAZNI
TUN
ACRE
BABYLON
TIGRIS
ISFAHAN
DASHT-E LUT
SIJISTAN
LAHORE
AMRITSAR
TIBET
JERUSALEM
EUPHRATES
SUSA
YAZD
SISTAN
AFGHANISTAN
SIMLA
PUNJAB
HIMALAYA MOUNTAINS
KANDAHAR
MULTAN
AL BASRAH
KERMAN
SHIRAZ
INDUS
DELHI
NEPAL
BRAHMAPUTRA
PERSIAN GULF
FARS
ORMUZ
AGRA
JAIPUR
AL-HASA
SIND
CAWNPORE
GANGES
KARACHI
PATNA
MEDINA
OMAN
MUSCAT
GUJERAT
BARODA
BENGAL
ARABIA
YAMAMA
ARABIAN SEA
UJJAIN
JEDDAH
MECCA
INDIA
RUB' AL KHALI
RED SEA
BAY OF BENGAL
HYDERABAD
YEMEN
ADEN
See enlargement overleaf
NELLORE
MADRAS
INDIAN OCEAN
CEYLON
MALDIVE ISLANDS
625 miles
1000 kms

HISTORICAL SYNOPSIS OF THE MIDDLE EAST

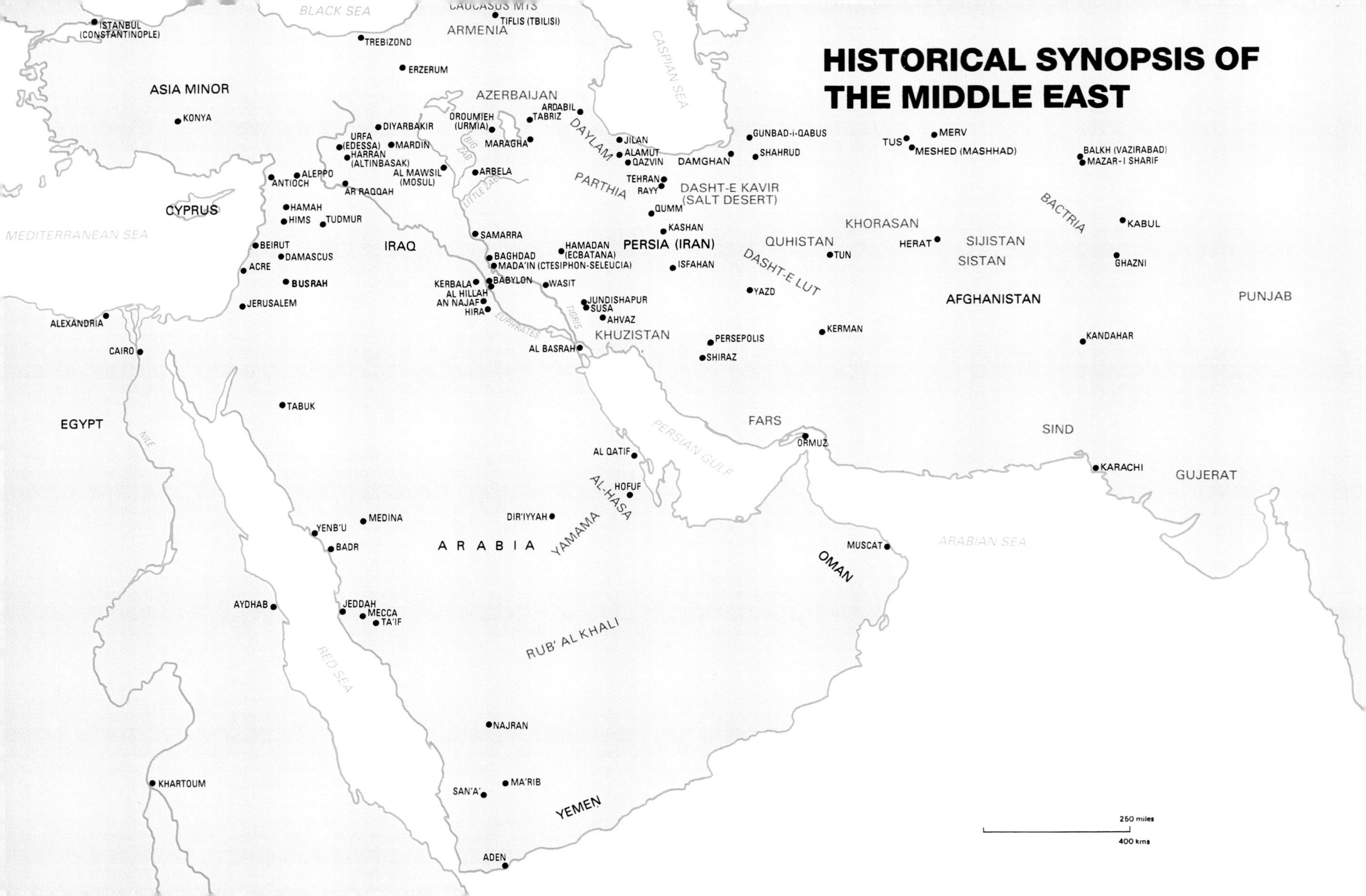

ARABIA AND ITS NEIGHBORS AT THE TIME OF THE PROPHET'S BIRTH

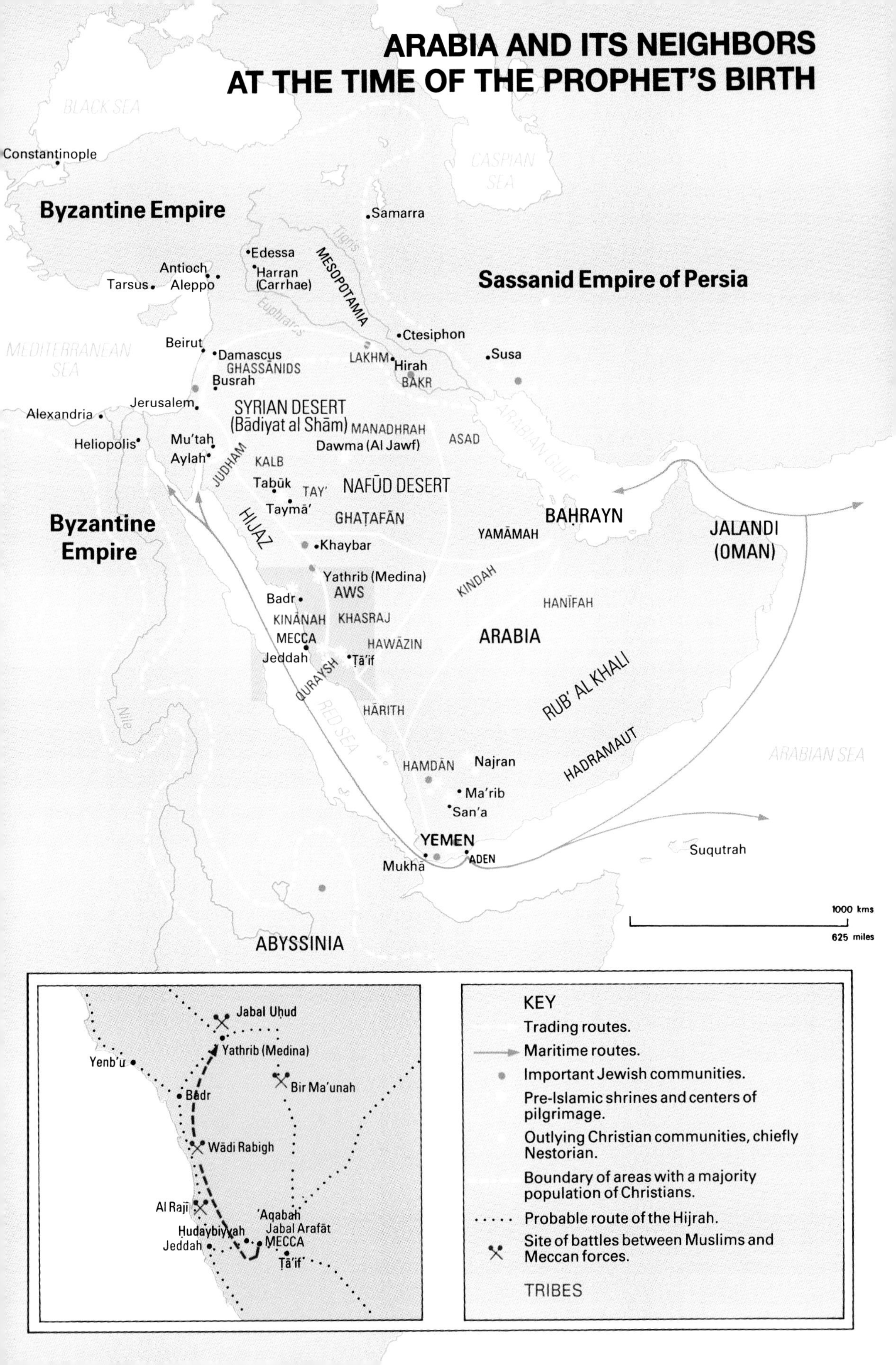
BLACK SEA
CASPIAN SEA
Constantinople
Byzantine Empire
Samarra
Tigris
Edessa
MESOPOTAMIA
Antioch
Harran (Carrhae)
Tarsus
Aleppo
Sassanid Empire of Persia
Euphrates
Ctesiphon
MEDITERRANEAN SEA
Beirut
Damascus
GHASSANIDS
LAKHM
Hirah
Susa
Busrah
BAKR
Jerusalem
Alexandria
SYRIAN DESERT (Bādiyat al Shām)
MANADHRAH
ASAD
ARABIAN GULF
Heliopolis
Mu'tah
Dawma (Al Jawf)
Aylah
JUDHAM
KALB
Tabūk
TAY'
NAFŪD DESERT
Taymā'
GHAṬAFĀN
HIJAZ
Byzantine Empire
BAHRAYN
YAMĀMAH
JALANDI (OMAN)
Khaybar
Yathrib (Medina)
KINDAH
AWS
Badr
HANĪFAH
KINĀNAH
KHASRAJ
MECCA
HAWĀZIN
ARABIA
Jeddah
Ṭā'if
QURAYSH
RUB' AL KHALI
Nile
RED SEA
HĀRITH
ARABIAN SEA
HADRAMAUT
HAMDĀN
Najran
Ma'rib
San'a
YEMEN
Suqutrah
ADEN
Mukhā
1000 kms
625 miles
ABYSSINIA
Jabal Uḥud
Yathrib (Medina)
Yenb'u
Bir Ma'unah
Badr
Wādi Rabigh
Al Rajī
'Aqabah
Ḥudaybiyyah
Jabal Arafāt
MECCA
Jeddah
Ṭā'if
KEY
Trading routes.
Maritime routes.
Important Jewish communities.
Pre-Islamic shrines and centers of pilgrimage.
Outlying Christian communities, chiefly Nestorian.
Boundary of areas with a majority population of Christians.
Probable route of the Hijrah.
Site of battles between Muslims and Meccan forces.
TRIBES

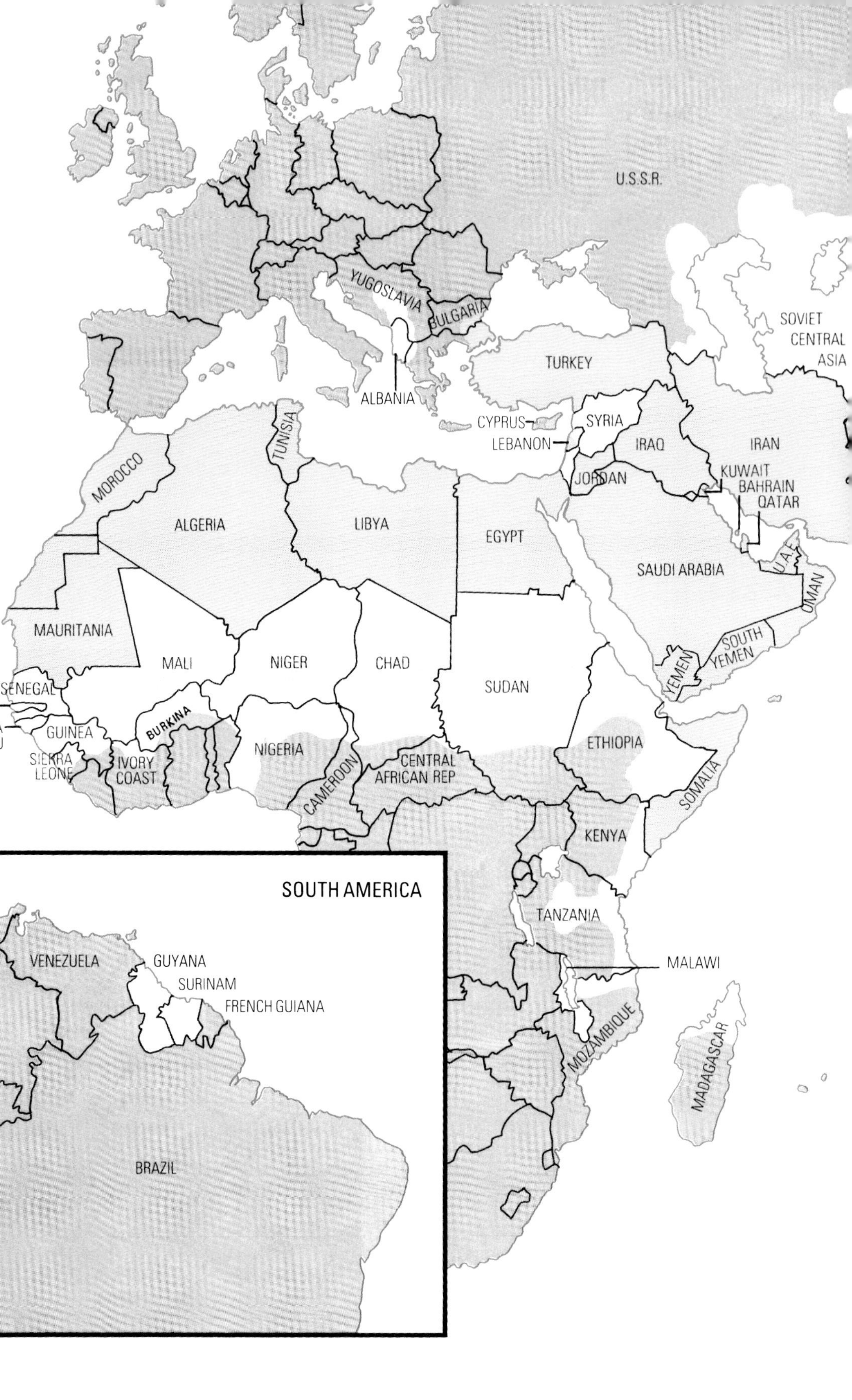
U.S.S.R.
SOVIET CENTRAL ASIA
YUGOSLAVIA
BULGARIA
TURKEY
ALBANIA
CYPRUS
SYRIA
LEBANON
IRAQ
IRAN
JORDAN
KUWAIT
BAHRAIN
QATAR
MOROCCO
TUNISIA
ALGERIA
LIBYA
EGYPT
SAUDI ARABIA
U.A.E.
OMAN
MAURITANIA
MALI
NIGER
CHAD
SUDAN
SOUTH YEMEN
YEMEN
SENEGAL
GAMBIA
GUINEA BISSAU
GUINEA
BURKINA
SIERRA LEONE
IVORY COAST
NIGERIA
CAMEROON
CENTRAL AFRICAN REP
ETHIOPIA
SOMALIA
KENYA
TANZANIA
MALAWI
MOZAMBIQUE
MADAGASCAR
SOUTH AMERICA
VENEZUELA
GUYANA
SURINAM
FRENCH GUIANA
BRAZIL

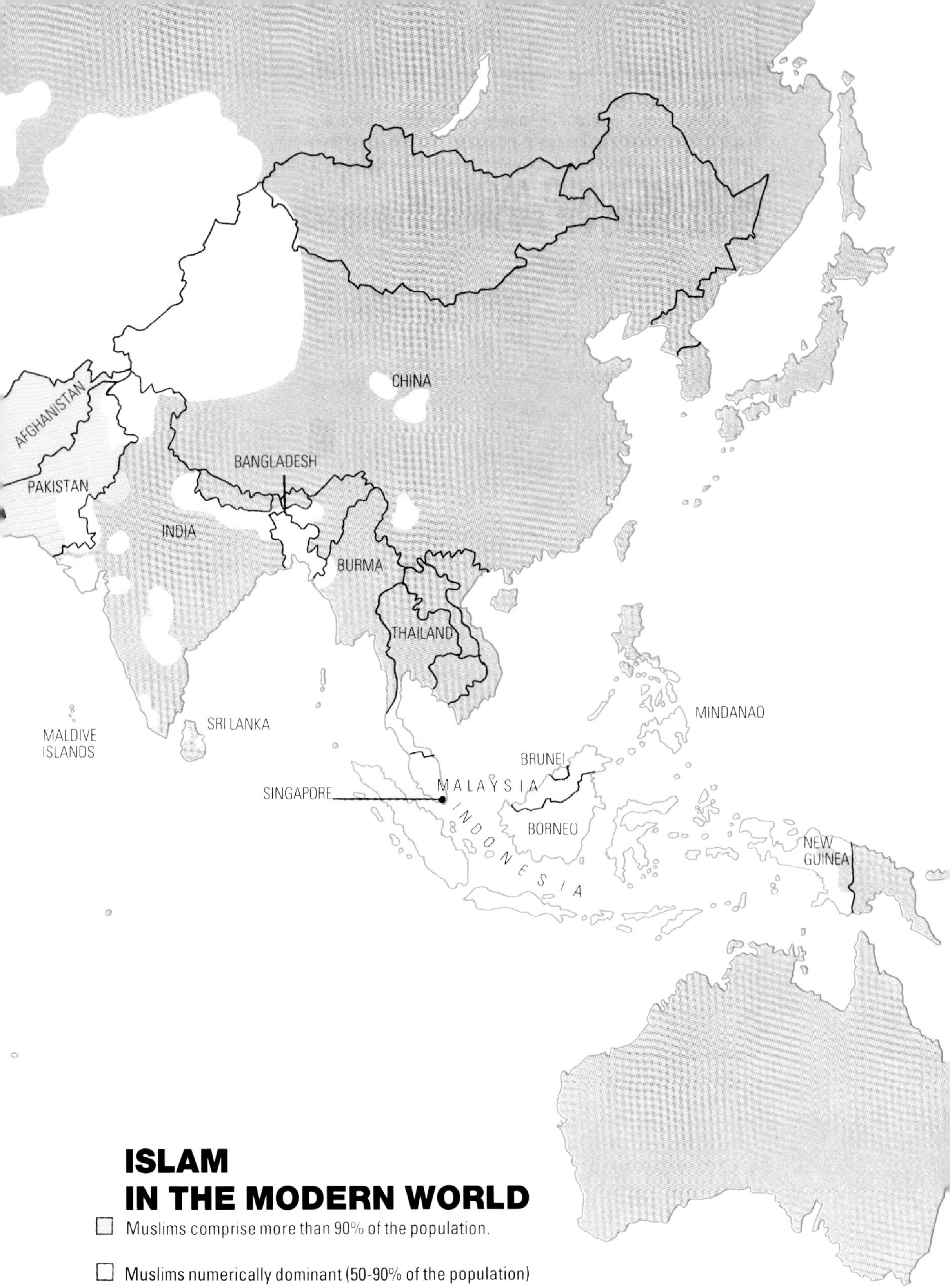

ISLAM IN THE MODERN WORLD

- ☐ Muslims comprise more than 90% of the population.
- ☐ Muslims numerically dominant (50-90% of the population)
- ☐ Muslims a substantial minority (10-50% of the population).

THE ḤAJJ the pilgrimage to Mecca

Before arrival in Mecca the pilgrim puts on *iḥrām* (consecration and pilgrim clothing) at one of the *mawāqīt* (see box below), or before, even at the point of departure, and the appropriate intentions (*an-niyyāt*) are formulated.

Note: a day runs from sunset to sunset

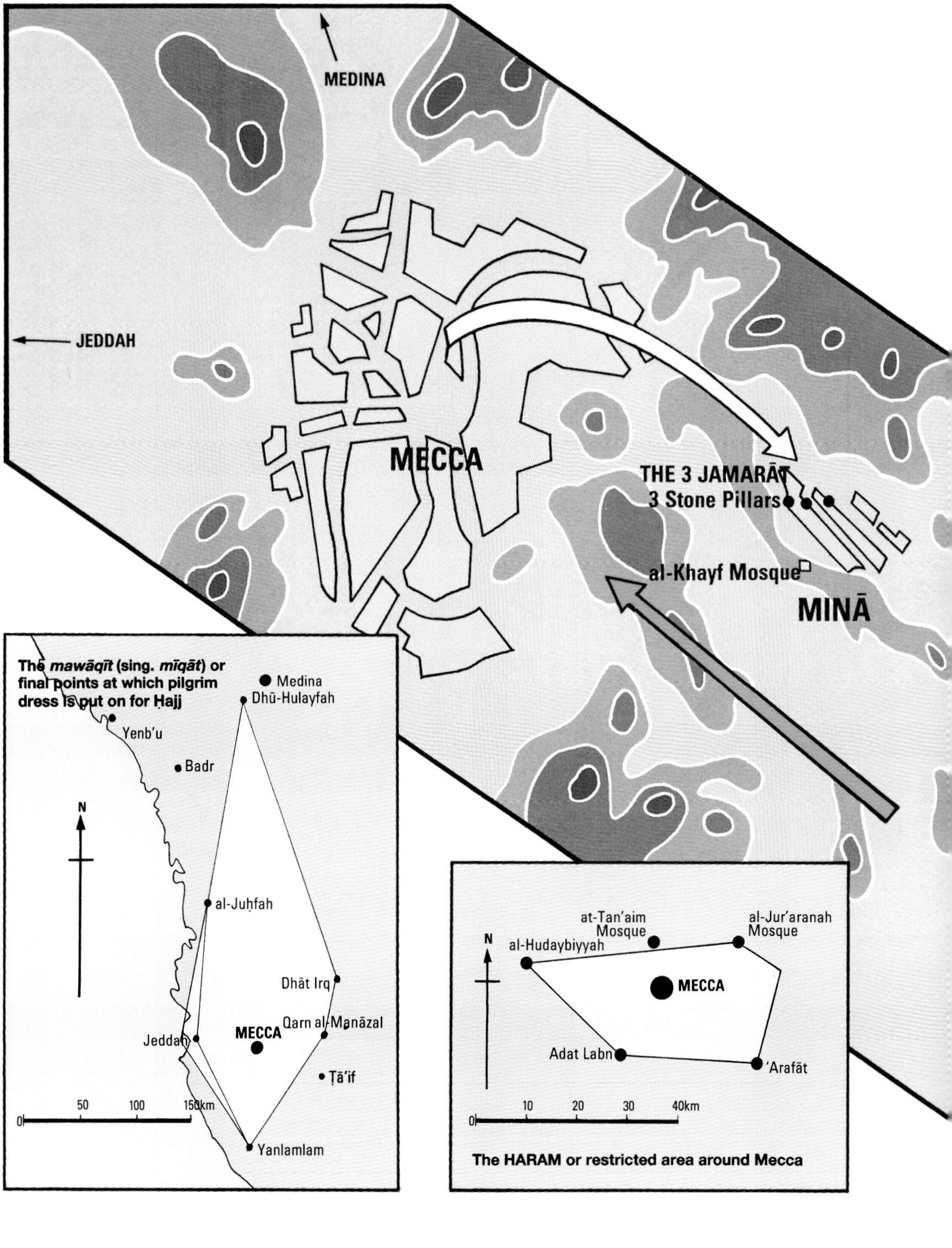

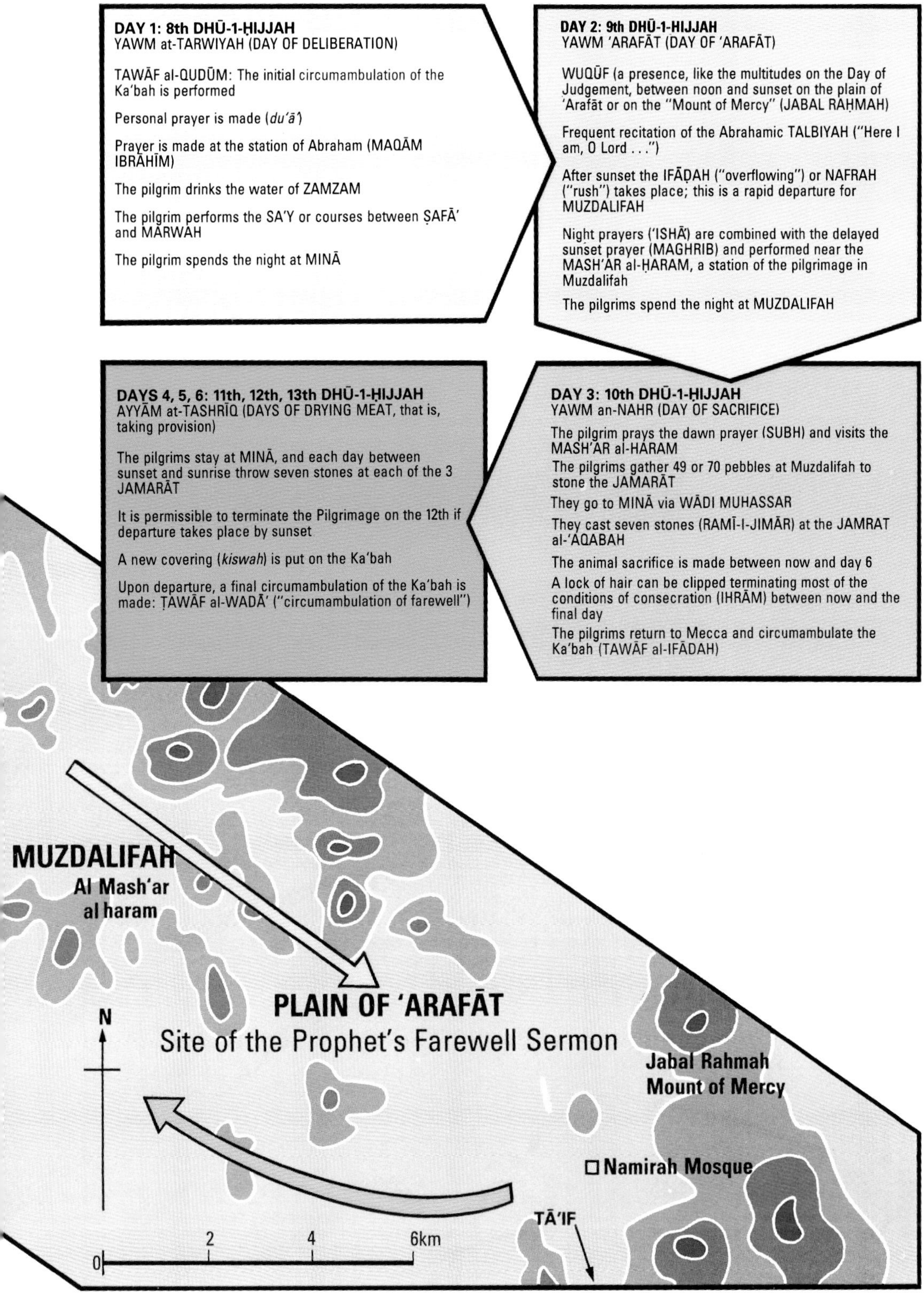
DAY 1: 8th DHŪ-1-ḤIJJAH
YAWM at-TARWIYAH (DAY OF DELIBERATION)
TAWĀF al-QUDŪM: The initial circumambulation of the Ka'bah is performed
Personal prayer is made (du'ā')
Prayer is made at the station of Abraham (MAQĀM IBRĀHĪM)
The pilgrim drinks the water of ZAMZAM
The pilgrim performs the SA'Y or courses between ṢAFĀ' and MARWAH
The pilgrim spends the night at MINĀ
DAY 2: 9th DHŪ-1-HIJJAH
YAWM 'ARAFĀT (DAY OF 'ARAFĀT)
WUQŪF (a presence, like the multitudes on the Day of Judgement, between noon and sunset on the plain of 'Arafāt or on the "Mount of Mercy" (JABAL RAḤMAH)
Frequent recitation of the Abrahamic TALBIYAH ("Here I am, O Lord . . .")
After sunset the IFĀḌAH ("overflowing") or NAFRAH ("rush") takes place; this is a rapid departure for MUZDALIFAH
Night prayers ('ISHĀ') are combined with the delayed sunset prayer (MAGHRIB) and performed near the MASH'AR al-ḤARAM, a station of the pilgrimage in Muzdalifah
The pilgrims spend the night at MUZDALIFAH
DAY 3: 10th DHŪ-1-ḤIJJAH
YAWM an-NAHR (DAY OF SACRIFICE)
The pilgrim prays the dawn prayer (SUBH) and visits the MASH'AR al-HARAM
The pilgrims gather 49 or 70 pebbles at Muzdalifah to stone the JAMARĀT
They go to MINĀ via WĀDI MUHASSAR
They cast seven stones (RAMĪ-I-JIMĀR) at the JAMRAT al-'AQABAH
The animal sacrifice is made between now and day 6
A lock of hair can be clipped terminating most of the conditions of consecration (IHRĀM) between now and the final day
The pilgrims return to Mecca and circumambulate the Ka'bah (TAWĀF al-IFĀDAH)
DAYS 4, 5, 6: 11th, 12th, 13th DHŪ-1-ḤIJJAH
AYYĀM at-TASHRĪQ (DAYS OF DRYING MEAT, that is, taking provision)
The pilgrims stay at MINĀ, and each day between sunset and sunrise throw seven stones at each of the 3 JAMARĀT
It is permissible to terminate the Pilgrimage on the 12th if departure takes place by sunset
A new covering (kiswah) is put on the Ka'bah
Upon departure, a final circumambulation of the Ka'bah is made: ṬAWĀF al-WADĀ' ("circumambulation of farewell")
MUZDALIFAH
Al Mash'ar al haram
PLAIN OF 'ARAFĀT
Site of the Prophet's Farewell Sermon
Jabal Rahmah
Mount of Mercy
Namirah Mosque
TĀ'IF
N
0
2
4
6km

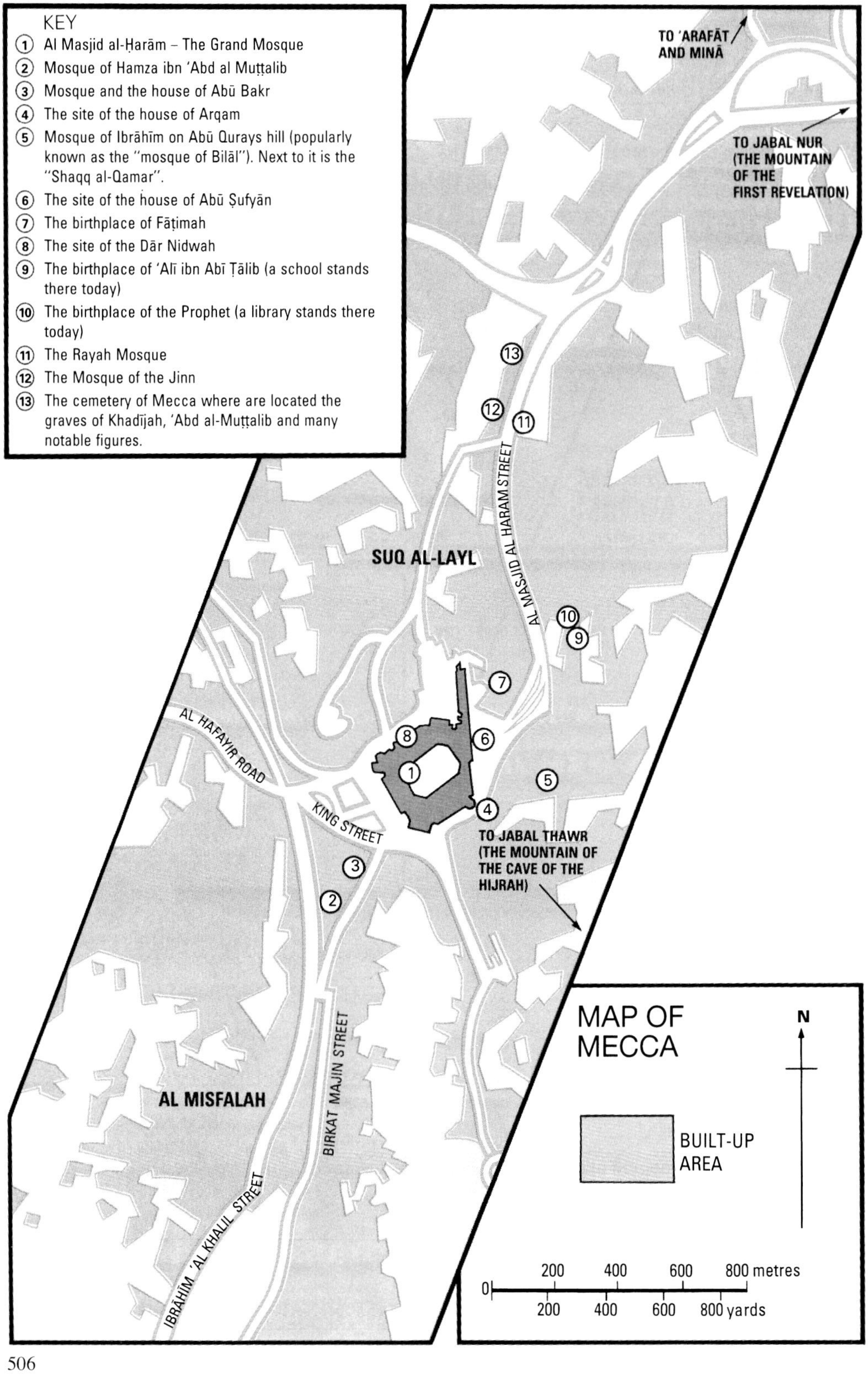
KEY
1 Al Masjid al-Ḥarām – The Grand Mosque
2 Mosque of Hamza ibn 'Abd al Muṭṭalib
3 Mosque and the house of Abū Bakr
4 The site of the house of Arqam
5 Mosque of Ibrāhīm on Abū Qurays hill (popularly known as the "mosque of Bilāl"). Next to it is the "Shaqq al-Qamar".
6 The site of the house of Abū Ṣufyān
7 The birthplace of Fāṭimah
8 The site of the Dār Nidwah
9 The birthplace of 'Alī ibn Abī Ṭālib (a school stands there today)
10 The birthplace of the Prophet (a library stands there today)
11 The Rayah Mosque
12 The Mosque of the Jinn
13 The cemetery of Mecca where are located the graves of Khadījah, 'Abd al-Muṭṭalib and many notable figures.
TO 'ARAFĀT AND MINĀ
TO JABAL NUR (THE MOUNTAIN OF THE FIRST REVELATION)
SUQ AL-LAYL
AL MASJID AL HARAM STREET
AL HAFAYIR ROAD
KING STREET
TO JABAL THAWR (THE MOUNTAIN OF THE CAVE OF THE HIJRAH)
BIRKAT MAJIN STREET
AL MISFALAH
IBRĀHĪM 'AL KHALIL STREET
MAP OF MECCA
N
BUILT-UP AREA
0
200 400 600 800 metres
200 400 600 800 yards

PLAN OF THE GRAND MOSQUE
AL-MASJID AL-ḤARĀM

1. The well of Zamzam
2. The Maqām Ibrāhīm
3. The Hatim, or semi-circular wall round the Ḥijr Ismā'īl
4. The Maṭāf, or open circumambulation area round the Ka'bah
5. The Ka'bah
6. The door to the Ka'bah. The Multazam ("the place of holding") is the area between the door and the Black Stone
7. The Black Stone
8. The Mas'ā between Ṣafā and Marwah
9. Steps down to Zamzam faucets
10. The portion of the Sa'y which is run, not walked
11. Ṣafā (the hill is enclosed in the Mosque)
12. King 'Abd al-'Azīz Gate
13. Marwah (the hill is enclosed in the Mosque)
14. Gate of the 'Umrah
15. Salām Gate

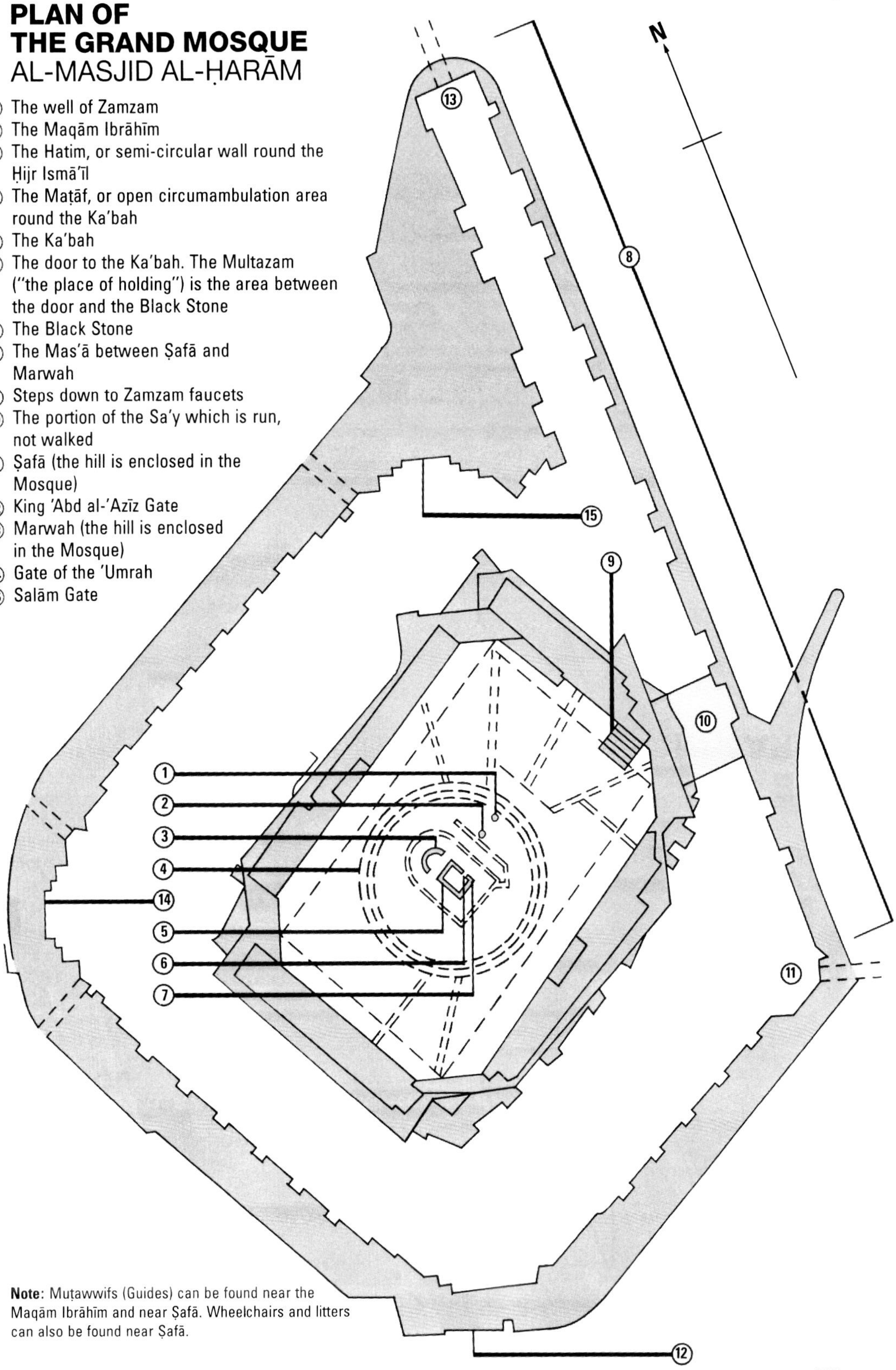

Note: Muṭawwifs (Guides) can be found near the Maqām Ibrāhīm and near Ṣafā. Wheelchairs and litters can also be found near Ṣafā.

BRANCHES OF ISLAM

SCHEMATIC REPRESENTATION OF THE BRANCHES OF ISLAM FROM THE REVELATION TO THE PRESENT

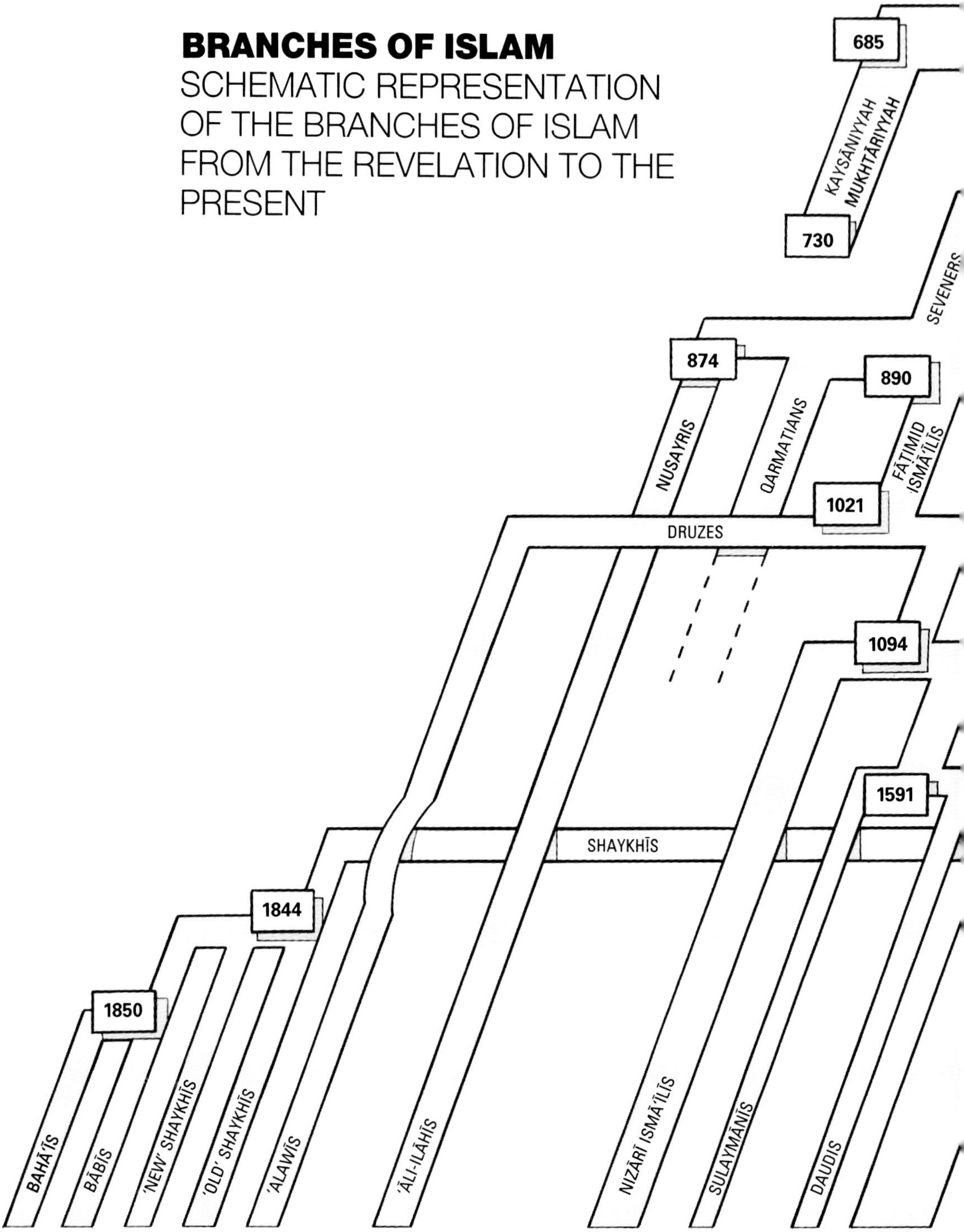

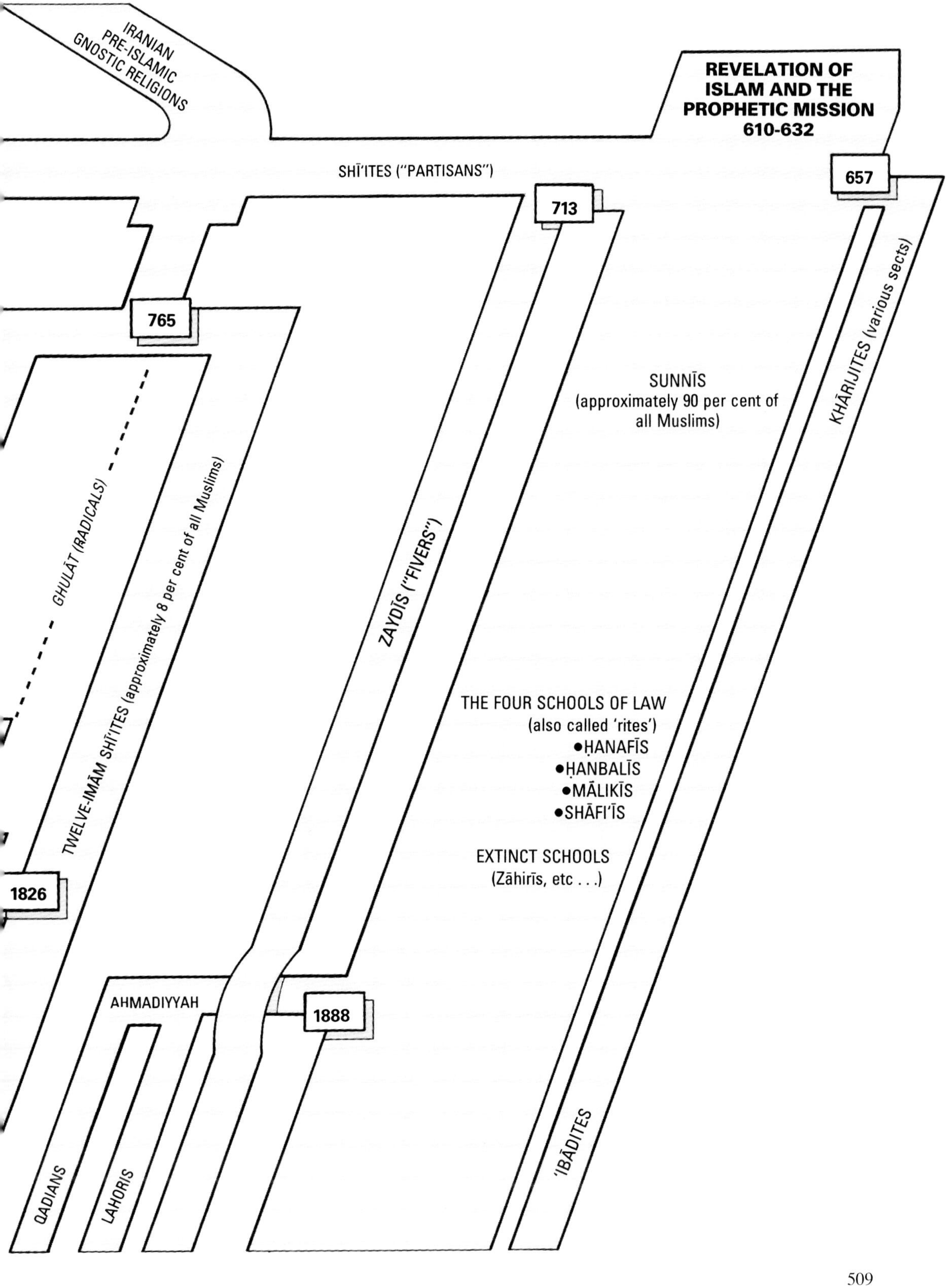
IRANIAN
PRE-ISLAMIC
GNOSTIC RELIGIONS
REVELATION OF
ISLAM AND THE
PROPHETIC MISSION
610-632
SHĪ'ITES ("PARTISANS")
657
713
765
KHĀRIJITES (various sects)
SUNNĪS
(approximately 90 per cent of
all Muslims)
GHULĀT (RADICALS)
TWELVE-IMĀM SHĪ'ITES (approximately 8 per cent of all Muslims)
ZAYDĪS ("FIVERS")
THE FOUR SCHOOLS OF LAW
(also called 'rites')
•ḤANAFĪS
•ḤANBALĪS
•MĀLIKĪS
•SHĀFI'ĪS
EXTINCT SCHOOLS
(Ẓāhirīs, etc . . .)
1826
AHMADIYYAH
1888
QADIANS
LAHORIS
'IBĀDITES

THE QURAYSH

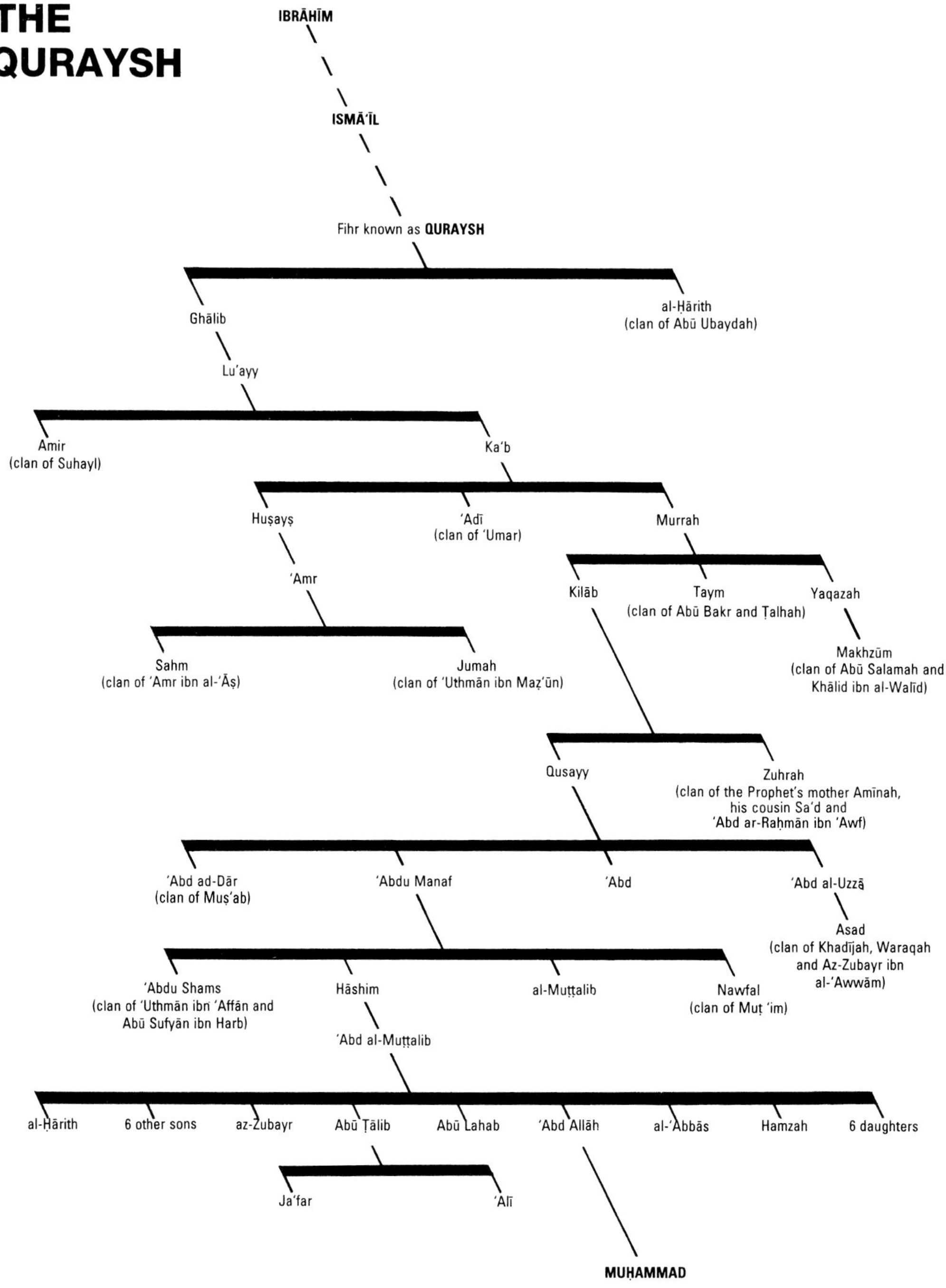
IBRĀHĪM
ISMĀ'ĪL
Fihr known as QURAYSH
Ghālib
al-Ḥārith
(clan of Abū Ubaydah)
Lu'ayy
Amir
(clan of Suhayl)
Ka'b
Huṣayṣ
'Adī
(clan of 'Umar)
Murrah
'Amr
Kilāb
Taym
(clan of Abū Bakr and Ṭalhah)
Yaqazah
Sahm
(clan of 'Amr ibn al-'Āṣ)
Jumah
(clan of 'Uthmān ibn Maẓ'ūn)
Makhzūm
(clan of Abū Salamah and
Khālid ibn al-Walīd)
Qusayy
Zuhrah
(clan of the Prophet's mother Amīnah,
his cousin Sa'd and
'Abd ar-Raḥmān ibn 'Awf)
'Abd ad-Dār
(clan of Muṣ'ab)
'Abdu Manaf
'Abd
'Abd al-Uzzā
Asad
(clan of Khadījah, Waraqah
and Az-Zubayr ibn
al-'Awwām)
'Abdu Shams
(clan of 'Uthmān ibn 'Affān and
Abū Sufyān ibn Harb)
Hāshim
al-Muṭṭalib
Nawfal
(clan of Muṭ 'im)
'Abd al-Muṭṭalib
al-Ḥārith
6 other sons
az-Zubayr
Abū Ṭālib
Abū Lahab
'Abd Allāh
al-'Abbās
Hamzah
6 daughters
Ja'far
'Alī
MUḤAMMAD

THE UMMAYAD CALIPHS OF DAMASCUS AND CORDOVA

The Caliphs are numbered sequentially

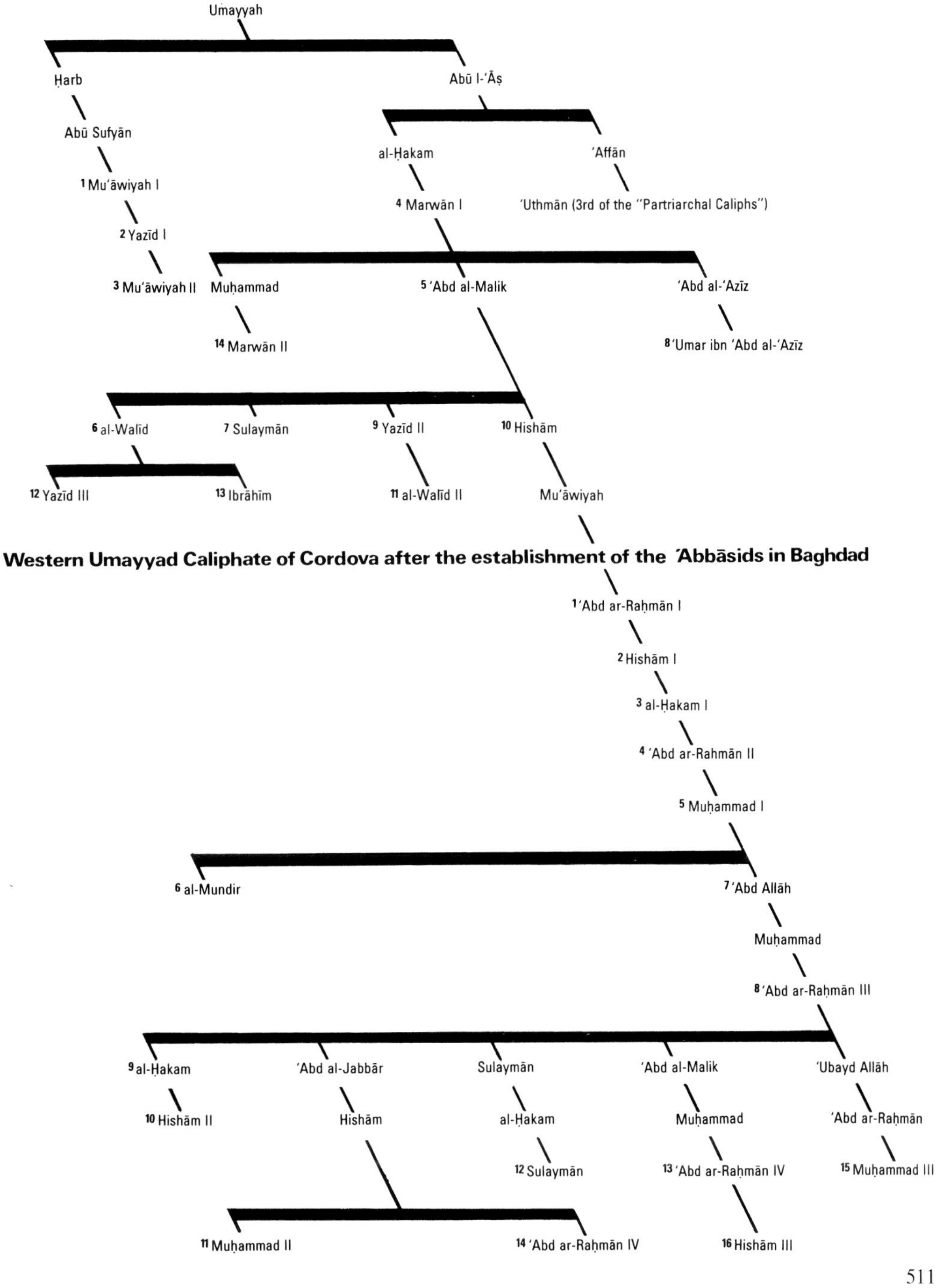

THE 'ABBĀSID CALIPHS IN BAGHDAD

The Caliphs are numbered sequentially

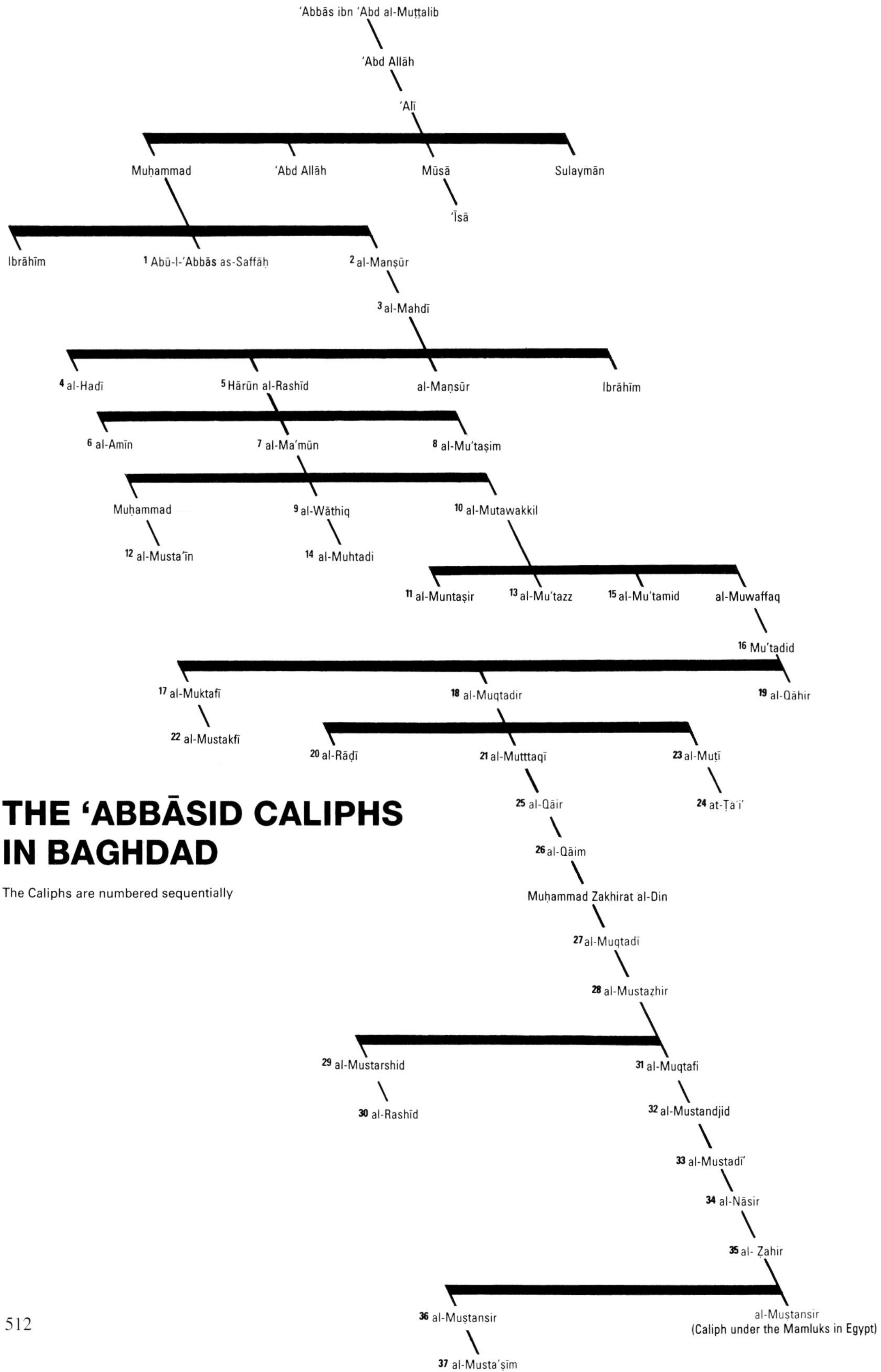
'Abbās ibn 'Abd al-Muṭṭalib
'Abd Allāh
'Alī
Muḥammad
'Abd Allāh
Mūsā
Sulaymān
'Īsā
Ibrāhīm
1 Abū-l-'Abbās as-Saffāḥ
2 al-Manṣūr
3 al-Mahdī
4 al-Hadī
5 Hārūn al-Rashīd
al-Manṣūr
Ibrāhīm
6 al-Amīn
7 al-Ma'mūn
8 al-Mu'taṣim
Muḥammad
9 al-Wāthiq
10 al-Mutawakkil
12 al-Musta'īn
14 al-Muhtadi
11 al-Muntaṣir
13 al-Mu'tazz
15 al-Mu'tamid
al-Muwaffaq
16 Mu'tadid
17 al-Muktafī
18 al-Muqtadir
19 al-Qāhir
22 al-Mustakfī
20 al-Rāḍī
21 al-Mutttaqī
23 al-Muṭī
25 al-Qāir
24 at-Ṭā'i'
26 al-Qāim
Muḥammad Zakhirat al-Din
27 al-Muqtadī
28 al-Mustaẓhir
29 al-Mustarshid
31 al-Muqtafi
30 al-Rashīd
32 al-Mustandjid
33 al-Mustadī'
34 al-Nāsir
35 al- Ẓahir
36 al-Muṣtansir
al-Muṣtansir
(Caliph under the Mamluks in Egypt)
37 al-Musta'ṣīm

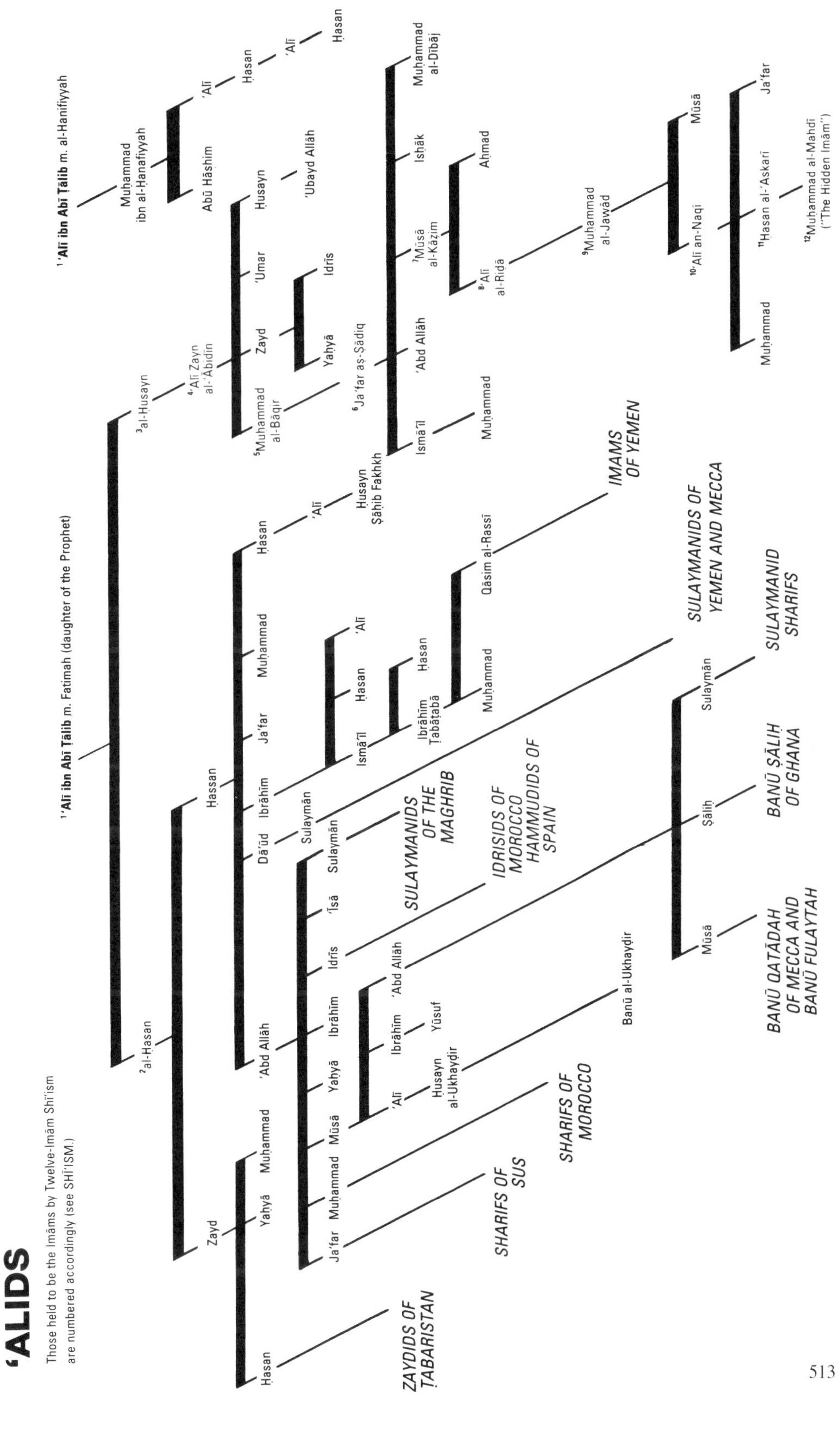
'ALIDS
Those held to be the Imāms by Twelve-Imām Shī'ism are numbered accordingly (see SHĪ'ISM.)
¹'Alī ibn Abī Ṭālib m. Fatimah (daughter of the Prophet)
¹'Alī ibn Abī Ṭālib m. al-Hanifiyyah
²al-Ḥasan
³al-Ḥusayn
Zayd
Ḥassan
Ḥasan
Yaḥyā
Muḥammad
'Abd Allāh
Dā'ūd
Ibrāhīm
Ja'far
Muḥammad
Ḥasan
Sulaymān
Ja'far
Muḥammad
Mūsā
Yaḥyā
Ibrāhīm
Idrīs
'Īsā
Sulaymān
'Alī
Ibrāhīm
'Abd Allāh
Yūsuf
Ḥusayn al-Ukhayḍir
Banū al-Ukhayḍir
Ismā'īl
Ḥasan
'Alī
Ibrāhīm Ṭabāṭabā
Ḥasan
Muḥammad
Qāsim al-Rassī
'Alī
Ḥusayn Ṣāḥib Fakhkh
ZAYDIDS OF ṬABARISTAN
SHARIFS OF SUS
SHARIFS OF MOROCCO
SULAYMANIDS OF THE MAGHRIB
IDRISIDS OF MOROCCO HAMMUDIDS OF SPAIN
IMAMS OF YEMEN
SULAYMANIDS OF YEMEN AND MECCA
SULAYMANID SHARIFS
Mūsā
Ṣāliḥ
Sulaymān
BANŪ QATĀDAH OF MECCA AND BANŪ FULAYTAH
BANŪ ṢĀLIḤ OF GHANA
⁴'Alī Zayn al-'Ābidīn
⁵Muḥammad al-Bāqir
Zayd
'Umar
Ḥusayn
Yaḥyā
Idrīs
'Ubayd Allāh
⁶Ja'far aṣ-Ṣādiq
Ismā'īl
Muḥammad
'Abd Allāh
⁷Mūsā al-Kāẓim
Isḥāk
Muḥammad al-Dībāj
⁸'Alī al-Riḍā
Aḥmad
⁹Muḥammad al-Jawād
¹⁰'Alī an-Naqī
Mūsā
Muḥammad
¹¹Ḥasan al-'Askarī
Ja'far
¹²Muḥammad al-Mahdī ("The Hidden Imām")
Muḥammad ibn al-Ḥanafiyyah
Abū Hāshim
'Alī
Ḥasan
'Alī
Ḥasan

CHRONOLOGY

516 Dhū Nuwāṣ is King of the Yemen.

523 Massacre of the Christians of Najrān in southern Arabia by Dhū Nuwāṣ. The martyrs of Najrān are mentioned in Koran 85: 4-11. Those who refuse conversion to Judaism, the religion of Dhū Nuwāṣ, are thrown into a burning pit. One survivor escapes to Byzantium and, holding up a half-burnt gospel, calls upon the Emperor to avenge the martyrs.

525 The Christian Abyssinians, at the request of Justin I, Emperor of Byzantium, send an army to punish Dhū Nuwāṣ and conquer the Yemen.

531 Beginning of the reign of the Sassanid Chosroes I (Anūshīrwān) in Persia, following the suppresion of the Mazdakites.

535 Abrahah, Christian king in the Yemen, viceroy of the Abyssinians.

570 "The Year of the Elephant", in which occurred the attack on Mecca by Abrahah (although some modern scholars say it must have taken place earlier); it is traditionally accepted as the year of the Prophet's birth.

575 The Persians conquer the Yemen under the general Wahriz, and Abrahah is killed.

579 Chosroes I is succeeded by Hormazd IV in Persia.

c.580 Collapse of the dam of Ma'rib symbolizing, for the desert Arabs, the end of the great age of South Arabian kingdoms.

Ghassanīs devastate Hirah, capital of the Lakhmids. A group of Meccans, among them Muḥammad, take an oath jointly to defend the rights of those without recourse – the Oath of Chivalry (*Ḥilf al-Fuḍūl*).

580-585 The "Sacrilegious War" (*Ḥarb al-Fijār*) between the Quraysh and Hawāzin over the trade in Yemen perfumes, against the background of Persian and Byzantine economic politics; the traditional yearly truce is breached and the war continues during the month of Ramaḍān; whence the name.

589-628 Reign of Chosroes II in Persia.

590 'Uthmān ibn Ḥuwayrith attempts to create an alliance with Byzantium and rule Mecca.

595 The Prophet marries his first wife, Khadījah.

608 The Ka'bah is rebuilt. The Prophet, before his mission, is chosen by destiny to put the Black Stone into the new Ka'bah.

610 The beginning of the Prophet's mission; the revelation of the Koran descends upon him in a cave at the summit of a mountain outside Mecca during the month of Ramaḍān.

Accession of Heraclius as Emperor of Byzantium.

611 The Battle of Dhū Qār in which an Arab tribe, the Banū Bakr, defeats a Persian army.

613 The public preaching of Islam begins.

614 The Persians capture Damascus.

615 The first emigration of Muslims to Abyssinia to escape Meccan persecution. They are received by the Negus and allowed to remain, despite attempts by the Meccans to turn the Abyssinians against the emigrants.

The Persians sack Jerusalem and take the "True Cross" to Ctesiphon.

616-618 Conversion of 'Umar. The Prophet is continually satirized and insulted by the pagan Quraysh who then proclaim a ban against the Banū Hāshim because of the Prophet's preaching. The ban is lifted two years later through growing opposition to it by Meccan sympathizers.

617 Civil war at Yathrib (later to be renamed Medina); the fourth and inconclusive battle of Bu'āth, between the tribes of Aws and Khazraj.

619 "The Year of Sadness": deaths of Khadījah, the Prophet's first wife, and of Abū Ṭālib, his uncle and protector, head of the Banū Hāshim.

Constantinople under siege from an alliance of the Persians and the Avars.

620 The Prophet goes to Ṭā'if to seek haven and converts, and is successful in neither. On the return journey the Prophet recites the Koran at night in Nakhlah; seven passing Jinn stop and listen.

The "Night Journey" in which the Prophet is taken in one night from Mecca to Jerusalem, mounted on the steed Burāq brought to him by the Angel Gabriel. From Temple Mount the Prophet, accompanied by Gabriel, ascends to the Divine Presence.

In the great pilgrimage (*Ḥajj*) of that year, six men of the tribe of Khazraj of Yathrib (Medina) enter Islam at the hand of the Prophet.

621 The First 'Aqabah covenant with twelve men of Khazraj and Aws of Yathrib (Medina).

622 The Second 'Aqabah covenant. The converted Medinans pledge to defend the Prophet.

In the Byzantine-Persian wars, the tide turns in favor of the Byzantines. Heraclius undertakes successful campaigns against the Persians.

15/16 July, 1st *Muḥarram*, the beginning of the Arab (and later Islamic) calendar year in which the emigration to Mecca (Hijrah) takes place. It becomes the first year of the Islamic era when the Prophet emigrates to Medina, arriving on 17 September, having fled Mecca some two weeks earlier, narrowly escaping assassination.

623 The Prophet concludes the marriage with 'Ā'ishah which had been contracted earlier in Mecca. (After the death of Khadījah he has already married a widow, Sawdah.)

624 (*Rajab AH 2*); Muslim raid by 'Abd Allāh ibn Jahsh on Nakhlah, when he captures a Meccan caravan on the last day of Rajab, traditionally a sacred month in which fighting was prohibited. The Koranic verse is revealed: "They will question thee concerning the holy month, and fighting in it. Say: 'Fighting in it is a heinous thing, but to bar from God's way, and disbelief in Him, and the Holy Mosque, and to expel its people from it – that is more heinous in God's sight; and persecution is more heinous than slaying. . .'" (Koran 2: 217).

624 February? (*Sha'bān? AH 2*); the direction of prayer is changed from Jerusalem to Mecca.

17 March (*19 Ramaḍān AH 2*); an outnumbered Muslim army defeats a Meccan force at Badr.

(*15 Shawwal AH 2*); the Muslims attack the Jewish tribe of the Banū Qaynuqā'.

625 March (*7 Shawwal AH 3*); the Muslims are defeated at Jabal Uḥud outside Medina.

(*Rabi' al-Awwal AH 4*); Muslim campaign against the Jewish tribe of Banū Nādir, who are expelled.

626 (*Sha'bān AH 5*); Muslim campaign against the Banū Musta'liq.

627 April (*Dhū-l-Qa'dah AH 5*); Medina is besieged by a combined Meccan and Beduin army: Battle of the Trench, also called "War of the Confederates" (*Ḥarb al-Aḥzāb*), followed by the destruction of the treacherous Banū Qurayẓah.

628 March (*Dhū-l-Qa'dah AH 6*); the Treaty of Ḥudaybiyyah; the Meccans compromise with the Muslims.

(*6 or 7 AH*); Messengers are sent to the Muqawqīs, ruler of Egypt, Chosroes of Persia, Heraclius of Byzantium, the rulers of the Yemen, and others, calling them to Islam. The Muqawqis sends gifts by way of return, the Persian Shah Siroes, who has succeeded Chosroes in the meantime, tears up the letter. The ruler of the Yemen, seeing certain prophecies made by the Prophet fulfilled regarding the death of Chosroes in Persia, revolts against Persian suzerainty, and enters Islam.

(*Jumādā-l-Ūlā AH 7*); the Jewish citadels of Khaybar are conquered, and the growing strength of the Muslims becomes apparent.

Siroes (Kobad II) of Persia makes peace with Heraclius and returns the "True Cross".

629 March (*Dhū-l-Qa'dah AH 7*); the Muslims make the pilgrimage to Mecca, agreed by the Treaty of Ḥudaybiyyah, and Bilāl calls the prayer from the top of the Ka'bah; thus the *shahādah* echoes in the valley of Mecca, while the Quraysh watch and listen from the hill of Abū Qubays.

(*Jumādā-l-Ūlā AH 8*); the Byzantines repulse a Muslim excursion at Mu'tah, and Khālid ibn Walīd takes command of Muslim armies for the first time. The Prophet sees the events in a vision and calls Khālid the "Sword of God".

The death of Siroes in Persia and the beginning of a period of anarchy.

630 January (*20 Ramaḍān AH 8*); the conquest of Mecca. The Ka'bah is purified of idols.

The Battle of Ḥunayn, and the attack on Ṭā'if.

9th year of Hijrah, the "Year of Deputations", when tribes from all over Arabia accept Islam. In *Muḥarram*/April messengers are sent out to collect the poor-tax from the converted tribes.

October to December (*Rajab*); the Prophet leads a military expedition to Tabūk in North Arabia.

631 (*Ramaḍān*) 'Alī is sent on a mission to Yemen.

The pilgrimage that year is led by Abū Bakr. Idolators are henceforth prohibited from making the pilgrimage to Mecca.

632 27 January; the death of the Prophet's son Ibrāhīm.

March (*Dhū-l-Ḥijjah AH 10*); the "Farewell Pilgrimage". While preaching at 'Arafāt to the multitude the Prophet receives the final revelation of the Koran (5:3).

16 March (*18 Dhū-l-Ḥijjah AH 10*); returning from the pilgrimage, the Prophet joins a Muslim army led by 'Alī at Ghadīr Khumm. 'Alī, criticised for excessive severity when in command, is defended by the Prophet. (These events and statements will later be taken by Shī'ites as designating 'Alī's succession to the Prophet.)

8 June (*12 Rabi' al-Awwal AH 11*); the Prophet dies, and is succeeded by Abū Bakr as *khalīfah*, the "one who is left behind", the Caliph.

Some Beduin tribes repudiate Islam and repulse the collectors of the poor-tax; false prophets arise: the "Wars of Apostasy" (*Ḥurūb ar-Riddah*). Abū Bakr refuses to turn Usāmah aside from a campaign to Syria which the Prophet had ordered, and instead himself takes the field against the apostates.

Yazdagird III becomes King in Persia.

633 The end of the "Wars of Apostasy". The false prophet Musaylamah is killed in a battle with a Muslim army led by Khālid ibn Walīd.

Southern Mesopotamia conquered.

634 The Byzantines are defeated by Muslims at the Battle of Ajnadayn in Palestine.

Abū Bakr dies, having designated 'Umar as his successor.

635 The conquest of Syria. Damascus is taken.

Jews and Christians are expelled from Arabia.

636 The Persian Sassanids are defeated at the Battle of Qādisiyyah.

637 The Byzantines are defeated at the river Yarmuk. In this battle Khālid ibn Walīd orders the veterans of Badr, some one hundred men, not to fight but to stand on the sidelines and perform the ritual prayer.

The Caliph 'Umar formalizes the convention of dating the Islamic era from the Hijrah and the establishment of the Islamic community (*Ummah*) at Medina.

The founding of Kufah as a garrison town.

The conquest of Jerusalem. 'Umar leaves Medina in the charge of 'Alī, and visits Jerusalem. He orders the clearing of the Temple Mount left in ruins after the Temple's destruction by the Romans in accordance with Jesus' prophecies concerning the destruction of Jerusalem.

638 The Byzantines find the Monophysite

Christians of Syria allying themselves with the Muslims. To win back their support they offer the compromise formula of *monothelitism*. This fails to win back the support of the Monophysite Christians, but is the origin of the Maronites.

640 'Amr ibn al-'Asī begins conquest of Egypt.

641 'Amr ibn al-'Asī founds Fuṣṭāṭ (outskirts of present day Cairo).

The end of the reign of Heraclius as Emperor of Byzantium.

642 The Persians are beaten decisively at Nihawand.

644 'Umar assassinated and 'Uthmān elected Caliph.

649 Cyprus is conquered.

650 The Koran is collated and edited in the canonical recension.

651 Yazdagird III, the last Sassanid Emperor, is assassinated near Merv.

'Uthmān loses the ring of the Prophet in a well in Medina; the beginning of discord.

656 'Uthmān is assassinated by the son of Abū Bakr and his compatriots amidst general insurrection in Medina. 'Alī becomes Caliph. Ṭalḥāh, Zubayr, and 'Ā'ishah revolt against him, and are defeated at the Battle of the Camel. Ṭalḥāh and Zubayr are killed, 'Ā'ishah is sent back to Medina, and 'Alī settles at the camp-city of Kufah.

657 The Battle of Ṣiffīn. Mu'āwiyah, under pretext of revenging 'Uthmān's death, attacks 'Alī, a stalemate ensuing between the armies, offers of negotiation are accepted; the Khārijites abandon 'Alī's army.

658 Mu'āwiyah is declared Caliph by the treachery of the negotiators at Adhruh, and is repudiated by 'Alī.

'Alī crushes the Khārijites at the Battle of Nahrawān.

661 'Alī is assassinated by the Khārijite Ibn Muljam. The brief Caliphate of Ḥasan, son of 'Alī, who cedes his title to Mu'āwiyah. Beginning of the Umayyad dynasty.

662-675 Ziyād is Umayyad governor in Iraq.

667 Arab armies reach Central Asia.

669 The Companion Abū Ayyūb dies before the walls of Constantinople in an unsuccessful Muslim attack.

670 Ḥasan, son of 'Alī, dies.

Kairouan/Qayrawān is founded and 'Uqbah ibn Nāfi' is militarily successful in North Africa, although he sends back the message, speaking of the Berbers: "We have met our match". 'Uqbah rides his horse into the Atlantic Ocean with his sword unsheathed and says: "Lord, thou art my witness that I can go no farther."

674-679 Constantinople is unsuccessfully besieged by Muslim armies.

678 'Ā'ishah dies.

680-683 Reign of the Caliph Yazīd I.

680 10 Oct (*10 Muḥarram AH 61*); Ḥusayn, son of 'Alī is killed by Yazīd's troops at Kerbala in Iraq. (This "martyrdom" will become the mythic "passion" and historic tragedy of Twelve-Imām Shī'ism.)

Schism of the 'Ibādites from the Khārijites.

683 Medina is sacked by Umayyads because of uprisings.

683-692 'Abd Allāh ibn az-Zubayr, declaring himself Caliph, holds Mecca in defiance of the Umayyads.

684 During a siege of Mecca the Ka'bah catches fire from a flaming arrow (AH *64*). It is rebuilt on a larger scale by 'Abd Allāh ibn az-Zubayr who, upon examination of the foundations, concludes that the Ka'bah had once been larger before rebuildings by the Quraysh.

685-687 Mukhtār, promoting Muḥammad ibn al-Ḥanafiyyah, a son of 'Alī, as the Mahdī, leads a revolt in Iraq (the "Kaysāniyyah" movement).

691 The Dome of the Rock and the al-Aqṣā' mosque are built in Jerusalem.

692 Al-Ḥajjāj ibn Yūsuf captures Mecca; 'Abd Allāh ibn az-Zubayr is killed (AH *73*), thus bringing to an end what the Umayyads call the "revolt" (*fitnah*), i.e. the old conservative, non-'Alid, opposition. Al-Ḥajjāj pulls down the enlarged Ka'bah built by 'Abd Allāh ibn az-Zubayr after the fire, and rebuilds it on the previous scale.

693 The Umayyad 'Abd al-Malik mints the first coins of the Islamic state in Damascus, followed by al-Ḥajjāj ibn Yūsuf in Iraq, thus replacing the previous Byzantine coinage.

705 The Great Umayyad Mosque of Damascus is built.

711 Ṭāriq ibn Ziyād, a Berber, under the Arab general Mūsā ibn Nuṣayr, invades Spain.

711-712 Muslim armies make conquests in Transoxiana and Sind.

713 The death of 'Alī Zayn al-'Abidin, Shī'ite Imām; some Shī'ites follow his son Zayd, instead of his older brother Muḥammad al-Baqir. Zayd takes up military resistance against the Umayyads. Beginning of Zaydī ("Fiver") Shī'ism.

717-718 Unsuccessful Muslim siege of Constantinople.

717 Muslim raids across the Pyrenees.

718 Resistance to Muslim rule begins in the Asturias in Spain.

719 Narbonne in France is captured by the Muslims.

728 Ḥasan of Basra, the great Sufi, dies. Mu'tazilite rationalist doctrines are diffused.

732 The Muslim advance into France is checked by Charles Martel in a battle between Tours and Poitiers.

738 Khārijite revolts in Iraq.

740 Death of Zayd, Imām of the Zaydīs; end of the Zaydī revolt in Iraq.

746 Abū Muslim incites a revolt against the Umayyads in Khorasan.

750 The Umayyad Caliph Marwān is defeated at the Zab river, and the 'Abbasid dynasty is founded by Abu-l-'Abbas aṣ-Ṣaffāḥ.

751 The first 'Ibādite Imām.

755 'Abd ar-Raḥmān I ad-Dākhil, Emir of Cordova founds the Umayyad dynasty of Spain. First construction of the Great Mosque of Cordova.

757 The death of Ibn al-Muqaffa', translator of the political allegory *Kalīlah and Dimnah*.

762 The 'Abbāsids found Baghdad.

The death of Ismā'īl, son of Ja'far aṣ-Ṣādiq (sixth Shī'ite Imām); using Ismā'īl as a cover, Iranian dualist religions penetrate Islam and the Sevener Movement emerges which, later, produces the Qarmatians and Fāṭimids.

765 The death of Ja'far aṣ-Ṣādiq, scholar and sixth Shī'ite Imām.

767 The death of Abū Ḥanīfah, founder of Ḥanafī School of Law.

778 Charlemagne leads a campaign against the Muslims in Spain.

780 The end of the revolt of al-Muqanna', "the veiled one".

795 The death of Mālik ibn Anas, founder of the Mālikī School of Law.

801 The death of the famous female Sufi, Rābi'ah al-'Adawiyyah.

803 The fall of the Barmecides.

808 The Moroccan city of Fez is founded by Idris II.

809 The death of Hārūn ar-Rashīd.

813 Al-Ma'mūn becomes Caliph; the flowering of scholarship and translation of Greek works into Arabic.

817 The uprising against al-Ḥakam I in Cordova. Part of the population emigrates to Fez, creating the city's "Andalusian quarter".

820 The death of ash-Shāfi'ī, founder of the Shāfi'ī School of Law.

822 The musician Ziryāb arrives in Cordova and establishes a grand style and high degree of elegance in the arts of living.

827 The Caliph al-Ma'mūn adopts Mu'tazilite doctrines and proclaims that the Koran is created.

830 The *Bayt al-Ḥikmah*, an academy for the sciences and the translation of Greek works into Arabic, is founded in Baghdad by the Caliph al-Ma'mūn.

831 Palermo is taken by the Arabs.

833 The Caliph al-Ma'mūn institutes the *miḥnah* (inquisition) to enforce adherence to Mu'tazilite doctrines on the part of Judges and scholars.
Al-Ma'mūn dies, al-Mu'taṣim becomes Caliph.

836 The 'Abbāsids make the camp-city of Samarra' their capital.

839 Diplomatic exchanges between Cordova and Constantinople.

847 The *miḥnah* (inquisition) ends.

855 The death of Ibn Ḥanbal, founder of the Ḥanbalī School of Law.

861 The death of al-Mutawakkil, first Caliph to be murdered by his Turkish troops.

864 Zaydī Shī'ism spreads in Daylam (Azerbaijan), and the Zaydī state is founded by Ḥasan ibn Zayd. (Zaydī-type Shī'ism will persist sporadically in the region until 1126.)

869-883 The Zanj (slaves from East Africa) revolt in Iraq.

870 Malta is conquered by the Muslims.
Al-Bukhārī, author of the *Ṣaḥīḥ*, a canonical collection of Ḥadīth, dies.

873 The eleventh Shī'ite Imām dies aged twenty-eight, leaving no successor. (Twelve-Imām Shī'ites will believe that his son by a concubine then disappeared, and that he, as the "Hidden Imām", is represented by chosen deputies (*wakīl*) until 940. The period 873-940 will be called "the Lesser Occultation"; the "Greater Occultation" will last until the coming of the Mahdī.)
The death of Abū-l-Ḥusayn Muslim, compiler of one of the two great collections of Ḥadīth jointly called the *Ṣaḥīḥān*.

874 Ismā'īli propagandist Muḥammad ibn Nuṣayr agitates in the Levant.
The death of Abū Yazīd al-Bisṭāmī, first of the so-called "drunken Sufis".

877 The Ibn Tulūn mosque in Cairo is built.

885 Dāwūd ibn Khalāf, founder of the Ẓāhirī School of Law, dies.

890 The rise of the populist revolutionary sect, the Qarmatians, an offshoot of the Ismā'īlis/ Seveners but without Imāms. Their leader, Ḥamdān Qarmāṭ, establishes his center, which he calls the "Abode of Exile" (*Dār al-Hijrah*) in southern Iraq.

The Arabs settle in Provence and carry out raids as far north as Switzerland.

892 Muḥammad at-Tirmidhī, the historian, dies.

898 A Zaydī Shī'ite state is established in the Yemen by the Imām al-Hādi Yaḥyā ibn al-Ḥusayn ar-Rassī.

The death of Ḥakim at-Tirmidhī, biographer of Sufis.

909 The Fāṭimid dynasty, claiming to be a Caliphate, is founded in North Africa.

910 The death of the Sufi al-Junayd.

922 The Persian Sufi al-Ḥallaj is executed.

923 The death of aṭ-Ṭabarī, the historian.

925 The death of Abū Bakr Muḥammad ar-Rāzī, physician and alchemist.

929 'Abd ar-Raḥmān III, the Umayyad ruler of Spain, takes the title of Caliph.

930 The Qarmatians raid Mecca and take the Black Stone from the Ka'bah to al-Ḥāsa' or to Baḥrayn.

932 The Buyid Mu'iz ad-Dawlah assumes control as "Prince of Princes" and makes the 'Abbāsid Caliph into figurehead.

935 The great theologian al-Ash'arī dies.

936 The royal city of Medīnat az-Zahrah is founded at Cordova.

940 The Fourth "representative" (*wakīl*) of the "Hidden Imām" refuses to name a successor as he dies, saying: "the matter now rests with God." The "Greater Occultation" begins.

950 The death of the philosopher al-Fārābī.

951 In Iraq the mysterious Brotherhood of Purity (*Ikhwān aṣ-Ṣafā'*) compile an encyclopedia of universal knowledge.

The Qarmatians return the Black Stone to Mecca.

953 John of Grötz sent to Cordova as Otto I's ambassador.

956 The death of al-Mas'udi, the historian.

961 Extension of the Great Mosque of Cordova by al-Ḥakam II.

962 The Buyid ruler Mu'izz ad-Dawlah institutes the observance of the 'Īd al-Ghadīr and public mourning for the death of Ḥusayn on 10 *Muḥarram*, as Shī'ite holy days.

965 The death of al-Mutannabi, the poet.

969 The Fāṭimid general Jawhar conquers Egypt and founds Cairo.

972 The founding of al-Azhar university, as a school for the training of Ismā'īli propagandists. (Later it will become one of the most renowned Muslim universities.)

976 The Spanish Umayyad Sultan al-Ḥakam II dies, and is succeeded by Hishām II, but the real power behind the throne is the chamberlain al-Manṣūr bi-Llāh.

985 Al-Manṣūr conducts campaigns in Spain and captures Coimbra in Portugal.

987 Al-Manṣūr further extends the Great Mosque of Cordova.

1009 The destruction of the Church of the Holy Sepulcher in Jerusalem by the Fāṭimid ruler al-Ḥākim.

1020 The death of Firdawsī, author of the *Shāh-nameh*.

1030 The death of Maḥmūd of Ghazna in Afghanistan.
The Spanish Caliphate comes to an end.

1037 The philosopher and physician Ibn Sīnā (Avicenna) dies.

1048 Al-Birūnī, scientist, philosopher, scholar, translator of works into and out of Sanskrit, dies.

1055 Saljūq Toghrul Beg enters Baghdad, and rules in the name of the ʿAbbāsids, taking the title of Sultan.

1058 The death of the poet Abū-l-Aʿlā al-Maʿarrī.

1062 The Almoravids under Yūsuf ibn Tashfīn conquer Morocco.

1063 Marrakesh is founded by the Almoravids.

1064 The death of the philosopher, theologian and poet, Ibn Ḥazm.

1065 The Vizier Niẓām al-Mulk founds the Niẓāmiyyah *Madrasah* in Baghdad.

1071 The Byzantines are defeated at Manzikert on 26 August by the Saljūq Alp Arslan. Most of Asia Minor is conquered by the Saljūqs.

1085 Toledo is taken from the Muslims by Alfonso VI.

1086 Yūsuf ibn Tashfīn comes to the help of Muslim princes in Spain and defeats the Christians at the Battle of az-Zallaqah.

1090 Ḥasan aṣ-Ṣabbāḥ seizes the Alamūt fortress in Northern Persia; the beginning of the Nizārī branch of the Ismāʿīlis (who will be called the "Assassin" sect by the Crusaders).
The third Almoravid landing in Spain; the king of Granada is deposed by Yūsuf ibn Tashfīn.

1092 Niẓām al-Mulk is murdered by Nizārī "Assassins".

1094 Valencia is captured by al-Cid.

1095 Pope Urban calls the first Crusade.

1097 Konya becomes the capital of the Saljūqs of Rūm.

1098 The Crusaders capture Antioch.

1099 15 July; Jerusalem is captured by the Crusaders.

1100 Baldwin becomes king of the Latin kingdom of Jerusalem.

1106 Yūsuf ibn Tashfīn, Almoravid ruler, dies.

1111 Death of al-Ghazālī, theologian, jurist, mystic. The "Renewer" (*Mujaddid*) of the age.
Almoravids capture Santarem, Badajoz, Porto, Evora, and Lisbon.

1121 The beginning of the Almohad movement in Morocco.

1124 Ḥasan aṣ-Ṣabbāḥ, the chief of the Assassins, dies.
The birth of Ibn Rushd (Averroes).

1130 The death of Ibn Tumart, the founder of the Almohad movement.

1135 The birth of Maimonides in Cordova.

1145 The end of Almoravid rule in Spain.

1146 The Almohads capture Fez.

1147 The Second Crusade, led by Conrad II and Louis VII.

1157 The Almohads capture Granada and Almeria.

1164 Ḥasan, the Assassin chief in Alamūt,

assumes the function of Ismā'īli Imām and declares the *Qiyāmah* ("the Resurrection"), dropping the cover of the Islamic law (*sharī'ah*).

1166 Death of 'Abd al-Qādir al-Jīlānī, a celebrated Sufi.

1167 The great Almohad mosque of Seville is built (today a cathedral).

1171 Ṣalāḥ ad-Dīn (Saladin) takes control of Egypt; the beginning of the Ayyūbid dynasty and the end of the Fāṭimids.
The death of the Spanish philosopher Ibn Ṭufayl.

1187 4 July; Ṣalāḥ ad-Dīn (Saladin) defeats the Crusaders at the Battle of the Horn of Hattin, and later captures Jerusalem.

1189 The Third Crusade, led by Frederick Barbarossa and Richard the Lion Heart.

1193 The death of Ṣalāḥ ad-Dīn (Saladin) and the division of the Ayyūbid Empire.

1195 The Almohad al-Manṣūr defeats the Castilians at the Battle of Alarcos.

1198 The death of Ibn Rushd (Averroes).

1200 The death of the Persian poet 'Aṭṭār.
The beginning of the Islamization of archipelagic South East Asia.

1203 The Persian poet Niẓāmī dies.

1204 The Fourth Crusade; the Doge Dandolo of Venice leads the Crusaders to sack Constantinople.
Maimonides dies.

1206 Temujin, having taken the name Jenghiz Khān ("universal ruler"), becomes the leader of the united Mongol tribes at an assembly in Qaraqorum.

1210 Jalāl ad-Dīn, Master of Alamūt and Chief of the Assassins, closes the curtain opened by Ḥasan in 1164, resumes observance of the Islamic religious law, and professes to be a Sunnī Muslim. The end of the "Resurrection" (*al-Qiyāmah*) and the resumption of the "Veiling" (*as-Satr*).

1212 The Almohads are defeated in Spain at the Battle of Las Navas de Tolosa.

1218 The Fifth Crusade.
At the Otrar river, a Khwarazmian governor massacres one hundred Mongol emissaries as spies. Mongol attacks against Muslim countries begin.

1220 The Khwarizm-Shāhīs are defeated by Mongols under Jenghiz Khān.

1223 The death of the historian Ibn al-Athīr.

1227 The death of Jenghiz Khān, and the partitioning of the empire among his sons and grandson.

1230 The end of Almohad rule in Spain.

1235 The death of the Sufi poet Ibn al-Fāriḍ.

1240 The death of the Sufi Ibn 'Arabī in Damascus.

1249 The Seventh Crusade.

1250 The Mamlūk dynasty arises in Egypt.

1256 Hūlāgū Khān conquers the Assassin fortress of Alamūt, and the last Grand Master Rukn ad-Dīn is put to death. The beginning of the Mongol dynasty in Persia, the Il-Khanids.

1258 Hūlāgū Khān sacks Baghdad; the end of the 'Abbāsids in Baghdad, but figurehead 'Abbāsids continue in Cairo under the Mamlūks.

1260 3 Sept; Mamlūks led by Qutuz and his lieutenant Baybars defeat the Mongols at the Battle of 'Ayn Jalūt. Baybars murders Qutuz and

becomes Sultan.
Kubilai, declared Great Khān by his army, founds the Mongol Yüan dynasty in China.

1264 Kubilai founds Khanbaliq (Peking) as his capital.

1265 The death of Hūlāgū Khān.

1271 Marco Polo begins his journey to China.

1273 The death of the Sufi Jalāl ad-Dīn ar-Rūmī.

1291 The last Crusader stronghold falls to the Mamlūks. The death of the Persian poet Sa'dī.

1294 Marco Polo returns to Italy.

c.1297 The first establishment of small Islamic states in the north of Sumatra.

1316 The death of Uljaytu, the Il-Khanid ruler who entered Islam as Muḥammad Khudabanda.

1317 The execution of the historian and Vizier Rashīd ad-Dīn at-Ṭabīb.

1326 The Ottoman Turks capture Bursa.

1328 The death of Ibn Taymiyyah, traditionalist theologian.

1349 The *Madrasah* founded at Granada.

1361 The Ottomans capture Adrianople (Edirne).

1369 Timur (Tamerlane) conquers Khorasan and Transoxiana.

1385 Ottoman conquests in the Balkans (Rumelia).

1389 The Ottomans defeat the Serbians at Kosovo.
The death of the Persian poet Ḥāfiẓ.

1391 The first Ottoman siege of Constantinople.

1399 Timur (Tamerlane) sacks Delhi.

1402 Timur (Tamerlane) captures Ottoman Sultan Bayezid.

1405 The death of Timur (Tamerlane).

1406 The death of the historian Ibn Khaldūn in Cairo.

1416 Chinese Muslim colonies are founded in Java.

1444 The Ottomans defeat the Hungarian King Ladislas.

1453 6 April- 29 May: the siege and fall of Constantinople.

1479 The Mosque of Demak, oldest in Indonesia, is built.

1487 Bartolomeu Diaz rounds the Cape of Storms which is then renamed "Cape of Good Hope".

1492 Granada and its dependencies, the last Muslim kingdom in Spain, falls to the "Catholic Kings" Ferdinand and Isabella.
Columbus lands in the New World.

1497 Bābur, founder of the Moghul Empire, captures Samarkand.

1501 Ismā'īl I establishes the Safavid dynasty in Persia, and Twelve-Imām Shī'ism becomes the state religion.

1507 The Portuguese under d'Albuquerque establish strongholds in the Persian Gulf.

1511 D'Albuquerque conquers Malacca from the Muslims.

1517 The Ottoman Sultan Selim Yavuz ("the Grim") defeats the Mamlūks and conquers Egypt.

1520 The reign of Sulaymān the Magnificent begins.

1526 Louis of Hungary dies at the Battle of Mohacs.

The Battle of Panipat in India, and the Moghul conquest; Bābur makes his capital at Delhi and Agra.

1528 The Ottomans take Buda in Hungary.

1529 Unsuccessful Ottoman siege of Vienna.

1550 The architect Sīnān builds the Süleymaniye mosque in Istanbul.

The rise of the Muslim kingdom of Atjeh in Sumatra.

Islam spreads to Java, the Moluccas, and Borneo.

1556 The death of Sulaymān the Magnificent.

1568 Alpujarra uprising of the Moriscos (Muslims forcibly converted to Catholicism) in Spain.

1571 The Ottomans are defeated at the naval Battle of Lepanto, and their dominance in the Mediterranean is brought to a close.

1578 The Battle of the Three Kings at Qaṣr al-Kabīr in Morocco. King Sebastian of Portugal is killed.

1588-1628 The reign of the Ṣafavid Sultan Shāh 'Abbas I.

1591 Musta'ili Ismā'īlis split into Sulaymānīs and Dāūdīs.

1602 Shāh 'Abbas captures Baḥrayn from the Portuguese.

1605 The Moghul Emperor Akbar dies.

1609 The expulsion of the Moriscos from Spain.

1640 Death of Mulla Ṣadrā, Persian theologian and philosopher. The great age of Sufism in Atjeh in Sumatra; Ibn 'Arabī, 'Abd al-Karīm al-Jīlī, and Ibn 'Aṭā' Allāh are studied.

1677 The first Russo-Ottoman war.

1683 The Ottomans unsuccessfully besiege Vienna, and are routed by the King of Poland, Jan Sobieski.

1686 The Ottomans lose Hungary to the Austrians.

1687 The Turks are defeated at Mohacs.

1688 The Austrians take Belgrade.

1689 Mustafa Köprülü becomes grand Vizier in Istanbul.

1690 The Turks retake Belgrade.

1696 Peter the Great of Russia captures the Turkish fortress of Azov.

1707 The death of 'Alamgīr (Awrangzeb), "last of the Great Moghuls".

1710-1711 The Russo-Ottoman war.

1730 Nādir Shāh of Persia drives out the Afghans.

1739 Nādir Shāh sacks Delhi.

1745 Muḥammad 'Abd al-Wahhāb is received in Dir'iyyah by Muḥammad ibn Sa'ud.

1757 The Wahhābīs take al-Ḥasā'.

1768-1774 The Russo-Ottoman war, and the Peace of Kuchuk Kaynarja.

1783 Russia conquers the Crimea.

1785 Muslims rebel against the Chinese Emperor.

1787-1792 The Russo-Ottoman War.

1791 The death of Ma (Muḥammad) Ming-hsin, founder of the "New Sect" in China, a militant Chinese Muslim movement directed against the Manchus.

1792 The death of Vahīd Bihbahānī, a Mulla who forced the Akhbarī school of Shī'ism out of Persia by declaring them unbelievers, thus definitively establishing the ascendancy of the Uṣūlī school and opening the way for a spectacular growth in the power of the religious authorities in Persia.

1798 Napoleon's victory at the Battle of the Pyramids in Cairo. Nelson destroys the French Fleet at Aboukir.

1801 Wahhābīs raid Kerbala.

1803 Wahhābīs capture Mecca and Medina.

1804 Muḥammad 'Alī is viceroy of Egypt.

1806-1812 The Russo-Ottoman War.

1809 The founding of the Sokoto Caliphate in Nigeria by Usumanu dan Fodio.

1811 The massacre of the Mamlūks by Muḥammad 'Alī.

1818 Muḥammad 'Alī's son Ibrāhīm Pasha campaigns against the Wahhābīs; Dir'iyyah is destroyed.

1821 The Muslim revolt in Sinkiang, China.

1821-1830 The Greek War of Independence from the Ottomans.

1826 The revolt of the Janissaries.

1826 The death of Aḥmad al-Aḥṣā'ī, founder of the Shaykhīs in Persia.

1827 The Triple Alliance against Turkey, and the naval battle of Navarino.

1828-1829 The Russo-Ottoman War.

1830 The French occupy Algeria.

1831 Ibrāhīm Pasha conquers Syria.

1835 'Abd al-Qādir defeats the French at Macta.

1837 The Sanūsī Order is founded.

1838-1842 The Anglo-Afghan war, in which the Afghans are victorious.

1839 The beginning of Tanẓīmāt proclamations in Turkey: *Hatt-i-Sharīf Gülhane*.

1843 The first Sanūsī *zāwiyyah* is founded in Libya.

1844 The Bābī sect establishes itself in Persia.

1850 The execution of the Bāb in Persia and the massacre of his followers; the beginning of the Bahā'i movement.

The reform movement of Khayr ad-Dīn Pasha in Tunisia.

The commercial code is revised along Western lines in Turkey, and secular Nizamiyyah courts are inaugurated.

1853 The spread of the Tijānī *Ṭarīqah* in West Africa.

1854-1856 The Crimean War.

1855 The Muslim revolt in Yunnan, China.

1856 Modernizing Tanẓīmāt reforms in Turkey: *Hatt-i Hümayun*.

1857 The Alexandria-Cairo railroad completed.

1858 The end of the Moghul dynasty.

1859 Imām Shāmil is captured by Russian troops, marking the end of the Muslim resistance in the Caucusus which began in 1834.

1869 The Suez canal is opened.

1873 The Dutch attack the Muslim kingdom of Atjeh in Sumatra and capture the Sultan.

1874 The Aligarh school (later to become a university) is founded by Sir Sayyid Ahmed Khan.

1875 The introduction of mixed civil and *sharī'ah* legal systems in Egypt.

1876 The Majalla, a uniform compilation of the laws of obligation based upon the Ḥanafī School of Law, begun in 1869, is completed.

1878-1879 The Second Anglo-Afghan war.

1880 Ismā'īl Pasha of Egypt assumes the title of Khedive.

1881 The French occupy Tunisia and the British occupy Egypt; the emergence of the Mahdī in the Sudan.

1884 Muḥammad 'Abduh publishes a magazine in Paris advocating Islamic reform.

1885 Khartum is seized by the Mahdī's forces, and General Gordon is killed (the Mahdī dies shortly thereafter).

1888 Ghulam Mirza Ahmad starts the Ahmadiyyah movement.

1896 Kitchener defeats the Mahdists at Omdurman.

1901 'Abd al-'Azīz (Ibn Sa'ūd) takes Riyāḍ.
The French invade Morocco.

1904 The Conference of Algeciras prepares the way for a French protectorate in Morocco.
The Persian constitution is promulgated.

1905 The beginning of the Salafiyyah movement.

1907 The Young Turks movement in Turkey.

1912 The Muḥammadiyyah reform movement emerges in Indonesia.

1914 Secret Arab nationalist societies are organized in Ottoman possessions.
Outbreak of World War I.

1916 The Arab revolt against the Turks, in which Lawrence leads attacks on the Hejaz Railway.

1917 Allenby enters Jerusalem.

1918 Damascus is taken, and an armistice with the Ottomans is signed on 30 October.
World War I ends 11 November.
Zaghlūl and the *wafd* movement in Egypt.

1921 The sons of Ḥusayn, the Sharīf of Mecca, 'Abd Allāh and Fayṣāl, are made Kings of Transjordan and Iraq respectively.

1921-1926 'Abd al-Karim leads a revolt against colonial rule in Moroccan Rif, and declares the "Republic of the Rif".

1922 Mustafa Kemal abolishes the Turkish Sultanate.

1924 The Turkish Caliphate is abolished. King 'Abd al-'Azīz conquers Mecca and Medina; the Kingdom of the Najd is unified with the Hejaz.

1925 Reza Khān seizes the government in Persia and establishes the Pahlavi dynasty.

1926 The King of the Najd, 'Abd al-'Azīz (Ibn Sa'ud), assumes the title "King of Najd and Hejaz".

1927 The death of the Egyptian nationalist leader Zaghlūl.

1928 Turkey is declared a secular state.
Ḥasan al-Banna founds the Muslim Brotherhood.

1934 War between King ʻAbd al-ʻAzīz and Imām Yahyā of the Yemen; the peace treaty of Ṭā'if. ʻAsīr becomes part of Saudi Arabia.

1935 Iran becomes the official name of Persia.

1939-1945 World War II.

1941 Reza Shah is forced to abdicate in favor of his son Mohammad Reza Shah in Iran.

1949 Ḥasan al-Banna, leader of the Muslim Brotherhood, is assassinated.

1951 Libya becomes independent.

1952 King Faruq of Egypt forced to abdicate.

1953 The death of King ʻAbd al-ʻAzīz (Ibn Saʻud) of Saudi Arabia.

In November the foundation stone is laid to enlarge the Prophet's mosque in Medina.

1956 the end of the French Protectorate in Morocco.

Tunisia becomes independent.

1957 The Bey of Tunisia is deposed, and Bourguiba becomes president.

1962 Algeria becomes independent.

On the death of Aḥmad, Zaydī Imām of the Yemen, his successor, Crown Prince Baḥr, takes the name Imām Manṣūr Bi-Llāh Muḥammad.

1965 Malcom X is assassinated.

1968 The enlargement of the Grand Mosque of Mecca, begun in 1957, is completed; the *saʻy* and *ṭawāf* can now be performed on two levels. (124,000 can pray at one time under normal conditions and, under the conditions of the greater pilgrimage, 275,000 have been accommodated at one time with another 100,000 outside around the mosque.)

1969 King Idris of Libya is ousted by a coup led by Colonel Qadhdhāfī.

1973 King Zahir Shāh of Afghanistan is overthrown.

1975 Elijah Muhammad dies; Wallace Warith Deen Muhammad becomes leader of the "Nation of Islam" among Blacks in the United States; the movement shifts towards Islamic orthodoxy, and is renamed the American Muslim Mission.

1978 Imām Mūsā Ṣadr, religious leader of the Lebanese Twelve-Imām Shīʻites, after promoting the resurgence of Shīʻites in Lebanon and the foundation of *Amal*, disappears on a trip to Libya, apparently assassinated.

1979 The Shah leaves Iran on January 15, thus bringing the Pahlavi dynasty to a close.

1979 On *1 Muḥarram AH 1400*/21 November, the first day of the 15th Islamic century, fanatics led by students of the Theological University of Medina attempt to promote one of their group as Mahdī and thus fulfill a certain prophetic Ḥadīth: "A man of the people of Medina will go forth, fleeing to Mecca, and certain of the people of Mecca will come to him and will lead him forth against his will and swear fealty to him between the *rukn* [Black Stone corner of the Kaʻbah] and the Maqam Ibrāhīm." They hold the Grand Mosque of Mecca against the army for two weeks. Sixty-three of the 300 fanatics are captured alive, the mosque is recovered, and the conspirators are all put to death.

1990-1991 Military annexation of Kuwait by Iraq, under Ba'athist leader Saddam Hussain, is reversed by a coalition of US-led Western and Muslim forces.

1980 Israel opens its first embassy in the Arab world, in Cairo.

Soviet and Afghan troops attack Mujahidin strongholds in Afghanistan.

The Shah of Iran, Mohamed Reza Pahlevi dies in Egypt.

Iraq invades Iran.

President Anwar as-Sadat is assassinated by Islamic fundamentalists.

1982 Uprising in Hama against the Alawite regime of Hafez al-Assad; Syrian troops kill 10,000 and level half the town.

Israel returns the Sinai to Egypt in accordance with the Camp David agreements.

Israel invades Lebanon with 20,000 troops.

Four hundred and twenty die in Mecca during the pilgrimage in a riot caused by an Iranian political demonstration.

Beginning of the Intifada, the Palestinian uprising in the occupied West Bank.

1988 Afghanistan and Pakistan sign an accord clearing the way for the Soviet Army's departure but guerrillas continue fighting.

Iran accepts the United Nations ceasefire plan in the Iran-Iraq war.

The Palestine National Council in exile in Algiers proclaims an independent Palestinian state and accepts UN Security Council resolution 242 implicitly recognising the existence of the state of Israel. The council rejects all forms of terrorism.

1989 Khomeini urges the execution of Salman Rushdie, Indian-born British author of *The Satanic Verses*. The book, which describes the wives of the Prophet of Islam as prostitutes, and the Prophet himself as a contemptuous scoundrel, is universally viewed by Muslims as blasphermy. Rushdie is forced into hiding.

The last of 15,000 soldiers, the Soviet 40th Army, withdraws from Afghanistan.

Two bombs explode in Mecca. One person dead and 16 wounded. The Saudi authorities blame Iranian-inspired terrorists.

The Prophet's Mosque in Medina is enlarged to accommodate 98,000 worshippers (from 16,000).

Ayatollah Khomeini dies.

1990 The Grand Mosque of Mecca is e nlarged to a capacity of 695,000 worshippers, (from 313,000)

North and South Yemen unite.

In Mecca 1,426 pilgrims are killed in a stampede in a pedestrian underpass at Mina.

Saddam Hussein of Iraq invades and annexes Kuwait, making it a province of Iraq.

Chechen independence movement led by Jakar Dudayev calls for sovereignty.

1991 January: Coalition forces led by the United States begin aerial bombardments of Iraq leading to 100 hours of ground fighting in which Iraqi forces are routed and Iraq is forced to give up Kuwait.

The war between the Moroccan government and the Polisario in the Western Sahara comes to a standstill awaiting a UN sponsored referendum.

The UN General Assembly votes to rescind the resolution naming Zionism a form of racism.

1992 A committee of clerics from Al-Azhar University confiscate eight books on religious topics at the Cairo book fair.

Bosnia and Herzogovina declares independence and Bosnian Serbs declare a separate state. Fighting spreads and Sarajevo is soon surrounded.

The Congress Government in New Delhi fails to prevent a Hindu nationalist mob from destroying a 16th century mosque, the Babri Masjid, built by Mogul Emperor Babur in Ayohya in North India on the site of an earlier Hindu temple.

1993 Israel announces an agreement with the PLO on autonomy for the Gaza strip and Jericho.

"Declaration of Principles" agreement signed in Washington for partial Palestinian autonomy. Yasir 'Arafat and Israeli Prime Minister Yitzhak Rabin shake hands on the White House lawn.

1994 'Arafat and Rabin sign a self-rule agreement in Cairo.

Israel and the PLO sign an agreement in Cairo on Israeli withdrawal from the Gaza strip and Jericho.

In a stampede at Mina during the casting of the stones, 207 pilgrims die.

In Turkey, 37 writers and intellectuals are burned to death after Islamic fundamentalists set fire to a hotel where the translator of Salman Rushdie's

The Satanic Verses was addressing a conference.

Russian troops launch a full-scale invasion of Chechnya, taking control of the capital Grozny.

Shimon Peres shares the Nobel Peace Prize with Yizhak Rabin and Yassir 'Arafat.

Jordan signs a peace agreement with Israel.

1995 Yizhak Rabin assassinated by Israeli rightist; Shimon Peres becomes Prime Minister.

1996 The population of Iran reaches 60 million (from 35 million in 1979 when the Ayatollahs reduced the legal age of marriage to 9 and exhorted the people to make babies for the revolution).

The Taliban, a fundamentalist military group in Afghanistan, capture Kabul.

The US Congress passes a law prohibiting female genital cutting, making it punishable by up to five years in prison and requiring US representatives to the World Bank to oppose loans to 28 African countries where the practice exists.

1997 Chinese authorities impose a curfew on a town in the northwestern Xinjiang region after at least 10 people are killed in a riot.

Bands of Buddhist monks vandalize mosques in Mandalay and Rangoon.

Fire sweeps through a pilgrim encampment at Mina. The death toll reaches 217 with more than 1,290 injured in the resulting panic. Most victims are from the Indian sub-continent. Some 70,000 tents are destroyed in the blaze.

Prime Minister Erbakan of Turkey resigns under pressure form the military.

Taliban agree to enforce a world ban on opium trade and in 2001 opium cultivation ceases.

1998 Massacres of villagers by Islamic militants continue in Algeria. The death toll in the war since 1991 is estimated at 76,000.

A stampede in Mina during the pilgrimage to Mecca kills over 100 pilgrims.

India explodes five atomic bombs.

After violent student demonstrations in Indonesia, Suharto steps down as head of state.

Pakistan detonates five atomic devices.

Fighting breaks out between Muslim separatists in Kosovo and Yugoslav police and army.

The US attacks Ousama Bin Ladin's training camps in Afghanistan and a pharmaceutical factory in Khartoum, Sudan, which it claims was used in the manufacture of nerve gas. Around seventy cruise missiles are used in the attacks which are retaliation for earlier attacks on US embassies.

Palestinian airport at Gaza opens.

1999 Religious rioting in Indonesia claims 45 lives. On the Island of Ambon, four days of rioting breaks out between Christian and Muslims.

King Hussein of Jordan dies and is succeeded by his son, Abdallah.

The massacre of ethnic Albanians by the Serb military in Kosovo continues. NATO talks in France break down and NATO attacks Serbia to force Slobodan Milosevic to accept terms regarding the province (pop. 90% Albanian Muslims). Serbia drives half a million ethnic Albanians out of Kosovo. One hundred thousand ethnic Albanians disappear and hundreds of thousands are forced into hiding.

The 2,500-strong Israeli-backed "South Lebanon Army", a Christian militia, begins pulling out of Jezzin in South Lebanon.

The Kashmir war between India and Pakistan reaches its highest level for thirty years.

Fundamentalist attacks continue in Algeria.

Serb forces complete withdrawal from Kosovo as NATO forces occupy Kosovo.

A Turkish court sentences the Kurdish leader Ocalan to death.

King Hassan of Morocco dies. He is succeeded by his son Muhammad.

The death toll in the Algerian civil war since 1992 reaches 100,000.

The Israel High Court prohibits the use of torture by the security organizations.

General Pervez Musharraf, relieved as Chief of Staff because of his aggressive handling of the border fighting with India over Kashmir, stages a *coup d'état* in Pakistan and places Prime Minister Nawaz Sharif under house arrest.

October 25: A "safe passage" road link is opened between the Gaza Strip and the Palestinian West Bank.

2001 The Palestinian Intifada resumes anew after the election of Ariel Sharon in Israel.

BIBLIOGRAPHY

Koranic passages are from the translation by A.J. Arberry, *The Koran Interpreted*, Oxford University Press, 1964. Excerpts from al-Hujwīrī's *Kashf al-Mahjūb*, Niffarī, Imru'-l-Qays, al-Ḥallāj and reports of him, the end of Yazdagird, the letter to the Muqawqīs, the Khārijite Sermon, the Creed of al-Ash'arī; the Sermon on Jihād, and some selected stories, are from Eric Schroeder's *Muhammad's People*. The quotations from Ibn 'Aṭā' Allāh are from Victor Danner's *Ibn 'Aṭā'illāh's Sufi Aphorisms*. Excerpts from the *Khamriyyah* are from *The Mystical Poems of Ibn al-Farid* by A.J. Arberry, Abū Sa'id on love is from his translation of the *Book of Truthfulness*, Ḥasan Basrī on the world and the conversion of al-Ghazālī is from his book *Sufism*. Quotations of the sayings of Muslim thinkers are also taken from Whitall N. Perry's *The Treasury of Traditional Wisdom*. The *Burdah* of Ka'b is from *The Life of Muhammad* translated by A. Guillaume. The Chinese description of the Arabs in *Ta Shih* is from Bretschneider, *Ancient Chinese Knowledge of Arabs* quoted in Broomhall, *Islam in China*. The writings of the Shaykh ad-Darqawi are from *Letters of a Sufi Master*, and the *as-Salāt al-Mashīshiyyah* is from the *Prayer of Ibn Mashish*, both translated by Titus Burkhardt. Ibn al-'Arif on *istridrāj* is from the translation of the *Maḥāsin al-Majālis* by Elliot and Abdulla. The Chinese *Three-Character Rhymed Classic of the Ka'bah* was translated by J. Peter Hobson.

In addition, the following books were principally consulted:

Ansari, Muhammad Abdul Haq. *Sufism and Sharī'ah*. Leicester: The Islamic Foundation, 1986.

Arberry, A.J. *The Book of Truthfulness* (trans. of the *Kitab as-Sidq*, by Abū Sa'id al-Kharraz). London: Oxford University Press, 1937.

Arberry, A.J. *Muslim Saints and Mystics*. London: Routledge and Kegan Paul, 1966.

Arberry, A.J. *The Mystical Poems of Ibn al-Farid*. Dublin: Emery Walker (Ireland) Ltd., 1956.

Arberry, A.J. *Sufism*. London: George Allen and Unwin, 1950.

Austin, R.J.W. *Sufis of Andalusia*. London: George Allen and Unwin, 1971.

Baillie, Neil B.E. *A Digest of Moohumadan Law*. Lahore: Premier Book House.

Bell, Richard, and Watt, W. Montgomery. *Introduction to the Qur'an*. Edinburgh: Edinburgh University Press, 1972.

Bosworth, C.E. *The Islamic Dynasties*. Edinburgh: Edinburgh University Press, 1980.

Bouhdiba, Abdelwahab. *Sexuality in Islam*. London: Routledge and Kegan Paul, 1985.

Boyce, Mary. *Zoroastrians*. London: Routledge and Kegan Paul, 1979.

Boyle, J.A. *The History of the World Conqueror* (by 'Ata-Malik Juvaini). Manchester: Manchester University Press, 1958.

Boyle, J.A. *The Successors of Genghiz Khan* (the History of Rashīd ad-Dīn aṭ-Ṭabīb). New York and London: Columbia University Press, 1971.

Brocklemann, Carl. *History of the Islamic Peoples*. London: Routledge and Kegan Paul, 1948.

Burckhardt, Titus. *Art of Islam*. London: World of Islam Festival, 1976.

Burckhardt, Titus. *Fez, Stadt des Islam*. Olten: Urs Graf Verlag, 1960.

Burckhardt, Titus. *Introduction to Sufi Doctrine*. Wellingborough: Thorson's Publishers, 1976.

Burckhardt, Titus. *Letters of a Sufi Master*. London: Perennial Books, 1973.

Burckhardt, Titus. *Moorish Culture in Spain*. London: George Allen and Unwin, 1972.

Burckhardt, Titus. 'The Prayer of Ibn Mashish'. *Studies in Comparative Religion*, Winter-Spring 1978. Pates Manor, Bedfont, Middlesex.

Burton, Sir Richard. *Personal Narrative of a Pilgrimage to al-Madinah and Meccah*. London: Tyleston and Edwards, 1893.

Corbin, Henry. *Cyclical Time and Ismā'īli Gnosis*. London: Kegan Paul International, 1983.

Corbin, Henry. 'The Dramatic Element Common to the Gnostic Comogonies of the Religions of the Book'. *Studies in Comparative Religion*, Summer-Autumn, 1980. Pates Manor, Bedfont, Middlesex.

Coulson, N.J. *A History of Islamic Law*. Edinburgh: Edinburgh University Press, 1964.

Danner, Victor. *Ibn 'Aṭa'illah's Sufi Aphorisms*. Leiden: E.J. Brill, 1973.

Davis, F Hadland. *Jami*. Lahore: Sh. Muhammad Ashraf, 1968.

Dermenghem, Emile. *Vies des Saints Musulmans*. Alger: Editions Baconnier.

Donaldson, Dwight M. *The Shī'ite Religion*. London: Luzac and Company, 1933.

Doniach, N.S. *The Oxford English-Arabic Dictionary*. Oxford: The Clarendon Press, 1962.

Elliot, William and Abdulla, Adnan K. *Mahasin al-Majalis* by Ibn al-'Arif. Avebury, 1980.

Encyclopaedia of Islam. London and Leiden: E.J. Brill, 1913-1939.

Foerster, Werner. *Gnosis*. London: Oxford, the Clarendon Press, 1972.

Freeman-Grenville, G. S. P. *The Muslim and Christian Calendars*. London: Oxford University Press, 1963.

Friedlander, Ira. *The Whirling Dervishes*. New York: Macmillan, 1975.

Friedlander, Shems, with al-Hajj Shaikh Muzaffareddin. *Ninety-Nine Names of Allah*. New York: Harper and Row, 1978.

Fu-ch'u, Ma. 'The Three-Character Rhymed Classic on the Ka'bah (*the Cube of Heaven*)'; Translated by J. Peter Hobson. *Studies in Comparative Religion*, Summer-Autumn, 1980. Pates Manor, Bedfont, Middlesex.

Fyzee, Asaf A.A. *The Book of Faith* (The *Da'a'im al-Islam* of al-Qadi al-Nu'man). Bombay: Nachiketa Publications Ltd, 1974.

Gaudefroy-Demombynes, Maurice. *Muslim Institutions*. London: George Allen and Unwin, 1950.

Geijbels, M. *An Introduction to Islam*. Rawalpindi: Pakistan Committee for Theological Education, 1977.

Goldziher, Ignaz. *Streitshrift des Gazali gegen die Batinijja-Sekte*. Leiden: E.J. Brill, 1956.

Grousset, Ren. *Conqueror of the World*. New York: The Orion Press, 1966

von Grunebaum, Gustave, Ed. *Unity and Variety in Muslim Civilization*. Chicago: University of Chicago Press, 1955.

Guenon, Ren. *The Reign of Quantity and the Signs of the Times* (translation from the French by North Northbourne). Baltimore, Maryland: Penguin Books, 1974.

Guerdan, Ren. *Byzantium: Its Triumphs and Tragedy*. London: George Allen and Unwin, 1956.

Guillaume, A. *The Life of Muhammad* (Ibn Ishaq's *Sirat Rasul Allah*). Karachi: Oxford University Press, 1970.

Halkin, Abraham S. *Moslem Schisms and Sects* (*al-Farqbayn al-Firaq* of Abu Mansur 'Abd al-Qahir al-Baghdadi), part II. Tel Aviv, 1935.

Hollister, John Norman. *The Shi'a of India*.

London: Luzac and Company, 1953.

Hodgson, Marshall G.S. *The Order of the Assassins.* 'S-Gravenhage: Mouton & Co., 1955.

Hodgson, Marshall G.S. *The Venture of Islam.* Chicago: The University of Chicago Press, 1974.

Howard, I.K.A. *Kitab al-Irshad* (*The Book of Guidance* by Shaykh al-Mufid). Qum: Ansariyan Publications.

Howarth, David. *The Desert King.* New York: McGraw-Hill, 1964.

Hughes, Thomas Patrick. *A Dictionary of Islam.* W.H. Allen and Unwin, 1885.

Ibn 'Arabī, Muhyiddin. *La Sagesse des Prophtes* (*Fusus al-Hikam*), translated by Titus Burckhardt. Paris: Editions Albin Michel, 1955.

Ibn Khaldun. *The Muqadimmah* (translated by Franz Rosenthal). Princeton, New Jersey: The Princeton University Press (for the Bollingen Foundation), 1958.

Ibn Sa'd. *Kitab al-Tabaqat al-Kabir.* Karachi: Pakistan Historical Society.

Ivanow, W. *On the Recognition of the Imām* (*Fasl dar Bayan-i Shinakht-i Imām*). Bombay: Thacker & Co., Ltd., for the Ismaili Society, 1947.

Ivanow. W. *Studies in Early Persian Ismailism.* Bombay: The Ismaili Society Series, 1955.

Ivanow. W. *The Rawdatu't-Taslim, commonly called Tasawwurat* by Nasiru'd-din Tusi. Leiden: E.J. Brill, for the Ismaili Society, 1950.

Jafri, S. Husain M. *Origins and Early Development of Shī'ism.* London: Longman, Librairie du Liban, 1979.

Jameelah, Maryam. *Islam and Modernism.* Pakistan: Mohammad Yusuf Khan, 1968.

Jeffery, Arthur. *A Reader on Islam.* 'S-Gravenhage: Mouton & Co., 1962.

Jeffery, Arthur. *Islam: Muhammad and His Religion.* Indianapolis: Bobbs-Merrill Company, Inc. 1958.

Kaidi, Hamza with Najm ad-Din Bammate and al-Hashimi Tijani. *Mecca and Medina Today.* Paris: Les Editions Jeune-Afrique, 1980.

Kassis, Hanna E. *A Concordance of the Qur'an.* Berkeley: University of California Press, 1983.

Khalidi, Tarif. *Islamic Historiography.* Albany: State of New York University Press, 1975.

Kreiser, Klaus; Diem, Werner; Majer, Hans Georg, editors. *Lexikon der Islamischen Welt.* Stuttgart: Verlag W. Kohlhammer GmbH, 1974.

Kritzeck, James. *Anthology of Islamic Literature.* Middlesex: Penguin, 1964.

Lawrence, Bruce B. *Shahrastani on the Indian Religion.* The Hague: Mouton, 1976.

Lewis, Bernard. *The Assassins.* New York: Basic Books.

Lewis, Bernard. *The Origins of Ismā'īlism.* Cambridge: W. Heffer and Sons Ltd., 1940.

Lichtenstadter, Ilse. *Introduction to Classical Arabic Literature.* New York: Schocken Books, 1976.

Lieu, Samuel N.C. *Manichaeism.* Manchester: Manchester University Press, 1985.

Lings, Martin. *A Sufi Saint of the Twentieth Century.* London: George Allen and Unwin, 1971.

Lings, Martin. *Muhammad.* London: George Allen and Unwin, Islamic Texts Society, 1983.

Lubis, Hajj Muhammad Bukhari. *Qasidahs in Honor of the Prophet.* Malaysia: Penerbit University Kebangsaan Malaysia, 1983.

MacDonald, Duncan Black. *Development of Muslim Theology, Jurisprudence and Constitutional Theory*. Lahore: Premier Book House, 1963 (first published 1903).

Massignon, Louis. *Akhbar al-Hallaj*. Paris: Librairie Philosophique J. Vrin, 1957.

Massignon, Louis. *Al-Hallaj, Martyr Mystique de L'Islam*. Paris: Librairie Orientaliste Paul Geuthner, 1921.

Al-Mas'udi. *Les Prairies d'Or*. Traduction francaise de Barbier de Maynard et Paret de Courteille. Revue et corrige par Charles Pellat. Paris: Societ Asiatique, 1962.

Momen, Moojan. *An Introduction to Shī'i Islam*. New Haven and London: Yale University Press, 1985.

Nasr, Seyyid Hossein. *Ideals and Realities of Islam*. London: George Allen and Unwin Ltd, 1966.

Nasr, Seyyid Hossein. *An Introduction to Islamic Cosmological Doctrines*. Cambridge, Massachusetts: The Belknap Press, 1960.

Nasr, Seyyed Hossein. *Islamic Science*. London: World of Islam Festival, 1976.

Nicholson, Reynold A. *The Kashf al-Mahjub of al-Hujwīrī*. London, Luzac and Co., 1936.

Nicholson, Reynold A. *A Literary History of the Arabs*. London: Cambridge University Press, 1966 (originally published 1907).

Nicholson, Reynold A. *Studies in Islamic Mysticism*. Cambridge: Cambridge University Press, 1921.

Padwick, Constance E. *Muslim Devotions*. London: S.P.C.K., 1961.

Pareja, F.M. with L. Hertling, A. Bausani, Th. Bois. *Islamologie*. Beirut: Imprimerie Catholique, 1957-1963.

Perry, Whitall. *A Treasury of Traditional Wisdom*. London: George Allen and Unwin, 1971.

Pickthall, Muhammad Marmaduke. *The Glorious Koran*. London: George Allen and Unwin, 1976.

Al-Qaradawi, Yusuf. *The Lawful and the Prohibited in Islam*. London: Shorouk International, 1985.

Al-Qayrawani, Ibn Abi Ziyad. *La Risala*, translated by Lon Bercher. Alger: Editions Populaires de l'Armee, 1975.

Rahman, Fazlur. *Prophecy in Islam*. London: George Allen and Unwin, 1955.

Rizvi, Saiyid Athar Abbas. *A History of Sufism in India*. New Delhi: Mushiram Manoharlal Publishers Pvt. Ltd, 1983.

Ronart, Stephan and Nandy. *Concise Encyclopedia of Arabic Civilization*. Amsterdam and Djakarta: Djambatan, 1959.

Ronart, Stephan and Nandy. *Lexikon der Arabischen Welt* (revision of *The Concise Encyclopaedia of Arabic Civilization*). Zurich: Artemis Verlag, 1972.

Schimmel, Annemarie. *As Through a Veil, Mystical Poetry in Islam*. New York: Columbia University Press, 1982.

Schroeder, Eric. *Muhammad's People*. Portland, Maine: Bond Wheelwright, 1955.

Schuon, Frithjof. *Dimensions of Islam*. London: George Allen and Unwin, 1970.

Schuon, Frithjof. *Understanding Islam*. London: George Allen and Unwin Ltd., 1963.

Shacht, Joseph, and Bosworth, C.E. *The Legacy of Islam*. Oxford: the Clarendon Press, 1974.

Shahrastani, Muhammad ben 'Abd al-Karim. *Kitab al-Milal, Les Dissidences de l'Islam*, translated by Jean-Claude Vadet. Paris: Librairie Orientaliste Paul Geuthner S.A., 1984.

Smith, Margaret. *An Early Mystic of Baghdad*, A Study of the Life and Teaching of Harith B. Asad al-Muhasibi. London: Sheldon Press (reprinted), 1977.

Spuler, Bertold. *History of the Mongols*. Berkeley: University of California Press, 1971.

Stern, S.M. *Studies in Early Ismā'īlism*. Jerusalem and Leiden: The Magnes Press – Hebrew University – E.J. Brill, 1983.

Trimingham, J. Spencer. *The Sufi Orders in Islam*. London: Oxford University Press, 1971.

Van den Bergh, Simon. *Averroes' Tahafut al-Tahafut*. London: Luzac and Co., 1954.

Watt, W. Montgomery, and Cachia, Pierre. *A History of Islamic Spain*. Edinburgh: Edinburgh University Press, 1965.

Watt, M. Montgomery. *Islamic Political Thought*. Edinburgh: Edinburgh University Press, 1968.

Watt, W. Montgomery. *The Influence of Islam on Medieval Europe*. Edinburgh: Edinburgh University Press, 1972.

Watt, W. Montgomery. *Islamic Philosophy and Theology*. Edinburgh: Edinburgh University Press, 1962.

Watt, W. Montgomery. *A Companion to the Qur'an*. London: George Allen and Unwin Ltd., 1967.

Wehr, Hans. *Arabic English Dictionary*, edited by J.M. Cowan. Ithaca, New York: Cornell University Press, 1960.